DRAMATIC CRITICISM INDEX

DRAMATIC CRITICISM INDEX

A Bibliography of Commentaries on
Playwrights from Ibsen to the Avant-Garde

Compiled and edited by
PAUL F. BREED
and
FLORENCE M. SNIDERMAN

Wayne State University Library

GALE RESEARCH COMPANY • DETROIT

Library of Congress Catalog Card Number: 79-127598
Gale Research Company, Book Tower, Detroit, Michigan 48226
© 1972 by Gale Research Company. All rights reserved
Printed in the United States of America

CONTENTS

PREFACE

Approximately 630 books and over 200 periodicals have been examined
for this selective index to commentaries on modern playwrights and their
plays. It is a bibliography of nearly 12,000 entries in English on 300 or more
American and foreign playwrights, the majority of them from the twentieth
century, although some nineteenth-century playwrights were included if their
plays were still being performed.

Playwrights are organized in a single alphabetical listing. Under the name
of each playwright there is first a GENERAL section where full-length studies
are listed as well as references to briefer commentaries in other books, sometimes full chapters, sometimes only a few pages, but often extremely useful to
the student. Individual works of the playwright are then listed alphabetically,
with foreign play titles in English, unless there was no translation. All citations
are arranged alphabetically by their authors.

Sources consulted include the PMLA Annual Bibliography, Abstracts of
English Studies, the Annual Bibliography of English Language and Literature,
and many specialized bibliographies on the theatre in general or on individual
playwrights. Authors of the commentaries include scholars, critics, literary
and theatre historians, playwrights, directors and journalists. Some play reviews
have been included, usually for foreign playwrights on whom little source
material was available in English, or for plays so recent that little critical
material has appeared.

ACKNOWLEDGMENTS

We are indebted to the Wayne State University General Library for the use
of its resources. Special appreciation is due to Norman Hutchinson, Betty Ray,
and Michael Sniderman for their help in tracking source materials.

P.F.B.
F.M.S.

DRAMATIC CRITICISM INDEX

ANONYMOUS

The Concept

Kerr, Walter. "They Grow Their Own Hay." *The New York Times,* June 2, 1968, Sect. 2, pp. 1, 3.

Lester, Elenore. "...Or the Wave of the Future." *The New York Times,* June 30, 1968, Sect. 2, p. 3.

LIONEL ABEL

Absalom

Roston, Murray. *Biblical drama in England trom the Middle Ages to the present day,* pp. 306-307.

KJELD ABELL 1901-1961

General

Anonymous. "Rebel of Danish Drama." *Times Literary Supplement* (Jan. 18, 1963), p. 40.

Bredsdorff, Elias. "Abell." *In:* Sprinchorn, Evert, ed. *The genius of the Scandinavian theater,* pp. 466-468, 473-475.

Madsen, Børge G. "Leading Motifs in the Dramas of Kjeld Abell." *Scandinavian Studies,* vol. 33 (1961), pp. 127-136.

Mitchell, P.M. *A history of Danish literature,* pp. 262-264.

Days on a Cloud (Dage paa en sky)

Bredsdorff, Elias. "Abell." *In:* Sprinchorn, Evert, ed. *The genius of the Scandinavian theater,* pp. 468-473.

PETER ABRAHAM

A Wreath for Udomo (Adapted by William Branch)

Mitchell, Loften. *Black drama,* p. 168.

ANTONIO ACEVEDO HERNANDEZ 1886-1962

General

Jones, W.K. *Behind Spanish American footlights,* pp. 224-227.

MARCEL ACHARD 1899-

General

Knowles, Dorothy. *French drama of the inter-war years, 1918-39,* pp. 183-184, 187.

Mankin, Paul. "The Humor of Marcel Achard." *Yale French Studies,* no. 23 (Summer, 1959), pp. 33-38.

Moore, Harry T. *Twentieth-century French literature since World War II,* pp. 28-29.

Pronko, Leonard C. "Sunshine and Substance: The Comic Theater of Achard, Anouilh, Ayme, Roussin." *Modern Drama,* vol. 2, no. 3 (Dec., 1959), pp. 243-251.

La Belle Marinière

Knowles, Dorothy. *French drama of the inter-war years, 1918-39,* pp. 184-185.

Le Corsaire

Bishop, Thomas. *Pirandello and the French theater,* pp. 86-88.

Knowles, Dorothy. *French drama of the inter-war years, 1918-39,* pp. 186-187.

Domino

Bishop, Thomas. *Pirandello and the French theater,* pp. 83-86.

Knowles, Dorothy. *French drama of the inter-war years, 1918-39,* p. 185.

La Femme en Blanc

Knowles, Dorothy. *French drama of the inter-war years, 1918-39,* pp. 185-186.

Jean de la Lune

Bishop, Thomas. *Pirandello and the French theater,* pp. 82-83, 85.

ALFRED ADAM

La Fugue de Caroline

Bishop, Thomas. *Pirandello and the French theater,* pp. 140-142.

ARTHUR ADAMOV 1908-

General

Bishop, Thomas. *Pirandello and the French theater,* pp. 130-132.

Esslin, Martin. *The theatre of the absurd,* pp. 47-52, 76-78.

Fletcher, John. "Confrontations. II. Arnold Wesker, John Arden, and Arthur Adamov." *Caliban,* vol. 4 (1967), pp. 149-159.

Fowlie, Wallace. *Dionysus in Paris,* pp. 223-228.

Gelbard, Peter. "Peter Gelbard Interviews Arthur Adamov." *Drama Survey,* vol. 3, no. 2 (Oct., 1963), pp. 253-256.

Grossvogel, David I. *The self-conscious stage in modern French drama,* pp. 318-324.

Guicharnaud, Jacques. *Modern French theatre from Giraudoux to Genet* (rev. ed.), pp. 49, 180, 184, 196-205, 212, 282, 283, 286-288, 290, 319, 321, 347-348, 363-364.

Kuhn, Reinhard. "The Debasement of the Intellectual in Contemporary Continental Drama." *Modern Drama,* vol. 7, no. 4 (February, 1965). pp. 454-462.

Lennon, Peter. "An Interview with Adamov." Plays and *Players,* vol. 7, no. 6 (March, 1960), p. 9.

Lumley, Frederick. *New trends in 20th century drama,* pp. 216-217.

Lynes, Carlos, Jr. "Adamov or 'le sens litteral' in the theatre." *Yale French Studies,* No. 14 (Winter 1954-55), pp. 48-56.

Moore, Harry T. *Twentieth-century French literature since World War II,* pp. 161-164.

Pronko, Leonard C. *Avant-garde: the experimental theater in France,* pp. 131-140.

Wardle, Irving. "Adamov in England." *Encore,* vol. 6, no. 4 (Sept.-Oct., 1959), pp. 20-22.

Wellwarth, George. *The theatre of protest and paradox,* pp. 27-36.

All Against All (Tous Contre Tous)

Wellwarth, George. *The theatre of protest and paradox,* pp. 29-31.

As We Were (Comme Nous Avons Été)

Esslin, Martin. *The theatre of the absurd,* pp. 64-65.

The Direction of the March (The Meaning of the Way) (Le Sens de la Marche)

Esslin, Martin. *The theatre of the absurd,* pp. 59-60.

Wellwarth, George. *The theatre of protest and paradox,* pp. 27-28.

En Fiacre

Esslin, Martin. *The theatre of the absurd,* p. 75.

The Great and the Small Maneuver (La Grande et la Petite Manoeuvre)

Esslin, Martin. *The theatre of the absurd,* pp. 57-59.

Hatzfeld, Helmut. *Trends and styles in twentieth century French literature,* pp. 275-276.

Wellwarth, George. *The theatre of protest and paradox,* pp. 33-34.

The Invasion (L'Invasion)

Esslin, Martin. *The theatre of the absurd,* pp. 54-57.

Hatzfeld, Helmut. *Trends and styles in twentieth century French literature,* p. 275.

Pronko, Leonard C. *Avant-garde: the experimental theater in France,* pp. 136-139.

Sherrell, Richard E. "Arthur Adamov and Invaded Man." *Modern Drama,* vol. 7 (Feb., 1965), pp. 399-404.

Wellwarth, George. *The theatre of protest and paradox,* pp. 32-33.

Paolo Paoli

Esslin, Martin. *The theatre of the absurd,* pp. 69-74.

Gellert, Roger. "Sickness or Health." *New Statesman,* vol. 64 (Aug. 31, 1962), p. 265.

Hatzfeld, Helmut. *Trends and styles in twentieth century French literature,* pp. 276-277.

Rodger, Ian. "Ironic Dalliance," *Listener,* vol. 60, no. 1537 (Sept. 11, 1958), pp. 394-395.

Styan, J.L. *The dark comedy,* 2nd ed., p. 240.

Wellwarth, George. *The theatre of protest and paradox,* pp. 29, 31-32.

The Parody (Le Parodie)

Esslin, Martin. *The theatre of the absurd,* pp. 52-54.

Fowlie, Wallace. *Dionysus in Paris,* pp. 223-224.

Hatzfeld, Helmut. *Trends and styles in twentieth century French literature,* pp. 274-275.

Pronko, Leonard C. *Avant-garde: the experimental theater in France,* pp. 132-136.

Wellwarth, George. *The theatre of protest and paradox,* p. 32.

Ping Pong (Le Ping-Pong)

Bermel, Albert. "Adamov In New York...and Out Again." *Tulane Drama Rev.,* vol. 4, no. 1 (Sept., 1959), pp. 104-107.

Esslin, Martin. *The theatre of the absurd,* pp. 65-69.

Hatzfeld, Helmut. *Trends and styles in twentieth century French literature,* p. 276.

Styan, J.L. *The dark comedy,* 2nd ed., p. 240.

Wellwarth, George. *The theatre of protest and paradox,* pp. 35-36.

Printemps 71

Gelbard, Peter. *Drama Survey,* vol. 3, no. 2 (Oct., 1963), pp. 289-290.

Le Professeur Taranne

Esslin, Martin. *The theatre of the absurd,* pp. 60-63.

Fowlie, Wallace. *Dionysus in Paris,* pp. 225-226.

The Recoveries (Les Retrouvailles)

Esslin, Martin. *The theatre of the absurd,* pp. 64-65.

Wellwarth, George. *The theatre of protest and paradox,* p. 27.

ALEXANDER NIKOLAEVICH AFINOGENOV
1904-1941

General

Dana, H.W.L. "Afinogenov: Soviet Hero Playwright." *Theatre Arts,* vol. 26 (1942), pp. 168-176.

Fear (Strakh)

Block, Anita. *The changing world in plays and theatre,* pp. 390-397.

On the Eve

Macleod, Joseph. *Actors cross the Volga,* pp. 143, 157, 159, 184, 240.

DEMETRIO AGUILERA MALTA 1909-

General

Jones, W.K. *Behind Spanish American footlights,* pp. 312-314.

ISADORA AGUIRRE 1919-

General

Jones, W.K. *Behind Spanish American footlights,* pp. 236-237.

CONRAD POTTER AIKEN 1889-

Mr. Arcularis

Voaden, Herman, ed. *Human values in the drama,* pp. ix-x, xiv, 2-5, 88-92.

EDWARD ALBEE 1928-

General

Albee, Edward. (Interview with Michael Nardacci and Walter Chura). *In:* Wager, Walter, ed. *The playwrights speak,* pp. 36-44, 45-52, 54-65, 66-67.

"Albee." *New Yorker,* vol. 37 (March 25, 1961), pp. 30-32.

"Albee Revisited." *New Yorker,* vol. 40 (Dec. 19, 1964), pp. 31-33.

Baxandall, Lee. "The Theater of Edward Albee." *In:* Kernan, Alvin B., ed., *The modern American theater,* pp. 80-98. Reprinted from *Tulane Drama Rev.,* vol. 9, no. 4 (Summer, 1965), pp. 19-40.

Blau, Herbert. *The impossible theatre,* pp. 39-42.

Booth, John E. "Albee and Schneider Observe: 'Something's Stirring.'" *Theatre Arts* (Mar., 1961), pp. 22-24.

Brustein, Robert. "The New American Playwrights." *In:* Rahv, Philip, ed. *Modern occasions,* pp. 124-127.

Cappalletti, John. "Are You Afraid of Edward Albee?" *Drama Critique,* vol. 6, no. 2 (Spring, 1963), pp. 84-88.

Chester, Alfred. "Edward Albee: Red Herrings and White Whales." *Commentary,* vol. 35 (1963), pp. 296-301.

Debusscher, Gilbert. *Edward Albee, tradition and renewal,* pp. 82-84.

Dias, Earl J. "Full-Scale Albee." *Drama Critique,* vol. 8, no. 3 (Fall, 1965), pp. 107-112.

Diehl, Digby. "Edward Albee Interviewed." *Transatlantic Rev., no.* 13 (Summer, 1963), pp. 57-72.

Downer, Alan S. "An Interview with Edward Albee." *In:* Downer, Alan S., ed. *The American theater today,* pp. 111-123.

Driver, Tom F. "What's the Matter with Edward Albee?" *In:* Kernan, Alvin B., ed. *The modern American theater,* pp. 99-103. Reprinted from *The Reporter* (Jan. 2, 1964).

Duprey, Richard A. "Today's Dramatist." *In: American theatre,* pp. 209, 212-216.

Evans, Arthur. "Love, History and Edward Albee." *Renascence,* vol. 19 (1967), pp. 115-118, 131.

Freedman, Morris. *The moral impulse,* pp. 122-124.

Fruchter, N. "Albee's Broadway Break-Thru." *Encore,* vol. 10 (Jan.-Feb., 1963), pp. 44-48.

Goodman, Henry. "The New Dramatists: 4. Edward Albee." *Drama Survey,* vol. 2 (June, 1962), pp. 72-79.

Goodman, Randolph. "Playwatching with a Third Eye." *Columbia University Forum,* vol. 10, no. 1 (1967), pp. 18-22.

Gould, Jean. *Modern American playwrights,* pp. 273-286.

Harris, Wendell V. "Morality, Absurdity, and Albee." *Southwest Rev.,* vol. 49, no. 3 (Summer, 1964), pp. 249-256.

Hurley, Paul J. "France and America: Versions of the Absurd." *College English,* vol. 26 (1965), pp. 634-640.

Knepler, Henry. "Edward Albee: Conflict of Tradition." *Modern Drama,* vol. 10, no. 3 (Dec., 1967), pp. 274-279.

Kostelanetz, Richard. "The New American Theatre." *In:* Kostelanetz, Richard, *The new American arts,* pp. 52-62.

Lewis, Allan. "The Fun and Games of Edward Albee." *Educational Theatre J.,* vol. 16 (1964), pp. 29-39.

Lumley, Frederick. *New trends in 20th century drama,* pp. 319-324.

Nelson, Gerald. "Edward Albee and His Well-Made Plays." *Tri-Quarterly* (Evanston, Ill.), no. 5 (1966), pp. 182-188.

Oberg, Arthur K. "Edward Albee: His Language and Imagination." *Prairie Schooner,* vol. 40, no. 2 (Summer, 1966), pp. 139-146.

Paris Review. *Writers at work; The Paris Review interviews. Third series,* pp. 321-346.

Phillips, Elizabeth C. "Albee and the Theatre of the Absurd." *Tennessee Studies in Literature,* vol. 10 (1965), pp. 73-80.

Phillips, Elizabeth C. *Modern American drama,* pp. 124-125.

Plotinsky, M.L. "Transformations of Understanding: Edward Albee in the Theatre of the Irresolute." *Drama Survey,* vol. 4 (Winter, 1965), pp. 220-232.

Rutenberg, Michael E. *Edward Albee: playwright in protest,* pp. 3-11, 229-260.

Samuels, Charles Thomas. "Theatre of Edward Albee." *Massachusetts Rev.,* vol. 6 (Autumn, 1964), pp. 187-201. Reply: Hill, C.P., vol. 6 (Spring, 1965), pp. 649-650.

Smith, Michael. "Edward Albee." *Plays and Players* (Mar., 1964), pp. 12-14.

Spencer, Sharon D. "Edward Albee: The Anger Artist." *Forum* (Houston), vol. 4, no. 12 (1967), pp. 25-30.

Tallmer, Jerry. "Hold that Tiger." *Evergreen Rev.,* vol. 5, no. 18 (May-June, 1961), pp. 109-113.

Wager, Walter. "Edward Albee." *In:* Wager, Walter, ed. *The playwrights speak,* pp. 25-36.

Wellwarth, George E. "Hope Deferred: The New American Drama." *Literary Rev.,* vol. 7 (Autumn, 1963), pp. 7-15.

Wellwarth, George E. *Theater of protest and paradox,* pp. 275-284.

Wolfe, Peter. "The Social Theater of Edward Albee." *Prairie Schooner,* vol. 39 (Fall, 1965), pp. 248-262.

The American Dream

Balliett, Whitney. "Three Cheers for Albee." *New Yorker,* vol. 36 (Feb. 4, 1961), pp. 62-66.

Bigsby, C.W.E. *Confrontation and commitment,* pp. xvii, 71, 75-79, 90.

Brustein, Robert. "Fragments from a Cultural Explosion." *New Republic,* vol. 144 (Mar. 27, 1961), pp. 29-30.

Brustein, Robert. *Seasons of discontent,* pp. 46-48.

Clurman, Harold. *The naked image,* pp. 15-16.

Clurman, Harold. "Theatre." *Nation,* vol. 192 (Feb. 11, 1961), pp. 125-126.

Debusscher, Gilbert. *Edward Albee, tradition and renewal,* pp. 35-46.

Gardner, R.H. *The splintered stage; the decline of the American theater,* pp. 146-147.

Hamilton, Kenneth "Mr. Albee's Dream." *Queens Q.,* vol. 70 (Autumn, 1963), pp. 393-399.

Hewes, Henry. "On Our Bad Behavior." *Saturday Rev.,* vol. 44 (Feb. 11, 1961), p. 54.

Lewis, Allan. *American plays and playwrights of the contemporary theatre,* pp. 86-88.

Lewis, Theophilus. *"The Zoo Story* and *The American Dream." America,* vol. 108 (June 22, 1963), pp. 891-892.

Lukas, Mary. *"The Death of Bessie Smith* and *The American Dream." Catholic World,* vol. 193 (Aug., 1961), pp. 335-336.

Lumley, Frederick. *New trends in 20th century drama,* pp. 320-321.

Reinert, Otto, ed. *Drama; an introductory anthology* (alternate ed.), pp. 866-871.

Rutenberg, Michael E. *Edward Albee: playwright in protest,* pp. 61-76.

Samuels, Charles T. "The Theatre of Edward Albee." *Massachusetts Rev.,* vol. 6 (Autumn-Winter, 1964-65), pp. 191-193.

Way, Brian. "Albee and the Absurd: *The American Dream* and *The Zoo Story." In: American theatre,* pp. 194-195, 197-201, 204-207.

Wellwarth, George. *The theatre of protest and paradox,* pp. 278-282, 289.

Box-Mao-Box

Kerr, Walter. "Mao—But What Message?" *The New York Times,* March 17, 1968, Sec. 2, pp. D-1, D-3.

Rutenberg, Michael E. *Edward Albee: playwright in protest,* pp. 201-226.

The Death of Bessie Smith

Balliett, Whitney. "Empress of the Blues." *New Yorker,* vol. 37 (Mar. 11, 1961), p. 114.

Brustein, Robert. "Fragments from a Cultural Explosion." *New Republic,* vol. 144 (Mar. 27, 1961), pp. 29-30.

Brustein, Robert. *Seasons of discontent,* pp. 46-48.

Clurman, Harold. *The naked image,* pp. 17-18.

Clurman, Harold. "Theatre." *Nation,* vol. 192 (Mar. 18, 1961), p. 242.

Daniel, Walter C. "Absurdity in *The Death of Bessie Smith." College Language Assoc. J.,* vol. 8, no. 1 (Sept., 1964), pp. 76-80.

Debusscher, Gilbert. *Edward Albee, tradition and renewal,* pp. 21-30.

Grande, Luke M. "Edward Albee's *Bessie Smith:* Alienation, The Color-Problem." *Drama Critique,* vol. 5 (1962), pp. 66-69.

Lukas, Mary. *"The Death of Bessie Smith* and *The American Dream.' Catholic World,* vol. 193 (Aug., 1961), pp. 335-336.

Rutenberg, Michael E. *Edward Albee: playwright in protest,* pp. 79-92.

Samuels, Charles T. "The Theatre of Edward Albee." *Massachusetts Rev.,* vol. 6 (Autum-Winter, 1964-65), pp. 189-190.

Wellwarth, George. *The theatre of protest and paradox,* p. 278.

Witherington, Paul. "Language of Movement in Albee's *The Death of Bessie Smith." Twentieth Century Literature,* vol. 13 (1967), pp. 84-88.

A Delicate Balance

Bigsby, C.W.E. *Confrontation and commitment,* pp. 71, 91-92.

Gassner, John. "Broadway in Review." *Educational Theatre J.,* vol. 18, no. 4 (Dec., 1966), pp. 450-452.

Gottfried, Martin. *A theater divided; the postwar American stage,* pp. 272-274.

Rutenberg, Michael E. *Edward Albee: playwright in protest,* pp. 137-164.

Everything in the Garden (Adapted from a play by Giles Cooper)

Rutenberg, Michael E. *Edward Albee: playwright in protest,* pp. 185-198.

?am and Yam

Rutenberg, Michael E. *Edward Albee: playwright in protest,* pp. 51-57.

Malcolm

Bigsby, C.W.E. *Confrontation and commitment,* pp. 90-91, 92, 93.

Brustein, Robert. "Albee's Allegory of Innocence." *New Republic,* vol. 154 (Jan. 29, 1966), pp. 34, 36-37.

Debusscher, Gilbert. *Edward Albee, tradition and renewal,* pp. 66-70.

McCarten, John. "Innocent Astray." *New Yorker,* vol. 41 (Jan. 22, 1966), p. 74.

Rutenberg, Michael E. *Edward Albee: playwright in protest,* pp. 179-185.

Quotations from Chairman Mao Tse-tung

Rutenberg, Michael E. *Edward Albee: playwright in protest,* pp. 207-226.

The Sandbox

Cubeta, Paul M. *Modern drama for analysis,* pp. 598-604.

Debusscher, Gilbert. *Edward Albee, tradition and renewal,* pp. 30-35.

Rutenberg, Michael E. *Edward Albee: playwright in protest,* pp. 41-48.

Wellwarth, George. *The theatre of protest and paradox,* p. 278.

Tiny Alice

Albee, Edward. (Interview with Michael Nardacci and Walter Chura). *In:* Wager, Walter, ed. *The playwrights speak,* pp. 34-35, 37, 41-42, 44-45, 54, 61, 63.

Ballew, Leighton M. "Who's Afraid of *Tiny Alice?*" *Georgia Rev.,* vol. 20 (1966), pp. 292-299.

Bigsby, C.W.E. *Confrontation and commitment,* pp. 10, 18, 68, 71, 87-90, 92, 96, 99, 167.

Bigsby, C.W.E. "Curiouser and Curiouser: A Study of Edward Albee's *Tiny Alice.*" *Modern Drama,* vol. 10, no. 3 (Dec., 1967), pp. 258-266.

Brustein, Robert. *Seasons of discontent,* pp. 307-311.

Brustein, Robert. "Three Plays and a Protest." *New Republic,* vol. 152 (Jan. 23, 1965), pp. 33-34.

Cavenough, Arthur. *"Tiny Alice." Sign,* vol. 44 (March, 1965), p. 27.
Clurman, Harold. *The naked image,* pp. 21-24.

Clurman, Harold. *"Tiny Alice; Hughie." Nation,* vol. 200 (Jan. 18, 1965), p. 65.

Davison, Richard Alan. "Edward Albee's *Tiny Alice:* A Note of Re-examination." *Modern Drama,* vol. 11, no. 1 (May, 1968), pp. 54-60.

Debusscher, Gilbert. *Edward Albee, tradition and renewal,* pp. 71-81.

Dukore, Bernard F. "Tiny Albee." *Drama Survey,* vol. 5, no. 1 (Spring, 1966), pp. 60-66.

Finkelstein, Sidney. *Existentialism and alienation in American literature,* pp. 241-242.

Franzblau, Abraham N. *"Psychiatrist Looks at Tiny Alice." Saturday Rev.,* vol. 48 (Jan. 30, 1965), p. 39.

Gielgud, John, and Edward Albee. "Talk About the Theater." *Atlantic Monthly,* vol. 215 (April 1965), pp. 61-65.

Gottfried, Martin. *A theater divided; the postwar American stage,* pp. 268-271.

Hewes, Henry. "Through the Looking Glass Darkly." *Saturday Rev.,* vol. 48 (Jan. 16, 1965), p. 40.

Hewes, Henry. "The *Tiny Alice* Caper." *Saturday Rev.,* vol. 48 (Jan. 30, 1965), pp. 38-39, 65. Reply: Lipton, Edward, vol. 48 (Feb. 20, 1965), p. 21.

Hewes, Henry. "Upon Your Imaginary Forces, ACT!" *Saturday Rev.,* vol. 48 (Sept. 4, 1965), p. 43.

Lucey, William F. "Albee's *Tiny Alice:* Truth and Appearance." *Renascence,* vol. 21, no. 2 (Winter, 1969), pp. 76-80, 110.

Lumley, Frederick. *New trends in 20th century drama,* pp. 322-323, 324.

McCarten, John. "Mystical Manipulations." *New Yorker,* vol. 40 (Jan. 9, 1965), p. 84.

Markson, John W. *"Tiny Alice:* Edward Albee's Negative Oedipal Enigma." *American Imago,* vol. 23 (1966), pp. 3-21.

Markus, Thomas B. *"Tiny Alice* and Tragic Catharsis." *Educational Theatre J.,* vol. 17 (1965), pp. 225-233.

Rogoff, Gordon. "The Trouble with *Alice.*" *Reporter,* vol. 32 (Jan. 28, 1965), pp. 53-54.

Rutenberg, Michael E. *Edward Albee: playwright in protest,* pp. 119-134.

Terrien, Samuel. "Albee's Alice." *Christianity and Crisis,* vol. 25 (June 28, 1965), pp. 140-143.

Ulanov, Barry. *"Luv* and *Tiny Alice." Catholic World,* vol. 200 (Mar., 1965), pp. 383-384.

Valgemae, Mardi. "Albee's Great God *Alice." Modern Drama,* vol. 10, no. 3 (Dec., 1967), pp. 267-273.

⁄ho's Afraid of Virginia Woolf?

Albee, Edward. (Interview with Michael Nardacci and Walter Chura). *In:* Wager, Walter, ed. *The playwrights speak,* pp. 49, 53-54, 61, 65-66.

Bigsby, C.W.E. *Confrontation and commitment,* pp. xvi, 43-44, 56, 68, 71, 79-87, 91, 92, 152, 167.

Brustein, Robert. *Seasons of discontent,* pp. 145-148.

Chester, Alfred. "Red Herrings and White Whales." *Commentary,* vol. 35 (April, 1963), pp. 296-301.

Chiari, Joseph. *Landmarks of contemporary drama,* pp. 157-160.

Chiaromonte, Nicolo. *"Who's Afraid of Virginia Woolf?" New York Rev. of Books,* vol. 1, no. 1 (Special Issue) (1963), p. 16.

Clurman, Harold. *The naked image,* pp. 18-21.

Clurman, Harold. "Theatre." *Nation,* vol. 195 (Oct. 27, 1962), pp. 273-274.

Coleman, D.C. "Fun and Games: Two Pictures of Heartbreak House." *Drama Survey,* vol. 5, no. 3 (Winter, 1966-67), pp. 223-236.

Debusscher, Gilbert. *Edward Albee, tradition and renewal,* pp. 47-58.

Dozier, Richard. "Adultery and Disappointment in *Who's Afraid of Virginia Woolf?" Modern Drama,* vol. 11, no. 4 (Feb., 1969), pp. 432-436.

Dukore, Bernard F. "A Warp in Albee's *Woolf." Southern Speech Journal,* vol. 30, no. 2 (Winter, 1964), pp. 261-268.

Duprey, Richard A. *"Who's Afraid of Virginia Woolf?" Catholic World,* vol. 196 (Jan., 1963), pp. 263-264.

"Edward Albee on a Love-Hate Marriage." *Times,* Nov. 5, 1962, p. 14

Finkelstein, Sidney. *Existentialism and alienation in America literature,* pp. 234-239.

Flasch, Joy. "Games People Play in *Who's Afraid of Virginia Woolf? Modern Drama,* vol. 10, no. 3 (Dec., 1967), pp. 280-288.

Gardner, R.H. *The splintered stage; the decline of the America theater,* pp. 147-150, 151-153.

Gassner, John. *Educational Theatre J.,* vol. 15 (Mar., 1963), pp. 77-80

Gassner, John. *"Who's Afraid of Virginia Woolf?" Saturday Rev.,* vol 46 (June 29, 1963), pp. 39-40.

Gellert, Roger. "Sex-War Spectacular: *Who's Afraid of Virgini Woolf?" New Statesman,* vol. 67 (Feb. 14, 1964), p. 262.

Gilman, Richard. "Here We Go Round the Albee Bush." *Commonweal,* vol. 77 (Nov. 9, 1962), pp. 175-176.

Gottfried, Martin. *A theater divided; the postwar American stage* pp. 265-268.

Hankiss, Elemér. "Who's Afraid of Edward Albee?" *New Hungaria Q.,* vol. 5 (1964), pp. 168-174.

Hewes, Henry. "Who's Afraid of Big Bad Broadway?" *Saturday Rev.* vol. 45 (Oct. 27, 1962), p. 29.

Hilfer, Anthony C. "George and Martha: Sad, Sad, Sad." *In* Whitbread, Thomas B. ed. *Seven contemporary authors,* pp. 119-139

Hughes, C. "Edward Albee: Who's Afraid of What?" *Critic,* vol. 2 (March, 1963), pp. 16-19.

Irwin, Ray. "Who's Afraid of Virginia Woolf, Hunh?" *Atlantic,* vol 213 (Apr., 1964), pp. 122, 124.

Kaplan, Donald M. "Homosexuality and American Theatre." *Tulan Drama Rev.,* vol. 9, no. 3 (Spring, 1965), pp. 34-35.

Kerr, Walter. *The theater in spite of itself,* pp 122-126.

Kerr, Walter. *Tragedy and comedy,* pp. 325-327.

Kostelanetz, Richard. "The New American Theatre." *In:* Kostelanetz Richard. *The new American arts,* pp. 55-59.

Lewis, Allan. *American plays and playwrights of the contemporar theatre,* pp. 88-95, 98.

Lewis, Theophilus. *"Who's Afraid of Virginia Woolf?" America,* vol. 107 (Nov. 17, 1962), pp. 1105-1106.

Lumley, Frederick. *New trends in 20th century drama,* pp. 321-322.

McCarten, John. "Long Night's Journey Into Daze." *New Yorker,* vol. 38 (Oct. 20, 1962), pp. 85-86.

McDonald, Daniel. "Truth and Illusion in *Who's Afraid of Virginia Woolf?" Renascence,* vol. 17, no. 2 (Winter, 1964), pp. 63-69.

Matthews, Honor. *The primal curse,* pp. 204-205.

Paul, Louis. "A Game Analysis of Albee's *Who's Afraid of Virginia Woolf:* The Core of Grief." *Literature and Psychology* (U. of Hartford), vol. 17 (1967), pp. 47-51.

Phillips, Elizabeth C. *Modern American drama,* p. 123.

Pryce-Jones, David. "The Rules of the Game: *Who's Afraid of Virginia Woolf?" Spectator,* vol. 212 (Feb. 14, 1964), pp. 213-214.

Roy, Emil. *"Who's Afraid of Virginia Woolf?* and the Tradition." *Bucknell Rev.,* vol. 13, no. 1 (Mar., 1965), pp. 27-36.

Rutenberg, Michael E. *Edward Albee: playwright in protest,* pp. 95-115.

Sainer, Arthur. *The sleepwalker and the assassin, a view of the contemporary theatre,* pp. 26-27.

Samuels, Charles T. "The Theatre of Edward Albee." *Massachusetts Rev.,* vol. 6 (Autumn-Winter, 1964-65), pp. 194-199.

Schechner, Richard. "Who's Afraid of Edward Albee?" *Tulane Drama Rev.,* vol. 7, no. 3 (1963), pp. 7-10.

Schneider, Alan. "Why So Afraid?" *Tulane Drama Rev.,* vol. 7, no. 3 (1963), pp. 10-13.

Simon, John. *Hudson Rev.,* vol. 15, no. 4 (Winter, 1962-63), pp. 571-573.

Styan, J.L. *The dark comedy,* 2nd ed., pp. 214, 216-217.

Taylor, Marion A. "Edward Albee and August Strindberg: Some Parallels between *The Dance of Death* and *Who's Afraid of Virginia Woolf?" Papers on English Language and Literature,* vol. 1, no. 1 (Winter, 1965), pp. 59-71.

Taylor, Marion A. "A Note on Strindberg's *The Dance of Death* and Edward Albee's *Who's Afraid of Virginia Woolf." Papers on English Language and Literature,* vol. 2, no. 2 (Spring, 1966), pp. 187-188.

15

Trilling, Diana. "The Riddle of Albee's *Who's Afraid of Virgini Woolf?" In:* Trilling, Diana. *Claremont essays,* pp. 203-227.

Tynan, Kenneth. *Tynan right and left,* pp. 135-136.

Wellwarth, George. *The theatre of protest and paradox,* pp. 282-284

"*Who's Afraid of Virginia Woolf?" Listener,* vol. 71 (Feb. 20, 1964), p 313.

"*Who's Afraid of Virginia Woolf?" Theatre Arts,* vol. 46 (Nov., 1962) p. 10.

The Zoo Story

Bigsby, C.W.E. *Confrontation and commitment,* pp. xvii, 10, 2C 71-75, 82, 84-85, 88, 91.

Brustein, Robert. *Seasons of discontent,* pp. 28-29.

Clurman, Harold. *The naked image,* pp. 14-15.

Cohn, Ruby, ed. *Twentieth century drama,* pp. 650-652.

Debusscher, Gilbert. *Edward Albee, tradition and renewal,* pp. 9-2C

Gardner, R.H. *The splintered stage; the decline of the America theater,* pp. 150-151.

Gottfried, Martin. *A theater divided; the postwar American stage,* pp 264-265.

Hewes, Henry. "Benchmanship." *Saturday Rev.,* vol. 43 (Feb. 6, 1960) p. 32.

Kostelanetz, Richard. "The New American Theatre." *In:* Kostelanet; Richard. *The new American arts,* pp. 50-55.

Levine, Mordecai H. "Albee's Liebestod." *College Languag Association Journal* (Morgan State College, Baltimore), vol. 10 (1967) pp. 252-255.

Lewis, Allan. American *plays and playwrights of the contemporar theatre,* pp. 82-84.

Lewis, Theophilus. "*The Zoo Story* and *The American Dream. America,* vol. 108 (June 22, 1963), pp. 891-892.

Lyons, Charles R. "Two Projections of the Isolation of the Huma Soul: Brecht's *Im Dickicht Der Staedte* and Albee's *The Zoo Story. Drama Survey,* vol. 4, no. 2 (Summer, 1965), pp. 131-137.

Macklin, Anthony. "The Flagrant Albatross." *College English,* vol. 28 (1966), pp. 58-59.

Malcolm, Donald, "And Moreover...." *New Yorker,* vol. 35 (Jan. 23, 1960), pp. 75-76.

Matthews, Honor. *The primal curse,* pp. 201-204.

Plotinsky, M.L. "The Transformations of Understanding: Edward Albee in the Theatre of the Irresolute." *Drama Survey,* vol. 4, no. 3 (Winter, 1965), pp. 220-232.

Rutenberg, Michael E., *Edward Albee: playwright in protest,* pp. 15-37.

Samuels, Charles T. "The Theatre of Edward Albee." *Massachusetts Rev.,* vol. 6 (Autumn-Winter, 1964-65), pp. 187-189.

Sheed, Wilfred. "Back to the Zoo." *Commonweal,* vol. 82 (July 9, 1965), pp. 501-502.

Spielberg, Peter. "The Albatross in Albee's Zoo." *College English,* vol. 27 (1966), pp. 562-565.

Spielberg, Peter. "Reply: The Albatross Strikes Again!" *College English,* vol. 28 (1966), p. 59.

Way, Brian. "Albee and the Absurd: *The American Dream* and *The Zoo Story.*" *In:* Brown, J.R., and B. Harris, eds. *American theatre,* pp. 188-207.

Wellwarth, George. *The theatre of protest and paradox,* pp. 88n, 275-278, 280.

Zimbardo, Rose A. "Symbolism of Naturalism in Edward Albee's *The Zoo Story.*" *Twentieth Century Literature,* vol. 8, no. 1 (Apr., 1962), pp. 10-17.

RAFAEL ALBERTI 1902-

Night and War in the Prado Museum

Benedikt, M., and G. Wellwarth, eds. *Modern Spanish theatre: an anthology,* pp. 196-197.

WILLIAM ALFRED, 1923-

Hogan's Goat

Downer, Alan S. "Total Theatre and Partial Drama: Notes on the New York Theatre, 1965-66." *Q. J. of Speech,* vol. 52, no. 3 (Oct., 1966), p. 234.

Flaherty, Daniel L. *"Hogan's Goat." America,* vol. 114, no. 12 (March 19, 1966), pp. 378-381.

Gassner, John. "Broadway in Review." *Educational Theatre J.,* vol. 18 no. 1 (Mar., 1966), p. 65.

HUGHES ALLISON

The Trial

Abramson, Doris E. *Negro playwrights in the American theatre, 1925-1959,* pp. 63-65.

ARTURO ALSINA 1897-

General

Jones, W.K. *Behind Spanish American footlights,* pp. 38-39.

ANTONIO ALVAREZ LLERAS 1892-1956

General

Jones, W.K. *Behind Spanish American footlights,* pp. 328-330.

Lyday, Leon F. "The Dramatic Art of Antonio Alvarez Lleras." *Dissertation Abstracts,* vol. 27 (1967), 2534A (N.C.).

JOAQUIN ALVAREZ QUINTERO 1873-1944

General

Chandler, F.W. *Modern continental playwrights,* pp. 487-502.

SAMUEL ALYOSHIN

Alone (Odna)

Revutsky, V. "A New View of Don Juan: Samuel Alyoshin's Comedy *At That Time in Seville." Slavonic and East European Review,* vol. 44 (1966), p. 88.

At That Time in Seville (Togda v Sevil'ye, 1947; new version, 1960)

Revutsky, Valerian. "A New View of Don Juan: Samuel Alyoshin's Comedy *At That Time in Seville." Slavonic and East European Review,* vol. 44 (1966), pp. 88-97.

DENYS AMIEL 1884-

afé-Tabac

Daniels, May. *The French drama of the unspoken,* pp. 153-156.

e Couple

Daniels, May. *The French drama of the unspoken,* pp. 161-163.

a Femme en Fleur

Daniels, May. *The French drama of the unspoken,* pp. 164-168.

a Souriante Madame Beudet (co-author, André Obey)

Daniels, May. *The French drama of the unspoken,* pp. 156-158.

e Voyageur

Daniels, May. *The French drama of the unspoken,* pp. 145-153, 170-171.

Ir. & Mrs. So-and-So (Monsieur et Madame Un Tel)

Block, Anita. *The changing world in plays and theatre,* pp. 95-97.

Daniels, May. *The French drama of the unspoken,* pp. 159-161.

GARLAND ANDERSON

ppearances

Abramson, Doris E. *Negro playwrights in the American theatre, 1925-1959,* pp. 27-32, 39-40.

MAXWELL ANDERSON 1888-

eneral

Anderson, Maxwell. "The Essence of Tragedy." *In:* Oppenheimer, George, ed. *The passionate playgoer,* pp. 259-267 (reprinted from Anderson's *Off Broadway,* N.Y., Sloanc, 1939). *Also in:* Cassell, Richard A. *What is the play?* pp. 663-669.

Anderson, Maxwell, "Religion and the Theatre." *In:* Richards, Dick. *The curtain rises,* pp. 59-63.

Artz, Lloyd Charles. "An Aristotelian critique of Maxwell Anderson's dramas." M.A., University of Illinois, 1946.

Atkinson, Brooks. *Broadway scrapbook,* pp. 251-254.

Avery, Laurence G. "Maxwell Anderson: A Changing Attitude Toward Love." *Modern Drama,* vol. 10, no. 3 (Dec., 1967), pp 241-248.

Bailey, Mabel D. "Maxwell Anderson, the playwright as prophet." Ph.D., University of Iowa, 1955.

Bartlett, Patricia A. "The use of history in the plays of Maxwell Anderson." M.A., University of Idaho, 1957.

Blanchard, Fred C. "The place of Maxwell Anderson in the American theatre." Ph.D., New York University, 1939.

Block, Anita. *The changing world in plays and theatre,* pp. 230-244 306-310.

Brown, John Mason. *As they appear,* pp. 199-206.

Brown, John Mason. *Broadway in review,* pp. 67-81.

Brown, John Mason. *Still seeing things,* pp. 185-195, 207-213, 227-232.

Brown, John Mason. *Two on the aisle,* pp. 148-159, 208-211.

Buchanan, Randall John. "Maxwell Anderson's rules of playwriting and their application to his plays." *Dissertation Abstracts,* vol. 25 (1964), 3163-64. (Louisiana State Univ.)

Carmer, Carl. "Maxwell Anderson, Poet and Champion." *Theatre Arts,* vol. 17, no. 6 (June, 1933), pp. 431-436.

Childs, Herbert E. "Playgoer's Playwright, Maxwell Anderson." *English J.,* vol. 27, no. 6 (June, 1938), pp. 475-485.

Clark, Barrett H. *An hour of American drama,* pp. 89-95.

Clurman, H. *Lies like truth,* pp. 33-35.

Covington, W.P. "A Maxwell Anderson bibliography with annotations." M.A., University of North Carolina, 1950.

Cox, Martha H. "Maxwell Anderson and his critics." Ph.D., University of Arkansas, 1955.

Downer, Alan S. *Fifty years of American drama, 1900-1950,* pp. 105-110.

Dusenbury, Winifred L. "Myth in American Drama between the Wars." *Modern Drama,* vol. 6, no. 3 (Dec., 1963), pp. 294-308.

Flexner, Eleanor. *American playwrights 1918-1938,* pp. 78-129.

Foote, Ronald Crighton. "The verse dramas of Maxwell Anderson in the modern theatre." *Dissertation Abstracts,* vol. 16 (1956), 1452. (Tulane)

Foster, Edward. "Core of Belief; An Interpretation of the Plays of Maxwell Anderson." *Sewanee Rev.,* vol. 50, no. 1 (Jan.-March., 1942), pp. 87-100.

Frenz, Horst. "The contributions of Maxwell Anderson to the American drama." M.A., University of Illinois, 1939.

Gagey, Edmond M. *Revolution in American drama,* pp. 71-119.

Gassner, John W. "Poetry in the Contemporary Theatre." *One-Act Play Mag.,* vol. 1 (1937), pp. 466-470.

Gassner, John W "Prospectus on Playwrights." *Theatre Arts,* vol. 38, no. 11 (Nov., 1954), pp. 32, 93.

Gassner, John W. "The Theatre at the Crossroads." *One-Act Play Mag.,* vol. 1 (1937), pp. 273-275.

Gassner, John. *The theatre in our times,* pp. 233-239.

Geiger, Louis G. and Ashton, J.R. "UND in the Era of Maxwell Anderson." *North Dakota Q.,* vol. 25 (1957), pp. 55-60.

Gerstenberger, Donna. "Verse Drama in America: 1916-1939." *Modern Drama,* vol. 6, no. 3 (Dec., 1963), pp. 309-322.

Gerstenberger, Donna. "Verse Drama in America." *In:* Meserve, Walter J., ed. *Discussions of American drama, pp.* 40-43.

Gilbert, Vedder M. "The Career of Maxwell Anderson." Michigan Academy of Science, Arts, and Letters. *Papers,* vol. 44 (1959), pp. 386-394.

Gilbert, Vedder M. "Maxwell Anderson. His interpretation of tragedy in six poetical dramas." M.A., Cornell University, 1938.

Goldberg, Isaac. "The Later Maxwell Anderson." *One-Act Play Magazine,* vol. 1 (1937), pp. 89-90.

Goldstein, Malcolm. "Playwrights of the 1930's." *In:* Downer, Alan S., ed. *The American theatre today,* pp. 26-27.

Gould, Jean. *Modern American playwrights,* pp. 118-134.

Halline, Allan G. "Maxwell Anderson's Dramatic Theory." *American Literature,* vol. 16 (1944-45), pp. 63-81.

Harris, Ainslie. "Maxwell Anderson." *Madison Q.,* vol. 4 (1944), pp. 30-44.

Harris, Kenneth E. "Maxwell Anderson's critical theories and their application to his verse dramas." M.A., University of Pittsburgh, 1948

Hatcher, Harlan. "Drama in Verse: Anderson, Eliot, MacLeish. *English J.,* vol. 25, no. 1 (Jan., 1936), pp. 1-9.

Isaacs, Edith J.R. "Maxwell Anderson." *English J.,* vol. 25, no. 1 (Dec., 1936), pp. 795-804.

Isaacs, Edith J.R. "Range of Life in One Man's Plays." *Theatre Arts,* vol. 18 (1934), pp. 601-606.

Knepler, Henry W. "Maxwell Anderson: A Historical Parallel. *Queen's Q.,* vol. 64 (1957), pp. 250-263.

Krutch, Joseph Wood. *American drama since 1918,* pp. 286-318.

Krutch, Joseph Wood. *"Modernism" in modern drama,* pp. 117-124

Lee, Henry G. "Maxwell Anderson's Impact on the Theatre." *North Dakota Q.,* vol. 25 (1957), pp. 49-52.

McNiven, Kathleen E. "Idealism in the plays of Maxwell Anderson." M.A., Cornell, 1943.

Maloney, Martin J. "Maxwell Anderson's debt to Shakespeare." M.A., University of Kansas, 1938.

Mantle, Burns. *American playwrights today,* pp. 65-72.

Mantle, Burns. *Contemporary American playwrights,* pp. 37-46.

Mersand, J. *American drama: 1930-1940,* pp. 118-127.

Miller, Jordan Y. "Maxwell Anderson: Gifted Technician." *In:* French, Warren, ed. *The thirties: fiction, poetry, drama,* pp. 183-192.

Mitchell, Albert Orton. "A study of irony in the plays of Maxwell Anderson." Ph.D., University of Wisconsin, 1940.

Mordoff, Helen Lee. "Dramatic theories of Maxwell Anderson." M.A., Cornell University, 1942.

Morton, Frederick. "Playwright's Craft." *Theatre Arts,* vol. 23, no. 8 (Aug., 1939), pp. 612-613.

Nardin, James T. "Maxwell Anderson: A critical estimate." M.A., Leigh, 1947.

O'Hara, Frank H. *Today in American drama,* pp. 1-52.

Prior, Moody E. *The language of tragedy,* pp. 317-326.

Anderson

Rabkin, Gerald. *Drama and commitment,* pp. 263-288.

Reveaux, Edward C. "A study of contemporary verse drama with especial emphasis on Maxwell Anderson." M.A., University of Arizona, 1938.

Rice, Patrick J. "Maxwell Anderson and the Eternal Dream." *Catholic World,* vol. 177 (Aug., 1953), pp. 364-370.

Rice, Patrick J. "Maxwell Anderson and tragic drama." M.A., Loyola, 1950.

Rice, Robert. "Maxwell Anderson: A Character Study of the Most Talked of Playwright in America." *PM's Sunday Picture News,* III (November 29, 1942), pp. 23-27.

Riepe, Dale. "The Philosophy of Maxwell Anderson." *North Dakota Q.,* vol. 24 (Spring, 1956), pp. 45-50.

Rodell, John S. "Maxwell Anderson: A Criticism." *Kenyon Rev., vol.* 5, no. 2 (Spring, 1943), pp. 272-277.

Rosenberg, Harold. "Poetry and the Theatre." *Poetry,* vol. 57, no. 4 (Jan., 1941), pp. 258-263.

Sampley, Arthur M. "Theory and Practice in Maxwell Anderson's Poetic Tragedies." *College English,* vol. 5 (May, 1944), pp. 412-418.

Sanders, Melba Frances. "Maxwell Anderson and his dramas." M.A., University of Southern California, 1941.

Sandoe, James L. "The Case for Maxwell Anderson." *Colorado Coll. Pubn.,* vol. 30 (April 1, 1940), pp. 73-82.

Seabury, Lorna G. "The use of imagery in the plays of Maxwell Anderson." M.A., University of Wisconsin, 1937.

Seabury, Lorna G. "The use of imagery in the plays of Maxwell Anderson." Ph.D., Columbia University, 1938.

Sherwood, Robert F.. *"White Desert* to *Bad Seed." Theatre Arts,* vol. 39 (March, 1955), pp. 28-29, 93.

Shields, James Christie. "Dramatic irony, an essential supplement to Maxwell Anderson's views on recognition in tragedy." M.A., University of Pittsburgh, 1951.

Sievers, W.D. *Freud on Broadway,* pp. 171-179.

Skinner, Richard D. *Our changing theatre,* pp. 69-73.

Stevenson, Philip. "Concerning M. Anderson: A Word About the Career and Thoughts of the War Dramatist." *The New York Times* January 9, 1944, Sec. 2, p. 1.

Stevenson, Philip. "Maxwell Anderson, Thursday's Child." *New Theatre,* vol. 3 (Sept., 1936), pp. 5-7, 25-27.

Thompson, Alan R. *The anatomy of drama,* pp. 383-386.

Wall, Vincent. "Maxwell Anderson: The Last Anarchist." *Sewanee Rev.,* vol. 49, no. 3 (July-Sept., 1941), pp. 339-369.

Watts, Harold H. "Maxwell Anderson: The Tragedy of Attrition." *College English,* vol. 4, no. 4 (Jan., 1943), pp. 220-230.

Wilson, Edmund. *Shores of light,* pp. 674-680.

Woodbridge, Homer E. "Maxwell Anderson." *South Atlantic Q.,* vol. 44, no. 1 (Jan., 1945), pp. 55-68.

Bibliography

Gilbert, Vedder M. "The Career of Maxwell Anderson: A Check List of Books and Articles." *Modern Drama,* vol. 2, no. 4 (1960), pp. 386-394.

Anne of the Thousand Days

Brown, John Mason. *Still seeing things,* pp. 207-213.

Nathan, George Jean. *Theatre book of the year, 1948-1949,* pp. 197-205.

Bad Seed (Adapted from a novel by William March)

Bailey, M.D. *Maxwell Anderson,* pp. 171-182.

Barefoot in Athens

Bailey, M.D. *Maxwell Anderson,* pp. 83-97.

Brown, J.M. *As they appear,* pp. 199-206.

Nathan, G.J. *Theatre in the fifties,* pp. 40-42.

Both Your Houses

Bailey, M.D. *Maxwell Anderson,* pp. 58-61.

Brown, John Mason. *Two on the aisle,* pp. 208-211.

Himelstein, Morgan Y. *Drama was a weapon, the left-wing theatre in New York 1929-1941,* pp. 129-130.

Rabkin, Gerald. *Drama and commitment,* pp. 270-272.

andle in the Wind

Bailey, M.D. *Maxwell Anderson,* pp. 114-118.

Himelstein, Morgan Y. *Drama was a weapon, the left-wing theatre in New York 1929-1941,* p. 151.

lizabeth the Queen

Bailey, M.D. *Maxwell Anderson,* pp. 45-54.

Flexner, Eleanor. *American playwrights: 1918-1938,* pp. 88-93.

Knepler, Henry W. "Maxwell Anderson: A Historical Parallel." *Queen's Q.,* vol. 64 (1957), pp. 250-263.

Miller, Jordan Y., "Maxwell Anderson: Gifted Technician." *In:* French, Warren, ed. *The thirties: fiction, poetry, drama,* pp. 186-187.

Milstead, Marian M. "A study and presentation of character; Queen Elizabeth in Maxwell Anderson's play, *Elizabeth the Queen."* M.A., University of Wyoming, 1955.

Rabkin, G. *Drama and commitment,* pp. 274-276.

Watts, Harold H. "Maxwell Anderson: The Tragedy of Attrition." *College English,* vol. 4, no. 4 (Jan., 1943), pp. 220-230.

he Eve of St. Mark

Nathan, G.J. *Theatre book of the year, 1942-1943,* pp. 89-93.

Rodell, John S. "Maxwell Anderson: A Criticism." *Kenyon Rev.,* vol. 5, no. 2 (Spring, 1943), pp. 272-277.

"Social Drama." *Sociology & Social Research,* vol. 27 (Jan., 1943), p. 250.

east of Ortolans

Bailey, M.D. *Maxwell Anderson,* pp. 30-35.

Gods of the Lightning

Avery, Laurence G. "Maxwell Anderson: A Changing Attitude Toward Love." *Modern Drama,* vol. 10, no. 3 (Dec., 1967), pp. 241-248.

Block, Anita. *The changing world in plays and theatre,* pp. 230-239.

Flexner, Eleanor. *American playwrights: 1918-1938,* pp. 85-88.

Rabkin, Gerald. *Drama and commitment,* pp. 266-268.

Yeazell, Paul G. "Maxwell Anderson's treatment of historical material in *Gods of the Lightning* and *Winterset.*" M.A., Arizona, 1954.

Gypsy

Flexner, Eleanor. *American Playwrights: 1918-1938,* pp. 83-84.

Sievers, W. David. *Freud on Broadway,* pp. 173-174.

High Tor

Bailey, M.D. *Maxwell Anderson,* pp. 146-149.

Brown, John Mason. *Two on the aisle,* pp. 152-155.

Krutch, Joseph W. *The American drama since 1918,* pp. 301-305.

Miller, Jordan Y. "Maxwell Anderson: Gifted Technician." *In:* French, Warren, ed. *The thirties: fiction, poetry, drama,* p. 190.

Rabkin, Gerald. *Drama and commitment,* pp. 284-286.

Joan of Lorraine

Bailey, M.D. *Maxwell Anderson,* pp. 155-170.

Journey to Jerusalem

Watts, Harold H. "Maxwell Anderson: The Tragedy of Attrition." *College English,* vol. 4, no. 4 (Jan., 1943), pp. 220-230.

Key Largo

Bailey, M.D. *Maxwell Anderson,* pp. 106-114.

Brown, John Mason. *Broadway in review,* pp. 41-42, 67-71.

Miller, Jordan Y. "Maxwell Anderson: Gifted Technician." *In:* French, Warren, ed., *The thirties: fiction, poetry, drama,* p. 191.

Rabkin, Gerald. *Drama and commitment,* pp. 286-288.

Rodell, John S. "Maxwell Anderson: A Criticism." *Kenyon Rev.,* vol. 5, no. 2 (Spring, 1943), pp. 272-277.

Sievers, W. David. *Freud on Broadway,* pp. 177-178.

Watts, Harold H. "Maxwell Anderson: The Tragedy of Attrition." *College English,* vol. 4, no. 4 (Jan., 1943), pp. 220-230.

nickerbocker Holiday (Musical. Score by Kurt Weill)

Bailey, M.D. *Maxwell Anderson,* pp. 76-83.

Rabkin, Gerald. *Drama and commitment,* pp. 272-274.

st in the Stars (Musical. Score by Kurt Weill. Adapted from the novel Cry, the Beloved Country, by Alan Paton)

Bailey, M.D. *Maxwell Anderson,* pp. 182-193.

Brown, J.M. *Still seeing things,* pp. 227-232.

adonna and Child (Unpublished)

Avery, Laurence G. "Maxwell Anderson: A Changing Attitude Toward Love." *Modern Drama,* vol. 10, no. 3 (Dec., 1967), pp. 241-248.

ary of Scotland

Bailey, M.D. *Maxwell Anderson,* pp. 36-45.

Flexner, Eleanor. *American playwrights: 1918-1938,* pp. 93-97.

Gabriel, Gilbert W. "Maxwell Anderson's *Mary of Scotland.*" In: Moses, Montrose J. *The American theatre as seen by its critics, 1752-1934,* pp. 315-318. (Reprinted from *The New York American,* Nov. 28, 1933.)

Knepler, Henry W. "Maxwell Anderson: A Historical Parallel." *Queens Q.,* vol. 64 (1957), pp. 250-263.

Miller, Jordan Y. "Maxwell Anderson: Gifted Technician." *In:* French, Warren, ed., *The thirties: fiction, poetry, drama,* pp. 186-187.

Rabkin, G. *Drama and commitment,* pp. 274-276.

Watts, Harold H. "Maxwell Anderson: The Tragedy of Attrition." *College English,* vol. 4, no. 4 (Jan., 1943), pp. 220-230.

he Masque of Kings

Bailey, M.D. *Maxwell Anderson,* pp. 67-76.

Flexner, Eleanor. *American playwrights: 1918-1938,* pp. 120-125.

Himelstein, Morgan Y. *Drama was a weapon, the left-wing theatre in New York 1929-1941,* p. 140.

Rabkin G. *Drama and commitment,* pp. 279-281.

Night Over Taos

Avery, Laurence G. "The Conclusion of *Night Over Taos.*" *America* *Literature,* vol. 37 (Nov., 1965), pp. 318-321.

Bailey, M.D. *Maxwell Anderson,* pp. 128-131.

Miller, Jordan Y. "Maxwell Anderson: Gifted Technician." *In:* Frenc* Warren, ed. *The thirties: fiction, poetry, drama,* pp. 186-187.

Sievers, W. David. *Freud on Broadway,* pp. 174-175.

Weales, Gerald. "The Group Theatre and its Plays." *In: America* *theatre,* pp. 76-77, 83.

Outside Looking In (Adapted from Beggars of Life, by Jim Tul*

Bailey, M.D. *Maxwell Anderson,* pp. 124-126.

Saturday's Children

Bailey, M.D. *Maxwell Anderson,* pp. 126-128.

Flexner, Eleanor. *American playwrights: 1918-1938,* pp. 82-83.

Second Overture

Bailey, M.D. *Maxwell Anderson,* pp. 25-30.

Watts, Harold H. "Maxwell Anderson: The Tragedy of Attrition. *College English,* vol. 4, no. 4 (Jan., 1943), pp. 220-230.

The Star Wagon

Bailey, M.D. *Maxwell Anderson,* pp. 149-151.

Brown, John Mason. *Two on the aisle,* pp. 155-159.

McCarthy, M.T. *Sights and spectacles, 1937-1956,* pp. 3-8.

Storm Operation

Bailey, M.D. *Maxwell Anderson,* pp. 119-122.

Valley Forge

Bailey, M.D. *Maxwell Anderson,* pp. 61-67.

Flexner, Eleanor. *American playwrights: 1918-1938,* pp. 98-102.

Himelstein, Morgan Y. *Drama was a weapon, the left-wing theatre i* *New York 1929-1941,* p. 133.

Rabkin, Gerald. *Drama and commitment,* pp. 282-284.

Young, Stark. *Immortal shadows,* pp. 165-168.

Vhat Price Glory?

Bailey, M.D. *Maxwell Anderson,* pp. 98-102.

Block, Anita. *The changing world in plays and theatre,* pp. 306-310.

Krutch, Joseph W. *The American drama since 1918,* pp. 29-44.

Miller, Jordan Y. "Maxwell Anderson: Gifted Technician." *In:* French, Warren, ed. *The thirties: fiction, poetry, drama,* pp. 195-186.

The White Desert

Sievers, W. David. *Freud on Broadway,* pp. 171-172.

The Wingless Victory

Bailey, M.D. *Maxwell Anderson,* pp. 142-145.

Belli, Angela. "Lenormand's *Asie* and Anderson's *The Wingless Victory.*" *Comparative Literature,* vol. 19 (1967), pp. 226-239.

Conway, Anthony. *Spectator,* vol. 171 (Sept. 17, 1943), p. 263.

Flexner, Eleanor. *American playwrights: 1918-1938,* pp. 116-120.

MacCarthy, Desmond. "A Tragedy of Race." *New Statesman,* vol. 26 (Sept. 18, 1943), p. 184.

Young, Stark. *Immortal shadows,* pp. 185-187.

Winterset

Abernethy, Francis E. "*Winterset:* A Modern Revenge Tragedy." *Modern Drama,* vol. 7 (Sept., 1964), pp. 185-189.

Adler, Jacob H. "Shakespeare in *Winterset.*" *Educational Theatre J.,* vol. 6 (Oct., 1954), pp. 241-248.

Bailey, M.D. *Maxwell Anderson,* pp. 132-142.

Boyce, Benjamin. "Anderson's *Winterset.*" *Explicator,* vol. 2 (Feb., 1944), item 32.

Brown, John Mason. "Maxwell Anderson's *Winterset.*" *In:* Brown, John Mason. *Dramatis personae,* pp. 73-76.

Brown, John Mason. *Two on the aisle,* pp. 148-152.

Davenport, William H. *Explicator,* vol. 10 (Apr.-May, 1952), item 41.

Dusenbury, Winifred L. *The theme of loneliness in modern American drama*, pp. 119-125.

Fallon, Richard G. "The quest for tragedy by O'Neill and Anderson as evidenced by their plays *Beyond the Horizon* and *Winterset.*" M.A., Columbia University, 1952.

Flexner, Eleanor. American *playwrights: 1918-1938*, pp. 102-116.

Heilman, Robert B. *Tragedy and melodrama*, pp. 276-278.

Kliger, Samuel. "Hebraic Lore in Maxwell Anderson's *Winterset.*" *American Literature*, vol. 18, no. 3 (Nov., 1946), pp. 219-232.

Krutch, Joseph W. *The American drama since 1918*, pp. 295-301.

Krutch, Joseph Wood. *"Modernism" in modern drama*, pp. 120-122.

McCullen, J.T., Jr. "Two Quests for Truth: *King Oedipus* and *Winterset.*" *Laurel Rev.* (W. Va. Wesleyan College), vol. 5, no. 1 (1965), pp. 28-35.

McGee, Betty Ruth. "A production book for Maxwell Anderson's *Winterset.*" M.A., Stanford, 1948.

Miller, Jordan Y. "Maxwell Anderson: Gifted Technician." *In:* French, Warren, ed. *The thirties: fiction, poetry, drama*, pp. 188-190.

O'Hara, Frank H. *Today in American drama*, pp. 25-34, 150-152, 254-255.

Pearce, Howard D. "Job in Anderson's *Winterset.*" *Modern Drama*, vol. 6, no. 1 (May, 1963), pp. 32-41.

Phillips, Elizabeth C. *Modern American drama*, p. 105.

Prior, Moody E. *The language of tragedy*, pp. 320-325.

Rabkin, Gerald. *Drama and commitment*, pp. 268-270.

Roby, Robert C. "Two Worlds: Maxwell Anderson's *Winterset.*" *College English*, vol. 18, no. 4 (Jan., 1957), pp. 195-202.

Rodell, John S. "Maxwell Anderson: A Criticism." *Kenyon Rev.*, vol. 5, no. 2 (Spring, 1943), pp. 272-277.

Sievers, W. David. *Freud on Broadway*, pp. 175-176.

Watts, Harold H. "Maxwell Anderson: The Tragedy of Attrition." *College English*, vol. 4, no. 4 (Jan., 1943), pp. 220-230.

Yeazell, Paul G. "Maxwell Anderson's treatment of historical material in *Gods of the Lightning* and *Winterset.*" M.A., Arizona, 1954.

ROBERT ANDERSON 1917-

General

Lewis, Allan. *American plays and playwrights of the contemporary theater,* pp. 143-163.

ll Summer Long

Gassner, John. *Theatre at the crossroads,* pp. 288-293.

Never Sang for My Father

Clurman, Harold. "Theatre." *Nation,* vol. 206, no. 7 (Feb. 12, 1968), p. 221.

Loney, Glenn. "Broadway in Review." *Educational Theatre J.,* vol. 20, no. 2 (May, 1968), p. 235.

ea and Sympathy

Bentley, Eric. *The dramatic event,* pp. 150-153.

Gassner, J. *Theatre at the crossroads,* pp. 288-293.

Gottfried, Martin. *A theater divided; the postwar American stage,* pp. 246-247.

Sievers, W. David. *Freud on Broadway,* pp. 410-411.

Tynan, K. *Curtains,* p. 172.

Weales, Gerald. *American drama since World War II,* pp. 49-50, 51.

You Know I Can't Hear You When the Water's Running

Velde, Paul. "The Stage." *Commonweal,* vol. 86, no. 6 (Apr. 28, 1967), pp. 175-177.

JORGE ANDRADE

General

Sayers, Raymond. "Brazilian Literature: 1964." *Books Abroad,* vol. 39, no. 2 (Spring, 1965), p. 148.

LEONID NIKOLAEVICH ANDREYEV 1871-1919

General

Chandler, F.W. *Modern continental playwrights,* pp. 111-129.

Dahlstrom, Carl E.W.L. "Theomachy: Zola, Strindberg, Andreyev.' *Scandinavian Studies,* vol. 17, no. 4 (Nov., 1942), pp. 121-132.

Gassner, J.W. *Masters of the drama,* pp. 495-525.

Kaun, Alexander. *Leonid Andreyev.*

Kayden, E.M. "Work of Andreev." *Dial,* vol. 67 (Nov. 15, 1919), pp 425-428.

Seltzer, T. "The Life and Works of L. Andreyev." *Drama* (Feb., 1914) pp. 5-33.

Wiener, L. *Contemporary drama of Russia,* pp. 146-153.

Woodward, James B. "Leonid Andreev and *Russkaia Volia.*" *Etude Slaves et Est-Européenes,* vol. 10 (1965/66), pp. 26-35.

Anathema

Clark, B.H. *Continental drama of today,* pp. 66-71.

Clark, B.H. *Study of the modern drama,* pp. 62-67.

Kaun, Alexander. *Leonid Andreyev,* pp. 278-286.

Lewisohn, Ludwig. *"Anathema."* *Nation,* vol. 116 (Apr. 25, 1923), pp. 500-501.

Thompson, O.R.H. "Andreyev's *Anathema* and the Faust Legend." *North American Rev.,* vol. 194 (Dec., 1911), pp. 882-887.

The Black Masks

Woodward, James B. "The Theme and Structural Significance of Leonid Andreev's *The Black Masks.*" *Modern Drama,* vol. 10, no. 1 (May, 1967), pp. 95-103.

Devil in the Wind

Skinner, R.D. *"Devil in the Wind."* *Commonweal,* vol. 14 (May 13, 1931), pp. 48-49.

He Who Gets Slapped

Catholic World, vol. 163 (May, 1946), p. 168.

Commonweal, vol. 44 (April 19, 1946), p. 14.

Hobson, Harold. *Theatre,* pp. 96-97.

Kaun, Alexander. *Leonid Andreyev,* pp. 315-317.

Nathan, George Jean. *Theatre book of the year, 1945-46,* pp. 336-338.
Nathanson, W. *"He Who Gets Slapped." Open Court,* vol. 39 (Jan., 1925), pp. 7-20.

Parker, R.A. *"He Who Gets Slapped." Independent,* vol. 108 (Jan. 28, 1922), pp. 90-92.

Shipp, H. *"He Who Gets Slapped." English Review,* vol. 45 (Dec., 1927), pp. 728-730.

Young, Stark. *Flower in drama and glamour; theatre essays and criticism,* pp. 64-70.

Young, Stark. *"He Who Gets Slapped." New Republic,* vol. 29 (Feb. 1, 1922) pp. 283-284.

Zilboorg, G. *"He Who Gets Slapped." Drama,* vol. 11 (March, 1921), pp. 191-192.

Caterina

Dial, vol. 86 (May, 1929), pp. 440-442.

Kaun, Alexander. *Leonid Andreyev,* pp. 312-313.

Saturday Review, vol. 141 (April 10, 1926), pp. 472-473.

The Life of Man

Baring, M. "Russian Mystery Play: *Life of Man." Living Age,* vol. 258 (Sept. 26, 1908), pp. 786-792.

Kaun, Alexander. *Leonid Andreyev,* pp. 207-212.

Lake, K. *"The Life of Man." New Republic,* vol. 33 (Jan. 10, 1923), pp. 176-177.

Sabine Women

Firkins, O.W. *"Sabine Women." Review,* vol. 2 (Apr., 24, 1920), pp. 441-442.

Kaun, A. *Leonid Andreyev,* pp. 306-308.

JEAN ANOUILH 1910-

General

Anouilh, Jean. "To Jean Giraudoux." *In:* Corrigan, Robert W., ed. *Masterpieces of the modern French theatre,* pp. 231-234. *Also in: Tulane Drama Rev.,* vol. 3, no. 4 (May, 1959).

Aylen, Leo. *Greek tragedy and the modern world,* pp. 278-282.

Benedict, Stewart H. "Anouilh in America." *Modern Language J.,* vol 45 (1962), pp. 341-343.

Benson, Philip A. "The dramaturgy of Jean Anouilh." *Dissertatio Abstracts,* vol. 19 (1959), 3052 (Minnesota).

Bermel, Albert, ed., *The genius of the French theater,* pp. 438-44(

Black, Harvey. "The Incomparable Anouilh." *European,* no. 58 (Dec 1957), pp. 223-229.

Bree, Germaine. "The Innocent Amusements of Jean Anouilh. *Horizon,* vol. 3 (Nov., 1960), pp. 50-55.

Brown, John Mason. *Seeing things,* pp. 167-173.

Champigny, Robert. "Theatre in a Mirror: Anouilh." *Yale Frenc. Studies, no. 14* (Winter, 1954-55), pp. 57-64.

Chiari, Joseph. *The contemporary French theatre,* pp. 170-178 202-204.

Chiari, Joseph. *Landmarks of contemporary drama,* pp. 51-53.

Corrigan, Robert W., ed. *Masterpieces of the modern French theatre* pp. 228-229.

Curtis, Anthony. *New developments in the French theatre,* pp. 32-40

Della Fazia, Alba. "Pirandello and His French Echo Anouilh. *Modern Drama,* vol. 6, no. 4 (1964), pp. 346-367.

Fowlie, W. *Dionysus in Paris,* pp. 110-124.

Galstaun, Joan Alma. "Jean Anouilh, a disillusioned idealist." M.A., University of Washington, 1958.

Gascoigne, Bamber. *Twentieth-century drama,* pp. 144-151.

Grossvogel, David I. *The self-conscious stage in modern French drama,* pp. 147-204.

Guicharnaud, J. *Modern French theatre from Giraudoux to Beckett* pp. 112-130.

Guicharnaud, J. *Modern French theatre from Giraudoux to Genet* (rev. ed.), pp. 117-134, 145, 159, 231, 281, 287-288, 308, 321, 333-336, 359-360.

Handy, Robert Swift. "Theatre of Jean Anouilh." M.A., Emerson College, 1958.

Harvey, J. *Anouilh.*

Hatzfeld, Helmut. *Trends and styles in twentieth century French literature,* pp. 172-174.

Heiney, Donald. "Jean Anouilh: The Revival of Tragedy." *College English,* vol. 16 (1955), pp. 331-335.

Hobson, H. *French theatre of today,* pp. 198-207.

John, S. Beynon. "Obsession and Technique in the Plays of Jean Anouilh." *In:* Bogard, Travis and Oliver, William I., eds. *Modern drama; essays in criticism,* pp. 20-41. (Reprinted from *French Studies,* vol. 11, no. 2, Apr., 1957, pp. 97-116.)

Jones, Robert Emmet. *The alienated hero in modern French drama,* pp. 58-75.

Kerr, W. *Theater in spite of itself,* pp. 148 157.

Knowles, Dorothy. *French drama of the inter-war years, 1918-39,* pp. 175-177, 180-181.

Lenski, Branko A. "Jean Anouilh: variations in rebellion." *Dissertation Abstracts,* vol. 27 (1966), 777A (N.Y.U.).

LeSage, Laurence. "The Theatre of Jean Anouilh." *Amer. Society of Legion of Honor Mag.,* vol. 23, no. 4 (Winter, 1952), pp. 319-328.

Lumley, Frederick. *New trends in 20th century drama,* pp. 170-181.

Lumley, Frederick. *Trends in 20th century drama,* pp. 164-165, 175-183.

Manheim, Eleanor B. "Pandora's Box: Persistent Fantasies in Themes in the Plays of Jean Anouilh." *Literature and Psychology,* vol. 8, no. 1 (1958), pp. 6-10.

Marsh, E.O. *Jean Anouilh,* pp. 134-154.

Moore, Harry T. *Twentieth-century French literature since World War II,* pp. 17-22.

Moore, Harry T. *Twentieth-century French literature to World War II,* pp. 205-207.

Nelson, R.J. *Play within a play,* pp. 134-154.

Pronko, Leonard C. "The Prelate and the Pachyderm: Rear Guard and Vanguard Drama in the French Theater." *Modern Drama,* vol. 4, no. 1 (May 1961), pp. 63-71.

Pronko, Leonard C. "The Theatre of Jean Anouilh." *Dissertation Abstracts,* vol. 19 (1958), 329 (Tulane).

Pronko, Leonard C. *The world of Jean Anouilh.*

Sanderson, James L., ed. *Medea, myth and dramatic form,* pp. 95-96.

Sartre, Jean-Paul. "Forgers of Myths: The Young Playwrights of France." *Theatre Arts,* vol. 30 (1946), pp. 324-335.

Scott-James, Paul. "The Theatre of Anouilh." *Contemporary Review,* No. 1025 (May, 1951), pp. 302-308.

Styan, J.L. *Dark comedy,* pp. 193-217.

Styan, J.L. *Dark comedy,* 2nd ed., pp. 2, 6, 13, 47, 62, 64, 112, 116-117, 118, 142, 158, 187-192, 217, 260, 262, 267, 281, 289, 292, 297.

Thomas, Merlin. "Jean Anouilh." *Adelphi,* vol. 28, no. 3 (May, 1952), pp. 605-614.

Waters, Harold A. "Philosophic Progression in Anouilh's Plays." *Symposium,* vol. 16 (1962), pp. 122-129.

Williams, Raymond. *Drama from Ibsen to Eliot,* pp. 196-201.

Antigone (Adaptation from Sophocles)

Aylen, Leo. *Greek tragedy and the modern world,* pp. 280, 282-284, 289.

Barnes, Hazel E. *The literature of possibility,* pp. 24-26.

Baxter, Kay M. *Contemporary theatre and the Christian faith,* pp. 50-53, 64-66.

Brown, John Mason. *Seeing things,* pp. 167-173.

Calin, William. "Patterns of Imagery in Anouilh's *Antigone.*" *French Rev.,* vol. 41 (1967), pp. 76-83.

Chiari, Joseph. *The contemporary French theatre,* pp. 183-185, 199-200.

Clancy, James H., "The American *Antigone.*" *Educational Theatre J.,* vol. 6, no. 3 (Oct. 1954), pp. 249-253.

Clurman, Harold, "Theatre." *Nation,* vol. 182, no. 16 (April 21, 1956), pp. 347-349.

DeLaura, David J. "Anouilh's Other Antigone." *French Rev.,* vol. 35 (1961), pp. 36-41.

Donaldsen, Ian, *"Antigone* at the Oxford Playhouse." *Guardian, no.* 37,094 (Oct. 11, 1965), p. 9.

Evan, John. "The Two Antigones." *Drama,* vol. 26 (Autumn, 1952), pp. 15-17.

Flanner, Janet. *Paris journal, 1944-1965,* p. 21.

Fowlie, Wallace. *Dionysus in Paris,* pp. 114-116.

Harvey, J. *Anouilh,* pp. 98-100, 160-161.

Henn, T.R. *The harvest of tragedy,* pp. 130-131, 239-240.

Knowles, Dorothy. *French drama of the inter-war years, 1918-39,* pp. 171, 174-175.

Krutch, Joseph Wood. "Drama." *Nation,* vol. 142, no. 9 (Mar. 2, 1946), p. 269

Lumley, Frederick. *New trends in 20th century drama,* pp. 173-174, 176, 178.

Lumley, Frederick. *Trends in 20th century drama,* pp. 178-179.

McCollom, E. *Tragedy,* pp. 245-248.

Marsh, E.O. *Jean Anouilh,* pp. 107-120.

Nazareth, Peter. "Anouilh's *Antigone:* An Interpretation." *English Studies in Africa* (Johannesburg), vol. 6 (1963), pp. 51-69.

Pronko, Leonard C. "Jean Anouilh's Antigone." *In:* Cassell, Richard A. *What is the play?* pp. 719-724. (From Pronko, Leonard C. *The world of Jean Anouilh)*

Pronko, Leonard C. *The world of Jean Anouilh,* pp. 24-28, 200-207.

Sachs, Murray. "Notes on the Theatricality of Jean Anouilh's *Antigone." French Review,* vol. 36 (1962), pp. 3-11.

Saisselin, Remy G. "Is Tragic Drama Possible in the Twentieth Century?" *Theatre annual, 1960,* vol. 17, pp. 19-20.

Siepmann, E.O. "The New Pessimism in France." *Nineteenth Century,* vol. 143 (1948), pp. 275-278.

Thomas, Sister Marie, F.S.E. "About Reality in Anouilh's *Antigone* and Claudel's *L'Annonce Faite a Marie." French Rev.,* vol. 40, no. 1 (Oct., 1966), pp. 39-46.

Varty, K. "The Future Tense in Anouilh's *Antigone." Modern Languages* (London), vol. 33 (1957), pp. 99-101.

Walker, Roy. "Free Spirits." *Listener,* vol. 57, no. 1455 (Feb. 14, 1957), pp. 283-284.

Wardle, Irving, *"Antigone." Listener,* vol. 62, no. 1597 (Nov. 5, 1959), pp. 796-797.

Ardele, or The Daisy (Ardèle, ou La Marguerite)

Bishop, Thomas. *Pirandello and the French theater,* pp. 113-114.

Chiari, Joseph. *The contemporary French theatre,* pp. 199-202.

Clurman, Harold. *Lies like truth,* pp. 202-203.

Harvey, J. *Anouilh,* pp. 105-106.

Herbert, Hugh, "Anouilh's *Ardele* at Oxford Playhouse." *Guardian,* no. 37,696 (Sept. 20, 1967), p. 7.

Hope-Wallace, Philip. *"Ardele* Anouilh." *Time and Tide,* vol. 32, no. 36 (Sept. 8, 1951), p. 846.

Hobson, Harold, "A Fine Play." *Times,* no. 6654, (Oct. 29, 1950), p. 2.

Hobson, Harold. *The theatre now,* pp. 34-36.

Marsh, E.O. *Jean Anouilh,* pp. 139-149.

Pronko, Leonard C. *The world of Jean Anouilh,* pp. 44-45.

Styan, J.L. *The dark comedy,* pp. 199-206.

Styan, J.L. *The dark comedy,* 2nd ed., pp. 116, 153, 188, 190, 191-198, 199, 203, 237, 256, 259, 265, 267, 272, 273, 296.

Styan, J.L. *The elements of drama.* pp. 198-204.

Becket, or The Honor of God (Becket, ou L'Honneur de Dieu)

Amis, Kingsley. "Mysterious Martyr." *Observer* (March 29, 1964), p. 20.

Aylen, Leo. *Greek tragedy and the modern world,* pp. 224, 282, 290-292.

Browne, E. Martin. "The Two Beckets." *Drama,* no. 60 (Spring, 1961), pp. 27-30.

Cismaru, Alfred, *"Becket:* Anouilh as Devil's Advocate." *Renascence,* vol. 18, no. 2 (Winter 1966), pp. 81-88.

Clurman, Harold. *The naked image,* pp. 27-30.

Clurman, Harold. "Theatre." *Nation,* vol. 192, no. 21 (May 27, 1961), pp. 467-468.

Coleman, John. "Panavisions." *New Statesman,* vol. 67, no. 1724 (Mar. 27, 1964), pp. 499-500.

Cubeta, Paul M. *Modern drama for analysis,* pp. 513-522.

Evans, Gareth Lloyd, . "*Becket* at the Belgrade Theatre." *Guardian,* no. 36,907 (Mar. 5, 1965), p. 11.

Gatlin, J.C. "Becket and Honor: A Trim Reckoning." *Modern 'Drama,* vol. 8 (Dec., 1965), pp. 277-283.

Harvey, J. *Anouilh,* pp. 97-98.

Harvitt, Helene. "The Translation of Anouilh's *Becket* " *French Review,* vol. 34, no. 6 (May, 1961), pp. 569-571.

Kerr, Walter. *The theater in spite of itself,* pp. 154-157.

Knowles, Dorothy. *French drama of the inter-war years, 1918-39,* pp. 179.

Milne, Tom. "*Becket.*" *Encore,* vol. 8, no. 5 (Sept.-Oct., 1961), pp. 37-40.

Nightingale, Benedict. "Anouilh's *Becket* at the Theatre Royal, Lincoln." *Guardian,* no. 37,103 (Oct. 21, 1965), p. 9.

Pritchett, V.S. "1170 and All That." *New Statesman,* vol. 67, no. 1583 (July 14, 1961), pp. 64-65.

Pronko, Leonard C. *The world of Jean Anouilh,* pp. 56-61.

Quigly, Isabel. "Bishop and King." *Spectator* (April 3, 1964), p. 450, 452.

Roy, Emil. "The Becket Plays: Eliot, Fry, and Anouilh." *Modern Drama,* vol. 8, no. 3 (Dec., 1965), pp. 268-276.

Tynan, Kenneth. *Tynan right and left,* pp. 99-100.

he Cavern (La Grotte)

Hope-Wallace, Philip. "*The Cavern* at the Strand." *Guardian,* no. 37,123 (Nov. 13, 1965), p. 6.

Knowles, Dorothy. *French drama of the inter-war years, 1918-39,* pp. 180.

"Revelation of a Volcano." *Times,* no. 56,315 (May 7, 1965), p. 18.

Shearer, Ann, *"The Cavern* at the Nottingham Playhouse." *Guardia.* no. 36,960 (May 7, 1965), p. 11.

Colombe (Mademoiselle Colombe)

Bentley, Eric. *The dramatic event,* pp. 182-185.

Bishop, Thomas. *Pirandello and the French theater,* pp. 110-111.

Clurman, Harold, "Theatre." *Nation,* vol. 178, no. 5 (Jan. 30, 1954 pp. 98-99.

Cooke, Richard P. "Two-faced Theatre." *Wall Street J.,* vol. 165, nc 38 (Feb. 25, 1965), p. 18.

Gassner, J. *Theatre at the crossroads,* pp. 245-247.

Harvey, J. *Anouilh,* pp. 73-75, 86-88.

Hatch, Robert. "Theatre." *Nation,* vol. 178, no. 4 (Jan. 23, 1954), pr 77-78.

Marsh, E.O. *Jean Anouilh,* pp. 157-164.

Nelson, R.J. *Play within a play,* pp. 145-154.

Pickering, Jerry V. "The Several Worlds of Anouilh's *Colombe. Drama Survey,* vol. 5, no. 3 (Winter, 1966-67), pp. 267-275.

Pronko, Leonard C. *The world of Jean Anouilh,* pp. 47-49.

Scott-James, P. "The Theatre of Jean Anouilh." *Contemporary Rev* vol. 179 (1951), pp. 302-308.

Styan, J.L. *The dark comedy,* pp. 206-217.

Styan, J.L. *The dark comedy,* 2nd ed., pp. 25, 116, 153, 157, 187, 188 190-192, 198-207.

Dinner with the Family (La Rendez-vous de Senlis)

Bishop, Thomas. *Pirandello and the French theatre,* p. 117.

English, vol. 12 (Summer, 1958), pp. 59-60.

Harvey, J. *Anouilh,* pp. 129-130.

Marsh, E.O. *Jean Anouilh,* pp. 77-78.

Nelson, R.J. *Play within a play,* pp. 136-137.

Pronko, Leonard C. *The world of Jean Anouilh,* pp. 15-16, 185-188

he Ermine (L'Hermine)

Harvey, J. *Anouilh,* pp. 103-104.

Knowles, Dorothy. *French drama of the inter-war years, 1918-39,* pp. 167-168.

Lumley, Frederick. *New trends in 20th century drama,* p. 171.

Marsh, E.O. *Anouilh,* pp. 103-104.

Pronko, Leonard C. *The world of Jean Anouilh,* pp. 4-6.

Stevens, Linton C. "Hybris in Anouilh's *L'Hermine* and *La Sauvage.*" *French Review,* vol. 37 (1964), pp. 658-663.

urydice (Point of Departure) (Legend of Lovers)

Aylen, Leo. *Greek tragedy and the modern world,* pp. 286-288, 291.

Chiari, Joseph. *The contemporary French theatre,* 185-187.

Gascoigne, Bamber. *Twentieth-century drama,* p. 146.

Harvey, J. *Anouilh,* pp. 84-84, 119-120.

Henn, T.R. *The harvest of tragedy,* pp. 240-242.

Hobson, Harold. "Eurydice." *Times,* no. 6663 (Dec. 31, 1950), p. 2.

Hobson, Harold. "Jean Anouilh." *Times,* no. 6655 (Nov. 5, 1950), p. 2

Hobson, Harold. *The theatre now,* pp. 36-39.

Ingham, Patricia. "The Renaissance of Hell." *Listener,* vol. 62 (Sept. 3, 1959), pp. 349-351.

Lumley, Frederick. *Trends in 20th century drama,* pp. 177-178.

Marsh, E.O. *Jean Anouilh,* pp. 91-106.

Nathan, George Jean. *Theatre in the fifties,* pp. 161-164.

Pronko, Leonard C. *The world of Jean Anouilh,* pp. 22-28, 33-36, 81-87, 195-200.

Robinson, Kenneth. "Theatre: Very Nearly a Pessimist." *Public Opinion,* no. 4642 (Nov. 10, 1950), p. 20.

Styan, J.L. *The dark comedy,* 2nd ed. pp. 94, 116, 142, 187, 188, 190-191, 198, 265, 273.

Styan, J.L. *The elements of drama,* pp. 217-227.

Fading Mansions (Roméo et Jeannette)

"Anouilh in a New Version." *Times,* no. 56,254 (Feb. 24, 1965), p. 1

Donaldsen, Ian. "Romeo and Jeannette at Oxford." *Guardian,* no 36,899 (Feb. 24, 1965), p. 9.

Harvey, J. *Anouilh,* pp. 58-60, 85-86, 131-132.

Marsh, E.O. *Jean Anouilh,* pp. 121-131.

Pronko, Leonard C. *The world of Jean Anouilh,* pp. 28-30.

The Fighting Cock (L'Hurluberlu, ou Le Réactionnaire Amoureu

Brustein, Robert. "Please Pass the Plasma." *New Republic,* vol. 142 no. 1 (Jan. 4, 1960), p. 20.

Brustein, Robert. *Seasons of discontent,* pp. 101-104.

Clurman, Harold. *The naked image,* pp. 25-27.

Clurman, Harold. "Theatre." *Nation,* vol. 189, no. 22 (Dec. 26, 1959) pp. 495-496.

"The Decorative Invention of Jean Anouilh." *Times,* no. 56,653 (Jun 9, 1966), p. 8.

"A Harlequinade Plot in Anouilh Play." *Times,* no. 56,773 (Oct. 27 1966), p. 6.

Harvey, J. *Anouilh,* pp. 44-49, 149-150, 162-163.

Hewes, Henry. "Mildness in Great Ones." *Saturday Rev.* vol. 42 (June 20, 1959), pp. 29-30.

Hope-Wallace, Philip. *"The Fighting Cock* at Chichester." *Guardian* no. 37,298 (June 9, 1966), p. 9.

Knowles, Dorothy. *French drama of the inter-war years, 1918-39,* p 178.

Pronko, Leonard C. *The world of Jean Anouilh,* pp. 53-56.

La Foire d'Empoigne

Knowles, Dorothy. *French drama of the inter-war years, 1918-39,* pp. 178-179.

Jezabel

Marsh, E.O. *Jean Anouilh,* pp. 40-43.

Pronko, L.C. *The world of Jean Anouilh,* pp. 41-44.

The Lark (L'Alouette)

Aylen, Leo. *Greek tragedy and the modern world,* pp. 193, 224, 281, 285, 287-290.

Bermel, Albert, ed. *The genius of the French theater,* pp. 21-22, 443-444.

Brooking, Jack. "Jeanne D'Arc, the Trial Notes, and Anouilh." *Theatre annual, 1959,* vol. 16, pp. 20-29.

Brousse, Jacques. "Theatre in Paris: *L'Alouette* by M. J. Anouilh." *European,* vol. 12 (Feb., 1954), pp. 35-39.

Chiari, Joseph. *The contemporary French theatre,* pp. 187-195.

Fowlie, Wallace. *Dionysus in Paris,* pp. 119-122.

Gassner, John. *Theatre at the crossroads,* pp. 247-249.

Harvey, J. *Anouilh,* pp. 94-96.

Hatch, Robert. "Theatre and Films." *Nation,* vol. 181, no. 23 (Dec. 3, 1955), pp. 485-486.

Hunter, F.J. "The Value of Time in Modern Drama." *J. of Aesthetics and Art Criticism,* vol. 16 (1957), pp. 194-201.

Knepler, Henry. *"The Lark.* Translation vs. Adaptation: A Case History." *Modern Drama,* vol. 1 (1958), pp. 15-28.

Lumley, Frederick. *New trends in 20th century drama,* pp. 176-178.

Lumley, Frederick. *Trends in 20th century drama,* pp. 181-183.

Pronko, Leonard C. *The world of Jean Anouilh,* pp. 37-40.

Williamson, Audrey. *Contemporary theatre, 1953-1956,* pp. 51-53.

Medea (Médée)

Aylen, Leo. *Greek tragedy and the modern world,* pp. 280, 284-286.

Harvey, J. *Anouilh,* pp. 96-97.

Lapp, John C. "Anouilh's *Médée:* A Debt to Seneca." *In:* Sanderson, James L., ed. *Medea, myth and dramatic form,* pp. 309-313. *Also in: Modern Language Notes,* vol. 69 (1954), pp. 183-187.

Lyons, Charles R. "The Ambiguity of the Anouilh *Medea." French Rev.,* vol. 37 (1964), pp. 312-319.

Marsh, E.O. *Jean Anouilh,* pp. 131-134.

Pronko, Leonard C., "The Use of Myth in Anouilh's *Medea.*" In Sanderson, James L., ed. *Medea, myth and dramatic form,* pp. 314-320. (Reprinted from Pronko, Leonard C. *The world of Jean Anouilh,* Berkeley, Univ. of California Press, 1961)

Pronko, Leonard C. *The world of Jean Anouilh,* pp. 30-33, 207-210.

Ornifle, ou Le Courant d'Air

Harvey, J. *Anouilh,* pp. 78-79, 168-169.

Pronko, L.C. *The world of Jean Anouilh,* pp. 52-53.

Le Petit Bonheur

Marsh, E.O. *Jean Anouilh,* pp. 60-62.

Poor Bitos (Pauvre Bitos)

"Anouilh Play Does the Trick on Small Screen." *Times,* no. 56,241 (Feb. 9, 1965), p. 8.

Bishop, Thomas. *Pirandello and the French theater,* pp. 111-113.

Brousse, Jacques. "Theatre in Paris: Jean Anouilh's *Pauvre Bitos.*' *European,* no. 49 (March, 1957), pp. 49-54.

Brustein, Robert. "Love and Hate on Broadway." *New Republic,* vol. 151, no. 24 (Dec. 12, 1964), pp. 20-21.

Clurman, Harold. *The naked image,* pp. 33-36.

Clurman Harold. *Nation,* vol. 199, no. 17 (Nov. 30, 1964), pp. 415-417.

Cooke, Richard P. "First-rate Anouilh." *Wall Street J.,* vol. 164, no. 98 (Nov. 16, 1964), p. 16.

Ford, Peter. "Anouilh and Pinero at Bristol." *Guardian* (Oct. 15, 1964) p. 9.

Fowlie, Wallace. *Dionysus in Paris,* pp. 110-112.

Harvey, J. *Anouilh,* pp. 106-110, 163-164.

Knowles, Dorothy. *French drama of the inter-war years, 1918-39,* pp. 177-178.

Novick, Julius. "Hinterland Theatre IV Washington to Philadelphia." *Nation,* vol. 23, no. 1 (July 4, 1966), pp. 27-30.

"Outsider Among the Old Boys." *Times,* no. 56,504 (Dec. 14, 1965), p. 13.

Rosselli, John. "Poor Bitos at the Duke of York's." *Guardian* (Jan. 8, 1964) p. 9.

Seymour, Alan. *"Bitos."* *London Magazine,* vol. 3, no. 11 (Feb., 1964), pp. 61-64.

Tynan, K. *Curtains,* pp. 395-396.

he Rehearsal (La Répétition, ou L'Amour Puni)

Bentley, Eric. *The dramatic event,* pp. 66-69.

Bishop, Thomas. *Pirandello and the French theatre,* pp. 114-115.

Harvey, J. *Anouilh,* pp. 111-112, 130-131, 148-149.

Hobson, Harold. "Jean Anouilh." *Times,* no. 6655 (Nov. 5, 1950), p. 2.

Marsh, E.O. *Jean Anouilh,* pp. 152-156.

Marshall, Margaret. "Drama" *Nation,* vol. 175, no. 24 (Dec. 13, 1952), pp. 562-563.

Nelson, R.J. *Play within a play,* pp. 141-145.

Pronko, L.C. *The world of Jean Anouilh,* pp. 45-47.

ing Around the Moon (L'Invitation au Chateau)

Brook, Peter. "A Producer Compares." *World Rev.,* new series no. 13 (Mar. 1950), pp. 55-57.

Hobson, Harold. "Fry Again." *Times,* no. 6615 (Jan. 29, 1950), p. 2.

Larner, Gerald. *"Ring Around the Moon."* *Guardian* (April 10, 1964), p. 11.

Marsh, E.O. *Jean Anouilh,* pp. 135-139.

Marshall, Margaret. "Drama." *Nation,* vol. 171, no. 23 (Dec. 2, 1950), pp. 514-515.

Nelson, R.J. *Play within a play,* pp. 140-141.

Pronko, Leonard C. *The world of Jean Anouilh,* pp. 41-44.

Taylor, John Russell. "Anouilh: 'brilliant'." *Listener,* vol. 71, no. 1829 (Apr. 16, 1964), p. 647.

he Thieves' Carnival (Le Bal des Voleurs)

Knowles, Dorothy. *French drama of the inter-war years, 1918-39,* pp. 172-173.

Lumley, Frederick. *New trends in 20th century drama,* p. 171.

Marsh, E.O. *Jean Anouilh,* pp. 43-48.

Nelson, R.J. *Play within a play,* pp. 134-136.

Pronko, Leonard C. *The world of Jean Anouilh,* pp. 14-15.

Valency, Maurice. "The World of Jean Anouilh." *Theatre Arts,* vol. 41 (1957), pp. 31-32; 92-93.

Time Remembered (Léocadia)

Bishop, Thomas. *Pirandello and the French theatre,* pp. 118-119.

Kerr, Walter. *The theater in spite of itself,* pp. 151-154.

Marsh, E.O. *Jean Anouilh,* pp. 88-91.

Nelson, R.J. *Play within a play,* pp. 137-140.

Traveller Without Luggage (Le Voyageur sans Bagage)

Bishop, Thomas, *Pirandello and the French theater,* pp. 109-110.

Chiari, Joseph. *The contemporary French theatre,* pp. 195-196.

Clurman, Harold. *The naked image,* pp. 31-33.

Clurman, Harold. *Nation,* vol. 199, no. 9 (Oct. 5, 1964), pp. 202-203.

Cooke, Richard P. "Search for the Past." *Wall Street J.,* vol. 164, no. 58 (Sept. 21, 1964), p. 12.

Harvey, J. *Anouilh,* pp. 17-18.

Hobson, Harold. *The theatre now,* pp. 39-43.

Knowles, Dorothy. *French drama of the inter-war years, 1918-39.* pp. 169-170.

Marsh, E.O. *Jean Anouilh,* pp. 65-76.

Milne, Tom. "Traveller Without Commitment." *Encore,* vol. 6, no. 2 (Mar.-Apr., 1959), pp. 37-39.

Pronko, Leonard C. *The world of Jean Anouilh,* pp. 12-14.

The Waltz of the Toreadors (La Valse des Toréadors)

Clurman, Harold. "Theatre." *Nation,* vol. 186, no. 12 (Mar. 22, 1958), p. 261.

Fowlie, Wallace. *Dionysus in Paris,* pp. 116-119.

Gassner, John. *Theatre at the crossroads,* pp. 249-252.

Harvey, J. *Anouilh,* pp. 18-19, 25-26, 31-32, 110-111.

Hatch, Robert. "Theatre." *Nation,* vol. 184, no. 5 (Feb. 2, 1957), p. 106.

Kauffmann, Stanley. "Family Life Here and There." *New Republic,* vol. 147, no. 5 (July 30, 1962), pp. 29-30.

Mannes, Marya. "Three London Plays: Satire, Sex, and a Song." *Reporter,* vol. 15 (Nov. 1, 1956), p. 38.

Marsh, E.O. *Jean Anouilh,* pp. 164-175.

Pronko, Leonard C. *The world of Jean Anouilh,* pp. 59-62.

Valency, Maurice. "The World of Jean Anouilh." *Theatre Arts,* vol. 41 (1957), pp. 31-32, 92-93.

Walker, Roy. "Another Anouilh." *Theatre,* vol. 7, no. 164 (Jan. 17, 1953), pp. 8-10.

Williamson, Audrey. *Contemporary theatre, 1953-1956,* pp. 73-75.

he Wild One (Restless Heart) **(La Sauvage)**

Chiari, Joseph. *The contemporary French theatre,* pp. 179-183.

Gascoigne, Bamber. *Twentieth-century drama,* pp. 144-146.

Jones, Robert Emmet. *The alienated hero in modern French drama,* pp. 65-67.

Knowles, Dorothy. *French drama of the inter-war years, 1918-39,* pp. 170-172.

Lumley, Frederick. *Trends in 20th century drama,* pp. 176-177.

Marsh, E.O. *Jean Anouilh,* pp. 48-60.

Pronko, Leonard C. *The world of Jean Anouilh,* pp. 9-11.

Scott-James, Paule. "The Theatre of Jean Anouilh." *Contemporary Rev.,* vol. 179 (1951), pp. 302-308.

Stevens, Linton C. "Hybris in Anouilh's *L'Hermine* and *La Sauvage.*" *French Review,* vol. 37 (1964), pp. 658-663.

Y'Avait un Prisonnier

Knowles, Dorothy. *French drama of the inter-war years, 1918-39,* pp 168-169.

Marsh, E.O. *Jean Anouilh,* pp. 62-65.

Pronko, L. C. *The world of Jean Anouilh,* pp. 11-12.

S. ANSKY 1863-1920
(real name Solomon Rappoport)

The Dybbuk

Brown, I. " *Dybbuk.*" *Saturday Review,* vol. 143 (Apr. 9, 1927), pp 559-560.

Dial, vol. 80 (Mar. 1926), pp. 255-259.

Goldberg, I. *Drama of transition,* pp. 425-434.

Horsnell, H. *"Dybbuk."* *Outlook* (London), vol. 54 (Apr. 16, 1927), p 407.

Jennings, R. *"Dybbuk."* *Spectator,* vol. 138 (Apr. 9, 1927), p. 639

Lifson, D. *The Yiddish theatre in America,* pp. 103-117.

MacCarthy, Desmond. *"Dybbuk."* *New Statesman,* vol. 28 (Apr. 9 1927), pp. 797-798.

Powys, J.C. *"Dybbuk."* *Menorah J.,* vol. 13 (Aug., 1927), pp. 361-365

Samuel, M. *"Dybbuk."* *Menorah J.,* vol. 13 (Feb., 1927), pp. 63-67

Shipp, H. *"Dybbuk."* *English Rev.,* vol. 44 (May, 1927), pp. 632-634

Waldman, M. *"Dybbuk."* *London Mercury,* vol. 16 (May, 1927), pp 83-84.

Young, Stark. *Immortal shadows,* pp. 67-71.

GUILLAUME APOLLINAIRE 1880-1918

General

Cocteau, Jean. *The difficulty of being,* pp. 100-107.

Mackworth, C. *Guillaume Apollinaire and the Cubist life.*

The Breasts of Tiresias (Tiresias's Breasts) (Les Mamelles de Tirésias)

Adema, Marcel. *Apollinaire,* pp. 241-252.

Bates, Scott. *Guillaume Apollinaire,* pp. 127, 129-132, 137, 143-144.

Bentley, Eric. *The playwright as thinker,* pp. 190-192.

Davies, Margaret. *Apollinaire,* pp. 95-96, 99, 287-289.

Esslin, Martin. *The theatre of the absurd,* pp. 259-261.

Grossvogel, David I. *The self-conscious stage in modern French drama,* pp. 30-46. *Also: 20th Century French drama.* pp. 30-46.

Mackworth, C. *Guillaume Apollinaire and the Cubist life,* pp. 222-225, 227.

Pronko, Leonard C. *Avant-garde: the experimental theatre in France,* pp. 7-9.

Color of the Weather (Couleur de Temps)

Adema, Marcel. *Apollinaire,* pp. 252-254, 261, 265.

Bates, Scott. *Guillaume Apollinaire,* pp. 25, 27, 127, 136-137, 147-149, 150.

Davies, Margaret. *Apollinaire,* pp. 26, 103.

ALEKSEJ ARBUZOV 1908-

rkutskaja Istorija

Ferrer, Olga P. "Theater in the U.S.S.R.: Summer of 1964." *Books Abroad,* vol. 39, no. 3 (Summer, 1965), p. 300.

WILLIAM ARCHIBALD 1919-

The Innocents

See James, Henry. *The Turn of the Screw*

JOHN ARDEN 1930-

General

Arden, John. "Delusions of Grandeur." *Twentieth Century* (Feb., 1961), pp. 200-206.

Arden, John. (Interview with Tom Milne and Clive Goodwin, first published in *Encore* in 1961, followed by replies to further questions put by Simon Trussler in 1966). *In:* Marowitz, Charles, ed., *Theatre at work,* pp. 12, 17, 34, 36-57.

Arden John. (Interview with Walter Wager). *In:* Wager, Walter, ed. *The playwrights speak,* pp. 244-248, 250-257, 258-268.

Arden, John. "Telling a True Tale." *In:* Marowitz, Charles, ed. *Encore reader,* pp. 125-129 (Reprinted from *Encore,* May, 1960.)

Blindheim, Joan T. "John Arden's Use of the Stage." *Modern Drama,* vol. 11, no. 3 (Dec., 1968), pp. 306-316.

Chiari, Joseph. *Landmarks of contemporary drama,* pp. 118-119.

Cox, Frank. "Arden of Chichester." *Plays and Players* (Aug., 1963), pp. 16-18.

Fletcher, John. "Confrontations. II. Arnold Wesker, John Arden, and Arthur Adamov." Caliban, vol. 4 (1967), pp. 149-159.

Gilman, Richard. "Arden's Unsteady Ground." *In:* Brown, John Russell, *Modern British dramatists, a collection of critical essays,* pp. 104-107. (From *Tulane Drama Rev.,* vol. 11, no. 2 (1966), pp. 57-62.)

Hainsworth, J.D. "John Arden and the Absurd." *Rev. of English Literature,* vol. 7, no. 4 (Oct., 1966), pp. 42-49.

Hatch, Robert. "A Coming Talent Casts its Shadow Before." *Horizon,* vol. 4, no. 6 (July, 1962), pp. 91-94.

Lumley, Frederick. *New trends in 20th century drama,* pp. 260-266.

Rush, David. "Grief, But Good Order." *Moderna Sprak* (Stockholm), vol. 58 (1964), pp. 452-458.

Taylor, John Russell. *Anger and after,* pp. 72-86.

Taylor, John Russell. "John Arden." *In:* Brown, John Russell, ed. *Modern British dramatists, a collection of critical essays.* pp. 83-85, 97. (From Taylor, J.R. *Anger and after,* London, Methuen, published as *The angry theatre,* N.Y., Hill & Wang, 1962.)

Wager, Walter. "John Arden." *In:* Wager, Walter, ed. *The playwrights speak,* pp. 238-244.

Wager, Walter and Simon Trussler. "Who's for a Revolution? Two Interviews with John Arden." *Tulane Drama Rev.* vol. 11, no. 2 (1966), pp. 41-53. (Ed. Kelly Morris.)

Wellwarth, George. *The theatre of protest and paradox,* pp. 267-273.

Armstrong's Last Goodnight

Arden, John. (Interview with Tom Milne and Clive Goodwin, first published in *Encore* in 1961, followed by replies to further questions put by Simon Trussler in 1966). *In:* Marowitz, Charles, ed. *Theatre at work,* pp. 50, 51, 52-53, 56.

Gilman, Richard. "Arden's Unsteady Ground." *In:* Brown, John Russell, ed. *Modern British dramatists, a collection of critical essays,* pp. 114-116. (From *Tulane Drama Rev.,* vol. 11, no. 2 (1966), pp. 54-62.)

Lumley, Frederick. *New trends in 20th century drama,* pp. 13, 256, 261, 264-265, 266.

s Longa, Vita Brevis

Arden, John. (Interview with Tom Milne and Clive Goodwin, first published in *Encore* in 1961, followed by replies to further questions out by Simon Trussler in 1966). *In:* Marowitz, Charles, ed. *Theatre at work,* pp. 53-54.

e Business of Good Government

Arden, John. (Interview with Tom Milne and Clive Goodwin, first published in *Encore* in 1961, followed by replies to further questions out by Simon Trussler in 1966). *In:* Marowitz, Charles, ed. *Theatre at work,* pp. 46-47, 53-54.

Blindheim, Joan T. "John Arden's Use of the Stage." *Modern Drama,* vol. 11, no. 3 (Dec., 1968), pp. 310-311.

iday's Hiding

Arden, John. (Interview with Tom Milne and Clive Goodwin, first published in *Encore* in 1961, followed by replies to further questions out by Simon Trussler in 1966). *In:* Marowitz, Charles, ed. *Theatre at work,* pp. 54-55.

ppy Haven

Arden, John. (Interview with Tom Milne and Clive Goodwin, first published in *Encore* in 1961, followed by replies to further questions out by Simon Trussler in 1966). *In:* Marowitz, Charles, ed. *Theatre at work,* pp. 40-42, 46-47, 51, 56.

Blindheim, Joan T. "John Arden's Use of the Stage." *Modern Drama,* vol. 11, no. 3 (Dec., 1968), pp. 311-312.

Gilman, Richard. "Arden's Unsteady Ground." *In:* Brown, John Russell. *Modern British dramatists, a collection of critical essays,* pp. 108-109. (From *Tulane Drama Rev.,* vol. 11, no. 2 (1966), pp. 54-62.)

Hainsworth, J.D. "John Arden and the Absurd." *Rev. of English Literature,* vol. 7, no. 4 (Oct., 1966), pp. 43-45, 47.

Lumley, Frederick. *New trends in 20th century drama,* p. 263.

Taylor, John Russell. *Anger and after,* pp. 82-85.

Taylor, John Russell. "John Arden." *In:* Brown, John Russell, e
Modern British dramatists, a collection of critical essays, pp. 93-9
(From Taylor, J.R. *Anger and after,* London, Methuen, published
The angry theater, N.Y., Hill & Wang, 1962.)

Tynan, Kenneth. *Tynan right and left,* p. 21.

Wellwarth, George. *The theatre of protest and paradox,* pp. 271-27

Worth, Katharine J. "Avant Garde At The Royal Court Theatre: Joh
Arden and N.F. Simpson." *In:* Armstrong, William A., e
Experimental drama, pp. 211-214.

Left-Handed Liberty

Arden, John. (Interview with Tom Milne and Clive Goodwin, fir
published in *Encore* in 1961, followed by replies to further questio
put by Simon Trussler in 1966). *In:* Marowitz, Charles, ed. *Theatre*
work, pp. 50-52, 55.

Gilman, Richard. "Arden's Unsteady Ground." *In:* Brown, Joh
Russell, *Modern British dramatists, a collection of critical essays,* p
107-108. (From *Tulane Drama Rev.,* vol. 11, no. 2 (1966), pp. 54-62

Lumley, Frederick. *New trends in 20th century drama,* pp. 261-26

Live Like Pigs

Gilman, Richard. "Arden's Unsteady Ground." *In:* Brown, Joh
Russell, ed. *Modern British dramatists, a collection of critical essay*
pp. 109-112. (From *Tulane Drama Rev.,* vol. 11, no. 2, (1966), p
54-62.)

Hunt, Albert. "Arden's Stagecraft." *In:* Brown, John Russell, e
Modern British dramatists, a collection of critical essays, pp. 101-10
(From *Encore,* vol. 12, no. 5 (1965), pp. 9-12.)

Taylor, John Russell. *Anger and after,* pp. 77-79.

Taylor, John Russell. "John Arden." *In:* Brown, John Russell, e
Modern British dramatists, a collection of critical essays, pp. 87-9
(From Taylor J.R. *Anger and after,* London, Methuen, published
The angry theater, N.Y., Hill & Wang, 1962.)

Wellwarth, George. *The theatre of protest and paradox,* pp. 270-27

Serjeant Musgrave's Dance

Arden John. (Interview with Tom Milne and Clive Goodwin, fir
published in *Encore* in 1961, followed by replies to further questio
put by Simon Trussler in 1966). *In:* Marowitz, Charles, ed. *Theatre*
work, pp. 12, 34, 39-40, 42-50.

Arden, John. (Interview with Walter Wager). *In:* Wager, Walter, ed. *The playwrights speak,* pp. 248-250, 255.

Blau, Herbert. *The impossible theatre,* pp. 220-227.

Blindheim, Joan T. "John Arden's Use of the Stage." *Modern Drama,* vol. 11, no. 3 (Dec., 1968), pp. 309-310.

Brandt, G.W. "Realism and Parables." *In:* Brown, John Russell and Bernard Harris, eds. *Contemporary theatre,* pp. 49-54.

Gascoigne, Bamber. *Twentieth-century drama,* pp. 204-206.

Gilman, Richard. "Arden's Unsteady Ground." *In:* Brown, John Russell, ed. *Modern British dramatists, a collection of critical essays,* pp. 112-114. (From *Tulane Drama Rev.,* vol. 11, no. 2 (1966), pp. 54-62.)

Hainsworth, J.D. "John Arden and the Absurd." *Rev. of English Literature,* vol. 7, no. 4 (Oct., 1966), pp. 43, 45-46, 47.

Hunt, Albert. "Arden's Stagecraft." *In:* Brown, John Russell, ed. *Modern British dramatists, a collection of critical essays,* pp. 98-101. From *Encore,* vol. 12, no. 5 (1965), pp. 9-12.)

Lumley, Frederick. *New trends in 20th century drama,* pp. 260, 262-263.

Matthews, Honor. *The primal curse,* pp. 190-194.

Milne, Tom. "The Hidden Face of Violence." *In:* Brown, John Russell, ed. *Modern British dramatists, a collection of critical essays,* pp. 38-46. From *Encore,* vol. 7, no. 1 (1960), pp. 14-20.)

Milne, Tom. "The Hidden Face of Violence." *In:* Marowitz, Charles, ed. *Encore reader,* pp. 122-123.

Page, Malcolm. "The Motives of Pacifists: John Arden's *Serjeant Musgrave's Dance.*" *Drama Survey,* vol. 6 (1967), pp. 66-73.

Prickett, Stephen. "Three Modern English Plays." *Philologica Pragensia,* vol. 10 (1967), pp. 12-21.

Styan, J.L. *The dark comedy,* 2nd ed., pp. 172-173.

Taylor, John Russell. *Anger and after,* pp. 79-82.

Taylor, John Russell. "John Arden." *In:* Brown, John Russell, ed. *Modern British dramatists, a collection of critical essays,* pp. 90-93. From Taylor, J.R. *Anger and after,* London, Methuen, published as *The angry theater,* N.Y., Hill & Wang, 1962.)

Wellwarth, George. *The theatre of protest and paradox,* pp. 269-270.

Worth, Katharine J. "Avant Garde at the Royal Court Theatre: Joh
Arden and N.F. Simpson." *In:* Armstrong, William A., ed
Experimental drama, pp. 206-211.

Soldier, Soldier

Arden, John. (Interview with Tom Milne and Clive Goodwin, firs
published in *Encore* in 1961, followed by replies to further question
put by Simon Trussler in 1966). *In:* Marowitz, Charles, ed. *Theatre a
work,* pp. 40-42.

Taylor, John Russell. *Anger and after,* p. 79.

Taylor, John Russell. "John Arden." *In:* Brown, John Russell, ed
Modern British dramatists, a collection of critical essays, pp. 87-90
(From Taylor, J.R. *Anger and after,* London, Methuen, published a
The angry theater, N.Y., Hill & Yang, 1962.)

The Waters of Babylon

Arden, John. (Interview with Walter Wager). *In:* Wager, Walter, ed
The playwrights speak, pp. 257-258.

Blindheim, Joan T. "John Arden's Use of the Stage." *Modern Drama*
vol. 11, no. 3 (Dec., 1968), pp. 306-308.

Taylor, John Russell. *Anger and after,* pp. 73-77.

Taylor, John Russell. "John Arden," *In:* Brown, John Russell, ed
Modern British dramatists, a collection of critical essays, pp. 85-87
(From Taylor, J.R. *Anger and after,* London, Methuen, published a:
The angry theater, N.Y., Hill & Wang, 1962.)

Wet Fish

Taylor, John Russell. "John Arden," *In:* Brown, John Russell, ed
Modern British dramatists, a collection of critical essays, pp. 96-97
(From Taylor, J.R. *Anger and after,* London, Methuen, published a:
The angry theater, N.Y., Hill & Wang, 1962.)

The Workhouse Donkey

Arden, John. (Interview with Tom Milne and Clive Goodwin, firs
published in *Encore* in 1961, followed by replies to further questions
put by Simon Trussler in 1966). *In:* Marowitz, Charles, ed. *Theatre a
work,* p. 51.

Hainsworth, J.D. "John Arden and the Absurd." *Rev. of English
Literature,* vol. 7, no. 4 (Oct., 1966), pp. 43, 45, 46, 47.

Lumley, Frederick. *New trends in 20th century drama,* pp. 263-264.

Marowitz, Charles. *"The Workhouse Donkey."* In: Marowitz, Charles, ed. *Encore reader,* pp. 238-241. (Reprinted from *Encore,* Sept., 1963)

Wellwarth, George. *The theatre of protest and paradox,* pp. 272-273.

ROBERT ARDREY 1908-

adow of Heroes

Tynan, Kenneth. *Tynan right and left.* pp. 7-9.

under Rock

Dent, Alan. *Preludes and studies,* pp. 179-180.

Himelstein, Morgan Y. *Drama was a weapon, the left-wing theatre in New York, 1929-1941,* pp. 177-178.

ARTHUR ARENT 1904-

hiopia

Isaac, Dan. "Introduction" to *ETJ* publication (the first) of *Ethiopia. Educational Theatre J.,* vol. 20, no. 1 (Mar., 1968), pp. 15-19. Text of *Ethiopia,* pp. 19-31.

iple-A Plowed Under

Himelstein, Morgan Y. *Drama was a weapon, the left-wing theatre in New York, 1929-1941,* pp. 89-92.

ROBERTO ARLT 1900-1942

neral

Anderson Imbert, Enrique. *Spanish-American literature: a history,* pp. 507-508.

Jones, W.K. *Behind Spanish American footlights,* pp. 145-147.

CARLOS ARNICHES ?-1943

eneral

Marquerie, Alfredo. "A Centenary of Spanish Theatre." *Topic: A Journal of the Liberal Arts* (Wash. and Jeff. College, Washington, Penn.), no. 15 (Spring, 1968), pp. 30-32.

Señorita de Trevelez

Marquerie, Alfredo. "A Centenary of Spanish Theatre." *Topic: A Journal of the Liberal Arts* (Wash. and Jeff. College, Wash., Penn.), no. 15 (Spring, 1968), pp. 30-31.

ALEXANDRE ARNOUX 1884-

General

Knowles, Dorothy. *French drama of the inter-war years, 1918-39,* p
188-191.

FERNANDO ARRABAL 1932-

General

Benedikt, M. and Wellwarth, G. eds. *Modern Spanish theatre: a
anthology,* p. 310.

Esslin, Martin. *The theatre of the absurd,* pp. 186-190.

Guicharnaud, Jacques. *Modern French theatre from Giraudoux t
Genet* (rev. ed.), pp. 180-181, 184-187, 194, 250, 287, 344, 362.

Moore, Harry T. *Twentieth-century French literature since World Wa
II,* p. 164.

The Architect and the Emperor

Clurman, Harold. "Theatre in Europe, II." *Nation,* vol. 205, no.
(July 3, 1967), pp. 29-30.

The Automobile Graveyard (Le Cimetière des Voitures)

Esslin, Martin. *The theatre of the absurd,* pp. 188-189.

Serreau, Genevieve. "A New Comic Style: Arrabal." *Evergreen Rev
vol. 4 (Nov.-Dec., 1960), pp. 65-66.

Fando and Lis

Serreau, Genevieve. "A New Comic Style: Arrabal." *Evergreen Rev
vol. 4 (Nov.-Dec., 1960), pp. 66-67.

First Communion

Benedikt, M. and G.E. Wellwarth. *Modern Spanish theatre, a.
anthology of plays,* p. 310.

Orison

Serreau, Genevieve. "A New Comic Style: Arrabal." *Evergreen Rev
vol. 4 (Nov.-Dec., 1960), pp. 62-64.

Picnic on the Battlefield

Serreau, Genevieve. "A New Comic Style: Arrabal." *Evergreen Rev
vol. 4 (Nov.-Dec., 1960) pp. 68-69.

١e Two Executioners

Serreau, Genevieve. "A New Comic Style: Arrabal." *Evergreen Rev.,* vol. 4 (Nov.-Dec., 1960), pp. 64-65.

"A Short Play at Lunchtime." *Times,* no. 56,621 (May 3, 1966), p. 20.

FRANCISCO ARRIVI 1915-

eneral

Dauster, Frank. "Francisco Arrivi: The Mask and the Garden." *Hispania,* vol. 45 (1962), pp. 637-643.

Jones, W.K. *Behind Spanish American footlights,* pp. 372-373.

ANTONIN ARTAUD 1896-1948

eneral

Arnold, Paul. "The Artaud Experiment." *Tulane Drama Rev.,* vol. 8, no. 2 (1963), pp. 15-29.

Artaud, Antonin. "States of Mind: 1921-1945." *Tulane Drama Rev.,* vol. 8, no. 2 (1963), pp. 30-33.

Brustein, Robert. "No More Masterpieces." *Michigan Quarterly Rev.,* vol. 6 (1967), pp. 185-192.

Brustein, R. *The theatre of revolt,* pp. 363-411.

Chambers, Ross. "La magie du reel, Antonin Artaud and the Experience of the Theatre." *Australian J. of French Studies* (Monash U., Clayton, Victoria), vol. 3 (1966), pp. 51-65.

Chiaromonte, Nicola. "Antonin Artaud." *Encounter,* vol. 29, no. 2 (1967), pp. 44-50.

Fowlie, W. *Dionysus in Paris,* pp. 203-209.

Hauger, George. "When a Play Is Not a Play." *Tulane Drama Rev.,* vol. 5, no. 2 (Dec., 1960), pp. 54-64.

Hellman, Helen. "Hallucination and Cruelty in Artaud and Ghelderode." *French Rev.,* vol. 41 (1967), pp. 1-10.

Hivnor, Mary O. "Barrault and Artaud." *Partisan Rev.,* vol. 15 (Mar., 1948), pp. 332-338.

Weingarten, R. "Re-read Artaud." *Tulane Drama Rev.,* vol. 8, no. 2 (1963), pp. 74-84.

Wellwarth, G. "Antonin Artaud: Prophet of the Avant-gar Theatre." *Drama Survey,* vol. 2 (1963), pp. 276-286. *Also* Wellwarth, G., *Theatre of protest and paradox,* pp. 14-36.

Willison, Sheila. "The Language of the Absurd: Artaud and Ionesc $New Theatre Magazine$ (Bristol), vol. 7, no. 1 (1966), pp. 9-14.

Le Jet de Sang

Zeps, Betty S. "Artaud's *Le Jet de Sang* and His Theory of Dram *Semigallian Blazoon* (Madison, Wis.), vol. 1 (1967), pp. 13-17.

MICHEL PETROVICH ARTSYBASHEV 1878-1927

General

Chandler, F.W. *Modern continental playwrights,* pp. 94-110.

SHOLEM ASCH 1880-1957

General

Goldberg, Isaac. *The drama of transition,* pp. 373-379.

Lifson, D. *The Yiddish theatre in America,* pp. 89-93.

The God of Vengeance

Goldberg, Isaac. *The drama of transition,* pp. 375-379.

WINIFRED ASHTON ?-1965
(pseud. Clemence Dane)

Naboth's Vineyard

Roston, Murray. *Biblical drama in England from the Middle Ages the present day,* pp. 250-251.

MIGUEL ANGEL ASTURIAS

General

Lyon, Thomas E. "Miguel Angel Asturias: Timeless Fantasy." *Boo Abroad,* vol. 42, no. 2 (Spring, 1968), pp. 183-189.

WYSTAN HUGH AUDEN 1907-

General

Beach, Joseph W. *The making of the Auden Canon.*

Bruehl, William J. "The. Auden/Isherwood plays." *Dissertati Abstracts,* vol. 27 (1966), 1361A (Penn.).

)arlington, W.A. "Theorist in the Theatre." *Discovery,* vol. 16 (1935), p. 349-351.

.llmann, Eichard. "Gasebos and Gashouses." *In:* Ellmann, R. *Eminent domain* pp. 97-126.

lazard, Forrest Earl. "The Auden group and the group theatre: the ramatic theories and practices of Rupert Doone, W.H. Auden, :hristopher Isherwood, Louis MacNeice, Stephen Spender, and Cecil)ay Lewis." *Dissertation Abstracts,* vol. 25 (1964), 1913-14 (U. of Visconsin).

.night, G. Wilson. *The golden labyrinth,* pp. 367-368.

4itchell, Breon. "W.H. Auden and Christopher Isherwood: The jerman Influence. *Oxford German Studies,* vol. 1 (1966), pp. 163-172.

.pears, Monroe K. "Auden and Dionysus." *Shenandoah, vol. 18, no. 2* 1967), pp. 85-95.

.pender, Stephen. "The Poetic Dramas of W.H. Auden and :hristopher Isherwood." *New writing,* n. s. vol. 1 (1938), pp. 102-108.

ymons, J. "Auden and Poetic Drama." *Life and Letters Today,* vol. 0 (1939), pp. 70-79.

Veales, Gerald. *Religion in modern English drama,* pp. 224-225.

Villiams, R. *Drama from Ibsen to Eliot,* pp. 247-268.

)liography

3loomfield, B.C. *W.H. Auden: A bibliography. The Early Years Through 1955.* Charlottesville: The University Press of Virginia, 1964. Published for the Bibliographical Society of the University of 'irginia).

:lancy, J.P. "A. W.H. Auden Bibliography, 1924-1955." *Thought,* vol. 30 (Summer, 1955), pp. 260-270.

e Ascent of F6 (Christopher Isherwood, co-author)

3ruehl, William J. "Polus Naufrangia: A Key Symbol in *The Ascent of F6." Modern Drama,* vol. 10, no. 2 (Sept., 1967), pp. 161-164.

)onoghue, Denis. *The third voice: modern British and American verse drama,* pp. 62-70.

:verett, Barbara. *Auden,* pp. 55-59.

Forster, E.M. *Two cheers for democracy,* pp. 263-265.

59

Gerstenberger, Donna. "Verse Drama of Auden and Isherwood *Modern Drama,* vol. 5, no. 2 (Sept., 1962), pp. 123-132.

Lumley, Frederick. *New trends in 20th century drama,* p. 310.

McCollom, W.G. *Tragedy,* pp. 242-245.

Markan, Ronald. "Power and Conflict in *The Ascent of F(* *Discourse,* vol. 7 (1964), pp. 277-282.

Prior, Moody E. *The language of tragedy,* pp. 369-371.

Williams, Raymond. *Drama from Ibsen to Eliot,* pp. 251-255.

The Dance of Death

Everett, Barbara. *Auden,* pp. 49-51.

Gerstenberger, Donna. "Verse Drama of Auden and Isherwood *Modern Drama,* vol. 5, no. 2 (Sept., 1962), pp. 123-132.

The Dog Beneath the Skin

Everett, Barbara. *Auden,* pp. 52-55.

Gerstenberger, Donna. "Verse Drama of Auden and Isherwood *Modern Drama,* vol. 5, no. 2 (Sept., 1962), pp. 123-132.

Prior, Moody E. *The language of tragedy,* pp. 367-369.

Williams, Raymond. *Drama from Ibsen to Eliot,* pp. 247-251.

On the Frontier

Everett, Barbara. *Auden,* pp. 59-60.

Gerstenberger, Donna. "Verse Drama in Auden and Isherwood *Modern Drama,* vol. 5, no. 2 (Sept., 1962), pp. 123-132.

Prior, Moody E. *The language of tragedy,* pp. 371-372.

Williams, Raymond. *Drama from Ibsen to Eliot,* pp. 255-256.

Paid on Both Sides

Gerstenberger, Donna. "Verse Drama of Auden and Isherwood. *Modern Drama,* vol. 5, no. 2 (Sept., 1962), pp. 123-132.

The Rake's Progress

Weales, Gerald. *Religion in modern English drama,* pp. 224-225.

JACQUES AUDIBERTI 1899-1965

General

Cismaru, Alfred. "Audiberti's Quest for Eden." *Renascence,* vol. 19 (1967), pp. 122-130.

Cornell, Kenneth. "Audiberti and Obscurity." *Yale French Studies,* vol. 2, no. 2 (1949), pp. 100-104.

Gellert, Roger. *New Statesman,* vol. 64 (Dec. 21, 1962), pp. 908-909.

Guicharnaud, Jacques. *Modern French theatre from Giraudoux to Genet* (rev. ed.), pp. 26, 160-164, 169, 172, 176, 180, 282-283, 286, 288, 321, 338-339, 361.

Pronko, Leonard C. *Avant-garde: the experimental theater in France,* pp. 180-188.

Wellwarth, George. "Jacques Audiberti: The Drama of the Savage God." *Texas Studies in Literature and Language,* vol. 4 (1962), pp. 330-340.

Wellwarth, George. *The theatre of protest and paradox.* pp. 73-84.

The Black Feast (La Fête Noire)

Wellwarth, George. *The theatre of protest and paradox.* pp. 80-82.

The Evil Runs (Le Mal Court)

Wellwarth, George. *The theatre of protest and paradox.* p. 79.

The Hobby (La Hobereaute)

Pronko, Leonard C. *Avant-garde: the experimental theatre in France,* pp. 186-188.

Theatre Arts, vol. 43, no. 7 (July, 1959), p. 13.

The Landlady (La Logeuse)

Wellwarth, George. *The theatre of protest and paradox.* pp. 82-83.

The Natives of Bordelais (Les Naturels du Bordelais)

Wellwarth, George. *The theatre of protest and paradox,* p. 83.

Quoat-Quoat

"M. Audiberti's Aztec Symbol." *Times,* no. 56,228 (Jan. 25, 1965), p. 7.

Wellwarth, George. *The theatre of protest and paradox,* pp. 76-

Spoken Opera (Opéra Parlé)

Wellwarth, George. *The theatre of protest and paradox,* pp. 77-

ENRIQUE AVELLAN FERRES

General

Jones W.K. *Behind Spanish American footlights,* pp. 310, 311, 3 319.

GEORGE AXELROD 1922-

The Seven Year Itch

Gottfried, Martin. *A theater divided; the postwar American stage,* 215-216, 222-225.

Sievers, W. David. *Freud on Broadway,* pp. 446-447.

MARCEL AYME 1902-1967

General

Brodin, Dorothy. "A Fabulist for Our Times: Marcel Aymé *American Society of Legion of Honor Magazine,* vol. 38 (1967), ¡ 41-52.

Moore, Harry T. *Twentieth century French literature since World W II,* pp. 26-28.

Clérambard

Clurman, Harold. "Theatre." *Nation,* vol. 185, no. 19 (Dec. 7, 195 pp. 441-442.

La Convention Belzébir

"*La Convention Belzébir,* by Aymé." *World Theatre,* vol. 15, no. (Nov.-Dec., 1966), p. 561.

"Marcel Aymé's New Comedy About Legalized Homicide." *Times,* n 56,788 (Nov. 14, 1966), p. 14.

AZORIN 1873-1967
(real name José Martinez Ruiz)

General

Ayllon, Candido. "Experiments in the Theater of Unamun Valle-Inclán, and Azorin." *Hispania,* vol. 46 (1963), pp. 49-56.

Newberry, Wilma. "Pirandello and Azorin." *Italica,* vol. 44 (1967), pp. 41-60.

INGEBORG BACHMANN 1926-

General

Schoolfield, George C. "Ingeborg Bachmann." *In:* Keith-Smith, Brian, ed. *Essays on contemporary German literature* (German Men of Letters, vol. IV), pp. 187-212.

Der Gute Gott von Manhattan (radio play)

Schoolfield, George C. "Ingeborg Bachmann." *In:* Keith-Smith, Brian, ed. *Essays on contemporary German literature* (German Men of Letters. vol. IV), pp. 205-206.

Die Zikaden (radio play)

Schoolfield, George C. "Ingeborg Bachmann." *In:* Keith-Smith, Brian, ed. *Essays on contemporary German literature* (German Men of Letters, vol. IV), pp. 204-205.

HERMANN BAHR 1863-1934

General

Bauland, Peter. *The hooded eagle,* pp. 31-32, 56, 64.

Daviau, Donald G. *"Dialog vom Marsyas:* Hermann Bahr's Affirmation of Life over Art." *Modern Language Quarterly,* vol. 20 (Dec., 1959), pp. 360-370.

Daviau, Donald G. "The Friendship of Hermann Bahr and Arthur Schnitzler." *Journal of the International Arthur Schnitzler Research Association,* vol. 5, no. 1 (1966), pp. 4-36.

Garten, H.F. *Modern German drama,* pp. 62-63.

The Concert (Das Konzert)

Bauland, Peter. *The hooded eagle,* pp. 31-32.

JAMES BALDWIN 1924-

General

Bigsby, C.W.E. "The Committed Writer: James Baldwin as Dramatist." *Twentieth Century Literature,* vol. 13 (1967), pp. 39-48.

The Amen Corner

Lumley, Frederick. *New trends in 20th century drama,* p. 339.

Blues for Mister Charlie

Abramson, Doris E. *Negro playwrights in the American theatr 1925-1959,* pp. 274-275.

Bigsby, C.W.E. *Confrontation and commitment,* pp. 122, 129-137, 16‹

Brustein, Robert. *Seasons of discontent,* pp. 161-165.

Clurman, Harold. *The naked image,* pp. 37-39.

Lumley, Frederick. *New trends in 20th century drama,* pp. 339-34(

Mitchell, Loften. *Black drama,* pp. 200-201, 204.

Sontag, Susan. *Against interpretation and other essays,* pp. 151-15!

Turpin, Waters E. "The Contemporary American Negro Playwright. College Language Assn. J., vol. 9, no. 1 (Sept., 1965), pp. 20-21.

Tynan, Kenneth. *Tynan right and left,* pp. 144-145.

LUIS A. BARALT 1892-

General

Jones, W.K. *Behind Spanish American footlights,* pp. 403-404.

ERNST BARLACH 1870-1938

General

Chick, Edson M. "Comic and Grotesque Elements in Ernst Barlach." *Modern Language Q.,* vol. 20, no. 2, (June, 1959), pP. 173-180.

Chick, Edson M. *"Ernst Barlach,* pp. 13-29, 51-53, 102-107, 112-120‹

Chick, Edson M. "Ernst Barlach and the Theatre." *German Q.,* vo‹ 36, no. 1 (Jan., 1963), pp. 39-51.

Garten, H.F. *Modern German drama,* pp. 109-111.

Hatfield, Henry. *Modern German literature,* pp. 75-76.

Keiler, M.L. "Ernst Barlach, Sculptor and Dramatist." *College Art J.* vol. 15 (1956), pp. 313-326.

Keith-Smith, Brian. "Ernst Barlach." *In:* Natan, A., ed. *German mer of letters,* vol. 3, pp. 55-81.

McFarlane, J.W. "Plasticity in Language: Some Notes on the Pros‹ Style of Ernst Barlach." *Modern Language Rev.,* vol. 49 (Oct., 1954) pp. 451-460.

Synn, Ilhi. "The ironic rebel in the early dramatic works of Ernst Barlach." *Disertation Abstracts,* vol. 27 (1967), 3882A (Princeton).

The Blue Mr. Ball (Der Blaue Boll)

Chick, E.M. *"Der Blaue Boll* and the Problem of Vision in Barlach." *Germanic Rev.,* vol. 40, no. 1 (Jan., 1965), pp. 31-40.

Chick, Edson M. *Ernst Barlach,* pp. 44, 85-99, 106, 110, 111, 114-115, 122-123, 125, 127, 130-131.

Hauch, Edward Franklin. "Ernst Barlach and the Search for God." *Germanic Rev.,* vol. 2, no. 2 (April, 1927), pp. 157-166.

Keith-Smith, Brian. "Ernst Barlach." *In:* Natan, A., ed. *German men of letters,* vol. 3, pp. 67-68.

Lucas, W.I. "Barlach's *Der Blaue Boll* and the New Man." *German Life and Letters,* vol. 16 (1963), pp. 238-247.

The Count of Ratzburg (Der Graf Von Ratzeburg)

Chick, Edson M. *Ernst Barlach,* pp. 22, 83-84.

The Dead Day (Der Tote Tag)

Chick, Edson M. *Ernst Barlach,* pp. 30-31, 32, 58, 93-94, 121-122.

Hauch, Edward Franklin. "Ernst Barlach and the Search for God." *Germanic Rev.,* vol. 2, no. 2 (Apr. 1927), pp. 157-166.

Keith-Smith, Brian. "Ernst Barlach." *In:* Natan, A. ed. *German men of letters,* vol. 3 pp. 65.

The Flood (The Deluge) (Die Sündflut)

Chick, Edson M. "Diction in Barlach's *Sündflut." Germanic Rev.,* vol. 33, no. 4 (Dec., 1958), pp. 243-250.

Chick, Edson M. *Ernst Barlach,* pp. 68-82, 93, 98, 105, 127-129.

Hauch, Edward Franklin. "Ernst Barlach and the Search for God." *Germanic Rev.,* vol. 2, no. 2 (Apr., 1927), pp. 157-166.

Keiler, M.L. "Ernst Barlach, Sculptor and Dramatist." *College Art J.,* vol. 15 (1956), pp. 322-326.

Keith-Smith, Brian. "Ernst Barlach." *In:* Natan, A., ed. *German men of letters,* vol. 3 pp. 66-67.

The Foundling (Der Findling)

Chick, Edson M. *Ernst Barlach,* pp. 58-60, 72, 73, 94, 109.

Hauch, Edward Franklin. "Ernst Barlach and the Search for God" *Germanic Rev.,* vol. 2, no. 2 (Apr., 1927), pp. 157-166.

Keith-Smith, Brian. "Ernst Barlach." *In:* Natan, A., ed. *German m* *of letters,* vol. 3, pp. 66, 71.

The Good Time (Der Gute Zeit)

Chick, Edson M. *Ernst Barlach,* pp. 27, 82-83, 108, 117.

The Hundred Percenters (The Genuine Sedemunds) (Die Echte Sedemunds)

Chick, Edson M. *Ernst Barlach,* pp. 53-58, 63, 65, 71, 91, 103, 10 107, 119-120, 123-137.

Hauch, Edward Franklin. "Ernst Barlach and the Search for God" *Germanic Rev.,* vol. 2, no. 2 (Apr., 1927), pp. 157-166.

Keith-Smith, Brian. "Ernst Barlach." *In:* Natan, A., ed. *German m* *of letters,* vol. 3, pp. 65-66.

The Poor Relation (Der Arme Vetter)

Chick, Edson M. *Ernst Barlach,* pp. 30, 31-50, 57-58, 63, 91, 108-11 115, 116-118, 129-130.

Chick, E.M. "Ernst Barlach's *Der Arme Vetter:* A Study." *Moder* *Language Rev.,* vol. 57, no. 3 (July, 1962), pp. 373-384.

Hauch, Edward Franklin. "Ernst Barlach and the Search for God. *Germanic Rev.,* vol. 2 no. 2 (Apr., 1927), pp. 157-166.

Keith-Smith, Brian. "Ernst Barlach." *In:* Natan, A., ed. *German me* *of letters,* vol. 3, p. 65.

DJUNA BARNES 1892-

The Antiphon

Abel, Lionel. *Metatheatre, a new view of dramatic form,* pp. 116-121

Eberhart, Richard. "Outer and Inner Verse Drama." *Virginia Q. Rev* vol. 34, no. 4 (Autumn, 1958), pp. 618-623.

SIR JAMES M. BARRIE 1860-1937

General

Butler, Pierce. "Barrie: The Playwright." *South Atlantic Q.,* vol. 31 (1932), pp. 222-241.

Child, Harold. "J.M. Barrie as Dramatist." In: Hudson, Derek, ed. *English critical essays; twentieth century* (2nd series), pp. 1-10.

Darlington, W.A. *J.M. Barrie.*

Grotjohn, Martin. "The Defense Against Creative Anxiety in the Life and Work of James Barrie." *American Imago,* vol. 14, no. 2 (Summer, 1957), pp. 143-148.

Hamilton, Clayton. *Conversations on contemporary drama.* pp. 73-94.

Knight, G. Wilson. *The golden labyrinth,* pp. 329-330.

Miller, Nellie Burget. *The living drama,* pp. 310-313.

Nethercot, Arthur H. "The Quintessence of Idealism." *PMLA,* vol. 62 (1947), pp. 844-859.

Nicoll, Allardyce. *British drama,* pp. 287-289.

Phelps, William Lyon. *Essays on modern dramatists,* pp. 1-66.

Salerno, Henry F. *English drama in transition, 1880-1920,* pp. 277-279.

Skinner, John. "James M. Barrie or The Boy Who Wouldn't Grow Up." *American Imago,* vol. 14, no. 2 (Summer, 1957), pp. 111-141.

Williams, Harold *Modern English writers,* pp. 265-267.

Woodbridge, Homer E. "Barrie's Dual Personality." *South Atlantic Q.,* vol. 28 (1929), pp. 269-280.

he Admirable Crichton

Beerbohm, Max. *Around theatres,* pp. 231-234.

Clark, B.H. *A study of the modern drama,* pp. 316-320.

Darlington, W.A., *J.M. Barrie,* pp. 90-92.

McGraw, William R. "James M. Barrie's Concept of Dramatic Action." *Modern Drama,* vol. 5, no. 2 (Sept. 1962), pp. 133-141.

Phelps, William Lyon. *Essays on modern dramatists,* pp. 19-27.

Salerno, Henry F. *English drama in transition, 1880-1920,* pp. 279-280.

Walkley, A.B. *Drama and life,* pp. 198-208.

he Adored One

Darlington, W.A. *J.M. Barrie,* pp. 113-115.

Alice Sit-By-The-Fire

McGraw, William R. "James M. Barrie's Concept of Dramati Action." *Modern Drama,* vol. 5, no. 2 (Sept., 1962), pp. 133-141.

The Boy David

Darlington, W.A. *J.M. Barrie,* pp. 143-147.

Roston, Murray. *Biblical drama in England from the Middle Ages t the present day,* pp. 285-286.

Weales, Gerald. *Religion in modern English drama,* pp. 35-36.

Dear Brutus

Darlington, W.A. *J.M. Barrie,* pp. 123-128.

MacCarthy, Desmond. *Drama,* pp. 315-321.

MacCarthy, Desmond. *Theatre,* pp. 144-149.

Miller, Nellie Burget. *The living drama,* pp. 313-316.

Phelps, William Lyon. *Essays on modern dramatists,* pp. 61-66.

A Kiss for Cinderella

Young, Stark. *Immortal shadows,* pp. 227-229.

The Little Minister

Darlington, W.A. *J.M. Barrie,* pp. 77-79.

Phelps, William Lyon. *Essays on modern dramatists,* pp. 15-18.

Shaw, George Bernard. *Shaw's dramatic criticism (1895-98),* pp. 266-270.

Mary Rose

Baring, M. *Punch and Judy and other essays,* pp. 349-354.

Darlington, W.A. *J.M. Barrie,* pp. 130-134.

Karpe, Marietta. "The Meaning of Barrie's *Mary Rose.*" *Internationa Journal of Psycho-Analysis,* vol. 38 (1957), pp. 408-411.

The New Word

Darlington, W.A. *J.M. Barrie,* pp. 118-121.

ter Pan

Beerbohm, Max., *Around theatres,* pp. 357-361.

Darlington, W.A. *J.M. Barrie,* pp. 97-103, 148-150.

Karpe, Marietta. "The Origins of Peter Pan." *Pyschoanalytic Review,* vol. 43 (1956), pp. 104-110.

McGraw, William R. "James M. Barrie's Concept of Dramatic Action." *Modern Drama,* vol. 5, no. 2 (Sept., 1962), pp. 133-141.

Phelps, William Lyon. *Essays on modern dramatists,* pp. 31-34.

Stevenson, Lionel. "A Source for Barrie's *Peter Pan." Philological Q.,* vol. 8 (1929), pp. 210-214.

Walkley, A.B. *Drama and life,* pp. 209-213.

uality Street

Beerbohm, Sir Max. *Around theatres,* pp. 220-223.

Darlington, W.A. *J.M. Barrie,* pp. 87-90.

Walkley, A.B. *Drama and life,* pp. 194-197.

hall We Join the Ladies?

Darlington, W.A. *J.M. Barrie,* pp. 134-136.

he Twelve Pound Look

Darlington, W.A., *J.M. Barrie,* pp. 109-111.

Valker, London

Phelps, William Lyon. *Essays on modern dramatists,* pp. 13-15.

Vhat Every Woman Knows

Darlington, W.A. *J.M. Barrie,* pp. 104-105.

McGraw, William R. "James M. Barrie's Concept of Dramatic Action." *Modern Drama,* vol. 5, no. 2 (Sept., 1962), pp. 133-141.

Phelps, William Lyon. *Essays on Modern dramatists,* pp. 41-47.

PHILIP BARRY 1896-1949

eneral

Broussard, Louis. *American drama...,* pp. 56-68.

Brown, John Mason. *Still seeing things,* pp. 30-37.

Brown, John Mason. *Upstage,* pp. 19-30.

Clark, Barrett H. "Philip Barry." *Stage* vol. 7 (May, 1930), pp. 21-26

Dusenbury, Winifred L. "Myth in American Drama Between the Wars." *Modern Drama,* vol. 6, no. 3 (Dec., 1963), pp. 294-308.

Flexner, Eleanor. *American playwrights: 1918-1938,* pp. 249-256.

Gagey, E.M. "Comedy—American Plan." *Revolution in American drama,* pp. 175-231.

Gassner, John. *The theatre in our times,* pp. 322-328.

Gould, Jean. *Modern American playwrights,* pp. 78-98.

Hamm, Gerald. *The dramas of Philip Barry.*

Lavery, Emmet. "The World of Philip Barry." *Drama Critique,* vol. (Nov., 1960), pp. 98-107.

Lippman, Monroe. "Philip Barry and His Socio-Political Attitudes." *Q. J. of Speech,* vol. 42, no. 2 (April, 1956), pp. 151-156.

Morris, L.R. *Postscript to yesterday,* pp. 172-213.

Moses, Montrose J. "Philip Barry." *In:* Moses, Montrose J. *The American theatre as seen by its critics, 1752-1934,* pp. 223-228 (Reprinted from *Representative American dramas,* Boston, Little Brown. 1934.)

Phillips, Elizabeth C. *Modern American drama,* pp. 97-98.

Roppolo, J.P. *Philip Barry.*

The Animal Kingdom

Hutchens, John. "Broadway in Review." *Theatre Arts,* vol. 16 (Mar. 1932), pp. 187-188.

Krutch, Joseph W. *The American drama since 1918,* pp. 172-175.

Krutch, J.W. "Nice People." *Nation,* vol. 134 (Feb. 3, 1932), pp 151-152.

Sievers, W. David. *Freud on Broadway,* pp. 198-199.

Wyatt, Euphemia. "The Drama: *The Animal Kingdom.*" *Catholic World,* vol. 134 (March, 1932), pp. 714-715.

right Star

Krutch, J.W. "Dissenting Opinion." *Nation,* vol. 141 (Oct. 30, 1935), pp. 518-520.

oolish Notion

Brown, J.M. "Did You Ever See Some Dreams Walking?" *Saturday Rev. of Literature,* vol. 28 (Mar., 24, 1945), pp. 18-19.

Gilder, Rosamond. "Notions, Foolish and Otherwise: Broadway in Prospect." *Theatre Arts,* vol. 29 (May, 1945), pp. 269-270.

Krutch, J.W. "Drama." *Nation,* vol. 160 (Mar., 24, 1945), pp. 340-341.

Sievers, W. David. *Freud on Broadway,* pp. 205-208.

ere Come the Clowns

Broussard, Louis. *American drama...,* pp. 65-68.

Brown, John Mason. *Broadway in review,* pp. 165-169.

Downer, Alan S. *Fifty years of American drama, 1900-1950,* pp. 72-73.

Gilder, Rosamond. "Hell's Paving Stones: Broadway in Review." *Theatre Arts,* vol. 23 (Feb., 1939), pp. 87-98.

Krutch, Joseph W. *The American drama since 1918,* pp. 176-178.

Krutch, Joseph W. "Prodigal's Return." *Nation,* vol. 147 (Jan., 1939), pp. 700-701.

Sievers, W. David. *Freud on Broadway,* pp. 195-197.

Wyatt, Euphemia. "Drama." *Catholic Worker,* vol. 148 (Jan., 1939), pp. 473-474.

oliday

Flexner, Eleanor. *American playwrights: 1918-1938,* pp. 256-261.

Sievers, W. David. *Freud on Broadway,* pp. 197-198.

otel Universe

Broussard, Louis. *American drama...,* pp. 58-65.

Brown, John Mason. *Two on the aisle,* pp. 159-163.

Downer, Alan S. *Fifty years of American drama, 1900-1950.* pp. 70-72.

Flexner, Eleanor. *American playwrights: 1918-1938,* pp. 261-266.

Krutch, Joseph W. *The American drama since 1918,* pp. 169-172.

Krutch, Joseph W. "Weltschmertz on the Riviera." *Nation,* vol. 13 (Apr. 30, 1930), pp. 525-526.

Roppolo, J.P. *Philip Barry,* pp. 66-69.

Sievers, W. David. *Freud on Broadway,* pp. 190-195.

In a Garden

Sievers, W. David. *Freud on Broadway,* pp. 188-190.

The Joyous Season

Flexner, Eleanor. *American playwrights: 1918-1938,* pp. 268-270.

Krutch, Joseph W. "No Miracle." *Nation,* vol. 138 (Feb. 14, 1934), pp 200-202.

Sievers, W. David. *Freud on Broadway,* pp. 199-201.

Paris Bound

Krutch, Joseph W. *The American drama since 1918,* pp. 165-167.

Krutch, Joseph W. "A School of Wives." *Nation,* vol. 126 (Jan. 18 1928), pp. 75-76.

Young, Stark, "Dilations." *New Republic,* vol. 53 (Jan. 25, 1928), pp 272-273.

The Philadelphia Story

Brown, John Mason. *Broadway in review,* pp. 127-131.

Krutch, Joseph W. *The American drama since 1918,* pp. 178-180.

Krutch, Joseph W. "Miss Hepburn Pays up." *Nation,* vol. 148 (Apr. 8, 1939), pp. 410-411.

Sievers, W. David. *Freud on Broadway,* pp. 203-204.

Second Threshold (Robert E. Sherwood, co-author)

Brown, John Mason. "Success Story." *Saturday Rev. of Literature,* vol 34 (Jan. 27, 1951), pp. 25-27.

Clurman, Harold. "From Lorca Down." *New Republic,* vol. 124 (Feb. 5, 1951), pp. 22-23.

Downer, Alan S. *Fifty years of American drama, 1900-1950,* pp. 148-150.

Gassner, J. *Theatre at the crossroads,* pp. 130-132.

Gibbs, Wolcott. "Death and Honor." *New Yorker,* vol. 26 (Jan. 13, 1951), pp. 44.

Sievers, W. David. *Freud on Broadway,* pp. 208-211.

omorrow and Tomorrow

Dusenbury, Winifred. L. *The theme of loneliness in modern American drama,* pp. 87-93.

Flexner, Eleanor. *American playwrights: 1918-1938,* pp. 266-268.

Roppolo, J.P. *Philip Barry,* pp. 69-75.

Sievers, W. David. *Freud on Broadway,* pp. 201-203.

Van Doren, Mark. "The Comic Spirit Takes a Rest." *Nation,* vol. 132 (Jan. 28, 1931), pp. 107-108.

/ithout Love

Krutch, Joseph W. "A Vehicle for Miss Hepburn." *Nation,* vol. 155 (Nov. 21, 1942), pp. 553-554.

Sievers, W. David. *Freud on Broadway,* pp. 204-205.

Young, Stark. "Barry-Barrie." *New Republic,* vol. 107 (Nov. 23, 1942), pp. 679-680.

ou and I

Wilson, Edmund. *Dial,* vol. 85 (July, 1923), pp. 100-101.

ENRICO BASSANO 1899-

eneral

Pandolfi, Vito. "Italian Theatre Since the War." *Tulane Drama Rev.,* vol. 8, no. 3 (Spring, 1964), pp. 97-98.

EMANUEL JO BASSHE 1900-1939

eneral

Knox, George A. *Dos Passos and "The Revolting Playwrights."* pp. 59-60, 64-66.

The Centuries

Knox, George A. *Dos Passos and "The Revolting Playwrights."* pr
117-121, 168, 171-173, 194.

Earth

Knox, George A. *Dos Passos and "The Revolting playwrights."* pr
104-106, 157, 160, 167, 170, 193.

HENRY BATAILLE 1872-1922

General

Knowles, Dorothy. *French drama of the inter-war years, 1918-39,* pr
260-262.

VICKI BAUM 1888-1960

General

Bauland, Peter. *The hooded eagle,* pp. 110-111.

JAMES K. BAXTER

The Spots of the Leopard

Sainer, Arthur. *The sleepwalker and the assassin, a view of th*
contemporary theatre, pp. 82-83.

SAMUEL BECKETT 1906-

General

Abel, Lionel. *Metatheatre, a new view of dramatic form,* pp. 83-85

Allsop, Kenneth. *The angry decade,* pp. 37-42.

Barbour, Thomas. "Beckett and Ionesco". *Hudson Rev.,* vol. 1
(Summer, 1958), pp. 271-277.

Barrett, William. "How I Understand Less and Less Every Year."
Columbia University Forum (Winter, 1959), pp. 44-48.

Berlin, Normand. "Beckett and Shakespeare." *French Rev.,* vol. 4(
(1967), pp. 647-651.

Bree, Germaine. "Beckett's Abstractors of Quintessence." *French Rev.,*
vol. 36 (1963), pp. 567-576.

Butler, Michael. "Anatomy of Despair." *Encore,* vol. 8, no. 3
(May-June, 1961), pp. 17-24.

Chambers, Ross. "Beckett's Brinkmanship." *In:* Esslin, Martin, ed. *Samuel Beckett,* pp. 152-168. *(Also in:* AUMLA, *J. of the Australasian Language and Literature Association,* No. 19, (May, 1963), pp. 57-75.)

Chambers, Ross. "Samuel Beckett and the Padded Cell." *Meanjin Q.* (Univ. of Melbourne), vol. 21 (1962), pp. 451-462.

Cleveland, Louise O. "Trials in the Soundscape: The Radio Plays of Samuel Beckett." *Modern Drama,* vol. 11, no. 3 (Dec., 1968), pp. 267-282.

Coe, Richard N. *Samuel Beckett,* pp. 88-110.

Cohn, Ruby. "Beckett for Comparatists: A Review Essay of Books Published in the Last Two Years." *Comparative Lit. Studies* (U. of Ill.), vol.3 (1966), pp 451-457.

Cohn, Ruby. "A Comic Complex and a Complex Comic." *In:* Corrigan, Robert W., ed. *Comedy: meaning and form,* pp. 427-439.

Cohn, Ruby. "Joyce and Beckett, Irish Cosmopolitans." *In:* Jost, Francois, ed. *Proceedings of the IVth Congress of the International Comparative Literature Association.* Fribourg, 1964, vol. 1, pp. 109-113.

Cohn, Ruby. "Play and Player in the Plays of Samuel Beckett." *Yale French Studies, no. 29* (Spring-Summer, 1962), pp. 43-48.

Cohn, Ruby. "Preliminary Observations on Samuel Beckett." *Perspective* (Washington University), Autumn, 1959, pp. 119-131.

Cohn, Ruby. *Samuel Beckett: the comic gamut.*

Cohn, Ruby. "Samuel Beckett, Self Translator." *PMLA,* vol. 76 (1961), pp. 613-621.

Cohn, Ruby. *"Theatrum Mundi* and Contemporary Theater." *Comparative Drama,* vol. 1 (1967), pp. 28-35.

Driver, Tom F. "Beckett by the Madeleine." *Columbia University Forum,* 4, no. 3 (Summer, 1961), pp. 21-25. (Interview)

Esslin, Martin. "Godot and His Children: The Theatre of Samuel Beckett and Harold Pinter." *In:* Armstrong, W.A., ed. *Experimental drama,* pp. 128-146.

Esslin, Martin. *Samuel Beckett,* Introduction, pp. 1-15.

Esslin, Martin. *The theatre of the absurd,* pp. 1-13, 43-46.

Fletcher, John. "Action and Play in Beckett's Theatre." *Modern Drama,* vol. 9, no. 3 (Dec. 1966), pp. 242-250.

Fletcher, John. *Samuel Beckett's art,* pp. 11-23, 41-49, 55-58, 62-64, 66-67, 71-76, 138-146.

Fowlie, W. *Dionysus in Paris,* pp. 210-217.

Friedman, M.J. "The Achievement of Samuel Beckett." *Books Abroad,* vol. 33 (1959), pp. 278-281.

Frye, Northrop. "The Nightmare Life in Death." *Hudson Rev.,* vol. 13, no. 3 (Autumn, 1960), pp. 442-448.

Gaddis, Marilyn. "The Purgatory Metaphor of Yeats and Beckett." *London Magazine,* vol. 7, no. 5 (Aug. 1967) pp. 33-46.

Gottfried, Martin. *A theater divided; the postwar American stage,* pp. 280-283.

Guicharnaud, Jacques. *Modern French theatre from Giraudoux to Beckett,* pp. 212-220.

Guicharnaud, Jacques. *Modern French theatre from Giraudoux to Genet* (rev. ed.), pp. 161, 180, 184, 187, 190, 193, 196-197, 202, 212, 224, 228, 248-258, 259, 281-282, 288, 290.

Hamilton, Kenneth. "Negative Salvation in Samuel Beckett." *Queen's Q.,* vol. 69, no. 1 (Spring, 1962), pp. 102-111.

Hampton, Charles Christy. "The human situation in the plays of Samuel Beckett: A study in stratagems of inaction." *Dissertation Abstracts,* vol. 27, 206A (Stanford).

Hoffman, Frederick J. *Samuel Beckett: the language of self.*

Hooker, Ward. "Irony and Absurdity in the Avant-Garde Theater." *Kenyon Rev.,* vol. 12 (Summer, 1960), pp. 436-454.

Hubert, Renee R. "The Couple and the Performance in Samuel Beckett's Play." *L'Esprit Createur,* vol. 2, no. 4 (Winter, 1962), pp. 175-180.

Hughes, Catherine. "Beckett and the Game of Life." *Catholic World,* vol. 195 (June, 1962), pp. 163-168.

Hurley, Paul J. "France and America: Versions of the Absurd." *College English,* vol. 26 (1965), pp. 634-640.

Iser, Wolfgang. "Beckett's Dramatic Language." *Modern Drama, vol.* 9, no. 3 (Dec., 1966), pp. 251-259.

Jacobsen, Josephine. *Ionesco and Genet, playwrights of silence,* pp. 2 7, 9-12, 15-19, 21-25, 84-85, 88-89, 91, 96-97, 99-102, 104, 179, 193-194, 197, 212, 219-221, 224-231, 233.

Jacobsen, Josephine. *The testament of Samuel Beckett,* pp. 19-39.

Kenner, Hugh. "The Beckett Landscape." *Spectrum* (Winter, 1958), pp. 8-24.

Kenner, Hugh. "Progress Report, 1962-65." *In: Beckett at 60, a festschrift,* pp. 61-77.

Kern, Edith. "Beckett's Knight of Infinite Resignation." *Yale French Studies,* no. 29 (Spring-Summer 1962), pp. 49-56.

Lumley, Frederick. *New trends in 20th century drama,* pp. 167, 179, 200-201, 202-208, 211, 269, 366.

Mayoux, Jean-Jacques. "Beckett and Expressionism." *Modern Drama,* vol. 9, no. 3 (Dec., 1966), pp. 238-241.

Mayoux, Jean-Jacques. "The Theatre of Samuel Beckett." *Perspective,* 11, no. 3 (Autumn, 1959), pp. 142-155.

Metz, Mary S. "Existentialism and inauthenticity in the theater of Beckett, Ionesco, and Genet." *Dissertation Abstracts,* vol. 27 (1966), 1377A-78A (La. State).

Moore, J.R. "Some Night Thoughts on Beckett." *Massachusetts Rev.,* vol. 8 (1967), pp. 529-539.

Morse, J. Mitchell. "The Comtemplative Life According to Samuel Beckett." *Hudson Rev.* vol 15 (1962), pp. 512-524.

Mueller, William R. and Jacobsen, Josephine. "Samuel Beckett's Long Saturday: To Wait or Not to Wait? *In:* Scott, Nathan A. *Man in the modern theatre,* pp. 76-97.

O'Brien, Justin. "Samuel Beckett and Andre Gide: An Hypothesis." *French Rev.,* vol. 40 (1967), pp. 485-486.

O'Neill, Joseph P. "The Absurd in Samuel Beckett." *Personalist,* vol. 48, no. 1 (Jan., 1967), pp. 56-61.

Parker, R.B. "The Theory and Theatre of the Absurd." *Queen's Q.,* vol. 73, no. 3 (Autumn, 1966), pp. 420-441.

Pronko, Leonard C. *Avant-garde: the experimental theater in France,* pp. 22-58.

Pronko, Leonard C. *Theater East and West,* pp. 106-111.

Reid, Alec. "Beckett and the Drama of Unknowing." *Drama Survey,* 2, no. 2 (Fall 1962), pp. 130-138.

Renaud, Madeleine. "Beckett the Magnificent." *In: Beckett at 60, a festschrift,* pp. 81-83.

Rexroth, Kenneth. "The Point is Irrelevance." *Nation,* vol. 182 (Apr 14, 1956), pp. 325-328.

Scott, Nathan A. *Samuel Beckett.*

Simpson, Alan. *Beckett and Behan and a theatre in Dublin,* pp. 62-97 101-103.

Smith, R.D. "Back to the Text." *In:* Brown, John Russell and Bernard Harris, eds. *Contemporary theatre,* pp. 127-136.

Styan, J.L. *The dark comedy,* 2nd ed. 2, 13, 31, 47, 112, 117-118, 158 214, 217-223, 240, 244, 246, 250, 255, 281, 288, 289, 292.

Suvin, Darko. "Beckett's Purgatory of the Individual or the 3 Laws of Thermodynamics." *Tulane Drama Rev.* vol. 11 (1967), no. 4, pp 23-36.

Wellwarth, G.E. "Life in the Void: Samuel Beckett." *Univ. of Kansas City Rev.,* vol. 28 (1961), pp. 25-33.

Wellwarth, George. *The theatre of protest and paradox.* pp. 37-51.

Williams, Raymond. *Modern tragedy,* pp. 153-155.

Act Without Words I (Acte sans Paroles I)

Allison, Alexander W., ed. *Masterpieces of the drama,* 2nd ed., pp 782.

Bigsby, C.W.E. *Confrontation and commitment,* pp. 21, 54-55.

"Bleak Genius Is Honoured." *Times,* no. 56,528 (Jan. 13, 1966), p. 14

Bray, Barbara. "The New Beckett." *Observer,* no. 8,972 (June 16 1963), p. 29.

Hassan, Ihab. *The literature of silence; Henry Miller and Samuel Beckett,* pp. 192-193.

Kerr, Walter. *Tragedy and comedy,* pp. 320-321.

Pronko, Leonard C. *Avant-garde: the experimental theater in France* p. 48.

Styan, J.L. *The dark comedy,* 2nd ed., pp. 221, 225, 271-272.

Tynan, Kenneth. "A Philosophy of Despair." *Observer,* no. 8649 (April 7, 1957), p. 15.

Vos, Nelvin. *The drama of comedy: victim and victor,* p. 28.

ct Without Words II (Acte sans Paroles II)

Gascoigne, Bamber. "From the Head." *Spectator,* no. 6996 (July 27, 1962), p. 115.

Hassan, Ihab. *The literature of silence; Henry Miller and Samuel Beckett,* pp. 192-193.

Pronko, Leonard C. *Avant-guard: the experimental theater in France,* pp. 48-49.

"A Trifle from Beckett." *Times,* no. 56,537 (Jan. 24, 1966), p. 14.

ll That Fall (Tous Ceux Qui Tombent)

Allison, Alexander W., ed. *Masterpieces of the drama,* 2nd ed., pp. 781-782.

Alpaugh, David J. "The Symbolic Structure of Samuel Beckett's *All That Fall." Modern Drama,* vol. 9, no. 3 (Dec., 1966), pp. 324-332.

Barbour, Thomas. "Beckett and Ionesco." *Hudson Rev.* 11 (Summer, 1958), pp. 274-275.

Cleveland, Louise O. "Trials in the Soundscape: The Radio Plays of Samuel Beckett." *Modern Drama,* vol. 11, no. 3 (Dec., 1968), pp. 270-277.

Cohn, Ruby. *Samuel Beckett,* pp. 243-247.

Davie, Donald. "Kinds of Comedy." *Spectrum* (Winter, 1958), pp. 25-31.

Esslin, Martin. *The theatre of the absurd,* p. 40.

Friedman, Maurice. *To deny our nothingness,* pp. 313-315.

Hassan, Ihab. *The literature of silence; Henry Miller and Samuel Beckett,* pp. 189-191, 195.

Hawtrey, Freda. *"All That Fall." Listener,* vol. 57, no. 1453 (Jan. 31, 1957), p. 197.

Hutchinson, Mary. *"All That Fall." Listener,* vol. 57, no. 1454 (Feb. 7, 1957), p. 235.

Jacobsen, Josephine. *The testament of Samuel Beckett,* pp. 111, 158, 160, 166, 181, 187, 189, 191.

Kenner, Hugh. *Samuel Beckett, a critical study* (new ed.), pp. 167-174.

Logue, Christopher. "For Those Still Standing." *New Statesman,* vol. 54 (Sept. 14, 1957), p. 325.

Lumley, Frederick. *New trends in 20th century drama,* pp. 207-208

Metman, Eva. "Reflections on Samuel Beckett's Plays." *In:* Esslin Martin, ed. *Samuel Beckett,* pp. 137-139. *(Also in J. of Analytica Psychology,* vol. 5, no. 1 (Jan., 1960), pp. 60-62.)

Miller, Karl. "Beckett's Voices." *Encounter,* vol. 13, no. 3 (Sept. 1959), pp. 59-60.

Paul, Robert. *Northwest Rev.,* vol. 1, no. 2 (Fall, 1957), pp. 59-61

Pronko, Leonard C. *Avant-garde: the experimental theater in France* pp. 49-50.

Scott, Nathan A. *Samuel Beckett,* pp. 114-118.

Styan, J.L. *The dark comedy,* 2nd ed., pp. 60, 63, 234-235, 250 291-292, 296.

"A Trifle from Beckett." *Times,* no. 56,537 (Jan. 24, 1966), p. 14.

Wace, Michael. *"All That Fall." Listener* vol. 57, no. 1455 (Feb. 14 1957), p. 275.

Walker, Roy. "Shagreen Shamrock." *Listener,* vol. 57, no. 1452 (Jan 24, 1957), pp. 167-168.

Cascando

Cleveland, Louise O. "Trials in the Soundscape: The Radio Plays o Samuel Beckett." *Modern Drama,* vol. 11, no. 3 (Dec. 1968), pp 280-282.

Fletcher, John. *Samuel Beckett's art,* pp. 79-82.

Furbank, P. N., "A New Work by Beckett." *Listener,* vol. 72, no. 185! (Oct. 15, 1964), p. 604.

Holmstrom, John. "Come On!" *New Statesman,* vol. 68, no. 1753 (Oct 16, 1964), pp. 588-589.

Kenner, Hugh. *Samuel Beckett, a critical study* (new ed.), pp. 216-217

"Two Voices in New Play by Samuel Beckett." *Times,* no. 56,137 (Oct 8, 1964), p. 6.

Come and Go (Va et Vient)

Cohn, Ruby. "Theatre Abroad." *Drama Survey,* vol 5, no. 3 (Winter 1966-67), p. 289.

Hayter, Augy, "Beckett, Old and New." *Plays and Players,* vol. 13, no 9 (June, 1966), p. 69.

Kenner, Hugh. *Samuel Beckett, a critical study* (new ed.), pp. 224-225.

McAuley, Gay. "Samuel Beckett's *Come and Go.*" *Educational Theatre J.,* vol. 18, no. 4 (Dec., 1966), pp. 439-442.

Ricks, Christopher. "Mr. Artesian." *Listener,* vol. 78, no. 2001 (Aug. 3, 1967), pp. 148-149.

"A Trifle from Beckett." *Times,* no. 56,537 (Jan. 24, 1966), p. 14.

Wilson, Angus. "The Humanism of Beckett." *Observer,* no. 9183 (July 16, 1967), p. 20.

h Joe

Kenner, Hugh. *Samuel Beckett, a critical study* (new ed.), pp. 219-220.

Ricks, Christopher. "Mr. Artesian." *Listener,* vol. 78, no. 2001 (Aug. 3, 1967), pp. 148-149.

"When Joe Has a Voice." *Times,* no. 56,676 (July 6, 1966), p. 16.

leutheria

Kenner, Hugh. *Samuel Beckett, a critical study* (new ed.), pp. 139-143.

mbers

Cleveland, Louise O. "Trials in the Soundscape: The Radio Plays of Samuel Beckett." *Modern Drama,* vol. 11, no. 3 (Dec., 1968), pp. 277-279.

Cohn, Ruby, ed. *Twentieth century drama,* pp. 679-680.

Esslin, Martin. *The theatre of the absurd,* pp. 42-43.

Ferris, Paul. "Radio Notes." *Observer,* no. 8765 (June 28, 1959), p. 18.

Hassan, Ihab. *The literature of silence; Henry Miller and Samuel Beckett,* pp. 189, 191-192.

Kenner, Hugh. *Samuel Beckett, a critical study* (new ed.), pp. 25, 174-175, 183-184, 186-187.

Miller, Karl. "Beckett's Voices." *Encounter,* vol. 13, no. 3 (Sept., 1959), p. 60.

Pronko, Leonard C. *Avant-garde: the experimental theater in France,* pp. 51-52.

Rodger, Ian. "Perishing on the Shore." *Listener,* vol. 62, no. 1579 (July 2, 1959), pp. 35-36.

Sainer, Arthur. *The sleepwalker and the assassin, a view of the contemporary theatre, pp. 104*-105.

Scott, Nathan A. *Samuel Beckett,* pp. 119-121.

Endgame (Fin de Partie)

Abel, Lionel. *Metatheatre, a new view of dramatic form,* pp. 134-140

Banerjee, C. "Theatre. *Endgame.* By Samuel Beckett." *Though.* (Delhi), vol. 18, no. 17 (Apr. 23, 1966), pp. 20-21.

Barbour, Thomas. "Beckett and Ionesco." *Hudson Rev.,* vol. 11 (Summer, 1958), pp. 271-274.

Baxter, Kay M. *Contemporary theatre and the Christian faith,* pp. 103-106.

Blau, Herbert. *The impossible theatre,* pp. 240-251

"Bleak Genius Is Honoured." *Times,* no. 56,528 (Jan. 13, 1966), p. 14.

Brick, Allan. "A Note On Perception and Communication in Beckett's *Endgame.*" *Modern Drama,* vol. 4, no. 1 (May 1961), pp. 20-22.

Cohn, Ruby. "The Beginning of *Endgame.*" *Modern Drama,* vol. 9, no. 3 (Dec. 1966), pp. 319-323.

Cohn, Ruby. *"Endgame:* The Gospel According to Sad Sam Beckett." *Accent,* vol. 20, no. 4 (Autumn, 1960), pp. 223-234.

Cohn, Ruby. "Tempest in an *Endgame.*" *Symposium,* vol. 19, no. 4 (Winter, 1965), pp. 328-334.

Cook, Albert S. "Language and Action in the Drama." *College English,* vol. 28, no. 1 (Oct., 1966), pp. 23-24.

Cook, Albert. *Prisms, studies in modern literature,* pp. 100-107, 144-145.

Davison, Peter. "Contemporary Drama and Popular Dramatic Forms." *In: Aspects of drama and the theatre,* pp. 167-169.

Dobrée, Bonamy. "The London Theater, 1957." *Sewanee Rev.,* vol. 66 (Winter, 1958), pp. 146-152.

Eastman, Richard M. "The Strategy of Samuel Beckett's *Endgame.*" *Modern Drama,* vol. 2, no. 1 (May, 1959), pp. 36-44.

Easthope, Anthony. "Hamm, Clov, and Dramatic Method in *Endgame.*" *Modern Drama,* vol. 10, no. 4 (Feb., 1968), pp. 424-433.

Esslin, Martin. *The theatre of the absurd,* pp. 27-39.

Fletcher, John. *Samuel Beckett's art,* pp. 52-55, 60-62, 65-66, 70-71, 120-121, 124.

Fowlie, Wallace. *Dionysus in Paris,* pp. 214-216.

Frisch, Jack E. *"Endgame:* A Play As Poem." *Drama Survey,* 3, no. 2 Oct. 1963), pp. 257-263.

Gassner, John. *Theatre at the crossroads,* pp. 256-261.

Glicksberg, Charles I. *The self in modern literature,* pp. 120-121.

Gross, John. "Amazing Reductions." *Encounter,* 23 (Sept. 1964), pp. 51-52.

Grossvogel, David I. *Four playwrights and a postscript, Brecht, Ionesco, Beckett, Genet,* pp. 109-120.

Grossvogel, David I. *The self-conscious stage in modern French drama,* pp. 331-334.

Hassan, Ihab. *The literature of silence; Henry Miller and Samuel Beckett,* pp. 183-188.

Hatch, Robert. *Nation,* 186 (Feb. 15, 1958), pp. 145-146.

Hatzfeld, Helmut. *Trends and styles in twentieth century French literature,* p. 267.

Hoffman, F.J. *Samuel Beckett,* pp. 153-155.

Jacobsen, Josephine. *The testament of Samuel Beckett,* pp. 101, 111, 123, 160, 179, 181-184, 187, 189-191.

Kenner, Hugh. *Samuel Beckett, a critical study* (new ed.), pp. 44-45, 57, 95-96, 155-156.

Kott, Jan. *"King Lear* or *Endgame." Evergreen Review,* no. 33 Aug.-Sept., 1964), pp. 53-65. *(Also in: Polish Perspectives,* vol. 4, no. 3 (March 1961), pp. 20-35.)

Lamont, Rosette C. "The Metaphysical Farce: Beckett and Ionesco." *French Rev.,* vol. 32, no. 4 (Feb., 1959), pp. 324-328.

Lennon, Peter. "Beckett's *Endgame* in Paris." *Guardian,* no. 36,586 Feb. 21, 1964), p. 11.

Leventhal, A.J. "Close of Play." *Dublin Mag.* (Apr.-June, 1957), pp. 18-22.

Lyons, Charles R. "Beckett's *Endgame:* An Anti-Myth of Creation." *Modern Drama,* vol. 7 (Sept., 1964), pp. 204-209.

Matthews, Honor. *The primal curse,* pp. 160-163.

Metman, Eva. "Reflections on Samuel Beckett's Plays." *In:* Esslin Martin, ed. *Samuel Beckett,* pp. 132-136. *(Also in J. of Analytics Psychology,* vol. 5, no. 1 (Jan., 1960), pp. 55-60.)

Nightingale, Benedict. *"Endgame* at Liverpool." *Guardian,* no. 37,17 (Jan. 19, 1966), p. 9.

Nightingale, Benedict. *"Endgame* at the Aldwych." *Guardian,* no. 36,706 (July 11, 1964), p. 7.

O'Callaghan, John. *"The Mandrake* and *Endgame* at York." *Guardian* no. 36,382 (June 26, 1963), p. 9.

O'Neill, Joseph P. "The Absurd in Samuel Beckett." *Personalist,* vo 48, no. 1 (Jan., 1967), pp. 65, 74.

Pronko, Leonard C. *Avant-garde: the experimental theater in Franc* pp. 39-47.

Robbe-Grillet, Alain. "Samuel Beckett, or 'Presence in the Theatre.' *In:* Esslin, Martin, ed. *Samuel Beckett,* pp. 113-115.

Schneider, Alan. "Waiting for Beckett." *In: Beckett at 60, a festschrif* pp. 41-51.

Schoell, Konrad. "The Chain and the Circle: A Structural Compariso of *Waiting for Godot* and *Endgame." Modern Drama,* vol. 11, no. (May, 1968), pp. 48-53.

Scott, Nathan A. *Samuel Beckett,* pp. 94-98, 100, 101, 104-105, 10 110.

Sheedy, John J. "The Comic Apocalypse of King Hamm." *Moder Drama,* vol. 9, no. 3 (Dec., 1966), pp. 310-318.

Tynan, Kenneth. "A Philosophy of Despair." *Observer,* no. 864 (April 7, 1957), p. 15.

Walker, Roy. "Love, Chess and Death; Samuel Beckett's Double Bill. *Twentieth Century,* 164 (Dec., 1958), pp. 538-544.

Weales, Gerald. "The Language of *Endgame." Tulane Drama Rev* vol. 6, no. 4 (June, 1962), pp. 107-117.

Wellwarth, George. *The theatre of protest and paradox.* pp. 43, 44, 4: 48-49.

Film

Hampton, Charles C., Jr. "Samuel Beckett's *Film." Modern Dram* vol. 11, no. 3 (Dec., 1968), pp. 299-305.

Kenner, Hugh. *Samuel Beckett, a critical study* (new ed.), pp. 217-219.

appy Days (Oh! Les Beaux Jours)

Alpaugh, David J. "Negative Definition in Samuel Beckett's *Happy Days.*" *Twentieth Century Literature,* vol. 11, no. 4 (Jan., 1966), pp. 202-210.

"Beckett Play Acted by French Company." *Times,* no. 56,288 (April 5, 1965), p. 6.

Bourne, Richard, *"Happy Days* and *Bedlam Galore* at Manchester." *Guardian,* no. 36,674 (June 4, 1964), p. 9.

Brook, Peter. *"Happy Days* and *Marienbad." In:* Marowitz, Charles, ed. *Encore reader,* pp. 164-167. (Reprinted from *Encore,* Jan., 1962.)

Brustein, Robert. "An Evening of Deja Vu." *New Republic,* vol. 145, no. 14 (Oct. 2, 1961), pp. 45-46.

Brustein, Robert. *Seasons of discontent,* pp. 53-56.

Cain, Alex Matheson. "Far Lower than the Angels." *The Tablet,* 216, no. 6390 (Nov. 10, 1962), pp. 1082-1083.

Clurman, Harold, *"Happy Days." Nation,* vol. 201, no. 12 (Oct. 18, 1965), pp. 258-259.

Clurman, Harold. *Nation,* vol. 193, no. 11, (Oct. 7, 1961), pp. 234-235.

Clurman, Harold. *The naked image,* pp. 40-42.

Cooke, Richard P. "Beckett Downtown." *Wall Street J.,* vol. 166, no. 53 (Sept. 15, 1965), p. 16.

Dennis, Nigel. "No View From the Toolshed." *Encounter,* 20, no. 1 (Jan., 1963), pp. 37-39.

Driver, Tom F. *Christian Century,* vol. 78, no. 41 (Oct. 11, 1961), pp. 1208-1209.

Eastman, Richard M. "Samuel Beckett and *Happy Days." Modern Drama,* 6 (Feb. 1964), pp. 417-424.

Gassner, John. *Educational Theatre J.* vol. 13 (Dec. 1961), 293-294.

Gellert, Roger. "Long Pause for Gallantry." *New Statesman,* vol. 64, no. 1652 (Nov. 9, 1962), p 679.

Gilman, Richard. *Commonweal,* vol. 75, no. 3 (Oct. 13, 1961), pp. 69-71.

Grossvogel, David I. *Four playwrights and a postscript, Brech* *Ionesco, Beckett, Genet,* pp 128-131.

Hassan, Ihab. *The literature of silence; Henry Miller and Samu* *Beckett,* pp. 196-198.

Hope-Wallace, Philip. *"Oh! Les Beaux Jours." Guardian,* no. 36,93 (April 5, 1965), p. 9.

Jacobsen, Josephine. *The testament of Samuel Beckett,* pp. 123, 15ʼ 161, 174, 182, 186-187, 192.

Kenner, Hugh. *Samuel Beckett, a critical study* (new ed.), pp. 93-9 185.

Kerr, Walter. *Tragedy and comedy,* pp. 321-323.

Kott, Jan. "A Note on Beckett's Realism." *Tulane Drama Rev.,* vo 10, no. 3 (Spring, 1966), pp. 156-159.

Matthews, Honor. *The primal curse,* p. 167.

Pumphrey, Arthur. *Theatre arts,* vol. 45, no. 11 (Nov., 1961), pp 57-58.

R., M.H. *"Happy Days:* A Play in Two Acts." *Dubliner,* no. (Sept.-Oct., 1962), pp. 59-61.

Scott, Nathan A. *Samuel Beckett,* pp. 121-123.

Taylor, John Russell. "Do-it-yourself." *Plays and Players,* vol. 10, n 3 (Dec., 1962), pp. 54-55.

Tynan, Kenneth. "Intimations of Mortality." *Observer,* no. 8,94 (Nov. 4, 1962), p. 29.

Tynan, Kenneth. *Tynan right and left,* pp. 105-106.

Krapp's Last Tape

Brustein, Robert. "Krapp and a Little Claptrap." *New Republic,* vo 142, no. 8 (Feb. 22, 1960), pp. 21-22.

Brustein, Robert. *Seasons of discontent,* pp. 26-28.

Clurman, Harold. *The naked image,* pp. 13-14.

Clurman, Harold. "Theatre." *Nation,* vol. 190, no. 7 (Feb. 13, 1960 pp. 153-154.

Cohn, R. *Samuel Beckett,* pp. 248-250.

Driver, Tom F. *Christian Century,* vol. 77, no. 9 (Mar. 2, 1960), pp. 256-257.

Esslin, Martin. *The theatre of the absurd,* pp. 41-42.

Grossvogel, David I. *Four playwrights and a postscript, Brecht, Ionesco, Beckett, Genet,* pp. 124-127.

Hassan, Ihab. *The literature of silence; Henry Miller and Samuel Beckett,* pp. 193-195.

Hatzfeld, Helmut. *Trends and styles in twentieth century French literature,* pp. 267-268.

Hewes, Henry. *Saturday Rev.,* vol. 43, no. 5 (Jan. 30, 1960), pp. 28.

Hoffman, F.J. *Samuel Beckett,* pp. 155-158.

Jacobsen, Josephine. *The testament of Samuel Beckett,* pp. 32-33, 64, 57, 135-136, 177, 181, 183.

Kenner, Hugh. *Samuel Beckett, a critical study* (new ed.), pp. 184-185.

Moore, Harry T. *Twentieth-century French literature since World War II,* pp. 173-175.

Oberg, Arthur K. *"Krapp's Last Tape* and the Proustian Vision." *Modern Drama,* vol. 9, no. 3 (Dec., 1966), pp. 333-338.

Pronko, Leonard C. *Avant-garde: the experimental theater in France,* p. 51

Scott, Nathan A. *Samuel Beckett,* pp. 118-119.

Walker, Roy. "Love, Chess and Death; Samuel Beckett's Double Bill." *Twentieth Century,* vol. 164 (Dec., 1958), pp. 533-536.

ay

Bray, Barbara. "The New Beckett." *Observer,* no. 8,972 (June 16, 1963), p. 29.

Brustein, Robert. *Seasons of discontent,* pp. 56.

Bryden, Ronald. "Absurds." *New Statesman,* vol. 67, no. 1727 (Apr. 17, 1964), p. 616.

Clurman, Harold. *The naked image,* pp. 113-114.

Dukore, Bernard F. "Beckett's Play, *Play." Educational Theatre J.,* vol. 17, no. 1 (March, 1965), pp. 19-23.

Ewart, Gavin. *"Play* by Samuel Beckett." *London Magazine,* vol. 4, no. 2 (May, 1964), pp. 95-96.

Gascoigne, Bamber. "How Far Can Beckett Go?" *Observer,* no. 901 (Apr. 12, 1964), p. 24.

Hayter, Augy. "Beckett, Old and New." *Plays and Players,* vol. 13, no 9 (June, 1966), p. 69.

Hubert, Renee Riese. "Beckett's *Play* Between Poetry and Per formance." *Modern Drama,* vol. 9, no. 3 (Dec., 1966), pp. 339-34(

Kenner, Hugh. *Samuel Beckett, a critical study (new* ed.), pp. 209-21: 220-221.

Kitchin, Laurence, "Samuel Beckett's *Play." Listener,* vol. 71, no. 183 (Apr. 30, 1964), pp. 718-719.

Marowitz, Charles. *"Play." Encore,* vol. 11, no. 3 (May-June, 1964 pp. 48-52.

Trilling, Ossia. "Beckett's *Play* at Ulm." *Guardian,* no. 36,380 (Jun 24, 1963), p. 7

Waiting for Godot (En Attendant Godot)

Abel, Lionel. *Metatheatre, a new view of dramatic form,* pp. 134-4(

Anders, Gunther. "Being without Time: On Beckett's Play *Waiting fc Godot." In:* Esslin, Martin ed. *Samuel Beckett,* pp. 140-151.

Anouilh, Jean. "Godot or the Music-Hall Sketch of Pascal's *Pensées a* Played by the Fratellini Clowns." *In:* Cohn, Ruby, ed. *Casebook o Waiting for Godot,* pp. 12-13. (From *Arts,* no. 400, Jan. 27, 1953.

Ashmore, Jerome. "Philosophical Aspects of Godot." *Symposium,* vo 16, no. 4 (Winter, 1962), pp. 296-306.

Atkins, Anselm. "Lucky's Speech in Beckett's *Waiting for Godot: I* Punctuated Sense-Line Arrangement." *Educational Theatre J.,* vol. 1! no. 4 (Dec., 1967), pp. 426-432.

Atkins, Anselm. "A Note on the Structure of Lucky's Speech. *Modern Drama,* vol. 9, no. 3 (Dec., 1966), pp. 309.

Audiberti, Jacques. "At The Babylone a Fortunate Move on th Theater Checkerboard." *In:* Cohn, Ruby, ed. *Casebook on Waiting fo Godot,* pp. 13-14. (From *Arts,* no. 394, Jan. 16, 1953.)

Baxter, Kay M. *Contemporary theatre and the Christian faith,* pp 9-22.

Bentley, Eric. "The Talent of Samuel Beckett." *In:* Cohn, Ruby, ed *Casebook on Waiting for Godot,* pp. 59-66. (From *New Republic,* Ma 14, 1956.)

entley, Eric. *The theatre of commitment,* pp. 157, 190, 202-204.

igsby, C.W.E. *Confrontation and commitment,* pp. xviii, 8, 51-53, 59, 7.

ishop, Thomas. *Pirandello and the French theater,* p. 129.

lau, Herbert. "Notes from the Underground." *In:* Cohn, Ruby, ed. *asebook on Waiting for Godot,* pp. 113-121. (From Blau, Herbert. *he impossible theater,* N.Y., Macmillan, 1964, pp. 228-240.)

rereton, Geoffrey. *Principles of tragedy, a rational examination of the agic concept in life and literature,* pp. 244-265.

rooks, Curtis M. "The Mythic Pattern in *Waiting for Godot.*" *Iodern Drama,* vol. 9, no. 3 (Dec., 1966), pp. 292-299.

rown, John Russell. "Mr. Beckett's Shakespeare." *Critical Q.,* vol. 5, o. 4 (Winter, 1963), pp. 310-326.

ryden, Ronald. "Second Non-coming." *New Statesman,* vol. 69, no. 765 (Jan. 8, 1965), pp. 50-51.

ull, Peter. "Peter Bull as Pozzo." *In:* Cohn, Ruby, ed. *Casebook on Vaiting for Godot,* pp. 39-43. (From Bull, Peter. *I know the face but...* London, Peter Davies, 1959).

utler, Harry L. "Balzac and Godeau, Beckett and Godot: A Curious arallel." *Romance Notes,* vol. 3, no. 2 (Spring, 1962), pp. 13-20.

ase, Sue-Ellen. "Image and Godot." *In:* Cohn, Ruby, ed. *Casebook n Waiting for Godot,* pp. 155-159.

hadwick, C. *"Waiting for Godot:* A Logical Approach." *Symposium,* ol. 14, no. 4 (Winter, 1960), pp. 252-257.

hampigny, Robert. "Interpretation of *En Attendant Godot." PMLA,* ol. 75, no. 3 (1960).

hampigny, Robert. *"Waiting for Godot:* Myth, Words, Wait." *In:* ohn, Ruby, *Casebook on Waiting for Godot,* pp. 137-144. (From *MLA,* 1960.)

hase, N.C. "Images of Man: *Le Malentendu* and *En Attendant Godot." Wisconsin Studies in Contemporary Literature,* vol. 7, no. 3 Autumn, 1966), pp. 295-302.

haucer, Daniel. *Shenandoah,* vol. 6, no. 2 (Spring, 1955), pp. 80-82.

hiari, J. *Landmarks of contemporary drama,* pp. 68-80.

lurman, Harold. *Lies like truth,* pp. 220-222.

Clurman, Harold. *Nation,* vol. 182 (May 5, 1956), pp. 387, 390.

Clurman, Harold. "Theatre." *Nation,* vol. 182, no. 18 (May 5, 1956 pp. 387-390.

Cohen, Robert S. "Parallels and the Possibility of Influence Betwee Simone Weil's *Waiting for God* and Samuel Beckett's *Waiting f Godot.*" *Modern Drama,* vol. 6 (1964), pp. 425-436.

Cohn, Ruby. "The Absurdly Absurd: Avatars of Godot." *Comparati Literature, Studies,* vol. 2, no. 3 (1965), pp. 234-236, 237.

Cohn, Ruby, ed. *Casebook on Waiting for Godot.*

Cohn, Ruby Haykin. "Waiting Is All." *Modern Drama,* vol. 3, no. (Sept 1960), pp. 162-167.

Cook, Albert S. "Language and Action in the Drama." *Colle₂ English,* vol. 28, no. 1 (Oct., 1966), pp. 21-23.

Cook, Albert. *Prisms, studies in modern literature,* pp. 107-10 140-144.

Cowell, Raymond. *Twelve modern dramatists,* pp. 113-115.

Davison, Peter. "Contemporary Drama and Popular Dramat Forms." *In: Aspects of drama and the theatre,* pp. 188-192.

"Dialogue: The Free Southern Theatre" (Interview with Richar Schechner, Gil Moses, John O'Neal, Murray Levy and Deni Nicholas). *In:* Cohn, Ruby, ed. *Casebook on Waiting for Godot,* p 79-82. (From *Tulane Drama Rev.,* vol. 9, no. 4, Summer, 1965.)

Dubois, Jacques. "Beckett and Ionesco: The Tragic Awareness (Pascal and the Ironic Awareness of Flaubert." *Modern Drama,* vol. no. 3 (Dec., 1966), pp. 283-291.

Duckworth, Colin. "The Making of Godot." *In:* Cohn, Ruby, e *Casebook on Waiting for Godot,* pp. 89-100. (From Duckworth, Colir ed. *En attendant Godot,* London, George G. Harrap, 1966.) *Also i, Theatre Research,* vol. 7, no. 3 (1966), pp. 123-145.

Dukore, Bernard F. "Controversy. A Non-Interpretation of Godot *Drama Survey,* vol. 3, no. 1 (May 1963), pp. 117-119.

Dukore, Bernard F. "Gogo, Didi, and the Absent Godot." *Dram Survey,* vol. 1, no. 3 (Winter, 1962), pp. 301-307.

Eckersley, Peter. *"Waiting for Godot,* Victoria Theatre, Stoke on-Trent." *Guardian,* no. 36,287 (Mar. 6, 1963), p. 7.

"An Epoch-making Play." *Times,* no. 56,208 (Jan. 1, 1965), p. 13

sslin, Martin. "Godot and His Children: The Theatre of Samuel ₂ckett and Harold Pinter." *In:* Brown, John Russell, ed. *Modern ritish dramatists, a collection of critical essays,* pp. 58-65. (From rmstrong, W.A. *Experimental drama,* London, Bell, 1963.)

sslin, Martin. "Godot at San Quentin." *In:* Cohn Ruby, ed. *Casebook* ₁ *Waiting for Godot,* pp. 83-85. (From Esslin, Martin.. *The theatre of ›e absurd,* N.Y., Doubleday, 1961.)

sslin, Martin. "Roger Blin at Work." *Modern Drama,* vol. 8, no. 4 ›eb., 1966), pp. 403-408.

sslin, Martin. *The theatre of the absurd,* pp. 13-27.

anner, Janet. *Paris journal, 1944-1965,* pp. 197-198.

etcher, John. "Roger Blin at Work." *In:* Cohn, Ruby, ed. *Casebook* ₁ *Waiting for Godot,* pp. 21-26. (From Fletcher, John. *Modern rama,* Feb., 1966, modified by the author.)

etcher, John. *Samuel Beckett's art,* pp. 49-52, 58-59, 61-62, 64-65, ₃-70, 120-121.

lood, Ethelbert. "A Reading Of Beckett's *Godot.*" *Culture,* vol. 22, ᴐ. 3, (Sept., 1961), pp. 257-262.

ord, Peter. *"Waiting for Godot." Guardian,* no. 36,985 (June 5, ›65), p. 6.

owlie, Wallace. *Dionysus in Paris,* pp. 210-214.

raser, G.S. *The modern writer and his world,* pp. 61-63.

raser, G.S. *"Waiting for Godot." In:* Cohn, Ruby, ed. *Casebook on Waiting for Godot,* pp. 133-137. (From *Times Literary Supplement,* ₑb. 10, 1956, p. 84.) *Also in: English critical essays: twentieth ₑntury,* London, 1958, pp. 324-332.

riedman, Maurice. *To deny our nothingness,* pp. 310-312.

riedman, Melvin J. *"Critic!" Modern Drama, vol. 9,* no. 3 (Dec., ›66), pp. 300-308.

ascoigne, Bamber. *Twentieth-century drama,* pp. 184-188.

assner, John. *Theatre at the crossroads,* pp. 252-256.

ibbs, Wolcott. *New Yorker,* vol. 32 (May 5, 1956), pp. 89-90.

licksberg, Charles I. *The self in modern literature,* pp. 118-120.

ray, Ronald. *"Waiting for Godot,* A Christian Interpretation." istener, vol. 57, no. 1452 (Jan. 24, 1957), pp. 160-161.

Gray, Ronald. *"Waiting for Godot." Listener,* vol. 57, no. 1454 (Feb 7, 1957), p. 235.

Grossvogel, David I. *Four playwrights and a postscript, Brech Ionesco, Beckett, Genet,* pp. 88-110.

Grossvogel, David I. *The self-conscious stage in modern Frenc drama,* pp. 324-331.

Guicharnaud, Jacques. *Modern French theatre from Giraudoux t Beckett,* pp. 193-212.

Guicharnaud, Jacques. *Modern French theatre from Giraudoux t Genet* (rev. ed.), pp. 159, 197, 230-248, 253-257, 289.

Harvey, Lawrence E. "Art and the Existential in *Waiting for Godot. In:* Cohn, Ruby, ed. *Casebook on Waiting for Godot,* pp. 144-15 (From *PLMA,* 1960, vol 75, no. 1, pp. 137-146.)

Hassan, Ihab. *The literature of silence; Henry Miller and Samu Beckett,* pp. 114, 137-138, 174-183, 208-209.

Hatzfeld, Helmut. *Trends and styles in twentieth century Frenc literature,* p. 266.

Hayes, Richard. *Commonweal,* vol. 64. no. 8 (May 25, 1956), p. 203

Hewes, Henry. "Mankind in the Merdecluse." *In:* Cohn, Ruby, ed *Casebook on Waiting for Godot."* pp. 67-69 (From *Saturday Rev.* May 5, 1956, p. 32.)

Hobson, Harold. "The First Night of *Waiting for Godot." In: Becket at 60, a festschrift,* pp. 25-28.

Hobson, Harold. "Tomorrow." *In:* Cohn, Ruby, ed. *Casebook o Waiting for Godot,* pp. 27-29. (From *The Times,* London, Aug. 7 1955.)

Hoffman, F.J. *Samuel Beckett,* pp. 138-153.

Hooker, Ward. "Irony and Absurdity in the Avant-Garde Theatre. *In:* Freedman, Morris, ed. *Essays in the modern drama,* pp. 335-348 (Reprinted from *Kenyon Rev.,* vol. 22, no. 3, Summer, 1960, pp 436-454.)

Houfe, E.A.S. *"Waiting for Godot." Listener,* vol. 57, no. 1453 (Jan 31, 1957), p. 197.

Jacobsen, Josephine. *Ionesco and Genet, playwrights of silence,* pp. 1 2, 5-6, 19, 21-22, 99.

acobsen, Josephine. *The testament of Samuel Beckett,* pp. 19-21, 9-31, 33, 60, 71, 112, 136, 139-140, 149-150, 153, 161, 164-165, 169, 77, 179, 182-188, 190, 192.

anvier, Ludovic. "Cyclical Dramaturgy." *In:* Cohn, Ruby, ed. *Casebook on Waiting for Godot,* pp. 166-171. (From *Pour Samuel Beckett,* Paris, Les Éditions de Minuit, 1966, trans. by Ruby Cohn.)

essup, Bertram. "About Beckett, Godot and Others." *Northwest Rev.,* ol. 1, no. 1 (Spring, 1957), pp. 25-30.

ohnston, Denis. "Waiting with Beckett." *In:* Cohn, Ruby, ed. *Casebook on Waiting for Godot,* pp. 31-38. (From *Irish Writing,* pring, 1956, pp. 23-28.)

osbin, Raoul. *"Waiting for Godot." Cross Currents,* vol. 6, no. 1, Summer, 1956), pp. 204-207.

enner, Hugh. "Life in the Box." *In:* Cohn, Ruby, ed. *Casebook on Waiting for Godot,* pp. 107-113. (From Kenner, Hugh. A *critical tudy,* N.Y., Grove, 1961.)

enner, Hugh. *Samuel Beckett, a critical study* (new ed.), pp. 67, 74, 13, 133-139, 146-155, 185-186.

ern, Edith. "Beckett and the Spirit of the Commedia Dell'Arte." *Modern Drama,* vol. 9, no. 3 (Dec., 1966), pp. 260-267.

ern, Edith. "Drama Stripped for Inaction: Beckett's *Godot." Yale French Studies,* no. 14 (Winter, 1954-55), pp. 41-47.

olve, V.A. "Religious Language in *Waiting for Godot." Centennial Review* (Mich. State), vol. 11 (1967), pp. 102-127.

ee, Warren. "The Bitter Pill of Samuel Beckett." *Chicago Rev.,* vol. 0, no. 4 (Winter 1957), pp. 80-83.

ennon, Peter. "Arrival of Godot." *Guardian,* no. 36,456 (Sept. 20, 963). p. 11.

evy, Alan. "The Long Wait for Godot." *In:* Cohn, Ruby, ed. *Casebook on Waiting for Godot,* pp. 74-78. (From *Theatre Arts,* vol. 0 Aug., 1956, pp. 33-35, 96.)

ewis, Allan. *The contemporary theatre,* pp. 261-264.

umley, Frederick. *New trends in 20th century drama,* pp. 200-201, 03-206, 207, 211, 269.

umley, Frederick. *Trends in 20th century drama,* pp. 137-141.

cCoy, C.S. *"Waiting for Godot." Religion in Life,* vol. 28 (Fall, 959), pp. 595-603.

McCoy, Charles. *"Waiting for Godot:* A Biblical Approach." *Floric Rev.* (Spring, 1958), pp. 63-72.

Mailer, Norman. "A Public Notice on *Waiting for Godot."* *In:* Cohn Ruby, ed. *Casebook on Waiting for Godot,* pp. 69-74. (From Maile: Norman. *Advertisements for myself,* N.Y., G.P. Putnam's Sons, 195! and *The Village Voice,* May 7, 1966.)

Malcolm, Derek. "The Day the Malt Fused." *Guardian* no. 36,85 (Dec. 30, 1964), p. 7.

Mannes, Marya. "Two Tramps." *In:* Cohn, Ruby, ed. *Casebook o Waiting for Godot,* pp. 30-31. (From *The Reporter,* Oct. 20, 1955.

Marinello, Leone J. "Samuel Beckett's *Waiting for Godot." Dram Critique,* vol. 6, no. 2 (Spring, 1963), pp. 75-81.

Markus, Thomas B. "Bernard Dukore and *Waiting for Godot." Dram Survey,* vol. 2, no. 3 (Winter, 1963), pp. 360-363.

Matthews, Honor. *The primal curse,* pp. 139, 154-160.

Mercier, Vivian. "A Pyrrhonian Eclogue." *Hudson Rev.,* vol. 7, no. (Winter, 1955), pp. 620-624.

Metman, Eva. "Reflections on Samuel Beckett's Plays." *In:* Esslin Martin, ed. *Samuel Beckett,* pp. 117-132. *Also in J. of Analytica Psychology,* vol. 5, no. 1 (Jan., 1960), pp. 44-55.

Milalyi, Gabor. "Beckett's *Godot* and the Myth of Alienation.' *Modern Drama,* vol. 9, no. 3 (Dec., 1966), pp. 277-282.

Moore, Harry T. *Twentieth-century French literature since World Wa II,* pp. 170-173.

Moore, John R. "A Farewell to Something." *Tulane Drama Rev.,* vol 5, no. 1 (Sept., 1960), pp. 49-60.

O'Casey, Sean. "Not Waiting for Godot." *In:* O'Casey, Sean. *Blast. and benedictions,* pp. 51-52. (From *Encore: A quarterly review fo. students of the theatre,* Easter, 1956.)

Oliver, Cordelia. *"Waiting for Godot* at the Traverse Theatre Edinburgh." *Guardian,* no. 37,778 (Dec. 27, 1967), p. 5.

O'Neill, Joseph P. "The Absurd in Samuel Beckett." Personalis*t,* vol 48, no. 1 (Jan., 1967), pp. 61-62, 65-66, 68-73.

Politzer, Heinz. "The Egghead Waits for Godot." *Christian Scholar* vol. 42 (1959), pp. 46-50.

Pronko, Leonard C. *Avant-garde: the experimental theater in France* pp. 25-38, 57-58.

adke, Judith J. "The Theatre of Samuel Beckett: 'Une Durée à nimer'." *Yale French Studies,* no. 29 (Spring-Summer, 1962), pp. '-64.

attigan, Terence. "Aunt Edna Waits for Godot." *New Statesman,* ol. 50 (Oct. 15, 1955), pp. 468-470.

echtein, Brother John. "Time and Eternity Meet in the Present." *exas Studies in Literature and Language,* vol. 6 (1964), pp. 5-21.

hodes, S.A. "From Godeau to Godot." *French Rev.,* vol. 36, no. 3 an. 1963), pp. 260-265.

obbe-Grillet, Alain. "Samuel Beckett or Presence on the Stage." *In:* ohn, Ruby ed., *Casebook on Waiting for Godot,* pp. 15-21. (From obbe-Grillet, Alain. *For a new novel,* N.Y., Grove Press, 1965; and om *Critique,* Feb., 1953, since revised by the author.)

alacrou, Armand. "It Is Not an Accident but a Triumph." *In:* Cohn, uby, ed. *Casebook on Waiting for Godot,* pp. 14-15. (From *Arts,* no.)0, Jan. 27, 1953.)

astre, Alfonso. "Seven Notes on *Waiting for Godot.*" *In:* Cohn, Ruby, 1. *Casebook on Waiting for Godot,* pp. 101-107. (From *Primer Acto,* o. 1, April, 1957, translated by Leonard C. Pronko.)

chechner, Richard. "There's Lots of Time in *Godot.*" *In:* Cohn, uby, ed. *Casebook on Waiting for Godot,* pp. 175-187. (From *lodern Drama,* vol. 9, no. 3, Dec., 1966, pp. 268-276.)

chneider, Alan. "Waiting for Beckett." *In: Beckett at 60, a festschrift,* p. 34-41.

chneider, Alan. "Waiting for Beckett: A Personal Chronicle." *In:* ohn, Ruby, ed. *Casebook on Waiting for Godot,* pp. 51-57. (From *Chelsea Rev.,* no. 2, Sept. 1958, abridged.)

choell, Konrad. "The Chain and the Circle: A Structural Comparison f *Waiting for Godot* and *Endgame.*" *Modern Drama,* vol. 11, no. 1 May, 1968), pp. 48-53.

chumach, Murray. "Why They Wait for Godot." *New York Times Magazine* (Sept. 21, 1958), pp, 36, 38, 41.

chwartz, D.J. *Waiting for Godot.*" *Listener,* vol. 57, no. 1453 (Jan. 1, 1957), p. 197.

cott, Nathan A. *Samuel Beckett,* pp. 83-94, 100-101, 105-109, 111.

erreau, Genevieve. "Beckett's Clowns." *In:* Cohn, Ruby, ed. *Casebook n Waiting for Godot,* pp. 171-175. (From *Histoire du nouveau héâtre,* Paris, Gallimard, 1966.) (Trans. by Ruby Cohn.)

Sheedy, John J. "The Net." *In:* Cohn, Ruby, ed. *Casebook on Waitin* *for Godot,* pp. 159-166.

Simpson, Alan. *Beckett and Behan and a theatre in Dublin,* pp 121-137.

Simpson, Alan. "Producing *Godot* in Dublin." *In:* Cohn, Ruby, ed *Casebook on Waiting for Godot, pp. 45-49.* (From Simpson, Alan *Beckett and Behan,* London, Routledge & Kegan, 1962.)

Smith, H.A. "Dipsychus Among the Shadows." *In:* Brown, John Russell and Bernard Harris, eds. *Contemporary theatre,* pp. 156-163

Strauss, Walter. "Dante's Belacqua and Beckett's Tramps." *Comparative Literature,* vol. 11, no. 3 (Summer, 1959), pp. 250-261.

Styan, J.L. *The dark comedy,* 2nd ed., pp. 41, 46, 218-234, 235, 250 258-259, 271, 275, 288, 294, 295.

Suvin, Darko. "Preparing for Godot—or the Purgatory of Individualism." *In:* Cohn, Ruby, ed. *Casebook on Waiting for Godot,* pp 121-132. (From *Tulane Drama Rev.,* vol. 11, no. 4, Summer, 1967.

Tallmer, Jerry. "The Magic Box." *Evergreen Rev.,* vol. 5, no. 1 (July-Aug. 1961), pp. 117-122.

"They Also Serve." *In:* Gassner, John. *Directions in modern theatr* *and drama,* pp. 318-325. (Reprinted from *Times Literary Supplement* Feb. 10, 1956, p. 84.)

Todd, Robert E. "Proust and Redemption in *Waiting for Godot.* *Modern Drama,* vol. 10, no. 2 (Sept., 1967), pp. 175-181.

Torrance, Robert M. "Modes of Being and Time in the World o Godot." *Modern Language Q.,* vol. 28, no. 1 (Mar., 1967), pp. 77-95

Trousdale, Marion. "Dramatic Form: The Example of *Godot.* *Modern Drama,* vol. 11, no. 1 (May, 1968), pp. 1-9.

"Waiting for Godot." Times, no. 56,195 (Dec. 15, 1964), p. 6.

Weissman, Philip. *Creativity in the theater,* pp. 251-252.

Wellwarth, George. *The theatre of protest and paradox.* pp. 37-43 45-46.

Williams, Raymond. *Drama in performance* (new ed.), pp. 153-158 183.

Williams, Raymond. *Modern tragedy,* pp. 153-155.

Williams, Raymond. *New Statesman,* vol. 61, no. 1575 (May 19, 1961) p. 802.

Williamson, Audrey. *Contemporary theatre, 1953-1956,* pp. 69-70.

Worsley, T.C. *New Statesman,* vol 50, no. 1275 (Aug. 13, 1955), pp. 184-185.

Zegel, Sylvain. "The First Review, At the Theatre de Babylone: *Waiting for Godot,* by Samuel Beckett." *In:* Cohn, Ruby, ed., *Casebook on Waiting for Godot,* pp. 11-12. (From *La Liberation,* Jan 7, 1953.)

⁄ords and Music

Cleveland, Louise O. "Trials in the Soundscape: The Radio Plays of Samuel Beckett." *Modern Drama,* vol. 11, no. 3 (Dec., 1968), pp. 279-280.

Fletcher, John. *Samuel Beckett's art,* pp. 76-79, 81-82.

Kenner, Hugh. *Samuel Beckett, a critical study* (new ed.), pp. 212-215.

HENRY BECQUE 1837-1899

⁀eneral

Gassner, John. *The theatre in our times,* pp. 114-122.

Lamm, Martin. *Modern Drama,* pp. 59-62,

he Vultures (Les Corbeaux)

Ellehauge, Martin. *The position of Bernard Shaw in European drama and philosophy,* pp. 114-115.

Gassner, John. *The theatre in our times,* pp. 116-118.

Lamm, Martin. *Modern drama,* pp. 60-64.

he Woman of Paris (La Parisienne)

Gassner, John. *The theatre in our times,* pp. 118-120.

Lamm, Martin. *Modern drama,* pp. 64-66.

BRENDAN BEHAN 1923-1964

⁀eneral

Armstrong, William A. "The Irish Point of View: The Plays of Sean O'Casey, Brendan Behan, and Thomas Murphy." *In:* Armstrong, William A., ed. *Experimental drama,* pp. 93-99.

DeBurca, Seamus. "The Essential Brendan Behan." *Modern Drama,* vol. 8, no. 4 (Feb., 1966), pp. 374-381.

Hogan, Robert. *After the Irish renaissance,* pp. 198-207.

Jordan, John. "The Irish Theatre: Retrospect and Premonition." *I* Brown, J.R. and B. Harris, eds. *Contemporary theatre,* pp. 180-18

Lumley, Frederick. *New trends in 20th century drama,* pp. 303-30

The New York Times, Mar. 21, 1964, p. 25. (Obituary)

O'Neill, John Drew. "Brendan Go Bragh!" *Michigan Q. Rev.,* vol. no. 1 (Winter, 1965), pp. 19-22.

Simpson, Alan. *Beckett and Behan and a theatre in Dublin,* pp. 29-4(51-61, 98-101, 103-119, 168-193.

Taylor, John Russell. *Anger and after,* pp. 101-108.

The Hostage

Brustein, Robert. *Seasons of discontent,* pp. 177-180.

Clurman, Harold. *The naked image,* pp. 43-44.

Flanner, Janet. *Paris journal, 1944-1965,* p. 417.

Gilliat, Penelope. *"The Hostage."* In: Marowitz, Charles, ed. *Encor reader,* pp. 94-95. (Reprinted from *Encore,* Nov., 1958.)

Hogan, Robert. *After the Irish renaissance,* pp. 203-205.

Kerr, Walter. *The theater in spite of itself,* pp. 108-111.

Kitchin, Laurence. *Mid-century drama,* p. 111.

Simon, John. *Hudson Rev.,* vol. 13, no. 4 (Winter, 1960-61), pp 587-588.

Taylor, John Russell. *Anger and after,* pp. 104-108.

Wellwarth, George. *The theatre of protest and paradox,* pp. 258-26 269.

The Quare Fellow

Hogan, Robert. *After the Irish renaissance,* pp. 199, 200-203.

Taylor, John Russell. *Anger and after,* pp. 97-104.

Wellwarth, George. *The theatre of protest and paradox,* pp. 25 259-260, 261.

S. N. BEHRMAN 1893-

Bauland, Peter. *The hooded eagle,* pp. 140, 150-153.

Behrman, S.N. "S.N. Behrman: A Dialogue with John Simon." *In: Theatre; the annual of the Repertory Theatre of Lincoln Center,* vol. 1, 1964, pp. 35-47.

Clurman, Harold. *Lies like truth,* pp. 35-37.

Gassner, John. *The theatre in our times,* pp. 329-336.

Goldstein, Malcolm. "Playwrights of the 1930's." *In:* Downer, Alan S., ed. *The American theater today,* pp. 27-28

Krutch, Joseph W. *The American drama since 1918,* pp. 180-206.

Krutch, Joseph Wood. "The Comic Wisdom of S.N. Behrman." *In:* Moses, Montrose J. *The American theatre as seen by its critics, 1752-1934,* pp. 272-277. (Reprinted from *Nation,* vol. 137, July 19, 1933, pp. 74-76.) *Also in:* Zabel, M.D., ed. *Literary Opinion in America,* pp. 302-308.

Lewis, Allan. *American plays and playwrights of the contemporary theatre, pp. 129*-136.

Phillips, Elizabeth C. *Modern American drama,* pp. 98-100.

Rabkin, Gerald. *Drama and commitment,* pp. 215-234.

Weales, Gerald. "S.N. Behrman Comes Home." *Commentary,* vol. 27, no. 3 (Mar., 1959), pp. 256-260.

Flexner, Eleanor. *American playwrights: 1918-1938,* pp. 66-68.

Krutch, Joseph W. *The American drama since 1918,* pp. 188-189.

Lawson, John Howard. "The Social Framework." *In:* Frenz, Horst, ed. *American playwrights on drama,* pp. 31, 33, 34-37. (A somewhat shortened version of the chapter "The Social Framework" in John Howard Lawson's *Theory and technique of playwriting,* Putnam, 1936.)

Rabkin, Gerald. *Drama and commitment,* pp. 221-222.

Sievers, W. David. *Freud on Broadway,* pp. 325-327.

Brief Moment

Flexner, Eleanor. *American playwrights: 1918-1938,* pp. 65-66.

Krutch, Joseph W. *The American drama since 1918,* pp. 187-188.

Sievers, W. David. *Freud on Broadway,* pp. 324-325.

But for Whom, Charlie?

Gottfried, Martin. *A theater divided; the postwar American stage,* pp. 152-153.

Dunningan's Daughter

Rabkin, Gerald. *Drama and commitment,* pp. 227-229.

Sievers, W. David. *Freud on Broadway,* pp. 334-335.

End of Summer

Brown, John Mason. *Two on the aisle,* pp. 143-145.

Flexner, Eleanor. *American playwrights: 1918-1938,* pp. 72-75.

Krutch, Joseph W. *The American drama since 1918,* pp. 195-197.

Rabkin, Gerald. *Drama and commitment,* pp. 225-227.

Sievers, W. David. *Freud on Broadway,* pp. 329-330.

I Know My Love

Brown, John Mason. *Still seeing things,* pp. 127-131.

Meteor

Flexner, Eleanor. *American playwrights: 1918-1938,* pp. 62-65.

No Time for Comedy

Krutch, Joseph W. *The American drama since 1918,* pp. 202-205.

O'Hara, Frank H. *Today in American drama,* pp. 133-139, 251.

Rabkin, Gerald. *Drama and commitment* pp. 233-234.

Sievers, W. David. *Freud on Broadway,* pp. 331-332.

Rain from Heaven

Flexner, Eleanor. *American playwrights: 1918-1938,* pp. 68-72.

Himelstein, Morgan Y. *Drama was a weapon, the left-wing theatre in New York 1929-1941,* pp. 133-134.

Krutch, Joseph W. *The American drama since 1918,* pp. 191-195.

Lawson, John Howard. "The Social Framework." *In:* Frenz, Horst, ed. *American playwrights on drama,* pp. 31, 33, 34-37. (A somewhat shortened version of the chapter "The Social Framework" in John Howard Lawson's *Theory and technique of playwriting,* Putnam, 1936.)

Rabkin, Gerald. *Drama and commitment,* pp. 229-231.

Sievers, W. David. *Freud on Broadway,* pp. 327-329.

ᴛe Second Man

Flexner, Eleanor. *American playwrights; 1918-1938,* pp. 60-62.

Krutch, Joseph W. *Thc American drama since 1918,* pp. 180-186.

Rabkin, Gerald. *Drama and commitment,* pp. 218-220.

ᴛe Talley Method

Rabkin, Gerald. *Drama and commitment,* pp. 231-233.

Sievers, W. David. *Freud on Broadway,* pp. 332-333.

ine of Choice

Flexner, Eleanor. *American playwrights: 1918-1938,* pp. 75-77.

Rabkin, Gerald. *Drama and commitment,* pp. 222-224.

Sievers, W. David. *Freud on Broadway,* pp. 330-331.

DAVID BELASCO 1859-1931

ᴛe Heart of Maryland

Shaw, George Bernard. *Shaw's dramatic criticism (1895-98),* pp. 287-290.

JOSE-MARIA BELLIDO 1922-

ᴊotball

Benedikt, M. and G.E. Wellwarth. *Modern Spanish theatre, an anthology of plays,* pp. 330-331.

SAUL BELLOW 1915-

The Last Analysis

Bigsby, C.W.E. *Confrontation and commitment,* pp. 70, 93-99.

Brustein, Robert. *Seasons of discontent,* pp. 172-175.

Clurman, Harold. *The naked image,* pp. 45-47.

Finkelstein, Sidney. *Existentialism and alienation in America* *literature,* pp. 266-268.

JACINTO BENAVENTE 1866-1954

General

Boyd, E.A. *Studies from ten literatures,* pp. 96-105.

Carter, Sister Mary Reginald. "The image of woman in selected plays of Jacinto Benavente y Martinez." *Dissertation Abstracts,* vol. 2((1966), 4653-54 (St. Louis).

Corrigan, Robert W., ed. *Masterpieces of the modern Spanish theatre* pp. 34-35.

Duran, Manuel and Michael Nimetz. "Spain and Spanish America.' *Books Abroad,* vol. 41, no. 1 (Winter, 1967), pp. 24.

Goldberg, Isaac. *The drama of transition,* pp. 96-106.

Lumley, Frederick. *New trends in 20th century drama,* pp. 366-367.

Marble, Annie Russell. *The Nobel Prize winners in literature,* pp 247-252.

Marquerie, Alfredo. "A Centenary of Spanish Theatre." *Topic: A* Journal of the Liberal Arts (Wash. and Jeff. College, Wash., Penn.) no. 15 (Spring, 1968), pp. 32-35.

Miller, Nellie Burget. *The living drama,* pp. 361-362.

Oñate, José D. "The inner reality in the dramatic works of Benavente.'' *Dissertation Abstracts,* vol. 23 (1962), 1709-09 (Boston University).

Ortega J. "Jacinto Benavente." *Modern Language Journal,* vol. 8 (1923), pp. 1-21.

Sanchez, Roberto. "Jacinto Benavente, 1866-1955" *Books Abroad,* vol. 29 (1955), pp. 41-43.

Schwartz, Kessel. "Benavente and Shakespearian Drama." *Romance Notes,* vol. 1, no. 2 (1960), pp. 101-105.

Sheehan, Robert Louis. "Moraleda, Benavente's Urban Dimension to the Generation of '98." *In:* Bleiberg, German, and E. Inman Fox, eds. *Spanish thought and letters in the twentieth century,* pp. 483-496.

Starkie, W. "In Memoriam: Jacinto Benavente." *Bulletin of Hispanic Studies,* vol. 31 (1954), pp. 210-226.

Starkie, W. *Jacinto Benavente,* pp. 151-167.

Warren, L.A. *Modern Spanish literature,* vol. 2, pp. 556-565.

Young, Raymond A. "The Heroines of Benavente and Martinez Sierra." *In:* MacLean, J. Beattie and R.W. Baldner, eds. *Proceedings: Pacific Northwest Conference on Foreign Languages. Seventeenth Annual Meeting, April 15-16, 1966.* (U. of Victoria), vol. 17, pp. 193-200.

Zimmerman, Irene. "Benavente's picture of Spain in the early 1930's." M.A., Univ. of Chicago, 1937.

he Bonds of Interest (Los Intereses Creados)

Clark, B.H. *A study of the modern drama,* pp. 215-218.

Goldberg, I. *Drama of transition,* pp. 115-120.

Hamilton, Clayton. *Seen on the stage,* pp. 132-137.

Miller, Nellie Burget. *The living drama,* pp. 362-364.

he Governor's Wife (La Gobernadora)

Goldberg, Isaac. *The drama of transition,* pp. 107-110.

Starkie, W. *Jacinto Benavente,* pp. 59-63.

a Infanzona

Marquerie, Alfredo. "A Centenary of Spanish Theatre." *Topic:* A Journal of the Liberal Arts (Wash. and Jeff. College, Wash., Penn.), no. 15 (Spring, 1968), p. 34.

he Little Man (The Manikin) (El Hombrecito)

Starkie, W. *Jacinto Benavente,* pp. 68-71.

Warren, L.A. *Modern Spanish literature,* vol. 2, pp. 563-564.

he Passion Flower (La Malquerida)

Hamilton, Clayton. *Seen on the stage,* pp. 132-137.

Marquerie, Alfredo "A Centenary of Spanish Theatre." *Topic: A Journal of the Liberal Arts* (Wash. and Jeff. College, Wash., Penn.), no. 15 (Spring, 1968), p. 34.

Starkie, W. *Jacinto Benavente,* pp. 91-103.

Princess Bebe (La Princesa Bebé)

Starkie, W. *Jacinto Benavente,* pp. 132-137.

Warren, L.A. *Modern Spanish literature,* vol. 2, pp. 562-563.

Señora Ama

Marguerie, Alfredo. "A Centenary of Spanish Theatre." *Topic: A Journal of the Liberal Arts* (Wash. and Jeff. College, Wash., Penn.), no. 15 (Spring, 1968), p. 34.

Vulgarity (Lo Cursi)

Starkie, W. *Jacinto Benavente,* pp. 50-54.

Warren, L.A. *Modern Spanish literature,* vol. 2, pp. 558-561.

A Witches' Sabbath (La Noche del Sábado)

Goldberg, Isaac. *The drama of transition,* pp. 110-114.

Starkie, W. *Jacinto Benavente,* pp. 120-132.

WALTER BENEKE 1928-

Funeral Home

Jones, W.K. *Behind Spanish American footlights,* p. 443.

El Paraiso de los Imprudentes

Jones, W.K. *Behind Spanish American footlights,* p. 443.

BEN BENGAL

Plant in the Sun

Himelstein, Morgan Y. *Drama was a weapon, the left-wing theatre in New York 1929-1941,* pp. 46-47.

RENE BENJAMIN 1885-

Il Faut Que Chacun Soit à Sa Place

Knowles, Dorothy. *French drama of the inter-war years, 1918-39,* pp. 71-72.

Les Plaisirs du Hasard

Knowles, Dorothy. *French drama of the inter-war years, 1918-39,* p. 71.

ARNOLD BENNET 1867-1931

General

Williams, Harold. *Modern English writers,* p. 267.

Judith

Roston, Murray. *Biblical drama in England from the Middle Ages to the present day,* pp. 246-248.

GEORGES BERNANOS 1888-1948

General

Moore, Kathleen B. "Bernanos and the dream." *Dissertation Abstracts,* vol. 27 (1967), 3464A-65A (Pittsburgh).

Nettlebeck, C.W. "The Obsessional Dream World of Georges Bernanos." *J. of the Australasian Universities Lang. and Lit. Assoc.,* vol. 26 (1966), pp. 241-253.

Dialogue of the Carmelites (Dialogues de Carmelites)

Baxter, Kay M. *Contemporary theatre and the Christian faith,* pp. 95-99.

Fowlie, Wallace. *Dionysus in Paris,* pp. 149-151.

Hebblethwaite, Peter. *Bernanos; an introduction,* pp. 26-27, 33-34, 35, 37, 88-89, 114-115.

Moore, Harry T. *Twentieth-century French literature since World War II,* p. 25.

O'Sharkey, Eithne, "Bernanos and the Carmelite Martyrs." *Dublin Rev.,* no. 508 (Summer, 1966), pp. 181-189.

Sous le Soleil de Satan

Sonnenfeld, Albert. "The Art of Georges Bernanos: The Prologue of *Sous le soleil de Satan." Orbis Litterarum,* vol. 21 (1966), pp. 133-153.

Sonnenfeld, Albert. "The Hostile Phantoms of Georges Bernanos: *Sous le Soleil de Satan* and M. Ouine." *L'Esprit Createur* (Winter, 1964), pp. 208-221.

JEAN-JACQUES BERNARD 1888-

General

Daniels, May. *The French drama of the unspoken,* pp. 172-180 224-237.

Knowles, Dorothy. *French drama of the inter-war years, 1918-39,* pp 113-114.

Moore, Harry T. *Twentieth-century French literature to World War II,* pp. 131-132.

Palmer, John. "J.J. Bernard and the Theory of Silence." *Fortnightly Rev.,* vol. 121 (Jan., 1927), pp. 46-50, 58.

Palmer, John. *Studies in the contemporary theatre,* pp. 94-111.

Rhodes, S.A "Jean-Jacques Bernard." *Books Abroad,* vol. 16, no. 2 (Apr., 1942), pp. 134-138.

"A World of Elusive Things." *Times Literary Supplement,* no. 1982 (Jan. 27, 1940), p. 41.

Denise Marette

Knowles, Dorothy. *French drama of the inter-war years, 1918-39,* pp 117.

Invitation to a Voyage (Glamour) (L'Invitation au Voyage)

Cookman, A.V. *London Mercury,* vol. 35 (Mar., 1937), pp. 498-499.

Daniels, May. *The French drama of the unspoken,* pp. 181, 199-205, 229.

Knowles, Dorothy. *French drama of the inter-war years, 1918-39,* p. 115.

Palmer, John. "J.J. Bernard and the Theory of Silence." *Fortnightly Rev.,* vol. 121 (Jan., 1927), pp. 55-56.

Saturday Rev., vol. 141 (June 19, 1926), pp. 744-745.

Spectator, vol. 137 (July 3, 1926), p. 12.

Madeleine (Le Jardinier d'Ispahan)

Daniels, May. *The French drama of the unspoken,* pp. 221-224.

Knowles, Dorothy. *French drama of the inter-war years, 1918-39,* p. 118.

Martine

Daniels, May. *The French drama of the unspoken,* pp. 119, 139, 173, 182-191.

Knowles, Dorothy. *French drama of the inter-war years, 1918-39,* pp. 114-115.

Palmer, John. "J.J. Bernard and the Theory of Silence." *Fortnightly Rev.,* vol. 121 (Jan., 1927), pp. 53-55, 58.

Palmer, John. *Studies in the contemporary theatre,* pp. 104-107.

Young, Stark. "American Laboratory Theater." *New Republic,* vol. 54 (Apr. 18, 1928), pp. 272-273.

Nationale 6

Daniels, May. *The French drama of the unspoken,* pp. 218-221.

Knowles, Dorothy. *French drama of the inter-war years, 1918-39,* p. 115.

A la Recherche des Coeurs

Daniels, May. *The french drama of the unspoken,* pp. 214-218.

Knowles, Dorothy. *French drama of the inter-war years, 1918-39,* pp. 117-118.

Le Secret d'Arvers

Daniels, May. *The French drama of the unspoken,* pp. 191-193.

The Springtime of Others (Le Printemps des Autres)

Daniels, May. *The French drama of the unspoken,* pp. 166-167, 193-199, 202, 204.

Knowles, Dorothy. *French drama of the inter-war years, 1918-39,* pp. 115-116.

New Statesman, vol. 24 (Aug. 1, 1942), pp. 75-76.

Palmer, John. "J.J. Bernard and the Theory of Silence." *Fortnightly Rev.,* vol. 121 (Jan., 1927), pp. 50-53.

Palmer, John. *Studies in the contemporary theatre,* pp. 101-104.

Redfern, James. *Spectator,* vol. 1969 (July 24, 1942), p. 83.

Sulky Fire (Le Feu Qui Reprend Mal)

Brown, I. *Saturday Rev.,* vol. 141 (June 26, 1926), p. 776.

Daniels, May. *The French drama of the unspoken,* pp. 180-181.

Knowles, Dorothy. *French drama of the inter-war years, 1918-39,* p 116.

The Unquiet Spirit (L'Ame en Peine)

Daniels, May. *The French drama of the unspoken,* pp. 81, 205-21C 221, 232, 234.

Knowles, Dorothy. *French drama of the inter-war years, 1918-39,* pp 116-117.

New Statesman, vol. 14 (Nov. 6, 1937), pp. 717-718.

New Statesman, vol. 30 (Jan. 28, 1928), pp. 493-494.

Palmer, John. "J.J. Bernard and the Theory of Silence." *Fortnightl Rev.,* vol. 121 (Jan., 1927), pp. 56-57.

Pope-Hennessy, James. *Spectator,* vol. 182 (Mar. 4, 1949), p. 286.

Saturday Rev., vol. 145 (Jan. 28, 1928), pp. 98-99.

Saturday Rev., vol. 152 (Dec. 5, 1931), pp. 722-723.

RUDOLPH BERNAUER and CARL MEINHARD

Johannes Kreisler (Die Wunderlichen Geschichten des Kappelmeisters Kreisler)

Bauland, Peter. *The hooded eagle,* pp. 74-78.

HENRY BERNSTEIN 1876-

General

Knowles, Dorothy. *French drama of the inter-war years, 1918-39,* pp 262-264.

CHARLES BERTIN 1919-

Christophe Colomb

Mallinson, Vernon. *Modern Belgian literature, 1830-1960,* pp. 194-195

UGO BETTI 1892-1953

General

Betti, Ugo. "Essays, Correspondence, Notes." *Tulane Drama Rev.,* vol 8, no. 3 (Spring, 1964), pp. 51-86.

Betti, Ugo. "Religion and the Theatre." *In:* Corrigan, Robert W., ed., *The new theatre of Europe,* pp. 322-332, and Corrigan, Robert W., ed. *Masterpieces of the modern Italian theatre,* pp. 171-181. *Also in: Tulane Drama Rev.,* vol. 5, no. 2 (Dec., 1960), pp. 3-14.

Corrigan, Robert W. "Introduction." *In:* Corrigan, Robert W., ed. *The new theatre of Europe,* pp. 25-27.

Corrigan, Robert W. *Masterpieces of the modern Italian theatre,* p. 170.

Kovic, George. "Human Justice in the Theatre of Ugo Betti." *In:* Baldner, R.W., ed. *Proceedings. Pacific Northwest Conference on Foreign Languages,* vol. 18 (1967), pp. 91-93.

Lumley, Frederick. *New trends in 20th century drama,* pp. 362-365.

MacClintock, Lander. "Ugo Betti." *Modern Language J.,* vol. 35, no. 4 (Apr., 1951), pp. 251-257.

McWilliam, G.H. "Interpreting Betti." *Tulane Drama Rev.,* vol. 5, no. 2 (Dec., 1960), pp. 15-23.

McWilliam, G.H. "The Minor Plays of Ugo Betti." *Italian Studies,* vol. 20 (1965), pp. 78-107.

Mankin, Paul A. "The Role of Ugo Betti in the Modern Italian Theatre." *Books Abroad,* vol. 36 (1962), pp. 131-133.

Pandolfi, Vito. "Italian Theatre Since the War." *Tulane Drama Rev.,* vol. 8, no. 3 (Spring, 1964), pp. 92-94.

Rizzo, Gino. "Regression-Progression in Ugo Betti's Drama." *Tulane Drama Rev.,* vol. 8, no. 1 (Fall, 1963), pp. 101-129.

Scott, J.A. "The Message of Ugo Betti." *Italica,* vol. 37, no. 1 (Mar., 1960), pp. 44-57.

he Burnt Flower-Bed (L'Ainola Brusciata)

Williamson, Audrey. *Contemporary theatre, 1953-1956,* pp. 62-65.

orruption at the Palace of Justice (Corruzione al Palazzo di Giustizia)

Corrigan, Robert W., ed. *The new theatre of Europe,* pp. 25-27.

Lumley, Frederick. *New trends in 20th century drama,* p. 363.

oat's Island (Delitto all' Isola delle Capre)

Lumley, Frederick. *New trends in 20th century drama,* pp. 363-364.

The Mistress (La Padrona)

Betti, Ugo. "Preface to *The Mistress.*" Trans. G. Rizzo and W Meriwether. *Tulane Drama Rev.,* vol. 5, no. 2 (1960), pp. 13-14.

The Queen and the Rebels (La Regina e gli Insorti)

Lumley, Frederick. *New trends in 20th century drama,* pp. 363 364-365.

Wadsworth, Frank W. "Magnanimous Despair: Ugo Betti and *Th Queen and the Rebels.*" *Drama Survey,* vol. 1, no. 2 (Oct., 1961), pp 165-177.

Williamson, Audrey. *Contemporary theatre, 1953-1956,* pp. 65-67.

Troubled Waters (Aqua Turbate)

Salmon, Eric. "Ugo Betti's *Troubled Waters.*" *Modern Drama,* vol. 11 no. 1 (May, 1968), pp. 97-108.

FRANCOIS BILLETDOUX 1927-

General

Guicharnaud, Jacques. *Modern French theatre from Giraudoux to Genet* (rev. ed.), pp. 197, 209-211, 348-349, 364.

Lumley, Frederick. *New trends in 20th century drama,* pp. 349-350

Chin-Chin

Knapp, Bettina. "Two Plays of Billetdoux." *Modern Drama,* vol. 7 (1964), pp. 199-203.

Mankin, Paul. "Blue Note from Billetdoux." *Yale French Studies,* no. 29 (1962), pp. 121-124.

Tynan, Kenneth. *Tynan right and left,* pp. 42-44.

Il Faut Passer par les Nuages

Mankin, Paul A. "The Paris Stage in 1965-66." *Books Abroad,* vol. 41, no. 4 (Autumn, 1967), pp. 403-404.

Torpe's Hotel (Va Donc Chez Torpe) (Chez Torpe)

Hope-Wallace, Philip. "Torpe's Hotel." *Guardian,* no. 37,103 (Oct. 21, 1965), p. 9.

"Hotel as Haven for Suicide." *Times,* no. 56,458 (Oct., 1965), p. 16.

"New Billetdoux for Guilford." *Times,* no. 56,433 (Sept. 22, 1965), p. 14.

ANDRE BIRABEAU 1890-

General

Knowles, Dorothy. *French drama of the inter-war years, 1918-39,* pp. 286-287.

SAMUEL BIRNKRANT

Whisper in God's Ear

Sainer, Arthur. *The sleepwalker and the assassin, a view of the contemporary theatre,* pp. 46-47.

BJORNSTERNE BJORNSON 1832-1910

General

Clark, Barrett H. *A study of modern drama,* pp. 16-21.

Downs, Brian W. "Björnson and Tragedy." *Scandinavica,* vol. 1 (1962), pp. 17-28.

Dukes, Ashley. *Modern dramatists,* pp. 41-49.

Foster, George B. "The Message of Björnson." *Open Court,* vol. 38 (1924), pp. 321-338.

Gassner, John. "Scandinavian Succession and Strindberg." *Masters of the drama,* pp. 384-396.

Lamm, Martin. *Modern drama,* pp. 76-95.

The Bankruptcy

Lamm, Martin. *Modern drama,* pp. 82-83.

Beyond Human Power (Beyond our Strength)

Madsen, B.G. "Björnsterne Björnson's *Beyond Human Power* and Kaj Munk's *The Word." Modern Drama,* vol. 3, no. 1 (May, 1960), pp. 30-36.

Lamm, Martin. *Modern drama,* pp. 87-93.

The New System

Lamm, Martin. *Modern drama,* pp. 83-86.

Paul Lange and Tora Parsberg

Lamm, Martin. *Modern drama,* pp. 93-94.

MICHAEL BLANKFORT and MICHAEL GOLD

Battle Hymn

Himelstein, Morgan Y. *Drama was a weapon, the left-wing theatre i* *New York 1929-1941,* pp. 93-96.

MARC BLITZSTEIN 1905-1964

General

Bauland, Peter. *The hooded eagle,* pp. 93, 142-143, 155, 180-182.

The Cradle Will Rock

Bauland, Peter. *The hooded eagle,* pp. 142-143.

Himelstein, Morgan Y. *Drama was a weapon, the left-wing theatre i* *New York 1929-1941,* pp. 113-118.

JEAN-RICHARD BLOCH 1884-

Le Dernier Empereur

Knowles, Dorothy. *French drama of the inter-war years, 1918-39,* pp 228-229.

BERNICE BLOHM and ADELAIDE BEAN

Bless the Child

Novick, Julius. "Theatre in Cleveland: Who'll *Bless the Child.*" *Th* *New York Times,* May 5, 1968, Sec. 2, pp. 16, 36.

ALEKSANDR ALEKSANDROVICH BLOK 1880-1921

General

Erlich, Victor. *The double image: concepts of the poet in Slav* *literatures,* pp. 68-119.

EDWIN HARVEY BLUM

The Saving Grace

Sainer, Arthur. *The sleepwalker and the assassin, a view of th* *contemporary theatre,* pp. 75-78.

BRIDGET BOLAND 1913-

The Prisoner

Williamson, Audrey. *Contemporary theatre, 1953-1956,* pp. 39-41.

HEINRICH BOLL 1917-

Yeuill, W.E. "Heinrich Böll." *In:* Keith-Smith, Brian, ed. *Essays on contemporary German literature* (German Men of Letters, vol. IV), pp. 141-158.

ROBERT BOLT 1924-

eneral

Atkins, Anselm. "Robert Bolt: Self, Shadow, and the Theater of Recognition." *Modern Drama,* vol. 10 (1967), pp. 182-188.

Bolt, Robert. (An interview with Tom Milne and Clive Goodwin, first published in *Encore* in 1961, followed by replies to further questions put by Simon Trussler in 1966.) *In:* Marowitz, Charles, ed. *Theatre at work,* pp. 58-77.

Cleave, Maureen. "For Robert Bolt a Play Is Like a Clock." *In:* Richards, Dick. *The curtain rises,* pp. 194-195.

Gascoigne, Bamber. *Twentieth-century drama,* pp. 203-204.

Lumley, Frederick. *New trends in 20th century drama,* pp. 299-300.

Marowitz, Charles. "Some Conventional Words: An Interview with Robert Bolt." *Tulane Drama Rev.,* vol. 11, no. 2 (1966), pp. 138-140.

lowering Cherry

Bolt, Robert. (An interview with Tom Milne and Clive Goodwin, first published in *Encore* in 1961, followed by replies to further questions put by Simon Trussler in 1966.) *In:* Marowitz, Charles, ed. *Theatre at work,* pp. 61-62, 64, 70.

Kitchin, Laurence. *Mid-century drama,* pp. 103-104.

Price, Martin. "The London Season." *Modern Drama,* vol. 1, no. 1 (May, 1958), pp. 53-59.

Trewin, J.C. "Two Morality Playwrights: Robert Bolt and John Whiting." *In:* Armstrong, William A., ed. *Experimental drama,* pp. 119-120.

entle Jack

Bolt, Robert. (An interview with Tom Milne and Clive Goodwin, first published in *Encore* in 1961, followed by replies to further questions put by Simon Trussler in 1966.) *In:* Marowitz, Charles, ed. *Theatre at work,* pp. 69-73.

113

A Man for All Seasons

Atkins, Anselm. "Robert Bolt: Self, Shadow, and the Theater (Recognition." *Modern Drama,* vol. 10, no. 2 (Sept., 1967), p 182-188.

Bolt, Robert. (An interview with Tom Milne and Clive Goodwin, fir published in *Encore* in 1961, followed by replies to further question put by Simon Trussler in 1966.) *In:* Marowitz, Charles, ed. *Theatre* work, pp. 62, 66-68, 70, 73.

Bolt, Robert. "Preface to the Play." *In:* Corrigan, R.W., ed. *The ne theatre of Europe,* pp. 34-44.

Brustein, Robert. "Chronicle of a Reluctant Hero." *In:* Seltzer, Danie ed. *The modern theatre, readings and documents,* pp. 469-471.

Brustein, Robert. *Seasons of discontent,* pp. 184-186.

Clurman, Harold. *The naked image,* pp. 48-50.

Corrigan, Robert W. "Introduction." *In:* Corrigan, Robert W., ed. *Th new theatre of Europe,* pp. 27-31.

Dennis, Negel. "From Down Among the Dead Men." *In:* Seltze Daniel, ed. *The modern theatre, readings and documents,* pp. 471-47 (From Dennis, Negel. *Dramatic essays,* London, Weidenfeld.)

Fosberry, M.W. "*A Man for All Seasons.*" *English Studies in Afric* vol. 6 (1963), pp. 164-172.

Kerr, Walter. *The theater in spite of itself,* pp. 161-165.

Lumley, Frederick. *New trends in 20th century drama,* pp. 299-30(

Smith, H.A. "Dipsychus Among the Shadows." *In:* Brown, J.R. and I Harris, eds. *Contemporary theatre,* pp. 143-144.

Trewin, J.C. "Two Morality Playwrights: Robert Bolt and Joh Whiting." *In:* Armstrong, William A., ed. *Experimental drama,* p 120-124.

Tynan, Kenneth. *Tynan right and left,* pp. 26-32.

The Thwarting of Baron Bolligrew

Bolt, Robert. (An interview with Tom Milne and Clive Goodwin, fir published in *Encore* in 1961, followed by replies to further question put by Simon Trussler in 1966.) *In:* Marowitz, Charles, ed. *Theatre* work, pp. 73-76.

he Tiger and the Horse

Bolt, Robert. (An interview with Tom Milne and Clive Goodwin, first published in *Encore* in 1961, followed by replies to further questions put by Simon Trussler in 1966.) *In:* Marowitz, Charles, ed. *Theatre at work,* pp. 62-64, 70-71.

Trewin, J.C. "Two Morality Playwrights: Robert Bolt and John Whiting." *In:* Armstrong, William A., ed. *Experimental drama,* pp. 124-127.

VALENTINO BOMPIANI 1898-

eneral

Pandolfi, Vito. "Italian Theatre Since the War." *Tulane Drama Rev.,* vol. 8, no. 3 (Spring, 1964), p. 98.

WOLFGANG BORCHERT 1921-1947

eneral

Garten, H.F. *Modern German drama,* pp. 244-245, 264.

Popper, Hans. "Wolfgang Borchert." *In:* Natan, A., ed. *German men of letters* vol. 3, (1964), pp. 269-303.

he Man Outside

Weimar, Karl S. "No Entry, No Exit: A Study of Borchert with Some Notes on Sartre." *Modern Lang. Q.,* vol. 17, no. 2 (June, 1956), pp. 153-163.

utside the Door (Draussen vor der Tür)

Bauland, Peter. *The hooded eagle,* pp. 94, 167-168, 170.

Popper, Hans. "Wolfgang Borchert." *In:* Natan, A., ed. *German men of letters* vol. 3, (1964), pp. 282-283, 284-292.

he Outsider

Wellwarth, G.E. "Introduction." *In:* Benedikt, M. and G.E. Wellwarth, eds. *Postwar German theatre,* pp. xii-xvi.

GORDON BOTTOMLEY 1874-1948

he Acts of Saint Peter

Spanos, William V. *The Christian tradition in modern British verse drama,* pp. 54, 59-63.

SAINT-GEORGES DE BOUHELIER 1876-1947

General

Knowles, Dorothy. *French drama of the inter-war years, 1918-39,* pp. 302-304.

EDOUARD BOURDET 1887-1945

General

Knowles, Dorothy. *French drama of the inter-war years, 1918-39,* pp. 268-269.

Welton, Archibald J. "Edouard Bourdet: man of the theater. *Dissertation Abstracts,* vol. 27 (1966), 1067A (Columbia).

The Captive (Le Prisonniére)

Block, Anita. *The changing world in plays and theatre,* pp. 110-12.

Jones, Robert Emmet. *The alienated hero in modern French dram.* pp. 32-36.

Mauriac, François. "Edouard Bourdet's *The Captive* at the Theat. Femina." *In:* La Nouvelle Revue Française, pp. 141-144.

WILLIAM BOYLE 1853-1923

General

Malone, Andrew E. *The Irish drama,* pp. 234-235.

Williams, Harold. *Modern English writers,* p. 217.

The Building Fund

Malone, Andrew E. *The Irish drama,* pp. 230-232.

The Eloquent Dempsey

Malone, Andrew E. *The Irish drama,* pp. 232-233.

The Mineral Workers

Malone, Andrew E. *The Irish drama,* pp. 233-234.

ROBERTO BRACCO 1862-1943

General

Altrocchi, Rudolph. "Bracco and the Drama of the Subconscious. *North American Rev.* (1927), pp. 151-162.

Richardson, Ruth. *Florencio Sánchez and the Argentine theatre*, pp. 181-183.

VITALIANO BRANCATI 1907-1954

General

Pandolfi, Vito. "Italian Theatre Since the War." *Tulane Drama Rev.* vol. 8, no. 3 (Spring, 1964), pp. 95-97.

WILLIAM BRANCH 1927-

n Splendid Error

Abramson, Doris E. *Negro playwrights in the American theatre, 1929-1959*, pp. 179-188, 256, 257-258.

Mitchell, Loften. *Black drama*, pp. 167-168.

Medal for Willie

Abramson, Doris E. *Negro playwrights in the American theatre, 1925-1959*, pp. 171-179, 255-256.

Mitchell, Loften. *Black drama*, pp. 151-154.

BERTOLT BRECHT 1898-1956

General

Abel, Lionel. *Metatheatre, a new view of dramatic form*, pp. 86-107.

Adler, Henry. "Bertolt Brecht's Contribution to Epic Drama." *In:* Gassner, John. *Directions in modern theatre and drama*, pp. 309-312. (Reprinted from *The Listener* (Jan. 12, 1956), pp. 51-52.)

Adler, Henry. "Bertolt Brecht's Theatre." *Twentieth Century*, vol. 160 (Aug., 1956), pp. 114-123.

Allsop, Kenneth. *The angry decade*, pp. 48-49.

Alter, Maria P. "The Many Faces of Bertolt Brecht." *American-German Rev.*, vol. 30, no. 6 (Aug.-Sept., 1964), pp. 25-28.

Anderson, Michael. "From Epic to Alienation." *New Theatre Magazine* (Bristol), vol. 7, no. 2 (1967), pp. 19-25; no. 3, pp. 25-34.

Bauland, Peter. *The hooded eagle*, pp. 122, 123, 124-132, 141-143, 148, 154-155, 157-158, 159, 160, 162, 164-167, 171, 175, 177, 221.

Bentley, Eric R. "Bertolt Brecht and His Work." *Theatre Arts*, vol. 28, no. 9 (Sept., 1944), pp. 9-12.

117

Bentley, Eric. *The playwright as thinker,* pp. 213-231.

Bentley, Eric. *The theatre of commitment,* pp. 94-96, 132-134.

Blau, Herbert. *The impossible theatre,* pp. 87-112, 192-205.

Bornemann, Ernest. "The Real Brecht." *In:* Marowitz, Charles, ed *Encore reader,* pp. 135-152. (Reprinted from *Encore,* July, 1958.)

Brandt, G.W. "Realism and Parables." *In:* Brown, J.R. and Bernar Harris, eds. *Contemporary theatre,* pp. 33-37.

Brecht, Bertolt. "Alienation Effects in Chinese Acting." *In:* Seltzer Daniel ed. *The modern theatre, readings and documents,* pp. 276-28

Brecht, Bertolt. *Brecht on theatre.*

Brecht, Bertolt. "Theatre for Pleasure or Theatre for Instruction." *In* Corrigan, Robert W., ed. *Masterpieces of the modern German theatre* pp. 315-323. (Reprinted from Brecht, Bertolt. *Brecht on theatre,* N.Y. Hill & Wang, 1964.)

Brustein, Robert. *The theatre of revolt,* pp. 231-234, 237-241, 250-258 276-278.

Busacca, Basil. "Brecht and the Destruction of Theater." *In:* Armato Rosario and Spalek, John M., eds. *Medieval epic to the "Epic Theater of Brecht,* pp. 185-201.

Chiari, J. *Landmarks of contemporary drama,* pp. 161-183.

Clancy, James H. "Beyond Despair: A New Drama of Ideas." *In* Freedman, Morris, ed. *Essays in the modern drama,* pp. 160-173 (Reprinted from *Educational Theatre J.,* vol. 13, no. 3 (Oct., 1961).

Clurman, Harold. "The Achievment of Bertolt Brecht." *Partisan Rev.* vol. 26, no. 4 (Fall, 1959), pp. 624-628.

Clurman, Harold. "Bertolt Brecht." *In:* Freedman, Morris, ed. *Essay in the modern drama,* pp. 151-159. (Reprinted from *Lies like truth* by Harold Clurman.)

Clurman, Harold. *The naked image,* pp. 51-55, 203-209.

Coenen, F.E. "The Modern German Drama." *In:* Hammer, Carl, Jr. ed. *Studies in German literature,* pp. 110-112.

Cohn, Ruby. "*Theatrum Mundi* and Contemporary Theater." *Comparative Drama,* vol. 1 (1967), pp. 28-35.

Cook, Bruce A. "Bertolt Brecht and the Dialectical Jones." *Catholic World,* vol. 196 (Jan., 1963), pp. 250-256.

orrigan, Robert W., ed. *Masterpieces of the modern German theatre,* p. 312-313.

emetz, Peter, ed. *Brecht.*

evine, George. "The Berliner Ensemble." *In:* Marowitz, Charles, ed. *ncore reader,* pp. 14-18. (Reprinted from *Encore,* April, 1956.)

ukore, Bernard F. "The Temptation of Goodness." *Educational heatre J.,* vol. 15 (1963), pp. 105-111.

sslin, Martin. "Brecht and the English Theatre." *Tulane Drama Rev.,* ol. 11, no. 2 (1966), pp. 63-70.

sslin, Martin. "Brecht at Seventy." *Tulane Drama Rev.,* vol. 12, no. 1 967), pp. 36-43.

sslin, Martin. "Brecht, the Absurd, and the Future." *Tulane Drama ev.,* vol. 7, no. 2 (Winter, 1962), pp. 43-54.

sslin, Martin. "Brecht's Twists & Turns." *Encounter,* vol. 27, no. 2 966), pp. 58-62.

ergusson, Francis. *The human image in dramatic literature,* pp. -50.

reedman, Morris. *The moral impulse,* pp. 99-114.

riebert, Stuart. "Notes on Brecht: Disillusionment and After." *Prairie chooner,* vol. 40 (1966), pp. 49-54.

arten, H.F. *Modern German drama.* pp. 200-218.

ascoigne, Bamber. *Twentieth-century drama,* pp. 121-133.

assner, John. *Directions in modern theatre and drama,* pp. 290-299, 4-317.

assner, John. *The theatre in our times,* pp. 82-96.

ttleman, Sol. "Frank Wedekind and Bertolt Brecht; Notes on a elationship." *Modern Drama,* vol. 10, no. 4 (Feb., 1968), pp. 401-409.

oldsmith, Ulrich K. "Brecht as Adaptor of Moliere." *In:* Jost, ancois, ed. *Proceedings of the IVth Congress of the International omparative Literature Association,* Fribourg, 1964, vol. 2, pp. 5-881.

oodman, Henry. "Bertolt Brecht as 'Traditional Dramatist'." *ducational Theatre J.,* vol. 4, 1952, pp. 109-114.

Goodman, Henry. "Bertolt Brecht: Dualism and Tradition." *In* Armato, Rosario, and Spalek, John M., eds. *Medieval epic to the "Epic Theater" of Brecht,* pp. 219-231.

Gorelik, Mordecai. "Brecht. 'I am the Einstein of the New Stage Form.'" *Theatre Arts,* vol. 41, no. 3 (Mar., 1957), pp. 72-73, 86-87.

Grossvogel, David I. *Four playwrights and a postscript, Brecht, Ionesco, Beckett, Genet,* pp. 3-45.

Hatfield, Henry. *Modern German literature,* pp. 78-79, 135-138.

Hecht, Werner. "The Characteristics of the Berliner Ensemble: Remarks on Brecht's Method." *Theatre Research,* vol. 8 (1967), pp. 165-174.

Hecht, Werner. "The Development of Brecht's Theory of Epic Theatre: 1918-1933." The *Tulane Drama Rev.,* VI (1961), pp. 40-97.

Heller, Peter. "Nihilist Into Activist: Two Phases in the Development of Bertolt Brecht." *Germanic Rev.,* vol. 28, no. 2 (Apr., 1953), pp. 144-155.

Hiller, Robert L. "The Symbolism of *Gestus* in Brecht's Drama." *In* Slote, Bernice, ed. *Myth and symbol,* pp. 89-100.

Jones, Frank. "Three Modern Adaptors of Sophocles' *Antigone.*" *In* Jost, Francois, ed. *Proceedings of the IVth Congress of the International Comparative Literature Assoc.,* vol. 2, pp. 1079-1083.

Kantor, Robert E., and Hoffman, Lynn. "Brechtian Theatre as Model for Conjoint Family Therapy." *Family Process,* vol. 5, no. 2.

Kitchin, Laurence. *Mid-century drama,* pp. 72-80.

Kuhn, Reinhard. "The Debasement of the Intellectual in Contemporary Continental Drama." *Modern Drama,* vol. 7, no. 4 (Feb., 1965), pp. 454-462.

Lazzari, Arturo. "Brecht in Italy." *Tulane Drama Rev.,* vol. 12, no. (1967), pp. 149-154.

Lewis, Allan. *The contemporary theatre,* pp. 218-242.

Losey, Joseph. "The Individual Eye." *In:* Marowitz, Charles, ed. *Encore reader,* pp. 195-209. (Reprinted from *Encore,* Mar., 1961.)

Lumley, Frederick. *New trends in 20th century drama,* pp. 78-79, 83-90.

Lumley, Frederick. *Trends in 20th century drama,* pp. 94-97.

Luthy, Herbert. "Of Poor Bert Brecht." *Encounter,* vol. 7, no. 1 (July, 1956), pp. 33-53.

Mandel, Oscar. "Brecht's Unheroes and Heroines." *In:* Armato, Rosario and Spalek, John M., eds. *Medieval epic to the "Epic Theater" of Brecht,* pp. 233-242.

Merchant, W. Moelwyn. "The Irony of Bertolt Brecht." *In:* Scott, Nathan A. *Man in the modern theatre,* pp. 58-75.

Moore, Harry T. *Twentieth-century German literature.* pp. 3, 22, 16-43, 107-110, 118, 119, 127, 132, 143, 144, 145.

Mueller, Carl H. "Brecht and the Marxist Concept of the Nature of Man." *In:* Armato, Rosario and Spalek, John M., eds. *Medieval epic to the "Epic Theater" of Brecht,* pp. 203-208.

Politzer, Heinz. "How Epic Is Bertolt Brecht's Epic Theater?" *In:* Bogard, Travis and Oliver, William I. eds. *Modern drama; essays in criticism,* pp. 54-63, 68-71. (Reprinted from *Modern Language Q.,* vol. 3, no. 2, (June, 1962), pp. 99-114.)

Pronko, Leonard C. *Theater East and West,* pp. 55-61, 100-101.

Puknat, Siegfried B. "Brecht and Schiller: Nonelective Affinities." *Modern Language Q.,* vol. 26 (1965), pp. 558-570.

Ryan, Lawrence. "Bertolt Brecht: a Marxist Dramatist?" *In: Aspects of drama and the theatre,* pp. 73-92, 94-100, 104-111.

Siebenmann, Otto. "Bertolt Brecht's Didactic Plays *The Yea-Sayer* and *The Nay-Sayer."* *In:* Baldner, R.W., ed. *Proceedings, Pacific Northwest Conference on Foreign Languages,* pp. 225-231.

Spalter, Max. *Brecht's tradition,* pp. 157-200.

Styan, J.L. *The dark comedy,* 2nd ed., pp. 2, 47, 76, 112, 117-118, 160, 166-167, 238, 242, 244, 252, 256, 262, 267, 277-278, 290.

Subiotto, Arrigo. "Bertolt Brecht and the Dialectic of Tradition." *Forum for Modern Language Studies* (U. of St. Andrews, Scotland), vol. 2 (1966), pp. 123-140.

Suvin, Darko. "The Mirror and the Dynamo: On Brecht's Aesthetic Point of View." *Tulane Drama Rev.,* vol. 12, no. 1 (1967), pp. 56-67.

Thompson, Lawrence. "Bert Brecht." *Kenyon Rev.,* vol. 2, no. 3 (Summer, 1940), pp. 319-329.

Tynan, Kenneth. "Bertolt Brecht." *In:* Freedman, Morris, ed. *Essays in the modern drama,* pp. 137-150. (Reprinted from *Curtains* by Kenneth Tynan.)

Tynan, Kenneth. *Tynan right and left,* pp. 156-160.

Viertel, Berthold. "Bertolt Brecht, Dramatist." *Kenyon Rev.,* vol. 7 no. 3 (Summer, 1945), pp. 467-475.

Weales, Gerald. "Brecht and the Drama of Ideas." *In:* Englis. Institute. *Ideas in the drama...,* pp. 125-154.

Weber, Carl. "Brecht as Director." *Tulane Drama Rev.,* vol. 12, no. (1967), pp. 101-107.

Wekwerth, Manfred. "Brecht Today." *Tulane Drama Rev.,* vol. 12, nc 1 (1967), pp. 118-124.

Williams, Raymond. "The Achievement of Brecht." *Critical Q.,* vol. 3 no. 3 (Summer, 1961), pp. 153-162.

Williams, Raymond. *Modern tragedy,* pp. 190-204.

World Theatre, vol. 15 (May-June, July-Aug., 1966). Double issu devoted to Brecht on the tenth anniversary of his death.

Baal

Bauland, Peter. *The hooded eagle,* pp. 125, 195-196.

Bentley, Eric. "Bertolt Brecht's First Play." *Kenyon Rev.,* vol. 26, n< 100 (Winter, 1964), pp. 83-92.

Goldstein, Bluma. "Bertolt Brecht's *Baal:* A Crisis in Poeti Existence." *In:* Schwarz, Egon, *et al.,* eds. *Festschrift fur Bernhar Blume: Aufsatze zur deutschen und eruopaischen literatur,* pr 333-347.

Heller, Peter. "Nihilist into Activist: Two Phases in the Developmen of Bertolt Brecht." *Germanic Rev.,* vol. 28, no. 2 (Apr., 1953), pr 144-155.

Lyons, Charles R. *Bertolt Brecht, the despair and the polemic,* pr 3-24.

Lyons, Charles R. "Bertolt Brecht's *Baal:* The Structure of Images. *Modern Drama,* vol. 8 no. 3 (Dec., 1965), pp. 311-323.

Matthews, Honor. *The primal curse,* pp. 21, 184-186.

Spalter, Max. *Brecht's tradition,* pp. 106, 131, 132, 157, 158-164, 17(

Steer, W.A.J. *"Baal:* A Key to Brecht's Communism." *German li. and letters,* n.s., vol. 1911 (1965-66), pp. 40-51.

he Caucasian Chalk Circle (Der Kaukasische Kreidekreis)

Abel, Lionel. *Metatheatre, a new view of dramatic form,* pp. 97-98.

Allison, Alexander W., ed. *Masterpieces of the drama,* 2nd ed., pp. 701-702.

Bentley, Eric. *The playwright as thinker,* pp. 225-226.

Brecht, Bertolt. "Notes on *The Caucasian Chalk Circle.*" *Tulane Drama Rev.,* vol. 12, no. 1 (1967), pp. 88-100.

Clurman, Harold. *Lies like truth,* pp. 228-230.

Flanner, Janet. *Paris journal, 1944-1965,* pp. 281-282.

Gaskell, Ronald. "The Form of *The Caucasiun Chalk Circle.*" *Modern Drama,* vol. 10, no. 2 (Sept., 1967), pp. 195-201.

Gaskill, William. (Interview with Tom Milne; first appeared in *Encore* in 1962.) *In:* Marowitz, Charles, ed. *Theatre at work,* pp. 123-132.

Gottfried, Martin. *A theater divided; the postwar American stage,* pp. 136-138.

Gray, Ronald. "On Brecht's *The Caucasian Chalk Circle.*" *In:* Demetz, Peter, ed. *Brecht,* pp. 151-156.

Lumley, Frederick. *New trends in 20th century drama,* pp. 87-88.

Lyons, Charles R. *Bertolt Brecht, the despair and the polemic.* pp. 132-154.

Politzer, Heinz. "How Epic Is Bertolt Brecht's Epic Theater?" *In:* Bogard, Travis and Oliver, William I. *Modern drama; essays in criticism,* pp. 63-67. (Reprinted from *Modern Language Q.,* 23, no. 2 (June, 1962), pp. 99-114.)

Pronko, Leonard C. *Theater East and West,* pp. 61-63.

Reinert, Otto, ed. *Drama; an introductory anthology* (alternate ed), pp. 829-835.

Sagar, Keith M. "Brecht in Neverneverland: *The Caucasian Chalk Circle.*" *Modern Drama,* vol. 9, no. 1 (May, 1966), pp. 11-17.

Spalter, Max. *Brecht's tradition,* pp. 196-197.

Styan, J.L. *The dark comedy,* 2nd ed., pp. 115-116, 168, 169, 177, 271, 294.

Tynan, Kenneth. *Tynan right and left,* pp. 121-123.

Drums in the Night (Trommeln in der Nacht)

Spalter, Max. *Brecht's tradition,* pp. 164-166.

The Exception and the Rule (Die Ausnahme und die Regel)

Bauland, Peter. *The hooded eagle,* pp. 195-196.

Ryan, Lawrence. "Bertolt Brecht: A Marxist Dramatist?" *In: Aspec of drama and the theatre,* pp. 92-93.

Spalter, Max. *Brecht's tradition,* pp. 181-182.

Exiles' Dialogues (Flüchlingspräche)

Lumley, Frederick. *New trends in 20th century drama,* p. 89.

Galileo (Das Leben des Galilei)

Abel, Lionel. *Metatheatre, a new view of dramatic form,* pp. 98-10

Bauland, Peter. *The hooded eagle,* pp. 128, 155, 164-167, 196.

Blau, Herbert. *The impossible theatre.* pp. 93-112.

Fraser, G.S. *The modern writer and his world,* pp. 59-61.

Lyons, Charles R. *Bertolt Brecht, the despair and the polemic,* p 110-131.

Lyons, Charles R. *"The Life of Galileo:* The Focus of Ambiguity the Villain Hero." *Germanic Rev.,* vol. 41 (1966), pp. 57-71.

Rohrmoser, Gunter. "Brecht's *Galileo." In:* Demetz, Peter, ed. *Brecl* pp. 117-126.

Ryan, Lawrence. "Bretolt Brecht: A Marxist Dramatist?" *In: Aspec of drama and the theatre,* pp. 103-104.

Sorensen, Otto M. "Brecht's *Galileo:* Its Development from Ideation into Ideological Theater." *Modern Drama,* vol. 11, no. 4 (Feb., 1969 pp. 410-422.

Spalter, Max. *Brecht's tradition,* pp. 189-193.

Tynan, Kenneth *Tynan right and left,* pp. 23-24, 63.

Williams, Raymond. *Drama in performance* (new ed.), pp. 148-15

Williams, Raymond. *Modern tragedy,* pp. 199-202.

Wood, Frank. "Gertrud von Le Fort and Bertolt Brecht: Counter Reformation and Atomic Bomb." *In:* Hammer, Carl, Jr., ed., *Studies in German literature,* pp. 136-147.

he Good Woman of Setzuan (Der Gute Mensch von Sezuan)

Bauland, Peter. *The hooded eagle,* pp. 157, 184-185, 196.

Bentley, Eric. *The playwright as thinker,* pp. 222-225.

Cowell, Raymond. *Twelve modern dramatists,* pp. 79-81.

Gassner, John. *Theatre at the crossroads,* pp. 264-270.

Hodge, Francis. "German Drama and the American Stage." *In:* Shaw, Leroy R., ed. *The German theatre today,* pp. 83-88.

Lewis, Allan. *The contemporary theatre,* pp. 225-231.

Mueller, Carl H. "Brecht and the Marxist Concept of the Nature of Man." *In:* Armato, Rosario, and Spalek, John M., eds. *Medieval epic to the "Epic Theater" of Brecht,* pp. 212-217.

Reinert, Otto. *Drama, an introductory anthology,* pp. 546-548.

Reinert, Otto, ed. *Modern drama; nine plays,* pp. 384-386.

Spalter, Max. *Brecht's tradition,* pp. 110, 193-195.

Williams, Raymond. *Modern tragedy,* pp. 196-198.

n the Jungle of Cities (In the Swamp of the Cities) (Im Dickicht der Stadte)

Bauland, Peter. *The hooded eagle,* pp. 179, 187-188.

Bentley, Eric. "On Brecht's *In the Swamp, A Man's a Man,* and *St. Joan of the Stockyards."* *In:* Demetz, Peter, ed. *Brecht,* pp. 51-53.

Brustein, Robert. *Seasons of discontent,* pp. 39-42.

Brustein, Robert. *The theater of revolt,* pp. 241-250.

Clurman, Harold. *The naked image,* pp. 56-58.

Lyons, Charles R. *Bertolt Brecht, the despair and the polemic,* pp. 25-44.

Lyons, Charles R. "Two Projections of the Isolation of the Human Soul: Brecht and Albee." *Drama Survey,* vol. 4 (Summer, 1965), pp. 121-131.

Spalter, Max. *Brecht's tradition,* pp. 106, 131, 166-168, 169-170.

The Life of Edward the Second of England (Leben Eduards de Zweiten) (An adaptation of Marlowe's Edward II)

Spalter, Max. *Brecht's tradition,* pp. 168-169.

Svendsen, Juris. "The Queen is Dead: Brecht's Eduard II." *Tulan Drama Rev.,* vol. 10, no. 3 (Spring, 1966), pp. 160-176.

A Man's a Man (Mann Ist Mann)

Bauland, Peter. *The hooded eagle,* pp. 179, 189-190.

Bentley, Eric. "On Brecht's *In the Swamp, A Man's a Man,* and *S. Joan of the Stockyards*" *In:* Demetz, Peter, ed. *Brecht,* pp. 53-57.

Brustein, Robert. "Brecht on the Rampage." *In:* Seltzer, Daniel, ed *The modern theatre, readings and documents,* pp. 465-468. (Fron Brustein, Robert, *Seasons of discontent,* pp. 71-74.)

Clurman, Harold, *The naked image,* pp. 58-61.

Lyons, Charles R. *Bertolt Brecht, the despair and the polemic,* pp 45-67.

Sainer, Arthur. *The sleepwalker and the assassin, a view of th contemporary theatre,* pp. 28-29.

Spalter, Max. *Brecht's tradition,* pp. 132, 170-174.

The Measures Taken (Die Massnahme)

Abel, Lionel. *Metatheatre, a new view of dramatic form,* pp. 90-92

Lyons, Charles R. *Bertolt Brecht, the despair and the polemic,* pp 68-88.

Spalter, Max. *Brecht's tradition,* pp. 94, 180-181.

Mr. Puntila and His Hired Man, Matti (Herr Puntila und Seir Knecht Matti)

Lumley, Frederick. *New trends in 20th century drama,* pp. 87-88.

Spalter, Max. *Brecht's tradition,* pp. 195-196.

The Mother (Die Mutter)

Bauland, Peter. *The hooded eagle,* pp. 130-131.

Gascoigne, Bamber. *Twentieth-century drama,* pp. 124-128, 130.

Himelstein, Morgan Y. *Drama was a weapon, the left-wing theatre it New York 1929-1941,* pp. 65-68, 73.

Mueller, Carl H. "Brecht and the Marxist Concept of the Nature of Man." *In:* Armato, Rosario and Spalek, John M., eds. *Medieval Epic to the "Epic Theater" of Brecht,* pp. 208-212.

[other Courage and Her Children (Mutter Courage und Ihre Kinder)

Abel, Lionel. *Metatheatre, a new view of dramatic form,* pp. 95-97.

Barthes, Roland. "Seven Photo Models of Mother Courage." *Tulane Drama Rev.,* vol. no. 1 (1967), pp. 44-55.

Bauland, Peter. *The hooded eagle,* pp. 129, 190-193, 196.

Bentley, Eric. "The Songs in *Mother Courage.*" In: Burnshaw, Stanley, ed. *Varieties of literary experience,* pp. 45-74.

Bentley, Eric. *The theatre of commitment,* pp. 95-96, 154-157, 221-224.

Blau, Herbert. "Brecht's *Mother Courage:* the Rite of War and the Rhythm of Epic." *Educational Theatre J.,* vol. 9 (1957), pp. 1-10.

Blau, Herbert. "From Counterforce I: The Social Drama." *In:* Seltzer, Daniel, ed. *The modern theatre, readings and documents,* pp. 427-441. (From Blau, Herbert. *The impossible theatre: a manifesto,* N.Y., Macmillan 1964.)

Blau, Herbert. *The impossible theatre,* pp. 192-205.

Brecht, Bertolt. "Observation on *Mother Courage.*" *In:* Block, Haskell M. *The creative vision,* pp. 158-161.

Brustein, Robert. *Seasons of discontent,* pp. 152-155.

Brustein, Robert. *The theatre of revolt,* pp. 267-276.

Clurman, Harold. *Lies like truth,* pp. 236-238.

Clurman, Harold. *The naked image,* pp. 61-64.

Fergusson, Francis. *The human image in dramatic literature,* pp. 45-49.

Glade, Henry. "The Death of Mother Courage." *Tulane Drama Rev.,* vol. 12, no. 1 (1967), pp. 137-148.

Gray, Ronald. "Brecht's *Mother Courage.*" *Oxford Rev.,* no. 2 (1966), pp. 44-54.

Himelstein, Morgan Y. "The Pioneers of Bertolt Brecht in America." *Modern Drama,* vol. 9, no. 2 (Sept., 1966), pp. 178-189.

Lumley, Frederick. *New trends in 20th century drama,* pp. 85, 86-87

Lumley, Frederick. *Trends in 20th century drama,* pp. 95-97.

Lyons, Charles R. *Bertolt Brecht, the despair and the polemic,* pp. 89-109.

Matthews, Honor. *The primal curse,* pp. 24-26.

Mennemeier, Franz Norbert. *"Mother Courage and Her Children." In* Demetz, Peter, ed. *Brecht,* pp. 138-150.

Ryan, Lawrence. "Bertolt Brecht: A Marxist Dramatist?" *In: Aspects of drama and the theatre,* pp. 100-103.

Spalter, Max. *Brecht's tradition,* pp. 170, 184-189, 193.

Steiner, George. *The death of tragedy,* pp. 345-349, 353-354.

Styan, J.L. *The dark comedy,* 2nd ed., pp. 168-170, 174, 175, 178-187, 264.

Tynan, Kenneth. *Tynan right and left,* pp. 136-138.

Williams, Raymond. *Modern tragedy,* pp. 196-202.

The Private Life of the Master Race (Fear and Misery of the Third Reich) (Furcht und Elend des Dritten Reich)

Bauland, Peter. *The hooded eagle,* pp. 132, 148, 154-155, 183.

Heilman, Robert B. *Tragedy and melodrama,* pp. 36-37, 278-279.

Spalter, Max. *Brecht's tradition,* pp. 163, 182-183.

The Resistable Rise of Arturo Ui (Der Aufhaltsame Aufsteig des Arturo Ui)

Bauland, Peter. *The hooded eagle,* pp. 193-195.

Brustein, Robert. *Seasons of discontent,* pp. 144-145.

Clurman, Harold. *The naked image,* pp. 64-66.

Gottfried, Martin. *A theater divided; the postwar American stage,* pp. 275-276.

Spalter, Max, *Brecht's tradition,* p. 184.

The Rise and Fall of the City of Mahagonny (Aufstieg und Fall der Stadt Mahagonny)

Spalter, Max. *Brecht's tradition,* pp. 177-178.

he Roundheads and the Peakheads (Die Rundköpfe und die Spitzköpfe)

Spalter, Max. *Brecht's tradition,* p. 184.

aint Joan of the Stockyards (Die Heilige Johanna der Schlachthof)

Bentley, Eric. "On Brecht's *In the Swamp, A Man's a Man,* and *St. Joan of the Stockyards.*" *In:* Demetz, Peter, ed. *Brecht,* pp. 57-58.

Sainer, Arthur. *The sleepwalker and the assassin, a view of the contemporary theatre,* pp. 111-113.

Spalter, Max. *Brecht's tradition,* pp. 178-179.

he Threepenny Opera (Die Dreigroschenoper)

Bauland, Peter. *The hooded eagle,* pp. 125, 127, 128-129, 143, 155, 167, 170, 177, 179, 180-183.

Brecht, Bertolt. "Production Notes for the Threepenny Opera." *In:* Seltzer, Daniel, ed. *The modern theatre, readings and documents,* pp. 295-304. (From Bentley, Eric, ed. *From the modern repertoire,* series I, Indiana Univ. Press.)

Brustein, Robert. *The theatre of revolt,* pp. 259-267.

Dukore, Bernard F. "The Averted Crucifixion of Macheath." *Drama Survey,* vol. 4, no. 1 (Spring, 1965), pp. 51-56.

Henning, Roslyn Brogue. "Expressionist Opera." *American-German Rev.,* vol. 22, no. 6 (Aug./Sept., 1966), pp. 21-22.

Himelstein, Morgan Y. "The Pioneers of Bertolt Brecht in America." *Modern Drama,* vol. 9, no. 2 (Sept., 1966), pp. 178-189.

Spalter, Max. *Brecht's tradition,* pp. 95, 124, 173, 174-177.

Williams, Raymond. *Modern tragedy* pp. 191-194.

The Yea-Sayer (Der Jasager)

Bauland, Peter. *The hooded eagle,* pp. 129-130.

GEORGE BREWER 1899-

Tide Rising

Himelstein, Morgan Y. *Drama was a weapon, the left-wing theatre in New York, 1929-1941,* pp. 201-202.

JAMES BRIDIE 1888-1951
(real name Osborne Henry Mavor)
General

Bannister, Winifred. *James Bridie and his theatre.*

Greene, Anne. "Priestley, Bridie and Fry: the mystery of existence in their dramatic work." *Dissertation Abstracts,* vol. 17 (1957), Univ. of Wisc.

Knight, G. Wilson. *The golden labyrinth,* pp. 382-384.

Linklater, Eric. *The art of adventure,* pp. 25-43.

Lumley, Frederick. *New trends in 20th century drama,* pp. 292-294

Lumley, Frederick. *Trends in 20th century drama,* pp. 203-205.

Luyben, Helen L. "The Dramatic Method of James Bridie." *Educational Theatre J.,* vol. 15 (1963), pp. 332-342.

Luyben, Helen L. *James Bridie: clown and philosopher.*

Weales, Gerald. *Religion in modern English drama,* pp. 79-90.

The Baikie Charivari, or, The Seven Prophets

Luyben, Helen L. "Bridie's Last Play." *Modern Drama,* vol. 5, no. 4 (Feb., 1963), pp. 400-414.

Weales, Gerald. *Religion in modern English drama,* pp. 86, 88-90.

The Black Eye

Luyben, Helen L. "James Bridie and the Prodigal Son Story." *Modern Drama,* vol. 7, no. 1 (May, 1964), pp. 35-45.

Daphne Laureola

Marshall, Margaret. "Drama." *Nation,* vol. 171 (Sept. 30, 1950), p. 295.

Gog and Magog

Bentley, Eric. *In search of theatre,* pp. 42-43.

Holy Isle

Weales, Gerald. *Religion in modern English drama,* pp. 85-86.

onah and the Whale

Michie, James A. "Educating the Prophets." *Modern Drama,* vol. 11, no. 4 (Feb., 1969), pp. 429-431.

Roston, Murray. *Biblical drama in England from the Middle Ages to the present day,* pp. 281-282.

Weales, Gerald. *Religion in modern English drama,* pp. 82-83.

Verschoyle, Derek. "The Theatre." *Spectator,* vol. 149 (Dec. 16, 1932), p. 861.

1r. Bolfry

Weales, Gerald. *Religion in modern English drama,* pp. 80-81.

he Queen's Comedy

Weales, Gerald. *Religion in modern English drama,* pp. 86-88.

Sleeping Clergyman

Krutch, J.W. "A Fig From Thistles." *Nation,* vol. 139 (Oct. 24, 1934), pp. 486-487.

Weales, Gerald. *Religion in modern English drama,* p. 80.

he Sunlight Sonata

Weales, Gerald. *Religion in modern English drama,* pp. 80, 81.

usannah and the Elders

Roston, Murray. *Biblical drama in England from the Middle Ages to the present day,* pp. 282-283.

Weales, Gerald. *Religion in modern English drama,* p. 84.

obias and the Angel

Roston, Murray. *Biblical drama in England from the Middle Ages to the present day,* pp. 280-281.

Styan, J.L. *The elements of drama,* pp. 267-269.

Walter, Marie. "The Grateful Dead: An Old Tale Newly Told." *Southern Folklore J.,* vol. 23 (1959), pp. 190-195.

Weales, Gerald. *Religion in modern English drama,* p. 82.

EUGENE BRIEUX 1858-1932

General

Dukes, Ashley. *Modern dramatists,* pp. 224-241.

Jameson, Storm. *Modern drama in Europe,* pp. 147-152.

Blanchette

Dukes, Ashley. Modern dramatists. pp. 226-228.

Damaged Goods (Les Avariés)

Block, Anita. *The changing world in plays and theatre,* pp. 61-63.

La Foi

Ellehauge, Martin. *The position of Bernard Shaw in European dram and philosophy,* pp. 312-315.

La Française

Ellehauge, Martin. *The position of Bernard Shaw in European dram and philosophy,* pp. 324-26.

Maternité

Dukes, Ashley. *Modern dramatists,* pp. 233-239.

The Philanthropists (Les Bienfaiteurs)

Dukes, Ashley. *Modern dramatists,* pp. 228-231.

The Three Daughters of Monsieur Dupont (Les Trois Filles de M Dupont)

Dukes, Ashley. *Modern dramatists,* pp. 231-233.

Henn, T.R. *The harvest of tragedy,* pp. 113-115.

ARNOLT BRONNEN 1895-1959

General

Garten, H.F. *Modern German drama,* pp. 120-121, 179-180, 231.

Parricide (Vatermord)

Garten, H.F. *Modern German drama,* pp. 120-121.

JERZY BROSZKIEWICZ 1922-

he End of Book VI (Koniec Kniegi VI)

Czerwinski, Edward J. "Jerzy Broszkiewicz: Transfiguration and Transmutation." *Books Abroad,* vol. 42, no. 2 (Spring, 1968), p. 206.

he Historical Role of Quince (Dziejowa Rola Pigwy)

Czerwinski, Edward J. "Jerzy Broszkiewicz: Transfiguration and Transmutation." *Books Abroad,* vol. 42, no. 2 (Spring, 1968), pp. 206-207.

Come to Tell (Przychodze Opowiedziec)

Czerwinski, Edward J. "Jerzy Broszkiewicz: Transfiguration and Transmutation." *Books Abroad,* vol. 42, no. 2 (Spring, 1968), pp. 206-208.

candal in Hellberg (Skandal W Helbergu)

Czerwinski, Edward J. "Jerzy Broszkiewicz: Transfiguration and Transmutation." *Books Abroad,* vol. 42, no. 2 (Spring, 1968), p. 206.

he Two Adventures of Lemuel Gulliver (Dwie Przygody Lemuela Gulliwera)

Czerwinski, Edward J. "Jerzy Broszkiewicz: Transfiguration and Transmutation." *Books Abroad,* vol. 42, no. 2 (Spring, 1968), p. 206.

KENNETH H. BROWN 1936-

he Brig

Bigsby, C.W.E. *Confrontation and commitment,* pp. xviii, 20, 24, 59, 60, 61-70, 98, 101, 103.

Bigsby, C.W.E. "The Violent Image: The Significance of Kenneth Brown's *The Brig.*" *Wisconsin Studies in Contemporary Literature,* vol. 8, no. 3 (Summer 1967), pp. 421-430.

Brustein, Robert. *Seasons of discontent,* pp. 79-82.

Dukore, Bernard F. "The Noncommercial Theater in New York." *In:* Downer, Alan S., ed. *The American theater today,* pp. 162-165.

Frost, David. "How Real is Real?" *In:* Richards, Dick. *The curtain rises,* pp. 56-58.

Kostelanetz, Richard. "The New American Theatre." *In:* Kostelanetz, Richard. *The new American arts,* pp. 67-70.

Lumley, Frederick. *New trends in 20th century drama,* pp. 328-329.

Rogoff, Gordon. *"The Brig."* In: Marowitz, Charles, ed. *Encore reader,* pp. 268-274. (Reprinted from *Encore,* Sept., 1963.)

Sainer, Arthur. *The sleepwalker and the assassin, a view of the contemporary theatre,* pp. 23-24.

Schechner, Richard. "Interview with Kenneth Brown." *Tulane Drama Rev.,* vol. 8, no. 3 (Spring, 1964), pp. 212-219.

THEODORE BROWNE

Natural Man

Abramson, Doris E. *Negro playwrights in the American theatre, 1925-1959,* pp. 102-109, 159-160.

WYNYARD BROWNE 1911-

Dark Summer

Hobson, Harold. *Theatre,* pp. 146-148.

A Question of Fact

Williamson, Audrey. *Contemporary theatre, 1953-1956,* pp. 37-39.

FERDINAND BRUCKNER 1891-1958
(real name Theodor Tagger)

General

Bauland, Peter. *The hooded eagle,* pp. 109, 117-118, 119, 148-150, 153, 160, 164.

Garten, H.F. *Modern German drama,* pp. 186-188, 242.

The Criminals (Die Verbrecher)

Bauland, Peter. *The hooded eagle,* pp. 148-150.

Gloriana (Elizabeth von England)

Bauland, Peter. *The hooded eagle,* pp. 109, 118.

Races (Die Rassen)

Bauland, Peter. *The hooded eagle,* p. 119.

Sickness of Youth (Krankheit der Jugend)

Bauland, Peter. *The hooded eagle,* pp. 117-118.

Block, Anita. *The changing world in plays and theatre,* pp. 103-106.

Garten, H.F. *Modern German drama,* pp. 186-187.

GEORG BUCHNER 1813-1837

General

Baxandall, Lee. "Introduction." *In:* Büchner, Georg. *Woyzeck and Leonce and Lena,* pp. xi-xvii.

Buechner, Georg. "From Buechner's Letters." *In:* Corrigan, Robert W., ed. *Masterpieces of the modern German theatre,* pp. 33-36. *(Also in: Tulane Drama Rev.,* vol. 6, no. 3, Mar., 1962.)

Corrigan, Robert W., ed. *Masterpieces of the modern German theatre,* pp. 32.

Hamburger, Michael. *Reason and energy: studies in German literature,* pp. 179-208.

Hoffman, Theodore. "Introduction." *In:* Büchner, Georg. *Danton's Death,* pp. vii-xvi.

Lindenberger, Herbert. *Georg Büchner,* pp. 3-18, 115-144.

Mueller, Carl R. "Introduction." *In:* Büchner, Georg. *Complete plays and prose,* pp. xi-xxx.

Sly, Gerlinde H. "The role of social consciousness and fatalism in the works, life, and letters of Georg Büchner and the younger Ivan Sergeyevich Turgenev. (Two types of literary reactions to social conditions.)" *Dissertation Abstracts,* vol. 27 (1966), 1346A-47A (N.Y.U.).

Danton's Death (Dantons Tod)

Aylen, Leo. *Greek tragedy and the modern world,* pp. 202-203, 231-236.

Brown, John Mason. *Broadway in review,* pp. 226-230.

Clurman, Harold. *Lies like truth,* pp. 233-235.

Cowen, Roy C. "Grabbe's *Napoleon,* Büchner's *Danton,* and the Masses." *Symposium,* vol. 21, no. 4 (Winter, 1967), pp. 316-323.

Gottfried, Martin. *A theater divided; the postwar American stage,* pp. 156-158.

Hamburger, Michael. *Reason and energy,* pp. 182, 183, 184, 185-186, 190-195, 197, 199, 205, 206.

Himelstein, Morgan Y. *Drama was a weapon, the left-wing theatre in New York 1929-1941,* pp. 119-120.

Lindenberger, Herbert. *Georg Büchner,* pp. 19-53.

Leonce und Lena

Hamburger, Michael. *Reason and energy,* pp. 182, 183, 188-190 196-197, 201.

Lindenberger, Herbert. *Georg Büchner,* pp. 54-67.

Woyzeck

Brustein, Robert. *The theatre of revolt,* pp. 235-236.

Hamburger, Michael. *Reason and energy,* pp. 182, 183, 190, 195 201-202, 204, 205, 206.

Kayser, Wolfgang. *The grotesque in art and literature,* pp. 90-95 97-98, 99, 131.

Lindenberger, Herbert. *Georg Büchner,* pp. 85-114.

Steiner, George. *The death of tragedy,* pp. 272-281.

ENRIQUE BUENAVENTURA 1925-

General

Jones, W.K. *Behind Spanish American footlights,* p. 336.

ANTONIO BUERO VALLEJO 1916-

General

Corrigan, Robert W. ed. *Masterpieces of the modern Spanish theatre* pp. 124-125.

Halsey, Martha T. "Light and 'Darkness' as Dramatic Symbols in Tw Tragedies Of Buero Vallejo." *Hispania,* vol. 50 (1967), pp. 63-68.

Lott, Robert E. "Functional Flexibility and Ambiguity in Buer Vallejo's Plays." *Symposium,* vol. 20, no. 2 (Summer, 1966), pp 150-160.

Lott, Robert E. "Scandinavian Reminiscences in Antonio Buer Vallejo's Theater." *Romance Notes* (U. of N.C.), vol. 7 (1966), pp 113-116.

The Double Story of Doctor Valmy (La Doble Historia del Doctor Valmy)

O'Connor, Patricia. "Government Censorship in the Contemporar Spanish Theatre." *Educational Theatre J.,* vol. 18, no. 4 (Dec., 1966 p. 447.

MIKHAIL AFANAS'EVICH BULGAKOV 1891-1940

▸ays of the Turbins

Block, Anita. *The changing world in plays and theatre,* pp. 360-365.

LEO BULGAKOV 1889-1948

˙he White Guard

Dent, Alan. *Preludes and studies,* pp. 152-154.

DINO BUZZATI 1906-

;eneral

Biasin, Gian-Paolo. "The Secret Fears of Men: Dino Buzzati." *Italian Q.,* vol. 6 (1962), pp. 78-93.

Fornacca, Daisy. "Dino Buzzati." *Books Abroad,* vol. 25 (1951), pp. 19-20.

Jn Caso Clinico

Esslin, Martin. *The theatre of the absurd,* pp. 179-180.

SEAMUS BYRNE

;eneral

Hogan, Robert. *After the Irish renaissance,* pp. 74-76.

EDUARDO CALCANO 1913-

;eneral

Jones, W.K. *Behind Spanish American footlights,* p. 347.

GEORGE CALDERON 1868-1915

ountain

Norwood, Gilbert. *Euripides and Shaw with other essays,* pp. 104-105.

ERSKINE CALDWELL 1903-

ourneyman

Krutch, Joseph W. *The American drama since 1918,* pp. 125-128.

Tobacco Road (Adapted by Jack Kirkland)

Himelstein, Morgan Y. *Drama was a weapon, the left-wing theatre in New York 1929-1941,* pp. 191-192.

Krutch, Joseph W. *The American drama since 1918,* pp. 122-124.

Sievers, W. David. *Freud on Broadway,* pp. 237-238.

DAVID CAMPTON 1924-

The Lunatic View

Sainer, Arthur. *The sleepwalker and the assassin, a view of the contemporary theatre,* pp. 52-53.

ALBERT CAMUS 1913-1960

General

Batt, Jean C. "The Themes of the Novels and Plays of Albert Camus." *J. of the Australasian Universities Language and Literature Assn.,* no. 6 (May, 1957), pp. 47-57.

Camus, Albert. "Why I Work in the Theatre." *Theatre Arts,* vol. 44 no. 12 (Dec., 1960), pp, 58-59, 70-71.

Clancy, James H. "Beyond Despair: A New Drama of Ideas." *In* Freedman, Morris, ed. *Essays in the modern drama,* pp. 160-173 (Reprinted from *Educational Theatre J.,* vol. 13, no. 3 (Oct., 1961).

Couch, John Philip. "Albert Camus' Dramatic Adaptations and Translations. *"French Rev.,* vol. 33, no. 1 (Oct. 1959), pp. 27-36.

Cranston, Maurice. "Albert Camus." *Encounter,* vol. 28, no. 2 (1967) pp. 43-54.

Eigsti, Melly. "Camus." *New Theatre Magazine,* vol. 5, no. 1, (1964) pp. 5-9.

Fugazy, Sister Irene Mercedes, S.C. "The positive values in the work of Albert Camus." *Dissertation Abstracts,* vol. 26 (1965), 2210 (Fordham).

Garnham, B.G. "Albert Camus: Metaphysical Revolt and Historical Action." *Modern Lang. Rev.,* vol. 62 (1967), pp. 248-255.

Guicharnaud, Jacques. *Modern French theatre from Giraudoux to Beckett,* pp. 131-152.

Guicharnaud, Jacques. *Modern French theatre from Giraudoux to Genet* (rev. ed.), pp. 94, 132, 135-155, 159, 183, 216, 223, 281-282 286-288, 337-338, 361.

Leal, R.B. "Albert Camus and the Significance of Art." *Australian J. of French Studies* (Monash U., Clayton, Victoria), vol. 3 (1966), pp. 66-78.

Lumley, Frederick. *New trends in 20th century drama,* pp. 347-349.

Lumley, Frederick. *Trends in 20th century drama,* pp. 140-142.

Maurois, Andre: *From Proust to Camus,* pp. 349-353, 366-368.

Moore, Harry T. *Twentieth-century French literature since World War II,* pp. 58-62.

Popkin, Henry. "Camus as Dramatist." *Partisan Rev.,* vol. 26, no. 3 (Summer, 1959), pp. 499-503.

Simon, John Kenneth. "The Presence of Musset in Modern French Drama." *French Rev.,* vol. 40, no. 1 (Oct., 1966), pp. 27-38.

Sonnenfeld, Albert. "Albert Camus as Dramatist: The sources of His Failure." *Tulane Drama Rev.,* vol. 5, no. 4 (June, 1961), pp. 106-110.

Stokle, Norman. "Albert Camus in the Theater." *Dissertation Abstracts,* vol. 28, 695A, 1967 (Syracuse Univ.).

Williams, Raymond. "Tragic Despair and Revolt." *Critical Q.,* vol. 5, no. 2 (Summer, 1963), pp. 103-111.

The Assassins (The Just Assassins) (Les Justes) (The Just)

Baxter, Kay M. *Contemporary theatre and the Christian faith,* pp. 53-56.

Clurman, Harold. "The Moralist on Stage." *New York Times Book Rev.* (Sept. 14, 1958), p. 12.

Lewis, Allan. *The contemporary theatre,* p. 214.

Luppé, Robert de. *Albert Camus,* pp. 81-84.

Maurois, Andre: *From Proust to Camus,* pp. 365-366.

Reck, Rima Drell. "The Theatre of Albert Camus." *Modern Drama,* vol. 4, no. 1 (May, 1961), pp. 51-53.

Reed, Peter J. "Judges in the Plays of Albert Camus." *Modern Drama,* vol. 5, no. 1 (May, 1962), pp. 51-53.

St. Aubyn F.C. "Albert Camus and the Death of the Other: An Existentialist Interpretation." *French Studies,* vol. 16 (April, 1962), pp. 137-138.

Sonnenfeld, Albert. "Albert Camus as Dramatist: The Souces of His Failure." *Tulane Drama Rev.,* vol. 5, no. 4 (June, 1961), pp. 121-123.

Caligula

Abraham, Claude K. *"Caligula:* Drama of Revolt or Drama of Deception?" *Modern Drama,* vol. 5 (1963), pp. 451-453.

Ayer, A.J. "Novelist-Philosophers-VIII: Albert Camus." *Horizon,* vol 13, no. 75 (Mar., 1946), pp. 166-168.

Barnes, Hazel E. *The literature of possibility,* pp. 23-24, 162-164.

Bishop, Thomas. *Pirandello and the French theater,* pp. 128-129.

Bree, Germaine. "Camus' *Caligula:* Evolution of a Play." *Symposium* vol. 12, nos. 1-2 (Spring-Fall, 1958), pp. 43-51.

Brustein, Robert. *New Republic,* vol. 142, no. 8 (Feb. 29, 1960), pp 21-22.

Brustein, Robert. *Seasons of discontent,* pp. 104-107.

Bryden, Ronald. "Absurds." *New Statesman,* vol. 67, no. 1727 (Apr 17, 1964), p. 616.

Clurman, Harold. *The naked image,* pp. 67-69.

Clurman, Harold. *Nation,* vol. 190, no. 10 (Mar. 5, 1960), pp. 213-214

Cohn, Ruby. "Four Stages of Absurdist Hero." *Drama Survey,* vol. 4 no. 3 (Winter, 1965), pp. 195-199.

Curtis, Anthony. *New developments in the French theatre,* pp. 30-32

Driver, Tom F. *Christian Century,* vol. 77, no. 12 (Mar. 23, 1960), pp 352-354.

Flanner, Janet. *Paris journal, 1944-1965,* pp. 48-49.

Fowlie, Wallace. *Dionysus in Paris,* pp. 187-188.

Friedman, Maurice. *To deny our nothingness,* pp. 322-324, 331.

Glicksberg, Charles I. *The tragic vision in twentieth-century literature* pp. 58-59.

Hammer, Louis Z. "Impossible Freedom in Camus's *Caligula. Personalist,* vol. 44, no. 3 (July, 1963), pp. 322-336.

Hewes, Henry. *Saturday Rev.,* vol. 43, no. 10 (Mar. 5, 1960), p. 36

ones, Robert Emmet. *The alienated hero in modern French drama,* p. 111-115.

ones, Robert E. "*Caligula,* the Absurd, and Tragedy." *Kentucky Foreign Language Q., vol.* 5, no. 3 (1958), pp. 123-127.

ail, Andrée. "The Transformation of Camus' Heroes from the Novel o the Stage." *Educational Theatre J.* vol. 13, no. 3 (Oct. 1961), pp. 01-206.

amont, Rosette C. "The Anti-Bourgeois." *French Rev.,* vol. 34, no. 5 Apr., 1961), pp. 451-453.

ansner, Kermit. "Albert Camus." *Kenyon Rev.,* vol. 14, no. 4 Autumn, 1952), pp. 568-569.

ewis, Allan. *The contemporary theatre,* pp. 215-217.

ewis, R.W.B. "*Caligula:* or the Realm of the Impossible." *Yale French Studies,* no. 25 (1960), pp. 52-58.

uppé, Robert de. *Albert Camus,* pp. 77-79.

Maurois, Andre. *From Proust to Camus,* pp. 362-363.

Playful Camus." *Times Literary Supplement,* no. 3327 (Dec. 2, 1965), . 1104.

eck, Rima Drell. "The Theatre of Albert Camus." *Modern Drama,* ol. 4, no. 1 (May, 1961), pp. 44-48.

eed, Peter J. "Judges in the Plays of Albert Camus." *Modern Drama,* ol. 5, no. 1 (May, 1962), pp. 54-57.

t. Aubyn, F.C. "Albert Camus and the Death of the Other: An Existentialist Interpretation." *French Studies,* vol. 16 (Apr. 1962), pp. 25-128.

avage, Edward B. "Masks and Mummeries in *Enrico IV* and *Caligula.*" *Modern Drama,* vol. 6, no. 4 (Feb., 1964), pp. 397-401.

onnenfeld, Albert. "Albert Camus as Dramatist: The Souces of His Failure." *Tulane Drama Rev.,* vol. 5, no. 4 (June, 1961), pp. 111-114.

tockwell, H.R.C. "Albert Camus." *Cambridge J.,* vol. 7, no. 11 (Aug., 954), pp. 692-693.

trauss, Walter A. "Albert Camus' *Caligula:* Ancient Souces and Modern Parallels." *Comparative Literature,* vol. 3, no. 2 (Spring, 951), pp. 160-173.

ynan, Kenneth. *New Yorker,* vol. 36 (Feb. 27, 1960), pp. 100-104.

Walker, I.H. "The Composition of *Caligula.*" *Symposium, vol. 20, no* 3 (Fall, 1966), pp. 263-275.

Williams, Raymond. *Modern tragedy.* pp. 179-181.

Cross Purpose (The Misunderstanding) (Le Malentendu)

Barnes, Hazel E. *The literature of possibility,* pp. 157-162.

Behrens, Ralph. "Existential 'Character Ideas' in Camus' *Th Misunderstanding." Modern Drama,* vol. 7, no. 2 (Sept. 1964), p[210-212.

Bigsby, C.W.E. *Confrontation and commitment,* pp. 21-22.

Chase, N.C. "Images of Man: *Le Malentendu* and *En Attenda Godot." Wisconsin Studies in Contemporary Literature,* vol. 7, no. (Autumn, 1966), pp. 295-302.

Church, D.M. *"Le Malentendu:* Search for Modern Tragedy." *Frenc Studies,* vol. 20 (1966), pp. 33-46.

Clurman, Harold. "The Moralist on Stage." *New York Times Boc Rev.* (Sept. 14, 1958), p. 12.

Curtis, Anthony. *New developments in the French theatre,* pp. 2 29-30.

Friedman, Maurice. *To deny our nothingness,* pp. 322, 324-326.

John, S. "Image and Symbol in the Work of Albert Camus." *Frenc Studies,* vol. 9, no. 1 (Jan. 1955), pp. 48-49.

Lewis, Allan. *The contemporary theatre,* pp. 213-214.

Lumley, Frederick. *Trends in 20th century drama,* pp. 141-142.

Luppé, Robert de. *Albert Camus,* pp. 74-77.

Matthews, Honor. *The primal curse,* p. 22.

Maurois, André. *From Proust to Camus,* pp. 364-365.

"Playful Camus." *Times Literary Supplement,* no. 3327 (Dec. 2, 1965 p. 1104.

Reck, Rima Drell. "The Theatre of Albert Camus." *Modern Dram* vol. 4, no. 1 (May, 1961), pp. 48-50.

Reed, Peter J. "Judges in the Plays of Albert Camus." *Modern Dram* vol. 5, no. 1 (May, 1962), pp. 53-54.

St. Aubyn, F.C. "Albert Camus and the Death of the Other: An Existentialist Interpretation." *French Studies,* vol. 16 (Apr. 1962), pp. 133-134.

Sonnenfeld, Albert. "Albert Camus As Dramatist: The Sources of His Failure." *Tulane Drama Rev., vol.* 5, no. 4 (June, 1961), pp. 114-116.

Stockwell, H.R.C. "Albert Camus." *Cambridge J.,* vol. 7, no. 11 (Aug., 1954), pp. 697-700.

"A Treatise of Despair." *Times,* no. 56,355 (June 23, 1965), p. 17.

Virtanen, Reino. "Camus' *Le Malentendu* and Some Analogues." *Comparative Literature,* vol. 10, no. 3 (Summer, 1958), pp. 232-240.

Williams, Raymond. *Modern tragedy,* pp. 179-180, 183.

,'Hôte

Grobe, Edwin P. "The Psychological Structure of Camus's *L'Hôte."* *French Rev.,* vol. 40 (1966), pp. 357-376.

tate of Siege (The Plague) (L'Etat de Siège)

Clurman, Harold. "The Moralist on Stage." *New York Times Book Rev.* (Sept. 14, 1958), p. 12

Fowlie, Wallace. *Dionysus in Paris,* pp. 188-189.

Gerhard, Robert. *"The Plague." Listener* vol. 71, no. 1826 (Mar. 26, 1964), p. 533.

John, S. "The Characters of Albert Camus." *Univ. of Toronto Q.* vol. 23, no. 4 (July, 1954), pp. 371-379.

John, S. "Image and Symbol in the Work of Albert Camus." *French Studies,* vol. 9, no. 1 (Jan. 1955), pp. 51-53.

Lewis, Allan. *The contemporary theatre,* p. 215.

Luppé, Robert de. *Albert Camus,* pp. 79-81.

Mason, Colin. "Gerhard's *The Plague." Guardian,* no. 36,621 (Apr. 3, 1964), p. 9.

Reck, Rima Drell. "The Theatre of Albert Camus." *Modern Drama,* Vol. 4, no. 1 (May, 1961), pp. 50-51.

Reed, Peter J. "Judges in the Plays of Albert Camus." *Modern Drama,* vol. 5, no. 1 (May, 1962), pp. 47-51.

St. Aubyn, F.C. "Albert Camus and the Death of the Other: A Existentialist Interpretation." *French Studies,* vol. 16 (Apr. 1962), pr 136-137.

Sonnenfeld, Albert. "Albert Camus as Dramatist: The Sources of Hi Failure." *Tulane Drama Rev.,* vol. 5, no. 4 (June, 1961), pp. 118-121

Tracey, Edmund, "Nothing But Sound Effects." *Observer,* no. 901 (Apr. 5, 1964), p. 25.

Williams, Raymond. *Modern tragedy,* pp. 182-183.

DENIS CANNAN 1919-

General

Taylor, John Russell. "The Early Fifties." *In:* Brown, John Russell, ec *Modern British dramatists, a collection of critical essays,* pp. 19-21 (From Taylor, J.R. *Anger and after,* London, Methuen, published a *The angry theater,* N.Y., Hill & Wang, 1962.)

Misery Me

Williamson, Audrey. *Contemporary theatre, 1953-1956,* pp. 44-46.

KAREL CAPEK 1890-1938

General

Bradbrook, B.R. "A Čapek Revival." *Slavonic and East Europear Rev.,* vol. 42 (1963-64), pp. 434-439.

Dresler, Jaroslav. "Čapek and Communism." *In:* Rechcigl, Miloslav Jr., ed. *The Czechoslovak contribution to world culture,* pp. 68-75

Haman, Ales, and Paul I. Trensky. "Man Against the Absolute: Th Art of Karel Čapek!" *Slavic and East European J.,* vol. 11 (1967), pr 168-184.

Harkins, William E. "The Real Legacy of Karel Čapek." *In:* Rechcig Miloslav, Jr., ed. *The Czechoslovak contribution to world culture,* pr 60-67.

Matuška, A. *Karel Čapek: an essay.*

Moore, Harry T. *Twentieth-century German literature,* pp. 28-30.

Nemecek, Zdenek. "Karel Čapek." *World literatures,* pp. 53-65.

Wellek, René. *Essays on Czech literature,* pp. 46-51. (Originall published in *Slavonic Rev.,* vol. 15, no. 43 (July, 1936.)

Adam the Creator (Adam Stvoritel)

Harkins, W.E. *Karel Čapek,* pp. 115-118.

Matuška, Alexander, *Karel Čapek,* pp. 218, 219, 222.

Wellek, René. *Essays on Czech literature,* pp. 51-52.

The Fateful Game of Love (Lásky hra osudná) Josef Čapek, co-author

Harkins, W.E. *Karel Čapek,* pp. 43-44.

Matuška, Alexander. *Karel Čapek,* pp. 185-186, 197.

Wellek, René. *Essays on Czech literature,* p. 47.

The Insect Comedy (From the Insect World) (The World We Live In) (Life of the Insects) (Ze Života hmyze) Josef Čapek, co-author

Harkins, W.E. *Karel Čapek,* pp. 75-83.

MacCarthy, Desmond. *Drama,* pp. 110-117.

Matuška, Alexander. *Karel Čapek,* pp. 206-210

Wellek, René. *Essays on Czech literature,* p. 51.

The Makropulos Secret (The Makropoulos Affair) (Věc Makropulos)

Harkins, W.E. *Karel Čapek,* pp. 110-115.

Harkins, William E. "The Real Legacy of Karel Čapek." *In:* Rechcigl, Miloslav, Jr., ed. *The Czechoslovak contribution to world culture,* p. 62.

Matuška, Alexander. *Karel Čapek,* pp. 210-212.

Wellek, René. *Essays on Czech literature,* p. 51.

Mother (Matka)

Dresler, Jaroslav. "Čapek and Communism." *In:* Rechcigl, Miloslav, Jr., ed. *The Czechoslovak contribution to world culture,* pp. 70-71.

Harkins, W.E. *Karel Čapek,* pp. 151-154.

Matuška, Alexander. *Karel Čapek,* pp. 280-283, 327.

The Outlaw (Loupeznik)

Harkins, W.E. *Karel Čapek,* pp. 66-72.

Matuška, Alexander. *Karel Capek,* pp. 197, 198-200, 287-288, 298 317-318.

R.U.R.

Bradbrook, B. "Karel Čapek and the western world." Unpublished Master's Essay, Oxford, 1958.

Darlington, W.A. "Brothers Čapek." *Literature in the theatre,* pp 137-144.

Harkins, W.E. *Karel Čapek,* pp. 84-95.

Harkins, W.E. "The Real Legacy of Karel Čapek." *In:* Rechcigl Miloslav, Jr., ed. *The Czechoslovak contribution to world culture,* pp 60, 61-62, 64.

Matuška, Alexander. *Karel Čapek,* pp. 203-206, 216, 217, 326.

Moskowitz, Samuel. *Explorers of the infinite,* pp. 208-224.

Pletnev, Rostislav. "The Concept of Time and Space in *R.U.R.* by Karel Čapek." *Etudes Slaves et Est-Européennes,* vol. 12 (1967), pp 17-24.

Wellek, René. *Essays on Czech literature,* pp. 50-51.

The White Plague (The Power and Glory) (Bílá Nemoc)

Harkins, W.E. *Karel Čapek,* pp. 149-151.

Matuška, Alexander. *Karel Čapek,* pp. 273-276, 327.

TRUMAN CAPOTE 1924-

The Grass Harp

Bentley, Eric. *The dramatic event,* pp. 20-24.

LEWIS JOHN CARLINO

Epiphany

Gottfried, Martin. *A theater divided; the postwar American stage,* p 278.

Telemachus

Gottfried, Martin. *A theater divided; the postwar American stage,* pp 278-279.

PAUL VINCENT CARROLL 1900-1968

General

Coleman, Sister Ann Gertrude. "Paul Vincent Carroll's View of Irish Life." *Catholic World,* vol. 192 (Nov., 1960), pp. 87-93.

Hogan, Robert. *After the Irish renaissance,* pp. 52-63.

"Irish Eyes Are Smiling." *New York Times,* April 17, 1938, Sec. 10, p. 1.

Pallette, Drew B., "Paul Vincent Carroll—Since *The White Steed,"* *Modern Drama,* vol. 7, no. 4 (Feb., 1965), pp. 375-381.

"The Rebel Mind." *New York Times,* Jan. 24, 1960, Sec. 2, p. 3.

"Reforming a Reformer." *New York Times,* Feb. 13, 1935, Sec. 2, p. 3.

"The Substance of Paul Vincent Carroll." *New York Times,* Jan. 30, 1938, Sec. 10, p. 1.

The Bed of Procrustes (Things That Are Caesar's)

Hogan, Robert. *After the Irish renaisance,* pp. 53-54.

Coggerers (The Conspirators)

Hogan, Robert. *After the Irish renaissance,* p. 58.

The Devil Came from Dublin (The Chuckeyhead Story)

Hogan, Robert. *After the Irish renaissance,* pp. 60-61.

Green Cars Go East

Hogan, Robert. *After the Irish renaissance,* pp. 61-62.

The Old Foolishness

Hogan, Robert. *After the Irish renaissance,* pp. 68-60.

Shadow and Substance

Brown, John Mason. *Two on the aisle,* pp. 130-132.

Dent, Alan. *Preludes and studies,* pp. 160-163.

Hogan, Robert. *After the Irish renaissance,* pp. 54-55.

The White Steed

Brown, John Mason. *Broadway in review,* pp. 205-208.

Hogan, Robert. *After the Irish renaissance,* pp. 55-57.

W. F. CASEY

The Suburban Groove

Malone, Andrew E. *The Irish drama,* pp. 235-236.

ALEJANDRO CASONA 1903-

General

Leighton, Charles H. "Casona and Lorca; A Brief Comparison *Modern Drama,* vol. 7, no. 1 (May, 1964), pp. 28-34.

Moon, H. Kay. "Alejandro Casona and Henri Bergson." *In:* Bleiber German, and E. Inman Fox, eds. *Spanish thought and letters in t twentieth century,* pp. 345-359.

Toms, J. Frank. "The Reality-Fantasy Technique of Alejand Casona." *Hispania,* vol. 44, no. 2 (May, 1961), pp. 218-221.

Suicide Prohibited in Springtime

Benedikt, M., and G.E. Wellwarth. *Modern Spanish theatre, anthology of plays,* pp. 240-241.

AQUILES CERTAD 1914-

General

Jones, W.K. *Behind Spanish American Footlights,* pp. 348-349.

RENE CHAR 1907-

General

Aspel, Paulène. "The Poetry of René Char, or Man Reconciled *Books Abroad,* vol. 42, no. 2 (Spring, 1968), pp. 199-203. Also bo review, p. 236.

MARY COYLE CHASE 1907-

Bernardine

Sievers, W. David. *Freud on Broadway,* pp. 358-359.

Harvey

Sievers, W. David. *Freud on Broadway,* pp. 356-357.

Mrs. McThing

Sievers, W. David. *Freud on Broadway,* pp. 357-358.

PADDY CHAYEFSKY 1923-

General

Duprey, Richard A. "Today's Dramatists." *In: American theatre,* pp. 216-218.

Gardner, R.H. *The splintered stage; the decline of the American theater,* p. 101.

Goldstein, Malcolm. "Body and Soul on Broadway." *Modern Drama,* vol. 7, no. 4 (February, 1965), pp. 411-421.

Styan, J.L., *The dark comedy,* 2nd ed. pp. 106, 108, 110-111, 235.

Gideon

Brustein, Robert. *Seasons of discontent,* pp. 122-125.

Lewis, Allan. *American plays and playwrights of the contemporary theatre,* pp. 126-128.

Roston, Murray. *Biblical drama in England from the Middle Ages to the present day,* pp. 307-308.

The Tenth Man

Brustein, Robert. *Seasons of discontent,* pp. 94-97.

Downer, Alan S. *Recent American drama,* pp. 20, 40-41.

Kerr, Walter. *The theater in spite of itself,* pp. 165-168.

Lewis, Allan. *American plays and playwrights of the contemporary theatre,* pp. 125-126.

ANTON PAVLOVICH CHEKHOV 1860-1904

General

Brahms, Caryl. "Chekhov, Father of the Family." *In:* Richards, Dick. *The curtain rises,* pp. 35-37.

Brandon, James R. "Toward a Middle View of Chekhov." *Educational Theatre J.,* vol. 12 (1960), pp. 270-275.

Brereton, Geoffrey. *Principles of tragedy, a rational examination of the tragic concept in life and literature,* pp. 214-224.

Brustein, Robert. *The theatre of revolt,* pp. 137-155.

Chekhov, Anton. "Letters." *In:* Caputi, Anthony. *Modern drama,* pp 363-369. (From Chekhov, Anton. *The selected letters of Anton Chekhov,* N.Y., Farrar, Straus & Giroux, 1955, pp. 19, 20, 54, 55, 133 137-139.)

Chizhevsky, Dmitri. "Chekhov in the Development of Russian Literature." *In:* Jackson, Robert Louis, ed. *Chekhov, a collection of critical essays,* pp. 49-61.

Corrigan, Robert W. "The Drama of Anton Chekhov." *In:* Bogard, Travis, and Oliver, William I., eds. *Modern drama; essays in criticism,* pp. 73-98. (Reprinted from Corrigan's *Six plays of Chekhov,* N.Y., Holt, 1962.)

Corrigan, Robert W. "Stanislavski and the Playwright." *In:* Corrigan, Robert W. *Theatre in the twentieth century,* pp. 185-191.

Dukes, Ashley. *Modern dramatists,* pp. 190-210.

Eichenbaum, Boris. "Chekhov at Large." *In:* Jackson, Robert Louis, ed. *Chekhov, a collection of critical essays,* pp. 21-31.

Ganz, Arthur. "Arrivals and Departures: The Meaning of the Journey in the Major Plays of Chekhov." *Drama Survey,* vol 5, no. 1 (Spring, 1966), pp. 5-23.

Gassner, John. "The Duality of Chekhov." *In:* Jackson, Robert Louis, ed. *Chekhov, a collection of critical essays,* pp. 175-183.

Gerhardi, William. "The Effect of Chekhov's Work." *In:* Caputi, Anthony, ed. *Modern drama,* pp. 374-384. (From Gerhardi, William. *Anton Chekhov: a critical study,* London, 1923.)

Grossman, Leonid. "The Naturalism of Chekhov." *In:* Jackson, Robert Louis, ed. *Chekhov, a collection of critical essays,* pp. 32-48.

Hingley, Ronald. *Chekhov, a biographical and critical study,* pp. 112-117, 219-244.

Jackson, Robert Louis. "Introduction: Perspectives on Chekhov." *In:* Jackson, Robert Louis, ed. *Chekhov, a collection of critical essays,* pp. 1-20.

Kramer, Karl D. "Chekhov at the End of the Eighties: The Question of Identity." *Etudes Slaves et Est-Europeennes,* vol. 11 (1966), pp. 3-18.

Kuhn, Reinhard. "The Debasement of the Intellectual in Contemporary Continental Drama." *Modern Drama,* vol. 7, no. 4 (Feb., 1965), pp. 454-462.

Lavrin, Janko. "Chekhov and Maupassant." *In:* Lavrin, J. *Studies in European literature,* pp. 156-192.

Lawson, John Howard. "Chekhov's Drama: Challenge to Playwrights." *Masses & Mainstream,* vol. 7, no. 10 (Oct., 1954), pp. 11-26.

Leaska, Mitchell A. *The voice of tragedy,* pp. 231-232, 238-242.

Lewis, Allan. *The contemporary theatre,* pp. 59-80.

Lucas, F.L. *The drama of Chekhov, Synge, Yeats & Pirandello,* pp. 114-146.

McConkey, James. "In Praise of Chekhov." *Hudson Rev.,* vol. 20 (1967), pp. 417-428.

Macleod, Joseph. *Actors cross the Volga,* pp. 96-114.

Magarshack, David, "Chekhov the Dramatist." *In:* Freedman, Morris, ed. *Essays in the modern drama,* pp. 40-55. (Reprinted from *Chekhov the dramatist* by David Magarshack.)

Mann, Thomas. *Last essays,* pp. 178-203.

Meyerhold, Vsevolod. "Naturalistic Theater and Theater of Mood." *In:* Jackson, Robert Louis, ed. *Chekhov, a collection of critical essays,* pp. 52-68.

Moravcevich, Nicholas. "The Dark Side of the Chekhovian Smile." *Drama Survey,* vol. 5, no. 3 (Winter, 1966-67), pp. 237-251.

Nilsson, Nils Ake. "Intonation and Rhythm in Chekhov's Plays." *In:* Jackson, Robert Louis, ed. *Chekhov, a collection of critical essays,* pp. 161-174.

O'Casey, Sean, "One of the World's Dramatists." *In:* O'Casey, Sean. *Blasts and benedictions,* pp. 42-45.

Peacock, Ronald. "The poet in the Theatre: Chekhov." *In:* Caputi, Anthony, ed. *Modern drama,* pp. 384-391. (From Peacock, Ronald. *The poet in the theatre,* N.Y., Hill & Wang, 1960, pp. 94-104.)

Skaftymov, A. "Principles of Structure in Chekhov's Plays." *In:* Jackson, Robert Louis, ed. *Chekhov, a collection of critical essays,* pp. 69-87.

Simmons, Ernest J. *Introduction to Russian realism,* pp. 209-215.

Smith, J. Oates. "Chekhov and the Theatre of the Absurd." *Bucknell Rev.,* vol. 14, no. 3 (Dec., 1966), pp. 44-58.

States, Bert O. "Chekhov's Dramatic Strategy." *Yale Rev.,* vol. 56 (1967), pp. 212-224

Steiner, George. *The death of tragedy,* pp. 300-306.

Styan, J.L. *The dark comedy,* pp. 82-94.

Styan, J.L. *The dark comedy,* 2nd ed., pp. 2, 31, 47, 56, 58, 62-65, 74-84, 106, 109-112, 133, 158, 170, 190, 192, 212, 217, 224, 245, 250, 260, 273, 276, 280, 283, 287, 293, 295-296, 298.

Valency, Maurice. *The breaking string,* pp. 289-301.

Volpe, Edmond L., ed. *An introduction to literature: drama,* pp. 343-351.

Williams, Raymond. *Drama from Ibsen to Eliot,* pp. 126-137.

Williams, Raymond. *Modern tragedy,* pp. 139-146, 153, 163.

The Cherry Orchard

Allison, Alexander W., ed. *Masterpieces of the drama,* 2nd ed., pp. 451-452.

Barrault, Jean-Louis, "Why *The Cherry Orchard?*" *In:* Seltzer, Daniel, ed. *The modern theatre, readings and documents,* pp. 288-294.

Block, Anita. *The changing world in plays and theatre,* pp. 70-73.

Brustein, Robert. *The theatre of revolt,* pp. 167-178.

Bulukhaty, S.D. *"The Cherry Orchard:* A Formalist Approach." *In* Jackson, Robert Louis, ed. *Chekhov, a collection of critical essays,* pp 136-146.

Corbin, John. "Moscow and Broadway." *In:* Moses, Montrose J. *The American theatre as seen by its critics, 1752-1934,* pp. 178-184 (Reprinted from *The New York Times,* Jan. 28, 1923.)

Cubeta, Paul M. *Modern drama for analysis,* pp. 322-328.

Fergusson, Francis. *"The Cherry Orchard:* A Theater-Poem of the Suffering of Change." *In:* Jackson, Robert Louis, ed. *Chekhov, a collection of critical essays,* pp. 147-160.

Fergusson, Francis. *"Ghosts* and *The Cherry Orchard:* The Theatre of Modern Realism." *In:* Freedman, Morris, ed. *Essays in the modern drama,* pp. 19-34. (Reprinted from *The idea of a theatre* by Francis Fergusson.)

Fergusson, Francis. *The idea of a theater,* 174-188.

Freedman, Morris. "Chekhov's Morality of Work." *Modern Drama* vol. 5, no. 1 (May 1962), pp. 83-92.

Freedman, Morris. *The moral impulse,* pp. 31-35.

Ganz, Arthur. "Arrivals and Departures: The Meaning of the Journey in the Major Plays of Chekhov." *Drama Survey,* vol. 5, no. 1 (Spring, 1966), pp. 6, 7, 19-22.

Gerould, Daniel C. *"The Cherry Orchard* as a Comedy." *J. of General Education,* vol. 11, no. 2 (Apr., 1958), pp. 109-122.

Hingley, Ronald. *Chekhov, a biographical and critical study,* pp. 6, 30, 47, 176, 193, 195, 212, 223, 226, 229-232, 234-235, 237-238, 240, 243-244.

Kelson, John. "Allegory and Myth in *The Cherry Orchard." Western Humanities Rev.,* vol. 13, no. 3 (Summer, 1959), pp. 321-324.

Kerr, Walter. *Tragedy and comedy,* pp. 234-238.

Kitchin, Laurence. *Mid-century drama,* pp. 125-130.

Krutch, Joseph Wood. *"Modernism" in modern drama,* pp. 72-77.

Lamm, Martin. *Modern drama,* pp. 210-215.

Latham, Jacqueline E.M. *"The Cherry Orchard* as Comedy." *Education Theatre J.,* vol. 10 (Mar., 1958), pp. 21-29.

Lewis, Allan. *The contemporary theatre,* pp. 66-70, 74-80.

Lid, R.W., ed. *Plays, classic and contemporary,* pp. 300-301.

Lucas, F.L. *The drama of Chekhov, Synge, Yeats & Pirandello,* pp. 87-113.

MacCarthy, Desmond. *Drama,* pp. 84-90.

Mendelsohn, Michael J. "The Heartbreak Houses of Shaw and Chekhov." *Shaw Rev.,* vol. 6, no. 3 (Sept., 1963), pp. 89-95.

Perry, Henry Ten Eyck. *Masters of dramatic comedy and their social themes,* pp. 352-357.

Pettigrew, John. "Stratford's Festival Theatre: 1965." *Queen's Q.,* vol. 72, no. 3 (Autumn, 1965), pp. 573-575.

Reinert, Otto, ed. *Drama; an introductory anthology* (alternate ed.), pp. 642-649.

Silverstein, Norman. "Chekhov's Comic Spirit and *The Cherry Orchard." Modern Drama,* vol. 1 (Sept., 1958), pp. 91-100.

Styan, J.L. *The dark comedy,* pp. 95-119.

Styan, J.L. *The dark comedy,* 2nd ed., pp. 41, 53, 58, 60, 62, 64, 84-106, 264-265, 271, 274, 277, 280, 297, 298.

Styan, J.L. *The elements of drama,* pp. 73-85.

Valency, Maurice. *The breaking string,* pp. 251-288.

Williams, Raymond. *Drama from Ibsen to Eliot,* pp. 134-137.

Williams, Raymond. *Modern tragedy,* pp. 143-145.

Ivanov

Berdnikov, G. *"Ivanov:* An Analysis." *In:* Jackson, Robert Louis, ed. *Chekhov, a collection of critical essays,* pp. 88-98.

Brustein, Robert. *Hudson Rev.,* vol. 12, no. 1 (Spring, 1959), pp. 94-101.

Chekhov, Anton. *In:* Cole, Toby, ed. *Playwrights on playwriting,* pp. 184-192. (Reprinted from Anton Chekhov, *Letters on the Short Story, the Drama and Other Literary Topics,* selected and edited by Louis S. Friedland (New York: Minton, Balch & Co., 1924, pp. 119-41 *passim.)*

Hingley, Ronald. *Chekhov, a biographical and critical study,* pp. 102-106, 109, 114-116, 133, 146, 232, 233.

Kerr, Walter. *Tragedy and comedy,* pp. 238-240.

Lamm, Martin. *Modern drama,* pp. 197-198.

MacCarthy, Desmond. *Drama,* pp. 174-177.

MacCarthy, Desmond. *Theatre,* pp. 102-104.

Valency, Maurice. *The breaking string,* pp. 82-100.

Winner, Thomas G. "Speech Characteristics in Čexov's *Ivanov* and Čapek's *Loupeznik."* *In: American Contributions to the Fifth International Congress of Slavists,* vol. 2, pp. 403-431.

Platonov

Tynan, Kenneth. *Tynan right and left,* p. 39.

Valency, Maurice. *The breaking string,* pp. 48-81.

The Seagull (Chayka)

Balukhaty, S.D. "Notes on Stage Settings for Stanislavski's Production of *The Sea Gull." In:* Seltzer, Daniel, ed. *The modern theatre, readings and documents,* pp. 368-370. (From Balukhaty, S.D. *The Sea Gull produced by Stanislavski,* N.Y., Theatre Arts Books.)

Brooks, Cleanth. *Understanding drama,* pp. 466, 473-474, 489-502.

Brown, John Mason. *Two on the aisle,* pp. 88-91.

Clurman, Harold. *Lies like truth,* pp. 131-133.

Cook, Albert S. "Language and Action in the Drama." *College English,* vol. 28, no. 1 (Oct., 1966), pp. 20-21.

Cook, Albert, *Prisms, studies in modern literature,* pp. 138-139.

Dent, Alan. *Preludes and studies,* pp. 146-148.

Dukes, Ashley. *Modern dramatists,* pp. 192-206.

Ehrenburg, Ilya. *Chekhov, Stendhal, and other essays,* pp. 48-53.

Freedman, Morris. *The moral impulse,* pp. 40-43.

Ganz, Arthur. "Arrivals and Departures: The Meaning of the Journey in the Major Plays of Chekhov." *Drama Survey,* vol. 5, no. 1 (Spring, 1966), pp. 10-12.

Hingley, Ronald. *Chekhov, a biographical and critical study,* pp. 191, 192, 195, 226, 232, 234, 237, 239-241.

Jackson, Robert Louis. "Chekhov's *Seagull:* The Empty Well, the Dry Lake, and the Cold Cave." *In:* Jackson, Robert Louis, ed. *Chekhov, a collection of critical essays,* pp. 99-111.

Kernan, Alvin. "Truth and Dramatic Mode in the Modern Theater: Chekhov, Pirandello and Williams." *Modern Drama,* vol. 1 (Sept., 1958), pp. 103-107.

Krutch, Joseph Wood. " *Modernism" in modern drama, pp. 68-72.*

Lamm, Martin. *Modern drama,* pp. 200-203.

Lucas, F.L. *The drama of Chekhov, Synge, Yeats, and Pirandello,* pp. 38-65.

Perry, Henry Ten Eyck. *Masters of dramatic comedy and their social themes,* pp. 341-345.

Seyler, Dorothy A. *"The Sea Gull* and *The Wild Duck:* Birds of a Feather?" *Modern Drama,* vol. 8, no. 2 (Sept., 1965), pp. 167-173.

Stanislavski, Konstantin. "From the Director's Notebook for *The Sea Gull." In:* Seltzer, Daniel, ed. *The modern theatre, readings and documents,* pp. 203-215. (From Balukhaty, S.D. *The Sea Gull produced by Stanislavski,* N.Y. Theatre Arts Books.)

Styan, J.L. *The dark comedy,* 2nd ed., pp. 74-75, 79-81, 107, 236.

Valency, Maurice. *The breaking string,* pp. 119-178.

William, Raymond. *Drama from Ibsen to Eliot,* pp. 126-134.

Williams, Raymond. *Drama in performance.* pp. 84-101.

Williams, Raymond. *Drama in performance* (new. ed.), pp. 107-133, 174-175.

Winner, Thomas G. "Chekhov's *Seagull* and Shakespeare's *Hamlet:* A Study of a Dramatic Device." *American Slavic and East European Rev.,* vol. 15 (1956), pp. 103-111.

Young, Stark. *Immortal shadows,* pp. 200-205.

Young, Stark. *"The Sea Gull." In:* Freedman Morris, ed. *Essays in the modern drama,* pp. 35-39. (Reprinted from *Immortal Shadows.)*

The Three Sisters (Tri Sestry).

Brustein, Robert. *The theatre of revolt,* pp. 155-167.

Chekhov, Anton. "Chekhov's Comments on *Three Sisters." In:* Caputi, Anthony, ed. *Modern drama,* pp. 369-374. (From *The Oxford Chekhov,* ed. by Ronald Hingley. London, Oxford Univ. Press, 1964, vol. 3, pp. 313-116.)

Clurman, Harold. *The naked image,* pp. 280-282.

Dent, Alan. *Preludes and studies,* pp. 149-151.

Dukes, Ashley. *Modern dramatists,* pp. 207-210.

Dupee, F.W. *"The King of the Cats" and other remarks on writers and writing,* pp. 90-96.

Freedman, Morris. "Chekhov's Morality of Work." *Modern Drama,* vol. 5, no. 1 (May, 1962), pp. 83-92.

Freedman, Morris. *The moral impulse,* pp. 35-37, 39.

Hingley, Ronald. *Chekhov, a biographical and critical study,* pp. 65, 168, 177, 181, 194-195, 204, 226, 227, 232, 235, 236, 237, 238, 239, 242-244.

Kitchin, Laurence. *Mid-century drama,* pp. 126-127, 130-134.

Lamm, Martin. *Modern drama,* pp. 206-210.

Leaska, Mitchell A. *The voice of tragedy,* pp. 232-238.

Lucas, F.L. *The drama of Chekhov, Synge, Yeats and Pirandello,* pp. 82-96.

MacCarthy, Desmond. *Drama,* pp. 118-122.

MacCarthy, Desmond. *Theatre,* pp. 98-101.

McCarthy, Mary. *Sights and spectacles 1937-1956,* pp. 57-60.

Muller, Herbert J. *The spirit of tragedy,* pp. 283-286, 292.

Perry, Henry Ten Eyck. *Masters of dramatic comedy and their social themes,* pp. 348-352.

Reinert, Otto. *Drama, an introductory anthology,* pp. 425-429.

Reinert, Otto, ed. *Modern drama; nine plays,* pp. 211-215.

Stroyeva, M.N. *"The Three Sisters* at the MAT." *Tulane Drama Rev.,* vol. 9, no. 1 (1964), pp. 42-56.

Stroyeva, M.N. *"The Three Sisters* in the Production of the Moscow Art Theater." *In:* Jackson, Robert Louis, ed. *Chekhov, a collection of critical essays,* pp. 121-135.

Styan, J.L. *The dark comedy,* 2nd ed., pp. 58-60, 75, 77, 81-84, 263, 277, 289, 298.

Styan J.L. *The elements of drama,* pp. 206-250.

Valency, Maurice. *The breaking string,* pp. 206-250.

Williams, Raymond. *Modern tragedy,* pp. 143-145.

Uncle Vanya (The Wood Demon) (Dyadya Vanya)

Bordinat, Philip. "Dramatic Structure in Čexov's *Uncle Vanja."* *Slavic and East European J.,* vol. 16, no. 3 (Fall 1958), pp. 195-210.

Cowell, Raymond. *Twelve modern dramatists,* pp. 36-38.

Freedman, Morris. "Chekhov's Morality of Work." *Modern Drama,* vol. 5, no. 1 (May, 1962), pp. 83-92.

Freedman, Morris. *The moral impulse,* pp. 37-40, 44.

Ganz, Arthur. "Arrivals and Departures: The Meaning of the Journey in the Major Plays of Chekhov." *Drama Survey,* vol. 5, no. 1 (Spring, 1966), pp. 5, 7, 13-17.

Gassner, John *Theatre at the crossroads,* pp. 188-191.

Greenwood, Ormerod. *The playwright,* pp. 178-185.

Hingley, Ronald. *Chekhov, a biographical and critical study,* pp. 115, 169, 192-194, 197, 223, 226, 232, 234, 235, 237, 239-241.

Kitchin, Laurence. *Mid-century drama,* pp. 134, 150- 151.

Lewis, Allan. The co*ntemporary theatre,* pp. 71-74.

Lucas, F.L. *The drama of Chekhov, Synge, Yeats and Pirandello,* pp. 66-81.

MacCarthy, Desmond. "Desmond MacCarthy on Chekov's *Uncle Vanya." In:* Agate, James. *The English dramatic critics,* pp. 300-306. *(Also in: New Statesman* (May 16, 1914).)

MacCarthy, Desmond. *Drama,* pp. 123-130.

Muller, Herbert J. *The spirit of tragedy,* pp. 285-287, 291

Perry, Henry Ten Eyck. *Masters of dramatic comedy and their social themes,* pp. 345-348.

Tynan, Kenneth. *Tynan right and left,* pp. 110-111.

Valency, Maurice. *The breaking string,* pp. 101-118, 179-205.

Yermilov, V. *"Uncle Vanya:* The Play's Movement." *In:* Jackson, Robert Louis, ed. *Chekhov, a collection of critical essays,* pp. 112-120.

LUIGI CHIARELLI 1884-1947

The Mask and the Face (Mask and Face) (La Maschera e il Volto)

Block, Anita. *The changing world in plays and theatre,* pp. 98-101.

Kayser, Wolfgang. *The grotesque in art and literature,* pp. 135-137.

ALICE CHILDRESS

General

Mitchell, Loften. *Black drama,* pp. 122, 127, 130, 145-147, 154, 168-169, 215-217, 218, 224.

Trouble in Mind

Abramson, Doris E. *Negro playwrights in the American theatre, 1925-1959,* pp. 187-204, 258-259.

JOSE CHIOINO 1898-

General

Jones, W.K. *Behind Spanish American footlights,* pp. 267-268.

HANS VON CHLUMBERG 1897-1930

Miracle at Verdun (Wunder um Verdun)

Bauland, Peter. *The hooded eagle,* pp. 106-109.

Block, Anita. *The changing world in plays and theatre,* pp. 321-328.

Himelstein, Morgan Y. *Drama was a weapon, the left-wing theatre in New York 1929-1941,* pp. 128-129.

JOHN PEPPER CLARK 1935-

General

Astrachan, Anthony. "Like Goats to Slaughter." *Black Orpheus,* no. 16 (Oct., 1964), pp. 21-24.

The Masquerade

Ferguson, John. "Nigerian Drama in English." *Modern Drama,* vol. 11, no. 1 (May, 1968), p. 16.

The Raft

Ferguson, John. "Nigerian Drama in English." *Modern Drama,* vol. 11, no. 1 (May, 1968), pp. 16-18.

Song of a Goat

Ferguson, John. "Nigerian Drama in English." *Modern Drama,* vol. 11, no. 1 (May, 1968), pp, 10-26.

AUSTIN CLARKE 1896-

General

Hogan, Robert. *After the Irish renaissance,* pp. 151-154.

PAUL CLAUDEL 1868-1955

General

Barrault, Jean Louis. "Claudel as Producer." *World Theatre,* vol. 7, no. 1 (Spring, 1958), pp. 30-35.

Bateman, May. "Catholic Note in Modern Drama." *Catholic World,* vol. 104 (Nov., 1916), pp. 170-176.

Bateman, May. "Paul Claudel." *Fortnightly,* vol. 105, n.s. (May 1, 1919), pp. 785-791.

Bateman, May. "Paul Claudel, Mystic." *Catholic World,* vol. 104 (Jan., 1917), pp. 484-495.

Beaumont, Ernest. "Paul Claudel and the Problem of Love." *Dublin Rev.,* vol. 115 (First Quarter, 1951), pp. 31-48.

Bentley, Eric. "Theatre, Religion and Politics." *Theatre Arts,* vol. 34, no. 3 (Mar., 1950), pp. 30-35.

Bondy, L.S. "Claudel and the Catholic Revival." *Thomist,* vol. 5 (Jan., 1943), pp. 171-187.

Bregy, K. "Paul Claudel, Mystic and Dramatist." *Dublin Rev.,* vol. 175 (July, 1924), pp. 54-66.

Chatterton-Hill, G. "Writings of Claudel." *Fortnightly, vol. 102 (Dec.,* 1914), pp. 971-983.

Claude, Paul. "Modern Drama and Music." *Yale Rev.,* n.s. vol. 20, no. 1 (Sept., 1930), pp. 94-102.

Cocossa, Anthony A. "A Portrait of Paul Claudel." CLA J., vol 10, no. 1 (Sept., 1966), pp. 42-48.

Cornell, Kenneth. "Claudel and the Greek Classics. The Classical Line: Essays in Honor of Henri Peyre." *Yale French Studies,* vol. 38 (1967), pp. 195-204.

Cornell, Kenneth. "Claudel's Plays on the Stage." *Yale French Studies,* no. 5 (1950), pp. 82-87.

Cunneen, Joseph E."The Present State of Claudel Criticism." *Thought,* vol. 27, no. 107 (Winter, 1952), pp. 500-520.

Deuel, Mildred T. "The spiritual development of Paul Claudel as seen in his works from 1889-1905." *Dissertation Abstracts,* vol. 27 (1967), 3867A-68A (N.Y.U.).

Downs, Brian W. "Paul Claudel." *North American Rev.,* vol. 220, no. 1 (Sept., 1924), pp. 78-92.

Fowlie, Wallace. "Claudel and the Problem of Sacred Art." *Accent,* vol. 14 (Winter, 1954), pp. 3-21.

Fowlie, Wallace. "Claudel: the Tidings That Are the Poem." *Poetry,* vol. 87, no. 3 (Dec., 1955), pp. 169-175.

Fowlie, Wallace. *A guide to contemporary French literature from Valery to Sartre,* pp. 96-103, 191-193.

Galantiere, L. "Poetic Drama of Paul Claudel." *Dial,* vol. 65 (June 20, 1918), pp. 9-11.

Gerrard, Thomas J. "The Art of Paul Claudel." *Catholic World,* vol. 104 (Jan., 1917), pp. 471-477.

Gheon, Henri. *The art of theatre,* pp. 68-70.

Goldbeck, Edward. "Paul Claudel." *Bookman,* vol. 67, no. 5 (July, 1928), pp. 501-505.

Grossvogel, David I. *The self-conscious stage in modern French drama,* pp. 106-123.

Guicharnaud, Jacques. *Modern French theatre from Giraudoux to Beckett,* pp. 69-89.

Guicharnaud, Jacques. *Modern French theatre from Giraudoux to Genet* (rev. ed.), pp. 11, 26, 65-84, 101, 104, 159, 195, 211, 270, 280, 281, 282, 287, 290, 314, 321, 327-330, 358-359.

Heppenstall, Rayner. "Claudel Revisited." *International Literary Annual,* no. 3 (London, Calder, 1961), pp. 144-153.

Heppenstall, Rayner. *The double image,* pp. 80-121, 126-133.

Kemp, John A. "The Philosophy of Paul Claudel." *Dublin Rev.,* vol. 207, no. 414 (July, 1940), pp. 82-93.

Knowles, Dorothy, *French drama of the inter-war years, 1918-39,* pp. 229-235, 239-242.

Lamm, Martin. *Modern drama,* pp. 166-170.

Lavallée, M.Marthe. "Approaches to Claudel." *Renascence,* vol. 8, no. 4 (Summer, 1956), pp. 202-208.

Lehner, Frederick. "Paul Claudel." *Poet Lore, vol.* 51, no. 3 (Autumn, 1945), pp. 257-267.

Lumley, Frederick. *New trends in 20th century drama,* pp. 59, 61-77.

Lumley, Frederick. *Trends in 20th century drama,* pp. 63-79.

Lutyens, David B. "The Dilemma of the Christian Dramatist: Paul Claudel and Christopher Fry." *Tulane Drama Rev.,* vol. 6, no. 4 (June, 1962), pp. 118-124.

"M.Claudel at 80." *Times Literary Supplement* (Aug. 14, 1948), p. 456.

Manship, J.P. "Claudel: Musician-Dramatist; The Universal Artist." *Commonweal,* vol. 62, no. 8 (May 27, 1955), pp. 201-203.

Maurois, André. *From Proust to Camus,* pp. 139-141.

Moore, Harry T. *Twenieth-century French literature to World War II,* pp. 12-14.

Murry, John M. "Works of Paul Claudel." *Quarterly Rev.,* vol. 227 (Jan., 1917), pp. 78-94.

Naughton, A.E.A. "A Poet Looks at His Work, or Claudel Repond Ses Drames." *Romanic Rev.,* vol. 52, no. 1 (Feb., 1961), pp. 27-35.

O'Donnell, Donat. pseud. (Conor Cruise O'Brien) "A Pillar in the Cloud." *New Statesman and Nation,* vol. 49 (Apr. 30, 1955), pp. 617-618.

Peacock, Vera. "The Early Plays of Paul Claudel." *Modern Language Forum,* vol. 26, no. 3 (Sept., 1941), pp. 152-160.

Peyre, Henri. "The Drama of Paul Claudel." *Thought,* vol. 27, no. 105 (Summer, 1952), pp. 185-202.

Peyre, Henri, "Paul Claudel (1868-1955)." *Yale French Studies,* no. 14 (Winter, 1954/55), pp. 94-97.

Peyre, Henri. "Work of Paul Claudel." *Living Age,* vol. 343 (Nov., 1932), pp. 225-231.

"The Presence of Paul Claudel." *Times Literary Supplement,* no. 2,721 (Mar. 26, 1954), p. viii.

Roeder, Ralph. "Paul Claudel." *Theatre Arts,* vol. 11, no. 5 (May, 1927), pp. 335-340.

Ryan, Mary. "Claudel, Poet of Love." *Studies,* vol. 42, no. 168 (Winter, 1953), pp. 440-445.

Ryan, Mary. "Paul Claudel." *Studies,* vol. 44, no. 174 (Summer, 1955), pp. 143-150.

Speaight, Robert. "The Theatre of Paul Claudel." *Month,* n.s. vol. 2, no. 2 (Aug., 1949), pp. 120-131.

Steiner, George. *The death of tragedy,* pp. 333-341.

Strauss, Walter A. "A Poet in the Theater: Paul Claudel." *Emory University Q.,* vol. 12, no. 4 (Dec. 1956), pp. 206-219.

Turnell, Martin. "The Intolerance of Genius." *Commonweal,* vol. 62, no. 8 (May 27, 1955), pp. 204-207.

Vial, Fernand. "Paul Claudel, 1868-1955." *American Society Legion of Honor Mag.,* vol. 26, no. 2 (Summer, 1955), pp. 105-121.

"Wagner of Letters." *Times Literary Supplement* (Apr. 1, 1965), p. 254.

Waters, Harold A. "Justice as Theme in Claudel's Drama." *Renascence,* vol. 17, no. 1 (Fall, 1964), pp. 17-28.

Waters, Harold A. "Paul Claudel and the Sensory Paradox." *Modern Language Q.,* vol. 20, no. 3 (Sept., 1959), pp. 267-272.

Watson, Harold M. "The theme of death in three plays of Claudel." *Dissertation Abstracts,* vol. 27 (1966), 784A-85A (Colo.).

Wood, Michael. "A Study of Fire Imagery in Some Plays by Paul Claudel." *French Studies,* vol. 19, no. 2 (Apr. 1965), pp. 144-158.

Break of Noon (Partage de Midi)

Berchan, Richard. *The inner stage,* pp. 96, 99, 101-113.

Brereton, Geoffrey. *Principles of tragedy, a rational examination of the tragic concept in life and literature,* pp. 226-243.

Chiari, Joseph. *The contemporary French theatre,* pp. 66-69.

Duclaux, Mary. *Twentieth century French writers,* pp. 86-90.

Fowlie, Wallace. "Claudel as Dramatist." *Sewanee Rev.,* vol. 64 (1956), pp. 225-228, 235.

Fowlie, Wallace. *Dionysus in Paris,* pp. 133-137.

Hobson, Harold. *The theatre now,* pp. 74-79.

Lee, Vera. "The Revising of *Partage de Midi.*" *French Rev.,* vol. 38, no. 3 (Jan., 1965), pp. 337-348.

Lumley, Frederick. *New trends in 20th century drama,* pp. 59, 65, 66, 68-71, 74, 75, 134, 278.

Lumley, Frederick. *Trends in 20th century drama,* pp. 70-73.

Maurois, André. *From Proust to Camus,* p. 136.

Nugent, Robert. "A Reading of Claudel's *Cantique de Mesa.*" *Cithara,* vol. 2, no. 1 (1962), pp. 1-5.

Peyre, Henri. "A Dramatist of Genius." *Chicago rev.,* vol. 15, no. 2 (Autumn, 1961), pp. 73-78.

Christopher Columbus (Christophe Colomb)

Brien, Alan. "Theatre in Paris." *European,* no. 10 (Dec., 1953), pp. 39-43.

Claudel, Paul. "Modern Drama and Music." *Yale Rev.,* n.s., vol. 20, no. 1 (Sept., 1930), pp. 102-106.

Farrell, Isolde. "Paris Letter." *America,* vol. 90, no. 17 (Jan. 23, 1954), p. 420.

Flanner, Janet. *Paris journal, 1944-1965,* pp. 216-217.

Hewes, Henry. "Total Theatre." *Saturday Rev.,* vol. 40, no. 4 (Jan. 26, 1957), pp. 22-23.

Knowles, Dorothy, *French drama of the inter-war years, 1918-39,* pp. 238-239.

Lavallée, M. Marthe. "Staging Claudel." *Renascence,* vol. 8, no. 5 (Autumn, 1955), pp. 39-44.

The City (La Ville)

Berchan, Richard. *The inner stage,* pp. 21-29.

Fowlie, Wallace. "Claudel as Dramatist." *Sewanee Rev.,* vol. 64 (1956), pp. 220-222.

Fowlie, Wallace. *Dionysus in Paris,* pp. 129-130.

Lumley, Frederick. *New trends in 20th century drama,* p. 67.

Lumley, Frederick. *Trends in 20th century drama,* p. 69.

Maurois, André. *From Proust to Camus,* pp. 133-134.

Crusts (Le Pain Dur)

Lumley, Frederick. *New trends in 20th century drama,* pp. 71, 73.

L'Echange

Berchan, Richard. *The inner stage,* pp. 40-53.

Chiari, Joseph. *The contemporary French theatre,* pp. 63-66.

Duclaux, Mary. *Twentieth century French writers,* pp. 81-86.

Lumley, Frederick. *New trends in 20th century drama,* pp. 63-64, 67-68, 77.

Lumley, Frederick. *Trends in 20th century drama,* pp. 69-70.

Maurois, André. *From Proust to Camus,* pp. 135-136.

L'Endormie

Berchan, Richard. *The inner stage,* pp. 3-7, 11-12.

The Hostage (L'Otage)

Brégy, Katherine. "Claudel's Play of Paradox." *Commonweal,* vol. 10, no. 23 (Oct. 9, 1929), pp. 581-582.

Dewey, Stoddard. "French Drama Extraordinary; *L'Otage* of Paul Claudel." *Nation,* vol. 99 (July 2, 1914), pp. 25-26.

Duclaux, Mary. *Twentieth century French writers,* pp. 72, 73-74, 90-97.

Hatzfeld, Helmut. *Trends and styles in twentieth century French literature,* pp. 184-185.

Knowles, Dorothy, *French drama of the inter-war years, 1918-39,* pp. 240-241.

Lumley, Frederick. *New trends in 20th century drama,* pp. 71-72, 73, 77.

Lumley, Frederick. *Trends in 20th century drama,* pp. 73-74.

Maurois, André. *From Proust to Camus,* p. 137.

Le Père Humilié (The Humiliation of the Father)

Lumley, Frederick. *New trends in 20th century drama,* pp. 71, 73.

The Satin Slipper (Le Soulier de Satin)

Cattaui, George. "Paul Claudel and *The Satin Slipper." Dublin Rcv.,* vol. 190 (Apr., 1932), pp. 268-278.

Chiari, Joseph. *The contemporary French theatre,* pp. 69-82.

Chiari, J. *Landmarks of contemporary drama,* pp. 59-61.

Cox, Sister Fidelia M. "Prayer and Sacrifice in Claudel's *Satin Slipper." Renascence,* vol. 13, no. 2 (Winter, 1961), pp. 78-83.

Forkey, Leo O. "A Baroque 'Moment' in the French Contemporary Theater." *J. of Aesthetics & Art Criticism,* vol. 18, no. 1 (Sept., 1959), pp. 80-89.

Fowlie, Wallace. "Claudel as Dramatist." *Sewanee Rev.,* vol. 64 (1956), pp. 229-237.

Fowlie, Wallace. *Dionysus in Paris,* pp. 137-145.

Grossvogel, David I. *The self-conscious stage in modern French drama,* pp. 117-120.

Hatzfeld, Helmut. *Trends and styles in twentieth century French literature,* pp. 183-184.

Knowles, Dorothy, French d*rama of the inter-war years, 1918-39,* pp. 235-238.

Lambert, J.W. "A Speaking Temple of the Spirit." *Times,* no. 7403 (Apr. 4, 1965), p. 25.

Lumley, Frederick. *New trends in 20th century drama,* pp. 59, 62, 65, 73, 74-76.

Lumley, Frederick. *Trends in 20th century drama,* pp. 76-79.

Maurois, André. *From Proust to Camus,* p. 138.

Moore, Harry T. *Twentieth-century French literature to World War II,* pp. 200-201.

Porter, Alan. *"The Satin Slipper,* or The Worst Is Not the Surest." *Bookman,* vol. 74 (Dec., 1931), pp. 459-460.

Selna, Barbara. "Paul Claudel: Prison and *The Satin Slipper."* *Renascence,* vol. 7 (Summer, 1955), pp. 171-180.

Steiner, George. *The death of tragedy,* pp. 335-339.

"A Tragedy of Scruples." *Times,* no. 56,287 (Apr. 3, 1965), p. 12.

Wolfe, Henry C. "The Worst Is Not the Surest." *Saturday Rev., vol.* 28, no. 26 (June 30, 1945), p. 13.

The Seventh Day's Rest (Le Repos du Septiême Jour)

Bateman, May. "Claudel's Great Mystic Drama." *Catholic World,* vol. 105 (June, 1917), pp. 361-375.

Chiari, Joseph. *The contemporary French theatre,* pp. 61-63.

Le Testament d'Orphée (Film)

Fowlie, Wallace. *Jean Cocteau,* pp. 114-119.

Tête d'Or

Berchan, Richard. *The inner stage,* pp. 13-21.

Duclaux, Mary. *Twentieth century French writers,* pp. 70, 71, 74-76.

Fowlie, Wallace. "Claudel as Dramatist." *Sewanee Rev.,* vol. 64 (1956), pp. 218-220.

Fowlie, Wallace. *Dionysus in Paris,* pp. 128-129.

Horry, Ruth N. "Claudel's *Tete d'Or*" *French Rev.,* vol. 35, no. 3 (Jan. 1962), pp. 279-286.

Lumley, Frederick, *New trends in 20th century drama,* pp. 65, 66-67, 74.

Lumley, Frederick. *Trends in 20th century drama,* pp. 68-69.

Maurois, André. *From Proust to Camus,* pp. 132-133.

Vial, Fernand. "Two Highlights of the Theatrical Season in France: *Teté d'Or* and *Les Séquestrés d'Altona.*" *American Society Legion of Honor Mag.,* vol. 31, no. 1 (1960), pp. 15-32.

he Tidings Brought to Mary (L'Annonce Faite à Marie) (La Jeune Fille Violaine)

Berchan, Richard. *The inner stage,* pp. 30-39, 75-76.

Baxter, Kay M. *Contemporary theatre and the Christian faith,* pp. 41-42.

Duclaux, Mary. *Twentieth century French writers,* pp. 76-81.

Fitzgerald, Sister Rachel Marie, C.S.J. "Paul Claudel's *Tidings:* an Affirmation of Vocation." *Renascence,* vol. 16, no. 1 (Fall, 1963), pp. 29-33.

Fowlie, Wallace. *"Claudel as Dramatist."* *Sewanee Rev.,* vol. 64 (1956), pp. 222-225.

Fowlie, Wallace. *Dionysus in Paris,* pp. 130-133.

Gerrard, Thomas J. "The Art of Paul Claudel." *Catholic World,* vol. 104 (Jan., 1917), pp. 447-480.

Hatzfeld, Helmut. *Trends and styles in twentieth century French literature,* p. 183.

Jennings, Richard. *Spectator,* vol. 142 (Mar. 30, 1929), p. 503.

Lumley, Frederick. *New trends in 20th century drama,* pp. 61, 72-73, 134.

Lumlcy, Frederick. *Trends in 20th century drama,* pp. 74-75.

MacCarthy, Desmond. *New Statesman,* vol. 9 (June 16, 1917), pp. 254-256.

Maurois, André. *From Proust to Camus,* pp. 134-135.

Melcher, Edith. "A Study of *L'Annonce Faite à Marie.*" *French Rev.,* vol. 23, no. 1 (Oct., 1949), pp. 1-9.

Peyre, Henri. "A Dramatist of Genius." *Chicago Rev.,* vol. 15, no. 2 (Autumn, 1961), pp. 71-73.

Thomas, Sister Marie, F.S.E. "About Reality in Anouilh's *Antigone* and Claudel's *L'Annonce Faite à Marie." French Rev.,* vol. 40, no. 1 (Oct., 1966), pp. 39-46.

The Woman and Her Shadow (La Femme et Son Ombre)

Pronko, Leonard C. *Theater East and West,* pp. 131-132.

HERMAN CLOSSON 1901-

General

Mallinson, Vernon. *Modern Belgian literature, 1830-1960,* pp. 181-185.

HUMPHREY COBB 1899-1944

Paths of Glory (Adapted by Sidney Howard)

Flexner, Eleanor. *American playwrights: 1918-1938,* pp. 54-56.

JEAN COCTEAU 1889-1963

General

Aylen, Leo. *Greek tragedy and the modern world,* pp. 196, 224, 258-261, 271, 340.

Boorsch, Jean. "The Use of Myths in Claudel's Theatre." *Yale French Studies,* no. 5 (1950), pp. 75-81.

Chiari, Joseph. *The contemporary French theatre,* pp. 102-106.

Cocteau, Jean. *The difficulty of being,* pp. 37-43, 59-62.

Cutts, John P. "They Do It with Mirrors: Shakespeare and Cocteau." *Revue de Littérature Comparée,* vol. 38 (1964), pp. 121-127.

Fowlie, Wallace. *Dionysus in Paris,* pp. 74-78, 86-88.

Fowlie, Wallace. *Jean Cocteau,* pp. 28-38, 57-60, 78-79, 136-137.

Fowlie, Wallace. "Tragedy in the Plays of Cocteau." *French Rev.,* vol 15, no. 6 (May, 1942), pp. 463-467.

Grossvogel, David I. *The self-conscious stage in modern French drama,* pp. 47-67.

Guicharnaud, Jacques. *Modern French theatre from Giraudoux to Beckett,* pp. 48-68.

Guicharnaud, Jacques. *Modern French theatre from Giraudoux to Genet* (rev. ed.), pp. 11, 44-64, 87, 101, 110, 120, 133, 145, 159, 179, 282, 325-327, 358.

Laver, J. "The Theatre and Jean Cocteau." *Life and Letters* (Aug., 1928), pp. 201-207.

Lumley, Frederick. *New trends in 20th century drama,* pp. 91, 105-114.

Lumley, Frederick. *Trends in 20th century drama,* pp. 114-123.

Moore, Harry T. *Twentieth-century French literature to World War II,* pp. 120-125.

Oxenhandler, Neal."Jean Cocteau: Theatre as Parade." *Yale French Studies,* no. 14 (Winter, 1954/55), pp. 71-75.

Oxenhandler, Neal. "Poetry in Three Films of Jean Cocteau." *Yale French Studies,* no. 17 (Summer, 1956), pp. 14-20.

Oxenhandler, Neal. *Scandal and parade: the theater of Jean Cocteau.*

Oxenhandler, Neal. "The theatre of Jean Cocteau." Ph.D., Yale University, 1955.

Pilcher, Velona. "Jean Cocteau." *Theatre Arts, vol.* 31, no. 4 (Apr., 1947), pp. 60-66.

Rosselli, John. "Creative Wake" (Interview). *Guardian,* no. 36,499 (Nov. 9, 1963), p. 5.

Sanderson, James L., ed. *Oedipus, myth and dramatic form,* pp. 179-180.

Turnell, Martin. "The Achievement of Cocteau." *Commonweal,* vol. 65, no. 12 (1956), pp. 309-311.

Bacchus

Fowlie, Wallace. "The French Literary Scene." *Commonweal,* vol. 56, no. 8 (May 30, 1952), p. 202.

Fowlie, Wallace. *A guide to contemporary French literature from Valery to Sartre,* pp. 202-204.

Fowlie, Wallace. *Jean Cocteau,* pp. 76-78.

Grossvogel, David I. *The self-conscious stage in modern French drama,* pp 65-66.

Knowles, Dorothy. *French drama of the inter-war years, 1918-39,* pp. 63-64.

Lumley, Frederick. *New trends in 20th century drama,* pp. 108, 109, 112, 113-114, 360.

Lumley, Frederick. *Trends in 20th century drama,* pp. 122-123.

Oxenhandler, Neal. *Scandal and parade: the theater of Jean Cocteau,* pp. 114-125.

Beauty and the Beast (La Belle et la Bête) (Film)

Agee, James. "Films." *Nation,* no. 2 (Jan. 10, 1948), p. 53.

Fowlie, Wallace. *Jean Cocteau,* p. 106.

The Blood of a Poet (Le Sang d'un Poète)

Fowlie, Wallace. *Age of Surrealism,* pp. 129-137.

Fowlie, Wallace. *Jean Cocteau,* pp. 102-106.

Oxenhandler, Neal. *Scandal and parade: the theater of Jean Cocteau,* pp. 64-77.

Le Boeuf sur le Toit

Grossvogel, David I. *The self-conscious stage in modern French drama,* pp. 49-50.

Oxenhandler, Neal. *Scandal and parade: the theater of Jean Cocteau,* pp. 52-54.

The Eagle with Two Heads (The Eagle Has Two Heads) (L'Aigle A Deux Têtes)

Brown, John Mason. "Seeing Things—Grounded Eagle." *Saturday Rev.,* vol. 30, no. 15 (Apr. 12, 1947), pp. 40-44.

Cocteau, Jean. *The difficulty of being,* pp. 159-160.

Curtis, Anthony. "Three Foreign Dramatists." *New Statesman & Nation,* vol. 36 (Sept. 4, 1948), p. 198.

Fowlie, Wallace. *Jean Cocteau,* pp. 75-76.

Gilder, Rosamond. "Eagle and Highlanders." *Theatre Arts,* vol. 3, no. 5 (May, 1947), pp. 16, 19.

Grossvogel, David I. *The self-conscious stage in modern French drama,* pp. 64-65.

Hobson, Harold. *Theatre,* pp. 1-6.

Knowles, Dorothy. *French drama of the inter-war years, 1918-39,* pp. 62-63.

Krutch, Joseph W. *Nation,* vol. 164, no. 14 (Apr. 5, 1947), pp. 403, 405.

Lumley, Frederick. *New trends in 20th century drama,* pp. 109, 112-113, 278.

Lumley, Frederick. Trends in *20th century drama,* pp. 121-122.

Marcel, Gabriel. "In Love With Death." *Theatre Arts,* vol. 31, no. 5 (May, 1947), pp. 45-46.

Phelan, Kappo. *Commonweal,* vol. 45, no. 25 (Apr. 4, 1947), pp. 613-614.

Oxenhandler, Neal. *Scandal and parade: the theater of Jean Cocteau,* pp. 220-226.

Stokes, Sewell. *"Lear* and Cocteau. The English Spotlight." *Theatre Arts,* vol. 30, no. 12 (Dec., 1946), pp. 705-706.

he Eiffel Tower Wedding Party (Les Mariés de la Tour Eiffel)

Cocteau, Jean. *In:* Cole, Toby, ed. *Playwrights on playwriting,* pp. 240-246.

Grossvogel, David I. *The self-conscious stage in modern French drama,* pp. 50-52.

Knowles, Dorothy. *French drama of the inter-war years, 1918-39,* pp. 49-50; 88.

Oxenhandler, Neal. *Scandal and parade: the theater of Jean Cocteau,* pp. 49-52.

'Eternel Retour

Closs, Hannah. "Jean Cocteau's *Tristan." Adelphi,* vol. 23, no. 2 (Jan.-Mar., 1947), pp. 79-81.

Whitebait, William. "L'Eternel Retour." *New Statesman & Nation,* vol. 29 (Mar. 10, 1945), p. 155

he Holy Terrors (Les Enfants Sacrés) (Les Monstres Sacrés) (Les Enfants Terribles (Film))

Fowlie, Wallace. *Jean Cocteau,* pp. 106-110.

Furbank, P.N. "Maugham and Cocteau." *Listener,* vol. 71, no. 1818 (Jan. 30, 1964), pp. 209-210.

Knowles, Dorothy. *French drama of the inter-war years, 1918-39,* pp 60-61.

Mudrick, Marvin. "Cocteau's Poem of Childhood." *Spectrum,* vol. 1 no. 3 (Fall, 1957), pp. 25-33.

Oxenhandler, Neal. *Scandal and parade: the theater of Jean Cocteau* pp. 200-211.

The Human Voice (La Voix Humaine)

Bentley, Eric. *The playwright as thinker,* pp. 193-194.

"Telephonic Communication." *Times Literary Supplement,* no. 259 (Oct. 19, 1951), p. 662.

The Infernal Machine (La Machine Infernale)

Aylen, Leo. *Greek tragedy and the modern world,* pp. 260, 263-265

Bentley, Eric. *The playwright as thinker,* pp. 193, 202.

Bishop, Thomas. *Pirandello and the French theater,* pp. 106-107.

Brousse, Jacques. "Theatre in Paris: *La Machine Infernale* by Jea Cocteau." *European,* no. 23 (Jan., 1955), pp. 40-42.

Carter, John. *Spectator,* vol. 165 (Sept. 13, 1940), p. 267.

Chiari, Joseph. *The contemporary French theatre, 102-106.*

Chiari, J. *Landmarks of contemporary drama,* pp. 50-51, 53.

Fergusson, Francis. *"The Infernal Machine:* The Myth Behind th Modern City." *In:* Sanderson, James L., ed. *Oedipus, myth an dramatic form,* pp. 330-335. (Reprinted from Fergusson, Francis. *Th idea of a theatre,* Princeton Univ. Press, 1949, pp. 209-215)

Feynman, Alberta E. *"The Infernal Machine, Hamlet* and Erne Jones." *Modern Drama,* vol. 6, no. 1 (May, 1963), pp. 72-83.

Fowlie, Wallace. *Dionysus in Paris,* pp. 82-85.

Fowlie, Wallace. *Jean Cocteau,* pp. 64-70.

Gassner, John. *The theatre in our times,* pp. 184-194.

Grossvogel, David I. *The self-conscious stage in modern Frenc drama,* pp. 59-62.

"The Infernal Machine at the Chanticleer." *New Statesman & Natio* vol. 29 (Feb. 10, 1945), p. 92.

Knowles, Dorothy. *French drama of the inter-war years, 1918-39,* pp. 53-57.

Lumley, Frederick. *New trends in 20th century drama,* pp. 108, 109, 111. ✓

Lumley, Frederick. *Trends in 20th century drama,* p. 120.

MacCarthy, Desmond. *"The Infernal Machine." New Statesman & Nation,* vol. 20 (Sept. 21, 1940), pp. 281-282.

Moore, Marianne. "Ichor of Imagination." *Nation,* vol. 144, no. 6 (Feb. 6, 1937), pp. 126-129.

Oxenhandler, Neal. *Scandal and parade: the theatre of Jean Cocteau,* pp. 129-148, 216-220.

Schlumberger, Jean. Jean Cocteau's *Infernal Machine." In: La Nouvelle Revue Francaise,* pp. 199-201.

Wyatt, Euphemia. *"The Infernal Machine." Catholic World,* vol. 187 (Apr., 1958), p. 69

ntimate Relations (Problem Parents) (The Storm Within) (Les Parents Terribles)

"A Cocteau Revival." *Times,* no. 51,929 (Feb. 19, 1951) p. 9.

Forster, Peter. "Unholy Terrors." *Observer,* no. 8356 (July 29, 1951), p. 6.

Fowlie, Wallace *Dionysus in Paris,* pp. 85-86.

Fowlie, Wallace. *Jean Cocteau,* pp. 72-74.

Frank, Charles. *"Intimate Relations,* by Jean Cocteau." *Times,* no. 51, 956 (Mar. 22, 1951), p. 80

Grossvogel, David I. *The self-conscious stage in modern French drama,* pp. 63-64.

Knowles, Dorothy. *French drama of the inter-war years, 1918-39,* pp. 58-60.

Lumley, Frederick. *New trends in 20th century drama,* pp. 108, 109, 111-112.

Lumley Frederick. *Trends in 20th century drama,* pp. 120-121

MacCarthy, Desmond. "Cocteau at the Gate." *New Statesman & Nation* vol. 19 (May 25, 1940), pp. 666-667.

Oxenhandler, Neal. *Scandal and parade: the theatre of Jean Cocteau,* pp. 181-196.

Walker, Roy. "Cocteau Couples." *Theatre,* vol. 7, no. 161 (Dec. 6 1952), pp. 3-4.

Knights of the Round Table (Les Chevaliers de la Table Ronde)

Bishop, Thomas. *Pirandello and the French theater,* pp. 107-108.

Fowlie, Wallace. *Jean Cocteau,* pp. 70-72.

Knowles, Dorothy. *French drama of the inter-war years, 1918-39,* p 57.

Muir, Lynette. "Cocteau's *Les Chevaliers de la Table Ronde:* A Baroque Play." *Modern Languages,* vol. 40 (1959), pp. 115-120.

Oxenhandler, Neal. *Scandal and parade: the theater of Jean Cocteau* pp. 163-177.

Worsley, T.C. *New Statesman,* vol. 52 (Oct. 27, 1956), p. 516.

Oedipus Rex (Oedipe-Roi)

"Geneva Stages Cocteau's *Oedipus* in Thiriet's Setting." *Time* (London), no. 55,666 (Apr. 3, 1963), p. 17.

Heyworth, Peter. *"Oedipus." Observer,* no. 8785 (Nov. 15, 1959), p 25.

Kernochan, Marshall R. *Outlook,* vol. 158 (May 13, 1931), p. 60.

MacCarthy, Desmond. *Drama,* pp. 190-193.

Rosenfeld, Paul. *"Oedipus Rex,* Cocteau and Stravinsky." *Nev Republic,* vol. 66 (May 13, 1931), pp. 356-357.

Orpheus (Orphée)

Aylen, Leo. *Greek tragedy and the modern world,* pp. 260-263.

Bentley, Eric. *The playwright as thinker,* pp. 193, 195.

Chiari, Joseph. *The contemporary French theatre,* pp. 109-111.

Cutts, John P. "They Do It With Mirrors: Shakespeare and Cocteau." *Revue de Littérature Comparée,* vol. 38, no. 1 (Jan.-March, 1964), pp 121-127.

Fowlie, Wallace. *Age of surrealism,* pp. 125-129.

Fowlie, Wallace. *Dionysus in Paris,* pp. 78-82.

Fowlie, Wallace. *Jean Cocteau,* pp. 61-64, 110-114.

Grossvogel, David I. *The self-conscious stage in modern French drama,* pp. 54-59.

Ingham, Patricia. "The Renaissance of Hell." *Listener,* vol. 62 (Sept. 3, 1959), pp. 349-351.

Jennings, Richard. *Spectator,* vol. 140 (Apr. 21, 1928), p. 594.

Kauffmann, Stanley "The Truth and Where To Find It." *New Republic,* vol. 146, no. 20 (May 14, 1962), pp. 34, 36-37.

Knowles, Dorothy. *French drama of the inter-war years, 1918-39,* pp. 52-53.

Lee, M. Owen. "Orpheus and Eurydice: Some Modern Versions." *Classical J.,* vol. 56, no. 4 (1960/61), pp. 307-313.

Lumley, Frederick. *New trends in the 20th century drama,* pp. 107, 109-111.

Lumley, Fredrick. *Trends in 20th century drama,* pp. 118-119.

MacCarthy, Desmond. *Drama,* pp. 184-189.

New Statesman, vol. 31 (Apr. 21, 1928), pp. 45-46.

Oxenhandler Neal. *Scandal and parade: the theater of Jean Cocteau.* pp. 79-103.

Sainer, Arthur. *The sleepwalker and the assassin, a view of the contemporary theatre,* pp. 54-55.

arade

Bancroft, David. "A Critical Re-assessment of Cocteau's *Parade.*" *J. of the Australasian Universities Language and Literature Association,* no. 25 (May 1966), pp. 83-92.

Fowlie, Wallace. *Jean Cocteau,* pp. 60-61.

Grossvogel, David I. *The self-conscious stage in modern French drama,* pp. 47-49.

enaud et Armide

Oxenhandler, Neal. *Scandal and parade: the theater of Jean Cocteau,* pp. 232-246.

Romeo and Juliette (Roméo et Juliette)

Grossvogel, David I. *The self-conscious stage in modern Frenc: drama,* pp. 52-53.

The Typewriter (La Machine à Ecrire)

Fowlie, Wallace. *Jean Cocteau,* pp. 74-75.

Hayes, Richard. "Cocteau." *Commonweal,* vol. 62, no. 25 (Sept. 2? 1955), p. 613.

Knowles, Dorothy. *French drama of the inter-war years, 1918-39,* ƒ 61.

LENORE COFFEE and WILLIAM JOYCE COWEN

Family Portrait

O'Hara, Frank H. *Today in American drama,* pp. 108-124, 248, 26?

TOM COFFEY 1925-

General

Hogan, Robert. *After the Irish renaissance,* pp. 82-85.

VAL COLEMAN

The Jackhammer

Sainer, Arthur. *The sleepwalker and the assassin, a view of th contemporary theatre,* pp. 43-44.

PADRAIC COLUM 1881-

General

Boyd, Ernest. *Ireland's literary renaissance,* pp. 335-337, 341-343.

Malone, Andrew E. *The Irish drama,* pp. 164-166, 168-169.

Williams, Harold. *Modern English writers,* pp. 217-218.

The Fiddler's House

Boyd, Ernest. *Ireland's literary renaissance,* pp. 339-340.

Malone, Andrew E. *The Irish drama,* pp. 167-168.

The Land

Boyd, Ernest. *Ireland's literary renaissance,* pp. 337-339.

Malone, Andrew E. *The Irish drama,* pp. 166-167.

homas Muskerry

Boyd, Ernest. *Ireland's literary renaissance,* pp. 340-341.

Malone, Andrew E. *The Irish drama,* pp. 168-169.

NORREYS CONNELL

he Piper

Dorcey, Donal. "The Big Occasions." *In:* McCann, Sean, ed. *The story of the Abbey Theatre,* pp. 140-141.

MARCUS COOK CONNELLY 1890-

he Green Pastures

Atkinson, Brooks. *"The Green Pastures." In:* Moses, Montrose J. *The American theatre as seen by its critics, 1752-1934,* pp. 292-294, (Reprinted from *The New York Times,* (Feb. 27, 1929).

Brown, John Mason. "The Ever Green Pastures." *In:* Brown, John Mason. *Dramatis personae,* pp. 85-89.

Eastman, Fred. *Christ in the drama,* pp. 103-111.

Ford, Nick Aaron. "How Genuine Is *The Green Pastures?" Phylon,* vol. 20, no. 1 (Spring, 1959), pp. 67-70.

Garey, Doris B. *"The Green Pastures* Again." *Phylon,* vol. 20, no. 2 (Summer, 1959), pp. 193-194.

Krumpelmann, John T. "Marc Connelly's *The Green Pastures* and Goethe's *Faust." In:* McNeir, Waldo F. *Studies in comparative literature,* pp. 199-218.

Mitchell, Loften. *Black drama,* pp. 35, 94-96, 120.

Nolan, Paul T. "God on Stage: A Problem in Characterization: Marc Connelly's Green Past*ures." Xavier University Studies,* vol. 4 (May, 1965), pp. 75-84.

Skinner, R. Dana. *"The Green Pastures." In:* Moses, Montrose J. *The American theatre as seen by its critics, 1752-1934,* pp. 278-281.

Withington, Robert. "Notes on the Corpus Christi Plays and *The Green Pastures." Shakespeare Assoc. Bulletin,* vol. 9, no. 4 (Oct., 1934), pp. 193-197.

Young, Stark. *Immortal shadows,* pp. 119-122.

JOSEPH CONRAD 1857-1924

One Day More (Adaptation from a short story)

Beerbohm, Max. *Around theatres,* pp. 384-387.

GILES COOPER

General

Taylor, John Russell. "The Early Fifties." *In:* Brown, John Russell, ed
Modern British dramatists, a collection of critical essays, pp. 24-2'
(From Taylor, J.R. *Anger and after,* London, Methuen, published a
The angry theater, N.Y. Hill & Wang, 1962.)

DANIEL CORKERY 1878-1964

The Labour Leader

Malone, Andrew E. *The Irish drama,* pp. 275-276.

GABRIEL COUSIN

General

Pronko, Leonard C. *Theater East and West,* p. 33.

Le Drame du Fukuryu Maru

Pronko, Leonard C. *Theater East and West,* pp. 134-137.

NOEL COWARD 1899-

General

Brown, John Mason. "Richard Brinsley Sheridan to Noel Coward." *Ir*
Brown, John Mason. *Dramatis personae,* pp. 159-183.

MacCarthy, Desmond. *Theatre,* pp. 140-143.

O'Casey, Sean. *The green crow,* pp. 108-115.

Richards, Dick. "Coward—The First Noel." *In:* Richards, Dick. *Th*
curtain rises, pp. 96-101.

Taylor, John Russell. *The rise and fall of the well-made play,* p
126-130, 140-145, 148.

Tynan, Kenneth. *Tynan right and left,* pp. 86-88.

Cavalcade

O'Casey, Sean. *The green crow,* pp. 90-96.

Conversation Piece

MacCarthy, Desmond. *Drama,* pp. 261-265.

esign for Living

O'Casey, Sean. *The green crow,* pp. 99-107.

Sievers, W. David. *Freud on Broadway.* pp. 217-218.

asy Virtue

Taylor, John Russell. *The rise and fall of the well-made play,* pp. 137-139.

eace in Our Time

Hobson, Harold. *Theatre,* pp. 111-114.

oint Valaine

Hobson, Harold. *Theatre,* pp. 123-125.

resent Laughter

Brown, John Mason. *Seeing more things,* pp. 200-208.

rivate Lives

MacCarthy, Desmond. *Drama,* pp. 243-246.

Taylor, John Russell. *The rise and fall of the well-made play,* pp. 130-131.

Song at Twilight

Taylor, John Russell. *The rise and fall of the well-made play,* pp. 124-126.

he Vortex

Taylor, John Russell. *The rise and fall of the well-made play,* pp. 134-136.

he Young Idea

Taylor, John Russell. *The rise and fall of the well-made play,* pp. 132-134.

RON COWEN

Summertree

Funke, Lewis. "News at the Rialto: 'Quo Vadis', Driver?" *New Yor* *Times,* May 12, 1968, Sec. 2, p. 13.

FERNAND CROMMELYNCK 1885-

Les Amants Puérils

Knowles, Dorothy. *French drama of the inter-war years, 1918-1939,* ┌ 68.

Chaud et Froid

Knowles, Dorothy. *French drama of the inter-war years, 1918-39,* p┌ 69-70.

Mallinson, Vernon. *Modern Belgian literature, 1830-1960,* p. 176.

Le Cocu Magnifique

Knowles, Dorothy. *French drama of the inter-war years, 1918-193*┤ pp. 65-68.

Mallinson, Vernon. *Modern Belgian literature, 1830-1960,* pp. 174-175┤

Dardamelle, ou Le Cocu

Knowles, Dorothy. *French drama of the inter-war years, 1918-39,* ┌ 70.

La Folle Journee

Knowles, Dorothy. *French drama of the inter-war years, 1918-39,* pp┤ 70-71.

Tripes d'Or

Mallinson, Vernon. *Modern Belgian literature, 1830-1960,* p. 175.

Une Femme Qu'a le Coeur Trop Petit

Mallinson, Vernon. *Modern Belgian literature, 1830-1960,* pp. 175-176┤

RUSSEL CROUSE 1893-1966

General

Gould, Jean. *Modern American Playwrights,* pp. 140-150.

MART CROWLEY

he Boys in the Band

Kerr, Walter. "To Laugh At Oneself—Or Cry?" *New York Times,* Apr. 28, 1968, pp. 1, 3.

Reed, Rex. "Breakthrough By *The Boys in the Band." New York Times,* May 12, 1968, Sec. 2, pp. 1, 11.

GYULA CSAK

'eace Be with the Guilty

Weiss, Thomas. "The Guilt Complex in Communist Literature." *East Europe,* vol. 15, no. 7 (July, 1966), pp. 14-15.

PABLO ANTONIO CUADRA 1912-

'eneral

Anderson-Imbert, Enrique. *Spanish-American literature: a history,* pp. 435, 436.

Jones, W.K. *Behind Spanish American footlights,* pp. 429-430.

EDWARD ESTLIN CUMMINGS 1894-1962

nthropos

Friedman, Norman. *E.E. Cummings, the growth of a writer,* pp. 93-97.

Wegner, Robert E. *The poetry and prose of E.E. Cummings,* pp. 134-141.

lim

Friedman, Norman. *E.E. Cummings, the growth of a writer,* pp. 51-74, 99, 102.

Littell, Robert. "E.E. Cumming's *Him." In:* Moses, Montrose J. *The American theatre as seen by its critics, 1752-1934,* pp. 326-328. (Reprinted from *The New York Evening Post,* Apr. 21, 1928.)

Norman, Charles. *E.E. Cummings, a biography,* pp. 156-170.

Wegner, Robert E. *The poetry and prose of E.E. Cummings,* pp. 16-17, 26-36, 131-132.

Worth, Katharine J. "The Poets in the American Theatre." *In: American theatre,* pp. 89, 102-106.

Santa Claus

Donoghue, Denis. *The third voice: modern British and American vers drama.* pp. 70-75.

Friedman, Norman. *E.E. Cummings, the growth of a writer,* pp 140-151.

Norman, Charles. *E.E. Cummings, a biography,* pp. 171-172.

Wegner, Robert E. *The poetry and prose of E.E. Cummings,* pp. 16-17 66, 117-118, 120-121, 132.

FRANÇOIS DE CUREL 1854-1928

General

Knowles, Dorothy. *French drama of the inter-war years, 1918-39,* pp 245-246.

La Fille Sauvage

Ellehauge, Martin. *The position of Bernard Shaw in European dram. and philosophy,* pp. 257-259.

Le Repas du Lion

Ellehauge, Martin. *The position of Bernard Shaw in European dram. and philosophy,* pp. 119-121.

LOUIS D'ALTON 1900-1951

General

Hogan, Robert. *After the Irish renaissance,* pp. 45-51.

GABRIEL D'ANNUNZIO 1863-1938

General

Miller, Nellie Burget. *The living drama,* pp. 379-381.

Sharp, William. *Studies and appreciations,* pp. 309-314.

The Daughter of Jorio

Miller, Nellie Burget. *The living drama,* pp. 384-386.

The Dead City (La Citta Morta)

MacCarthy, Desmond. *Drama,* pp. 141-146.

Sharp, William. *Studies and appreciations,* pp. 326-331.

Dream of a Morning in Spring (Sogno d'un Mattino di Primavera)

Sharp, William. *Studies and appreciations,* pp. 314-320.

Dream of an Autumn Sunset (Sogno d'un Tramonto d'Autunno)

Sharp, William. *Studies and appreciations,* pp. 320-324.

Francesca da Rimini

Miller, Nellie Burget. *The living drama,* pp. 381-384.

La Gioconda

Sharp, William. *Studies and appreciations,* pp. 325-326.

La Gloria

Sharp, William. *Studies and appreciations,* pp. 331-336.

RUBEN DARIO 1867-1916

General

Anderson Imbert, Enrique. *Spanish-American literature: a history,* pp. 266-271.

Jones, W.K. *Behind Spanish American footlights,* pp. 427, 355, 441.

Woodbridge, Hensley C. "Rubén Darío: A Critical Bibliography." *Hispania,* vol. 50 (1967), pp. 982-985.

CAMILO DARTHES 1889-
Co-author, Carlos S. Damel, "Darthés y Damel"

General

Jones, W.K. *Behind Spanish American footlights,* pp. 142-144.

Los Chicos Crecen

Jones, W.K. *Behind Spanish American footlights,* pp. 142-143.

La Hermana Josefina

Jones, W.K. *Behind Spanish American footlights,* p. 144.

MARCELINO DAVALOS 1871-1923

General

González Peña, Carlos. *History of Mexican literature,* pp. 323-324.

Jones, W.K. *Behind Spanish American footlights,* pp. 486-487.

JOHN DAVIDSON 1857-1909

The Triumph of Mammon

Knight, G. Wilson. *The golden labyrinth,* pp. 312-317.

HUBERT HENRY DAVIES 1869-1917

General

Williams, Harold. *Modern English writers,* p. 269.

GORDON DAVIOT
(real name Elizabeth Mackintosh)

Leith Sands

Roston, Murray. *Biblical drama in England from the Middle Ages t* *the present day,* pp. 288-289.

Queen of Scots

MacCarthy, Desmond. *Drama,* pp. 290-293.

Richard of Bordeaux

MacCarthy, Desmond. *Drama,* pp. 286-289.

JULIA DAVIS 1904-

The Anvil

Sainer, Arthur. *The sleepwalker and the assassin, a view of th* *contemporary theatre,* p. 47.

OSSIE DAVIS 1917-

Alice in Wonder (The Big Deal)

Mitchell, Loften. *Black drama,* pp. 155-156.

Purlie Victorious

Davis, Ossie. "The Wonderful World of Law and Order." *In:* Hill Herbert. *Anger, and beyond,* pp. 154-180.

Mitchell, Loften. *Black drama,* pp. 188-190.

Turpin, Waters E. "The Contemporary American Negro Playwright." *College Language Assn. J.,* vol. 9, no. 1 (Sept., 1965), pp. 19-20.

OWEN DAVIS 1874-1956

General

Goff, Lewin. "The Owen Davis—Al Wood Melodrama Factory." *Educational Theatre J.,* vol. 11 (1959), pp. 200-207.

cebound

Sievers, W. David. *Freud on Broadway,* pp. 135-136.

TERESA DEEVY

General

Hogan, Robert. *After the Irish renaissance,* pp. 39-43.

Riley, J.D. "On Teresa Deevy's Plays." *Irish Writing.* no, 32 (Autumn, 1955).

FRANCISCO DEFILIPPIS NOVOA 1892-1930

General

Jones, W.K. *Behind Spanish American footlights,* pp. 132-134.

EDUARDO DE FILIPPO 1900-

General

Acton, Harold. "Eduardo de Filippo." *In:* Bentley, Eric, ed. *The genius of the Italian theatre,* pp. 551-563. (Reprinted from *The London Magazine,* June, 1962.)

Bentley, Eric. "Son of Pulcinella." *In:* Corrigan, Robert W., ed. *Masterpieces of the modern Italian theatre,* pp. 245-247. (Reprinted from Bentley, Eric. *In search of theatre,* N.Y., Knopf, 1951.)

Corrigan, Robert W., ed. *Masterpieces of the modern Italian theatre,* p. 244.

Codignola, Luciano. "Reading de Filippo." *Tulane Drama Rev.,* vol. 8, no. 3 (Spring, 1964), pp. 108-117.

he Boss

Codignola, Luciano. "Reading de Filippo." *Tulane Drama Rev.,* vol. 8, no. 3 (Spring, 1964), pp. 113-117.

Christmas in the Cupiello Home (Natale in Case Cupiello)

Codignola, Luciano. "Reading de Filippo." *Tulane Drama Rev.,* vol. 8, no. 3 (Spring, 1964), pp. 111-112.

185

Filumena Marturano

Bentley, Eric. "Son of Pulcinella." *In:* Corrigan, Robert W., ed. *Masterpieces of the modern Italian theatre,* pp. 247-249. (Reprinted from Bentley, Eric. *In search of theater,* N.Y., Knopf, 1951.)

The Mayor of the Sanita District (Il Sindaco del Rione Sanita)

Acton, Harold. "Eduardo de Filippo." *In:* Bentley, Eric, ed. *The genius of the Italian theatre,* pp. 358-363. (Reprinted from *The London Magazine,* June, 1962.)

Napoli Milionaria

Acton, Harold. "Eduardo de Filippo." *In:* Bentley, Eric, ed. *The genius of the Italian theatre,* pp. 552-556. (Reprinted from *The London Magazine,* June, 1962.)

Sabato, Domenica e Lunedi

Acton, Harold. "Eduardo de Filippo." *In:* Bentley, Eric, ed. *The genius of the Italian theatre,* pp. 556-558. (Reprinted from *The London Magazine,* June, 1962.)

SHELAGH DELANEY 1939-

General

Lumley, Frederick. *New trends in 20th century drama,* p. 310.

Taylor, John Russell. *Anger and after,* pp. 109-118.

The Lion in Love

Taylor, John Russell. *Anger and after,* pp. 114-118.

Tynan, Kenneth. *Tynan right and left,* pp. 20-21.

Wellwarth, George. *The theatre of protest and paradox,* pp. 252-253

A Taste of Honey

Clurman, Harold. *The naked image,* pp. 70-71.

Gillett, Eric. "Regional Realism: Shelagh Delaney, Alun Owen, Keith Watherhouse, and Willis Hall." *In:* Armstrong, William A., ed *Experimental drama,* pp. 189-192.

Ippolito, G.J. "The New Dramatists: Shelagh Delaney." *Drama Survey,* vol. 1, no. 1 (May, 1961), pp. 86-91.

Kerr, Walter. *The theater in spite of itself,* pp. 126-129.

Kitchin, Laurence. *Mid-century drama,* pp. 110-111.

McCarten, John. *New Yorker,* vol. 36 (Oct. 15, 1960), p. 73.

MacInnes, Colin. "A Taste of Reality." *Encounter,* vol. 12, no. 4 (1959), pp. 70-71.

Oberg, Arthur K. *"A Taste of Honey* and the Popular Play." *Wisconsin Studies in Contemporary Literature,* vol. 7. no. 2 (Summer, 1966), pp. 160-167.

Popkin, Henry. "Theatre Chronicle." *Sewanee Review,* vol. 69 (1961), pp. 337-338.

Taylor, John Russell. *Anger and after,* pp. 109-114.

Wellwarth, George. *The theatre of protest and paradox,* pp. 250-252.

NIGEL DENNIS 1912-

;eneral

Wellwarth, George. *The theatre of protest and paradox,* pp. 261-267.

:ards of Identity

Allsop, Kenneth. *The angry decade,* pp. 148-151.

Wellwarth, George. *The theatre of protest and paradox,* pp. 262, 265-267.

he Making of Moo

Allsop, Kenneth. *The angry decade,* pp. 151-153.

Wellwarth, George. *The theatre of protest and paradox,* pp. 262-265, 267.

MANUEL DE PEDROLO

:ruma

Esslin, Martin. *The theatre of the absurd,* pp. 183-184.

Iumans and No (Homes i No)

Esslin, Martin. *The theatre of the absurd,* pp. 184-185.

EZIO D'ERRICO

.a Foresta (The Forest)

Esslin, Martin, *The theatre of the absurd,* pp. 181-182.

JACQUES DEVAL 1894-

General

Knowles, Dorothy. *French drama of the inter-war years, 1918-39,* pp 283-286.

ROBERT DHERY

La Grosse Valise

Downer, Alan S. "Total Theatre and Partial Drama: Notes on the New York Theatre, 1965-1966." *Q. J. of Speech,* vol. 52. no. 3 (Oct., 1966, p. 226.

La Plume de Ma Tante

Downer, Alan S. "Total Theatre and Partial Drama: Notes on the New York Theatre, 1965-1966." *Q. J. of Speech,* vol. 52, no. 3 (Oct., 1966, p. 226.

CARLOS DIAZ DUFOO 1861-

General

González Peña, Carlos. *History of Mexican literature,* pp. 281, 31(377-378.

JORGE DIAZ GUTIERREZ 1930-

General

Jones, W.K. *Behind Spanish American footlights,* pp. 240-241.

RAFAEL ANGEL DIAZ SOSA 1926-

General

Jones, W.K. *Behind Spanish American footlights,* p. 348.

ANTONIO DIAZ VILLAMIL 1897-1948

General

Jones, W.K. *Behind Spanish American footlights,* pp. 283-284.

La Hoguera

Jones, W.K. *Behind Spanish American footlights,* p. 284.

JOACHIM DICENTA 1863-1917

General

Warren, L.A. *Modern Spanish literature,* vol. 2, pp. 549-554.

VICTOR MANUEL DIEZ BARROSO 1890-1936

General

González Peña, Carlos. *History of Mexican literature,* p. 376.

FRANKLIN DOMINGUEZ

Alberto y Ercilia

Jones, W.K. *Behind Spanish American footlights,* p. 389.

Espigas Maduras

Jones, W.K. *Behind Spanish American footlights,* pp. 389-390.

Exodo

Jones, W.K. *Behind Spanish American footlights,* p. 388.

El Vuelo de la Paloma

Jones, W.K. *Behind Spanish American footlights,* p. 389.

J.P. DONLEAVY 1926-

The Ginger Man (Adapted from his novel of the same title)

Hogan, Robert. *After the Irish renaisance,* pp. 230-231.

What They did in Dublin with "The Ginger Man." London, MacGibbon & Kee, 1961. (Contains the text of the play and a long introduction.)

TANKRED DORST 1925-

Freedom for Clemens

Wellwarth, G.E. "Introduction." *In:* Benedikt, M. and G.E. Wellwarth, eds. *Postwar German theatre,* pp. xxii-xxiii

Great Diatribe at the Town Wall (Grosse Schmahrede an der Stadtmauer)

Garten, H.F. *Modern German drama,* pp. 272-273.

Society in Autumn (Gesellschaft im Herbst)

Garten, H.F. *Modern German drama*, p. 272.

JOHN DOS PASSOS 1896-

General

Knox, George A. *Dos Passos and "The Revolting Playwrights"*, pp 56-59.

Airways, Inc.

Knox, George A. *Dos Passos and "The Revolting Playwrights"*, pp 142-146, 174-176.

The Garbage Man (The Moon Is a Gong)

Bauland, Peter. *The hooded eagle,* p. 93.

Knox, George A. *Dos Passos and "The Revolting Playwrights,"* pp. 35-36, 96-102.

Turner, Darwin T. "Jazz-Vaudeville Drama in the Twenties." *Educational Theatre J.,* vol. 11 (1959), pp. 112-113.

Valgemae, Mardi. "Civil War Among the Expressionists: John Howard Lawson and the *Pinwheel* Controversy." *Educational Theatre J.,* vol. 2O, no. 1 (Mar., 1968), p. 9..

FEDOR MIKHAILOVICH DOSTOEVSKII 1821-1881

The Idiot (Adapted by Robert Hogan)

MacCarthy, Desmond. *Drama,* pp. 91-94.

Les Possedes (The Possessed) (Adapted by Albert Camus)

Flanner, Janet "Letter from Paris." *New Yorker,* vol. 35 (Mar. 7, 1959), pp. 106-107.

Ramsey, Warren. "Albert Camus on Capital Punishment: His Adaptation of *The Possessed."* *Yale Rev.,* vol. 48, no. 4 (June, 1959), pp. 634-640

Ries, Joachim Schutmann. "Camus the adapter: an analysis of Camus' dramatization of Dostoevsky's novel *The Possessed."* *Dissertation Abstracts,* vol. 26, no. 8 (Feb. 1966), 4673 (Univ. of Washington).

JAMES DOUGLAS 1929-

General

Hogan, Robert. *After the Irish renaissance,* pp. 192-195.

Hogan, Robert, G., ed. *Seven Irish plays, 1946-1964,* pp. 413-415.

The Ice Goddess

Hogan, Robert. *After the Irish renaissance,* pp. 194-195.

North City Traffic Straight Ahead

Hogan, Robert. *After the Irish renaissance,* pp. 192, 193-194.

ROBERT DOWNEY

What Else Is There?

Sainer, Arthur. *The sleepwalker and the assassin, a view of the contemporary theatre,* pp. 95-96.

THEODORE DREISER 1871-1945

General

Biddle, Edmund Randolph. "The plays of Theodore Dreiser." *Dissertation Abstracts,* vol. 26 (1965), pp. 3325-26 (Penn.).

Szeliski, John J. von. "Dreiser's Experiment with Tragic Drama." *Twentieth Century Literature,* vol. 12 (1966), pp. 31-40.

American Tragedy (The Case of Clyde Griffiths) (Adapted by Erwin Piscator & Lena Goldschmidt)

Himelstein, Morgan Y. *Drama was a weapon, the left-wing theatre in New York 1929-1941,* pp. 171-172.

The Hand of the Potter

Sievers, W. David. *Freud on Broadway.* pp. 66-68.

Szeliski, John J. von. "Dreiser's Experiment with Tragic Drama." *Twentieth Century Literature,* vol. 12, no. 1 (Apr., 1966), pp. 31-40.

JOHN DRINKWATER 1882-1937

Robert E. Lee

Shaw, George Bernard. *In:* Henderson, Archibald. *Table-talk of G.B.S.,* pp. 86-88.

DONALD DRIVER

Status Quo Vadis?

Funke, Lewis. "News of the Rialto: 'Quo Vadis, Driver?," *New York Times,* May 12, 1968, Sec. 2, pp. 1, 13.

ROLAND DUBILLARD

General

Guicharnaud, Jacques. *Modern French theatre from Giraudoux to Genet* (rev. ed.), pp. 180-181, 195, 345, 363.

La Maison d'Os

Guicharnaud, Jacques. *Modern French theatre from Giraudoux to Genet* (rev. ed.), pp. 193-194.

Naives Hirondelles

Guicharnaud, Jacques. *Modern French theatre from Giraudoux to Genet* (rev. ed.), pp. 191-192.

ROGER MARTIN DU GARD 1881-1958

See Martin du Gard, Roger

GEORGES DUHAMEL 1884-1966

The Combat

Goldberg, Isaac. *The drama of transition,* pp. 263-266.

In the Shadow of the Statues

Goldberg, Isaac. *The drama of transition,* pp. 260-263.

The Light

Goldberg, Isaac. *The drama of transition,* pp. 256-261.

RONALD DUNCAN 1914-

This Way to the Tomb

Spanos, William V. *The Christian tradition in modern British verse drama,* pp. 282-293.

Welland, Dennis. "Some Post-War Experiments in Poetic Drama." *In:* Armstrong, William A., ed. *Experimental drama,* pp. 36-55.

LORD DUNSANY 1878-1957

General

Boyd, Ernest. *Ireland's literary renaissance,* pp. 360-362.

Malone, Andrew E. *The Irish drama,* pp. 246-247, 255-256.

The Glittering Gate

Malone, Andrew E. *The Irish drama,* pp. 248-250.

King Argimenes and the Unknown Warrior

Malone, Andrew E. *The Irish drama,* pp. 250-252.

A Night at the Inn

Malone, Andrew E. *The Irish drama,* pp. 254-255.

The Tents of the Arabs

Malone, Andrew E. *The Irish drama,* pp. 254-255.

MARGUERITE DURAS 1914-

General

Guicharnaud, Jacques. *Modern French theatre from Giraudoux to Genet* (rev. ed.), pp. 181, 187-191, 195, 345, 363.

Days in the Trees

Browne, E. Martin. "A Look Round the English Theatre: Summer and Fall, 1966." *Drama Survey,* vol. 5, no. 3 (Winter, 1966-67), pp. 298-299.

Hope-Wallace, Philip. *"Days in the Trees." Guardian,* no. 37,300 (June 11, 1966), p. 6.

"A Pattern with Little Force." *Times,* no. 56,655 (June 11, 1966), p. 7.

Worsley, T.C., *et al. "Days in the Trees."* Listener, vol. 75, no. 1944 (June 30, 1966), p. 947.

La Musica

"Good Moments in Double-bill." *Times,* no. 56,721 (Aug. 27, 1966), p. 6.

Hoyenga, Betty. "Arts As Music." *Prairie Schooner,* vol. 40, no. 2 (Summer 1966), pp. 174-175.

Jones, D.A.N. "Challenge to Optimists." *New Statesman,* vol. 72, no. 1851 (Sept. 2, 1966), p. 329.

Lambert, J.W. "Tis Pity She's a Bore." *Times,* no. 7475 (Aug. 28, 1966), p.26.

"Marguerite Duras Double Bill." *Times,* no. 56,699 (Aug. 2, 1966), p. 7.

Oliver, Cordelia. "Two Duras Plays at The Traverse, Edinburgh." *Guardian,* no. 37,268 (May 5, 1966) p. 9.

The Square

Edelstein, J.M. "The Surface to Things." *New Republic,* vol. 141, no. 20 (Nov. 16, 1959), p. 19.

"Good Moments in Double-bill." *Times,* no. 56,721 (Aug. 27, 1966), p. 6.

Jones, D.A.N. "Challenge to Optimists." *New Statesman,* vol. 72, no. 1851 (Sept. 2, 1966), p. 329.

Lambert, J.W. "'Tis Pity She's a Bore." *Times,* no. 7475 (Aug. 28, 1966), p. 26

"Marguerite Duras Double Bill." *Times,* no. 56,699 (Aug. 2, 1966), p. 7.

Oliver, Cordelia. "Two Duras Plays at The Traverse, Edinburgh." *Guardian,* no. 37,268 (May 5, 1966) p. 9.

The Viaduct

"Grand Guignol Cannot Save the Day." *Times,* no. 56,849 (Jan. 26, 1967). p. 6.

Hobson, Harold. "Nothing but the Truth." *Times,* no. 7496 (Jan. 29, 1967), p. 45.

Hope-Wallace, Philip. *"The Viaduct* at the Yvonne Arnaud Theatre" *Guardian,* no. 37,494 (Jan. 26, 1967), p. 7.

LAWRENCE DURRELL 1912-

An Irish Faustus

Cole, Douglas. "Faust and Anti-Faust in Modern Drama." *Drama Survey,* vol. 5, no. 1 (Spring, 1966), pp. 49-52.

FRIEDRICH DURRENMATT 1921-

General

Bauland, Peter. *The hooded eagle,* pp. 49, 94, 160, 173, 197-207,

Carew, Rivers. "The Plays of Friedrich Dürrenmatt." *The Dublin Magazine* (formerly *The Dubliner),* vol. 4 (1965), pp. 57-68.

Coenen, F.E. "The Modern German Drama." *In:* Hammer, Carl, Jr., ed. *Studies in German literature,* pp. 123-128.

Diller, Edward. "Aesthetics and the Grotesque: Friedrich Dürrenmatt." *Wisconsin Studies in Contemporary Literature,* vol. 7, no. 3 (Autumn, 1966), pp. 328-335.

Diller, Edward. "Despair and the Paradox: Friedrich Dürrenmatt." *Drama Survey,* vol. 5, no. 2 (Summer, 1966), pp. 131-136.

Diller, Edward. "Dürrenmatt's Use of the Stage as a Dramatic Element." *Symposium,* vol. 20, no. 3 (Fall, 1966), pp. 197-205.

Diller, Edward. "Friedrich Dürrenmatt's Theological Concept of History." *German Q.,* vol. 40 (1967), pp. 363-371.

Dürrenmatt, Friedrich. "From Problems of the Theatre." *In:* Seltzer, Daniel, ed. *The modern theatre, readings and documents,* pp. 54-73. (Reprinted from Preface to *Four plays* by Friedrich Dürrenmatt, N.Y., Grove, 1965.)

Dürrenmatt, Friedrich. (Interview with Horst Bienek.) *In:* Wager, Walter, ed. *The playwrights speak,* pp. 70-77, 80-81, 83-89.

Esslin, Martin. "Friedrich Dürrenmatt and the Neurosis of Neutrality." *In:* Freedman, Morris, ed. *Essays in the modern drama,* pp. 225-227. (Reprinted in *The Washington Post,* Feb. 17, 1963, from *The Manchester Guardian.)*

Esslin, Martin. "Merciless Observer." *Plays and Players* (Mar., 1963), pp. 15-16.

Garten, H.F. *Modern German drama,* pp. 246, 249-250, 255-262.

Goodman, Randolph. *Drama on stage,* pp. 378-380.

Hatfield, Henry. *Modern German literature,* pp. 140-142.

Helbling, Robert E. "The Function of the 'Grotesque' in Dürrenmatt." *Satire Newsletter* (State U. Coll., Oneonta, N.Y.) vol. 4 (1966), pp. 11-19.

Holzapfel, Robert. "The Divine Plan Behind the Plays of Friedrich Dürrenmatt." *Modern Drama,* vol. 8, no. 3 (Dec., 1965), pp. 237-246.

Johnson, Peter. "Grotesqueness and Injustice in Dürrenmatt," *German life and letters,* vol. 15 (1962), pp. 264-273.

Klarmann, Adolf D. "Friedrich Dürrenmatt and the Tragic Sense of Comedy." *In:* Bogard, Travis, and Oliver, William I., eds. *Modern drama; essays in criticism,* pp. 99-105. (Reprinted from *Tulane Drama Rev.,* vol. 4, no. 4 (May, 1960), pp. 77-104.)

Lumley, Frederick. *New trends in 20th century drama,* pp. 239-246.

Moore, Harry T. *Twentieth-century German literature,* pp. 143, 147-149, 151-152, 183, 185-187.

"Morality Plays." *Times Literary Supplement,* no. 3,176 (Jan. 11, 1963), pp. 17-19.

Peppard, Murray B. "The Grotesque in Dürrenmatt's Dramas." *Kentucky Foreign Language Q.,* vol. 9 (1962), pp. 36-44.

Seidmann, Peter. "Modern Swiss Drama: Frisch and Dürrenmatt," *Books Abroad,* vol. 34 (1960), pp. 112-114.

Sheppard, Vera. "Friedrich Dürrenmatt as a Dramatic Theorist." *Drama Survey,* vol. 4, no. 3 (Winter, 1965), pp. 244-263.

Wager, Walter. "Friedrich Dürrenmatt." *In:* Wager, Walter, ed. *The playwrights speak,* pp. 68-70.

Waidson, H.M. Friedrich Dürrenmatt." *In:* Natan, A., ed. *German men of letters* vol. 3 (1964), pp. 323-343.

Wellwarth, George E. "Friedrich Dürrenmatt and Max Frisch: Two Views of the Drama." *Tulane Drama Rev.,* vol. 6, no. 3 (Mar., 1962), pp. 14-42.

Wellwarth, George. *The theatre of protest and paradox,* pp. 134-161.

Wilbert-Collins, Elly. *A bibliography of four contemporary German-Swiss authors: Friedrich Dürrenmatt, Max Frish, Robert Walser, Albin Zollinger.* Bern: Francke, 1967.

An Angel Comes to Babylon (Ein Engel Kommt nach Babylon)

Klarmann, Adolf D. "Friedrich Dürrenmatt and the Tragic Sense of Comedy." *In:* Bogard, Travis and Oliver, William I., eds. *Modern drama; essays in criticism,* pp. 124-126 (Reprinted from *Tulane Drama Rev.,* vol. 4, no. 4 (May, 1960), pp. 77-104.)

Wellwarth, George E. "Friedrich Dürrenmatt and Max Frisch: Two Views of the Drama." *Tulane Drama Rev.,* vol. 6, no. 3 (Mar., 1962), pp. 14-42.

Wellwarth, George. *The theatre of protest and paradox,* pp. 149-153.

The Blind Man (Der Blinde)

Klarmann, Adolf D. "Friedrich Dürrenmatt and the Tragic Sense of Comedy." *In:* Bogard, Travis, and Oliver, William I., eds. *Modern drama; essays in criticism,* pp. 111-113. (Reprinted from *Tulane Drama Rev.,* vol. 4, no. 4 (May, 1960), pp. 77-104.)

Frank V--Opera of a Private Bank (Frank V--Oper Einer Privatbank)

Dürrenmatt, Friedrich. (Interview with Horst Bienek.) *In:* Wager, Walter, ed. *The playwrights speak,* pp. 72-76, 77-80

Wellwarth, George E. "Friedrich Dürrenmatt and Max Frisch: Two Views of the Drama." *Tulane Drama Rev.,* vol. 6, no. 3 (Mar., 1962), pp. 14-42.

Wellwarth, George. *The theatre of protest and paradox,* pp. 153-154.

Incident at Twilight

Wellwarth, G.E. "Introduction." *In:* Benedikt, M. and G.E. Wellwarth, eds. *Post-war German theatre,* pp. xxi-xxii.

It Is Written (Es Steht Geschrieben)

Diller, Edward. "Despair and the Paradox: Friedrich Dürrenmatt." *Drama Survey,* vol. 5, no. 2 (Summer, 1966), pp. 131-132.

Hirschback, Frank D. "New Directions in German Comedy." *Drama Survey,* vol. 1, no. 2 (Oct., 1961), pp. 195-213.

Klarmann, Adolf D. "Friedrich Dürrenmatt and the Tragic Sense of Comedy." *In:* Bogard, Travis, and Oliver, William I., eds. *Modern drama; essays in criticism,* pp. 105-111. (Reprinted from *Tulane Drama Rev.,* vol. 4, no. 4, (May, 1960), pp. 77-104.)

The Marriage of Milord Mississippi (Die Ehe des Herrn Mississippi)

Bauland, Peter. *The hooded eagle,* pp. 197, 198-199.

Diller, Edward. "Despair and the Paradox: Friedrich Dürrenmatt." *Drama Survey,* vol. 5, no. 2 (Summer, 1966), pp. 132-133.

Heilman, Robert B. "Tragic Elements in a Dürrenmatt Comedy." *Modern Drama,* vol. 10, no. 1 (May, 1967), pp. 11-16.

Hirschbach, Frank D. "New Directions in German Comedy." *Drama Survey,* vol. 1, no. 2 (Oct., 1961), pp. 195-213.

Klarmann, Adolf D. "Friedrich Dürrenmatt and the Tragic Sense of Comedy." *In:* Bogard, Travis, and Oliver, William I., eds. *Modern drama; essays in criticism,* pp. 114-123. (Reprinted from *Tulane Drama Rev.,* vol. 4, no. 4 (May, 1960), pp. 77-104.)

Lumley, Frederick. *New trends in 20th century drama,* pp. 241-242.

Phelps, Leland R. "Dürrenmatt's *Die Ehe des Herrn Mississippi:* The Revision of a Play." *Modern Drama,* vol. 8, no. 2 (Sept., 1965), pp. 156-160.

Wellwarth, George E. "Friedrich Dürrenmatt and Max Frisch: Two Views of the Drama." *Tulane Drama Rev.* vol. 6, no. 3 (Mar., 1962), pp. 14-42.

Wellwarth, George. *The theatre of protest and paradox,* pp. 140, 145-149, 162.

Der Meteor

Regensteiner, Henry. Review in English of the play published in German in Zurich (*Die Arche,* 1966). *Books Abroad,* vol. 41, no. 1 (Winter, 1967), p. 66.

Operation Wega (Das Unternehmen der Wega)

Wellwarth, George. *The theatre of protest and paradox,* pp. 154-157.

The Physicists (Die Physiker)

Bauland, Peter. *The hooded eagle,* pp. 205-206.

Chiari, J. *Landmarks of contemporary drama,* pp. 187-188.

Lumley, Frederick. *New trends in 20th century drama,* pp. 244-245.

Wellwarth, George. *The theatre of protest and paradox,* pp. 157-160.

Romulus the Great (Romulus der Grosse)

Bauland, Peter. *The hooded eagle,* pp. 204-205.

Klarmann, Adolf D. "Friedrich Dürrenmatt and the Tragic Sense of Comedy." *In:* Bogard, Travis and Oliver, William I., eds. *Modern drama; essays in criticism,* pp. 113-114. (Reprinted from *Tulane Drama Rev.,* vol. 4, no. 4 (May, 1960), pp. 77-104.)

Lumley, Frederick. *New trends in 20th century drama,* p. 241.

Wellwarth, George E. "Friedrich Dürrenmatt and Max Frisch: Two Views of the Drama." *Tulane Drama Rev.* vol. 6, no. 3 (Mar., 1962), pp. 14-42.

Wellwarth, George. *The theatre of protest and paradox,* pp. 141-145.

The Visit (The Visit of the Old Lady) (Der Besuch der Alten Dame)

Askew, Melvin W. "Dürrenmatt's *The Visit of the Old Lady.*" *Tulane Drama Rev.,* vol. 5 no. 4 (June, 1961), pp. 89-105.

Bauland, Peter. *The hooded eagle,* pp. 173, 198-202.

Cassell, Richard A. *What is the play?* pp. 562, 618-620.

Dürrenmatt, Friedrich, (Interview with Horst Bienek.) *In:* Wager, Walter, ed. *The playwrights speak,* pp. 80-83.

Dürrenmatt, Freidrich. "A Note on *The Visit of the Old Lady.*" *In:* Block, Haskell, and Salinger, Herman, eds. *Creative vision,* pp. 195-197.

Eustis, Morton. "The Actor Attacks His Part; Morton Eustis Interviews Lynn Fontanne and Alfred Lunt." *In:* Goodman, Randolph, *Drama on stage,* pp. 395-401. (Reprinted from *Theatre Arts,* 1936.)

Fickert, Kurt J. "Dürrenmatt's *The Visit* and Job." *Books Abroad,* vol. 41, no. 4 (Autumn, 1967), pp. 389-392.

Gascoigne, Bamber. *Twentieth-century drama,* pp. 194-195.

Gassner, John. *Theatre at the crossroads,* pp. 271-273.

Goodman, Randolph, "Claire Zachanassian in Norway; An Interview with Lillebil Ibsen." *In:* Goodman, Randolph. *Drama on stage,* pp. 418-419.

Goodman, Randolph. "Conceiving *The Visit;* An Interview with Friedrich Dürrenmatt." *In:* Goodman, Randolph. *Drama on stage,* pp. 386-389.

Goodman, Randolph. "Costumes for Lynn Fontanne; An Interview with Antonio del Castillo." *In:* Goodman, Randolph. *Drama on stage,* pp. 412-416.

Goodman, Randolph. "Creating the Role of Claire; An Interview with Therese Giehse." *In:* Goodman, Randolph. *Drama on stage,* pp. 416-419.

Goodman, Randolph. "Directing *The Visit;* An Interview with Peter Brook." *In:* Goodman, Randolph. *Drama on stage,* pp. 401-405.

Goodman, Randolph. *Drama on stage, pp.* 379-386.

Goodman, Randolph. "Publicizing *The Visit;* An Interview with Barry Hyams." *In:* Goodman, Randolph. *Drama on stage,* pp. 419-423.

Goodman, Randolph. "Scenery for *The Visit;* An Interview with Teo Otto." *In:* Goodman, Randolph. *Drama on stage,* pp. 410-412.

Goodman, Randolph. "Stage Managing *The Visit;* An Interview with Mary Lynn." In: Goodman, Randolph. *Drama on stage,* pp. 405-410.

Goodman, Randolph, *"The Visit* Undergoes a Sea Change; An Interview with Maurice Valency." *In:* Goodman, Randolph. *Drama on stage,* pp. 389-395.

Guth, Hans P. "Dürrenmatt's *Visit:* The Play Behind the Play." *Symposium,* vol. 16 (1962), pp. 94-102.

Heilman, Robert B. *Tragedy and melodrama,* pp. 42, 44-47, 60-61, 80, 229, 240, 291.

Klarmann, Adolf D. "Friedrich Dürrenmatt and the Tragic Sense of Comedy." *In:* Bogard, Travis, and Oliver, William I., eds. *Modern drama; essays in criticism, pp. 126-132.* (Reprinted from *Tulane Drama Rev.,* vol. 4, no. 4 (May, 1960), pp. 77-104.)

Loram, Ian C. *"Der Besuch der alten Dame* and *The Visit,"* *Monatshefte,* vol. 53 (1961), pp. 15-21.

Lumley, Frederick. *New trends in 20th century drama,* pp. 243-244.

Pfefferkorn, Eli. "Dürrenmatt's Mass Play." *Modern Drama,* vol. 12, no. 1 (May, 1969), pp. 30-37.

Rosenberg, James. "European Influences." *In: American theatre,* pp. 57, 62-63.

Wellwarth, George E. "Friedrich Dürrenmatt and Max Frisch: Two Views of the Drama." *Tulane Drama Rev.,* vol. 6, no. 3 (Mar., 1962), pp. 14-42.

Wellwarth, George. *The theatre of protest and paradox,* pp. 136-140.

SIDNEY EASTON

Miss Trudie Fair

Mitchell, Loften. *Black drama,* pp. 159-162.

RICHARD EBERHART 1904-

The Visionary Farms

Donoghue, Denis. *The third voice: modern British and American verse drama.* pp. 223-235.

JOSE ECHEGARAY 1832-1916

General

Duran, Manuel, and Michael Nimetz. "Spain and Spanish America." *Books Abroad,* vol. 41, no. 1 (Winter, 1967), pp. 23-24.

Goldberg, Isaac. *The drama of transition,* pp. 61-74.

Marble, Annie Russell. *The Nobel Prize winners in literature,* pp. 239-246.

Miller, Nellie Burget. *The living drama,* pp. 355-356.

Newberry, Wilma. "Echegaray and Pirandello." *PMLA,* vol. 81 (March, 1966), pp. 123-129.

Shaw, George Bernard. *Dramatic opinions and essays* (New York, 1906), vol. 2, pp. 186-187.

Warren, L.A. *Modern Spanish literature,* vol. 2, pp. 542-548.

Young, John Ripley. *José Echegaray: a study of his dramatic technique.* Ph.D. University of Illinois, 1938.

The Cleansing Stain (Mancha Que Limpia)

MacCarthy, Desmond. *Drama,* pp. 131-135.

The Great Galeoto

Miller, Nellie Burget. *The living drama,* pp. 356-360.

GUNTER EICH 1907-

General

Fowler, F.M. "Günter Eich." *In:* Keith-Smith, B., ed. *Essays on contemporary German literature* (German Men of Letters, Vol. IV), pp. 89-107.

Die Andere und Ich

Fowler, F.M. "Günter Eich." *In:* Keith-Smith, B., ed. *Essays on contemporary German literature* (German Men of Letters, Vol. IV), pp. 94-95.

Geh Nicht Nach El Kuwehd

Fowler, F.M. "Günter Eich." *In:* Keith-Smith, B., ed. *Essays on contemporary German literature* (German Men of Letters, Vol. IV), pp. 93-94.

Das Jahr Lazertis

Fowler, F.M. "Günter Eich." *In:* Keith-Smith, B., ed. *Essays or contemporary German literature* (German Men of Letters, Vol. IV) pp. 95-97.

Die Madchen aus Viterbo

Fowler, F.M. "Günter Eich." *In:* Keith-Smith B., ed. *Essays or contemporary German literature* (German Men of Letters, Vol. IV) pp. 97-98.

Traüme, 1951 (radio play)

Fowler, F.M. "Günter Eich." *In:* Keith-Smith, B., ed. *Essays or contemporary German literature* (German Men of Letters, Vol. IV) pp. 89-93.

SAMUEL EICHELBAUM 1894-

General

Anderson Imbert, Enrique. *Spanish-American literature: a history,* pp 419-420.

Apstein, Theodore. "Samuel Eichelbaum, Argentine Playwright." *Books Abroad,* vol. 19 (1945), pp. 237-241.

House, Roy Temple. *Books Abroad,* vol. 18 (1944), p. 68.

Jones, W.K. *Behind Spanish American footlights,* pp. 134-137.

THOMAS STEARNS ELIOT 1888-1965

General

Adler, Jacob H. "A Source for Eliot in Shaw." *Notes & Queries,* vol 14 (1967), pp. 256-257.

Arrowsmith, William. "The Comedy of T.S. Eliot." *In:* Bogard, Travis and Oliver, William I., eds. *Modern drama; essays in criticism,* pp 134-151. (Reprinted from *English Institute essays: English stag comedy,* W.K. Wimsatt, ed. N.Y., Columbia Univ. Press, 1954.)

Aylen, Leo. *Greek tragedy and the modern world,* pp. 201-202 216-217, 221-222, 320-323.

Bradbook, M.C. *English dramatic form,* pp. 162-177.

Broussard, Louis. *American drama...,* pp. 69-91.

Browne, E. Martin. "T.S. Eliot in the Theatre: The Director' Memories." *Sewanee Rev.,* vol. 74, no. 1 (Jan.-Mar., 1966), pp 136-152.

Carnell, Corbin S. "Creation's Lonely Flesh: T.S. Eliot and Christopher Fry on the Life of the Senses." *Modern Drama*, vol. 6 (1963-64), pp. 141-149.

Chiari, J. *Landmarks of contemporary drama*, pp. 85-101.

Ellmann, Richard. "Possum's Conversion." *In:* Ellmann, R. *Eminent domain*, pp. 89-95.

Fabricius, Johannes. *The unconscious and Mr. Eliot*, pp. 123-130.

Fergusson, Francis. *The human image in dramatic literature*, pp. 41-43, 60-71, 98-104.

Fraser, G.S. *The modern writer and his world*, pp. 219-220.

Gardner, Helen. "The Comedies of T.S. Eliot." *In:* Tate, Allen, ed. *T.S. Eliot*, pp. 159-163. *Essays by Divers Hands*, vol. 34 (1966), pp. 55-73, *Sewanee Rev.*, vol. 74, no. 1 (Jan.-Mar., 1966), pp. 153-175.

Gascoigne, Bamber. *Twentieth-century drama*, pp. 158-165.

Gassner, John. *The theatre in our times*, pp. 267-281.

Harding, D.W. "Progression of Theme in Eliot's Modern Plays." *Kenyon Rev.*, vol. 18, no. 3 (Summer, 1956), pp. 337-360.

Howarth, Herbert. "Eliot and Hofmannsthal." *South Atlantic Q.*, vol. 59 (Fall, 1960), pp. 500-509.

Johnston, William. "The Mysticism of T.S. Eliot." *In:* Hirai, Masao, ed. *T.S. Eliot, a tribute from Japan*, pp. 144-166.

Kaul, R.K. "Rhyme and Blank Verse in Drama: A Note on Eliot." *English*, vol. 15 (1964), pp. 96-99.

Knight, G. Wilson. *The golden labyrinth*, pp. 362-366.

Jarrett-Kerr, M. "The Poetic Drama of T.S. Eliot." *English Studies in Africa*, vol. 2, no. 1 (Mar., 1959), pp. 16-33.

Lewis, Allan. *The contemporary theatre*, pp. 143-168.

Lightfoot, Marjorie J. "Charting Eliot's Course in Drama." *Educational Theatre J.*, vol. 20, no. 2 (May, 1968), pp. 186-197.

Lumley, Frederick. *New trends in 20th century drama*, pp. 126-136.

Malawsky, Beryl Y. "T.S. Eliot. A Check-List: 1952-1964." *Bulletin of Bibliography*, vol. 25 (1967), pp. 59-61, 69.

Pallette, Drew B. "Eliot, Fry, and Broadway." *Arizona*, vol. 11 (1955), pp. 342-347.

Rahv, Philip. *The myth and the powerhouse,* pp. 185-190.

Rahv, Philip. "T.S. Eliot: The Poet as Playwright." *In:* Rahv. P. *Image and idea,* pp. 197-202.

Rillie, John A.M. "Melodramatic Device in T.S. Eliot." *Rev. of English Studies,* n.s., vol. 13, no. 51 (1962), pp. 267-281.

Roby, Robert C. "T.S. Eliot and the Elizabethan and Jacobean dramatists." Ph.D., Northwestern University, 1950.

Rometch, Carol Sue. "The search for form: the verse and dramas of T.S. Eliot." M.A., Montana State University, 1959.

Styan, J.L., *The dark comedy,* 2nd ed., pp. 12, 52, 118, 158-166, 217, 229, 230, 286.

Whitfield, J.H. "Pirandello and T.S. Eliot: An Essay in Counterpoint." *English Miscellany,* vol. 9 (1958), pp. 329-357.

Williams, Raymond. *Drama from Ibsen to Eliot,* pp. 223-246.

Williams, Raymond. *Drama in performance,* pp. 110-115.

Williams, Raymond. *Modern tragedy,* pp. 159-167, 173.

The Cocktail Party

Arrowsmith, William. "Transfiguration in Eliot and Euripides." *Sewanee Rev.,* vol. 63 (1955), pp. 421-442. (Reprinted in *English Institute essays, 1954,* pp. 148-172.)

Aylen, Leo. *Greek tragedy and the modern world,* pp. 201, 295, 323, 331-336.

Barth, J. Robert, S.J. "T.S. Eliot's Image of Man; A Thematic Study of His Drama." *Renascence,* vol. 14, no. 3 (Spring, 1962), pp. 126-138, 165.

Bentley, Eric. *The dramatic event,* pp. 230-233.

Brandt, G.W. "Realism and Parables." *In:* Brown, John Russell and Bernard Harris, eds. *Contemporary theatre,* pp. 44-49.

Broussard, Louis. *American drama...,* pp. 78-84.

Brown, John Mason. *Still seeing things,* pp. 167-174.

Brown, John Mason. "Two Plays by T.S. Eliot." *In:* Brown, John Mason. *Dramatis personae,* pp. 190-195.

Browne, E. Martin. *The making of a play: T.S. Eliot's The Cocktail Party.*

Browne, E. Martin. "T.S. Eliot in the Theatre." *In:* Tate, Allen, ed. *T.S. Eliot,* pp. 127-130.

Cattaui, Georges. *T.S. Eliot,* pp. 97-101.

Chiari, J. *Landmarks of contemporary drama,* pp. 96-98.

Clurman, Harold. *Lies like truth,* pp. 178-182.

Colby, Robert A. "The Three Worlds of *The Cocktail Party:* The Wit of T.S. Eliot." *Univ. of Toronto Q.,* vol. 24, no. 1, Oct., 1954, pp. 56-69.

Donoghue, Denis. *The third voice: modern British and American verse drama,* pp. 114-137, 238-240.

Eliot, T.S. *In* Cole, Toby, ed. *Playwrights on playwriting,* pp. 257-260. (Reprinted from T.S. Eliot, *Poetry and drama,* The First Theodore Spencer Memorial Lecture, November 12, 1950 (Cambridge, Mass.: Harvard University Press, c. 1951), pp. 23-44.)

Eliot, Thomas Stearns. *Poetry and drama,* pp. 38-40.

Fraser, G.S. *The modern writer and his world,* pp. 217-219.

Friedman, Maurice. *To deny our nothingness,* pp. 98-99, 103-104, 305.

Fukuda, Tsuneari. "God Present Though Absent, Reflections on *The Cocktail Party."* *In:* Hirai, Masao, ed. *T.S. Eliot, a tribute from Japan,* pp. 167-179.

Gardner, Helen. "The Comedies of T.S. Eliot." *In:* Tate, Allen, ed. *T.S. Eliot,* pp. 163-172.

Glicksberg, Charles I. "The Spirit of Irony in Eliot's Plays." *Prairie Schooner,* vol. 29 (1955), pp. 222-237.

Hanzo, Thomas. "Eliot and Kierkegaard: 'The Meaning of Happening in *The Cocktail Party."* *Modern Drama,* vol. 3, no. 1 (May, 1960), pp. 52-59.

Harding, D.W. *Experience into words; essays on poetry,* pp. 140-147, 155.

Heilman, Robert B. *"Alcestis* and *The Cocktail Party."* *Comparative Literature,* vol. 5, no. 2 (Spring, 1953), pp. 105-116.

Henn, T. R. *The harvest of tragedy,* pp. 225-231.

Hobson, Harold. *The theatre now,* pp. 5-12.

Hovey, Richard B. "Psychiatrist and Saint in *The Cocktail Party.*" *In:* Manheim, Leonard and Eleanor, *Hidden patterns,* pp. 230-242. *Also in: Literature and Psychology,* vol. 9 (1959), pp. 51-55.

Kline, Peter. "The Spiritual Center in Eliot's Plays." *Kenyon Rev.* vol. 21, no. 3 (1959), pp. 471-472.

Lawlor, John. "The Formal Achievement of *The Cocktail Party.*" *Virginia Q. Rev.,* vol. 30, no. 3 (Summer, 1954), pp. 431-451.

Lewis, Allan. *The contemporary theatre,* pp. 150-163, 165-169.

Lightfoot, Marjorie J. "The Uncommon Cocktail Party." *Modern Drama,* vol. 11, no. 4 (Feb., 1969), pp. 382-395.

Lumley, Frederick. *New trends in 20th century drama,* pp. 127, 133-134, 135, 136.

Lumley, Frederick. *Trends in 20th century drama,* pp. 87-89.

McCollom, William G. *Tragedy,* pp. 239-241.

Muller, Herbert J. *The spirit of tragedy,* pp. 299-300.

Rahv, Philip. *The myth and the power house,* pp. 190-192.

Reckford, Kenneth J. "Heracles and Mr. Eliot." *Comparative Literature,* vol. 16, no. 1 (Winter, 1964), pp. 1-18.

Rexine, John E. "Classical and Christian Foundations of T.S. Eliot's *Cocktail Party.*" *Books Abroad,* vol. 39, no. 1 (Winter, 1965), pp. 21-26.

Robins, Russell H. "A Possible Analogue for *The Cocktail Party.*" *English Studies,* vol. 34 (1953), pp. 165-167.

Schwartz, Edward. "Eliot's *Cocktail Party* and the New Humanism." *Philological Q.,* vol. 32, no. 1 (Jan., 1953), pp. 58-68.

Scott, Nathan A. "The Theatre of T.S. Eliot." *In:* Scott, Nathan A. *Man in the modern theatre,* pp. 22-36.

Scruggs, Charles E. "T.S. Eliot and J.-P. Sartre, Toward the Definition of the Human Condition." *Appalachian State Teachers College Faculty Publications,* 1965, pp. 24-29.

Shuman, R. Baird. "Buddhistic Overtones in Eliot's *The Cocktail Party.*" *Modern Language Notes,* vol. 72, no. 6 (June, 1957), pp. 426-427.

Sievers, W. David. *Freud on Broadway,* pp. 436-437.

Spanos, William V. *The Christian tradition in modern British verse drama,* pp. 194-195, 220-224, 238-240, 243-244.

Styan, J.L. *The dark comedy,* 2nd ed., pp. 4, 34, 164, 165, 265-266, 273, 283, 294.

Styan, J.L. *The elements of drama,* pp. 274-284.

Unger, Leonard. *T.S. Eliot, moments and patterns,* pp. 14, 29-30, 116, 119, 127-128, 135-139, 167.

Weales, Gerald. *Religion in modern English drama,* pp. 197-200, 202.

Williams, Raymond. *Drama from Ibsen to Eliot,* pp. 237-244.

Williams, Raymond. *Modern tragedy,* pp. 159-160, 163-167.

Winter, Jack. "Prufrockism in *The Cocktail Party.*" *Modern Language Q.,* vol. 22, no. 2 (June, 1961), pp. 135-148.

The Confidential Clerk

Arrowsmith, William. "Transfiguration in Eliot and Euripides," *Sewanee Rev.,* vol. 63 (1955), pp. 421-442. (Reprinted in *English Institute essays, 1954,* pp. 148-172.)

Aylen, Leo. *Greek tragedy and the modern world,* pp. 323, 331, 336.

Barth, J. Robert, S.J. "T.S. Eliot's Image of Man: A Thematic Study of His Drama." *Renascence,* vol. 14, no. 3 (Spring, 1962), pp. 126-138, 165.

Bentley, Eric. *The dramatic event,* pp. 195-199.

Broussard, Louis. *American drama...,* pp. 84-88.

Brown, John Mason. "Two Plays by T.S. Elliot." *In:* Brown, John Mason. *Dramatis personae,* pp. 195-199.

Brown, Spencer. "T.S. Eliot's Latest Poetic Drama." *Commentary,* vol. 17 (Apr., 1954), pp. 367-372.

Browne, E. Martin. "T.S. Eliot in the Theatre." *In:* Tate, Allen, ed. *T.S. Eliot,* P. 130.

Cattaui, Georges. *T.S. Eliot,* pp. 101-103.

Clurman, Harold. *Lies like truth,* pp. 182-184.

Dobree, Bonamy. *"The Confidential Clerk." Sewanee Rev.,* vol. 62, (1954), pp. 117-131.

Dobree, Bonamy. *The lamp and the lute, studies in seven authors,* 2nd ed., pp. 122-141. (Reprinted from *Sewanee Rev.* (Winter), 1954.)

Donoghue, Denis. *The third voice: modern British and American verse drama,* pp. 138-157, 269-271.

Fergusson, Francis. *The human image in dramatic literature,* pp. 60-67, 69.

Gardner, Helen. "The Comedies of T.S. Eliot." *In:* Tate, Allen, ed. *T.S. Eliot,* pp. 172-177.

Glicksberg, Charles I. "The Journey That Must Be Taken: Spiritual Quest in T.S. Eliot's Plays." *Southwest Rev.,* vol. 40 (1955), pp. 203-210.

Glicksberg, Charles I. "The Spirit of Irony in Elliot's Plays." *Prairie Schooner,* vol. 29 (1955), pp. 222-237.

Harding, D.W. *Experience into words; essays on poetry,* pp. 147-156.

Lumley, Frederick. *Trends in 20th century drama,* pp. 89-90.

Styan, J.L. *The dark comedy,* 2nd ed., pp. 165, 273.

Styan, J.L. *The elements of drama,* pp. 96-98.

Unger, Leonard. *T.S. Eliot, moments and patterns,* pp. 12, 14, 30, 32, 33, 116, 127-129, 136-140, 177-178.

Unger, Leonard. "T.S. Eliot's Images of Awareness." *In:* Tate, Allen, ed. *T.S. Eliot,* pp. 221-222.

Weales, Gerald. *Religion in modern English drama,* pp. 200-203, 204.

Williamson, Audrey. *Contemporary theatre, 1953-1956,* pp. 22-26.

The Elder Statesman

Aylen, Leo. *Greek tragedy and the modern world,* pp. 323-324, 332, 336-337.

Barth, J. Robert, S.J. "T.S. Eliot's Image of Man: A Thematic Study of His Drama." *Renascence,* vol. 14, no. 3 (Spring, 1962), pp. 126-138, 165.

Broussard, Louis. *American drama...,* pp. 89-91.

Browne, E. Martin. "T.S. Eliot in the Theatre." *In:* Tate, Allen, ed. *T.S. Eliot,* pp. 131-132.

Cattaui, Georges. *T.S. Eliot,* pp. 103-104.

Dobrée, Bonamy. *The lamp and the lute, studies in seven authors,* 2nd ed., pp. 141-149. (Reprinted from *Sewanee Rev.* (Winter), 1959.)

Donoghue, Denis. *The third voice: modern British and American verse drama,* pp. 158-168.

Fleming, Rudd. *"The Elder Statesman* and Eliot's Programme for the Metier of Poetry." *Wisconsin Studies in Contemporary Literature,* vol. 2, no. 1 (Winter, 1961), pp. 54-64.

Gardner, Helen. "The Comedies of T.S. Eliot." *In:* Tate, Allen, ed. *T.S. Eliot,* pp. 177-181.

Harding, D.W. *Experience into words; essays on poetry,* pp. 156-162.

Lumley, Frederick. *New trends in 20th century drama,* pp. 135-136.

Spanos, William V. *The Christian tradition in modern British verse drama,* pp. 230-238, 241-251.

Stanford, Derek. *Contemporary Rev.,* vol. 194 (Oct., 1958), pp. 199-201.

Unger, Leonard. *T.S. Eliot, moments and patterns,* pp. 15, 30, 183-184.

Weales, Gerald. *Religion in modern English drama,* pp. 203-204.

The Family Reunion

Avery, Helen P. *"The Family Reunion* Reconsidered." *Educational Theatre J.,* vol. 17 (1965), pp. 10-18.

Aylen, Leo. *Greek tragedy and the modern world,* pp. 224, 323-324, 332-334.

Barth, J. Robert, S.J. "T.S. Eliot's Image of Man; A Thematic Study of His Drama." *Renascence,* vol. 14, no. 3 (Spring, 1962), pp. 126-138, 165.

Broussard, Louis. *American drama...,* pp. 74-78, 81-84.

Browne, E. Martin. "T.S. Eliot in the Theatre." *In:* Tate, Allen, ed. *T.S. Eliot,* pp. 124-127.

Cattaui, Georges. *T.S. Eliot,* pp. 95-97.

Chiari, J. *Landmarks of contemporary drama,* pp. 95-96.

Dobrée, Bonamy. "T.S. Eliot; a Personal Reminiscence." *In:* Tate, Allen, ed. *T.S. Eliot,* pp. 84-85.

Donoghue, Denis. *The third voice: modern British and American verse drama,* pp. 94-113.

Eliot T.S. *In:* Cole, Toby, ed. *Playwrights on playwriting* pp. 254-257. (Reprinted from T.S. Eliot, *Poetry and drama,* The First Theodore Spencer Memorial Lecture, Nov. 12, 1950 (Cambridge, Mass., Harvard University Press, (1951), pp. 23-44.)

Eliot, Thomas Stearns. *Poetry and drama,* pp. 32-38.

Fraser, G.S. *The modern writer and his world,* pp. 214-217.

Gaskell, Ronald. *"The Family Reunion." Essays in Criticism,* vol. 12, no. 3 (July, 1962), pp. 292-301.

Glicksberg, Charles I. "The Journey That Must Be Taken: Spiritual Quest in T.S. Eliot's Plays." *Southwest Rev.,* vol. 40 (1955), pp. 203-210.

Glicksberg, Charles I. "The Spirit of Irony in Eliot's Plays." *Prairie Schooner,* vol. 29 (1955), pp. 222-237.

Greenwood, Ormerod. *The playwright,* pp. 103-109.

Harding, D.W. *Experience into words; essays on poetry,* pp. 134-140, 153, 155.

Heilman, Robert B. *Tragedy and melodrama,* pp. 14, 97, 120, 157-159, 231, 310.

Henn, T.R. The *harvest of tragedy,* pp. 222-225.

Isaacs, Jennifer I. "Eliot the Poet-Playwright as Seen in *The Family Reunion." English,* vol. 16, no. 93 (Autumn, 1966), pp. 100-105.

Kline, Peter. "The Spiritual Center in Eliot's Plays." *Kenyon Rev.* vol. 21, no. 3 (1959), pp. 469-471.

Leaska, Mitchell A. *The voice of tragedy,* pp. 256-261.

Lightfoot, Marjorie J. *"Purgatory and The Family Reunion:* In Pursuit of Prosodie Description." *Modern Drama,* vol. 7, no. 3 (Dec., 1964), pp. 256-266.

Lumley, Frederick. *New trends in 20th century drama,* pp. 126, 132-133, 135.

Matthiessen, F.O. "The Plays of T.S. Eliot." *In:* Freedman, Morris, ed. *Essays in the modern drama,* pp. 264-279. (Reprinted from *The achievement of T.S. Eliot* by F.O. Matthiessen, pp. 155-176.)

McCollom, William G. *Tragedy,* pp. 236-239, 243.

Merchant, W. Moelwyn. *Creed and drama,* pp. 88-97.

Muller, Herbert J. *The spirit of tragedy,* pp. 296-298.

Palmer, Richard E. "Existentialism in T.S. Eliot's *The Family Reunion.*" *Modern Drama*, vol. 5, no. 2 (Sept., 1962), pp. 174-186.

Peacock, Ronald. *The poet in the theatre*, pp. 3-25.

Peacock, Ronald. "Public and Private Problems in Modern Drama." *Tulane Drama Rev.*, vol. 3, no. 3 (Mar., 1959), pp. 69-72.

Prior, Moody E. *The language of tragedy*, pp. 360-367.

Ramsey, Warren. "The *Oresteia* since Hofmannsthal: Images and Emphases." *Revue de Littérature Comparée*, vol. 38 (1964), pp. 370-373.

Scrimgeour, C.A. *"The Family Reunion."* *Essays in Criticism*, vol. 13 (1963), pp. 104-106.

Spanos, William V. *The Christian tradition in modern British verse drama*, pp. 184-218, 220, 222-223.

Spanos, William V. "T.S. Eliot's *The Family Reunion:* The Strategy of Sacramental Transfiguration." *Drama Survey, vol. 4*, no. 1 (Spring, 1965), pp. 3-27.

Steiner, George. *The death of tragedy*, pp. 327-330.

Styan, J.L. *The dark comedy*, 2nd ed., pp. 3-4, 161-164, 165.

Unger, Leonard. *T.S. Eliot, moments and patterns*, pp. 12-14, 16, 32, 38, 82-87, 96, 116, 119, 120, 126, 132-137, 152, 181-183.

Unger, Leonard. "T.S. Eliot's Images of Awareness." *In:* Tate, Allen, ed. *T.S. Eliot*, pp. 226-228.

Ward, Anne. "Speculations on Eliot's Time-World: An Analysis of *The Family Reunion* in Relation to Hulme and Bergson." *American Literature*, vol. 21 (1949-50), pp. 18-34.

Weales, Gerald. *Religion in modern English drama*, pp. 194-197.

Williams, Raymond. *Drama from Ibsen to Eliot*, pp. 232-237.

Williams, Raymond. *Drama in performance* (new ed.), pp. 135-148.

Williamson, Audrey. *Contemporary theatre, 1953-1956*, pp. 98-100.

Murder in the Cathedral

Adams, John F. "The Fourth Temptation in *Murder in the Cathedral.*" *Modern Drama*, vol. 5, no. 4 (Feb., 1963), pp. 381-388.

Aylen, Leo. *Greek tragedy and the modern world*, pp. 162, 208, 224, 323-331, 334, 337.

Barth, J. Robert, S.J. "T.S. Eliot's Image of Man: A Thematic Study of His Drama." *Renascence,* vol. 14, no. 3 (Spring, 1962), pp. 126-138, 165.

Boulton, J.T. "The Use of Original Sources of the Development of a Theme: Eliot in *Murder in the Cathedral."* *English,* vol. 11, no. 61 (Spring, 1956), pp. 2-8.

Broussard, Louis. *American drama...,* pp. 71-74.

Browne, E. Martin. "T.S. Eliot in the Theatre." *In:* Tate, Allen, ed. *T.S. Eliot,* pp. 121-124.

Cattaui, Georges. *T.S. Eliot,* pp. 91-95.

Chiari, Joseph. *Landmarks of contemporary drama,* pp. 91-94, 95.

Cohn, Ruby, ed. *Twentieth century drama,* pp. 173-174.

Cubeta, Paul M. *Modern drama for analysis,* pp. 434-443.

Dobrée, Bonamy. "T.S. Eliot; a Personal Reminiscence." *In:* Tate, Allen, ed. *T.S. Eliot,* p. 84.

Donoghue, Denis. *The third voice: modern British and American verse drama,* pp. 76-93.

Eliot, T.S. *In:* Cole, Toby, ed. *Playwrights on playwriting,* pp. 250-254. (Reprinted from T.S. Eliot, *Poetry and drama,* The First Theodore Spencer Memorial Lecture, Nov., 12, 1950 (Cambridge Mass., Harvard University Press (1951), pp. 23-44.)

Eliot, Thomas Stearns. *Poetry and drama,* pp. 25-32.

Fergusson, Francis. *The idea of a theater,* pp. 222-234.

Fraser, G.S. *The modern writer and his world,* pp. 213-215.

Friedman, Maurice. *To deny our nothingness,* pp. 99, 104-108, 120.

Gassner, John. "Broadway in Review." *Educational Theatre J.,* vol. 18, no. 3 (Oct., 1966), p. 278.

Geraldine, Sister M., C.S.J. "The Rhetoric of Repetition in *Murder in the Cathedral."* *Renascence,* vol. 19 (1967), pp. 132-141.

Gerstenberger, Donna. "The Saint and the Circle: The Dramatic Potential of an Image." *Criticism,* vol. 2, no. 4 (Fall, 1960), pp. 336-341.

Glicksberg, Charles I. "The Journey That Must Be Taken: Spiritual Quest in T.S. Eliot's Plays," *Southwest Rev.,* vol. 40 (1955), pp. 203-210.

Glicksberg, Charles I. "The Spirit of Irony in Eliot's Plays." *Prairie Schooner,* vol. 29 (1955), pp. 222-237.

Hathorn, Richmond Y. "Eliot's *Murder in the Cathedral,* Myth and History." *In:* his *Tragedy, myth and mystery,* pp. 195-216.

Hathorn, Richmond Y. *Tragedy, myth, and mystery,* pp. 195-216.

Henn, T.R. *The harvest of tragedy,* pp. 220-222, 228-229.

Hobson, Harold. *Theatre,* pp. 45-46.

Kantra, Robert A. "Satiric Theme and Structure in *Murder in the Cathedral.*" *Modern Drama,* vol. 10, no. 4 (Feb., 1968), pp. 387-393.

Kline, Peter. "The Spiritual Center in Eliot's Plays." *Kenyon Rev.,* vol. 21, no. 3 (1959), pp. 457-469.

Leaska, Mitchell A. *The voice of tragedy,* pp. 249-256.

Lumley, Frederick. *New trends in 20th century drama,* pp. 126, 127-128, 132, 288.

Lumley, Frederick. *Trends in 20th century drama,* pp. 83-87.

Maccoby, H.Z. "The Notes on *Murder in the Cathedral.*" *Notes & Queries,* vol. 14 (1967), pp. 253-256.

McCollom, William G. *Tragedy,* pp. 232-236.

Martz, Louis L. "The Saint as Tragic Hero." *In:* Kaufmann, R.J. *G.B. Shaw, a collection of critical essays,* pp. 143-161. (Reprinted from Brooks, Cleanth, ed. *Tragic themes in Western literature,* pp. 150-177.) (Original title: "The Saint as Tragic Hero: *Saint Joan* and *Murder in the Cathedral.*")

Matthiessen, F.O. "The Plays of T.S. Eliot." *In:* Freedman, Morris, ed. *Essays in the modern drama,* pp. 264-279. (Reprinted from *The achievement of T.S. Eliot* by F.O. Matthiessen, pp. 155-176.)

Muller, Herbert J. *"The spirit of tragedy,* pp. 295-296.

Peacock, Ronald. *"The poet in the theatre,* pp. 3-25.

Phillips, Elizabeth C. *Modern American drama,* pp. 106-107.

Pickering, Jerry V. "Form as Agent: Eliot's *Murder in the Cathedral.*" *Educational Theatre J.,* vol. 20, no. 2 (May, 1968), pp. 198-207.

Prior, Moody E. *The language of tragedy,* pp. 353-360.

Roy, Emil. "The Becket Plays: Eliot, Fry, and Anouilh." *Modern Drama,* vol. 8, no. 3 (Dec., 1965), pp. 268-276.

213

Scott, Nathan A. "The Theatre of T.S. Eliot." *In:* Scott, Nathan A. *Man in the modern theatre,* pp. 16-22.

Siddiqui, M.N. "The Ambivalence of Motives in *Murder in the Cathedral." Osmania J. of English Studies,* Osmania Univ., Hyderabad, vol. 5 (1965), pp. 1-11.

Spanos, William V. *The Christian tradition in modern British verse drama,* pp. 39-40, 80-104, 187-190.

Speaight, Robert. "With Becket in *Murder in the Cathedral." Sewanee Rev.,* vol. 74, no. 1 (Jan.-Mar., 1966), pp. 176-187.

Tate, Allen, ed. *T.S. Eliot,* pp. 182-193.

Styan, J.L. *The dark comedy,* 2nd ed., pp. 33, 115, 160-161, 163.

Styan, J.L. *The elements of drama,* pp. 135-140.

Unger, Leonard. *T.S. Eliot, moments and patterns,* pp. 14, 107-108, 115, 119, 125-126, 132-134, 167-170, 181.

Unger, Leonard. "T.S. Eliot's Images of Awareness." *In:* Tate, Allen, ed. *T.S. Eliot,* pp. 225-226.

Weales, Gerald. *Religion in modern English drama,* pp. 189-194.

Williams, Raymond. *Drama from Ibsen to Eliot,* pp. 227-231.

The Rock

Cattaui, Georges. *T.S. Eliot,* pp. 91.

Spanos, William V. *The Christian tradition in modern British verse drama,* pp. 63-68, 331-332.

Weales, Gerald. *Religion in modern English drama,* pp. 187-9.

Sweeney Agonistes

Eliot, T.S. Letter to Hallie Flanagan dated March 18, 1933. *In:* H. Flanagan. *Dynamo,* New York, 1943, pp. 82-84.

Fabricius, Johannes. *The unconscious and Mr. Eliot,* p. 123 and note, pp. 123-124.

Holt, Charles Loyd. "On Structure and *Sweeney Agonistes." Modern Drama,* vol. 10, no. 1 (May, 1967), pp. 43-47.

Williams, Raymond. *Drama from Ibsen to Eliot,* pp. 224-225.

JOSE F. ELIZONDO 1880-

General

González Peña, Carlos. *History of Mexican literature,* pp. 323, 374-375.

SHUSAKU ENDO

Ogon No Kuni

Saito, Mother M. "Contemporary Japanese Theatre: Symbolism in Shusaku Endo's *Ogon No Kuni.*" *Modern Drama,* vol. 10, no. 4 (Feb., 1968), pp. 397-400.

MILTON ERSKINE

A Time of the Key

Sainer, Arthur. *The sleepwalker and the assassin, a view of the comtemporary theatre,* pp. 81-82.

ST. JOHN ERVINE 1883-

General

Hogan, Robert. *After the Irish renaissance,* pp. 30-31.

Malone, Andrew E. *The Irish drama,* pp. 198-199.

Nicoll, Allardyce. *British drama,* pp. 269-271.

Williams, Harold. *Modern English writers,* p. 220.

The Critics

Malone, Andrew E. *The Irish drama,* p. 202.

Jane Clegg

Hamilton, Clayton. *Seen on the stage,* pp. 164-175.

John Ferguson

Hamilton, Clayton. *Seen on the stage,* pp. 164-175.

Malone, Andrew E. *The Irish drama,* pp. 202-205.

The Magnanimous Lover

Malone, Andrew E. *The Irish drama,* pp. 200-201.

Mixed Marriage

Malone, Andrew E. *The Irish drama,* pp. 199-200.

Private Enterprise

Hobson, Harold. *Theatre,* pp. 169-171.

NIKOLAI EVREINOV

General

Budel, Oscar. *Pirandello,* pp. 96-98.

The Merry Death

Goldberg, Isaac. *The drama of transition,* pp. 446-449.

Theatre of the Soul

Goldberg, Isaac. *The drama of transition.* pp, 442-446.

DIEGO FABBRI 1911-

General

Pandolfi, Vito. "Italian Theatre Since the War." *Tulane Drama Rev.,* vol. 8, no. 3 (Spring, 1964), pp. 94-95.

ALEXIS FAIKO

Man with the Portfolio

Block, Anita. *The changing world in plays and theatre,* pp. 386-389.

PADRAIC FALLON

General

Hogan, Robert. *After the Irish renaissance,* pp. 159-163.

Hogan, Robert G., ed. *Seven Irish plays, 1946-1964,* pp. 12-13.

FRANCIS EDWARDS FARAGOH

General

Knox, George A. *Dos Passos and "The Revolting Playwrights,"* p. 60.

Pinwheel

Faragoh, F.E. "Faragoh, Author of *Pinwheel,* Explains Himself." New York *Evening Post,* Mar. 4, 1927.

216

Knox, George A. *Dos Passos and "The Revolting Playwrights,"* pp. 106-113, 157, 162, 165, 170-171.

Lawson, John Howard. *Theory and technique of playwriting,* p. 241. *"Pinwheel* Through Other Eyes." *New York Sun,* Feb. 12, 1927.

Valgemae, Mardi. "Civil War Among the Expressionists: John Howard Lawson and the *Pinwheel* Controversy." *Educational Theatre J.,* vol. 20, no. 1 (Mar., 1968), pp. 8-14.

Watts, Richard, Jr. "Expressionism Again Becomes a Dramatic Form of Interest: With Opening of John Howard Lawson's New Play and the Controversy Over *Pinwheel,* the Theatrical Radicals Again Assume Importance." New York *Herald-Tribune,* Feb. 27, 1927, Sec. 6, p. 5.

CONOR FARRINGTON 1928-

General

Hogan, Robert. *After the Irish renaissance,* pp. 158-159.

RENE FAUCHOIS 1882-

General

Knowles, Dorothy. *French drama of the inter-war years, 1918-39,* pp. 280-281.

WILLIAM FAULKNER 1897-1962

Requiem for a Nun (Requiem pour une Nonne) (Adapted by Albert Camus)

Coenen, F.E. "The Modern German Drama." *In:* Hammer, Carl, Jr., ed. *Studies in German literature,* p. 114.

Couch, John Philip. "Camus and Faulkner: The Search for the Language of Modern Tragedy." *Yale French Studies,* no. 25 (1960), pp. 120-125.

PHILIPPE FAURE-FREMIET

General

Knowles, Dorothy. *French drama of the inter-war years, 1918-39,* pp. 304-305.

CARLOS FELIPE

ee Fernandez, Carlos

217

LAWRENCE FERLINGHETTI 1919-

The Soldiers of No Country

Ianni, L.A. "Lawrence Ferlinghetti's Fourth Person Singular and the Theory of Relativity." *Wisconsin Studies in Contemporary Literature,* vol. 8, no. 3 (Summer, 1967), pp. 392-406.

The Three Thousand Red Ants

Ianni, L.A. "Lawrence Ferlinghetti's Fourth Person Singular and the Theory of Relativity." *Wisconsin Studies in Contemporary Literature,* vol. 8, no. 3 (Summer, 1967), pp. 392-406.

The Victims of Amnesia

Ianni, L.A. "Lawrence Ferlinghetti's Fourth Person Singular and the Theory of Relativity." *Wisconsin Studies in Contemporary Literature,* vol. 8, no. 3 (Summer, 1967), pp. 392-406.

CARLOS FERNANDEZ 1914-

General

Jones, W.K. *Behind Spanish American footlights,* pp. 407-408.

AURELIO FERRETTI 1907-

General

Jones, W.K. *Behind Spanish American footlights,* pp. 154-155.

GEORGES FEYDEAU 1862-1921

General

"M. Charon on the Feydeau Behind the Farces." *Guardian,* no 56,546 (Feb. 3, 1966), p. 18.

Glenville, Peter. "Feydeau, Father of Pure Farce." *Theatre Arts,* vol. 41, no. 4 (Apr., 1957), pp. 66-67, 86-87.

Shapiro, Norman R. "Suffering and Punishment in the Theatre of Georges Feydeau." *Tulane Drama Rev.,* vol. 5, no. 1 (Sept., 1960), pp. 117-126.

Steiner, Robert J. "The Perennial Georges Feydeau." *Symposium,* vol 15, no. 1 (Spring, 1961), pp. 49-54.

The Birdwatcher

"Buoyant French Farce." *Times,* no. 56,527 (Jan. 12, 1966), p. 13.

he Dupe (Le Dindon)

Brien, Alan. "Quelle Heure Est-Il?" *Spectator,* vol. 202 (Mar. 20, 1959), p. 401.

Weightman, J.G. "What Price 'la Gloire?'" *Observer,* no. 8751 (Mar. 22, 1959), p. 23.

eu la Mère de Madame

Theatre Arts, vol. 41 (April, 1957), p. 82.

Flea in Her Ear

Billington, Michael. *"A Flea in Her Ear." Listener,* vol. 75, no. 1927 (Mar. 3, 1966), p. 315.

"Feydeau Performed on the Grand Scale." *Times,* no. 56,552 (Feb. 10, 1966), p. 16.

Hope-Wallace, Philip. *"A Flea in Her Ear* at The Old Vic." *Guardian,* no. 37,197 (Feb. 10, 1966), p. 9

Hotel Paradise (Hotel Paridiso)

Clurman, Harold. "Theatre." *Nation,* vol. 184, no. 17 (Apr. 27, 1957), p. 377.

Gibbs, Wolcott. "Cuckolds, Cats, and Cockroaches." *New Yorker,* vol. 33 (Apr. 20, 1957), pp. 75-76.

Hayes, Richard. "The Mathematics of Farce." *Commonweal,* vol. 66 (May 10, 1957), p. 154.

"Missing Element in World of Farce." *Times,* no. 56,654 (June 10, 1966), p. 18.

Wyatt, Euphemia V.R. "Theater." *Catholic World,* vol. 185 (June, 1957), p. 228.

An Italian Straw Hat

"Farce Acted With Relish." *Times,* no. 56,527 (Jan. 12, 1966), p. 13.

A Laxative for Baby

Van Druten, John. "A Gem from the French Crown." *Theatre Arts,* vol. 42, no. 3 (Mar., 1958), pp. 19-21.

Look After Lulu (Occupe-Toi d'Amélie)

Clurman, Harold. "Theatre." *Nation,* vol. 183, no. 12 (March 21, 1959), pp. 262-263.

Hewes, Henry. "Broadway Postscript." *Saturday Rev.,* vol. 35 (Dec. 13, 1952), p. 26.

Marshall, Margaret. "Drama." *Nation,* vol. 175, no. 24 (Dec. 13, 1952), p. 562.

Pryce-Jones, Alan. "Palm Beach Puppetry." *Observer,* no. 8770 (Aug. 2, 1959), p. 13

Theatre Arts, vol. 43, no. 5 (May 1959), pp. 24, 65.

Tynan, Kenneth. "Putting on the Style." *New Yorker,* vol. 35 (Mar. 14, 1959), pp. 80-83.

RUDOLPH FISHER

Conjur Man Dies

Abramson, Doris E. *Negro playwrights in the American theatre, 1925-1959,* pp. 59-63, 86-87.

CLYDE FITCH 1865-1909

General

Phelps, William Lyon. *Essays on modern dramatists,* pp. 142-178.

Beau Brummel

Phelps, William Lyon. *Essays on modern dramatists,* pp. 156-158.

The City

Phillips, Elizabeth C. *Modern American drama,* pp. 46-50, 53-54.

The Truth

Gassner, John. "Introduction." *Best plays of the early American theatre from the beginning to 1916,* pp. XLI-XLII.

GEORGE FITZMAURICE 1877-1963

General

Boyd, Ernest. *Ireland's literary renaissance,* pp. 356-360.

Hogan, Robert. *After the Irish renaissance,* pp. 164-175.

Hogan, Robert. "The Genius of George Fitzmaurice." *Drama Survey,* vol. 5, no. 3 (Winter, 1966-67), pp. 199-212.

Slaughter, Howard K. "A biographical study of Irish dramatist George Fitzmaurice, together with critical editions of his folk and realistic plays." *Dissertation Abstracts,* vol. 27 (1967), 3975A-76A (Pittsburgh).

The Country Dressmaker

Hogan, Robert. *After the Irish renaissance,* pp. 164, 165, 166-167.

Malone, Andrew E. *The Irish drama,* pp. 170-171.

The Dandy Dolls

Hogan, Robert. *After the Irish renaissance,* p. 169.

The Enchanted Land

Hogan, Robert. *After the Irish renaissance,* p. 174.

The Moonlighter

Hogan, Robert. *After the Irish renaissance,* pp. 167-168.

Malone, Andrew E. *The Irish drama,* p. 172.

The Ointment Blue, or, The Ring of the Barna Men

Hogan, Robert. *After the Irish renaissance,* pp. 170-171.

One Evening Gleam

Hogan, Robert *After the Irish renaissance,* p. 173.

The Pie Dish

Malone, Andrew E. *The Irish drama,* p. 171.

MARIO FLORES 1901-

General

Jones, W.K. *Behind Spanish American footlights,* pp. 287-288.

ROLF FORSBERG

A Tenth of an Inch Makes the Difference

Sainer, Arthur. *The sleepwalker and the assassin, a view of the contemporary theatre,* pp. 48-49.

GIOVACCHINO FORZANO

Sly

Goldberg, Isaac. *The drama of transition,* pp. 152-160.

PAUL FOSTER 1931-

Hurrah for the Bridge

Sainer, Arthur. *The sleepwalker and the assassin, a view of the contemporary theatre,* pp. 116-118.

Tom Paine

Kerr, Walter. "I'm Glad You Got Back In, Anne." *The New York Times,* May 12, 1968, Sec. 2, pp. 1, 3.

Lester, Elenore. "...Or the Wave Of the Future?" *The New York Times,* June 30, 1968, p. 3.

BRUNO FRANK 1887-1945

Storm in a Teacup (Storm Over Patsy) (Sturm im Wasserglas)

Bauland, Peter. *The hooded eagle,* p. 135.

LEONHARD FRANK 1882-1961

Karl und Anna

Garten, H.F. *Modern German drama,* pp. 180-181.

ROSE FRANKEN 1898-

Another Language

Sievers, W. David. *Freud on Broadway,* pp. 275-276.

The Hallams

Sievers, W. David. *Freud on Broadway,* pp. 276-277.

Outrageous Fortune

Sievers, W. David. *Freud on Broadway,* p. 278.

MARIO FRATTI 1927-

General

Corrigan, Robert W., ed. *Masterpieces of the modern Italian theatre,* p. 308.

Fratti, Mario. "My Theatre." *In:* Corrigan, Robert W., ed. *Masterpieces of the modern Italian theatre,* pp. 309-311.

Sainer, Arthur. *The sleepwalker and the assassin, a view of the contemporary theatre,* p. 23.

BRUCE JAY FRIEDMAN 1930-

Scuba Duba

Barthel, Joan. *"Scuba Duba* Makes Him Manic." *New York Times,* June 2, 1968, Sec. 2, pp. 1, 3.

Loney, Glenn. "Broadway in Review." *Educational Theatre J.,* vol. 19, no. 4 (Dec., 1967), pp. 511-512.

Weales, Gerald. *Reporter,* vol. 38, no. 2 (Jan. 25, 1968), pp. 43-44.

BRIAN FRIEL 1929-

General

Hogan, Robert. *After the Irish renaissance,* pp. 195-197.

Philadelphia, Here I Come!

Hogan, Robert. *After the Irish renaissance,* pp. 196-197.

MAX FRISCH

General

Barlow, D. *"Ordnung* and *Das Wirkliche Leben* in the Work of Max Frisch." *German Life and Letters,* n.s., vol. 19 (1965-66), pp. 52-60.

Bauland, Peter. *The hooded eagle,* pp. 94, 160, 169-170, 197-198, 207-209.

Bradley, Brigitte L. "Max Frisch's *Homo Faber:* Theme and Structural Devices." *Germanic Rev.,* vol. 41 (1966), pp. 279-290.

Coenen, F.E. "The Modern German Drama." *In:* Hammer, Carl, Jr., ed. *Studies in German literature,* pp. 121-123.

Esslin, Martin. "Max Frisch." *In:* Natan, A. ed. *German Men of Letters,* vol. 3 (1964), pp. 307-320.

Garten, H.F. *Modern German drama,* pp. 246, 249-255, 257.

Glaettli, Walter E. "Max Frisch, A New German Playwright." *German Q.,* vol. 25, no. 4 (Nov., 1952), pp. 248-254.

Gontrum, Peter. "Max Frisch's *Don Juan:* A New Look at a Traditional Hero." *Comparative Literature Studies,* vol. 3, no. 2 (1965), pp. 117-123.

Hatfield, Henry. *Modern German literature,* pp. 138-140.

Heilman, Robert B. "Max Frisch's Modern Moralities." *Univ. of Denver Q.,* vol. 1, no. 1 (1966), pp. 42-60.

Juergensen, Manfred. "Symbols as Leitmotifs in the Dramas of Max Frisch." *J. of the Australasian Universities Lang. and Lit. Assoc.,* vol. 27 (1967), pp. 59-70.

Kustow, Michael. "No Graven Image." *In:* Marowitz, Charles, ed. *Encore reader,* pp. 178-185, 190-194. (Reprinted from *Encore,* May, 1962.)

Lumley, Frederick. *New trends in 20th century drama,* pp. 233-239, 245-246.

Moore, Harry T. *Twentieth-century German literature,* pp. 143-147, 152, 181, 183, 186-187.

"Morality Plays." *Times Literary Supplement,* no. 3,176 (Jan. 11, 1963), pp. 17-19.

Wellwarth, George E. "Friedrich Duerrenmatt and Max Frisch: Two Views of the Drama." Tulane *Drama Rev.,* vol. 6, no. 3 (Mar., 1962), pp. 14-42.

Wellwarth, George. *The theatre of protest and paradox,* pp. 161-183.

Wilbert-Collins, Elly. *A bibliography of four contemporary German-Swiss authors: Friedrich Dürrenmatt, Max Frisch, Robert Walser, Albin Zollinger.*

Ziolkowski, Theodore. "Max Frisch: Moralist without a Moral." *Yale French Studies,* no. 29 (1962), pp. 132-141.

And Now They Sing Once More (Nun Singen Sie Wieder)

Weisstein, Ulrich. *Max Frisch,* pp. 102-109.

Wellwarth, George E. "Friedrich Duerrenmatt and Max Frisch: Two Views of the Drama." *Tulane Drama Rev.,* vol. 6, no. 3 (Mar., 1962), pp. 14-42.

Wellwarth, George. *The theatre of protest and paradox,* pp. 169-170.

Andorra

Bauland, Peter. *The hooded eagle,* pp. 207-208.

Bryden, Ronald. "Plaything." *New Statesman,* vol. 67 (Apr. 3, 1964), p. 536.

Brustein, Robert. *Seasons of discontent,* pp. 187-190.

Chiari, J. *Landmarks of contemporary drama,* pp. 184-187.

Gellert, Roger. "Paris-Andorra." *New Statesman,* vol. 67 (Feb. 7, 1964), p. 221.

Weisstein, Ulrich. *Max Frisch,* pp. 155-164.

Wellwarth, George. *The theatre of protest and paradox,* pp. 181-183.

The Chinese Wall (Die Chinesische Mauer)

Weisstein, Ulrich. *Max Frisch,* pp. 117-125.

Wellwarth, George E. "Friedrich Duerrenmatt and Max Frisch: Two Views of the Drama." *Tulane Drama Rev.,* vol. 6, no. 3 (Mar., 1962), pp. 14-42.

Wellwarth, George. *The theatre of protest and paradox,* pp. 170-176.

Count Oderland (Graf Öderland)

Barlow, D. " *Ordnung* and *Das Wirkliche Leben* in the Work of Max Frisch" *German Life and Letters,* n.s., vol. 19 (1965-66), pp. 55-57.

Weisstein, Ulrich. *Max Frisch,* pp. 126-136.

Wellwarth, George E. "Friedrich Duerrenmatt and Max Frisch: Two Views of the Drama." *Tulane Drama Rev.,* vol. 6, no. 3 (Mar., 1962), pp. 14-42.

Wellwarth, George. *The theatre of protest and paradox,* pp. 164-167.

Don Juan, or The Love of Geometry (Don Juan, oder Die Liebe zur Geometrie)

Gontrum, Peter. "Max Frisch's *Don Juan.*" *Comparative Literature Studies,* vol. 2, no. 2 (1965), pp. 117-123.

Weisstein, Ulrich. *Max Frisch,* pp. 136-143.

Wellwarth, George E. "Friedrich Duerrenmatt and Max Frisch: Two views of the Drama." *Tulane Drama Rev.,* vol. 6, no. 3 (Mar., 1962), pp. 14-42.

Wellwarth, George. *The Theater of protest and paradox,* pp. 167-169.

The Firebugs (Mr. Biedermann and the Arsonists) (The Fire Raisers) (Biedermann und die Brandstifter)

Brustein, Robert. *Seasons of discontent,* pp. 187-190.

Cohn, Ruby. "Hell on the Twentieth Century Stage." *Wisconsin Studies in Contemporary Literature,* vol. 5, no. 1 (Winter-Spring, 1964), pp. 52-53.

Esslin, Martin. *The theatre of the absurd,* pp. 191-193.

Gascoigne, Bamber. "Mushroom Soup." *Spectator,* vol. 207 (Dec. 29, 1961), p. 951.

Gascoigne, Bamber. *Twentieth-century drama,* pp. 195-196.

Gellert, Roger. *New Statesman,* vol. 62 (Dec. 29, 1961), p. 997.

Kustow, Michael. "No Graven Image." *In:* Marowitz, Charles, ed. *Encore reader,* pp. 187-190. (Reprinted from *Encore,* May, 1962.)

Sainer, Arthur. *The sleepwalker and the assassin, a view of the contemporary theatre,* pp. 21-22, 67-69.

Weisstein, Ulrich. *Max Frisch,* pp. 143-152.

Wellwarth, George E. "Friedrich Duerrenmatt and Max Frisch: Two Views of the Drama." *Tulane Drama Rev.,* vol. 6, no. 3 (Mar., 1962), pp. 14-42.

Wellwarth, George. *The theatre of protest and paradox,* pp. 176-181, 183.

The Great Wrath of Philipp Hotz (The Great Fury of Philip Hotz) (Die Grosse Wut des Philipp Hotz)

Weisstein, Ulrich. *Max Frisch,* pp. 152-155.

Wellwarth, G.E. "Introduction." *In:* Benedikt, M. and G.E. Wellwarth, eds. *Postwar German theatre,* p. xxiii.

A House in Berlin (Als der Krieg zu Ende War)

Bauland, Peter. *The hooded eagle, pp. 169-170.*

Weisstein, Ulrich. *Max Frisch,* pp. 109-117.

Santa Cruz

Barlow, D. "*Ordnung* and *Das Wirkliche Leben* in the Work of Max Frisch." *German Life and Letters,* n.s., vol. 19 (1965-66), pp. 54-55.

Weisstein, Ulrich, *Max Frisch,* pp. 96-102.

Wellwarth, George E. "Friedrich Duerrenmatt and Max Frisch: Two Views of the Drama." *Tulane Drama Rev.,* vol. 6, no. 3 (Mar., 1962), pp. 14-42.

Wellwarth, George. *The theatre of protest and paradox,* pp. 163-164.

CHRISTOPHER FRY 1907-

General

Alexander, John. "Christopher Fry and Religious Comedy." *Meanjin,* vol. 15 (Autumn, 1956), pp. 77-81.

Barnes, Lewis W. "Christopher Fry: The Chestertonian Concept of Comedy." *Xavier Univ. Studies,* vol. 2 (1963), pp. 30-47.

Bullough, Geoffrey. "Christopher Fry and the 'Revolt' Against Eliot." *In:* Armstrong, William A., ed. *Experimental drama,* pp. 56-78.

Carnell, Corbin S. "Creation's Lonely Flesh: T.S. Eliot and Christopher Fry on the Life of the Senses." *Modern Drama,* vol. 6 (1963-64), pp. 141-149.

Chiari, J. *Landmarks of contemporary drama,* pp. 101-105.

Donoghue, Denis. *The third voice: modern British and American verse drama,* pp. 180-187.

Fraser, G.S. *The modern writer and his world,* pp. 220-223.

Greene, Anne. "Fry's Cosmic Vision." *Modern Drama,* vol. 4, no. 4 (Feb., 1962), pp. 355-364.

Kerr, Walter. "Christopher Fry." In: Freedman, Morris, ed. *Essays in the modern drama,* pp. 294-299.

Lumley, Frederick. *New trends in 20th century drama,* pp. 283-289.

Lumley, Frederick. *Trends in 20th century drama,* pp. 198-203.

Mandel, O. "Theme in the Drama of Christopher Fry." *Etudes Anglaises,* vol. 10 (Oct.-Dec., 1957), pp. 335-349.

Merchant, W. Moelwyn. *Creed and drama,* pp. 98-108.

Prater, Eugene G. "Christopher Fry: Reconsidered." *Ball State Univ. Forum,* vol. 6, no. 3 (Autumn, 1965), pp. 69-79.

Redman, Ben R. "Christopher Fry: Poet-Dramatist." *College English,* vol. 14, no. 4 (Jan., 1953), pp. 191-197.

Roy, Emil. *Christopher Fry.*

Roy, Emil. "Christopher Fry as Tragicomedian." *Modern Drama,* vol. 11, no. 1 (May, 1968), pp. 40-47.

Roy, Emil. "Imagery in the Comedies of Christopher Fry." *Modern Drama,* vol. 7, no. 1 (May, 1964), pp. 79-88.

Spears, Monroe K. "Christopher Fry and the Redemption of Joy." *Poetry,* vol. 78 (Apr., 1951), pp. 23-43. (Reprinted in *Vanderbilt Studies in the Humanities,* vol. 1 (1951).)

Stanford, Derek. *Christopher Fry: an appreciation.*

Stanford, Derek. "Comedy and Tragedy in Christopher Fry." *Modern Drama,* vol. 2, no. 1 (May, 1959), pp. 3-7.

Vos, Nelvin. "The Comedy of Faith: The Drama of Christopher Fry." *Gordon Rev.,* vol. 8 (1965), pp. 139-150.

Vos, Nelvin. *The drama of comedy: victim and victor,* pp. 74-80, 93-99.

Weales, Gerald. *Religion in modern English drama,* pp. 206-224.

Bibliography

Schear, Bernice, and Eugene Prater. "A Bibliography on Christopher Fry." *Tulane Drama Rev.,* vol. 4 (Mar., 1960), pp. 88-98.

The Boy with a Cart

Ferguson, John. *"The Boy With a Cart." Modern Drama,* vol. 8, no. 3 (Dec., 1965), pp. 284-292.

Roy, Emil. *Christopher Fry,* pp. 31-36.

Weales, Gerald. *Religion in modern English drama,* pp. 208-210.

Curtmantle

Baxter, Kay M. *Contemporary theatre and the Christian faith,* p. 94.

Chiari, J. *Landmarks of contemporary drama,* pp. 103-104.

Donoghue, Denis. *The third voice: modern British and American verse drama,* pp. 187-192.

Louis, Dolores Gros. "Tragedy in Christopher Fry and in Shakespeare: A Comparison of *Curtmantle* and *Richard II." CLA J.,* vol. 9, no. 2 (Dec., 1965), pp. 151-158.

Merchant, W. Moelwyn. *Creed and drama,* pp. 103-108.

Roy, Emil. "The Becket Plays: Eliot, Fry, and Anouilh." *Modern Drama,* vol. 8, no. 3 (Dec., 1965), pp. 268-276.

Roy, Emil. *Christopher Fry,* pp. 122-139.

The Dark Is Light Enough

Lumley, Frederick. *New trends in 20th century drama,* pp. 285, 286, 287-288.

Lumley, Frederick. *Trends in 20th century drama,* pp. 201-202.

Roy, Emil. *Christopher Fry,* pp. 110-121.

Vos, Nelvin. *The drama of comedy: victim and victor,* pp. 83-84.

Weales, Gerald. *Religion in modern English drama,* pp.220-222.

Williamson, Audrey. *Contemporary theatre, 1953-1956,* pp. 30-32.

The Firstborn

Roston, Murray. *Biblical drama in England from the Middle Ages to the present day,* pp. 299-301.

Roy, Emil. *Christopher Fry,* pp. 37-48.

Weales, Gerald. *Religion in modern English drama,* pp. 200-213.

The Lady's Not for Burning

Bullough, Geoffrey. "Christopher Fry and the 'Revolt' Against Eliot." *In:* Armstrong, William A., ed. *Experimental drama,* pp. 67-70.

Clurman, Harold. *Lies like truth,* pp. 184-187.

Lumley, Frederick. *Trends in 20th century drama,* pp. 200-201.

Roy, Emil. *Christopher Fry,* pp. 59-75.

Styan, J.L. *The elements of drama,* pp. 263-267.

Urang, Gunnar. "The Climate Is the Comedy: A Study of Christopher Fry's *The Lady's Not for Burning." Christian Scholar,* vol. 46 (1963), pp. 61-86.

Vos, Nelvin. "The Comedy of Faith: The Drama of Christopher Fry." *Gordon Rev.,* vol. 8, no. 4 (Spring, 1965), pp. 139-150.

Vos, Nelvin. *The drama of comedy: victim and victor,* pp. 84-93.

Weales, Gerald. *Religion in modern English drama,* 1961, pp. 218-219.

Williams, Raymond. *Drama from Ibsen to Eliot,* pp. 262-268.

A Phoenix Too Frequent

Roy, Emil. *Christopher Fry,* pp. 49-58.

Vos, Nelvin. *The drama of comedy: victim and victor,* pp. 80-82.

Weales, Gerald. *Religion in modern English drama,* pp. 217-218.

Wiersma, Stanley M. "Christopher Fry's *A Phoenix Too Frequent;* A Study in Source and Symbol." *Modern Drama,* vol. 8, no. 3 (Dec., 1965), pp. 293-302.

A Sleep of Prisoners

Heilman, Robert B. *Tragedy and melo-drama,* pp. 8, 91, 105-106.

Hobson, Harold. *The theatre now,* 82-85.

Lumley, Frederick. *New trends in 20th century drama,* pp. 286-287.

Lumley, Frederick. *Trends in 20th century drama,* p. 201.

Matthews, Honor. *The primal curse,* pp. 187-189.

Roston, Murray. *Biblical drama in England from the Middle Ages to the present day,* pp. 301-306.

Roy, Emil. *Christopher Fry,* pp. 98-109.

Spanos, William V. *The Christian tradition in modern British verse drama,* pp. 304-324.

Spanos, William V. "Christopher Fry's *A Sleep of Prisoners:* The Choreography of Comedy." *Modern Drama,* vol. 8, no. 1 (May, 1965), pp. 58-72.

Styan, J.L. *The elements of drama,* pp. 39-44.

Weales, Gerald. *Religion in modern English drama,* pp. 215-217.

Thor with Angels

Roy, Emil. *Christopher Fry,* pp. 76-82.

Weales, Gerald. *Religion in modern English drama,* pp. 213-215.

Venus Observed

Clurman, Harold. *Lies like truth,* pp. 188-189, 192-194.

Hobson, Harold. *The theatre now,* pp. 13-20.

Roy, Emil. *Christopher Fry,* pp. 83-97.

Vos, Nelvin. *The drama of comedy: victim and victor,* pp. 82-83.

Weales, Gerald. *Religion in modern English drama,* pp. 219-220.

Williams, Raymond. *Drama from Ibsen to Eliot,* pp. 262-268.

JAMES FULLER

Rebel Without a Cause

Voaden, Herman. ed. *Human values in the drama,* pp. x-xi, xv, 198-199, 278-284.

FRANKLIN FYLES and DAVID BELASCO

The Girl I Left Behind Me

Shaw, George Bernard. *Shaw's dramatic criticism (1895-98),* pp. 48-52.

BENITO PEREZ GALDOS

General

Goldberg, Isaac. *The drama of transition,* pp. 74-92, 114-121.

Miller, Nellie Burget. *The living drama,* pp. 365-366.

The Grandfather

Miller, Nellie Burget. *The living drama,* pp. 366-368.

ZONA GALE 1874-1938

Miss Lulu Bctt

Lewisohn, Ludwig. "Native Plays." *Nation,* vol. 112 (Feb. 2, 1921), p. 189.

Simonson, Harold P. *Zona Gale,* pp. 84-87.

The Neighbors

Simonson, Harold P. *Zona Gale,* pp. 43, 50.

MANUEL GALICH 1913-

General

Jones, W.K. *Behind Spanish American footlights,* pp, 457-459.

G. P. GALLIVAN 1920-

General

Hogan, Robert. *After the Irish renaissance,* pp. 189-192.

Decision at Easter

Hogan, Robert. *After the Irish renaissance,* p. 190.

Mourn the Ivy Leaf

Hogan, Robert. *After the Irish renaissance,* pp. 190-191.

JOHN GALSWORTHY 1869-1933

General

Coats, R.H. *John Galsworthy as a dramatic artist.*

Dukes, Ashley. *Modern dramatists,* pp. 141-150.

Eaker, J. Gordon. "Galsworthy and the Modern Mind." *Philological Q.,* vol. 29, no. 1 (Jan., 1950), pp. 31-48.

Hamilton, Clayton. *Conversations on contemporary drama,* pp. 124-137, 146-149.

Henderson, Archibald. *European dramatists,* pp. 469-479.

Herrick, Marvin T. "Current English Usage and the Dramas of Galsworthy." *American Speech,* vol. 7 (1932), pp. 412-419.

Lamm, Martin. *Modern Drama,* pp. 285-292.

Miller, Nellie Burget. *The living drama,* pp. 304-307.

Nicoll, Allardyce. *British drama,* pp. 254-258.

Phelps, William Lyon. *Essays on modern dramatists,* pp. 99-141.

Salerno, Henry F. *English drama in transition, 1880-1920,* pp. 341-342.

Scrimgeour, Gary J. "Naturalist Drama and Galsworthy." *Modern drama, vol. 7,* no. 1 (May, 1964), pp. 65-78.

Williams, Harold. *Modern English writers,* pp. 253-259.

The Eldest Son

Norwood, Gilbert. *Euripides and Shaw with other essays,* pp. 80-82.

Taylor, John Russell. *The rise and fall of the well-made play,* p. 116.

The Fugitive

MacCarthy, Desmond. *Drama,* pp. 194-199.

Justice

Bache William B. *"Justice:* Galsworthy's Dramatic Tragedy." *Modern Drama,* vol. 3, no. 2 (Sept., 1960), pp. 138-142.

Beerbohm, Max. *Around theatres,* pp. 565-568.

Dukes, Ashley. *Modern dramatists,* pp. 146-150.

Hamilton, Clayton. *Conversations on contemporary drama,* pp. 144-146.

Norwood, Gilbert. *Euripides and Shaw with other essays,* pp. 83-85.

Phelps, William Lyon. *Essays on modern dramatists,* pp. 122-128.

Taylor, John Russell. *The rise and fall of the well-made play,* pp. 116-117.

The Little Man

Weales, Gerald. *Religion in modern English drama,* pp. 16-17.

Loyalties

Eastman, Fred. *Christ in the drama,* pp. 70-72.

Shanks, Edward. *Second essays on literature,* pp. 48-50.

Taylor, John Russell. *The rise and fall of the well-made play,* pp. 118-119.

The Mob

MacCarthy, Desmond. *Drama,* pp. 200-205.

MacCarthy, Desmond. *Theatre,* pp. 107-112.

The Pigeon

Eastman, Fred. *Christ in the drama,* pp. 69-70.

Hamilton, Clayton. *Conversations on contemporary drama,* pp. 142-144.

Phelps, William Lyon. *Essays on modern dramatists,* pp. 129-135.

Weales, Gerald. *Religion in modern English drama,* p. 16.

The Silver Box

Norwood, Gilbert. *Euripides and Shaw with other essays,* pp. 82-83.

Phelps, William Lyon. *Essays on modern dramatists,* pp. 106-111.
Salerno, Henry F. *English drama in transition, 1880-1920,* pp. 342-344.

Shanks, Edward. *Second essays on literature,* pp. 45-47.

Taylor, John Russell. *The rise and fall of the well-made play,* p. 116.

The Skin Game

Balmforth, Ramsden. *The problem-play and its influence on modern thought and life,* pp. 38-41.

Taylor, John Russell. *The rise and fall of the well-made play,* pp. 117-118.

Strife

Eastman, Fred. *Christ in the drama,* pp. 65-68.

Hamilton, Clayton. *Conversations on contemporary drama.* pp. 137-142.

Miller, Nellie Burget. *The living drama,* pp. 307-309.

Phelps, William Lyon. *Essays on modern dramatists,* pp. 114-122.

Taylor, John Russell. *The rise and fall of the well-made play,* pp. 117.

DON FEDERICO GAMBOA 1864-1939

General

González Peña, Carlos. *History of Mexican literature,* pp. 312-313.

JOSE JOAQUIN GAMBOA 1878-1931

General

González Peña, Carlos. *History of Mexican literature,* pp. 323, 324-325, 375.

Jones, W.K. *Behind Spanish American footlights,* 493-494.

The Gentleman, Death, and the Devil (El Caballero, la Muerte, y el Diablo)

Anderson Imbert, Enrique. *Spanish-American literature: a history,* p. 323.

Jones, W.K. *Behind Spanish American footlights,* pp. 493-494.

JOAQUIN GANTIER 1903-

General

Jones, W.K. *Behind Spanish America footlights,* pp. 288-289.

SIMON GANTILLON

General

Knowles, Dorothy. *French drama of the inter-war years, 1918-39,* p. 107-108.

Cyclone

Knowles, Dorothy. *French drama of the inter-war years, 1918-39,* pp. 107.

Maya

Knowles, Dorothy. *French drama of the inter-war years, 1918-39,* pp. 106-107.

ENRIQUE GARCES

General

Jones, W.K. *Behind Spanish American footlights,* p. 315.

FEDERICO GARCIA LORCA 1899-1936

General

Aratari, Anthony. "The Tragedies of García Lorca." *Commonweal,* vol. 62 (Aug. 12, 1955), pp. 472-476.

Barea, Arturo. *Lorca: the poet and his people.*

Blackburn, Susan Smith. "Humor in the Plays of Federico García Lorca." *In:* Duran, M., ed., *Lorca,* pp. 155-166.

Carrier, Warren. "Poetry in the Drama of Lorca." *Drama Survey,* vol. 2, no. 3 (1963), pp. 297-304.

Cobb, Carl W. *Federico García Lorca*

Colecchia, Francesca. "The treatment of woman in the theatre of Federico García Lorca." *Dissertation Abstracts,* vol. 14 (1954), 1406 (Univ. of Pittsburgh).

Corrigan, Robert W., ed. *Masterpieces of the modern Spanish theatre,* p. 352.

Duran, Manuel. ed., *Lorca.*

Fergusson, Francis. "Don Perlimplín: Lorca's Theatre-Poetry." *Kenyon Rev.,* vol. 17, no. 3 (Summer, 1955), pp. 337-348. *Also in:* Bogard T. and Oliver, W., eds. Mode*rn drama: essays in criticism,* pp. 209-218. *Also in:* Fergusson, F. *The human image in dramatic literature,* pp. 85-97.

García Lorca, Federico. "Lorca Discusses His Plays." *Tulane Drama Rev.,* vol. 7, no. 2 (Winter, 1962), pp. 111-119.

Gassner, John. *The theatre in our times,* pp. 224-226.

Graham-Lujan, James. "Federico García Lorca: His Heroines." *Chrysalis,* vol. 2, nos. 6-8 (1949), pp. 3-15.

Higginbotham, Virginia. "The comic spirit of Federico García Lorca." *Dissertation abstracts,* vol. 27 (1966), 1368A (Tulane).

Honig, Edwin. *García Lorca.*

Honig, Edwin. "Lorca To Date." *Tulane Drama Rev.,* vol. 7, no. 2 (Winter, 1962), pp. 120-126.

Lamm, Martin. *Modern drama,* pp. 344-351.

Lewis, Allan. *The contemporary theatre,* pp. 242-258.

Lima, Robert. *Theatre of García Lorca.*

Lumley, Frederick. *New trends in 20th century drama, pp. 91,* 92-104.

Lumley, Frederick. *Trends in 20th century drama,* pp. 101-113.

Oliver, William I. "Lorca: The Puppets and the Artist." *Tulane Drama Rev.,* vol. 7, no. 2 (Winter, 1962), pp. 76-95.

Oliver, William I. "The Trouble With Lorca." *Modern Drama,* vol. 7, no. 1 (May, 1964), pp. 2-15.

Salinas, P. "Lorca and the Poetry of Death.". *In: Tulane Drama Rev. Theatre in the twentieth century,* pp. 273-281.

Blood Wedding (Bodas de Sangre)

Barea, A. *Lorca,* pp. 34-42.

Barnes, Robert. "The Fusion of Poetry and Drama in *Blood Wedding." Modern Drama,* vol. 2, no. 2 (Feb., 1960), pp. 395-402.

Bierman, Judah. *The dramatic experience,* pp. 461-464.

Cobb, Carl W. *Federico García Lorca,* pp. 130-135.

Dickson, Ronald J. "Archetypal Symbolism in Lorca's *Bodas de sangre.*" *Literature and Psychology,* vol. 10, no. 3 (Summer, 1960), pp. 76-79.

Freedman, Morris. *The moral impulse,* pp. 89-92, 94-96.

Gaskell, Ronald. "Theme and Form: Lorca's *Blood Wedding.*" *Modern Drama,* vol. 5, no. 4 (Feb., 1963), pp. 431-439.

Henn, T.R. *The harvest of tragedy,* pp. 116-118.

Honig, E. *García Lorca,* pp. 153-163.

Honig, Edwin. "Lorca's Folk Tragedies." *In:* Freedman, Morris, ed. *Essays in the modern drama,* pp. 245-263. (Reprinted from *García Lorca,* by Edwin Honig. Copyright 1944 by New Directions.)

Lewis, Allan. *The contemporary theatre,* pp. 248-256.

Lima, R. *Theatre of García Lorca,* pp. 188-216.

Lumley, Frederick. *New trends in 20th century drama,* pp. 99-101.

Lumley, Frederick. *Trends in 20th century drama,* pp. 108-110.

Mullikin, Mildred Bailey. "The philosophy and designs for the play *Blood Wedding* by Federico García Lorca." M.A., University of Alabama, 1952.

Palley, Julian. "Archetypal Symbols in *Bodas de sangre.*" *Hispania,* vol. 50 (1967). pp. 74-79.

Touster, Eva K. "Thematic Patterns in Lorca's *Blood Wedding.*" *Modern Drama,* vol. 7, no. 1 (May, 1964), pp. 16-27.

Zimbardo, R.A. "The Mythic Pattern in Lorca's *Blood Wedding.*" *Modern Drama,* vol. 10, no. 4 (Feb., 1968), pp. 364-371.

The Butterfly's Evil Spell (El Maleficio de la Mariposa)

Honig, E. *García Lorca,* pp. 111-114.

Lima, R. *Theatre of García Lorca,* pp. 55-66.

Lumley, Frederick. *New trends in 20th century drama,* pp. 92, 97.

Doña Rosita the Spinster, or The Language of the Flowers (Doña Rosita la Soltera, o El Lenguaje de las Flores)

Barea, A. *Lorca,* pp. 27-30.

Cobb, Carl W. *Federico García Lorca,* pp. 127-130.

Correa, Gustavo. "Honor, Blood and Poetry in *Yerma.*" *Tulane Drama Rev.,* vol. 7, no. 2 (Winter, 1962), pp. 96-110.

Honig, E. *García Lorca,* pp. 178-193.

Lima, R. *Theatre of García Lorca,* pp. 241-262.

Lumley, Frederick. *New trends in 20th century drama,* pp. 99-100, 102.

Lumley, Frederick. *Trends in 20th century drama,* pp. 108, 110-111.

The House of Bernarda Alba (La Casa de Bernarda Alba)

Allison, Alexander W., ed. *Masterpieces of the drama,* 2nd ed., pp. 581-582.

Barea, A. *Lorca,* pp. 51-56.

Bluefarb, Sam. "Life and Death in García Lorca's *House of Bernarda Alba.*" *Drama Survey,* vol. 4, no. 2 (Summer, 1965), pp. 109-120.

Cobb, Carl W. *Federico García Lorca,* pp. 138-141, 142, 143.

Fergusson, Francis. *The human image in dramatic literature,* p. 95.

Freedman, Morris. *The moral impulse,* pp. 89, 94-98.

Greenfield, Sumner M. "Poetry and Stagecraft in *La casa de Bernarda Alba.*" *Hispania,* vol. 38, no. 4 (Dec., 1955), pp. 456-461.

Henn, T.R. *The harvest of tragedy,* 118-121.

Honig, E. *García Lorca,* pp. 193-196, 219-226.

Lewis, Allan. *The contemporary theatre,* pp. 256-258.

Lima, R. *Theatre of García Lorca,* pp. 263-287.

Lumley, Frederick. New trends *in 20th century drama,* pp. 100, 102-103.

Lumley, Frederick. *Trends in 20th century drama,* pp. 111-113.

Sharp, Thomas F. "The Mechanics of Lorca's Drama in *"La Casa de Bernarda Alba."* *Hispania,* vol. 44, no. 2 (May, 1961), pp. 230-233.

Love of Don Perlimplín with Belisa in the Garden (Amor de Don Perlimplin con Belisa en su Jardin)

Cobb, Carl W. *Federico García Lorca,* p. 122.

Fergusson, Francis. "Don Perlimplín: Lorca's Theatre-Poetry." *Kenyon Rev.,* vol. 17 (Summer, 1955), pp. 337-348. *Also in:* Bogard, T. and Oliver, W., eds. *Modern Drama,* pp. 209-218; Duran, M., ed. *Lorca,* pp. 167-175; Fergusson, F., *Human image in dramatic literature,* pp. 85-97.

Honig, E. *García Lorca,* pp. 123-129.

Lima, R. *Theatre of García Lorca,* pp. 141-156.

Lumley, Frederick. *New trends in 20th century drama,* pp. 98, 99.

Mariana Pineda

Barea, A. *Lorca,* pp. 21-27.

Cobb, Carl W. *Federico García Lorca,* pp. 119-121.

García Lorca, Federico. *In:* Cole, Toby, ed. *Playwrights on playwriting,* pp. 228-231.

Honig, E. *García Lorca,* pp. 114-123.

Lima, R. *Theatre of García Lorca,* pp. 96-119.

Lumley, Frederick. *New trends in 20th century drama,* pp. 97-98.

The Public (The Audience) (El Público)

Cobb, Carl W. *Federico García Lorca,* p. 122.

Lumley, Frederick. *New trends in 20th century drama,* p. 99.

The Puppet Farce of Don Cristobal (Pantomime of Don Christopher) (Sketch of Don Christopher) (Retablillo de Don Cristobal)

Cobb, Carl W. *Federico García Lorca,* pp. 122-123.

Honig, E. *García Lorca,* pp. 131-134.

Lumley, Frederick. *New trends in 20th century drama,* pp. 98, 99.

Oliver, William I. "Lorca: The Puppets and the Artist." *Tulane Drama Rev.,* vol. 7, no. 2 (Winter, 1962), pp. 76-95.

Puppet Show of the Cachiporra (Los Títeres de Cachiporra)

Cobb, Carl W. *Federico García Lorca,* p. 123.

Lima, R. *Theatre of García Lorca,* pp. 67-95.

Thus Five Years Pass (Así Que Pasen Cinco Años)

Cobb, Carl W. *Federico García Lorca,* p. 121.

Honig, E. *García Lorca,* pp. 135-149.

Lima, R. *Theatre of García Lorca,* pp. 157-187

Lumley, Frederick. *New trends in 20th century drama,* p. 99.

The Shoemaker's Prodigious Wife (La Zapatera Prodigiosa)

Benedikt, M. and G.E. Wellwarth. *Modern Spanish theatre, an anthology of plays,* pp. 80-81.

Cobb, Carl W. *Federico García Lorca,* pp. 124-127.

García Lorca, Federico. *In:* Cole, Toby, ed. *Playwrights on playwriting,* pp. 231-232.

Honig, E. *García Lorca,* pp. 129-131.

Lima, R. *Theatre of García Lorca,* pp. 120-140.

Lumley, Frederick. *New trends in 20th century drama,* pp. 98, 99.

Picciotto, Robert S. *"La zapatera prodigiosa* and Lorca's Poetic Credo." *Hispania,* vol. 49 (1966), pp. 250-257.

Yerma

Barea, A. *Lorca,* pp. 42-51.

Cannon, Calvin. "The Imagery of Lorca's *Yerma." Modern Lang. Q.,* vol. 21, no. 2 (June, 1960), pp. 122-130.

Cobb, Carl W. *Federico García Lorca,* pp. 135-138.

Correa, Gustavo. "Honor, Blood, and Poetry in *Yerma." Tulane Drama Rev.,* vol. 6, no. 2 (1962), pp. 96-110.

Freedman, Morris. *The moral impulse,* pp. 89, 92-94, 97.

Honig, E. *García Lorca,* pp. 163-178.

Honig, Edwin. "Lorca's Folk Tragedies." *In:* Freedman, Morris, ed. *Essays in the modern drama,* pp. 245-263. (Reprinted from *García Lorca* by Edwin Honig. Copyright 1944 by New Directions.)

Lima, R. *Theatre of García Lorca,* pp. 217-240.

Lott, Robert E. *"Yerma:* The Tragedy of Unjust Barrenness." *Modern Drama,* vol. 8, no. 1 (May, 1965), pp. 20-27.

Lumley, Frederick. *New trends in 20th century drama,* pp. 99, 101-102.

Skloot, Robert. "Theme and Image in Lorca's *Yerma." Drama Survey,* vol. 5, no. 2 (Summer, 1966), pp. 151-161.

ENRIQUE GARCIA VELLOSO 1880-1938

General

Jones, W.K. *Behind Spanish American footlights,* pp. 155-157.

ELENA GARRO 1917-

A Solid Home (Un Hogar Solido)

Anderson Imbert, Enrique. *Spanish-American literature: a history,* p. 550.

Jones, W.K. *Behind Spanish American footlights,* p. 490.

McMahon, Dorothy. "Changing trends in Spanish American Literature." *Books Abroad,* vol. 39, no. 1 (Winter, 1965), p. 17.

ARMAND GATTI

General

Guicharnaud, Jacques. *Modern French theatre from Giraudoux to Genet* (rev. ed.), pp. 89, 197, 206-208, 210, 212, 290, 319, 348, 364.

Chant Publique Devant Deux Chaises Electriques

"Gatti Play Asks Great Things of the Audience." *Times,* no. 56,655 (Feb. 14, 1966), p. 14.

Le Crapaud-Buffle

Merrick, Gordon. "The Toad in the Ointment." *New Republic,* vol. 142, no. 7 (Feb. 15, 1960), p. 20.

V Comme Vietnam

Kustow, Michael. "French Play about the Vietnam War." *Times,* no. 56, 972 (June 20, 1967), p. 6.

FRANCISCO GAVIDIA 1864-1955

General

Anderson-Imbert, Enrique. *Spanish-American literature: a history,* pp. 266, 271.

Jones, W.K. *Behind Spanish-American footlights,* pp. 437-440.

MICHAEL GAZZO 1923-

A Hatful of Rain

Gassner, John. *Theatre at the crossroads,* pp. 159-161.

VIRGIL GEDDES

The Earth Between

Block, Anita. *The changing world in plays and theatre,* pp. 128-132.

JACK GELBER 1932-

General

Hurley, Paul J. "France and America: Versions of the Absurd." *College English,* vol. 26 (1965), pp. 634-640.

The Apple

Abel, Lionel. *Metatheatre, a new view of dramatic form,* pp. 128-134.

Bigsby, C.W.E. *Confrontation and commitment,* pp. 59, 145.

Dukore, Bernard F. "The New Dramatists: 5. Jack Gelber." *Drama Survey,* vol. 2, no. 2 (Oct., 1962), pp. 146-157.

Kerr, Walter. *The theater in spite of itself,* pp. 178-182.

Kostelanetz, Richard. "The New American Theatre." *In:* Kostelanetz, Richard. *The new American arts,* pp. 66-67.

Lumley, Frederick. *New trends in 20th century drama,* p. 328.

Wellwarth, George. *The theatre of protest and paradox,* pp. 294-295.

The Connection

Abel, Lionel. *Metatheatre, a new view of dramatic form,* pp. 122-127.

Bigsby, C.W.E. *Confrontation and commitment,* pp. xviii, 5, 10, 20, 50-61, 69, 71, 99-100.

Brook, Peter. "From Zero to the Infinite." *In:* Marowitz, Charles, ed. *Encore reader,* pp. 245-251. (Reprinted from *Encore,* Nov., 1960)

Brustein, Robert. "The New American Playwrights," *In:* Rahv, Philip, ed. *Modern occasions,* pp. 128-129.

Brustein, Robert. *Seasons of discontent,* pp. 23-26.

Dukore, Bernard F. "The New Dramatists: 5. Jack Gelber." *Drama Survey,* vol. 2, no. 2 (Oct., 1962), pp. 146-157.

Dukore, Bernard F. "The Noncommercial Theater in New York." *In:* Downer, Alan S., ed. *The American theater today,* pp. 158-162.

Eskin, Stanley G. "Theatricality in the Avant-Garde Drama: A Reconsideration of a Theme in the Light of *The Balcony* and *The Connection." Modern Drama,* vol. 7, no. 2 (Sept. 1964), pp. 213-222.

Kerr, Walter. *The theater in spite of itself,* pp. 182-185.

Kostelanetz, Richard C. "*The Connection:* Heroin As Existential Choice." Texas Q., vol. 5, no. 4 (Winter, 1962), pp. 159-162.

Kostelanetz, Richard. "The New American Theatre." *In:* Kostelanetż, Richard. *The new American arts,* pp. 62-66.

Lewis, Allan. *American plays and playwrights of the contemporary theatre,* pp. 202-204.

Lumley, Frederick. *New trends in 20th century drama,* pp. 327-328.

Mee, Charles L., Jr. "The Beck's Living Theatre." *Tulane Drama Rev.,* vol. 7, no. 2 (Winter, 1962), pp. 194-205.

Tynan, Kenneth. *Tynan right and left,* pp. 71-73.

Wellwarth, George. *The theatre of protest and paradox,* pp. 293-295.

Weales, Gerald. "Off-Broadway: Its Contribution to American Drama." *Drama Survey,* vol. 2, no. 1 (June, 1962), pp. 16-18.

Square in the Eye

Brustein, Robert. "The New American Playwrights." *In:* Rahv, Philip, ed. *Modern occasions,* pp. 129-130.

JEAN GENET 1910-

General

Barnes, Hazel E. *The litcrature of possibility,* pp. 340-361.

Blau, Herbert. *The impossible theatre,* pp. 261-276.

Brustein, Robert. *The theatre of revolt,* pp. 378-394.

Coe, Richard N. "All Done with Mirrors or The Solitude of Jean Genet." *Australian J. of French Studies* (Monash U., Clayton, Victoria), vol. 3 (1966), pp. 79-104.

Coe, Richard N. "Genetflexions, L. The Small Boy Who Was Night: Introduction to the Theatre of Jean Genet." *Cambridge Rev.,* vol. 89a, no. 2158 (Nov. 18, 1967), pp. 109-113.

Coe, Richard N. *The vision of Jean Genet,* pp. 3-31, 213-225, 251-261, 282-284.

Cohn, Ruby. *"Theatrum Mundi* and Contemporary Theater." *Comparative Drama,* vol. 1 (1967), pp. 28-35.

Ehrmann, Jacques. "Genet's Dramatic Metamorphoses: From Appearance to Freedom." *Yale French Studies,* no. 29 (1963), pp. 33-42.

Elsom, John. "Genet and the Sadistic Society." *London Mag.,* vol. 3, no. 5 (Aug., 1963), pp. 61-67.

Esslin, Martin. *The theatre of the absurd,* pp. 140-144, 165-167.

Fowlie, Wallace. "The Case of Jean Genet." *Commonweal,* vol. 73, no. 5 (Oct. 28, 1960), pp. 111-113.

Gascoigne, Bamber. *A theatre divided; the postwar American stage,* pp. 283-286.

Guicharnaud, Jacques. *Modern French theatre from Giraudoux to Genet* (rev. ed.), pp. 13, 19, 26, 58-59, 159, 177, 187, 197, 212, 259-264, 267, 286-288, 318, 321, 352-353, 365-366.

Hatzfeld, Helmut. *Trends and styles in twentieth century French literature,* pp. 268-269.

Hobson, Harold. *The French theatre of today,* pp. 120-127.

Jacobsen, Josephine. *Ionesco and Genet, playwrights of silence,* pp. 126-127, 128-130, 174-186.

Killinger, John. "Jean Genet and Scapegoat Drama." *Comparative Literature Studies,* vol. 3, no. 2 (1966), pp. 207-221.

Knapp, Bettina. "An Interview With Roger Blin." *Tulane Drama Rev.,* vol. 7, no. 3 (Spring, 1963), pp. 111-124.

Knapp, Bettina L. *Jean Genet,* pp. 88-91, 156-157.

Lumley, Frederick. *New trends in 20th century drama,* pp. 214-216, 309, 382.

Markus, Thomas B. "Jean Genet; The Theatre of the Perverse." *Educational Theatre J.,* vol. 14, no. 3 (Oct., 1962), pp. 209-214.

Marowitz, Charles. "The Revenge of Jean Genet." *In:* Marowitz, Charles, ed. *Encore reader,* pp. 174-178. (Reprinted from *Encore,* Sept., 1961.)

Matthews, Honor. *The primal curse,* pp. 168-171.

Metz, Mary S. "Existentialism and inauthenticity in the theater of Beckett, Ionesco, and Genet." *Dissertation Abstracts,* vol. 27 (1966), 1377A-78A (La. State).

Moore, Harry T. *Twentieth-century French literature since World War II,* pp. 151-154.

"A Note on Theatre." *Tulane Drama Rev.,* vol. 7, no. 3 (Spring, 1963), pp. 37-41.

Parker, R.B. "The Theory and Theatre of the Absurd." *Queen's Q.,* vol. 73, no. 3 (Autumn, 1966), pp. 420-441.

Pronko, Leonard C. *Avant-garde: the experimental theatre in France,* pp. 140-153.

Pronko, Leonard C. *Theater East and West,* pp. 63-67.

Sartre, Jean-Paul. "Saint Genet: Actor and Martyr." *Tulane Drama Rev.,* vol. 7, no. 3 (Spring, 1963), pp. 19-36.

Svendsen, J.M. "Corydon Revisited: A Reminder on Genet." *Tulane Drama Rev.,* vol. 7, no. 3 (Spring, 1963), pp. 98-110.

Thody, Philip. *Jean Genet, a study of his novels and plays,* pp. 3-54.

Adame Miroir

Knapp, Bettina L. *Jean Genet,* pp. 91-93.

Albert Giacometti's Studio

Knapp, Bettina L. *Jean Genet,* pp. 95-97.

The Balcony (Le Balcon)

Abel, Lionel. *Metatheatre, a new view of dramatic form,* pp. 80-83.

Abel, Lionel. *Partisan Rev.,* vol. 27, no. 2 (Spring, 1960), pp. 324-330.

Blau, Herbert. *The impossible theatre,* pp. 268-273.

Brustein, Robert. "The Brothel and the Western World." *New Republic,* vol. 142, no. 13 (Mar. 28, 1960), pp. 21-22.

Brustein, Robert. *Seasons of discontent,* pp. 33-36.

Brustein, Robert. *The theatre of revolt,* pp. 394-402.

Chiari, J. *Landmarks of contemporary drama,* pp. 63-64.

Clurman, Harold. *The naked image,* pp. 72-73.

Clurman, Harold. "Theatre." *Nation,* vol. 190, no. 13 (March 26, 1960), pp. 282-283.

Coe, Richard N. *The vision of Jean Genet,* pp. 261-277.

Driver, Tom F. "House of Illusions." *Christian Century,* vol. 77 (May 4, 1960), pp. 546-548.

Eskin, Stanley G. "Theatricality in the Avant-Garde Drama: A Reconsideration of a Theme in the Light of *The Balcony* and *The Connection.*" *Modern Drama, vol. 7,* no. 2 (Sept. 1964), pp. 213-222.

Esslin, Martin. *The theatre of the absurd,* pp. 152-160.

Grossvogel, David I. *Four playwrights and a postscript, Brecht, Ionesco, Beckett, Genet,* pp. 157-167.

Hewes, Henry. *Saturday Rev.,* vol. 43 (Mar. 26, 1960), p. 34.

Jacobsen, Josephine. *Ionesco and Genet, playwrights of silence,* pp. 1-2, 17, 20, 23-24, 128-129, 146-157, 162, 164, 170, 182, 186-191, 193, 203, 210, 215.

Knapp, Bettina L. *Jean Genet,* pp. 118-128.

Lewis, Allan. *The contemporary theatre,* pp. 280-281.

Malcolm, Donald. *New Yorker,* vol. 36 (Mar., 1960), pp. 112, 114-115.

Mares, F.H. "Jean Genet's *The Balcony.*" *Meanjin,* vol. 24, no. 3 (1965), pp. 354-356.

Marowitz, Charles. "The Revenge of Jean Genet." *In:* Marowitz, Charles, ed. *Encore reader,* pp. 170-174. (Reprinted from *Encore,* Sept., 1961.)

Melcher, Edith. "The Pirandellism of Jean Genet." *French Rev.,* vol. 36, no. 1 (Oct., 1962), pp. 32-35.

Nelson, Benjamin. *"The Balcony* and Parisian existentialism." *Tulane Drama Rev.,* vol. 7, no. 3 (Spring, 1963), pp. 60-79.

Pronko, Leonard C. *Avant-garde: the experimental theater in France,* pp. 147-149.

Reck, Rima D. "Appearance and Reality in Genet's *Le Balcon.*" *Yale French Studies,* no. 29 (1962), pp. 20-25.

Stewart, Harry E. "Jean Genet's Saintly Pre-occupation in *Le Balcon.*" *Drama Survey,* vol. 6 (1967), pp. 24-30.

Styan, J.L. *The dark comedy,* 2nd ed., pp. 142, 242-243, 255, 256.

Thody, Philip. *Jean Genet, a study of his novels and plays,* pp. 179-195.

"Undergraduates' Taste of Power." *Times,* no. 56,558, (Feb. 17, 1966), p. 15.

Wellwarth, George. *The theatre of protest and paradox,* pp. 118-126.

Zadek, Peter. "Acts of Violence." *New Statesman, vol. 53* (May 4, 1957), pp. 568-570.

The Blacks (Les Negres)

Alvarez, A. *New Statesman,* vol. 58 (Nov. 21, 1959), p. 706.

Balliett, Whitney. *New Yorker,* vol. 37 (May 13, 1961), pp. 93-94.

Bonosky, Phillip. *Mainstream,* vol. 15, no. 2 (Feb., 1962), pp. 61-62.

Brustein, Robert. *New Republic,* vol. 144, no. 22 (May 29, 1961), pp. 21-22.

Brustein, Robert. *Seasons of discontent,* pp. 49-52.

Brustein, Robert. *The theatre of revolt,* pp. 402-410.

Chiaromonte, Nicola. *Partisan Rev.,* vol. 28, no. 5-6 (1961), pp. 662-668.

Clurman, Harold. *The naked image,* pp. 74-76.

Clurman, Harold. *Nation,* vol. 192, no. 20 (May 20, 1961), pp. 447-448.

Coe, Richard N. *The vision of Jean Genet,* pp. 284-296.

Driver, Tom F. "Criticism in the Modern World-Drama." *Christian Century,* vol. 78, no. 24 (June 14, 1961), pp. 744-745.

Esslin, Martin. *The theatre of the absurd,* pp. 160-164.

Fowlie, Wallace. "New Plays of Ionesco and Genet." *Tulane Drama Rev.,* vol. 5, no. 1 (Sept. 1960), pp. 46-48.

Gascoigne, Bamber. *Spectator,* vol. 206, no. 6937 (June 9, 1961), pp. 835-837.

Gassner, John. *Educational Theater J.,* vol. 13, no. 3 (Oct., 1961), pp. 217-220.

Grossvogel, David I. *Four playwrights and a postscript, Brecht, Ionesco, Beckett, Genet,* pp. 166-172.

Guicharnaud, Jacques. *Modern French theatre from Giraudoux to Genet* (rev. ed.), pp. 259, 261, 262, 264-266, 270-271.

Hatch, Robert. "Disturbing? Jean Genet Is Downright Terrifying." *Horizon,* vol. 4, no. 2 (Nov., 1961), pp. 98-102.

Hewes, Henry. *Saturday Rev.,* vol. 44, (June 3, 1961), p. 29.

Jacobsen, Josephine. *Ionesco and Genet, playwrights of silence,* pp. 20-21, 23-24, 85, 128, 147, 156-166, 168, 177, 182, 186-187, 191-193, 195, 202, 210-211, 221, 226.

Kerr, Walter. *The theater in spite of itself,* pp. 119-122.

Knapp, Bettina L. *Jean Genet,* pp. 129-139.

Lewis, Allan. *The contemporary theatre,* pp. 279-280.

Lewis, Theophilus. *America,* vol. 105, no. 22 (Aug. 26, 1961), pp. 671-672.

Lukas, Mary. *Catholic World,* vol. 194, no. 1 (Oct., 1961), pp. 63-64.

Mailer, Norman. *The Presidential papers,* pp. 200-212

Matthews, Honor. *The primal curse,* pp. 171, 179-183.

Melcher, Edith. "The Pirandellism of Jean Genet." *French Rev.,* vol. 36, no. 1 (Oct., 1962), pp. 35-36.

Mitchell, Loften. *Black drama,* pp. 76, 186-187.

Pritchett, V.S. "Black and White Murder Show." *New Statesman,* vol. 61 (June 9, 1961), p. 928.

Pronko, Leonard C. *Avant-garde: the experimental theater in France,* pp. 149-153.

Pryce-Jones, Alan. *Theatre Arts,* vol. 45, no. 7 (July, 1961), pp. 8-9.

Styan, J.L. *The dark comedy,* 2nd ed., pp. 220, 242, 243-244.

Swander, Homer D. "Shakespeare and the Harlem Clowns: Illusion and Comic Form in Genet's *The Blacks." Yale Rev.,* vol. 55, no. 2 (Dec., 1965), pp. 209-226.

Taubes, Susan. "The White Mask Falls." *Tulane Drama Rev.,* vol. 7, no. 3 (Spring, 1963), pp. 85-92.

Thody, Philip. *Jean Genet, a study of his novels and plays,* pp. 196-204.

"To a Would-Be Producer." *Tulane Drama Rev.,* vol. 7, no. 3 (Spring, 1963), pp. 80-81.

Tynan, Kenneth. *Tynan right and left,* pp. 85-86.

Wellwarth, George. *The theatre of protest and paradox,* pp. 126-127.

Zimbardo, R.A. "Genet's Black Mass." *Modern Drama,* vol. 8, no. 3 (Dec., 1965), pp. 253-258.

Deathwatch (Haute Surveillance)

Coe, Richard N. *The vision of Jean Genet,* pp. 225-236.

Esslin, Martin. *The theatre of the absurd,* pp. 144-146.

Fowlie, Wallace. *Dionysus in Paris,* pp. 219-222.

Grossvogel, David I. *Four playwrights and a postscript, Brecht, Ionesco, Beckett, Genet,* pp. 151-157.

Hewes, Henry. *Saturday Rev.,* vol. 41 (Nov. 1, 1958), p. 28.

Jacobsen, Josephine. *Ionesco and Genet, playwrights of silence,* pp. 12, 20, 23, 26, 37, 128, 130-138, 140-141, 143, 158, 161, 182, 184-188, 191, 193, 195, 198, 210, 226.

Knapp, Bettina L. *Jean Genet,* pp. 98-108.

Lewis, Allan. *The contemporary theatre,* pp. 278-279

McCarthy, Mary. "Odd Man In." *Partisan Rev.,* vol. 26, no. 1 (Winter, 1959), pp. 100-106.

Matthews, Honor. *The primal curse,* pp. 170-172.

Pronko, Leonard C. *Avant-garde: the experimental theater in France,* pp. 142-145.

Thody, Philip. *Jean Genet, a study of his novels and plays,* pp. 155-162.

Wellwarth, George. *The theatre of protest and paradox,* pp. 116-118.

The Maids (Les Bonnes)

Barbour, Thomas. *Hudson Rev.,* vol. 7, no. 3 (Autumn, 1954), pp. 474-475.

Bartholomew, Rati. "Theatre. *The Maids.* By Jean Genet, Directed by Harbhajan Virdi. Presented by Youth of India." *Thought* (Delhi), vol. 18, no. 22 (May, 28, 1966), p. 20.

Bishop, Thomas. *Pirandello and the French theater,* pp. 138-139.

Coe, Richard N. *The vision of Jean Genet,* pp. 236-245.

Donaldson, Ian. "Brecht and Genet at Oxford." *Guardian,* no. 36,597 (Mar. 5, 1964), p. 9.

Esslin, Martin. *The theatre of the absurd,* pp. 146-151.

Fowlie, Wallace. *Dionysus in Paris,* pp. 218-222.

Grossvogel, David I. *Four playwrights and a postscript, Brecht, Ionesco, Beckett, Genet,* pp. 140-151.

Hatch, Robert. "Theatre." *Nation,* vol. 180, no. 22 (May 28, 1955), pp. 469-470.

Hobson, Harold. *The French theatre of today,* pp. 125-128.

Hoy, Peter. "Jean Genet: *The Maids." Ripple,* vol. 10, no. 2 (Oct. 27, 1966), p. 4.

Jacobsen, Josephine. *Ionesco and Genet, playwrights of silence,* pp. 1, 3, 12, 23-24, 26, 128, 130, 137-148, 156, 177, 182, 186-190, 193, 197, 202, 210, 214.

Knapp, Bettina L. *Jean Genet,* pp. 109-117.

Lewis, Allan. *The contemporary theatre,* pp. 277-278.

Matthews, Honor. *The primal curse,* pp. 172-179.

Oliver, Edith. *New Yorker,* vol. 39 (Nov. 23, 1963), pp. 143-144, 146.

Pronko, Leonard C. *Avant-garde: the experimental theater in France,* pp. 145-147.

Pucciani, Oreste F. "Tragedy, Genet and *The Maids." Tulane Drama Rev.,* vol. 7, no. 3 (Spring, 1963), pp. 42-59.

Sartre, Jean-Paul. *"The Maids." In:* Bogard, Travis and Oliver, William I., eds. *Modern drama; essays in criticism,* pp. 152-167. (Reprinted from Sartre, Jean-Paul. *Saint Genet, actor and martyr,* N.Y., Braziller, 1963.)

Sartre, Jean-Paul. *Saint Genet, actor and martyr,* pp. 611-625.

Thody, Philip. *Jean Genet, a study of his novels and plays,* pp. 163-178.

Wellwarth, George. *The theatre of protest and paradox,* pp.114-116.

Zimbardo, R.A. "Genet's Black Mass." *Modern Drama,* vol. 8, no. 3 (Dec., 1965), pp. 247-253.

Paolo Paoli

Fowlie, Wallace. *Dionysus in Paris.* pp. 226-228.

The Screens (Les Paravents)

Abel, Lionel. "Don't Sing Your Crap." *New York Review of Books,* vol. 1, no. 1 (1963), "Special Issue," p. 17.

Calarco, N. Joseph. "Vision Without Compromise: Genet's *The Screens." Drama Survey,* vol. 4, no. 1 (Spring, 1965), pp. 44-50.

Clements, Robert J. "The European Literary Scene." *Saturday Rev.,* (July 2, 1966), p. 23.

Coe, Richard N. *The vision of Jean Genet,* pp. 296-315.

Cohn, Ruby. "Four Stages of Absurdist Hero." *Drama Survey,* vol. 4, no. 3 (Winter, 1965), pp. 204-208.

Cohn, Ruby. "Theatre Abroad." *Drama Survey,* vol. 5, no. 3 (Winter, 1966-67), pp. 289-290.

Esslin, Martin. *The theatre of the absurd,* pp. 164-165.

Grossvogel, David I. *Four playwrights and a postscript, Brecht, Ionesco, Beckett, Genet,* pp. 171-174.

Guicharnaud, Jacques. *Modern French theatre from Giraudoux to Genet* (rev. ed.), pp. 160, 260, 265-266, 268, 277, 289.

Jacobsen, Josephine. *Ionesco and Genet, playwrights of silence,* pp. 1, 3, 12, 18, 21, 23-24, 26, 128-130, 156-157, 165-173, 182, 192-193, 195, 200, 204, 209, 211, 215.

Knapp, Bettina L. *Jean Genet,* pp. 140-155.

Knapp, Bettina. *"The Screens." Tulane Drama Rev.,* vol. 11, no. 4, (Summer, 1967), pp. 105-112.

McMahon, Joseph H. "Keeping Faith and Holding Firm." *Yale French Studies,* no. 29 (1962), pp. 26-32.

Marowitz, Charles. ed. *Theatre at work,* pp. 180-182.

Pierret, Marc. "Genet's New Play: *The Screens." Tulane Drama Rev.,* vol. 7, no. 3 (Spring, 1963), pp. 93-97.

Pronko, Leonard C. *L'Esprit Createur,* vol. 2, no. 4 (Winter, 1962), pp. 181-188.

Thody, Philip. *Jean Genet, a study of his novels and plays,* pp. 205-219.

Wellwarth, George. *The theatre of protest and paradox,* pp. 128-131.

The Tight Rope Walker

Knapp, Bettina L. *Jean Genet,* pp. 93-95.

PAUL GERALDY 1885-

General

Knowles, Dorothy. *French drama of the inter-war years, 1918-39,* pp. 264-266.

Moore, Harry T. *Twentieth-century French literature to World War II,* pp. 130-131.

Palmer, John. *Studies in the contemporary theatre,* pp. 151-162.

Robert et Marianne

Palmer, John. *Studies in the contemporary theatre,* pp. 155-158.

The War, Madame (La Guerre, Madame)

Palmer, John. *Studies in the contemporary theatre,* pp. 158-160.

MICHEL DE GHELDERODE 1898-1962

General

Abel, Lionel. "Our Man in the 16th Century: Michel de Ghelderode." *Tulane Drama Rev.,* vol. 8, no. 1 (Fall, 1963), pp. 62-71.

Brady, Leo. "The Showcase." *The Critic* (Feb., Mar., 1961), p. 66.

Columbia Encyclopedia, 3rd ed., New York, 1963, p. 822.

Corrigan, Robert W., ed. *Masterpieces of the modern French theatre,* pp. 88-89.

Draper, Samuel and Lois Alworth. "Bibliography on Michel de Ghelderode." *Modern Drama,* vol. 8, no. 3 (Dec., 1965), pp. 332-334.

Draper, Samuel. *Commonweal,* vol. 73, no. 5 (Oct. 28, 1960), pp. 113-115.

Draper, Samuel. *Commonweal,* vol. 76, no. 7 (May 11, 1962), pp. 166-168.

Draper, Samuel. "Infernal Theater." *Commonweal,* vol. 71, no. 10 (Dec. 4, 1959), pp. 279-282.

Draper, Samuel. "An Interview With Michel de Ghelderode." *Tulane Drama Rev.,* vol. 8, no. 1 (Fall, 1963), pp. 39-50.

Draper, Samuel. "Michel de Ghelderode; A Personal Statement." *Tulane Drama Rev., vol.* 8, no. 1 (Fall, 1963), pp. 33-38.

Draper, Samuel. "Michel de Ghelderode: More Life than Death." *Drama Critique,* vol. 8, no. 1 (Winter, 1965)

Draper, Samuel, *et al.* "Modern Dramatist." *New York Times Book Review,* April 22, 1962.

Funke, Lewis. "Theatre: 3 One Act Plays at the Gate." *New York Times* (July 23, 1960).

Ghelderode, Michel de. "The Ostend Interviews." *In:* Corrigan, Robert W., ed. *Masterpieces of the modern French theatre,* pp. 91-114. *(Also in: Tulane Drama Rev.,* vol. 3, no. 3 (March, 1959), pp. 3-23; Corrigan, R.W., ed. *The new theatre of Europe,* pp. 220-247.)

Ghelderode, Michel de. "To Directors and Actors: Letters, 1948-1959." *Tulane Drama Rev.,* vol. 9, no. 4 (Summer, 1965), pp. 41-62.

Grossvogel, David I. "Plight of the Comic Author...and Some New Departures in Contemporary Comedy." *Romanic Rev.,* vol. 45, no. 4 (Dec., 1954), pp. 268-270.

Grossvogel, David I. *The self-conscious stage in modern French drama,* pp. 254-310.

Guicharnaud, Jacques. *Modern French theatre from Giraudoux to Genet* (rev. ed.), pp. 160, 164-169, 172, 176, 181, 195, 287, 321, 339-341, 361.

Harris, Leonard. "Ghelderode Let Down." *New York World Telegram* (Dec. 3, 1963).

Hauger, George. "Dispatches from the Prince of Ostreland." *Tulane Drama Rev.,* vol. 8, no. 1 (Fall, 1963), pp. 24-32.

Hauger, George. "Notes on the Plays of Michel de Ghelderode." *Tulane Drama Rev.,* vol. 14, no. 1 (Sept., 1959), pp. 19-30.

Hellman, Helen. "Hallucination and Cruelty in Artaud and Ghelderode." *French Rev.,* vol. 41 (1967), pp. 1-10.

Hellman, Helen. *"Splendors of Hell:* A Tragic Force." *Renascence,* vol. 20 (1967), pp. 30-38.

Herz, Micheline. "Tragedy, Poetry, and the Burlesque in Ghelderode's Theatre." *Yale French Studies,* no. 29 (Spring-Summer, 1962), pp. 92-101.

Jacobi, Peter. "Chicago Samples the Absurd." *Christian Science Monitor* (March 25, 1963).

Kliewer, Warren. "Ghelderode and the Cure of Sin." *Drama Critique,* vol. 8, no. 1 (Winter, 1965).

Lilar, Suzanne. "The Belgian Theatre." *Theatre Arts,* vol. 35, no. 2 (Feb., 1951), pp. 34-35.

Lilar, Suzanne. "The Sacred and the Profane in the Work of Belgian Dramatists." *World Theatre,* vol. 9, no. 1 (Spring, 1960), pp. 11-12.

Maddocks, Melvin. "Image Theatre's Ghelderode." *Christian Science Monitor* (Nov. 10, 1961).

Mallinson, Vernon. *Modern Belgian literature, 1830-1960,* pp. 177-179.

Moore, Harry T. *Twentieth-century French literature since World War II,* pp. 30-33.

Pronko, Leonard C. *Avant-garde: the experimental theater in France,* pp. 165-180.

Richardson, Jack. "Neglected Playwrights I: Michel de Ghelderode." *Theatre Arts,* vol. 46 (August, 1962), pp. 28-52.

Share, Peter. "Theatre: Three by Ghelderode." *Village Voice,* (Dec. 5, 1963), p. 12.

Tallmer, Jerry. "3 by Ghelderode Opens at the Stage 73 Theater." *New York Post* (Dec. 23, 1963).

Taubman, Harold. "Theatre: by Ghelderode." *New York Times* (May 8, 1962).

Time, "Playwrights, Smoke, Froth, Snort!" vol. 80 (October 5, 1962), p. 72.

Trousson, Raymond. "The Fool-Hero of Michel de Ghelderode." *Drama Survey,* vol. 4, no. 3 (Winter 1965), pp. 264-271.

Vibert, Trevor. "Michel de Ghelderode." *New Theatre Magazine,* vol. 5, no. 3 (1964), pp. 2-10.

Weiss, Aureliu. "The Theatrical World of Michel de Ghelderode." *Tulane Drama Rev.,* vol. 8, no. 1 (Fall, 1963), pp. 51-61.

Wellwarth, George E. "Ghelderode's Theatre of the Grotesque." *Tulane Drama Rev.,* vol. 8, no. 1 (Fall, 1963), pp. 11-23.

Obituary

New York Herald Tribune (April 2, 1962).

New York Times (April 2, 1962).

Time (April 13, 1962), p. 92.

Barabbas

Mallinson, Vernon. *Modern Belgian literature, 1830-1960,* pp. 179-180.

Scheff, Aimee. "Introducing Michel de Ghelderode: Loyola University Presentation of *Barabbas."* *Theatre Arts,* vol. 37, no. 4 (Apr., 1953), p. 83.

Wellwarth, George. *The theatre of protest and paradox,* pp. 109-110.

The Blind Men (Les Aveugles)

Wellwarth, George. *The theatre of protest and paradox,* pp. 100-101.

Christopher Columbus

Cassell, Richard A. *What is the play?* pp. 623, 642-643.

Chronicles of Hell (The Pomps of Hell) (Fastes d'Enfer)

Clurman, Harold. "Theatre." *Nation,* vol. 205, no. 21 (Dec. 18, 1967), p. 669-670.

Hellman, Helen. "The Fool-Hero of Michel de Ghelderode." *Drama Survey,* vol. 4, no. 3 (Winter, 1965), pp. 269-270.

Wellwarth, George. *The theatre of protest and paradox,* pp. 107-108.

The Death of Doctor Faust (Le Mort du Docteur Faust)

Cole, Douglas. "Faust and Anti-Faust in Modern Drama." *Drama Survey,* vol. 5, no. 1 (Spring, 1966), pp. 39-44.

Pronko, Leonard C. *Avant-garde: the experimental theater in France,* pp. 169-171.

Wellwarth, George. *The theatre of protest and paradox,* p. 111.

Don Juan

Pronko, Leonard C. *Avant-garde: the experimental theater in France,* pp. 172-173.

Wellwarth, George. *The theatre of protest and paradox,* pp. 111-112.

Escurial

Hellman, Helen. "The Fool-Hero of Michel de Ghelderode." *Drama Survey,* vol. 4, no. 3 (Winter, 1965), pp. 265-266, 267.

Kelly, Kevin. "De Ghelderode's *Escurial* Cryptic, Grim, Fascinating." *Boston Globe* (Nov. 10, 1961).

New Yorker. "*Escurial.*" *Criticism,* vol. 38 (May 19, 1962), p. 104.

Richardson, Jack. "Ghelderode's *Escurial.*" *The Second Coming Magazine* (Jan.-Feb., 1961).

The Grand Macabre's Stroll (La Balade du Grand Macabre)

Wellwarth, George. *The theatre of protest and paradox,* pp. 103, 104-105.

Hop, Signor!

Gilman, Richard. *Commonweal,* vol. 76, no. 10 (June 1, 1962), pp. 259-260.

Harris, Leonard. "*Signor* Opens at the Cricket." *New York World Telegram* (May 8, 1962).

Hellman, Helen. "The Fool-Hero of Michel de Ghelderode." *Drama Survey,* vol. 4, no. 3 (Winter, 1965), p. 267.

Kerr, Walter. "Off Broadway Report: *Hop Signor.*" *New York Herald Tribune,* (May 8, 1962).

New Yorker, "*Hop Signor!*" *Criticism,* vol. 38 (May 19, 1962), p. 104.

Simon, John. *Theatre Arts,* vol. 46, no. 8 (Aug., 1962), p. 58.

Mademoiselle Jaïre

Wellwarth, George. *The theatre of protest and paradox,* pp. 106-107.

Worsley, T.C. "A Modern Miracle." *New Statesman,* vol. 54 (Nov. 16, 1957), p. 648.

The Magpie on the Gallows (La Pié sur la Gibet)

Wellwarth, George. *The theatre of protest and paradox,* pp. 101-102.

Marie la Miserable

Wellwarth, George. *The theatre of protest and paradox.* pp. 99-100, 107.

Of a Devil Who Preached Wonders (D'Un Diable Qui Precha Merveilles)

Wellwarth, George. *The theatre of protest and paradox,* pp. 105-106.

Pantagleize

Clurman, Harold. "Theatre." *Nation,* vol. 205, no. 21 (Dec. 18, 1967), pp. 669-670.

Corrigan, Robert W. "Introduction." *In:* Corrigan, Robert W., ed. *The new theatre of Europe,* pp. 23-25.

Ghelderode, Michel de. "Epitaph for *Pantagleize.*" *In:* Corrigan, Robert W., ed. *The new theatre of Europe,* pp. 244-247; *Theatre Arts,* vol. 46, no. 8 (Aug., 1962), pp. 22-24.

Mallinson, Vernon. *Modern Belgian literature, 1830-1960,* p. 181.

Pronko, Leonard C. *Avant-garde: the experimental theater in France,* pp. 173-174.

Wellwarth, George. *The theatre of protest and paradox,* pp. 112-113.

Red Magic (Magie Rouge)

Fraidstern, Iska. "Ghelderode's *Red Magic:* Gold and the Use of the Christian Myth." *Modern Drama,* vol. 11, no. 4 (Feb., 1969), pp. 376-381.

Wellwarth, George. *The theatre of protest and paradox,* pp. 103-104.

Saint François d'Assise

Ghelderode, M. de. "The Ostend Interviews." *In:* Corrigan, R.W., ed. *The new theatre of Europe,* pp. 239-240.

School for Buffoons (Ecole des Bouffons)

Hellman, Helen. "The Fool-Hero of Michel de Ghelderode." *Drama Survey,* vol. 4, no. 3 (Winter, 1965), pp. 265, 266-267, 268, 270.

Sortie de l'Acteur

Grossvogel, David I. *The self-conscious stage in modern French drama,* pp. 254-259.

The Strange Rider (La Cavalier Bizarre)

Wellwarth, George. *The theatre of protest and paradox,* pp. 102-103.

Trois Auteurs, un Drame

Bishop, Thomas. *Pirandello and the French theater,* pp. 75-78.

The Women at the Tomb (Les Femmes au Tombeau)

Wellwarth, George. *The theatre of protest and paradox,* pp. 109, 110.

HENRI GHEON 1875-1944

General

Aylen, Leo. *Greek tragedy and the modern world,* pp. 219, 225, 227, 312-313.

Knowles, Dorothy. *French drama of the inter-war years, 1918-39,* pp. 299-301.

Le Mystère de l'Invention de la Croix

Aylen, Leo. *Greek tragedy and the modern world,* pp. 313-316, 318.

Oedipe

Aylen, Leo. *Greek tragedy and the modern world,* pp. 316-318.

Les Trois Miracles de Saint Cécile

Chiari, Joseph. *The contemporary French theatre,* pp. 49-53.

GUISEPPE GIACOSA

General

Miller, Nellie Burget. *The living drama,* pp. 376-377.

Like Falling Leaves

Miller, Nellie Burget. *The living drama,* p. 377-378.

WILLIAM GIBSON 1914-

The Miracle Worker

Kerr, Walter. *The theater in spite of itself,* pp. 255-257.

Two for the Seesaw

Gassner, John. *Theatre at the crossroads,* pp. 211-216.

ANDRE GIDE 1869-1951

General

Knowles, Dorothy. *French drama of the inter-war years, 1918-39,* pp. 218-220.

McLaughlin, Richard. *Theatre Arts,* vol. 36, no. 1 (Jan., 1952), p. 2.

Peyre, Henri. "Intellectual Drama." *Saturday Rev.,* vol. 35, no. 5 (Feb. 2, 1952), p. 18.

Sanderson, James L., ed. *Oedipus, myth and dramatic form,* pp. 149-150, 177-178.

San Juan, E., Jr. "The Idea of André Gide's Theatre." *Educational Theatre J.,* vol. 17, no. 3 (Oct., 1965), pp. 220-224.

The Immoralist (L'Immoraliste) (Adapted by Ruth and Augustus Goetz)

Bentley, Eric. *The dramatic event,* pp. 205-208.

Bentley, Eric. *New Republic,* vol. 130 (Mar. 22, 1954), p. 21.

Clurman, Harold. *Nation,* vol. 178, no. 8 (Feb. 20, 1954), pp. 156-157.

Fowlie, Wallace. *André Gide: his life and art,* pp. 46-56.

Gibbs, Wolcott. *New Yorker,* vol. 29, (Feb. 13, 1954), pp. 61-62.

Hewes, Henry. "The Serpent in the Orchard." *Saturday Rev.,* vol. 37, no. 9 (Feb. 27, 1954), p. 28.

Theatre Arts, vol. 38, no. 4 (Apr., 1954), p. 17.

Worsley, T.C. *New Statesman & Nation,* vol. 48 (Nov. 13, 1954), p. 610.

King Candaules (Le Roi Candaule)

Fowlie, Wallace. *Dionysus in Paris,* pp. 163-164.

San Juan, E., Jr. "Pattern and Significance in Two Plays of André Gide." *Discourse,* vol. 8 (1965), pp. 350-361.

Watson-Williams, Helen. *André Gide and the Greek myth,* pp. xi, 62-63, 68-69, 70, 72-81, 82-84, 88-89, 103, 114, 124, 132-133, 135, 142, 149, 151, 153-154, 155-156, 159-161, 164-165, 173, 187.

Oedipus (Oedipe)

Aylen, Leo. *Greek tragedy and the modern world,* pp. 265-267.

Conacher, D.J. "Theme and Technique in the *Philoctètes* and *Oedipus* of André Gide." *Univ. of Toronto Q.,* vol. 24 (1965), pp. 126-135.

Fowlie, Wallace. *André Gide: his life and art,* pp. 107-110.

Fowlie, Wallace. *Dionysus in Paris,* pp. 164-165.

Knowles, Dorothy. *French drama of the inter-war years, 1918-39,* pp. 215-218.

San Juan, E., Jr. "The Significance of André Gide's *Oedipus." In:* Sanderson, James L., ed. *Oedipus, myth and dramatic form,* pp. 321-329. *(Also in: Modern Drama,* vol. 7, no. 4 (Feb., 1965), pp. 422-430.)

Watson-Williams, Helen. *André Gide and the Greek myth, a critical study,* pp. xi, xiii, 69, 84, 103-104, 110-116, 117-125, 126, 132-133, 135-136, 138, 140, 142, 144, 148, 150-156, 158-159, 161-166, 168, 172-173, 175-177, 180, 184, 186-189.

Persephone

Rosenfeld, Paul. "The Mystery of *Persephone." New Republic,* vol. 82 (Apr. 3, 1935), pp. 213-214.

Watson-Williams, Helen. *André Gide and the Greek myth, a critical study,* pp. 45, 69, 103, 105-110, 125, 136, 158-159, 165, 184, 187-188.

Philoctetes (Philoctète)

Conacher, D.J. "Theme and Technique in the *Philoctètes* and *Oedipus* of André Gide." *Univ. of Toronto Q.,* vol. 24 (1965), pp. 121-126.

Watson-Williams, Helen. *André Gide and the Greek myth, a critical study,* pp. 39-40, 57-68, 74-75, 88, 92, 103, 118-119, 124, 132, 136, 140, 142, 149, 153, 158-159, 165-166, 168, 172-174, 186, 193.

The Return of the Prodigal (Le Retour de l'Enfant Prodique)

Fowlie, Wallace. *André Gide: his life and art,* pp. 57-61.

Fowlie, Wallace. *Dionysus in Paris,* p. 160.

Knowles, Dorothy. *French drama of the inter-war years, 1918-39,* p. 215.

Robert, ou l'Interet General

Knowles, Dorothy. *French drama of the inter-war years, 1918-39,* p. 218.

Saul

Fowlie, Wallace. *Dionysus in Paris,* pp. 161-163.

Knowles, Dorothy. *French drama of the inter-war years, 1918-39,* pp. 214-215.

San Juan, E., Jr. "Pattern and Significance in Two Plays of André Gide." *Discourse,* vol. 8 (1965), pp. 350-361.

Stolzfus, Ben F. " *Saul:* A Germinating Gide." *French Rev.,* vol. 39, no. 1 (Oct. 1965), pp. 49-56.

Watson-Williams, Helen. *André Gide and the Greek myth,* pp. xi, 62-63, 68-72, 74-75, 81-83, 112, 122, 124, 133, 135, 148-149, 159-160, 180, 187.

W. S. GILBERT 1836-1911

General

Siney, Marion C. "Victorian England through Gilbert's Eyes." *Michigan Q. Rev.,* vol. 2, no. 2 (Spring, 1963), pp. 94-101.

Stedman, Jane W. "Introduction." *In:* Stedman, J.W., ed. *Gilbert before Sullivan: six comic plays by W.S. Gilbert.*

FRANK D. GILROY

The Subject Was Roses

Duprey, Richard A. "Today's Dramatists." *In: American theatre,* pp. 221-222.

Gilroy, F.D. *About those roses or how not to do a play and succeed and the text of The Subject Was Roses.*

JEAN GIONO 1895-

General

Knowles, Dorothy. *French drama of the inter-war years, 1918-39,* pp. 227-228.

Le Bout de la Route

Smith, Maxwell A. *Jean Giono,* pp. 68-70.

Domitien

Smith, Maxwell A. *Jean Giono,* pp. 126-128.

La Femme du Boulanger

Smith, Maxwell A. *Jean Giono,* pp. 72-74.

Lanceurs de Graines

Smith, Maxwell A. *Jean Giono,* pp. 70-72.

Le Voyage en Caleche

Smith, Maxwell A. *Jean Giono,* pp. 123-26.

SILVIO GIOVANINETTI 1901-1962

General

Pandolfi, Vito. "Italian Theatre Since the War." *Tulane Drama Rev.,* vol. 8, no. 3 (Spring, 1964), p. 99.

JEAN GIRAUDOUX 1882-1944

General

Aylen, Leo. *Greek tragedy and the modern world,* pp. 267-269, 276-277.

Bermel, Albert, ed. *The genius of the French theater,* pp. 407-410.

Calvin, Judith S. "The GBS sense of Giraudoux." *Shaw Rev.,* vol. 5, no. 1 (Jan., 1962), pp. 21-35.

Cohen, Robert. *Giraudoux; three faces of destiny,* pp. 131-155.

Corrigan, Robert W., ed. *Masterpieces of the modern French theatre,* pp. 140-141.

Fowlie, Wallace. *Dionysus in Paris,* pp. 59-63, 72-73.

Fowlie, Wallace. "Giraudoux's Approach to Tragedy." *Tulane Drama Rev.,* vol. 3, no. 4 (May, 1959), pp. 6-16.

Gascoigne, Bamber. *Twentieth-century drama,* pp. 134-143.

Giraudoux, Jean. "Two Laws." *In:* Corrigan, Robert W. ed. *Masterpieces of the modern French theatre,* pp. 143-145. *Also in:* Cole, Toby. *Playwrights on playwriting.*

Grossvogel, David I. *The self-conscious stage in modern French drama,* pp. 68-105.

Guicharnaud, Jacques. *Modern French theatre from Giraudoux to Beckett,* pp. 19-47. *Also in:* Bogard, Travis, and Oliver, William I., eds. *Modern drama; essays in criticism,* pp. 168-191.

Guicharnaud, Jacques. *Modern French theatre from Giraudoux to Genet* (rev. ed.), pp. 8, 13, 16-43, 44, 48, 61, 66, 67, 80, 87, 100, 101, 117, 120, 121, 133, 137, 155, 159, 179, 231, 282, 287, 321, 323-325, 357-358.

Hatzfeld, Helmut. *Trends and styles in twentieth century French literature,* pp. 135-138.

Jones, Robert Emmet. *The alienated hero in modern French drama,* pp. 76-83, 88-94.

Knowles, Dorothy. *French drama of the inter-war years, 1918-39,* pp. 213-214.

Leefmans, Bert M.P. "Giraudoux's Other Muse." *Kenyon Rev.,* vol. 16, no. 4 (Autumn, 1954), pp. 611-627.

LeSage, Laurence. "Jean Giraudoux, Surrealism, and the German Romantic Ideal." *Illinois Studies in Language and Literature,* vol. 36, no. 3 (1952), pp. 1-37.

LeSage, Laurent. "Jean Giraudoux's Case Against Germany." *French Rev.,* vol. 17, no. 6 (May, 1944), pp. 353-357.

Lewis, Allan. *The contemporary theatre,* pp. 194-201.

Lumley, Frederick. *New trends in 20th century drama,* pp. 35-58.

Lumley, Frederick. *Trends in 20th century drama,* pp. 36-59.

Maclean, Mary. "Jean Giraudoux and Frank Wedekind." *Australian J. of French Studies* (Monash U., Clayton, Victoria), vol. 4 (1967), pp. 107-108.

McLendon, Will L. "Giraudoux and the Impossible Couple." *PMLA,* vol. 82 (1967), pp. 197-205.

May, Georges. "Jean Giraudoux: Diplomacy and Dramaturgy." *Yale French Studies,* no. 5 (1950), pp. 88-99.

May, Georges. "Marriage vs. Love in the World of Giraudoux." *Yale French Studies,* no. 11 (1953), pp. 106-115.

Moore, Harry T. *Twentieth-century French literature to World War II,* pp. 144-149.

Peacock, Ronald. "Public and Private Problems in Modern Drama." *In:* Corrigan, Robert W. *Theatre in the twentieth century,* pp. 312-316.

Pucciani, Oreste. "The 'Infernal Dialogue' of Giraudoux and Sartre." *Tulane Drama Rev.,* vol. 3, no. 4 (May, 1959), pp. 57-75.

Simon, John Kenneth. "The Presence of Musset in Modern French Drama." *French Rev.,* vol. 40, no. 1 (Oct., 1966), pp. 27-38.

Stansburg, Milton H. *Bookman,* vol. 76, no. 3 (Mar., 1933), pp. 246-251.

Valency, Maurice. "Playwright Who Kept His Rendez-vous." *Theatre Arts,* vol. 33, no. 7 (Aug., 1949), pp. 12-13.

Wahl, Charles Z. "Jean Giraudoux, a twentieth century humanist." Ph.D., Yale University, 1950.

Amphitryon 38

Cohen, Robert. *Giraudoux; three faces of destiny,* pp. 45-51.

Fowlie, Wallace. *Dionysus in Paris,* pp. 71-72.

Garapon, Robert. "Classical and Contemporary French Literature." *Univ. of Toronto Q.,* vol. 36, no. 2 (Jan., 1967), pp. 103-104, 105.

Gearin-Tosh, Michael. *Amphitryon 38* at the Oxford Playhouse." *Guardian,* no. 37,265 (May 2, 1966), p. 7.

"Giraudoux on Marital Bliss." *Times,* no. 56,896 (Mar. 22, 1967), p. 10.

Grossvogel, David I. *The self-conscious stage in modern French drama,* pp. 89-91.

Knowles, Dorothy. *French drama of the inter-war years, 1918-39,* pp. 198-199.

Lumley, Frederick. *New trends in the 20th century drama,* pp. 38, 41, 45-48.

Lumley, Frederick. *Trends in 20th century drama,* pp. 46-49.

Nathan, George Jean. *Scribner's Mag.,* vol. 102 (Oct., 1937), pp. 66, 68.

Wyatt, Euphemia. *Catholic World,* vol. 146 (Dec., 1937), pp. 338-339.

Young, Stark. *New Republic,* vol. 93 (Nov. 17, 1937), p. 44.

Young, Stark. *New Republic,* vol. 94 (Mar. 9, 1938), p. 132.

The Apollo of Bellac (L'Apollon de Bellac)

Cohen, Robert. *Giraudoux; three faces of destiny,* pp. 76-81.

Duel of Angels (For Lucretia) (Pour Lucrèce)

Chiari, Joseph. *The contemporary French theatre,* 127-131.

Clurman, Harold. *The naked image,* pp. 77-79.

Clurman, Harold. *Nation,* vol. 190, no. 19 (May, 1960), pp. 411-412.

Clurman, Harold. "Theatre." *Nation,* vol. 178, no. 23 (June 5, 1954), pp. 488-490.

Cohen, Robert. *Giraudoux; three faces of destiny,* pp. 30-40.

Dirks, Mary D. "Buskin and Farce; Notes on *Pour Lucrèce.*" *Tulane Drama Rev.,* vol. 3, no. 4 (May, 1959), pp. 76-87.

Driver, Tom F. *Christian Century,* vol. 77, no. 22 (June 1, 1960), pp. 672-673.

Gascoigne, Bamber. *Twentieth-century drama,* pp. 140-142.

Hewes, Henry. *Saturday Rev.,* vol. 43 (May 7, 1960), p. 26.

Hooker, Ward. "Giraudoux's Last Play." *Hudson Rev.,* vol. 12, no. 4 (Winter, 1959-60), pp. 604-611.

Knowles, Dorothy. *French drama of the inter-war years, 1918-39,* pp. 212-213.

Lumley, Frederick. *New Trends in 20th century drama,* pp. 54, 55-57.

Tynan, Kenneth. *New Yorker,* vol. 36 (Apr. 30, 1960), pp. 83-84.

Electra (Electre)

Aylen, Leo. *Greek tragedy and the modern world,* pp. 269-271, 273-277.

Burdick, Delores M. "Concept of Character in Giraudoux's *Electre* and Sartre's *Les Mouches.*" *French Rev.,* vol. 33, no. 2 (Dec., 1959), pp. 131-136.

Chiari, Joseph. *The contemporary French theatre,* 119, 121-125, 137.

Cohen, Robert. *Giraudoux; three faces of destiny,* pp. 104-116.

Force, William M., ed. *Orestes and Electra, myth and dramatic form,* pp. 135-136.

Gascoigne, Bamber. *Twentieth-century drama,* pp. 138-140.

Gassner, John. "At War with Electra." *In:* Force, William M., ed. *Orestes and Electra, myth and dramatic form,* pp. 315-323. *(Also in: Tulane Drama Rev.,* vol. 3, no. 4 (May 1959).)

Gassner, John. *Theatre at the crossroads,* pp. 95-99.

Gassner, John. *The theatre in our times,* pp. 257-266.

Grossvogel, David I. *The self-conscious stage in modern French drama,* pp. 93-97.

Jones, Robert Emmet. *The alienated hero in modern French drama,* pp. 84-88.

Knowles, Dorothy. *French drama of the inter-war years, 1918-39,* pp. 206-208.

Lumley, Frederick. *New trends in 20th century drama,* pp. 35, 51-52, 54.

Lumley, Frederick. *Trends in 20th century drama,* pp. 52-53.

Ramsey, Warren. "The Oresteia Since Hofmannsthal: Images and Emphases." *Revue de Littérature Comparée."* vol. 38 (1964), pp. 366-369.

The Enchanted (Intermezzo)

Beyer, William. *School and Society,* vol. 71 (Feb. 25, 1950), pp. 118-119.

Bishop, Thomas. *Pirandello and the French theatre,* p. 97.

Cohen, Robert. *Giraudoux; three faces of destiny,* pp. 51-63.

Knowles, Dorothy. *French drama of the inter-war years, 1918-39,* pp. 201-203.

Lumley, Frederick. *New trends in 20th century drama,* pp. 41, 49-50, 51, 52, 54, 286.

Lumley, Frederick, *Trends in 20th century drama,* pp. 50-51.

Reilly, John Hurford. "Giraudoux's *Intermezzo:* Its Elaboration." *French Rev.,* vol. 39, no. 3 (Dec. 1965), pp. 410-417.

Sievers, W. David. *Freud on Broadway,* pp. 427-428.

Valency, Maurice. *Theatre Arts,* vol. 34, (Oct., 1950), p. 56.

Judith

Brustein, Robert. "Bagatelles and Jacks." *New Republic,* vol. 152 (Apr. 10, 1965), pp. 23-24.

Chiari, Joseph. *The contemporary French theatre,* 115-120, 138-139.

Clurman, Harold. "A Director Prepares." *Theatre Arts,* vol. 47, no. 4 (Apr., 1963), pp. 16-19, 75-76.

Clurman, Harold. *"Judith."* *Nation,* vol. 200, no. 15 (Apr. 12, 1965), pp. 403-404.

Cohen, Robert. *Giraudoux; three faces of destiny,* pp. 5-15.

Dirks, Mary D. "The Problem of *Judith." Tulane Drama Rev.,* vol. 3, no. 4 (May, 1959), pp. 31-41.

Gascoigne, Bamber. *Spectator,* no. 6993 (July 6, 1962), pp. 17-18.

Gascoigne, Bamber. *Twentieth-century drama,* pp. 135-137.

Grossvogel, David I. *The self-conscious stage in modern French drama,* pp. 87-89.

Hewes, Henry. *Saturday Rev.,* vol. 48 (Apr. 10, 1965), p. 58.

Knowles, Dorothy. *French drama of the inter-war years, 1918-39,* p. 199.

Lumley, Frederick. *New trends in the 20th century drama, pp. 48-*49.

Lumley, Frederick. *Trends in 20th century drama,* pp. 49-50.

Oliver, Edith. *New Yorker,* vol. 41 (Apr. 3, 1965), p. 86.

Roston, Murray. *Biblical drama in England from the Middle Ages to the present day,* pp.251-252.

The Madwoman of Chaillot (La Folle de Chaillot)

Allison, Alexander W. ed. *Masterpieces of the drama,* 2nd ed., pp. 629-630.

Beyer, William. *School and Society,* vol. 69 (Jan. 29, 1949), pp. 83-84.

Bishop, Thomas. *Pirandello and the French theater,* pp. 97-99.

Breé, Germaine. *"The Madwoman of Chaillot:* A Modern Masque." *Tulane Drama Rev.,* vol. 3, no 4 (May, 1959), pp. 51-56.

Brown, John Mason. *Saturday Rev.,* vol. 32, no. 3 (Jan. 15, 1949), pp. 32-34.

Brown, John Mason. *Still seeing things,* pp. 214-221.

Clurman, Harold. *Lies like truth,* pp. 213-218.

Clurman, Harold. *New Republic,* vol. 120 (Jan. 17, 1949), pp. 28-29.

Cohen, Robert. *Giraudoux; three faces of destiny,* pp. 116-129.

Downer, Alan S. *Furioso,* vol. 4, no. 4 (Fall, 1949), pp. 79-84.

Fay, Gerard. "Lunatics on the War-Path." *Public Opinion, no. 4657* (Feb. 23, 1951), p. 24.

Flanner, Janet. *Paris journal, 1944-1965,* pp. 52, 54-56.

Knowles, Dorothy. *French drama of the inter-war years, 1918-39,* pp. 211-212.

Krutch, Joseph Wood. *Nation,* vol. 168, no. 2 (Jan. 8, 1949), pp. 53-54.

LeSage, Laurent. "Giraudoux and Big Business: An Element of Reminiscence in *La Folle de Chaillot.*" *French Rev.,* no. 4 (Feb., 1958), pp. 278-282.

Lewis, Allan. *The contemporary theatre,* pp. 198-201.

Lumley, Frederick. *New trends in 20th century drama,* pp. 40, 41-42, 54-55.

Lumley, Frederick. *Trends in 20th century drama,* pp. 55-57.

Phelan, Kappo. *Commonweal,* vol. 49, no. 14 (Jan. 14, 1949), pp. 351-352.

"Play by Jean Giraudoux." *Times,* no. 51,899 (Jan. 15, 1951), p. 6.

Reboussin, Marcel. "Giraudoux and *The Madwoman of Chaillot.*" *Educational Theatre J.,* vol. 13, no. 1 (Mar., 1961), pp. 11-17.

Sievers, W. David. *Freud on Broadway,* p. 415.

Wall, Stephen. "Giraudoux's Goodies and Baddies." *Guardian,* no. 37,756 (Nov. 29, 1967), p. 7.

Worsley, T.C. *New Statesman,* vol. 41 (Feb. 24, 1951), pp. 214-215.

Wyatt, Euphemia. *Catholic World,* vol. 168 (Feb., 1949), pp. 401-402.

Ondine

Bentley, Eric. *The dramatic event,* pp. 200-204.

Bentley, Eric. *New Republic,* vol. 130 (Mar. 8, 1954), p. 21.

Clurman, Harold. "Theatre." *Nation,* vol. 178, no. 10 (Mar. 6, 1954), p. 206.

Cohen, Robert. *Giraudoux; three faces of destiny,* pp. 64-76.

Fowlie, Wallace. *Dionysus in Paris,* pp. 67-69.

Gascoigne, Bamber. *Spectator,* no. 6917 (Jan. 20, 1961), p. 76.

Gibbs, Wolcott. *New Yorker,* vol. 30 (Feb. 27, 1954), pp. 74-78.

Grossvogel, David I. *The self-conscious stage in modern French drama,* pp. 80-86.

Knowles, Dorothy. *French drama of the inter-war years, 1918-39,* pp. 208-210.

Lumley, Frederick. *New trends in 20th century drama,* pp. 52-53, 54.

Lumley, Frederick. *Trends in 20th century drama,* pp. 53-55.

Milne, Tom. "Neither Sprite nor Woman." *Time and Tide,* vol. 42, no. 3 (Jan. 20, 1961), p. 110.

Siepmann, Eric O. "The Plays of Giraudoux." *Nineteenth Century and After,* vol. 127 (June, 1940), pp. 732-736.

Theatre Arts, vol. 38, no. 5 (May, 1954), pp. 18-20.

Valency, Maurice. "Some Facts About a Myth." *Theatre Arts,* vol. 38, no. 12 (Dec., 1954), pp. 32-33.

Wyatt, Euphemia. *Catholic World,* vol. 179 (Apr., 1954), pp. 67-68.

Siegfried

Bishop, Thomas. *Pirandello and the French theater,* pp. 100-101.

Cohen, Robert. *Giraudoux; three faces of destiny,* pp. 85-93.

Cremieux, Benjamin. "Jean Giraudoux's *Siegfried." In:* La Nouvelle Revue Francaise. *From the N.R.F.,* pp. 166-168.

Grossvogel, David I. *The self-conscious stage in modern French drama,* pp. 75-80.

Inskip, Donald P. "Jean Giraudoux and 'Le Merite des Femmes,' An Interesting Allusion in *Siegfried." Modern Language Q.,* vol. 18, no. 3 (Sept., 1957), pp. 211-214.

Inskip, Donald P. "Some Notes on the First Production of Jean Giraudoux's *Siegfried* (May 3rd, 1928)." *French Studies,* vol. 12, no. 2 (Apr., 1958), pp. 143-146.

Inskip, Donald P. "The Stylist in the Theater. Some Remarks on a Passage of Jean Giraudoux's *Siegfried." Modern Language Rev.,* vol. 53, no. 2 (Apr., 1958), pp. 218-221.

Knowles, Dorothy. *French drama of the inter-war years, 1918-39*, pp. 195-198.

Lumley, Frederick. *New trends in the 20th century drama*, pp. 40, 42-45.

Lumley, Frederick. *Trends in the 20th century drama*, pp. 43-47.

Sodom and Gomorrah (Sodome et Gomorrhe)

Chiari, Joseph. *The contemporary French theatre*, pp. 125-127.

Cohen, Robert. *Giraudoux; three faces of destiny*, pp. 21-30.

Knowles, Dorothy. *French drama of the inter-war years, 1918-39*, pp. 210-211.

Lumley, Frederick. *New trends in 20th century drama*, pp. 41, 54, 55.

Lumley, Frederick. *Trends in 20th century drama*, pp. 55-56.

Fowlie, Wallace. *Dionysus in Paris*, pp. 69-71.

Grossvogel, David I. *The self-conscious stage in modern French drama*, pp. 97-101.

Song of Songs (Cantiques des Cantiques)

Bermel, Albert. ed. *The genius of the French theater*, pp. 19-20.

Cohen, Robert. *Giraudoux; three faces of destiny*, pp. 16-21.

Kemp, Robert. "Thoughts on *Song of Songs.*" *In:* Bermel, Albert, ed. *The genius of the French theater*, pp. 558-562.

Tiger at the Gates (La Guerre de Troie N'Aura Pas Lieu)

Aylen, Leo. *Greek tragedy and the modern world*, pp. 218, 221, 267, 269-277.

Becker, William. "Some French Plays in Translation." *Hudson Rev.,* vol. 9, no. 2 (Summer, 1956), pp. 280-283.

Bentley, Eric. *New Republic,* vol. 133 (Oct. 24, 1955), p. 22.

Bourgeois, André. "La Curieuse Helene de Jean Giraudoux dans *La Guerre de Troie N'Aura Pas Lieu.*" *Rice Institute pamphlet,* vol. 44, no. 2 (July, 1957), pp. 26-47.

Brockway, James. *"Tiger at the Gates." Guardian,* no. 37,357 (Aug 17, 1966), p. 7.

Chiari, Joseph. *The contemporary French theatre*, pp. 131-136.

Cohen, Robert. *Giraudoux; three faces of destiny,* pp. 94-104.

Falk, Eugene H. "Theme and Motif in *La Guerre de Troie n'aura pas lieu.*" *Tulane Drama Rev.,* vol. 3, no. 4 (May, 1959), pp. 17-30.

Fowlie, Wallace. Dionysus in Paris, pp. 64-65.

Garapon, Robert. "Classical and Contemporary French Literature." *Univ. of Toronto Q.,* vol. 36, no. 2 (Jan., 1967), pp. 104-105.

Gascoigne, Bamber. *Twentieth-century drama,* pp. 137-138.

Gibbs, Wolcott. *New Yorker,* vol. 31, (Oct. 15, 1955), pp. 76, 78-79.

Grossvogel, David I. *The self-conscious stage in modern French drama,* pp. 91-93.

Hayes, Richard. *"Tiger at the Gates."* *Commonweal,* vol. 63, no. 8 (Nov. 25, 1955), pp. 200-201.

Hivnor, Mary. *Kenyon Rev.,* vol. 18, no. 1 (Winter, 1956), pp. 128-130.

Knowles, Dorothy. *French drama of the inter-war years, 1918-39, pp.* 203-206.

Living Age, vol. 349, no. 4432 (Jan. 1936), pp. 457-458.

Lumley, Frederick. *New trends in 20th century drama,* pp. 41, 43, 50-51, 353.

Lumley, Frederick. *Trends in 20th century drama,* pp. 51-52.

Peacock, Ronald. "Public and Private Problems in Modern Drama." *Tulane Drama Rev.,* vol. 3, no. 3 (Mar., 1959), pp. 65-69.

Sainer, Arthur. *The sleepwalker and the assassin, a view of the contemporary theatre,* pp. 96-97.

Stanford, W.B. *The Ulysses theme; a study of a traditional hero,* pp. 173-174.

Worsley, T.C. *New Statesman,* vol. 49 (June 11, 1955), p. 811.

Wyatt, Euphemia. *Catholic World,* vol. 182 (Dec., 1955), pp. 223-234.

SUSAN GLASPELL 1882-1948

General

Goldberg, Isaac. *The drama of transition,* pp. 472-481.

Gould, Jean. *Modern American playwrights,* pp. 26-49.

Waterman, Arthur E. "Susan Glaspell and the Provincetown." *Modern Drama,* vol. 7, no. 2 (Sept., 1964), pp. 174-184.

Alison's House

Waterman, Arthur E. *Susan Glaspell,* pp. 74, 75, 84, 85, 86-89, 92, 103, 118.

Bernice

Waterman, Arthur E. *Susan Glaspell,* pp. 60, 73-76, 79, 84.

Chains of Dew (Unpublished)

Waterman, Arthur E. *Susan Glaspell,* pp. 63-64, 83-84, 100.

Close the Book

Waterman, Arthur E. *Susan Glaspell,* pp. 60, 69-70.

The Comic Artist

Waterman, Arthur E. *Susan Glaspell,* pp. 85-86, 92.

The Inheritors

Waterman, Arthur E. *Susan Glaspell,* pp. 53-54, 61, 63, 76-79, 84, 103, 111, 114, 118.

The Outside

Waterman, Arthur E. *Susan Glaspell,* pp. 71-72, 75.

The People

Waterman, Arthur E. *Susan Glaspell,* pp. 70-71.

Suppressed Desires

Sievers, W. David. *Freud on Broadway,* pp. 53-55.

Waterman, Arthur E. *Susan Glaspell,* pp. 57, 59, 67-68.

Tickless Time

Waterman, Arthur E. *Susan Glaspell,* p. 72.

Trifles

Waterman, Arthur E. *Susan Glaspell,* pp. 29, 58, 59, 68-69.

The Verge

Sievers, W. David. *Freud on Broadway,* pp. 70-71.
Waterman, Arthur E. *Susan Glaspell,* pp. 28, 39, 63, 79-83, 84.

Young, Stark. "Susan Glaspell's *The Verge.*" *In:* Moses, Montrose J. *The American theatre as seen by its critics, 1752-1934,* pp. 252-255.

Woman's Honor

Waterman, Arthur E. *Susan Glaspell,* p. 69.

ANATOL GLEBOV

Inga

Block, Anita. *The changing world in plays and theatre,* pp. 382-385.

REINHARD GOERING 1887-1936

Naval Battle (Seeschlacht)

Garten, H.F. *Modern German drama,* 128-130.

NIKOLAY VASILYEVICH GOGOL 1809-1852

General

Kropotkin, P. *Russian literature,* pp. 67-86.

Lavrin, Janko. *Nikolai Gogol (1809-1852) a centenary survey,* pp. 92-94.

Strong, Robert L., Jr. "The Soviet Interpretation of Gogol." *American Slavic and East European Rev.,* vol. 14, no. 4 (1955), pp. 528-539.

Alfred (Fragment. Unpublished)

Setchkarev, Vsevolod. *Gogol: his life and works,* pp. 166-167.

The Gamblers (Igrokhi)

Coleman, Arthur P. *Humor in the Russian comedy from Catherine to Gogol,* pp. 13-14, 65.

The Inspector-General (The Revizor)

Coleman, Arthur P. *Humor in the Russian comedy from Catherine to Gogol,* pp. 15, 25-26, 35-37, 47-48, 56-58, 66-68, 74-78, 82-83, 87, 88.

Kropotkin, P. *Russian literature,* pp. 73-79.

Lavrin, Janko. *Nikolai Gogol (1809-1852), a centenary survey,* pp. 79-89, 124.

Macleod, Joseph. *Actors cross the Volga,* pp. 25-28.

Nabokov, Vladimir. *Nikolai Gogol,* pp. 35-60.

Perry, Henry Ten Eyck. *Masters of dramatic comedy and their social themes,* 319-325.

Setchkarev, Vsevolod. *Gogol: his life and works,* pp. 167-172, 177-178.

Simmons, Ernest J. *Introduction to Russian realism,* pp. 61-65.

Valency, Maurice. *The breaking string,* pp. 26-28.

The Marriage

Coleman, Arthur P. *Humor in the Russian comedy from Catherine to Gogol,* pp. 14-15, 25, 35, 46-47, 54-55.

Dent, Alan. *Preludes and studies,* pp. 151-152.

Lavrin, Janko. *Nikolai Gogol (1809-1852), a centenary survey,* pp. 89-92.

Setchkarev, Vsevolod. *Gogol: his life and works,* pp. 42, 43-44, 115, 172-177.

MIKE GOLD

General

Knox, George A. *Dos Passos and "The Revolting Playwrights,"* pp. 55-56.

Fiesta

Knox, George A. *Dos Passos and "The Revolting Playwrights,"* pp. 127-140, 176-177.

Hoboken Blues

Knox, George A. *Dos Passos and "The Revolting Playwrights,"* pp. 124-127, 173-174, 191, 194.

WILLIAM GOLDING 1911-

The Brass Butterfly

Baker, James R. *William Golding; a critical study,* pp. 48-54.

Barnet, Sylvan ed. *The genius of the later English theater,* pp. 439-442.

Dick, Bernard F. *William Golding,* pp. 16, 63-66, 92.

Oldsey, Bernard S. *The art of William Golding,* pp. 150-158.

JAMES GOLDMAN
The Lion in Winter

Downer, Alan S. "Total Theatre and Partial Drama: Notes on the New York Theatre, 1965-1966." *Q. J. of Speech,* vol. 52, no. 3 (Oct., 1966), pp. 235-236.

CLIFFORD GOLDSMITH
What a Life

O'Hara, Frank H. *Today in American drama,* pp. 56-57, 195-202.

IVAN GOLL
Mathusalem

Knowles, Dorothy. *French drama of the inter-war years, 1918-39,* p. 88.

MAXIM GORKI 1868-1936
General

Dukes, Ashley, *Modern dramatists,* pp. 185-190.

Lewis, Allan. *The contemporary theatre,* pp. 111-127.

Lindstrom, Thais. "Pirandellian Masks in the Gorky Theatre." *Theatre annual, 1960,* pp. 1-11.

Macleod, Joseph. *Actors cross the Volga,* pp. 88-91, 92-94, 100-114.

O'Casey, Sean. "Great Man, Gorki!" *In:* O'Casey, Sean. *Blasts and benedictions,* pp. 230-233.

The Lower Depths

Beerbohm, Max. *Around theatres,* pp. 302-305.

Borras, F.M. *Maxim Gorky the writer; an interpretation,* pp. 167-178.

Dukes, Ashley. *Modern dramatists,* pp. 185-190.

Heilman, Robert B. *Tragedy and melodrama,* pp. 47-50, 55-56, 80.

Lamm, Martin. *Modern drama,* pp. 217-219.

Lewis, Allan. *The contemporary theatre,* pp. 115-119.

Muchnic, Helen. "Circe's Swine: Plays by Gorky and O'Neill." *In:* Gassner, John, ed. *O'Neill,* pp. 99-109. (From *Comparative Literature,* vol. 3, no. 2 (Spring, 1951), pp. 119-128.)

Rowe, Kenneth Thorpe. *A theatre in your head,* pp. 127-135.

Night Lodging

Hamilton, Clayton. *Seen on the stage,* pp. 140-143.

Vassa Zheleznova

Borras, F.M. *Maxim Gorky the writer; an interpretation,* pp. 181-182.

Yegor Bulychov

Block, Anita. *The changing world in plays and theatre,* pp. 409-411.

Borras, F.M. *Maxim Gorky the writer; an interpretation,* pp. 178-181.

Lewis, Allan. *The contemporary theatre,* pp. 119-124.

CELESTINO GOROSTIZA 1904-

The Color of our Skin (El Color de Nuestra Piel)

Anderson Imbert, Enrique. *Spanish-American literature: a history,* p. 513.

Jones, W.K. *Behind Spanish American footlights,* p. 501.

JAMES GOW and ARNAUD d'USSEAU

Deep Are the Roots

Mitchell, Loften. *Black drama,* pp. 123-124.

IDA GRAMKO 1924-

General

Jones, W.K. *Behind Spanish American footlights,* p. 352.

HARLEY GRANVILLE-BARKER 1877-1946

General

Knight, G. Wilson. *The golden labyrinth,* pp. 317-318.

Henderson, Archibald. *European dramatists,* pp. 373-406.

Miller, Nellie Burget. *The living drama,* pp. 317-319.

Nicoll, Allardyce. *British drama,* pp. 258-261.

Taylor, John Russell. The *rise and fall of the well—made play,* pp. 112-115

Weales, Gerald. "Edwardian Theatre and the Shadow of Shaw." *In: English Institute essays,* 1959, pp. 160-187.

Williams, Harold. *Modern English writers,* pp. 248-250.

Ann Leete

Norwood, Gilbert. *Euripides and Shaw with other essays,* pp. 87-88, 93.

The Madras House

MacCarthy, Desmond, *Drama,* pp. 214-220.

MacCarthy, Desmond. *Theatre,* pp. 113-118.

Norwood, Gilbert. *Euripides and Shaw with other essays,* pp. 90-92, 94-95.

Weales, Gerald. "Edwardian Theatre and the Shadow of Shaw." *In: English Institute essays,* 1959, pp. 160-187.

The Voysey Inheritance

Norwood, Gilbert. *Euripides and Shaw with other essays,* pp. 88-89, 91-95.

Weales, Gerald. "Edwardian Theatre and the Shadow of Shaw." *In: English Institute essays,* 1959, pp. 160-187.

Waste

Miller, Nellie Burget. *The living drama,* pp. 319-321.

Norton, Roger C. "Hugo von Hofmannsthal's *Der Schwierige* and Granville-Barker's *Waste." Comparative Literature,* vol. 14 (Summer, 1962), pp. 272-279.

Norwood, Gilbert. *Euripides and Shaw with other essays,* pp. 89-90, 92, 94-95.

Weales, Gerald. "Edwardian Theatre and the Shadow of Shaw." *In: English Institute essays,* 1959, pp. 160-187.

GUNTER GRASS 1927-

General

Subiotto, Arrigo. "Günter Grass." *In:* Keith-Smith, Brian, ed. *Essays on contemporary German literature* (German Men of Letters, vol. IV), pp. 215-235.

The Plebians Rehearse the Uprising (Die Plebejer Proben den Aufstand)

Cunliffe, W.G. "Aspects of the Absurd in Günter Grass." *Wisconsin Studies in Contemporary Literature,* vol. 7, no. 3 (Autumn 1966), pp. 311-327.

Luft, Friedrich. "Theatre: Documentaries Roll On But Lose Steam." *American-German Rev.,* vol. 32, no. 4 (Apr.-May, 1966), p. 30.

Rey, Marta. "Letter from Berlin." *American German Rev.,* vol. 32, no. 6 (Aug.-Sept., 1966), pp. 12-13.

Triesch, Manfred. "Not in the Reviews." *Books Abroad,* vol. 40, no. 3 (Summer, 1966), pp. 285-286.

JACINTO GRAU 1877-1958

General

Warren, L.A. *Modern Spanish literature,* vol. 2, pp. 584-593.

El Conde Alarcos

Warren, L.A. *Modern Spanish literature,* vol. 2, pp. 590-592.

En Ildaria

Warren, L.A. *Modern Spanish literature,* vol. 2, pp. 585-590.

JULIEN GREEN

General

Gellert, Roger. "A Survey of the Treatment of the Homosexual in Some Plays." *Encore,* vol. 8, no. 1 (Jan.-Feb., 1961), pp. 29-39.

Moore, Harry T. *Twentieth-century French literature since World War II,* pp. 25-26.

Rose, Marilyn G. "Julien Green, Novelist as Playwright." *Modern Drama,* vol. 6 no. 2 (Sept., 1963), pp. 195-203.

Rose, Marilyn G. "The Production of Julien Green: Microcosm of Mid-Century Writing." *French Rev.,* vol. 34, n9. 2 (Dec., 1960), pp. 164-169.

L'Ombre

Meyer, John H. "Out of Focus." *Renascence,* vol. 11, no. 1 (Autumn, 1958), pp. 33-36.

South (Sud)

Craig, H.A.L. *New Statesman,* vol. 61 (Apr. 14, 1961), pp. 598-599.

Flanner, Janet. "Letter from Paris." *New Yorker,* vol. 29 (Apr. 18, 1953), pp. 127-128.

Fowlie, Wallace. *Dionysus in Paris,* pp. 191-193.

Matthews, Honor. *The primal curse,* pp. 196-198, 201.

Meyer, John H. "Heat, Horror, and Mr. Green." *Renascence,* vol. 7 (Winter, 1954), pp. 80-84.

Williamson, Audrey. *Contemporary theatre, 1953-1956,* pp. 70-71.

Worsley, T.C. *New Statesman,* vol. 49 (Apr. 9, 1955), pp. 502-503.

PAUL GREEN 1894-

General

Green, Paul. "Symphonic Drama." *In:* Frenz, Horst, ed. *American playwrights on drama,* pp. 68-78. (Reprinted from Green, P. *Dramatic heritage,* pp. 14-27. Shorter version first appeared in *College English,* vol. 10 (Apr. 1949), pp. 359-365.)

The Field God

Sievers, W. David. *Freud on Broadway,* pp. 312-313.

The House of Connelly

Dusenbury, Winnifred L. *The theme of loneliness in modern American drama,* pp. 149-154.

Himelstein, Morgan Y. *Drama was a weapon, the left-wing theatre in New York 1929-1941,* p. 157.

Sievers, W. David. *Freud on Broadway,* pp. 313-314.

Weales, Gerald. "The Group Theatre and its Plays." *In: American theatre,* pp. 74, 75-76, 83.

Young, Stark. *Immortal shadows,* pp. 127-131.

Hymn to the Rising Sun

Himelstein, Morgan Y. *Drama was a weapon, the left-wing theatre in New York 1929-1941,* pp. 43-45.

In Abraham's Bosom

Block, Anita. *The changing world in plays and theatre,* pp. 245-250.

Downer, Alan S. *Fifty years of American drama, 1900-1950,* pp. 81-85.

Sievers, W. David. *Freud on Broadway,* pp. 311-312.

Young, Stark. *Immortal shadows,* pp. 88-90.

Johnny Johnson

Himelstein, Morgan Y. *Drama was a weapon, the left-wing theatre in New York 1929-1941,* pp. 173-174.

Sievers, W. David. *Freud on Broadway,* pp. 314-315.

Native Son

See Wright, Richard

Shroud My Body Down

Sievers, W. David. *Freud on Broadway,* pp. 318-319.

Tread the Green Grass

Sievers, W. David. *Freud on Broadway,* pp. 315-318.

GRAHAM GREENE 1904-

General

Lumley, Frederick. *New trends in 20th century drama,* pp. 289-292.

Stratford, Philip. "Graham Greene, Master of Melodrama." *Tamarack Review,* no. 19 (1961), pp. 67-86.

Stratford, Philip. "The Uncomplacent Dramatist: Some Aspects of Graham Greene's Theatre." *Wisconsin Studies in Contemporary Literature,* vol. 2, no. 3 (Fall, 1961), pp. 5-19.

Turnell, Martin. *Graham Green,* pp. 38-42.

Carving a Statue

Lumley Frederick. *New trends in 20th century drama,* pp. 291-292.

Turnell, Martin. *Graham Greene,* pp. 41-42.

The Complaisant Lover

Kerr, Walter. *The theatre in spite of itself,* pp. 157-160.

Lumley, Frederick. *New trends in 20th century drama,* pp. 290-291.

Turnell, Martin. *Graham Greene,* pp. 40-41.

The Living Room

Atkins, John. *Graham Greene, pp. 217-222.*

Baxter, Kay M. *Contemporary theatre and the Christian faith,* pp. 22-32.

Lumley, Frederick. *New trends in 20th century drama,* pp. 289-290.

Robertson, Roderick. "Towards a Definition of Religious Drama." *Educational Theatre J.,* vol. 9 (1957), pp. 99-100.

Sainer, Arthur. *The sleepwalker and the assassin, a view of the contemporary theatre,* pp. 50-51.

Turnell, Martin. *Graham Greene,* pp. 38-40.

The Potting Shed

Gassner, John. *Theatre at the crossroads,* pp. 155-157.

Lumley, Frederick. *New trends in 20th century drama,* p. 290.

Turnell, Martin. *Graham Greene,* p. 40.

The Power and the Glory (Adapted by Denis Canan and Pierre Bost)

Williamson, Audrey. *Contemporary theatre, 1953-1956,* pp. 96-98.

LADY ISABELLA AUGUSTA GREGORY 1859-1932

General

Bowen, Anne. "Lady Gregory's Use of Proverbs in Her Plays." *Southern Folklore Q.,* vol. 3, no. 4 (Dec., 1939), pp. 231-243.

Boyd, Ernest. *Ireland's literary renaissance,* pp. 345-348.

Coxhead, Elizabeth. *J.M. Synge and Lady Gregory,* pp. 24-29.

Edwards, A.C. "The Lady Gregory Letters to Sean O'Casey." *Modern Drama,* vol. 8, no. 1 (May, 1965), pp. 95-111.

Hoare, Dorothy M. *The works of Morris and of Yeats in relation to early saga literature,* pp. 78-79, 81, 87, 91, 92, 93, 100, 103-105.

Malone, Andrew E. *The Irish drama,* pp. 52-60, 156, 158-160, 162-164.

Miller, Nellie Burget. *The living drama,* pp. 335-337.

Murphy, Daniel J. "The Lady Gregory Letters to G.B. Shaw." *Modern Drama,* vol. 10, no. 4 (Feb., 1968), pp. 331-345.

O'Casey, Sean. "A Sprig of Rosemary Among the Laurel." *In:* O'Casey, Sean. *Blasts and benedictions, pp. 213-215.* (From foreword to *Lady Gregory: selected plays,* N.Y., Putnam, 1962.)

O'Donovan, Michael. *A short history of Irish literature,* pp. 178-179, 189-193.

Saddlemyer, Ann. "Image-Maker for Ireland: Augusta, Lady Gregory." *In:* Skelton, Robin, ed. *The world of W.B. Yeats,* pp. 195-202.

Saddlemyer, Ann. *In defence of Lady Gregory, playwright,* pp. 9-28, 31-39, 46-53, 63, 72-77, 87-102.

Williams, Harold. *Modern English writers,* pp. 202-206.

Aristotle's Bellows

Saddlemyer, Ann. *In defence of Lady Gregory, playwright,* p. 57.

The Caravans

Barnet, Sylvan, ed. *The genius of the Irish theatre,* pp. 108-110.

Dervorgilla

Saddlemyer, Ann. *In defence of Lady Gregory, playwright,* pp. 65, 68-71.

The Dragon

Saddlemyer, Ann. *In defence of Lady Gregory, playwright,* pp. 55-57.

The Full Moon

Saddlemyer, Ann. *In defence of Lady Gregory, playwright,* pp. 39-46.

The Golden Apple

Saddlemyer, Ann. *In defence of Lady Gregory, playwright,* pp. 53-55.

Grania

Malone, Andrew E. *The Irish drama,* pp. 160-161.

Saddlemyer, Ann. *In defence of Lady Gregory, playwright,* pp. 65-68.

The Image

Saddlemyer, Ann. *In defence of Lady Gregory, playwright,* pp. 28-30, 78-86, 88.

The Jester

Saddlemyer, Ann. *In defence of Lady Gregory, playwright,* pp. 58-62.

Kincora

Saddlemyer, Ann. *In defence of Lady Gregory, playwright,* p. 64.

Spreading the News

Malone, Andrew E. *The Irish drama,* pp. 157-158.

The Wrens

Saddlemyer, Ann. *In defence of Lady Gregory, playwright,* pp. 32-34.

HERMANN GRESSIEKER 1903-

The Emperor

Bauland, Peter. *The hooded eagle,* pp. 212.

Royal Gambit (Heinrich VIII und Seine Frauen)

Bauland, Peter. *The hooded eagle,* pp. 210-212.

ANGEL GUIMERA 1847-1924

Marta of the Lowlands

Miller, Nellie Burget. *The living drama,* pp. 370-372.

SACHA GUITRY 1885-1957

General

Knowles, Dorothy, *French drama of the inter-war years, 1918-39,* pp. 275-279

Quand Jouons-Nous la Comedie

Bishop, Thomas. *Pirandello and the French theatre,* pp. 104-106.

HANS-JOACHIM HAECKER 1910-

Don't Turn Around (Dreht Euch Nicht Um)

Garten, H.F. *Modern German drama,* p. 271.

OLIVER HAILEY 1932-

Hey You, Light Man!

Sainer, Arthur. *The sleepwalker and the assassin, a view of the contemporary theatre,* pp. 70-71.

WILLIAM WISTER HAINES 1908-

Command Decision

Dusenbury, Winifred L. *The theme of loneliness in modern American drama,* pp. 191-196.

MAX HALBE 1865-1945

Youth (Jugend)

Bauland, Peter. *The hooded eagle,* pp. 16-18, 52.

Witkowski, Georg. *German drama of the nineteenth century,* p. 176.

WILLIS HALL 1929-

General

Gillett, Eric. "Regional Realism: Shelagh Delaney, Alun Owen, Keith Waterhouse and Willis Hall." *In:* Armstrong, William A., ed. *Experimental drama,* pp. 198-203.

The Long and the Short and the Tall

Kitchin, Laurence. *Mid-century drama,* pp. 107-109.

PIERRE HAMP 1876-

General

Knowles, Dorothy. *French drama of the inter-war years, 1918-39,* pp. 272-273.

ST. JOHN EMILE CLAVERING HANKIN 1860-1909

General

Norwood, Gilbert. *Euripides and Shaw with other essays,* pp. 76-80.

Williams, Harold. *Modern English writers,* pp. 248-250.

WILLIAM HANLEY 1931-

Mrs. Dally

Duprey, Richard A. "Today's Dramatists." *In: American theatre,* p. 221.

Slow Dance on the Killing Ground

Brustein, Robert. *Seasons of discontent,* pp. 304-306.

Brustein, Robert. "Three Plays and a Protest." *New republic,* vol. 152 (Jan. 23, 1965), p. 32.

Duprey, Richard A. "Today's Dramatists." *In: American theatre,* pp. 220-221.

LORRAINE HANSBERRY 1930-1965

General

Zietlow, Edward R. "Wright to Hansberry: The evolution of outlook in four Negro writers." *Dissertation Abstracts,* vol. 28 (1967), 701A (U. of Washington).

Raisin in the Sun

Abramson, Doris E. *Negro playwrights in the American theatre, 1925-1959,* pp. 239-254, 263-266.

Alvarez, A. "That Evening Sun." *New Statesman,* vol. 58 (Aug. 15, 1959), p. 190.

Bigsby, C.W.E. *Confrontation and commitment,* pp. 122, 156-161, 168, 172.

Brien, Alan. "Suspected Persons." *Spectator,* vol. 203, no. 6842 (Aug. 14, 1959), pp. 189, 191.

Isaacs, Harold R. "Five Writers and Their African Ancestors." *Phylon,* vol. 21 (Winter, 1960), pp. 329-333.

Lumley, Frederick. *New trends in 20th century drama,* p. 339.

Mitchell, Loften. *Black drama,* pp. 180-182, 202, 204, 208.

Trewin, J.C. "Promise and Performance." *Illustrated London News,* vol. 235 (Sept. 12, 1959), p. 246.

Turpin, Waters E. "The Contemporary American Negro Playwright." *College Language Assn. J.,* vol. 9, no. 1 (Sept., 1965), pp. 18-19.

Weales, Gerald. "Thoughts on *A Raisin in the Sun.*" *Commentary, vo.* 27, no. 6 (June, 1959), pp. 527-530.

The Sign in Sidney Brustein's Window

Bigsby, C.W.E. *Confrontation and commitment,* pp. 54, 122-123, 138 154, 156, 162-173.

Mitchell, Loften. *Black drama,* pp. 202-204.

MOSS HART 1904-1961

General

Gould, Jean. *Modern American playwrights,* pp. 154-167.

Christopher Blake

Sievers, W. David. *Freud on Broadway,* pp. 294-295.

The Climate of Eden (Adapted from the novel Shadows Move Among Them, by Edgar Mittelholzer)

Sievers, W. David. *Freud on Broadway,* pp. 296-298.

Lady in the Dark

Sievers, W. David. *Freud on Broadway,* pp. 291-294.

WALTER HASENCLEVER 1890-1940

General

Garten, H.F. *Modern German drama,* pp. 119-121, 130-133, 169, 186, 241.

Antigone

Garten, H.F. *Modern German drama,* pp. 130-132.

Beyond (Jenseits)

Bauland, Peter. *The hooded eagle,* pp. 82-83.

Goldberg, Isaac. *The drama of transition,* pp. 299-302.

Her Man on Wax (Napoleon Greift Ein)

Bauland, Peter. *The hooded eagle,* pp. 119-120.

Men (Die Menschen)

Goldberg, Isaac. *The drama of transition,* pp. 296-299.

The Saviour (Der Retter)

Sokel, Walter. *The writer in extremis,* pp. 146, 171-172.

The Son (Der Sohn)

Garten, H.F. *Modern German drama,* pp. 119-121.

Goldberg, Isaac. *The drama of transition,* pp. 287-295.

Sokel, Walter. *The writer in extremis,* pp. 39-40, 99-100, 170, 217.

CHRISTOPHER HASSALL 1912-

Christ's Comet

Spanos, William V. *The Christian tradition in modern British verse drama,* pp. 146-155.

GERHART HAUPTMANN 1862-1946

General

Bauland, Peter. *The hooded eagle,* pp. 4-9, 10, 15, 19-22, 24-25, 53-54, 160, 175-176.

Corrigan, Robert W., ed. *Masterpieces of the modern German theatre,* p. 132.

Cunningham, Horace Milton. "How Gerhart Hauptmann produces the sensation of pathos." M.A., University of Chicago, 1913.

Dukes, Ashley. *Modern dramatists,* pp. 78-94.

Ficks, Edna. "The art of exposition in the dramas of Gerhart Hauptmann." M.A., University of California, 1925.

Garten, H.F. *Modern German drama, pp. 34-48.*

Hatfield, Henry. *Modern German literature,* pp. 11-15, 110-112.

Hauptmann, Gerhart. "On the Drama." *In:* Corrigan, Robert W., ed. *Masterpieces of the modern German theatre,* pp. 133-138. (Reprinted from Corrigan, Robert W., ed. *The modern theatre,* N.Y., Macmillan, 1964.)

Heller, Otto. *Studies in modern German literature,* pp. 119-134.

Heuser, Frederick W.J. "Gerhart Hauptmann and Frank Wedekind." *Germanic Rev.,* vol. 20, no. 1 (Feb. 1945), pp. 54-68.

Keefer, L.B. "Woman's Mission in Hauptmann's Dramas." *Germanic Rev.,* vol. 9, no. 1 (Jan. 1934), pp. 35-53.

Klemm, Frederick A. "The death problem in the life and works of Gerhart Hauptmann." Ph.D., University of Pennsylvania, 1938-39.

Lamm, Martin. *Modern drama,* pp. 225-227, 233-236.

McInnes, Edward. "The Image of the Hunt in Hauptmann's Dramas." *German Life and Letters,* n.s., vol. 19 (1965-66), pp. 190-195.

McMillan, Dougald. "Influences of Gerhart Hauptmann in Joyce's *Ulysses." James Joyce Q.* (U. of Tulsa, Oklahoma), vol. 4 (1967), pp. 107-119.

Marble, Annie Russell. *The Nobel Prize winners in literature,* pp. 133-147.

Miller, Nellie Burget. *The living drama,* pp. 253-257, 259-260.

Nabholz, Johannes. "The Clergymen in Gerhart Hauptmann's Contemporary Plays." *Monatshefte,* vol. 39, no. 7 (Nov., 1947), pp. 463-476.

Reichart, Walter A. "Gerhart Hauptmann, War Propaganda, and George Bernard Shaw." *Germanic Rev.,* vol. 33, no. 3 (Oct., 1958), pp. 176-180.

Reichart, Walter A. "Hauptmann Before *Vor Sonnenaufgang." J. of English and Germanic Philology,* vol. 28 (1929), pp. 518-531.

Salpeter, Harry. "Gerhart Hauptmann." *Bookman,* vol. 67, no. 6 (August, 1928), pp. 662-666.

Schutze, Martin. "Gerhart Hauptmann's plays and their literary relations." M.A., University of Pennsylvania, 1899.

Sinden, Margaret. "Gerhart Hauptmann." *Univ. of Toronto Q.,* vol. 19, no. 1 (Oct., 1949), pp. 17-34.

Van Duren, Arthur. "Ibsen and Hauptmann." Ph. D., University of Michigan, 1930.

Wahr, Fred B. "Hauptmann's Hellenism." *J. of English and Germanic Philology,* vol. 33, no. 3 (July, 1934), pp. 421-451.

Wahr, F.B. "Theory and Composition of the Hauptmann Drama." *Germanic Rev.* vol. 17, no. 3 (Oct., 1942), pp. 163-173.

Weigand, Hermann J. *Surveys and soundings in European literature,* pp. 223-242. (Reprinted from *Monatshefte,* vol. 44 (1952), pp. 317-332.)

Witkowski, Georg. *German drama of the nineteenth century,* pp. 187-189.

Agamemnon (Agamemnons Tod)

Kayser, Rudolf. "Iphigenia's Character in Gerhart Hauptmann's Tetralogy of the Atrides." *Germanic Rev.,* vol. 28, no. 3 (Oct., 1953), pp. 190-194.

Reichart, Walter A. "The Genesis of Hauptmann's Iphigenia Cycle." *Modern Language Q.,* vol. 9, no. 4 (Dec., 1948), pp. 467-477.

The Assumption of Hannele (Hannele) (Hanneles Himmelfahrt)

Bauland, Peter. *The hooded eagle,* pp. 4-8, 15, 164.

Block, Anita. *The changing world in plays and theatre,* pp. 37-38.

Ellehauge, Martin. *The position of Bernard Shaw in European drama and philosophy,* pp. 315-317.

Heller, Otto. *Studies in modern German literature,* pp. 166-174.

Witkowski, Georg. *German drama of the nineteenth century,* pp. 197-198.

The Beaver Coat (Der Biberpelz)

Bauland, Peter. *The hooded eagle,* pp. 175-176.

Heller, Otto. *Studies in modern German literature,* pp. 210-214.

Witkowski, Georg. *German drama of the nineteenth century,* pp. 197-198.

Before Sunrise (Vor Sonnenaufgang)

Ellehauge, Martin. *The position of Bernard Shaw in European drama and philosophy,* pp. 109-110.

Heller, Otto. *Studies in modern German literature,* pp. 134-140.

Lamm, Martin. *Modern drama* pp. 226-227.

Witkowski, Georg. *German drama of the ninetenth century,* pp. 189-192.

The Bow of Ulysses

Stanford, W.B. *The Ulysses theme; a study of a traditional hero,* pp. 195-199.

Colleague Crampton (Kollege Crampton)

Heller, Otto. *Studies in modern German literature,* pp. 161-165.

Elektra

Kayser, Rudolph. "Iphigenia's Character in Gerhart Hauptmann's Tetralogy of the Atrides." *Germanic Rev.,* vol. 28, no. 3 (Oct., 1953), pp. 190-194.

Weisert, John J. "Two Recent Variations on the Orestes Theme." *Modern Language J.,* vol. 35, no. 5 (May, 1951), pp. 356-363.

The Feast of Peace (Das Friedensfest)

Heller, Otto. *Studies in modern* German literature, pp. 140-144.

Witkowski, Georg. *German drama of the nineteenth century,* pp. 192-193.

Festspiel in Deutschen Reimen

Braun, Frank. "Hauptmann's *Festspiel* and Frenssen's *Bismarck:* A Study in Political Contrasts." *Germanic Rev.,* vol. 22, no. 2 (Apr., 1947), pp. 106-116.

Die Finsternisse

Stirk, S.D. "Gerhart Hauptmann's Play *Die Finsternisse.*" *Modern Language Q.,* vol. 9, no. 2 (June, 1948), pp. 146-151.

Florian Geyer

Heller, Otto. *Studies in modern German literature,* pp. 175-180.

Weigand, Hermann J. "Gerhart Hauptmann's Range as Dramatist: A Lecture." *Monatshefte Fur Deutschen Unterricht,* vol. 44, no. 7 (Nov., 1952), pp. 323-325.

Witkowski, Georg. *German drama of the nineteenth century,* pp. 196-197.

Gabriel Schillings Flucht

Ellehauge, Martin. *The position of Bernard Shaw in European drama and philosophy,* pp. 134-136.

Germanen und Romer

Heuser, Frederick W.J. "Hauptmann's *Germanen und Romer.*" *Germanic Rev.,* vol. 17, no. 3 (Oct., 1942), pp. 174-196.

Reichart, Walter A. "Hauptmann's *Germanen und Romer.*" *PMLA,* vol. 44, no. 3 (Sept., 1929), pp. 901-910.

Griselda

Ellehauge, Martin. *The position of Bernard Shaw in European drama and philosophy,* pp. 133-134, 316.

Henschel the Teamster (Fuhrmann Henschel)

Ellehauge, Martin. *The position of Bernard Shaw in European drama and philosophy,* pp. 153.

Heller, Otto. *Studies in modern German literature,* pp. 195-199.

Witkowski, Georg. *German drama of the nineteenth century,* p. 200.

Herbert Engelmann

See Zuckmayer, Carl

Indipohdi

Weigand, Hermann J. "Gerhart Hauptmann's Range as Dramatist: A Lecture." *Monatshefte Fur Deutschen Unterricht,* vol. 44, no. 7 (Nov., 1953), pp. 329-331.

Iphigenie in Aulis

Kayser, Rudolf. "Iphigenia's Character in Gerhart Hauptmann's Tetralogy of the Atrides." *Germanic Rev.,* vol. 28, no. 3 (Oct., 1953), pp. 190-194.

Iphigenie in Delphi

Reichart, Walter A. "The Genesis of Hauptmann's Iphigenia Cycle." *Modern Language Q.,* vol. 9, no. 4 (Dec., 1948), pp. 467-477.

Reichart, W. A. "Iphigenie in Delphi." *Germanic Rev.,* vol. 17, no. 3 (Oct., 1942), pp. 221-237.

Lonely Men (Einsame Menschen)

Ellehauge, Martin. *The position of Bernard Shaw in European drama and philosophy,* pp. 145-146.

Fehlau, U.E. "Another Look at Hauptmann's *Einsame Menschen.*" *Monatshcftc,* vol. 42. no. 8 (Dec., 1950), pp. 409-413.

Heller, Otto. *Studies in modern German literature,* pp. 144-149.

Heuser, Frederick W.J. "Biographic and Autobiographic Elements in Gerhart Hauptmann's *Einsame Menschen.*" *Germanic Rev.,* vol. 22, no. 3 (Oct., 1947), pp. 218-225.

Lamm, Martin. *Modern drama,* pp. 228-229.

Witkowski, Georg. *Germanic drama of the nineteenth century,* p. 193

Michael Kramer

Heller, Otto. *Studies in modern German literature,* pp. 202-209.

Poor Heinrich (Der Arme Heinrich)

Heller, Otto. *Studies in modern German literature,* pp. 218-224.

Die Ratten

Loney, Glenn. "Broadway and Off-Broadway Supplement." *Educational Theatre J.,* vol. 18, no. 3 (Oct., 1966), pp. 281-282.

The Red Cock (Der Rote Hahn)

Heller, Otto. *Studies in modern German literature,* pp. 215-218.

Rose Berndt

Bauland, Peter. *The hooded eagle,* pp. 53-54.

Heller, Otto. *Studies in modern German literature,* pp. 224-226.

Miller, Nellie Burget. *The living drama,* pp. 257-259.

Witkowski, Georg. *German drama of the nineteenth century,* pp. 201-202.

Schluck und Jau

Heller, Otto. *Studies in modern German literature,* pp. 199-202.

The Sunken Bell (Die Versunkene Glocke)

Bauland, Peter. *The hooded eagle,* pp. 8, 24-25.

Ellehauge, Martin. *The position of Bernard Shaw in European drama and philosophy,* pp. 145-146, 261-266.

Gunvaldsen, K.M. *"The Master Builder* and *Die Versunkene Glocke." Monatshefte fur Deutschen Unterricht,* vol. 33, no. 4 (Apr., 1941), pp. 153-162.

Heller, Otto. *Studies in modern German literature,* pp. 180-194.

Miller, Nellie Burget. *The living drama,* pp. 260-264.

Weisert, John J. "Critical Reception of Gerhart Hauptmann's *The Sunken Bell* on the American Stage." *Monatshefte,* vol. 43 (1951), pp. 221-234.

Witkowski, Georg. *German drama of the nineteenth century,* p. 199.

The Thieves' Comedy

Beerbohm, Max. *Around theatres,* pp. 365-369.

Und Pippa Tanzt

Ellehauge, Martin. *The position of Bernard Shaw in European drama and philosophy,* pp. 266-267.

Weigand, Hermann J. "Gerhart Hauptmann's Range as Dramatist: A Lecture." *Monatshefte Fur Deutschen Unterricht,* vol. 44, no. 7 (Nov., 1952), pp. 325, 327-328.

The Weavers (Die Weber)

Bauland, Peter. *The hooded eagle,* pp. 19-22.

Blankenagel, John C. "Early Reception of Hauptmann's *Dic Weber* in the United States." *Modern Language Notes,* vol. 68, no. 5 (May, 1953), pp. 334-340.

Block, Anita. *The changing world in plays and theatre,* pp. 18-19, 33-36.

Ellehauge, Martin. *The position of Bernard Shaw in European drama and philosophy,* pp. 109-110.

Heller, Otto. *Studies in modern German literature,* pp. 149-158.

Lamm, Martin. *Modern drama,* pp. 229-233.

Moore, Charles H. "A Hearing on *Germinal* and *Die Weber.*" *Germanic Rev.,* vol. 33, no. 1 (Feb., 1958), pp. 30-40.

Williams, Raymond. *Drama from Ibsen to Eliot,* pp. 175-179.

Witkowski, Georg. *German drama of the nineteenth century,* pp. 194-196.

The White Redeemer (Der Weisse Heiland)

Ellehauge, Martin. *The position of Bernard Shaw in European drama and philosophy,* pp. 310-312.

Goldberg, Isaac. *The drama of transition,* pp. 279-286.

VACLAV HAVEL 1936-

General

Grossman, Jan. "A Preface to Havel." *Tulane Drama Rev.,* vol. 11, no. 3 (Spring, 1967), pp. 117-120.

The Garden Party (Zahradni Slavnost)

Den, Petr. "Notes on Czechoslovakia's Young Theater of the Absurd." *Books Abroad,* vol. 41, no. 2 (Spring, 1967), p. 160.

Grossman, Jan. "A Preface to Havel." *Tulane Drama Rev.,* vol. 11, no. 3 (Spring, 1967), pp. 118-120.

The Memorandum (Notification) (Vyrozumeni)

Den, Petr. "Notes on Czechoslovakia's Young Theater of the Absurd." *Books Abroad,* vol. 41, no. 2 (Spring, 1967), pp. 160-161.

Funke, Lewis. "It's All Action at APA." *The New York Times,* Apr. 28, 1968, Sec. 2, pp. 1, 11.

Grossman, Jan. "A Preface to Havel." *Tulane Drama Rev.,* vol. 11, no. 3 (Spring, 1967), pp. 118-119.

Kerr, Walter. "Not in Despair, But Hope." *The New York Times,* May 19, 1968, Sec. 2, p. 3.

Tigrid, Pavel. "Frost and Thaw: Literature in Czechoslovakia." *East Europe,* vol. 15, no. 9 (Sept., 1966), pp. 9-10.

IAN HAY 1876-1952
(real name John Hay Beith)

Hattie Stowe

Hobson, Harold. *Theatre,* pp. 48-50.

JULIUS HAY 1900-

General

Michalski, John. "German Drama and Theater in 1965." *Books Abroad,* vol. 40 (1966), p. 138.

JOSEPH HAYES 1918-

The Desperate Hours

Bierman, Judah. *The dramatic experience,* pp. 16-22.

Hayes, Joseph. "Several Aspects of a Complex Problem." *In:* Bierman, Judah. *The dramatic experience,* pp. 72-78.

BEN HECHT 1893-1964

To Quito and Back

Himelstein, Morgan Y. *Drama was a weapon, the left-wing theatre in New York 1929-1941,* p. 140.

McCarthy, Mary. *Sights and spectacles 1937-1956,* pp. 3-6.

Sievers, W. David. *Freud on Broadway,* pp. 304-305.

THOMAS HEGGEN 1919-1949

Mister Roberts

Brown, John Mason. *Seeing more things,* pp. 282-288.

Brown, John Mason. "The Order of the Palm." *In:* Oppenheimer, George, ed. *The passionate playgoer,* pp. 574-580. (Reprinted from *Saturday Review of Literature,* Mar. 6, 1948.)

HERMANN HEIJERMANS 1864-1924

General

Dukes, Ashley. *Modern dramatists,* pp. 254-263.

Ghetto

Dukes, Ashley. *Modern dramatists,* pp. 262-263.

The Good Hope (Op Hoop van Zegen)

Dukes, Ashley. *Modern dramatists,* pp. 259-261.

Ora et Labora

Dukes, Ashley. *Modern dramatists,* pp. 261-262.

LUIS ALBERTO HEIREMANS 1928-1964

General

Jones, W.K. *Behind Spanish American footlights,* pp. 239-240.

JOSEPH HELLER 1923-

We Bombed in New Haven

Loney, Glenn. "Broadway in Review." *Educational Theatre J.,* vol. 20, no. 1 (Mar., 1968), p. 99.

Weales, Gerald. *Reporter,* vol. 38, no. 2 (Jan. 25, 1968), p. 44.

LILLIAN HELLMAN 1905-

General

Gassner, John. *Theatre at the crossroads,* pp. 132-139.

Goldstein, Malcolm. "Body and Soul on Broadway." *Modern Drama,* vol. 7, no. 4 (Feb., 1965), pp. 411-421.

Gould, Jean *Modern American playwrights,* pp. 168-185.

Hellman, Lillian. "An Introduction to *Four Plays." In:* Oppenheimer, George, ed. *The passionate playgoer,* pp. 294-301. (Reprinted from introduction to Hellman's *Four plays,* N.Y., Random House, 1942.)

Isaacs, Edith J.R. "Lillian Hellman: A Playwright on the March." *In:* Meserve, Walter J., ed. *Discussions of American drama,* pp. 46-51.

Keller, Alvin Joseph. "Form and Content in the Plays of Lillian Hellman." *Dissertation Abstracts,* vol. 26 (1966), 6715 (Stanford).

Krutch, Joseph W. *The American drama since 1918,* pp. 130-133.

Lewis, Allan. *American plays and playwrights of the contemporary theatre,* pp. 101-109.

Paris Review. *Writers at work; the Paris Review interviews. Third series,* pp. 117-140.

Another Part of the Forest

Dusenbury, Winifred L. *The theme of loneliness in modern American drama,* pp. 144-149.

Sievers, W. David. *Freud on Broadway,* pp. 283-285.

Triesch, Manfred. "Hellman's *Another Part of the Forest." Explicator,* vol. 24, no. 1 (Sept., 1965), Item 20.

The Autumn Garden

Clurman, Harold. *Lies like truth,* pp. 47-49.

Downer, Alan S. *Fifty years of American drama, 1900-1950,* pp. 139-140.

Felheim, Marvin. *"The Autumn Garden:* Mechanics and Dialectics." *Modern Drama,* vol. 3, no. 2 (Sept., 1960), pp. 191-195.

Gassner, John. *Theatre at the crossroads,* p. 132.

Sievers, W. David. *Freud on Broadway,* pp. 287-289.

The Children's Hour

Bentley, Eric. *The dramatic event,* pp. 74-77.

Bentley, Eric. *The theatre of commitment,* pp. 39-40.

Block, Anita. *The changing world in plays and theatre,* pp. 122-126.

Goldstein, Malcolm. "The Playwrights of the 1930's." *In:* Downer, Alan S., ed. *The American theatre today,* pp. 34-35.

New Statesman, vol. 12 (Nov. 21, 1936), p. 180.

Sievers, W. David. *Freud on Broadway,* pp. 279-281.

Verschoyle, Derek. *Spectator,* vol. 157 (Nov. 20, 1936), p. 905.

Days to Come

Himelstein, Morgan Y. *Drama was a weapon, the left-wing theatre in New York, 1929-1941,* pp. 200-201.

Sievers, W. David. *Freud on Broadway,* pp. 281.

The Little Foxes

Dusenbury, Winifred L. *The theme of loneliness in modern American drama,* pp. 144-149.

Freedman, Morris. *The moral impulse,* pp. 101-104.

Goldstein, Malcolm. "The Playwrights of the 1930's." *In:* Downer, Alan S., ed. *The American theater today,* pp. 35-36.

Himelstein, Morgan Y. *Drama was a weapon, the left-wing theatre in New York 1929-1941,* pp. 208-209.

New Statesman, vol. 24 (Nov. 7, 1942), p. 304.

O'Hara, Frank H. *Today in American drama,* pp. 83-101, 152-153, 248-249.

Sievers, W. David. *Freud on Broadway,* pp. 282-283.

The Searching Wind

Sievers, W. David. *Freud on Broadway,* pp. 285-287.

Toys in the Attic

Adler, Jacob H. "Miss Hellman's Two Sisters." *Educational Theatre J.,* vol. 15 (1963), pp. 112-117.

Gardner, R.H. *The splintered stage; the decline of the American theater,* p. 102.

Kerr, Walter. *The theater in spite of itself,* pp. 235-238.

Watch on the Rhine

Heilman, Robert B. *Tragedy and melodrama,* pp. 76-78, 80-81, 85.
Himelstein, Morgan Y. *Drama was a weapon, the left-wing theatre in New York 1929-1941,* pp. 213-214.

Martin, Kingsley. *New Statesman,* vol. 23 (May 2, 1942), p. 288.

Sievers W. David. *Freud on Broadway,* pp. 285.

Wright, Basil. *Spectator,* vol. 168 (May 1, 1942), p. 419.

ERNEST HEMINGWAY 1899-1961

The Fifth Column

Himelstein, Morgan Y. *Drama was a weapon, the left-wing theatre in New York 1929-1941,* pp. 146-147, 220-221.

ALFRED HENSCHKE 1891-1928
(pseud. Alfred Klabund)

The Circle of Chalk (The Chalk Circle) (Der Kreidekreis)

Bauland, Peter. *The hooded eagle,* pp. 119, 146-148, 169.

HERWIG HENSEN 1917-

General

Mallinson, Vernon. *Modern Belgian literature, 1830-1960,* pp. 170-172.

FERENC HERCZEG 1863-

General

Remenyi, Joseph. "Ferenc Herczeg: Hungarian Playwright and Novelist." *Slavonic and East European Rev.,* vol. 30 (1951/52), p. 175-184.

LUISA JOSEFINA HERNANDEZ 1928-

General

Jones, W.K. *Behind Spanish American footlights,* pp. 510-511.

The Real Guests (Los Huespedes Reales)

Anderson Imbert, Enrique. *Spanish-American literature: a history,* p. 550.

ERNESTO HERRERA 1886-1917

General

Anderson Imbert, Enrique. *Spanish-American literature: a history,* pp. 375, 419.

Jones, W.K. *Behind Spanish American footlights,* pp. 63-65.

Schanzer, George O. "A Great National Drama of Uruguay." *Modern Language J.,* vol. 38 (1954), pp. 220-223.

GERHART HERRMANN
See Mostar, Gerhart Herrmann

RICHARD HEY 1926-

The Fish with the Gold Dagger (Der Fisch mit dem Goldenen Dolch)

Garten, H.F. *Modern German drama,* pp. 271-272.

Thymian und Drachentod

Garten, H.F. *Modern German drama,* p. 271.

Woe to Him Who Doesn't Lie (Weh dem der Nicht Lügt)

Garten, H.F. *Modern German drama,* p. 272.

PAUL HEYSE 1830-1914

Mary of Magdala (Maria von Magdala)

Bauland, Peter. *The hooded eagle,* pp. 13-14.

DOROTHY HEYWARD and DUBOIS HEYWARD

Mamba's Daughter

O'Hara, Frank H. *Today in American drama,* pp. 154-164.

Mitchell, Loften. *Black drama,* pp. 95, 108-109.

WOLFGANG HILDESHEIMER 1916-

General

Coenen, F.E. "The Modern German Drama." *In:* Hammer, Carl, Jr., ed. *Studies in German literature,* p. 118.

Taeni, Rainer. "W. Hildesheimer and H.G. Michelson: The Absurd Play as Mirroring a Fundamental Condition of Reality." *Komos, A Quarterly of Drama and Arts of the Theatre,* vol. 1 (1967), pp. 76-83.

The Delay (Die Verspätung)

Garten, H.F. *Modern German drama,* pp. 270-271.

Nightpiece

Wellwarth, G. E. "Introduction." *In:* Benedikt, M. and G.E. Wellwarth, eds. *Postwar German theatre,* pp. xi-xii.

Plays in Which Darkness Falls (Plays in Which It Grows Dark) (Spiele in Denen Es Dunkel Wird)

Garten, H.F. *Modern German drama,* p. 270.

Wellwarth, G.E. "Introduction." *In:* Benedikt, M., and G.E. Wellwarth, eds. *Postwar German theatre,* pp. xix-xx.

Wegener, Adolph H. "The Absurd in Modern Literature." *Books Abroad,* vol. 41, no. 2 (Spring, 1967), pp. 150-156.

ABRAM HILL

See Silvera, John (co-author Liberty Deferred)

ROLF HOCHHUTH 1933-

General

Moore, Harry T. *Twentieth-century German literature,* pp. 153, 157, 158, 159-160.

The Deputy (The Representative) (Der Stellvertreter)

Bauland, Peter. *The hooded eagle,* pp. 214-220.

Bentley, Eric., ed. *The storm over The Deputy.* (Essays and articles about Hochhuth's drama.)

Bentley, Eric. *The theatre of commitment,* pp. 197, 205-220, 224-228.

Brustein, Robert. *Seasons of discontent,* pp. 204-207.

Butler, James A. *"The Deputy* in Retrospect." *Four Quarters* (La Salle Coll.), vol. 15, no. 3 (1966), pp. 19-21.

Chiari, J. *Landmarks of contemporary drama,* pp. 188-195.

Clurman, Harold. *The naked image,* pp. 80-82.

Garten, H.F. *Modern German drama,* pp. 267-268.

Gong, Alfred. "Rolf Hochhuth's *The Deputy." American-German Review,* vol. 30, no. 3 (Feb.-Mar., 1964), pp. 38-40.

Graef, Hilda. "The Play That Indicts Pope Pius XII." *Catholic World,* vol. 197 (Sept., 1963), pp. 380-385.

Lumley, Frederick. New trends *in 20th century drama,* pp. 361-362.

Roubiczek, Hjordis. *"Der Stellvertreter* and Its Critics." *German Life and Letters,* vol. 17, n.s., no. 3 (Apr., 1964), pp. 193-199.

Schwarz, Egon. "Rolf Hochhuth's *The Representative." Germanic Rev.,* vol. 39, no. 3 (May, 1964), pp. 211-230.

Sontag, Susan. *Against interpretation and other essays,* pp. 124-131, 145-147.

Zipes, Jack D. "Documentary Drama in Germany: Treading the Circuit." *Germanic Rev.,* vol. 42, no. 1 (Jan., 1967), pp. 49-62.

Soldiers

Alvarez, A. "Churchill, Figure of Tragedy?" *The New York Times,* April 28, Sec. 2, pp. 1, 5.

Kerr, Walter. "Kerr: *Soldiers* and *New Faces." The New York Times,* May 12, 1968, Sec. 2, p. 3.

FRITZ HOCHWALDER 1911-

General

Coenen, F.E. "The Modern German Drama." *In:* Hammer, Carl, Jr., ed. *Studies in German literature,* pp. 120-121.

Garten, H.F. *Modern German drama,* pp. 246-249.

Loram, Ian C. "Fritz Hochwalder." *Monatshefte,* vol. 57, no. 1 (Jan., 1965), pp. 8-16.

Lumley, Frederick. *New trends in 20th century drama,* pp. 359-361.

Moore, Harry T. *Twentieth-century German literature,* pp. 141-142.

Theobald, Erika. "An Austrian Playwright Confronts the Past." *American-German Rev.,* vol. 32, no. 6 (Aug.-Sept., 1966), pp. 9-10.

Wellwarth, George E. "The Drama Within the Self." *Q.J. of Speech,* vol. 49 (1963), pp. 274-281.

Wellwarth, George. *The theatre of protest and paradox,* pp. 184-195.

Donadieu

Loram, Ian C. "Fritz Hochwalder." *Monatshefte,* vol. 57, no. 1 (Jan., 1965) p. 12.

Wellwarth, George. *The theatre of protest and paradox,* pp. 192-193.

Donnerstag (Thursday)

Loram, Ian C. "Fritz Hochwalder." *Monatshefte,* vol. 57, no. 1 (Jan., 1965), pp. 13-14.

Lumley, Frederick. *New trends in 20th century drama,* p. 360.

Esther

Loram, Ian C. "Fritz Hochwalder." *Monatshefte,* vol. 57, no. 1 (Jan. 1965), p. 9.

The Fugitive (Der Flüchtling)

Loram, Ian C. "Fritz Hochwalder." *Monatshefte,* vol. 57, no. 1 (Jan., 1965) pp. 10-11.

Lumley, Frederick. *New trends in 20th century drama,* pp. 359-360.

Wellwarth, George. *The theatre of protest and paradox,* pp. 188-192, 194.

Die Herberge

Loram, Ian C. "Fritz Hochwalder." *Monatshefte,* vol. 57, no. 1 (Jan., 1965) pp. 12-13.

Hotel du Commerce

Loram, Ian C. "Fritz Hochwalder." *Monatshefte,* vol. 57, no. 1 (Jan., 1965), p. 10.

Liebe in Florenz

Loram, Ian C. "Fritz Hochwalder." *Monatshefte,* vol. 57, no. 1 (Jan., 1965), p. 9.

Meier Helmbrecht

Wellwarth, George. *The theatre of protest and paradox,* pp. 193-194.

Der Offentliche Anklager

Loram, Ian C. "Fritz Hochwalder." *Monatshefte,* vol. 57, no. 1 (Jan., 1965), pp. 11-12.

Wellwarth, George. *The theatre of protest and paradox,* pp. 194-195.

1003

Loram, Ian C. "Fritz Hochwalder." *Monatshefte,* vol. 57., no. 1 (Jan. 1965), p. 14.

The Raspberry Picker (Der Himbeerpflucker)

Lumley, Frederick. *New trends in 20th century drama,* pp. 360-361.

The Strong Are Lonely (Faith Is Not Enough) (Crown Colony) (Das Heilige Experiment)

Bauland, Peter. *The hooded eagle,* pp. 164, 171-172.

Garten, H.F. *Modern German drama,* p. 246.

Loram, Ian C. "Fritz Hochwalder." *Monatshefte,* vol. 57, no. 1 (Jan., 1965), pp. 9-10.

Lumley, Frederick. *New Trends in 20th century drama,* p. 359.

Wellwarth, George. *The theatre of protest and paradox,* pp. 184-188.

Williamson, Audrey. *Contemporary theatre, 1953-1956,* pp. 88-90.

HUGO VON HOFMANNSTHAL 1874-1926

General

Bednall, J.B. "The Slav Symbol in Hofmannsthal's Post-War Comedies." *German Life and Letters,* vol. 14 (1961), pp. 34-44.

Burger, Hilda. "Hofmannsthal's Debt to Moliere: Monsieur de Pourceaugnac and Baron von Lerchenau." *Modern Languages,* vol. 39 (1958), pp. 56-61.

Dodd, H.R. "A study of the dramas of Hugo von Hofmannsthal" D. Phil., Oxford University, 1953.

Doswald, Herman K. "Hofmannsthal's Plays in the Austrian Theater." *J. of the International Arthur Schnitzler Research Assoc.,* vol. 6, no. 2 (1967), pp. 2-31.

Garten H.F. *Modern German drama* pp. 63-76.

Hatfield, Henry. *Modern German literature,* pp. 18, 19, 21, 24, 26-32, 112-114.

Howarth, Herbert. "Eliot and Hofmannsthal." *South Atlantic Q.,* vol. 59 (Fall, 1960), pp. 500-509.

Lewis, Hanna Ballin. "English and American influences on Hugo von Hofmannsthal." *Dissertation Abstracts,* vol. 25, 1916 (Rice Univ.) 1964.

Lewis, Hanna B. "Hofmannsthal and Browning." *Comparative Literature,* vol. 19 (1967), pp. 142-159.

Oswald, Victor A., Jr. "Hofmannsthal's Collaboration with Moliere." *Germanic Rev.,* vol. 29, no. 1 (Feb., 1954), pp. 18-30.

Peacock, Ronald. *The poet in the theatre,* pp. 129-150.

Roe, Virginia Matilda. "Hugo von Hofmannsthal's *Elektra, Oedipus* and *Alkestis* compared with corresponding dramas of the ancient Greek playwrights." M.A., University of Cincinnati, 1934.

Schwarz, Egon. "Hofmannsthal and the Problem of Reality." *Wisconsin Studies in Contemporary Literature,* vol. 8, no. 4 (Autumn, 1967), pp. 484-504.

Witkowski, Georg. *German drama of the nineteenth century,* pp. 185-186.

Arabella

Bednall, J.B. "The Slav Symbol in Hofmannsthal's Post-War Comedies." *German Life and Letters,* vol. 14 (1961), pp. 35, 39-43.

Death and the Fool (The Fool and Death)

Schwartz, Alfred. "Introduction." *In:* Schwartz, A., translator, *Hugo von Hofmannsthal: three plays.*

Lamm, Martin. *Modern drama,* pp. 245-247.

The Difficult Man (Der Schwierige)

Bednall, J.B. "The Slav Symbol in Hofmannshal's Post-War Comedies." *German Life and Letters,* vol. 14 (1961), pp. 35-36, 39.

Carter, T.E. "Structure in Hofmannsthal's *Der Schwierige." German Life and Letters* n.s., vol. 18, no. 1 (Oct., 1964), pp. 15-24.

Gray, Ronald. *The German tradition in literature,* pp. 301-326.

Norton, Roger C. "Hugo von Hofmannsthal's *Der Schwierige* and Granville-Barker's *Waste.*" *Comparative Literature,* vol. 14 (Summer, 1962), pp. 272-279.

Norton, Roger C. "The Inception of Hofmannsthal's *Der Schwierige:* Early Plans and Their Significance." *PMLA,* vol. 79 (1964), pp. 97-103.

Schultz, H. Stefan. "Hofmannsthal's *Der Schwierige* and Goethe's *Torquato Tasso.*" English Goethe Society. *Publications,* vol. 33 (1963), pp. 130-149.

Schwarz, Egon. "Hofmannsthal and the Problem of Reality." *Wisconsin Studies in Contemporary Literature,* vol. 8, no. 4 (Autumn, 1967), pp. 499-500.

White, John J. "A Note on the Significance of the Game of Bridge as an Image in Hugo von Hofmannsthal's *Der Schwierige.*" *German Life and Letters,* n.s., vol. 19 (1965-66), pp. 197-200.

Electra

Corrigan, Robert W. "Character as Destiny in Hofmannsthal's *Electra.*" *Modern Drama,* vol. 2, no. 1 (May, 1959), pp. 17-28.

Ramsey, Warren. "The *Oresteia* Since Hofmannsthal: Images and Emphases." *Revue de Literature Comparee,* vol. 38 (1964), pp. 359-363.

Schwartz, Alfred. "Introduction." *In:* Schwartz, A., translator, *Hugo von Hofmannsthal: three plays.*

Everyman (Via Crusis) (Jedermann)

Adolf, Helen. "From *Everyman* and *Elckerlije* to Hofmannsthal and Kafka." *Comparative Literature,* vol. 9, no. 3 (Summer, 1957), pp. 204-212.

Bauland, Peter. *The hooded eagle* pp. 34, 58, 61-62, 156.

Doswald, Herman K. "The Reception of *Jedermann* in Salzburg." *German Q.,* vol. 40 (1967), pp: 212-225.

Das Gerettete Venedig

Kleineberger, H.R. "Otways's *Venice Preserved* and Hofmannsthal's *Das Gerettete Venedig.*" *Modern Language Rev.,* vol. 62, no. 2 (Apr., 1967), pp. 292-297.

The Phantom Lady (Dame Kobold)

Schwarz, Egon. "Hofmannsthal and the Problem of Reality." *Wisconsin Studies in Contemporary Literature,* vol. 8, no. 4 (Autumn, 1967), pp. 496-499.

Der Rosenkavalier

Giordano, Charles B. "On the Significance of Names in Hofmannsthal's *Rosenkavalier." German Q.,* vol. 36, no. 3 (May, 1963), pp. 258-268.

Schwarz, Egon. "Hofmannsthal and the Problem of Reality." *Wisconsin Studies in Contemporary Literature,* vol. 8, no. 4 (Autumn, 1967), pp. 492-496.

The Salzburg Great Theater of the World (The Great Theatre of the World) (Salzburger Grosse Weltheater)

Best, A.J. "The Mystery Plays in a Leeds Church." *Spectator,* vol. 132 (Jan. 19, 1924), p. 80.

Schwarz, Egon. "Hofmannsthal and the Problem of Reality." *Wisconsin Studies in Contemporary Literature,* vol. 8, no. 4 (Autumn, 1967), pp. 487-492.

The Tower (Der Turm)

Schwartz, Alfred. "Introduction." *In:* Schwartz, A., translator, *Hugo von Hofmannsthal: three plays.*

Schwarz, Egon. "Hofmannsthal and the Problem of Reality." *Wisconsin Studies in Contemporary Literature,* vol. 8, no. 4 (Autumn, 1967), pp. 503-504.

Llewellyn, R.T. "Hofmannsthal's Nihilism." *Modern Language Rev.,* vol. 61, no. 2 (Apr., 1966), pp. 250-259.

The White Fan

Schwarz, Egon. "Hofmannsthal and the Problem of Reality." *Wisconsin Studies in Contemporary Literature,* vol. 8, no. 4 (Autumn, 1967), pp. 484-485.

Der Unbestechliche

Bednall, J.B. "The Slav Symbol in Hofmannsthal's Post-War Comedies." *German Life and Letters,* vol. 14 (1961), pp. 35, 36-39.

JOHN HAYNES HOLMES 1879- and REGINALD LAWRENCE

If This Be Treason

Block, Anita. *The changing world in plays and theatre,*pp. 333-337.

Himelstein, Morgan Y. *Drama was a weapon, the left-wing theatre in New York 1929-1941,* pp. 137-138.

WILLIAM DOUGLAS HOME 1912-

The Chiltern Hunters

Hobson, Harold. *Theatre,* pp. 118-121.

Now Barabbas

Hobson, Harold. *Theatre,* pp. 50-52.

ISRAEL HOROVITZ

The Indian Wants the Bronx

Kerr, Walter. "'Futz--Is it a Fiasco...'" *The New York Times,* June 30, 1968, Sec. 2, p. 5.

OEDON VON HORVATH 1901-1938

General

Garten, H.F. *Modern German drama,* pp. 191-192.

STANLEY HOUGHTON 1881-1913

General

Williams, Harold. *Modern English writers,* pp. 259-261.

Hindle Wakes

Block, Anita. *The changing world in plays and theatre,* pp. 79-82.

LAURENCE HOUSMAN 1865-1959

Bethlehem

Weales, Gerald. *Religion in modern English drama,* pp. 122-124.

Jacob's Ladder

Weales, Gerald. *Religion in modern English drama,* p. 132.

Little Plays of St. Francis (1st series)

Weales, Gerald. *Religion in modern English drama,* pp. 125-131, 134.

Old Testament Plays

Roston, Murray. *Biblical drama in England from the Middle Ages to the present day,* pp. 286-288.

St. Martin's Pageant

Weales, Gerald. *Religion in modern English drama,* pp. 124-125.

Victoria Regina

Weales, Gerald. *Religion in modern English drama,* p. 131.

SIDNEY HOWARD 1891-1939

General

Brown, John Mason. *Upstage.* pp. 51-59.

Dusenbury, Winifred L. "Myth in American Drama Between the Wars." *Modern Drama,* vol. 6, no. 3 (Dec., 1963), pp. 294-308.

Gould, Jean. *Modern American playwrights,* pp. 21-25.

Krutch, Joseph Wood. *The American drama since 1918,* pp. 56-60.

Krutch, Joseph Wood. "The Dramatic Variety of Sidney Howard." *In:* Zabel, Morton Dauwen. *Literary opinion in America,* pp. 539-543. (Reprinted from *The Nation,* vol. 137 (Sept. 13, 1933), pp. 294-295.)

Meserve, Walter J. "Sidney Howard and the Social Drama of the Twenties." *Modern Drama,* vol. 6, no. 3 (Dec., 1963), pp. 256-266. *Also in:* Meserve, Walter J., ed. *Discussions of American drama,* pp. 8-17.

Alien Corn

Flexner, Eleanor. *American playwrights: 1918-1938,* pp. 42-44.

Sievers, W. David. *Freud on Broadway,* pp. 169-170.

Dodsworth

See Sinclair Lewis

Ghost of Yankee Doodle

Flexner, Eleanor. *American playwrights: 1918-1938,* pp. 56-58.

Himelstein, Morgan Y. *Drama was a weapon, the left-wing theatre in New York 1929-1941,* p. 141.

Half Gods

Sievers, W. David. *Freud on Broadway,* pp. 168-169.

Lucky Sam McCarver

Brown, John Mason. *Upstage.* pp. 51-59.

Downer, Alan S. *Fifty years of American drama, 1900-1950,* pp. 48-49.

Flexner, Eleanor. *American playwrights: 1918-1938,* pp. 34-36.

Meserve, Walter J. "Sidney Howard and the Social Drama of the Twenties." *Modern Drama,* vol. 6, no. 3 (Dec., 1963), pp. 256-266. *Also in:* Meserve, Walter J., ed. *Discussions of American drama,* pp. 8-17.

Madam, Will You Walk?

Sievers, W. David. *Freud on Broadway,* pp. 170-171.

Ned McCobb's Daughter

Flexner, Eleanor. *American playwrights: 1918-1938,* pp. 38-40.

Meserve, Walter J., "Sidney Howard and the Social Drama of the Twenties." *Modern Drama,* vol. 6, no. 3 (Dec., 1963), pp. 256-266. *Also in:* Meserve, Walter J., ed. *Discussions of American drama,* pp. 8-17.

Paths of Glory

See Cobb, Humphrey

The Silver Cord

Downer, Alan S. *Fifty years of American drama, 1900-1950,* pp. 58-60.

Dusenbury, Winifred L. *The theme of loneliness in modern American drama,* pp. 67-74.

Flexner, Eleanor. *American playwrights: 1918-1938,* pp. 36-38.

Gabriel, Gilbert W. "Sidney Howard's *The Silver Cord.*" *In:* Moses, Montrose J. *The American theatre as seen by its critics, 1752-1934,* pp. 313-315. (Reprinted from *The New York Sun,* Dec. 21, 1926.) *Also in:* Oppenheimer, George, ed. *The passionate playgoer,* N.Y., Viking, 1958, pp. 562-564.

MacCarthy, Desmond. *Drama,* pp. 221-224.

Meserve, Walter J. "Sidney Howard and the Social Drama of the Twenties." *Modern Drama,* vol. 6, no. 3 (Dec., 1963), pp. 256-266. *Also in:* Meserve, Walter J., ed. *Discussions of American drama,* pp. 8-17.

O'Hara, Frank H. *Today in American drama,* pp. 78-81, 246-248.

Sievers, W. David. *Freud on Broadway,* pp. 165-168.

Young, Stark. *Immortal shadows,* pp. 76-79.

They Knew What They Wanted

Flexner, Eleanor. *American playwrights: 1918-1938,* pp. 32-33.

Krutch, Joseph W. *The American drama* since 1918, pp. 44-56.

Meserve, Walter J. "Sidney Howard and the Social Drama of the Twenties." *Modern Drama,* vol. 6, no. 3 (Dec., 1963), pp. 256-266. *Also in:* Meserve, Walter J., ed. *Discussions of American drama,* pp. 8-17.

Yellow Jack

Flexner, Eleanor. *American playwrights: 1918-1938,* pp. 44-51.

Lawson, John Howard. "The Social Framework." *In:* Frenz, Horst, ed. *American playwrights on drama,* pp. 37-40. (Shortened version of the chapter on "The Social Framework" in John Howard Lawson's *The theory and technique of playwriting.*)

LANGSTON HUGHES 1902-1967

General

Emanuel, James A. *Langston Hughes.*

Presley, James. "The American Dream of Langston Hughes." *Southwest Rev.,* vol. 48 (Autumn, 1963), pp. 380-386.

Smalley, Webster, ed. "Introduction" to *Five plays of Langston Hughes,* Bloomington: Indiana Univ. Pres, 1963.

Spencer, T.J., and Clarence J. Rivers. "Langston Hughes: His Style and Optimism." *Drama Critique,* vol. 7, no. 2 (Spring, 1964), pp. 99-102.

Turner, Darwin T. "Langston Hughes as Playwright." *College Language Assn. J.,* vol. 11, no. 4 (June, 1968) (Special Langston Hughes Number), pp. 297-309.

Turner, Darwin T. "The Negro Dramatist's Image of the Universe, 1920-1960." *College Language Assn. Journal,* vol. 5 (Dec., 1961), pp. 106-120.

Wertz, I.J. "Langston Hughes: Profile." *Negro History Bulletin* (Mar., 1964), pp. 146-147.

Bibliography

Babb, Inez Johnson. "Bibliography of Langston Hughes, Negro poet." Unpublished Master's Thesis, Pratt Institute Library School, 1947.

Dickinson, Donald C. *A bio-bibliography of Langston Hughes, 1902-1967.* Hamden, Conn., Archon Books, The Shoe String Press, 1967.

Kaiser, Ernest. "Selected Bibliography of the Published Writings of Langston Hughes." *Freedomways,* vol. 8 (Spring, 1968), pp. 185-191.

O'Daniel, Therman B. "A Langston Hughes Bibliography." *College Language Assn. Bulletin,* vol. 7 (Spring, 1951), pp. 12-13.

O'Daniel, Therman B. "Langston Hughes: A Selected Classified Bibliography." *College Language Assn. J.,* vol. 11, no. 4 (June, 1968), pp. 349-366.

Ballad of the Brown King (Christmas cantata with music by Margaret Bonds, dedicated to Martin Luther King)

Emanuel, James A. *Langston Hughes,* p. 168.

The Barrier

Davis, Arthur P. "The Tragic Mulatto Theme in Six Works of Langston Hughes." *Phylon,* vol. 16 (Winter, 1955), pp. 195-204.

Emanuel, James A. *Langston Hughes,* pp. 43, 114.

Black Nativity

Emanuel, James A. *Langston Hughes,* p. 168.

Don't You Want To Be Free?

Abramson, Doris E. *Negro playwrights in the American theatre, 1925-1959,* pp. 79-83, 88.

Emanuel, James A. *Langston Hughes,* pp. 39, 40.

MacLeod, Norman. "The Poetry and Argument of Langston Hughes." *The Crisis,* vol. 45 (Nov., 1938), pp. 358-359.

Mitchell, Loften. *Black drama,* pp. 103-105.

Turner, Darwin T. "Langston Hughes as Playwright." *College Language Assn. J.,* vol. 11, no. 4 (June, 1968), p. 304.

Drums of Haiti (Emperor of Haiti) (Troubled Island)

Emanuel, James A. *Langston Hughes,* pp. 38, 42, 43.

Turner, Darwin T. "Langston Hughes as Playwright." *College Language Assn. J.,* vol. 11, no. 4 (June, 1968), pp. 307-308.

Esther (An opera, music by Jan Meyerowitz)

Emanuel, James A. *Langston Hughes,* p. 43.

Front Porch

Emanuel, James A. *Langston Hughes,* p. 39.

Gospel Glow

Emanuel, James A. *Langston Hughes,* p. 168.

Jerico-Jim Crow

Emanuel, James A. *Langston Hughes,* p. 169.

Just a Little Simple (Adapted by Alice Childress from Simple Speaks his Mind)

Mitchell, Loften. *Black drama,* pp. 145-147.

Little Ham

Hughes, Langston. *Five plays,* ed. by Webster Smalley, pp. xii-xiii.

Turner, Darwin T. "Langston Hughes As Playwright." *College Language Assn. J.,* vol. 11, no. 4 (June, 1968), pp. 301-304.

Mulatto

Abramson, Doris E. *Negro playwrights in the American theatre, 1925-1959,* pp. 69-79, 87.

Emanuel, James A. *Langston Hughes,* pp. 37, 38, 43, 44.

Hughes, Langston. *Five plays,* ed. by Webster Smalley, pp. x-xi.

Mitchell, Loften. *Black drama,* p. 97.

Turner, Darwin T. "Langston Hughes As Playwright." *College Language Assn. J.* vol. 11, no. 4 (June, 1968), pp. 297-301.

Port Town (One-act opera, with music by Jan Meyerowitz)

Emanuel, James A. *Langston Hughes,* pp. 167-168.

The Prodigal Son

Emanuel, James A. *Langston Hughes,* p. 169.

Simply Heavenly

Emanuel, James A. *Langston Hughes,* pp. 44, 155, 178.

Hughes, Langston. *Five plays,* ed. by Webster Smalley, pp. xiii-xv, 115.

Turner, Darwin T. "Langston Hughes as Playwright." *College Language Assn. J.,* vol. 11, no. 4 (June, 1968), pp. 305-307.

Soul Gone Home

Emanuel, James A. *Langston Hughes,* pp. 38, 39.

Hughes, Langston. *Five plays,* ed. by Webster Smalley, pp. xi-xii.

The Sun Do Move

Turner, Darwin T. "Langston Hughes as Playwright." *College Language Assn. J.,* vol. 11, no. 4 (June, 1968), pp. 304-305.

Tambourines to Glory

Emanuel, James A. *Langston Hughes,* pp. 168-169.

Hughes, Langston. *Five plays,* ed. by Webster Smalley, pp. xv-xvi, 184.

Mitchell, Loften. *Black drama,* pp. 197-198, 230.

Nichols, Lewis. "Langston Hughes Describes the Genesis of His *Tambourines to Glory." The New York Times,* Oct., 27, 1963, Sec. 2, p. 3.

Turner, Darwin T. "Langston Hughes as Playwright." *College Language Assn. J.,* vol. 11, no. 4 (June, 1968), pp. 308-309.

When the Jack Hollers

Emanuel, James A. *Langston Hughes,* pp. 38, 39.

RICHARD HUGHES 1900-

A Comedy of Good and Evil

MacCarthy, Desmond. *Drama,* pp. 338-342.

N. C. HUNTER
A Day by the Sea

Williamson, Audrey. *Contemporary theatre, 1953-1956*, pp. 35-37.

WILLIAM HURLBURT

Bride of the Lamb

Sievers, W. David. *Freud on Broadway*, pp. 137-138.

Recessional

Sievers, W. David. *Freud on Broadway*, pp. 139-140.

ALDOUS HUXLEY 1894-1963

The World of Light

MacCarthy, Desmond. *Drama*, pp. 327-333.

DOUGLAS HYDE 1860-1949

The Twisting of the Rope

Dent, Alan. *Preludes and studies*, pp. 159-160.

HENRIK IBSEN 1828-1906

General

Abel, Lionel. *Metatheatre, a new view of dramatic form*, pp. 107-110.

Adams, Robert M. "Ibsen on the Contrary." *In:* Caputi, Anthony, ed. *Modern drama*, pp. 344-353. (Earlier version in *Hudson Rev.* vol. 10, no. 3 (Autumn, 1957) with title "Henrik Ibsen: The Fifty-first Anniversary.")

Amble, Kjell. "The spirit of Ibsen: problems of English translation in three of his plays." *Dissertation Abstracts*, vol. 26 (1965), 2381-82 (Northwestern).

Archer, William. "The Point of Attack: Shakespeare and Ibsen." *In:* Archer, W. *Play-making: a manual of craftsmanship*, pp. 98-110.

Arup, Jens. "Narrative and Symbol in Ibsen." *In:* McFarlane, James Walter ed. *Discussions of Henrik Ibsen*, pp. 99-103. (From *Listener* (June 18, 1959).)

Aylen, Leo. *Greek tragedy and the modern world*, pp. 221-222, 230-231, 236-237, 241-242.

Bentley, Eric. "Ibsen, Pro and Con." *In:* McFarlane, James Walter, ed. *Discussions of Henrik Ibsen, pp. 11*-18. (From Bentley, Eric. *In search of theatre,* N.Y., Knopf, 1950.)

Bentley, Eric. *The playwright as thinker,* pp. 90-106.

Bentley, Eric. *The theatre of commitment,* pp. 98-118.

Blindheim, Joan T. "Bringing Ibsen to Life." *The Norseman* (Oslo, 1966), pp. 155-159.

Bockstahler, O.L. "Sudermann and Ibsen." *German Q,* vol. 5, no. 2 (Mar., 1932), pp. 54-57.

Bradbrook, M.C. *Ibsen, the Norwegian, a revaluation,* pp. 1-25, 148-158.

Brustein, Robert. "Ibsen and Revolt." *Tulane Drama Rev.,* vol. 7, no. 1 (Fall, 1962), pp. 113-154.

Brustein, Robert. *The theatre of revolt,* pp. 37-50.

Cornaby, Paul G. "A study of tragic elements in the works of Henrik Ibsen." M.A., Brigham Young University, 1953.

Courtney, W.L. *The idea of tragedy in ancient and modern drama,* pp. 111-126.

Cram, Clara. "Ibsen's idea of tragedy." M.A., Stanford University, 1915.

Dobrée, Bonamy. *The lamp and the lute, studies in seven authors,* 2nd ed., pp. 1-17.

Dukes, Ashley. *Modern dramatists,* pp. 20-40.

Ellis-Fermor, Una. "Ibsen and the Artist." *Queen's Q.,* vol. 53, no. 2 (Summer, 1946), pp. 200-208.

Fischer, F.G. "Ibsen: His Background." *Anglo-Welsh Rev.,* vol. 10, no. 25 (1959), pp. 42-47.

Forster, E.M. "Ibsen the Romantic." *In:* McFarlane, James Walter, ed. *Discussions of Henrik Ibsen,* pp. 66-70. (From Forster, E.M. *Abinger harvest,* N.Y., Harcourt, 1936.)

Gassner, John. *The theatre in our times,* pp. 105-113.

Gilman, Richard. "The Search for Ibsen." *Commonweal,* vol. 74 (Aug. 25, 1961), pp. 473-475.

Grene, David. *Reality and the heroic pattern, last plays of Ibsen, Shakespeare, and Sophocles,* pp. 1-9.

Haakonsen, Daniel. "Ibsen the Realist." *In:* McFarlane, James Walter, ed. *Discussions of Henrik Ibsen, pp. 70*-82. (From Haakonsen, Daniel. *Henrik Ibsens realisme,* Oslo, Aschhoug, 1957, translated by the author.)

Hamilton, Clayton. *Seen on the stage,* pp. 154-163.

Henderson, Archibald. *European dramatists,* pp. 75-195.

Hofmannsthal, Hugo von. "The People in Ibsen's Dramas." *In:* McFarlane, James Walter, ed. *Discussions of Henrik Ibsen,* pp. 83-88.

Ibsen, Henrik. "Letters and Speeches." *In:* Caputi, Anthony. ed. *Modern drama,* pp. 338-344. (From *Ibsen, letters and speeches,* ed. by Evert Sprinchorn. N.Y., Hill & Wang, 1964, pp. 105-107, 108-109, 114-116, 226-227, 337-338.)

Jacobs, Elizabeth. "Henrik Ibsen and the Doctrine of Self-Realization." *J. of English and Germanic Philology,* vol. 38, no. 3 (July, 1939), pp. 416-430.

Kaufmann, F.W. "Ibsen's Conception of Truth." *Germanic Rev.,* vol. 32, no. 2 (Apr., 1959), pp. 83-92.

Kaufmann, F.W. "Ibsen's Search for the Authentic Self." *Monatshefte,* vol. 45, no. 4 (Apr.-May, 1953), pp. 232-239.

Knight, G. Wilson. *The golden labyrinth,* pp. 282-297.

Knudsen, Trygve. "Phrases of Style and Language in the Works of Henrik Ibsen." *In:* Skrifttradisjon og litteraturmal: Artikler og avhandlinger i utvalg, pp. 143-172.

Krutch, Joseph Wood. *"Modernism" in modern drama,* pp. 36-41.

Lamm, Martin. *Modern drama,* pp. 97-134.

Lavrin, Janko. "Ibsen and Shaw." *In:* Lavrin, J. *Studies in European literature,* pp. 80-98.

Leaska, Mitchell A. *The voice of tragedy,* pp. 204-205, 208-212.

Lewis, Allan. The *contemporary theatre,* pp. 8-41.

Lund, Mary Graham. "The Existentialism of Ibsen." *Personalist,* vol. 41, no. 3 (July, 1960), pp. 310-317.

MacCarthy, Desmond. *Theatre,* pp. 77-80.

McCarthy, Mary. "The Will and Testament of Ibsen." *Partisan Rev.,* vol. 23 no. 1 (Winter, 1956), pp. 74-80.

McCollom, William G. *Tragedy,* pp. 215-226.

McFarlane, James Walter. "Revaluations of Ibsen." *In:* McFarlane, James Walter, ed. *Discussions of Henrik Ibsen,* pp. 19-27. (From *Ibsen and the temper of Norwegian literature,* London, Oxford Univ. Press, 1960.)

McInnes, Edward. "Ibsen and Poetic Drama." *Forum for Modern Language Studies* (U. of St. Andrews, Scotland), vol. 2 (1966), pp. 141-149.

Mencken, Henry L. "From *Introduction to Ibsen's Plays.*" *In:* Levin Richard. *Tragedy: plays, theory, and criticism,* pp. 202-205. (Reprinted from Mencken's introduction to a Modern Library Edition of Ibsen's plays, N.Y., Boni & Liveright, n.d.)

Mencken, H.L. "Ibsen." *In:* Freedman, Morris, ed. *Essays in the modern drama,* pp. 3-8. (Reprinted from *Eleven plays of Henrik Ibsen,* Random House.)

Mencken, H.L. "The Technical Quality of the Plays." *In:* McFarlane, James Walter, ed. *Discussions of Henrik Ibsen,* pp. 7-10. (From Ibsen, H. *Eleven plays of Henrik Ibsen,* N.Y., Random House, 1935.)

Meyer, Michael. "Ibsen: The Years of Failure." *Listener,* vol. 77 (1967), pp. 225-227.

Miller, Arthur. "The 'Real' in Ibsen's Realism." *In:* McFarlane, James Walter, ed. *Discussions of Henrik Ibsen,* pp. 104-105. (From Miller, Arthur *Collected plays,* N.Y., Viking, 1957.)

Montague, Charles E. *Dramatic values,* pp. 139-159.

Norwood, Gilbert. *Euripides and Shaw with other essays,* pp. 52-59.

O'Casey, Sean. "Dramatis Personae Ibsenisensis." *In:* O'Casey, Sean. *Blasts and benedictions,* pp. 46-50. (Reprinted from *The American Spectator,* New York, (July, 1933).)

O'Donnell, Norbert F. "Ibsen and Shaw: The Tragic and the Tragi-Comic." *Theatre annual, 1957-58,* vol. 15, pp. 15-27.

Orr, Stella. "Good and evil in the plays of Ibsen and Strindberg." M.A., University of Kansas, 1917.

Peacock, Ronald. "Effects of Ibsen." *In:* McFarlane, James Walter, ed. *Discussions of Henrik Ibsen,* pp. 106-110 (From Peacock, Ronald. *The poet in the theatre,* N.Y., Hill & Wang, 1960.)

Peacock, Ronald. *The poet in the theatre,* pp. 77-85.

Popperwell, Ronald G. "The Problem of Inflence—A Specific Case." *Proceedings of the Fifth Internat. Study Conference on Scand. Lit. held at Univ. College, London, 1964.*

Raphael, Robert. "From *Hedda Gabler* to *When We Dead Awaken:* The Quest for Self-Realization." *Scandinavian Studies,* vol. 36, no. 1 (1964).

Reichardt, Konstantin. "Tragedy of Idealism: Henrik Ibsen." *In:* Brooks, Cleanth, ed. *Tragic themes in western literature,* pp. 128-149.

Reinert, Otto. "Archetypes of Ambiguity." *Edda,* vol. 54 (1967), pp. 288-294. (Rev. of *Ibsen yearbook,* vol. 8.)

Schechner, Richard. "The Unexpected Visitor in Ibsen's Late Plays." *Educational Theatre J.,* vol. 14, no. 2 (May, 1962), pp. 120-127.

Setterquist, Jan. *Ibsen and the beginnings of Anglo-Irish drama. I. John Millington Synge,* pp. 76-91.

Shaw, George Bernard. "Ibsen Triumphant." *In:* Sprinchorn, Evert, ed. *The genius of the Scandinavian theatre,* pp. 548-554.

Shaw, George Bernard. "The Lesson of the Plays." *In:* McFarlane, James Walter ed. *Discussions of Henrik Ibsen,* pp. 1-6. (From Shaw, G.B. *The quintessence of Ibsenism,* London, 1913.)

Shaw, George Bernard. *The quintessence of Ibsenism,* pp. 159-210.

Shaw, George Bernard. "The Technical Novelty in Ibsen's Plays." *In:* Freedman, Morris, ed. *Essays in the modern drama,* pp. 9-18. (Reprinted from *The quintessence of Ibsenism.)*

Steiner, George. *The death of tragedy,* pp. 290-297.

Street, Gertrude. "A comparison of Greek tragedy and modern drama as shown by Ibsen." M.A., University of Southern California, 1931.

Styan, J.L. *The dark comedy,* 2nd ed., pp. 35, 52, 53, 58, 64-68, 74, 161, 208, 212, 220, 280, 296.

Thompson, Alan Reynolds. *The dry mock,* pp. 197-244.

Volpe, Edmond L., ed. *An introduction to literature: drama,* pp. 245-253.

Von Klenze, Henriette B. "Paul Ernst and Henrik Ibsen: A Study in Dramatic Revolution." *Germanic Rev.,* vol. 16, no. 2 (Apr., 1941), pp. 134-145.

Willey, Norman L. "Factual Inadvertencies in Ibsen's Dramas." *Scandinavian Studies,* vol. 17, no. 6 (May, 1943), pp. 185-194.

Williams, Raymond. *Drama from Ibsen to Eliot,* pp. 41-97.

Williams, Raymond. "Ibsen's Non-Theatrical Plays." *In:* McFarlane, James Walter, ed. *Discussions of Henrik Ibsen,* pp. 35-38. (From *Listener* (Dec. 22, 1949) and adapted from *Drama from Ibsen to Eliot,* London, Chatto & Windus, 1952.)

Williams, Raymond. *Modern tragedy,* pp. 96-103.

Winter, William. "Ibsenites and Ibsenism." *In:* Moses, Montrose J. *The American theatre as seen by its critics, 1752-1934,* pp. 94-101. (Reprinted from *The wallet of time,* Moffat, Yard & Co., 1913.)

Brand

Arestad, Sverre. "Ibsen's Concept of Tragedy." *PLMA,* vol. 74, no. 3 (June, 1959), pp. 286-289.

Auden, W.H. "Genius and Apostle." *In:* Auden, W.H. *The dyer's hand and other essays,* pp. 441-450.

Bradbrook, M.C. *Ibsen, the Norwegian, a revaluation,* pp. 6-7, 42-53, 62, 64, 90, 125-126, 146.

Brustein, Robert. "Ibsen and Revolt." *Tulane Drama Rev.,* vol. 7, no. 1 (Fall, 1962), pp. 125-132.

Brustein, Robert. *The theatre of revolt,* pp. 50-59.

Dahlstrom, Carl E.W.L. "Brand—Ibsen's Bigot?" *Scandinavian Studies,* vol. 22, no. 1 (Feb., 1950), pp. 1-13.

Deer, Irving. "Ibsen's Brand: Paradox and the Symbolic Hero." *Lock Haven Bulletin,* no. 3 (1961), pp. 7-18.

Glicksberg, Charles I. *The self in modern literature,* pp. 12-20.

Henn, T.R. *The harvest of tragedy,* pp. 175-178.

McCollom, William G. *Tragedy,* pp. 216-223.

Matthews, Honor. *The primal curse,* pp. 86, 89-95, 118, 205.

Myers, Henry A. *Tragedy: a view of life,* pp. 141-142.

Setterquist, Jan. *Ibsen and the beginnings of Anglo-Irish drama, II. Edward Martyn,* pp. 29-30, 54-55.

Shaw, George Bernard. *The quintessence of Ibsenism.* pp. 44-47.

Smith, H.A. "Dipsychus Among the Shadows." *In:* Brown, J.R. and B. Harris, eds. *Contemporary theatre,* pp. 147-151.

Thompson, Alan Reynolds. *The dry mock,* pp. 212-215.

Williams, Raymond. *Drama from Ibsen to Eliot,* pp. 51-56.

Williams, Raymond. *Modern tragedy.* pp. 96-98.

Catiline

Meyer, Michael. *Henrik Ibsen; the making of a dramatist, 1828-1864,* pp. 59-62, 64-65, 73-75.

Pearce, John C. Hegelian Ideas in Three Tragedies by Ibsen." *Scandinavian Studies,* vol. 34, (1962), pp. 245-257.

A Doll's House

Block, Anita. *The changing world in plays and theatre,* pp. 25-28, 77.

Bradbrook, M.C. *Ibsen, the Norwegian, a revaluation,* pp. 1, 76-89, 100.

Ellehauge, Martin. *The position of Bernard Shaw in European drama and philosophy,* pp. 10, 65-66.

Freedman, Morris. *The moral impulse,* pp. 3-5, 58.

"The First Ibsen in America—Modjeska's *Thora* In Louisville." *In:* Moses, Montrose J. *The American theatre as seen by its critics, 1752-1934,* pp. 101-103. (Reprinted from *The Louisville Courier-Journal,* Dec. 8, 1883.)

Ibsen, Henrik. *"A Doll's House:* Notes for the Modern Tragedy." *In:* Cole, Toby, ed. *Playwrights on playwriting,* pp. 151-154.

Jameson, Storm. *Modern drama in Europe,* pp. 93-96.

Peacock, Ronald. "Public and Private Problems in Modern Drama." *In:* Corrigan, Robert W. *Theatre in the twentieth century* pp. 304-308. *Also in: Tulane Drama Rev.,* vol. 3, no. 3 (Mar., 1959), pp. 59-62.

Rowe, Kenneth Thorpe. *A theatre in your head,* pp. 117-122.

Setterquist, Jan. *Ibsen and the beginnings of Anglo-Irish drama. I. John Millington Synge,* pp. 17-19, 22-26, 87-88. *II. Edward Martyn,* pp. 18, 45-46, 94-95.

Shaw, George Bernard. *The quintessence of Ibsenism.* pp. 77-81.

Spacks, Patricia Meyer. "Confrontation and Escape in Two Social Dramas." *Modern Drama,* vol. 11, no. 1 (May, 1968), pp. 61-72.

Thompson, Alan Reynolds. *The dry mock,* pp. 217-218.

Williams, Raymond. *Drama from Ibsen to Eliot.* pp. 66-69.

Zucker, A.E. "The Forgery in Ibsen's *Doll's House.*" *Scandinavian Studies,* vol. 17, no. 8 (Nov., 1943), pp. 309-312.

Emperor and Galilean

Arestad, Sverre. "Ibsen's Concept of Tragedy." *PMLA,* vol. 74, no. 3 (June, 1959), pp. 288-289.

Bradbrook, M.C. *Ibsen, the Norwegian, a revaluation,* pp. 64-67.

Brustein, Robert. *The theatre of revolt,* pp. 61-65.

Knight, G. Wilson. *The golden labyrinth,* pp. 285-289.

Pearce, John C. "Hegelian Ideas in Three Tragedies by Ibsen." *Scandinavian Studies,* vol. 34 (1962), pp. 245-257.

Shaw, George Bernard. *The quintessence of Ibsenism,* pp. 55-70.

Williams, Raymond. *Drama from Ibsen to Eliot,* pp. 60-65.

Williams, Raymond. *Modern tragedy,* pp. 99-100.

An Enemy of the People

Adamczewski, Zygmunt. *The tragic protest,* pp. 143-171.

Bradbrook, M.C. *Ibsen, the Norwegian, a revaluation,* pp. 10, 11, 94-95.

Brustein, Robert. "Ibsen and Revolt." *Tulane Drama Rev.,* vol. 7, no. 1 (Fall, 1962), pp. 140-141.

Cassell, Richard A. *What is the play?* pp. 171-173, 243-244.

Ellehauge, Martin. *The position of Bernard Shaw in European drama and philosophy,* pp. 58-59, 78-79.

Freedman, Morris. *The moral impulse,* pp. 9-14.

Heilman, Robert B. *Tragedy and melodrama,* pp. 42-44, 47.

Krutch, Joseph Wood. "Arthur Miller Bowdlerizes Ibsen." *Nation,* vol. 172 (May 5, 1951), pp. 423-424.

Krutch, Joseph Wood. *"Modernism" in modern drama,* pp. 11-13.

Lambert, Robert G. *"An Enemy of the People:* A Friend of the teacher." *English J.,* vol. 54 (1965), pp. 626-628.

Lepke, Arno K. "Who Is Doctor Stockmann?" *Scandinavian Studies,* vol. 32, no. 2 (May, 1960), pp. 57-75.

Setterquist, Jan. *Ibsen and the beginnings of Anglo-Irish drama, II. Edward Martyn,* pp. 29, 58-61, 99.

Styan, J.L. *The dark comedy,* 2nd ed., pp. 2-3, 35, 65, 66.

The Feast at Solhang

Meyer, Michael. *Henrik Ibsen; the making of a dramatist, 1828-1864,* pp. 141-145, 148-149.

Williams, Raymond. *Drama in performance* (new ed.), pp. 101-106.

Ghosts (Gengangere)

Archer, William. "From *Introduction to Ghosts.*" *In:* Levin. Richard. *Tragedy: plays, theory, and criticism,* pp. 201-202. (Reprinted from the Viking Edition of the *Works of Ibsen,* vol, 7, N.Y., Scribner's, 1917.)

Arestad, Sverre. "Ibsen's Concept of Tragedy." *PMLA* vol. 74, no. 3 (June, 1959) pp. 289-291.

Barnet, Sylvan, ed. *Eight great tragedies,* pp. 228-230.

Block, Anita. *The changing world in plays and theatre,* pp. 28-31.

Bradbrook, M.C. *Ibsen, the Norwegian, a revaluation,* pp. 89-93, 94.

Brereton, Geoffrey. *Principles of tragedy, a rational examination of the tragic concept in life and literature,* pp. 200-201.

Brustein, Robert. "Ibsen and Revolt." *Tulane Drama Rev.,* vol. 7, no. 1 (Fall, 1962), pp. 136-140.

Brustein, Robert. *Seasons of discontent,* pp. 57-60.

Brustein, Robert. *The theater of revolt,* pp. 67-71.

Cook, Albert. *Prisms, studies in modern literature,* pp. 137-138.

Corrigan, Robert W. "The Sun Always Rises: Ibsen's *Ghosts* as Tragedy?" *Educational Theatre J.,* vol. 11 (1959), pp. 171-180.

Cowell, Raymond. *Twelve modern dramatists,* pp. 15-17.

Downer, Alan S. *The art of the play,* pp. 163-166, 170-172, 184-194.

Ellehauge, Martin. *The position of Bernard Shaw in European drama and philosophy,* pp. 68.

Ellis-Fermor, Una. "Ibsen and Shakespeare as Dramatic Artists." *In:* McFarlane, James Walter, ed. *Discussions of Henrik Ibsen,* pp. 91-94. (From Muir, Kenneth, ed. *Shakespeare the dramatist,* London, Methuen, 1961.)

Fergusson, Francis. "Ghosts." *In* McFarlane, James Walter, ed. *Discussions of Henrik Ibsen,* pp. 39-46. (From *The idea of a theater,* Princeton Univ. Press. 1949.)

Fergusson, Francis. *The idea of a theater, pp. 161-174. Also in:* Freedman, Morris, ed. *Essays in the modern drama,* pp. 19-34.

Fergusson, Francis. "The Plot of *Ghosts:* Thesis, Thriller, and Tragedy." *In: Le*vin, Richard. *Tragedy: plays, theory, and criticism,* pp. 207-211. (Reprinted from Fergusson, Francis. *The idea of a Theatre.)*

Freedman, Morris. *The moral impulse,* pp. 4-8.

Gassner, John. *The theatre in our times,* pp. 66-68.

Ibsen, Henrik. *In:* Cole, Toby, ed. *Playwrights on playwriting,* pp. 154-155.

Ibsen, Henrik. "Ibsen on *Ghosts." In:* Levin, Richard. *Tragedy: plays, theory, and criticism,* pp. 127-129. (Reprinted from the Viking Edition of the *Works of Ibsen,* vol. 12, N.Y., Scribner's, 1917.)

Krutch, Joseph Wood. *"Modernism" in modern drama,* pp. 9-11, 40-41.

Lamm, Martin. *Modern drama,* pp. 129-132.

Leaska, Mitchell A. *The voice of tragedy,* pp. 199-204, 205-206, 208-209.

Lecky, Eleazer. *"Ghosts* and *Mourning Becomes Electra:* Two Versions of Fate." *Arizona Q.,* vol. 13, no. 4 (Winter, 1957), pp. 320-338.

Lewis, Allan. *The contemporary theatre,* pp. 16-29.

MacCarthy, Desmond. *Drama,* pp. 61-67.

Muller, Herbert J. *The spirit of tragedy,* 260-267.

Sedgewick, G.G. *Of irony especially in drama,* pp. 44-48, 120.

Shaw, George Bernard. *The quintessence of Ibsenism,* pp. 81-90.

Stanislavski, K. "Director's Diary, 1905." *In:* Munk, Erika, ed. *Stanislavski and America,* pp. 30-45.

Swanson, C.A. "Ibsen's *Ghosts* at the Theatre-Libre." *Scandinavian Studies,* vol. 16, no. 8 (Nov., 1941), pp. 281-290.

Thompson, Alan Reynolds. *The dry mock,* pp. 218-219.

Williams, Raymond. *Drama from Ibsen to Eliot,* pp. 69-72.

Williams, Raymond. *Modern tragedy,* pp. 98-99.

Hedda Gabler

Allison, Alexander W., ed. *Masterpieces of the drama,* 2nd ed., pp. 365-366.

Aylen, Leo. *Greek tragedy and the modern world,* p. 241.

Blau, Herbert. "Hedda Gabler: The Irony of Decadence." *Educational Theatre J.,* vol. 5 (1953), pp. 112-116.

Bradbrook, M.C. *Ibsen, the Norwegian, a revaluation,* pp. 16, 24-25, 87-88, 97, 116-121.

Brereton, Geoffrey. *Principles of tragedy, a rational examination of the tragic concept in life and literature,* pp. 198-200, 204.

Dorcy, Michael M. "Ibsen's *Hedda Gabler:* Tragedy as Denouement." *College English,* vol. 29, no. 3 (Dec., 1967), pp. 223-227.

Ellehauge, Martin. *The position of Bernard Shaw in European drama and philosophy,* pp. 152-153.

Freedman, Morris. *The moral impulse,* pp. 8-9.

Henn, T.R. *The harvest of tragedy,* 180-181.

Ibsen, Henrik. *In:* Cole, Toby, ed. *Playwrights on playwriting,* pp. 156-170.

James, Henry. "On the Occasion of *Hedda Gabler." In:* McFarlane, James Walter, Ed. *Discussions of Henrik Ibsen,* pp. 54-60. (Wade, Allan, ed. *The scenic art,* Rutgers Univ. Pres, 1948. First Published in *New Review,* (June, 1891).)

Kildahl, Erling E. "The Social Conditions and Principles of *Hedda Gabler." Educational Theatre J.,* vol. 13, no. 3 (Oct., 1961), pp. 207-213.

Krutch, Joseph Wood. *"Modernism" in modern drama,* pp. 17-22.

McCollom, William G. *Tragedy,* pp. 73-79, 110, 225.

Mayerson, Caroline W. "Thematic Symbols in *Hedda Gabler." Scandinavian Studies,* vol. 22, no. 4 (Nov., 1950), pp. 151-160.

Reinert, Otto, ed. *Drama; an introductory anthology* (alternate ed.), pp. 458-463.

Setterquist, Jan. *Ibsen and the beginnings of Anglo-Irish drama, II. Edward Martyn,* pp. 59, 78, 83-92.

Shaw, George Bernard. *The quintessence of Ibsenism.* pp. 110-118.

Spacks, Patricia Meyer. "The World of *Hedda Gabler." Tulane Drama Rev.* vol. 7, no. 1 (Fall, 1962), pp. 155-164.

Williams, Raymond. *Drama from Ibsen to Eliot,* pp. 82-84.

Williamson, Audrey. *Contemporary theatre, 1953-1956,* pp. 143-145.

Zucker, A.E. "Ibsen's Barach Episode and *Hedda Gabler." Philological Q,* vol. 8, no. 3 (July, 1929), pp. 288-295.

John Gabriel Borkman

Aylen, Leo. *Greek tragedy and the modern world,* pp. 239-240. 242, 302.

Bradbrook, M.C. *Ibsen, the Norwegian, a revaluation,* pp. 3, 30, 137-147.

Ellehauge, Martin. *The position of Bernard Shaw in European drama and philosophy,* pp. 143-144.

Grene, David. *Reality and the heroic pattern, last plays of Ibsen, Shakespeare, and Sophocles,* pp. 24-27.

Heilman, Robert B. *Tragedy and melodrama,* pp. 158. 233-234.

Henn, T.R. *The harvest of tragedy,* 182-184.

MacCarthy, Desmond. *Drama,* pp. 74-78.

MacCarthy, Desmond. *Theatre,* pp. 78-79.

Matthews, Honor. *The primal curse,* pp. 88, 91, 114-115.

Muller, Herbert J. *The spirit of tragedy,* pp. 271-272.

Setterquist, Jan. *Ibsen and the beginnings of Anglo-Irish drama, II. Edward Martyn,* pp. 33-34, 36.

Shaw, George Bernard. *The quintessence of Ibsenism,* pp. 139-146.

Williams, Raymond. *Drama from Ibsen to Eliot,* p. 91.

Lady from the Sea (The Sea Woman)

Bradbrook, M.C. *Ibsen, the Norwegian, a revaluation,* pp. 102-103, 108-109, 133-134, 136, 140.

Ellehauge, Martin. *The position of Bernard Shaw in European drama and philosophy,* p. 63.

Meyer, Michael. *Henrik Ibsen; the making of a dramatist, 1828-1864,* pp. 134-138, 183.

Setterquist, Jan. *Ibsen and the beginnings of Anglo-Irish drama. I. John Millington Synge,* pp. 19-20, 21, 23, 29-32, 34-35, 37, 49, 69, 88. *II. Edward Martyn,* pp. 34-35, 50, 52, 69-70, 72-76, 78-79, 94-95.

Shaw, George Bernard. *The quintessence of Ibsenism,* pp. 107-110.

Tynan, Kenneth. *Tynan right and left,* pp. 93-95.

Williams, Raymond. *Drama from Ibsen to Eliot,* pp. 81-82.

Young, Stark. *Immortal shadows,* pp. 29-32.

The League of Youth

Bradbrook, M.C. *Ibsen, the Norwegian, a revaluation,* pp. 9, 68-71.

Lamm, Martin. *Modern drama,* pp. 106-111.

Setterquist, Jan. *Ibsen and the beginnings of Anglo-Irish drama. I. John Millington Synge,* pp. 41, 77. *II. Edward Martyn,* pp. 95-96.

Little Eyolf

Arestad, Sverre. *"Little Eyolf* and Human Responsibility." *Scandinavian Studies,* vol. 32 (1960), pp. 140-152.

Bradbrook, M.C. *Ibsen, the Norwegian, a revaluation,* pp. 29, 59, 133-137.

Grene, David. *Reality and the heroic pattern, last plays of Ibsen, Shakespeare and Sophocles,* pp. 20-24.

Henn, T.R. *The harvest of tragedy,* 181-182.

Kerans, James E. "Kindermord and Will in *Little Eyolf." In:* Bogard, Travis, and Oliver, William I., eds. *Modern drama; essays in criticism,* pp. 192-207.

Lid, R.W., ed. *Plays, classic and contemporary,* pp. 589-606.

Matthews, Honor. *The primal curse,* pp. 110-113.

Shaw, George Bernard. *The quintessence of Ibsenism.* pp. 127-139.

Shaw, George Bernard. *Shaw's dramatic criticism (1895-98),* pp. 193-206.

Thompson, Alan Reynolds. *The dry mock,* pp. 231-238.

Williams, Raymond. Drama from *Ibsen to Eliot,* pp. 88-91.

Love's Comedy

Bradbrook, M.C. *Ibsen, the Norwegian, a revaluation,* pp. 23, 31-32, 33, 35-42, 125-126, 146.

Downs, Brian W. *"Love's Comedy* and Ibsen's Humour." *In:* McFarlane, James Walter, ed. *Discussions of Henrik Ibsen,* pp. 28-34. (From Downs, B.W. *A study of six plays by Ibsen,* Cambridge Univ. Pres, 1950.)

Ellehauge, Martin. *The position of Bernard Shaw in European drama and philosophy,* pp. 63.

Meyer, Michael. *Henrik Ibsen; the making of a dramatist, 1828-1864,* pp. 218, 221-225, 228-229.

The Master Builder (Bygmester Solness)

Arestad, Sverre. "Ibsen's Concept of Tragedy." *PMLA,* vol. 74 (1959), pp. 292-296.

Arup, Jens. "Narrative and Symbol in Ibsen." *Listener,* vol. 61 (June 18, 1959), pp. 1063-1065.

Bentley, Eric. *The playwright as thinker,* pp. 98-100.

Bradbrook, M.C. *Ibsen, the Norwegian, a revaluation,* pp. 3, 15, 92, 121, 126-133, 134.

Brereton, Geoffrey. *Principles of tragedy, a rational examination of the tragic concept in life and literature,* pp. 204-209.

Brustein, Robert. "Ibsen and Revolt." *Tulane Drama Rev.,* vol. 7, no. 1 (Fall, 1962), pp. 143-147.

Brustein, Robert. *The theatre of revolt,* pp. 75-78.

Ellehauge, Martin. *The position of Bernard Shaw in European drama and philosophy,* p. 143.

Grene, David. *Reality and the heroic pattern, last plays of Ibsen, Shakespeare, and Sophocles,* pp. 10-19.

Gunvaldsen, K.M. "The *Master Builder* and *Dene Glocke.*" *Monatshefte fur Deutschen Unterricht,* vol. 33, no. 4 (Apr., 1941), pp. 153-162.

Herford, C.H. "On Ibsen's *The Master Builder.*" *In:* Agate, James. *The English dramatic critics,* pp. 283-287. *Also in: The Manchester Guardian,* Apr., 23, 1909.

Hobson, Harold. *Theatre,* pp. 41-42.

Lyons, Charles R. "*The Master Builder* as Drama of the Self." *Scandinavian Studies,* vol. 39 (1967), pp. 329-339.

Matthews, Honor. *The primal curse,* pp. 20, 88, 106-110, 119.

Muller, Herbert J. *The spirit of tragedy,* 270-271.

Sehmsdorf, Henning K. "Two Legends about St. Olaf, the Masterbuilder: A Clue to the Dramatic Structure of Henrik Ibsen's *Bygmester Solness.*" *Edda,* vol. 54 (1967), pp. 263-271.

Setterquist, Jan. *Ibsen and the beginnings of Anglo-Irish drama. I. John Millington Synge,* pp. 66-70, 73, 77, 80. *II. Edward Martyn, pp.* 23, 32-33, 37, 44, 50-51, 52-53, 97.

Shaw, George Bernard. *The quintessence of Ibsenism,* pp. 121-127.

Sprinchorn, Evert, ed. *The genius of the Scandinavian theater,* pp. 82-83.

Thompson, Alan Reynolds. *The dry mock,* pp. 227-228, 230-231.

Weigand, Hermann J. "*The Master Builder.*" *In:* Sprinchorn, Evert, ed. *The genius of the Scandinavian theater,* pp. 555-582.

Williams, Raymond. *Drama from Ibsen to Eliot,* pp. 84-88.

Olaf Liljekrans

Meyer, Michael. *Henrik Ibsen; the making of a dramatist, 1828-1864,* pp. 153-156.

Peer Gynt

Arestad, Sverre. "*Peer Gynt* and the Idea of Self." *Modern Drama,* vol. 3, no. 2 (Sept., 1960), pp. 103-122.

Auden, W.H. "Genius and Apostle." *In:* Auden, W.H. *The dyer's hand and other essays,* pp. 435-441.

Bradbrook, M.C. *Ibsen the Norwegian, a revaluation,* pp. 10, 39, 53-63, 64, 69, 90, 110, 111, 122, 153.

Brereton, Geoffrey. *Principles of tragedy, a rational examination of the tragic concept in life and literature,* pp. 192-197.

Brustein, Robert. "Ibsen and Revolt." *Tulane Drama Rev.,* vol. 7, no. 1 (Fall, 1962), pp. 132-134.

Brustein, Robert. *Seasons of discontent,* pp. 218-221.

Edwards, Lee Rosenblum. "A Structural Analysis of *Peer Gynt.*" *Modern Drama,* vol. 8, no. 1 (May, 1965), pp. 28-38.

Gaskell, Ronald. "Symbol and Reality in *Peer Gynt.*" *Drama Survey,* vol. 4, no. 1 (Spring, 1965), pp. 57-64.

Glicksberg, Charles I. The *self in modern literature,* pp. 12-13, 18, 20-26.

Hurt, James R. "Fantastic Scenes in *Peer Gynt.*" *Modern Drama,* vol. 5, no. 1 (May, 1962), pp. 37-41.

Lamm, Martin. *Modern drama,* 103-106.

Matthews, Honor. *The primal curse,* pp. 87, 91, 93-100, 118.

Reed, Robert R. "Boss Mangan, *Peer Gynt,* and *Heartbreak House.*" *Shaw Rev.,* vol. 2, no. 7 (1959), pp. 6-12.

Setterquist, Jan. *Ibsen and the beginnings of Anglo-Irish drama. I. John Millington Synge,* pp. 42, 55-65. *II. Edward Martyn,* pp. 30, 51, 96-97.

Shaw, George Bernard. *The quintessence of Ibsenism,* pp. 47-54.

Thompson, Alan Reynolds. *The dry mock,* pp. 215-216.

Williams, Raymond. *Drama from Ibsen to Eliot,* pp. 56-60.

Zucker, A.E. "Goethe and Ibsen's Buttonmoulder." *PMLA,* vol. 57, no. 4, pt. 1 (Dec., 1942), pp. 1101-1107.

Pillars of Society

Aylen, Leo. *Greek tragedy and the modern world,* pp. 237-238.

Bradbrook, M.C. *Ibsen, the Norwegian, a revaluation,* pp. 67, 71-76, 86, 87.

Ellehauge, Martin. *The position of Bernard Shaw in European drama and philosophy,* pp. 56-57.

Jameson, Storm. *Modern drama in Europe,* pp. 73-75.

The Pretenders

Meyer, Michael. *Henrik Ibsen; the making of a dramatist, 1828-1864,* pp. 230-235.

Pearce, John C. "Hegelian Ideas in Three Tragedies by Ibsen." *Scandinavian Studies,* vol. 34 (1962), pp. 245-257.

Thompson, Alan Reynolds. *The dry mock,* pp. 211-212.

Rosmersholm

Arestad, Sverre. "Ibsen's Concept of Tragedy." *PMLA,* vol. 74, (1959), pp. 291-292.

Aylen, Leo. *Greek tragedy and the modern world,* pp. 231, 239-241.

Beerbohm, Max. *Around theatres,* pp. 497-501.

Bradbrook, M.C. *Ibsen, the Norwegian, a revaluation,* pp. 1, 2, 92, 109-115, 124, 150-151.

Brereton, Geoffrey. *Principles of tragedy, a rational examination of the tragic concept in life and literature,* pp. 202-204.

Brooks, Cleanth. *Understanding drama,* pp. 269-271, 283-288, 307-317.

Cubeta, Paul M. *Modern drama for analysis,* pp. 143-150.

Ellehauge, Martin. *The position of Bernard Shaw in European drama and philosophy,* p. 143.

Ellis-Fermor, Una. "Ibsen and Shakespeare as Dramatic Artists." *In:* McFarlane, James Walter, ed. *Discussions of Henrik Ibsen,* pp. 96-98. (From Muir, Kenneth, ed, *Shakespeare the dramatist,* London, Methuen, 1961.)

Gustafson, Alrik. "Aspects of Theme and Form in *Rosmersholm.*" *In:* American-Scandinavian Foundation, New York. *Scandinavian studies,* pp. 213-226.

Heilman, Robert B. *Tragedy and melodrama,* pp. 12, 18, 117-119, 229, 230, 253.

Henn, T.R. *The harvest of tragedy,* pp. 174, 179-180, 182.

Hurrell, John D. "*Rosmersholm,* The Existential Drama, and the Dilemma of Modern Tragedy." *Educational Theatre J.,* vol. 15 (1963), pp. 118-124.

Jameson, Storm. *Modern drama in Europe,* pp. 75-80, 84-88.

Johnston, Brian. "The Dialectic of *Rosmersholm." Drama Survey,* vol. 6 (1967), pp. 181-220.

Krutch, Joseph, Wood. *"Modernism" in modern drama,* pp. 15-17.

MacCarthy, Desmond. *Drama,* pp. 95-100.

McCollom, William G. *Tragedy,* pp. 223-226.

McFarlane, J.W. "A Note in Ibsen's *Vildanden* and *Rosmersholm." Modern Language Rev.,* vol. 54, (1959), pp. 244-245.

Matthews, Honor. *The primal curse,* pp. 20, 88, 100-106, 109, 118.

Muller, Herbert J. *The spirit of tragedy,* 269-270.

Setterquist, Jan. *Ibsen and the beginnings of Anglo-Irish drama. I. John Millington Synge,* pp. 17, 20, 32-35, 37, 77, 85. *II. Edward Martyn,* pp. 23, 35, 51-52, 54, 75, 78, 83, 87, 90-92, 95, 100.

Shaw, George Bernard. *The quintessence of Ibsenism.* pp. 99-106.

Steene, Birgitta. *"Macbeth* and *Rosmersholm:* A Comparison." *Proceedings of the Fifth International Study Conference on Scandinavian Literature* (1966), pp. 198-216.

Styan, J.L. *The elements of drama,* pp. 14-20, 249-254.

Thompson, Alan Reynolds. *The dry mock,* pp. 238-243.

Van Laan, Thomas F. "Art and Structure in *Rosmersholm." Modern Drama,* vol. 6, no. 2 (Sept., 1963), pp. 150-163.

Williams, Raymond. *Drama from Ibsen to Eliot,* pp. 78-81.

St. John's Night

Meyer, Michael. *Henrik Ibsen; the making of a dramatist, 1828-1864,* pp. 117-122.

The Vikings at Helgeland

Meyer, Michael. *Henrik Ibsen; the making of a dramatist, 1828-1864,* pp. 170-172, 174-178, 181-182.

The Warrior's Barrow

Meyer, Michael. *Henrik Ibsen; the making of a dramatist, 1828-1864,* pp. 78-80, 86, 133.

When We Dead Awaken

Arestad, Sverre. *"When We Dead Awaken* Reconsidered." *Scandinavian Studies,* vol. 30, no. 3 (Aug., 1958), pp. 117-130.

Balmforth, Ramsden. *The problem-play and its influence on modern thought and life,* pp. 63-70.

Bradbrook, M.C. *Ibsen, the Norwegian, a revaluation,* pp. 93, 137-147.

Brustein, Robert. "Ibsen and Revolt." *Tulane Drama Rev.,* vol. 7, no. 1 (Fall, 1962), pp. 147-151.

Brustein, Robert. *The theatre of revolt,* pp. 78-83.

Fergusson, Francis. *The human image in dramatic literature,* pp. 73-76, 79.

Grene, David. *Reality and the heroic pattern, last plays of Ibsen, Shakespeare, and Sophocles,* pp. 27-34.

Henn, T.R. *The harvest of tragedy,* 184-187.

Joyce, James. *"When We Dead Awaken." In:* McFarlane, James Walter, ed. *Discussions of Henrik Ibsen,* pp. pp. 61-65. (Joyce, James. *The critical essays of James Joyce,* ed. R. Ellmann. London, Faber, 1959. First published in *Fortnightly Rev.,* 1900.)

Matthews, Honor. *The primal curse,* pp. 88, 91, 109, 115, 118.

Muller, Herbert J. *The spirit of tragedy,* 272-273.

Shaw, George Bernard. *The quintessence of Ibsenism,* pp. 146-158.

Williams, Raymond. *Drama from Ibsen to Eliot,* pp. 92-95.

The Wild Duck (Vildanden)

Arestad, Sverre. *"The Iceman Cometh* and *The Wild Duck." Scandinavian Studies,* vol. 20, no. 1 (Feb., 1948), pp. 1-11.

Aylen, Leo. *Greek tragedy and the modern world,* pp. 238-239.

Bierman, Judah. *The dramatic experience,* pp. 148-155.

Bigsby, C.W.E. *Confrontation and commitment,* pp. 13-14, 17, 28-30.

Bradbrook, M.C. *Ibsen, the Norwegian, a revaluation,* pp. 28, 98-107, 113, 150, 156-158.

Bradbrook, M.C. *"The Wild Duck." In:* Caputi, Anthony, ed. *Modern drama,* pp. 357-362. (From Bradbrook, M.C. *Ibsen the Norwegian,* London, Chatto & Windus, 1946, pp. 102-107.)

Bradbrook, M.C. *"The Wild Duck."* In: McFarlane, James Walter, ed. *Discussions of Henrik Ibsen,* pp. 47-53.

Brustein, Robert. "Ibsen and Revolt." *Tulane Drama Rev.,* vol. 7, no. 1 (Fall, 1962), pp. 141-142.

Brustein, Robert. The the*atre of revolt,* pp. 72-74.

Cook, Albert S. "Language and Action in the Drama." *College English,* vol. 28, no. 1 (Oct., 1966), pp. 18-19.

Cook, Albert. *Prisms, studies in modern literature,* pp. 133-137.

Crompton, Louis. "The Demonic in Ibsen's *The Wild Duck." Tulane Drama Rev.,* vol. 4, no. 1 (Sept., 1959), pp. 96-103.

Freedman, Morris. *The moral impulse,* pp. 14-18.

Gutkke, Karl S. *Modern tragicomedy,* pp. 144-165.

Heilman, Robert B. *Tragedy and melodrama,* pp. 18, 53-54, 115, 144, 231, 290.

Krutch, Joseph Wood. *"Modernism" in modern drama,* pp. 13-15.

McCarthy, Mary. *Sights and spectacles 1937-1956,* pp. 168-178.

McFarlane, J.W. "A Note on Ibsen's *Vildanden* and *Rosmersholm." Modern Language Rev.,* vol. 54 (1959), pp. 244-245.

Matthews, Honor. *The primal curse,* pp. 117-118.

Mueller, Janet M. "Ibsen's Wild Duc*k." Modern Drama,* vol. 11, no. 4 (Feb., 1969), pp. 347-355.

Reinert, Otto. *Drama, an introductory anthology,* pp. 297-300.

Reinert, Otto, ed. *Modern drama; nine plays,* pp. 83-86.

Reinert, Otto. "Sight Imagery in *The Wild Duck." J. of English and Germanic Philology,* vol. 55 (1956), pp. 457-462.

Roberts, R. Ellis. *"The Wild Duck."* In: Caputi, Anthony, ed. *Modern drama,* pp. 354-357. *Also in:* Roberts, R. Ellis. *Henrik Ibsen, a critical study,* London, 1912, pp. 130-137.

Setterquist, Jan. *Ibsen and the beginnings of Anglo-Irish drama. I. John Millington Synge,* pp. 11, 23, 42, 44-51, 64-65, 87-88. *II. Edward Martyn,* pp. 28-32, 36-37, 44, 59, 77-78, 96, 100.

Shaw, George Bernard. *The quintessence of Ibsenism.* pp. 95-99.

Smith, John E. "When Should We Not Tell theTruth?" *In:* MacIver,

R.M. *Great moral dilemmas,* pp. 47-60.

Sprinchorn, Evert, ed. *The genius of the Scandinavian theater,* pp. 80-82.

Styan, J.L. *The dark comedy,* 2nd ed., pp. 35-36, 64, 66-68, 252-253, 274, 280-281, 295.

Styan, J.L. *The elements of drama,* pp. 149-152.

Sydney, Mendel. "The Revolt Against the Father: The Adolescent Hero in *Hamlet* and *The Wild Duck." Essays in Criticism,* vol. 14, no. 2 (April, 1964), pp. 171-178.

Thompson, Alan Reynolds. *The dry mock,* pp. 221-225.

Williams, Raymond. *Drama from Ibsen to Eliot,* pp. 76-78.

JORGE ICAZA 1906-

General

Anderson Imbert, Enrique. *Spanish—American literature: a history,* p. 500.

Franklin, Albert. "A Versatile Ecuadorean." *Inter—America,* vol. 1 (nov., 1942), pp. 33-35.

Jones, W.K. *Behind Spanish American footlights,* pp. 309-311.

WILLIAM INGE 1913-

General

Boxandall, Lee. "Theatre and Affliction." *Encore,* vol. 10 (May-June, 1963), pp. 8-13.

Downer, Alan S. *Recent American drama,* pp. 25-28.

Driver, Tom F. "Psychologism: Roadblock to Religious Drama." *Religion in Life,* vol. 29 (Winter, 1959-60), pp. 107-109.

Goldstein, Malcolm. "Body and Soul on Broadway." *Modern Drama,* vol. 7, no. 4 (Feb., 1965), pp. 411-421.

Gould, Jean. *Modern American playwrights,* pp. 264-272.

Inge, William. (Interview with Walter Wager.) *In:* Wager, Walter, ed. *The playwrights speak,* pp. 114-139.

Lumley, Frederick. *New trends in 20th-century drama,* pp. 329-33∶.

Manley, Frances. "William Inge: A Bibliography." *American Book Collector,* vol. 16, no. 2 (Oct., 1965), pp. 13-21.

Phillips, Elizabeth C. *Modern American drama,* pp. 93-95.

Shuman, R. Baird. *William Inge.*

Wager, Walter. "William Inge." In: Wager, Walter, ed. *The playwrights speak,* pp. 110-114.

Weales, Gerald. *American drama since World War II,* pp. 41-49.

Williams, Tennessee. "The Writing Is Honest." *In:* Oppenheimer, George, ed. *The passionate playgoer,* pp. 246-249. (Reprinted from preface to Inge's *Dark at the top of the stairs,* N.Y., Random House, 1958.)

Wolfson, Lester M. "Inge, O'Neill and the Human Condition." *Southern Speech J.* vol. 22, no. 4 (Summer, 1957), pp. 221-232.

The Boy in the Basement

Shuman, R. Baird. *William Inge,* pp. 135-140.

Bus Riley's Back in Town

Shuman, R. Baird. *William Inge,* pp. 146-150.

Bus Stop

Shuman, R. Baird. *William Inge,* pp. 58-70.

Weales, Gerald. *American drama since World War II,* pp. 41, 43-46, 48.

Wolfson, Lester M. "Inge, O'Neill and the Human Condition." *Southern Speech J.,* vol. 22, no. 4 (Summer, 1957), pp. 226-227.

Come Back, Little Sheba

Beyer, William H. *School & Society,* vol. 71 (June 3, 1950), pp. 345-346.

Clurman, Harold. *Lies like truth,* pp. 59-60.

Dusenbury, Winifred L. *The theme of loneliness in modern American drama,* pp. 9-16, 200, 203.

Gardner, R.H. *The splintered stage; the decline of the American theater,* pp. 97-98.

Gottfried, Martin. *A theater divided; the postwar American stage,* pp. 257-258, 260.

Lumley, Frederick. *New trends in 20th-century drama,* pp. 329-330.

Nathan, George Jean. *Theatre book of the year, 1949-50,* pp. 232-236.

Shuman, R. Baird. *William Inge,* pp. 36-48.

Sievers, W. David. *Freud on Broadway,* pp. 352-354.

Weales, Gerald. *American drama since World War II,* pp. 41, 43-47, 199.

Wolfson, Lester M. "Inge, O'Neill and the Human Condition." *Southern Speech J.,* vol. 22, no. 4 (Summer, 1957), pp. 224-225.

The Dark at the Top of the Stairs

Barbour, Thomas. *Hudson Rev.,* vol. 11, no. 1 (Spring, 1958), pp. 122-123.

Brustein, Robert. "The Men-Taming Women of William Inge: *The Dark at the Top of the Stairs." In:* Kernan, Alvin B., ed. *The Modern American theater,* pp. 70-79. (Reprinted from Brustein, R. *Seasons of discontent* (N.Y. and London, 1965). Originally published in *Harper's Magazine* (Nov., 1958).)

Brustein, Robert. *Seasons of discontent,* pp. 83-93.

Gardner, R.H. *The splintered stage; the decline of the American theater,* p. 99.

Gassner, John. *Theatre at the crossroads,* pp. 167-173.

Gottfried, Martin. *A theater divided; the postwar American stage,* pp. 259-261.

Shuman, R. Baird. *William Inge,* pp. 70-85.

Weales, Gerald. *American drama since World War II,* pp. 41-48, 49, 56, 187.

Glory in the Flower

Shuman, R. Baird. *William Inge,* pp. 150-153.

An Incident at the Standish Arms

Shuman, R. Baird. *William Inge,* pp. 158-160.

A Loss of Roses

Brustein, Robert. *Seasons of discontent,* pp. 97-100.

Gardner, R.H. *The splintered stage; the decline of the American theater,* pp. 99-100.

Kerr, Walter. *The theater in spite of itself,* pp. 239-242.

Shuman, R. Baird. *William Inge,* pp. 86-99.

Weales, Gerald. *American drama since World War II,* pp. 41, 44-46, 51.

The Mall

Shuman, R. Baird. *William Inge,* pp. 155-158.

Memory of Summer

Shuman, R. Baird. *William Inge,* pp. 143-146.

Natural Affection

Brustein, Robert. *Seasons of discontent,* pp. 100-101.

Gassner, John. *Educational Theatre J.,* vol. 15 (May, 1963), pp. 185-186.

Gottfried, Martin. *A theater divided; the postwar American stage,* pp. 260, 261-262.

Shuman, R. Baird. *William Inge,* pp. 109-121.

People in the Wind

Shuman, R. Baird. *William Inge,* pp. 58-70.

Picnic

Bentley, Eric. *The dramatic event,* pp. 103-106.

Clurman, Harold. *Lies like truth,* pp. 60-62.

Gardner, R.H. *The splintered stage; the decline of the American theater,* pp. 98-99.

Gottfried, Martin. *A theater divided; the postwar American stage,* pp. 258-259.

Shuman, R. Baird. *William Inge,* pp. 48-57.

Sievers, W. David. *Freud on Broadway,* pp. 354-356.

Weales, Gerald. *American drama since World War II,* pp. 41, 43-48.

Wolfson, Lester M. "Inge, O'Neill and the Human Condition." *Southern Speech J.,* vol. 22, no. 4 (Summer, 1957), pp. 225-226.

The Rainy Afternoon

Shuman, R. Baird. *William Inge,* pp. 153-155.

A Social Event

Shuman, R. Baird. *William Inge,* pp. 131-135.

Splendor in the Grass

Shuman, R. Baird. *William Inge,* pp. 87, 99-109.

The Strains of Triumph

Shuman, R. Baird. *William Inge,* pp. 160-163.

Summer Brave

Shuman, R. Baird. *William Inge,* pp. 46-57.

The Tiny Closet

Shuman, R. Baird. *William Inge,* pp. 140-143.

To Bobolink, for Her Spirit

Shuman, R. Baird. *William Inge,* pp. 128-131.

EUGENE IONESCO 1912-

General

Barbour, Thomas. "Beckett and Ionesco." *Hudson Rev.,* vol. 11 (Summer, 1958), pp. 271-277.

Bishop, Thomas. *Pirandello and the French theater,* pp. 133-134.

Chiari, J. *Landmarks of contemporary drama,* pp. 64-68.

Coe, Richard N. "Eugene Ionesco and the Tragic Farce." Leeds Philosophical and Literary Society. *Proceedings,* vol. 9, (Mar. 1962), pp. 219-235.

Coe, Richard N. "Eugene Ionesco, the Meaning of Un—Meaning." *In: Aspects of drama and the theatre,* pp. 3-32

Coe, Richard N. *Ionesco,* pp. 1-113.

Cohn, Ruby. "Berenger, Protagonist of an Anti—playwright." *Modern Drama,* vol. 8, no. 2 (Sept. 1965), pp. 127-133.

Cook, Albert. *Prisms, studies in modern literature,* pp. 108-109.

Corrigan, Robert W., ed. *Masterpieces of the modern French theatre,* pp. 388-389.

Daniel, John T. "Ionesco and the Ritual of Nihilism." *Drama Survey,* I, no. 1 (1961), pp. 54-65.

Demaitre, Ann. "The idea and the technique of the absurd in Eugene Ionesco's theater." *Dissertation Abstracts,* vol. 27, no. 12 (June 1967), 4246a. (Brooklyn Univ.).

Doubrovsky, J.S. "Ionesco and the Comic of Absurdity." *Yale French Studies,* no. 23 (1959), pp. 3-10.

Eastman, Richard M. "Experiment and Vision in Ionesco's Plays." *Modern Drama,* vol. 4, no. 1 (May, 1961), pp. 3-19.

Ellis, Mary Hamrick. "The Work of Eugene Ionesco." *Southern Q.,* vol. 2 (1964), pp. 220-235.

Esslin, Martin. "Ionesco and the Creative Dilemma." *Tulane Drama Rev.,* vol. 7, no. 3 (Spring, 1963), pp. 169-179.

Esslin, Martin. *The theatre of the absurd,* pp. 79-87, 127-139.

Fletcher, John. "Confrontations: I. Harold Pinter, Roland Dubillard, and Eugene Ionesco." *Caliban,* vol. 4 (1967), pp. 149-159.

Fowlie, Wallace. *Dionysus in Paris,* pp. 229-237.

Freedman, Morris. *The moral impulse,* pp. 119-122.

Gascoigne, Bamber. *Twentieth-century drama,* pp. 188-191.

Girard, Denis. "L'Anti-Theatre d'Eugene Ionesco." *Modern Languages,* vol. 40 (1959), pp. 45-53.

Glicksberg, Charles I. "Ionesco and the Aesthetic of the Absurd." *Arizona Q.,* vol. 18, no. 4 (Winter, 1962), pp. 293-303.

Glicksberg, Charles I. *The self in modern literature,* pp. 106-112.

Gottfried, Martin. *A theater divided; the postwar American stage,* pp. 286-288.

Grossvogel, David I. *Four playwrights and a postscript, Brecht, Ionesco, Beckett, Genet,* pp. 49-83.

Grossvogel, David I. *The self-conscious stage in modern French drama,* pp. 313-318.

Guicharnaud, Jacques. *Modern French theatre from Giraudoux to Beckett,* pp. 178-192.

Guicharnaud, Jacques. *Modern French theatre from Giraudoux to Genet.* (rev. ed.), pp. 49, 159, 161, 180, 181, 187, 190, 193, 196-199, 202-203, 212, 215-229, 234, 282, 286, 288, 290.

Guicharnaud, Jacques. "A World Out of Control: Eugene Ionesco." *American Society Legion of Honor Mag.,* vol. 31, no. 2 (1960), pp. 105-115.

Hurley, Paul J. "France and America: Versions of the Absurd." *College English,* vol. 26 (1965), pp. 634-640.

Ionesco, Eugene. "The Avant-Garde Theatre." *Tulane Drama Rev.,* vol. 5, no. 2 (Dec., 1960), 44-53. *Also in: World Theatre,* vol. VIII, no. 3 (Autumn, 1959), pp. 171-202.

Ionesco, Eugene. "Discovering the Theatre." *Tulane Drama Rev.,* vol. 4, no. 1 (Sept., 1959), pp. 3-18 *Also in: Tulane Drama Rev. Theatre in the twentieth century,* pp. 77-93.

Ionesco, Eugene. "A Discussion on the Avant-Garde Theatre—Eugene Ionesco Opens Fire." *World Theatre,* vol. 8, no. 3 (Autumn, 1959), pp. 171-202.

Ionesco, Eugene. "Essays by Eugene Ionesco." *Theatre Arts,* vol. 42, no. 6 (June, 1958), pp. 17-18, 77.

Ionesco, Eugene. "Interview." *New Yorker,* vol. 36 (Dec. 10, 1960), pp. 46-47.

Ionesco, Eugene, "An Interview With Eugene Ionesco." Ed. by Vieri Tucci. *Mademoiselle,* vol. 52 (Apr. 1961), pp. 137, 185-189.

Ionesco, Eugene. "The Marvelous Come To Life." *Theatre Arts,* vol. 45 (Sept. 1961), pp. 18-19, 78.

Ionesco, Eugene. "My Thanks To the Critics." *Theatre Arts,* vol. 44, no. 10 (Oct., 1960), pp. 18-19.

Ionesco, Eugene. "Notes on My Theatre." *Tulane Drama Rev.,* vol. 7, no. 3 (Spring, 1963), pp. 127-159.

Ionesco, Eugene. "Outrageous Ionesco." (Interview) *Horizon,* vol. 3 (May, 1961), pp. 89-91, 93-97.

Ionesco, Eugene. "Selections from the Journals." *Yale French Studies,* no. 29 (1962), pp. 3-9.

Ionesco, Eugene. "Still About Avant-Garde Theatre." *In:* Seltzer, Daniel, ed. *The modern theatre, readings and documents,* pp. 90-99. (Reprinted from Ionesco, Eugene. *Notes and counter notes,* N.Y., Grove, 1964.)

Jacobsen, Josephine. *Ionesco and Genet, playwrights of silence,* pp. 4, 7, 10, 16-17, 20, 62, 73-74, 86, 88, 91, 95, 100-101, 103, 111-117, 120, 122, 124, 220.

Knowles, Dorothy. "Ionesco and the Mechanisms of Language." *Modern Drama,* vol. 5, no. 1 (May, 1962), pp. 7-10.

Kuhn, Reinhard. "The Debasement of the Intellectual in Contemporary Continental Drama." *Modern Drama,* vol. 7, no. 4 (Feb. 1965), pp. 454-462.

Lamont, Rose. "Eugene Ionesco." *In:* Wager, Walter, ed. *The playwrights speak,* pp. 149-151.

Lamont, Rosette C. "Hero in Spite of Himself." *Yale French Studies,* no. 29 (1962), pp. 73-81.

Lamont, Rosette C. "The Proliferation of Matter in Ionesco's Plays." *L'Esprit Createur,* vol. 2, no. 4 (Winter, 1962), pp. 189-197.

Lumley, Frederick. *New trends in 20th century drama,* pp. 179, 209-214, 357, 382.

Marowitz, Charles. "Anti-Ionesco Theatre." *In:* Marowitz, Charles, ed. *Encore reader,* pp. 160-164. (Reprinted from *Encore,* July, 1960.)

Metz, Mary S. Existentialism and inauthenticity in the theater of Beckett, Ionesco, and Genet." *Dissertation Abstracts,* vol. 27 (1966), 1377A-78A (La. State).

Moore, Harry T. *Twentieth-century French literature since World War II,* pp. 154-161.

Murray, Jack. "Ionesco and the Mechanics of Memory." *Yale French Studies,* no. 29 (1962), pp. 82-87.

Norin, Luc. "Ionesco's Confession." *In:* Richards, Dick. *The curtain rises,* pp. 115-121.

Onnen, Frank. "An Interview with Eugene Ionesco." *Approach,* no. 30 (Autumn, 1959), pp. 29-32.

Parker, R.B. "The Theory and Theatre of the Absurd." *Queen's Q.,* vol. 73, no. 3 (Autumn, 1966), pp. 420-441.

Pronko, Leonard C. "The Anti-Spiritual Victory in the Modern Theatre of Ionesco." *Modern Drama,* v.2, no. 1 (May, 1959), pp. 29-35.

Pronko, Leonard C. *Avant—garde: the experimental theater in France,* pp. 59-111.

Pronko, Leonard C. *Eugene Ionesco,* pp. 3-6, 9-13, 22-23.

Roud, Richard. "Ionesco: the Opposite of Sameness." *In:* Marowitz, Charles, ed. *Encore reader,* pp. 18-26. (Reprinted from *Encore,* June, 1957.)

Schechner, Richard. "The Inner and the Outer Reality." *Tulane Drama Rev.,* vol. 7, no. 3 (Spring, 1963), pp. 187-217.

Schechner, Richard. "An Interview With Ionesco." *Tulane Drama Rev.,* vol. 7, no. 3 (Spring, 1963), pp. 163-168.

"A School of Vigilance," *Times Literary Supplement,* (Mar. 4, 1960), p. 144.

Smith, R.D. "Back to the Text." *In:* Brown, J. R., B. Harris, eds. *Contemporary theatre,* pp. 121-133.

Sontag, Susan. *Against interpretation and other essays,* pp. 115-123.

Strem, George, "The Anti-Theatre of Eugene Ionesco." *Twentieth Century* (Melbourne), vol. 16 (1962), pp. 70-83.

Strem, George, "Ritual and Poetry in Eugene Ionesco's Theatre." *Texas Q.,* vol. 5, no. 4 (1962), pp. 149-158.´

Vannier, Jean. "A Theatre of Language." *Tulane Drama Rev.,* vol. 7, no. 3 (Spring, 1963), pp. 180-186.

Vos, Nelvin. *"The drama of comedy: victim and victor,* pp. 53-56, 65-73.

Wager, Walter. "Eugene Ionesco." *In:* Wager, Walter, ed. *The playwrights speak,* pp. 140-149.

Watson, Donald. "The Plays of Ionesco." *Tulane Drama Rev.,* vol. 3, no. 1 (Oct., 1958), pp. 48-53.

Wegener, Adolph H. "The Absurd in Modern Literature." *Books Abroad,* vol. 41, no. 2 (Spring, 1967), pp. 150-156.

Wilbur, R.H. "Ionesco in Paris: Sopranos to Rhinoceroses." *Northwest Rev.,* vol. 3, no. 2, (Spring, 1960), pp. 5-17.

Williams, Raymond. Modern t*ragedy,* pp. 152-153.

Willison, Sheila. "The Language of the Absurd: Artaud and Ionesco." *New Theatre Magazine* (Bristol), vol. 7, no. 1 (1966), pp. 9-14.

The Aerial Pedestrian (The Airborne Pedestrian) (The Pedestrian of the Air) (A Stroll in the Air) (Le Piéton de l'Air)

"Barrault Acts Ionesco." *Times,* no. 56,281 (Mar. 27, 1965), p. 6.

Cate, Curtis. "Eugene Ionesco." *Atlantic,* vol. 217, no. 4 (Apr., 1966), p. 119.

Jacobsen, Josephine. *Ionesco and Genet, playwrights of silence,* pp. 60, 68-69, 72, 82, 91-92, 119.

Lamont, Rosette C. "Air and Matter: Ionesco's *Le Piéton de l'air* and *Victims du Devoir.*" *French Rev.,* vol. 38, no. 3 (Jan., 1965), pp. 349-361.

Pronko, Leonard C. *Eugene Ionesco,* pp. 36-40.

Wellwarth, George. *The theatre of protest and paradox.* pp. 71-72.

Amédée, or How To Get Rid of It (Amédée, ou Comments s'en Debarrasser)

Cate, Curtis. "Eugene Ionesco." *Atlantic,* vol. 217, no. 4 (Apr. 1966), pp. 114, 117.

Esslin, Martin. *The theatre of the absurd,* pp. 107-110.

Ionesco, Eugene. "Reality in Depth." *In:* Marowitz, Charles, ed. *Encore reader,* pp. 26-28. (Reprinted from *Encore,* May, 1958.)

Jacobsen, Josephine..*Ionesco and Genet, playwrights of silence,* pp. 22, 26, 28-30, 53, 97, 102, 104, 231.

Matthews, Honor. *The primal curse,* pp. 147, 209-215.

Pronko, Leonard C. *Avant-garde: the experimental theater in France,* pp. 93-96.

Pronko, Leonard C. *Eugene Ionesco,* pp. 21-22.

Vos, Nelvin. *The drama of comedy: victim and victor,* pp. 61-62.

Wellwarth, George. *The theatre of protest and paradox.* pp. 62-63.

The Bald Soprano (La Cantatrice Chauve)

Cate, Curtis. "Eugene Ionesco." *Atlantic,* vol. 217, no. 4 (Apr., 1966), pp. 115, 116, 120.

Clurman, Harold. *The naked image,* pp. 83.

Dukore, Bernard F. "The Theatre of Ionesco: a Union of Form and Substance." *Educational Theatre J.,* vol. 13 (1961), pp. 174-179.

Esslin, Martin. *The theatre of the absurd,* pp. 87-93.

Grossvogel, David I. *Four playwrights and a postscript, Brecht, Ionesco, Beckett, Genet,* pp. 52-56.

Hatzfeld, Helmut. *Trends and styles in twentieth century French literature,* pp. 270-271.

Ionesco, Eugene. *In:* Cole, Toby, ed. *Playwrights on playwriting,* pp. 282-284. (Reprinted from "The World of Eugene Ionesco." *The New York Times,* June 1, 1958.)

Ionesco, Eugene. "The Tragedy of Language. How an English Primer Became My First Play." *Tulane Drama Rev., vol. 4, no. 3 (Mar., 1960), pp. 10-13.

Ionesco, Eugene. "The Tragedy of Language." *In:* Corrigan, Robert W., ed. *Masterpieces of the modern French theatre,* pp. 391-395. (Reprinted from Ionesco, Eugene. *Notes and counter notes: writings on the theatre,* N.Y. Grove Press, 1964.)

Jacobsen, Josephine. *Ionesco and Genet, playwrights of silence,* pp. 3, 7, 10, 20, 26, 33, 47-51, 54-58, 84-85, 88, 101-102, 107-108.

Lewis, Allan. *The contemporary theatre,* pp. 266, 269-272.

Miller, H. "Ionesco's Soprano Punched a Time Clock." *Between Worlds,* vol. 1 (Summer, 1960), pp. 99-112.

O'Casey, Sean. "The Bald Primaqueera." *In:* O'Casey, Sean. *Blasts and benedictions,* p. 64.

Pronko, Leonard C. *Avant-garde: the experimental theater in France,* pp. 68-71.

Pronko, Leonard C. *Eugene Ionesco,* pp. 6-9.

Vos, Nelvin. *The drama of comedy: victim and victor,* pp. 57-58.

Wellwarth, George, *The theatre of protest and paradox.* pp. 54-57.

The Chairs (Les Chaises)

Brown, James L. "Ionesco's *The Chairs." Explicator,* vol. 24, no. 8 (Apr. 1966) p. 73.

Cate, Curtis. "Eugene Ionesco." *Atlantic,* vol. 217, no. 4 (Apr., 1966), pp. 116-117.

Clurman, Harold. "Theatre." *Nation,* vol. 186, no. 4 (Jan. 25, 1958), pp. 86-87.

Cohn, Ruby. "Four Stages of Absurdist Hero." *Drama Survey,* vol. 4, no. 3 (Winter, 1965), pp. 201-204.

Cook, Albert S. "Language and Action in the Drama." *College English,* vol. 28, no. 1 (Oct., 1966), pp. 24.

Cook, Albert. *Prisms, studies in modern literature,* pp. 145-146.
Dubois, Jacques. "Beckett and Ionesco: The Tragic Awareness of Pascal and the Ironic Awareness of Flaubert." *Modern Drama,* vol. 9, no. 3 (Dec., 1966), pp. 283-291.

Esslin, Martin. *The theatre of the absurd,* pp. 99-101.

Flanner, Janet. *Paris journal, 1944-1965,* p. 311.

Gardner, R.H. The *splintered stage; the decline of the American theater,* pp. 11-12.

Hatzfeld, Helmut. *Trends and styles in twentieth-century French literature,* pp. 271-272.

Ionesco, Eugene. *In:* Cole, Toby, ed. *Playwrights on playwriting,* pp. 284. (Reprinted from "The World of Eugene Ionesco." *The New York Times,* June 1, 1958.)

Isaacs, Neil D. "Ionesco's *The Chairs.*" *Explicator,* vol. 24, no. 3 (Nov., 1965), p. 30.

Jacobs, Willis D. "Ionesco's *The Chairs.*" *Explicator,* vol. 22 (1964), item 42.

Jacobsen, Josephine. *Ionesco and Genet, playwrights of silence,* pp. 8, 20, 50-51, 55, 60-62, 64, 72, 89; 102, 105.

Lamont, Rosette. "The Metaphysical Farce: Beckett and Ionesco." *French Rev.,* vol. 32, no. 4 (Feb., 1959), pp. 319-324.

Lewis, Allan. *The contemporary theatre,* pp. 272-274.

Pronko, Leonard C. *Avant-garde: the experimental theater in France,* pp. 78-85.

Pronko, Leonard C. *Eugene Ionesco,* pp. 16-19.

Schechner, Richard. "The Enactment of the 'Not' in Ionesco's *Les Chaises.*" *Yale French Studies,* no. 29 (1962), 65-72.

Styan, J.L. *The dark comedy,* 2nd ed., pp. 220, 236-237, 294.

Warnke, Frank J. "Letter from Holland." *Nation,* vol. 185, no. 6 (Sept. 7, 1957), pp. 117-119.

Wellwarth, Geroge. *The theatre of protest and paradox.* p. 59.

Exit the King (The King Dies) (Le Roi se Meurt)

Batholemew, Rati. "Theatre; *Exit the King.* By Eugene Ionesco. Presented by Theatre Group, Bombay." *Thought* (Delhi), vol. 17, no. 1, (Jan. 2, 1965), p. 18.

Cate, Curtis. "Eugene Ionesco." *Atlantic,* vol. 217, no. 4 (Apr. 1966), p. 119.

Gellert, Roger *New Statesman,* vol. 66, no. 1696, (Sept. 13, 1963), p. 330.

Jacobsen, Josephine. *Ionesco and Genet, playwrights of silence,* pp. 16, 60, 68-72, 89-91, 119, 124.

"An Ornate Parable of Mortality." *Times,* no. 56,870 (Feb. 20, 1967), p. 10.

Pronko, Leonard C. *Eugene Ionesco,* pp. 40-44.

Reeves, Geoffrey. "Conversation with Ionesco." *New Theatre Magazine,* vol. 6, no. 3 (1965), pp. 4-7.

Styan, J.L. *The dark comedy,* 2nd ed., pp. 219, 236, 239.

Theatre arts, vol. 48, no. 1 (Jan., 1964), pp. 31-32.

Wellwarth, George. *The theatre of protest and paradox.* pp. 69-71.

Zavada, Mary. "The Play's the Thing." *America,* vol. 109, no. 18 (Nov. 2, 1963), pp. 512-514.

Frenzy for Two

Jacobsen, Josephine. *Ionesco and Genet, playwrights of silence.* pp. 82.

The Future Is in the Eggs, or It Takes Everything To Make a World (L'Avenir est dans les Oeufs, ou Il Faut de Tout pour Faire un Monde)

Jacobsen, Josephine. *Ionesco and Genet, playwrights of silence,* pp. 33, 35, 38, 40-41, 105.

Pronko, Leonard C. *Avant-garde: the experimental theater in France,* pp. 73-78.

Pronko, Leonard C. *Eugene Ionesco,* pp. 15-16.

Hunger and Thirst (La Soif et la Faim)

Cate, Curtis. "Eugene Ionesco." *Atlantic,* vol. 217, no. 4 (Apr. 1966), p. 120.

Cismaru, Alfred. "Ionesco's Latest: *Hunger and Thirst.*" *Laurel Review* (West Va. Wesleyan Coll.), vol. 7, no. 2 (1967), pp. 63-70.

Cohn, Ruby. "Theater Abroad." *Drama Survey,* vol. 5, no. 3 (Winter, 1966-67), p. 289.

"Ionesco's New Play Proves To Be His Most Didactic." *Times,* no. 56,208 (Jan. 1, 1965), p. 13.

Lennon, Peter. "New Ionesco Play in Paris." *Guardian,* no. 37,217 (Mar. 5, 1966), p. 6.

"Success for Ionesco at Comedie-Francaise." *Times,* no. 56,569 (Mar. 2, 1966), p. 15.

Trilling, Ossia. "Ionesco at Dusseldorf." *Guardian,* no. 36,863 (Jan. 13, 1965), p. 9.

Tynan, Kenneth. *Tynan right and left,* pp. 192-193.

Improvisation, or The Shepherd's Chameleon (L'Impromptu de l'Alma, or Le Cameleon du Berger)

Esslin, Martin. *The theatre of the absurd,* pp. 114-177.

Jacobsen, Josephine. *Ionesco and Genet, playwrights of silence,* pp. 50-51, 74-75, 86, 94, 122.

Pronko, Leonard C. *Avant-garde: the experimental theater in France,* pp. 64-67.

Pronko, Leonard C. *Eugene Ionesco,* pp. 23-25.

Tynan, Kenneth. *Tynan right and left,* pp. 36-37.

Jack, or The Submission (Jacques, ou La Soumission)

Clurman, Harold. *The naked image,* pp. 83-85.

Esslin, Martin. *The theatre of the absurd,* pp. 97-98.

Jacobsen, Josephine. *Ionesco and Genet, playwrights of silence,* pp. 20, 33, 35, 38-40, 45, 53, 93, 102, 222.

Pronko, Leonard C. *Avant-garde: the experimental theater in France,* pp. 72-73.

Pronko, Leonard C. *Eugene Ionesco,* pp. 14-15.

Wellwarth, George. *The theatre of protest and paradox,* pp. 63-64.

The Killer (Tueur sans Gages)

Cate, Curtis. "Eugene Ionesco." *Atlantic,* vol. 217, no. 4 (Apr. 1966), p. 118.

Clurman, Harold. "Theatre." *Nation,* vol. 190, no. 16 (Apr. 16, 1960), pp. 343-344.

Esslin, Martin. *The theatre of the absurd,* pp. 119-124.

Glicksberg, Charles I. *The self in modern literature,* pp. 113-114.

Hatzfeld, Helmut. *Trends and styles in twentieth-century French literature,* pp. 272-273.

Hewes, Henry. "Here Without Portfolio." *Saturday Rev.,* vol. 43 (Apr. 19, 1960), 37.

Hughes, Catherine. "Ionesco's Plea for Man." *Renascence,* vol. 14, no. 3 (Spring, 1962), 121-123.

Jacobsen, Josephine. *Ionesco and Genet, playwrights of silence,* pp. 1-2, 8-10, 23, 26, 30-32, 52-53, 58-60, 62-65, 68, 71-72, 75-84, 86-93, 102-103, 113, 118-119, 121-122, 124-125.

Matthews, Honor. *The primal curse,* pp. 23-24.

Pronko, Leonard C. *Avant-garde: the experimental theater in France,* pp. 96-102.

Pronko, Leonard C. *Eugene Ionesco,* pp. 25-31.

Purdy, Strother B. "A Reading of Ionesco's *The Killer.*" *Modern Drama,* vol. 10, no. 4 (Feb. 1968), pp. 416-423.

Smith, H.A. "Dipsychus Among the Shadows." *In:* Brown, J.R., and B. Harris, eds. *Contemporary Theatre,* pp. 141-142.

Styan, J.L. *The dark comedy,* 2nd ed., pp. 237-238, 239.

Wellwarth, George. *The theatre of protest and paradox,* pp. 64-67.

The Lesson (La Leçon)

Clurman, Harold. "Theatre," *Nation,* vol. 186, no. 4 (Jan. 25, 1958), pp. 86-87.

Dukore, Bernard F. "The Theatre of Ionesco: a Union of Form and Substance." *Educational Theatre J.,* vol. 13 (1961), pp. 179-181.

Esslin, Martin. *The theatre of the absurd,* pp. 94-97.

Hatzfeld, Helmut. *Trends and styles in twentieth-century French literature,* p. 271.

Jacobsen, Josephine. *Ionesco and Genet, playwrights of silence,* pp. 20, 22, 33, 35-38, 40-41, 46, 95, 102, 105, 108.

Matthews, Honor. *The primal curse,* p. 23.

Pronko, Leonard C. *Avant-garde: the experimental theater in France,* pp. 71-72.

Pronko, Leonard C. *Eugene Ionesco,* pp. 13-14.

Reinert, Otto. *Drama, an introductory anthology,* pp. 575-577.

Reinert, Otto, ed. *Modern drama; nine plays,* pp. 477-479.

Vos, Nelvin. *The drama of comedy: victim and victor,* pp. 58-59.

Warnke, Frank J. "Letter from Holland." *Nation,* vol. 185, no. 6 (Sept. 7, 1957), pp. 117-119.

Wellwarth, George. *The theatre of protest and paradox,* pp. 57-58.

Maid to Marry

Jacobsen, Josephine. *Ionesco and Genet, playwrights of silence,* pp. 53-54.

Lid, R.W. ed. *Plays, classic and contemporary,* pp. 514-517.

The New Tenant (Le Nouveau Locataire)

Esslin, Martin. *The theatre of the absurd,* pp. 110-111.

Jacobsen, Josephine. *Ionesco and Genet, playwrights of silence,* pp. 47, 57-58, 102.

Pronko, Leonard C. *Avant-garde: the experimental theater in France,* pp. 90-92.

Pronko, Leonard C. *Eugene Ionesco,* pp. 20-21.

Wellwarth, George. *The theatre of protest and paradox,* p. 64.

The Picture (Le Tableau)

Esslin, Martin. *The theatre of the absurd,* pp. 112-114.

Pronko, Leonard C. *Eugene Ionesco,* p. 23.

Rhinoceros (Le Rhinoceros)

Brustein, Robert. "The Enormous Sum of Zero." *New Republic,* vol. 144, no. 5 (Jan. 30, 1961), pp. 22-23.

Brustein, Robert. *Seasons of discontent,* pp. 119-122.

Cate, Curtis. "Eugene Ionesco." *Atlantic,* vol. 217, no. 4 (Apr., 1966), p. 118.

Clurman, Harold. *The naked image,* pp. 85-87.

Clurman, Harold. "Theatre." *Nation,* vol. 192, no. 4 (Jan. 28, 1961), pp. 85-86.

Coxwell, Raymond. *Twelve modern dramatists,* pp. 124-126.

Driver, Tom F. "A Milestone and a Fumble." *Christian Century,* vol. 78 (Mar. 1, 1961), pp. 274-275.

Esslin, Martin. *The theatre of the absurd,* pp. 124-127.

Fowlie, Wallace. "New Plays of Ionesco and Genet." *Tulane Drama Rev.,* vol. 5, no. 1 (Sept., 1960), pp. 43-46.

Glicksberg, Charles I. *The self in modern literature,* pp. 115-117.

Hatzfeld, Helmut. *Trends and styles in twentieth century French literature,* pp. 273-274.

Hewes, Henry. "Watch on the *Rhinoceros." Saturday Rev.,* vol. 44 (Jan. 21, 1961), p. 51.

Hughes, Catherine. "Ionesco's Plea for Man." *Renascence,* vol. 14, no. 3 (Spring, 1962), pp. 124-125.

Jacobsen, Josephine. *Ionesco and Genet, playwrights of silence,* pp. 10-11, 20, 23, 33, 35, 41-47, 51, 60, 62-63, 65-68, 71-72, 83, 89-90, 93, 102, 105, 109, 111-112, 116, 118, 121-122, 124.

Kerr, Walter. *The theater in spite of itself,* pp. 112-116.

Knowles, Dorothy. "Ionesco's Rhinoceros." *Drama,* no. 58 (Autumn, 1960), pp. 35-39.

Lewis, Allan. *The contemporary theatre,* pp. 274-276.

McCarten, John. "Charging Through the Bogs." *New Yorker,* vol. 36 (Jan. 21, 1961), pp. 66-67.

Pronko, Leonard C. *Avant-garde: the experimental theater in France,* pp. 102-111.

Pronko, Leonard C. *Eugene Ionesco,* pp. 31-36.

Pryce-Jones, Alan. *Theater Arts,* vol. 45 (Mar. 1961), pp. 9-10.

Tynan, Kenneth. *Tynan right and left,* pp. 33-34.

Ulanov, Barry. *"Rhinoceros." Catholic World,* vol. 192 (Mar., 1961), pp. 380-381.

Vos, Nelvin. *The drama of comedy: victim and victor,* pp. 63-65.

Wellwarth, George. *The theatre of protest and paradox,* pp. 67-68.

Victims of Duty (Victimes du Devoir)

Cate, Curtis. "Eugene Ionesco." *Atlantic,* vol. 217, no. 4 (Apr., 1966), p. 117.

Chambers, Ross. "Detached Committal: Eugene Ionesco's *Victims of Duty." Meanjin Q.,* vol. 22 (1963), pp. 23-33.

Esslin, Martin. *The theatre of the absurd,* pp. 101-106.

Grossvogel, David I. *The self-conscious stage in modern French drama,* pp. 314-316.

Hatzfeld, Helmut. *Trends and styles in twentieth century French literature,* p. 271.

Jacobsen, Josephine. *Ionesco and Genet, playwrights of silence,* pp. 22, 26-28, 30, 34-35, 38, 50, 53, 55, 60, 94-95, 102, 104-105, 222.

Lamont, Rosette C. "Air and Matter: Ionesco's *Le Piéton de l'air* and *Victimes du Devoir." French Rev.,* vol. 38, no. 3 (Jan., 1965), pp. 349-361.

Matthews, Honor. *The primal curse,* pp. 208-209.

Pronko, Leonard C. *Avant-garde: the experimental theater in France,* pp. 85-90.

Pronko, Leonard C. *Eugene Ionesco, pp. 19-20.*

Wellwarth, George. *The theatre of protest and paradox,* pp. 59-62.

CHRISTOPHER ISHERWOOD 1904-

General

Hazard, Forrest Earl. "The Auden Group and the Group Theatre: the dramatic theories and practices of Rupert Doone, W.H. Auden, Christopher Isherwood, Louis MacNeice, and Cecil Day Lewis." *Dissertation Abstracts,* vol. 25 (1964) (U. of Wisconsin).

I Am a Camera (Adapted by John Van Druten from The Berlin Stories)

Gassner, John. *Theatre at the crossroads,* pp. 144-146.

VSEVOLOD IVANOV 1895-

Armored Train No. 14-69

Block, Anita. *The changing world in plays and theatre,* pp. 358-360.

RICARDO JAIMES FREYRE 1868-1933

Los Conquistadores

Jones, W.K. *Behind Spanish American footlights,* p. 279.

HENRY JAMES 1843-1916

General

Peacock, Ronald. *The poet in the theatre,* pp. 26-46.

The American

King, Kimball. "Theory and Practice in the Plays of Henry James." *Modern Drama,* vol. 10, no. 1 (May, 1967), pp. 24-33.

Daisy Miller

King, Kimball. "Theory and Practice in the Plays of Henry James." *Modern Drama,* vol. 10, no. 1 (May, 1967), pp. 24-33.

Mendelsohn, Michael J. "'Drop a tear...' Henry James Dramatizes *Daisy Miller.*" *Modern Drama,* vol. 7, no. 1 (May, 1964), pp. 60-64.

Guy Domville

Shaw, George Bernard. *Shaw's dramatic criticism (1895-98),* pp. 1-3.

Wells, H.G. "Review." *Pall Mall Gazett,* Jan. 7, 1895.

The High Bid

King, Kimball. "Theory and Practice in the Plays of Henry James." *Modern Drama,* vol. 10, no. 1 (May, 1967), pp. 24-33.

The Innocents

See The Turn of the Screw

The Other House

King, Kimball. "Theory and Practice in the Plays of Henry James." *Modern Drama,* vol. 10, no. 1 (May, 1967), pp. 24-33.

The Outcry

King, Kimball. "Theory and Practice in the Plays of Henry James." *Modern Drama,* vol. 10, no. 1 (May, 1967), pp. 24-33.

The Saloon

Knight, G. Wilson. *The golden labyrinth,* pp. 321-322.

The Turn of the Screw (The Innocents) (Adapted by William Archibald)

Brown, John Mason. *Still seeing things,* pp. 175-182.

Sievers, W. David. *Freud on Broadway,* pp. 426-427.

MARIA ELENA JAMES DE TERZA 1913-

Una Mujer Libre

Jones, W.K. *Behind Spanish American footlights,* p. 172.

ALFRED JARRY 1873-1907

General

Davies, Margaret. *Apollinaire,* pp. 93-96.

Grossman, Manuel L. "Alfred Jarry and the Theatre of the Absurd." *Educational Theatre J.,* vol. 19, no. 4 (Dec., 1967), pp. 473-477.

Jarry, Alfred. "Of the Futility of the 'Theatrical' in the Theater." *In:* Jarry, Alfred. *Selected works,* pp. 69-75.

Jarry, Alfred. "Theater Questions." *In:* Jarry, Alfred. *Selected works,* pp. 82-85.

Jarry, Alfred. "Twelve Theatrical Questions." *In:* Jarry, Alfred. *Selected works,* pp. 86-90.

Mayne, Richard. "Ubu and the Absurd." *New Statesman,* vol. 70, (Sept. 3, 1965), p. 323.

Shattuck, Roger. *The banquet years,* pp. 146-158, 164-176, 178-194.

Shattuck, Roger. "Introduction." *In:* Jarry, Alfred. *Selected works,* pp. 9-20.

Updike, John. *New Yorkcr,* vol. 41 (Oct. 2, 1965), pp. 221-228.

Wellwarth, G.E. "Alfred Jarry: The Seed of the Avant-Garde Drama." *Criticism,* vol. 4, no. 2 (Spring, 1962), pp. 108-119.

Wellwarth, George. *The theatre of protest and paradox,* pp. 1-14.

César-Antéchrist

Shattuck, Roger. *The banquet years,* pp. 175-176.

Cuckold Ubu (Ubu Cocu)

Hughes, Pennethorne. "The Savage God." *Listener,* vol. 74, no. 1918 (Dec. 30, 1965), p. 1090.

Wellworth, George. *The theatre of protest and paradox,* pp. 6-7.

King Ubu (Ubu Roi)

Baro, Gene. "Hickney's *Ubu." Art and Artists,* vol. 1, no. 2 (May 1966), pp. 8-13.

Blakeston, Oswell. "Surrealist Ancestor." *Time and Tide,* vol. 32, no. 37 (Sept. 15, 1951), p. 878.

Brabazon, James. "Quite Unnecessary." *New Christian,* no. 23, (Aug. 11, 1966), pp. 21-22.

Bryden, Ronald. "On the Altar of Antiart." *Observer,* no. 9,133 (July 24, 1966), p. 20.

Church, Dan M. "Pere Ubu: The Creation of a Literary Type." *Drama Survey,* vol. 4, no. 3 (Winter, 1965), pp. 233-243.

Cuthbertson, Ian. "Let's Forget the Labels." *Plays and Players,* vol. 13, no. 9 (June 1966), pp. 54-55.

Esslin, Martin. "Ooboo in Chelsea." *Plays and Players,* vol. 13, no. 12 (Sept. 1966), pp. 16-17.

Esslin, Martin. *The theatre of the absurd,* pp. 255-258.

Ford, Peter. *Guardian,* no. 36,484 (Oct. 23, 1963), p. 9.

Grossvogel, David I. *The self-conscious stage in modern French drama,* pp. 20-30.

Grubbs, Henry A. "Alfred Jarry's Theories of Dramatic Technique." *Romantic Rev.,* vol. 26, no. 4 (Oct.-Dec., 1935), pp. 340-345.

Hartley, Anthony. "Father of Ubu." *Guardian,* no. 37,038 (Aug. 6, 1965), p. 5.

Jarry, Alfred. "A Letter to Lugné-Poe." *In:* Jarry, Alfred. *Selected works,* pp. 67-68.

Jarry, Alfred. "Preliminary Address at the First Performance of *Ubu Roi,* December 10, 1896." *In:* Jarry, Alfred, *Selected works,* pp. 76-78.

Jarry, Alfred. *"Ubu Roi." In:* Jarry, Alfred. *Selected works,* pp. 79-81, (Program Notes).

Oliver, Cordelia. *"Ubu Roi* at the Gateway Theatre." *Guardian,* no. 37,685. (Sept. 7, 1967), p. 9.

Pronko, Leonard C. *Avant-garde: the experimental theater in France,* pp. 4-7.

"Prototype of Pataphysics." *Times Literary Supplement,* no. 3,364 (Aug. 18, 1966), p. 736.

Schnurer, Herman. "Alfred Jarry." *Sewanee Rev.,* vol. 40 (July, 1932), pp. 350-353.

Shattuck, Roger. *The banquet years,* pp. 158-164.

Shearer, Ann. *"Ubu Roi* at the Royal Court." *Guardian,* no. 37,336 (July 23, 1966), p. 6.

Wardle, Irving. "Arts in Society: King Ubu's New Clothes." *New Society,* vol. 8, no. 200 (July 28, 1966), p. 164.

Wellwarth, George. *The theatre of protest and paradox,* pp. 1-14, 15-16.

York, Ruth B. "Ubu Revisited: The Reprise of 1922." *French Rev.,* vol. 35, no. 4 (Feb., 1962), pp. 408-411.

Ubu Enchained (Ubu Enchaine)

Shattuck, Roger. *The banquet years,* pp. 176-177.

Wellwarth, George. *The theatre of protest and paradox,* pp. 7-8.

ROBINSON JEFFERS 1887-1962

General

Carpenter, Frederic I. *Robinson Jeffers.*

Monjian, Mercedes. *Robinson Jeffers, a study in inhumanism.*

Sanderson, James L. ed. *Medea, myth and dramatic form,* pp. 127-129.

Sanderson, James L. ed. *Phaedra and Hippolytus, myth and dramatic form,* pp. 167-168.

Squires, Radcliffe. *The loyalties of Robinson Jeffers.*

Weales, Gerald. *American drama since World War II,* pp. 182-202.

The Cretan Woman

Gregory, Horace. *The dying gladiators,* p. 19.

Reviews: The Atlantic Monthly, Sept. 1954, p. 69; *Catholic World,* July 1954, pp. 270-273; *Commonweal,* Sept. 10, 1954, p. 142; *Poetry,* July 1954, pp. 266-231; *Saturday Rev. of Literature,* Jan. 16 and June 5, 1954, pp. 17 and 142; *New York Times Book Review,* Jan. 10, 1954, p. 18.

Weales, Gerald. *American drama since World War II,* pp. 193-195.

Medea

Brown, John Mason. *Dramatis personae,* pp. 208-213.

Brown, John Mason. *Seeing more things,* pp. 231-237.

Fitts, Dudley. "The Hellenism of Robinson Jeffers." *In:* Sanderson, James L., ed. *Medea, myth and dramatic form,* pp. 321-325. *Also in: Kenyon Rev.,* vol. 8 (Autumn 1946).

Floyd, Harold Wayne. "A comparative study of Seneca's and Robinson Jeffers' versions of the *Medea* as related to the *Medea* of Euripides." M.A., University of Southern California, 1952.

Stevens, Virginia. (Account of Gielgud's rehearsal of the play.) *Theatre Arts,* Nov. 1947), pp. 31-34.

Weales, Gerald. *American drama since World War II,* pp. 190-193.

The Tower Beyond Tragedy

Jeffers, Robinson. *"The Tower Beyond Tragedy." In:* Frenz, Horst, ed. *American playwrights on drama,* pp. 94-97. (Reprinted from *The New York Times,* Nov. 26, 1950.)

ANN JELLICOE 1927-

General

Taylor, John Russell. *Anger and after,* pp. 65-71.

The Knack

Clurman, Harold. *The naked image,* pp. 88-89.

Gottfried, Martin. *A theater divided; the postwar American stage,* pp. 218-225.

Kustow, Michael. *"The Knack* at the Theater Royal, Bath." *In:* Marowitz, Charles, ed. *Encore reader,* pp. 220-223. (Reprinted from *Encore,* Jan., 1962.)

Prickett, Stephen. "Three Modern English Plays." *Philologica Pragensia,* vol. 10 (1967), pp. 12-21.

Taylor, John Russell. *Anger and after,* pp. 69-71.

The Rising Generation

Taylor, John Russell. *Anger and after,* pp. 68-69.

The Sport of My Mad Mother

Lumley, Frederick. *New trends in 20th-century drama,* pp. 311-312.

Price, Martin. "The London Season." *Modern Drama,* vol. 1, no. 1 (May, 1958), pp. 53-59.

Taylor, John Russell. *Anger and after,* pp. 65-68.

JULIO JIMINEZ RUEDA, 1898-1960

General

Jones, W.K. *Behind Spanish American footlights,* p. 488.

HERMOGENES JOFRE 1841-1890

Los Martires

Jones, W.K. *Behind Spanish American footlights,* pp. 280-281.

HALL JOHNSON 1888-

Run, Little Chillun

Abramson, Doris E. *Negro playwrights in the American theatre, 1925-1959,* pp. 49-54, 85-86.

DENIS JOHNSTON 1901-

General

Fraser, G.S. *The modern writer and his world,* pp. 209-210.

Hogan, Robert. *After the Irish renaissance,* pp. 133-146.

Blind Man's Buff

Hogan, Robert. *After the Irish renaissance,* pp. 140-141.

A Bride for the Unicorn

Hogan, Robert. *After the Irish renaissance,* pp. 138-139.

The Dreaming Dust

Hogan, Robert. *After the Irish renaissance,* pp. 142-143.

The Golden Cuckoo

Hogan, Robert. *After the Irish renaissance,* pp. 143-144.

The Moon in the Yellow River

Hogan, Robert. *After the Irish renaissance,* pp. 137-138.

Jordan, John. "The Irish Theatre: Retrospect and Premonition." *In:* Brown, J.R. and B. Harris, eds. *Contemporary theatre,* pp. 173-175.

The Old Lady Says "No!"

Hogan, Robert. *After the Irish renaissance,* pp. 135-137.

Jordan, John. "The Irish Theatre: Retrospect and Premonition." *In:* Brown, J.R. and B. Harris, eds. *Contemporary theatre,* pp. 171-173.

The Scythe and the Sunset

Hogan, Robert. *After the Irish renaissance,* pp. 144-146.

Storm Song

Hogan, Robert. *After the Irish renaissance,* pp. 139-140.

Strange Occurrence on Ireland's Eye

Hogan, Robert. *After the Irish renaissance,* pp. 141-142.

HENRY ARTHUR JONES 1851-1929

General

Archer, William. "Pinero, Jones, and Wilde." *In:* Freedman, Morris, ed. *Essays in the modern drama,* pp. 107-121. (Reprinted from *The old drama and the new,* by William Archer.)

Ellehauge, Martin. *The position of Bernard Shaw in European drama and philosophy,* pp. 54-56, 58.

Nicoll, Allardyce. *British drama,* pp. 237-241

Salerno, Henry F. *English drama in transition, 1880-1920,* pp. 23-24.

Williams, Harold. *Modern English writers,* pp. 232-235.

The Lackey's Carnival

Beerbohm, Max. *Around theatres,* pp. 104-109.

The Liars

Salerno, Henry F. *English drama in transition, 1880-1920,* pp. 24-25.

Michael and His Lost Angel

Shaw, George Bernard. *Shaw's dramatic criticism (1895-98)*, pp. 138-144.

The Physician

Shaw, George Bernard. *Shaw's dramatic criticism (1895-98)*, pp. 225-232.

JACK JONES

Rhonda Roundabout

Dent, Alan. *Preludes and studies*, pp. 175-177.

LE ROI JONES 1934-

General

Abramson, Doris E. *Negro playwrights in the American theatre, 1925-1949*, pp. 275-278.

Brustein, Robert. "The New American Playwrights." *In:* Rahv, Philip, ed. *Modern occasions*, pp. 134-135.

Lumley, Frederick. *New trends in 20th-century drama*, pp. 339-340.

Mitchell, Loften. *Black drama*, pp. 103, 127, 130, 202, 204, 231, 205-207, 212, 214-217.

The Dutchman

Bigsby, C.W.E. *Confrontation and commitment*, pp. 122, 142-147, 148, 150-151, 154, 155.

Clurman, Harold. *The naked image*, pp. 90-91.

Dukore, Bernard F. "The Noncommercial Theater in New York." *In:* Downer, Alan S., ed. *The American theater today*, pp. 165-166.

Gottfried, Martin. *A theater divided: the postwar American stage*, pp. 78-79.

Mitchell, Loften. *Black drama*, pp. 199, 205, 216.

Nelson, Hugh. "LeRoi Jones' *Dutchman:* A Brief Ride on a Doomed Ship." *Educational Theatre J.*, vol. 20, no. 1 (Mar., 1968), pp. 53-59.

Sontag, Susan. *Against interpretation and other essays*, pp. 152, 155-157.

Turpin, Waters E. "The Contemporary American Negro Playwright." *College Language Assn. J.,* vol. 9, no. 1 (Sept., 1965), pp. 21-22, 24.

The Slave

Bigsby, C.W.E. *Confrontation and commitment,* pp. 122, 140, 147-151, 152, 154, 155.

Brustein, Robert. *Seasons of discontent,* pp. 306-307.

Brustein, Robert. "Three Plays and a Protest." *New Republic,* vol. 152 (Jan. 23, 1965), pp. 32-33.

Clurman, Harold. *The naked image,* pp. 92-93.

Dennison, George. "The Demagogy of LeRoi Jones." *Contemporary,* vol. 39, no. 2 (Feb., 1965), pp. 67-70.

Gottfried, Martin. *A theater divided; the postwar American stage,* pp. 79-80.

Turpin, Waters E. "The Contemporary American Negro Playwright." *College Language Assn. J.,* vol. 9, no. 1 (Sept., 1965), pp. 22-23, 24.

The Toilet

Bigsby, C.W.E. *Confrontation and commitment,* pp. 109, 122, 138, 140.

Brustein, Robert. *Seasons of discontent,* pp. 306-307.

Brustein, Robert. *"Three Plays and a Protest." New Republic,* vol. 152 (Jan. 23, 1965), pp. 32-33.

Clurman, Harold. *The naked image,* pp. 91-92.

Dennison, George. "The Demagogy of LeRoi Jones." *Commentary,* vol. 39. no. 2 (Feb., 1965), pp. 67-70.

Gottfried, Martin. *A theater divided; the postwar American stage,* pp. 79-80.

Turpin, Waters E. "The Contemporary American Negro Playwright." *College Language Assn. J.,* vol. 9, no. 1 (Sept., 1965), pp.123-24.

ANDRE JOSSET

Elizabeth la Femme sans Homme

Knowles, Dorothy. *French drama of the inter-war years, 1918-39,* pp. 266-267.

JAMES JOYCE 1882-1941

General

Ellmann, Richard. "The Hawklike Man." *In:* Ellmann, R. *Eminent domain*, pp. 29-56.

Exiles

Douglas, James W. "James Joyce's *Exiles:* A Portrait of the Artist." *Renascence,* vol. 15, no. 2 (Winter, 1963), pp. 82-87.

Ellmann, Richard. "The Hawklike Man." *In:* Ellmann, R. *Eminent domain.* p. 48.

Fergusson, Francis. *The human image in dramatic literature,* pp. 72-84.

MacCarthy, Desmond. *Drama,* pp. 206-213.

Metzger, Deena P. "Variations on a Theme: A Study of *Exiles* by James Joyce and *The Great God Brown* by Eugene O'Neill." *Modern Drama,* vol. 8, no. 2 (Sept., 1965), pp. 174-184.

O'Connor, Frank. *A short history of Irish literature,* pp. 207, 208.

FRANZ KAFKA 1883-1924

The Trial (Le Procès) (Der Prozess)

Bentley, Eric. "Jean-Louis Barrault." *Kenyon Rev.,* vol. 12, no. 2 (Spring, 1950), pp. 224-235.

Pasley, J.M. "Two Literary Sources of Kafka's *Der Prozess.*" *Forum for Modern Language Studies,* vol. 3 (1967), pp. 142-147.

Vallette, Rebecca M. *"Der Prozess* and *Le Procès:* A Study in Dramatic Adaptation." *Modern Drama,* vol. 10, no. 1 (May, 1967), pp. 87-94.

GEORG KAISER 1878-1945

General

Bauland, Peter. *The hooded eagle,* pp. 68-74, 91-94, 103-104, 111, 153-154, 160, 164, 167.

Frenz, Horst. "Georg Kaiser." *Poet Lore,* vol. 52, no. 4 (Winter, 1946), pp. 363-369.

Garten, H.F. "Georg Kaiser." *In:* Natan, A., ed. *German men of letters,* vol. 2, pp. 157-172.

Garten, H.F. "Georg Kaiser and the Expressionist Movement." *Drama,* no. 37 (Summer, 1955), pp. 18-21.

Garten, H.F. *Modern German drama,* pp. 147-165.

Goldberg, Isaac. *The drama of transition,* pp. 302-313.

Hatfield, Henry. *Modern German literature,* pp. 69, 70, 72-74.

Jones, Robert Alston. "German Drama on the American Stage: The Case of Georg Kaiser." *German Q.,* vol. 37, no. 1 (Jan., 1964), pp. 17-25.

Kaiser, Georg. "The Head Is Stronger Than the Heart." (Interview.) *Tulane Drama Rev.,* vol. 7, no. 1 (Fall, 1962), pp. 183-187.

Kauf, Robert. "Georg Kaiser's Social Tetralogy and the Social Ideas of Walther Rathenau." *PMLA,* vol. 77 (1962), pp. 311-317.

Reichart, Herbert W. "Nietzsche and Georg Kaiser." *Studies in Philology,* vol. 61, no. 1 (Jan., 1964), pp. 85-108.

Sokel, Walter. *The writer in extremis,* pp. 62, 63, 107-108, 173-175.

Alkibiades Saved (Der Gerettete Alkibiades)

Reichart, Herbert W. "Nietzsche and Georg Kaiser." *Studies in Philology,* vol. 61, no. 1 (Jan., 1964), pp. 87-93.

Sokel, Walter. "Thorn of Socrates." *Germanic Rev.,* vol. 30, no. 1 (Feb., 1955), pp. 72-76.

Sokel, Walter. *The writer in extremis,* pp. 104-110, 117.

Bellerophon

Loram, Ian C. "Georg Kaiser's Swan Song: 'Griechische Dramen.'" *Monatshefte,* vol. 49, no. 1 (Jan., 1957), pp. 29-30.

Burghers of Calais (Die Bürger von Calais)

Garten, H.F. "Georg Kaiser." *In:* Natan, A., ed. *German men of letters,* vol. 2, pp. 160-161.

Sokel, Walter. *The writer in extremis,* pp. 108, 172-175.

Last, R.W. "Symbol and Struggle in Georg Kaiser's *Die Bürger von Calais." German Life and Letters,* n. s., vol. 19 (1965-66), pp. 201-209.

Flight to Venice (Flucht nach Venedig)

Sokel, Walter. *The writer in extremis,* pp. 127-128.

From Morn to Midnight (Von Morgens bis Mitternacht)

Bauland, Peter. *The hooded eagle,* pp. 68-74, 91, 111, 167.

Crawford, Jack. "Expressionism on Broadway." *Drama,* vol. 12, no. 10 (Sept., 1922), p.342.

Garten, H.F. "Georg Kaiser." *In:* Natan, A., ed. *German men of letters,* vol. 2, pp. 162-163.

Jones, Robert Alston. "German Drama on the American Stage: The Case of Georg Kaiser." *German Q.,* vol. 37, no. 1 (Jan., 1964), pp. 19-22.

Gas Trilogy (The Coral; Gas I; Gas II) (Die Koralle)

Bauland, Peter. *The hooded eagle,* pp. 68-69, 74, 92-93, 153-154, 164.

Garten, H.F. "Georg Kaiser." *In:* Natan, A., ed. *German men of letters,* vol. 2, pp. 163-165.

Peacock, Ronald. "Public and Private Problems in Modern Drama." *In:* Corrigan, Robert W. *Theatre in the twentieth century,* pp. 309-312. *Also in: Tulane Drama Rev.,* vol. 3, no. 3 (Mar., 1959), pp. 62-65.

Sokel, Walter. *The writer in extremis,* pp. 96, 130, 192-195, 201-202.

Holle Weg Erde

Sokel, Walter. *The writer in extremis,* pp. 171n, 183-184, 195, 201.

The Jewish Widow (Die Judische Witwe)

Sokel, Walter. *The writer in extremis,* pp. 108, 121.

The Phantom Lover (Oktobertag)

Bauland, Peter. *The hooded eagle,* pp. 103-104.

Jones, Robert Alston. "German Drama on the American Stage: The Case of Georg Kaiser." *German Q.,* vol. 37, no. 1 (Jan., 1964), p. 21.

The Protagonist (Der Protagonist)

Sokel, Walter. *The writer in extremis,* pp. 128-129.

Pygmalion

Loram, Ian C. "Georg Kaiser's Swan Song: 'Griechische Dramen.'" *Monatshefte,* vol. 49, no. 1 (Jan., 1957), pp. 23-27.

The Raft of the Medusa

Wellwarth, G.E. "Introduction." *In:* Benedikt, M., and Wellwarth, G.E., eds. *Post-war German theatre,* pp. xi-xii.

Rektor Kleist

Reichart, Herbert W. "Nietzsche and Georg Kaiser." *Studies in Philology,* vol. 61, no. 1 (Jan., 1964), pp. 93-99.

Sokel, Walter. *The writer in extremis,* pp. 88, 104, 121.

Schellenkonig

Kauf, R. *"Schellenkonig:* An Unpublished Early Play by Georg Kaiser." *J. of English & Germanic Philology,* vol. 55 (July, 1956), pp. 439-450.

Twice Oliver (Zweimal Oliver)

Sokel, Walter. *The writer in extremis,* pp. 96-97, 129.

Zweimal Amphitryon

Jetter, Marianne R. "Some Thoughts on Kleist's *Amphytryon* and Kaiser's *Zweimal Amphytryon." German Life & Letters,* n.s., vol. 13, no. 1 (Oct., 1959), pp. 178-189.

Loram, Ian C. "Georg Kaiser's Swan Song: 'Griechische Dramen.'" *Monatshefte,* vol. 49, no. 1 (Jan., 1957), pp. 27-28.

LEE H. KALCHIEM

The Morning After

Sainer, Arthur, *The sleepwalker and the assassin, a view of the contemporary theatre,* p. 103.

ERICH KASTNER 1899-

Die Schule der Diktatoren

Coenen, F.E. "The Modern German Drama." *In:* Hammer, Carl, Jr., ed. *Studies in German Literature,* pp. 114-115.

VALENTIN KATAYEV 1897-

The Blue Scarf

Macleod, Joseph. *Actors cross the Volga,* pp. 147, 216, 225, 243, 252, 313.

The Path of Flowers

Himelstein, Morgan Y. *Drama was a weapon, the left-wing theatre in New York 1929-1941,* pp. 97-98.

Squaring the Circle

Block, Anita. *The changing world in plays and theatre,* pp. 378-381.

Himelstein, Morgan Y. *Drama was a weapon, the left-wing theatre in New York, 1929-1941,* pp. 195-197.

GEORGE S. KAUFMAN 1889-1962

General

Flexner, Eleanor. *American playwrights: 1918-1938,* pp. 198-206, 214-216, 220-233.

Freedley, George. "George S. Kaufman, 1889-1962." *Modern Drama,* vol. 6, no. 3 (Dec., 1963), pp. 241-244.

Gould, Jean. *Modern American playwrights,* pp. 154-167.

Krutch, Joseph W. *The American drama since 1918,* pp. 139-151.

Lembke, Russell. "The George S. Kaufman Plays as Social History." *Q. J. of Speech,* vol. 33, no. 3 (Oct., 1947), pp. 341-347.

The American Way

Himelstein, Morgan Y. *Drama was a weapon, the left-wing theatre in New York, 1929-1941,* p. 208.

The Beggar on Horseback (Marc Connelly, co-author)

Belloc, Hilaire. "Drama and Dream." *Saturday Rev.,* vol. 140 (June 18, 1925), pp. 63-64.

Brown, Ivor. "Furious Fashions." *Saturday Rev.,* vol. 139 (May 23, 1925), p. 552.

Flexner, Eleanor. *American playwrights: 1918-1938,* pp. 206-213.

Sievers, W. David. *Freud on Broadway,* pp. 86-87.

The Dark Tower (Alexander Woollcott, co-author)

Fleming, Peter. *Spectator,* vol. 152 (May 18, 1934), p. 774.

Dinner at Eight (Edna Ferber, co-author)

Fleming, Peter. *Spectator,* vol. 150 (Jan. 13, 1933), p. 40.

G.D.N. "Social Drama Notes." *Sociology and Social Research,* vol. 17 (Jan., 1933), p. 297.

Gassner, John. "Broadway in Review." *Educational Theatre J.,* vol. 18, no. 4 (Dec., 1966), pp. 453-454.

MacCarthy, Desmond. *Drama,* pp. 249-254.

MacCarthy, Desmond. "Excitement, Satire, Speed." *New Statesman,* vol. 5 (Jan. 14, 1933), pp. 41-42.

The Man Who Came to Dinner (Moss Hart, co-author)

New Statesman, vol. 22 (Dec. 13, 1941), p. 492.

Turner, W.J. *Spectator,* vol. 167 (Dec. 12, 1941), p. 555.

Once in a Lifetime (Moss Hart, co-author)

Fleming, Peter. *Spectator,* vol. 150 (Mar. 3, 1933), pp. 284-285.

Flexner, Eleanor. *American playwrights: 1918-1938,* pp. 216-220.

The Small House (Leueen MacGrath, co-author)

Sievers, W. David. *Freud on Broadway,* p. 413.

Theatre Royal (Edna Ferber, co-author)

Verschoyle, Derek. *Spectator,* vol. 153 (Nov. 2, 1934), p. 670.

You Can't Take It with You (Moss Hart, co-author)

Brown, John Mason. *Two on the aisle,* pp. 177-180.

O'Hara, Frank H. *Today in American drama,* pp. 224-232, 249-250.

Sievers, W. David. *Freud on Broadway,* pp. 289-291.

JOHN B. KEANE 1928-

General

Hogan, Robert. *After the Irish renaissance,* pp. 208-220.

Hogan, Robert G., ed. *Seven Irish plays, 1946-1964,* pp. 307-310.

The Field

Hogan Robert. *After the Irish renaissance,* pp. 219-220.

The Highest House on the Mountain

Hogan, Robert. *After the Irish renaissance,* pp. 214-215.

Many Young Men of Twenty

Hogan, Robert. *After the Irish renaissance,* pp. 215-217.

No More in Dust

Hogan, Robert. *After the Irish renaissance,* p. 217.

Sharon's Grave

Hogan, Robert. *After the Irish renaissance,* pp. 213-214.

Sive

Hogan, Robert. *After the Irish renaissance,* pp. 210-213.

The Year of the Hiker

Hogan, Robert. *After the Irish renaissance,* pp. 218-219.

GEORGE KELLY 1887-

General

Atkinson, Brooks. "Several Matters of Craft." *The New York Times,* Mar. 8, 1931, Sec. 8, p. 1.

Brown, John Mason. *Upstage,* pp. 31-39.

Carmer, Carl. "George Kelly." *Theatre Arts,* vol. 15 (Apr., 1931), pp. 322-330.

Clark, Barrett. "George Kelly." *In:* Clark, B. *An hour of American drama,* pp. 50-61.

Downer, Alan. S. *Fifty years of American drama,* pp. 49-51, 121-125.

Gabriel, Gilbert W. "A Playwright You Should Know and Why." *Mentor,* vol. 14 (June 1926), pp. 36-37.

Gagey, E.M. *Revolution in American drama,* pp. 120-174.

Hartley, L., and Arthur Ladu, eds. *Patterns in modern drama,* pp. 248-251.

Krutch, Joseph Wood. *The American drama since 1918,* pp. 60-72.

Krutch, Joseph Wood. "The Austerity of George Kelly." *Nation,* vol. 137 (Aug. 30, 1933), pp. 240-242. (Reprinted in Zabel, M. *Literary opinion in America,* pp. 535-539.)

McCarthy, Mary. *Sights and spectacles 1937-1956,* pp. 97-104.

McCarthy, Mary. "Something About the Weather." *In:* Partisan Review. *New Partisan Reader,* 1945-1953, pp. 531-536. *Also in: Partisan Rev.,* vol. 14 (Mar., Apr., 1947), pp. 174-178.

Maisel, Edward. "The Theatre of George Kelly." *Theatre Arts,* vol. 31 (Feb., 1937), pp. 39-43.

Mantle, Burns. *American playwrights of today,* pp. 21-30.

Mantle, Burns. *Contemporary American playwrights,* pp. 78-82.

Morris, Lloyd. *Postscript to yesterday,* pp. 192-195.

Morris, Ruth. "Mr. Kelly to the Defense." *The New York Times, Feb.* 8, 1931, Sec. 8, p. 3.

Moses, Montrose J. "George Kelly." *Theatre Guild Magazine,* vol. 7 (July, 1930), pp. 15-17.

Nathan, George Jean. *Theatre book of the year, 1946-47,* pp. 197-200.

Skinner, R. Dana. *Our changing theatre,* pp. 110-113, 166-168.

VanDruten, John. "Small Souls and Great Plays." *Theatre Arts,* vol. 11 (July, 1927), pp. 493-498.

Wills, Arthur. "The Kelly Play." *Modern Drama,* vol. 6 (1963-64), pp. 245-255.

Behold the Bridegroom

Downer, Alan S. *Fifty years of American drama, 1900-1950,* pp. 49-51.

Krutch, Joseph W. *The American drama since 1918,* pp. 66-69.

Krutch, Joseph Wood. "Drama." *Nation,* vol. 126 (Jan. 11, 1928), p. 51.

Sayler, Oliver M. "The Play of the Week." *Saturday Rev. of Literature,* vol. 4 (Jan. 28, 1928), pp. 547-548.

Sievers, W. David. *Freud on Broadway,* pp. 162-163.

White, Kenneth. "George Kelly and Dramatic Device." *Hound & Horn,* vol. 4 (Apr.-June, 1931), pp. 384-400.

Young, Stark. "Migratory Souls." *New Republic,* vol. 53 (Jan. 18, 1928), pp. 246-247.

Craig's Wife

Atkinson, Brooks. *"Craig's Wife."* *The New York Times,* Mar. 30, 1947, Sec. 2, p. 1.

Atkinson, Brooks. "Endorsing Mr. Kelly." *The New York Times,* May 9, 1926, Sec. 8, p. 1.

Brown, John Mason. "Inhospitality Hall." *Saturday Rev. of Literature,* vol. 30 (Mar. 8, 1947), pp. 32-34.

Dusenbury, Winifred L. *The theme of loneliness in modern American drama,* pp. 164-171.

Flexner, Eleanor. *American playwrights: 1918-1938,* pp. 236-238.

Gilder, Rosamond. "Broadway in Review." *Theatre Arts,* vol. 31 (Apr., 1947), pp. 19-20.

Krutch, Joseph Wood. "Drama." *Nation,* vol. 169 (Mar. 1, 1947), pp. 256-257.

Lardner, John. "Not All She Used To Be." *New Yorker,* vol. 23 (Feb. 22, 1947), p. 53.

Nathan, George Jean. "An American Play." *American Mercury,* vol. 6 (Dec., 1925), pp. 504-505.

Nathan, George Jean. *Theatre book of the year, 1946-47, pp. 307-*310.

O'Hara, Frank H. *Today in American drama,* pp. 82-83.

"Old Play in Manhattan." *Time,* vol. 49 (Feb. 24, 1947), p. 58.

Phelan, Kappo. *"Craig's Wife."* *Commonweal,* vol. 45 (Feb. 28, 1947), p. 492.

Sievers, W. David. *Freud on Broadway,* pp. 161-162.

Walcutt, Charles C. *American literary naturalism, a divided stream,* pp. 63-64.

Daisy Mayme

Atkinson, Brooks. "Americans All." *The New York Times,* Oct. 26, 1926, p. 24.

Atkinson, Brooks. "Americans All." *The New York Times,* Oct. 31, 1926, Sec. 8, p. 1.

Young, Stark. "The Shine of Life." *New Republic,* vol. 48 (Nov. 17, 1926), pp. 375-376.

The Deep Mrs. Sykes

Gilder, Rosamond. "Broadway in Review." *Theatre Arts,* vol. 29 (May, 1945), pp. 270-271.

Krutch, Joseph Wood. "Drama." *Nation,* vol. 160 (April 7, 1945), p. 395.

Nathan, George Jean. *Theatre book of the year, 1944-45,* pp. 305-309.

Nichols, Lewis. *"The Deep Mrs. Sykes." The New York Times,* Mar. 20, 1945, p. 22.

Sievers, W. David. *Freud on Broadway,* p. 163.

Young, Stark. "Varieties of Legend." *New Republic,* vol. 112 (Apr. 2, 1945), p. 447.

The Fatal Weakness

Atkinson, Brooks. "The Play in Review." *The New York Times,* Nov. 20, 1946, p. 43.

Gilder, Rosamond. "Broadway in Review." *Theatre Arts,* vol. 31 (Jan., 1947), p. 21.

Krutch, Joseph Wood. "Drama." *Nation,* vol. 164 (Jan. 18, 1947), p. 81.

Sievers, W. David. *Freud on Broadway,* pp. 163-164.

Young, Stark. "Weaknesses." *New Republic,* vol. 115, (Dec. 9, 1946), p. 764.

Maggie the Magnificent

Atkinson, Brooks. "On An Unpopular Theme." *The New York Times,* Nov. 3, 1929, Sec. 9, p. 1.

Hutchens, John. "Mid-Season Show Shop." *Theatre Arts Monthly,* vol. 14 (Jan., 1930), pp. 17-18.

Moses, Montrose J. "Dramatist of the Middle Classes." *Rev. of Reviews,* vol. 80 (Dec., 1929), pp. 158-159.

Young, Stark. "An Actress and a Dramatist." *New Republic,* vol. 60 (Nov. 6, 1929), pp. 323-325.

Philip Goes Forth

"As the Provinces See Three New Plays." *The New York Times,* Jan. 4, 1931, Sec. 8, p. 2.

Atkinson, Brooks. "Going Forth." *The New York Times,* Jan. 18, 1931, Sec. 8, p. 1.

"Craft and Mr. Kelly." *The New York Times,* Mar. 15, 1931, Sec. 9, p. 4.

Hutchens, John. "Playwrights' Parade." *Theatre Arts Monthly,* vol. 15 (Mar. 1931), pp. 183-185.

"Philip Goes Forth." *Theatre Magazine,* vol. 53 (Mar., 1931), pp. 24-25.

Young, Stark. *"Philip Goes Forth."* *New Republic,* vol. 65 (Jan. 28, 1931), pp. 301-302.

Reflected Glory

Isaacs, Edith J. "Broadway in Review." *Theatre Arts,* vol. 20 (Nov., 1936), pp. 849-850.

Krutch, Joseph Wood. "Drama." *Nation,* vol. 143 (Oct. 3, 1936), pp. 401-402.

Nichols, Lewis. *"Reflected Glory."* *The New York Times,* Sept. 22, 1936, p. 30.

Vernon, Grenville. *"Reflected Glory."* *Commonweal,* vol. 24 (Oct. 2, 1936), p. 352.

Young, Stark. *"Reflected Glory."* *New Republic,* vol. 88 (Oct. 7, 1936), p. 257.

The Show-Off

Atkinson, Brooks. "First Night at the Theatre." *The New York Times,* June 1, 1950, p. 24.

Broun, Heywood. George Kelly's *The Show-Off." In:* Moses, Montrose J. *The American theatre as seen by its critics, 1752-1934, pp. 211-213.* (Reprinted from *The Show-Off,* Little, Brown, 1925.)

Broun, Heywood. "Preface." *The Show-Off.* pp. ix-xi.

Downer, Alan S. *Fifty years of American drama, 1900-1950,* pp. 122-125.

Eaton, Walter P. *"The Show-Off." In:* Eaton, W.P. *The drama in English,* pp. 317-319.

Kellock, Harold. "A Comedy of Wind." *The Freeman,* vol. 8 (Feb. 27, 1924), pp. 592-593.

Marshall, Margaret. "Drama." *Nation,* vol. 170 (June 17, 1950), p. 603.

"Revival." *Newsweek,* vol. 35 (June 12, 1950), p. 83.

Skinner, Richard Dana. "The Play." *Commonweal,* vol. 17 (Dec. 28, 1932), p. 245.

The Torchbearers

Macgowan, Kenneth. "Preface." *The torchbearers,* New York, American Library Service, 1923, pp. xiii-xix.

Parker, Robert A. "New Playwrights and New Producers." *The Independent* (New York), vol. 109 (Dec. 23, 1922), pp. 397-398.

Young, Stark. *Immortal shadows,* pp. 5-7.

Young, Stark. "The So So and the Future." *New Republic,* vol. 32 (Sept. 20, 1922), pp. 100-101.

TIM KELLY 1935-

A Darker Flower

Sainer, Arthur. *The sleepwalker and the assassin, a view of the contemporary theatre,* pp. 71-72.

ADRIENNE KENNEDY

The Funny House of a Negro

Mitchell, Loften. *Black drama,* pp. 198-199, 216.

LUDOVIC KENNEDY 1919-

Murder Story

Williamson, Audrey. *Contemporary theatre, 1953-1956,* pp. 92-94.

SHEPPARD KERMAN

Mr. Simian

Sainer, Arthur. *The sleepwalker and the assassin, a view of the contemporary theatre,* pp. 86-88.

JOSEPH KESSELRING 1902-

Arsenic and Old Lace

Browne, E. Martin. "Theatre Abroad." *Drama Survey,* vol. 5, no. 2 (Summer, 1966), p. 193.

Sievers, W. David. *Freud on Broadway,* pp. 414-415.

NORMAN KING

The Shadow of Doubt

Williamson, Audrey. *Contemporary theatre, 1953-1956,* pp. 90-92.

SIDNEY KINGSLEY 1906-

Darkness at Noon

See Koestler, Arthur

Dead End

Himelstein, Morgan. Y. *Drama was a weapon, the left-wing theatre in New York, 1929-1941,* pp. 197-198.

Sievers, W. David. *Freud on Broadway,* pp. 299-300.

Detective Story

Sievers, W. David. *Freud on Broadway,* pp. 301-302.

Men in White

Dusenbury, Winifred L. *The theme of loneliness in modern American drama,* pp. 185-190.

Himelstein, Morgan Y. *Drama was a weapon, the left-wing theatre in New York 1929-1941,* pp. 161-162.

The World We Make

Sievers, W. David. *Freud on Broadway,* pp. 300-301.

HEINAR KIPPHARDT 1922-

General

Moore, Harry T. *Twentieth-century German literature,* pp. 153, 157-158.

The Adventures of Joel Brand (Joel Brand: Geschichte Eines Geschäfts)

Luft, Friedrich. "Documentaries Roll On But Lose Steam." *American-German Rev.,* vol. 32, no. 4 (Apr.-May, 1966), pp. 29-30.

Michalski, John. "German Drama and Theater in 1965." *Books Abroad,* vol. 40 (1966), p. 138.

Zipes, Jack D. "Documentary Drama in Germany: Mending the Circuit." *Germanic Rev.,* vol. 42, no. 1 (Jan., 1967), p. 59.

The Case of J. Robert Oppenheimer (In der Sache J. Robert Oppenheimer)

Gong, Alfred. *"The Case of J. Robert Oppenheimer." American-German Rev.,* vol. 31, no. 5 (June-July, 1965), pp. 27-28, 39.

Luft, Fredrich. "Documentaries Roll On But Lose Steam." *American-German Rev.,* vol. 32, no. 4 (Apr.-May, 1966), p. 29.

Michalski, John. "German Drama and Theater in 1965." *Books Abroad,* vol. 40 (1966), pp. 137-138.

Zipes, Jack D. "Documentary Drama in Germany: Mending the Circuit." *Germanic Rev.,* vol. 42, no. 1 (Jan., 1967), pp. 49-62.

Der Hand des Generals

Zipes, Jack D. "Documentary Drama in Germany: Mending the Circuit." *Germanic Rev.,* vol. 42, no. 1 (Jan., 1967), p. 59.

VLADIMIR KIRCHON

Red Dust (André Uspenski, co-author)

Block, Anita. *The changing world in plays and theatre,* pp. 375-378.

Himelstein, Morgan Y. *Drama was a weapon, the left-wing theatre in New York 1929-1941,* pp. 126-127.

HENRI KISTEMAECKERS 1872-1938

General

Knowles, Dorothy. *French drama of the inter-war years, 1918-39,* pp. 287-288.

ALEXANDER KNOX

The Closing Door

Sievers, W. David. *Freud on Broadway,* pp. 420-421.

KENNETH KOCH 1925-

Washington Crossing the Delaware

Gottfried, Martin. *A theater divided; the postwar American stage,* pp. 234-236.

ARTHUR KOESTLER 1905-

Darkness at Noon (Adapted by Sidney Kingsley)

Bentley, Eric. *The theatre of commitment,* pp. 34-35.

Brown, John Mason. "The Iron Transparency." *In:* Brown, John Mason. *Dramatis personae,* pp. 328-401.

Heilman, Robert B. *Tragedy and melodrama,* pp. 143, 278-282.

Sievers, W. David. *Freud on Broadway,* pp. 302-303.

OSKAR KOKOSCHKA 1886-

General

Garten, H.F. *Modern German drama,* pp. 108-109.

Lucas, W.I. "Oskar Kokoschka." *In:* Natan, A., ed. *German men of letters,* vol. 3 (1964), pp. 37-52.

Natan, Alex. "Introduction." *In:* Natan, A., ed. *German men of letters,* vol. 3 (1964), pp. 2-3.

The Burning Bush (Schauspiel der Brennende Dornbusch)

Lucas, W.I. "Oskar Kokoschka." *In:* Natan, A., ed. *German men of letters,* vol. 3 (1964), pp. 44-45, 48.

Hiob (new longer version of Sphinx und Strohmann)

Lucas, W.I. "Oskar Kokoschka." *In:* Natan, A., ed. *German men of letters,* vol. 3 (1964), pp. 45-46.

Mörder, Hoffnung der Frauen

Henning, Roslyn Brogue. "Expressionist Opera." *American-German Rev.,* vol. 32, no. 6 (Aug.-Sept., 1966), p. 20.

Lucas, W.I. "Oskar Kokoschka." *In:* Natan, A., ed. *German men of letters,* vol. 3 (1964), pp. 40-42.

Natan, Alex. "Introduction." *In:* Natan, A., ed. *German men of letters,* vol. 3 (1964), p. 3.

Orpheus und Euridike

Henning, Roslyn Brogue. "Expressionist Opera." *American-German Rev.,* vol. 32, no. 6 (Aug.-Sept., 1966), p. 20.

Lucas, W.I. "Oskar Kokoschka." *In:* Natan, A., ed. *German men of letters,* vol. 3 (1964), pp. 46-48.

Sphinx and Strawman (Sphinx und Strohmann)

Lucas, W.I. "Oskar Kokoschka." *In:* Natan, A. ed. *German men of letters,* vol. 3 (1964), pp. 42-43.

ARTHUR KOPIT 1937-

General

Hurley, Paul J. "France and America: Versions of the Absurd." *College English,* vol. 26 (1965), pp. 634-640.

The Day the Whores Came Out To Play Tennis

Brustein, Robert. "The New American Playwrights." *In:* Rahv, Philip, ed. *Modern occasions,* p. 134.

Oh Dad, Poor Dad, Mama's Hung You in the Closet and I'm Feelin' So Sad

Brustein, Robert. "The New American Playwrights." *In:* Rahv, Philip, ed. *Modern occasions,* p. 133.

Lumley, Frederick. *New trends in 20th-century drama,* pp. 331-332.

Wellwarth, George. *The theatre of protest and paradox,* pp. 711n, 291-293.

BERNARD KOPS 1926-

General

Taylor, John Russell. *Anger and after,* pp. 123-129.

Wellwarth, George. *The theatre of protest and paradox,* pp. 244-248.

Change for an Angel

Taylor, John Russell. *Anger and after,* pp. 126-127.

The Dream of Peter Mann

Lumley, Frederick. *New trends in 20th-century drama,* p. 316.

Taylor, John Russell. *Anger and after,* pp. 127-128.

Wellwarth, George. *The theatre of protest and paradox,* pp. 246-247.

Enter Solly Gold

Wellwarth, George. *The theatre of protest and paradox,* pp. 247-248.

Goodbye, World

Taylor, John Russell. *Anger and after,* pp. 125-126.

The Hamlet of Stepney Green

Lumley, Frederick. *New trends in 20th-century drama,* p. 316.

Taylor, John Russell. *Anger and after,* pp. 123-125.

Wellwarth, George. *The theatre of protest and paradox,* pp. 245-246.

Stray Cats and Empty Bottles

Taylor, John Russell. *Anger and after,* pp. 128-129.

ALEXANDER KORNEICHUK 1905-

Partisans in the Steppes of the Ukraine

Macleod, Joseph. *Actors cross the Volga,* pp. 240-242.

PAUL KORNFELD 1889-1942

General

Sokel, Walter. *The writer in extremis,* pp. 35, 52-53, 217-218, 220-222.

Heaven and Hell (Himmel und Hölle)

Garten, H.F. *Modern German drama,* p. 119.

Sokel, Walter. *The writer in extremis,* pp. 153-154.

The Seduction (Die Verführung)

Garten, H.F. *Modern German drama,* pp. 117-119.

Sokel, Walter. *The writer in extremis,* pp. 39, 40, 52, 66-67.

JOSEPH KRAMM 1908-

The Shrike

Sievers, W. David. *Freud on Broadway,* pp. 439-440.

KARL KRAUS 1874-1936

General

Hatfield, Henry. *Modern German literature,* pp. 119-122.

Spalter, Max. *Brecht's tradition,* pp. 137-155, 162, 163.

Stern, J.P. "Karl Kraus's Vision of Language." *Modern Language Rev.,* vol. 61 (1966), pp. 71-84.

Die Fackel

Spalter, Max. *Brecht's tradition,* pp. 137-138, 154.

The Last Days of Mankind (Die Letzten Tage der Menschheit)

Garten, H.F. *Modern German drama,* pp. 126-128.

Hatfield, Henry. *Modern German literature,* pp. 120-121.

Spalter, Max. *Brecht's tradition,* pp. 137n, 138-155, 162, 163, 182; text of a scene, pp. 237-261.

GREGORIO DE LAFERRERE 1867-1913

General

Anderson Imbert, Enrique. *Spanish-American literature: a history,* pp. 319-320.

Jones, W.K. *Behind Spanish American footlights,* pp. 127-129.

The Crackpots (Locos de Overano)

Jones, W.K. *Behind Spanish American footlights,* p. 128.

The Women of Barranco (Las de Barranco)

Jones, W.K. *Behind Spanish American footlights,* pp. 128-129.

PAR LAGERKVIST 1891-

General

Buckman, Thomas R. "Introduction." *In:* Lagerkvist, Pär. *Modern theatre, seven plays and an essay,* pp. ix-xv, xxi-xxii.

Lagerkvist, Pär. "Modern Theatre: Points of View and Attack." *In:* Lagerkvist, Pär. *Modern theatre, seven plays and an essay,* pp. 3-24, 32-38.

Lagerkvist, Pär. "Modern Theater: Points of View and Attack." *In:* Sprinchorn, Evert, ed. *The genius of the Scandinavian theater,* pp. 604-624, 632-637.

Spector, Robert Donald. "Pär Lagerkvist's Dialogue of the Soul." *In:* American-Scandinavian Foundation, New York, *Scandinavian studies,* pp. 302-310.

Sprinchorn, Evert, ed. *The genius of the Scandinavian theater,* pp. 428-435.

Swanson, Roy Arthur. "Evil and Love in Lagerkvist's Crucifixion Cycle." *Scandinavian Studies,* vol. 38 (1966), pp. 302-317.

The Difficult Hour I-III (Den Svåra Stunden I-III)

Buckman, Thomas R. "Introduction." *In:* Lagerkvist, Pär. *Modern theatre, seven plays and an essay,* pp. xv-xviii.

The Dwarf

Jackson, Naomi. "The Fragmented Mirror: Lagerkvist's *The Dwarf.*" *Discourse* (Concordia Coll.), vol. 8 (1965), pp. 185-193.

The Hangman (Bodeln)

Buckman, Thomas R. "Introduction." *In:* Lagerkvist, Pär. *Modern theatre, seven plays and an essay,* pp. xx, xxii-xxiii.

The King (Konungen)

Buckman, Thomas R. "Introduction." *In:* Lagerkvist, Pär. *Modern theatre, seven plays and an essay,* pp. xix-xx, xxii.

The Philosopher's Stone (De Vises Sten)

Buckman, Thomas R. "Introduction." *In:* Lagerkvist, Pär. *Modern theatre, seven plays and an essay,* pp. xx-xxi, xxiii.

The Secret of Heaven (Himlens Hemlighet)

Buckman, Thomas R. "Introduction." *In:* Lagerkvist, Pär. *Modern theatre, seven plays and an essay,* pp. xviii-xix.

LAWRENCE LANGNER 1890-1962

Moses

Roston, Murray. *Biblical drama in England from the Middle Ages to the present day,* pp. 261-263.

MARGHANITA LASKI 1915-

The Offshore Island

Voaden, Herman, ed. *Human values in the drama,* pp. xi, xvi, 286-288, 347-352.

ARTHUR LAURENTS 1918-

General

Weales, Gerald. *American drama since World War II*, pp. 51-56.

The Bird Cage

Sievers, W. David. *Freud on Broadway*, pp. 349-350.

A Clearing in the Woods

Cerf, Walter. "Psychoanalysis and the Realistic Drama." *J. of Aesthetics and Art Criticism*, vol. 16, no. 3 (Mar., 1958), pp. 328-336.

The Home of the Brave

Sievers, W. David. *Freud on Broadway*, pp. 347-349.

Invitation to a March

Brustein, Robert. *Seasons of discontent*, pp. 114-116.

The Time of the Cuckoo

Sievers, W. David. *Freud on Broadway*, p. 351.

RAY LAWLER 1921-

Summer of the Seventeenth Doll

Kitchin, Laurence. *Mid-century drama*, pp. 111-112.

DAVID HERBERT LAWRENCE 1885-1930

General

Mahnken, Harry E. "The Plays of D.H. Lawrence: Addenda." *Modern Drama*, vol. 7, no. 4 (Feb., 1965), pp. 431-432.

Waterman, Arthur E. "The Plays of D.H. Lawrence." *Modern Drama*, vol. 2, no. 4 (Feb., 1960), pp. 349-357.

Williams, Raymond. *Modern tragedy*, pp. 121-138.

David

Panichas, George A. "D.H. Lawrence's Biblical Play *David.*" *Modern Drama*, vol. 6, no. 2 (Sept., 1963), pp. 164-176.

Roston, Murray. *Biblical drama in England from the Middle ages to the present day*, pp. 275-279.

Weales, Gerald. *Religion in modern English drama*, pp. 34-35.

JOHN HOWARD LAWSON 1895-

General

Knox, George A. *Dos Passos and "The Revolting Playwrights,"* pp. 30-31, 37-39, 47-51, 53-55, 69, 181-182, 197-200.

Krutch, Joseph Wood. *The American drama since 1918,* pp. 256-262.

Mendelsohn, Michael J. "The Social Critics on Stage." *Modern Drama,* vol. 6, no. 3 (Dec., 1963), pp. 277-285.

Rabkin, Gerald. *Drama and commitment,* pp. 127-165.

Valgemae, Mardi. "Civil War Among the Expressionists: John Howard Lawson and the *Pinwheel* Controversy." *Educational Theatre J.,* vol. 20, no. 1 (Mar., 1968), pp. 8-14.

Gentlewoman

Himelstein, Morgan Y. *Drama was a weapon, the left-wing theatre in New York 1929-1941,* pp. 162-164.

Rabkin, Gerald. *Drama and commitment,* pp. 148-150.

The Internationals

Knox, George A. *Dos Passos and "The Revolting Playwrights,"* pp. 34-35, 121-124, 163-165, 174, 183-189, 194.

Rabkin, Gerald. *Drama and commitment,* pp. 139-142.

Turner, Darwin T. "Jazz-Vaudeville Drama in the Twenties." *Educational Theatre J.,* vol. 11 (1959), pp. 115-116.

Loud Speaker

Knox, George A. *Dos Passos and "The Revolting Playwrights,"* pp. 102-104, 157, 158-159, 163, 166-167, 168-170, 193.

Rabkin, Gerald. *Drama and commitment,* pp. 138-139.

Marching Song

Himelstein, Morgan Y. *Drama was a weapon, the left-wing theatre in New York 1929-1941,* pp. 70-72.

Rabkin, Gerald. *Drama and commitment,* pp. 157-160.

Nirvana

Rabkin, Gerald. *Drama and commitment,* pp. 137-138.

Parlor Magic

Rabkin, Gerald. *Drama and commitment,* pp. 163-164.

The Processional

Block, Anita. *The changing world in plays and theatre,* pp. 225-229.

Gabriel, Gilbert W. "Rhapsody in Red—John Howard Lawson's *Processional." In:* Moses, Montrose J. *The American theatre as seen by its critics, 1752-1934,* pp. 311-313. (Reprinted from *The Telegram Mail,* Jan. 13, 1925.)

Himelstein, Morgan Y. *Drama was a weapon, the left-wing theatre in New York 1929-1941,* pp. 104-105.

Knox, George A. *Dos Passos and "The Revolting Playwrights,"* pp. 27-31.

Krutch, Joseph W. *The American drama since 1918,* pp. 240-242.

Rabkin, Gerald. *Drama and commitment,* pp. 134-137.

Turner, Darwin T. "Jazz-Vaudeville Drama in the Twenties." *Educational Theatre J.,* vol. 11 (1959), pp. 110-112.

The Pure in Heart

Rabkin, Gerald. *Drama and commitment,* pp. 146-148.

Roger Bloomer

Broussard, Louis. *American drama...,* pp. 50-55.

Rabkin, Gerald. *Drama and commitment,* pp. 127-134.

Sievers, W. David. *Freud on Broadway,* pp. 140-142.

Success Story

Himelstein, Morgan Y. *Drama was a weapon, the left-wing theatre in New York 1929-1941,* pp. 160-161.

Rabkin, Gerald. *Drama and commitment,* pp. 143-145.

Sievers, W. David. *Freud on Broadway,* pp. 143-145.

CARL LAZIO

Let's Eat Hair! The Chinese Icebox (Two playlets)

Wellwarth, G.E. "Introduction." *In:* Benedikt, M., and G.E. Wellwarth, ed. *Post-war German theatre,* pp. xxiii-xxv.

HENRI-RENE LENORMAND 1882-1951

General

Arlin Lubard, Henriette d'. "Lenormand's drama in the light of his confessions." *Dissertation Abstracts,* vol. 14 (1954), 128 (Columbia).

Behrens, Ralph. "L'Inconnu As Object of Desire in the Plays of Lenormand." *French Rev.,* vol. 31, no. 2 (Dec., 1957), pp. 152-154.

Hatzfeld, Helmut. *Trends and styles in twentieth-century French literature,* pp. 102-105.

Jones, Robert Emmet. *The alienated hero in modern French drama,* pp. 43-57.

Jones, Robert Emmet. "Desire and Death in the Plays of Lenormand." *French Rev.,* vol. 30, no. 2 (Dec., 1956), pp. 138-142.

Knowles, Dorothy. *French drama of the inter-war years, 1918-39,* pp. 90-91, 104-106.

Moore, Harry T. *Twentieth-century French literature to World War II,* pp. 125-129.

Palmer, John. "H.R. Lenormand and the Play of Psychoanalysis." *Nineteenth Century and After,* vol. 100 (Oct., 1926), pp. 594-596, 606-607.

Palmer, John. *Studies in contemporary theatre,* pp. 65-93.

Posen, R. "Aspects of the Work of Henri-René Lenormand." *Nottingham French Studies,* vol. 6 (1967), pp. 30-44.

Sper, F. "Lenormand and the Dark Wish." *Drama,* vol. 18, no. 4 (Jan., 1928), pp. 100-103.

Stewart, Nancy. "The Dramatic Themes of Henri-René Lenormand." *South Atlantic Bulletin,* vol. 19, no. 3 (Jan. 1954), p. 13.

White, Kenneth S. "The development of Lenormand's principles and purposes as a dramatist." *Dissertation Abstracts,* vol. 19 (1958), 331.

White, Kenneth S. "Toward a New Interpretation of Lenormand's Theatrical Ethos." *Modern Drama,* vol. 2, no. 4 (Feb., 1960), pp. 334-348.

L'Amour Magicien

Knowles, Dorothy. *French drama of the inter-war years, 1918-39,* pp. 98-99.

Asie

Knowles, Dorothy. *French drama of the inter-war years, 1918-39,* pp. 100-101.

The Coward (Le Lache)

"French-Fright Goes Behind the Footlights." *Literary Digest,* vol. 120, no. 4 (July 27, 1935), pp. 22, 31.

Knowles, Dorothy. *French drama of the inter-war years, 1918-39,* p. 99.

La Dent Rouge

Knowles, Dorothy. *French drama of the inter-war years, 1918-39,* p. 94.

Palmer, John. "H.R. Lenormand and the Play of Psychoanalysis." *Nineteenth Century and After,* vol. 100 (Oct., 1926), pp. 604-605.

The Dream Doctor (Le Mangeur des Reves)

Knowles, Dorothy. *French drama of the inter-war years, 1918-39,* pp. 96-97.

New Statesman, vol. 34 (Nov. 23, 1929), pp. 226-227.

Palmer, John. "H.R. Lenormand and the Play of Psychoanalysis." *Nineteenth Century and After,* vol. 100 (Oct., 1926), pp. 602-604.

Palmer, John. *Studies in contemporary theatre, pp. 86-92.*

Equator (L'Ombre du Mal)

Knowles, Dorothy. *French drama of the inter-war years, 1918-39,* pp. 95-96.

Palmer, John. "H.R. Lenormand and the Play of Psychoanalysis." *Nineteenth Century and After,* vol. 100 (Oct., 1926), pp. 596-599.

Palmer, John. *Studies in the contemporary theatre,* pp. 75-81.

Saturday Rev., vol. 145 (Mar. 3, 1928), pp. 254-255.

The Failures (Les Rates)

Knowles, Dorothy. *French drama of the inter-war years, 1918-39,* pp. 91-92.

Lewisohn, Ludwig. *Nation,* vol. 117 (Dec. 12, 1923), pp. 692-693.

Malcolm, Donald. "Off Broadway." *The New Yorker,* Jan. 17, 1959, p. 66.

Palmer, John. "H.R. Lenormand and the Play of Psychoanalysis." *Nineteenth Century and After,* vol. 100 (Oct., 1926), pp. 601-602.

Young, Stark, *New Republic,* vol. 37 (Dec. 5, 1923), p. 46.

La Folle du Ciel

Knowles, Dorothy. *French drama of the inter-war years, 1918-39,* pp. 103-105.

The House on the Ramparts (La Maison des Ramparts)

Knowles, Dorothy. *French drama of the inter-war years, 1918-39* pp. 101-103.

White, Kenneth S. "Visions of a Transfigured Humanity: Strindberg and Lenormand." *Modern Drama,* vol. 5, no. 3 (Dec., 1962), pp. 327-330.

In Theatre Street (Crépuscle du Théâtre)

Fleming, Peter. *Spectator,* vol. 158 (May 14, 1937), p. 903.

Knowles, Dorothy. *French drama of the inter-war years, 1918-39,* p. 104.

Man and His Phantoms (L'Homme et Ses Fantômes)

Knowles, Dorothy. *French drama of the inter-war years, 1918-39,* pp. 97-98.

Orrok, Douglas Hall. "Lenormands's Don Juan." *Literature and Psychology,* vol. 6, no. 3 (Aug., 1956), pp. 87-89.

Palmer, John. "H.R. Lenormand and the Play of Psychoanalysis." *Nineteenth Century and After,* vol. 100 (Oct., 1926), pp. 605-606.

Mixture

Knowles, Dorothy. *French drama of the inter-war years, 1918-39,* pp. 99-100.

The Possessed (Les Possédés)

Sheffer, Eugene. "H.R. Lenormand As a Student of the Personality." *French Rev.,* vol. 7, no. 1 (Nov., 1933), pp. 50-55.

A Secret Life (Une Vie Secrète)

Knowles, Dorothy. *French drama of the inter-war years, 1918-39,* p. 96.

Palmer John. "H.R. Lenormand and the Play of Psychoanalysis." *Nineteenth Century and After,* vol. 100 (Oct., 1926), pp. 599-601.

Sheffer, Eugene. "H.R. Lenormand as a Student of the Personality." *French Rev.,* vol. 7, no. 1 (Nov., 1933), pp. 55-57.

Le Simoun

Knowles, Dorothy. *French drama of the inter-war years, 1918-39,* pp. 94-95.

Time Is a Dream (Le Temps Est un Songe)

Knowles, Dorothy. *French drama of the inter-war years, 1918-39,* pp. 92-93.

White, Kenneth S. "Toward a New Interpretation of Lenormand's Theatrical Ethos." *Modern Drama,* vol. 2, no. 4 (Feb., 1960), pp. 337-342.

Terre de Satan

Knowles, Dorothy. *French drama of the inter-war years, 1918-39,* pp. 100-101.

SIEGFRIED LENZ 1926-

Time of the Guiltless (Zeit der Schuld-Losen)

Garten, H.F. *Modern German drama,* pp. 265-266.

HUGH LEONARD 1926-

Pseud. of John Keyes Byrne

General

Hogan, Robert. *After the Irish renaissance,* p. 186-189.

The Big Birthday

Hogan, Robert. *After the Irish renaissance,* p. 186.

Mick and Mick (All the Nice People)

Hogan, Robert. *After the Irish renaissance,* p. 189.

The Poker Session

Loney, Glenn. "Broadway in Review." *Educational Theatre J.,* vol. 19, no. 4 (Dec., 1967), p. 512.

Stephen D (Adaptation of James Joyce's Portrait of the Artist as a Young Man and Stephen Hero)

Hogan, Robert. *After the Irish renaissance,* 182, 187-188.

Loney, Glenn. "Broadway in Review." *Educational Theatre J.,* vol. 19, no. 4 (Dec., 1967), pp. 512-513.

LEONID LEONOV 1899-

Invasion

Macleod, Joseph. *Actors cross the Volga,* pp. 236-238.

DORIS LESSING 1919-

Each His Own Wilderness

Wellwarth, George. *The theatre of protest and paradox,* p. 249.

BENN LEVY 1900-

The Rape of the Belt

Price, Martin. "The London Season." *Modern Drama,* vol. 1, no. 1 (May, 1958), pp. 53-59.

MELVIN LEVY 1902-

Gold Eagle Guy

Himelstein, Morgan Y. *Drama was a weapon, the left-wing theatre in New York 1929-1941,* pp. 164-166.

SINCLAIR LEWIS 1885-1951

It Can't Happen Here

Himelstein, Morgan Y. *Drama was a weapon, the left-wing theatre in New York 1929-1941,* pp. 98-100.

Dodsworth (Adapted by Sidney Howard)

Flexner, Eleanor. *American playwrights: 1918-1938,* pp. 51-54.

SUZANNE LILAR 1901-

Le Burlador

Mallinson, Vernon. *Modern Belgian literature, 1830-1960,* pp. 191-192.

MANUEL LINARES RIVAS 1867-1938
General

Warren, L.A. *Modern Spanish literature,* vol. 2, pp. 565-571.

Aire de Fuera

Warren, L.A. *Modern Spanish literature,* vol. 2, pp. 567-570.

La Fuerza del Mal

Warren, L.A. *Modern Spanish literature,* vol. 2, pp. 566-567.

La Garra

Warren, L.A. *Modern Spanish literature,* vol. 2, p. 566.

HOWARD LINDSAY 1889-1968
General

Gould, Jean. *Modern American playwrights,* pp. 140-150.

HENRY LIVINGS 1929-
General

Taylor, John Russell. *Anger and after,* pp. 129-135.

The Arson Squad

Taylor, John Russell. *Anger and after,* pp. 130-131.

Big Soft Nellie

Taylor, John Russell. *Anger and after,* pp. 133-135.

Eh?

Gassner, John. "Broadway in Review." *Educational Theatre J.,* vol. 19, no. 1 (Mar., 1967), pp. 82-83.

Giannetti, Louis D. "Henry Livings: A Neglected Voice in the New Drama." *Modern Drama,* vol. 12, no. 1 (May, 1969), pp. 39-44.

Lumley, Frederick. *New trends in 20th-century drama,* pp. 312-313.

Jack's Horrible Luck

Taylor, John Russell. *Anger and after,* pp. 131-133.

Kelly's Eye

Giannetti, Louis D. "Henry Living: A Neglected Voice in the New Drama." *Modern Drama*, vol. 12, no. 1 (May, 1969), pp. 44-48.

Stop It, Whoever You Are

Taylor, John Russell. *Anger and after*, pp. 129-130.

Taylor, John Russell. "Parables in Farce." *Encore*, vol. 9 (May-June, 1962), pp. 33-38.

LADY CHRISTINE LONGFORD

General

Hogan, Robert. *After the Irish renaissance*, pp. 126-132.

FREDERICK LONSDALE 1881-1954

Aren't We All?

Taylor, John Russell. *The rise and fall of the well-made play*, pp. 120-121.

But for the Grace of God

Hobson, Harold. *Theatre*, pp. 6-8.

The Last of Mrs. Cheyney

Taylor, John Russell. *The rise and fall of the well-made play*, pp. 121-122.

On Approval

Taylor, John Russell. *The rise and fall of the well-made play*, pp. 122-123.

JOSE LOPEZ-RUBIO

General

Holt, Marion P. "Lopèz-Rubio's Venture Into Serious Drama." *Hispania*, vol. 49 (1966), pp. 764-768.

Alberto

Holt, Marion P. "Lopèz-Rubio's *Alberto:* Character Revelation and Form." *Modern Drama*, vol. 10, no. 3 (Sept., 1967), pp. 144-150.

TRACY LORD

The Philadelphia Story

O'Hara, Frank H. *Today in American drama,* pp. 127-129.

PIERRE LOUYS 1870-1925
The Girl and the Puppet

MacCarthy, Desmond. *Drama,* pp. 136-140.

ROBERT LOWELL 1917-

Endecott and the Red Cross

Gilman, Richard. "Life Offers No Neat Conclusions." *The New York Times,* May 5, 1968, Sec. 2, pp. 1, 5.

My Kinsman, Major Molineux

Cassell, Richard A. *What is the play?* pp. 459-460, 483-485.

Worth, Katharine J. "The Poets in the American Theatre." *In: American theatre,* pp. 96-97.

The Old Glory

Brustein, Robert. "The New American Playwrights." *In:* Rahv, Philip, ed. *Modern occasions,* pp. 137-138.

Clurman, Harold. *The naked image,* pp. 94-97.

Hochman, Baruch. "Robert Lowell's *The Old Glory." Tulane Drama Rev.,* vol. 11, no. 4 (1967), pp. 127-138.

LAZARO LOZANO GARCIA and CARLOS LOZANO GARCIA

General

Gonzáles Peña, Carlos. *History of Mexican literature,* p. 375.

FRANK LAWRENCE LUCAS 1894-
Land's End

Dent, Alan. *Preludes and studies,* pp. 166-168.

CLAIRE BOOTH LUCE 1903-

Kiss the Boys Goodbye

O'Hara, Frank H. *Today in American drama,* pp. 202-204.

The Women

Sievers, W. David. *Freud on Broadway,* pp. 221-222.

GERMAN LUCO CRUCHAGO 1894-1936

General

Jones, W.K. *Behind Spanish American footlights,* pp. 229-230.

La Viuda de Apablaza

Jones, W.K. *Behind Spanish American footlights,* pp. 229-230.

DOROTHY MacARDLE 1889-

The Old Man

Malone, Andrew E. *The Irish drama,* pp. 269-270.

JOHN BERNARD MacCARTHY

General

Malone, Andrew E. *The Irish drama,* pp. 279-280.

Kinship

Malone, Andrew E. *The Irish drama,* pp. 276-279.

CARSON McCULLERS 1917-1967

General

Dusenbury, Winifred L. *The theme of loneliness in modern American drama,* pp. 57-85.

Phillips, Robert S. "Carson McCullers, 1956-1964: A Selected Checklist." *Bulletin of Bibliography,* vol. 24, no. 5 (Sept.-Dec., 1964), pp. 113-116.

Stewart, Stanley. "Carson McCullers, 1940-1956; A Selected Checklist." *Bulletin of Bibliography (Jan.-April, 1959), pp. 182-185.*

The Ballad of the Sad Cafe (Adapted by Edward Albee)

Anonymous. *America,* vol. 110 (Jan. 4, 1964), p. 26.

Anonymous. "Lonesome Lovers." *Time,* vol. 82, no. 19 (Nov. 8, 1963), p. 67.

Anonymous. *Life* (Feb. 14, 1964), pp. 43-50.

Anonymous. "Too, Too Solid Flesh." *Newsweek* (Nov. 11, 1963), p. 76.

Brustein, Robert. *New Republic,* vol. XLXIX (Nov. 16, 1963), p. 76.

Chapman, John. "Albee's *Ballad of the Sad Cafe* Beautiful, Exciting." New York *Daily News* (Oct. 31, 1963), p. 66.

Clurman, Harold. *The Nation,* vol. 197 (Nov. 23, 1963), pp. 353-354.

Debusscher, Gilbert. *Edward Albee, tradition and renewal,* pp. 60-66.

Gilman, Richard. "Albee's Sad *Ballad." Commonweal,* vol. 74, no. 9 (Nov. 22, 1963), pp. 256-257.

Gottfried, Martin. *A theater divided; the postwar American stage,* pp. 268, 272.

Guernesy, O. *Show* (Jan., 1964), p. 32.

Hardwick, Elizabeth. "One Play, Unbelievably Decadent." *Vogue,* vol. 143, no. 1 (Jan., 1964), p. 20.

Hewes, Henry. "Dismemberment of the Wedding." *Saturday Rev.,* (Nov. 16, 1963), p. 54.

Kerr, Walter. "The Barrier of *The Sad Cafe." The New York Sunday Herald Tribune* Magazine, (Nov. 17, 1963), p. 31.

Kerr, Walter. "Kerr's Critique." New York *Herald Tribune* (Oct. 31, 1963), p. 13.

Kostelanetz, Richard. "Albee's *Sad Cafe." Sewanee Rev.,* vol. 72, no. 4 (Autumn, 1964), pp. 724-726.

Lask, Thomas. "Edward Albee at Ease." *New York Times* (Oct. 27, 1963), p. 3.

Levy, A. "The ABC of Alan Schneider." *New York Times Magazine* (Oct. 20, 1963).

Lewis, Allan. *American plays and playwrights of the contemporary theatre,* pp. 95-96.

McCarten, John. "Tormented Trio." *New Yorker,* vol. 39 (Nov. 9, 1963), p. 95.

McClain, John. "Albee's *Ballad* Sings Rugged Drama of Love." New York *Journal-American* (Oct. 31, 1963), p. 22.

Miller, Jonathan. "A Plausible Forgery." *The New Leader* (Nov. 25, 1963), p. 27.

Nadel, Norman. *"Ballad of the Sad Cafe* Paints Poignant Tale of Loneliness." New York *World-Telegram and Sun* (Oct. 31, 1963), p. 22.

Phillips, Robert S. "Painful Love: Carson McCullers Parable." *Southwest Rev.,* vol. 51 (1966), pp. 80-86.

Rutenberg, Michael E. *Edward Albee: playwright in protest,* pp. 167-179.

Skow, John. "Edward Albee." *Saturday Evening Post* (Jan. 18, 1964), pp. 32-33.

Smith, Michael. "Albee's McCullers." *The Village Voice,* vol. 9, no. 3 (Nov. 7, 1963), pp. 14, 18.

Sontag, Susan. "Going to Theatre." *Partisan Rev.,* vol. 31, no. 1 (Winter, 1964), pp. 95-102.

Taubman, Howard. "Nature of Love: *Sad Cafe* Explores It in Strange Triangle." *New York Times* (Nov. 10, 1963), p. ix.

Taubman, Howard. "Theatre: *Ballad of the Sad Cafe."* *New York Times,* (Oct. 31, 1963), p. 27.

Ulanov, Barry. "Brecht and Albee." *Catholic World, vol. 198* (Jan., 1964), p. 264.

Van Dreele, W.H. "A Master Carpenter." *National Review,* vol. 16 (Jan. 14, 1964), pp. 34-35.

The Member of the Wedding (Adapted by Edward Albee)

Anonymous. *U.S. quarterly book list,* vol. 2 (Sept., 1946), pp. 180-181.

Anonymous. *English,* vol. 11 (Summer, 1957), pp. 185-186.

Baker, W. *School and Society,* vol. 66 (Apr. 8, 1950), pp. 213-214.

Beauvoir, Simone de. *The second sex.* pp. 280, 285-286.

Brown, John Mason. *Saturday Rev.,* vol. 33 (Jan. 28, 1950), pp. 27-29.

Clurman, Harold. *Lies like truth,* pp. 62-64.

Dusenbury, Winifred L. *The theme of loneliness in modern American drama,* pp. 58-67.

Hewes, Henry. "Dismemberment of the Wedding." *Saturday Rev.,* vol. 46 (Nov. 16, 1963), p. 54.

Phillips, Robert S. "The Gothic Architecture of *The Member of the Wedding."* *Renascence,* vol. 16, no. 2 (Winter, 1964), pp. 59-72.

Sievers, W. David. *Freud on Broadway,* pp. 431-433.

Trewin, J.C. *Illustrated London News,* vol. 230 (Feb. 16, 1957), p. 276.

Worsley, T.C. *New Statesman and Nation,* vol. 53 (Feb. 16, 1957), p. 276.

The Square Root of Wonderful

Anonymous. *Booklist,* vol. 55 (Sept. 1, 1958) p. 16.

Anonymous. *Catholic World,* vol. 186 (Jan., 1958), p. 306.

Anonymous. *Kirkus,* vol. 26 (May 1, 1958), p. 348.

Anonymous. *Times Literary Supplement* (London), Feb. 27, 1959.

Freedley, George. *Library J.,* vol. 83 (June 1, 1958), p. 1800.

DONAGH MacDONAGH 1912-

General

Hogan, Robert. *After the Irish renaissance,* pp. 154-158.

Hogan, Robert G., ed. *Seven Irish plays, 1946-1964,* pp. 11-12.

Happy As Larry

Hobson, Harold. *Theatre,* pp. 130-132.

Hogan, Robert. *After the Irish renaissance,* pp. 154-156.

J. P. McEVOY

God Loves Us

Turner, Darwin T. "Jazz-Vaudeville Drama in the Twenties." *Educational Theatre J.,* vol. 11 (1959), pp. 113-115.

PERCY McKAYE 1875-1956

General

Miller, Nellie Burget. *The living drama,* pp. 400-401.

The Scarecrow

Downer, Alan S. *Fifty years of American drama, 1900-1950,* pp. 35-38.

Gassner, John. "Introduction." *Best plays of the early American theatre from the beginning to 1916,* pp. xlv-xlvi.

Miller, Nellie Burget. *The living drama,* pp. 401-404.

WALTER MACKEN 1915-

General

Hogan, Robert. *After the Irish renaissance,* pp. 65-70.

ARCHIBALD MacLEISH 1892-

General

Gerstenberger, Donna. "Verse Drama in America: 1916-1939." *Modern Drama,* vol. 6, no. 3 (Dec., 1963), pp. 309-322.

Gerstenberger, Donna. "Verse Drama in America. *"In:* Meserve, Walter J., ed. *Discussions of American drama,* pp. 43-46.

Sickels, E.M. "MacLeish and the Fortunate Fall." *American Literature,* vol. 35 (May, 1963), pp. 205-217.

J.B.

Abel Lionel. *Metatheatre, a new view of dramatic form,* pp. 116-118.

Broussard, Louis. *American drama...,* pp. 122-127.

Campbell, Colin C. "The Transformation of Biblical Myth: MacLeish's Use of Adam and Job Stories." *In:* Slote, Bernice, ed. *Myth and symbol,* pp. 82-88.

Christensen, Parley A. *"J. B.,* the Critics, and Me." *Western Humanities Rev.,* vol. 15, no. 2 (Spring, 1961), pp. 111-126.

D'Arcy, Martin C. *"J. B.,* Wrong Answer to the Problem of Evil." *Catholic World,* vol. 190, no. 1,136 (Nov., 1959), pp. 81-85.

Donoghue, Denis. *The third voice: modern British and American verse drama,* pp. 207-212.

Eberhart, Richard. "Outer and Inner Verse Drama." *Virginia Q., Rev.,* vol. 34, no. 4 (Autumn, 1958), pp. 618-623.

Fickert, Kurt J. "Durrenmatt's *The Visit* and Job." *Books Abroad,* vol. 41, no. 4 (Autumn, 1967), pp. 389-392.

Gassner, John. *Theatre at the crossroads,* pp. 298-305.

Grebstein, Sheldon Norman. *"J.B.* and the Problems of Evil." *Univ. of Kansas City Rev.,* vol, 24, no. 4 (Summer, 1963), pp. 253-261.

Hamilton, Kenneth. "The Patience of *J.B.* " Dalhousie Rev., vol. 41 (Spring, 1961), pp. 32-39.

Lewis, Allan. *American plays and playwrights of the contemporary theatre,* pp. 120-125.

MacLeish, Andrew. "The Poet's Three Comforters: *J. B.* and the Critics." *Modern Drama,* vol. 2, no. 3 (Dec. 1959), pp. 224-230.

MacLeish, Archibald. "About a Trespass on a Monument." *In:* Frenz, Horst. *American playwrights on drama,* pp. 154-159. (Reprinted from the drama section of *The New York Times,* Dec. 7, 1958).

Montgomery, Marion. "On First Looking Into Archibald MacLeish's Play in Verse, *J. B.*" *Modern Drama,* vol. 2, no. 3 (Dec. 1959), pp. 231-242.

Phillips, Elizabeth C. *Modern American drama,* pp. 107-108.

Roston, Murray. *Biblical drama in England from the Middle Ages to the present day,* pp. 308-310, 313-321.

Siegel, Ben. "Miracle on Broadway: On the Box-Office Magic of the Bible." *Modern Drama,* vol. 2 (May, 1959), pp. 45-46.

Weales, Gerald. *American drama since World War II,* pp. 186-190.

• Weiner, Herbert. "Job on Broadway: MacLeish's Man and the Bible's." *Commentary,* vol. 27, no. 2 (Feb., 1959), pp. 153-158.

Worth, Katharine J. "The Poets in the American Theatre." *In: American Theatre,* pp. 94-95.

Nobodaddy

Campbell, Colin C. "The Transformation of Biblical Myth: MacLeish's Use of Adam and Job Stories." *In:* Slote, Bernice, ed. *Myth and symbol,* pp. 79-81.

Matthews, Honor. *The primal curse,* pp. 189-190.

Panic

Himelstein, Morgan Y. *Drama was a weapon, the left-wing theatre in New York, 1929-1941,* pp. 194-195.

Worth, Katharine J. "The Poets in the American Theatre." *In: American theatre,* p. 92.

This Music Crept by Me on the Water

Donoghue, Denis. *The third voice: modern British and American verse drama,* pp. 195-205.

Worth, Katharine J. "The Poets in the American Theatre." *In: American theatre,* pp. 89-90, 91-92, 93-94.

MICHAEL MacLIAMMOIR 1909-

General

Hogan, Robert. *After the Irish renaissance,* pp. 112-119.

Ill Met by Moonlight

Hobson, Harold. *Theatre,* pp. 43-45.

Hogan, Robert. *After the Irish renaissance,* pp. 116-118.

BRYAN MacMAHON 1909-

General

Hogan, Robert. *After the Irish renaissance,* pp. 70-74.

Hogan, Robert G., ed. *Seven Irish plays, 1946-1964,* pp. 183-185.

The Honey Spike

Hogan, Robert. *After the Irish renaissance,* pp. 73-74.

Song of the Anvil

Hogan, Robert. *After the Irish renaissance,* pp. 71-73.

BRINSLEY MacNAMARA 1891-1963
(real name John Weldon)

General

Hogan, Robert. *After the Irish renaissance,* pp. 32-33.

The Glorious Uncertainty

Malone, Andrew E. *The Irish drama,* p. 207.

The Land for the People

Malone, Andrew E. *The Irish drama,* pp. 206-207.

Look at the Heffermans!

Malone, Andrew E. *The Irish drama,* p. 207.

The Master

Malone, Andrew E. *The Irish drama,* pp. 207-209.

LOUIS MacNEICE 1907-1963

General

Hazard, Forrest Earl. "The Auden Group and the Group Theatre: the dramatic theories and practices of Rupert Doone, W.H. Auden, Christopher Isherwood, Louis MacNeice, and Cecil Day Lewis." *Dissertation Abstracts,* vol. 25 (1964), (U. of Wisconsin).

EDWARD McNULTY

The Lord Mayor

Malone, Andrew E. *The Irish drama,* pp. 236-237.

TERENCE MacSWINEY

The Revolutionist

Malone, Andrew E. *The Irish drama,* pp. 270-271.

MAESTRO SOLNES
See Planchart, Julio

MAURICE MAETERLINCK 1862-1949

General

Anonymous. "Maeterlinck's New Type of Heroine." *Current Literature,* vol. 48, no. 5 (May, 1910), pp. 554-558.

Brashear, Robert. "Maurice Maeterlinck and His *Musee Grevin.*" *French Rev.,* vol. 40, no. 3 (Dec., 1966), pp. 347-351.

Burton, Richard. "Maurice Maeterlinck: A Dramatic Impressionist." *Atlantic Monthly,* vol. 74 (Nov., 1894), pp. 672-680.

Cooper, Frederic T. "Maeterlinck and the Forbidden Play." *Bookman,* vol. 16 (Sept., 1902), pp. 46-49.

Chandler, Frank Wadleigh. *The contemporary drama of France,* pp. 294-306.

Daniels, May. *The French drama of the unspoken,* pp. 46-55, 92-99.

Dukes, Ashley. *Modern dramatists,* pp. 242-254.

Hamilton, Clayton. *Conversations on contemporary drama,* pp. 150-159, 166-170, 172-174.

Heller, Otto. *Prophets of dissent,* pp. 3-68.

Henderson, Archibald. *European dramatists,* pp. 199-250.

Henderson, Archibald. "Maurice Maeterlinck as a Dramatic Artist." *Sewanee Rev.,* vol. 12, no. 2 (Apr., 1904), pp. 207-216.

Jervey, Huger. "Maeterlinck Versus the Continental Drama." *Sewanee Rev.,* vol. 11, no. 2 (Apr., 1903), pp. 187-204.

Lamm, Martin. *Modern drama,* pp. 152-166.

Leblanc-Maeterlinck, Georgette (Mme). "The Later Heroines of Maurice Maeterlinck." *Fortnightly Rev.,* vol. 87, n.s. (Jan., 1910), pp. 48-56.

Mahony, Patrick. "The Maeterlinck Centenary, 1862-1962." *Personalist,* vol. 43, no. 4 (Oct., 1962), pp. 487-492.

Malcolm, J.E. "Maeterlinck and Static Drama." *English,* vol. 6, no. 34 (Spring, 1947), pp. 183-186.

Mallinson, Vernon. *Modern Belgian literature, 1830-1960,* pp. 79-87.

Marble, Annie Russell. *The Nobel Prize winners in literature,* pp. 148-158.

Miller, Nellie Burget. *The living drama,* pp. 237-242.

Palleske, S.O. "The Dramatic Technique of Maurice Maeterlinck." *French Rev.,* vol. 14, no. 6 (May, 1941), pp. 500-504.

Phelps, William Lyon. *Essays on modern dramatists,* pp. 179-228.

Phelps, William Lyon. "An Estimate of Maeterlinck." *North American Rev.,* vol. 213, no. 1 (Jan., 1921), pp. 98-108.

Scott, Evelyn. "A Critic of the Threshold." *Dial,* vol. 68 (Mar., 1920), pp. 311-325.

Smith, Hugh A. *Main currents, modern French drama,* pp. 283-307.

Soissons, S.C. de. "Maeterlinck as a Reformer of the Drama." *Contemporary Rev.,* vol. 86 (Nov., 1904), pp. 699-708.

Strindberg, August. *Open letters to the intimate theater,* pp. 299-301, 305.

Turquet-Milnes, G. *Some modern Belgian writers,* pp. 25-45.

Witkowski, Georg. *German drama of the nineteenth century,* pp. 182-184.

Aglavaine et Selysette

Anonymous. "Maeterlinck Propounds the Emotional Triangle." *Current Literature,* vol. 52 (Mar. 1912), pp. 332-335.

Daniels, May. *The French drama of the unspoken,* pp. 89-92.

Falk, Eugene H. *Renunciation as a tragic focus,* pp. 73-81.

Freeman, John. *The moderns; essays in literary criticism;* pp. 175-176.

Alladine and Palomides

Daniels, May. *The French drama of the unspoken,* pp. 78-83.

The Betrothal (Les Fiançailles)

Anonymous. "Maeterlinck's New Plan for Picking a Wife." *Literary Digest,* vol. 59, no. 10 (Dec. 7, 1918), pp. 28-29.

Anonymous. *New Republic,* vol. 17 (Jan. 11, 1919) p. 313.

Anonymous. *Spectator,* vol. 126 (Jan. 15, 1921), pp. 78-79.

Gilman, Lawrence. *North American Rev.,* vol. 209 (Jan., 1919), pp. 117-123.

Hamilton, Clayton. *Seen on the stage. pp. 114-121.*

The Blind (Les Aveugles)

Daniels, E.D. "A Cursory View of Symbolism in Maeterlinck's *The Blind." Poet Lore,* vol. 13, no. 4 (1901), pp. 554-560.

Daniels, May. *The French drama of the unspoken,* pp. 67-70.

Rose, H. *The Quest,* vol. 3 (1911), pp. 120-133.

The Blue Bird (L'Oiseau Bleu)

Anonymous. *Current Literature,* vol. 49 (Nov., 1910), pp. 548-551.

Anonymous. *Dial,* vol. 46 (May 1, 1909), pp. 296-297.

Anonymous. *Everybody's Mag.,* vol. 24, no. 1 (Jan., 1911), pp. 119-120.

Anonymous. *Nation,* vol. 88 (Apr. 8, 1909), pp. 366-367.

Anonymous. *Spectator,* vol. 104 (Jan. 1, 1910), pp. 18-19.

Chaudhury, J. *Calcutta Rev.* (July, 1933), pp. 106-123.

Freeman, John. *The moderns; essays in literary criticism,* pp. 185-186.

Gilder, Jeannette L. "The American Production of Maeterlinck's *Blue Bird." Rev. of Reviews,* vol. 42, no. 6 (Dec. 1910) pp. 689-697.

Hamblen, Emily S. "The Significance of Maeterlink's *Bluebird.*" *Poet Lore,* vol. 22 (Nov., 1911), pp. 460-468.

Phelps, William Lyon. *Essays on modern dramatists,* pp. 219-224.

Roof, Katharine M. *"The Blue Bird:* Maeterlinck's Symbolic Fairy Story: The Production at the New Theater." *Craftsman,* vol. 19. no. 3 (Dec., 1910), pp. 249-261.

Stanislavsky, Constantin S. "Stanislavsky to His Players at the First Rehearsal of *The Blue Bird.*" *Theatre Arts,* vol. 7 (Jan., 1923), pp. 29-40.

Syford, Ethel. *New England Mag.,* n.s., vol. 43, no. 1 (Sept., 1910), pp. 36-42.

Bluebeard and Aryan (Ariane et Barbebleu)

Soissons, S.C. de. *Fortnightly Rev.,* vol. 74 (Dec. 1900), pp. 994-997.

The Burgomaster of Stilemonde (Le Bourgmestre de Stilmonde)

Anonymous. "Maeterlinck's War Play." *Literary Digest,* vol. 60, no. 8 (Feb. 22, 1919), pp. 31-32.

Anonymous. *Nation,* vol. 108 (Apr. 5, 1919), p. 511.

Anonymous. "A War Play by Maeterlinck." *Living Age,* vol. 299 (Nov. 16, 1918), pp. 440-442.

The Death of Tintagiles (La Mort de Tintagiles)

Daniels, May. *The French drama of the unspoken,* pp. 86-88.

Hamilton, Clayton. *Conversations on contemporary drama,* pp. 170-172.

MacCarthy, Desmond. *Drama,* pp. 54-60.

The Home (L'Interieur)

Daniels, May. *The French drama of the unspoken,* pp. 83-85.

Freeman, John. *The moderns; essays in literary criticism,* p. 184.

The Intruder (L'Intruse)

Daniels, May. *The French drama of the unspoken,* pp. 62-67.

Joyzelle

Freeman, John. *The moderns; essays in literary critism,* pp. 169-173.

Gerothwohl, Maurice. *Fortnightly Rev.,* vol. 80 (July, 1903), pp. 76-87.

Huneker, James G. *Lamp,* vol. 27 (Jan., 1904), pp. 581-586.

Mukherji, M. *Calcutta Rev.* (Oct., 1935), pp. 50-57.

Mary Magdaleine (Marie Magdeleine)

Anonymous. *Current Literature,* vol. 49 (Dec., 1910), pp. 667-669.

Davis, Hartley. *Everybody's Mag.,* vol. 24, no. 3 (Mar., 1911), pp. 408-412.

Freeman, John. *The moderns; essays in literary criticism,* pp. 161-169.

Hamilton, Clayton. *Bookman,* vol. 32, no. 6 (Feb., 1911), pp. 602-604.

Syford, Ethel. "Maeterlinck's *Mary Magdaleine.*" *New England Mag.,* n.s., vol. 43, no. 4 (Jan., 1911), pp. 485-491.

Monna Vanna

Dukes, Ashley. *Modern dramatists,* pp. 246-254.

Freeman, John. *The moderns; essays in literary criticism,* pp. 173-175.

Gerothwohl, Maurice A. "M. Maeterlinck's New Play." *Monthly Rev.,* vol. 8 (June, 1902), pp. 121-134.

Hale, Edward E., Jr. "A Drama of Justice and Humanity." *Dial,* vol. 35 (Oct. 16, 1903), pp. 257-258.

Lamm, Martin. *Modern drama,* pp. 163-164.

Lord, Walter F. "The Reader of Plays to the Rescue." *Nineteenth Century and After,* vol. 52 (July, 1902), pp. 72-75; (Aug., 1902), pp. 289-291.

Phelps, William Lyon. *Essays on modern dramatists,* pp. 183-190, 214-218.

Pelleas and Melisande (Pélleas et Mélisande)

Beerbohm, Max. *Saturday Rev.,* vol. 85 (June 18, 1898), pp. 843-846.

Brainerd, Gertrude G. "The Paolo and Francesca Theme in Modern Drama; D'Annunzio, Phillips, Maeterlinck, Echegaray." *Poet Lore,* vol. 27, no. 4 (July, 1916), pp. 391-395.

Daniels, May. *The French drama of the unspoken,* pp. 73-78.

Evans, Calvin. "Maeterlinck and the Quest for a Mystic Tragedy of the Twentieth Century." *Modern Drama,* vol. 4, no. 1 (May, 1961), pp. 54-59.

Freeman, John. *The moderns; essays in literary criticism,* pp. 180-183.

Kellock, Harold. *Freeman,* vol. 8 (Dec. 19, 1923), pp. 353-354.

Kosove, Joan P. "Maeterlinck's *Pélleas et Mélisande." French Rev.,* vol. 40 (1967), pp. 781-784.

Leblanc-Maeterlinck, Georgette (Mme). "Our Production of Pelleas and Melisande." *Century,* vol. 81, no. 3 (Jan., 1911), pp. 325-337.

Lewisohn, Ludwig. *Nation,* vol. 117 (Dec. 26, 1923), pp. 746-747.

Lilley, George."Debussy's *Pélleas et Mélisande." Contemporary Rev.,* vol. 99 (Jan., 1911), pp. 61-70. *Also in: Living Age,* vol. 268 (Feb. 25, 1911), pp. 475-483.

Miller, Nellie Burget. *The living drama,* pp. 242-244.

Porter, Charlotte. "Maurice Maeterlinck: Dramatist of a New Method." *Poet Lore,* vol. 5, no. 3 (1893), pp. 151-157.

Woollcott, Alexander. *Enchanted aisles,* pp. 224-226.

La Princesse Maleine

Daniels, May. *The French drama of the unspoken,* pp. 55-62.

Freeman, John. *The moderns; essays in literary criticism,* pp. 176-180.

Lamm, Martin. *Modern drama,* pp. 157-158.

Phelps, William Lyon. *Essays on modern dramatists,* pp. 194-196.

The Seven Princesses (Les Sept Princesses)

Daniels, May. *The French drama of the unspoken,* pp. 70-72.

Sister Beatrice (Soeur Béatrice)

Phelps, William Lyon. *Essays on modern dramatists,* pp. 209-214.

MILES MALLESON 1888-

The Fanatics

Balmforth, Ramsden. *The problem-play and its influence on modern thought and life,* pp. 55-62.

ALBERT MALTZ 1908-

Black Pit

Himelstein, Morgan Y. *Drama was a weapon, the left-wing theatre in New York 1929-1941,* pp. 63-65.

Private Hicks

Himelstein, Morgan Y. *Drama was a weapon, the left-wing theatre in New York 1929-1941,* p. 43.

WILLIAM MANHOFF

The Owl and the Pussycat

Gottfried, Martin. *A theater divided; the postwar American stage,* pp. 76-77.

KLAUS MANN 1906-1949

Anja und Esther

Garten, H.F. *Modern German drama,* p. 184.

MARY MANNING

General

Hogan, Robert. *After the Irish renaissance,* pp. 119-122.

Youth's The Season

Hogan, Robert. *After the Irish renaissance,* pp. 120-121.

FELICIEN MARCEAU

The Egg

Brustein, Robert. *Seasons of discontent,* pp. 130-132.

GABRIEL MARCEL 1887-

General

Cooper, Nina Ruth. "A study of the theatre of Gabriel Marcel." *Dissertation Abstracts,* vol. 26, no. 12 (June, 1966) (Univ. of Texas).

Farraher, Anne T. "The nature of man's relationships as exemplified in the plays of Gabriel Marcel." *Dissertation Abstracts,* vol. 20, no. 11 (May, 1960), pp. 4394-4395.

Knowles, Dorothy. *French drama of the inter-war years, 1918-39,* pp. 247-250.

Lumley, Frederick. *New trends in 20th century drama,* pp. 350-353.

Lumley, Frederick. *Trends in 20th century drama,* pp. 236-239.

McGowan, F.A. "Marcel's Early Drama: A Mediation." *Renascence,* vol. 15, no. 4 (Summer, 1963), pp. 183-194.

Speaight, Robert. "Philosophy in the French Theatre Today." *Listener,* vol. 49, no 1251 (Feb. 19, 1953), pp. 308-309.

Ariadne

Worsley, T.C. *New Statesman,* vol. 56 (Aug. 30, 1958), p. 246.

La Chapelle Ardente

Geissman, Erwin W. *Renascence,* vol. 6 (Autumn, 1953), p 53.

Hatzfeld, Helmut. *Trends and styles in twentieth-century French literature,* p. 203.

Jarrett-Kerr, Martin. "The Dramatic Philosophy of Gabriel Marcel." *Dublin Rev.,* vol. 222 (Spring, 1949), pp. 47-48.

Knowles, Dorothy. *French drama of the inter-war years, 1918-39,* pp. 250-251, 253.

Marcel, Gabriel. *The existential background of human dignity,* pp. 103-107.

Le Chemin de Crete

Allen, E.L. "Gabriel Marcel, a Theatre of Sincerity." *Contemporary Rev.,* vol. 181, no. 1034 (Feb., 1952), p. 101.

Hatzfeld, Helmut. *Trends and styles in twentieth-century French literature,* p. 203.

Jarrett-Kerr, Martin. "The Dramatic Philosophy of Gabriel Marcel." *Dublin Rev.,* vol. 222 (Spring, 1949), pp. 46-47.

Le Coeur des Autres

Hatzfeld, Helmut. *Trends and styles in twentieth-century French literature,* p. 205.

Les Coeurs Avides (La Soif)

Geissman, Erwin W. "Marcel's Limitations." *Renascence,* vol. 7 (Spring, 1955), pp. 156-157.

Le Dard

Jarrett-Kerr, Martin. "The Dramatic Philosophy of Gabriel Marcel." *Dublin Rev.,* vol. 222 (Spring, 1949), pp. 52-53.

Marcel, Gabriel. *The existential background of human dignity,* pp. 116-122.

L'Emissaire

Allen E.L. "Gabriel Marcel, a Theatre of Sincerity." *Contemporary Rev.,* vol. 181, no 1034 (Feb., 1952), pp. 102-103.

Le Fanal

Jarrett-Kerr, Martin. "The Dramatic Philosophy of Gabriel Marcel." *Dublin Rev.,* vol. 222 (Spring, 1949), pp. 49-50.

La Grace

Hatzfeld, Helmut. *Trends and styles in twentieth-century French literature,* p. 202.

Un Homme de Dieu

Allen, E.L. "Gabriel Marcel, a Theatre of Sincerity." *Contemporary Rev.,* vol. 181, no. 1034 (Feb., 1952), pp. 99-101.

Jarrett-Kerr, Martin. "The Dramatic Philosophy of Gabriel Marcel." *Dublin* Rev., vol. 222 (Spring, 1949), pp. 45-46.

Knowles, Dorothy. *French drama of the inter-war years, 1918-39,* pp. 251-253.

Marcel, Gabriel. *The existential background of human dignity,* pp. 108-111.

L'Horizon

Jarrett-Kerr, Martin. "The Dramatic Philosophy of Gabriel Marcel." *Dublin Rev.,* vol. 222 (Spring, 1949), pp. 50-52.

Knowles, Dorothy. *French drama of the inter-war years, 1918-39,* pp. 253-254.

L'Iconoclaste

Hatzfeld, Helmut. *Trends and styles in twentieth-century French literature,* p. 204.

Marcel, Gabriel. *The existential background of human dignity,* pp. 50-53.

Mon Temps N'est Pas le Vôtre

Knowles, Dorothy. *French drama of the inter-war years, 1918-39,* pp. 257.

Le Monde Cassé

Allen, E.L. "Gabriel Marcel; a Theatre of Sincerity." *Contemporary Rev.,* vol. 181, no. 1034 (Feb., 1952), pp. 101-102.

Knowles, Dorothy. *French drama of the inter-war years, 1918-39,* pp. 254-255.

Marcel, Gabriel. *The existential background of human dignity,* pp. 90-93.

Le Mort de Demain

Hatzfeld, Helmut. *Trends and styles in twentieth-century French literature,* pp. 202-203.

Le Quatuor en la Dièse

Hatzfeld, Helmut. *Trends and styles in twentieth century French literature,* p. 204.

Jarrett-Kerr, Martin. "The Dramatic Philosophy of Gabriel Marcel." *Dublin Rev.,* vol. 222 (Spring, 1949), pp. 48-49.

Marcel, Gabriel. *The existential background of human dignity,* pp. 48-50.

Le Regard Neuf

Hatzfeld, Helmut. *Trends and styles in twentieth-century French literature,* p. 204.

Rome N'est Plus dans Rome

Geissman, Erwin W. *Renascence,* vol. 5 (Autumn, 1952), pp. 91-93.

Hatzfeld, Helmut. *Trends and styles in twentieth-century French literature,* p. 205.

Knowles, Dorothy. *French drama of the inter-war years, 1918-39,* p. 256.

Lumley, Frederick. *New trends in 20th century drama,* pp. 351-353.

Le Signe de la Croix

Knowles, Dorothy. *French drama of the inter-war years, 1918-39,* p. 256.

La Soif

Ralston, Zachary Taylor. *Gabriel Marcel's paradoxical expression of mystery; a stylistic study of La Soif.* Dissertation, Catholic Univ. Washington, D.C., 1961.

FRANK MARCUS

The Killing of Sister George

Browne, E. Martin. "Theatre Abroad." *Drama Survey,* vol. 5, no. 2 (Summer, 1966), pp. 193-194.

Gassner, John. "Broadway in Review." *Educational Theatre J.,* vol. 19, no. 1 (Mar., 1967), pp. 83-84.

FRANCESCO T. MARINETTI

General

Goldberg, Isaac. *The drama of transition,* pp. 160-172.

LEO MARKS

The Girl Who Couldn't Quite

Hobson, Harold. *Theatre,* pp. 115-118.

JOHN P. MARQUAND 1893-1960

Point of No Return (Adapted by Paul Osborn)

Gassner, John. *Theater at the crossroads,* pp. 146-149.

Sievers, W. David. *Freud on Broadway,* pp. 339-340.

RENE MARQUES

General

Franco, Jean. *The modern culture of Latin America,* pp. 234-235, 248.

Jones, W.K. *Behind Spanish American footlights,* pp. 373-376.

Pilditch, Charles R. "A study of the literary works of René Marqués from 1948 to 1962." *Dissertation Abstracts,* vol. 27 (1966), 1833A (Rutgers).

The Little Cart (La Carreta)

Anderson Imbert, Enrique. *Spanish-American literature: a history,* p. 539.

Jones, W.K. *Behind Spanish American footlights,* p. 374.

Un Niño Azul para Esa Sombra

Jones, W.K. *Behind Spanish American footlights,* pp. 375-376.

Palm Sunday

Jones, W.K. *Behind Spanish American footlights,* p. 374.

The Sun and the MacDonalds (El Sol y los MacDonald)

Jones, W.K. *Behind Spanish American footlights,* pp. 373-374.

ROGER MARTIN DU GARD 1881-1958

Un Taciturne

Jones, Robert Emmet. *The alienated hero in modern French drama,* pp. 36-43.

Knowles, Dorothy. *French drama of the inter-war years,* p. 110.

GREGORIO MARTINEZ SIERRA 1881-1947

General

Boyd, E.A. *Studies from ten literatures,* pp. 114-119.

Chandler, F.W. *Modern continental playwrights,* pp. 487-502.

Corrigan, Robert W., ed. *Masterpieces of the modern Spanish theatre,* pp. 276-277.

Douglas, Frances. "Gregorio Martinez Sierra, Stylist and Romantic Interpreter. " *Hispania,* vol. 5 (Nov., 1922), pp. 257-268.

Mercer, Lucille E. "Martinez Sierra's conception of woman's role in modern society." *Dissertation Abstracts,* no. 34 (1941), 415-420 (Ohio State Univ.).

O'Connor, Patricia Walker. *Women in the theatre of Gregorio Martinez Sierra.*

Starkie, Walter. "Gregorio Martinez Sierra and Modern Spanish Drama." *Contemporary Rev.,* vol. 125 (Feb., 1924), pp. 198-205.

Underhill, John Garrett. "An Introduction to the Plays of G. Martinez Sierra." *In:* Corrigan, Robert W., Ed. *Masterpieces of modern Spanish theatre,* pp. 279-288. (Reprinted from Introduction by John Garret Underhill to *The plays of G. Martinez Sierra,* Dutton, 1951.)

Warren, L.A. *Modern Spanish literature,* vol. 2, pp. 577-584.

Young, Raymond A. "The Heroines of Benavente and Martinez Sierra." *In:* MacLean, J. Beattie, and R. W. Baldner, eds. *Proceedings: Pacific Northwest Conference on Foreign Languages. Seventeenth Annual Meeting, April 15-16, 1966.* (U. of Victoria), vol. 17, pp. 193-200.

Cradle Song

MacCarthy, Desmond. *Drama,* pp. 334-337.

The Kingdom of God (El Reino de Dios)

MacCarthy, Desmond. *Drama,* pp. 106-109.

Young, Stark. *Immortal shadows,* pp. 101-105.

Nuestra Esperanza

Warren, L.A. *Modern Spanish literature,* vol. 2, pp. 583-584.

Primavera en Otoño

Warren, L.A. *Modern Spanish literature,* vol. 2, pp. 582-583.

FAUSTO MARIA MARTINI 1886-1931

Ridi, Pagliaccio

Goldberg, Isaac. *The drama of transition,* pp. 175-179.

EDWARD MARTYN 1859-1923

General

Boyd, Ernest. *Ireland's literary renaissance,* pp. 289-294, 302-306.

Malone, Andrew E. *The Irish drama,* pp. 61-69, 256-257

Saddlemyer, Ann. "All Art Is a Collaboration? George Moore and Edward Martyn." *In:* Skelton, Robin, ed. *The world of W.B. Yeats,* pp. 203-208, 212-213.

Setterquist, Jan. *Ibsen and the beginnings of Anglo-Irish drama. II. Edward Martyn,* pp. 13-23.

Williams, Harold. *Modern English writers,* pp. 199-200.

The Bending of the Bough (Adapted by George Moore and W.B. Yeats)

Boyd, Ernest. *Ireland's literary renaissance,* pp. 298-299.

Saddlemyer, Ann. "All Art Is a Collaboration? George Moore and Edward Martyn." *In:* Skelton, Robin, ed. *The world of W.B. Yeats,* pp. 210-212.

The Dream Physician

Malone, Andrew E. *The Irish drama,* pp. 261-262.

The Enchanted Sea

Boyd, Ernest. *Ireland's literary renaissance,* pp. 299-300.

Malone, Andrew E. *The Irish drama,* pp. 260-261.

Setterquist, Jan. *Ibsen and the beginning of Anglo-Irish drama. II. Edward Martyn,* pp. 65-79, 99.

Grangecolman

Boyd, Ernest. *Ireland's literary renaissance,* pp. 300-302.

Malone, Andrew E. *The Irish drama,* p. 261.

Setterquist, Jan. *Ibsen and the beginnings of Anglo-Irish drama. II. Edward Martyn,* pp. 80-92; 100.

The Heather Field

Boyd, Ernest. *Ireland's literary renaissance,* pp. 294-296.

Malone, Andrew E. *The Irish drama,* pp. 257-258.

Saddlemyer, Ann. "All Art Is a Collaboration? George Moore and Edward Martyn." *In:* Skelton, Robin, ed. *The world of W.B. Yeats,* pp. 208-209.

Setterquist, Jan. *Ibsen and the beginnings of Anglo-Irish drama. II. Edward Martyn,* pp. 24-40, 44, 51, 71, 99, 101.

Maeve

Boyd, Ernest. *Ireland's literary renaissance,* pp. 296-297.

Malone, Andrew E. *The Irish drama,* pp. 258-260.

Saddlemyer, Ann. "All Art Is a Collaboration? George Moore and Edward Martyn." *In:* Skelton, Robin, ed. *The world of W.B. Yeats,* pp. 209-210.

Setterquist, Jan. *Ibsen and the beginnings of Anglo-Irish drama. II. Edward Martyn,* pp. 41-55, 75, 99.

The Place Hunters

Boyd, Ernest. *Ireland's literary renaissance,* p. 300.

The Tale of a Town

Saddlemyer, Ann. "All Art Is a Collaboration? George Moore and Edward Martyn." *In:* Skelton, Robin, ed. *The world of W.B. Yeats,* p. 210.

Setterquist, Jan. *Ibsen and the beginnings of Anglo-Irish drama. II. Edward Martyn,* pp. 56-64, 99, 100.

HENRY MARX

L'Homme en Marche

Knowles, Dorothy. *French drama of the inter-war years, 1918-39,* p. 247.

JOHN MASEFIELD 1878-1967

General

Montague, Charles E. *Dramatic values,* pp. 197-206.

Williams, Harold. *Modern English writers,* pp. 262-263.

The Coming of Christ

Eastman, Fred. *Christ in the drama,* pp. 73-78.

Spanos, William V. *The Christian tradition in modern British verse drama,* pp. 137-145.

A King's Daughter

Roston, Murray. *Biblical drama in England from the Middle Ages to the present day,* pp. 248-250.

EDGAR LEE MASTERS 1869-1950

General

Hartley, Lois. "The Early Plays of Edgar Lee Masters." *Ball State Univ. Forum,* vol. 7, no. 2 (Spring, 1966), pp. 26-38.

Althea

Hartley, Lois. "The Early Plays of Edgar Lee Masters." *Ball State Univ. Forum,* vol. 7, no. 2 (Spring, 1966), pp. 28-29.

The Bread of Idleness

Hartley, Lois. "The Early Plays of Edgar Lee Masters." *Ball State Univ. Forum* vol. 7, no. 2 (Spring, 1966), pp. 36-37.

Eileen

Hartley, Lois. "The Early Plays of Edgar Lee Masters." *Ball State Univ. Forum,* vol. 7, no. 2 (Spring, 1966), pp. 32-34, 35.

The Leaves of the Tree

Hartley, Lois. "The Early Plays of Edgar Lee Masters." *Ball State Univ. Forum,* vol. 7, no. 2 (Spring, 1966), pp. 30-32, 38.

The Locket

Hartley, Lois. "The Early Plays of Edgar Lee Masters." *Ball State Univ. Forum,* vol. 7, no. 2 (Spring, 1966), pp. 32, 35-36.

Maximilian

Hartley, Lois. "The Early Plays of Edgar Lee Masters." *Ball State Univ. Forum,* vol. 7, no. 2 (Spring, 1966), pp. 26-28, 37.

The Trifler

Hartley, Lois. "The Early Plays of Edgar Lee Masters." *Ball State Univ. Forum,* vol. 7, no. 2 (Spring, 1966), pp. 29-30.

WILLIAM SOMERSET MAUGHAM 1874-1965

General

Barnes, Ronald E. *The dramatic comedy of William Somerset Maugham,* pp. 9-44, 51-53, 59-60, 64-67, 76-82, 84-86, 89-96, 98-100, 102-114, 116-117, 130-132, 135-140, 141-144, 146-158.

Ervine, St. John. "Maugham the Playwright." *In:* Jonas, Klaus W., ed. *The world of Somerset Maugham,* pp. 142-148, 150-153.

Fielden, John Seward. "The Ibsenite Maugham." *Modern Drama,* vol. 4, no. 2 (Sept., 1961), pp. 138-151.

Montague, Clifford M. "William Somerset Maugham—Dramatist." *Poet Lore,* vol. 47, no. 1 (Spring, 1941), pp. 40-55.

Naik, M.K. *W. Somerset Maugham,* pp. 28-45, 66-72, 102-107, 165-170.

Nicoll, Allardyce. *British drama,* pp. 296-298.

Salerno, Henry F., ed. *English drama in transition, 1880-1920,* pp. 464-466.

Taylor, John Russell. *The rise and fall of the well-made play,* pp. 92-96, 99-101, 108-109.

Williams, Harold. *Modern English writers, pp. 267*-269.

Winn, Godfrey. "Maugham—A Literary God." *In:* Richards, Dick. *The curtain rises,* pp. 78-81.

The Breadwinner

Barnes, Ronald E. *The dramatic comedy of William Somerset Maugham,* pp. 50, 59, 70-72, 146, 177-179.

MacCarthy, Desmond. *Drama,* pp. 246-248.

Taylor, John Russell. *The rise and fall of the well-made play,* pp. 106-107.

Caesar's Wife

Taylor, John Russell. *The rise and fall of the well-made play,* pp. 102-103.

The Circle

Barnes, Ronald E. *The dramatic comedy of William Somerset Maugham,* pp. 71, 123-127, 133-135, 173-175.

Fielden, John S. "Mrs. Bramish and *The Circle." Boston Univ. Studies in English,* vol. 2 (1956), pp. 113-123.

Kronenberger, Louis. *The thread of laughter,* pp. 294-298.

Lewisohn, Ludwig. "Somerset Maugham Himself." *In:* Jonas, Klaus W., ed. *The Maugham enigma,* pp. 104-106.

MacCarthy, Desmond. *Theatre,* pp. 129-131.

Taylor, John Russell. *The rise and fall of the well-made play,* pp. 104-105.

Thompson, A.R. *Dry mock,* pp. 40-42.

The Constant Wife

Barnes, Ronald E. *The dramatic comedy of William Somerset Maugham,* pp. 46, 68-69, 127-129, 144, 175-177.

Block, Anita. *The changing world in plays and theatre,* pp. 82-94.

Cordell, Richard A. *"The Constant Wife."* *In:* Jonas, Klaus W., ed. *The Maugham enigma,* pp. 111-113.

Taylor, John Russell. *The rise and fall of the well-made play,* pp. 105-106.

East of Suez

Jonas, Klaus W. "Maugham and the East." *In:* Jonas, Klaus W., ed. *The world of Somerset Maugham,* pp. 132-137.

MacCarthy, Desmond. *Theatre,* pp. 131-134.

Taylor, John Russell. *The rise and fall of the well-made play,* pp. 101-102.

For Services Rendered

Block, Anita. *The changing world in plays and theatre,* pp. 328-333.

Ervine, St. John. "Maugham the Playwright." *In:* Jonas, Klaus W., ed. *The world of Somerset Maugham,* pp. 157-159.

MacCarthy, Desmond. *Theatre,* pp. 134-139.

Taylor, John Russell. *The rise and fall of the well-made play,* pp. 107-108.

Home and Beauty

Barnes, Ronald E. *The dramatic comedy of William Somerset Maugham,* pp. 55-58, 171-173.

Jack Straw

Barnes, Ronald E. *The dramatic comedy of William Somerset Maugham,* pp. 60-63, 82-83, 161-162.

Lady Frederick

Barnes, Ronald E. *The dramatic comedy of William Somerset Maugham,* pp. 45-48, 50-51, 53-54, 76, 84, 96-97, 159-160.

Ervine, St. John. "Maugham the Playwright." *In:* Jonas, Klaus W., ed. *The world of Somerset Maugham,* pp. 148-150.

Hobson, Harold. *Theatre,* pp. 30-31.

Taylor, John Russell. *The rise and fall of the well-made play,* pp. 93-94, 97-99.

The Land of Promise

Barnes, Ronald E. *The dramatic comedy of William Somerset Maugham,* pp. 55, 67, 85, 87-88, 114-116, 165-167.

A Man of Honour

Barnes, Ronald E. *The dramatic comedy of William Somerset Maugham,* pp. 100-101.

The Mob

Block, Anita. *The changing world in plays and theatre,* pp. 59-60.

The Noble Spaniard

Sainer, Arthur. *The sleepwalker and the assassin, a view of the contemporary theatre,* pp. 91-93.

Our Betters

Barnes, Ronald E. *The dramatic comedy of William Somerset Maugham,* pp. 67-70, 71, 74-75, 117-120, 122-123, 132-133, 145-146, 167-170.

Cordell, Richard A. *"Our Betters." In:* Jonas, Klaus W., ed. *The Maugham enigma,* pp. 107-110.

Ervine, St.John. "Maugham the Playwright." *In:* Jonas, Klaus W., ed *The world of Somerset Maugham,* pp. 154-155.

Greenwood, Ormerod. *The playwright,* pp. 165-169.

Hobson, Harold. *Theatre,* pp. 20-22.

Kronenberger, Louis. *The thread of laughter,* 290-294.

MacCarthy, Desmond. *Drama,* pp. 233-239.

MacCarthy, Desmond. *Theatre,* pp. 119-124.

Salerno, Henry F., ed. *English drama in transition, 1880-1920,* pp. 464-466.

Penelope

Barnes, Ronald E. *The dramatic comedy of William Somerset Maugham,* pp. 48-49, 54, 68-69, 73-74, 75, 76, 86-87, 162-164.

Sheppey

Ervine, St. John. "Maugham the Playwright." *In:* Jonas, Klaus W., ed. *The world of Somerset Maugham,* pp. 159-160.

MacCarthy, Desmond. *Drama,* pp. 343-348.

MacCarthy, Desmond. *Theatre,* pp. 124-128.

Taylor, John Russell. *The rise and fall of the well-made play,* p. 108.

Weales, Gerald. *Religion in modern English drama,* pp. 17, 20.

Smith

Barnes, Ronald E. *The dramatic comedy of William Somerset Maugham,* pp. 54, 67-68, 83-84, 120-122, 140-141, 164-165.

Ervine, St. John. "Maugham the Playwright. " *In:* Jonas, Klaus W., ed. *The world of Somerset Maugham,* pp. 152-154.

The Unattainable

Barnes, Ronald E. *The dramatic comedy of William Somerset Maugham,* pp. 58-59, 68, 88-89, 170-171.

The Unknown

Balmforth, Ramsden. *The problem-play and its influence on modern thought and life,* pp. 108-121.

Barnes, Ronald E. *The dramatic comedy of William Somerset Maugham,* pp. 72-73.

Ervine, St. John. "Maugham the Playwright." *In:* Jonas, Klaus W., ed. *The world of Somerset Maugham,* pp. 155-157.

Taylor, John Russell. *The rise and fall of the well-made play,* pp. 103-104.

Weales, Gerald. *Religion in modern English drama,* pp. 19-21.

THIERRY MAULNIER 1909-

La Maison de la Nuit

Giraud, Raymond. "Maulnier: In and Above the Conflict." *Yale French Studies,* no. 14 (Winter, 1954-55), pp. 79-84.

FRANCOIS MAURIAC 1885-

General

Jenkins, Cecil. *Mauriac,* pp. 100-104, 108-111.

Moore, Harry T. *Twentieth-century French literature to World War II,* pp. 135-136.

Smith, Maxwell A. "Mauriac and the Theatre." *American Society Legion of Honor Magazine*, vol. 37, no. 2 (1966), pp. 101-110.

Asmodee

Fowlie, Wallace. *Dionysus in Paris*, pp. 151-153.

Jenkins, Cecil. *Mauriac*, pp. 104-105.

Knowles, Dorothy. *French drama of the inter-war years, 1918-39*, pp. 108-109.

Feu sur la Terre, ou Le Pays sans Chemin

Jenkins, Cecil. *Mauriac*, pp. 107-108.

Knowles, Dorothy. *French drama of the inter-war years, 1918-39*, pp. 109-110.

Les Mal Aimés

Jenkins, Cecil. *Mauriac*, pp. 105-106.

Passage du Malm

Jenkins, Cecil. *Mauriac*, pp. 106-107, 110.

O.H. MAVOR
See Bridie, James

VLADIMIR MAYAKOVSKI 1894-1930

General

Erlich, Victor. *The double image: concepts of the poet in Slavic literatures*, pp. 120-132.

Moser, Charles A. "Mayakovsky and America." *Russian Rev.*, vol. 25 (1966), pp. 242-256.

The Bedbug (La Punaise)

Block, Anita. *The changing world in plays and theatre*, pp. 397-400.

Flanner, Janet. *Paris journal, 1944-1965*, pp. 411-413.

The Bug (Klop)

Ferrer, Olga P. "Theater in the U.S.S.R.: Summer of 1964." *Books Abroad*, vol. 39, no. 3 (Summer, 1965), pp. 297, 298.

EDWIN JUSTUS MAYER 1897-1960

Children of Darkness

Krutch, Joseph W. *The American drama since 1918*, pp. 209-213.

JULIAN MAYFIELD 1928-

The Other Foot

Mitchell, Loften. *Black drama*, pp. 155-156.

RUTHERFORD MAYNE 1878-
(real name Samuel J. Waddell)

General

Hogan, Robert. *After the Irish renaissance*, pp. 31-32.

Williams, Harold. *Modern English writers*, p. 219.

The Drone

Boyd, Ernest. *Ireland's literary renaissance*, pp. 368-369.

The Troth

Boyd, Ernest. *Ireland's literary renaissance*, pp. 369-370.

The Turn of the Road

Boyd, Ernest. *Ireland's literary renaissance*, pp. 366-368.

CARL MEINHARD

Johannes Kreisler (Die Wunderlichen Geschichten des Kappelmeisters Kreisler) (Rudolph Bernauer, co-author)

Bauland, Peter. *The hooded eagle*, pp. 74-78.

MAURICE MELDON

Aisling

Hogan, Robert. *After the Irish renaissance*, pp. 227-228.

HECTOR MENDOZA 1932-

General

Jones, W.K. *Behind Spanish American footlights*, pp. 511-512.

419

FRANK MERLIN

I Got Shoes

Sainer, Arthur. *The sleepwalker and the assassin, a view of the contemporary theatre*, pp. 58-59.

HANS GUNTER MICHELSEN 1920-

General

Michalski, John. "German Drama and Theater in 1965." *Books Abroad*, vol. 40 (1966), p. 138.

MIGUEL MIHURA 1903-

General

Arjona, Doris K. "Beyond Humor: The Theatre of Miguel Mihura." *Kentucky Foreign Language Q.*, vol. 6 (1959), p. 65.

Boring, Phyllis Z. "Incongruous Humor in the Contemporary Spanish Theatre." *Modern Drama*, vol 11,. no. 1 (May, 1968), pp. 82-86.

Three Top Hats

Benedikt, M., and G. E. Wellwarth. *Modern Spanish theatre, an anthology of plays*, pp. 128-129.

EDNA ST. VINCENT MILLAY 1892-1950

General

McGraw, Gertrude H., Sr. "Edna St. Vincent Millay, poet, dramatist, and propagandist." Unpublished M.A. thesis, Villanova University, 1956.

Parks, Edd Winfield. "Edna St. Vincent Millay." *Sewanee Rev.*, vol. 38 (Jan., 1930), pp. 42-49.

Patton, John Joseph. "Edna St. Vincent Millay as a verse dramatist." *Dissertation Abstracts*, vol. 23 (1963), 4363 (Colorado).

Preston, John H. "Edna St. Vincent Millay." *Virginia Q. Rev.*, vol. 3 (1927), pp. 342-355.

Quinn, Arthur H. "Edna St. Vincent Millay." *In:* Quinn, A. H. *A history of the American drama from the Civil War to the present day*, pp. 148-150.

Bibliography

Brenni, Vito J., and John E. James. "Edna St. Vincent Millay: Selected Criticism." *Bulletin of Bibliography,* vol. 23 (May-Aug., 1962), pp. 177-178.

Aria da Capo

Britten, Norman A. *Edna St. Vincent Millay,* pp. 96-102.

Gerstenberger, Donna. "Verse Drama in America." *In:* Meserve, Walter J., ed. *Discussions of American drama,* pp. 38-40.

Gray, James. *Edna St. Vincent Millay,* p. 35.

McKee, Mary J. "Millay's *Aria Da Capo:* Form and Meaning." *Modern Drama,* vol. 9, no. 2 (Sept., 1966), pp. 165-169.

Conversations at Midnight

Gray, James. *Edna St. Vincent Millay,* pp. 35-36.

The King's Henchman

Britten, Norman A. *Edna St. Vincent Millay,* pp. 107-109.

Gray, James. *Edna St. Vincent Millay,* pp. 36-38.

Watkins, Mary F. "Operatic Events of the Past Month." *Musical Observer,* vol. 26 (Apr., 1927), pp. 12, 38-39.

The Lamp and the Bell

Britten, Norman A. *Edna St. Vincent Millay,* pp. 102-106.

The Princess Marries the Page

Britten, Norman A. *Edna St. Vincent Millay,* pp. 93-94.

Two Slatterns and a King

Britten, Norman A. *Edna St. Vincent Millay,* pp. 94-95.

The Wall of Dominoes

Britten, Norman A. *Edna St. Vincent Millay,* pp. 95-96.

ARTHUR MILLER 1915-

General

"Arthur Miller Talks." *Michigan Q. Rev.,* vol. 6 (1967), pp. 153-184. (Trans. of talk and panel discussion.)

Bannerjee, Chinmoy. "Arthur Miller: The Prospect of Tragedy." *An English Miscellany* (St. Stephens College, Delhi), vol. 3 (1965), pp. 66-76.

Barksdale, Richard K. "Social Background in the Plays of Miller and Williams." *College Language Assn. J.,* vol. 6 (1963), pp. 161-169.

Blau, Herbert. *The impossible theatre,* pp. 186-192.

Brandon, Henry. "Conversation with Arthur Miller." *World Theatre,* vol. 11, no. 3 (Autumn, 1962), pp. 229-240.

Brandon, Henry. "The State of the Theatre: A Conversation with Arthur Miller." *Harper Mag.,* vol. 221 (Nov., 1960), pp. 63-69.

Brien, Alan. "There Was a Jolly Miller." *Spectator,* vol. 201 (Aug. 8, 1958), pp. 191-192.

Chiari, J. *Landmarks of contemporary drama,* pp. 146-157.

Clurman, Harold. "Arthur Miller: Theme and Variations." *In: Theatre; the annual of the Repertory Theatre of Lincoln Center,* vol. 1 (1964), pp. 13-19.

Dillingham, William B. "Arthur Miller and the Loss of Conscience." *Emory Univ. Q.,* vol. 16, no. 1 (Spring, 1960), pp. 40-50.

Downer, Alan S. *Recent American drama,* pp. 8, 11, 33-39.

Downer, Alan S. "The Two Worlds of Arthur Miller and Tennessee Williams." *In:* Seltzer, Daniel, ed. *The modern theatre, readings and documents,* pp. 410-422. (Reprinted from *Princeton Alumni Weekly,* vol. 52, no. 5 [Oct. 20, 1961].)

Driver, Tom F. "Strength and Weakness in Arthur Miller." *In:* Meserve, Walter J., ed. *Discussions of American drama,* pp. 105-133. *Tulane Drama Rev.,* vol. 4, no. 4 (May, 1960), pp. 45-52.

Ganz, Arthur. "Arthur Miller: After the Silence." *Drama Survey,* vol. 3, no. 4 (Spring-Fall, 1964), pp. 520-530.

Gascoigne, Bamber. *Twentieth-century drama.* pp. 174-183.

Goldstein, Malcolm. "Body and Soul on Broadway." *Modern Drama,* vol. 7, no. 4 (Feb., 1965), pp. 411-421.

Goodsell, Gilbert Dean. "Tragic elements in the major plays of Arthur Miller." M.A., University of Utah, 1953.

Gould, Jean. *Modern American playwrights,* pp. 247-263.

Groff, Edward. "Point of View in Modern Drama." *Modern Drama,* vol. 2, no. 3 (Dec. 1959), pp. 274-276, 282.

Hayashi, Tetsumaro. "Arthur Miller: The Dimension of His Art and a Checklist of His Published Works." *Serif,* vol. 4 no. 2 (1967), pp. 26-32.

Hurrell, John D. *Two modern American tragedies, reviews and criticism of "Death of a Salesman" and "A Streetcar Named Desire."*

James, Stuart B. "Pastoral Dreamer in an Urban World." *University of Denver Q.,* vol. 1, no. 3 (1966), pp. 45-57.

Krutch, Joseph W. *The American drama since 1918,* pp. 324-329.

Lumley, Frederick. *New trends in 20th-century drama,* pp. 137-138, 183-185, 194-199.

Lumley, Frederick. *Trends in 20th-century drama,* pp. 184-187.

McCarthy, Mary. "Americans, Realists, Playwrights." *Encounter,* vol. 17, no. 1 (July, 1961), pp. 24-31.

Martin, Robert Allen. "The major plays and critical thought of Arthur Miller to the *Collected Plays." Dissertation Abstracts,* vol. 26 (1965) 2755 (Mich.).

Miller, Arthur. "The Family in Modern Dress." *Atlantic Monthly,* vol. 97, no. 4 (Apr., 1956), pp. 35-41.

Miller, Arthur. (Interview by Phillip Gelb.) "Morality and Modern Drama." *Educational Theatre J.,* vol. 10 (1958), pp. 190-202.

Miller, Arthur. (Interview with Walter Wager.) *In:* Wager, Walter, ed. *The playwrights speak,* pp. 6-12, 14-24.

Miller, Arthur. "On Recognition." *Michigan Q. Rev.,* vol. 2, no. 4, (Oct., 1963), pp. 213-220.

Miller, Arthur. "On Social Plays." *In:* Cassell, Richard A. *What is the play?* pp. 670-679. (From Miller, Arthur. *A view from the bridge,* N.Y., Viking, 1955.)

Miller Arthur. "Tragedy and the Common Man." *In:* Caputi, Anthony, ed. *Modern drama,* pp. 328-331. (From *New York Times,* Feb. 27, 1949, Sec. 2, pp. 1, 3.) *In:* Levin, Richard. *Tragedy: plays, theory and criticism,* pp. 171-173. (Reprinted from *New York Times,* Feb. 27, 1949, Sec. 2.) *Also in: Theatre Arts,* vol. 35, no. 3 (Mar., 1951), pp. 48-50.

Moss, Leonard. *Arthur Miller.*

Moss, Leonard. "Arthur Miller and the Common Man's Language." *Modern Drama,* vol. 7 no. 1 (May, 1964), pp. 52-59.

Mottram, Eric. "Arthur Miller: the Development of a Political Dramatist in America." *In: American theatre*, pp. 127-131.

Murray, Edward. *Arthur Miller, dramatist*, pp. 179-182.

Murray, Edward James. "Structure, character, and theme in the plays of Arthur Miller." *Dissertation Abstracts*, vol. 27 (1966), 1061A-62A (So. Calif.).

Newman, William J. "The Plays of Arthur Miller." *Twentieth Century*, vol. 164 (Nov., 1958), pp. 491-496.

Paris Review. *Writers at work; The Paris Review interviews. Third series*, pp. 199-230.

Phillips, Elizabeth C. *Modern American drama*, pp. 110-113, 116.

Popkin, Henry. "Arthur Miller: the Strange Encounter." *Sewanee Rev.*, vol. 68, no. 1 (Winter, 1960), pp. 34-60.

Prudhoe, John. "Arthur Miller and Tradition of Tragedy." *English Studies*, vol. 43, no. 1-6 (1962), pp. 430-439.

Rovere, Richard H. "Arthur Miller's Conscience." *New Republic,* vol. 136, no. 24 (June 17, 1957), pp. 13-15.

Seager, Allan. "The Creative Agony of Arthur Miller." *In:* Miller, Arthur. *Death of a salesman. Text and criticism,* ed. by Gerald Weales, pp. 326-338. (From *Esquire,* vol. 52 (Oct., 1959) pp. 123-126.)

Sharpe, Robert Boies. *Irony in the drama*, pp. 195-204.

\ Stambusky, Alan. "Three plays by Arthur Miller examined as tragedy in the light of Aristole's *Poetics,* and Miller's theory." M.A., Catholic University of America, 1955.

Steinberg, M.W. "Arthur Miller and the Idea of Modern Tragedy." *Dalhousie Rev.* vol. 40, no. 3 (Fall, 1960), pp. 329-340.

Swett, Tamie Waters. "An appraisal of Arthur Miller's concept of tragedy." M.A., University of Southern California, 1953.

Trowbridge, Clinton W. "Arthur Miller: Between Pathos and Tragedy." *Modern Drama*, vol. 10, no. 3 (Dec., 1967), pp. 221-232.

Tynan, Kenneth. "American Blues: The Plays of Arthur Miller and Tennessee Williams." *In:* Kernan, Alvin B., ed *The modern American theater,* pp. 34-44. (Reprinted from Tynan, K. *Curtains,* (Atheneum, 1961).) *Also in: Encounter,* vol. 2, no. 5 (May, 1954), pp. 13-16.

Wager, Walter. "Arthur Miller." *In:* Wager, Walter, ed. *The playwrights speak,* pp. 1-6.

Weales, Gerald. *American drama since World War II,* pp. 3-17.

Weales, Gerald. "Arthur Miller." *In:* Downer, Alan S. *The American theater today,* pp. 85-98.

Weales, Gerald. "Arthur Miller: Man and His Image." *Tulane Drama Rev.,* vol. 7, no. 1 (Fall, 1962), pp. 165-180.

Wiegand, William. "Arthur Miller and the Man Who Knows." *In:* Miller, Arthur. *Death of a salesman. Text and criticism,* ed. by Gerald Weales, pp. 296-312. (From *Western Rev.* vol. 21, no. 2 (Winter, 1957), pp. 85-103.)

Williams, Raymond. *Modern tragedy,* pp. 103-105.

Williams, Raymond. "The Realism of Arthur Miller." *Critical Q.,* vol. 1, no. 2 (Summer, 1949), pp. 140-149.

After the Fall

Bigsby, C.W.E. *Confrontation and commitment,* pp. 27, 31, 34, 36-47, 48, 49, 68, 84, 166.

Bigsby, C.W.E. "The Fall and After—Arthur Miller's Confession." *Modern Drama,* vol. 10, no. 2 (Sept., 1967), pp. 124-136.

Brashear, William R. "The Empty Bench: Morality, Tragedy, and Arthur Miller." *Michigan Q. Rev.,* vol. 5 (1966), pp. 270-278.

Brustein, Robert. *Seasons of discontent,* pp. 243-247.

Chiari, J. *Landmarks of contemporary drama,* pp. 151-157.

Clurman, Harold. "Arthur Miller: Theme and Variations." *In;* *Theatre; the annual of the Repertory Theatre of Lincoln Center,* vol. 1 (1964), pp. 20-22.

Finkelstein, Sidney. *Existentialism and alienation in American literature,* pp. 258-263.

Gassner, John. "Broadway in Review." *Educational Theatre J.,* vol. 16 (1964), pp. 177-179.

Gottfried, Martin. *A theater divided; the postwar American stage,* pp. 150-152.

Heilman, Robert B. *Tragedy and melodrama,* pp. 18, 104, 141.

Koppenhaver, Allen J. *"The Fall* and After: Albert Camus and Arthur Miller." *Modern Drama,* vol. 9, no. 2 (Sept., 1966), pp. 206-209.

Lewis, Allan. *American plays and playwrights of the contemporary theatre,* pp. 35-51.

Meyer, Nancy and Richard. *"After the Fall:* A View from the Director's Notebook." *In: Theatre; the annual of the Repertory Theatre of Lincoln Center,* vol. 2 (1965), pp: 43-73.

Miller, Arthur. "Apropos of *After the Fall."* (Interview, ed. by Oriana Fallaci.) *World Theatre,* vol. 14, no. 1 (Jan.-Feb., 1965), pp. 79.81.

Moss, Leonard. *Arthur Miller,* pp. 79-86, 102, 107-110, 112-114.

Moss, Leonard. "Biographical and Literary Allusion in *After the Fall." Educational Theatre J.,* vol. 18, no. 1 (Mar., 1966), pp. 34-40.

Mottram, Eric. "Arthur Miller: the Development of a Political Dramatist in America." *In: American theatre,* pp. 150-156.

Murray, Edward. *Arthur Miller, dramatist,* pp. 125-157.

Murray, Edward. "Point of View in *After the Fall." College Language Assn. J.* (Morgan State College, Baltimore), vol. 10, no. 2 (Dec. 1966), pp. 135-142.

Nolan, Paul T. "Two Memory Plays: *The Glass Menagerie* and *After the Fall." McNeese Rev.* (McNeese State Coll., La.), vol. 17 (1966), pp. 27-38.

Phillips, Elizabeth C. *Modern American drama,* p. 115.

Simon, John. *Hudson Rev.,* vol. 17, no. 2 (Summer, 1964), pp. 234-236.

Sontag, Susan. *Against interpretation and other essays,* pp. 140-145.

Sontag, Susan. "Going to Theater (and the Movies)." *Partisan Rev.,* vol. 31, no. 2 (Spring, 1964), pp. 284-287.

Stinson, John J. "Structure in *After the Fall:* The Relevance of the Maggie Episodes to the Main Themes and the Christian Symbolism." *Modern Drama,* vol. 10, no. 3 (Dec., 1967), pp. 233-240.

Tynan, Kenneth. *Tynan right and left,* pp. 143-144.

Weales, Gerald. "Arthur Miller." *In:* Downer, Alan S., ed. *The American theater today,* pp. 92-95, 97-98.

All My Sons

Bigsby, C.W.E. *Confrontation and commitment,* pp. 26-32, 36, 41, 45.

Boggs, W. Arthur. *"Oedipus* and *All My Sons." Personalist,* vol. 42, no. 4 (Oct., 1961), pp. 555-560.

Clurman, Harold. *Lies like truth,* pp. 66-68.

Dillingham, William B. "Arthur Miller and the Loss of Conscience." *In:* Miller, Arthur. *Death of a salesman. Text and criticism,* ed. by Gerald Weales, pp. 339-343. (From *Emory University Q.,* vol. 16, (Spring, 1960), pp. 40-50.)

Downer, Alan S. *Fifty years of American drama, 1900-1950,* pp. 52-53.

Finkelstein, Sidney. *Existentialism and alienation in American literature,* pp. 252-253.

Fleming, Peter. "The Theatre." *Spectator* vol. 180 (May 21, 1948), p. 612.

Ganz, Arthur. "The Silence of Arthur Miller." *Drama Survey,* vol. 3, no. 2 (Oct., 1963), pp. 231-233.

Gassner, John. *The theatre in our times,* pp. 344-346.

Hagopian, John V., and Dolch, Martin. *Insight I; analysis of American literature,* pp. 166-174.

Loughlin, Richard L. "Tradition and Tragedy in *All My Sons.*" *English Record,* vol. 14 (Feb., 1964), pp. 23-27.

Moss, Leonard. *Arthur Miller,* pp. 37-43, 45-47, 52, 54, 59, 62-63, 65-66, 69, 71-72, 92-93, 102, 106, 108-116.

Mottram, Eric. "Arthur Miller: the Development of a Political Dramatist in America." *In: American theatre,* pp. 131-133.

Murray, Edward. *Arthur Miller, dramatist,* pp. 1-21.

Phillips, Elizabeth C. *Modern American drama,* pp. 113-114.

Sievers, W. David. *Freud on Broadway,* pp. 389-391.

Stevens, Virginia. "Seven Young Broadway Artists." *Theatre Arts,* vol. 31, no. 6 (June, 1947), pp. 53, 56.

Weales, Gerald. *American drama since World War II,* pp. 3, 6-7, 10-11, 13, 16, 17, 230.

Weales, Gerald. "Arthur Miller." *In:* Downer, Alan S., ed. *The American theater today,* p. 87.

Weales, Gerald. "Arthur Miller: Man and His Image." *In:* Miller Arthur. *Death of a salesman. Text and criticism,* ed. by Gerald Weales, pp. 353-354. (From Weales, Gerald. *American drama since World War II,* N.Y., Harcourt, Brace & World, 1962, pp. 3-17.) *Also in: Tulane Drama Rev.,* vol. 7, no. 1 (Fall, 1962) pp. 168-169.

Wells, Arvin R. "The Living and the Dead in *All My Sons.*" *Modern Drama,* vol. 7, no. 1 (May, 1964), pp. 46-51.

Whittey, Alvin. "Arthur Miller: An Attempt at Modern Tragedy." *Wisconsin Academy of Sciences, Arts, and Letters. Transactions,* vol. 42 (1953), pp. 257-260.

Williams, Raymond. *Modern tragedy.* pp. 103-104.

Williams, Raymond. "The Realism of Arthur Miller." *In:* Miller, Arthur. *Death of a salesman. Text and criticism,* ed. by Gerald Weales, pp. 315-319. (From *Critical Q.,* 1 (Summer, 1959), pp. 140-149.)

Yorks, Samuel A. "Joe Killer and His Sons." *Western Humanities Rev.,* vol. 13, no. 4 (Autumn, 1959), pp. 401-407.

The Crucible

Aylen, Leo. *Greek tragedy and the modern world,* pp. 193, 253, 256.

Bentley, Eric. *The dramatic event,* pp. 90-94.

Bentley, Eric. "Miller's Innocence." *New Republic,* vol. 128, no. 7 (Feb. 16, 1953), pp. 22-23.

Bentley, Eric. *The theatre of commitment,* pp. 36-40, 51-52.

Blau, Herbert. "From Counterforce I: The Social Drama." *In:* Seltzer, Daniel, ed. *The modern theatre, readings and documents,* pp. 422-427. (From Blau, Herbert. *The impossible theatre: a manifesto,* N.Y., Macmillan, 1964.)

Blau, Herbert. *The impossible theatre,* pp. 188-192.

Cohn, Ruby, ed. *Twentieth-century drama,* pp. 537-538.

Dillingham, William B. "Arthur Miller and the Loss of Conscience." *In:* Miller, Arthur. *Death of a salesman. Text and criticism,* ed. by Gerald Weales, pp. 346-348. (From *Emory University Q.,* vol. 16 (Spring, 1960), pp. 40-50.)

Douglass, James W. "Miller's *The Crucible:* Which Witch Is Which?" *Renascence,* vol. 15, no. 3 (Spring, 1953), pp. 145-151.

Downer, Alan S. *Recent American drama,* pp. 36-37.

Fender, Stephen. "Precision and Pseudo Precision in *The Crucible." J. of American Studies,* vol. 1 (1967), pp. 87-98.

Finkelstein, Sidney. *Existentialism and alienation in American literature,* pp. 255-258.

Freedman, Morris. *The moral impulse,* pp. 107-108, 110-111.

Ganz, Arthur. "The Silence of Arthur Miller." *Drama Survey,* vol. 3, no. 2 (Oct., 1963), pp. 233-235.

Gassner, John. *Theatre at the crossroads,* pp. 274-278.

Gottfried, Martin. *A theater divided; the postwar American stage,* pp. 243-244.

Hartley, Anthony. "Good Melodrama." *Spectator,* vol. 196 (Apr. 20, 1956), p. 547.

Heemann, Paul Warren. "Arthur Miller's *The Crucible: a study of* the playwright's dramatic theory and method." M.A., University of North Carolina, 1959.

Hill, Philip G. *"The Crucible:* A Structural View." *Modern Drama* vol. 10, no. 3 (Dec., 1967), pp. 312-317.

Lumley, Frederick. *Trends in 20th-century drama,* p. 192.

McElroy, Davis Dunbar. *The study of literature; an existential appraisal,* p. 85.

Moss, Leonard. *Arthur Miller,* pp. 59-66, 69, 71, 77, 89, 91, 94, 97, 102, 107-108, 111-116.

Mottram, Eric. "Arthur Miller: the Development of a Political Dramatist in America." *In: American theater,* pp. 138-142.

Murray, Edward. *Arthur Miller, dramatist,* pp. 52-75.

Nathan, George Jean. *"The Crucible." Theatre Arts,* vol. 37, no. 4 (Apr., 1953), pp. 24-26.

Popkin, Henry. "Arthur Miller's *The Crucible." College English,* vol. 26, no. 2 (Nov., 1964), pp. 139-146.

Rowe, Kenneth Thorpe. *A theatre in your head,* pp. 149-150, 239-240.

Small, Christopher. *Spectator,* vol. 193, no. 6595 (Nov. 19, 1954), p. 608.

Sievers, W. David. *Freud on Broadway,* pp. 397-399.

Warshow, Robert. "The Liberal Conscience in *The Crucible." Commentary,* vol. 15 (1953), pp. 265-271. Also in: Freedman, Morris, ed. *Essays in the modern drama,* pp. 195-205. (Reprinted from *The immediate experience* by Robert Warshow, 1953.)

Weales, Gerald. *American drama since World War II,* pp. 3, 10-13, 16-17.

Weales, Gerald. "Arthur Miller." *In:* Downer, Alan S., ed. *The American theater today,* pp. 89-90.

Weales, Gerald. "Arthur Miller: Man and His Image." *In:* Miller, Arthur. *Death of a salesman. Text and criticism,* ed. by Gerald Weales, pp. 358-360. (From Weales, Gerald. *American drama since World War II,* N.Y., Harcourt, Brace & World, 1962, pp. 3-17.) *Also in: Tulane Drama Rev.,* vol. 7, no. 1 (Fall, 1962), pp. 172-174.

West, Paul. "Arthur Miller & the Human Mice." *Hibbert J.,* vol. 61, no. 241 (Jan., 1963), pp. 84-86.

Williams, Raymond. *Modern tragedy,* pp. 104-105.

Williams, Raymond. "The Realism of Arthur Miller." *In:* Miller, Arthur. *Death of a salesman. Text and criticism,* ed. by Gerald Weales, pp. 321-322. (From *Critical Q., 1,* (Summer, 1959), pp. 140-149.)

Williamson, Audrey. *Contemporary theatre, 1953-1956,* pp. 53-55.

Death of a Salesman

Adamczewski, Zygmunt. *The tragic protest,* pp. 172-192.

Aylen, Leo. *Greek tragedy and the modern world,* pp. 248-251.

Bentley Eric. "Back to Broadway." *Theatre Arts,* vol. 33, no. 10 (Nov., 1949), pp. 12-14.

Bettina, Sister M. "Willy Loman's Brother Ben: Tragic Insight in *Death of a Salesman." Modern Drama,* vol. 4, no. 2 (Feb., 1962), pp. 409-412.

Beyer, William. "The State of the Theatre: The Season Opens." *In:* Miller, Arthur. *Death of a salesman. Text and criticism.* ed. by Gerald Weales, pp. 228-230. (From *School and Society,* vol. 70 (Dec., 1949), pp. 363-364.)

Bierman, Judah. "Arthur Miller: *Death of a Salesman." In:* Miller Arthur. *Death of a salesman. Text and criticism,* ed. by Gerald Weales, pp. 265-271. (From Bierman, Judah. *The dramatic experience,* Englewood Cliffs, N.J., Prentice-Hall, 1958, pp. 490-493.)

Bigsby, C.W.E. *Confrontation and commitment,* pp. 27, 32-36, 41, 45, 49.

Bliquez, Guerin. "Linda's Role in *Death of a Salesman." Modern Drama,* vol. 10, no. 4 (Feb., 1968), pp. 383-386.

Broussard, Louis. *American drama...,* pp. 117-121.

Brown, Ivor. "As London Sees Willy Loman" *In:* Miller Arthur. *Death of a salesman. Text and criticism,* ed. by Gerald Weales, pp. 244-249. (From *The New York Times Magazine* (Aug. 28, 1949), pp. 11, 59.)

Brown, John Mason. "Even as You and I." *In:* Miller, Arthur. *Death of a salesman. Text and criticism,* ed. by Gerald Weales, pp. 205-211. (From Brown, John Mason. *Dramatis Personae,* N.Y., Viking, 1963, pp. 94-100.)

Brown, John Mason. "Seeing Things: Even As You and I." *Sat. Rev.,* vol. 32, no 9 (Feb. 26, 1949), pp. 30-32.

Brown, John Mason. *Still seeing things,* pp. 195, 197-204.

Chiari, J. *Landmarks of contemporary drama,* pp. 146-148, 150.

Clark, Eleanor. "Old Glamour, New Gloom." *In:* Miller, Arthur. *Death of a salesman. Text and criticism,* ed. by Gerald Weales, pp. 217-223. (from *Partisan Rev.* "Theatre Chronicle." vol. 16 no. 6 (June 1949), pp. 631-635).

Clurman, Harold. "The Success Dream on the American Stage." *In:* Miller, Arthur. *Death of a salesman. Text and criticism,* ed. by Gerald Weales, pp. 212-216. (From Clurman, Harold. *Lies like truth,* N.Y., Macmillan, 1958, pp. 68-72.)

Clurman, Harold. "Theatre: Attention!" *New Republic,* vol. 120, no. 9 (Feb. 28, 1949), pp. 26-28.

Couchman, Gordon W. "Arthur Miller's Tragedy of Babbitt." *Educational Theatre J.,* vol. 7 (1955), pp. 206-211.

Cowell, Raymond, *Twelve modern dramatists,* pp. 93-95.

DeSchweinitz, George. *"Death of a Salesman:* A Note on Epic and Tragedy." *Western Humanities Rev.,* vol. 14, no. 1 (Winter, 1960), pp. 91-96.

Dillingham, William B. "Arthur Miller and the Loss of Conscience." *In:* Miller, Arthur. *Death of a salesman. Text and criticism,* ed. by Gerald Weales, pp. 343-346. (From *Emory University Q.,* vol. 16 (Spring, 1960), pp. 40-50.)

Downer, Alan S. *Fifty years of American drama, 1900-1950.* pp. 73-75.

Downer, Alan S. "Mr. Williams and Mr. Miller." *Furioso,* vol. 4, no. 3 (Summer, 1949), pp. 68-70.

Dusenbury, Winifred L. *The theme of loneliness in modern American drama,* pp. 16-26.

Finkelstein, Sidney. *Existentialism and alienation in American literature,* pp. 253-255.

Freedman, Morris. *The moral impulse,* pp. 107-111, 115.

Fuller, A. Howard. "A Salesman Is Everybody." *In:* Miller, Arthur. *Death of a salesman. Text and criticism,* ed. by Gerald Weales, pp. 240-243. (From *Fortune,* vol. 39 (May 1949), pp. 79-80.)

Ganz, Arthur. "The Silence of Arthur Miller." *Drama Survey,* vol. 3, no. 2 (Oct., 1963), pp. 226-231, 235-237.

Gardner, R.H. *The splintered stage; the decline of the American theater,* pp. 123-134.

Garland, Robert. "Audience Spellbound by Prize Play of 1949." *In:* Miller, Arthur. *Death of a salesman. Text and criticism,* ed. by Gerald Weales, pp. 199-201. (From the *New York Journal-American* (Feb. 11, 1949), p. 24.)

Gassner, John. *"Death of a Salesman:* First Impressions, 1949." *In:* Miller, Arthur. *Death of a salesman. Text and criticism,* ed. by Gerald Weales, pp. 231-239. (From Gassner, John. *The theatre in our times,* N.Y., Crown, 1954, pp. 368-373.)

Gassner, John. *The theatre in our times,* pp. 346-348, 366-373.

Gassner, John. "Tragic Perspectives: A Sequence of Queries." *Tulane Drama Rev.,* vol. 2, no. 3 (May, 1958), pp. 20-22.

Gottfried, Martin. *"A theater divided; the postwar American stage,* pp. 241-242, 244-245, 246, 247.

Gross, Barry Edward. "Peddler and Pioneer in *Death of a Salesman.*" *Modern Drama,* vol. 7, no. 4 (Feb., 1965), pp. 405-410.

Hagopian, John V. "Arthur Miller: The Salesman's Two Cases." *Modern Drama,* vol. 6, no. 2 (Oct., 1963), pp. 117-125.

Hagopian, John V., and Dolch, Martin. *Insight I; analysis of American literature,* pp. 174-185.

Hawkins, William. *"Death of a Salesman,* Powerful Tragedy." *In:* Miller, Arthur. *Death of a salesman. Text and criticism,* ed. by Gerald Weales, pp. 202-204. (From *The New York World-Telegram.* (Feb. 11, 1949), p. 16.)

Heilman, Robert B. *Tragedy and melodrama,* pp. 102-103, 233-237, 243, 250.

Hurrell, John D. *Two modern American tragedies, reviews and criticism of "Death of a Salesman" and "A Streetcar Named Desire."*

Hynes, Joseph A. "Arthur Miller and the Impasse of Naturalism." *South Atlantic Q.,* vol. 62, no. 3 (Summer, 1963), pp. 327-334.

Hynes, Joseph A. "Attention Must Be Paid." *In:* Miller, Arthur. *Death of a salesman. Text and criticism,* ed. by Gerald Weales, pp. 280-289. (From *College English,* vol. 23, no. 7 (Apr., 1962), pp. 574-578.)

Jackson, Esther M. *"Death of a Salesman:* Tragic Myth in the Modern Theatre." *College Language Assn. J.,* vol. 7 (1963), pp. 63-76.

Kazan, Elia. "From Notebook Made in Preparation for Directing *Death of a Salesman." In:* Seltzer, Daniel, ed. *The modern theatre, readings and documents,* pp. 257-268. (From Rowe, Kenneth Thorpe. *A theatre in your head.* N.Y., Funk and Wagnalls, 1960.)

Kennedy, Sighle. "Who Killed the Salesman?" *Catholic World,* vol. 171 (May, 1950), pp. 110-116.

Kitchin, Laurence. *Mid-century drama,* pp. 60-63.

Krutch, Joseph W. *The American drama since 1918,* pp. 328-329.

Krutch, Joseph Wood. "Drama." *Nation,* vol. 168, no. 10 (Mar. 5, 1949), pp. 283-284.

Krutch, Joseph Wood. *"Modernism" in modern drama,* pp. 123-126.

Lawrence, Stephen A. "The Right Dream in Miller's *Death of a Salesman." College English,* vol. 25, no. 7 (Apr., 1964), pp. 547-549.

Leaska, Mitchell A. *The voice of tragedy,* pp. 273-278.

Lewis, Allan. *The contemporary theatre,* pp. 295-303.

Lumley, Frederick. *Trends in 20th-century drama,* pp. 191-192.

McAnany, Emile G. "The Tragic Commitment: Some Notes on Arthur Miller." *Modern Drama,* vol. 5, no. 1 (May, 1962), pp. 11-20.

McCollom, William G. *Tragedy.* pp. 16-17.

McElroy, Davis Dunbar. *The study of literature; an existential appraisal,* pp. 6-7.

Mander, John. *The writer and commitment,* pp. 138-152.

Mielziner, Jo. "Designing a Play: *Death of a Salesman." In:* Miller, Arthur. *Death of a salesman. Text and criticism,* ed. by Gerald Weales, pp. 187-198. (From Mielziner, Jo. *Designing for the theatre,* N.Y., Atheneum, 1965.)

Miller, Arthur. "The American Theater." *In:* Miller, Arthur. *Death of a salesman. Text and criticism,* ed. by Gerald Weales, pp. 151-155. (Reprinted from *Holiday,* vol. 17 (Jan., 1955), pp. 90-104.)

Miller, Arthur. "From An Introduction to *Collected plays.*" *In:* Seltzer, Daniel, ed. *The modern theatre, readings and documents,* pp. 13-22. (Reprinted from Miller, Arthur. Introduction to *Death of a salesman,* N.Y., Viking, 1957.)

Miller, Arthur. "From the Introduction to Arthur Miller's *Collected Plays.*" *In:* Meserve, Walter J., ed. *Discussions of American drama,* pp. 141-145.

Miller, Arthur. *In:* Cole, Toby, ed. *Playwrights on playwriting,* pp. 261-276. (Reprinted from Arthur Miller, Introduction, *Collected plays* (New York: the Viking Press, 1958), pp. 23-38.)

Miller, Arthur. "Introduction to *Collected Plays.*" *In:* Miller, Arthur. *Death of a salesman. Text and criticism,* ed. by Gerald Weales, pp. 155-171. (From *Collected plays,* N.Y., Viking, 1957, pp. 23-28.)

Miller, Arthur. "Morality and Modern Drama: Interview with Philip Gelb." *In:* Miller, Arthur. *Death of a salesman. Text and criticism,* ed. by Gerald Weales, pp. 172-186. (From *Educational Theatre J.,* vol. 10 (Oct., 1958), pp. 190-202.)

Miller, Arthur. " The *Salesman* Has a Birthday." *In:* Miller, Arthur. *Death of a Salesman. Text and criticism,* ed. by Gerald Weales, pp. 147-150. (Reprinted from *The New York Times* (Feb. 5, 1950), II, pp. 1, 3.)

Miller, Arthur. "Tragedy and the Common Man." *In:* Miller, Arthur. *Death of a salesman. Text and criticism,* ed. by Gerald Weales, pp. 143-147. (Reprinted from *The New York Times* (Feb. 27, 1949), II, pp. 1, 3.)

Miller, Arthur, Gore Vidal, *et al.* "*Death of a Salesman,* a Symposium." *Tulane Drama Rev.,* vol. 2, no. 3 (May, 1958), pp. 63-69.

Moss, Leonard. *Arthur Miller,* pp. 45-59, 63, 66, 69, 75-76, 83-84, 91-93, 102, 106, 108-110, 112-116.

Mottram, Eric. "Arthur Miller: the Development of a Political Dramatist in America." *In: American theatre,* pp. 133-138.

Muller, Herbert J. *The spirit of tragedy,* pp. 316-317.

Murray, Edward. *Arthur Miller, dramatist,* pp. 22-51.

Oberg, Arthur K. "*Death of a Salesman* and Arthur Miller's Search for Style." *Criticism, vol. 9, no.* 4 (Fall, 1967), pp. 303-311.

Parker, Brian. "Point of View in *Death of a Salesman.*" *Univ. of Toronto Q.,* vol. 35, no. 2 (Jan., 1966), pp. 144-157.

Phillips, Elizabeth C. *Modern American drama,* p. 114.

Ranald, Margaret Loftus. *"Death of a Salesman:* Fifteen Years After." *Comment,* vol. 3, no. 1 (May, 1965), pp. 28-35.

Ross, George. *"Death of a Salesman* in the Original." *In:* Miller Arthur. *Death of a salesman. Text and criticism,* ed. by Gerald Weales, pp. 259-264. (From *Commentary,* vol. 11 (Feb., 1951), pp. 184-186.)

Saisselin, Remy G. "Is Tragic Drama Possible in the Twentieth Century?" *Theatre annual, 1960,* vol. 17, pp. 20-21.

Schneider, Daniel E. "Play of Dreams." *In:* Miller, Arthur. *Death of a salesman. Text and criticism,* by Gerald Weales, pp. 250-258. (From Schneider, Daniel E. *The psychoanalyst and the artist,* N.Y., Farrar, Straus, 1950, pp. 246-255.) *Also in: Theatre Arts,* vol. 33, no. 9 (Oct., 1949), pp. 18-21.

Schweinitz, George de. *"Death of a Salesman:* A Note on Epic and Tragedy." *In:* Miller, Arthur. *Death of a salesman. Text and criticism,* ed. by Gerald Weales, pp. 272-279. (From *Western Humanities Rev.,* vol. 14 (Winter 1960), pp. 91-96.)

Sears, Forest. "Production and production book of *Death of a Salesman,* by Arthur Miller." M.F.A., Yale University, 1958.

Siegel, Paul N. "Willy Loman and King Lear." *College English,* vol. 17, no. 6 (Mar., 1956), pp. 341-345.

Sievers, W. David. *Freud on Broadway,* pp. 391-396.

Weales, Gerald. *American drama since World War II,* pp. 3, 5, 7-10, 13-17, 43, 69, 103.

Weales, Gerald. "Arthur Miller." *In:* Downer, Alan S., ed. *The American theater today,* pp. 87-89, 91, 97.

Weales, Gerald. "Arthur Miller: Man and His Image." *In:* Miller, Arthur. *Death of a salesman. Text and criticism,* ed. by Gerald Weales, pp. 354-358, 363-364. (From Weales, Gerald. *American drama since World War II,* N.Y., Harcourt, Brace and World, 1962, pp. 3-17.) *Also in: Tulane Drama Rev.,* vol. 7, no. 1 (Fall, 1962), pp. 169-172, 177, 178, 180.

Weales, Gerald. "Introduction." *In:* Miller Arthur. *Death of a salesman. Text and criticism,* ed. by Gerald Weales, pp. vii-xx.

Whittey, Alvin. "Arthur Miller: An Attempt at Modern Tragedy." Wisconsin Academy of Sciences, Arts, and Letters. *Transactions,* vol. 42 (1953), pp. 260-262.

Wiegand, William. "Arthur Miller and the Man Who Knows." *In:* Miller, Arthur. *Death of a Salesman. Text and criticism,* ed. by Gerald Weales, pp. 290-295. (From *Western Humanities Rev.* (Winter, 1957), pp. 85-102.)

Williams, Raymond. *Modern tragedy,* pp. 104-105, 159-160.

Williams, Raymond. "The Realism of Arthur Miller." *In:* Miller, Arthur. *Death of a salesman. Text and criticism,* ed. by Gerald Weales, pp. 319-321. (From *Critical Q.,* 1 (Summer, 1959), pp. 140-149)

Worsley, T.C. "Poetry Without Words." *In:* Miller, Arthur. *Death of a salesman. Text and criticism,* ed. by Gerald Weales, pp. 224-227. (From *New Statesman & Nation,* n.s. vol. 38 (Aug. 6, 1949), pp. 146-147)

Worth, Deane. "An examination of Arthur Miller's play *Death of a Salesman* in the light of Aristotle's ideas of action, plot, and the tragic hero." M.A., Smith College, 1950.

Honors at Dawn

Wiegand, William. "Arthur Miller and the Man Who Knows." *In:* Miller, Arthur. *Death of a salesman. Text and criticism,* ed. by Gerald Weales, pp. 295. (From *Western Humanities Rev.* (Winter, 1957), pp. 85-102.)

Incident at Vichy

Bigsby, C.W.E. *Confrontation and commitment,* pp. 41, 47-49.

Brustein, Robert. *Seasons of discontent,* pp. 259-263.

Clurman, Harold. "Director's Notes: *Incident at Vichy.*" *Tulane Drama Rev.,* vol. 9, no. 4 (Summer, 1965), pp. 77-90.

Lewis, Allan. *American plays and playwrights of the contemporary theatre,* pp. 51-52.

Miller, Arthur. (Interview with Walter Wager.) *In:* Wager, Walter, ed. *The playwrights speak,* pp. 12-14, 16, 19.

Moss, Leonard. *Arthur Miller,* pp. 96-99, 102, 108-110, 114.

Mottram, Eric. "Arthur Miller: the Development of a Political Dramatist in America." *In: American theatre,* pp. 156-161.

Murray, Edward. *Arthur Miller, dramatist,* pp. 158-178.

Rahv, Philip. *The myth and the power-house,* pp. 225-233.

Roth, Martin. "Sept-d'un-coup." *Chicago Rev.,* vol. 19, no. 1 (1966), pp. 108-111.

Weales, Gerald. "Arthur Miller." *In:* Downer, Alan S., ed. *The American theatre today.* pp. 92-95, 97-98.

The Man Who Had All the Luck

Moss, Leonard. *Arthur Miller,* pp. 32-33, 76, 91-93, 102, 106, 108-110, 114.

Mottram, Eric. "Arthur Miller: the Development of a Political Dramatist in America." *In: American theatre,* p. 131.

Sievers, W. David. *Freud on Broadway,* pp. 388-389.

Weales, Gerald. "Arthur Miller: Man and His Image." *Tulane Drama Rev.,* vol. 7 no. 1 (Fall, 1962), pp. 167-168.

Wiegand, William. "Arthur Miller and the Man Who Knows." *In:* Miller, Arthur. *Death of a salesman. Text and Criticism,* ed. by Gerald Weales, pp. 296-297. (From *Western Humanities Rev.* (Winter, 1957), pp. 85-102.)

A Memory of Two Mondays

Hewes, Henry. "Death of a Longshoreman." *Sat. Rev. of Lit.,* vol. 38, no. 42 (Oct. 15, 1955), p. 25.

Moss, Leonard. *Arthur Miller,* pp. 71-75, 93, 109, 114.

Murray, Edward. *Arthur Miller, dramatist,* pp. 76-94.

Williams, Raymond. "The Realism of Arthur Miller." *In:* Miller, Arthur. *Death of a salesman. Text and criticism,* ed. by Gerald Weales, p. 322. (From *Critical Q.,* 1 (Summer, 1959), pp. 140-149.)

The Misfits

Ganz, Arthur. "The Silence of Arthur Miller." *Drama Survey,* vol. 3, no. 2 (Oct., 1963), pp. 224-226.

Moss, Leonard. *Arthur Miller,* pp. 75-78, 86, 91-93, 102, 108-109.

Mottram, Eric. "Arthur Miller: the Development of a Political Dramatist in America." *In: American theatre,* pp. 146-150.

Weales, Gerald. *American drama since World War II,* pp. 14-16.

Weales, Gerald. "Arthur Miller: Man and His Image." *In:* Miller, Arthur. *Death of a salesman. Text and criticism,* ed. by Gerald Weales, pp. 363-365. (From Weales, Gerald. *American drama since World War II,* N.Y., Harcourt, Brace and World, 1962, pp. 3-17.)

The Price

Bermel, Albert. "Right, Wrong, and Mr. Miller." *The New York Times* (Apr. 14, 1968), pp. 1, 7D.

"Drama Mailbag." *The New York Times* (May 12, 1968), p. 5.

Loney, Glenn. "Broadway in Review." *Educational Theatre J.,* vol. 20, no. 2 (May, 1968), p. 235.

The Pussycat and the Expert Plumber Who Was a Man.

Moss, Leonard. *Arthur Miller,* pp. 31-32.

They Too Arise

Wiegand, William. "Arthur Miller and the Man Who Knows." *In:* Miller, Arthur. *Death of a salesman. Text and criticism,* ed. by Gerald Weales, pp. 295-296. (From *Western Humanities Rev.* (Winter, 1957), pp. 85-102.)

A View from the Bridge

Aylen, Leo. *Greek tragedy and the modern world,* pp. 251-256.

Bentley, Eric. "Theatre." *New Republic,* vol. 133, no. 25 (Dec. 19, 1955), pp. 21-22.

Chiari, J. *Landmarks of contemporary drama,* pp. 150-151.

Cubeta, Paul M. *Modern drama for analysis,* pp. 382-390.

Dillingham, William B. "Arthur Miller and the Loss of Conscience." *In:* Miller, Arthur. *Death of a salesman. Text and criticism,* ed. by Gerald Weales, pp. 348-349. (From *Emory University Q.,* vol. 16 (Spring, 1960), pp. 40-50.)

Epstein, Arthur D. "A Look at *A View from the Bridge.*" *Texas Studies in Literature and Language,* vol. 7, no. 1 (Spring, 1965), pp. 109-122.

Findlater, Richard. "No Time for Tragedy?" *Twentieth Century,* vol. 161 (Jan., 1957), pp. 56-62.

Gottfried, Martin. *A theater divided; the postwar American stage,* pp. 244-246.

Hewes, Henry. "Death of a Longshoreman." *Saturday Rev.,* vol. 38, no. 42 (Oct. 15, 1955), pp. 25-26.

Lumley, Frederick. *Trends in 20th-century drama,* pp. 192-193.

Miller, Arthur. "Viewing *A View from the Bridge." Theatre Arts,* vol. 40, no. 9 (Sept. 1956), pp. 31-32.

Moss, Leonard. *Arthur Miller,* pp. 66-71, 74, 86, 91, 93, 102, 107, 110-114, 116.

Mottram, Eric. "Arthur Miller: the Development of a Political Dramatist in America." *In: American theatre,* pp. 142-146.

Murray, Edward. *Arthur Miller, dramatist,* pp. 95-124.

Phillips, Elizabeth C. *Modern American drama,* pp. 114-115.

Reinert, Otto. *Drama, an introductory anthology,* pp. 636-639.

Weales, Gerald. "Arthur Miller." *In:* Downer, Alan S., ed. *The American theater today,* p. 90.

Weales, Gerald. "Arthur Miller: Man and His Image." *In:* Miller, Arthur. *Death of a salesman. Text and criticism,* ed. by Gerald Weales, pp. 360-362, 365-366. (From Weales, Gerald. *American drama since World War II,* N.Y., Harcourt, Brace and World, 1962, pp. 3-17.) *Also in: Tulane Drama Rev.,* vol. 7, no. 1 (Fall, 1962), pp. 174-175.

Williams, Raymond. "The Realism of Arthur Miller." *In:* Miller, Arthur. *Death of a salesman. Text and criticism,* ed. by Gerald Weales, pp. 323-325. (From *Critical Q.,* 1 (Summer, 1959), pp. 140-149.

Worsley, T.C. "Realistic Melodrama." *New Statesman,* vol. 52 (Oct. 20, 1956), p. 482.

ROGER MILNER

How's the World Treating You?

Browne, E. Martin. "Theatre Abroad." *Drama Survey,* vol. 5, no. 2 (Summer, 1966), p. 194.

LANGDON MITCHELL 1862-1935

The New York Idea

Downer, Alan S. *Fifty years of American drama, 1900-1950,* pp. 33-35.

Gassner, John. "Introduction." *Best plays of the early American theatre from the beginning to 1916,* pp. xxxix-xl.

Metcalfe, James. "Langdon Mitchell's *The New York Idea.*" *In:* Moses, Montrose J. *The American theatre as seen by its critics, 1752-1934,* pp. 167-169. (Reprinted from *Life,* Nov. 29, 1906.)

LOFTEN MITCHELL

A Land Beyond The River

Abramson, Doris E. *Negro Playwrights in the American theatre, 1925-1959,* pp. 204-221, 259-260.

Mitchell, Loften. *Black drama,* pp. 7, 170-180.

EDGAR MITTELHOLZER

Shadows Move Among Them

See Hart, Moss. The Climate of Eden

HERMANN MOERS 1930-

When the Thistle Blooms (Zur Zeit der Distelblute)

Garten, H.F. *Modern German drama,* p. 271.

JEAN MOGIN 1921-

A Chacun Selon Sa Faim

Mallinson, Vernon. *Modern Belgian literature, 1830-1960,* pp. 195-196.

La Fille a la Fontaine

Mallinson, Vernon. *Modern Belgian literature, 1830-1960,* pp. 196-197.

MICHAEL MOLLOY 1917-

General

Hogan Robert. *After the Irish renaissance,* pp. 86-98.

Hogan, Robert G., ed. *Seven Irish plays, 1946-1964,* pp. 29-31.

Lane, Temple. "The Dramatic Arrival of M.J. Molloy." *Irish Writing,* no. 11 (May, 1950), pp. 59-65.

FERENC MOLNAR 1878-1952

General

Behrman, S.N. *The suspended drawing room,* pp. 191-253.

Carnival

Gergely, Emro Joseph. *Hungarian drama in New York,* pp. 37-39.

The Devil

Gergely, Emro Joseph. *Hungarian drama in New York,* pp. 12-17.

The Glass Slipper

Gergely, Emro Joseph. *Hungarian drama in New York,* pp. 39-42.

The Good Fairy

Gergely, Emro Joseph. *Hungarian drama in New York,* pp. 34-36.

The Guardsman (Where Ignorance Is Bliss)

Gergely, Emro Joseph. *Hungarian drama in New York,* pp. 48-50, 50-51.

Launze

Gergely, Emro Joseph. *Hungarian drama in New York,* pp. 27-31.

Liliom

Clark, Barrett. *Study of the modern drama,* pp. 113-118.

Gergely, Emro Joseph. *Hungarian drama in New York,* pp. 23-27.

Strangnel, Gregory. "A Psychological Study of Ferenc Molnar's *Liliom." Psychoanalytic Rev.,* vol. 9 (1922), p. 40.

Olympia

Gergely, Emro Joseph. *Hungarian drama in New York,* pp. 45-48.

The Phantom Rival (The Tale of the Wolf)

Gergely, Emro Joseph. *Hungarian drama in New York,* pp. 31-34.

The Red Mill (Adapted by David Belasco as Mima)

Gergely, Emro Joseph. *Hungarian drama in New York,* pp. 17-23.

The Swan

Gergely, Emro Joseph. *Hungarian drama in New York,* pp. 42-45.

HENRY DE MONTHERLANT 1896-

General

Batchelor, J.W. "Religious Experiences in Henry de Montherlant's Dramatic Characters." *Australian J. of French Studies* (Monash U., Clayton, Victoria), vol. 3 (1966), pp. 180-195.

Beauvoir, Simone de. "Novelist-Philosophers XV—Montherlant." *Horizon,* vol. 20, no. 119 (Nov., 1949), pp. 292-307.

Becker, Lucille. "Pessimism and Nihilism in the Plays of Henry de Montherlant." *Yale French Studies,* no. 29 (Spring-Summer, 1962), pp. 88-91.

Corrigan, Robert W., ed. *Masterpieces of the modern French theatre,* pp. 302-303.

Cruickshank, John. *Montherlant,* pp. 101-121.

"A Displaced Person." *Times Literary Supplement,* (June 16, 1950), p. 372.

Guicharnaud, Jacques. *Modern French theatre from Giraudoux to Beckett,* pp. 93-111.

Guicharnaud, Jacques. *Modern French theatre from Giraudoux to Genet* (rev. ed.), pp. 19, 26, 98-116, 135, 159, 281, 332-333, 359.

Hartley, A.A. "The Heroic Drama of Henry de Montherlant." *Mandrake,* vol. 2, no. 8 (Spring-Summer, 1952), pp. 164-174.

"Henry de Montherlant—The Christian Vein." *Times Literary Supplement,* no. 2778 (May 27, 1955), p. xi.

Hobson, Harold. *The French theatre of today,* pp. 169-197.

Johnson, Robert B. "Definitions of Youth in the Theatre of Montherlant." *Modern Language J.,* vol. 47, no. 4 (Apr., 1963), pp. 149-154.

Johnson, Robert B. *Henry de Montherlant,* pp. 82-83, 100-101, 136-138.

Jones, Robert Emmet. *The alienated hero in modern French drama,* pp. 17-26.

Lumley, Frederick. *New trends in 20th-century drama,* pp. 342-347.

Lumley, Frederick. *Trends in 20th-century drama,* pp. 231-236.

Moore, Harry T. *Twentieth-century French literature since World War II,* pp. 22-25.

Morreale, Gerald. "'Alternance' and Montherlant's Aesthetics." *French Rev., vol.* 37 (1964), pp. 626-636.

Norrish, P.J. "Montherlant's Conception of the Tragic Hero." *French Studies,* vol. 14, no. 1 (Jan., 1960), pp. 18-37.

Price, Jonathan R. "Montherlant: The Jansenist Libertine." *Renascence,* vol. 19 (1967), pp. 208-216.

Price, Jonathan R. "Montherlant's Aesthetics." *Modern Drama,* vol. 8 (Dec., 1965), pp. 324-331.

Rosenbaum, Sidonia C. "Henry de Montherlant and Spain." *Bulletin of Hispanic Studies,* vol. 29, no. 115 (July-Sept., 1952), pp. 138-147.

Turnell, M. "Adventurer Montherland." *Commonweal,* vol. 74, no. 7 (May 12, 1961), pp. 171-173.

Vial, Fernand. "The Last Plays of Henry de Montherlant." *American Society Legion of Honor Mag.,* vol. 32, no. 1 (1961), pp. 31-47.

Vial, Fernand. "Montherlant and the Post-War Drama in France." *American Society Legion of Honor Mag.,* vol. 22, no. 1 (Spring, 1951), pp. 59-74.

Vial, Fernand. "Montherlant's Farewell to the Stage." *American Society Legion of Honor Mag.,* vol. 27, no. 1 (Spring, 1956), pp. 33-54.

Les Bestiaires

Hobson, Harold. *The French theatre of today,* pp. 174-175.

Broceliande

Johnson, Robert B. *Henry de Montherlant,* pp. 96-99.

The Cardinal of Spain

Flanner, Janet (Genet). "Letters from Paris." *New Yorker,* vol. 36 (Jan. 21, 1961), p. 94.

Johnson, Robert B. *Henry de Montherlant,* pp. 120-123.

Celles Qu'on Prend dans Ses Bras

Fowlie, Wallace. *Dionysus in Paris,* pp. 102-104.

Gobert, David L. "Identity in Diversity: Montherlant's *Celles qu'on prend dans Ses Bras* and *La Ville dont le Prince Est Un Enfant.*" *Symposium,* vol. 21, no. 1 (Spring, 1967), pp. 22-28.

Hobson, Harold. *The French theatre of today,* pp. 185-187.

Johnson, Robert B. *Henry de Montherlant,* pp. 94-96.

Don Juan

Johnson, Robert B. *Henry de Montherlant,* pp. 118-120, 133-134.

L'Exil

Johnson, Robert B. *Henry de Montherlant,* pp. 86-88.

La Guerre Civile

Johnson, Robert B. *Henry de Montherlant,* pp. 123-126.

Un Incompris

Johnson, Robert B. *Henry de Montherlant,* pp. 93-94.

Malatesta

Fowlie, Wallace. *Dionysus in Paris,* pp. 96-98.

Hobson, Harold. *The French theatre of today,* pp. 182-185.

Johnson, Robert B. *Henry de Montherlant,* pp. 107-110.

Rey, John B. "The Search for the Absolute: The Plays of Henry de Montherlant." *Modern Drama,* vol. 3, no. 2 (Sept., 1960) pp. 184-185.

"Theatre Marigny: M. de Montherlant's New Plays." *Times* no. 51,888 (Jan. 2, 1951), p. 7.

The Master of Santiago (Le Maître de Santiago)

Chiari, Joseph. *The contemporary French theatre, pp. 215-218.*

Fowlie, Wallace. *Dionysus in Paris,* pp. 98-101.

Gobert, David L. "Structural Identity of *La Reine Morte* and *Le Maître de Santiago, French Rev.,* vol. 38 (1964), pp. 30-33.

Hobson, Harold. *The French theatre of today,* pp. 176-181.

Johnson, Robert B. *Henry de Montherlant,* pp. 110-114, 135.

Lumley, Frederick. *New trends in 20th-century drama,* pp. 345-346.

Rey, John B. "The Search for the Absolute: The Plays of Henry de Montherlant." *Modern Drama,* vol. 3, no. 2 (Sept., 1960), pp. 185-187.

Taylor, John Russell. "Complex Ambiguity." *Listener,* vol. 71, no. 1823 (Mar. 5, 1964), p. 407.

Worsley, T.C. "A Hateful Play." *New Statesman,* vol. 53 (Mar. 2, 1957), pp. 275-276.

No Man's Son (Fils de Personne)

Chiari, Joseph. *The contemporary French theatre,* pp. 213-215.

Fowlie, Wallace. *Dionysus in Paris.* pp. 93-96.

Johnson, Robert B. *Henry de Montherlant,* pp. 89-93, 131.

Rey, John B. "The Search for the Absolute: The Plays of Henry de Montherlant." *Modern Drama,* vol. 3, no. 2 (Sept., 1960), pp. 181-183.

Port Royal

Chiari, Joseph. *The contemporary French theatre,* pp. 220-221.

Farrell, Isolde. *America,* vol. 93, no. 6 (May 7, 1955), pp. 155-156.

Flanner, Janet (Genet). "Letters from Paris." *New Yorker,* vol. 30 (Jan. 1, 1955), pp. 54-55.

Fowlie, Wallace. *Dionysus in Paris,* pp. 107-109.

Johnson, Robert B. *Henry de Montherlant,* pp. 114-118.

Rey, John B. "The Search for the Absolute: The Plays of Henry de Montherlant." *Modern Drama,* vol. 3, no. 2 (Sept., 1960), pp. 188-190.

Vial, Fernand. "Paris Letter." *Renascence,* vol. 7 (1955), pp. 192-194.

Queen After Death (La Reine Morte)

Chiari, Joseph. *The contemporary French theatre,* 208-213.

Craig, H.A.L. "Life—Anti-Life." *New Statesman,* vol. 61 (Feb. 17, 1961), p. 275.

Fowlie, Wallace. *Dionysus in paris,* pp. 91-93.

Gobert, David L. "Structural Identity of *La Reine Morte* and *Le Maître de Santiago.*" *French Rev.,* vol. 38 (1964), pp. 30-33.

Hobson, Harold. *The French theatre of today,* pp. 170-174.

Johnson, Robert B. "The Ferrante Image in Montherlant's *La Reine Morte.*" *French Rev.,* vol. 36, no. 3 (Jan., 1963), pp. 255-259.

Johnson, Robert B. *Henry de Montherlant,* pp. 101-107, 129-131.

Lumley, Frederick. *New trends in 20th-century drama,* pp. 343, 344-345.

Montherlant, Henry de. "Notes on the Theatre." *In:* Corrigan, Robert W., ed. *Masterpieces of the modern French theatre,* pp. 305-313.

Moore, Harry T. *Twentieth-century French literature to World War II,* pp. 198-200.

O'Brien, Justin. "A Man Absent from Himself." *Reporter,* vol. 34, no. 5 (Mar. 10, 1966), p. 50.

Rey, John B. "The Search for the Absolute: The Plays of Henry de Montherlant." *Modern Drama,* vol. 3, no. 2 (Sept., 1960), pp. 179-181.

Tynan, Kenneth. *Tynan right and left,* pp. 88-90.

Warnke, Frank J. "Poetic Drama on European Stages." *New Republic,* vol. 141, nos. 8-9 (Aug. 24, 1959), pp. 30-31.

Tomorrow the Dawn (Demain il Fera Jour)

Fowlie, Wallace. *Dionysus in Paris,* pp. 101-102.

Johnson, Robert B. *Henry de Montherlant,* pp. 89-94.

Rey, John B. "The Search for the Absolute: The Plays of Henry de Montherlant." *Modern Drama,* vol. 3, no. 2 (Sept., 1960), pp. 183-184.

La Ville Dont le Prince Est un Enfant

Chiari, Joseph. *The contemporary French theatre,* pp. 218-220.

Fowlie, Wallace. *Dionysus in Paris,* pp. 104-107.

Gobert, David L. "Identity in Diversity: Montherlant's *Celles Qu'on Prend Dans Ses Bras* and *La Ville Dont Le Prince Est Un Enfant.*" *Symposium,* vol. 21 no. 1 (Spring, 1967), pp. 22-28.

Hobson, Harold. *The French theatre of today,* pp. 193-197.

Johnson, Robert B. *Henry de Montherlant,* pp. 83-86, 131-132.

Rey, John B. "The Search for the Absolute: The Plays of Henry de Montherlant." *Modern Drama,* vol. 3, no. 2 (Sept., 1960), pp. 187-188.

ARMANDO MOOCK 1894-1942.

General

Jones, W.K. "Armando Moock, Forgotten Chilean Dramatist." *Hispania,* vol. 22 (Feb., 1939), pp. 41-50.

WILLIAM VAUGHN MOODY 1869-1910.

General

Halpern, Martin. *William Vaughn Moody,* pp. 15-23.

Henry, David D. *William Vaughn Moody, a study,* pp. 111-140, 214-218.

Miller, Nellie Burget. *The living drama,* pp. 394-395.

The Death of Eve

Halpern, Martin. *William Vaughn Moody,* pp. 51, 114, 158, 166-181, 182, 183.

Henry, David D. *William Vaughn Moody, a study,* pp. 162-170.

The Faith Healer

Halpern, Martin. *William Vaughn Moody,* pp. 46, 48, 95, 116-117, 159-166, 181, 183.

Henry, David D. *William Vaughn Moody, a study,* pp. 195-214.

The Fire Bringer

Halpern, Martin. *William Vaughan Moody,* pp. 51, 93-114, 130, 151, 166, 172, 175.

Henry, David D. *William Vaughan Moody, a study,* pp. 148-162.

The Great Divide

Gassner, John. "Introduction." *In: Best plays of the early American theatre from the beginning to 1916,* pp. xxxviii-xxxix.

Halpern, Martin. *William Vaughan Moody,* pp. 115-133, 158, 159, 166, 181, 182.

Henry, David D. *William Vaughan Moody, a study,* pp. 170-195.

Miller, Nellie Burget. *The living drama,* pp. 395-397.

GEORGE MOORE 1852-1933

General

Malone, Andrew E. *The Irish drama,* pp. 69-76.

Saddlemyer, Ann. "All Art is a Collaboration? George Moore and W.B. Yeats." *In:* Skelton, Robin, ed. *The world of W.B. Yeats,* pp. 213-220.

Williams, Harold. *Modern English writers,* pp. 200-201.

THOMAS STURGE MOORE 1870-1944

Daimonassa

Winters, Yvor. "The Poetry of T. Sturge Moore." *Southern Rev.,* vol. 2, no. 1 (Winter, 1966), pp. 1-16.

Judith

Roston, Murray. *Biblical drama in England from the Middle Ages to the present day,* pp. 244-246.

Mariamne

Roston, Murray. *Biblical drama in England from the Middle Ages to the present day,* pp. 119, 173-175, 242-243.

ALBERTO MORAVIA 1907-
(real name Alberto Pincherle)

General

Mastrangelo, Aida. "Alberto Moravia as Dramatist." *Quarterly J. of Speech,* vol. 53 (1967), pp. 127-134.

Pandolfi, Vito. "Italian Theatre Since the War." *Tulane Drama Rev.* vol. 8, no. 3 (Spring, 1964), pp. 102-104.

Beatrice Cenci

Mastrangelo, Aida. "Alberto Moravia as Dramatist." *Q. J. of Speech,* vol. 53, no. 2 (Apr., 1967), pp. 127-134.

Pandolfi, Vito. "Italian Theatre Since the War." *Tulane Drama rev.* vol. 8, no. 3 (Spring, 1964), pp. 102-104.

CHARLES MORGAN 1894-1958

General

Lumley, Frederick. *Trends in 20th century drama,* pp. 210-211.

The Burning Glass

Williamson, Audrey. *Contemporary theatre, 1953-1956,* pp. 33-35.

The Flashing Stream

Dent, Alan. *Preludes and studies,* pp. 168-172.

PETER MORRELL

See Smith, J. Augustus (co-author)

ENRICO LUIGI MORSELLI

General

Goldberg, Issac. *The drama of transition,* pp. 145-152.

JOHN MORTIMER 1923-

General

Taylor, John Russell. *Anger and after,* pp. 214-226.

Wellwarth, George. *The theatre of protest and paradox,* pp. 253-257, 258.

Call Me a Liar

Taylor, John Russell. *Anger and after,* pp. 219-220.

David and Broccoli

Taylor, John Russell. *Anger and after,* pp. 223-224.

The Dock Brief

Taylor, John Russell. *Anger and after,* pp. 216-217.

Wellwarth, George. *The theatre of protest and paradox,* pp. 255-256.

I Spy

Taylor, John Russell. *Anger and after,* pp. 218-219.

Two Stars for Comfort

Taylor, John Russell. *Anger and after,* pp. 224-226.

What Shall We Tell Caroline?

Taylor, John Russell. *Anger and after,* pp. 218-219.

Wellwarth, George. *The theatre of protest and paradox,* pp. 255-257.

The Wrong Side of the Park

Taylor, John Russell. *Anger and after,* pp. 220-222.

Wellwarth, George. *The theatre of protest and paradox,* p. 254.

LUIS A. MOSCOSO VEGA 1909-
General

Jones, W.K. *Behind Spanish American footlights,* p. 312.

GERHART HERRMANN MOSTAR 1901-
General   (pseud. Gerhart Herrmann)

Samelson, William. *Gerhart Herrmann Mostar: a critical profile,* pp. 66-181.

The Birthday (Die Geburt)

Samelson, William. *Gerhart Herrmann Mostar: a critical profile,* pp. 149-171.

Bis Der Schnee Schultz

Samelson, William. *Gerhart Herrmann Mostar: a critical profile,* pp. 179-181.

Meier Helmbrecht

Samelson, William. *Gerhart Herrmann Mostar: a critical profile,* pp. 171-179.

Putsch Imx Paris

Samelson, William. *Gerhart Herrmann Mostar: a critical profile,* pp. 112-149.

Der Zimmerherr

Samelson, William. *Gerhart Herrmann Mostar: a critical profile,* pp. 67-112.

SLAWOMIR MROZEK 1930-
General

Tarn, Adam. "Plays." *Polish Perspectives,* vol. 8, no. 10 (Oct., 1965), pp. 6-7, 10-11.

Tango

Grodzicki, August. "Mrozek's Danse Macabre." *Polish Perspectives,* vol. 8, no. 11 (Nov., 1965), pp. 62-65.

Knott, Jan. "Mrozek's Family." *Encounter,* vol. 25 (July-Dec., 1965), pp. 54-58.

RICARDO MUJIA 1861-1934

Bolívar en Junín

Jones, W.K. *Behind Spanish American footlights,* p. 279.

KAJ MUNK 1898-1944

General

Schmidt, Robert. "Kaj Munk, a New Danish Dramatist." *American-Scandinavian Rev.,* vol. 21 (1933), pp. 227-232.

Thompson, Lawrence. "A Voice Death Has Not Silenced." *Books Abroad,* vol. 18 (1944), pp. 126-127.

Thompson, Lawrence. "The Actuality of Kaj Munk's Dramas." *Books Abroad,* vol. 15 (1941), pp. 267-272.

He Sits at the Melting Pot

Arestad, Sverre. "Kaj Munk as a Dramatist." *Scandinavian Studies,* vol. 26, no. 4 (Nov., 1954), pp. 151-176.

An Idealist

Arestad, Sverre. "Kaj Munk as a Dramatist." *Scandinavian Studies,* vol. 26, no. 4 (Nov., 1954), pp. 151-176.

The Word

Arestad, Sverre. "Kaj Munk as a Dramatist." *Scandinavian Studies,* vol. 26, no. 4 (Nov., 1954), pp. 151-176.

JOHN MURPHY

General

Hogan, Robert. *After the Irish renaissance,* pp. 81-82.

THOMAS MURPHY

A Whistle in the Dark

Armstrong, William A. "The Irish Point of View; The Plays of Sean O'Casey, Brendan Behan, and Thomas Murphy." *In:* Armstrong William A., ed. *Experimental drama,* pp. 99-101.

THOMAS C. MURRAY 1873-1958

General

Hogan, Robert. *After the Irish renaissance,* pp. 27-29.

Malone, Andrew E. *The Irish drama,* pp. 308-309.

Aftermath

Malone, Andrew E. *The Irish drama,* pp. 191-192.

Autumn Fire

Malone, Andrew E. *The Irish drama,* pp. 192-193.

Birthright

Malone, Andrew E. *The Irish drama,* pp. 187-189.

The Blind Wolf

Malone, Andrew E. *The Irish drama,* pp. 193-194.

Maurice Harte

Malone, Andrew E. *The Irish drama,* pp. 189-190.

The Pipe in the Fields

Malone, Andrew E. *The Irish drama,* p. 193.

Sovereign Love

Malone, Andrew E. *The Irish drama,* pp. 185-187.

Spring

Malone, Andrew E. *The Irish drama,* pp. 190-191.

ROBERT MUSIL 1880-1942

Die Schwärmer

Braun, Wilhelm. "An Approach to Musil's *Die Schwärmer.*" *Monatshefte,* vol. 54 (1962), pp. 156-170.

Braun, Wilhelm. "Musil's Anselm and 'The Motivated Life." *Wisconsin Studies in Contemporary Literature,* vol. 8, no. 4 (Autumn, 1967), pp. 517-527.

Braun, Wilhelm "Musil's *Die Schwärmer.*" PMLA, vol. 80 (1965), 292-298.

VLADIMIR NABOKOV 1899-

General

Bryer, Jackson R. "Vladimir Nabokov's Critical Reputation in English: A Note and a Checklist." *Wisconsin Studies in Contemporary Literature,* vol. 8, no. 2 (Spring, 1967), pp. 312-364.

Darack, Arthur. "Trouble With Doubles." *Saturday Rev.,* vol. 49 (May 21, 1966), pp. 32-33.

"Selected Bibliography of Nabokov's Work." *Wisconsin Studies in Contemporary Literature,* vol. 8, no. 2 (Spring 1967), pp. 310-311.

Death (Smert')

Field, Andrew. *Nabokov, his life in art,* pp. 75-76, 166.

The Event (Sobytie)

Field, Andrew. *Nabokov, his life in art,* pp. 208, 212-218.

Karlinsky, Simon. "Illusion, Reality, and Parody in Nabokov's Plays." *In:* Dembo, L.S., ed. *Nabokov, the man and his work,* pp. 184-191, 193-194. *Also in: Wisconsin Studies in Contemporary Literature,* vol. 8, no. 2 (Spring, 1967), pp. 268-279.

The Grandfather (Dedushka)

Field, Andrew. *Nabokov, his life in art,* pp. 77-78.

The Pole (Polius)

Field, Andrew. *Nabokov, his life in art,* pp. 76-77.

The Tragedy of Mister Morn (Tragediya Gospodina Morna)

Field, Andrew. *Nabokov, his life in art,* pp. 78-79.

The Waltz Invention (Izobretenie Val'sa)

Brophy, Brigid. "Lolita and Other Games." *Book Week (Wash. Post, Chicago Sun-Times),* May 15, 1966, pp. 2, 10.

Darack, Arthur. "Trouble With Doubles." *Saturday Rev.,* vol. 49 (May 21, 1966), pp. 32-33.

Davis, Douglas M. "Perils Are Apparent in Reissuing Early Nabokov, Vonnegut Works." *National Observer* (May 23, 1966), p. 23.

Fanning, Garth. "Nabokov Play Deals With Power and the Fantasies It Can Produce." Sacramento *Bee* (Apr. 17, 1966), p. 128.

Field, Andrew. *Nabokov, his life in art,* pp. 208-213.

Hayes, E. Nelson. "Theme of Early Nabokov Play Predicts Nuclear Blackmail." New Haven *Register* (Apr. 17, 1966), Sec. 4, p. 4.

Hobby, Diana. "2 Nabokovs." Houston *Post* (June 5, 1966), Spotlight Section, p. 13.

Jackson, Paul R. "Artistic Perfection of a Crime." *Chicago Sunday Tribune Books Today* (May 29, 1966), p. 3.

Karlinsky, Simon. "Illusion, Reality, and Parody in Nabokov's Plays." *In:* Dembo, L.S., ed. *Nabokov, the man and his work,* pp. 184-185, 191-194. *Also in: Wisconsin Studies in Contemporary Literature,* vol. 8, no. 2 (Spring, 1967), pp. 268-279.

"The Nabokov Defense." *Time,* vol. 87 (Apr. 29, 1966), pp. 118, 120.

Newman, Vivian D. *Library J.,* vol. 91 (June 1, 1966), p. 2869.

Root, Bertram. "Within the Spacious Circle." *North American Rev.,* n.s., vol. 3 (May, 1966), p. 36.

Stuart, Reece. "A Nabokov Pre-Lolita." Des Moines *Sunday Register* (Apr. 24, 1966), p. 23-G.

Williams, Vera. Orange County *Evening News* (Garden Grove, Cal.), Apr. 17, 1966, *Southland Magazine,* p. 19. *See also:* Long Beach (Cal.) *Independent Press-Telegram,* Apr. 17, 1966.

The Wanderers (Skital'tsy)

Field, Andrew. *Nabokov, his life in art,* pp. 73-75.

CONRADO NALE ROXLO 1898-

General

Anderson Imbert, Enrique. *Spanish-American literature: a history,* pp. 513-515.

Jones, W.K. *Behind Spanish American footlights,* pp. 140-142.

Tull, John Frederick. "Nalé Roxlo's 'Chamico' Stories: A Dramatist's Apprenticeship." *Hispania,* vol. 44, no. 2 (May, 1961), pp. 245-249.

Tull, John F. "Unifying Characteristics in Nalé Roxlo's Theatre." *Hispania,* vol. 44, no. 4 (Dec., 1961), pp. 643-646.

Cristina's Pact (El Pacto de Cristina)

Anderson Imbert, Enrique. *Spanish-American literature: a history,* pp. 514-515.

Mazzara, Richard A. "Dramatic Variations of Themes of *El sombrero de tres picos: La zapatera prodigiosa* and *Una viuda difícil." Hispania,* vol. 41 (1958), pp. 186-189.

The Mermaid Tail (La Cola de la Sirena)

Anderson Imbert, Enrique. *Spanish-American literature: a history,* p. 514.

Mazzara, Richard A. "Dramatic Variations of Themes of *El sombrero de tres picos: La zapatera prodigiosa* and *Una viuda dificil.*" *Hispania,* vol. 41 (1958), pp. 186 189.

Judith y las Rosas

Mazzara, Richard A. "Dramatic Variations of Themes of *El sombrero de tres picos: La zapatera prodigiosa* and *Una viuda dificil.*" *Hispania,* vol. 41 (1958), pp. 186-189.

Una Viuda Dificil

Mazzara, Richard A. "Dramatic Variations of Themes of *El sombrero de tres picos: La zapatera prodigiosa* and *Una viuda dificil.*" *Hispania,* vol. 41 (1958), pp. 186-189.

JACQUES NATANSON

General

Knowles, Dorothy. *French drama of the inter-war years, 1918-39,* pp. 140-141.

L'Eté

Knowles, Dorothy. *French drama of the inter-war years, 1918-39,* pp. 142-143.

Le Greluchon Délicat

Knowles, Dorothy. *French drama of the inter-war years, 1918-39,* pp. 141-142.

GEORGES NEVEUX

General

Bishop, Thomas. *Pirandello and the French theater,* pp. 135-138.

Bree, Germaine. "Georges Neveux: A Theatre of Adventure." *Yale French Studies,* no. 14 (Winter, 1954-55), pp. 65-70.

Pronko, Leonard C. "Georges Neveux: The Theatrical Voyage." *Drama Survey,* vol. 3, no. 2 (Oct., 1963), pp. 244-252.

ROBERT NICHOLS

The Decapitated Taxi

Sainer, Arthur. *The sleepwalker and the assassin, a view of the contemporary theatre,* pp. 106-107.

The Wax Engine

Sainer, Arthur. *The sleepwalker and the assassin, a view of the contemporary theatre,* pp. 107-108.

Wings over Europe (Maurice Brown, Co-author)

Block, Anita. *The changing world in plays and theatre,* pp. 310-321.

Smith, Winifred. "The Dying God in the Modern Theatre." *Rev. of Religion,* vol. 5 (Mar., 1941), pp. 273-275.

NORMAN NICHOLSON 1914-

A Match for the Devil

Roston, Murray. *Biblical drama in England from the Middle Ages to the present day,* pp. 293-294.

The Old Man of the Mountains

Roston, Murray. *Biblical drama in England from the Middle Ages to the present day,* p. 293.

Spanos, William V. *The Christian tradition in modern British verse drama,* pp. 269-281.

Welland, Dennis. "Some Post-War Experiments in Poetic Drama." *In:* Armstrong, William A., ed. *Experimental drama,* pp. 36-55.

GREGORY NOBIKOV

Newsboy

Himelstein, Morgan Y. *Drama was a weapon, the left-wing theatre in New York 1929-1941,* pp. 15-17.

CARLOS NORIEGA HOPE 1896-1934

General

Gonzalez Pena, Carlos. *History of Mexican literature,* pp. 376-377.

HANS ERICH NOSSACK 1901-

General

Keith-Smith, Brian. "Hans Erich Nossack." *In:* Keith-Smith, B., ed. *Essays on contemporary German literature* (German Men of Letters, Vol. IV), pp. 63-85.

Prochnik, Peter. "Controlling Thoughts in the Work of Hans Erich Nossack." *German Life and Letters,* vol. 19 (1965), pp. 68-74.

Die Rotte Kain

Keith-Smith, Brian. "Hans Erich Nossack." *In:* Keith-Smith, B., ed. *Essays on contemporary German literature* (German Men of Letters, Vol. IV), p. 67.

Ein Sonderfall

Keith-Smith, Brian. "Hans Erich Nossack." *In:* Keith-Smith, B., ed. *Essays on contemporary German literature* (German Men of Letters, Vol. IV), p. 68.

Puppe, Heinz W. (Review.) *Books Abroad,* vol. 39, no. 1 (Winter, 1965), p. 54.

ELLIOTT NUGENT 1900-

General

Gould, Jean. *Modern American playwrights,* pp. 151-154.

RENE DE OBALDIA

L'Air du Large

"*L'Air du Large* by Obaldia." *World Theatre,* vol. 15, no. 6 (Nov.-Dec. 1966), pp. 562-563.

Du Vent dans les Branches de Sassafras

Mankin, Paul A. "The Paris Stage in 1965-66." *Books Abroad,* vol. 41, no. 4 (Autumn 1967), p. 404.

ARCH OBELER 1909-

Night of the Auk

Weales, Gerald. *American drama since World War II,* pp. 183-184.

ANDRE OBEY 1892-

General

Knowles, Dorothy. *French drama of the inter-war years, 1918-39,* pp. 220-221.

Bataille de la Marne

Knowles, Dorothy. *French drama of the inter-war years, 1918-39,* pp. 223-224.

Une Fille Pour du Vent

Knowles, Dorothy. *French drama of the inter-war years, 1918-39,* pp. 226-227.

Lazare

Knowles, Dorothy. *French drama of the inter-war years, 1918-39,* p. 226.

Loire

Knowles, Dorothy. *French drama of the inter-war years, 1918-39,* pp. 224-225.

Noah (Noé)

Fergusson, Francis. *The idea of a theater,* pp. 215-222.

Gassner, John. *The theatre in our times,* pp. 214-215.

Knowles, Dorothy. *French drama of the inter-war years, 1918-39,* pp. 221-222.

Roston, Murray. *Biblical drama in England from the Middle Ages to the present day,* pp. 283-285.

Venus and Adonis

Gassner, John. *The theatre in our times,* pp. 213-214.

Le Viol de Lucrèce (Lucrèce)

Knowles, Dorothy. *French drama of the inter-war years, 1918-39,* pp. 222-223.

Young, Stark. *Immortal shadows,* pp. 145-149.

SEAN O'CASEY 1880-1964

General

Armstrong, William A., ed. *Experimental drama,* pp. 79-95.

Armstrong, William A. "The Irish Point of View: The Plays of Sean O'Casey, Brendan Behan, and Thomas Murphy." *In:* Armstrong, William A., ed. *Experimental drama,* pp. 79-102.

Benstock, Bernard. "A Covey of Clerics in Joyce and O'Casey." *James Joyce Q.,* vol. 2, no. 1 (Fall, 1964), pp. 18-32.

Blau, Herbert. *The impossible theatre,* pp. 205-210.

Boas, Guy. "The Drama of Sean O'Casey." *College English,* vol. 10, no. 2 (Nov., 1948), pp. 80-86.

Butler, Anthony. "The Abbey Daze." *In:* McCann, Sean, ed. *The world of Sean O'Casey,* pp. 92-105.

Casey, Anna McGinley. "The development of Sean O'Casey as a dramatist." M.A., University of Colorado, 1949.

Coston, Herbert. "Sean O'Casey: Prelude to Playwriting." *In:* Freedman, Morris ed. *Essays in the modern drama,* pp. 125-136. (Reprinted from the *Tulane Drama Rev.,* Sept., 1960, pp. 102-112.)

Coston, Herbert. "Sean O'Casey: Prelude to Playwriting." *Tulane Drama Rev.,* vol. 5, no. 1 (Sept., 1960), pp. 102-112.

Cowasjee, Saros. "The Juxtaposition of Tragedy and Comedy in the Plays of Sean O'Casey." *Wascana Rev.* (Regina, Sask.), vol. 2, no. 1 (1967), pp. 75-89.

Cowasjee, Saros. *O'Casey,* pp. 1-14, 67-70, 85-87, 99-101.

Cowasjee, Saros. "O'Casey Seen Through Holloway's Diary." *Rev. of English Literature,* vol. 6, no. 3 (July, 1965), pp. 58-69.

Coxhead, Elizabeth. *Lady Gregory, a literary portrait,* pp. 196-206.

Edwards, A.C. "The Lady Gregory Letters to Sean O'Casey." *Modern Drama,* vol. 8, no. 1 (May, 1965), pp. 95-111.

Fallon, Gabriel. "Pathway of a Dramatist." *Theatre Arts,* vol. 34, no. 1 (Jan., 1950), pp. 36-39.

Fraser, G.S. *The modern writer and his world,* pp. 206-209.

Freedman, Morris. "The Modern Tragicomedy of Wilde and O'Casey." *College English,* vol. 25, no. 7 (Apr., 1964), pp. 518-522, 527.

Freedman, Morris. *The moral impulse,* pp. 67-73.

Gassner, John. "Introduction." *In:* O'Casey, Sean. *Selected plays of Sean O'Casey,* pp. v-xxi.

Gassner, John. *The theatre in our times,* pp. 240-248.

Hogan, Robert. *After the Irish renaissance,* pp. 235-252.

Hogan, Robert. "O'Casey and the Archbishop." *New Republic,* vol. 138, no. 20 (May 19, 1958), pp. 29-30.

Hogan, Robert Goode. "Sean O'Casey's experiments in dramatic form." Ph.D., University of Missouri. 1956.

Howse, K.F. "The plays of Sean O'Casey." M.A., University of Liverpool, 1950-51.

Jordan, John. "The Irish Theatre: Retrospect and Premonition." *In:* Brown, J.R. and B. Harris, eds. *Contemporary theatre,* pp. 168-170, 175-178.

Kavanagh, Peter. *The story of the Abbey Theatre from its origins to the present,* pp. 129-133.

Knight, G. Wilson. *The golden labyrinth,* pp. 373-380.

Koslow, Jules. *Sean O'Casey, the man and his plays,* pp. 9-10, 13-22, 29, 32-33, 36-37, 40-42, 43-44, 109-110.

Krause, David. "O'Casey and Yeats and the Druid." *Modern Drama,* vol. 11, no. 3 (Dec., 1968), pp. 252-262.

Krause, David. "Prometheus of Dublin, a study of the plays of Sean O'Casey." Ph.D., New York University, 1954.

Krause, David. "The Rageous Ossean." *Modern Drama,* vol. 4, no. 3 (Dec., 1961), pp. 268-291.

Krause, David. "Sean O'Casey: 1880-1964." *In:* Skelton, Robin and David R. Clark, eds. *Irish renaissance,* pp. 139-157. (From an essay read in a series of Lectures in the Humanities at Clark University, Worcester, Massachusetts on Feb. 19, 1965). *Massachusetts Rev.,* vol. 6 (Winter-Spring, 1965).

Krutch, Joseph Wood. *"Modernism" in modern drama,* pp. 98-101.

Lewis, Allan. *The contemporary theatre,* pp. 169-191.

Lumley, Frederick. *New trends in 20th-century drama,* pp. 294-296.

Lumley, Frederick. *Trends in 20th-century drama,* pp. 208-210.

McHugh, Roger. "The Legacy of Sean O'Casey." *Texas Q.,* vol. 8, no. 1 (Spring, 1965), pp. 123-137.

Malone, Andrew E. *The Irish drama,* pp. 209-214, 214-216, 306-308.

Nordell, H.R. "The dramatic theory and practice of Sean O'Casey." B. Litt., Trinity College, Dublin, 1951-52.

O'Casey, Sean. *The green crow,* pp. 177-190.

O'Casey, Sean. "An Irishman's Plays." *In:* O'Casey, Sean. *Blasts and benedictions,* pp. 82-84. (From *Radio Times* (Jan. 25, 1957) with title: *The Drama of the Future.)*

O'Casey, Sean. "On the Banks of the Ban." *In:* O'Casey, Sean. *Blasts and benedictions,* pp. 146-149. (From *The New York Times,* (Jan. 5, 1964.)

O'Casey, Sean. "A Word Before Curtain-Rise." *In:* O'Casey, Sean. *Blasts and benedictions,* pp. 85-87. (From foreword to *Selected plays of Sean O'Casey,* N.Y., Braziller, 1954.)

O'Donovan, Michael. *A short history of Irish literature,* pp. 154, 213, 216-221, 224.

O'Riley, Margaret Catherine. "The dramaturgy of Sean O'Casey." Ph.D., University of Wisconsin, 1955.

O'Shaughnessy, John. "O'Casey: Forever Fare Thee Well." *Nation,* vol. 184, (Mar. 16, 1957), pp. 237-239.

Parker, R.B. "Bernard Shaw and Sean O'Casey." *Queen's Q.,* vol. 73, no. 1 (Spring, 1966), pp. 13-34.

Ritchie, Harry M. "The Influence of Melodrama on the Early Plays of Sean O'Casey." *Modern Drama,* vol. 5, no. 1 (May, 1962), pp. 164-173.

Rollins, Ronald G. "Shaw and O'Casey: John Bull and His Other Island." *Shaw Rev.,* vol. 10 (1967), pp. 60-69.

Rudin, Seymour. "Playwright to Critic: Sean O'Casey's Letters to George Jean Nathan." *In:* Skelton, Robin and David R. Clark, eds. *Irish renaissance,* pp. 130-138.

Woodbridge, Homer E. "Sean O'Casey." *South Atlantic Q.,* vol. 40, no. 1 (Jan., 1941), pp. 50-59.

Worth, Katherine J. "O'Casey's Dramatic Symbolism." *Modern Drama,* Vol. 4, no. 3 (Dec., 1961), pp. 260-267.

Bibliography

Carpenter, Charles A. "Sean O'Casey Studies Through 1964." *Modern Drama,* vol. 1, no. 1 (May, 1967), pp. 17-23.

Bedtime Story

O'Casey, Sean. "Bedtime Story." *In:* O'Casey, Sean. *Blasts and benedictions,* pp. 132-134.

Smith, Bobby L. "The Hat, the Whore, and the Hypocrite in O'Casey's *Bedtime Story." The Serif* (Kent, Ohio), vol. 4, no. 2 (1967), pp. 3-5.

Behind the Green Curtain

Armstrong, William A. *Sean O'Casey,* pp. 29-30.

Cowasjee, Saros. *O'Casey,* pp. 97-98.

Hogan, Robert. *After the Irish renaissance* pp. 249-250.

The Bishop's Bonfire

Armstrong, William A., ed. *Experimental drama,* pp. 87-88.

Armstrong, William A. *Sean O'Casey,* pp. 27-28.

Carroll, Niall. "The Bonfire." *In:* McCann, Sean, ed. *The world of Sean O'Casey,* pp. 129-131.

Casey, Kevin. "The Excitements and the Disappointments." *In:* McCann. Sean, ed. *The world of Sean O'Casey,* pp. 230-231.

Cowasjee, Saros. *O'Casey,* pp. 93-95.

Hogan, Robert. *After the Irish renaissance* pp. 244-247.

Koslow, Jules. *Sean O'Casey, the man and his plays,* pp. 111-115.

O'Casey, Sean. *The green crow,* pp. 130-159.

O'Casey, Sean. "O'Casey's Drama—Bonfire." *In:* O'Casey, Sean. *Blasts and benedictions,* pp. 138-141.

Williamson, Audrey. *Contemporary theatre, 1953-1956,* pp. 75-77.

Cock-A-Doodle Dandy

Armstrong, William A. *Sean O'Casey,* pp. 25-27.

Casey, Kevin. "The Excitements and the Disappointments." *In:* McCann, Sean, ed. *The world of Sean O'Casey,* pp. 228-230.

Cowasjee, Saros. *O'Casey,* pp. 90-92.

Hogan, Robert. *After the Irish renaissance,* pp. 241-243.

Koslow, Jules. *Sean O'Casey, the man and his plays,* pp. 101-107.

O'Casey, Sean. "Cockadoodle Doo." *In:* O'Casey, Sean. *Blasts and benedictions,* pp. 142-145.

O'Casey, Sean. *In:* Cole, Toby, ed. *Playwrights on playwriting,* pp. 247-249. (Reprinted from Sean O'Casey. "O'Casey's Credo." *The New York Times,* Nov. 9, 1958, Drama Section.

Smith, Bobby L. "Satire in O'Casey's *Cock-A-Doodle-Dandy."* *Renascence,* vol. 19 (1967), pp. 64-73.

Styan, J.L. *The dark comedy,* 2nd ed., p. 136.

The Crimson in the Tri-Colour

Hogan, Robert. "O'Casey's Apprenticeship." *Modern Drama,* vol. 4, no. 3 (Dec., 1961), pp. 243-253.

The Drums of Father Ned

Armstrong, William A. *Sean O'Casey, pp. 28-29.*

Carroll, Niall. "The Bonfire." *In:* McCann, Sean, ed. *The world of Sean O'Casey,* pp. 133-134.

Casey, Kevin. "The Excitements and the Disappointments." *In:* McCann, Sean, ed. *The world of Sean O'Casey,* pp. 231-232.

Cowasjee, Saros. *O'Casey,* pp. 95-97.

Hogan, Robert. *After the Irish renaissance,* pp. 247-249.

Koslow, Jules. *Sean O'Casey, the man and his plays,* pp. 115-117.

Figure in the Night

Hogan, Robert. *After the Irish renaissance.* pp. 249, 250-251.

The Frost in the Flower

Hogan, Robert. "O'Casey's Apprenticeship." *Modern Drama,* vol. 4, no. 3 (Dec., 1961), pp. 243-253.

The Harvest Festival

Hogan, Robert. "O'Casey's Apprenticeship." *Modern Drama,* vol. 4, no. 3 (Dec., 1961), pp. 243-253.

Juno and the Paycock

Allison, Alexander W., ed. *Masterpieces of the drama,* 2nd ed., pp. 519-520.

Armstrong, William A. *Sean O'Casey,* pp. 13-15, 17.

Cohn, Ruby, ed. *Twentieth-century drama,* pp. 168-169.

Cowasjee, Saros. *O'Casey,* pp. 21-27.

Cowell, Raymond. *Twelve modern dramatists,* pp. 66-67.

Dorcey, Donal. "The Great Occasions." *In:* McCann, Sean, ed. *The world of Sean O'Casey,* pp. 54-55.

Fallon, Gabriel. "The Man in the Plays." *In:* McCann, Sean, ed. *The world of Sean O'Casey,* pp. 206-208.

Henn, T.R. *The harvest of tragedy,* pp. 212-213.

Koslow, Jules. *Sean O'Casey, the man and his plays,* pp. 23-25, 30-32.

McCollom, William G. *Tragedy,* pp. 102-103.

McHugh, Roger. "The Legacy of Sean O'Casey." *Texas Q.,* vol. 8, no. 1 (1965), pp. 123-137.

Malone, Andrew E. *The Irish drama,* pp. 214-216.

O'Casey, Sean. "O'Casey in Hungarian Costume." *In:* O'Casey, Sean. *Blasts and benedictions,* pp. 135-137.

O'Donovan, John. "The Big Three." *In:* McCann, Sean, ed. *The world of Sean O'Casey,* pp. 189-192.

Rollins, Ronald G. "Form and Content in Sean O'Casey's Dublin Trilogy." *Modern Drama,* vol. 8, no. 4 (Feb., 1966), pp. 419-425.

Styan, J.L. *The dark comedy,* 2nd ed., pp. 132, 133, 174-175, 263, 267, 268.

Kathleen Listens In

Dorcey, Donal. "The Great Occasions." *In:* McCann, Sean, ed. *The world of Sean O'Casey,* pp. 53-54.

Hogan, Robert. "O'Casey's Apprenticeship." *Modern Drama,* vol. 4, no. 3 (Dec., 1961), pp. 243-253.

The Moon Shines on Kylenamoe

Hogan, Robert. *After the Irish renaissance,* p. 249.

Nannie's Night Out

Ayling, Ronald. *"Nannie's Night Out." Modern Drama,* vol. 5, no. 1 (May, 1962), pp. 154-163.

Dorcey, Donal. "The Great Occasions." *In:* McCann, Sean, ed. *The world of Sean O'Casey,* pp. 56-57.

Hogan, Robert. "O'Casey's Apprenticeship." *Modern Drama,* vol. 4, no. 3 (Dec., 1961), pp. 243-253.

Oak Leaves and Lavender

Armstrong, William A. *Sean O'Casey,* pp. 22-23.

Casey, Kevin. "The Excitements and the Disappointments." *In:* McCann, Sean, ed. *The world of Sean O'Casey,* pp. 227-228.

Cowasjee, Saros. *O'Casey,* pp. 82-84.

Hobson, Harold. *Theatre,* pp. 83-85.

Koslow, Jules. *Sean O'Casey, the man and his plays,* pp. 95-101.

The Plough and the Stars

Armstrong, William A. *Sean O'Casey,* pp. 15-17.

Armstrong, W.A. "The Sources and Themes of *The Plough and the Stars." Modern Drama,* vol. 4, no. 3 (Dec., 1961), pp. 234-242.

Colum, Padraic. "Review of *The Plough and the Stars." Saturday Rev. of Literature,* vol. 2 (June 12, 1926), p. 854.

Cowasjee, Saros. *O'Casey,* pp. 27-39.

DeBaun, Vincent C. "Sean O'Casey and the Road to Expressionism." *Modern Drama,* vol. 4 no. 3 (Dec., 1961), pp. 254-259.

Dorcey, Donal. "The Big Occasions." *In:* McCann, Sean, ed. *The story of the Abbey Theatre,* pp. 148-152.

Dorcey, Donal. "The Great Occasions." *In:* McCann, Sean, ed. *The world of Sean O'Casey,* pp. 58-72.

Fallon, Gabriel. "The Man in the Plays." *In:* McCann, Sean, ed. *The world of Sean O'Casey,* pp. 208-209.

Kavanagh, Peter. *The story of the Abbey Theatre from its origins to the present,* pp. 134-138.

Koslow, Jules. *Sean O'Casey, the man and his plays,* pp. 25-30, 33-36, 37-40.

McHugh, Roger. "The Legacy of Sean O'Casey." *Texas Q.,* vol. 8, no. 1 (1965), pp. 123-137.

Malone, Andrew E. *The Irish drama,* pp. 216-218.

O'Casey, Sean. "Nationalism and *The Plough and the Stars.*" *In:* O'Casey, Sean. *Blasts and benedictions,* pp. 92-94. (From a letter to the *Irish Independent* (Feb. 26, 1926).)

O'Casey, Sean. "*The Plough and the Stars:* A Reply to the Critics." *In:* O'Casey, Sean. *Blasts and benedictions,* pp. 88-91. (From *Irish Times* (Feb. 19, 1926) and *Irish Independent* (Feb. 20, 1926).)

O'Casey, Sean. "*The Plough and the Stars in Retrospect.*" *In:* O'Casey, Sean. *Blasts and benedictions,* pp. 95-98. (From *The New York Times* (Dec. 4, 1960), with title: "Memories of a Farewell to Ireland.")

O'Donovan, John. "The Big Three." *In: McC*ann, Sean, ed. *The world of Sean O'Casey,* pp. 192-195.

O'Donovan, Michael. *A short history of Irish literature,* pp. 219-220, 222.

Rollins, Ronald G. "Form and Content in Sean O'Casey's Dublin Trilogy." *Modern Drama,* vol. 8, no. 4 (Feb., 1966), pp. 419-425.

Shipp, Horace. "The Art of Sean O'Casey." *English Rev.,* vol. 42 (June, 1926), pp. 851-853.

Styan, J.L. *The dark comedy,* 2nd ed., pp. 132-133, 267, 275, 284.

Styan, J.L. *The elements of drama,* pp. 190-195.

Purple Dust

Armstrong, William A. *Sean O'Casey,* pp. 21-22.

Barnet, Sylvan, ed. *The genius of the Irish theater,* pp. 262-264.

Casey, Kevin. "The Excitements and the Disappointments." *In:* McCann, Sean, ed. *The world of Sean O'Casey,* pp. 222-225.

Cowasjee, Saros. *O'Casey,* pp. 87-90.

Hogan, Robert. *After the Irish renaissance,* pp. 239-241.

Koslow, Jules. *Sean O'Casey, the man and his plays,* pp. 69-75.

Rollins, Ronald G. "O'Casey's *Purple Dust.*" *Explicator,* vol. 26 (1967), item 19.

Red Roses for Me

Armstrong, William A. *Experimental drama,* pp. 84-87.

Armstrong, William A. *Sean O'Casey,* pp. 23-24.

Casey, Kevin. "The Excitements and the Disappointments." *In:* McCann, Sean, ed. *The world of Sean O'Casey,* pp. 225-227.

Clurman, Harold. *Lies like truth,* pp. 122-124.

Cowasjee, Saros. *O'Casey,* pp. 75-82.

Esslinger, Pat M. "Sean O'Casey and the Lockout of 1913: *Materia Poetica* of the Two Red Plays." *Modern Drama,* vol. 6 (1963-64), pp. 53-63.

Koslow, Jules. *Sean O'Casey, the man and his plays,* pp. 85-94.

Lewis, Allan. *The contemporary theatre,* pp. 176-191.

Malone, Maureen. *"Red Roses for Me:* Fact and Symbol." *Modern Drama,* vol. 9, no. 2 (Sept., 1966), pp. 147-152.

The Robe of Rosheen

Hogan, Robert. "O'Casey's Apprenticeship." *Modern Drama,* vol. 4, no. 3 (Dec., 1961), pp. 243-253.

The Shadow of a Gunman

Armstrong, William A. "History, Autobiography and *The Shadow of a Gunman." Modern Drama,* vol. 2, no. 4 (Feb., 1960), pp. 417-424.

Armstrong, William A. *Sean O'Casey,* pp. 11-13, 17.

Cowasjee, Saros. *O'Casey,* pp. 15-31.

Dorcey, Donal. "The Great Occasions." *In:* McCann, Sean, ed. *The world of Sean O'Casey,* pp. 50-52.

Fallon, Gabriel. "The Man in the Plays." *In:* McCann, Sean, ed. *The world of Sean O'Casey,* pp. 199-205.

Fitzgerald, John J. "Sean O'Casey's Dramatic Slums." *Descant,* vol. 10, no. 1 (Fall, 1965), pp. 26-34.

Freedman, Morris. "The Modern Tragicomedy of Wilde and O'Casey," *College English,* vol. 25, no. 7 (Apr., 1964), pp. 518-527.

Koslow, Jules. *Sean O'Casey, the man and his plays.* pp. 22-23, 42-43.

McHugh, Roger. "The Legacy of Sean O'Casey." *Texas Q.,* vol. 8, no. 1 (1965), pp. 123-137.

Malone, Andrew E. *The Irish drama,* p. 216.

O'Donovan, John, "The Big Three." *In:* McCann, Sean, ed. *The world of Sean O'Casey,* pp. 186-189.

O'Donovan, Michael. *A short history of Irish literature,* pp. 217-218, 219, 222.

Rollins, Ronald G. "Form and Content in Sean O'Casey's Dublin Trilogy." *Modern Drama,* vol. 8, no. 4 (Feb., 1966), pp. 419-425.

The Silver Tassie

Armstrong, William A. *Sean O'Casey,* pp. 18-20.

Brandt, G.W. "Realism and Parables." *In:* Brown, John Russell and Bernard Harris, eds. *Contemporary theatre,* pp. 36-40.

Casey, Kevin. "The Excitements and the Disapointments." *In:* McCann, Sean, ed. *The world of Sean O'Casey,* pp. 212-218.

Cowasjee, Saros. *O'Casey,* pp. 42-56.

Dorcey, Donal. "The Big Occasions." *In:* McCann, Sean, ed. *The story of the Abbey Theatre,* pp. 152-153.

Edwards, A.C. "The Lady Gregory Letters to Sean O'Casey." *Modern Drama,* vol. 8, no. 1 (May, 1965), pp. 95, 98, 99, 106, 107, 108.

Henn, T.R. *The harvest of tragedy,* pp. 213-214.

Kavanagh, Peter. *The story of the Abbey Theatre from its origins to the present,* pp. 139-143.

Koslow, Jules. *Sean O'Casey, the man and his plays,* pp. 45-54.

McHugh, Roger. "The Legacy of Sean O'Casey." Texas Q., vol. 8, no. 1 (1965), pp. 123-137.

Morgan, Charles. "On Sean O'Casey's *The Silver Tassie.*" *In:* Agate, James. *The English dramatic critics,* pp. 347-349. *Also in: The Times* (Oct. 12, 1929).

O'Casey, Sean. "Blasphemy and *The Silver Tassie.*" *In:* O'Casey, Sean. *Blasts and benedictions,* pp. 108-110.

O'Casey, Sean. *"The Silver Tassie." In:* O'Casey, Sean. *Blasts and benedictions,* pp. 103-107. (Published in *The Nineteenth Century* (Sept. 1928), with title "The Plays of Sean O'Casey, A Reply.")

O'Casey, Sean. "W.B. Yeats and *The Silver Tassie.*" (Letter) *In:* O'Casey, Sean. *Blasts and benedictions,* pp. 99-102. (From *The Letters of W.B. Yeats,* pp. 740-742.) (Full Correspondence in *The Irish Statesman* (Dublin), (June 9, 1928), pp. 268-272.)

Smith, Winifred. "The Dying God in the Modern Theatre." *Rev. of Religion,* vol. 5, (Mar. 1941) pp. 269-273.

Styan, J.L. *The dark comedy,* 2nd ed., pp. 3, 133-136, 264.

The Star Turns Red

Armstrong, William A. *Sean O'Casey,* pp. 20-21.

Casey, Kevin. "The Excitements and the Disappointments." *In:* McCann, Sean, ed. *The world of Sean O'Casey,* p. 222.

Cowasjee, Saros. *O'Casey,* pp. 70-75.

Esslinger, Pat. M. "Sean O'Casey and the Lockout of 1913: *Materia poetica* of the Two Red Plays." *Modern Drama,* vol. 6 (1963-64), pp. 53-63.

Koslow, Jules. *Sean O'Casey, the man and his plays,* pp. 77-85.

Rollins, Ronald G. "*The Star Turns Red:* A Political Philosophy." *Mississippi Q.,* vol. 16 (1963), pp. 67-75.

Time To Go

Hogan, Robert. *After the Irish renaissance* pp. 243-244.

Within the Gates

Armstrong, William A. *Sean O'Casey,* p. 20.

Brown, John Mason. *Two on the aisle,* pp. 126-130.

Casey, Kevin. "The Excitements and the Disappointments." *In:* McCann, Sean, ed. *The world of Sean O'Casey,* pp. 218-222.

Cowasjee, Saros. *O'Casey,* pp. 56-65.

Goldstone, Herbert. "The Unevenness of O'Casey: A Study of *Within the Gates.*" *Forum* (Houston), vol. 4, no. 4 (1965), pp. 37-42.

Knight, G. Wilson. *The golden labyrinth,* pp. 376-378.

Koslow, Jules. *Sean O'Casey, the man and his plays,* pp. 55-68.

MacCarthy, Desmond. *Drama,* pp. 349-354.

O'Casey, Sean. "The Church Tries to Close the Gates." *In:* O'Casey, Sean. *Blasts and benedictions,* pp. 124-131.

O'Casey, Sean. "From *Within the Gates." In:* O'Casey, Sean. *Blasts and benedictions,* pp. 111-117. (From *The New York Times,* Oct. 21, 1934.)

O'Casey, Sean. *"Within the Gates* and Without." *In:* O'Casey, Sean. *Blasts and benedictions,* pp. 118-123.

Rollins, Ronald G. "O'Casey, O'Neill, and Expressionism in *Within the Gates." West Virginia University Philological Papers,* vol. 13 (1961: pub. 1962), pp. 76-81.

Todd, R. Mary. "The Two Published Versions of Sean O'Casey's *Within the Gates." Modern Drama,* vol. 10, no. 4 (Feb., 1968), pp. 346-355.

FRANK O'CONNOR 1903-
(real name Michael O'Donovan)

General

Hogan, Robert. *After the Irish renaissance,* pp. 44-45.

In the Train

Barnet, Sylvan, ed. *The genius of the Irish theater,* pp. 245-247.

CLIFFORD ODETS 1906-1963

General

Clurman, Harold. "The First 15 Years." *New Republic,* vol. 123 (Dec. 11, 1950), pp. 29-30.

Clurman, Harold. *The naked image,* pp. 270-273.

Gassner, John. "The Long Journey of Talent." *Theatre Arts,* vol. 33, no. 7 (July, 1949), pp. 25-30.

Gassner, John. *The theatre in our times,* pp. 303-310.

Goldstein, Malcolm. "Body and Soul of Broadway." *Modern Drama,* vol. 7, no. 4 (Feb. 1965), pp. 411-421.

Goldstein, Malcolm. "Clifford Odets and the Found Generation." *In:* Downer, Alan. S. *American drama and its critics: A collection of critical essays.*

Goldstone, Richard H. "The Making of Americans: Clifford Odets's Implicit Theme." *In:* Jost, Francois, ed. *Proceedings of the IVth Congress of the International Comparative Lit. Assoc. Fribourg, 1964.* vol. 1, pp. 654-660.

Gould, Jean. *Modern American playwrights,* pp. 186-201.

Griffin, Robert J. "On the Love Songs of Clifford Odets." *In:* French, W., ed. *The thirties: fiction, poetry, drama,* pp. 193-200.

Hughes, Catharine. "Odets: The Prince of Success." *Commonweal,* vol. 78, no. 21 (Sept. 20, 1963), pp. 558-560.

Hunt, Albert. "Only Soft-Centered Left: Odets and Social Theatre." *Encore,* vol. 8 (May-June, 1961), pp. 5-12.

Hyams, Barry. "Twenty Years on a Tightrope." *Theatre Arts,* vol. 39, no. 4 (Apr., 1955), pp. 68-70, 86.

Isaacs, Edith J.R. "Clifford Odets." *Theatre Arts,* vol. 23, no. 4 (Apr. 1939), pp. 257-264.

Lumley, Frederick. *New trends in 20th-century drama,* pp. 335-337.

McCarten, John. "Revolution's Number One Boy." *New Yorker,* vol. 14 (Jan. 22, 1938), pp. 21-27.

McCarthy, Mary. *Sights and spectacles 1937-1956,* pp. 9-12.

Mendelsohn, Michael J. "Clifford Odets and the American Family." *Drama Survey,* vol. 3 (Fall, 1963), pp. 238-243.

Mendelsohn, Michael J. "Clifford Odets: The Artist's Commitment." *Literature and Society,* vol. 12, (1964), pp. 142-152.

Mendelsohn, Michael J. "Odets at Center Stage." (Interview.) *Theatre Arts,* vol. 47, no. 5 (May, 1963), pp. 16-19, 74-76; (June, 1963), pp. 28-30, 78-80.

Mendelsohn, Michael J. "The Social Critics on Stage." *Modern Drama,* vol. 6, no. 3 (Dec., 1963), pp. 277-285.

Mersand, Joseph. *The American drama since 1930,* pp. 61-90.

Murray, Edward. *Clifford Odets: the thirties and after,* pp. 3-32, 97-118, 219-224.

Rabkin, Gerald. *Drama and commitment,* pp. 169-212.

Awake and Sing

Block, Anita. *The changing world in plays and theatre,* pp. 286-290.

Brown, John Mason. *"Awake and Sing." In:* Brown, John Mason. *Dramatis personae,* pp. 71-72.

Brown, John Mason. *Two on the aisle,* pp. 217-219.

Clurman, Harold. *"Awake and Sing* and the Group Theatre." *In:* Freedman, Morris. ed. *Essays in modern drama,* pp. 174-185. (Reprinted from *The fervent years* by Harold Clurman (1945).)

Cohn, Ruby, ed. *Twentieth-century drama,* pp. 221-222.

Downer, Alan S. *Fifty years of American drama 1900-1950,* pp. 61-63.

Flexner, Eleanor. *American playwrights: 1918-1938,* pp. 296-299.

Freedman, Morris. *The moral impulse,* pp. 105-107, 111.

Goldstein, Malcolm. "The Playwrights of the 1930's." *In:* Downer, Alan S., ed. *The American theater today,* pp. 32-33.

Griffin, Robert J. "On the Love Songs of Clifford Odets." *In:* French, Warren, ed. *The thirties: fiction, poetry, drama,* pp. 196-198; 199.

Hart-Davis, Rupert. *Spectator,* vol. 160 (Feb. 25, 1938), p. 311.

Haslam, Gerald W. "Odets' Use of Yiddish-English in *Awake and Sing." Research Studies* (Wash. State Univ.), vol. 34 (1966), pp. 161-164.

Himelstein, Morgan Y. *Drama was a weapon, the left-wing theatre in New York 1929-1941,* pp. 166-167.

Krutch, Joseph W. *The American drama since 1918,* pp. 267-271.

Mersand, Joseph. *The American drama since 1930,* pp. 63-66, 76-80.

Murray, Edward. *Clifford Odets: the thirties and after,* pp. 33-52.

O'Hara, Frank H. *Today in American drama,* pp. 68-75, 78, 247-248.

Rabkin, Gerald. *Drama and commitment,* pp. 182-186. Sievers, W. David. *Freud on Broadway,* pp. 262-264.

Warshow, Robert S. "Poet of the Jewish Middle Class." *Commentary,* vol. 1, no. 7 (May, 1946), pp. 17-22. *Also in:* Freedman, Morris, ed. *Essays in the modern drama,* pp. 186-194. (Reprinted from *The immediate experience* by Robert Warshow, 1953.)

Weales, Gerald. "The Group Theatre and Its Plays." *In: American theatre,* pp. 80-81, 84.

Wright, Basil. *Spectator,* vol. 168 (May 29, 1942), p. 507.

The Big Knife

Brown, John Mason. *Still seeing things,* pp. 222-226.

Clurman, Harold. *Lies like truth,* pp. 49-53.

Hartley, Anthony. *Spectator,* vol. 192 (Jan. 8, 1954), p. 37.

Murray, Edward. *Clifford Odets: the thirties and after,* pp. 160-181.

Rabkin, Gerald. *Drama and commitment,* pp. 196-199.

Sievers, W. David. *Freud on Broadway,* pp. 271-272.

Worsley, T.C. *New Statesman,* vol. 47 (Jan. 9, 1954), p. 40.

Clash by Night

Murray, Edward. *Clifford Odets: the thirties and after,* pp. 136-159.

Rabkin, Gerald. *Drama and commitment,* pp. 206-209.

Sievers, W. David. *Freud on Broadway,* pp. 270-271.

The Country Girl

Clurman, Harold. *Lies like truth,* pp. 53-54.

Murray, Edward. *Clifford Odets: the thirties and after,* pp. 182-203.

Rabkin, Gerald. *Drama and commitment,* pp. 201-203.

Sievers, W. David. *Freud on Broadway,* pp. 272-274.

The Flowering Peach

Becker, William. "Reflections on Three New Plays." *Hudson Rev.,* vol. 8 (Summer, 1955), pp. 263-268.

Clurman, Harold. *Lies like truth,* pp. 54-57.

Gassner, John. *Theatre at the crossroads,* pp. 153-155.

Murray, Edward. *Clifford Odets: the thirties and after,* pp. 204-218.

Rabkin, Gerald. *Drama and commitment,* pp. 209-212.

Golden Boy

Block, Anita. *The changing world in plays and theatre,* pp. 295-300.

Brown, John Mason. *Two on the aisle,* pp. 220-222.

Flexner, Eleanor. *American playwrights: 1918-1938,* pp. 299-302, 313-314.

Goldstein, Malcolm. "The Playwrights of the 1930's." *In:* Downer, Alan S., ed. *The American theater today,* pp. 33-34.

Griffin, Robert J. "On the Love Songs of Clifford Odets." *In:* French, Warren, ed. *The thirties: fiction, poetry, drama,* pp. 199-200.

Himelstein, Morgan Y. *Drama was a weapon, the left-wing theatre in New York 1929-1941,* pp. 174-176.

Krutch, Joseph W. *The American drama since 1918,* pp. 271-274.

McCarthy, Mary. *Sights and spectacles 1937-1956,* pp. 10-12.

Mersand, Joseph. *The American drama since 1930,* pp. 86-88.

Murray, Edward. *Clifford Odets: the thirties and after,* pp. 53-71.

Rabkin, Gerald. *Drama and commitment,* pp. 193-196.

Sievers, W. David. *Freud on Broadway,* pp. 265-267.

Verschoyle, Derek. *Spectator,* vol. 161 (July 1, 1938), p. 16.

Night Music

Brown, John Mason. *Broadway in review,* pp. 181-184.

Dusenbury, Winifred L. *The theme of loneliness in modern American drama,* pp. 38-45.

Himelstein, Morgan Y. *Drama was a weapon, the left-wing theatre in New York 1929-1941,* p. 178.

Murray, Edward. *Clifford Odets: the thirties and after,* pp. 119-135.

Rabkin, Gerald. *Drama and commitment,* pp. 203-206.

Sievers, W. David. *Freud on Broadway,* pp. 268-270.

Paradise Lost

Block, Anita. *The changing world in plays and theatre,* pp. 290-300.

Himelstein, Morgan Y. *Drama was a weapon, the left-wing theatre in New York 1929-1941,* pp. 169-171.

Mersand, Joseph. *The American drama since 1930,* pp. 82-86.

New Statesman, vol. 16 (Dec. 17, 1938), pp. 1044-1045.

Rabkin, Gerald. *Drama and commitment,* pp. 186-190.

Sievers, W. David. *Freud on Broadway,* pp. 264-265.

Weales, Gerald. "The Group Theatre and Its Plays." *In: American theatre,* pp. 81-82.

Rocket to the Moon

Brown, John Mason. *Broadway in review,* pp. 176-179.

Dusenbury, Winifred L. *The theme of loneliness in modern American drama,* pp. 93-100.

Foster, Peter. *Spectator,* vol. 180 (Mar. 26, 1948), p. 373.

Goldstein, Malcolm. "The Playwrights of the 1930's." *In:* Downer, Alan S., ed. *The American theater today,* p. 34.

Krutch, Joseph W. *The American drama since 1918,* pp. 274-277.

Murray, Edward. *Clifford Odets: The thirties and after,* pp. 72-93.

O'Hara, Frank H. *Today in American drama,* pp. 130-132.

Rabkin, Gerald. *Drama and commitment,* pp. 199-201.

Sievers, W. David. *Freud on Broadway,* pp. 267-268.

Till the Day I Die

Himelstein, Morgan Y. *Drama was a weapon, the left-wing theatre in New York 1929-1941,* pp. 167-168.

Mersand, Joseph. *The American drama since 1930,* pp. 80-81.

New Statesman, vol. 20 (Aug. 3, 1940), p. 111.

Rabkin, Gerald. *Drama and commitment,* pp. 176-178.

Waiting for Lefty

Block, Anita. *The changing world in plays and theatre,* pp. 280-286.

Brown, John Mason. *"Waiting for Lefty." In:* Brown, John Mason. *Dramatis personae,* pp. 69-71.

Flexner, Eleanor. *American playwrights: 1918-1938,* pp. 290-295.

Goldstein, Malcolm. "The Playwrights of the 1930's." *In:* Downer, Alan S., Ed. *The American theater today,* p. 31.

Griffin, Robert J. "On the Love Songs of Clifford Odets." *In:* French, Warren, ed. *The thirties: fiction, poetry, drama,* pp. 193-197.

Himelstein, Morgan Y. *Drama was a weapon, the left-wing theatre in New York 1929-1941,* pp. 37-43.

Krutch, Joseph W. *The American drama since 1918,* pp. 264-267.

Krutch, Joseph Wood. "Mr. Odets Speaks His Mind." *Nation,* vol. 140 (Apr. 10, 1935), pp. 427-428.

Lewis, Allan. *American plays and playwrights of the contemporary theatre,* pp. 110-112.

Rabkin, Gerald. *Drama and commitment,* pp. 169-176.

Shuman, R. Baird. *"Waiting for Lefty:* A Problem of Structure." *Revue des Langues Vivantes,* vol. 28 (Nov.-Dec., 1962), pp. 521-526.

FRANK J. HUGH O'DONNELL

Anti-Christ

Malone, Andrew E. *The Irish drama,* pp. 271-272.

The Shaws of Synge Street

Hogan, Robert. *After the Irish renaissance,* pp. 78-79.

JOHN O'DONOVAN 1921-

General

Hogan Robert G., ed. *Seven Irish plays, 1946-1964,* pp. 247-249.

The Less We Are Together

Hogan, Robert. *After the Irish renaissance,* pp. 78-79.

FRANK O'HARA 1926-

The General Returns from One Place to Another

Sontag, Susan. *Against interpretation and other essays,* pp. 157-158.

SEUMAS O'KELLY

General

Boyd, Ernest. *Ireland's literary renaissance,* 355-356.

Malone, Andrew E. *The Irish drama,* pp. 197-198.

The Bribe

Malone, Andrew E. *The Irish drama,* pp. 196-197.

The Parnellite

Malone, Andrew E. *The Irish drama,* p. 197.

The Shuiler's Child

Malone, Andrew E. *The Irish drama,* pp. 195-196.

EUGENE O'NEILL 1888-1953

General

Alexander, Doris M. "Eugene O'Neill, 'The Hound of Heaven,' and the 'Hell Hole'" *Modern Language O.,* vol. 20, no. 4 (Dec., 1959), pp. 307-314.

Anonymous. "Counsels of Despair." *In:* Miller, J. Y. *Playwright's progress: O'Neill and the critics,* pp. 137-146. (Reprinted from *The Times Literary Supplement* (London) (Apr. 10, 1948), pp. 197-199.) *Also in:* Cargill *et al. O'Neill and his plays,* pp. 369-376.

Anonymous. "Mr. Eugene O'Neill: An Iconoclast in the Theatre." *In:* Cargill *et al. O'Neill and his plays,* pp. 358-368. (From *The Times Literary Supplement* (May 8, 1937).)

Azzarito, Bettina. "Tragic values in Eugene O'Neill's plays." M.A., Cornell University, 1943.

Bab, Julius. "As Europe Sees America's Foremost Playwright." *In:* Cargill *et al. O'Neill and his plays,* pp. 347-352. (From the *Theatre Guild Magazine* (Nov., 1931).)

Baldwin, Mary Louise. "The influence of Greek tragedy on the dramas of Eugene O'Neill: a selective study." M.A., University of Southern California, 1945.

Bell, Wayne E. "Forms of religious awareness in the late plays of Eugene O'Neill." *Dissertation Abstracts,* vol. 28 (1967), 222A (Emory).

Bjork, Lennart A. "The Swedish Critical Reception of O'Neill's Posthumous Plays." *Scandinavian Studies,* vol. 38 (1966), pp. 231-250.

Blackburn, Clara. "Continental Influences on Eugene O'Neill's Expressionistic Drama." *American Literature,* vol. 13, no. 2 (May, 1941), pp. 109-133.

Brashear, William R. "O'Neill and Shaw: The Play as Will and Idea." *Criticism,* vol. 8 (1966), pp. 155-169.

Broussard, Louis. *American drama...,* pp. 9-38.

Brown, John Mason. "O'Neill and God's Angry Eye." *In:* Brown, John Mason. *Dramatis personae,* pp. 39-52.

Brown, John Mason. "O'Neill in Retrospect." *In:* Brown, John Mason. *Dramatis personae,* pp. 63-66.

Brown, John Mason. *Upstage,* pp. 60-77.

Brustein, Robert. *The theatre of revolt, pp. 321-336.*

Burns, M. Vincentia, Sister. "The Wagnerian theory of art and its influence on the drama of Eugene O'Neill." Ph.D., University of Pennsylvania, 1943.

Cargill, Oscar. "Fusion-Point of Jung and Nietzsche." *In:* Cargill *et al. O'Neill and his plays,* pp. 408-414. (From *Intellectual America* by Oscar Cargill (1941).)

Carpenter, Frederic I. "Eugene O'Neill, the Orient, and American Transcendentalism." *In:* Simon, Myron and Thornton H. Parsons, eds. *Transcendentalism and its legacy,* pp. 204-213.

Carpenter, Frederic I. "The Romantic Tragedy of Eugene O'Neill." *College English,* vol. 6, no. 5 (Feb., 1945), pp. 250-258.

Casseres, Benjamin de. "The Triumphant Genius of Eugene O'Neill." *In:* Miller, J.Y. *Playwright's progress: O'Neill and the critics,* pp. 88-91. (Reprinted from *Theatre,* vol. 47 (Jan. 1928), pp. 12, 62.)

Chaitin, Norman C. "The Power of Daring." *Modern Drama,* vol. 3, no. 3 (Dec. 1960), pp. 231-241.

Chiari, J. *Landmarks of contemporary drama,* pp. 135-142.

Clark, Barrett H. "Aeschylus and O'Neill." *English J.,* vol. 21, no. 9 (Nov., 1932), pp. 699-710.

Clark, Barrett H. "The Plays of Eugene O'Neill." *In:* Cargill *et al. O'Neill and his plays,* pp. 230-233. (From *New York Sun* (May 18, 1919).)

Daiches, David. "Mourning Becomes O'Neill." *Encounter,* vol. 16, no. 6 (June, 1961), pp. 74-78.

Debusscher, Gilbert. *Edward Albee, tradition and renewal,* pp. 1-5.

DeVoto, Bernard. "Minority Report." *In:* Miller, J.Y. *Playwright's progress: O'Neill and the critics,* pp. 108-113. (Reprinted from *Saturday Rev.* vol. 15 (Nov., 21, 1936), pp. 3-4, 16. Also reprinted by the author in his book *Minority report* (Little, Brown, 1943) and in Cargill *et al.* eds., *O'Neill and his plays, pp. 301-306.)

Dobrée, Bonamy. "The Plays of Eugene O'Neill." *Southern Rev.,* vol. 2 (1936-37), pp. 435-446.

Downer, Alan S. "Eugene O'Neill As Poet of the Theatre." *In:* Cargill *et al. O'Neill and his plays,* pp. 468-471. (From *Theatre Arts* (Feb., 1951).)

Downer, Alan S. *Fifty years of American drama, 1900-1950,* pp. 64-70.

Downer, Alan S. *Recent American drama,* pp. 6, 7, 8, 16-18, 42-43.

Driver, Tom F. "On the Late Plays of Eugene O'Neill." *Tulane Drama Rev.,* vol. 3, no. 2 (Dec., 1958), pp. 8-20. (Reprinted in Scott, Nathan A. *Man in the modern theatre,* pp. 40-57.)

Eaton, Walter P. "O'Neill: New Risen Attic Stream." *American Scholar,* vol. 6, no. 3 (Summer, 1937), pp. 304-312.

Ellis, Seth Howard. "Classical influences on O'Neill's plays." M.A. University of Missouri, 1954.

Engel, Edwin A. "Eugene O'Neill as a writer of tragedy." Dissertation, Michigan, 1948.

Engel, Edwin A. "Eugene O'Neill's Long Day's Journey into Light." *Michigan Alumnae Q. Rev.,* vol. 63 (1957), pp. 348-354.

Engel, Edwin A. *Haunted heroes of Eugene O'Neill.*

Engel, Edwin A. "Ideas in the Plays of Eugene O'Neill." *In:* Gassner, J., ed. *Ideas in the drama,* pp. 101-124.

Engel, Edwin A. "O'Neill, 1960." *Modern Drama,* vol. 3, no. 3 (Dec., 1960) pp. 219-223.

Fagin, N. "Eugene O'Neill." *Antioch Rev.,* vol. 14, (Mar., 1954), pp. 14-26.

Fagin, N.B. "Eugene O'Neill Contemplates Mortality." *Open Court,* vol. 45 (Apr., 1931), pp. 208-231. *Also in:* Cargill *et al.,* eds. *O'Neill and his plays,* pp. 124-130.

Falk, Doris V. *"Eugene O'Neill and the tragic tension.*

Falk, Doris V. "That Paradox, O'Neill." *Modern Drama,* vol. 6, no. 3 (Dec., 1963), pp. 221-238.

Falk, Signi. "Dialogue in the Plays of Eugene O'Neill." *Modern Drama,* vol. 3, no. 3 (Dec., 1960), pp. 314-325.

Fergusson, Francis. "Melodramatist." *In:* Cargill *et al.,* eds., *O'Neill and his plays,* pp. 271-282. *Also in:* Zabel, M.D., ed., *Literary opinion in America,* pp. 513-521. (Originally entitled "Eugene O'Neill" in *Hound and Horn,* vol. 3 (Jan., 1930), pp. 145-160.)

Fish, Margaret. "A comparative study of Eugene O'Neill and the decadent Elizabethan dramatists." M.A., Brigham Young University, 1934.

Fiskin, A.M.I. "The Basic Unity of Eugene O'Neill." *In:* Fiskin, A.M.I., ed., *Writers of our years,* pp. 101-117.

Fitzgerald, John J. "The Bitter Harvest of O'Neill's Projected Cycle." *New England Q.* vol. 40 (1967), pp. 364-374.

Fleisher, Frederic. "Strindberg and O'Neill." *Symposium,* vol. 10 (1956), pp. 84-94.

Fleisher, Frederic. "Swedes in the Published Plays of O'Neill." *Orbis Litterarum,* vol. 12 (1957), pp. 99-103.

Fleisher, Frederic, and Frenz, Horst. "Eugene O'Neill and the Royal Dramatic Theatre of Stockholm: The Later Phrase." *Modern Drama,* vol. 10, no. 3 (Dec., 1967), pp. 300-311.

Flexner, Eleanor. *American playwrights: 1918-1938,* pp. 130-141, 155-156, 165-166.

Fox, Josef. "Probability in the plays of Eugene O'Neill." Ph.D., University of Chicago, 1953.

Freedman, Morris. "O'Neill and the Contemporary Drama." *College English,* vol. 23 (1962) pp. 570-574.

Frenz, Horst. "Eugene O'Neill ọn the German Stage." *Theatre annual, 1953,* vol. 11, pp. 24-34.

Frenz, H. "Eugene O'Neill on the London Stage." *Queen's Q.* vol. 54 (1947), pp. 223-230.

Frenz, H. "Notes on Eugene O'Neill in Japan." *Modern Drama,* vol. 3 (1960), pp. 306-313.

Gagey, E.M. *Revolution in American drama,* pp. 39-70.

Gallup, Donald, ed. "Eugene O'Neill's *The Ancient Mariner.*" *Yale Univ. Library Gazette,* vol. 35 (Oct., 1960), pp. 61-86.

Gascoigne, Bamber. *Twentieth-century drama,* pp. 109-120.

Gassner, John. *Eugene O'Neill.*

Gassner, John. "Eugene O'Neill: The Course of a Modern Dramatist." *Critique: Rev. of Theatre Arts and Literature,* vol. 1, no. 1 (1958), pp. 5-14.

Gassner, John. "Homage to O'Neill." *Theatre Time,* vol. 3 (Summer, 1951), pp. 17-21. *Also in:* Cargill *et al.,* eds. *O'Neill and his plays,* pp. 321-330.

Gassner, John. "The Nature of O'Neill's Achievement: A Summary and Appraisal." *In:* Gassner, John, ed. *O'Neill,* pp. 165-171. (Shortened and revised version of an essay in his *Theatre at the crossroads* (N.Y., Holt, Rinehart & Winston, 1960), pp. 65-76.)

Gassner, John, ed. *O'Neill.*

Gassner, John. *Theatre at the crossroads,* pp. 66-76.

Gassner, John. *The theatre in our times,* pp. 249-266

Geddes, Virgil. "Eugene O'Neill." *Theatre Arts,* vol. 15 (Nov., 1931), pp. 943-946.

Gelb, Arthur. "O'Neill's Hopeless Hope for a Giant Cycle." *New York Times* (Sept. 29, 1958), Sec. 2, pp. 1, 4.

Gelb, Arthur and Barbara. "As O'Neill Saw the Theatre." *New York Times Mag.* (Nov. 12, 1961), p. 32.

Gierow, Karl-Ragnar. "Eugene O'Neill's Posthumous Plays." *In:* Cargill *et al. O'Neill and his plays,* pp. 377-379. (From *World Theatre* (Spring 1958), pp. 46-52.)

Glicksberg, Charles I. *The tragic vision in twentieth-century literature,* pp. 83-84, 92-96, 152-153.

- Goldberg, Georgine Hablewitz. "A character story of the heroines of *The Great God Brown, Strange Interlude,* and *Mourning Becomes Electra."* M.A., University of Colorado, 1957.

Goldberg, Isaac. "At the Beginning of a Career." *In:* Cargill *et al. O'Neill and his plays,* pp. 234-243. (From Goldberg, I. *The drama of transition,* 1922, pp. 457-471.)

Goldberg, Isaac. *The drama of transition,* pp. 457-471.

Golden, Joseph. *The death of Tinker Bell,* pp. 30-51.

Goldman, Arnold. "The Vanity of Personality: The Development of Eugene O'Neill." *In:* Brown, J. R., and Bernard Harris, eds. *American theatre,* pp. 28-51.

Gould, Jean. *Modern American playwrights,* pp. 50-77.

Granger, Bruce I. "Illusion and Reality in Eugene O'Neill." *Modern Language Notes,* vol. 73, no. 3 (Mar., 1958), pp. 179-186.

Groff, Edward. "Point of View in Modern Drama." *Modern Drama,* vol. 2, no. 3 (Dec., 1959), pp. 268-282.

Gump, Margaret. "From Ape to Man and from Man to Ape." *Kentucky Foreign Language Q.,* vol. 14 (1957), pp. 177-185.

Hahn, Vera T. "The plays of Eugene O'Neill: a psychological analysis." Ph.D., University of Louisiana, 1939.

Halman, Doris F. "O'Neill and the Untrained Playwright." *Writer,* vol. 40 (July, 1928), pp. 215-217.

Hamilton, Clayton. *Conversations on contemporary drama,* pp. 198-218.

Hamilton, Clayton. "O'Neill's First Book." *In:* Cargill *et al. O'Neill and his plays,* p. 229. (From *The Bookman,* Apr., 1915.)

Hartman, Murray. "Strindberg and O'Neill." *Educational Theatre J.,* vol. 18, no. 3 (Oct., 1966), pp. 216-223.

Hayes, Richard. "Eugene O'Neill: The Tragic in Exile." *In:* Gassner, John, ed. *O'Neill,* pp. 52-56. (Reprinted from *Theatre Arts* (Oct., 1963), p. 16.

Hayward, Ira N. "Strindberg's Influence on Eugene O'Neill." *Poet Lore,* vol. 39 (Winter, 1928), pp. 596-604.

Heideman, Joanna. "The influence of Greek tragedy upon Eugene O'Neill." M.A., University of Southern California, 1933.

Hensley, Donald Melton. "Eugene O'Neill's use of Greek dramatic types." M.A., University of North Carolina, 1954.

Herndon, Geneva. "American criticism of Eugene O'Neill: 1917-1948." Ph.D., Northwestern University, 1949.

Hofmannsthal, Hugo von. "Eugene O'Neill." *In:* Corrigan, Robert W. *Theatre in the twentieth century,* pp. 125-130.

Hofmannsthal, Hugo von. "Eugene O'Neill." (The TDR Document Series, edited by Bernard Hewitt.) *Tulane Drama Rev.,* vol. 5, no. 1 (September, 1960), pp. 169-173.

Hofmannsthal, Hugo von. "Eugene O'Neill." *In:* Miller, J.Y. *Playwright's progress: O'Neill and the critics,* pp. 44-48. (Reprinted from *The Freeman,* vol. 7 (Mar., 21, 1923), pp. 39-41.) *Also in:* Cargill *et al.,* eds. *O'Neill and his plays,* pp. 249-255, and in Gassner, J., ed. *O'Neill,* pp. 23-28.

Isaacs, Edith J. "Meet Eugene O'Neill." *Theatre Arts,* vol. 30 (Oct., 1946), pp. 576-587.

Jenkins, Lloyd Harold. "Dramatic technique and tragic values in the works of Eugene O'Neill." M.A., McGill University, Canada, 1930.

Jones, C. "A Sailor's O'Neill." *Revue Anglo-Americane,* vol. 12 (Feb., 1935), pp. 226-229.

Kaucher, Dorothy. *Modern dramatic structure,* pp. 125-158.

Kemelman, H.G. "Eugene O'Neill and the Highbrow Melodrama." *In:* Miller, J.Y., *Playwright's progress: O'Neill and the critics,* pp. 94-105. (Reprinted from *The Bookman,* vol. 75 (Sept., 1932), pp. 482-491.)

Klavsons, Janis. "O'Neill's Dreamer: Success and Failure." *Modern Drama,* vol. 3, no. 3 (Dec., 1960), pp. 268-272.

Kommer, Rudolf. "Eugene O'Neill in Europe." *In:* Cargill *et al. O'Neill and his plays,* pp. 266-269. (From the *Greenwich Playbill,* 1924-25 season.)

Koplik, Irwin J. "Jung's Psychology in the Plays of O'Neill." *Dissertation Abstracts,* vol. 27 (1967), 3872A (New York Univ.).

Krutch, Joseph W. *The American drama since 1918,* pp. 75-133.

Krutch, Joseph Wood. "Eugene O'Neill." *In:* Oppenheimer, George, ed. *The passionate playgoer,* pp. 268-279. (Reprinted from introduction to O'Neill's *Nine plays,* N.Y., Random House, 1932.)

Krutch, Joseph Wood. "Eugene O'Neill's Claim to Greatness." *In:* Cargill *et al. O'Neill and his plays,* pp. 472-476. (From a review of *A touch of the poet, New York Times Book Rev.* (Sept., 22, 1957), p. 1.) *Also in:* Freedman, Morris, ed. *Essays in the modern drama,* pp. 91-95.

Krutch, Joseph Wood. "Eugene O'Neill, the Lonely Revolutionary." *In:* Miller, J.Y., *Playwright's progress: O'Neill and the critics,* pp. 158-161. (Reprinted from *Theatre Arts,* vol. 36 (Apr., 1952), pp. 29-30, 78.)

Krutch, Joseph Wood. *"Modernism" in modern drama,* pp. 117-122.

Krutch, Joseph Wood. "O'Neill the Inevitable" *Theatre Arts,* vol. 38 (Feb., 1954), pp. 66-69.

Krutch, Joseph Wood. "O'Neill's Tragic Sense." *American Scholar,* vol. 16 (1947), pp. 283-290.

Krutch, Joseph Wood. "Why the O'Neill Star Is Rising." *In:* Miller, J.Y., *Playwright's progress: O'Neill and the critics,* pp. 174-179. (Reprinted from *The New York Times Magazine* (Mar. 19, 1961), pp. 36, 108, 111.)

Lamm, Martin. *Modern drama,* pp. 315-333.

Lang, Marie Elizabeth, Sister. "A study of the influence of the Greek tragedians on the dramatic work of Eugene O'Neill." M.A., University of Hawaii, 1949.

Langford, Richard E. "Eugene O'Neill: The Mask of Illusion." *In:* Langford, R.E., *et al. Essays in modern American literature,* pp. 65-75.

Laverty, Carroll D. "The dramatic presentation of Eugene O'Neill's ideas." M.A., University of Colorado, 1934.

Lawson, John Howard. "Eugene O'Neill." *In:* Gassner, John, ed. *O'Neill,* pp. 42-51. (Reprinted from Chapter V. of *Theory and technique of playwriting* (N.Y., Putnam's Sons, 1936, by John Howard Lawson, pp. 129-141.)

Lawson, John Howard. "Eugene O'Neill and His Plays." *Critical Q.,* vol. 3 (1961), pp. 242-256, 339-353.

Lawson, John Howard. "The Tragedy of Eugene O'Neill." *Masses and Mainstream,* vol. 7 (Mar., 1954), pp. 7-18.

Lee, Robert C. "Eugene O'Neill's Rememberance: The Past Is the Present." *Arizona Q.* vol. 23 (1967), pp. 293-305.

Lee, Robert C. "Eugene O'Neill: a grapple with a ghost." *Dissertation Abstracts,* vol. 26 (1965), 2754-55 (Mich.).

Lee, Robert C. "The Lonely Dream." *Modern Drama,* vol. 9, no. 2 (Sept., 1966), pp. 127-135.

Leech, Clifford. *Eugene O'Neill.*

Leech, Clifford. "Eugene O'Neill and His Plays." *Critical Q.* vol. 3, no. 4 (Winter, 1961), pp. 339-353.

Lewis, Allan. *American plays and playwrights of the contemporary theatre,* pp. 15-34.

Lewisohn, Ludwig. "Eugene O'Neill." Nation, vol. 113 (Nov. 30, 1921), p. 626.

Lewisohn, Ludwig. *Expressionism in America,* 1932; rev. ed., *The story of American literature,* 1939, pp. 543-553.

Loggins, Vernon. *I hear America,* pp. 143-174.

Long, Chester Clayton. *The role of nemesis in the structure of selected plays by Eugene O'Neill,* pp. 216-225.

Lovell, John, Jr. "Eugene O'Neill's Darker Brother." *Theatre Arts,* vol. 32 (1948), pp. 45-48.

Loving, Pierre. "Eugene O'Neill." *Bookman,* vol. 53 (Aug., 1921), pp. 511-520.

Lumley, Frederick. *New trends in 20th-century drama,* pp. 91, 115-125.

Lumley, Frederick. *Trends in 20th-century drama,* pp. 124-132.

MacDonald, James Gilbert. "Eugene O'Neill's method in tragedy." M.A., Acadia University, Canada, 1941.

McDonnell, Thomas P. O'Neill's Drama of the Psyche." *Catholic World,* vol. 197 (May, 1963), pp. 120-125.

Macgowan, Kenneth. "The O'Neill Soliloquy." *In:* Cargill *et al. O'Neill and his plays,* pp. 449-453. (From *Theatre Guild Magazine* (Feb., 1929).)

Malone, Andrew E. "Eugene O'Neill's Limitations." *In: O'Neill and his plays,* pp. 256-265. (From *Dublin Magazine* (Dec., 1923), pp. 401-409.)

Malone, Andrew E., "The Plays of Eugene O'Neill." *Contemporary Rev.,* vol. 129 (Mar., 1926), pp. 363-372.

Masters, Robert William. "Fate as it appears in the works of Eugene O'Neill." M.A., University of Indiana, 1933.

Mayfield, John S. "Eugene O'Neill and the Senator from Texas." *Yale Univ. Library Gazette,* vol. 35 (1960), pp. 87-93.

Mersand, J. *Play's the thing; enjoying the plays of today,* pp. 41-48.

Meserve, Walter J. "Sidney Howard and the Social Drama of the Twenties." *Modern Drama,* vol. 6 (1963-64), pp. 256-266.

Micklc, Alan D. *Studies on six plays of Eugene O'Neill.*

Miller, Jordan Y. "The Georgia Plays of Eugene O'Neill." *Georgia Rev.,* vol. 12, no. 3 (Fall, 1958), pp. 278-290.

Miller, Nellie Burget. *The living drama,* pp. 409-411.

Morris, L.R. *Postscript to yesterday,* pp. 172-213.

Moses, Montrose J. "The 'New' Eugene O'Neill." *North American Rev.,* vol. 236 (1933), pp. 543-549.

Motherwell, H. "O'Neill: What Next?" *In: Essay annual, 1936,* pp. 202-211.

Muchnic, Helen. "Circe's Swine: Plays by Gorky and O'Neill." *Comparative Literature,* vol. 3 (1951), pp. 119-128.

Muller, H.J. *Spirit of tragedy,* pp. 311-319.

Mullett, Mary B. "The Extraordinary Story of Eugene O'Neill." *American Magazine,* vol. 94 (Nov., 1922), pp. 34, 112-120.

Nathan, George Jean. "The Case of O'Neill." *In:* Miller, J.Y. *Playwright's progress: O'Neill and the critics,* pp. 91-94. (Reprinted from *American Mercury,* vol. 13 (Apr., 1928), pp. 500-502.)

Nathan, G.J. "O'Neill: A Critical Summation." American Me*rcury,* vol. 63 (1946), pp. 713-719.

Nathan, George Jean. "Our Premier Dramatist." *In:* Cargill *et al. O'Neill and his plays,* pp. 283-291. (From *The intimate notebooks of George Jean Nathan,* Knopf, 1931, pp. 188-198.)

Nathan, G.J. *The world of George Jean Nathan,* pp. 30-43.

Nethercot, Arthur H. "The Psychoanalyzing of Eugene O'Neill." Part I. *Modern Drama,* vol. 3, no. 3 (Dec., 1960), pp. 242-256. Part II. *Modern Drama,* vol. 3, no. 4 (Feb., 1961), pp. 357-372.

Nethercot, Arthur H. "The Psychoanalyzing of Eugene O'Neill; Postscript." *Modern Drama,* vol. 8 (1965), pp. 150-155.

Norwood, Gilbert. "The Art of Eugene O'Neill." *Dalhousie Rev.,* vol. 21 (1941), pp. 143-157.

O'Hara, F.H. *Today in American drama,* pp. 1-52.

Olson, Esther J. "An analysis of the Nietzschean elements in the plays of Eugene O'Neill." *Dissertation Abstracts,* vol. 17 (1957), 695 (Minnesota).

O'Neill, Eugene. *In:* Cole, Toby, ed. *Playwrights on playwriting,* pp. 233-234. (Reprinted from Barrett H. Clark. *Eugene O'Neill: the man and his plays* (New York: Dover Publications, 1947).)

O'Neill, Eugene. "From an Interview with Oliver M. Sayler." *In:* Caputi, Anthony, ed. *Modern drama,* pp. 451-452. (From *Century Magazine,* (Jan., 1922) and Saylor, Oliver M. *Our American theatre,* N.Y., 1923.)

O'Neill, Eugene. "A Letter to Arthur Hobson Quinn." *In:* Caputi, Anthony, ed. *Modern drama,* pp. 450-451. (From Quinn, Arthur Hobson. *History of the American drama,* N.Y., Crofts, 1945.)

O'Neill, E. "Sea Plays." *In:* Cole, T., ed. *Playwrights on playwriting,* pp. 233-234.

O'Neill, Joseph P., S.J. "The Tragic Theory of Eugene O'Neill." *Texas Studies in Literature and Language,* vol. 4 (1963), pp. 481-498.

Opper, Hylbert Norman. "Exposition in the plays of Eugene O'Neill." M.A., Northwestern University, 1937.

Pallette, Drew B. "O'Neill and the Comic Spirit." *Modern Drama,* vol. 3, no. 3 (Dec., 1960), pp. 273-279.

Pallette, Drew B. "O'Neill's *A Touch of the Poet* and His Other Last Plays." *Arizona Q.,* vol. 13, no. 4 (Winter, 1957), pp. 308-319.

Parks, Edd Winfield. "Eugene O'Neill's Quest." *In:* Meserve, Walter J., ed., *Discussions of American drama,* pp. 96-105. *Also in: Tulane Drama Rev.,* vol. 4, no. 3 (1960), pp. 99-107.

Parks, E.W. "Eugene O'Neill's Symbolism." *Sewanee Rev.,* vol. 43 (1935), pp. 436-451. *Also in:* Parks, E.W. *Segments of Southern thought,* Athens, Univ. of Georgia Press, 1938, pp. 293-313.

Pellizzi, Camillo. "Irish-Catholic Anti-Puritan." *In:* Cargill *et al. O'Neill and his plays,* pp. 353-357. (From Rowan Williams' translation of *English Drama: the last great phase* by Camillo Pellizzi, 1935.)

Perosh, George. "A study of the tragic theory of Eugene O'Neill." M.A., Catholic University of America, 1950.

Perry, William. "Does the Buskin Fit O'Neill?" *Univ. of Kansas City Rev.,* vol. 15 (Summer, 1949), pp. 281-287.

Pettegrove, James P. "Eugene O'Neill as Thinker." *Maske und Kothurn* (Jan. 10, 1964), pp. 617-624.

Phillips, Elizabeth C. *Modern American drama,* pp. 56-64, 74-76, 77-79.

Pommer, Henry F. "The Mysticism of Eugene O'Neill." *Modern Drama,* vol. 9, no. 1 (May, 1966), pp. 26-39.

Pratt, Norman T., Jr. "Aeschylus and O'Neill: Two Worlds." *Classic J.,* vol. 51 (1956), pp. 163-167.

Quinn, Arthur Hobson. "Eugene O'Neill." *In:* Meserve, Walter J., ed. *Discussions of American drama,* pp. 5-7.

Quinn, Arthur Hobson. "Eugene O'Neill, Poet and Mystic." *In:* Miller, J.Y. *Playwright's progress: O'Neill and the critics,* pp. 82-88. (Reprinted from *Scribner's Magazine* (Oct., 1926), pp. 368-372.)

Quinn, Arthur H. *History of American Drama from the Civil War to the present day,* rev. ed., 1936, vol. 2, pp. 165-206.

Quinn, Arthur H. "Modern American Drama II." *English J.,* vol. 13 (Jan., 1924), pp. 1-10.

Quinn, Arthur H. "The Real Hope for the American Theatre." *Scribners,* vol. 97 (Jan., 1935), pp. 30-35.

Raghavacharyulu, D.V.K. *Eugene O'Neill a study,* pp. 1-19, 21-23, 35-36, 36-45, 76-81, 85-93, 131-139, 170-175, 180-196, 198-218.

Raleigh, John H. "Eugene O'Neill." *Ramparts,* vol. 2, no. 5 (1964), pp. 74.

Raleigh, John Henry. "Eugene O'Neill and the Escape from the Chateau d'If." *In:* Gassner, John, ed. *O'Neill,* pp. 7-22.

Raleigh, John H. *The plays of Eugene O'Neill.*

Ray, Helen Houser. "The relation between man and man in the plays of Eugene O'Neill." *Dissertation Abstracts,* vol. 26, 7324 (Kan.)

Reardon, William R. "O'Neill Since World War II: Critical Reception in New York." *Modern Drama,* vol. 10, no. 3 (Dec., 1967), pp. 289-299.

Rhodes, Raymond Hayden. "The influence of Greek tragedy on Eugene O'Neill." M.A., Stanford University, 1939.

Rosenberg, James. "European Influences." *In: American theatre,* pp. 53-55, 58-59, 60.

Rubinstein, Annette. "The Dark Journey of Eugene O'Neill." *Mainstream,* vol. 10 (Apr., 1957), pp. 29-33.

Salem, James M. "Eugene O'Neill and the Sacrament of Marriage." *The Serif* (Kent, Ohio), vol. 3, no. 2 (1966), pp. 23-35.

Sanderson, James L., ed. *Phaedra and Hippolytus, myth and dramatic form,* pp. 211-212.

Sayler, Oliver M. *Our American theatre,* pp. 27-43.

Sayler, Oliver M. "The Real Eugene O'Neill." The Century *Magazine,* vol. 103 (Jan., 1922), pp. 351-359.

Seiler, Conrad. "Los Angeles Must Be Kept Pure." *In:* Cargill *et al. O'Neill and his plays,* pp. 443-448. (From *The Nation* (May 19, 1926).)

Sergeant, Elizabeth S. "O'Neill: The Man With a Mask." *New Republic,* vol. 50 (Mar., 16, 1927), pp. 91-95. *Also in:* Sergeant, E., *Fire under the Andes.* New York, Knopf, 1927.

Sharpe, Robert Boies. *Irony in the drama,* pp. 183-189.

Shipley, Joseph T. *The art of Eugene O'Neill.*

Sievers, W. David. *Freud on Broadway,* pp. 97-133.

Skinner, R. D. *Eugene O'Neill: a poet's quest.*

Skinner, R.D. *Our changing theatre,* pp. 76-96.

Slater, Montagu. "Eugene O'Neill." *Nation,* vol. 178 (Feb., 1954), pp. 174-175.

Slochower, Harry. "Eugene O'Neill's Lost Moderns." *In:* Cargill *et al. O'Neill and his plays,* pp. 383-389. (From *No voice is wholly lost* by Harry Slochower (1945). Originally published in *The University Rev.,* (Autumn 1943), pp. 32-37.)

Snapp, Edwin Robert. "The dramatic technique of Eugene O'Neill." M.A. University of New Mexico, 1934.

Stamm, Rudolf. "The Dramatic Experiments of Eugene O'Neill." *English Studies,* vol. 28 (Feb., 1947), pp. 1-15.

Stamm, Rudolf. "Faithful Realism: Eugene O'Neill and the Problem of Style." *English Studies,* vol. 40 (Aug., 1959), pp. 242-250.

Steinhauer, H. "Eros & Psyche: A Nietzschean Motif in Anglo-American Literature." *Modern Language Notes,* vol. 64, no. 4 (Apr., 1949), pp. 225-228.

Stevens, Thomas W. "How Good Is Eugene O'Neill?" *English J.,* vol. 26 (Mar., 1937), pp. 179-187.

Straumann, Heinrich. "The Philosophical Background of the Modern American Drama." *English Studies,* vol. 26 (June, 1944), pp. 65-78.

Sutton, G. *Some contemporary dramatists,* pp. 167-183.

Tapper, Bonno. "Eugene O'Neill's World View." *Personalist,* vol. 18 (Winter, 1937), pp. 40-48.

Thomas, Ruth Bartlett. "The use of obsessions and delusions as a tragic device in the major plays of Eugene O'Neill." M.A., College of the Pacific, 1942.

Thompson, A.R. *Anatomy of drama,* pp. 291-315.

Thorpe, W. *American writing in the twentieth century,* pp. 63-109.

Thurman, William R. "Journey into Night: Elements of Tragedy in Eugene O'Neill." *Q. J. of Speech,* vol. 52, no. 2 (Apr., 1966), pp. 139-145.

Tiusanen, Timo. *O'Neill's scenic images,* pp. 3-45, 49-56, 331-348.

Tornquist, Egil. "Personal Nomenclature in the Plays of O'Neill." *Modern Drama,* vol. 8, no. 4 (Feb., 1966), pp. 362-373.

Trilling, Lionel. "Eugene O'Neill." *In:* Miller, J.Y. *Playwright's progress: O'Neill and the critics,* pp. 113-119. (Reprinted from *The New Republic,* vol. 88 (Sept. 23, 1936), pp. 176-179.) *Also in:* Cargill et al. *O'Neill and his plays,* pp. 292-300, and Cowley, M., ed. *After the genteel tradition,* pp. 127-140. (Reprinted in Freedman, Morris, ed. *Essays in the modern drama,* pp. 96-103.)

Trilling, Lionel. "Eugene O'Neill." *In:* Meserve, Walter J., ed. *Discussions of American drama,* pp. 18-25.

Valgemae, Mardi. "O'Neill and German Expressionism." *Modern Drama,* vol. 10, no. 2 (Sept., 1967), pp. 111-123.

Volpe, Edmond L., ed. *An introduction to literature: drama,* pp. 403-410.

Vunovich, Nancy W. "The women in the plays of Eugene O'Neill." *Dissertation Abstracts,* vol. 28 (1967), 1089A-90A (Kansas).

Waith, Eugene M. "Eugene O'Neill: An Exercise in Unmasking." *In:* Gassner, John, ed. *O'Neill,* pp. 229-41. (Reprinted from *Educational Theatre J.,* vol. 13, no. 3 (Oct., 1961), pp. 182-191.)

Walker, Roy. "The Right Kind of Pity." *Twentieth Century,* vol. 155 (1954), pp. 79-86.

Walton, Ivan. "Eugene O'Neill and the Folklore and Folkways of the Sea." *Western Folklore,* vol. 14 (1955), pp. 153-169.

Weales, Gerald. *American drama since World War II,* pp. 76-96.

Weathers, Winston. "Communication and Tragedy in Eugene O'Neill." *ETC.: A Review of General Semantics,* vol. 14 (July, 1962), pp. 148-160.

Weissman, Philip. "Conscious and Unconscious Autobiographical Dramas of Eugene O'Neill." *J. of the Psychoanalytical Assoc.,* vol. 5 (1957), pp. 432-460.

Weissman, Philip. *Creativity in the theater,* pp. 114-117, 129-136.

Welch, Mary. "Softer Tones for Mr. O'Neill's Portrait." *Theatre Arts,* vol. 41 (May, 1957), pp. 67-68.

Whicher, G.F. "Vitalizers of the Drama." *In:* Quinn, A.H., ed. *Literature of the American people,* pp. 927-941.

Whipple, Thomas K. *Spokesmen, modern writers, and American life,* pp. 230-253.

White, Arthur F. "The Plays of Eugene O'Neill." *Western Reserve Univ. Bulletin,* vol. 26 (1923), pp. 20-36.

White, Jackson E. "Existential themes in selected plays of Eugene O'Neill." *Dissertation Abstracts,* vol. 27 (1967), 4270A-71A (Arizona State).

Whitman, Robert F. "O'Neill's Search for a 'Language of the Theatre.'" *In:* Gassner, John, ed. *O'Neill,* pp. 142-164. (From *Q. J. of Speech,* vol. 16, no. 2 (Apr., 1960), pp. 154-170.)

Williams, Raymond. *Modern tragedy,* pp. 115-119.

Wilson, Edmund. "Eugene O'Neill As a Prose Writer." *In:* Cargill *et al. O'Neill and his plays,* pp. 464-467. (From *The shores of light,* Farrar, Straus and Young, 1952. Originally the following articles: "Eugene O'Neill as Prose Writer," *Vanity Fair,* Nov., 1922; "All God's Chillun Got Wings and Others" *New Republic,* May 28, 1924; "The All-Star Literary Vaudeville," *American Criticism,* Harcourt, Brace, 1926.)

Winther, Sophus K. *Eugene O'Neill, a critical study* (rev., enl. ed.)

Winther, Sophus K. "Eugene O'Neill—The Dreamer Confronts His Dream." *Arizona Q.,* vol. 21, no. 3 (Autumn, 1965), pp. 221-233.

Winther, Sophus K. "O'Neill's Posthumous Plays." *Prairie Schooner,* vol. 32 (Spring, 1958), pp. 7-12.

Winther, Sophus K. "Strindberg and O'Neill: A Study of Influence." *Scandinavian Studies,* vol. 31, no. 3 (Aug., 1959), pp. 103-120.

Wolfson, Lester M. "Inge, O'Neill and the Human Condition." *Southern Speech J.,* vol. 22, no. 4 (Summer, 1957), pp. 221-232.

Woodbridge, Homer E. "Eugene O'Neill." *South Atlantic Q.,* vol. 37, no. 1 (Jan., 1938), pp. 22-25. (Entitled "Beyond Melodrama," and reprinted in Cargill *et al. O'Neill and his plays,* pp. 307-320.)

Young, Stark. "Eugene O'Neill: Notes from a Critic's Diary." *Harpers,* vol. 214 (June, 1957), pp. 66-74.

Zwinggi, Antoinette. "Certain aspects of similarity between the Greek dramatists and the plays of Eugene O'Neill." M.A., Northwestern University, 1929.

Bibliography

Miller, Jordan Y. *Eugene O'Neill and the American critic: a summary and bibliographical checklist.*

Bryer, Jackson R. "Forty Years of O'Neill Criticism: A Selected Bibliography." *Modern Drama,* vol. 4 (1961), pp. 196-216.

Abortion

Long, Chester Clayton. *The role of nemesis in the structure of selected plays by Eugene O'Neill,* pp. 29-44, 68-69, 71-74.

Raghavacharyulu, D.V.K. *Eugene O'Neill, a study,* pp. 19-20.

Ah, Wilderness!

Adler, Jacob H. "The Worth of *Ah, Wilderness!*" *Modern Drama,* vol. 3, no. 3 (Dec., 1960), pp. 280-288.

Atkinson, Brooks. "In Which Eugene O'Neill Recaptures the Past in a Comedy with George M. Cohan." *In:* Miller, J.Y. *Playwright's progress: O'Neill and the critics,* pp. 74-75. (Reprinted from *The New York Times,* Oct., 3, 1933.)

Brustein, Robert. *The theatre of revolt,* pp. 336-339.

Burr, Eugene. *"Ah, Wilderness!" In:* Miller, J.Y., *Playwright's progress: O'Neill and the critics,* pp. 78-80. (Reprinted from *Billboard,* vol. 45 (Oct., 14, 1933), pp. 16-17.)

Engel, E.A. *The haunted heroes of Eugene O'Neill,* pp. 270-277.

Gabriel, Gilbert W. *"Ah, Wilderness!" In:* Cargill *et al. O'Neill and his plays,* pp. 194-196. (From the *New York American,* Oct., 3, 1933. Also reprinted in Miller, J.Y. *Playwright's progress: O'Neill and the critics,* pp. 76-77.)

Krutch, Joseph W. *The American drama since 1918,* pp. 113-115.

Leech, Clifford. *Eugene O'Neill,* pp. 94-96.

Moses, Montrose J. "The 'New Eugene O'Neill." *North American Rev.,* vol. 236 (Dec., 1933), pp. 543-549.

O'Hara, F.H. *Today in American drama,* pp. 53-141.

Phillips, Elizabeth C. *Modern American drama,* pp. 66-67.

Raghavacharyulu, D.V.K. *Eugene O'Neill, a study,* pp. 114-116.

Shawcross, John T. "The Road to Ruin: The Beginning of O'Neill's Long Day's Journey." *Modern Drama,* vol. 3, no. 3 (Dec., 1960), pp. 289-296.

Sievers, W. David. *Freud on Broadway,* pp. 124-125.

Skinner, Richard Dana. *Eugene O'Neill, a poet's quest,* pp. 227-233.

Tiusanen, Timo. *O'Neill's scenic images,* pp. 241-245.

All God's Chillun Got Wings

Bigsby, C.W. *Confrontation and commitment,* pp. 117-118, 149.

Block, Anita. *The changing world in plays and theatre,* pp. 147-149, 242.

Eliot, T.S. *"All God's Chillun Got Wings." New Criterion,* vol. 4 (Apr., 1926), pp. 395-396. *Also in:* Cargill *et al. O'Neill and his plays,* pp. 168-169.

Engel, E.A. *The haunted heroes of Eugene O'Neill,* pp. 117-126.

Falk, Doris V. *Eugene O'Neill and the tragic tension,* pp. 87-90.

Flexner, Eleanor. *American playwrights: 1918-1938,* pp. 152-155.

Goldman, Arnold. "The Vanity of Personality: the Development of Eugene O'Neill." *In: American theatre,* pp. 30-31.

Leech, Clifford. *Eugene O'Neill,* pp. 43-44.

Lewisohn, Ludwig. *"All God's Chillun." In:* Miller, J.Y. *Playwright's progress: O'Neill and the critics,* pp. 39-40. (Reprinted from *The Nation, vol. 11*8 (June 4, 1924), p. 664.)

Mitchell, Loften. *Black drama,* p. 83.

Phillips, Elizabeth C. *Modern American drama,* p. 65.

Pollock, Arthur. *"All God's Chillun." In:* Miller, J.Y. *Playwright's progress: O'Neill and the critics,* pp. 37-39. (Reprinted from *Brooklyn Daily News* (May 16, 1924).)

Raghavacharyulu, D.V.K. *Eugene O'Neill, a study,* pp. 53-55.

Rice, Elmer. "Sex in the Modern Theatre." *Harpers,* vol. 164 (May, 1932), pp. 665-673.

Skinner, Richard Dana. *Eugene O'Neill, a poet's quest,* pp. 131-141.

Tiusanen, Timo. *O'Neill's scenic images,* pp. 174-182.

Zabel, Morton Dauwen. *Literary opinion in America,* pp. 515-517.

Anna Christie

Atkinson, Brooks. "Eugene O'Neill's *Anna Christie* Performed at the City Center with Celeste Holm." *In:* Miller, J.Y. *Playwright's progress: O'Neill and the critics,* pp. 130-131. (Reprinted from *The New York Times* (Jan., 10, 1952).)

Bogard, Travis. *"Anna Christie:* Her Fall and Rise." *In:* Gassner, John, ed. *O'Neill,* pp. 62-71.

Dale, Alan. *"Anna Christie* Is Offered at the Vanderbilt." *In:* Miller, J.Y. *Playwright's progress: O'Neill and the critics,* pp. 26-27. (Reprinted from *New York American* (Nov., 3, 1921).)

Dusenbury, Winifred L. *The theme of loneliness in modern American drama,* pp. 50-56.

Engel, E.A. *The haunted heroes of Eugene O'Neill,* pp. 39-45.

Falk, Doris V. *Eugene O'Neill and the tragic tension,* pp. 27-28, 45, 48-52.

Flexner, Eleanor. *American playwrights: 1918-1938,* pp. 144-146.

Hackett, Francis. *"Anna Christie." In:* Cargill *et al. O'Neill and his plays,* pp. 152-154. (Reprinted from *The New Republic* (November 30, 1921).)

Leech, Clifford. *Eugene O'Neill,* pp. 29-33.

McAleer, John J. "Christ Symbolism in *Anna Christie." Modern Drama,* vol. 4, no. 4 (Feb., 1962), pp. 389-396.

Macgowan, Kenneth. "Eugene O'Neill's *Anna Christie* a Notable Drama Notably Acted at the Vanderbilt Theatre." *In:* Miller, J.Y. *Playwright's progress: O'Neill and the critics,* pp. 27-28. (Reprinted from *New York Globe and Commercial Advertiser* (Nov., 3, 1921).)

Mickle, Alan D. *Studies on six plays of Eugene O'Neill,* pp. 15-31.

O'Hara, Frank H. *Today in American drama,* pp. 14-20, 149-150.

Parker, Robert Allerton. "An American Dramatist Developing." *In:* Miller, J.Y. *Playwright's progress: O'Neill and the critics,* pp. 28-31. (Reprinted from *The Independent and The Weekly Review,* vol. 107 (Dec., 3, 1921), p. 236.)

Phillips, Elizabeth C. *Modern American drama,* pp. 64-65.

Raghavacharyulu, D.V.K. *Eugene O'Neill, a study,* pp. 25-26.

Skinner, Richard Dana. *Eugene O'Neill, a poet's quest,* pp. 76-84.

Tiusanen, Timo. *O'Neill's scenic images,* pp. 86-89.

Before Breakfast.

Deutsch, Helen. *"Before Breakfast." In:* Cargill *et al. O'Neill and his plays,* p. 131. (Reprinted from Deutsch, H., *The Provincetown,* 1931.)

Beyond the Horizon

Broun, Heywood. "Eugene O'Neill's *Beyond the Horizon." In:* Moses, Montrose J. *The American theatre as seen by its critics, 1752-1934,* pp. 209-211. (Reprinted from *The New York Tribune* (Feb. 4, 1920).) *Also in:* Miller, J.Y., *Playwright's progress: O'Neill and the critics,* pp. 17-18.

Engel, E.A. *The haunted heroes of Eugene O'Neill,* pp. 15-18.

Falk, Doris V. *Eugene O'Neill and the tragic tension,* pp. 19, 27-28, 37-45, 47, 51, 58, 60, 193, 194.

Flexner, Eleanor. *American playwrights: 1918-1938,* pp. 147-148.

Goldman, Arnold. "The Vanity of Personality: the Development of Eugene O'Neill." *In: American theatre,* pp. 39-40.

Hagopian, John V. and Dolch, Martin. *Insight I; analysis of American literature,* pp. 187-193.

Hamilton, Clayton. *Seen on the stage.* pp. 184-191.

Kozelka, Edwin Paul. "A production of Eugene O'Neil's *Beyond the Horizon."* M.A., Northwestern University, 1937.

Krutch, J.W. "A Note on Tragedy." *Nation,* vol. 123 (Dec. 15, 1926), pp. 646-647.

Leech, Clifford. *Eugene O'Neill,* pp. 20-24.

O'Neill, Eugene. *In:* Cole, Toby, ed. *Playwrights on playwriting,* pp. 234-235. (Reprinted from Barrett H. Clark. *Eugene O'Neill: the man and his plays* (New York: Dover Publications, 1947).)

Phillips, Elizabeth C. *Modern American drama,* p. 64.

Raghavacharyulu, D.V.K. *Eugene O'Neill, a study,* pp. 24-25.

Roy, Emil. "Tragic Tension in *Beyond the Horizon." Ball State Univ. Forum,* vol 8, no. 1 (Winter, 1967), pp. 74-79.

Shipp, Horace. "Conviction and the Drama." *English rev.,* vol 42 (May, 1926), pp. 701-703.

Skinner, Richard Dana. *Eugene O'Neill, a poet's quest,* pp. 49-60.

Tiusanen, Timo. *O'Neill's scenic images,* pp. 73-81.

Woollcott, Alexander. *"Beyond the Horizon." In:* Cargill *et al. O'Neill and his plays,* pp. 135-139. (Reprinted from *The New York Times* (Feb., 8, 1920).)

Woollcott, Alexander. "Eugene O'Neill's Tragedy." *In:* Miller, J.Y. *Playwright's progress: O'Neill and the critics,* pp. 19-20. (Reprinted from *The New York Times* (Feb., 4, 1920).)

Bound East for Cardiff

Broun, Heywood. Review. *New York Tribune* (Jan., 30, 1917). (Reprinted in Miller, J.Y. *Playwright's progress: O'Neill and the critics,* pp. 4-5. Also in Cargill *et al.,* eds. *O'Neill and his plays,* pp. 129-130.)

Falk, Doris V. *Eugene O'Neill and the tragic tension,* pp. 15, 20-22, 24, 43, 45, 164.

Goldman, Arnold. "The Vanity of Personality: the Development of Eugene O'Neill." *In: American theatre,* pp. 44-45.

Skinner, Richard Dana. *Eugene O'Neill, a poet's quest,* pp. 37-45.

Tiusanen, Timo. *O'Neill's scenic images,* pp. 45-49.

Bread and Butter

Tiusanen, Timo. *O'Neill's scenic images,* pp. 57-63.

Chris

Anonymous. *"Chris." In:* Cargill *et al. O'Neill and his plays,* pp. 140-141. (Reprinted from The Stage, Mar., 27, 1920).)

Days Without End

Anderson, John. "O'Neill's *Days Without End." In:* Moses, Montrose J. *The American theatre as seen by its critics, 1752-1934,* pp. 287-289. (Reprinted from *The New York Evening Journal* (Jan. 9, 1934). *Also in:* Cargill *et al.* eds. *O'Neill and his plays,* pp. 200-202.

Block, Anita. *The changing world in plays and theatre,* pp. 190-193.

Broussard, Louis. *American drama...,* pp. 27-30.

Brown, John Mason. "The Theatre Guild Presents Earle Larimore and Stanley Ridges in Mr. O'Neill's *Days Without End!" In:* Miller, J.Y. *Playwright's progress: O'Neill and the critics,* pp. 80-82. (Reprinted from *New York Post* (Jan., 9, 1934).)

Eastman, Fred. *Christ in the drama,* pp. 97-102.

Engel, E.A. *The haunted heroes of Eugene O'Neill,* pp. 265-270.

Falk, Doris V. *Eugene O'Neill and the tragic tension,* pp. 18, 79, 114, 145-155, 194. (Reprinted in Cargill *et al.,* eds. *O'Neill and his plays,* pp. 415-423.)

Flexner, Eleanor. *American playwrights: 1918-1938,* pp. 192-197.

Fergusson, Francis. *American Rev.,* vol. 2 (Feb., 1934), pp. 491-495.

Goldman, Arnold. "The Vanity of Personality: the Development of Eugene O'Neill." *In: American theatre,* pp. 37, 45-46.

Leech, Clifford. *Eugene O'Neill,* pp. 92-94.

Parks, Edd W. "Eugene O'Neill's Symbolism." *Sewanee Rev.,* vol. 43, no. 4 (Oct.-Dec., 1935), pp. 436-451.

Peck. M.W. "A Psychiatrist Views the Drama." *Psychoanalytic Rev.,* vol. 22 (1935), pp. 306-313.

Raghavacharyulu, D.V.K. *Eugene O'Neill, a study,* pp. 116-127.

Reekie, A.G. "Eugene O'Neill: the Dilemma of the Intellectual." *In: The rationalist annual,* 1949. Ed. by Frederick Watts. London, Watts & Co., 1949, pp. 9-13.

Sievers, W. David. *Freud on Broadway,* pp. 125-127.

Skinner, Richard Dana. *Eugene O'Neill, a poet's quest,* pp. 234-242.

Tiusanen, Timo. *O'Neill's scenic images,* pp. 197-206.

Desire Under the Elms

Atkinson, Brooks. "At the Theatre." *In:* Miller, J.Y. *Playwright's progress: O'Neill and the critics,* pp. 131-132. (Reprinted from *The New York Times* (Jan. 17, 1952).)

Barnet, Sylvan, ed. *Eight great tragedies,* pp. 350-352.

Beyer, William H. "The State of the Theatre: Classics Revisited." *School and Society,* vol. 75 (Feb. 16, 1952), pp. 106-107.

Block, Anita. *The changing world in plays and theatre,* pp. 149-151.

Conlin, Matthew T. "The Tragic Effect in *Autumn Fire* and *Desire Under the Elms.*" *Modern Drama,* vol. 1 (Feb., 1959), pp. 228-235.

Cubeta, Paul M. *Modern drama for analysis,* pp. 202-209.

Downer, Alan S. *Fifty years of American drama, 1900-1950,* pp. 68-70.

Engel, E.A. *The haunted heroes of Eugene O'Neill,* pp. 126-134.

Falk, Doris V. *Eugene O'Neill and the tragic tension,* pp. 93-99, 177.

Flexner, Eleanor. *American playwrights: 1918-1938,* pp. 155-159.

Frenz, Horst. "Eugene O'Neill's *Desire Under the Elms* and Henrik Ibsen's *Rosmersholm.*" *Jahrbuch für Amerikastudien,* Bd. 9 (1964), pp. 160-165.

Goldman, Arnold. "The Vanity of Personality: the Development of Eugene O'Neill." *In: American theatre,* pp. 41-42, 50-51.

Hammond, Percy. *"Desire Under the Elms." In:* Cargill *et al. O'Neill and his plays,* pp. 170-171. (From the *New York Herald Tribune* (Nov., 12, 1924).)

Hartman, Murray. *"Desire Under the Elms* in the Light of Strindberg's Influence." *American Literature,* vol. 33 (1961-62), pp. 360-369.

Hays, Peter L. "Biblical Perversions in *Desire Under the Elms." Modern Drama,* vol. 11, no. 4 (Feb., 1969), pp. 423-428.

Krutch, Joseph W. *The American drama since 1918,* pp. 94-100.

Krutch, Joseph Wood. *"Desire Under the Elms." In:* Caputi, Anthony, ed. *Modern drama,* pp. 452-455. (From Krutch, Joseph Wood. *The American drama since 1918,* N.Y., Braziller, 1957, pp. 94-100.)

Krutch, Joseph Wood. "The God of Stumps." *In:* Miller, J.Y. *Playwright's progress: O'Neill and the critics,* pp. 42-44. (Reprinted from *The Nation,* vol. 119 (Nov., 26, 1924), pp. 578, 580.)

Leaska, Mitchell A. *The voice of tragedy,* pp. 264-268.

Leech, Clifford. *Eugene O'Neill,* pp. 47-55.

Long, Chester Clayton. *The role of nemesis in the structure of selected plays by Eugene O'Neill,* pp. 97-116.

McCollom, William G. *Tragedy,* pp. 229-230.

Macgowan, K. "O'Neill and a Mature Hollywood Outlook." *Theatre Arts,* vol. 42 (Apr., 1958), pp. 79-81.

Meyers, Jay R. "O'Neill's Use of the Phaedre Legend in *Desire Under the Elms." Revue de Litterature Comparee,* vol. 41 (1967), pp. 120-125.

Niblo, Fred, Jr. "New O'Neill Play Sinks to Depths." *In:* Miller, J.Y., *Playwright's progress: O'Neill and the critics,* pp. 40-41. (Reprinted from *New York Morning Telegraph* (Nov., 12, 1924).)

O'Hara, Frank H. *Today in American drama,* pp. 21-22.

O'Neill, Eugene. "Letters to George Jean Nathan." *In:* Caputi, Anthony, ed. *Modern drama,* p. 450.

Phillips, Elizabeth C. *Modern American drama,* p. 66.

Racey, Edgar F., Jr. "Myth as Tragic Structure in *Desire Under the Elms." In:* Sanderson, James L., ed. *Phaedra and Hippolytus, myth and dramatic form,* pp. 329-334. *Also in: Modern Drama,* vol. 5, no. 1 (May 1962), pp. 42-46, and Gassner, J., ed. *O'Neill,* pp. 57-61.

Raghavacharyulu, D.V.K. *Eugene O'Neill, a study,* pp. 55-60.

Sievers, W. David. *Freud on Broadway,* pp. 112-115.

Skinner, Richard Dana. *"Desire Under the Elms:* Dragons of Youth." *In:* Caputi, Anthony, ed. *Modern drama,* pp. 455-462. (From Skinner, Richard Dana. *Eugene O'Neill, a poet's quest,* N.Y., Longmans, Green, 1935, pp. 143-156.)

Taubman, Howard. "Theatre: New *Desire." In:* Miller, J.Y. *Playwright's progress: O'Neill and the critics,* pp. 171-172. (Reprinted from *The New York Times* (Jan., 11, 1963).)

Tiusanen, Timo. *O'Neill's scenic images,* pp. 151-162.

Weissman, Philip. *Creativity in the theater,* pp. 136-145, 235-236.

Weissman, Philip. "Eugene O'Neill's Autobiographical Dramas." *American Psychoanalytic Assoc. J.,* vol. 5, no. 3 (July, 1957), pp. 451-459.

Winther, Sophus Keith. *"Desire Under the Elms:* A Modern Tragedy." *Modern Drama,* vol. 3, no. 3 (Dec., 1960), pp. 326-332. (Reprinted in Caputi, Anthony, ed. *Modern drama,* pp. 462-469.)

Young, Stark. "Eugene O'Neill's Latest Play." *In:* Miller, J.Y. *Playwright's progress: O'Neill and the critics,* pp. 41-42. (Reprinted from *The New York Times* (Nov., 12, 1924).)

Diff'rent

Engel, E.A. *The haunted heroes of Eugene O'Neill,* pp. 29-36.

Falk, Doris V. *Eugene O'Neill and the tragic tension,* pp. 61, 71-72.

Krutch, Joseph W. *The American drama since 1918,* pp. 84-87.

Leech, Clifford. *Eugene O'Neill,* pp. 24-25.

Macgowan, Kenneth. *"Diff'rent."* In: Miller, J. Y. *Playwright's progress: O'Neill and the critics,* pp. 10-12. (Reprinted from *Vogue,* vol. 57 (Mar., 15, 1921), pp. 80-82.) *Also in:* Cargill *et al.,* eds. *O'Neill and his plays,* pp. 147-149.

O'Neill, Eugene. "From the *New York Tribune,* February 13, 1921." In: Caputi, Anthony, ed. *Modern drama,* pp. 447-449.

Raghavacharyulu, D.V.K. *Eugene O'Neill, a study,* p. 23.

Sayler, Oliver. "Eugene O'Neill, Master of Naturalism." *Drama,* vol. 11 (Mar., 1921), pp. 189-190.

Sievers, W. David. *Freud on Broadway,* pp. 101-102.

Skinner, Richard Dana. *Eugene O'Neill, a poet's quest,* pp. 91-95.

Taubman, Howard. "O'Neill Drama Revived at New Mermaid." In: Miller, J.Y. *Playwright's progress: O'Neill and the critics,* pp. 170-171. (Reprinted from *The New York Times* (Oct., 18, 1961).)

Tiusanen, Timo. *O'Neill's scenic images,* pp. 89-91

The Dreamy Kid

Engel, E.A. *The haunted heroes of Eugene O'Neill,* pp. 46-48.

Woollcott, Alexander. *"The Dreamy Kid."* In: Cargill *et al.,* eds. *O'Neill and his plays,* p. 134. (Reprinted from *The New York Times* (Nov., 9, 1919).)

Dynamo

Benchley, Robert. *"Dynamo."* In: Cargill *et al. O'Neill and his plays,* pp. 187-189. (From *Life* vol. 93 (Mar. 8, 1929), pp. 24, 37.

Block, Anita. *The changing world in plays and theatre,* pp. 188-190.

Broussard, Louis. *American drama...,* pp. 23-27.

Clark, Barrett H. "O'Neill's *Dynamo* and the Village Experiments." *Drama,* vol. 19 (Apr., 1929), pp. 199-201.

Colum, Padraic. "The Theatre." *Dial,* vol. 86 (Apr., 1929), pp. 349-350.

Dahlstrom, Carl E.W.L. *"Dynamo* and *Lazarus Laughed:* Some Limitations." *Modern Drama,* vol. 3, no. 3 (Dec., 1960), pp. 224-230.

Engel, E.A. *The haunted heroes of Eugene O'Neill,* pp. 229-239.

Falk, Doris V. *Eugene O'Neill and the tragic tension,* pp. 19, 121, 126-129, 148.

Flexner, Eleanor. *American playwrights: 1918-1938,* pp. 179-181.

Garland, Robert. "Eugene O'Neill's *Dynamo* Displayed in 45th Street." *In:* Miller, J.Y. *Playwright's progress: O'Neill and the critics,* pp. 62-64. (Reprinted from *New York Telegram* (Feb., 12, 1929).)

Hammond, Percy. "The Theaters: *Dynamo." In:* Miller, J.Y. *Playwright's progress: O'Neill and the critics,* pp. 64-65. (Reprinted from *New York Herald Tribune* (Feb., 12, 1929).)

Leech, Clifford. *Eugene O'Neill,* pp. 90-92.

Raghavacharyulu, D.V.K. *Eugene O'Neill, a study,* pp. 100-103.

Sievers, W. David. *Freud on Broadway,* pp. 120-121.

Simonson, Lee. "A Memo From O'Neill On the Sound Effects for *Dynamo." In:* Cargill *et al. O'Neill and his plays,* pp. 454-458. (Reprinted from *The stage is set* by Lee Simonson, Harcourt, Brace, 1932.)

Skinner, Richard Dana. *Eugene O'Neill, a poet's quest,* pp. 203-210.

Tiusanen, Timo. *O'Neill's scenic images,* pp. 162-167.

Young, Stark. *Immortal shadows.* pp. 91-95.

The Emperor Jones

Block, Anita. *The changing world in plays and theatre,* pp. 140-143.

Broun, Heywood. *"The Emperor Jones." In:* Cargill et al. *O'Neill and his plays,* pp. 144-146. (Reprinted from the *New York Tribune* (Nov. 4, 1920).)

Castellun, Maida. "O'Neill's *The Emperor Jones* Thrills and Fascinates." *In:* Miller, J.Y. *Playwright's progress: O'Neill and the critics,* pp. 22-23. (Reprinted from *New York Call* (Nov. 10, 1920).)

Chen, David Y. "Two Chinese Adaptations of Eugene O'Neill's *The Emperor Jones." Modern Drama,* vol. 9 (1967), pp. 431-439.

Downer, Alan S. *The art of the play,* pp. 327-329.

Downer, Alan S. *"Fifty Years of American drama, 1900-1950,* pp. 93-95.

Engel, E.A. *The haunted heroes of Eugene O'Neill,* pp. 48-53.

Falk, Doris V. *Eugene O'Neill and the tragic tension,* pp. 52, 61, 66-71, 198.

Flexner, Eleanor. *American playwrights: 1918-1938,* pp. 141-144.

Gilman, Lawrence. "*The Emperor Jones* as Opera." *In:* Cargill et al. *O'Neill and his plays,* pp. 197-199. (From *New York Herald Tribune* (Jan. 8, 1933).)

Leech, Clifford. *Eugene O'Neill,* pp. 34-46.

McCollom, Willam G. *Tragedy,* pp. 86-87, 229.

Miller, Nellie Burget. *The living drama,* pp. 411-413.

Mitchell, Loften. *Black drama,* pp. 75-76, 83-84.

O'Neill, Eugene. *In:* Cole, Toby, ed. *Playwrights on playwriting,* pp. 234-235. (Reprinted from Barrett H. Clark. *Eugene O'Neill: the man and his plays* (New York: Dover Publications, 1947).)

Phillips, Elizabeth C. *Modern American drama,* pp. 67-68.

Raghavacharyulu, D.V.K. *Eugene O'Neill, a study,* pp. 27-28.

Shand, John. "*The Emperor Jones.*" *In:* Miller, J.Y. *Playwright's progress: O'Neill and the critics,* pp. 23-26. (Reprinted from *New Statesman,* vol. 25 (Sept. 19, 1925), pp. 628-629.)

Sievers, W. David. *Freud on Broadway,* pp. 105-106.

Skinner, Richard Dana. *Eugene O'Neill, a poet's quest,* pp. 85-91.

Tiusanen, Timo. *O'Neill's scenic images,* pp. 97-112.

Woollcott, Alexander. "The New O'Neill Play." *In:* Miller, J.Y. *Playwright's progress: O'Neill and the critics,* pp. 20-22. (Reprinted from *The New York Times* (Nov. 7, 1920).)

Exorcism

Woollcott, Alexander. "*Exorcism.*" *In:* Cargill *et al. O'Neill and his plays,* pp. 142-143. (Reprinted from *The New York Times* (Apr. 4, 1920).)

Woollcott, Alexander. "Second Thoughts on First Nights." *The New York Times* (Apr. 4, 1920). (Reprinted in Miller, J.Y. *Playwright's progress: O'Neill and the critics,* pp. 6-7.)

The First Man

Castellun, Maida. "*The First Man.*" *In:* Cargill *et al. O'Neill and his plays,* pp. 157-159. (Reprinted from *New York Call* (Mar. 9, 1922).)

Dale, Alan. "*The First Man,* Eugene O'Neill Play Staged." *In:* Miller, J.Y. *Playwright's progress: O'Neill and the critics,* pp. 13-14. (Reprinted from *New York American* (Mar. 6, 1922).)

Falk, Doris V. *Eugene O'Neill and the tragic tension,* pp. 61, 72-75.

Leech, Clifford. *Eugene O'Neill,* pp. 28-29.

Raghavacharyulu, D.V.K. *Eugene O'Neill: a study,* pp. 26-27.

Skinner, Richard Dana. *Eugene O'Neill, a poet's quest,* pp. 96-102.

Tiusanen, Timo. *O'Neill's scenic images,* pp. 91-92.

Fog

Falk, Doris V. *Eugene O'Neill and the tragic tension,* p. 19.

The Fountain

Andreach, Robert J. "O'Neill's Use of Dante in *The Fountain* and *The Hairy Ape.*" *Modern Drama,* vol. 10, no. 1 (May, 1967), pp. 48-56.

Engel, E.A. *The haunted heroes of Eugene O'Neill,* pp. 95-107.

Falk, Doris V. *Eugene O'Neill and the tragic tension,* pp. 79-84.

Gabriel, Gillbert W. "DeLeon in Search of His Spring." *In:* Miller, J.Y. *Playwright's progress: O'Neill and the critics,* pp. 15-16. (Reprinted from *The New York Sun* (Dec. 11, 1925).)

Leech, Clifford. *Eugene O'Neill,* pp. 56-62.

Mickle, A.D. *Studies on six plays of Eugene O'Neill,* pp. 91-109.

Pommer, Henry F. "The Mysticism of Eugene O'Neill." *Modern Drama,* vol. 9, no. 1 (May, 1966), pp. 26-39.

Raghavacharyulu, D.V.K. *Eugene O'Neill, a study,* pp. 45-48.

Skinner, Richard Dana. *Eugene O'Neill, a poet's quest,* pp. *1*14-123.

Tiusanen, Timo. *O'Neill's scenic images,* pp. 129-139.

Young, Stark. "The Fountain." *In:* Cargill *et al. O'Neill and his plays,* pp. 172-174. (Reprinted from *The New Republic,* Dec. 30, 1925).)

Gold

Broun, Heywood. "Gold." *In:* Cargill *et al. O'Neill and his plays,* pp. 150-151. (Reprinted from *New York Tribune* (June 2, 1921).)

Engel, E.A. *The haunted heroes of Eugene O'Neill,* pp. 24-29.

Falk, D.V. *Eugene O'Neill and the tragic tension,* pp. 62-65.

Leech, Clifford. *Eugene O'Neill,* pp. 25-27.

Sievers, W. David. *Freud on Broadway*, pp. 102-103.

Skinner, Richard Dana. *Eugene O'Neill, a poet's quest*, pp. 68-75.

The Great God Brown

Anderson, John. "O'Neill's Newest Play Opens at the Greenwich Village." *In:* Miller, J.Y. *Playwright's progress: O'Neill and the critics,* pp. 51-52. (Reprinted from *New York Post* (Jan. 25, 1926).)

Atkinson, Brooks. "Symbolism in an O'Neill tragedy." *In:* Miller, J.Y. *Playwright's progress: O'Neill and the critics,* pp. 53-55. (Reprinted from *The New York Times* (Jan. 25, 1926).)

Atkinson, Brooks. "Theatre: O'Neill's *Great God Brown.*" *In:* Miller, J.Y. *Playwright's progress: O'Neill and the critics,* pp. 169-170. (Reprinted from *The New York Times* (Oct. 7, 1959).)

Berkelman, Robert. "O'Neill's Everyman—*The Great God Brown.*" *South Atlantic Q.,* vol. 58 (Fall, 1959), pp. 609-616.

Block, Anita. *The changing world in plays and theatre,* pp. 159-162.

Clurman, Harold. *The naked image,* pp. 98-100.

Day, Cyrus. "*Amor Fati:* O'Neill's Lazarus as Superman and Savior." *In:* Gassner, John, ed. *O'Neill,* pp. 72-81. (Reprinted from *Modern Drama,* vol. 3, no. 3 (Dec., 1960), pp. 297-305.)

Downer, Alan S. *Fifty years of American drama, 1900-1950,* pp. 96-97.

Dusenbury, Winifred L. *The theme of loneliness in modern American drama,* pp. 171-178.

Engel, E.A. *The haunted heroes of Eugene O'Neill,* pp. 152-175.

Falk, Doris V. *Eugene O'Neill and the tragic tension,* pp. 19, 26, 99-108, 117, 193.

Flexner, Eleanor. *American playwrights: 1918-1938,* pp. 159-165.

Gabriel, Gilbert W. "*The Great God Brown.*" *In:* Cargill *et al. O'Neill and his plays,* pp. 175-177. (From *New York Sun* (Jan. 25, 1926).)

Krutch, Joseph. W. *The American drama since 1918,* pp. 90-94.

Leech, Clifford. *Eugene O'Neill,* pp. 62-66.

Metzger, Deena P. "Variations on a Theme: Study of *Exiles* by James Joyce and *The Great God Brown* by Eugene O'Neill." *Modern Drama,* vol. 8 (1965-66), pp. 174-184.

Mickle, A.D. *Studies on six plays of Eugene O'Neill,* pp. 61-87.

O'Neill, Eugene. *In:* Cole, Toby, ed. *Playwrights on playwriting,* pp. 237-239. (Reprinted from Barrett H. Clark. *Eugene O'Neill: the man and his plays* (New York: Dover Publications, 1947)).)

O'Neill, Eugene. "An Explanation of *The Great God Brown.*" *In:* Meserve, Walter J., ed. *Discussions of American drama.* pp. 130-131.

Phillips, Elizabeth C. *Modern American drama,* pp. 69-71.

Raghavacharyulu, D.V.K. *Eugene O'Neil, a study,* pp. 60-68.

Sievers, W. David. *Freud on Broadway,* pp. 108-112.

Skinner, Richard Dana. *Eugene O'Neill, a poet's quest,* pp. 167-179.

Sogliuzzo, A. Richard. "The Uses of the Mask in *The Great God Brown* and *Six Characters in Search of an Author.*" *Educational Theatre J.,* vol. 18, no. 3 (Oct., 1966), pp. 224-229.

Tiusanen, Timo. *O'Neill's scenic images,* pp. 182-197.

Tynan, K. *Curtains,* pp. 322-324.

Young, Stark. *Immortal shadows,* pp. 61-66.

The Hairy Ape

Andreach, Robert J. "O'Neill's Use of Dante in *The Fountain* and *The Hairy Ape.*" *Modern Drama,* vol. 10, no. 1 (May, 1967), pp. 48-56.

Baum, Bernard. "*Tempest* and *Hairy Ape;* The Literary Incarnation of Mythos." *Modern Language Q.,* vol. 14, no. 3 (Sept., 1953), pp. 258-273.

Bierman, Judah. *The dramatic experience,* pp. 155-156.

Block, Anita. *The changing world in plays and theatre,* pp. 143-147.

Broussard, Louis. *American drama...,* pp. 14-23.

Clark, Marden J. "Tragic Effect in *The Hairy Ape.*" *Modern Drama,* vol. 10, no. 4 (Feb., 1968), pp. 372-382.

Downer, Alan S. *Fifty years of American* drama, 1900-1950, pp. 95-96.

Dusenbury, Winifred L. *The theme of loneliness in modern American drama,* pp. 125-134.

Eaton, Walter Prichard. "*The Hairy Ape.*" *In:* Miller, J.Y. *Playwright's progress: O'Neill and the critics,* pp. 32-35. (Reprinted from *The Freeman,* vol. 5 (Apr. 26, 1922), pp. 160-161.)

Engel, E.A. *Haunted heroes of Eugene O'Neill,* pp. 54-60.

Falk, Doris V. *Eugene O'Neill and the tragic tension,* pp. 10, 27-35, 36, 52, 55, 57, 58, 98, 198.

Flexner, Eleanor. *American playwrights: 1918-1938,* pp. 148-151.

Gump, Margaret. "From Ape to Man and from Man to Ape." *Kentucky Foreign Language Q.,* vol. 4, no. 4 (1957), pp. 177-185.

Kahan, Gerald. "Eugene O'Neill's *The Hairy Ape.*" M.A., University of Wisconsin, 1948.

James, Patterson. "Off the Record." *In:* Miller, J.Y. *Playwright's progress: O'Neill and the critics,* pp. 35-37. (Reprinted from *Billboard,* vol. 34 (Apr. 15, 1922), p. 18.)

Krutch, Joseph W. *The American drama since 1918,* pp. 87-89.

Leech, Clifford. *Eugene O'Neill,* pp. 34-46.

Long, Chester Clayton. *The role of nemesis in plays by Eugene O'Neill,* pp. 75-96.

McCollom, William G. *Tragedy,* pp. 49, 98-99, 229, 231.

Macgowan, K. "Experiment on Broadway." *Theatre Arts,* vol. 7 (July, 1923), pp. 175-185.

Mickle, A.D. *Studies on six plays of Eugene O'Neill,* pp. 35-57.

O'Neill, Eugene. *In:* Cole, Toby, ed. *Playwrights on playwriting,* pp. 235-237. (Reprinted from Barrett H. Clark. *Eugene O'Neill: the man and his plays* (New York: Dover Publications, 1947).)

O'Neill, Eugene. "O'Neill on *The Hairy Ape.*" *In:* Levin, Richard. *Tragedy: plays, theory, and criticism,* pp. 129-130. (Excerpt reprinted from Mary B. Mullett's interview with O'Neill published as "The Extraordinary Story of Eugene O'Neill." *American Mag.,* vol. 94, no. 5 (Nov., 1922).)

Phillips, Elizabeth C. *Modern American drama,* pp. 68-69.

Raghavacharyulu, D.V.K. *Eugene O'Neill, a study,* pp. 28-35.

Skinner, Richard Dana. *Eugene O'Neill, a poet's quest,* pp. 103-113.

Styan, J.L. *The element of drama,* pp. 245-248.

Tiusanen, Timo. *O'Neill's scenic images,* pp. 113-128.

Woollcott, Alexander. "*The Hairy Ape.*" *In:* Cargill *et al. O'Neill and his plays,* pp. 160-162. (Reprinted from *The New York Times* (Mar. 10, 1922).)

Woollcott, Alexander. "Eugene O'Neill at Full Tilt." *In:* Miller, J.Y. *Playwright's progress: O'Neill and the critics,* pp. 31-32 (Reprinted from *The New York Times* (Mar. 10, 1922).)

Hughie

Alexander, Doris. "The Missing Half of *Hughie.*" *Tulane Drama Rev.,* vol. 11 (1967), no. 4, pp. 125-126.

Cassell, Richard A. *What is the play?* pp. 7-8, 27-28.

Clurman, Harold. "*Tiny Alice, Hughie.*" *Nation,* vol. 200 (Jan. 18, 1965), p. 65.

Goldman, Arnold. "The Vanity of Personality: the Development of Eugene O'Neill." *In: American theatre,* pp. 44-45, 49.

Hewes, Henry. "*Hughie.*" *In:* Cargill *et al. O'Neill and his plays,* pp. 224-226. (From *The Saturday Rev.* (Oct. 4, 1958).)

Hewes, Henry. "Through the Looking Glass Darkly." *Saturday Rev.,* vol. 48 (Jan. 16, 1965), p. 40.

Krutch, J.W. "And Now—*Hughie.*" *Theatre Arts,* vol. 43 (Aug., 1959), pp. 14-15.

Leech, Clifford. *Eugene O'Neill,* p. 116.

Tiusanen, Timo. *O'Neill's scenic images,* pp. 316-321.

Weales, Gerald. "Variation on an O'Neill Theme." *Commonweal,* vol. 70 (May, 15, 1959), pp. 187-188.

The Iceman Cometh

Andreach, Robert J. "O'Neill's Women in *The Iceman Cometh.*" *Renascence,* vol. 18, no. 2 (Winter, 1966), pp. 89-98.

Arestad, Sverre. *The Iceman Cometh and The Wild Duck.*" *Scandinavian Studies,* vol. 20, no. 1 (Feb., 1948), pp. 1-11.

Atkinson, Brooks. "*The Iceman Cometh.*" *In:* Cargill *et al. O'Neill and his plays,* pp. 212-213. (From *The New York Times* (May 9, 1956).)

Atkinson, Brooks. "*Iceman Cometh,* Mr. O'Neill's New Work with Four-hour Running Time, Has Its World Premiere at the Martin Beck." *In:* Miller, J.Y. *Playwright's progress: O'Neill and the critics,* pp. 122-123. (Reprinted from *The New York Times* (Oct. 10, 1946).)

Bentley, Eric. "The Return of Eugene O'Neill." *In:* Miller, J.Y. *Playwright's progress: O'Neill and the critics,* pp. 125-130. (Reprinted from *The Atlantic Monthly,* vol. 178 (Nov., 1946), pp. 64-66.)

Bentley, Eric. "Trying to Like O'Neill." *In:* Gassner, John, ed. *O'Neill,* pp. 89-98. (Abbreviated and reprinted from Eric Bentley's *In search of theater* (N. Y., Knopf, 1952), pp. 233-247.)

Bigsby, C.W.E. *Confrontation and commitment,* pp. 12-15, 18.

Bowen, Croswell. "Rehearsing *The Iceman Cometh.*" *In:* Cargill *et al. O'Neill and his plays,* pp. 459-461. (Reprinted from *The curse of the misbegotten* by Croswell Bowen.)

Brashear, William R. "The Wisdom of Silenus in O'Neill's *Iceman.*" *American Literature,* vol. 36 (Mar.-June, 1964/65), pp. 180-188.

Broussard, Louis. *American Drama...,* pp. 30-35.

Brown, John Mason. "Moaning at the Bar." *In:* Brown, John Mason. *Dramatis personae,* pp. 57-63. *Also in:* Brown, J.M., *Seeing more things,* pp. 257-265.

Brustein, Robert. *The theatre of revolt,* pp. 339-348.

Chabrowe, Leonard. "Dionysus in *The Iceman Cometh.*" *Modern Drama,* vol. 4, no. 4 (Feb., 1962), pp. 377-388.

Chiari, J. *Landmarks of contemporary drama,* pp. 139-141, 142.

Cohn, Ruby, ed. *Twentieth-century drama,* pp. 405-407.

Coleman, Robert. "*The Iceman Cometh* a Terrific Hit." *In:* Miller, J.Y. *Playwright's progress: O'Neill and the critics,* pp. 124-125. (Reprinted from *New York Mirror* (Oct. 11, 1946).)

Day, Cyrus. "The Iceman and the Bridegroom." *Modern Drama,* vol. 1, no. 1 (May, 1958), pp. 3-9.

Dobrée, Bonamy. "Mr. O'Neill's Latest Play." *Sewanee Rev.,* vol. 56 (1948), pp. 118-126.

Dusenbury, Winifred L. *The theme of loneliness in modern American drama,* pp. 26-37.

Engel, E.A. *The haunted heroes of Eugene O'Neill,* pp. 281-296.

Falk, Doris V. *Eugene O'Neill and the tragic tension,* pp. 15, 28, 94, 156-166, 194, 197, 199.

Frazer, Winifred Dusenbury. *Love as death in "The Iceman Cometh:" a modern treatment of an ancient theme.* University of Florida Monographs, Humanities Series, no. 27. Gainesville, Univ. of Florida Press, 1967.

Gassner, John. "Broadway in Review." *Educational Theatre J.,* vol. 8 (Oct., 1956), pp. 224-225.

Gilder, Rosamond. *"The Iceman Cometh." In:* Cargill *et al. O'Neill and his plays,* pp. 203-208. (From *Theatre Arts* (Dec., 1946).)

Goldman, Arnold. "The Vanity of Personality: the Development of Eugene O'Neill." *In: American theatre,* pp. 37-38.

Heilman, Robert B. *Tragedy and melodrama,* pp. 15, 49-56, 72-73, 80, 103, 128, 155, 160.

Hopkins, Vivian C. *"The Iceman* Seen Through *The Lower Depths." College English,* vol. 11, no. 2 (Nov., 1949), pp. 81-87.

Kitchin, Laurence. *Mid-century drama,* pp. 69-71.

Leaska, Mitchell A. *The voice of tragedy,* pp. 269-271.

Leech, Clifford. *Eugene O'Neill,* pp. 98-108.

Long, Chester Clayton. *The role of nemesis in the structure of selected plays by Eugene O'Neill,* pp. 175-197.

Lumley, Frederick. *New trends in 20th-century drama,* pp. 122-124.

Lumley, Frederick. *Trends in 20th-century drama,* pp. 130-132.

McCarthy, Mary. *Sights and spectacles 1937-1956,* pp. 81-85.

Muchnic, Helen. "Circe's Swine: Plays by Gorky and O'Neill." *In:* Gassner, John, ed. *O'Neill,* pp. 99-109. (From *Comparative Literature,* vol. 3, no. 2 (Spring, 1951), pp. 119-128.)

Muchnic, Helen. "The Irrelevancy of Belief: *The Iceman* and *The Lower Depths." In:* Cargill *et al. O'Neill and his plays,* pp. 431-442. (From *Comparative Literature* (Spring, 1951).) Revised version; originally entitled "Circe's Swine: Plays by Gorky and O'Neill."

Myers, Henry A. *Tragedy: a view of life,* pp. 100-102.

Phillips, Elizabeth C. *Modern American drama,* pp. 73-74.

Raghavacharyulu, D.V.K. *Eugene O'Neill, a study,* pp. 139-150.

Sievers, W. David. *Freud on Broadway,* pp. 127-129.

Silverberg, William V. "Notes on *The Iceman Cometh." Psychiatry,* vol. 10 (1947), pp. 27-29.

Stamm, Rudolf. "A New Play by Eugene O'Neill." *English Studies,* vol. 29 (Oct., 1948), pp. 138-145.

Tiusanen, Timo. *O'Neill's scenic images,* pp. 264-284.

Tynan, K. *Curtains,* pp. 198-200.

Watts, Richard,Jr. "The Revival of O'Neill's *Iceman.*" *In:* Miller, J.Y. *Playwright's progress: O'Neill and the critics,* pp. 132-133. (Reprinted from *New York Post.* (May 9, 1956).)

Weales, Gerald. *American drama since World War II,* pp. 82-83.

Winther, Sophus. "*The Iceman Cometh:* A Study in Technique." *Arizona Q.,* vol. 3 (Winter, 1947), pp. 293-300.

Wolfson, Lester M. "Inge, O'Neill and the Human Condition." *Southern Speech J.,* vol. 22, no. 4 (Summer, 1957), pp. 227-229.

Wright, Robert C. "O'Neill's Universalizing Technique in *The Iceman Cometh.*" *Modern Drama,* vol. 8 (1965-66), pp. 1-11.

Young, Stark. *Immortal shadows,* pp. 271-274.

Ile

Engel, E.A. *The haunted heroes of Eugene O'Neill,* pp. 19-21.

Falk, Doris V. *Eugene O'Neill and the tragic tension,* pp. 15, 22-24.

Mantle, Burns. "Greenwich Village Players Offer Three Short Plays." *New York Mail* (Apr. 19, 1918). (Reprinted in Miller, J.Y. *Playwright's progress: O'Neill and the critics,* pp. 5-6.)

Sherwin, Louis. "*Ile.*" *In:* Cargill *et al.,* eds. *O'Neill and his plays,* pp. 132-133. (Reprinted from *New York Globe* (Apr. 19, 1918).)

Skinner, Richard Dana. *Eugene O'Neill, a poet's quest,* pp. 45-46.

In the Zone

Anonymous. "New Season of Short Plays at the Comedy." *New York World* (Nov. 1, 1917). (Reprinted in Miller, J.Y. *Playwright's progress: O'Neill and the critics,* p. 5.)

Goldhurst, William. "A Literary Source for O'Neill's *In the Zone.*" *American Literature,* vol. 35, no. 4 (Jan., 1964), pp. 530-534.

Lazarus Laughed

Alexander, Doris M. "*Lazarus Laughed* and Budda." *Modern Language Q.,* vol. 17 (Dec., 1956), pp. 357-365. *Also in:* Gassner, John, ed. *O'Neill,* pp. 72-81.

Block, Anita. *The changing world in plays and theatre,* pp. 151-158.

Chabrowe, Leonard. "Dionysus in *The Iceman Cometh.*" *Modern Drama,* vol. 4, no. 4 (Feb., 1962), pp. 377-388.

Dahlstrom, Carl E.W.L. "*Dynamo* and *Lazarus Laughed:* Some Limitations." *Modern Drama,* vol. 3, no. 3 (Dec., 1960), pp. 224-230.

Day, Cyrus. "*Amor Fati:* O'Neill's Lazarus as Superman and Savior." *In:* Gassner, John, ed. *O'Neill,* pp. 72-81. (Reprinted from *Modern Drama,* vol. 3, no. 3 (Dec., 1960), pp. 297-305.)

Engel, E.A. *The haunted heroes of Eugene O'Neill,* pp. 175-196.

Falk, Doris V. *Eugene O'Neill and the tragic tension,* pp. 108-114.

Flexner, Eleanor. *American playwrights: 1918-1938,* pp. 167-172.

Hersey, F.W. "*Lazarus Laughed:* A World Premiere at Pasadena." *Drama,* vol. 18 (May, 1928), pp. 244-246.

Leech, Clifford. *Eugene O'Neill,* pp. 70-72.

Phillips, Elizabeth C. *Modern American drama,* pp. 69-71.

Pommer, Henry F. "The Mysticism of Eugene O'Neill." *Modern Drama,* vol. 9, no. 1 (May, 1966), pp. 26-39.

Raghavacharyulu, D.V.K. *Eugene O'Neill, a study,* pp. 68-76.

Skinner, Richard Dana. *Eugene O'Neill, a poet's quest,* pp. 180-190.

Stechan, H.O. "*Lazarus Laughed.*" *In:* Miller, J.Y. *Playwright's progress: O'Neill and the critics,* pp. 61-62. (Reprinted from *Billboard,* vol. 40 (Apr. 21, 1928), p. 11.)

Tiusanen, Timo. *O'Neill's scenic images,* pp. 141-150.

Warren, George C. "*Lazarus Laughed.*" *In:* Cargill *et al. O'Neill and his plays,* pp. 178-180. (From *San Francisco Chronicle* (Apr. 10, 1928).)

Long Day's Journey Into Night

Bigsby, C.W.E. *Confrontation and commitment,* pp. 12, 15-16.

Brustein, Robert. *The theatre of revolt,* pp. 348-359.

Cerf, Walter. "Psychoanalysis and the Realistic Drama." *J. of Aesthetics and Art Criticism,* vol. 16, no. 3 (Mar., 1958), pp. 328-336.

Chapman, John. "*Long Day's Journey Into Night,* a Drama of Sheer Magnificence." *In:* Miller, J.Y. *Playwright's progress: O'Neill and the critics,* pp. 133-134. (Reprinted from *New York Daily News* (Nov. 8, 1956).)

Chapman, John. "O'Neill's *Long Day's Journey Into Night.*" *In:* Oppenheimer, George, ed. *The passionate playgoer,* pp. 281-288. (Reprinted from *Broadway's best,* N.Y., Doubleday, 1957.)

Chiari, J. *Landmarks of contemporary drama,* pp. 138-139, 158-159.

Clurman, Harold. "*Long Day's Journey Into Night.*" *Nation* (Mar. 3, 1956). *Also in:* Clurman, H. *Lies like truth,* pp. 24-33. (Reprinted in Cargill *et al. O'Neill and his plays,* pp. 214-216.)

Dash, Thomas R. "*Long Day's Journey Into Night.*" *In:* Miller, J.Y. *Playwright's progress: O'Neill and the critics,* pp. 134-136. (Reprinted from *Women's Wear Daily* (Nov. 8, 1956).)

Downer, Alan S. "Tragedy and 'The Pursuit of Happiness'; *Long Day's Journey Into Night.*" *Jahrbuch,* no. 6 (1961), pp. 114-121.

Falk, Doris V. *Eugene O'Neill and the tragic tension,* pp. 15, 19-20, 149, 165, 170-171, 179-195, 198.

Finkelstein, Sidney. *Existentialism and alienation in American literature,* pp. 149-153.

Finkelstein, Sidney. "O'Neill's *Long Day's Journey.*" *Mainstream* vol. 16, no. 6 (June, 1963), pp. 47-51.

Fraser, G.S. *The modern writer and his world,* pp. 65-66.

Gassner, John. *Theatre at the crossroads,* pp. 235-238.

Golden, Joseph. *The death of Tinker Bell,* pp. 44-45.

Goldman, Arnold. "The Vanity of Personality: the Development of Eugene O'Neill." *In: American theatre,* pp. 31-32, 38-39, 48.

Hewes, Henry. "*Long Day's Journey Into Night.*" *In:* Cargill *et al. O'Neill and his plays,* pp. 217-220. (From *The Saturday Rev.* (Nov. 24, 1956).)

Hilfer, Anthony C. "George and Martha: Sad, Sad, Sad." *In:* Whitbread, Thomas B., ed. *Seven contemporary authors,* pp. 124-130, 134-135.

Kerr, Walter. "*Long Day's Journey Into Night.*" *In:* Miller, J.Y. *Playwright's progress: O'Neill and the critics,* pp. 136-137. (Reprinted from *New York Herald Tribune* (Nov. 8, 1956).)

Krutch, Joseph W. *The American drama since 1918,* pp. 332-336.

Lawrence, Kenneth. "Dionysus and O'Neill." *Univ. Rev.,* vol. 33, no. 1 (Oct., 1966), pp. 67-70.

Leech, Clifford. *Eugene O'Neill,* pp. 108-111.

Long, Chester Clayton. *The role of nemesis in the structure of selected plays by Eugene O'Neill,* pp. 198-215.

Matthews, Honor. *The primal curse,* pp. 194-196.

Nagarajan, S. "A Note on O'Neill's *Long Day's Journey Into Night.*" *Literary Criterion* (U. of Mysore, India), vol. 7, no. 3 (1966), pp. 52-54.

Phillips, Elizabeth C. *Modern American drama,* pp. 76-77.

Raghavacharyulu, D.V.K. *Eugene O'Neill, a study,* pp. 157-170.

Raleigh, John H. "O'Neill's *Long Day's Journey Into Night* and New England Irish-Catholicism." *Partisan Rev.,* vol. 26 (Fall, 1959), pp. 573-592. *Also in:* Bogard, T. and W. Oliver, eds. *Modern drama,* pp. 234-254, and Gassner, J., ed. *O'Neill,* pp. 124-141.

Redford, Grant H. "Dramatic Art vs. Autobiography: A Look at *Long Day's Journey Into Night.*" *College English,* vol. 25, no. 7 (Apr., 1964), pp. 527-535.

Rubinstein, Annette. "The Dark Journey of Eugene O'Neill." *Mainstream,* vol. 10 (Apr. 1957), pp. 29-33.

Shawcross, John T. "The Road to Ruin: The Beginning of O'Neill's Long Day's Journey." *Modern Drama,* vol. 3, no. 3 (Dec., 1960), pp. 289-296.

Tiusanen, Timo. *O'Neill's scenic images,* pp. 285-303.

Tynan, K. *Curtains,* pp. 223-225.

Weales, Gerald. *American drama since World War II,* pp. 81-82.

Weissman, Philip. *Creativity in the theater,* pp. 117-129, 132-133, 238-239.

Weissman, Philip. "Eugene O'Neill's Autobiographical Dramas." *American Psychoanalytic Assoc. J.,* vol. 5, no. 3 (July, 1957), pp. 432-451.

Williams, Raymond. *Modern tragedy,* pp. 117-118.

Winther, Sophus K. "O'Neill's Tragic Themes: *Long Day's Journey Into Night.*" *Arizona Q.,* vol. 13, no. 4 (Winter, 1957), pp. 295-307.

Wolfson, Lester M. "Inge, O'Neill and the Human Condition." *Southern Speech J.,* vol. 22, no. 4 (Summer, 1957), pp. 230-232.

Marco Millions

Allen, Kelcey. "*Marco Millions* Is Poignant O'Neill Satire." *In:* Miller, J.Y. *Playwright's progress: O'Neill and the critics,* pp. 55-57. (Reprinted from *Women's Wear Daily* (Jan. 10, 1928).)

Brown, John Mason. *"Marco Millions." In:* Cargill *et al. O'Neill and his plays,* pp. 181-183. (From *Theatre Arts,* Mar. 1928, pp. 163-166.)

Engel, E.A. *The haunted heroes of Eugene O'Neill,* pp. 135-152.

Falk, Doris V. *Eugene O'Nell and the tragic tension,* pp. 19, 90-93.

Farquhar, E.F. *"Marco Millions." Letters* (U. of Kentucky), vol. 1 (Nov., 1928), pp. 33-40.

Gelb, Arthur and Barbara. "Eugene O'Neill and *Marco Millions." In: Theatre: the annual of the Repertory Theatre of Lincoln Center,* vol. 1 (1964), pp. 25-33.

Krutch, J.W. "Marco the Westerner." *Nation,* vol. 124 (May 18, 1927), pp. 562-564.

Leech, Clifford. *Eugene O'Neill,* pp. 66-69.

Mickle, A.D. *Studies on six plays of Eugene O'Neill,* pp. 113-137.

Nathan, G.J. "O'Neill's New Play." *American Mercury,* vol. 8 (Aug., 1926), pp. 499-505.

Raghavacharyulu, D.V.K. *Eugene O'Neill, a study,* pp. 48-51.

Skinner, Richard Dana. *Eugene O'Neill, a poet's quest,* pp. 157-166.

Taubman, Howard. "O'Neill Revisted." *In:* Miller, J.Y. *Playwright's progress: O'Neill and the critics,* pp. 172-174. (Reprinted from *The New York Times* (Mar. 1, 1964).)

Tiusanen, Timo. *O'Neill's scenic images,* pp. 136-141.

A Moon for the Misbegotten

Bentley, Eric. *The dramatic event,* pp. 30-33.

Clurman, Harold "Theatre." *Nation,* vol. 178 (May 8, 1954), p. 409. *Also in:* Clurman, H. *Lies like truth,* pp. 24-33.

Donnelly, Tom. "A Long Night's Moongazing." *In:* Miller, J.Y. *Playwright's progress: O'Neill and the critics,* pp. 163-166. (Reprinted from *New York World-Telegram, and Sun* (May 3, 1957).)

Falk, Doris V. *Eugene O'Neill and the tragic tension,* pp. 15, 94, 156-157, 171-177, 197, 199.

Goldman, Arnold. "The Vanity of Personality: the Development of Eugene O'Neill." *In: American theatre,* pp. 33-34.

Kerr, Walter. "Futz—Is It a Fiasco..." *The New York Times* (June 30, 1968), Sec. 2, p. 5.

Krutch, J.W. "Genius Is Better Than Talent." *Theatre Arts,* vol. 39 (Oct., 1954), pp. 22-23.

Leech Clifford. *Eugene O'Neill,* pp. 111-112.

McCarthy, Mary. *"A Moon for the Misbegotten." In:* Cargill *et al. O'Neill and his plays,* pp. 209-211. (From McCarthy, M. *Sights and spectacles.* Originally appeared in *New York Times Book Review,* (Aug. 31, 1952).)

Raghavacharyulu, D.V.K. *Eugene O'Neill, a study,* pp. 150-153.

Sievers, W. David. *Freud on Broadway,* pp. 129-132.

Tiusanen, Timo. *O'Neill's scenic images,* pp. 304-315.

Wolfson, Lester M. "Inge, O'Neill and the Human Condition." *Southern Speech J.,* vol. 22, no. 4 (Summer, 1957), pp. 229.

The Moon of the Caribbees

Engel, E.A. *The haunted heroes of Eugene O'Neill,* pp. 11-13.

Long, Chester Clayton. *The role of nemesis in the structure of selected plays by Eugene O'Neill,* pp. 59-67, 70-74.

More Stately Mansions

Falk, Doris V. *Eugene O'Neill and the tragic tension,* pp. 156-157, 199.

Hartman, Murray. "The Skeletons in O'Neill's *Mansions." Drama Survey,* vol. 5, no. 3 (Winter, 1966-67), pp. 276-279.

Loney, Glenn. "Broadway in Review." *Educational Theatre J.* vol. 20, no. 1 (Mar., 1968), p. 102.

Tiusanen, Timo. *O'Neill's scenic images,* pp. 249-263.

Mourning Becomes Electra

Alexander, Doris M. "Captain Brant and Captain Brassbound: The Origin of an O'Neill Character." *Modern Language Notes,* vol. 74 (Apr., 1959), pp. 306-310.

Alexander, Doris M. "Psychological Fate in *Mourning Becomes Electra." PMLA,* vol. 68, no. 5 (Dec., 1953), pp. 923-934.

Asselineau, Roger. *Mourning Becomes Electra* as a Tragedy." *Modern Drama,* vol. 1, no. 3 (Dec., 1958), pp. 143-150.

Atkinson, Brooks. "Strange Images of Death in Eugene O'Neill's Masterpiece." *In:* Miller, J.Y. *Playwright's progress: O'Neill and the critics,* pp. 65-67. (Reprinted from *The New York Times* (Oct. 27, 1931).)

Barron, Samuel. "The Dying Theatre." *Harpers,* vol. 172 (Dec., 1935), pp. 108-117.

Benchley, Robert C. "O'Neill's *Mourning Becomes Electra.*" *In:* Moses, Montrose J. *The American theatre as seen by its critics, 1752-1934,* pp. 262-265. (Reprinted from *New Yorker* (Nov. 7, 1931).) *Also in:* Oppenheimer, George, ed. *The passionate playgoer,* pp. 580-584.

Block, Anita. *The changing world in plays and theatre,* pp. 178-188.

Brown, John Mason. *"Mourning Becomes Electra."* *In:* Brown, John Mason. *Dramatis personae,* pp. 53-57.

Brown, John Mason. *"Mourning Becomes Electra,* Eugene O'Neill's Exciting Trilogy, Is Given an Excellent Production at the Guild." *In:* Miller, J.Y. *Playwright's progress: O'Neill and the critics,* pp. 67-71. (Reprinted from *New York Post* (Oct. 27, 1931).)

Brown, John Mason. *Two on the aisle,* pp. 136-142.

Burr, Eugene. *"Mourning Becomes Electra."* *In:* Miller, J.Y. *Playwright's progress: O'Neill and the critics,* pp. 71-73. (Reprinted from *Billboard,* vol. 43 (Nov. 7, 1931), pp. 17, 19.)

Clark, Barrett H. "Aeschylus and Eugene O'Neill." *English J.,* vol. 21 (Nov., 1932), pp. 699-710.

Corrigan, Robert. 'The Electra' theme in the history of drama." *Dissertation Abstracts,* vol. 15 (1955), 1612 (Minnesota).

Dukes, Ashley. "The English Scene: O'Neill Succeeds." *Theatre Arts,* vol. 22 (Feb., 1938), pp. 101-107.

Dusenbury, Winifred L. *The theme of loneliness in modern American drama,* pp. 74-85.

Eastman, Fred. *Christ in the drama,* pp. 93-97.

Engel, E.A. *The haunted heroes of Eugene O'Neill,* pp. 199-229, 241-259.

Falk, Doris V. *Eugene O'Neill and the tragic tension,* pp. 98, 121, 177, 189-190, 198, 199.

Feldman, Abraham. "The American Aeschylus?" *Poet Lore,* vol. 52 (Summer, 1946), pp. 149-155.

Fergusson, Francis. "A Month of the Theatre." *Bookman,* vol. 74 (Dec., 1931), pp. 440-445.

Flexner, Eleanor. *American playwrights: 1918-1938,* pp. 182-193.

Frenz, Horst, and Martin Mueller. "More Shakespeare and Less Aeschylus in Eugene O'Neill's *Mourning Becomes Electra." American Literature,* vol. 38, no. 1 (Mar., 1966), pp. 85-100.

Gassner, John. *The theatre in our times,* pp. 260-266.

Goldman, Arnold. "The Vanity of Personality: the Development of Eugene O'Neill." *In: American theatre,* pp. 42-44, 50.

Greenwood, Ormerod. *The playwright,* pp. 100-103.

Hall, Philip G. Dramatic Irony in *Mourning Becomes Electra." Southern Speech J.,* vol. 31, no. 1 (Fall, 1965), pp. 42-55.

Hanzeli, Victor E. "The Progeny of Atreus." *Modern Drama,* vol. 3, no. 1 (May, 1960), pp. 79-81.

Hutchens, John. *"Mourning Becomes Electra." In:* Cargill *et al. O'Neill and his plays,* pp. 190-193. From *Theatre Arts* (Jan. 1932).

Kirstein, Lincoln. "Theatre Chronicle." *Hound and Horn,* vol. 5 (Jan.-Mar., 1932), pp. 280-282.

Knickerbocker, Frances W. "A New England House of Atreus." *Sewanee Rev.,* vol. 40 (Apr.-June, 1932), pp. 249-254.

Krutch, Joseph W. *The American drama since 1918,* pp. 106-113.

Lecky, Eleazer. *"Ghosts* and *Mourning Becomes Electra:* Two Versions of Fate." *Arizona Q.,* vol. 13, no. 4 (Winter, 1957), pp. 320-338.

Leech, Clifford. *Eugene O'Neill,* pp. 82-89.

Long, Chester Clayton. *The role of nemesis in the structure of selected plays by Eugene O'Neill,* pp. 117-174.

McCollom, William G. *Tragedy,* pp. 230-232.

Mickle, A.D. *Studies on six plays of Eugene O'Neill,* pp. 141-166.

Muller, Herbert J. *The spirt of tragedy,* pp. 313-315.

Myers, Henry A. *Tragedy: a view of life,* pp. 22-23.

Nagarajan, S. "Eugene O'Neill's *Mourning Becomes Electra:* The Classical Aspect." *Literary Criterion* (Mysore, India), vol. 5, no. 3 (1962), pp. 148-154.

Olson, Elder. *Tragedy and the theory of drama,* pp. 237-243.

O'Neill, Eugene. "Language in a Faithless Age: A Letter to Arthur Hobson Quinn." *In:* Cargill *et al. O'Neill and his plays,* p. 463. (From *A history of the American drama,* vol. II, by Arthur Hobson Quinn, Crofts, 1945.)

Phillips, Elizabeth C. *Modern American drama,* pp. 71-73.

Ponich, Emil. "The Greek Atreidae dramas and Eugene O'Neill's *Mourning Becomes Electra:* a study in contrasts." M.A., Montana State University, 1959.

Pratt, Norman T., Jr. "Aeschylus and O'Neill: Two Worlds." *Classic J.,* vol. 51 (Jan., 1956), pp. 163-167.

Raghavacharyulu, D.V.K. *Eugene O'Neill, a study,* pp. 104-114.

Ramsey, Warren. "The *Oresteia* Since Hofmannsthal: Images and Emphases." *Revue de Litterature Comparee,* vol. 38 (1964), pp. 363-366.

Sievers, W. David. *Freud on Broadway,* pp. 121-124.

Skinner, Richard Dana. *Eugene O'Neill, a poet's quest,* pp. 211-226.

Smith, John. "If I Had Written *Mourning Becomes Electra.*" *Modern Thinker,* vol. 1 (Aug., 1932), pp. 359-363.

Stafford, John. "Mourning Becomes America." *Texas Studies in Literature and Language,* vol. 3, no. 4 (Winter, 1962), pp. 549-556.

Stamm, Rudolf. "The Orestes Theme in Three Plays by Eugene O'Neill, T.S. Eliot & Jean-Paul Sartre." *English Studies,* vol. 30 (Nov., 1949), pp. 244-247.

Tapper, Bonno. "Eugene O'Neill's World View." *Personalist,* vol. 18, no. 1 (Jan., 1937), pp. 40-48.

Tiusanen, Timo. *O'Neill's scenic images,* pp. 225-240.

Van Bark, Bella S. "The Alienated Person in Literature." *American J. of Psychoanalysis,* vol. 21 (1961), pp. 183-197.

Vincent, W. Ernest. "Five Electras—Aeschylus to Sartre." *Southern Speech J.,* vol. 24 (Summer, 1959), pp. 225-235.

Weissman, Philip. *Creativity in the theater,* pp. 204-209.

Weissman Philip. *"Mourning Becomes Electra and The Prodigal." In:* Force, William M., ed. *Orestes and Electra, myth and dramatic form,* pp. 324-327. *Also in: Modern Drama,* vol. 3, no. 3 (Dec., 1960), pp. 257-259.

Williams, Raymond. *Modern tragedy,* pp. 117-119.

Young, Stark. "American Drama in Production." *In:* Zabel, Morton Dauwen. *Literary opinion in America,* pp. 522-529. (Reprinted from *The New Republic,* vol. 68 (Nov. 11, 1931), pp. 352-355.) *Also in:* Young, S. *Immortal shadows,* N.Y., Scribner's, 1948.

Young, Stark. "Eugene O'Neill's New Play." *In:* Gassner, John, ed. *O'Neill,* pp. 82-88. (Reprinted from *Immortal shadows* by Stark Young (N. Y., Scribner's, 1948), pp. 132-139.)

Now I Ask You

Tiusanen, Timo. *O'Neill's scenic images,* pp. 63-66.

The Rime of the Ancient Mariner (Adapted from Samuel Taylor Coleridge)

Nathan, George Jean. *"The Rime of the Ancient Mariner." In:* Cargill *et al. O'Neill and his plays,* pp. 166-167. (From *The American Mercury* (June 1924).)

Tiusanen, Timo. *O'Neill's scenic images,* pp. 170-174.

The Rope

Skinner, Richard Dana. *Eugene O'Neill, a poet's quest,* pp. 46-48.

Servitude

Falk, Doris V. *Eugene O'Neill and the tragic tension,* pp. 15-19, 24, 45, 48, 60.

S.S. Glencairn

Rust, R. Dilworth. "The Unity of O'Neill's *S.S. Glencairn." American Literature,* vol. 35, no. 3 (Sept.,1966), pp. 280-290.

Shell Shock

Tiusanen, Timo. *O'Neill's scenic images,* pp. 66-72.

Strange Interlude

Alexander, Doris. M. "Freud and O'Neill: an analysis of *Strange Interlude."* Dissertation, New York University, 1952.

Alexander, Doris M. *"Strange Interlude* and Schopenhauer." *American Literature,* vol. 25 (May, 1953), pp. 213-228.

Anderson, John. *"Strange Interlude* Profound Drama of Subconscious." *In:* Miller, J.Y. *Playwright's progress: O'Neill and the critics,* pp. 57-59. (Reprinted from *New York Evening Journal* (Jan. 31, 1928).)

Battenhouse, Roy W. *"Strange Interlude* Restudied." *Religion in Life,* vol. 15 (Spring, 1946), pp. 202-213.

Block, Anita. *The changing world in plays and theatre,* pp. 162-177.

Brashear, William R. "O'Neill's Schopenhauer Interlude." *Criticism,* vol. 6 (Summer, 1964), pp. 256-265.

Brustein, Robert. *Seasons of discontent,* pp. 141-143.

Dusenbury, Winifred L. *The theme of loneliness in modern American drama,* pp. 101-112.

Falk, Doris V. *Eugene O'Neill and the tragic tension,* pp. 110, 121-126, 197, 198, 199.

Flexner, Eleanor. *American playwrights: 1918-1938,* pp. 172-179.

Goldman, Arnold. "The Vanity of Personality: the Development of Eugene O'Neill." *In: American theatre,* pp. 29-30, 32-33, 48-49.

Krutch, Joseph W. *The American drama since 1918,* pp. 100-106.

Krutch, John Wood. "A Modern Heroic Drama." *In:* Miller, J.Y. *Playwright's progress: O'Neill and the critics,* pp. 59-61. (Reprinted from *New York Herald Tribune* (Mar. 11, 1928).)

Krutch, Joseph Wood. *"Strange Interlude." In:* Cargill *et al. O'Neill and his plays,* pp. 184-186. (From *The Nation* (Feb., 15, 1928).)

Leech, Clifford. *Eugene O'Neill,* pp. 73-82.

Malone, Kemp. "The Diction of *Strange Interlude." American Speech,* vol. 6 (Oct., 1930), pp. 19-28.

Montgomery, Guy. *"Strange Interlude." Univ. of California Chronicles,* vol. 30 (July, 1928), pp. 364-368.

Phillips, Elizabeth C. *Modern American drama,* p. 71.

Raghavacharyulu, D.V.K. *Eugene O'Neill, a study,* pp. 93-100.

Reekie, A.G. "Eugene O'Neill: the Dilemma of the Intellectual." *In: The rationalist annual,* 1949, ed. by Frederick Watts. London, Watts & Co. pp. 6-8.

Sievers, W. David. *Freud on Broadway,* pp. 115-119.

Skinner, Richard Dana. *Eugene O'Neill, a poet's quest,* pp. 191-202.

Tiusanen, Timo. *O'Neill's scenic images,* pp. 212-224.

Waton, Harry. *The historic significance of Eugene O'Neill's Strange Interlude.*

The Straw

Engel, E.A. *The haunted heroes of Eugene O'Neill,* pp. 36-39.

Falk, Doris V. *Eugene O'Neill and the tragic tension,* pp. 27-28, 45-48, 51, 58, 97.

Leech, Clifford. *Eugene O'Neill,* pp. 27-28.

Parker, Robert Allerton. "An American Dramatist Developing." *In:* Miller, J.Y. *Playwright's progress: O'Neill and the critics,* pp. 28-31. (Reprinted from *The Independent and The Weekly Review,* vol. 107 (Dec. 3, 1921), p. 236.)

Raghavacharyulu, D.V.K. *Eugene O'Neill, a study,* p. 26.

Skinner, Richard Dana. *Eugene O'Neill, a poet's quest,* pp. 61-67.

Tiusanen, Timo. *O'Neill's scenic images,* pp. 82-86.

Woollcott, Alexander. "The Straw." In: Cargill *et al. O'Neill and his plays,* pp. 155-156. (Reprinted from *The New York Times* (Nov. 11, 1921).)

Thirst

Long, Chester Clayton. *The role of nemesis in the structure of selected plays by Eugene O'Neill,* pp. 44-59, 69-70, 73-74.

A Touch of the Poet

Alexander, Doris. "Eugene O'Neill and Charles Lever." *Modern Drama,* vol. 5, no. 4 (Feb., 1963), pp. 415-420.

Atkinson, Brooks. "Theatre: Eugene O'Neill's *A Touch of the Poet.*" *In:* Miller, J.Y. *Playwright's progress: O'Neill and the critics,* pp. 166-167. (Reprinted from *The New York Times* (Oct. 3, 1958).)

Bigsby, C.W.E. *Confrontation and commitment,* pp. 16-17.

Brustein, Robert. "Theatre Chronicle." *Hudson Rev.,* vol. 12 (Spring, 1959), pp. 96-98.

Falk, Doris V. *Eugene O'Neill and the tragic tension,* pp. 28, 156-157, 165-170.

Gassner, John. *Theatre at the crossroads,* pp. 238-241.

Hewes, Henry. *"A Touch of the Poet."* In: Cargill *et al. O'Neill and his plays,* pp. 221-223. (From *The Saturday Review* (Apr. 13. 1957).)

Krutch, Joseph Wood. "The O'Neills on Stage Once More." *Theatre Arts,* vol. 42 (Oct., 1958), pp. 16-17.

Leech, Clifford. *Eugene O'Neill,* pp. 112-116.

McCarthy, Mary. "Odd Man In." *Partisan Rev.,* vol. 26 (Winter, 1959), pp. 100-106.

McClain, John. "O'Neill Again Proves He's Incomparable." *In:* Miller, J.Y. *Playwright's progress: O'Neill and the critics,* pp. 167-168. (Reprinted from *New York Journal-American* (Oct. 3, 1958).)

Marcus, Mordecai. "Eugene O'Neill's Debt to Thoreau in *A Touch of the Poet." J. of English and Germanic Philology,* vol. 62 (1963), pp. 270-279.

Pallette, Drew B. "O'Neill's *A Touch of the Poet* and His Other Last Plays." *Arizona Q.,* vol. 13 (1957), pp. 308-319.

Raghavacharyulu, D.V.K. *Eugene O'Neill, a study,* pp. 153-157.

Rogoff, Gordon. "From Tall Acorns Little Acorns Grow." *Encore,* vol. 6 (Jan.-Feb., 1959), pp. 30-33.

Tiusanen, Timo. *O'Neill's scenic images,* pp. 321-330.

Tynan, K. *Curtains,* pp. 445-446.

Vidal, Gore. *Rocking the boat.* pp. 118-123. *Also in: Nation,* vol. 187, no. 13 (Oct. 25, 1958), pp. 298-299.

The Web

Fish, Charles. "Beginnings: O'Neill's *The Web." Princeton University Library Chronicle,* vol. 27, no. 1 (Autumn, 1965), pp. 3-20.

Welded

Engel, E.A. *The haunted heroes of Eugene O'Neill,* pp. 107-116.

Falk, Doris V. *Eugene O'Neill and the tragic tension,* pp. 85-87, 117, 148.

Goldman, Arnold. "The Vanity of Personality: the Development of Eugene O'Neill." *In: American theatre,* pp. 35-36.

Leech, Clifford. *Eugene O'Neill,* pp. 44-46.

Lewisohn, Ludwig. *"Welded."* In: Cargill *et al. O'Neill and his plays,* pp. 163-165. (From *The Nation* (Apr. 2, 1924).)

O'Neill, Eugene. "Letters to George Jean Nathan." *In:* Caputi, Anthony, ed. *Modern drama,* pp. 449-450.

Raghavacharyulu, D.V.K. *Eugene O'Neill, a study,* pp. 51-53.

Skinner, Richard Dana. *Eugene O'Neill, a poet's quest,* pp. 124-130.

Tiusanen, Timo. *O'Neill's scenic images,* pp. 207-212.

Whittaker, James. "Eugene O'Neill's Play Shown at 37th Street." *In:* Miller, J.Y. *Playwright's progress: O'Neill and the critics,* pp. 14-15. (Reprinted from *New York American,* Mar. 18, 1924).)

Where the Cross Is Made

Engel, E.A. *The haunted heroes of Eugene O'Neill,* pp. 21-24.

Leech, Clifford. *Eugene O'Neill,* pp. 26-27.

JOE ORDWAY

Entertaining Mrs. Sloane

Kerr, Walter. *Tragedy and comedy,* pp. 317-319.

O'Casey, Sean. "The Bald Primaqueera." *In:* O'Casey, Sean. *Blasts and benedictions,* pp. 74-75.

CONAL O'RIORDAN

The Piper

Malone, Andrew E. *The Irish drama,* p. 267.

PAUL OSBORN 1901-

Point of No Return

See Marquand, John P.

JOHN OSBORNE 1929-

General

Allsop, Kenneth. *The angry decade,* pp. 104-132, 135-140.

Baxter, Kay M. *Contemporary theatre and the Christian faith,* pp. 79-89.

Blau, Herbert. *The impossible theatre,* pp. 213-220.

Bode, Carl. "The Redbrick Cinderellas." *College English,* vol. 20, no. 7 (Apr., 1959), pp. 331-333.

Brown, John Russell. "Introduction." *In:* Brown, John Russell, ed. *Modern British dramatists, a collection of critical essays,* pp. 9-10.

Carter, A.V. "John Osborne: A Re-appraisal." *Revue Belge de Philologie et d'Histoire,* vol. 44 (1966), pp. 971-976.

Chiari, J. *Landmarks of contemporary drama,* pp. 109-115.

Fraser, G.S. *The modern writer and his world,* pp. 323-233.

Gascoigne, Bamber. *Twentieth-century drama,* pp. 196-198.

Gersh, Gabriel. "The Theatre of John Osborne." *Modern Drama,* vol. 10, no. 3 (Sept., 1967), pp. 137-143.

Lumley, Frederick. *New trends in 20th-century drama,* pp. 219, 221-232.

Nathan, David. "John Osborne—Is His Anger Simmering?" *In:* Richards, Dick. *The curtain rises,* pp. 244-247.

Osborne, John. (Interview with John Freeman.) *In:* Wager, Walter, ed. *The playwrights speak,* pp. 96-109.

Taylor, John Russell. *Anger and after,* pp. 39-57.

Wager, Walter. "John Osborne." *In:* Wager, Walter, ed. *The playwrights speak,* pp. 90-96.

Wellwarth, George. *The theatre of protest and paradox,* pp. 52, 197, 221, 222-234.

The Blood of the Bambergs

Wellwarth, George. *The theatre of protest and paradox,* pp. 231-233.

A Bond Honoured

Browne, E. Martin. "A Look Round the English Theatre: Summer and Fall, 1966." *Drama Survey,* vol. 5, no. 3 (Winter, 1966-67), pp. 297-298.

The Entertainer

Allsop, Kenneth. *The angry decade,* pp. 120-130.

Blau, Herbert. *The impossible theatre,* pp. 217-220.

Davison, Peter. "Contemporary Drama and Popular Dramatic Forms." *In: Aspects of drama and the theatre,* pp. 152-157.

Deming, Barbara. "John Osborne's War Against the Philistines." *Hudson Rev.,* vol. 11, no. 3 (Autumn, 1958), pp. 411-419.

Kitchin, Laurence. *Mid-century drama,* pp. 104-106.

Lumley, Frederick. *New trends in 20th-century drama,* pp. 224-226.

Price, Martin. "The London Season." *Modern Drama,* vol. 1, no. 1 (May, 1958), pp. 53-59.

Styan, J.L. *The dark comedy,* 2nd ed., pp. 63, 116-117, 223, 256, 265, 270, 271, 296.

Taylor, John Russell. *Anger and after,* pp. 47-50.

Wellwarth, George. *The theatre of protest and paradox,* pp. 226, 227.

Worth, Katharine J. "The Angry Young Man: John Osborne." *In:* Armstrong, William A., cd. *Experimental drama,* pp. 156 163.

Epitaph for George Dillon

Brustein, Robert. *Hudson Rev.,* vol. 12, no. 1 (Spring, 1959), pp. 94-101.

Gassner, John. *Theatre at the crossroads,* pp. 175-177.

Nicoll, Allardyce. "Somewhat in a New Dimension." *In:* Brown, J.R., and B. Harris, eds. *Contemporary theatre,* pp. 83-84.

Taylor, John Russell. *Anger and after,* pp. 45-47.

Tynan, Kenneth. *Tynan right and left,* pp. 5-6.

Wellwarth, George. *The theatre of protest and paradox,* pp. 226, 254.

Hotel in Amsterdam

Kennedy, Andrew K. "Old and New in London Now." *Modern Drama,* vol. 11, no. 4 (Feb., 1969), pp. 444-445.

Inadmissible Evidence

Clurman, Harold. *The naked image,* pp. 101-104.

Downer, Alan S. "Total Theatre and Partial Drama: Notes on the New York Theatre, 1965-1966." *Q. J. of Speech,* vol. 52, no. 3 (Oct., 1966), pp. 232-234.

Gassner, John. "Broadway in Review." *Educational Theatre J.,* vol. 18, no. 1 (Mar., 1966), pp. 59-60.

Lumley, Frederick. *New trends in 20th-century drama,* pp. 229-230, 231.

Look Back in Anger

Allsop, Kenneth. *The angry decade,* pp. 112-121.

Barbour, Thomas. *Hudson Rev.,* vol. 11, no. 1 (Spring, 1958), pp. 118-120.

Chiari, J. *Landmarks of contemporary drama,* pp. 109-110, 111.

Clurman, Harold. *Lies like truth,* pp. 190-192.

Cohn, Ruby, ed. *Twentieth-century drama,* pp. 542-544.

Deming, Barbara. "John Osborne's War Against the Philistines." *Hudson Rev.,* vol. 11, no. 3 (Autumn, 1958), pp. 411-419.

Dupee, F.W. *"The King of the Cats" and other remarks on writers and writing,* pp. 198-200.

Dyson, A.E. "Look Back in Anger." In: Brown, John Russell, ed. *Modern British dramatists, a collection of critical essays,* pp. 47-57. (From *Critical Q.,* vol. 1, no. 4 (1959), pp. 318-326.)

Fraser, G.S. *The modern writer and his world,* pp. 227-232.

Gascoigne, Bamber. *Twentieth-century drama,* pp. 196-197.

Gassner, John. *Theatre at the crossroads,* pp. 173-175.

Granger, Derek. "Themes for New Voices." *London Mag.,* vol. 3, no. 12 (Dec., 1956), pp. 41-47.

Heilman, Robert B. *Tragedy and melodrama,* pp. 138, 146-148, 297-298.

Huss, Roy. "John Osborne's Backward Halfway Look." *Modern Drama,* vol. 6 (1963-64), pp. 20-25.

Kerr, Walter. *The theater in spite of itself,* pp. 129-131.

Kerr, Walter. *Tragedy and comedy,* pp. 325-327.

Kitchin, Laurence. *Mid-century drama,* pp. 99-101.

Lumley, Frederick. *New trends in 20th-century drama,* pp. 222-224, 229, 255.

Mander, John. *The writer and commitment,* pp. 179-188.

Nicoll, Allardyce. "Somewhat in a New Dimension." *In:* Brown, John Russell, and Bernard Harris, eds. *Contemporary theatre,* pp. 77-79.

Spacks, Patricia Meyer. "Confrontation and Escape in Two Social Dramas." *Modern Drama,* vol. 11, no. 1 (May, 1968), pp. 61-72.

Styan, J.L. *The dark comedy,* 2nd ed., pp. 73, 106, 167, 256, 257-258, 271, 273, 276, 280, 293, 296.

Taylor, John Russell. *Anger and after,* pp. 39-49.

Tynan, Kenneth. "The Angry Young Movement." *In:* Barnet, Sylvan, ed. *The genius of the later English theater,* pp. 524-527.

Wellwarth, George. *The theatre of protest and paradox,* pp. 222-227, 233, 258, 274, 293.

Worth, Katharine J. "The Angry Young Man: John Osborne." *In:* Armstrong, William A., ed. *Experimental drama,* pp. 147-155.

Luther

Brustein, Robert. "The Backwards Birds." *New Republic* (Oct. 19, 1963), pp. 28, 30-31.

Brustein, Robert. *Seasons of discontent,* pp. 196-198.

Chapman, John. "Two Strong New Dramas: *Luther* and *Chips With.*" *Sunday News* (Oct. 20, 1963), Sec. 2, p. 1.

Lumley, Frederick. *New trends in 20th-century drama,* pp. 226-229.

Marowitz, Charles. "The Ascension of John Osborne." *Tulane Drama Rev.,* vol. 7, no. 2 (Winter, 1962), pp. 175-179.

O'Brien, Charles H. "Osborne's Luther and the Humanistic Tradition." *Renascence,* vol. 21, no 2 (Winter, 1969), pp. 59-63.

Taylor, John Russell. *Anger and after,* pp. 54-57.

Tynan, Kenneth. *Tynan right and left,* pp. 77-79.

Wellwarth, George. *The theatre of protest and paradox,* pp. 226, 229-231, 233.

Worth, Katherine J. "The Angry Young Man: John Osborne." *In:* Armstrong, William A., ed. *Experimental drama,* pp. 163-168.

A Patriot for Me

Lumley, Frederick. *New trends in 20th-century drama,* pp. 230-231.

Plays for England (Under Plain Cover)

Tynan, Kenneth. *Tynan right and left,* pp. 109-110.

Wellwarth, George. *The theatre of protest and paradox,* pp. 231-233.

A Subject of Scandal and Concern (Television play)

Taylor, John Russell. *Anger and after,* pp. 52-54.

Wellwarth, George. *The theatre of protest and paradox,* p. 229.

Time Present

Esslin, Martin. "Angry Young Woman." *The New York Times* (June 2, 1968), Sec. 2, pp. 3, 26.

Kennedy, Andrew K. "Old and New in London Now." *Modern Drama,* vol. 11, no. 4 (Feb., 1969), pp. 442-443.

The World of Paul Slickey

Marowitz, Charles. "The Ascension of John Osborne." *In:* Brown, John Russell, ed. *Modern British dramatists, a collection of critical essays,* pp. 117-121. (From *Tulane Drama Rev.,* vol. 7, no. 2 (1962), pp 175-179.)

Marowitz, Charles. *"The World of Paul Slickey." In:* Marowitz, Charles, ed. *Encore reader,* pp. 103-105. (Reprinted from *Encore,* Sept., 1959.)

Taylor, John Russell. *Anger and after,* pp. 50-52.

Wellwarth, George. *The theatre of protest and paradox,* pp. 227-230, 233.

LUIS ENRIQUE OSORIO 1896-

General

Jones, W.K. *Behind Spanish American footlights,* pp. 331-333, 334-335.

ALEXANDER NIKOLAEVICH OSTROVSKY 1823-1886

General

Valency, Maurice. *The breaking string,* pp. 32-40.

ALUN OWEN 1926-

General

Gillette, Eric. "Regional Realism: Shelagh Delaney, Alun Owen, Keith Waterhouse, and Willis Hall." *In:* Armstrong, William A., ed. *Experimental drama,* pp. 193-197.

ROCHELLE OWENS 1936-

Futz

Gottfried, Martin. *A theater divided; the postwar American stage,* p. 300.

Kerr, Walter. *"Futz,—Is It a Fiasco..."* The New York Times (June 30, 1968), Sec. 2, pp. 1, 5.

Kroll, Jack. "Theatre: The Human Animal." *Newsweek* (July 1, 1968), p. 95.

Lester, Elenore. "...Or the Wave of the Future." *The New York Times* (June 30, 1968), Sec. 2, p. 1, 3.

MARCEL PAGNOL 1899-

General

Knowles, Dorothy. *French drama of the inter-war years, 1918-39,* pp. 269-271.

DOROTHY PARKER 1893-1967

Ladies of the Corridor

Bentley, Eric. *The dramatic event,* pp. 154-158.

GIOVANNI PASCOLI 1855-1912

General

Cecchetti, Giovanni. "Giovanni Pascoli As Playwright." *Modern Language Forum,* vol. 36 (1951), pp. 118-125.

STEVE PASSEUR

Je Vivrai un Grand Amour

Knowles, Dorothy. *French drama of the inter-war years, 1918-39,* pp. 133, 140.

N'Importe Quoi pour Elle

Knowles, Dorothy. *French drama of the inter- war years, 1918-39,* pp. 136-138.

No Fury (L'Acheteuse)

Knowles, Dorothy. *French drama of the inter-war years, 1918-39,* pp. 134-135, 139-140.

Une Vilaine Femme

Knowles, Dorothy. *French drama of the inter-war years, 1918-39*, pp. 135-136, 139.

ALAN PATON 1903-

Too Late the Phalarope (Adapted by Robert Yale Libott)

Gassner, John. *Theatre at the crossroads;* pp. 177-180.

JOHN PATRICK 1907–
Pseud. of John Patrick Goggan

The Curious Savage

Sievers, W. David. *Freud on Broadway,* pp. 361-362.

The Hasty Heart

Sievers, W. David. *Freud on Broadway,* pp. 360-361.

Teahouse of the August Moon

Bentley, Eric. *The dramatic event,* pp. 222-225.

Sievers, W. David. *Freud on Broadway,* pp. 362-363.

JEAN-VICTOR PELLERIN 1885-

Terrain Vague

Knowles, Dorothy. *French drama of the inter-war years, 1918-39.* pp. 127-128.

Têtes de Rechange

Knowles, Dorothy. *French drama of the inter-war years, 1918-39,* pp. 125-127.

LUIS PERAZA 1908-

El Hombre Que Se Fue

Jones, W.K. *Behind Spanish American footlights,* pp. 346-347.

S. J. PERELMAN 1904-

The Beauty Part

Brustein, Robert. *Seasons of discontent,* pp. 149-151.

CAMILO PEREZ DE ARCE 1912-

General

Jones, W.K. *Behind Spanish American footlights,* pp. 241-242.

BENITO PEREZ GALDOS 1843-1920

General

Warren, L.A. *Modern Spanish literature,* vol. 2, pp. 554-555.

NOTIS PERYALIS

Masks of Angels

Peryalis, Notis. "The Birds We Kill." *In:* Corrigan, Robert W., ed. *The new theatre of Europe,* pp. 194-197.

PAUL PETERS

Stevedore (George Sklar, co-author)

Block, Anita. *The changing world in plays and theatre,* pp. 264-275.

Flexner, Eleanor. *American playwrights: 1918-1938,* pp. 302-304.

Himelstein, Morgan Y. *Drama was a weapon, the left-wing theatre in New York 1929-1941,* pp. 59-61, 73.

Krutch, Joseph W. *The American drama since 1918,* pp. 251-256.

Mitchell, Loften. *Black drama,* pp. 97-98.

LOUIS PETERSON 1922-

General

Mitchell, Loften. *Black drama,* pp. 163-166, 170.

Take a Giant Step

Abramson, Doris E. *Negro playwrights in the American theatre, 1925-1959,* pp. 221-238, 260-263.

Turpin, Waters E. "The Contemporary American Negro Playwright." *College Language Assn. J.,* vol. 9, no. 1 (Sept., 1965), pp. 16-18.

HENRI PICHETTE 1924-

The Epiphanies (Les Epiphanies)

Pronko, Leonard C. *Avant-Garde: the experimental theater in France,* pp. 164-165.

PEDRO E. PICO 1882-1945

General

Anderson Imbert, Enrique. *Spanish-American literature:a history,* p. 322.

Jones, W.K. *Behind Spanish American footlights,* pp. 129-130.

RAFAEL PINEDA 1926-
See Diaz Sosa, Rafael Angel

VIRGILI PINERA 1914-

General

Jones, W.K. *Behind Spanish American footlights,* pp. 441-412.

SIR ARTHUR WING PINERO 1855-1934

General

Archer, William. "Pinero, Jones, and Wilde." *In* Freedman, Morris, ed. *Essays in the modern drama,* pp. 107-121. (Reprinted from *The old drama and the new* by William Archer, c. 1923 by Dodd, Mead, renewal copyright 1950 by Frank Archer.)

Meisel, Martin. *Shaw and the nineteenth-century theatre,* pp. 67, 71, 75-80, 84, 86, 96, 156-157, 439.

Nicoll, Allardyce. *British drama,* pp. 235-237.

Salerno, Henry F. *English drama in transition, 1880-1920,* pp. 81-82.

Williams, Harold. *Modern English writers,* pp. 229-232.

The Benefit of the Doubt

Shaw, George Bernard. *Shaw's dramatic criticism (1895-98),* pp. 106-110.

The Notorious Mrs. Ebbsmith

Archer, William. "On Pinero's *The Notorious Mrs. Ebbsmith." In:* Agate, James. *The English dramatic critics,* pp. 229-240. *Also: in Theatrical world of 1894,* London, Walter Scott, 1894.

Shaw, George Bernard. *Shaw's dramatic criticism (1895-98),* pp. 24-29.

The Princess and the Butterfly, or The Fanatics

Shaw, George Bernard. *Shaw's dramatic criticism, (1895-98),* pp. 226-232.

The Second Mrs. Tanqueray

Burns, Winifred. "Certain Women Characters of Pinero's Serious Drama." *Poet Lore,* vol. 54, no. 3 (Autumn, 1948), pp. 195-219.

Kornbluth, Martin L. "Two Fallen Women: Paula Tanqueray and Kitty Warren." *Shavian,* no. 14 (1959), pp. 14-15.

Salerno, Henry F. *English drama in transition, 1880-1920,* pp. 82-83.

Shaw, George Bernard. *Shaw's dramatic criticism (1895-98),* pp. 21-24.

ROBERT PINGET 1920-

Dead Letter (Lettre Morte)

Esslin, Martin. *The theatre of the absurd,* pp. 196-197.

The Inquisitory (L'Inquisitoire)

Bishop, Thomas. "Life In the Labyrinth." *Saturday Rev.* (Feb. 11, 1967), pp. 41, 54.

Brook-Rose, Christine. "Making It New." *Observer,* no. 9143 (Oct. 2, 1966), p. 26.

Mercier, Vivian. "With a Cast of Hundreds." *New York Times Book Rev.* (Feb. 19, 1967), pp. 4, 49.

Steisel, Marie-Georgette. "Pinget's Method in *L'Inquisitoire.*" *Books Abroad* (Summer 1966), pp. 267-271.

The Old Tune (La Manivelle)

Esslin, Martin. *The theatre of the absurd,* pp. 198.

HAROLD PINTER 1930-

General

Amend, Victor E. "Harold Pinter—Some Credits and Debits." *Modern Drama,* vol. 10, no. 2 (Sept., 1967), pp. 165-174.

Bernhard, F.J. "Beyond Realism: The Plays of Harold Pinter." *Modern Drama,* vol. 8, no. 2 (Sept., 1965), pp. 185-191.

Brown, John Russell. "Dialogue in Pinter and Others." *In:* Brown John Russell, ed. *Modern British dramatists, a collection of critical essays,* pp. 122-144. *Also in: Critical Q.,* vol. 7, no. 3 (Autumn, 1965), pp. 225-243.

Brown, John Russell. "Introduction." *In:* Brown, John Russell, ed. *Modern British dramatists, a collection of critical essays,* pp. 10-12.

Brown, John Russell. "Mr. Pinter's Shakespeare." *In:* Freedman, Morris, ed. *Essays in the modern drama,* pp. 352-366. (Reprinted from *Critical Q.* (Autumn, 1963).)

Chiari, J. *Landmarks of contemporary drama,* pp. 119-126.

Cohn, Ruby. "The World of Harold Pinter." *Tulane Drama Rev.,* vol. 6, no. 3 (Mar., 1962), pp. 55-68.

Dukore, Bernard. "The Theatre of Harold Pinter." *Tulane Drama Rev.,* vol. 6, no. 3 (Mar., 1962), pp 43-54.

Esslin, Martin. "Godot and His Children: The Theatre of Samuel Beckett and Harold Pinter." *In:* Brown, John Russell, ed. *Modern British dramatists, a collection of critical essays,* pp. 68-70. (From Armstrong, W.A. *Experimental drama,* pp. 139-146.)

Evans, Gareth Lloyd. "Pinter's Black Magic." *In:* Richards, Dick. *The curtain rises,* pp. 69-72.

Fletcher, John. "Confrontations: I. Harold Pinter, Ronald Dubillard, and Eugene Ionesco." *Caliban,* vol. 4 (1967), pp. 149-159.

Fraser, G.S. *The modern writer and his world,* pp. 238-239.

Freedman, Morris. *The moral impulse,* pp. 124-126.

Gascoigne, Bamber. *Twentieth-century drama,* pp. 206-207.

Hinchliffe, Arnold P. *Harold Pinter.*

Kerr, Walter. *Harold Pinter.* Columbia Essays on Modern Writers, 1967.

Leech, Clifford. "Two Romantics: Arnold Wesker and Harold Pinter." *In:* Brown, John Russell and Bernard Harris, eds. *Contemporary theatre,* pp. 11-31.

Lumley, Frederick. *New trends in 20th-century drama,* pp. 266-273.

Malpas, Edward R. "A critical analysis of the stage plays of Harold Pinter." *Dissertation Abstracts,* vol. 27 (1966): 1955A (Wisconsin).

Paris Review. *Writers at work; The Paris Review interviews. Third series,* pp. 347-368.

Pesta, John. "Pinter's Usurpers." *Drama Survey,* vol. 6 (1967), pp. 54-65.

Pinter, Harold. (An Interview with Lawrence M. Bensky, first published in the *Paris review,* 1966.) *In:* Marowitz, Charles, ed. *Theatre at work,* pp. 96-109. *Also in:* Wager, Walter, ed. *The playwrights speak,* pp. 179-180, 181-188.

Storch, R.F. "Harold Pinter's Happy Families." *Massachusetts Rev.,* vol. 8 (1967), pp. 703-712.

Sykes, Arlene. "Harold Pinter's *Dwarfs.*" *Komos: A Quarterly of Drama and Arts of the Theatre,* vol. 1 (1967), pp. 70-75.

Taylor, John Russell. *Anger and after,* pp. 233-261.

Wager, Walter. "Harold Pinter." *In:* Wager, Walter, ed. *The playwrights speak,* pp. 171-178.

Wellwarth, George. *The theatre of protest and paradox,* pp. 197-211, 221, 233.

The Basement (Originally, The Compartment)

Hinchliffe, Arnold P. *Harold Pinter,* pp. 126, 135-138.

The Birthday Party

Boulton, James T. "Harold Pinter: *The Caretaker* and Other Plays." *Modern Drama,* vol. 6 (1963-64), pp. 131-140.

Chiari, Joseph. *Landmarks of contemporary drama,* pp. 202-207.

Davison, Peter. "Contemporary Drama and Popular Dramatic Forms." *In: Aspects of drama and the theatre,* pp. 181-185.

Esslin, Martin. *The theatre of the absurd,* pp. 202-207.

Gottfried, Martin. *A theater divided; the postwar American stage,* pp. 289-290, 291.

Hinchliffe, Arnold P. *Harold Pinter,* pp. 38, 40, 41, 48-63, 64, 68, 73, 74, 75, 81, 87, 106, 107, 108, 117, 118, 152, 163.

Hoefer, Jacqueline. "Pinter and Whiting: Two Attitudes Towards the Alienated Artist." *Modern Drama,* vol. 4, no. 4 (Feb., 1962), pp. 402-408.

Leech, Clifford. "Two Romantics: Arnold Wesker and Harold Pinter." *In:* Brown, John Russell, and Bernard Harris, eds. *Contemporary theatre,* pp. 24-26.

Loney, Glenn. "Broadway in Review." *Educational Theatre J.,* vol. 19, no. 4 (Dec., 1967), p. 514.

Lumley, Frederick. *New trends in 20th-century drama,* pp. 268-269.

Milne, Tom. "The Hidden Face of Violence." *In:* Brown, John Russell, ed. *Modern British dramatists, a collection of critical essays,* pp. 38-46. (From *Encore,* vol. 7, no. 1 (Jan., 1960), pp. 14-20.) *Also in:* Marowitz, Charles, ed. *Encore reader,* pp. 120-123.

O'Casey, Sean. "The Bald Primaqueera." *In:* O'Casey, Sean. *Blasts and benedictions,* pp. 71-72.

Pinter, Harold. (An Interview with Lawrence M. Bensky, first published in the *Paris Review* 1966.) *In:* Marowitz, Charles, ed. *Theatre at work,* pp. 97-98, 100, 103, 105. *Also in:* Wager, Walter, ed. *The playwrights speak,* pp. 180-181.

Rosenberg, James. "European Influences." *In: American theatre,* pp. 59-60.

Styan, J.L. *The dark comedy,* 2nd ed., pp. 247, 250, 296.

Taylor, John Russell. Anger and *after,* pp. 236-239.

Wellwarth, George. *The theatre of protest and paradox,* pp. 199, 201-205, 209.

The Caretaker

Boulton, James T. "Harold Pinter: *The Caretaker* and Other Plays." *Modern Drama,* vol. 6 (1963-64), pp. 131-140.

Brustein, Robert. *Seasons of discontent,* pp. 180-183.

Chiari, J. *Landmarks of contemporary drama,* pp. 119-121.

Clurman, Harold. *The naked image,* pp. 105-107.

Cook, David, and Harold F. Brooks. "A Room With Three Views: Harold Pinter's *The Caretaker.*" *Komos: A Quarterly of Drama and Arts of the Theatre,* vol. 1 (1967), pp. 62-69.

Cowell, Raymond. *Twelve modern dramatists,* pp. 134-135.

Davison, Peter. "Contemporary Drama and Popular Dramatic Forms." *In: Aspects of drama and the theatre,* pp. 164-166, 185-187.

Esslin, Martin. "Godot and His Children: The Theatre of Samuel Beckett and Harold Pinter." *In:* Brown, John Russell, ed. *Modern British dramatists, a collection of critical essays,* pp. 67-68. (From Armstrong, W.A. *Experimental drama.)*

Esslin, Martin. *The theatre of the absurd,* pp. 210-214.

Fraser, G.S. *The modern writer and his world,* pp. 239-242.

Gallagher, Kent G. "Harold Pinter's Dramaturgy." *Q. J. of Speech,* vol. 52, no. 3 (Oct., 1966), pp. 242-248.

Gottfried, Martin. *A theater divided; the postwar American stage,* p. 291.

Hinchliffe, Arnold P. *Harold Pinter,* pp. 31, 37, 42, 61, 63, 70, 71, 74, 75, 78, 85, 86, 87-107, 108, 146, 153, 156, 160, 161, 162, 164, 165.

Kerr, Walter. *The theater in spite of itself,* pp. 116-119.

Leech Clifford. "Two Romantics: Arnold Wesker and Harold Pinter." *In:* Brown, John Russell, and Bernard Harris, eds. *Contemporary theater,* pp. 27-31.

Lumley, Frederick. *New trends in 20th-century drama,* pp. 269-270.

Pinter, Harold. (An Interview with Lawrence M. Bensky, first published in the *Paris Review* 1966.) *In:* Marowitz, Charles, ed. *Theatre at work,* pp. 98, 100, 102-105, 109.

Prickett, Stephen. "Three Modern English Plays." *Philologica Pragensia,* vol. 10 (1967), pp. 12-21.

Styan, J.L. *The dark comedy,* 2nd ed., pp. 245, 246, 248, 250.

Taylor, John Russell. *Anger and after,* pp. 246-249.

Tynan, Kenneth. *Tynan right and left,* pp. 21-33.

Walker, Augusta. "Messages from Pinter." *Modern Drama,* vol. 10, no. 1 (May, 1967), pp. 1-10.

Wardle, Irving. "There's Music in that Room." *In:* Marowitz, Charles, ed. *Encore reader,* pp. 130-132. (Reprinted from *Encore,* (July, 1960).)

Wellwarth, George. *The theatre of protest and paradox,* pp. 199, 205-207.

The Collection

Clurman, Harold. *The naked image,* pp. 101-110.

Gottfried, Martin. *A theater divided; the postwar American stage,* p. 292.

Hinchliffe, Arnold P. *Harold Pinter,* pp. 71, 86, 110, 111, 114-118, 142, 160.

Matthews, Honor. *The primal curse,* pp. 198-201.

Styan, J.L. *The dark comedy,* 2nd ed., pp. 248-249.

Walker, Augusta. "Messages from Pinter." *Modern Drama,* vol. 10, no. 1 (May, 1967), pp. 1-10.

Wellwarth, George. *The theatre of protest and paradox,* pp. 207-210.

The Dumb Waiter

Boulton, James T. "Harold Pinter: *The Caretaker* and Other Plays." *Modern Drama,* vol. 6 (1963-64), pp. 131-140.

Clurman, Harold. *The naked image,* pp. 108.

Cohn, Ruby. "The Absurdly Absurd: Avatars of Godot." *Comparative Literature Studies,* vol. 2, no. 3 (1965), pp. 235, 236-238.

Cohn, Ruby, ed. *Twentieth-century drama,* pp. 619-620.

Davison, Peter. "Contemporary Drama and Popular Dramatic Forms." *In: Aspects of drama and the theatre,* pp. 175-179.

Esslin, Martin. *The theatre of the absurd,* pp. 201-202.

Hinchliffe, Arnold P. *Harold Pinter,* pp. 33, 38, 50, 51, 55, 63-68, 69, 73, 75, 79, 89, 164.

Matthews, Honor. *The primal curse,* pp. 22-23.

Taylor, John Russell. *Anger and after,* pp. 239-240.

Tynan, Kenneth. *Tynan right and left,* pp. 75-76.

Walker Augusta. "Messages from Pinter." *Modern Drama,* vol. 10, no. 1 (May, 1967), pp. 1-10.

Wellwarth, George. *The theatre of protest and paradox,* pp. 200-202, 204, 209.

The Dwarfs

Esslin, Martin. *The theatre of the absurd,* pp. 214-215.

Hinchliffe, Arnold P. *Harold Pinter,* pp. 28, 68, 70, 73, 75, 78-86. 87, 101, 117, 159.

Wellwarth, George. *The theatre of protest and paradox,* pp. 207-208.

The Homecoming

Dukore, Bernard F. "A Woman's Place." *Q. J. of Speech,* vol. 52, no. 3 (Oct., 1966), pp. 237-241.

Gottfried, Martin. *A theater divided; the postwar American stage,* pp. 293-295.

Hinchliffe, Arnold P. *Harold Pinter,* pp. 138, 144, 146-162.

Morris, Kelly. "*The Homecoming.*" *Tulane Drama Rev.,* vol. 11, no. 2 (1966). pp. 185-191.

Nelson, Hugh. "*The Homecoming:* Kith and Kin." *In:* Brown, John Russell, ed. *Modern British dramatists, a collection of critical essays,* pp. 145-163.

Styan, J.L. *The dark comedy,* 2nd ed., pp. 245-246, 248, 249-250.

Landscape (Radio play for two voices)

Kennedy, Andrew K. "Old and New in London Now." *Modern Drama,* Vol. 11, no. 4 (Feb., 1969), pp. 445-446.

The Lover

Clurman, Harold. *The naked image,* pp. 112-113.

Gottfried, Martin. *A theater divided; the postwar American stage,* pp. 291, 292-293.

Hinchliffe, Arnold P. *Harold Pinter,* pp. 33, 71, 83, 84, 109, 110, 111, 114, 117, 118-124, 134, 142, 160, 161.

Wellwarth, George. *The theatre of protest and paradox,* pp. 207-211.

A Night Out (Radio play)

Esslin, Martin. *The theatre of the absurd,* p. 209.

Hinchliffe, Arnold P. *Harold Pinter,* pp. 75-78, 108, 110, 112, 114, 144.

Wellwarth, George. *The theatre of protest and paradox,* p. 207.

Night School

Esslin, Martin. *The theatre of the absurd,* pp. 209-210.

The Room

Boulton, James T. "Harold Pinter: *The Caretaker* and Other Plays." *Modern Drama,* vol. 6 (1963-64), pp. 131-140.

Esslin, Martin. "Godot and His Children: The Theatre of Samuel Beckett and Harold Pinter." *In:* Brown, John Russell, ed. *Modern British dramatists, a collection of critical essays,* pp. 66-67. (From Armstrong, W.A. *Experimental drama,* pp. 140-141.)

Esslin, Martin. *The theatre of the absurd,* pp. 199-201.

Hinchiffe, Arnold P. *Harold Pinter,* pp. 38, 40, 41-48, 50, 52, 67, 68, 73, 88, 106, 137, 146, 147, 160, 164.

Taylor, John Russell. *Anger and after,* pp. 233-236.

Walker, Augusta. "Messages from Pinter." *Modern Drama,* vol. 10, no. 1 (May, 1967), pp. 1-10.

Wellwarth, George. *The theatre of protest and paradox,* pp. 199-200, 204, 209.

A Slight Ache

Burkman, Katherine H. "Pinter's *A Slight Ache* As Ritual." *Modern Drama,* vol. 11, no. 3 Dec., 1968) pp. 326-335.

Clurman, Harold. *The naked image,* pp. 111-112.

Esslin Martin. *The theatre of the absurd,* p. 208.

Gottfried, Martin. *A theater divided; the postwar American stage,* pp. 290-291.

Hinchliffe, Arnold P. *Harold Pinter,* pp. 68-71, 73, 75, 84, 85, 89, 109, 125, 126, 144.

Sainer, Arthur, *The sleepwalker and the assassin, a view of the contemporary theatre,* pp. 99-102.

Taylor, John Russell. *Anger and after.* pp. 240-242.

Walker, Augusta. "Messages from Pinter." *Modern Drama;* Vol. 10, no. 1 (May, 1967), pp. 1-10.

Wellwarth, George. *The theatre of protest and paradox,* pp. 207-208.

Tea Party

Hinchliffe, Arnold P. *Harold Pinter,* pp. 138-145, 146, 148, 153, 157, 160.

LUIGI PIRANDELLO 1867-1936

General

Bentley, Eric. *In search of theatre,* pp. 296-314.

Bentley, Eric. *The playwright as thinker,* pp. 145-154.

Bishop, Thomas. "Pirandello's Influence on French Drama." *In:* Cambon, Glauco, ed. *Pirandello: a collection of critical essays,* pp. 43-65. (Reprinted from Bishop, T. *Pirandello and the French theater.)*

Bradbrook, M.C. *English dramatic form,* pp. 149-152.

Brustein, Robert. "Pirandello's Drama of Revolt." *In:* Cambon, Glauco, ed. *Pirandello: a collection of critical essays,* pp. 103-133. (Reprinted from Brustein, R. *The theatre of revolt.)*

Brustein, Robert. *The theatre of revolt,* pp. 281-293, 303-308.

Budel, Oscar. *Pirandello.*

Corrigan, Beatrice. "Pirandello and the Theatre of the Absurd." *Cesare Barbieri Courier,* vol. 8, no. 1 (1966), pp. 3-6.

Corrigan, Robert W., ed. *Masterpieces of the modern Italian theatre,* p. 32.

Erhard, Thomas A. "The dramatic technique of Luigi Pirandello." *Dissertation Abstracts,* vol. 22, (1961), 573-574. (Univ. of New Mexico).

Fiskin, A.M.I. "L. Pirandello: The Tragedy of the Man Who Thinks." *Italica,* vol. 25, no. 1 (Mar., 1948), pp. 44-51.

Freedman, Morris. "Moral Perspective in Pirandello. "*Modern Drama,* vol. 6, no. 4 (Feb., 1964), pp. 368-377.

Gascoigne, Bamber. *Twentieth-century drama,* pp. 98-108.

Glicksberg, Charles I. *The self in modern literature,* pp. 75-79.

Hamilton, Clayton. *Conversations on comtemporary drama,* pp. 159-166.

Heffner, Hubert C. "Pirandello and the Nature of Man." *In:* Bogard, Travis, and Oliver, William I., ed. *Modern drama; essays in criticism,* pp. 255-275. (Reprinted from *Tulane Drama Rev.,* vol. 1, no. 3 (June, 1957), pp. 23-40.)

Herman, William. "Pirandello and Possibility." *Tulane Drama Rev.,* vol. 10, no. 3 (1966), pp. 91-111.

Illiano, Antonio. "Pirandello in England and the United States: A Chronological List of Criticism." *Bulletin of the New York Public Library,* vol. 71 (1967), pp. 105-130.

Krutch, Joseph Wood. "Pirandello and the Dissolution of Ego." *In:* Caputi, Anthony, ed. *Modern drama,* pp. 485-492. (From Krutch, Joseph Wood. "*Modernism" in modern drama: a definition and an estimate*

Lamm, Martin. *Modern drama,* pp. 334-342.

Lewis, Allan *The contemporary theatre,* pp. 127-143.

Lucas, F.L. *The drama of Chekhov, Synge, Yeats & Pirandello,* pp. 359-368, 403-409, 423-438.

Lumley, Frederick. *New trends in 20th-century drama,* pp. 17-34.

Lumley, Frederick. *Trends in twentieth-century drama,* pp. 19-35.

Maurino, Ferdinando D. "Pirandello: The Plausible Absurd." *In: A Homage to Pirandello. Forum Italicum 1* (1967), pp. 259-266.

May, Frederick. "Polyaretus: Some Notes on Ulysses in the Dramatic Works of Luigi Pirandello." *Komos, A Quarterly of Drama and Arts of the Theatre,* vol. 1 (1967), pp. 105-114.

Nelson, R.J. *Play within a play,* pp. 122-133.

Newberry, Wilma. "Echegaray and Pirandello." *PMLA,* vol. 81 (1966), pp. 123-129.

Newberry, Wilma. "Luca de Tena, Pirandello, and the Spanish Tradition." *Hispania,* vol. 50 (1967), pp. 253-261.

Newberry, Wilma. "Pirandello and Azorin." *Italica,* vol. 44 (1967), pp. 41-60.

Norwood, W.D., Jr. "Zen Themes in Pirandello." *In: A homage to Pirandello. Forum Italicum 1* (1967), pp. 349-356.

Palmer, John. *Studies in the contemporary theatre,* pp. 45-64.

Pirandello, Luigi. "From Unorismo." *In:* Caputi, Anthony, ed. *Modern drama,* pp. 470-479. (From Pirandello, Luigi. *Unorismo,* Rome, The Pirandello Estate, 1960, pp. 145-157.)

Pirandello, Luigi. "The New Theatre and the Old." *In:* Corrigan, Robert W., ed. *Masterpieces of the modern Italian theatre,* pp. 33-48. (Reprinted from Block, Haskell M. *The creative vision: modern European writers on their art.* New York, Grove Press, 1960.)

Radcliff-Umstead, Douglas. "Pirandello and the Puppet World." *Italica,* vol. 44 (1967), pp. 13-27.

Ragusa, Olga. "Carducci; Deledda; Pirandello; Quasimodo." *Books Abroad, vol. 41,* no. 1 (Winter, 1967), pp. 28-29.

Rosenberg, Marvin. "Pirandello's Mirror." *Modern Drama,* vol. 6, no. 4 (Feb., 1964), pp. 331-345.

Smith, H.A. "Dipsychus Among the Shadows." *In:* Brown, J.R. and B. Harris, eds. *Contemporary theatre,* pp. 151-152.

Squarzina, Luigi, and Gino Rizzo. "Directing Pirandello Today." *In:* Cambon, Glauco, ed. *Pirandello: a collection of critical essays,* pp. 141-152. (An interview reprinted from *Tulane Drama Review,* vol. 10, no. 3 (T31, Spring 1966), pp. 76-90. Translated in part by Joseph Williman.)

Styan, J.L. *The dark comedy,* 2nd ed., pp. 2, 15, 22, 31, 43, 47-48, 62-64, 112, 118, 122, 137-143, 158, 186-189, 194-195, 204, 212, 217, 219, 244, 249, 260, 287, 289, 291, 293-294.

Tilgher, Adriano. "Life Versus Form." *In:* Cambon, Glauco, ed. *Pirandello: a collection of critical essays,* pp. 19-34. (Reprinted from *Studi sul teatro contemporaneo.* (Rome, Libreria di Scienze e Lettere, 1923, 1928), translated by G. Cambon, pp. 186-195, 230-248.)

Vittorini, Domenico. "Luigi Pirandello As I Saw Him." *Symposium,* vol. 8, no. 1 (Summer, 1954), pp. 113-123.

Vittorini, Domenico. "Pirandello's Philosophy of Life." *In:* Freedman, Morris, ed. *Essays in the modern drama,* pp. 80-90. (Reprinted from *The drama of Luigi Pirandello* by Domenico Vittorini (1957).)

Weiss, Aureliu. "The Remorseless Rush of Time." Tr. by Simone Sanzenbach. *Tulane Drama Rev.,* vol. 10, no. 3 (Spring, 1966), pp. 30-45.

Weiss, Auréliu. "The Technique of the Un-Seizable." *In:* Cambon, Glauco, ed., *Pirandello: a collection of critical essays,* pp. 135-139. (Reprinted from *Le theatre de Luigi Pirandello dans le mouvement dramatique contemporain* (Paris: Librairie 73, 1965).) Tr. by Glauco Cambon.

Whitfield, J.H. "Pirandello and T.S. Eliot: An Essay in Counterpoint." *English Miscellany,* vol. 9 (1958), pp. 329-357.

Williams, Raymond. *Drama from Ibsen to Eliot,* pp. 185-195.

Williams, Raymond. *Modern tragedy,* pp. 139, 146-152, 163.

Young, Stark. "The Pirandello Play." *In:* Cambon, Glauco, ed. *Pirandello: a collection of critical essays,* pp. 11-18. (Reprinted from Young, S. *Immortal shadows)*

Bibliography

Illiano, Antonio. "Pirandello in England and the United States: A Chronological List of Criticism." *Bulletin of the New York Public Library,* vol. 71 (1967), pp. 105-130.

All for the Best (Tutto per Bene)

Lucas, F.L. *The drama of Chekhov, Synge, Yeats & Pirandello,* pp. 385-387.

Lumley, Frederick. *Trends in 20th-century drama*, pp. 28-29.

As at First But Better Than at First (Come Prima, Meglio di Prima)

Lucas, F.L. *The drama of Chekhov, Synge, Yeats & Pirandello,* pp. 384-387.

Cap and Bells (Il Berretto a Sonagli)

Gascoigne, Bamber. *Twentieth-century drama,* p. 102.

Lucas, F.L. *The drama of Chekhov, Synge, Yeats & Pirandello,* pp. 373-374.

Cece

Styan, J.L. *The dark comedy,* 2nd ed., p. 62.

Clothing the Naked (To Clothe the Naked) (Naked) (Vestire gli Ignudi)

Herman, William. "Pirandello and Possibility." *In:* Cambon, Glauco, ed. *Pirandello: a collection of critical essays,* pp. 153-172. (Reprinted from *Tulane Drama Rev.,* vol. 10, no. 3 (T31, Spring, 1966), pp. 91-111.)

Herman, William. "Pirandello and Possibility." *Tulane Drama Rev.,* vol. 10, no. 3 (Spring, 1966), pp. 91-111.

Lucas, F.L. *The drama of Chekhov, Synge, Yeats & Pirandello,* pp. 390-392.

Styan, J.L. *The dark comedy,* 2nd ed., pp. 62-63, 140.

Diana and Tuda (Diana e la Tuda)

Blankner, Fredericka. "The New Pirandello in *Diana e la Tuda.*" *Poet Lore,* vol. 40 (1929), pp. 215-222.

Feng, Carole B. "Reconciliation of Movement and Form in *Diana and Tuda.*" *Modern Drama,* vol. 10, no. 4 (Feb., 1968), pp. 410-415.

Sinicropi, Giovanni. "The Later Phase: Towards Myth." *In:* Cambon, Glauco, ed. *Pirandello: a collection of critical essays,* pp. 73-81. (Reprinted from *Italica,* vol. 38, no. 4 (Dec., 1961), pp. 265-295.) Tr. by Glauco Cambon.

Each in His Own Way (Ciascuno a Suo Modo)

Freedman, Morris. *The moral impulse,* pp. 81-84.

Freedman, Morris. "Moral Perspective in Pirandello." *Modern Drama,* vol. 6, no. 4 (Feb., 1964), pp. 368-377.

Herman, William. "Pirandello and Possibility." *In:* Cambon, Glauco, ed. *Pirandello: a collection of critical essays,* pp. 153-172. (Reprinted from *Tulane Drama Rev.,* vol. 10, no. 3 (T31, Spring 1966), pp. 91-111.)

Lucas, F.L. *The drama of Chekhov, Synge, Yeats & Pirandello,* pp. 394-402.

Lumley, Frederick. *Trends in 20th-century drama,* pp. 32-33.

Squarzina, Luigi. "Notes for *Each in His Own Way.*" *Tulane Drama Rev.,* vol. 10, no. 3 (Spring, 1966), pp. 87-90.

Styan, J.L. *The dark comedy,* 2nd ed., pp. 137, 142, 153, 155, 187, 237, 243.

Each in His Role (The Game As He Played It) (Il Giuoco Delle Parti)

Lucas, F.L. *The drama of Chekhov, Synge, Yeats & Pirandello,* pp. 380-383.

Lumley, Frederick. *Trends in 20th-century drama,* pp. 27-28.

Styan, J.L. *The dark comedy,* 2nd ed., pp. 140-142.

Grafting (L'Innesto)

Lucas, F.L. *The drama of Chekhov, Synge, Yeats & Pirandello,* pp. 383-384.

Henry IV (Enrico IV)

Bentley, Eric. "Il Tragico Imperatore." *Tulane Drama Rev.,* vol. 10, no. 3 (Spring, 1966), pp. 60-75.

Brustein, Robert. *The theatre of revolt,* pp. 296-303.

Freedman, Morris. *The moral impulse,* pp. 84-85.

Greenwood, Ormerod. *The playwright,* pp. 187-192.

Lewis, Allan. *The contemporary theatre,* pp. 137-143.

Lucas, F.L. *The drama of Chekhov, Synge, Yeats & Pirandello,* pp. 417-422.

Lumley, Frederick. *Trends in 20th-century drama,* pp. 33-35.

May, Frederick. "Three Major Symbols in Four Plays by Pirandello." *Modern Drama,* vol. 6, no. 4 (Feb., 1964), pp. 378-396.

Palmer, John. *Stuaies in the contemporary theatre,* pp. 58-63.

Savage, Edward B. "Masks and Mummeries in *Enrico IV* and *Caligula.*" *Modern Drama,* vol. 6, no. 4 (Feb., 1964), pp. 397-401.

Styan, J.L. *The dark comedy,* pp. 161-177.

Styan, J.L. The *dark comedy,* 2nd ed., pp. 137, 141, 143-157, 187, 235, 237, 259-260, 261, 271, 273, 297, 298.

Tynan, Kenneth. *Tynan right and left,* pp. 138-139.

Vittorini, Domenico. "Being and Seeming: *Henry IV.*" *In:* Caputi Anthony, ed. *Modern drama,* pp. 479-485. (From Vittorini, Domenico. *The drama of Luigi Pirandello,* pp. 89-94, 157-159.)

Young, Stark. *Immortal shadows.* pp. 48-51.

It Is Only in Jest (But It's Not in Earnest) (Ma Non È una Cosa Seria)

Lucas, F.L. *The drama of Chekhov, Synge, Yeats & Pirandello,* pp. 379-380.

The Life I Gave You (La Vita Che Ti Diedi)

Lucas, F.L. *The drama of Chekhov, Synge, Yeats & Pirandello,* pp. 392-393.

Liolà

Freedman, Morris. *The moral impulse,* pp. 79-80.

Gascoigne, Bamber. *Twentieth-century drama, p. 99.*

Man, Beast, and Virtue (L'Uomo, la Bestia e la Virtu)

Lumley, Frederick. *Trends in 20th-century drama,* p. 28.

May, Frederick. "Three Major Symbols in Four Plays by Pirandello." *Modern Drama,* vol. 6, no. 4 (Feb., 1964), pp. 378-396.

Styan, J.L. *The dark comedy,* 2nd ed., pp. 138.

The Mountain Giants (I Giganti Della Montagna)

Büdel, Oscar. *Pirandello,* pp. 45, 55-57, 96.

Freedman, Morris. *The moral impulse,* pp. 85-87.

Naked Masks

Cecchetti, Giovanni. "Beneath Pirandello's *Naked Masks.*" *In: A homage to Pirandello. Forum Italicum* 1 (1967), pp. 244-258.

The New Colony

Freedman, Morris. *The moral impulse,* pp. 85-86.

The Pleasure of Honesty (The Pleasure of Respectability) (Il Piacere dell' Onesta)

Gascoigne, Bamber. *Twentieth-century drama,* pp. 101-102.

Lucas, F.L. *The drama of Chekhov, Synge, Yeats & Pirandello,* pp. 377-379.

Lumley, Frederick. *Trends in 20th-century drama,* p. 27.

The Reason of Others (La Ragione degli Altri)

Lucas, F.L. *The drama of Chekhov, Synge, Yeats & Pirandello,* pp. 369-370.

Right You Are (If You Care To Think So) It Is So (If You Think So) (Così È, Se Vi Pare)

Bentley, Eric. *The playwright as thinker,* pp. 146-157.

Bentley, Eric. *In search of theatre,* pp. 296-314.

Brustein, Robert. *The theatre of revolt,* pp. 293-296.

Freedman, Morris. *The moral impulse,* pp. 74-79, 83-87.

Freedman, Morris. "Moral Perspective in Pirandello." *Modern Drama,* vol. 6, no. 4 (Feb., 1964), pp. 368-377.

Gascoigne, Bamber. *Twentieth-century drama,* pp. 102-104.

Goldberg, Isaac. *The drama of transition,* pp. 184-189.

Leo, Ulrich. "Pirandello Between Fiction and Drama." *In:* Cambon, Glauco, ed. *Pirandello: a collection of critical essays,* pp. 83-90. (Reprinted from *Romanistisches Jahrbuch,* XIV, Band (1963), pp. 133-169.) Tr. by Glauco Cambon.

Lewis, Allan. *The contemporary theatre,* pp. 132-134.

Lucas, F.L. *The drama of Chekhov, Synge, Yeats & Pirandello,* pp. 374-376.

Lumley, Frederick. *Trends in 20th-century drama,* p. 26-27.

Nelson, R.J. *Play within a play,* pp. 122-125.

Sticca, Sandro. "The Drama of Being and Seeming in Schnitzler's *Anatol* and Pirandello's *Cosi è se vi Pare.*" *J. of the International Arthur Schnitzler Research Assoc.,* vol. 5, no. 2 (1966), pp. 4-28.

Williams, Raymond. *Modern tragedy,* pp. 146-149.

Young, Stark. *Immortal shadows.* pp. 84-87.

Young, Stark. "Pirandello's Commedia." *In:* Cambon, Glauco, ed. *Pirandello: a collection of critical essays,* pp. 15-18. (Reprinted from Young, S. *Immortal shadows.)*

Signòra Morli, The First and the Second (La Signòra Morli, Una e Due)

Lucas, F.L. *The drama of Chekhov, Synge, Yeats & Pirandello,* pp. 388-390.

Six Characters in Search of an Author (Sei Personaggi in Cerca d'Autore)

Bentley, Eric. *Father's day.* New York: Instituto Italiano di Cultura, 1968.

Brustein, Robert. *The theatre of revolt,* pp. 308-315.

Büdel, Oscar. *Pirandello,* pp. 10, 14, 21, 25, 26, 27, 40, 56, 57, 77, 80, 85, 87, 90, 91, 92, 98-99, 105.

Clark, Hoover W. "Existentialism and Pirandello's *Sei Personaggi.*" *Italica,* vol. 43, no. 3 (Sept., 1966), pp. 276-284.

Clurman, Harold. *Lies like truth,* pp. 129-131.

Fergusson, Francis. "Action as Theatrical: *Six Characters in Search of an Author.*" *In:* Cambon, Glauco, ed. *Pirandello: a collection of critical essays,* pp. 35-42. (Reprinted from Fergusson, F. *The idea of a theater.)*

Fergusson, Francis. *The idea of a theatre,* 198-206.

Freedman, Morris. *The moral impulse,* pp. 74-75, 80-81.

Gascoigne, Bamber. *Twentieth-century drama,* pp. 104-106.

Gassner, John. *Theatre at the crossroads,* pp. 242-245.

Gassner, John. *The theatre in our times,* pp. 194-198.

Goldberg, Isaac. *The drama of transition,* pp. 189-197.

Herman, William. "Pirandello and Possibility." *In:* Cambon, Glauco, ed. *Pirandello: a collection of critical essays,* pp. 153-172. (Reprinted from *Tulane Drama Rev.* vol. 10, no. 3 (T31, Spring 1966), pp. 91-111.)

Illiano, Antonio. "Pirandello's *Six Characters in Search of an Author:* A Comedy in the Making." *Italica,* vol. 44 (1967), pp. 1-12.

Kayser, Wolfgang. *The grotesque in art and literature,* pp. 137-139.

Kennedy, Andrew K. *"Six Characters:* Pirandello's Last Tape." *Modern Drama,* vol. 12, no. 1 (May, 1969). pp. 1-9.

Kernan, Alvin. "Truth and Dramatic Mode in the Modern Theater: Chekhov, Pirandello and Williams." *Modern Drama,* vol. 1 (Sept., 1958), pp. 107-111.

Krutch, Joseph Wood. *"Modernism" in modern drama,* pp. 80-84.

Lewis, Allan. *The contemporary theatre,* pp. 134-137.

Lucas, F.L. *The drama of Chekhov, Synge, Yeats & Pirandello,* pp. 410-416.

Lumley, Frederick. *Trends in 20th-century drama,* pp. 29-32.

MacCarthy, Desmond. *Drama,* pp. 161-165.

MacCarthy, Desmond. *Theatre,* pp. 94-97.

May, Frederick. "Three Major Symbols in Four Plays by Pirandello." *Modern Drama,* vol. 6, no. 4 (Feb., 1964), pp. 378-396.

Nelson, R.J. *Play within a play,* pp. 125-130.

Palmer, John. *Studies in the contemporary theatre,* pp. 52-57.

Pirandello Luigi. "Preface to *Six Characters in Search of an Author." In:* Corrigan, Robert W., ed. *Masterpieces of the modern Italian theatre,* pp. 49-61. (Reprinted from Pirandello, Luigi. *Naked masks: five plays,* N.Y., E.P. Dutton, 1952.)

Pirandello, Luigi. *In:* Cole, Toby, ed. *Playwrights on playwriting,* pp. 204-217. (Reprinted from Luigi Pirandello, Preface, *Six characters in search of an author, Naked masks* (New York: E.P. Dutton & Co.), pp. 363-75.)

Reinert, Otto, ed. *Drama; an introductory anthology* (alternate ed.), pp. 749-753.

Reinert, Otto, ed. *Modern drama; nine plays,* pp. 300-304.

Sogliuzzo, A. Richard. "The Uses of the Mask in *The Great God Brown* and *Six Characters in Search of an Author.*" *Educational Theatre J.,* vol. 18, no. 3 (Oct., 1966), pp. 224-229.

Styan, J.L. *The dark comedy,* 2nd ed., pp. 137, 142, 153, 155, 187, 237, 243.

Styan, J.L. *The elements of drama,* pp. 180-187.

Sypher, Wylie. "Cubist Drama." *In:* Cambon, Glauco, ed. *Pirandello: a collection of critical essays,* pp. 67-71. (Reprinted from Sypher, W. *Rococo to Cubism in art and literature* (New York, Random House, 1960).)

Thompson, Alan Reynolds. *The dry mock,* pp. 73-74.

Williams, Raymond. *Drama from Ibsen to Eliot,* pp. 185-195.

Williams, Raymond. *Modern tragedy,* pp. 149-150.

Think It Over, Giacomino (Think, Giacomino) (Think of It, Giacomino) (Pensaci, Giacomino)

Gascoigne, Bamber. *Twentieth-century drama,* pp. 99-100.

Lucas, F.L. *The drama of Chekhov, Synge, Yeats & Pirandello,* pp. 370-372.

Lumley, Frederick. *Trends in 20th-century drama,* pp. 25-26.

Tonight We Improvise (Questa Sera Si Recita a Soggetto)

Brustein, Robert. *Seasons of discontent,* pp. 30-33.

Büdel, Oscar. *Pirandello,* pp. 27, 76, 78, 80, 85, 88-89, 93-95, 98.

Lumley, Frederick. *Trends in 20th-century drama,* p. 33.

Nelson, R.J. *Play within a play,* pp. 130-133.

Trovarsi

Sinicropi, Giovanni. "The Later Phase: Towards Myth." *In:* Cambon, Glauco, ed. *Pirandello: a collection of critical essays,* pp. 78-80. (Reprinted from *Italica,* vol. 38, no. 4 (Dec., 1961), pp. 265-295.) Tr. by Glauco Cambon.

When Someone Is Somebody (Quando Si È Qualcuno)

Freedman, Morris. *The moral impulse,* pp. 85-86.

IRWIN PISCATOR 1893-

General

Lumley, Frederick. *Trends in 20th-century drama,* pp. 93-94.

JOSEFINA PLA 1907-

General

Jones, W.K. *Behind Spanish American footlights,* pp. 38-41, 51.

JULIO PLANCHART 1885-1948

La Republica de Cain

Jones, W.K. *Behind Spanish American footlights,* p. 346.

NIKOLAI POGODIN 1900-1962

Aristocrats

Block, Anita. *The changing world in plays and theatre,* pp. 400-405.

ENRIQUE JARDIEL PONCELA 1901-

General

Boring, Phyllis Z. "Incongruous Humor in the Contemporary Spanish Theater." *Modern Drama,* vol. 11, no. 1 (May, 1968), pp. 82-86.

FRANÇOIS PORCHE 1877-

General

Knowles, Dorothy, *French drama of the inter-war years, 1918-39,* pp. 309-310.

EZRA POUND 1885-

Women of Trachis

Donoghue, Denis. *The third voice: modern British and American verse drama,* pp. 213-222.

J. B. PRIESTLEY 1894-

General

Evans, Gareth Lloyd. *J.B. Priestley— the dramatist,* pp. 3-71, 151-159, 177-185, 214-223.

Knight, G. Wilson. *The golden labyrinth,* pp. 386-389.

Lumley, Frederick. *New trends in 20th-century drama,* pp. 296-299.

Lumley, Frederick. *Trends in 20th-century drama,* pp. 205-208.

Priestley, J.B. "Why the Theatre?" *In:* Richards, Dick. *The curtain rises,* pp. 7-9.

Taylor, John Russell. *The rise and fall of the well-made play,* p. 147.

Bees on the Deck

Evans, Gareth Lloyd. *J.B. Priestley—the dramatist,* pp. 154-155, 162-164.

Cornelius

Evans, Gareth Lloyd. *J.B. Priestley—the dramatist,* pp. 185-189.

Dangerous Corner

Dent, Alan. *Preludes and studies,* pp. 173-174.

Evans, Gareth Lloyd. *J.B. Priestley—the dramatist,* pp. 72-82.

Eden End

Evans, Gareth Lloyd. *J.B. Priestley—the dramatist,* pp. 82-91.

Ever Since Paradise

Evans, Gareth Lloyd. *J.B. Priestley—the dramatist,* pp. 170-176.

Hobson, Harold. *Theatre,* pp. 89-91.

The Golden Fleece

Evans, Gareth Lloyd. *J.B. Priestley—the dramatist,* pp. 156-157, 159-162.

Home Is Tomorrow

Evans, Gareth Lloyd. *J.B. Priestley—the dramatist,* pp. 201-203.

I Have Been Here Before

Dent, Alan. *Preludes and studies,* pp. 164-166.

Evans, Gareth Lloyd. *J.B. Priestley—the dramatist,* pp. 103-121.

An Inspector Calls

Evans, Gareth Lloyd. *J.B. Priestley—the dramatist,* pp. 206-209.

Hobson, Harold. *Theatre,* pp. 18-20.

Johnson over Jordan

Dent, Alan. *Preludes and studies,* pp. 184-186.

Evans, Gareth Lloyd. *J.B. Priestley—the dramatist,* pp. 122-136.

Laburnum Grove

Evans, Gareth Lloyd. *J.B. Priestley—the dramatist,* pp. 164-167.

The Linden Tree

Evans, Gareth Lloyd. *J.B. Priestley—the dramatist,* pp. 209-213.

Greenwood, Ormerod. *The playwright,* pp. 204-207.

Lumley, Frederick. *New trends in 20th-century drama,* p. 298.

Music at Night

Evans, Gareth Lloyd. *J.B. Priestley—the dramatist,* pp. 136-147.

People at Sea

Evans, Gareth Lloyd. *J.B. Priestley—the dramatist,* pp. 189-193.

Summer Day's Dream

Evans, Gareth Lloyd. *J.B. Priestley—the dramatist,* pp. 203-205.

They Came to the City

Evans, Gareth Lloyd. *J.B. Priestley—the dramatist,* pp. 193-201.

Lumley, Frederick. *New trends in 20th-century drama,* pp. 297-298.

Time and the Conways

Evans, Gareth Lloyd. *J.B. Priestley—the dramatist,* pp. 91-103.

When We Are Married

Evans, Gareth Lloyd. *J.B. Priestley—the dramatist,* pp. 167-170, 176.

SERAFIN QUINTERO 1871-1938

General

Warren, L.A. *Modern Spanish literature,* vol. 2, pp. 571-577.

La Prisa

Warren, L.A. *Modern Spanish literature,* vol. 2, pp. 575-577.

REINHARD RAFFALT 1920-

The Successor (Der Nachfolger)

Garten, H.F. *Modern German drama,* p. 268.

GEROME RAGNI and JAMES RADO

Hair

Bender, Marylin. "Topless, and No Bottoms Either." *New York Times* (Apr. 28, 1968), Sec. 2, pp. 1, 3.

Kloman, William. "*2001* and *Hair*—Are They the Groove of the Future?" *The New York Times* (May 12, 1968), Sec. 2, p. 15.

Lester, Elenore. "Of Course, There Were Some Limits." *The New York Times* (May 19, 1968), Sec. 2, pp. 1, 14.

Lester, Elenore. "...Or the Wave of the Future?" *The New York Times* (June 30, 1968), Sec. 2, p. 3.

JOSE ANTONIO RAMOS

General

Goldberg, Isaac. *The drama of transition,* pp. 237-243.

Jones, W. K. *Behind Spanish American footlights,* pp. 399-402.

SAMSON RAPHAELSON 1899-

Accent on Youth

Sievers, W. David. *Freud on Broadway,* pp. 342-343.

Hilda Crane

Sievers, W. David. *Freud on Broadway,* pp. 344-346.

Jason

Sievers, W. David. *Freud on Broadway,* pp. 343-344.

The Perfect Marriage

Sievers, W. David. *Freud on Broadway,* pp. 344.

Young Love

Block, Anita. *The changing world in plays and theatre,* pp. 106-108.

Sievers, W. David. *Freud on Broadway,* pp. 341-342.

TERENCE M. RATTIGAN 1911-

General

Lumley, Frederick. *New Trends in 20th-century drama,* pp. 306-310.

Lumley, Frederick. *Trends in 20th-century drama,* pp. 211-213.

Watts, Stephen. "Rattigan's Image." *In:* Richards, Dick. *The curtain rises,* pp. 133-135.

The Browning Version

Taylor, John Russell. *The rise and fall of the well-made play,* p. 152.

The Deep Blue Sea

Taylor, John Russell. *The rise and fall of the well-made play* pp. 153-154.

Flare Path

Taylor, John Russell. *The rise and fall of the well-made play,* pp. 149-150.

French Without Tears

Taylor, John Russell. *The rise and fall of the well-made play,* pp. 148-149, 154-155.

Heart to Heart

Taylor, John Russell. *The rise and fall of the well-made play,* pp. 157-158.

Love in Idleness

Taylor, John Russell. *The rise and fall of the well-made play,* p. 150.

Man and Boy

Taylor, John Russell. *The rise and fall of the well-made play,* pp. 158-159.

Nelson: A Portrait in Miniature

Taylor, John Russell. *The rise and fall of the well-made play,* p. 159.

Ross

Taylor, John Russell. *The rise and fall of the well-made play,* pp. 156-157.

Tynan, Kenneth. *Tynan right and left,* pp. 90-92.

Separate Tables

Clurman, Harold. *Lies like truth,* pp. 174-176.

Taylor, John Russell. *The rise and fall of the well-made play,* p. 155.

Williamson, Audrey. *Contemporary theatre, 1953-1956,* pp. 42-44.

Variation on a Theme

Taylor, John Russell. *The rise and fall of the well-made play,* pp. 155-156.

Who Is Sylvia?

Taylor, John Russell. *The rise and fall of the well-made play,* p. 153.

The Winslow Boy

Brown, John Mason. "Let Right Be Done." *In:* Brown, John Mason. *Dramatis personae,* pp.·313-322.

Brown, John Mason. *Seeing more things,* pp. 37-42.

Taylor, John Russell. *The rise and fall of the well-made play,* pp. 150-151, 160-161.

A. R. RAWLINSON

Birthmark

Hobson, Harold. *Theatre,* pp. 67-68.

R. J. RAY

The Gombeen Man

Malone, Andrew E. *The Irish drama,* p. 273.

DAVID RAYFIEL

Nathan Weinstein, Mystic, Connecticut

Gottfried, Martin. *A theatre divided; the postwar American stage,* pp. 274-275.

PAUL RAYNAL 1890-

General

Moore, Harry T. *Twentieth-century French literature to World War II,* p. 131.

Le Maître de Son Coeur

Knowles, Dorothy. *French drama of the inter-war years, 1918-39,* pp. 305.

Le Matériel Humain

Knowles, Dorothy, *French drama of the inter-war years, 1918-39,* p. 307.

Le Tombeau sous l'Arc de Triomphe

Hatzfeld, Helmut. *Trends and styles in twentieth-century French literature,* p. 111.

Knowles, Dorothy. *French drama of the inter-war years, 1918-39,* pp. 306.

MARK REED 1893-

Yes, My Darling Daughter

Block, Anita. *The changing world in plays and theatre,* pp. 108-110.

O'Hara, Frank H. *Today in American drama,* pp. 217-224.

Sievers, W. David. *Freud on Broadway,* pp. 219-220.

LEON REGIS (François de Vegnes, co-author)

Bastos le Hardi

Knowles, Dorothy. *French drama of the inter-war years, 1918-39,* pp. 72-73.

Le Grande Pénitence

Knowles, Dorothy. *French drama of the inter-war years, 1918-39,* p. 73.

CESAR RENGIFO 1911-

General

Jones, W.K. *Behind Spanish American footlights,* pp. 347-348.

MARIA ASUNCION REQUENA 1915-

General

Jones, W.K. *Behind Spanish American footlights,* pp. 235-236.

Jones, W.K. "Chile's Dramatic Renaissance." *Hispania,* vol. 44 (Mar., 1961), pp. 89-94.

Jones, W.K. "New Life in Chile's Theater." *Modern Drama,* vol. 2, no. 1 (May, 1959), pp. 60-61.

JOSE TRINIDAD REYES

General

Hoffman, E. Lewis. "The Pastoral Drama of José Trinidad Reyes." *Hispania,* vol. 46 (1963), pp. 93-101.

GEORGES RIBEMONT-DESSAIGNES 1884-

Le Bourreau du Pérou

Knowles, Dorothy. *French drama of the inter-war years, 1918-39,* pp. 87-88.

RONALD RIBMAN 1932-

The Ceremony of Innocence

Loney, Glenn. "Broadway in Review." *Educational Theatre J.,* vol. 20, no. 1 (Mar., 1968), p. 102.

Harry, Noon and Night

Gottfried, Martin. *A theatre divided; the postwar American stage,* pp. 72-73.

The Journey of the Fifth Horse

Gottfried, Martin. *A theatre divided; the postwar American stage,* pp. 74-75.

ELMER RICE 1892-1967

General

Collins, Ralph L. "The Playwright and the Press: Elmer Rice and His Critics." *In: Theater Annual,* vol. 7 (1948-49), pp. 35-38.

Dusenbury, Winifred L. "Myth in American Drama Between the Wars." *Modern Drama,* vol. 6, no. 3 (Dec., 1963), pp. 294-308.

Gould, Jean. *Modern American playwrights,* pp. 8-11, 13-15, 17-21.

Hogan, Robert. *The independence of Elmer Rice,* pp. 138-152.

Levin, Meyer. "Elmer Rice." *Theatre Arts* (Jan., 1932), pp. 54-63.

Hogan, Robert. "Rice: The Public Life of a Playwright." *Modern Drama,* vol. 8, no. 4 (Feb., 1966), pp. 426-439.

Lewis, Allan. *American plays and playwrights of the contemporary theatre,* pp. 136-140.

Lumley, Frederick. *New trends in 20th-century drama,* pp. 333-334.

Mendelsohn, Michael J. "The Social Critics on Stage." *Modern Drama,* vol. 6, no. 3 (Dec., 1963), pp. 277-285.

Mersand, Joseph. *The American drama since 1930,* pp. 35-45.

Rabkin, Gerald. *Drama and commitment,* pp. 237-259.

Rice, Elmer. *Minority report: an autobiography.*

Weales, Gerald. *American drama since World War II,* pp. 77-78.

Bibliography

Hogan, Robert. "Elmer Rice: A Bibliography." *Modern Drama,* vol. 8, no. 4 (Feb., 1966), pp. 440-443.

The Adding Machine

Bauland, Peter. *The hooded eagle,* pp. 74, 92.

Block, Anita. *The changing world in plays and theatre,* pp. 216-224.

Broussard, Louis. *American drama...,* pp. 41-50.

Downer, Alan S. *Fifty years of American drama, 1900-1950.* pp. 98-99.

Elwood, William R. "An Interview with Elmer Rice on Expressionism." *Educational Theatre J.,* vol. 20, no. 1 (Mar., 1968), pp. 1-7.

Gould, Jean. *Modern American playwrights,* pp. 14-15.

Hogan, Robert. *The independence of Elmer Rice,* pp. 30-38.

Jennings, Richard. "The Theatre." *Spectator,* vol. 140 (Jan. 14, 1928), p. 42.

Krutch, Joseph W. *The American drama since 1918,* pp. 230-233.

Lewisohn, Ludwig. "Creative Irony—Mr. Rice's *The Adding Machine.*" *In:* Moses, Montrose J. *The American theatre as seen by its critics, 1752-1934,* pp. 196-198. (Reprinted from *The Nation,* Apr. 4, 1923.)

McElroy, Davis Dunbar. *The study of literature; an existential appraisal,* pp. 39-43.

New Statesman, vol. 30 (Jan. 21, 1928), pp. 462-463.

Rabkin, Gerald. *Drama and commitment,* pp. 242-245, 259.

Sievers, W. David. *Freud on Broadway,* pp. 146-149.

Wright, Ralph. "Expressionism." *New Statesman,* vol. 22 (Mar. 22, 1924), pp. 699-700.

American Landscape

Himelstein, Morgan Y. *Drama was a weapon, the left-wing theatre in New York 1929-1941,* pp. 145-146.

Hogan, Robert. *The independence of Elmer Rice,* pp. 92-95.

Rabkin, Gerald. *Drama and commitment,* pp. 255-257.

Between Two Worlds

Himelstein, Morgan Y. *Drama was a weapon, the left-wing theatre in New York 1929-1941,* pp. 193-194.

Hogan, Robert. *The independence of Elmer Rice,* pp. 74-80.

Rabkin, Gerald. *Drama and commitment,* pp. 253-255.

Black Sheep

Hogan, Robert. *The independence of Elmer Rice,* pp. 63-65.

Close Harmony

Hogan, Robert. *The independence of Elmer Rice,* pp. 42-43.

Cock Robin

Hogan, Robert. *The independence of Elmer Rice,* pp. 43-44.

Counsellor-at-Law

Hogan, Robert. *The independence of Elmer Rice,* pp. 60-63.

Verschoyle, Derek. "The Theatre." *Spectator,* vol. 152 (Apr. 20, 1934), p. 618.

Cue for Passion

Hogan, Robert. *The independence of Elmer Rice,* pp. 111, 118-121.

Dream Girl

Hogan, Robert. *The independence of Elmer Rice*, pp. 106-110, 145-146.

Sievers, W. David. *Freud on Broadway*, pp. 153-154.

Flight to the West

Himelstein, Morgan Y, *Drama was a weapon, the left-wing theatre in New York 1929-1941*, pp. 150.

Hogan, Robert. *The independence of Elmer Rice*, pp. 100-104.

Rabkin, Gerald. *Drama and commitment*, pp. 257-259.

The Grand Tour

Hogan, Robert. *The independence of Elmer Rice*, pp. 111-115.

The Home of the Free

Hogan, Robert. *The independence of Elmer Rice*, pp. 22-23.

The House in Blind Alley

Hogan, Robert. *The independence of Elmer Rice*, pp. 25-26.

Judgment Day

Fleming, Peter. "Totalitarian Justice on the Stage." *Spectator*, vol. 158 (May 28, 1937), pp. 987-988.

Himelstein, Morgan Y. *Drama was a weapon, the left-wing theatre in New York 1929-1941*, pp. 192-193.

Hogan, Robert. *The independence of Elmer Rice*, pp. 70-74.

Rabkin, Gerald. *Drama and commitment*, pp. 251-253.

The Left Bank

Hogan, Robert. *The independence of Elmer Rice*, pp. 57-60.

Krutch, Joseph W. *The American drama since 1918*, pp. 235-238.

Sievers, W. David. *Freud on Broadway*, pp. 150-152.

Love Among the Ruins

Hogan, Robert. *The independence of Elmer Rice*, pp. 122-137.

A New Life

Hogan, Robert. *The independence of Elmer Rice,* pp. 104-106.

Not for Children

Hogan, Robert. *The independence of Elmer Rice,* pp. 80-87.

Rabkin, Gerald. *Drama and commitment,* pp. 239-242.

Verschoyle, Derek. "The Theatre." *Spectator,* vol. 155 (Nov. 29, 1935), p. 900.

On Trial

Gould, Jean. *Modern American playwrights,* pp. 11-13.

Hogan, Robert. *The independence of Elmer Rice,* pp. 4-5, 17-21.

Rice, Elmer. "Author! Author! Or, How to Write a Smash Hit the First Time You Try." *American Heritage,* vol. 16 (Apr. 1965), pp. 46-49, 84-86.

The Passing of Chow-Chow

Hogan, Robert. *The independence of Elmer Rice,* pp. 17, 23-24.

See Naples and Die

Hogan, Robert. *The independence of Elmer Rice,* pp. 54-57.

Verschoyle, Derek. "The Theatre." *Spectator,* vol. 148 (Apr. 2, 1932), p. 476.

The Sidewalks of New York

Hogan, Robert. *The independence of Elmer Rice,* pp. 44-45.

Street Scene

Anderson, John. "Elmer Rice's *Street Scene.*" *In:* Moses, Montrose J. *The American theatre as seen by its critics, 1752-1934,* pp. 281-283. (Reprinted from *The New York Evening Journal* (Jan. 11, 1929).) *Also in:* Oppenheimer, George, ed. *The passionate playgoer,* pp. 564-567.

Downer, Alan S. *Fifty years of American drama 1900-1950,* pp. 63-64.

Dusenbury, Winifred L. *The theme of loneliness in modern American drama,* pp. 114-119.

Gould Jean. *Modern American playwrights,* pp. 16-17.

Hogan, Robert. *The independence of Elmer Rice,* pp. 46-54.

Jennings, Richard. "The Theatre." *Spectator,* vol. 145 (Sept. 27, 1930), p. 407.

Krutch, Joseph W. *The American drama since 1918,* pp. 233-235.

McCarthy, Mary. *Sights and spectacles 1937-1956,* pp. 113-115.

New Statesman, vol. 35 (Sept. 20, 1930), p. 733.

Young, Stark. "American Drama in Production." *In:* Zabel, Morton Dauwen. *Literary opinion in America.* pp. 529-532. (Reprinted from *The New Republic,* vol. 57 (Jan. 30, 1929), pp. 296-298.)

Young, Stark. *Immortal shadows,* pp. 106-109.

The Subway

Elwood, William R. "An Interview with Elmer Rice on Expressionism." *Educational Theatre J.,* vol. 20, no. 1 (Mar., 1968), pp. 1-7.

Hogan, Robert, *The independence of Elmer Rice,* pp. 36-41.

Rabkin, Gerald. *Drama and commitment,* pp. 245-247.

Sievers, W. David. *Freud on Broadway,* pp. 149-150.

Valgemae, Mardi. "Rice's *The Subway." Explicator,* vol. 25 (1967), Item 62.

Two on an Island

Hogan, Robert. *The independence of Elmer Rice,* pp. 95-100.

Wake Up, Jonathan

Hogan, Robert. *The independence of Elmer Rice,* pp. 27-29.

We, the People

Brown, John Mason. *Two on the aisle,* pp. 204-208.

Himelstein, Morgan Y. *Drama was a weapon, the left-wing theatre in New York 1929-1941,* pp. 187-188.

Hogan, Robert. *The independence of Elmer Rice,* pp. 66-70.

Krutch, Joseph W. *The American drama since 1918,* pp. 248-249.

Rabkin, Gerald. *Drama and commitment,* pp. 249-251.

The Winner

Hogan, Robert. *The independence of Elmer Rice,* pp. 111, 115-118.

JACK RICHARDSON 1935-

General

Brustein, Robert. "The New American Playwrights." *In:* Rahv, Philip, ed. *Modern occasions,* pp. 130-131.

Lumley, Frederick. *New trends in 20th-century drama,* pp. 333.

Gallows Humor

Downer, Alan S. "Total Theatre and Partial Drama: Notes on the New York Theatre, 1965-1966." *Q. J. of Speech,* vol. 52, no. 3 (Oct., 1966), p. 231.

Wellwarth, George. *The theatre of protest and paradox,* pp. 287-289.

Lorenzo

Wellwarth, George. *The theatre of protest and paradox,* pp. 289-290.

The Prodigal

Force, William M., ed. *Orestes and Electra, myth and dramatic form,* p. 209.

Weissman, Philip. *"Mourning Becomes Electra and The Prodigal." In:* Force, William M., ed. *Orestes and Electra, myth and dramatic form,* pp. 324-327. *Also in: Modern Drama,* vol. 3, no. 3 (Dec., 1960), pp. 257-259.

Wellwarth, George. *The theatre of protest and paradox,* pp. 284-287, 289.

Xmas in Las Vegas

Downer, Alan S. "Total Theatre and Partial Drama: Notes on the New York Theatre, 1965-1966. *Q. J. of Speech,* vol. 52, no. 3 (Oct., 1966), pp. 231-232.

RANSOM RIDEOUT

Goin' Home

O'Hara, Frank H. *Today in American drama,* pp. 164-170.

ANNE RIDLER 1912-

General

Welland, Dennis, "Some Post-War Experiments in Poetic Drama." *In:* Armstrong, William A., ed. *Experimental drama,* pp. 36-55.

The Shadow Factory

Spanos, William V. *The Christian tradition in modern British verse drama,* pp. 253-269.

LYNN RIGGS 1899-1954

The Cream in the Well

Sievers, W. David. *Freud on Broadway,* pp. 309-311.

Green Grow the Lilacs

Brown, John Mason. *Two on the aisle,* pp. 168-171.

Lockridge, Richard. "Lynn Rigg's Southwest— *Green Grow the Lilacs." In:* Moses, Montrose J. *The American theatre as seen by its critics, 1752-1934,* pp. 328-330. (Reprinted from *The New York Sun,* Jan. 27, 1931)

Russet Mantle

Sievers, W. David. *Freud on Broadway,* p. 308-309.

JUAN RIOS 1914-

General

Jones, W.K. *Behind Spanish American footlights,* p. 270.

Tamayo Vargas, Augusto. "Peruvian Literature in 1961." *Books Abroad,* vol. 36 (1962), p. 269.

THOMAS WILLIAM ROBERTSON 1829-1871

General

Meisel, Martin. *Shaw and the nineteenth-century theatre,* pp. 70-76, 95-95, 327.

Caste

Williams, Raymond. *Drama in performance* (new. ed.), pp. 90-95.

Ours

O'Casey, Sean. *The green crow,* pp. 74-77.

LENNOX ROBINSON 1886-1958

General

Hogan, Robert. *After the Irish renaissance,* pp. 22-27.

Malone, Andrew E. *The Irish drama,* pp. 175-176, 184-185, 308-309.

Miller, Nellie Burget. *The living drama,* pp. 350-351.

Williams, Harold. *Modern English writers,* pp. 218-219.

The Big House

Malone, Andrew E. *The Irish drama,* pp. 183-184.

The Clancy Name

Malone, Andrew E. *The Irish drama,* pp. 176-177.

Crabbed Youth and Age

Malone, Andrew E. *The Irish drama,* p. 182.

The Dreamers

Malone, Andrew E. *The Irish drama,* p. 179.

Harvest

Malone, Andrew E. *The Irish drama,* pp. 177-178.

The Lost Leader

Malone, Andrew E. *The Irish drama,* pp. 180-181.

Patriots

Malone, Andrew E. *The Irish drama,* pp. 178-179.

Portrait

Malone, Andrew E. *The Irish drama,* p. 183.

The Round Table

Malone, Andrew E. *The Irish drama,* pp. 181-182.

The Whiteheaded Boy

Malone, Andrew E. *The Irish drama,* pp. 179-180.

Miller, Nellie Burget. *The living drama,* pp. 351-352.

EMMANUEL ROBLES

Montserrat

Clurman, Harold. *Lies like truth,* pp. 260-266.

HERNAN ROBLETO 1893-

General

Jones, W.K. *Behind Spanish American footlights,* pp. 428-429.

JOHN ROC

Fire

Novick, Julius. "Theatre at Brandeis: Who Will Vote for *Fire?" New York Times* (May 12, 1968), Sec. 2, p. 7.

GUILLAUME ROCHE
(real name Denys Amiel, q.v.)

General

Knowles, Dorothy. *French drama of the inter-war years, 1918-39,* pp. 120-122.

La Souriante Madame Beudet (André Obey, co-author)

Knowles, Dorothy. *French drama of the inter-war years, 1918-39,* p, 120.

Le Voyageur

Knowles, Dorothy. *French drama of the inter-war years, 1918-39,* pp. 119-120.

GABRIELA ROEPKE 1920-

General

Jones, W.K. *Behind Spanish American footlights,* pp. 237-238.

The White Butterfly (Mariposa Blanca)

Jones, W.K. *Behind Spanish American footlights,* p. 238.

BELISARIO ROLDAN 1873-1922

El Bronce

Jones, W.K. *Behind Spanish American footlights,* pp. 124-125, 169.

La Niña a la Moda

Jones, W.K. *Behind Spanish American Footlights,* pp. 168-169.

JULES ROMAINS 1885-

General

Knowles, Dorothy. *French drama of the inter-war years, 1918-39*, pp. 81-82.

Moore, Harry T. *Twentieth-century French literature to World War II*, pp. 137-143.

Palmer, John. *Studies in the contemporary theatre*, pp. 137-150.

Amedée et les Messieurs en Rang

Knowles, Dorothy. *French drama of the inter-war years, 1918-39*, pp. 79-80.

L'Armée dans la Ville

Knowles, Dorothy. *French drama of the inter-war years, 1918-39*, pp. 74-76.

Boën

Knowles, Dorothy. *French drama of the inter-war years, 1918-39*, pp. 80-81.

Cromedeyre-le-Vieil

Knowles, Dorothy. *French drama of the inter-war years, 1918-39*, p. 75.

The Dictator (Le Dictateur)

Block, Anita. *The changing world in plays and theatre*, pp. 212-214.

Knowles, Dorothy. *French drama of the inter-war years, 1918-39*, pp. 76-77.

Donogoo

Knowles, Dorothy. *French drama of the inter-war years, 1918-39*, p. 77.

Grâce Encore pour la Terre

Knowles, Dorothy. *French drama of the inter-war years, 1918-39*, p. 81.

Jean le Maufranc

Knowles, Dorothy. *French drama of the inter-war years, 1918-39*, p. 80.

Jean Musse, ou L'École de l'Hypocrisie

Knowles, Dorothy. *French drama of the inter-war years, 1918-39,* p. 80.

Knock, ou Le Triomphe de la Médicine

Knowles, Dorothy. *French drama of the inter-war years, 1918-39,* pp. 78-79.

Le Mariage de M. Le Trouhadec

Knowles, Dorothy. *French drama of the inter-war years, 1918-39,* p. 78.

REGINALD ROSE 1920-

The Porcelain Year

Downer, Alan S. "Total Theatre and Partial Drama; Notes on the New York Theatre, 1965-1966." *Q. J. of Speech,* vol. 52, no. 3 (Oct., 1966), pp. 225-226.

ISAAC ROSENBERG

Moses

Roston, Murray. *Biblical drama in England from the Middle Ages to the present day,* pp. 255-257.

EDMOND ROSTAND 1868-1918

General

Bermel, Albert, ed. *The genius of the French theatre,* pp. 371-374.

Phelps, William Lyon. *Essays on modern dramatists,* pp. 229-278.

L'Aiglon

Chiari, Joseph. *The contemporary French theatre,* pp. 44-46.

Duclaux, Mary. *Twentieth-century French writers,* p. 59.

Miller, Nellie Burget. *The living drama,* pp. 246.

Chantecler

Chiari, Joseph. *The contemporary French theatre,* pp. 42-44.

Duclaux, Mary. *Twentieth-century French writers,* pp. 59-66.

Lamm, Martin. *Modern drama,* pp. 176-177.

Cyrano de Bergerac

Butler, Mildred Allen. "The Historical Cyrano de Bergerac as a Basis for Rostand's Play." *Educational Theatre J.,* vol. 6, no. 3 (Oct. 1954), pp. 231-240.

Chiari, Joseph. *The contemporary French theatre, pp. 36-42.*

Clurman, Harold. "Theatre." Nation, vol. 177, no. 23 (Dec. 5, 1953), pp. 473, 475.

Duclaux, Mary. *Twentieth-century French writers,* pp. 57-59.

Hamilton, Clayton. *Conversations on contemporary drama.,* pp. 33-38.

Lamm, Martin. *Modern drama,* pp. 171-174.

Miller, Nellie Burget. *The living drama,* pp. 247-250.

Myers, Henry A. *Tragedy: a view of life,* pp. 146-47.

La Princesse Lointaine

Shaw, George Bernard. *Shaw's dramatic criticism (1895-98),* pp. 86-94.

The Romantics

Bermel, Albert ed. *The genius of the French theater,* pp. 18-19.

LEO ROSTEN 1908-

The Education of H*Y*M*A*N K*A*P*L*A*N

Kerr, Walter. "Skin Deep Is Not Enough." *The New York Times* (Apr. 14, 1968), pp. 1, 3D.

NORMAN ROSTEN 1914-

Mister Johnson

Sainer, Arthur. *The sleepwalker and the assassin, a view of the contemporary theatre,* pp. 118-120.

RAYMOND ROUSSEL 1877-1933

General

Knowles, Dorothy. *French drama of the inter-war years, 1918-39,* p. 87.

VICTOR ROZANOV

General

Weiss, Thomas. "The Guilt Complex in Communist Literature." *East Europe,* vol. 15, no. 7 (July, 1966), pp. 13-14.

DAVID RUDKIN 1936-

General

"An Affiction of Images: An Interview with David Rudkin." *Encore,* vol. 11, no. 4 (July, August, 1964), pp. 6-16.

Afore Night Come

Heilman, Robert B. *Tragedy and melodrama,* pp. 40-42, 238-239.

Lumley, Frederick. *New trends in 20th-century drama,* pp. 313-314.

Milne, Tom. "Afore Night Come." *In:* Marowitz, Charles, ed. *Encore reader,* pp. 234-238. (Reprinted from *Encore* (July, 1962).)

O'Casey, Sean. "The Bald Primaqueera." *In:* O'Casey, Sean. *Blasts and benedictions,* pp. 67-70.

Tynan, Kenneth. *Tynan right and left,* pp. 114-115.

JOSE MARTINEZ RUIZ (Azorin) 1873-1967

General

Abbott, James H. "Ya Es Tarde, Se Tenia Que Morir: Azorin and Death." *Books Abroad,* vol. 41, no. 4 (Autumn, 1967), pp. 409-412.

GUENTHER RUTENBORN 1912-

The Sign of Jonah (Das Zeichen des Jona)

Bauland, Peter. *The hooded eagle,* pp. 212-213.

ALBERTO SAAVEDRA PEREZ 1895-

General

Jones, W.K. *Behind Spanish American footlights,* pp. 282-283.

HOWARD SACKLER

The Great White Hope

Loney, Glenn. "Broadway in Review." *Educational Theatre J.,* vol. 20, no. 1 (Mar., 1968), pp. 98-99.

ARMAND SALACROU 1899-

General

Cunard, Nancy. "On Some Plays in Paris." *Our Time,* vol. 5, no. 10 (May, 1946), pp. 209-210, 215.

Curtis, Anthony. "Drama and Ventriloquism in Paris." *World Rev.,* n.s., no. 27 (May, 1951), pp. 66-69.

Fauve, Jacques. "A Drama of Essences: Salacrou and Others." *Yale French Studies,* no. 14 (Winter, 1954-55), pp. 31-39.

Guicharnaud, Jacques. *Modern French theatre from Giraudoux to Genet* (rev. ed.), pp. 87-90, 91, 94-97, 117, 121, 132, 135, 159, 211, 281, 298, 330-332, 359.

Guicharnaud, Jacques. *Modern French theatre from Giraudoux to Beckett,* pp. 112-130.

Hahn, Paul. "Introducing Armand Salacrou." *Educational Theatre J.,* vol. 3, no. 1 (Mar., 1951).

Hobson, Harold. *The French theatre of today,* pp. 128-168.

Knowles, Dorothy. *French drama of the inter-war years, 1918-39,* pp. 143-146, 153-154, 157-158.

Lumley, Frederick. *New trends in 20th-century drama,* pp. 159-170.

Lumley, Frederick. *Trends in 20th-century drama,* pp. 164-175.

Moore, Harry T. *Twentieth-century French literature since World War II,* pp. 16-17.

Silenieks, Juris. "Circularity of Plot in Salacrou's Plays." *Symposium,* vol. 20, no. 1 (Spring, 1966), pp. 56-62.

Silenieks, Juris. "Themes and dramatic forms in the plays of Armand Salacrou." *Dissertation Abstracts,* vol. 24 (1964), 3342-44 (Nebraska).

Stokle, Norman. "Armand Salacrou and His Theatre." *In:* Salacrou, Armand. *Three plays,* pp. 3-9.

Vial, Fernand. "Montherlant and the Post-War Drama in France." *American Society Legion of Honor Magazine,* vol. 22, no. 1 (Spring, 1951).

L'Archipel Lenoir

Arnold, Paul. "Actor-Directors in Paris." *Theatre Arts,* vol. 32, no. 2 (Feb., 1948), pp. 29-30.

Bishop, Thomas. *Pirandello and the French theater,* pp. 93-94.

Hobson, Harold. *The French theatre of today,* pp. 166-167.

Knowles, Dorothy. *French drama of the inter-war years, 1918-39,* pp. 154-155.

Atlas-Hotel

Bishop, Thomas. *Pirandello and the French theater,* p. 91.

Hobson, Harold. *The French theatre of today,* pp. 138-140.

Lumley, Frederick. *New trends in 20th-century drama,* pp. 163, 164.

Lumley, Frederick. *Trends in 20th-century drama,* pp. 168-169.

Boulevard Durand

Knowles, Dorothy. *French drama of the inter-war years, 1918-39,* pp. 156-157.

Knowles, Dorothy. "Popular Drama in France. " *Drama,* n.s., no. 65 (Summer, 1962), pp. 37-39.

Dieu le Savait

Hobson, Harold. *The French theatre of today,* pp. 167-168.

Une Femme Libre

Hobson Harold. *The French theatre of today,* pp. 147-148.

Knowles, Dorothy. *French drama of the inter-war years, 1918-39,* pp. 147-148.

Lumley, Frederick. *New trends in 20th-century drama,* pp. 164-166.

Lumley, Frederick. *Trends in 20th-century drama,* pp. 169-171.

Les Frénétiques

Lumley, Frederick. *New trends in 20th-century drama,* pp. 163, 164.

Un Homme Comme les Autres

Lumley, Frederick. *New trends in 20th-century drama,* p. 167.

La Marguerite

Bishop, Thomas. *Pirandello and the French theater,* pp. 92-93.

Stokle, Norman. "Armand Salacrou and His Theatre." *In:* Salacrou, Armand. *Three plays,* pp. 21-23.

Nights of Wrath (Les Nuits de la Colère)

Bishop, Thomas. *Pirandello and the French theater,* p. 93.

Hobson, Harold. *The French theatre of today,* pp. 162-166.

Hobson, Harold. *The theatre now,* pp. 64-69.

Knowles, Dorothy. *French drama of the interwar years, 1918-39,* pp. 149-150.

Lloyd, Celine. *"Les Nuits de la Colère:* Barrault's Avant-Garde Production." *Theatre Newsletter,* vol. 1, no. 23 (May 31, 1947), p. 6.

Lumley, Frederick. *New trends in 20th-century drama,* pp. 168-169.

Lumley, Frederick. *Trends in 20th-century drama,* pp. 173-174.

Marcel, Gabriel. "In Love with Death." *Theatre Arts,* vol. 31, no. 5 (May, 1947), p. 46.

Tynan, K. *Curtains,* pp. 383-384.

Patchouli, ou Les Desordres de l'Amour

Hobson Harold. *The French theatre of today,* pp. 133-137.

Lumley, Frederick. *New trends in 20th-century drama,* p. 163.

Pont de l'Europe

Bishop, Thomas. *Pirandello and the French theater,* pp. 89-91.

Hobson, Harold. *The French theatre of today,* pp. 131-133.

Poof

Bishop, Thomas. *Pirandello and the French theater,* pp. 94-95.

The Unknown Women of Arras (L'Inconnue d'Arras)

Bishop, Thomas. *Pirandello and the French theater,* pp. 91-92.

Guicharnaud, Jacques. *Modern French theatre from Gir. doux to Genet* (rev. ed.), pp. 90-91, 92-94.

Hobson, Harold. *The French theatre of today,* pp. 148-156.

Knowles, Dorothy. *French drama of the inter-war years, 1918-39,* pp. 150-151.

Lumley, Frederick. *New trends in 20th-century drama,* pp. 161, 164, 166-167, 168.

Lumley, Frederick. *Trends in 20th-century drama,* pp. 171-172.

When the Music Stops (Histoire de Rire)

Hobson, Harold. *The French theatre of today,* pp. 156-161.

Porter, Stephen. "Introduction." *In:* Salacrou, Armand. *Three plays,* pp. ix-x.

Stokle, Norman. "Armand Salacrou and His Theatre." *In:* Salacrou, Armand. *Three plays,* pp. 17-21.

The World Is Round (La Terre Est Ronde)

Bishop, Thomas. *Pirandello and the French theater,* p. 92.

Knowles, Dorothy. *French drama of the inter-war-years, 1918-39,* pp. 151-153.

Lumley, Frederick. *New trends in 20th-century drama,* pp. 167-168.

Lumley, Frederick. *Trends in 20th-century drama,* pp. 172-173.

Porter, Stephen. "Introduction." *In:* Salacrou, Armand. *Three plays,* pp. vi-ix.

Stokle, Norman. "Armand Salacrou and His Theatre." *In:* Salacrou, Armand. *Three plays,* pp. 9-17.

SEBASTIAN SALAZAR BONDY 1924-

General

Jones, W.K. *Behind Spanish American footlights,* p. 271.

FLORENCIO SANCHEZ 1875-1910

General

Anderson Imbert, Enrique. *Spanish-American literature: a history,* pp. 320-323.

Downing, G.T. "The life and works of Florencio Sánchez." Unpublished Master's Thesis, U. of Oklahoma, 1928.

Goldberg, Isaac. *The drama of transition,* pp. 218-237.

House, Roy Temple. "Florencio Sánchez, A Great Uruguayan Dramatist." *Poet Lore,* vol. 34 (Summer, 1923), pp. 278-282.

Jones, W.K. *Behind Spanish American footlights,* pp. 105-116.

Jones, Willis K. "The Gringo Theme in River Plate Drama." *Hispania,* vol. 25 (1942) pp. 326-332.

Richardson, Ruth. *Florencio Sánchez and the Argentine theatre.*

Richardson, Ruth. "Introduction." *In:* Jones, Willis Knapp. *Representative plays of Florencio Sánchez,* Wash., D.C., Pan American Union, 1961.

Canillita

Richardson, Ruth. *Florencio Sánchez and the Argentine theatre,* pp. 77-82.

Los Curdas

Richardson, Ruth. *Florencio Sánchez and the Argentine theatre,* pp. 129-132.

Los Derechos de la Salud

Richardson, Ruth. *Florencio Sánchez and the Argentine theatre,* pp. 145-155.

El Desalojo

Richarson, Ruth. *Florencio Sánchez and the Argentine theatre,* pp. 122-123.

Down Hill (Barranca Abajo)

Anderson Imbert, Enrique. *Spanish-American literature: a history,* pp. 321-322.

Jones, W.K. *Behind Spanish American footlights,* pp. 111-112.

Richardson, Ruth. *Florencio Sánchez and the Argentine theatre,* pp. 95-103.

En Familia

Richardson, Ruth. *Florencio Sánchez and the Argentine theatre,* pp. 105-113.

The Immigrant's Daughter (La Gringa)

Anderson Imbert, Enrique. *Spanish-American literature, a history,* pp. 320-321.

Jones, W.K. *Behind Spanish American footlights,* pp. 110-111, 118-119.

Richardson, Ruth. *Florencio Sánchez and the Argentine theatre,* pp. 85-95.

Mano Santa

Richardson, Ruth. *Florencio Sánchez and the Argentine theatre,* pp. 103-105.

Marta Gruni

Richardson, Ruth. *Florencio Sánchez and the Argentine theatre,* pp. 155-161.

Moneda Falsa

Richardson, Ruth. *Florencio Sánchez and the Argentine theatre,* pp. 133-137.

Los Muertos

Richardson, Ruth. *Florencio Sánchez and the Argentine theatre,* pp. 113-121.

My Son the Doctor (M'Hijo el Dotor)

Anderson Imbert, Enrique. *Spanish-American literature: a history,* p. 320.

Jones, W.K. *Behind Spanish American footlights,* pp. 107-110.

Richardson, Ruth. *Florencio Sánchez and the Argentine theatre,* pp. 71-77.

Nuestros Hijos

Richarson, Ruth. *Florencio Sánchez and the Argentine theatre,* pp. 137-145.

El Pasado de una Vida

Richardson, Ruth. *Florencio Sánchez and the Argentine theatre,* pp. 124-129.

La Pobre Gente

Richardson, Ruth. *Florencio Sánchez and the Argentine theatre,* pp. 82-85.

La Tigra

Richardson, Ruth. *Florencio Sánchez and the Argentine theatre,* pp. 132-133.

MALENA SANDOR

See James de Terza, Maria Elena

ROSSO DI SAN SECONDO

The Desired Guest (L'Ospite Desiderato)

Goldberg, Isaac. *The drama of transition,* pp. 201-203.

ROBERTO SARAH 1918-

General

Jones, W.K. *Behind Spanish American footlights,* pp. 242-243.

Some Day

Jones, W.K. "New Life in Chile's Theater." *Modern Drama,* vol. 2, no. 1 (May, 1959), pp. 59-60.

VICTORIEN SARDOU 1831-1908

Delia Harding

Shaw, George Bernard. *Shaw's dramatic criticism (1895-98),* pp. 52-54.

Divorçons

Ellehauge, Martin. *The position of Bernard Shaw in European drama and philosophy,* pp. 67-68.

Fédora

Shaw, George Bernard. *Shaw's dramatic criticism (1895-98),* pp. 71-74.

Gismonda

Shaw, George Bernard. *Shaw's dramatic criticism (1895-98),* pp. 74-76.

JEAN SARMENT 1897-

General

Knowles, Dorothy. *French drama of the inter-war years, 1918-39,* pp. 165-167.

Moore, Harry T. *Twentieth-century French literature to World War II,* pp. 133-135.

Palmer, John. *Studies in the contemporary theatre,* pp. 112-136.

La Couronne de Carton

Knowles, Dorothy. *French drama of the inter-war years, 1918-39,* pp. 162-163.

Palmer, John. *Studies in the contemporary theatre,* pp. 125-127.

Facilité

Knowles, Dorothy. *French drama of the inter-war years, 1918-39,* pp. 161-162.

Je Suis Trop Grand pour Moi

Knowles, Dorothy. *French drama of the inter-war years, 1918-39,* pp. 164-165.

Palmer, John. *Studies in the contemporary theatre,* pp. 129-131.

Madelon

Knowles, Dorothy. *French drama of the inter-war years, 1918-39,* p. 165.

Le Mariage d'Hamlet

Knowles, Dorothy. *French drama of the inter-war years, 1918-39,* pp. 163-164.

Palmer, John. *Studies in the contemporary theatre,* pp. 120-125.

Le Pecheur d'Ombres

Knowles, Dorothy. *French drama of the inter-war years, 1918-39,* p. 163.

Palmer, John. *Studies in the contemporary theatre,* pp. 127-129.

WILLIAM SAROYAN 1908-

General

Fisher, William J. "What Ever Happened to Saroyan?" *College English,* vol. 16, no. 6 (Mar., 1955), pp. 336-340.

Gould, Jean. *Modern American playwrights,* pp. 201-203.

Justus, James H. "William Saroyan and the Theatre of Transformation." *In:* French, Warren, ed. *The thirties: fiction, poetry, drama,* pp. 211-219.

Krutch, Joseph Wood. *The American drama since 1918,* pp. 322-324.

Lewis, Allan. *American plays and playwrights of the contemporary theatre,* pp. 75-80.

Saroyan, William. "How and Why to Be a Playwright." *In:* Oppenheimer, George, ed. *The passionate playgoer,* pp. 254-259. (Reprinted from *Three plays,* N.Y., Harcourt, 1939.)

Across the Board on Tomorrow Morning

Floan, Howard R. *William Saroyan,* pp. 114-117.

The Beautiful People

Floan, Howard R. *William Saroyan,* pp. 110-114.

Hobson, Harold. *Theatre,* pp. 54-56.

Justus, James H. "William Saroyan and the Theatre of Transformation." *In:* French, Warren, ed. *The thirties: fiction, poetry, drama,* pp. 215-216.

The Cave Dwellers

Floan, Howard R. *William Saroyan,* pp. 121-122.

Don't Go Away Mad

Sievers, W. David. *Freud on Broadway,* pp. 252-253.

Get Away Old Man

Floan, Howard R. *William Saroyan,* p. 119.

Hello Out There

Floan, Howard R. *William Saroyan,* pp. 117-120.

Jim Dandy

Justus, James H. "William Saroyan and the Theatre of Transformation." *In:* French, Warren, Ed. *The thirties: fiction, poetry, drama,* pp. 218-219.

Sievers, W. David. *Freud on Broadway,* pp. 249-250.

Love's Old Sweet Song

Brown, John Mason. *Broadway in review,* pp. 194-197.

Floan, Howard R. *William Saroyan,* pp. 106-110.

Himelstein, Morgan Y. *Drama was a weapon, the left-wing theatre in New York 1929-1941,* p. 149.

Young, Stark. *Immortal shadows,* pp. 215-217.

My Heart's in the Highlands

Floan, Howard R. *William Saroyan,* pp. 92-97, 100-101.

Justus, James H. "William Saroyan and the Theatre of Transformation." *In:* French, Warren, ed. *The thirties, fiction, poetry, drama,* pp. 212, 215.

McCarthy, Mary. *Sights and spectacles 1937-1956,* pp. 46-52.

Sam Ego's House

Sievers. W. David. *Freud on Broadway,* p. 251.

Subway Circus

Floan, Howard R. *William Saroyan,* pp. 98-99.

Talking to You

Floan, Howard R. *William Saroyan,* pp. 114, 117, 120.

The Time of Your Life

Bierman, Judah. *The dramatic experience,* pp. 217-219.

Brown, John Mason. *Broadway in review,* pp. 189-194.

Clurman, Harold. *Lies like truth,* pp. 57-59.

Dusenbury, Winifred L. *The theme of loneliness in modern American drama,* pp. 157-164.

Floan, Howard R. *William Saroyan,* pp. 101-106.

Gassner, John. *The theatre in our times,* pp. 297-302.

Justus, James H. "William Saroyan and the Theatre of Transformation." *In:* French, Warren, ed. *The thirties, fiction, poetry, drama,* pp. 213, 215, 217.

McCarthy, Mary. *Sights and spectacles 1937-1956,* pp. 46-52.

Sievers, W. David. *Freud on Broadway,* p. 247.

JEAN PAUL SARTRE 1905-

General

Aylen, Leo. *Greek tragedy and the modern world,* pp. 176-178, 214-215, 222-224, 293-297, 310-311.

Bentley, Eric. "Sartre's Struggle for Existenz." *Kenyon Rev.,* Vol. 10, no. 2 (Spring, 1948), pp. 332-334.

Brombert, Victor. "Sartre and the Drama of Ensnarement." *In:* English Institute. *Ideas in the drama...,* pp. 155-174.

Carrandang, Amado I. "Jean-Paul Sartre and his atheism." *Dissertation Abstracts,* vol. 27 (1967), 2555A-56A (Notre Dame).

Chiari, J. *Landmarks of contemporary drama,* pp. 53-58.

Cranston, Maurice. "Jean-Paul Sartre." *Encounter,* vol. 18, no. 4 (Apr., 1962), pp. 34-45. (Cf. *Monat,* vol. 14, no. 164, 1962, pp. 32-44.)

Curtis, Anthony. *New developments in the French theatre,* pp. 3-8.

Fergusson, Francis. "Sartre as Playwright." *Partisan Rev.,* vol. 16 (Apr., 1949), pp. 407-411.

Fowlie, Wallace. "Sartre." *In:* Freedman, Morris, ed. *Essays in the modern drama,* pp. 206-218. (Reprinted from *Dionysus in Paris: a guide to contemporary French theater,* by Wallace Fowlie (1960).)

Galler, Dieter. "The Relationship Between Soma and Psyche in Jean-Paul Sartre's Drama *Les Sequestres d'Altona." Language Q.* (U. of So. Fla.), vol. 6, no. 1, 2 (1967), pp. 35-38.

Gascoigne, Bamber. *Twentieth-century drama,* pp. 152-157.

Glicksberg, Charles I. *The tragic vision in twentieth-century literature,* pp. 87-88, 100-103, 108-109, 126-136.

Gore, Keith O. "The Theatre of Sartre: 1940-65." *Books Abroad,* vol. 41, no. 2 (Spring, 1967), pp. 133-149.

Grossvogel, David I. *The self-conscious stage in modern French drama,* pp. 123-146.

Guicharnaud, Jacques. *Modern French theatre from Giraudoux to Beckett,* pp. 131-152.

Guicharnaud, Jacques. *Modern French theatre from Giraudoux to Genet* (rev. ed.), pp. 19, 24, 26, 91, 94, 102, 110, 135-155, 159, 179, 189, 215, 222, 223, 231, 238, 246, 269, 270, 271, 281-282, 286-290, 336-337, 360.

Hatzfeld, Helmut. *Trends and styles in twentieth-century French literature,* pp. 156-160.

Heppenstall, Rayner. "Jean-Paul Sartre." *Q. Rev. of Literature,* vol. 4, no. 4 (1949), pp. 416-427.

Hobson, Harold. *The French theatre of today,* pp. 75-127.

Jackson, R.F. "Sartre's Theatre and the Morality of Being." *In: Aspects of drama and the theatre,* pp. 35-39.

Jarrett-Kerr, Martin. The Dramatic Philosophy of Jean-Paul Sartre." *Tulane Drama Rev.,* vol. 1, no. 3 (June, 1957), pp. 41-48.

Jeanson, Francis. "Hell and Bastardy." *Yale French Studies,* no. 30 (Fall-Winter, 1962-63), pp. 5-20.

John, S. "Sacrilege and Metamorphosis: Two Aspects of Sartre's Imagery." *Modern Language Q.,* vol. 20, no, 1 (Mar., 1959), pp. 57-66.

Leavitt, Walter. "Sartre's Theatre." *Yale French Studies,* vol. 1, no. 1 (Spring-Summer, 1948), pp. 102-105.

Lewis, Allan. *The contemporary theatre,* pp. 201-211.

Lumley, Frederick. *Trends in 20th-century drama,* pp. 145-163.

Lumley, Frederick. *New trends in 20th-century drama,* pp. 139-158.

McCall, Dorothy Kaufmann. "Action and its image: a critical study of the plays of Jean-Paul Sartre." *Dissertation Abstracts,* vol. 28, no. 2 (Aug., 1967), 684-685 (Series A.) (Brooklyn Univ.).

McMahon, Joseph H. "A Reader's Hesitations." *Yale French Studies,* no. 30 (Fall-Winter, 1962-63), pp. 66-97, 102-107.

Magnan, Henri. "Said Jean-Paul Sartre." *Yale French Studies,* no. 16 (Winter, 1955-56), pp. 3-7.

Maurois, André. *From Proust to Camus,* pp. 299-315, 322-324.

Mendel, Sydney. "From Solitude to Salvation: A Study in Development." *Yale French Studies, no. 30* (Fall-Winter, 1962-63), pp. 45-55.

Pucciani, Oreste F. "An Interview with Jean-Paul Sartre." *Tulane Drama Rev.,* vol. 5, no. 3 (Mar., 1961), pp. 12-18.

Ridge, George R. "Meaningful Choice in Sartre's Drama." *French Rev.,* vol. 30, no. 6 (May, 1957), pp. 435-441.

Rose, M.G. "Sartre and the Ambiguous Thesis Play." *Modern Drama,* vol. 8 (May, 1965), pp. 12-19.

Simon, John Kenneth. "The Presence of Musset in Modern French Drama." *French Rev.,* vol. 40, no. 1 (Oct., 1966), pp. 27-38.

Stockwell, H.C.R. "Jean-Paul Sartre." *Cambridge J.,* vol. 6, no. 12 (Sept., 1953), pp. 753-760.

Upchurch, Norma. "The theatre of Jean-Paul Sartre: myth, freedom and commitment." *Dissertation Abstracts,* vol. 27, no. 11 (May 1967), 3885A. (Brookly. Univ.)

Wardman, H.W. "Sartre and the Theatre of Catharsis." *Essays in French Literature,* (U. of Western Australia), no. 1 (1964), pp. 72-88.

Weales, Gerald. "Whatever Happened to Jean-Paul Sartre?" *In:* Freedman, Morris, ed. *Essays in the modern drama,* pp. 219-224. (Reprinted from *The Hudson Review,* vol. 13, no. 3 (Autumn, 1960).)

Will, Frederic. "Sartre and the Question of Character in Literature. " *PMLA,* vol. 76, no. 4 (Sept., 1961), pp. 455-460.

Williams, Raymond. *Modern tragedy,* pp. 185-189.

Williams, Raymond. "Tragic Despair and Revolt." *Critical Q.,* vol. 5, no. 2 (Summer, 1963), pp. 111-115.

Wreszin, Michael. "Jean-Paul Sartre: Philosopher as Dramatist." *Tulane Drama Rev.,* vol. 5, no. 3 (Mar. 31, 1961), pp. 34-57.

Bariona

Stenstrom, Thure. "Jean-Paul Sartre's First Play." *Orbis Litterarum,* vol. 22 (1967), pp. 173-190.

The Condemned of Altona (Altona) (The Loser Wins) (Les Sequestres d'Altona)

Adereth, Maxwell, *Commitment in modern French literature,* pp. 165-167, 182, 195-196.

Aylen, Leo. *Greek tragedy and the modern world,* pp. 297, 302-304.

Brustein, Robert. "Sartre: the Janus of Modern Dramatists. *New Republic,* vol. 154, no. 9 (Feb. 26, 1966), pp. 42-43.

Chapsal, Madeleine. "To Show, To Demonstrate...." *Yale French Studies,* no. 30 (Fall-Winter, 1962-63), pp. 30-44.

Clurman, Harold. "Theatre." *Nation,* vol. 202, no. 8 (Feb. 21, 1966), pp. 222-224.

Cooke, Richard P.- "Black Illusion." *Wall Street J.,* vol. 167, no. 26 (Feb. 7, 1966), p. 14.

Craig, H.A.L. "Come to Judgment." *New Statesman,* vol. 61 (Apr. 28, 1961), pp. 680-681.

Dallas, Ian. "The New Sartre." *In:* Marowitz, Charles, ed. *Encore reader,* pp. 153-160. (Reprinted from *Encore* (Jan., 1960).)

Findlater, Richard. "Trial by Theatre." *Time and Tide,* vol. 42, no. 18 (May 4, 1961), p. 735.

Gascoigne, Bamber. "A Share in Guilt." *Spectator,* vol. 206 (Apr. 28, 1961), p. 608.

Glicksberg, Charles I. *The tragic vision in twentieth-century literature,* pp. 107-108.

Hardwick, Elizabeth. "We Are All Murderers." *New York Review of Books,* vol. 6, no. 3 (Mar. 3, 1966), pp. 6-7.

Heilman, Robert B. *Tragedy and melodrama,* pp. 149, 240, 246-247, 249, 256-259.

Jackson, R.F. "Sartre's Theatre and the Morality of Being." *In: Aspects of drama and the theatre,* pp. 62-70.

Lewis, Allan. *The contemporary theatre,* pp. 206-208.

Lumley, Frederick. *New trends in 20th-century drama,* pp. 137, 146, 156-158.

Matthews, Honor. *The primal curse,* pp. 141-147.

Maurois, André. *From Proust to Camus,* pp. 321-322.

Moore, Harry T. *Twentieth-century French literature since World War II,* pp. 50-51.

Pucciani, Oreste F. "Letter from Paris." *Nation,* vol. 189, no. 22 (Dec. 26, 1959), pp. 492-493.

Pucciani, Oreste F. *"Les Séquestres d'Altona* of Jean-Paul Sartre." *Tulane Drama Rev.,* vol. 5, no. 3 (Mar., 1961), pp. 19-33.

Roberts, Peter. "*Altona* in England." *Plays and Players,* vol. 8, no. 9 (June 1961), pp. 5, 18.

Sartre, Jean-Paul. "The Theatre." (Interview.) *Evergreen Rev.,* vol. 4, no. 11 (Jan.-Feb., 1960), pp. 143-152.

Simon, John K. "Madness in Sartre: Sequestration and the Room." *Yale French Studies,* no. 30 (Fall-Winter, 1962-63), pp. 63-67.

Tembeck, Robert, "Dialectic and Time in *The Condemned of Altona."* *Modern Drama,* vol. 12, no. 1 (May, 1969), pp. 10-17.

Tynan, Kenneth. *Tynan right and left,* pp. 58-60.

Vial, Fernand. "Two Highlights of the Theatrical Season in France: *Tête d'Or* and *Les Séquestres d'Altona." American Legion of Honor Society Mag.,* vol. 31, no. 1 (1960), pp. 15-32.

Wilbur, Richard. *"Les Séquestres d'Altona."* *Partisan Rev.,* no. 4 (1962), pp. 603-608.

Williams, Raymond. *Modern tragedy.* pp. 187-188.

Dirty Hands (Red Gloves) (Les Mains Sales) (Crime Passionnel)

Adereth, Maxwell. *Commitment in modern French literature,* pp. 136, 159-164.

Aylen, Leo. *Greek tragedy and the modern world,* pp. 297, 300-302.

Beyer, William. *School & Society,* vol. 698 (Jan. 29, 1949), pp. 84-86.

Bishop, Thomas. *Pirandello and the French theater,* pp. 125-126.

Brown, John Mason. "The Boudoir vs. the Kremlin." *Saturday Rev.,* vol. 32, no. 1 (Jan. 1, 1940), pp. 24-27.

Chiari, Joseph. *The contemporary French theatre,* pp. 155-162.

Clurman, Harold. "Red Faces." *New Republic,* vol. 119 (Dec. 20, 1948), pp. 28-29.

Curtis, Anthony. *New developments in the French theatre,* pp. 14-16.

Fergusson, Francis. "Sartre as Playwright." *In:* Bermel, Albert, ed. *The genius of the French theater,* pp. 570-572.

Fowlie, Wallace. *Dionysus in Paris,* pp. 177-179.

Gabriel, Gilbert. *Theatre Arts,* vol. 33, no. 1 (Jan., 1949), pp. 18, 20.

Gibbs, Wolcott. "Communism in Graustark." *New Yorker,* vol. 24 (Dec. 11, 1948), pp. 57-58.

Glicksberg, Charles I. *The tragic vision in twentieth-century literature,* pp. 128-131.

Gore, Keith O. "The Theater of Sartre: 1940-65." *Books Abroad,* vol. 41, no. 2 (Spring, 1967), pp. 140-141.

Grossvogel, David I. *The self-conscious stage in modern French drama,* pp. 129-138.

Hobson, Harold. *The French theatre of today,* pp. 103-110.

J.G.W. "Les Mains Sales." (Film.) *Twentieth Century,* vol. 152, no. 908 (Oct., 1952), pp. 362-364.

Jackson, R.F. "Sartre's Theatre and the Morality of Being." *In: Aspects of drama and the theatre,* pp. 52-59. (Five Kathleen Robinson lectures delivered at the University of Sydney, 1961-1963.)

Jameson, Fredric. "The Problem of Acts." *In:* Bogard, Travis, and Oliver, William I., ed. *Modern drama; essays in criticism,* pp. 280-287. (From Jameson's *Sartre: the origins of a style, New Ha*ven, Yale Univ. Press, 1961.)

Jones, Robert Emmet. *The alienated hero in modern French drama,* pp. 103-107.

Krutch, Joseph Wood. "Drama." *Nation,* vol. 167, no. 26 (Dec. 25, 1948), pp. 731-732.

Lumley, Frederick. *New trends in 20th-century drama,* pp. 147, 153-154.

Lumley, Frederick. *Trends in 20th-century drama,* pp. 159-160.

MacArthur, Roderick. *Theatre Arts,* vol. 33, no. 2 (Mar., 1949), pp. 11-13.

Matthews, Honor. *The primal curse,* p. 140.

Maurois, André. *From Proust to Camus,* pp. 318-320.

Mendel, Sydney. "The Ambiguity of the Rebellious Son. Observations on Sartre's Play *Dirty Hands." Forum* (Houston), vol. 4, no. 9 (Spring 1966), pp. 32-36.

Moore, Harry T. *Twentieth-century French literature since World War II,* pp. 46-47.

Sauvage, Leo. "*Red Gloves* and *Dirty Hands." Nation,* vol. 168, no. 1 (Jan. 1, 1949), p. 19.

Schneider, Isidor. "*Dirty Hands." Masses and Mainstream,* vol. 2, no. 1 (Jan., 1949), pp. 88-92.

Scruggs, Charles E. "T.S. Eliot and J.-P. Sartre Toward the Definition of the Human Condition." *Appalachian State Teachers College Faculty Publication,* 1965, pp. 24-29.

Styan, J.L. *The elements of drama,* pp. 239-243.

Travers, P.L. *"Crime Passionnel." New English Weekly,* vol. 33, no. 14 (July 15, 1948), pp. 152-153.

Worsley, T.C. *New Statesman,* vol. 35 (June 26, 1948), p. 520.

The Flies (Les Mouches)

Adamczewski, Zygmunt. *The tragic protest,* pp. 193-225.

Adereth, Maxwell. *Commitment in modern French literature,* pp. 138-139, 157-158.

Aylen, Leo. *Greek tragedy and the modern world,* pp. 295-297, 304-306, 309.

Barnes, Hazel E. *The literature of possibility,* pp. 1824.

Bentley, Eric. "Jean-Paul Sartre, Dramatist: The Thinker as Playwright." *Kenyon Rev.,* vol. 8, no. 1 (Winter, 1946), pp. 71-79.

Bentley, Eric. *The playwright as thinker,* pp. 195, 201-203, 204-208.

Bishop, Thomas. *Pirandello and the French theater,* pp. 123-124.

Burdick, Delores Mann. "Imagery of the 'Plight' in Sartre's *Les Mouches."* *French Rev,* vol. 32, no. 3 (Jan., 1959), pp. 242-246.

Chiari, Joseph. *The contemporary French theatre,* 150-155.

Cohn, Ruby. "Four Stages of Absurdist Hero." *Drama Survey,* vol. 4, no. 3 (Winter, 1965), pp. 199-201.

Conacher, D.J. "Orestes as Existentialist Hero." *Philological Q.,* vol. 33, no. 4 (Oct., 1954), pp. 404-417.

Curtis, Anthony. *New developments in the French theatre,* pp. 9-12.

Fowlie, Wallace. *Dionysus in Paris,* pp. 170-173.

Friedman, Maurice. *To deny our nothingness,* pp. 252-253.

Gassner, John. *The theatre in our times,* pp. 337-341.

Gore, Keith O. "The Theater of Sartre: 1940-65." *Books Abroad,* vol. 41, no. 2 (Spring, 1967), pp. 136, 138, 139.

Grossvogel, David I. *The self-conscious stage in modern French drama,* pp. 138-142.

Hanzeli, Victor E. "The Progeny of Atreus." *Modern Drama,* vol. 3, no. 1 (May, 1960), pp. 75-81.

Heilman, Robert B. *Tragedy and melodrama,* pp. 253-256, 259, 289.

Henn, T.R. *The harvest of tragedy,* 237-238.

Hobson, Harold. *The French theatre of today,* pp. 83-91.

Hobson, Harold. *The theatre now,* pp. 89-93.

Jackson, R.F. "Sartre's Theater and the Morality of Being." *In: Aspects of drama and the theatre,* pp. 39-45.

Jones, Robert Emmet. *The alienated hero in modern French drama,* pp. 96-99.

Kahn, Ludwig W. "Freedom: An Existentialist and an Idealist View." *PMLA,* vol. 64, no. 1 (Mar., 1949), pp. 5-15.

Lerner, Max. "Sartre's Orestes: The Free Man in an Age of Fear." *In: Actions and passions,* pp. 49-51.

Lewis, Allan. *The contemporary theatre,* pp. 202-204.

Lumley, Frederick. *New trends in 20th-century drama,* pp. 143, 146-150.

Lumley, Frederick. *Trends in 20th-century drama,* pp. 153-156.

McCollom, William G. *Tragedy,* pp. 37-40.

Matthews, Honor. *The primal curse,* pp. 137-140.

Maurois, André. *From Proust to Camus,* pp. 316-317.

Moore, Harry T. *Twentieth-century French literature to World War II,* pp. 202-203.

Muller, Herbert J. *The spirit of tragedy,* pp. 304-306.

Phelan, Kappo. *"The Flies." Commonweal,* vol. 46, no. 4 (May 9, 1947), pp. 93-94.

Ramsey, Warren. "The *Oresteia* Since Hofmannsthal: Images and Emphases." *Revue de Litterature Comparee,* vol. 38 (1964), pp. 369-370.

Reinhardt, Kurt F. *The existentialist revolt,* pp. 170-174.

Rickman, H.P. "The Death of God." *Hibbert J.,* vol. 59 (Apr., 1961), pp. 220-226.

Slochower, Harry. "The Function of Myth in Existentialism." *Yale French Studies,* no. 1 (Spring-Summer, 1948), pp. 42-52.

Williams-Ellis, Amabel. "Paris Faces the Winter." *Spectator,* vol. 175 (Sept. 21, 1945), p. 264.

Worsley, T.C. *New Statesman,* vol. 42 (Dec. 1, 1951), pp. 620-622.

Kean

Jackson, R.F. "Sartre's Theatre and the Morality of Being." *In: Aspects of drama and the theatre,* pp. 61-62.

Nelson, R.J. *Play within a play,* pp. 100-114.

Lucifer and the Lord (The Devil and the Good Lord) (Le Diable et le Bon Dieu)

Arnold, Paul. "Jean-Paul Sartre's New Play." *Theatre Arts,* vol 35, no. 10 (Oct., 1951), pp. 24, 87.

Aylen, Leo. *Greek tragedy and the modern world,* pp. 297, 306-309.

Chiari, Joseph. *The contemporary French theatre,* pp. 162-169.

Churman, Harold. "French Immorality." *New Republic,* vol. 125 (July 23, 1951), p. 22. "The New Moralities." *New Republic,* vol. 125 (Aug. 6, 1951), pp. 21-22.

Douglas, Kenneth. "Sartre and the Self-Inficted Wound." *Yale French Studies,* no. 9 (1952), pp. 123-131.

Flanner, Janet. *Paris journal, 1944-1965,* pp. 151-152.

Fowlie, Wallace. *Dionysus in Paris,* pp. 179-181.

Frank, Joseph. "God, Man, and Jean-Paul Sartre." *Partisan Rev.,* vol. 19 (Mar.-Apr., 1952), pp. 202-210.

Friedman, Maurice. *To deny our nothingness, pp. 252-253.*

Glicksberg, Charles I. *The tragic vision in twentieth-century literature,* pp. 104-107, 113, 130.

Gore, Keith O. "The Theater of Sartre: 1940-65." *Books Abroad,* vol. 41, no. 2 (Spring 1967), pp. 141-142.

Grossvogel, David I. *The self-conscious stage in modern French drama,* pp. 142-143.

Heinemann, F.H. "Theologic Diaboli." *Hibbert J.,* vol. 52 (Oct., 1953), pp. 65-72.

Hobson, Harold. *The French theatre of today,* pp. 110117.

Jackson, R.F. "Sartre's Theatre and the Morality of Being." *In: Aspects of drama and the theatre,* pp. 59-61.

Jones, Robert Emmet. *The alienated hero in modern French drama,* pp. 107-111.

Lewis, Allan. *The contemporary theatre,* pp. 208-211.

Lumley, Frederick. *New trends in 20th-century drama,* pp. 113, 141, 146, 147, 154-156.

Luthy, Herbert. "Jean-Paul Sartre and God." *Twentieth Century,* vol. 150, no. 895 (Sept., 1951), pp. 221-230.

Maurois, André. *From Proust to Camus,* pp. 320-321.

Moore, Harry T. *Twentieth-century French literature since World War II,* pp. 48-49.

Pendennis. "Le Bon Sartre." *Observer,* no. 8351 (June 24, 1951), p. 5.

Peyre, Henri. "Jean-Paul Sartre: the Philosopher as Playwright." *New York Times Book Rev.* (Mar. 6, 1960), pp. 5, 34.

Ricoeur, Paul. "Sartre's *Lucifer and the Lord.*" *Yale French Studies,* no. 14 (Winter 1954-55), pp. 85-93.

Ridge, George R. *"Le Diable et le Bon Dieu:* Sartre's Concept of Freedom." *Shenandoah,* vol. 9, no. 2 (1958), pp. 35-38.

Speaight, Robert. "Philosophy in the French Theatre Today." *Listener,* vol. 49, no. 1251 (Feb. 19, 1953), pp. 308-309.

Winner, Percy. "Tract for the Times." *New Republic,* vol. 125 (Sept. 10, 1951), p.9.

Men Without Shadows (The Victors) (Morts sans Sépultures)

Abraham, Claude K. "A Study in Autohypocrisy: *Morts Sans Sépultures.* " *Modern Drama,* vol. 3, no. 4 (Feb., 1961), pp. 343-347.

Adereth, Maxwell, *Commitment in modern French literature,* pp. 159, 188-189.

Aylen, Leo. *Greek tragedy and the modern world,* pp. 190, 297, 299-300.

Barnes, Hazel E. *The literature of possibility,* pp. 222-224.

Bentley, Eric. "Sartre's Struggle for Existenz." *Kenyon Rev.,* vol. 10, no. 2 (Spring, 1948), pp. 330-332.

Bishop, Thomas. *Pirandello and the French theater,* p. 125.

Clurman, Harold. *Lies like truth,* pp. 212-213.

Fergusson, Francis. "Sartre as Playwright." *In:* Bermel, Albert, ed. *The genius of the French theater,* pp. 569-570.

Flanner, Janet. *Paris journal, 1944-1965,* p. 72.

Fowlie, Wallace. *Dionysus in Paris,* pp. 175-177.

Jones, Robert Emmet. *The alienated hero in modern French drama,* pp. 100-103.

Lumley, Frederick. *New trends in 20th-century drama,* pp. 146, 147, 150-151.

Lumley, Frederick. *Trends in 20th-century drama,* pp. 156-157.

McMahon, Joseph H. "A Reader's Hesitations." *Yale French Studies,* no. 30 (Fall-Winter, 1962-63), pp. 98-101.

Marcel, Gabriel. "Sartre and Barrault." *Theatre Arts,* vol. 31, no. 2 (Feb., 1947), p. 45.

Milroy, Vivian. "Two Plays by Jean-Paul Sartre." *New English Weekly,* vol. 31, no. 16 (July 31, 1947), pp. 142-143.

Muller, Herbert J. *The spirit of tragedy,* 308-310.

Nekrassov

Adereth, Maxwell, *Commitment in modern French literature,* pp. 168-169.

Moore, Harry T. *Twentieth-century French literature since World War II,* pp. 49-50.

Oxenhandler, Neal. "*Nekrassov* and the Critics." *Yale French Studies,* no. 16 (Winter, 1955-56), pp. 8-12.

Worsley, T.C. *New Statesman,* vol. 51 (Jan. 14, 1956), pp. 40-41.

No Exit (Huis Clos)

Adereth, Maxwell, *Commitment in modern French literature,* pp. 144, 158-159.

Astruc, Alexandre. "The European Audience: Jean-Paul Sartre and *Huis Clos.*" *New Writing and Daylight,* vol. 6, (1945) pp. 136-142.

Ayer, A.J. "Secret Session." *Polemic,* no. 2 (Jan. 1946), pp. 60-63.

Aylen, Leo. *Greek tragedy and the modern world,* pp. 297-299.

Barnes, Hazel E. *The literature of possibility,* pp. 26-28.

Bentley, Eric. "Jean-Paul Sartre, Dramatist: The Thinker as Playwright." *Kenyon Rev.,* vol. 8, no. 1 (Winter, 1946), pp. 66-71.

Bentley, Eric. *The playwright as thinker,* pp. 196-201.

Bishop, Thomas. *Pirandello and the French theater,* pp. 124-125, 136.

Blitgen, Sister M.J. Carol, BVM. "No Exit: The Sartrean Idea of Hell." *Renascence,* vol. 19 (1967), pp. 59-63.

Brown, John Mason. *Seeing more things,* pp. 85-91.

Brown, John Mason. "The Unbeautiful and the Damned." *Saturday Rev.,* vol. 29, no. 52 (Dec. 28, 1946), pp. 26-28.

Cargo, Robert T. "Sartre's *Huis Clos* (No Exit)." *Explicator,* vol. 24, no. 9 (May 1966), p. 96.

Chiari, Joseph. *The contemporary French theatre, 149-150.*

Curtis, Anthony. *New developments in the French theatre,* pp. 12-14.

Fergusson, Francis. "Sartre as Playwright." *In:* Bermel, Albert, ed. *The genius of the French theater,* p. 569.

Fowlie, Wallace. *Dionysus in Paris,* pp. 173-175.

Friedman, Maurice. *To deny our nothingness,* pp. 261.

Grossvogel, David I. *The self-conscious stage in modern French drama,* pp. 143-146.

Hobson, Harold. *The French theatre of today,* pp. 96-103.

Jackson, R.F. "Sartre's Theater and the Morality of Being." *In: Aspects of drama and the theatre,* pp. 45-52.

Jameson, Frederic. "The Problem of Acts." *In:* Bogard, Travis, and Oliver, William I., eds. *Modern drama; essays in criticism,* pp. 276-280. (From Jameson's *Sartre: the origins of a style,* New Haven, Yale Univ. Press, 1961.)

Kern, Edith. "Abandon Hope All Ye..." *Yale French Studies,* no. 30 (Fall-Winter, 1962-63), pp. 56-60.

Krutch, Joseph Wood. "Drama." *Nation,* vol. 163, no. 24 (Dec. 14, 1946), p. 708.

Lejeune, C.A. "Hotel in Hell." *Observer,* no. 8788 (Dec. 6, 1959), p. 24.

Lewis, Allan. *The contemporary theatre,* pp. 204-206.

Loeb, Ernst. "Sartre's *No Exit* and Brecht's *The Good Woman of Setzuan:* A Comparison." *Modern Language Q.,* vol. 22, no. 3 (Sept., 1961), pp. 283-291.

Lumley, Frederick. *New trends in 20th-century drama,* pp. 150, 152.

Lumley, Frederick. *Trends in 20th-century drama,* p. 156.

Mankowitz, Wolf. "Hell Is Other People." *Politics and Letters,* vol. 1, no. 1 (Summer, 1947), pp. 68-70.

Maurois, André. From P*roust to Camus,* pp. 317-318.

Moore, Harry T. *Twentieth-century French literature to World War II,* pp. 203-204.

Muller, Herbert J. *The spirit of tragedy,* 303-304.

Weimar, Karl S. "No Entry, No Exit: A Study of Borchert with Some Notes on Sartre." *Modern Language Q.,* vol. 17, no. 2 (June, 1956), pp. 161-165.

Young, Stark. "Weaknesses." *New Republic,* vol. 115 (Dec. 9, 1946), p. 764.

The Respectful Prostitute (La Putaine Respectueuse)

Adereth, Maxwell. *Commitment in modern French literature,* pp. 151, 167-168.

Bentley, Eric. "Sartre's Struggle for Existenz." *Kenyon Rev.,* vol. 10, no. 2 (Spring, 1948), pp. 328-330.

Beyer, William. *School & Society,* vol. 67 (Feb. 28, 1948), p. 166.

Brown, John Mason. "Guignal a la Sartre." *Saturday Rev.,* vol. 31, no. 11 (Mar. 13, 1948), pp. 26-27.

Clurman, Harold. *Lies like truth,* pp. 208-211.

Flanner, Janet. *Paris journal, 1944-1965,* pp. 72-73.

Gassner, John *The theatre in our times,* pp. 385-386.

Jack, Homer A. "Censoring Sartre." *Nation,* vol. 168, no. 11 (Mar. 12, 1949) p. 305.

Lumley, Frederick. *New trends in 20th-century drama,* p. 151.

Lumley, Frederick. *Trends in 20th-century drama,* pp. 157-159.

Marcel, Gabriel. "Sartre and Barrault." *Theatre Arts,* vol. 31, no. 2 (Feb., 1947), pp. 44-45.

Marshall, Margaret. *Nation,* vol. 166, no. 9 (Feb. 28, 1948), pp. 257-258.

Milroy, Vivian. "Two Plays by Jean-Paul Sartre." *New English Weekly,* vol. 31, no. 16 (July 31, 1947), pp. 142-143.

Moore, Harry T. *Twentieth-century French literature since World War II,* pp. 45-46.

O'Keefe, Winston. "Tis Pity She's Respectful." *Theater Arts,* vol. 33 no. 2 (Mar., 1949), pp. 49-50.

Shaw, Irwin. *New Republic,* Vol. 118 (Feb. 23, 1948), pp. 29-30.

Troubled Sleep

Milano, Paolo. "The Men of Bad Will." *Nation,* vol. 172, no. 6, (Feb. 10, 1951), pp. 136-137.

ALFONSO SASTRE 1927-

General

Corrigan, Robert W., ed. *Masterpieces of the modern Spanish theatre,* p. 200.

De Coster, Cyrus C. "Alfonso Sastre." *Tulane Drama Rev.,* vol. 5, no. 2 (Dec., 1960), pp. 121-132.

Pronko, Leonard C. "The Revolutionary Theatre of Alfonso Sastre." *Tulane Drama Rev.,* vol. 5, no. 2 (Dec., 1960), pp. 111-120.

Sastre, Alfonso. "Drama and Society." *In:* Corrigan, Robert W. ed. *The new theatre of Europe,* pp. 136-145.

Schwartz, Kessel. "Tragedy and the Criticism of Alfonso Sastre." *Symposium,* vol. 21, no. 4 (Winter, 1967), pp. 338-345.

Anna Kleiber

Corrigan, Robert W., ed. *The new theatre of Europe,* pp. 21-23.

The Condemned Squad

Pronko, Leonard C. "The 'Revolutionary' Theatre of Alfonso Sastre." *Tulane Drama Rev.,* vol. 5, no. 2 (Dec., 1960), pp. 111-120.

Death in the Neighborhood

Pronko, Leonard C. "The 'Revolutionary' Theatre of Alfonso Sastre." *Tulane Drama Rev.,* vol. 5, no. 2 (Dec., 1960), pp. 111-120.

Every Man's Bread

Pronko, Leonard C. "The 'Revolutionary' Theatre of Alfonso Sastre." *Tulane Drama Rev.,* vol. 5, no. 2 (Dec., 1960), pp. 111-120.

Pathetic Prologue

Pronko, Leonard C. "The 'Revolutionary' Theatre of Alfonso Sastre." *Tulane Drama Rev.*, vol. 5, no. 2 (Dec., 1960), pp. 111-120.

OSCAR SAUL

Medicine Show

Himelstein, Morgan Y. *Drama was a weapon, the left-wing theatre in New York 1929-1941*, pp. 210-211.

The Revolt of the Beavers

Himelstein, Morgan Y. *Drama was a weapon, the left-wing theatre in New York 1929-1941*, pp. 102-103.

HENRI SAUMAGNE 1891-1951

L'Autre Messie

Mallinson, Vernon. *Modern Belgian literature, 1830-1960*, pp. 186-187.

Bas-Noyard

Mallinson, Vernon. *Modern Belgian literature, 1830-1960*, p. 187.

Madame Marie

Mallinson, Vernon. *Modern Belgian literature, 1830-1960*, pp. 188-190.

Terminus

Mallinson, Vernon. *Modern Belgian literature, 1830-1960*, pp. 187-188.

ALFRED SAVOIR

General

Knowles, Dorothy. *French drama of the inter-war years, 1918-39*, pp. 281-283.

DOROTHY LEIGH SAYERS 1893-1957

The Man Born To Be King (Radio play)

Roston, Murray. *Biblical drama in England from the Middle Ages to the present day*, pp. 296-298.

The Zeal of Thy House

Spanos, William V. *The Christian tradition in modern British verse drama*, pp. 124-134.

GEORGES SCHEHADE

General

Guicharnaud, Jacques. *Modern French theatre from Giraudoux to Genet* (rev. ed.), pp. 172-176, 177, 342, 361-362.

Kuhn, Reinhard. "The Debasement of the Intellectual in Contemporary Continental Drama." *Modern Drama,* vol. 7, no. 4 (Feb., 1965), pp. 454-462.

Pronko, Leonard C. *Avant-Garde: the experimental theater in France,* pp. 188-196.

Pronko, Leonard. "Poetry and Purity: the Theatre of Georges Schehadé, *French Rev.,* vol. 31, no. 5 (Apr., 1958), pp. 378-386.

L'Emigré de Brisbane

Silenieks, Juris. "Georges Schehadé: The Transfiguration of a Poetic Theatre." *Modern Drama,* vol. 10, no. 2 (Sept., 1967), pp. 151-160.

The History of Vasco (Vasco) (L'Histoire de Vasco)

Bean, David. *"Vasco* at Newcastle." *Guardian,* no. 36,502 (Nov. 13, 1963), p. 7.

Brien, Alan, *Spectator,* vol. 205, no. 6998 (Sept. 9, 1960), p. 371.

Fowlie, Wallace. *Dionysus in Paris,* p. 241.

Rodger, Ian. "The Coming of *Vasco." Listener,* vol. 60, no. 1538 (Sept. 18, 1958), pp. 437-438.

Silenieks, Juris. "Georges Schehadé: The Transfiguration of a Poetic Theatre." *Modern Drama,* vol. 10, no. 2 (Sept., 1967), pp. 151-160.

Stein, Elliott. "Letter from Paris." *Nation,* vol. 185, no. 19 (Dec. 7, 1957), pp. 439-441.

Monsieur Bob'le

Fowlie, Wallace. *Dionysus in Paris,* pp. 238-240.

Knapp, Bettina. "Georges Schehadé: 'He Who Dreams Diffuses into Air...'" *Yale French Studies,* no. 29 (Spring-Summer, 1962), pp. 108-112, 115.

Silenieks, Juris. "Georges Schehadé: The Transfiguration of a Poetic Theatre." *Modern Drama,* vol. 10, no. 2 (Sept., 1967), pp. 151-160.

La Soirée des Proverbes

Fowlie, Wallace. *Dionysus in Paris,* pp. 240-241.

Pronko, Leonard C. *Avant-garde: the experimental theater in France,* pp. 191-196.

Silenieks, Juris. "Georges Schehadé: The Transfiguration of a Poetic Theatre." *Modern Drama,* vol. 10, no. 2 (Sept., 1967), pp. 151-160.

Les Violettes

Silenieks, Juris. "Georges Schehadé: The Transfiguration of a Poetic Theatre." *Modern Drama,* vol. 10, no. 2 (Sept., 1967), pp. 151-160.

The Voyage (Le Voyage)

Davies, Oliver. *"The Voyage* at the Oxford Playhouse." *Guardian,* no. 36,257 (Jan. 30, 1963), p. 7.

Knapp, Bettina. "Georges Schehadé: 'He who dreams diffuses into air...'" *Yale French Studies,* vol. 29 (Spring, Summer, 1962), pp. 108, 112-115.

"Sea Fable That Travels Well." *Times,* no. 55,612 (Jan. 30, 1963), p. 13.

Silenieks, Juris. "Georges Schehadé: The Transfiguration of a Poetic Theatre." *Modern Drama,* vol. 10, no. 2 (Sept., 1967), pp. 151-160.

RENE SCHICKELE 1883-1940

General

Ackermann, Paul Kurt. "Excerpts from an Unpublished Diary of René Schickele." *Monatshefte,* vol. 46, no. 6 (Nov., 1954), pp. 332-338.

Ackermann, Paul Kurt. *René Schickele, a critical study.* Typewritten dissertation, Harvard University, 1953.

Mann, Thomas. "René Schickele." *The New York Times* (May 26, 1940), Sec. VI, pp. 8, 19.

Schickele, Rainer. "René Schickele." *Books Abroad,* vol. 15, no. 3 (Summer, 1941), pp. 273-275.

MURRAY SCHISGAL 1926-

General

"An Interview With Murray Schisgal." *In:* Downer, Alan S., ed. *The American theater today,* pp. 124-135.

Duprey, Richard A. "Today's Dramatists." *In: American theatre,* pp. 219-220.

Luv

Clurman, Harold. *The naked image,* pp. 115-116.

Gottfried, Martin. *A theater divided; the postwar American stage,* pp. 66, 217-218, 222.

Kerr, Walter. *Tragedy and comedy,* pp. 329-332.

Lumley, Frederick. *New trends in 20th-century drama,* p. 333.

Ulanov, Barry. *"Luv and Tiny Alice." Catholic World,* vol. 200 (Mar., 1965), pp. 383-384.

The Tiger

Brustein, Robert. "The New American Playwrights." *In:* Rahv, Philip, ed. *Modern occasions,* p. 132.

Sainer, Arthur. *The sleepwalker and the assassin, a view of the contemporary theatre,* p. 65.

The Typists

Brustein, Robert. "The New American Playwrights." *In:* Rahv, Philip, ed., *Modern occasions,* pp. 131-132.

Sainer, Arthur. *The sleepwalker and the assassin, a view of the contemporary theatre,* pp. 65-66.

EDOUARD SCHNEIDER 1880-

General

Knowles, Dorothy. *French drama of the inter-war years, 1918-39,* pp. 246-247.

LEONARD A. SCHNEIDER (Pseud. Lenny Bruce)

General

Marowitz, Charles. "The Confessions of Lenny Bruce." *In:* Marowitz, Charles, ed. *Encore reader,* pp. 251-260. (Reprinted from *Encore* (July, 1962).)

ARTHUR SCHNITZLER 1862-1931

General

Alexander, Theodore W. "Schnitzler and the Interior Monologue: A Study in Technique." *J. of the International Arthur Schnitzler Research Assoc.,* vol. 6, no. 2 (1967), pp. 4-20.

Allen, Richard H. "Schnitzler and His Early Critics." *J. of the International Arthur Schnitzler Research Assoc.,* vol. 5, no. 3 (1966), pp. 17-21.

Apsler, Alfred. "A Sociological View of Arthur Schnitzler." *Germanic Rev.,* vol. 18, no. 2 (Apr., 1943), pp. 90-106.

Beharriel, Frederick J. "Arthur Schnitzler's Range of Theme." *Monatshefte,* vol. 43, no. 7 (Nov., 1951), pp. 301-311.

Beharriel, Frederick J. "Schnitzler's Vienna." *J. of the International Arthur Schnitzler Research Assoc.,* vol. 6, no. 1 (1967), pp. 4-13. Dukes, Ashley. *Modern dramatists,* pp. 151-159.

Ellehauge, Martin. *The position of Bernard Shaw in European drama and philosophy,* pp. 148-150, 170-173, 177-178, 323-324.

Ewing, Blair. "The Politics of Nihilism: Schnitzler's 'Last Man'." *J. of the International Arthur Schnitzler Research Assoc.,* vol. 5, no. 3 (1966), pp. 4-16.

Garland, H.B. "Arthur Schnitzler." *In:* Natan, A., ed. *German men of letters,* vol. 2 (1963), pp. 57-75.

Garten, H.F. *Modern German drama,* pp. 55-63.

Henderson, Archibald. *European dramatists,* pp. 409-465.

Hill, Claude. "The Stature of Arthur Schnitzler. " *Modern Drama,* vol. 4, no. 1 (May, 1961), pp. 80-91.

Ilmer, Freda. "Schnitzler's Attitude with Regard to the Transcendental." *Germanic Rev.,* vol. 10, no. 2 (Apr., 1935), pp. 114-125.

Kann, Robert A. "Arthur Schnitzler: Reflections on the Evolution of His Image." *Wisconsin Studies in Contemporary Literature,* vol. 8, no. 4 (Autumn, 1967), pp. 548-555.

Lamm, Martin. *Modern drama,* pp. 238-244.

Lederer, Herbert. "Arthur Schnitzler's Typology: An Excursion into Philosophy." *PMLA,* vol. 78 (1963), pp. 394-406.

Liptzin, Sol. "The Call of Death and the Lure of Love." *German Q.,* vol. 5, no. 1 (Jan., 1932), pp. 21-36.

Plant, Richard. "Notes on Arthur Schnitzler's Literary Technique." *Germanic Rev.,* vol. 25, no. 1 (Feb., 1950), pp. 13-25.

Politzer, Heinz. "Arthur Schnitzer: The Poetry of Pschology." *Modern Lang. Notes,* vol. 78 (1963), pp. 353-372.

Richert, Herbert. "Schnitzler and Jung-Wien." *J. of the International Arthur Schnitzler Research Assoc.,* vol. 5, no. 3 (1966), pp. 27-32.

Swales, M.W. "Arthur Schnitzler as a Moralist." *Modern Language Rev.,* vol. 62 (1967), pp. 462-475.

Von Nardorff, Ernest H. "Aspects of symbolism in the works of Arthur Schnitzler." *Dissertation Abstracts,* vol. 27 (1966), 1842A (Columbia).

Witkowski, Georg. *German drama of the nineteenth century,* pp. 180-181.

Bibliography

Allen, Richard H. *An annotated ˋArthur Schnitzler bibliography: editions and criticism in German, French and English 1879-1965.* U. of N.C. Studies in Germanic Languages and Literature, 56 (Chapel Hill: U. of N.C. Press, 1966).

Anatol (The Affairs of Anatole)

Bauland, Peter. *The hooded eagle,* pp. 29-31.

Ellehauge, Martin. *The position of Bernard Shaw in European drama and philosophy,* pp. 167-168.

Garland, H.B. "Arthur Schnitzler." *In:* Natan, A., ed. *German men of letters,* vol. 2, pp. 57-60.

Hill, Claude. "The Stature of Arthur Schnitzler." *Modern Drama,* vol. 4, no. 1 (May, 1961), pp. 80-91.

Sticca, Sandro. "The Drama of Being and Seeming in Schnitzler's *Anatol* and Pirandello's *Cosi è se vi pare."* *J. of the International Arthur Schnitzler Research Assoc.,* vol. 5, no. 2 (1966), pp. 4-28.

The Call of Life (Der Ruf des Lebens)

Bauland, Peter. *The hooded eagle,* pp. 56-57.

Flirtation (Light-o'-Love) (The Reckoning) (Liebelei)

Bauland, Peter. *The hooded eagle,* pp. 26-27.

Ellehauge, Martin. *The position of Bernard Shaw in European drama and philosophy,* pp. 155-157.

Garland, H.B. "Arthur Schnitzler." *In:* Natan, A., ed. *German men of letters,* pp. vol. 2, pp. 60-62.

Liptzin, Sol. "The Call of Death and the Lure of Love." *German Q.,* vol. 5, no. 1 (Jan., 1932), pp. 21-36.

Freiwild

Liptzin, Sol. "The Call of Death and the Lure of Love." *German Q.,* vol. 5, no. 1 (Jan., 1932), pp. 21-36.

Die Gefährtin

Ellehauge, Martin. *The position of Bernard Shaw in European drama and philosophy,* pp. 168-169.

The Green Cockatoo (Der Grüne Kakadu)

Bauland, Peter. *The hooded eagle,* pp. 28-29.

Büdel, Oscar. *Pirandello,* pp. 85-86.

Kayser, Wolfgang. *The grotesque in art and literature,* pp. 134-135.

Nelson, R.J. *Play within a play,* pp. 116-122.

Hands Around (Round Dance) (Riegen) (La Ronde)

Bauland, Peter. *The hooded eagle,* pp. 26, 173-175.

Bentley, Eric. *The dramatic event,* pp. 209-212.

Block, Anita. *The changing world in plays and theatre,* pp. 65-67.

Garland, H.B. "Arthur Schnitzler." *In:* Natan, A., ed. *German men of letters,* vol. 2, p. 60.

Hill, Claude. "The Stature of Arthur Schnitzler." *Modern Drama,* vol. 4, no. 1 (May, 1961), pp. 80-91.

Nelson, R.J. *Play within a play,* pp. 115-116.

Schinnerer, Otto P. "The History of Schnitzler's *Reigen.*" *PMLA,* vol. 46 (1931), pp. 839-859.

Der Junge Medarus

Ellehauge, Martin. *The position of Bernard Shaw in European drama and philosophy,* pp. 164-165.

Literature (The Literary Sense) (Literatur)

Bauland, Peter. *The hooded eagle,* pp. 27-28.

Ellehauge, Martin. *The position of Bernard Shaw in European drama and philosophy,* pp. 136-138.

The Lonely Way (Der Einsame Weg)

Garland, H.B. "Arthur Schnitzler." *In:* Natan, A., ed. *German men of letters,* vol. 2, p. 62.

Liptzin, Sol. "The Genesis of Schnitzler's *Der Einsame Weg.*" *J. of English and Germanic Philology,* vol. 30 (1931), pp. 392-404.

Miller, Nellie Burget. *The living drama,* pp. 271-274.

Das Marchen

Ellehauge, Martin. *The position of Bernard Shaw in European drama and philosophy,* pp. 71-74.

Professor Bernhardi

Ellehauge, Martin. *The position of Bernard Shaw in European drama and philosophy,* pp. 59-61.

Garland, H.B. "Arthur Schnitzler." *In:* Natan, A., ed. *German men of letters,* vol. 2, pp. 63-65.

Hill, Claude. "The Stature of Arthur Schnitzler." *Modern Drama,* vol. 4, no. 1 (May, 1961), pp. 80-91.

Liptzin, Sol. "The Genesis of Schnitzler's *Professor Bernhardi.*" *Philological Q.,* vol. 10 (1931), pp. 348-355.

Das Vermachtnis

Liptzin, Sol. "The Call of Death and the Lure of Love." *German Q.,* vol. 5, no. 1 (Jan., 1932), pp. 21-36.

Das Weite Land

Garland, H.B. "Arthur Schnitzler." *In:* Natan, A., ed. *German men of letters,* vol. 2, pp. 62-63.

Liptzin, Sol. "The Genesis of Schnitzler's *Des Weite Land.*" *PMLA,* vol. 46 (1931), pp. 860-866.

Der Zug der Schatten

Reiss, H.S. "A Note on *Der Zug der Schatten,* an unpublished play by Arthur Schnitzler." *German Life and Letters,* n.s., vol. 2, no. 1 (Oct., 1948), pp. 222-224.

603

SEAMUS DE BRUCE 1912-
(real name Jimmy Bourke)

General

Hogan, Robert. *After the Irish renaissance,* pp. 221-224.

PETER SHAFFER 1926-

General

Lumley, Frederick. *New trends in 20th-century drama,* pp. 279-283.

Taylor, John Russell. *Anger and after,* pp. 227-230.

Black Comedy

Browne, E. Martin. "Theatre Abroad." *Drama Survey,* vol. 5, no. 2 (Summer, 1966), pp. 192-193.

Five Finger Exercise

Lumley, Frederick. *New trends in 20th-century drama,* pp. 279-280.

Taylor, John Russell. *Anger and after,* pp. 227-230.

Vidal, Gore. *Rocking the boat,* pp. 148-152. *Also in: Reporter,* vol. 22, no. 1, (Jan. 7, 1960), pp. 36-37.

The Royal Hunt of the Sun

Downer, Alan S. "Total Theatre and Partial Drama: Notes on the New York Theatre, 1965-1966." *Q. J. of Speech,* vol. 52, no. 3 (Oct., 1966), pp. 229-231.

Gassner, John. "Broadway in Review." *Educational Theatre J.,* vol. 18, no. 1 (Mar., 1966), pp. 57-58.

Lumley, Frederick. *New trends in 20th-century drama,* pp. 280-282.

Pronko, Leonard C. *Theater East and West,* pp. 175-177.

Shaffer, Peter. "In Search of a God." *Plays and Players* (Oct., 1964), p. 22.

Taylor, John Russell. "Shaffer and the Incas." *Plays and Players* (Apr., 1964), pp. 12-13.

MORDAUNT SHAIRP 1887-

The Green Bay Tree

Block, Anita. *The changing world in plays and theatre,* pp. 120-122.

Sievers, W. David. *Freud on Broadway,* pp. 218-219.

GEORGE BERNARD SHAW 1856-1950

General

Adams, Elsie B. "Bernard Shaw's Pre-Raphaelite Drama." PMLA, vol. 81, no. 5 (Oct., 1966), pp. 428-438.

Adler, Henry. "29 Fitzroy Square." *Shavian,* vol. 2, no. 4 (1961), pp. 12-14.

Albert, Sidney P. "Bernard Shaw: The Artist as Philosopher." *J. of Aesthetics and Art Criticism,* vol. 14, no. 4 (June, 1956), pp. 419-438.

Allen, Walter. "Bernard Shaw." *In:* Hudson, Derek, ed. *English critical essays; twentieth century* (2nd series), pp. 307-315. *Also in:* Times Literary Supplement (July 27, 1956).

Anderson, Maxwell. "St. Bernard." *In:* Anderson, M. *Off Broadway: essays about the theatre,* pp. 12-17.

Armstrong, William A. "George Bernard Shaw: The Playwright as Producer." *Modern Drama,* vol. 8, no. 4 (Feb., 1966), pp. 347-361.

Atkinson, Brooks "Ideas and the Theatre: A G. B. S. Symposium." *Shaw Bulletin,* vol. 2, no. 6 (1958), pp. 15-20.

Auchincloss, Katherine L. "Shaw and the Commissars: The Lenin Years 1917-1924." *Shaw Rev.,* vol. 6, no. 2 (1963), pp. 51-59.

Austin, Don DeForest. "The comic structure in five plays of Bernard Shaw." *Dissertation Abstracts,* vol. 20, 4658 (Univ. of Washington).

Baker, A.E. "Christianity and Bernard Shaw." *Church Times,* vol. 130 (1950), p. 826.

Barnet, Sylvan. "Bernard Shaw on Tragedy." *PMLA,* vol. 71 (1956), pp. 888-899.

Barzun, Jacques. *The energies of art: studies of authors classic and modern,* pp. 245-280.

Barzun, Jacques. "Love and the Playwright." *New Republic,* vol. 127 (Nov. 3, 1952), pp. 17-18.

Barzun, Jacques. "Shaw and Rousseau: No Paradox." *Shaw Bulletin,* vol. 1 (May, 1955), pp. 1-6.

Batson, Eric J. "G.B.S.: The Orator and the Man." *English,* vol. 14 (1962), pp. 97-100.

Batson, Eric J. "Hyperion and the Yahoos." *Shaw Bulletin,* vol. 1 (Jan., 1955), pp. 16-18.

Batson, Eric J. "The Quintessence of Winstenism." *Shaw Bulletin,* vol. 1 (May, 1955), pp. 19-21.

Bax, Clifford. "A Criticism." *Drama,* vol. 20 (Spring, 1951), pp. 19-22.

Beerbohm, Sir Max et al. *In:* Winsten, Stephen, ed., *G.B.S. 90: aspects of Bernard Shaw's life and work.*

Bentley, Eric. *Bernard Shaw,* 2nd British ed., pp. ix-xviii, 30-34, 43-63, 64-69, 79-82, 101-104, 108-110, 118-125, 126-140, 143-150, 151-159, 160-163, 171-175.

Bentley, Eric. *Bernard Shaw: a reconsideration.*

Bentley, Eric. "The Making of a Dramatist (1892-1903)." *In:* Corrigan, Robert, ed. *Laurel British drama: the nineteenth century,* pp. 305-308, 316-320, 326-328.

Bentley, Eric. *The playwright as thinker,* pp. 107-126, 154-157.

Bentley, Eric R. "The Theory and Practice of Shavian Drama." *Accent,* vol. 5, no. 1 (Autumn, 1944), pp. 5-18. (Reprinted in *Accent anthology* (N.Y., Harcourt, 1946), pp. 447-466).

Bernd, Daniel W. "The dramatic theory of George Bernard Shaw." *Dissertation Abstracts,* vol. 23 (1963), 2910-2911. University of Nebraska.

Besant, Lloyd. "Shaw's women characters." *Dissertation Abstracts,* vol. 25 (1964), 2661-2662. University of Wisconsin.

Black, Matthew W. "Shaw to Arliss." *Shaw Rev.,* vol. 6, no. 1 (1963), pp. 28-29.

Block, Anita. *The changing world in plays and theatre,* pp. 15-75.

Block, Toni. "Shaw's Women." *Modern Drama,* vol. 2, no. 2 (Sept., 1959), pp. 133-138.

Bosworth, R.F. "Shaw Recordings at the B. B. C." *Shaw Rev.,* vol. 7, no. 2 (1964), pp. 42-46.

Brailsford, H.N. "Shaw on Himself." *Listener,* vol. 41 (Apr., 21, 1949), pp. 663-664.

Brashear, William R. "O'Neill and Shaw: The Play as Will and Idea." *Criticism,* vol. 8 (1966), pp. 155-169.

Brecht, Bertolt. "Ovation for Shaw." *In:* Kaufmann, R.J. *G.B. Shaw, a collection of critical essays,* pp. 26-41. (Reprinted from *Modern Drama,* vol. 2, no. 2 (Sept., 1959), pp. 184-187.

Bridie, James. "Play of Ideas." *New Statesman and Nation,* vol. 39 (Mar. 11, 1950), p. 270.

Bridie, James. "Shaw as Playwright." *New Statesman and Nation,* vol. 40 (Nov. 11, 1950), p. 422.

Brinser, Ayers. *The respectability of Mr. Bernard Shaw.*

Brooks, Harold F. and J.R. "Dickens in Shaw." *Dickensian,* vol. 59 (1963), pp. 93-99.

Brower, R.A. *In:* Harrison, G.B. *Major British writers,* vol. 2, pp. 521-534.

Brown, Allison M. "The George Bernard Shaw Papers." *California Shavian,* vol. 3 (Nov.-Dec., 1962).

Brown, John Mason. *As they appear,* pp. 59-97.

Brown, John Mason. "Professional Man of Genius." *In:* Brown, John Mason. *Dramatis personae,* pp. 148-156.

Brown, John Mason. "Satan, Saint, and Superman." *In:* Brown, John Mason. *Dramatis personae,* pp. 103-112.

Brustein, Robert. "Bernard Shaw: The Face Behind the Mask." *In:* Kaufmann, R.J. *G.B. Shaw, a collection of critical essays,* pp. 100-107. (Reprinted from Brustein, Robert. *The theatre of revolt.*)

Brustein, Robert. *The theatre of revolt,* pp. 183-195, 204-212.

Bullough, G. "Bernard Shaw, the Dramatist: a Centenary Tribute." *Cairo Studies in English* (1959), pp. 59-75.

Burton, Richard. *Bernard Shaw, the man and the mask,* pp. 1-33, 189-294.

Cardigan, Robert. "The Bearded Ancient." *Twentieth Century,* vol. 3 (Dec., 1948), pp. 32-43.

Carpenter, Charles A., Jr. "Bernard Shaw's development as a dramatic artist." *Dissertation Abstracts,* vol. 24 (1963), 295. (Cornell University.)

Carpenter, Charles A. "The Quintessence of Shaw's Ethical Position." *In:* Caputi, Anthony, ed. *Modern drama,* pp. 402-408.

Carpenter, Charles A. "Shaw's Collected Letters." *Modern Drama,* vol. 9, no. 2 (Sept., 1966, pp. 190-194.

Carpenter, Charles A., Jr. "Shaw's Cross Section of Anti-Shavian Opinion." *Shaw Rev.,* vol. 7, no. 3 (1964), pp. 78-86.

Cathey, Kenneth C. "George Bernard Shaw's drama of ideas." *Dissertation Abstracts,* vol. 17 (1957), 2606.

Caudwell, Christopher (pseud. of Christopher St. John Sprigg). *Studies in a dying culture,* pp. 1-19.

Chappelow, Allan, ed. *Shaw the villager and human being; a biographical symposium.*

Chase, Harrison V. "A Note on Spiritual Meagreness." *Shaw Bulletin,* vol. 1 (Summer, 1953), pp. 15-16.

Cherry, D.R. "The Fabianism of Shaw." *Queen's Q.,* vol. 69 (1962), pp. 83-93.

Chesterton, Gilbert K. *George Bernard Shaw* (1910 ed.), pp. 90-117, 171-196, 234-258.

Chesterton, G.K. *Bernard Shaw* (7th ed.), 1950.

Chislett, William. "G.B.S., or from Bashville to Methusaleh." *In:* Chislett, William. *Moderns and near-moderns,* pp. 129-137, 144-145.

Church, Richard. *British authors,* pp. 25-28.

Clark, Eleanor. "Shaw, Fry, and Others." *Partisan Rev.,* vol. 19 (1952), pp. 217-224.

Clark, William R. *Literary Aspects of Fabian Socialism. Dissertation Abstracts,* vol. 12 (1952), 615-16.

Clarke, Arthur C. "Shaw and the Sound Barrier." *Virginia Q. Rev.,* vol. 36 (1960), pp. 72-77.

Clarke, David Waldo. *Modern English writers,* pp. 53-59.

Clarke, Winifred. *George Bernard Shaw.*

Coates, J.B. *Leaders of modern thought,* pp. 23-39.

Colbourne, Maurice Dale. *The real Bernard Shaw.*

Cole, Margaret. "G.B. Shaw and Fabian Socialism." *Fabian J.,* vol. 3 (Feb., 1951), pp. 11-14.

Cole, Toby, and H.K. Chinoy, eds. *Actors on acting,* pp. 346-352.

Coleman, D.C. "Bernard Shaw and *Brave New World." Shaw Rev.,* vol. 10 (1967), pp. 6-8.

Collins, A.S. *English literature of the twentieth century,* pp. 314-327.

Collis, J.S. "John Bull's Other Islander." *Shavian,* vol. 2, no. 2 (1960), pp. 20-23.

Collis, J.S. "The Two Bernard Shaws." *Dublin Magazine,* vol. 31, no. 3 (1956), pp. 36-40.

Connolly, Thomas E. "On the Consistency of Joan's Use of Archaic Speech." *Explicator,* vol. 14 (Dec., 1955), Item 19.

Corrigan, Robert W. *Theatre in the twentieth century,* pp. 283-303.

Coxe, Louis O. "You Never Can Tell: G. B. Shaw Reviewed." *Western Humanities Rev.,* vol. 4 (1955), pp. 313-325.

Crompton, Louis. "Shaw's Challenge to Liberalism." *Prairie Schooner,* vol. 37 (1963), pp. 229-244. (Reprinted in Slote, Bernice, ed. *Literature and society.)*

d'Agostino, Nemi. "Bernard Shaw." *Belfagor* (1952), pp. 188-204.

D'Amato, Guy Albert. *Portraits of ideas,* pp. 43-44.

D'Angelo, Evelyn. "George Bernard Shaw's Theory of Stage Representation." *Q. J. of Speech,* vol. 15 (1929), pp. 330-349.

Demaray, John G. "Bernard Shaw and C.E.M. Joad: The Adventure of Two Puritans in Their Search for God." *PMLA,* vol. 78 (1963), pp. 262-270.

DeSelincourt, Aubrey. *Six great playwrights,* pp. 161-190.

Donaghy, Henry J. "Chesterton on Shaw's Views of Catholicism." *Shaw Rev.,* vol. 10 (1967), pp. 108-116.

Dougherty, Joseph Charles. *The political thought of G. B. Shaw as expressed in his drama.* Thesis. (Washington, 1948).

Doyle, P.A. "Shaw on Immortality and on Illustrating His Dramatis Personae: Two Unpublished Letters." *Bulletin of the New York Public Library,* vol. 71 (1967), pp. 59-60.

Duerksen, Roland A. "Shelley and Shaw." *PMLA,* vol. 78 (1963), pp. 114-127.

Duffin, H.C. "The Bourgois Moralist in Shaw." *Shavian,* vol. 2, no. 1 (1960), pp. 12-14.

Duffin, H.C. Creative Evolution (rev. by Shaw). London, Staddon's (Shaw Society: Shavian Tract no. 1), 1950.

Dukes, Ashley. *Modern dramatists,* pp. 118-135.

Dukore, Bernard F. "Brecht's Shavian Saint." *Q. J. of Speech,* vol. 50 (1964), pp. 136-139.

Dukore, Bernard F. "The Fabian and the Freudian." *Shavian,* vol. 2, no. 4 (1961), pp. 8-11.

Dukore, Bernard F. "Shaw Improves Shaw." *Modern Drama,* vol. 6, no. 1 (1963), pp. 26-31.

Dunkel, Wilbur D. "Bernard Shaw's Religious Faith." *Theology Today,* vol. 6 (Oct., 1949), pp. 367-377.

Dunkel, Wilbur D. "The Essence of Shaw's Dramaturgy." *College English,* vol. 10 (Mar., 1949), pp. 307-312.

Dunkel, Wilbur D. "George Bernard Shaw." *Sewanee Rev.,* vol. 50, no. 2 (1942), pp. 255-262.

Dupler, Dorothy. "An analytic study of the use of rhetorical devices in three selected plays of George Bernard Shaw: *St. Joan, Androcles and the Lion,* and *Candida." Dissertation Abstracts,* vol. 22, 359 (University of Southern California, 1961).

Eastman, Fred. "From Shakespeare to Shaw." *In:* Eastman, F. *Christ in the drama,* pp. 40-60.

Eaton, W.P. "Bernard Shaw as a Playwright." *Bulletin of the Shaw Society of America,* vol. 1 (Autumn, 1951), pp. 6-7.

Ellehauge, Martin. *The position of Bernard Shaw in European drama and philosophy,* pp. 40-44, 186-191, 215-220, 223-236, 270-271, 340-383.

Ellis, Havelock. *From Marlowe to Shaw,* pp. 291-296.

Erikson, Erik H. "Identity and Totality: Psychoanalytic Observations on the Problems of Youth." *Human Development Bulletin,* (1954).

Ervine, St. John. *Bernard Shaw.*

Fergusson, F. "The Theatricality of Shaw and Pirandello." *Partisan Rev.,* vol. 16 (June, 1949), pp. 589-603. (Reprinted in *Idea of a theatre,* pp. 178-193.)

Fiske, Irving. "Bernard Shaw and William Blake." *In:* Kaufmann, R.J. *G.B. Shaw, a collection of critical essays,* pp. 170-178. (From *The Shavian,* Tract no. 2, The Shaw Society, 1951, Original title: "Bernard Shaw's Debt to William Blake.")

Fiske, Irving. *Bernard Shaw's Debt to William Blake* (foreword and notes by G.B.S.). Shavian Tract no. 2, London, Shaw Society, 1951.

Fiske, Irving. "My Correspondence with GBS." *Shavian,* no. 11 (1957), pp. 12-15.

Forter, Elizabeth T. "A study of the dramatic technique of Bernard Shaw." Doctoral Dissertation (Univ. of Wisc., 1955).

Fraser, George S. "Bernard Shaw: 1950." *Shaw Bulletin,* vol. 1 (May, 1954), pp. 13-14.

Fraser, George S. *The modern writer and his world,* pp. 191-197.

Freeman, John. *The moderns; essays in literary criticism,* pp. 1-51.

Fremantle, Anne. "Shaw and Religion." *Commonweal,* vol. 67 (1957), pp. 249-251.

Fuller, Edmund. *George Bernard Shaw, critic of Western morale.*

Furlong, William B. "Shaw and Chesterton: The Link Was Magic." *Shaw Rev.,* vol. 10 (1967), pp. 100-107.

Fyfe, W.H. "George Bernard Shaw." *Queen's Q.,* vol. 39 (Feb., 1932), pp. 29-45.

Gassner, John. "Bernard Shaw and the Making of the Modern Mind." *In:* Freedman, Morris, ed. *Essays in the modern drama,* pp. 64-75. (Reprinted from *College English,* vol. 23, no. 7 (Apr., 1962), pp. 517-525.)

Gassner, J.W. "Bernard Shaw and the Puritan in Hell." *In:* Gassner, J. W. *Theatre in our time,* pp. 156-162.

Gassner, John. "Shaw on Ibsen and the Drama of Ideas." *In:* English Institute. *Ideas in the drama...,* pp. 71-100.

Gassner, John. *The theatre in our times,* pp. 134-169.

Gatch, Katherine Haynes. "The Last Plays of Bernard Shaw: Dialectic and Despair." *In: English Institute essays,* 1954, pp. 126-147.

Gatch, Katherine H. "The Real Sorrow of Great Men: Mr. Bernard Shaw's Sense of Tragedy." *College English,* vol. 8 (Feb., 1947), pp. 230-240.

Geduld, H.M. "Bernard Shaw and Leo Tolstoy: The Shavian Critique of Tolstoy." *California Shavian,* vol. 4 (Mar.-Apr., 1963), pp. 1-9; (May-June, 1963), pp. 1-4.

Geduld, H.M. "The Comprehensionist." *Shavian,* vol. 2, no. 7 (1963), pp. 22-26.

Gerould, Daniel Charles. "George Bernard Shaw's Criticism of Ibsen." *Comparative Literature,* vol. 15 (1963), pp. 130-145.

Gerould, Daniel Charles. *"Saint Joan* In Paris." *Shaw Rev.,* vol. 7, no. 1 (1964), pp. 11-23.

Gilder, Rosamond. *Theatre arts anthology,* pp. 265-77, 639-41.

Gilenson, Boris. "Shaw in the Soviet Union." *Shavian,* vol. 2, no. 7 (1963), pp. 11-13.

Glicksberg, Charles I. "Criticism of Bernard Shaw." *South Atlantic Q.,* vol. 50 (Jan., 1951), pp. 96-108.

Glicksberg, Charles I. "Shaw Versus Science." *Dalhousie Rev.,* vol. 28 (1948-49), pp. 271-283.

Gray, James. *On second thought,* pp. 36-58.

Green, P. "Mystical Bernard Shaw." *In:* Green, P. *Dramatic heritage,* pp. 112-131.

Gregory, Isabella Augusta, Lady. *Lady Gregory's journals, 1916-1930,* pp. 199-216.

Hackett, Francis. *On judging books,* pp. 201-204.

Hackett, Francis. "Shaw and Wells." *Atlantic Monthly,* vol. 177 (May, 1951), pp. 73-76.

Hales, John. "Shaw's comedy." *Dissertation Abstracts,* vol. 24 (1964), 3324. (University of Texas).

Hamilton, Clayton. *Conversations on contemporary drama,* pp. 49-67.

Harris, Frank. *Bernard Shaw,* pp. 144-155, 162-176, 187-193, 246-273, 409-417.

Harris, Harold J. "Shaw, Chekhov, and Two Great Ladies of the Theatre." *Shaw Rev.,* vol. 7, no. 3 (1963), pp. 96-99.

Harrison, George B., ed. *Major British writers,* vol. 2, pp. 521-552, 651-656.

Henderson, Archibald. *European dramatists,* pp. 323-369.

Henderson, Archibald. "Bernard Shaw and France: Gaelic Triumph or Gallic Repulse?" *Carolina Q.,* vol. 3 (Mar., 1951), pp. 42-56.

Henderson, Archibald. "Collectors and Collections of Shaviana in the U. S. A." *Shaw Bulletin,* vol. 1 (May, 1952), pp. 7-9.

Henderson, Archibald. "Creative Evolution." *Shaw Society of America, Inc. Bulletin,* vol. 1 (Feb., 1951), pp. 4-5.

Henderson, Archibald. *George Bernard Shaw: man of the century.*

Henderson, Archibald. "Shaw and Shakespeare." *Shaw Bulletin,* vol. 1 (Sept., 1954), pp. 1-6.

Henderson, Archibald. "Shaw's Stature." *Queen's Q.,* vol. 58, no. 1 (1951), pp. 14-22.

Henderson, Archibald. "Where Shaw Stands Today." *Shaw Bulletin,* vol. 1 (Autumn, 1951), pp. 1-6. *Also in:* supplement to *Shaw Society Bulletin,* no. 39 (June, 1951).

Henson, Janice. "Bernard Shaw's Contribution to the Wagner Controversy in England." *Shaw Rev.,* vol. 4, no. 1 (1961), pp. 21-26.

Herrin, Virginia T. "Bernard Shaw and Richard Wagner: a study of their intellectual kinship as artist philosophers." Doctoral Dissertation. University of North Carolina, 1955.

Hickin, R.A. "The Christian Debt to G.B. Shaw." *London Q. and Holborn Rev.,* (Jan., 1954), pp. 46-50.

Hildeman, Per-Axel. "Shaw and the Anglo-Swedish Literary Foundation." *Shavian,* vol. 2, no. 3 (1961), pp. 34-37.

Hill, Eldon C. "Shaw's 'Biographer-in-Chief.'" *Modern Drama,* vol. 2, no. 2 (Sept., 1959), pp. 164-172.

Hobsbawm, E.J. "Bernard Shaw's Socialism." *Science and Society,* vol. 40 (1947), pp. 305-326.

Hobson, Harold. "George Bernard Shaw." *In:* Russell, Leonard, ed. *English wits.*

Hodess, J. "Shaw and the Jews." *Zion,* vol. 2 (Dec., 1950), pp. 1-14.

Holberg, Stanley Marquis. "The Economic Rogue in the Plays of Bernard Shaw." *University of Buffalo Studies,* vol. 21 (1953).

Hudson, Lynton. *The twentieth-century drama,* pp. 17-22.

Hummert, Paul A. "Bernard Shaw's Marxist Utopias." *Shaw Review,* vol. 2 (Sept., 1959), pp. 7-26.

Hummert, Paul A. "Marxist elements in the works of George Bernard Shaw." Doctoral Dissertation, Northwestern University, 1953. *Dissertation Abstracts,* vol. 13 (1953), 1183-84.

Huss, Roy. "Max the 'Incomparable' on G.B.S. the 'Irrepressible'." *Shaw Rev.,* vol. 5 (1962), pp. 10-20.

Irvine, William. "G. B. Shaw and Karl Marx." *J. of Economic History,* vol. 6 (May, 1946) pp. 53-72.

Irvine, William. "Shaw and Chesterton." *Virginia Q. Rev.,* vol. 23 (Apr., 1947), pp. 273-281.

Irvine, William. "Shaw, the Fabians, and the Utilitarians." *J. of the History of Ideas,* vol. 8 (Apr., 1947), pp. 218-231.

Irvine, William. "Shaw, War and Peace, 1894-1919." *Foreign Affairs,* vol. 25 (Jan., 1947), pp. 314-327.

Irvine, William. "Shaw's *Quintessence of Ibsenism.*" *South Atlantic Q.,* vol. 46 (Apr., 1947), pp. 252-262.

Irvine, William. *The universe of G.B.S.*

Isaacs, J. "Bernard Shaw and the Jews." *Jewish Chronicle* (London) (Nov. 10, 1950).

James, Eugene N. "The Critic as Dramatist: Bernard Shaw, 1895-1898." *Shaw Rev.,* vol. 5 (1962), pp. 97-108.

Jameson, Storm. *Modern drama in Europe,* pp. 137-147.

Joad, C.E.M. *Shaw.*

Jones, A.R. "George Bernard Shaw." *In:* Brown, John Russell, and Bernard Harris, eds. *Contemporary theatre,* pp. 57-75.

Kaufmann, R.J. *G.B. Shaw, a collection of critical essays.*

Kaufmann, R.J. "Introduction." *In:* Kaufmann, R.J. *G.B. Shaw, a collection of critical essays,* pp. 1-13.

Kaufmann, R.J. "Shaw's Elitist Vision: A Serial Criticism of the Plays of the First Decade." *Komos: A Q. of Drama and Arts of the Theatre,* vol. 1 (1967), pp. 97-104.

Kaye, Julian B. *Bernard Shaw and the nineteenth century tradition.*

Kerr, Allison. *Bernard Shaw: an exhibition of books and manuscripts from the collection presented by Mr. Bernard Burgunder.*

Ketels, Violet B. "Shaw, Snow and the New Men." *The Personalist,* vol. 47 (1966), pp. 520-531.

Klein, John W. "Shaw and Brieux: an Enigma." *Drama,* vol. 67 (Winter, 1962), pp. 33-35.

Knight, G. Wilson. "Shaw's Integral Theatre." *In:* Kaufmann, R.J. *G.B. Shaw, a collection of critical essays,* pp. 119-129. (Reprinted from Knight, G. Wilson. *The golden labyrinth,* pp. 342-354.)

Kornbluth, Martin L. "Shaw and Restoration Comedy." *Shaw Bulletin,* vol. 2, no. 4 (1958), pp. 9-17.

Kronenberger, Louis. *The thread of laughter,* pp. 227-278.

Krutch, Joseph Wood. "The Loss of Confidence." *American Scholar,* vol. 22 (1953), pp. 141-153.

Krutch, Joseph Wood. *"Modernism" in modern drama,* pp. 49-55.

Krutch, Joseph Wood. "Shaw the Shavian." *Nation,* vol. 175 (Dec. 6., 1952), pp. 524-525.

Krutch, Joseph Wood. "Two Scholars: Wells and Shaw." *Nation,* vol. 171 (Dec. 16, 1950), pp. 648 ff.

Lamm, Martin. "George Bernard Shaw." *Modern Drama,* pp. 251-284.

Langner, Lawrence. *G. B. S and the lunatic: reminiscences of the long, lively and affectionate friendship between George Bernard Shaw and the author.*

Laurence, Dan H. "Shaw's Life Force: The Superpersonal Need." *Shaw Society Bulletin,* vol. 48 (Mar., 1953), pp. 14-17.

Lavrin, Janko. "Ibsen and Shaw." *In:* Lavrin, J. *Studies in European literature,* pp. 80-98.

Leavis, F.R. "Shaw against Lawrence." *Spectator,* vol. 194 (Apr. 1, 1955), pp. 397-399; *Discussion (Apr. 8, 1955), pp. 437-471.*

Lewis, Allan. *The contemporary theatre,* pp. 80-111.

Lewis, Arthur O., Jr. "Bernard Shaw—Ten Years After (1950-1960): A Transcript of the Second MLA Conference of Scholars on Shaw. *Shaw Rev.,* vol. 4, no. 2 (1961), pp. 29-32.

Lewis, A.O., Jr., and S. Weintraub, eds. "Bernard Shaw—Aspects and Problems of Research." *Shaw Rev.,* vol. 3, no. 2 (1960), pp. 18-26.

Ludeke, H. "Some Remarks on Shaw's History Plays." *English Studies,* vol. 36 (1955), pp. 239-246.

Lynch, Vernon E. "George Bernard Shaw and the Comic." Dissertation. Univ. of Texas, 1951.

McDowell, Frederick P.W. "Another Look at Bernard Shaw: A Reassessment of His Dramatic Theory, His Practice and His Achievement." *Drama Survey,* vol. 1, no. 1 (May, 1961), pp. 34-53.

McDowell, Frederick P.W. "Shaw's Increasing Stature." *Drama Survey,* vol. 3 (1964), pp. 423-441.

McDowell, Frederick P.W. "Shaw's 'Real, Creative, Material World': The Correspondence." *Drama Survey,* vol. 5, no. 1 (Spring, 1966), pp. 78-86.

McKee, Irving. "Bernard Shaw's Beginnings on the London Stage." *PMLA,* vol. 74 (Sept., 1959), 470-481.

Mann, Thomas. "G. B. S. Mankind's Friend." *Yale Rev.,* vol. 40 (Mar., 1951), pp. 412-420.

Mann, Thomas. "George Bernard Shaw." *Shaw Bulletin,* vol. 1 (Feb., 1951), p. 2.

Mark Twain J. (Bernard Shaw Memorial Number), Summer, 1954.

Mayer, David. "The Case for Harlequin: A Footnote on Shaw's Dramatic Method." *Modern Drama,* vol. 3, no. 1 (May, 1960), pp. 60-74.

Mayne, Fred. "Consonance and Consequence." *English Studies in Africa,* vol. 2, no. 1 (Mar., 1959), pp. 59-72.

Mayne, Fred. "The Real and the Ideal: Irony in Shaw." *Southern Rev.,* (University of Adelaide, Australia), No. 1 (1963), pp. 15-26.

Mayne, Fred. "Types and Contrasts in Shaw." *English Studies in Africa,* vol. 7, no. 2 (Sept., 1964), pp. 187-194.

Mayne, Fred. *The wit and satire of Bernard Shaw.*

Meisel, Martin. *Shaw and the nineteenth century theatre.*

Meister, Charles W. "Comparative Drama: Chekhov, Shaw, Odets." *Poet Lore,* vol. 55, no. 3 (Autumn, 1950), pp. 249-257.

Mierow, Herbert E. "A Modern Euripides." *Sewanee Rev.,* vol. 36 (1928), pp. 24-26.

Miller, Joseph W. "Working methods of modern playwrights." *Cornell University abstracts of theses,* 1944 (1945), pp. 47-51.

Miller, Nellie Burget. *The living drama,* pp. 297-301.

Mills, John A. "The Comic in Words: Shaw's Cockneys." *Drama Survey,* vol. 5, no. 2 (Summer, 1966), pp. 137-150.

Mills, John A. "Language and laughter in Shavian Comedy." *Q. J. of Speech,* vol. 51, no. 4 (Dec., 1965), pp. 433-441.

Mills, John A. "Shaw's Linguistic Satire." *Shaw Rev.,* vol. 8, no. 1 (Jan., 1965), pp. 2-11.

Mix, Katherine Lyon. "Max on Shaw." *Shaw Rev.,* vol. 6, no. 3 (1963), pp. 100-104.

Molnar, J. "Shaw's Four Kinds of Women." *Theatre Arts,* vol. 36 (Dec., 1952), pp. 18-21, 92. (Adapted as "Shaw's Living Women." *Shaw Society Bulletin,* vol. 49 (June, 1953), pp. 7-11.)

Montague, Charles E. *Dramatic values,* pp. 75-99.

Morgan, L.N. "Bernard Shaw as Playwright." *Books Abroad,* vol. 25, no. 2 (1951), pp. 101-104.

Morgan, Margery M. "Bernard Shaw on the Tightrope." *Modern Drama,* vol. 4 (1962), pp. 243-254.

Murphy, Daniel J. "The Lady Gregory Letters to G. B. Shaw." *Modern Drama,* vol. 10, no. 4 (Feb., 1968), pp. 331-345.

Nathan, George Jean. "Sample British Imports: Bernard Shaw." *In:* Nathan, G.J. *Theatre in the fifties,* pp. 157-160.

Nethercot, Arthur H. "Bernard Shaw and Psychoanalysis." *Modern Drama,* vol. 11, no. 4 (Feb., 1969), pp. 356-375.

Nethercot, Arthur H. "Bernard Shaw, Ladies and Gentlemen." *Modern Drama,* vol. 2, no. 2 (Sept., 1959), pp. 84-98.

Nethercot, Arthur H. "Bernard Shaw, Philosopher." *PMLA,* vol. 69 (Mar., 1954), pp. 57-75.

Nethercot, Arthur H. "The Quintessence of Idealism." *PMLA,* vol. 62 (Sept., 1947), pp. 844-859.

Nethercot, Arthur H. "Schizophrenia of Bernard Shaw." *American Scholar,* vol. 21 (Oct., 1952), pp. 455-467.

Nickson, Joseph R. "The art and politics of the later plays of Bernard Shaw." Ph.D., 1957. (Southern California).

Nickson, Richard. "The World Betterer: Shaw versus Shaw." *Shaw Rev.,* vol. 2 (Sept., 1959), pp. 39-44.

Nicoll, Allardyce. *British drama,* pp. 280-289.

Norwood, Gilbert. *Euripedes and Shaw with other essays,* pp. 1-48, 95-96, 98-104.

O'Casey, Sean. "Bernard Shaw: An Appreciation of a Fighting Idealist." *New York Times Book Rev.,* (Nov. 12, 1950), p. 41.

O'Casey, Sean. *The green crow,* pp. 197-211.

O'Casey, Sean. "Shaw's Corner." *Shavian,* no. 4 (May, 1955), pp. 2-5.

O'Casey, Sean. "A Whisper About Bernard Shaw." *In:* Barnet, Sylvan, ed. *The genius of the Irish theater,* pp. 359-364.

O'Donnell, Norbert F. "The Conflict of Wills in Shaw's Tragicomedy." *In:* Kaufmann, R.J. *G.B. Shaw, a collection of critical essays,* pp. 76-87. (Reprinted from *Modern Drama,* vol. 4, no. 4 (Feb., 1962) pp. 413-425.)

O'Donnell, Norbert F. "Ibsen and Shaw: The Tragic and the Tragi-Comic." *Theatre annual, 1957-58,* vol. 15, pp. 15-27.

O'Donnell, Norbert F. "Shaw, Bunyan, and Puritanism." *PMLA,* vol. 72 (1957), pp. 520-523.

Ohmann, Richard M. "Born To Set It Right: The Roots of Shaw's Styles." *In:* Kaufman R.J. *G.B. Shaw, a collection of critical essays,* pp. 26-41. (Reprinted from Ohmann, Richard M. *Shaw: the style and the man,* pp. 74-90, 101-108).

Ostergaard, G. "G. B. S.—Anarchist." *New Statesman and Nation,* vol. 46 (Nov. 21, 1953), p. 628.

Park, Bruce R. "A Mote in the Critic's Eye: Bernard Shaw and Comedy." *In:* Kaufmann, R.J. *G.B. Shaw, a collection of critical essays,* pp. 42-56. (Reprinted from *Texas Studies,* vol. 37 (1958), pp. 195-210.)

Parker, R.B. "Bernard Shaw and Sean O'Casey." *Queen's Q.,* vol. 73, no. 1 (Spring, 1966), pp. 13-34.

Parmenter, Ross. "Shaw and Mozart." *Shaw Bulletin,* vol. 1 (May, 1952), pp. 3-5.

Peacock, Ronald. *The poet in the theatre,* pp. 86-93.

Pease, Edward R. "Personal Recollections of Shaw." *Fabian J.,* vol. 3 (Feb., 1951), pp. 9-11.

Perry, Henry Ten Eyck. *Masters of dramatic comedy and their social themes,* pp. 366-408.

Pettet, Edwin Burr. "Shavian socialism and the Shavian life force: an analysis of the relationship between the philosophic and economic systems of G. B. S." *Dissertation Abstracts,* vol. 12 (1952), 622-23 (New York University).

Pettet, Edwin Burr. "Shaw's Socialist Life Force." *Educational Theatre J.,* vol. 3 (May, 1951), pp. 109-114.

Phelps, William Lyon. *Essays on modern dramatists,* pp. 67-98.

Pollock, Ellen. "The Lightness in Shaw." *Modern Drama,* vol. 2, no. 2 (Sept., 1959), pp. 130-132.

Priestley, J.B. "Shaw as a Social Critic." *Saturday Rev. of Literature,* vol. 29 (July 27, 1946), pp. 5-7.

Pritzker, Lee. "What Shaw Did." *Shaw Bulletin,* vol. 1 (Autumn, 1951), p. 9.

Purcell, Victor. "Shaw, Russell, Toynbee, and the Far East." *Shavian,* vol. 4 (May, 1955), pp. 15-19.

Purdom, C.B. "An Appreciation." *Drama,* vol. 20 (Spring, 1951), pp. 16-19.

Purdom, C.B. *A guide to the plays of Bernard Shaw.*

Purdom, C.B. "Shaw and Granville-Barker." *Shavian,* vol. 3 (Autumn, 1954), pp. 16-18.

Rattray, R.F. *Bernard Shaw: a chronicle.*

Rattray, R.F. "Bernard Shaw's Origins." *Q. Rev.,* vol. 288 (Jan., 1950), pp. 46-61.

Rattray, R.F. "The Shavian Religion I Believe In." *Shavian,* vol. 5 (Sept., 1955), pp. 7-9.

Rattray, R.F. "Shaw as the Sorcerer's Apprentice." *Shavian,* vol. 11 (1957), pp. 9-12.

Rattray, R.F. "The Subconscious and Shaw." *Q. Rev.,* vol. 291 (Apr., 1953), pp. 210-222.

"The Rediscovery of Bernard Shaw." *In:* Richards, Dick. *The curtain rises,* pp. 130-132.

Robinson, Lennox, ed. *Lady Gregory's journals,* pp. 119-216.

Roppen, Georg. *Evolution and poetic belief,* pp. 447-457.

Rosset, B.C. *Shaw of Dublin: the formative years.*

Russell, Bertrand. "George Bernard Shaw." *Virginia Q. Rev.,* vol. 27 (Jan., 1951), pp. 1-7.

Sadleir, Michael. "George Bernard Shaw." *Nineteenth Century,* vol. 140 (August, 1946), pp. 62-66.

Salerno, Henry F. *English drama in transition, 1880-1920,* pp. 195-200.

Schlauch, Margaret. "Symbolic Figures and the Symbolic Technique of George Bernard Shaw." *Science and Society,* vol. 21 (1957), pp. 210-221.

Sharp, William L. "The relation of dramatic structure to comedy in the plays of George Bernard Shaw." *Dissertation Abstracts,* vol. 14, 1007-1008 (Stanford University, 1954).

Sharpe, Robert Boies. *Irony in the drama,* pp. 164-176.

Shaw, George Bernard. *In:* Henderson, Archibald. *Table-talk of G.B.S.,* pp. 38-41, 60-70.

Shaw, G.B. "Mr. Shaw's Method and Secret." *Shaw Rev.,* vol. 8, no. 2 (May, 1965), pp. 65-67. (Reprinted from London *Daily Chronicle* (Apr., 30, 1898).)

Shaw, George Bernard. *The rationalization of Russia.*

Silverman, Albert H. "Bernard Shaw's political extravaganzas." Ph.D., Tulane University, 1955.

Smith, J. Percy. *The unrepentant pilgrim; a study of the development of Bernard Shaw,* pp. 199-266.

Smith, Robert M. "Modern dramatic censorship: George Bernard Shaw." *Dissertation Abstracts,* vol. 14, pp. 133-134. Indiana University, 1953.

Smith, Winifred. "Bernard Shaw and His Critics (1892-1938)." *Poet Lore,* vol. 47, no. 1 (Summer, 1941), pp. 76-83.

Speckhard, Robert R. "Shaw and Aristophanes: How the Comedy of Ideas Works." *Shaw Rev.,* vol. 8, no. 3 (Sept., 1965), pp. 82-92.

Spender, Stephen. "Riddle of Shaw." *Nation,* vol. 168 (Apr. 30, 1949), pp. 503-505.

Spenker, Lenyth. "The Dramatic Criteria of G. B. S." *Speech Monographs,* vol. 17 (Mar., 1950), pp. 24-36.

Spink, Judith B. "The Image of the Artist in the Plays of Bernard Shaw." *Shaw Rev.,* vol. 6, no. 3 (Sept., 1963), pp. 82-88.

Stanton, Stephen S. "English drama and the French well-made play." *Dissertation Abstracts,* vol. 15, 2194-95.

Stanton, Stephen S. "Shaw's Debt to Scribe." *PMLA,* vol. 76 (1961), pp. 575-585.

Stewart, J.I.M. *Eight modern writers,* pp. 122-183.

Stokes, E.E., Jr. "Jonson's 'Humour' Plays and Some Later Plays of G. B. Shaw." *Shavian,* vol. 2, no. 10 (1964), pp. 13-18.

Stokes, E.E., Jr. "Shaw and William Morris." *Shaw Bulletin,* vol. 1 (Summer, 1953), pp. 16-19.

Stoppel, Hans. "Shaw and Sainthood." *English Studies,* vol. 36 (Apr., 1955), pp. 49-63.

Styan, J.L., *The dark comedy,* 2nd ed., pp. 36, 40, 52-54, 63, 65, 70, 118, 124-130, 157-158, 169, 186, 244, 255, 290-291, 295.

Taylor, John Russell. *The rise and fall of the well-made play,* pp. 81-90.

Thompson, Alan R. *The dry mock: a study of irony in drama,* pp. 103-127.

Thompson, Alan R. "Shaw: Ironist or Paradoctor?" *Pacific Spectator,* vol. 1 (1947), pp. 113-129.

Tulane Drama Rev., vol. 5, no. 1 (Sept., 1960) pp. 3-21.

Tynan, K. *Curtains,* pp. 150-152.

Ussher, Arland. *Three great Irishmen: Shaw, Yeats, Joyce.*

Veilleux, Jere. "Shavian Drama: A Dialectical Convention for the Modern Theatre." *Twentieth Century Literature,* vol. 3, no. 4 (Jan., 1958), pp. 170-176.

Ward, A.C. *Bernard Shaw* (Longman's *Writers and Their Work* series, 1960).

Wardle, Irving. "Back to Shaw." *Listener,* vol. 75, no. 1920 (Jan. 13, 1966), pp. 56-58.

Watson, Barbara Bellow. *A Shavian guide to the intelligent woman.*

Weales, Gerald. "Edwardian Theatre and the Shadow of Shaw." *In: English Institute essays,* 1959, pp. 160-187.

Weintraub, Stanley. "The Garnetts, the Fabians, and *The Paradox Club.*" *Shaw Bulletin,* vol. 2, no. 2 (1957), pp. 9-12.

Weintraub, Stanley. "How History Gets Rewritten: Lawrence of Arabia in the Theatre." *Drama Survey,* vol. 2, no. 3 (1963), pp. 269-275.

Weintraub, Stanley. ed. "St. Pancras Manifesto." *Shaw Rev.,* vol. 3, no. 1 (1960), pp. 21-31.

Weisert, John J. "One Amongst So Many: A Minority Report from Germany." *Shaw Rev.,* vol. 7, no. 2 (1964), pp. 64-65.

West, Alick. "Debate and Comedy: A Note on the Unresolved Dissonance in Bernard Shaw's Early Plays." *Arena,* no. 1 (1950), pp. 37-41.

West, Alick. *George Bernard Shaw, "A Good Man Fallen Among Fabians."* pp. 101-105, 121-126, 142-150, 154-160.

West, E.J. "Bernard Shaw and His Critics." *Q. J. of Speech,* vol. 38 (1952), pp. 81-85.

West, E.J. "G. B. S. and the Rival Queens—Duse and Bernhardt." *Q. J. of Speech,* vol. 43 (1957), pp. 365-373.

West, E.J. "G. B. S., Music and Shakespearean Blank Verse." *Elizabethan studies and other essays in honor of George F. Reynolds,* pp. 344-356.

West, E.J. "G. B. S. on Shakespearean Production." *Studies in Philology,* vol. 45 (1948), pp. 216-245.

West, E.J. "Shaw's Criticism of Ibsen: A Reconsideration." *Univ. of Colorado Studies, Series in Language and Literature, IV* (July, 1953), pp. 101-127.

West, E.J. "Some Uncollected Shaviana on Theatre and Drama." *Shavian,* vol. 5 (Sept., 1955), pp. 24-26.

Williams, Harold. *Modern English writers,* pp. 238-247.

Williams, Raymond. *Drama from Ibsen to Eliot,* pp. 138-153.

Williams, Raymond. *Modern tragedy,* pp. 102-103.

Williamson, Audrey. *Bernard Shaw: man and writer.*

Wilson, Angus. "The Living Dead—IV Bernard Shaw." *London Mag.,* vol. 3, no. 12 (Oct., 1956), pp. 53-58.

Wilson, Colin. *Religion and the rebel,* pp. 242-289.

Wilson, Colin. "Shaw's Existentialism." *Shavian,* vol. 2, no. 1 (1960), pp. 4-6.

Wilson, Edmund. *Triple thinkers,* pp. 165-196.

Woodbridge, B.M. "Bernard Shaw's Spiritual Forbear, A. Dumas fils." *Harvard Graduate Magazine,* vol. 36 (1928), pp. 533-538.

Woodbridge, Homer. *G. B. Shaw, creative artist.*

Woolf, Leonard. "Shaw and Fabians." *New Statesman and Nation,* vol. 46 (Nov. 14, 1953), p. 601.

Woolf, Virginia. "Virginia Woolf on Shaw." *Shaw Bulletin,* vol. 1 (Jan., 1955), p. 9.

Worth, Katharine J. "Shaw and John Osborne." *Shavian,* vol. 2, no. 10 (1964), pp. 29-35.

Yeats, William Butler. "Unity of Being: Unity of Culture." Harrison, G.B. et al., eds. *Major British writers,* vol. 2, pp. 651-656.

The Admirable Bashville, or Constancy Rewarded

Burton, Richard. *Bernard Shaw, the man and the mask,* pp. 106-107.

Purdom, C.B. *A guide to the plays of Bernard Shaw,* pp. 191-194.

Androcles and the Lion

Atkinson, Brooks. *Broadway scrapbook,* pp. 261-264.

Brown, John Mason. *Seeing more things,* pp. 181-187.

Burton, Richard. *Bernard Shaw, the man and the mask,* pp. 167-173.

Eastman, Fred. *Christ in the drama,* pp. 44-54.

Ellehauge, Martin. *The position of Bernard Shaw in European drama and philosophy,* pp. 326-330, 332-335.

Ervine, St. John. *Bernard Shaw,* pp. 435-443.

Haussler, Franz. *"Androcles:* Shaw's Fable Play." *Shaw Bulletin,* vol. 1 (May, 1954), pp. 8-9.

Himelstein, Morgan Y. *Drama was a weapon, the left-wing theatre in New York, 1929-1941,* p. 108.

Kronenberger, Louis. *The thread of laughter,* pp. 260-263.

MacCarthy, Desmond. "On Bernard Shaw's *Androcles and the Lion." In:* Agate, James. *The English dramatic critics,* pp. 295-299.

Meisel, Martin. *Shaw and the nineteenth-century theatre,* pp. 324-348.

Pearson, Hesketh. "The Origins of *Androcles and the Lion." Listener* (Nov. 13, 1953).

Purdom, C.B. *A guide to the plays of Bernard Shaw,* pp. 242-245.

Stewart, J.I.M. *Eight modern writers,* pp. 166-167.

Weales, Gerald. *Religion in modern English drama,* pp. 70-71.

Williamson, Audrey. *Bernard Shaw: man and writer,* pp. 156-158.

Annajanska, the Bolshevik Empress

Chislett, William. "G.B.S., or from Bashville to Methusaleh." *In:* Chislett, William. *Moderns and near-moderns,* pp. 139-140.

Meisel, Martin. *Shaw and the nineteenth-century theatre,* p. 113.

Purdom, C.B. *A guide to the plays of Bernard Shaw,* pp. 259-260.

The Apple Cart

Bentley, Eric. *Bernard Shaw,* 2nd British ed., pp. 81, 97, 104, 141-142, 148, 153, 174.

Clurman, Harold. *Lies like truth,* pp. 142-144.

Coward, Noel. "Coward Upsets His Apple Cart." *Theatre Arts,* vol. 37 (Sept., 1953), pp. 30-32.

Croome, H. "The Show Goes on." *Spectator,* vol. 190 (June 5, 1953), p. 724.

Ervine, St. John. *Bernard Shaw,* pp. 516-518.

Harris, Frank. *Bernard Shaw,* pp. 406-408.

MacCarthy, Desmond. *Drama,* pp. 225-232.

McDowell, Frederick P. W. "The Eternal Against the Expedient: Structure and Theme in Shaw's *The Apple Cart." Modern Drama,* vol. 2, no. 2 (Sept., 1959), pp. 99-113.

Meisel, Martin. *Shaw and the nineteenth-century theatre,* pp. 399-403, 407, 439.

Morgan, Margery M. "Two Varieties of Political Drama: *The Apple Cart* and Granville-Barker's *His Majesty." Shavian,* vol. 2, no. 6 (1962), pp. 9-16.

Pearson, Hesketh. "The Origins of *The Apple Cart." Listener* (June 4, 1953).

Perry, Henry Ten Eyck. *Masters of dramatic comedy and their social themes,* pp. 400-403.

Purdom, C.B. *A guide to the plays of Bernard Shaw,* pp. 285-289.

Silverman, Albert H. "Bernard Shaw's Political Extravaganzas." *Drama Survey,* vol. 5, no. 3 (Winter, 1966-67), pp. 213-222.

Stewart, J.I.M. *Eight modern writers,* p. 182.

Styan, J.L. *The elements of drama,* pp. 101-103.

Woodbridge, H.E. *G. B. Shaw,* pp. 127-131.

Arms and the Man

Archer, William. "On George Bernard Shaw's *Arms and the Man.*" *In:* Agate, James. *The English dramatic critics,* pp. 223-228. *Also in: Theatrical world of 1894,* London. Walter Scott, 1894.

Beerbohm, Max. *"Arms and the Man* (Review)." *In:* Cassell, Richard A. *What is the play?* pp. 687-688. (From Beerbohm, Max. *Around theatres,* N.Y., Simon & Schuster, 1954.)

Beerbohm, Max. *Around theatres,* pp. 491-493.

Bentley, Eric. *Bernard Shaw,* 2nd British ed., pp. 99-100, 160, 162, 166-171.

Bentley, Eric. "The Making of a Dramatist (1892-1936)." *In:* Bogard, Travis, and Oliver, William I., eds. *Modern drama; essays in criticism,* pp. 292, 296-298. (Reprinted from Shaw's *plays,* N.Y., New American Library, 1963 (Foreword).) *In:* Corrigan, Robert, ed. *Laurel British drama: the nineteenth century,* pp. 307, 311-316, 327. *Tulane Drama Rev.,* vol. 5, no. 1 (Sept., 1960), pp. 3-21. Kaufmann, R.J. *G.B. Shaw, a collection of critical essays,* pp. 59, 62.

Brown, Jack R. "Two Notes on Shaw's *Advice to a Young Critic: You Never Can Tell* and *Arms and the Man.*" *Shaw Rev.,* vol. 7, no. 1 (1964), pp. 25-27.

Burton, Richard. *Bernard Shaw, the man and the mask,* pp. 58-65.

Cassell, Richard A. *What is the play?* pp. 31-32, 86-87.

Chesterton, Gilbert K. *George Bernard Shaw* (1910 ed.), pp. 118-123.

Chesterton, G.K. *George Bernard Shaw* (1950 ed.), pp. 114-119.

Elliott, R.C. "Shaw's Captain Bluntschli: A Latter-Day Falstaff." *Modern Language Notes,* vol. 67 (Nov., 1952), pp. 461-464.

Ervine, St. John. *Bernard Shaw,* pp. 264-269.

Henderson, A. *George Bernard Shaw,* pp. 536-543.

Meisel, Martin. *Shaw and the nineteenth-century theatre,* pp. 127-128, 134-136, 186-194, 222, 381-383.

Mills, John A. "Shaw's Linguistic Satire." *Shaw Rev.,* vol. 8, no. 1 (Jan., 1965), pp. 2-11.

Nethercot, A.H. *Men and supermen: The Shavian portrait gallery,* pp. 57-60.

Perrine, Laurence. "Shaw's *Arms and the Man.*" *Explicator,* vol. 15 (1957), Item 54.

Purdom, C.B. *A guide to the plays of Bernard Shaw,* pp. 157-163.

Quinn, Michael. "Form and Intention: A Negative View of *Arms and the Man." Critical Q.,* vol. 5 (1963), pp. 148-154.

Reinert, Otto. *Drama, an introductory anthology,* pp. 361-363.

Reinert, Otto, ed. *Modern drama; nine plays,* pp. 147-149.

Stewart, J.I.M. *Eight modern writers,* pp. 133-134.

Styan, J.L. *The elements of drama,* pp. 100-101, 169-174.

West, Alick. *George Bernard Shaw, "A Good Man Fallen Among Fabians."* pp. 80-88.

West, E.J. "'Arma Virumque' Shaw Did Not Sing." *Colorado Q.* vol. 1 (1953), pp. 267-280.

As Far As Thought Can Reach

Rankin, H.D. "Plato and Bernard Shaw, Their Ideal Communities." *Hermathena,* vol.. 93 (1959), pp. 71-77.

Augustus Does His Bit

Purdom, C.B. *A guide to the plays of Bernard Shaw,* pp. 256-257.

Back to Methuselah

Bentley Eric. *Bernard Shaw,* 2nd British ed., pp. 34, 35-37, 40-41, 43-44, 49, 57, 72, 83, 106, 111, 116, 124, 147.

Brustein, Robert. *The theatre of revolt,* pp. 195-204.

Chislett, William. "G.B.S., or from Bashville to Methusaleh." *In:* Chislett, William. *Moderns and near-moderns,* pp. 140-144.

Ellehauge, Martin. *The position of Bernard Shaw in European drama and philosophy,* pp. 274-279, 281, 283-291.

Geduld, Harry M. *"Back to Methuselah,* and the Birmingham Repertory Company." *Modern Drama,* vol. 2, (1959/60), pp. 115-129.

Geduld, H.M. "The Lineage of Lilith." *Shaw Rev.,* vol. 7, no. 2 (1964), pp. 58-61.

Geduld, H.M. "The Premiere of the Pentateuch." *California Shavian,* vol. 4 (Jan. Feb., 1963), pp. 1-17.

Hamilton, R. "Philosophy of Bernard Shaw; a Study of *Back to Methuselah." London Q. and Holborn Rev.,* vol. 170 (July, 1945), pp. 333-341.

Hobson, Harold. *Theatre,* pp. 53-54, 63-66.

Jennings, Richard. "Nearly Methuselah and Shaw versus Shake-speare." *Nineteenth Century,* vol. 140 (1946), pp. 39-40.

Knepper, Bill G. *Back to Methuselah* and the Utopian tradition." *Dissertation Abstracts,* vol. 28 (1967), 681A (Neb.).

Krutch, Joseph Wood. *"Modernism."* in *modern drama,* pp. 61-64.

Krutch, Joseph Wood. "Why not *Methuselah?"* Theatre Arts, vol. 38 (June, 1954).

Langner, Lawrence. "Shaw and *Back to Methuselah." Theatre Arts,* vol. 35 (Nov., 1951), pp. 22-23.

Meisel, Martin. *Shaw and the nineteenth-century theatre,* pp. 31, 33, 57-58, 60-61, 140, 245-246, 380-381, 396, 406-407, 412-422, 442-443.

Morgan, Margery M. *"Back to Methuselah:* The Poet and the City." *In:* Kaufmann, R.J. *G.B. Shaw, a collection of critical essays,* pp. 130-142. (From *Essays and studies,* vol. 13 (1960), pp. 82-98.)

Perry, Henry Ten Eyck. *Masters of dramatic comedy and their social themes,* pp. 393-396.

Purdom, C.B. *A guide to the plays of Bernard Shaw,* pp. 265-276.

Roppen, Georg. *Evolution and poetic belief,* pp. 371-402.

Roston, Murray. *Biblical drama in England from the Middle Ages to the present day,* pp. 257-260.

Stewart, J.I.M. *Eight modern writers,* pp. 175-179.

Weales, Gerald. *Religion in modern English drama,* pp. 71-72, 74, 79.

Williams, Raymond. *Drama from Ibsen to Eliot,* pp. 147-149.

Williamson, Audrey. *Bernard Shaw: man and writer,* pp. 176-182.

Buoyant Billions

Anonymous. "G.B.S. Writing New Play." Christian Science Monitor Magazine Section (Aug. 10, 1946), p. 14.

Grendon, Felix, *"Buoyant Billions." Shaw Bulletin,* vol. 1 (May, 1952), pp. 9-10.

Krutch, Joseph Wood. "Shaw's Last Play." *Nation,* vol. 172 (June 16, 1951), p. 565.

McDowell, Frederick P. "The World, God, and World Bettering: Shaw's *Buoyant Billions.*" *Boston Univ. Studies in English,* vol. 3 (1957), pp. 167-176.

Purdom, C.B. *A guide to the plays of Bernard Shaw,* pp. 319-322.

Shaw, G.B. "The Author Explains." *World Rev.,* vol. 7, n.s. (Sept., 1949), pp. 17-22.

Caesar and Cleopatra

Atkinson, Brooks. "About the Play." *Theatre Arts,* vol. 34 (Sept., 1950), p. 52.

Austin, Don. "Dramatic Structure in *Caesar and Cleopatra.*" *California Shavian,* vol 3. (Sept.-Oct., 1962)

Bentley, Eric. *Bernard Shaw,* 2nd British ed., pp. 10, 74, 77-79, 109, 111-113, 116, 118, 122, 160.

Bierman, Judah. *The dramatic experience,* pp. 260-262.

Brown, John Mason. "Hail, Caesar — and Cleopatra." *In* Brown, John Mason. *Dramatis personae,* pp. 136-141.

Brown, John Mason. "O Eastern Star! Shaw and Shakepeare's *Anthony and Cleopatra.*" *Saturday Rev., of Literature,* vol. 30 (Dec. 20, 1947), p. 22.

Brown, John Mason. *Still seeing things,* pp. 160-166.

Burton, Richard. *Bernard Shaw, the man and the mask,* pp. 95-100.

Carrington, Norman T. *G.B. Shaw: Caesar and Cleopatra.*

Chesterton, Gilbert K. *George Bernard Shaw,* (1910 ed.) pp. 154-170.

Chesterton, G.K. *George Bernard Shaw* (1950 ed.), pp. 148-159.

Couchman, Gordon W. "Comic Catharsis in *Caesar and Cleopatra.*" *Shaw Rev.,* vol. 3, no. 1 (1960), pp. 11-14.

Couchman, Gordon W. "Here Was a Caesar: Shaw's Comedy Today." *PMLA,* vol. 72 (1957), pp. 272-285.

Couchman, Gordon W. "Shaw, Caesar, and the Critics." *Speech Monographs,* vol. 23 (1956), pp. 262-271.

Deans, Marjorie. *Meeting at the Sphinx.*

Ellehauge, Martin. *The position of Bernard Shaw in European drama and philosophy,* pp. 337-339.

Ervine, St. John. *Bernard Shaw,* pp. 332-335.

Greenwood, Ormerod. *The playwright,* pp. 124-128.

Kronenberger, Louis. *The thread of laughter,* pp. 235-239.

Leary, Daniel J. "The Moral Dialectic in *Caesar and Cleopatra." Shaw Rev.,* vol. 5, no. 2 (May, 1962), pp. 42-53.

MacCarthy, Desmond. *Drama,* pp. 266-275.

Meisel, Martin. "Cleopatra and 'The Flight Into Egypt.'" *Shaw Rev.* vol. 7, no. 2 (1964), pp. 62-63.

Meisel, Martin. *Shaw and the nineteenth-century theatre,* pp. 114-117, 359-365, 370-371, 373-375, 378-379, 439.

Nathan, George Jean. "Two Cleopatras." *Theatre Arts,* vol. 36 (Mar., 1952), pp. 18-19.

Norwood, Gilbert. *Euripides and Shaw with other essays,* pp. 97-98.

Purdom, C.B. *A guide to the plays of Bernard Shaw,* pp. 184-188.

Reinhert, Otto, ed. *Drama; an introductory anthology* (alternate ed.), pp. 590-596.

Reinert, Otto. "Old History and New: Anachronism in *Caesar and Cleopatra." Modern Drama,* vol. 3, no. 1 (May, 1960), pp. 37-41.

Stewart, J.I.M. *Eight modern writers,* pp. 139-142.

Tynan, K. *Curtains,* pp. 8-10.

Weales, Gerald. *Religion in modern English drama,* pp. 62-63.

Whiting, George W. "The Cleopatra Rug Scene: Another Source." *Shaw Rev.* vol. 3, no. 1 (1960), pp. 15-17.

Williamson, Audrey. *Bernard Shaw: man and writer,* pp. 122-126.

Woodbridge, Homer E. *G.B. Shaw,* pp. 48-53.

Young, Stark. *Immortal shadows,* pp. 57-60.

Candida

Adams, Elsie B. "Bernard Shaw's Pre-Raphaelite Drama." *PMLA,* vol. 81, no. 5 (Oct., 1966), pp. 428-438.

Adler, Jacob H. "Ibsen, Shaw, and *Candida." J. of English and Germanic Philology,* vol. 59 (1960), pp. 50-58.

Bentley, Eric. *Bernard Shaw,* 2nd British ed., pp. 76, 108, 115, 173, 175-178, 182.

Bentley, Eric. "The Making of a Dramatist (1892-1903)." *In:* Corrigan, Robert, ed. *Laurel British drama: the nineteenth century,* pp. 320-324. *Tulane Drama Rev.,* vol. 5, no. 1 (Sept. 1960), pp. 3-21. Kaufmann, R.J. *G.B. Shaw, a collection of critical essays,* pp. 69-71. Bogard, Travis and Oliver, William I., eds. *Modern drama; essays in criticism,* pp. 304-308. (Reprinted from Shaw's *Plays,* New York, New American Library, 1963 (Foreword).)

Bentley, Eric. *The playwright as thinker,* pp. 132-136.

Burton, Richard. *Bernard Shaw, the man and the mask,* pp. 66-74. pp. 33-34, 127-128, 226-234, 241.

Miller, Nellie Burget. *The living drama,* pp. 301-302.

Mills, John A. "The Comic in Words: Shaw's Cockneys." *Drama Survey,* vol. 5, no. 2 (Summer, 1966), pp. 137-138.

Mills, John A. "Shaw's Linguistic Satire." *Shaw Rev.,* vol. 8, no. 1 (Jan., 1965), pp. 2-11.

Nethercot, Arthur H. "Shaw's Women and 'The Truth About *Candida.'" Shavian,* vol. 1 (Dec., 1953), pp. 12-13.

Nethercot, Arthur H. "The Truth about *Candida." PMLA,* vol. 64 (Sept., 1949), pp. 639-647.

Purdom, C.B. *A guide to the plays of Bernard Shaw,* pp. 164-169.

Riding, George A. "The *Candida* Secret." *Spectator,* vol. 185 (Nov. 17, 1950), p. 506.

Spink, Judith B. "The Image of the Artist in the Plays of Bernard Shaw." *Shaw Rev.,* vol. 6, no. 3 (Sept., 1963), pp. 82-88.

Stanton, Stephen S. *A Casebook on Candida.*

Stanton, Stephen S. "Shaw's Debt to Scribe." *PMLA,* vol. 76 (Dec., 1961), pp. 575-585.

Stewart, J.I.M. *Eight modern writers,* pp. 134-136.

Tynan, Kenneth. *Tynan right and left,* pp. 24-25.

West, Alick. *George Bernard Shaw, "A Good Man Fallen Among Fabians."* pp. 105-114.

Williams, Raymond. *Drama from Ibsen to Eliot,* pp. 144-147.

Woodbridge, Homer E. *G.B. Shaw,* pp. 34-40.

Young, Stark. *Immortal shadows,* pp. 193-195.

Captain Bluntschli

Elliott, Robert C. "Shaw's Captain Bluntschli: A Latter-Day Falstaff." *In:* Cassell, Richard A. *What is the play?* pp. 698-700. (From *Modern Language Notes,* vol. 67 (Nov., 1952).

Captain Brassbound's Conversion

Alexander, Doris M. "Capt. Brant and Capt. Brassbound: The Origin of an O'Neill Character." *Modern Language Notes,* vol. 74 (Apr., 1959), pp. 306-310.

Bentley, Eric. *Bernard Shaw,* 2nd British ed., pp. 74, 76-77, 78, 153, 160, 174.

Bentley, Eric. *The playwright as thinker,* pp. 136-140.

Bentley, Eric R. "The Theory and Practice of Shavian Drama." *Accent,* vol. 5, no. 1 (Autumn, 1944), pp. 5-18.

Burton, Richard. *Bernard Shaw, the man and the mask,* pp. 100-105.

Chesterton, Gilbert K. *George Bernard Shaw* (1910 ed.), pp. 151-154.

Chesterton, G.K, *George Bernard Shaw* (1950 ed.), pp. 146-148.

Mason, Michael. "Captain Brassbound and Governor Eyre." *Shavian,* vol. 2 (1963), pp. 20-22.

Meisel, Martin. *Shaw and the nineteenth-century theatre,* pp. 31-32, 206-215, 347.

Mills, John A. "The Comic in Words: Shaw's Cockneys." *Drama Survey,* vol. 5, no. 2 (Summer, 1966), pp. 139-143.

Mills, John A. "Shaw's Linguistic Satire." *Shaw Rev.,* vol. 8, no. 1 (Jan., 1965), pp. 2-11.

Purdom, C.B. *A guide to the plays of Bernard Shaw,* pp. 188-191.

Stanton, Stephen S. "Shaw's Debt to Scribe." *PMLA,* vol. 76 (Dec., 1961), pp. 575-585.

Stewart, J.I.M. *Eight modern writers,* pp. 142-143.

West, Alick. *George Bernard Shaw, "A Good Man Fallen Among Fabians."* pp. 92-95.

Woodbridge, H.E. *G.B. Shaw,* pp. 53-55.

Cymbeline Refinished

Mortimer, R. *"Geneva, Cymbeline Refinished* and *Good King Charles.* A Review." *New Statesman and Nation,* vol. 33 (May 3, 1947), p. 317.

Purdom. C.B. *A guide to the plays of Bernard Shaw,* pp. 310-311.

The Dark Lady of the Sonnets.

Burton, Richard. *Bernard Shaw, the man and the mask,* pp. 160-162.

Purdom, C.B. *A guide to the plays of Bernard Shaw,* pp. 237-238.

The Devil's Disciple

Beerbohm, Max. *Around theatres,* pp. 38-41.

Bentley, Eric. *Bernard Shaw,* 2nd British ed., pp. 74-76, 77, 78, 83, 88, 91, 104.

Bentley, Eric. "Melodrama and Education." *In:* Caputi, Anthony, ed. *Modern drama,* pp. 408-411. (From Bentley, Eric. *Bernard Shaw,* N.Y., New Directions, 1947, pp. 108-111, 115-117.)

Burton, Richard. *Bernard Shaw, the man and the mask,* pp. 89-95.

Chesterton, Gilbert K. *George Bernard Shaw* (1910 ed), pp. 147-151.

Chesterton, G.K. *George Bernard Shaw* (1950 ed.), pp. 142-146.

Cubeta, Paul M. *Modern drama for analysis,* pp. 70-81.

Ellehauge, Martin. *The position of Bernard Shaw in European drama and philosophy,* pp. 195-197, 279.

Henderson, A. *George Bernard Shaw,* pp. 445-454, 549-552.

Kronenberger, Louis. *The thread of laughter,* pp. 233-235.

Lamm, Martin. *Modern drama,* pp. 263-265.

Meisel, Martin. "Rebels and Redcoats." *In:* Caputi, Anthony, ed. *Modern drama,* pp. 411-419. (From ·Meisel, Martin. *Shaw and the nineteenth-century theater,* pp. 194-206.)

Meisel, Martin. *Shaw and the nineteenth-century theatre,* pp. 194-206, 347-348. 443-444.

Norwood, Gilbert. *Euripides and Shaw with other essays,* pp. 96-97.

Purdom, C.B. *A guide to the plays of Bernard Shaw,* pp. 178-184.

Shaw, George Bernard. "Ideals and Idealists." *In:* Caputi, Anthony, ed. *Modern drama,* pp. 392-404. (From Shaw, George Bernard. *The quintessence of Ibsenism,* London, 1891, pp. 19-30.)

Stanton, Stephen S. "Shaw's Debt to Scribe." *PLMA,* vol. 76 (Dec., 1961, pp. 575-585.

Stewart, J.I.M. *Eight modern writers,* pp. 137-139.

Weales, Gerald. *Religion in modern English drama,* p. 62.

West, Alick. *George Bernard Shaw, "A Good Man Fallen Among Fabians."* pp. 95-97.

Williamson, Audrey. *Bernard Shaw: man and writer,* pp. 119-122.

Woodbridge, H.E. *G. B. Shaw,* pp. 45-48.

The Doctor's Dilemma

Beerbohm, Max. *Around theatres,* pp. 442-446.

Burton, Richard. *Bernard Shaw, the man and the mask,* pp. 129-139.

Chesterton, Gilbert K. *George Bernard Shaw,* pp. 221-223.

Downer, Alan S. *"The Doctor's Dilemma:* Notes on the New York Theatre, 1966-67." *Q. J. of Speech,* vol. 53 (1967), pp. 213-223.

Ellehauge, Martin. *The position of Bernard Shaw in European drama and philosophy,* pp. 17, 293-294.

Ervine, St. John. *Bernard Shaw,* pp. 350-351, 406-409.

Freedman, Morris. *The moral impulse,* pp. 49-50.

Grendon, Felix. "Theatre Notes: The Phoenix's Dilemma." *Shaw Bulletin,* vol. 1 (May, 1955), pp. 22-24.

Henderson, A. *George Bernard Shaw,* pp. 606-609.

Henn, T.R. "The Shavian Machine." *In:* Kaufmann, R.J. *G.B. Shaw, a collection of critical essays,* pp. 163-165. (From Henn, T.R. *The harvest of tragedy, pp. 190-*192.)

Lid, R.W., ed. *Plays, classic and contemporary,* pp. 352 353.

McCarthy, Mary. "Shaw at the Phoenix." *Partisan Rev.,* vol. 22 (Spring, 1955), pp. 252-259.

McCarthy, Mary. *Sights and spectacles 1937-1956,* pp. 151-159.

Meisel, Martin. *Shaw and the nineteenth-century theatre,* pp. 233-239, 241, 292, 444.

O'Donnell, Norbert F. "Dr. Ridgeon's Deceptive Dilemma." *Shaw Rev.,* vol. 2, no. 7 (1959), pp. 1-5.

Purdom, C.B. *A guide to the plays of Bernard Shaw,* pp. 215-221.

Smith, J. Percy. "A Shavian Tragedy: *The Doctor's Dilemma." Univ. of Calif. Publications, English Studies,* 11 (1955), pp. 189-207.

Spink, Judith B. "The Image of the Artist in the Plays of Bernard Shaw." *Shaw Rev.,* vol. 6, no. 3 (Sept., 1963), pp. 82-88.

Stewart, J.I.M. *Eight modern writers,* pp. 163-164.

Walkley, A.B. "On Bernard Shaw's *The Doctor's Dilemma." In:* Agate, James. *The English dramatic critics,* pp. 261-264. *Also in: The Times* (Nov. 21, 1906), and *Drama and life,* by A. B. Walkley, London, Methuen & Co., 1907.

Weisert, John J. "Oh, Bottom, Thou Art Translated!" *Shaw Rev.,* vol. 3, no. 1 (1960) pp. 18-20.

Williamson, Audrey. *Bernard Shaw: man and writer,* pp. 144-147.

Woodbridge, Homer E. *G. B. Shaw,* pp. 68-72.

Fanny's First Play

Burton, Richard. *Bernard Shaw, the man and the mask,* pp. 162-167.

Carpenter, Charles. "Shaw's Cross-section of Anti-Shavian Opinion." *Shaw Rev.,* vol. 7 (1964), pp. 78-86.

Ellehauge, Martin. *The position of Bernard Shaw in European drama and philosophy,* pp. 193-194, 195, 197-198, 206.

Ervine, St. John. *Bernard Shaw,* pp. 429-435.

Meisel, Martin. *Shaw and the nineteenth-century theatre,* pp. 259-260.

Purdom, C.B. *A guide to the plays of Bernard Shaw,* pp. 238-242.

Woodbridge, Homer E. *G. B. Shaw,* pp. 83-85.

Far Fetched Fables

Cerf, B. "Trade Winds: Notices Accorded Premiere of *Far Fetched Fables., Saturday Rev. of Literature,* vol. 33 (Sept. 30, 1950), p. 4.

Meisel, Martin. *Shaw and the nineteenth-century theatre,* pp. 380, 422n, 443.

Purdom, C.B. *A guide to the plays of Bernard Shaw,* pp. 135, 323-324.

The Fascinating Foundling

Purdom, C.B. *A guide to the plays of Bernard Shaw,* pp. 230-231.

Geneva

Ervine, St. John. *Bernard Shaw,* pp. 564-568.

Henderson, A. *George Bernard Shaw,* pp. 650-656.

Meisel, Martin. *Shaw and the nineteenth-century theatre,* pp. 380-381, 399, 403, 407-409, 427.

Mortimer, R. *"Geneva, Cymbeline Refinished* and *Good King Charles. A Review."* *New Statesman and Nation,* vol. 33 (May 3, 1947), p. 317.

Pilecki, Gerard Anthony. *Shaw's Geneva.*

Purdom. C.B. *A guide to the plays of Bernard Shaw,* pp. 311-315.

Sharp, Sister M. Carona, O.S.U. "The Theme of Masks in *Geneva."* *Shaw Rev,* vol. 5, no. 3 (Sept., 1962), pp. 82-91.

Silverman, Albert H. "Bernard Shaw's Political Extravaganzas." *Drama Survey,* vol. 5, no. 3 (Winter, 1966-67), pp. 213-222.

Woodbridge, Homer E. *G.B. Shaw,* pp. 144-146.

Getting Married

Archer, William. "The First Act." *In: Play-making: a manual of craftsmanship,* pp. 132-136.

Beerbohm, Max. *Around theatres,* pp. 508-512.

Bentley, Eric. *Bernard Shaw,* 2nd British ed., pp. 81, 83, 87-90, 91-93, 96-97, 104, 148.

Burton, Richard. *Bernard Shaw, the man and the mask,* pp. 140-146.

Chesterton, Gilbert K. *George Bernard Shaw,* pp. 223-225.

Ellehauge, Martin. *The position of Bernard Shaw in European drama and philosophy,* pp. 18-20, 236-238.

Ervine, St. John. *Bernard Shaw,* pp. 421-424.

Henderson, A. *George Bernard Shaw,* pp. 609-610.

Kronenberger, Louis. *The thread of laughter,* pp. 256-260.

Meisel, Martin. *Shaw and the nineteenth-century theatre,* pp. 224, 243, 264-266, 268, 293, 303-307, 318-319, 440.

Purdom, C.B. *A guide to the plays of Bernard Shaw,* pp. 221-226.

Sharp, William. *"Getting Married:* New Dramaturgy in Comedy." *Educational Theatre J.,* vol. 11 (1959), pp. 103-109.

Solomon, Stanley J. "Theme and Structure in *Getting Married." Shaw Rev.,* vol. 5, no. 3 (Sept., 1962), pp. 92-96.

Stewart, J.I.M. *Eight modern writers,* pp. 165-166.

The Glimpse of Reality

Purdom, C.B. *A guide to the plays of Bernard Shaw,* pp. 231-232.

Great Catherine

Burton, Richard. *Bernard Shaw, the man and the mask,* pp. 183-185.

Purdom, C.B. *A guide to the plays of Bernard Shaw,* pp. 251-253.

Heartbreak House

Agate, J.E. *Alarums and excursions,* pp. 187-192.

Bentley, Eric. *Bernard Shaw,* 2nd British ed., pp. 90-91, 93-98, 115, 122, 140-141.

Brustein, Robert. "Bernard Shaw: The Face Behind the Mask." *In:* Kaufmann, R.J. *G.B. Shaw, a collection of critical essays,* pp. 113-118. (Reprinted from Brustein, Robert. *The theatre of revolt,* pp. 220-227.)

Chislett, William. "G.B.S., or from Bashville to Methusaleh." *In:* Chislett, William. *Moderns and near-moderns,* p. 139.

Clurman, Harold. "Notes for a Production of *Heartbreak House." Tulane Drama Rev.,* vol. 5, no. 3 (1961), pp. 58-67.

Coleman, D.C. "Fun and Games: Two Pictures of *Heartbreak House." Drama Survey,* vol. 5, no. 3 (Winter, 1966-67), pp. 223-236.·

Corrigan, R.W. *"Heartbreak House:* Shaw's Elegy for Europe." *Shaw Rev.* vol. 2 (Sept., 1959), pp. 2-6.

Crompton, Louis. "Shaw's *Heartbreak House." Prairie Schooner, vol.* 39, no. 1 (Spring, 1965), pp. 17-32.

Ellehauge, Martin. *The position of Bernard Shaw in European drama and philosophy,* pp. 291-292.

Ervine, St. John. *Bernard Shaw,* pp. 474-477.

Fergusson, Francis. *The idea of a theater,* pp. 194-197.

Henderson, A. *George Bernard Shaw,* pp. 625-629.

Jordan, John. "Shaw's *Heartbreak House.*" *Threshold,* vol. 1, no. 1 (1957), pp. 50-56.

Kozelka, Paul. *"Heartbreak House* Revived." *Shaw Rev.,* vol. 3, no. 1 (1960), pp. 38-39.

Kronenberger, Louis. *The thread of laughter,* pp. 266-272.

Krutch, Joseph Wood. *"Modernism" in modern drama,* pp. 58-60.

Lewis, Allan. The *contemporary theatre,* pp. 93-100.

McCarthy, Mary. *Sights and spectacles 1937-1956,* pp. 39-43.

McDowell, Frederick P.W. "Technique, Symbol, and Theme in *Heartbreak House." PMLA,* vol. 68, no. 3 (June, 1953), pp. 335-356.

Meisel, Martin. *Shaw and the nineteenth-century theatre,* pp. 20-21, 295-296, 314-323, 437-438.

Mendelsohn, Michael J. "The Heartbreak Houses of Shaw and Chekhov." *Shaw Rev.,* vol. 6, no. 3 (Sept., 1963), pp. 89-95.

Perry, Henry Ten Eyck. *Masters of dramatic comedy and their social themes,* pp. 291-393.

Purdom, C.B. *A guide to the plays of Bernard Shaw,* pp. 260-265.

Reed, Robert R. "Boss Mangan, Peer Gynt, and *Heartbreak House." Shaw Rev.,* Vol. 2, no. 7 (1959), pp. 6-12.

Stewart, J.I.M. *Eight modern writers,* pp. 169-175.

Styan, J.L. *The dark comedy,* pp. 144-146.

Styan, J.L. *The dark comedy,* 2nd ed., pp. 46, 63, 106, 128-130, 253, 271, 274-275, 281.

Tynan, K. *Curtains,* pp. 327-330.

Vidal, Gore. *Rocking the boat.* pp. 124-135. *Also in: Reporter,* vol. 21, no. 9 (Nov. 26, 1959), pp. 33-35.

Webster, Grant. "Smollett and Shaw: A Note on a Source for *Heartbreak House." Shaw Rev.,* vol. 4, no. 3 (1961), pp. 16-17.

West, Alick. *George Bernard Shaw. "A Good Man Fallen Among Fabians."* pp. 150-154.

Williamson, Audrey. *Bernard Shaw: man and writer,* pp. 170-177.

Woodbridge, Homer E. *G. B. Shaw,* pp. 102-108.

Young, Stark. "Heartbreak Houses." *In:* Freedman, Morris, ed. *Essays in the modern drama,* pp. 76-79. (Reprinted from *Immortal shadows* by Stark Young (1948).)

Young, Stark. *Immortal shadows,* pp. 206-210.

How He Lied to Her Husband.

Burton, Richard. *Bernard Shaw, the man and the mask,* pp. 74-76.

Dukore, Bernard F. "Shaw Improves Shaw." *Modern Drama,* vol. 6, no. 1 (May, 1963), pp. 26-31.

Meisel, Martin. *Shaw and the nineteenth-century theatre,* p. 233.

Purdom, C.B. *A guide to the plays of Bernard Shaw,* pp. 206-207.

In Good King Charles's Golden Days

Ervine, St. John. *Bernard Shaw,* pp. 568-570.

Henderson, A. *George Bernard Shaw,* pp. 656-660.

Meisel, Martin. *Shaw and the nineteenth-century theatre,* pp. 349, 370, 376-379.

Mortimer, R. *"Geneva, Cymbeline Refinished* and *Good King Charles.* A Review." *New Statesman and Nation,* vol. 33 (May 3, 1947), p. 317.

Purdom, C.B. *A guide to the plays of Bernard Shaw,* pp. 315-319.

O'Donnell, Norbert F. "Harmony and Discord in *Good King Charles." Shaw Bulletin,* vol. 2, no. 4 (1958), pp. 5-8.

Weales, Gerald. *Religion in modern English drama,* pp. 59, 75, 77-78.

The Inca of Perusalem

Chislett, William. "G.B.S., or from Bashville to Methusaleh." *In:* Chislett, William. *Moderns and near-moderns,* pp. 137-138.

Purdom, C.B. *A guide to the plays of Bernard Shaw,* pp. 257-259.

The Interlude at the Playhouse

Burton, Richard. *Bernard Shaw, the man and the mask,* pp. 139-140.

Matlaw, Myron. "Bernard Shaw and The Interlude at the Playhouse." *Shaw Rev.,* vol. 3, no. 2 (1960), pp. 9-17.

Purdom, C.B. *A guide to the plays of Bernard Shaw*, p. 221.

Jitta's Atonement

Bentley, Eric. *Bernard Shaw*, 2nd British ed., p. 119.

Purdom, C.B. *A guide to the plays of Bernard Shaw*, pp. 276-278.

John Bull's Other Island

Barnet, Sylvan, ed. *The genius of the Irish theater*, pp. 12-14.

Beerbohm, Max. *Around theatres*, pp. 353-357.

Bentley, Eric. *Bernard Shaw*, 2nd British ed., pp. 59, 81, 113-114, 115, 122, 138, 142-143, 148, 150.

Burton, Richard. *Bernard Shaw, the man and the mask*, pp. 114-118.

Chesterton, Gilbert K. *George Bernard Shaw*, pp. 200-203.

Gassner, John. *The theatre in our times*, pp. 387-389.

Henderson, A. *George Bernard Shaw*, pp. 618-625.

Kronenberger, Louis. *The thread of laughter*, pp. 247-250.

McDowell, Frederick P.W. "Politics, Comedy, Character and Dialectic: The Shavian World of *John Bull's Other Island.*" *PMLA*, vol. 82, no. 7 (Dec., 1967), pp. 542-553.

Meisel, Martin. *Shaw and the nineteenth-century theatre*, pp. 269-289, 290-291, 444.

Purdom, C.B. *A guide to the plays of Bernard Shaw*, pp. 201-206.

Sidnell, M.J. *"John Bull's Other Island*—Yeats and Shaw." *Modern Drama*, vol. 11, no. 3 (Dec., 1968), pp. 245-251.

Stewart, J.I.M. *Eight modern writers*, pp. 153-155.

West, Alick. *George Bernard Shaw, "A Good Man Fallen Among Fabians."* pp. 114-120.

Williamson, Audrey. *Bernard Shaw: man and writer*, pp. 137-140.

Woodbridge, Homer E. *G. B. Shaw*, pp. 64-66.

Major Barbara

Albert, Sidney P. "In More Ways than One: *Major Barbara's* Debt to Gilbert Murray." *Educational Theatre J.*, vol. 20, no. 2 (May, 1968), pp. 123-140.

Balmforth, Ramsden. *The problem-play and its influence on modern thought and life,* pp. 34-37.

Barnet, Sylvan, ed. *The genius of the later English theater,* pp. 309-312.

Beerbohm, Max. *Around theatres,* pp. 409-414.

Bentley, Eric. *Bernard Shaw,* 2nd British ed., pp. 81, 114-115, 116, 179.

Blau, Herbert. *The impossible theatre,* pp. 210-213.

Burton, Richard. *Bernard Shaw, the man and the mask,* pp. 120-128.

Chesterton, Gilbert K. *George Bernard Shaw,* pp. 177-178, 197-200.

Clurman, Harold. *Lies like truth,* pp. 144-146.

Cohn, Ruby, ed. *Twentieth-century drama,* pp. 5-6.

Crompton, Louis. *"Major Barbara:* Shaw's Challenge to Liberalism." *In:* Slote, Bernice, ed. *Literature and society,* pp. 121-141.

Dukore, Bernard F. "Toward an Interpretation of *Major Barbara."* *Shaw Rev.,* vol. 6, no. 2 (May, 1963), pp. 62-70.

Dukore, Bernard F. "The Undershaft Maxims." *Modern Drama,* vol. 9, no. 1 (May, 1966), pp. 90-100.

Ellehauge, Martin. *The position of Bernard Shaw in European drama and philosophy,* pp. 15, 24, 194-195, 199, 203-204, 221-223, 330, 332.

Ervine, St. John. *Bernard Shaw,* pp. 398-404.

Fergusson, Francis. *The idea of a theater,* pp. 192-194.

Frank, Joseph. *"Major Barbara*—Shaw's Divine Comedy." *PMLA,* vol. 71 (1956), pp. 61-74.

Frankel, Charles. "Efficient Power and Inefficient Virtue." *In:* MacIver, R. M. *Great moral dilemmas,* pp. 15-23.

Freedman, Morris. *The moral impulse,* pp. 47-48.

Henderson, A. *George Bernard Shaw,* pp. 583-587.

Irvine, William. *"Major Barbara."* *Shavian,* vol. 7 (1956), pp. 43-47.

Kaufmann, R.J. *G.B. Shaw, a collection of critical essays,* pp. 88-99. (Reprinted from *Prairie Schooner,* vol. 37, no 3 (Fall, 1963), pp. 229-244.)

Kronenberger, Louis. *The thread of laughter,* pp. 250-256.

Krutch, Joseph Wood. *"Modernism" in modern drama,* pp. 55-58.

Lamm Martin. *Modern drama,* pp. 274-277.

Lewis, Allan. *The contemporary theatre,* pp. 88-91.

Meisel, Martin. *Shaw and the nineteenth-century theatre,* pp. 32-33, 178-180, 293-303, 439, 444.

Mills, John A. "The Comic in Words: Shaw's Cockneys." *Drama Survey,* vol. 5, no. 2 (Summer, 1966), p. 143.

Nethercot, Arthur H. *"Major Barbara:* Rebuttal and Addendum." *Shaw Bulletin,* vol. 2, no. 5 (1958), pp. 20-21.

Purdom, C.B. *A guide to the plays of Bernard Shaw,* pp. 208-214.

Salerno, Henry F. *English drama in transition, 1880-1920,* pp. 200-202.

Shaw, George Bernard. "Preface to *Major Barbara." In:* Barnet, Sylvan, ed. *The genius of the later English theater,* pp. 314-348.

Stewart, J.I.M. *Eight modern writers,* pp. 155-163.

Watson, Barbara Bellow. "Sainthood for Millionaires: *Major Barbara." Modern Drama,* vol. 11, no. 3 (Dec., 1968), pp. 227-244.

Weales, Gerald. *Religion in modern English drama,* pp. 65-69.

West, Alick. *George Bernard Shaw, "A Good Man Fallen Among Fabians."* pp. 127-141.

Williamson, Audrey. *Bernard Shaw: man and writer,* pp. 140-143.

Woodbridge, Homer E. *G.B. Shaw,* pp. 66-68.

Man and Superman

Barzun, J. "In Hell Again." *Shaw Society Bulletin,* vol. 48 (Mar., 1953), pp. 11-13.

Beerbohm, Max. *Around theatres,* pp. 268-272.

Bentley, Eric. *Bernard Shaw,* 2nd British ed., pp. 15, 34-40, 44-45, 49, 59, 79, 81, 83, 91, 104-108, 112, 114, 116, 124, 138, 142, 160, 168, 170-171, 181-182.

Bentley, Eric. "The Making of a Dramatist (1892-1903)." *In:* Bogard, Travis, and Oliver, William I., ed. *Modern drama; essays in criticism,* pp. 298-301, 311-312. (Reprinted from Shaw's *Plays,* N.Y., New American Library, 1963 (Foreword).) *Tulane Drama Rev.,* vol. 5, no. 1 (Sept., 1960), pp. 3-21. Kaufmann, R.J. *G.B. Shaw, a collection of critical essays,* pp. 64-66, 74-75.

Blanch, Robert L. "The Myth of Don Juan in *Man and Superman.*" *Revue des Langues Vivantes* (Bruxelles), vol. 33 (1967), pp. 158-163.

Brower, R.A. *"Man and Superman." In:* Harrison, G. B., ed. Major *British writers,* vol. 2, pp. 535-537.

Brown, John Mason. "Progress and the Superman." *In:* Brown, John Mason. *Dramatis personae,* pp. 121-135.

Brown, John Mason. *Seeing more things,* pp. 90-91, 188-199.

Brown, John Mason. "What, Shaw Again?" *Saturday Rev. of Literature,* vol. 34 (Nov. 10, 1951), pp. 22ff.

Brustein, Robert. "Bernard Shaw: The Face Behind the Mask." *In:* Kaufmann, R.J. *G. B. Shaw, a collection of critical essays,* pp. 108-113. (Reprinted from Brustein, Robert. *The theatre of revolt,* pp. 213-220.)

Burton, Richard. *Bernard Shaw, the man and the mask,* pp. 108-114.

Chesterton, Gilbert K. *George Bernard Shaw,* pp. 196, 203-221.

Cohn, Ruby. "Hell on the Twentieth-Century Stage." *Wisconsin Studies in Contemporary Literature,* vol. 5, no. 1 (Winter-Spring, 1964), pp. 49-50.

Ellehauge, Martin. *The position of Bernard Shaw in European drama and philosophy,* pp. 20, 29, 193, 208-214, 272-274, 280-283.

Freedman, Morris. *The moral impulse,* pp. 51-54.

Gassner, John. "Puritan in Hell." *Theatre Arts,* vol. 36 (Apr., 1952), pp. 67-70. (Reprinted in *Shaw Society Bulletin,* vol. 47 (Dec., 1952), pp. 7-14.)

Grendon, Felix. "The Quartette in John Tanner's Dream." *Shaw Bulletin,* vol. 1 (Summer, 1953), pp. 21-23.

Henderson, A. *George Bernard Shaw,* pp. 578-583.

Irvine, William. *"Man and Superman.* A Step in Shavian Disillusionment." *Huntington Library Q.,* vol. 10, no. 2 (Feb., 1947), pp. 209-224.

Kronenberger, Louis. *The thread of laughter,* pp. 239-247.

Lamm, Martin. *Modern drama,* pp. 271-274.

Leary, Daniel J. "Shaw's Use of Stylized Characters and Speech in *Man and Superman.*" *Modern Drama,* vol. 5, no. 4 (Feb., 1963), pp. 477-490.

Lewis, Allan. *The contemporary theatre,* pp. 87-88.

McDowell, F.P.W. "Heaven, Hell, and Turn-of-the-Century London: Reflections upon Shaw's *Man and Superman.*" *Drama Survey,* vol. 2 (1962), pp. 245-268.

Meisel, Martin. *Shaw and the nineteenth-century theatre,* pp. 32-33, 35, 46-47, 50, 56-57, 160-161, 168-169, 177-183, 218-219, 444-445.

Nathan, George Jean. *"Don Juan in Hell."* *Theatre Arts,* vol. 36 (Jan., 1952), p. 80.

Nethercot, Arthur H. *Men and supermen; the Shavian portrait gallery,* pp. 90-94, 135-136, 278-282.

Perry, Henry Ten Eyck. *Masters of dramatic comedy and their social themes,* pp. 379-381.

Purdom, C.B. *A guide to the plays of Bernard Shaw,* pp. 195-201.

Roppen, Georg. *Evolution and poetic belief,* pp. 352-371.

Spink, Judith B. "The Image of the Artist in the Plays of Bernard Shaw." *Shaw Rev.,* vol. 6, no. 3 (Sept., 1963), pp. 82-88.

Stanton, Stephen S. "Shaw's Debt to Scribe. *PMLA,* vol. 76 (Dec., 1961), pp. 575-585.

Stewart, J.I.M. *Eight modern writers,* pp. 143-153.

Styan, J.L. *The dark comedy,* 2nd ed., pp. 29, 46, 124-125, 128, 248, 249.

Weales, Gerald. *Religion in modern English drama,* pp. 63-65.

West, Alick. *George Bernard Shaw, "A Good Man Fallen Among Fabians."* pp. 97-101.

Williamson, Audrey. *Bernard Shaw: man and writer,* pp. 129-134, 136-137.

Woodbridge, Homer E. *G. B. Shaw,* pp. 56-63.

Worthington, Mabel Parker. "Don Juan: theme and development in the nineteenth century." *Dissertation Abstracts,* vol. 13 (1953), 399.

The Man of Destiny

Bentley, Eric. *Bernard Shaw,* 2nd British ed., pp. 72, 109, 110-111, 160.

Burton, Richard. *Bernard Shaw, the man and the mask,* pp. 82-89.

Chesterton, Gilbert K. *George Bernard Shaw* (1910 ed.), pp. 130-131.

Ervine, St. John. *Bernard Shaw,* pp. 288-292.

Henderson, A. *George Bernard Shaw,* pp. 546-548.

Meisel, Martin. *Shaw and the nineteenth-century theatre,* pp. 127, 134, 355-359, 439-440.

Purdom, C.B. *A guide to the plays of Bernard Shaw,* pp. 169-172.

The Millionairess

Bentley, Eric R. *Dramatic event,* pp. 50-53.

Brown, John Mason. "Katherine Without Petruchio." *Saturday Rev., of Literature,* vol. 35 (Nov. 1, 1952), pp. 24-25.

Ervine, St. John. *Bernard Shaw,* pp. 558-563.

Meisel, Martin. *Shaw and the nineteenth-century theatre,* pp. 161, 175, 179, 247, 423.

Purdom, C.B. *A guide to the plays of Bernard Shaw,* pp. 306-310.

Tynan, K. *Curtains,* pp. 26-28.

Misalliance

Beerbohm, Max. *Around theatres,* pp. 561-565.

Bentley, Eric. *Bernard Shaw,* 2nd British ed., pp. 87, 91, 92-93, 96-97, 148, 154.

Burton, Richard. *Bernard Shaw, the man and the mask,* pp. 157-160.

Ervine, St. John. *Bernard Shaw,* pp. 427-429.

Gassner, John. *The theatre in our times,* pp. 163-169.

Gassner, John. "When Shaw Boils the Pot: *Misalliance."* *Theatre Arts,* vol. 37 (July, 1953), pp. 63-64.

Meisel, Martin. *Shaw and the nineteenth-century theatre,* pp. 36, 60, 106, 160-161, 308-311, 307-314, 318-319, 439.

Purdom, C.B. *A guide to the plays of Bernard Shaw,* pp. 233-237.

Sharp, William L. *"Misalliance:* An Evaluation." *Educational Theatre J.,* vol. 8 (1956), pp. 9-16.

Stewart, J.I.M. *Eight modern writers,* pp. 165-166.

Woodbridge, Homer E. *G. B. Shaw,* pp. 74-79.

Mrs. Warren's Profession

Beerbohm, Max. *Around theatres,* pp. 191-195.

Beerbohm, Max. "Mr. Shaw's Profession." *Shaw Rev.,* vol. 5, no. 1 (Jan., 1962), pp. 5-9.

Bentley, Eric. *Bernard Shaw,* 2nd British ed., pp. 64, 69, 71-73, 114, 147, 160, 173, 179-181.

Bentley, Eric. "The Making of a Dramatist." *In:* Bogard, Travis, and Oliver, William I., ed., *Modern drama; essays in criticism,* pp. 308-310. (Reprinted from Shaw's *Plays,* New York, New American Library, 1963 (Foreword). Corrigan, Robert, ed. *Laurel British drama; the nineteenth century,* pp. 324-326. Kaufmann, R.J. *G.B. Shaw, a collection of critical essays,* pp. 72-73.)

Berst, Charles A. "Propaganda and Art in *Mrs. Warren's Profession."* ELH, vol. 33, no. 3 (Sept., 1966), pp. 390-404.

Block, A. *Changing world in plays and theatre,* pp. 49-52.

Bullough, Geoffrey. "Literary Relations of Shaw's Mrs. Warren." *Philological Q.,* vol. 12 (1962), pp. 339-358.

Burton, Richard. *Bernard Shaw, the man and the mask,* pp. 49-57.

Chesterton, Gilbert K. *George Bernard Shaw,* pp. 137-146.

Ellehauge, Martin. *The position of Bernard Shaw in European drama and philosophy,* pp. 202-206.

Ervine, St. John. *Bernard Shaw,* pp. 251-256.

Harris, Frank. *Bernard Shaw,* pp. 176-181.

Henderson, A. *George Bernard Shaw,* pp. 460-465.

Henn, T.R. "The Shavian Machine." *In:* Kaufmann, R.J. *G.B. Shaw, a collection of critical essays,* pp. 165-166. (From Henn, R.R. *The harvest of tragedy,* pp. 192-193.)

Kornbluth, Martin L., "Two Fallen Women: Paula Tanqueray and Kitty Warren." *Shavian,* no. 14 (1959), pp. 14-15.

Lamm, Martin. *Modern drama,* pp. 259-261.

"The Limit of Stage Indecency" — Shaw's *Mrs. Warren's Profession. In:* Moses Montrose J. *The American theatre as seen by its critics, 1752-1934,* pp. 163-166. (Reprinted from *The New York Herald,* Oct. 31, 1905.)

Meisel, Martin. *Shaw and the nineteenth-century theatre,* pp. 36, 52-54, 123, 127-131, 133-138, 141-159.

Nethercot, Arthur. "The Vivie-Frank Relationship in *Mrs. Warren's Profession." Shavian,* no. 15 (1959), pp. 7-9.

Purdom, C.B. *A guide to the plays of Bernard Shaw,* pp. 152-157.

Sainer, Arthur. *The sleepwalker and the assassin, a view of the contemporary theatre,* pp. 78-80.

Stewart, J.I.M. *Eight modern writers,* pp. 130-133.

Strozier, Robert. "The Undramatic Dramatist: Mrs. Warren's Shaw." *Shavian,* vol. 3, no. 2 (Summer, 1965), pp. 11-14.

Wellwarth, George. "Mrs. Warren Comes to America; or the Blue-noses, the Politicians and the Procurers." *Shaw Rev.,* vol. 2 (May, 1959), pp. 8-16.

West, Alick. *George Bernard Shaw, "A Good Man Fallen Among Fabians."* pp. 55-66.

Williamson, Audrey. *Bernard Shaw: man and writer,* pp. 111-112.

Woodbridge, Homer E. *G. B. Shaw,* pp. 28-30.

The Music Cure

Burton, Richard. *Bernard Shaw, the man and the mask,* pp. 185-188.

Purdom C.B. *A guide to the plays of Bernard Shaw,* pp. 253-254.

O'Flaherty, V.C.

Chislett, William. "G.B.S., or from Bashville to Methusaleh." *In:* Chislett, William. *Moderns and near-moderns,* p. 138.

Purdom, C.B. *A guide to the plays of Bernard Shaw,* pp. 254-256.

On the Rocks

Block, Anita. *The changing world in plays and theatre,* pp. 52-57.

Ervine, St. John. *Bernard Shaw,* pp. 533-535, 551-555.

Himelstein, Morgan Y. *Drama was a weapon, the left-wing theatre in New York 1929-1941,* pp. 106-107.

Hummert, Paul A. "Bernard Shaw's *On the Rocks." Drama Critique,* vol. 2, no. 1 (Feb., 1959), pp. 34-41.

Meisel, Martin. *Shaw and the nineteenth-century theatre,* pp. 380, 403, 405-406, 427.

McDowell, Frederick P.W. "Crisis and Unreason: Shaw's *On the Rocks." Educational Theatre J.,* vol, 13 (1961), pp. 162-200.

O'Casey, Sean. "G.B.S. Speaks Out of the Whirlwind." *In:* O'Casey, Sean. *Blasts and benedictions,* pp. 198-200. (From *The Listener,* (Mar. 7, 1934).)

Purdom, C.B. *A guide to the plays of Bernard Shaw,* pp. 295-299.

Silverman, Albert H. "Bernard Shaw's Political Extravaganzas." *Drama Survey,* vol. 5, no. 3 (Winter, 1966-67), pp. 213-222.

Stewart, J.I.M. *Eight modern writers,* p. 182.

Woodbridge, Homer E. *G. B. Shaw,* pp. 134-136.

Overruled

Burton, Richard. *Bernard Shaw, the man and the mask,* pp. 173-176.

Meisel, Martin. *Shaw and the nineteenth-century theatre,* pp. 55, 224, 243, 260-263, 267.

Purdom, C.B. *A guide to the plays of Bernard Shaw,* pp. 245-246.

Passion, Poison, and Petrifaction, or The Fatal Gazogene

Burton, Richard. *Bernard Shaw, the man and the mask,* pp. 119-120.

Purdom, C.B. *A guide to the plays of Bernard Shaw,* pp. 214-215.

The Philanderer

Beerbohm, Max. *Around theatres,* pp. 449-451.

Burton, Richard. *Bernard Shaw, the man and the mask,* pp. 45-49.

Chesterton, Gilbert K. *George Bernard Shaw* (1910 ed.), pp. 131-134.

Ellehauge, Martin. *The position of Bernard Shaw in European drama and philosophy,* pp. 210-212.

Ervine, St. John. *Bernard Shaw,* pp. 327-332.

Harris, Frank. *Bernard Shaw,* pp. 160-161.

Henderson, A. *George Bernard Shaw,* pp. 529-530.

Meisel, Martin. *Shaw and the nineteenth-century theatre,* pp. 29, 52, 96, 127-128, 132-134, 251-254.

Purdom, C.B. *A guide to the plays of Bernard Shaw,* pp. 147-152.

Smith, J. Percy. *The unrepentant pilgrim; a study of the development of Bernard Shaw,* pp. 165-197.

Stewart, J.I.M. *Eight modern writers,* pp. 129-130.

Tyson, Brian. "One Man and His Dog: A Study of a Deleted Draft of Bernard Shaw's *The Philanderer." Modern Drama,* vol. 10, no. 1 (May, 1967), pp. 69-78.

Williams, Raymond. *Drama from Ibsen to Eliot,* pp. 142-144.

Press Cuttings

Burton, Richard. *Bernard Shaw, the man and the mask,* pp. 153-157.

Purdom, C.B. *A guide to the plays of Bernard Shaw,* pp. 226-228.

Pygmalion

Adams, Elsie B. "Bernard Shaw's Pre-Raphaelite Drama." *PMLA,* vol 81, no. 5 (Oct., 1966), pp. 435-436.

Bentley, Eric. *Bernard Shaw,* 2nd British ed., pp. 82-87, 107, 114, 147, 179, 181-182.

Bentley, Eric. "The Making of a Dramatist." *In:* Kaufmann, R.J. *G.B. Shaw, a collection of critical essays,* pp. 73-74.

Burton, Richard. *Bernard Shaw, the man and the mask,* pp. 176-183.

Crane, Milton. *"Pygmalion:* Bernard Shaw's Dramatic Theory and Practice." *PMLA,* vol. 66 (Dec., 1951), pp. 879-885.

Crompton, Louis. "Improving *Pygmalion." Prairie Schooner,* vol. 41, no. 1 (Spring, 1967), pp. 73-83.

Drew, Arnold P. *"Pygmalion* and Pickwick." *Notes and Queries,* n.s., vol. 2 (1955), pp. 221-22.

Ervine, St. John. *Bernard Shaw,* pp. 457-460.

Henderson, A. *George Bernard Shaw,* pp. 614-617.

Freedman, Morris. *The moral impulse,* pp. 48-49, 60-61.

Kronenberger, Louis. *The thread of laughter,* pp. 263-266.

Lauter, Paul. *"Candida* and *Pygmalion:* Shaw's Subversion of Stereotypes." *Shaw Rev.,* vol. 3, no. 3 (1960), pp. 14-19.

Matlaw, Myron. "The Denouement of *Pygmalion." Modern Drama,* vol. 1, no. 1 (May, 1958), pp. 29-34.

Meisel, Martin. *Shaw and the nineteenth-century theatre,* pp. 169-177.

Mills, John A. "The Comic in Words: Shaw's Cockneys." *Drama Survey,* vol. 5, no. 2 (Summer, 1966), pp. 143-149.

O'Donnell, Norbert F. "On the 'Unpleasantness' of *Pygmalion." Shaw Bulletin,* vol. 1 (May, 1955), pp. 7-10.

Purdom, C.B. *A guide to the plays of Bernard Shaw,* pp. 247-251.

Roll-Hansen, Diderik. "Shaw's *Pygmalion:* The Two Versions of 1916 and 1941." *Rev. of English Literature* (Leeds), vol. 8, no. 3 (1967), pp. 81-90.

Solomon, Stanley J. "The Ending of *Pygmalion:* A Structural View." *Educational Theatre J.,* vol. 16 (1964), pp. 59-63.

Stewart, J.I.M. *Eight modern writers,* pp. 167-169.

Styan, J.L. *The dark comedy,* 2nd ed., pp. 117, 127-128, 261.

Styan, J.L. *The elements of drama,* pp. 87-92.

Weissman, Philip. *Creativity in the theater,* pp. 146-170.

Williamson, Audrey. *Bernard Shaw: man and writer,* pp. 168-170.

Woodbridge, Homer E. *G. B. Shaw,* pp. 87-89.

Saint Joan

Austin, Don. "Comedy Through Tragedy: Dramatic Structure in *Saint Joan." Shaw Rev.,* vol. 8, no. 2 (May, 1965), pp. 52-62.

Ayling, Ronald. "The Ten Birthplaces of *Saint Joan:* a Letter from G. B. S." *Shaw Rev.,* vol. 7, no. 1 (1964), p. 24.

Bentley, Eric. *Bernard Shaw,* 2nd British ed., pp. xviii, 97, 101, 109, 115-118, 121-122, 182.

Blankenagel, J.C. "Shaw's *St. Joan* and Schiller's *Jungfrau von Orleans." In:* Wagenknecht, E. C., ed. *Joan of Arc,* pp. 279-292.

Boas, F.S. "Joan of Arc in Shakespeare, Schiller, and Shaw." *Shakespeare Q.,* vol. 2 (Jan., 1951), pp. 35-45.

Bosler, Jean. "Was Joan of Arc Charles VII's Sister?" *Chamber's J.,* vol. 7 (1954), pp. 756-776.

Brown, John Mason. "Miss Cornell's *Saint Joan.*" *In:* Brown, J.M. *Two on the aisle,* pp. 102-106.

Brown, John Mason. "The Prophet and the Maid." *In:* Brown, John Mason. *Dramatis personae,* pp. 141-148.

Campbell, Douglas. "Canadian Players on the Snowplow Circuit." *Theatre Arts,* vol. 39 (Apr., 1955), pp. 71-73. Appendix by Ann Casson, reprinted as *"Saint Joan* of the Snows." *Shavian,* vol. 5 (Sept., 1955), pp. 19-21.

— Carrington, Norman T. *G. B. Shaw: Saint Joan.*

Clurman, Harold. *Lies like truth,* pp. 138-142.

Connolly, Thomas E. "Shaw's *Saint Joan.*" *Explicator,* vol. 14 (1955), Item 18.

Cowell, Raymond. *Twelve modern dramatists,* pp. 49-50.

Eastman, Fred. *Christ in the drama,* pp. 154-160.

Eells, G. "Third *Saint Joan.*" *Theatre Arts,* vol. 35 (Nov., 1951), pp. 32-33.

Ellehauge, Martin. *The position of Bernard Shaw in European drama and philosophy,* pp. 331, 335-337, 339.

Ervine, St. John. *Bernard Shaw,* pp. 496-504.

Fielden, John. "Shaw's *Saint Joan* as Tragedy." Twentieth *Century Literature,* vol. 3, no. 2 (July, 1957), pp. 59-67.

Gassner, John. *The theatre in our times,* pp. 143-147.

Gorelik, Mordecai. "Metaphorically Speaking." *Theatre Arts,* vol. 38 (Nov., 1954), pp. 78-80.

Griffin, Alice. "The New York Critics and *Saint Joan.*" *Shaw Bulletin,* vol. 1 (Jan., 1955), pp. 10-15.

Hamilton, Clayton. *Conversations on contemporary drama,* pp. 42-48.

Harris, Frank. *Bernard Shaw,* pp. 371-379.

Henderson, A. *George Bernard Shaw,* pp. 598-604.

Henn, T.R. *The harvest of tragedy,* pp. 193-195.

Henn, T.R. "The Shavian Machine." *In:* Kaufmann, R.J. *G.B. Shaw, a collection of critical essays,* pp. 166-169. (From Henn, T.R. *The harvest of tragedy.*)

Hobson, Harold. *Theatre,* pp. 173-175.

Honan, William. "A Presentational *Saint Joan." Shaw Bulletin,* vol. 1 (Jan., 1955), pp. 19-21.

Kronenberger, Louis. *The thread of laughter,* pp. 272-277.

Lamm, Martin. *Modern drama,* pp. 280-283.

Landsdale, Nelson. "Joans of London." *Theatre Arts,* vol. 39 (Sept., 1955), pp. 70-71.

Leary, Daniel J. "The Rest Could Not Be Silence." *Independent Shavian,* vol. 3, no. 3 (Spring, 1965), pp. 40-42.

MacCarthy, Desmond. *Drama,* pp. 276-285.

Martz, Louis L. "The Saint as Tragic Hero: *St. Joan* and *Murder in the Cathedral." In:* Brooks, Cleanth, ed. *Tragic themes in Western literature,* pp. 150-177. Kaufmann, R.J. *G.B. Shaw, a collection of critical essays,* pp. 143-161.

Meirow, Herbert E. "A Modern Euripedes." *Sewanee Rev.,* vol. 36, no. 1 (Jan., 1928), pp. 24-26.

Meisel, Martin. *Shaw and the nineteenth-century theatre,* pp. 50-52, 365-370, 372-373, 438-439, 446.

Perry, Henry Ten Eyck. *Masters of dramatic comedy and their social themes,* pp. 396-400.

Purdom, C.B. *A guide to the plays of Bernard Shaw,* pp. 278-285.

Rosselli, J. "Right Joan and the Wrong One." *Twentieth Century,* vol. 157 (Apr., 1955), pp. 374-383.

Shaw, George Bernard. *In:* Henderson, Archibald. *Table-talk of G.B.S., pp. 32-*36.

Shaw, G.B. *"Saint Joan." Listener* (Jan. 14, 1954), pp. 79-81. (Reprinted from *Listener* (1931).)

Solomon, Stanley J. "*Saint Joan* as Epic Tragedy." *Modern Drama,* vol. 6, no. 4 (Feb., 1964), pp. 437-449.

Stewart, J.I.M. *Eight modern writers,* pp. 179-182.

Stokes, Sewell. "Shaw, Frank Harris and *Saint Joan." John O'London's Weekly* (May 28, 1954).

Styan, J.L. *The dark comedy,* 2nd ed., pp. 4, 126-127, 128, 149, 186, 253, 281.

Styan, J.L. *The elements of drama,* pp. 146-148.

Weales, Gerald. *Religion in modern English drama,* pp. 72-74, 78.

Weintraub, Stanley. "Bernard Shaw's Other *Saint Joan." Shavian,* vol. 2, no. 10 (1964), pp. 7-13. *South Atlantic Q.,* vol. 64 (1965), pp. 194-205.

West, Alick. *George Bernard Shaw, "A Good Man Fallen Among Fabians."* pp. 160-166.

West, E.J. *"Saint Joan: A Mod*ern Classic Reconsidered." *Q. J. of Speech,* vol. 40 (Oct., 1954), pp. 249-259.

Williams, Raymond. *Drama from Ibsen to Eliot,* pp. 149-152.

Williams, Raymond. *Modern tragedy,* pp. 102-103.

Williamson, Audrey. *Bernard Shaw: man and writer,* pp. 186-190.

Witman, Wanda. "Shaw and Shakespeare on Saint Joan." *Independent Shavian,* vol. 2 (1963), p. 6.

Woodbridge, Homer E. *G. B. Shaw,* pp. 116-126.

Shakes Versus Shav

Douglas, James. *"Shakes versus Shav:* Battle Across the Centuries." *UNESCO Courier,* vol. 8 (June, 1955), pp. 8-9.

Jennings, Richard. "Nearly Methuselah, and Shaw vs. Shakespeare." *Nineteenth Century and After,* vol. 140 (July, 1946), pp. 39-40.

Purdom, C.B. *A guide to the plays of Bernard Shaw,* pp. 322-323.

The Shewing Up of Blanco Posnet

Balmforth, Ramsden. *The problem-play and its influence on modern thought and life,* pp. 94-108.

Burton, Richard. *Bernard Shaw, the man and the mask,* pp. 147-153.

Dorcey, Donal. "The Big Occasions." *In:* McCann, Sean, ed. *The story of the Abbey Theatre,* pp. 142-148.

Ellehauge, Martin. *The position of Bernard Shaw in European drama and philosophy,* pp. 279-281.

Gregory, Isabella Augusta (Lady). *Our Irish theatre,* pp. 140-168.

Henderson, A. *George Bernard Shaw,* pp. 587-591.

Laurence, Dan H. "The *Blanco Posnet* Controversy." *Shaw Bulletin,* vol. 1 (Jan., 1955), pp. 1-9.

Meisel, Martin. *Shaw and the nineteenth-century theatre,* pp. 215-222, 347.

"The Nation on *"Blanco Posnet." In:* Gregory, Isabella Augusta (Lady). *Our Irish theatre,* pp. 267-274.

Purdom, C.B. *A guide to the plays of Bernard Shaw,* pp. 228-230.

Shaw, George Bernard. "Letter from W.G. Bernard Shaw to Lady Gregory after the Production of *Blanco Posnet. In:* Gregory, Isabella Augusta (Lady). *Our Irish theatre,* pp. 274-279.

Stewart, J.I.M. *Eight modern writers,* pp. 164-165.

Weales, Gerald. *Religion in modern English drama,* pp. 69-70.

The Simpleton of the Unexpected Isles

Anonymous. "Desperate Remedies." *New Statesman and Nation,* vol. 29 (Mar. 24, 1945), pp. 187-188.

Dukore, Bernard F. "Shaw's Doomsday." *Educational Theatre J.,* vol. 19, no. 1 (Mar., 1967), pp. 61-71.

Ervine, St. John. *Bernard Shaw,* pp. 556-558.

Henderson, A. *George Bernard Shaw,* pp. 639-643.

Himelstein, Morgan Y. *Drama was a weapon, the left-wing theatre in New York 1929-1941,* pp. 134-135.

McDowell, Frederick P.W. "Spiritual and Political Reality: *The Simpleton of the Unexpected Isles." Modern Drama,* vol. 3, no. 2 (Sept., 1960), pp. 196-210.

Meisel, Martin. *Shaw and the nineteenth-century theatre,* pp. 380, 383, 403, 410, 423-427, 445.

Purdom, C.B. *A guide to the plays of Bernard Shaw,* pp. 300-304.

Silverman, Albert H. "Bernard Shaw's Political Extravaganzas." *Drama Survey,* vol. 5, no. 3 (Winter, 1966-67), pp. 213-222.

Stewart, J.I.M. *Eight modern writers,* p. 182.

Weales, Gerald. *Religion in modern English drama,* pp. 76-77.

Woodbridge, Homer E. *G. B. Shaw,* pp. 140-142.

The Six of Calais

Purdom, C.B. *A guide to the plays of Bernard Shaw,* pp. 304-306.

Too True To Be Good

Anderson, John. "Shaw's *Too True to be Good."* In: Moses, Montrose J. *The American theatre as seen by its critics, 1752-1934,* pp. 283-286. (Reprinted from *The Arts Weekly* (Apr. 16, 1932).)

Brustein, Robert. *Seasons of discontent,* pp. 143-144.

Ervine, St. John. *Bernard Shaw,* pp. 526-529.

Henderson, A. *George Bernard Shaw,* pp. 632-634.

McDowell, Frederick P.W. "The Pentacostal Flame and the Lower Centers: *Too True To Be Good." Shaw Rev.,* vol. 2 (Sept., 1959), pp. 27-38.

Meisel, Martin. *Shaw and the nineteenth-century theatre,* pp. 247, 380, 399, 403-405, 427, 439, 440.

O'Casey, Sean. "G.B.S. Speaks Out of the Whirlwind." *In:* O'Casey, Sean. *Blasts and benedictions,* pp. 195-198. (From *The Listener,* (Mar. 7, 1934).)

Purdom, C.B. *A guide to the plays of Bernard Shaw,* pp. 290-293.

Silverman, Albert H. "Bernard Shaw's Political Extravaganzas." *Drama Survey,* vol. 5, no. 3 (Winter, 1966-67), pp. 213-222.

Stewart, J.I.M. *Eight modern writers,* p. 182.

Weales, Gerald. *Religion in modern English drama,* pp. 75-76.

Weintraub, Stanley. "The Two Sides of Lawrence of Arabia: Aubrey and Meek." *Shaw Rev.,* vol. 7, no. 2 (May, 1964), pp. 54-57.

Williamson, Audrey. *Bernard Shaw: man and writer,* pp. 198-202.

Village Wooing

Purdom, C.B. *A guide to the plays of Bernard Shaw,* pp. 293-295.

Why She Would Not

Purdom, C.B. *A guide to the plays of Bernard Shaw,* pp. 324-326.

Widowers' Houses

Archer, William, and Bernard Shaw. *"Widowers' Houses:* A Collaboration (1893)." *In:* Cole, Toby, ed. *Playwrights on playwriting,* pp. 193-200. (Reprinted from Bernard Shaw. *Prefaces* (London: Constable & Co. Ltd., 1934), pp. 667-71.)

Bentley, Eric. *Bernard Shaw,* 2nd British ed., pp. 46, 69-70, 72, 73, 104, 163-166, 179.

Bentley, Eric. "The Making of a Dramatist." *In:* Bogard, Travis, and Oliver, William I., eds. *Modern drama; essays in criticism,* pp. 293-296. (Reprinted from Shaw's *Plays,* New York, New American Library, 1963 (Foreword). Corrigan, Robert, ed. *Laurel British drama: the nineteenth century,* pp. 308-311. Kaufmann, R.J. *G.B. Shaw, a collection of critical essays,* pp. 60-63.)

Burton, Richard. *Bernard Shaw, the man and the mask,* pp. 39-45.

Chesterton, Gilbert K. *George Bernard Shaw* (1910 ed.), pp. 135-137.

Ellehauge, Martin. *The position of Bernard Shaw in European drama and philosophy,* pp. 192, 200-202.

Ervine, St. John. *Bernard Shaw,* pp. 244-250.

Harris, Frank. *Bernard Shaw,* pp. 155-160.

Lewis, Allan. *The contemporary theatre,* pp. 80-83.

Meisel, Martin. *Shaw and the nineteenth-century theatre,* pp. 29-30, 32, 37, 89, 124, 134-138, 161-168.

Purdom, C.B. *A guide to the plays of Bernard Shaw,* pp. 143-147.

Shattuck, Charles H. "Bernard Shaw's 'Bad Quarto.'" *In:* Illinois University Dept. of English. *Studies by members of the English Department, University of Illinois, in memory of John Jay Parry,* pp. 170-182. *J. of English and Germanic Philology,* vol. 54 (Oct., 1955), pp. 651-663.

Stewart, J.I.M. *Eight modern writers,* pp. 127-129.

West, Alick. *George Bernard Shaw, "A Good Man Fallen Among Fabians."* pp. 48-54.

Woodbridge, Homer E. *G. B. Shaw,* pp. 25-27.

You Never Can Tell

Burton, Richard. *Bernard Shaw, the man and the mask,* pp. 76-82.

Chesterton, Gilbert K. *George Bernard Shaw* (1910 ed.), pp. 134-135.

Coxe, Louis O. *"You Never Can Tell:* G. B. Shaw Reviewed." *Western Humanities Rev.,* vol. 9 (1955), pp. 313-325.

Henderson, A. *George Bernard Shaw,* pp. 545-546.

Meisel, Martin. *Shaw and the nineteenth-century theatre,* pp. 32, 34, 36, 58-59, 113, 127-128, 253-259, 265, 267.

Purdom, C.B. *A guide to the plays of Bernard Shaw,* pp. 172-178.

Stewart, J.I.M. *Eight modern writers,* pp. 136-137.

West, Alick. *George Bernard Shaw, "A Good Man Fallen Among Fabians."* pp. 88-92.

IRWIN SHAW 1913-

General

Evans, Bergen, "Irwin Shaw." *College English,* vol. 13, no. 2 (Nov., 1951), pp. 71-77.

Bury the Dead

Himelstein, Morgan Y. *Drama was a weapon, the left-wing theatre in New York 1929-1941,* pp. 45-46.

O'Hara, Frank H. *Today in American drama,* pp. 260-263.

The Gentle People

Himelstein, Morgan Y. *Drama was a weapon, the left-wing theatre in New York 1929-1941,* pp. 176-177.

O'Hara, Frank H. *Today in American drama,* pp. 61-65, 76, 182-189.

EDWARD SHELDON 1886-1946

Salvation Nell

Gassner, John. "Introduction." *Best plays of the early American theatre from the beginning to 1916,* pp. xlii-xliii.

ARCHIE SHEPP 1937-

June Bug Graduates Tonight

Abramson, Doris E. *Negro playwrights in the American theatre, 1925-1959,* pp. 281-283.

ROBERT CEDRIC SHERRIFF 1896-

Journey's End.

Block, Anita. *The changing world in plays and theatre,* pp. 304-306.

Casey, Kevin. "The Excitements and the Disappointments." *In:* McCann, Sean, ed. *The world of Sean O'Casey,* pp. 211-212.

Knight, G. Wilson. *The golden labyrinth,* pp. 358-361.

Young, Stark. *Immortal shadows,* pp. 110-113.

ROBERT EMMET SHERWOOD 1898-1955

General

Anderson, Maxwell. "Robert E. Sherwood." *Theatre Arts,* vol. 40, no. 2 (Feb., 1956), pp. 26-27.

Behrman, Samuel N. "Old Monotonous." *New Yorker,* vol. 16 (June 1, 1940), pp. 33-40; (June 8, 1940), pp. 26-33.

Behrman, S.N. *The suspended drawing room,* pp. 137-165.

Brown, John Mason. *Still seeing things,* pp. 13-23.

Campbell, Oscar J. "Robert Sherwood and His Time." *College English,* vol. 4, no. 5 (Feb., 1943), pp. 275-280.

Dusenbury, Winifred L. "Myth in American Drama Between the Wars." *Modern Drama,* vol. 6, no. 3 (Dec. 1963), pp. 294-308.

Flexner, Eleanor. *American playwrights: 1918-1938,* pp. 272-276.

Gassner, John. "Robert Emmett Sherwood." *Atlantic Monthly,* vol. 169 (Jan., 1942), pp. 26-33.

Gassner, John. *The theatre in our times,* pp. 311-321.

Goldstein, Malcolm. "Playwrights of the 1930's." *In:* Downer, Alan S., ed. *The American theater today,* pp. 28-29.

Gould, Jean. *Modern American playwrights,* pp. 99-117.

Isaacs, Edith J.R. "Robert Sherwood; Man of the Hour." *Theatre Arts,* vol. 23, no. 1 (Jan., 1939), pp. 31-40.

Lausch, Anne N. "Robert Sherwood's Heartbreak Houses." *Shaw Rev.,* vol. 6, no. 2 (May, 1963), pp. 42-50.

Lumley, Frederick, *New trends in 20th-century drama,* pp. 334-335.

Shuman, R. Baird. "The Shifting Pacifism of Robert E. Sherwood." *South Atlantic Q.,* vol. 65 (1966). pp. 382-389.

Abe Lincoln in Illinois

Atkinson, Brooks. *"Abe Lincoln in Illinois." In:* Oppenheimer, George, ed. *The passionate playgoer,* pp. 537-540. (Reprinted from *The New York Times* (Oct. 23, 1938).)

Bierman, Judah. *The dramatic experience,* pp. 98-102.

Brown, John Mason. *Broadway in review,* pp. 147-154.

Brown, John Mason. "The Worlds of Robert E. Sherwood." *Saturday Rev.* vol. 48 (Aug. 14, 1965), pp. 16-18, 20, 63-64.

Brown, John Mason. *The worlds of Robert E. Sherwood, mirror to his times, 1896-1939,* pp. 366-386.

Campbell, Oscar J. "Robert Sherwood and His Times." *College English,* vol. 4, no. 5 (Feb., 1943), pp. 275-280.

Dusenbury, Winifred L. *The theme of loneliness in modern American drama,* pp. 181-185.

Fergusson, Francis. *"Abe Lincoln in Illinois." Southern Rev.,* vol. 5, no. 3 (Winter, 1940), pp. 560-562.

Himelstein, Morgan Y. *Drama was a weapon, the left-wing theatre in New York 1929-1941,* pp. 143-144.

O'Hara, Frank H. *Today in American drama,* pp. 102-107, 253.

Sainer, Arthur. *The sleepwalker and the assassin, a view of the contemporary theatre,* pp. 55-57.

Shuman, R. Baird. *Robert E. Sherwood,* pp. 83-92.

Acropolis

Brown, John Mason. *The worlds of Robert E. Sherwood, mirror to his times, 1896-1939,* pp. 294-307, 312.

Verschoyle, Derek. *Spectator,* vol. 151 (Dec. 1, 1933), p. 801.

Idiot's Delight

Brown, John Mason. *The worlds of Robert E. Sherwood, mirror to his times, 1896-1939,* pp. 325-236, 328-248.

Campbell, Oscar J. "Robert Sherwood and His Times." *College English,* vol. 4, no. 5 (Feb., 1943), pp. 275-280.

Flexner, Eleanor. *American playwrights: 1918-1938*, pp. 279-282.

Himelstein, Morgan Y. *Drama was a weapon, the left-wing theatre in New York 1929-1941*, pp. 138-139.

Krutch, Joseph W. *The American drama since 1918*, pp. 221-225.

Shuman, R. Baird. *Robert E. Sherwood.* pp. 67-74.

Verschoyle, Derek. *Spectator*, vol. 160 (Apr. 1, 1938), p. 583.

The Petrified Forest

Broussard, Louis. *American drama...*, pp. 106-110.

Brown, John Mason. "Allegory and Mr. Sherwood." *In:* Brown, John Mason. *Dramatis personae*, pp. 77-79.

Brown, John Mason. *Two on the aisle*, pp. 163-165.

Brown, John Mason. *The worlds of Robert E. Sherwood, mirror to his times, 1896-1939*, pp. 316-319.

Campbell, Oscar J. "Robert Sherwood and His Times." *College English*, vol. 4, no. 5 (Feb., 1943), pp. 275-280.

Flexner, Eleanor. *American playwrights: 1918-1938*, pp. 276-279.

Krutch, Joseph, W. *The American drama since 1918*, pp. 217-221.

Lausch, Anne N. "Robert Sherwood's Heartbreak Houses." *Shaw Rev.*, vol. 6, no. 2 (May, 1963), pp. 42-50.

Shuman, R. Baird. *Robert E. Sherwood*, pp. 59-67.

Sievers, W. David. *Freud on Broadway*, pp. 182-184.

The Queen's Husband

Brown, John Mason. *The worlds of Robert E. Sherwood, mirror to his times, 1896-1939*, pp. 238, 240, 245-248.

Shuman, R. Baird. *Robert E. Sherwood*, pp. 123-132.

Wakefield, Gilbert, *Saturday Rev.*, vol. 152 (Oct. 17, 1931), p. 498.

Reunion in Vienna

Brown, John Mason. *The worlds of Robert E. Sherwood, mirror to his times, 1896-1939*, pp. 262-279.

Campbell, Oscar J. "Robert Sherwood and His Times." *College English*, vol. 4, no. 5 (Feb., 1943), pp. 275-280.

Krutch, Joseph Wood. *The American drama since 1918,* pp. 214-217.

MacCarthy, Desmond. "American Acting." *New Statesman,* vol. 7 (Jan. 13, 1934), p. 41.

Shuman, R. Baird. *Robert E. Sherwood,* pp. 132-141.

Sievers, W. David. *Freud on Broadway,* pp. 180-181.

The Road to Rome

Brown, Ivor. *Saturday Rev.,* vol. 145 (May 26, 1928), p. 660.

Brown, John Mason. *The worlds of Robert E. Sherwood, mirror to his times, 1896-1939,* pp. 210-222, 255-257.

Jennings, Richard. *Spectator,* vol. 140 (June 2, 1928), pp. 826-827.

Lausch, Anne N. "*The Road to Rome* by Way of Alexandria and Tavazzano." *Shaw Rev.,* vol. 6, no. 1 (Jan., 1963), pp. 2-12.

Shuman, R. Baird. *Robert E. Sherwood.* pp. 36-46.

Sievers, W. David. *Freud on Broadway,* pp. 180.

Verschoyle, Derek. *Spectator,* vol. 158 (Mar. 19, 1937), p. 516.

The Rugged Path

Shuman, R. Baird. *Robert E. Sherwood.* pp. 103-111.

Small War on Murray Hill

Bronstein, Arthur J. "Footnote to a Broadway Play." *Educational Theatre J.,* vol. 10 (1958), pp. 120-121.

Shuman, R. Baird. *Robert E. Sherwood,* pp. 36-37, 46-51.

There Shall Be No Night

Brown, John Mason. *Broadway in review,* pp. 154-165.

Campbell, Oscar J. "Robert Sherwood and His Times." *College English,* vol. 4, no. 5 (Feb., 1943), pp. 275-280.

Heilman, Robert B. *Tragedy and melodrama,* pp. 56-58, 77, 80, 85.

Himelstein, Morgan Y. *Drama was a weapon, the left-wing theatre in New York 1929-1941,* pp. 147-149.

MacCarthy, Desmond. *New Statesman,* vol. 26 (Dec. 25, 1943), p. 415.

Redfern, James. *Spectator,* vol. 171 (Dec. 24, 1943), p. 598.

Shuman, R. Baird. *Robert E. Sherwood,* pp. 92-102.

Sievers, W. David. *Freud on Broadway,* pp. 184-185.

"Social Drama." *Sociology and Social Research,* vol. 25 (Jan., 1941), p. 295.

This Is New York

Brown, John Mason. *The worlds of Robert E. Sherwood, mirror to his times, 1896-1939,* pp. 251-252.

Shuman, R. Baird. *Robert E. Sherwood,* pp. 52-59.

Tovarich

Brown, John Mason. *The worlds of Robert E. Sherwood, mirror to his times, 1896-1939,* pp. 324-325.

The Virtuous Knight

Shuman, R. Baird. *Robert E. Sherwood,* pp. 112-120.

Waterloo Bridge

Brown, John Mason. *The worlds of Robert E. Sherwood, mirror to his times, 1896-1939,* pp. 248-250.

Shuman, R. Baird. *Robert E. Sherwood,* pp. 77-83.

BURT SHEVELOVE 1915-

Too Much Johnson

Gottfried, Martin. *A theater divided; the postwar American stage,* pp. 218, 226-227.

GEORGE SHIELS 1886-1949

General

Hogan, Robert. *After the Irish renaissance,* pp. 33-39.

Malone, Andrew E. *The Irish drama,* pp. 239-240.

Paul Twying

Malone, Andrew E. *The Irish drama,* pp. 237-238.

Professor Tim

Malone, Andrew E. *The Irish drama,* p. 239.

The Rugged Path

Hogan, Robert. *After the Irish renaissance,* pp. 33, 36.

The Summit

Hogan, Robert. *After the Irish renaissance,* p. 37.

ALEJANDRO SIEVEKING 1934-

General

Jones, W.K. *Behind Spanish American footlights,* pp. 240-241.

PAUL SIFTON

General

Knox, George A. *Dos Passos and "The Revolting Playwrights,"* pp. 60-61.

The Belt

Knox, George A. *Dos Passos and "The Revolting Playwrights,"* pp. 114-117, 177-179, 182, 193-194.

1931

Himelstein, Morgan Y. *Drama was a weapon, the left-wing theatre in New York 1929-1941,* pp. 19-20, 157-159.

Weales, Gerald. "The Group Theatre and Its Plays." *In: American theatre,* pp. 74-75, 83.

JOHN SILVERA (Abram Hill, co-author)

Liberty Deferred

Abramson, Doris E. *Negro playwrights in the American theatre, 1925-1959,* pp. 65-66.

On Strivers Row

Abramson, Doris E. *Negro playwrights in the American theatre, 1925-1959,* pp. 95-102, 159.

KONSTANTIN SIMONOV

Wait for Me

Macleod, Joseph. *Actors cross the Volga,* p. 242.

NORMAN FREDERICK SIMPSON 1919-

General

Lumley, Frederick. *New trends in 20th-century drama,* pp. 300-303.

Smith, R.D. "Back to the Text." *In:* Brown, John Russell, and Bernard Harris, eds. *Contemporary theatre,* pp. 124-126.

Taylor, John Russell. *Anger and after,* pp. 58-64.

Wellwarth, George. *The theatre of protest and paradox,* pp. 197, 211, 212-220, 221, 254.

Worth, Katharine J. "Avant Garde at The Royal Court Theatre: John Arden and N.F. Simpson." *In:* Armstrong, William A., ed. *Experimental drama,* pp. 214-223.

The Cresta Run

Lumley, Frederick. *New trends in 20th-century drama,* pp. 302-303.

The Hole

Esslin, Martin. *The theatre of the absurd,* pp. 220-221.

Velde, Paul. "The Stage." *Commonweal,* vol. 86, no. 6 (Apr. 28, 1967), pp. 176-177.

Wellwarth, George. *The theatre of protest and paradox,* pp. 212, 215-218.

One Way Pendulum

Esslin, Martin. *The theatre of the absurd,* pp. 221-224.

Lumley, Frederick. *New trends in 20th-century drama,* pp. 301-302.

Swanson, Michele A. *"One Way Pendulum:* A New Dimension in Farce." *Drama Survey,* vol. 2, no. 3 (Fall, 1963), pp. 322-332.

Wellwarth, George. *The theatre of protest and paradox,* pp. 212, 218-220.

A Resounding Tinkle

Esslin Martin. *The theatre of the absurd,* pp. 217-220.

Lumley, Frederick. *New trends in 20th-century drama,* pp. 300-301.

O'Casey, Sean. "The Bald Primaqueera." *In:* O'Casey, Sean. *Blasts and benedictions,* pp. 72-73.

663

Velde, Paul. "The Stage." *Commonweal,* vol. 86, no. 6 (Apr. 28, 1967), pp. 176.

Wellwarth, George. *The theatre of protest and paradox,* pp. 212-216, 218, 254.

UPTON SINCLAIR 1878-1968

Singing Jailbirds

Knox, George A. *Dos Passos and "The Revolting Playwrights,"* pp. 140-142, 179-181, 196-197.

GEORGE SION 1913-

Charles le Téméraire

Mallinson, Vernon. *Modern Belgian literature, 1830-1960,* pp. 192-193.

GEORGE SKLAR 1908- (Albert Maltz, co-author)

Life and Death of an American

Himelstein, Morgan Y. *Drama was a weapon, the left-wing theatre in New York 1929-1941,* pp. 109-110.

Peace on Earth

Block, Anita. *The changing world in plays and theatre,* pp. 337-351.

Himelstein, Morgan Y. *Drama was a weapon, the left-wing theatre in New York 1929-1941,* pp. 57-59.

ART SMITH (Elia Kazan, co-author)

Dimitroff

Himelstein, Morgan Y. *Drama was a weapon, the left-wing theatre in New York 1929-1941,* pp. 26-28.

DODIE SMITH

Bonnet over the Windmill

Dent, Alan. *Preludes and studies,* pp. 181-182.

J. AUGUSTUS SMITH (Peter Morrell, co-author)

Turpentine

Abramson, Doris E. *Negro playwrights in the American theatre, 1925-1959,* pp. 63-64.

LILLIAN SMITH 1897-1966
Strange Fruit

Mitchell, Loften. *Black drama,* pp. 125-126.

MICHAEL TOWNSEND SMITH 1935-
I Like It

Sainer, Arthur. *The sleepwalker and the assassin, a view of the contemporary theatre,* pp. 109-111.

RAFAEL SOLANA 1915-
General

Jones, Willis K. *Behind Spanish American footlights,* pp. 509-510.

Smith, John David. "Humor in the short stories and plays of Rafael Solana." *Dissertation Abstracts,* vol. 27 (1966), 216A (So. Calif.).

JOSE ANTONIO SOLDIAS 1891-1946
General

Jones, W.K. *Behind Spanish American footlights,* pp. 169-170.

CARLOS SOLORZANO 1922-
General

Franco, Jean. *The modern culture of Latin America,* p. 235.

Jones, W.K. *Behind Spanish American footlights,* pp. 456-457.

Los Fantoches

McMahon, Dorothy. "Changing Trends in Spanish American Literature." *Books Abroad,* vol. 39, no. 1 (Winter, 1965), p. 19.

REINHARD JOHANNES SORGE 1892-1916
General

Sokel, Walter. *The writer in extremis,* pp. 155-156, 159, 162, 229.

The Beggar (Der Bettler)

Garten, H.F. *Modern German drama,* pp. 115-117.

Güntwar

Sokel, Walter. *The writer in extremis,* pp. 157, 158-159.

GETHA SOWERBY

General

Williams, Harold. *Modern English writers,* pp. 261-262.

WOLE SOYINKA 1934-

General

Maclean, Una. "Soyinka's International Drama." *Black Orpheus,* no. 15 (Aug. 1964), pp. 46-51.

A Dance of the Forests

Ferguson, John. "Nigerian Drama in English." *Modern Drama,* vol. 11, no. 1 (May, 1968), pp. 22-24.

Kongi's Harvest

Ferguson, John. "Nigerian Drama in English." *Modern Drama,* vol. 11, no. 1 (May, 1968), pp. 25-26.

Kroll, Jack. "Caesar in Africa." *Newsweek* (Apr. 29, 1968), p. 93.

The Lion and the Jewel

Ferguson, John. "Nigerian Drama in English." *Modern Drama,* vol. 11, no. 1 (May, 1968), pp. 18-19.

The Road

Ferguson, John. "Nigerian Drama in English." *Modern Drama,* vol. 11, no. 1 (May, 1968), pp. 24-25.

The Strong Breed

Ferguson, John. "Nigerian Drama in English." *Modern Drama,* vol. 11, no. 1 (May, 1968), p. 22.

Kroll, Jack. "Caesar in Africa." *Newsweek* (Apr. 29, 1968), p. 93.

The Swamp-Dwellers

Ferguson, John. "Nigerian Drama in English." *Modern Drama,* vol. 11, no. 1 (May, 1968), pp. 19-20.

The Trials of Brother Jero

Ferguson, John. "Nigerian Drama in English." *Modern Drama,* vol. 11, no. 2 (May, 1968), pp. 20-22.

Kroll, Jack. "Caesar in Africa." *Newsweek* (Apr. 29, 1968), p. 93.

STEPHEN SPENDER 1909-

Trial of a Judge

Fraser, G.S. *The modern writer and his world,* pp. 223-224.

Knight, G. Wilson. *The golden labyrinth,* pp. 368-369.

Prior, Moody E. *The language of tragedy,* pp. 372-376.

BELLA SPEWACK 1899- (Samuel Spewack, co-author)

General

Gould, Jean. *Modern American playwrights,* pp. 135-140.

Boy Meets Girl

O'Hara, Frank II. *Today in American drama,* pp. 204-212.

LUIGI SQUARZINA 1922-

General

Pandolfi, Vito. "Italian Theatre Since the War." *Tulane Drama Rev.,* vol. 8, no. 3 (Spring, 1964), pp. 101-102.

LAURENCE STALLINGS (Maxwell Anderson, co-author)

What Price Glory

See Anderson, Maxwell

DAVID STARKWEATHER

The Love Affair

Sainer, Arthur. *The sleepwalker and the assassin, a view of the contemporary theatre,* pp. 108-109.

BARRIE STAVIS

The Man Who Never Died

Mitchell, Loften. *Black drama,* p. 180.

The Sun and I

Himelstein, Morgan Y. *Drama was a weapon, the left-wing theatre in New York 1929-1941,* p. 101.

GERTRUDE STEIN 1874-1946

Four Saints in Three Acts

Garvin, Harry R. "Sound and Sense in *Four Saints in Three Acts.*" *Bucknell Rev.,* vol. 5 no. 1 (1954), pp. 1-11.

Sievers, .W. David. *Freud on Broadway,* pp. 243-244.

Young, Stark. *Immortal shadows,* pp. 150-152.

JOSEPH STEIN 1912-

Enter Laughing

Sainer, Arthur. *The sleepwalker and the assassin, a view of the contemporary theatre,* p. 36-39.

JOHN STEINBECK 1902-1968

Bibliography

Hayashi, Tetsumaro. *John Steinbeck: a concise bibliography (1930-1965).*

The Moon Is Down

Gassner, John. *"The Moon Is Down* as a Play." *Current History,* new series, vol. 2 (May, 1942), pp. 228-231.

Gilder, Rosamond. "Moon Down. Theatre Rises." *Theatre Arts,* vol. 26 (May, 1942), pp. 237, 270.

Of Mice and Men

Brown, John Mason. *Two on the aisle,* pp. 183-187.

Dusenbury, Winifred L. *The theme of loneliness in modern American drama,* pp. 45-50.

Krutch, Joseph W. *The American drama since 1918,* pp. 128-130.

Lisca, Peter. "Motif and Pattern in *Of Mice and Men." Modern Fiction Studies,* vol. 2 (1956), pp. 228-234.

O'Hara, Frank H. *Today in American drama,* pp. 172-182, 250-251.

Roane, Margaret C. "John Steinbeck as a Spokesman for the Mentally Retarded." *Wisconsin Studies in Contemporary Literature,* vol. 5 (Summer, 1964), pp. 127-132.

Shedd, Margaret. *"Of Mice and Men." Theatre Arts,* vol. 17 (Oct., 1937), pp. 774-780.

Sievers, W. David. *Freud on Broadway,* pp. 239-240.

CARL STERNHEIM 1878-1942

General

Beckley, R. "Carl Sternheim." *In:* Natan, A., ed. *German men of letters,* vol. 2, pp. 133-154.

Garten, H.F. *Modern German drama,* pp. 96-101.

Hatfield, Henry. *Modern German literature,* pp. 71-72.

Sokel, Walter. *The writer in extremis,* pp. 62, 63, 92, 108, 123, 176.

The Bloomers (The Underpants) (Die Hose)

Beckley, R. "Carl Sternheim." *In:* Natan, A., ed. *German men of letters,* vol. 2, pp. 134, 137-140.

Sainer, Arthur. *The sleepwalker and the assasin, a view of the contemporary theatre,* pp. 113-115.

Sokel, Walter. *The writer in extremis,* pp. 121-123.

Citizen Schippel (Burger Schippel)

Beckley, R. "Carl Sternheim." *In:* Natan, A. ed. *German men of letters,* vol. 2, pp. 146-147.

Hirschbach, Frank D. "New Directions in German Comedy." *Drama Survey,* vol. 1, no. 2 (Oct., 1961), pp. 195-213.

The Mask of Virtue (Die Marquise von Arcis)

Beckley, R. "Carl Sternheim." *In:* Natan, A., ed. *German men of letters,* vol. 2, pp. 149-151.

1913

Beckley, R. "Carl Sternheim." *In:* Natan, A., ed. *German men of letters,* vol. 2, pp. 134, 144-146.

The Snob (Der Snob)

Beckley, R. "Carl Sternheim." *In:* Natan, A., ed. *German men of letters,* vol. 2, pp. 140-143.

Tabula Rasa

Beckley, R. "Carl Sternheim." *In:* Natan, A., ed. *German men of letters,* vol. 2, pp. 147-148.

WALLACE STEVENS 1879-1955

Three Travelers Watch a Sunrise

Gerstenberger, Donna. "Verse Drama in America." *In:* Meserve, Walter J., ed. *Discussions of American drama*, pp. 36-38.

Gerstenberger, Donna. "Verse Drama in America: 1916-1939." *Modern Drama*, vol. 6, no. 3 (Dec., 1963), pp. 309-322.

TOM STOPPARD 1937-

The Real Inspector Hound

Kennedy, Andrew K. "Old and New in London Now." *Modern Drama*, vol. 11, no. 4 (Feb., 1969), pp. 437-439.

Rosencrantz and Guildenstern Are Dead

Kennedy, Andrew K. "Old and New in London Now." *Modern Drama*, vol. 11, no. 4 (Feb., 1969), pp. 438-442.

Loney, Glenn. "Broadway in Review." *Educational Theatre J.,* vol. 20, no. 1 (Mar., 1968), p. 103.

AUGUST STRINDBERG 1849-1912

General

Benston, Alice N. "From Naturalism to *The Dream Play:* A Study of the Evolution of Strindberg's Unique Theatrical Form." *Modern Drama*, vol. 7, no. 4 (Feb., 1965), pp. 382-398.

Bentley, Eric. "August Strindberg" *Kenyon Rev.,* vol. 7, no. 4 (Autumn, 1945), pp. 540-560.

Bentley, Eric. *The playwright as thinker,* pp. 158-180.

Bradbrook, M.C. *English dramatic form,* pp. 144-149.

Brustein, Robert. "Male and Female in August Strindberg." *Tulane Drama Rev.,* vol. 7, no. 2 (Winter, 1962), pp. 130-174.

Brustein, Robert. *The theatre of revolt,* pp. 87-104. *Also in:* Bogard, Travis, and Oliver, William I., eds. *Modern drama; essays in criticism,* pp. 313-326, 339-344.

Dahlstrom, Carl E.W.L. "Strindberg and the Problems of Naturalism." *Scandinavian Studies,* vol. 16, no. 6 (May, 1941), pp. 212-219.

Dahlstrom, Carl E.W.L. "Theomachy: Zola, Strindberg, Andreyev." *Scandinavian Studies,* vol. 17, no. 4 (Nov., 1942), pp. 121-132.

Dukes, Ashley. *Modern dramatists,* pp. 49-64.

Freedman, Morris. "Strindberg's Positive Nihilism." *In:* Freedman, Morris, ed. *Essays in the modern drama,* pp. 56-63. (Reprinted from *Drama Survey,* vol. 2, no. 3 (Winter, 1963).)

Gassner, John. "The Influence of Strindberg in the U.S.A." *World Theatre,* vol. 11, no. 1 (Spring 1962), pp. 21-29.

Gassner, John. *The theatre in our times,* pp. 170-181.

Grant, Vernon W. *Great abnormals; the pathological genius of Kafka, van Gogh, Strindberg and Poe,* pp. 127-129, 142-180.

Gravier, Maurice. "Strindberg and the French Drama." *World Theatre,* vol. 11 no. 1 (Spring 1962), pp. 45-60.

Henderson, Archibald. *European dramatists,* pp. 3-73.

Hartman, Murray. "Strindberg and O'Neill." *Educational Theatre J.,* vol. 18, no. 3 (Oct., 1966), pp. 216-223.

Hoogland, Claes. "How to Produce Strindberg?" *World Theatre,* vol. 11, no. 1 (Spring 1962), pp. 67-79.

Johnson, Walter. "Fifth Letter—Introduction." *In:* Strindberg, August. *Open letters to the intimate theater,* pp. 234-245.

Krutch, Joseph Wood. *"Modernism" in modern drama,* pp. 23-35, 42.

Lagerkvist, Pär. "Modern theater: Points of View and Attack." *In:* Sprinchorn, Evert, ed. *The genius of the Scandinavian theater,* pp. 624-632.

Lagerkvist, Pär. *Modern theatre, seven plays and an essay,* pp. 24-32.

Lamm, Martin. *Modern drama,* pp. 135-151.

Lamm, Martin. "Strindberg and the Theatre." *Tulane Drama Rev.,* vol. 6, no. 2 (Nov., 1961), pp. 132-139.

Lavrin, Janko. "Huysmans and Strindberg." *In:* Lavrin, J. *Studies in European literature,* pp. 118-130.

Leaska, Mitchell A. *The voice of tragedy, pp. 212-*217, 228-231.

Lewis, Allan. *The contemporary theatre,* pp. 42-59.

Lind af Hageby, Lizzy. *August Strindberg: the spirit of revolt; studies and impressions,* pp. 202-209, 211-219, 298-306, 315-324, 328-350.

MacCarthy, Desmond. *Theatre,* pp. 84-93.

Melchinger, Siegfried. "German People Face to Face with Strindberg." *World Theatre,* vol. 11, no. 1 (Spring 1962), pp. 31-44.

Ollen, Gunnar. "Strindberg, 1962." *World Theatre,* vol. 11. no. 1 (Spring, 1962), pp. 4-17.

O'Neill, Eugene. "Strindberg and Our Theatre." *In:* Frenz, Horst, ed. *American playwrights on drama,* pp. 1-2. (First printed in Provincetown Playbill, no. 1, season 1923-24.) *Also in:* Cargill, O., ed. *O'Neill and his plays,* pp. 108-109.

Orr, Stella. "Good and evil in the plays of Ibsen and Strindberg." M.A., University of Kansas, 1917.

Palmblad, H.V.E. "A 'Conscious Will' in History: Summary." *In:* Caputi, Anthony, ed. *Modern drama,* pp. 426-427. (From Palmblad, H.V.E. *Strindberg's conception of history,* N.Y., Columbia Univ. Press, 1927, pp. 88-90.)

Raphael, Robert. "Strindberg and Wagner." *In:* American-Scandinavian Foundation, New York. *Scandinavian studies,* pp. 260-268.

Scobbie, Irene. "Strindberg and Lagerkvist." *Modern Drama,* vol. 7, no. 2 (Sept., 1964), pp. 126-134.

Sprinchorn, Evert, ed. *The genius of the Scandinavian theater,* pp. 267-270.

Steene, Birgitta. "Shakespearean Elements in Historical Plays of Strindberg." *Comparative Literature,* vol. 11 (Summer, 1959), pp. 209-220.

Strindberg, Ausust. *Open letters to the intimate theater,* pp. 15-53.

Strindberg, August. "Paradise Regained." *In:* Caputi, Anthony, ed., *Modern drama,* pp. 420-425. (From: Strindberg, August. *Inferno,* London, Hutchinson, 1962, pp. 42-44, 164-168)

Styan, J.L. *The dark comedy,* 2nd ed., pp. 29, 53, 58, 61-64, 68-73, 74, 118-124, 212, 217, 241, 294.

Uppvall, Axel Johan. "Strindberg in the Light of Psychoanalysis." *Scandinavian Studies,* vol. 21, no. 3 (Aug., 1949), pp. 133-150.

Wescher, Paul. "Strindberg and the Chance-Images of Surrealism: A Study in the Interrelationship Between Art and Literature." *Art Q.,* vol. 16, no. 2 (Summer, 1953), pp. 93-105.

Williams, Raymond. *Drama from Ibsen to Eliot,* pp. 98-125.

Williams, Raymond. *Modern tragedy,* pp. 107-117.

Williams, Raymond. "Strindberg and the New Drama in Britain." *World Theatre,* vol. 11, no. 1 (Spring 1962), pp. 61-66.

The Bond

Madsen, Borge Gedso. "Naturalism in Transition: Strindberg's 'Cynical Tragedy', *The Bond* (1892)." *Modern Drama,* vol. 5, no. 3 (December, 1962), pp. 291-298.

Charles XII

Johnson, Walter. *Strindberg and the historical drama.* pp. 155-174.

Strindberg, August. *Open letters to the intimate theater,* pp. 127, 259-262.

Comrades

Grant, Vernon W. *Great abnormals; the pathological genius of Kafka, van Gogh, Strindberg and Poe,* pp. 138-140.

Lind af Hageby, Lizzy. *August Strindberg: the spirit of revolt; studies and impressions,* pp. 184-195.

The Creditors.

Dukore, Bernard F. "Strindberg: The Real and the Surreal." *Modern Drama,* vol. 5, no. 3 (Dec., 1962), pp. 331-334.

Grant, Vernon W. *Great abnormals; the pathological genius of Kafka, van Gogh, Strindberg and Poe,* pp. 136-138.

Jameson, Storm. *Modern drama in Europe,* pp. 34-38.

Johnson, Walter. *"Creditors* Re-examined." *Modern Drama,* vol. 5, no. 3 (Dec., 1962), pp. 281-290.

Lind af Hageby, Lizzy. *August Strindberg: the spirit of revolt; studies and impressions,* pp. 195-202.

Styan, J.L. *The dark comedy,* 2nd ed., pp. 69, 71.

The Dance of Death

Blau, Herbert. *The impossible theatre,* pp. 258-261.

Dukore, Bernard F. "Strindberg: The Real and the Surreal." *Modern Drama,* vol. 5, no. 3 (Dec., 1962), pp. 331-334.

Grant, Vernon W. *Great abnormals; the pathological genius of Kafka, van Gogh, Strindberg and Poe,* pp. 140-142.

Jameson, Storm. *Modern drama in Europe,* pp. 56-61.

Johnson, Walter. "Strindberg and the *Danse Macabre"* *Modern Drama,* vol. 3, no. 1, (May, 1960), pp. 8-15.

Lind af Hageby, Lizzy. *August Strindberg: the spirit of revolt; studies and impressions,* pp. 310-311.

Taylor, Marion A. "Edward Albee and August Strindberg: Some Parallels Between *The Dance of Death* and *Who's Afraid of Virginia Woolf?" Papers on English Language and Literature,* vol. 1, no. 1 (Winter, 1965), pp. 59-71.

Taylor, Marion A. "A Note on Strindberg's *The Dance of Death* and Edward Albee's Who's A*fraid of Virginia Woolf?" Papers on Language and Literature,* vol. 2, no. 2 (Spring, 1966), pp. 187-188.

Williams, Raymond. *Drama from Ibsen to Eliot,* pp. 118-119.

Debit and Credit

Styan, J.L. *The dark comedy,* 2nd ed., pp 71-72.

A Dream Play

Benston, Alice N. "From Naturalism to the *Dream Play:* A Study of the Evolution of Strindberg's Unique Theatrical Form." *Modern Drama,* vol. 7, no. 4 (Feb., 1965), pp. 382-398.

Brustein, Robert. "August Strindberg: *A Dream Play." In:* Caputi, Anthony, ed. *Modern drama,* pp. 440-446. (From Brustein, Robert. *The theatre of revolt,* pp. 126-133.) *Also in:* Bogard, Travis, and Oliver, William I., eds. *Modern drama; essays in criticism,* pp. 344-349

Brustein, Robert. "Male and Female in August Strindberg." *Tulane Drama Rev.,* vol. 7, no. 2 (Winter, 1962). pp.167-173.

Greenwood, Ormerod. *The playwright,* pp. 197-203.

Lamm, Martin. *Modern drama,* pp. 144-148.

Lewis, Leta Jane. "Alchemy and the Orient in Strindberg's *Dream Play." Scandinavian Studies,* vol. 35, no. 3 (Aug., 1963) pp. 208-222.

Lind af Hageby, Lizzy. August *Strindberg: the spirit of revolt; studies and impressions,* pp. 314-315.

Matthews, Honor. *The primal curse,* pp. 124-125, 133-134.

Milton, John R. "The Esthetic Fault of Strindberg's *Dream Play." Drama Rev.,* vol. 4, no. 3 (Mar., 1960), pp. 108-116.

Muller, Herbert J. *The spirit of tragedy,* p. 280.

Sokel, Walter. *The writer in extremis,* pp. 38, 39, 161.

Sprinchorn, Evert. "The Logic of *A Dream Play." Modern Drama,* vol. 5, no. 3 (Dec., 1962), pp. 352-365.

Strindberg, August. "Author's Note to *A Dream Play.*" *In:* Caputi, Anthony, ed. *Modern drama,* pp. 425-426. (From Strindberg, August. *Six plays of Strindberg,* Willis Kingsley Wing, 1955.)

Strindberg, August. *In:* Cole, Toby, ed. *Playwrights on playwriting,* pp. 182-183.

Valency, Maurice. "*A Dream Play:* The Flower and the Castle." *In:* Caputi, Anthony, ed. Mod*ern drama,* pp. 427-440. (From Valency, Maurice. *The flower and the castle,* N.Y., Macmillan, 1963, pp. 326-342.)

Williams, Raymond. *Drama from Ibsen to Eliot,* pp. 120-121.

Earl Birger of Bjalbo (Bjalbojarlen)

Johnson, Walter. *Strindberg and the historical drama,* pp. 267-278.

Strindberg, August. *Open letters to the intimate theatre,* pp. 303-304.

Easter

Bergeron, David M. "Strindberg's *Easter:* A Musical Play." *Univ. Rev.,* vol. 33, no. 3 (Mar., 1967), pp. 219-225.

Freedman, Morris. *The moral impulse,* pp. 23-27.

Lind af Hageby, Lizzy. *August Strindberg: the spirit of revolt; studies and impressions,* pp. 306-308.

White, Kenneth S. "Visions of a Transfigured Humanity: Strindberg and Lenormand." *Modern Drama,* vol. 5, no. 3 (Dec., 1962), pp. 323-330.

Williams, Raymond. *Drama from Ibsen to Eliot,* pp. 119-120.

Englebrekt

Johnson, Walter. *Strindberg and the historical drama.* pp. 175-190.

Strindberg, August. *Open letters to the intimate theatre,* pp. 253-255.

Erik XIV

Johnson, Walter. *Strindberg and the historical drama,* pp. 114-130.

Lind af Hageby, Lizzy. *August Strindberg: the spirit of revolt; studies and impressions,* pp. 295-297.

Strindberg, August. *Open letters to the intimate theater,* pp. 127, 256-257.

The Father (Fadren)

Benston, Alice N. "From Naturalism to the *Dream Play:* A Study of the Evolution of Strindberg's Unique Theatrical Form." *Modern Drama,* vol. 7, no. 4 (Feb., 1965), pp. 382-398.

Brustein, Robert. "Male and Female in August Strindberg." *Tulane Drama Rev.,* vol. 7, no. 2 (Winter, 1962), pp. 146-154.

Brustein, Robert. *The theatre of revolt.* pp. 104-113. *Also in:* Bogard, Travis, and Oliver, William I., eds. *Modern drama; essays in criticism,* pp. 326-333.)

Clurman, Harold. *Lies like truth,* pp. 126-127.

Dahlstrom, Carl E.W.L. "Is Strindberg's *Fadren* Naturalistic?" *Scandinavian Studies,* vol. 15 (1939), pp. 257-265.

Dahlstrom, Carl E.W.L. "Strindberg and Naturalistic Tragedy." *Scandinavian Studies,* vol. 30, no. 1 (Feb., 1958), pp. 1-18.

Dahlstrom, Carl E.W.L. "Strindberg's *Fadren* as an Expressionistic Drama." *Scandinavian Studies,* vol. 16 (1940-41), pp. 83-94.

Freedman, Morris. *The moral impulse,* pp. 19-23.

Grant, Vernon W. *Great abnormals; the pathological genius of Kafka, van Gogh, Strindberg and Poe,* pp. 132-136.

Jameson, Storm. *Modern drama in Europe,* pp. 41-45.

Lamm, Martin. *Modern drama,* pp. 137-139.

Leaska, Mitchell A. *The voice of tragedy,* pp. 217-228.

Lind af Hageby, Lizzy. *August Strindberg: the spirit of revolt; studies and impressions,* pp. 171-176, 210-211.

Lyons, Charles L. "The Archetypal Action of Male Submission in Strindberg's *The Father."* *Scandinavian Studies,* vol. 36, no. 3 (Aug., 1964), pp. 218-232.

MacCarthy, Desmond. *Drama,* pp. 101-105.

MacCarthy, Desmond. *Theatre,* pp. 84-88.

Matthews, Honor. *The primal curse,* pp. 72, 126.

Paulson, Arvid. *"The Father:* A Survey of Critical Opinion of August Strindberg's Tragedy and Leading American Performances of It During the Past Half Century." *In:* American-Scandinavian Foundation, New York. *Scandinavian studies,* pp. 247-259.

Styan, J.L. *The elements of drama,* pp. 158-162.

Williams, Raymond. *Drama from Ibsen to Eliot,* pp. 101-104.

Williams, Raymond. *Modern tragedy,* pp. 108-109.

The Ghost Sonata

Bentley, Eric. *The playwright as thinker,* pp. 169-174.

Freedman, Morris. *The moral impulse,* pp. 28-29.

Lamm, Martin. *Modern drama,* pp. 149-150.

Lewis, Allan. *The contemporary theatre,* pp. 52-56.

Matthews, Honor. *The primal curse,* p. 134.

Mays, Milton A. "Strindberg's *Ghost Sonata:* Parodied Fairy Tale On Original Sin." *Modern Drama,* vol. 10, no. 2 (Sept., 1967), pp. 189-194.

Milton, John R. "The Esthetic Fault of Strindberg's *Dream Play."* *Drama Rev.,* vol. 4, no. 3 (Mar., 1960), pp. 108-116.

Muller, Herbert J. *The spirit of tragedy,* 279-280.

Reinert, Otto. *Drama, an introductory anthology,* pp. 461-465.

Reinert, Otto, ed. *Modern drama; nine plays,* pp. 247-251.

Styan, J.L. *The dark comedy,* 2nd ed., pp. 122-124, 255.

Williams, Raymond. *Drama from Ibsen to Eliot,* pp. 121-125.

Gustav Adolf

Ellehauge, Martin. *The position of Bernard Shaw in European drama and philosophy,* pp. 307-309.

Johnson, Walter. *"Gustav Adolf* Revised." *In:* American-Scandinavian Foundation, New York. *Scandinavian studies,* pp. 236-246.

Johnson, Walter. *Strindberg and the historical drama.* pp. 131-154.

Johnson, Walter. "Strindberg's *Gustav Adolf* and Lessing." *Scandinavian Studies,* vol. 28, no. 1 (Feb., 1956), pp. 1-8.

Lind af Hageby, Lizzy. *August Strindberg: the spirit of revolt; studies and impressions* pp. 301-302.

Strindberg, August. *Open letters to the intimate theater,* pp. 242, 257-258.

Gustav III

Johnson, Walter. *Strindberg and the historical drama,* pp. 208-225.

Strindberg, August. *Open letters to the intimate theater,* pp. 242, 258-259.

Gustav Vasa

Johnson, Walter. *Strindberg and the historical drama,* pp. 94-113.

Lind af Hageby, Lizzy. *August Strindberg: the spirit of revolt; studies and impressions,* pp. 289-295.

Strindberg, August. *Open letters to the intimate theater,* pp. 137, 255-256.

The Highway

Nydahl, Bertil. *"The Highway:* Strindberg's Last Drama." *Bul. of the Amer. Inst. of Swedish Arts, Lit. and Science,* vol. 4, no. 2 (1949), pp. 19-21.

In Rome

Lind af Hageby, Lizzy. *August Strindberg: the spirit of revolt; studies and impressions,* pp. 74-77.

Isle of the Dead

Vowles, Richard B. "Strindberg's *Isle of the Dead." Modern Drama,* vol. 5, no. 3 (Dec., 1962), pp. 366-378.

The Journey of Lucky Peter

Lind af Hageby, Lizzy. *August Strindberg: the spirit of revolt; studies and impressions,* pp. 143-144.

The Last of the Knights (Siste Riddaren)

Johnson, Walter. *Strindberg and the historical drama,* pp. 247-257.

Strindberg, August. *Open letters to the intimate theater,* pp. 265-266.

The Link

Lind af Hageby, Lizzy. *August Strindberg: the spirit of revolt; studies and impressions,* pp. 224-225.

Lord Bengt's Wife

Johnson, Walter. *Strindberg and the historical drama,* pp. 68-72.

Lind af Hageby, Lizzy. *August Strindberg: the spirit of revolt; studies and impressions,* pp. 144-146.

Master Olaf (Mäster Olaf)

Ellehauge, Martin. *The position of Bernard Shaw in European drama and philosophy,* pp. 305-307.

Johnson, Walter. *Strindberg and the historical drama,* pp. 32-55.

Lind af Hageby, Lizzy. *August Strindberg: the spirit of revolt; studies and impressions,* pp. 98-103, 142-143.

Miss Julie

Aylen, Leo. *Greek tragedy and the modern world,* pp. 231, 242-247.

Barnet, Sylvan, ed. *Eight great tragedies,* pp. 286-288.

Brustein, Robert. "Male and Female in August Strindberg." *Tulane Drama Rev.,* vol. 7, no. 2 (Winter, 1962), pp. 154-160.

Brustein, Robert. *The theatre of revolt,* pp. 113-119. *Also in:* Bogard, Travis, and Oliver, William I., eds. *Modern drama; essays in criticism,* pp. 333-339.

Clurman, Harold. *Lies like truth,* pp. 127-129.

Cowell, Raymond. *Twelve modern dramatists,* pp. 27-29.

Dahlstrom, Carl E.W.L. "Strindberg and Naturalistic Tragedy." *Scandinavian Studies,* vol. 30, no. 1 (Feb., 1958), pp. 1-18.

Ellehauge, Martin. *The position of Bernard Shaw in European drama and philosophy,* pp. 127-28.

Jameson, Storm. *Modern drama in Europe,* pp. 46-48.

Lamm, Martin. *Modern drama,* pp. 140-142.

Hind af Hageby, Lizzy. *August Strindberg: the spirit of revolt; studies and impressions,* pp. 176-184, 209-210.

MacCarthy, Desmond. *Drama,* pp. 178-182.

MacCarthy, Desmond. *Theatre,* pp. 90-91.

Matthews, Honor. *The primal curse,* pp. 127-128.

Muller, Herbert J. *The spirit of tragedy,* pp. 276-277, 294.

Reinert, Otto, ed. *Drama; an introductory anthology* (alternate ed.), pp. 495-501.

Strindberg, August. *In:* Cole, Toby, ed. *Playwrights and playwriting,* pp. 171-182.

Strindberg, August. "The Author's Preface to *Miss Julie." In:* Gassner, John. *Directions in modern theatre and drama,* pp. 259-277. (Reprinted from *Seven plays* by August Strindberg, N.Y., Bantam Books, 1960.)

Styan, J.L. *The dark comedy,* 2nd ed., pp. 61-62, 69-71.

Williams, Raymond. *Drama from Ibsen to Eliot,* pp. 104-110.

Williams, Raymond. *Modern tragedy, pp. 107-*111.

Moses, Socrates, and Christ

Johnson, Walter. *Strindberg and the historical drama,* pp. 237-246.

The Nightingale of Wittenberg

Johnson, Walter. *Strindberg and the historical drama,* pp. 226-236.

The Outlaw

Lind af Hageby, Lizzy. *August Strindberg: the spirit of revolt; studies and impressions,* pp. 81, 85-87.

Pariah

Lind af Hageby, Lizzy. *August Strindberg: the spirit of revolt; studies and impressions,* pp. 220-222.

MacCarthy, Desmond. *Drama,* pp. 182-183.

MacCarthy, Desmond. *Theatre,* pp. 91-93.

Queen Christina

Johnson, Walter. *Strindberg and the historical drama.* pp. 191-207.

The Regent

Johnson, Walter. *Strindberg and the historical drama.* pp. 257-266.

The Road to Damascus (To Damascus) (Till Damaskus)

Brandell, Gunnar. "Toward a New Art Form." *In:* Sprinchorn, Evert, ed. *The genius of the Scandinavian theater,* pp. 583-598.

Brustein, Robert. *The theatre of revolt,* pp. 119-124.

Glicksberg, Charles I. *The self in modern literature,* pp. 27-35, 67-68.

Kristensen, Sven M. "Strindberg's *Damascus.*" *Orbis Litterarum,* vol. 22 (1967), pp. 363-377.

Lind af Hageby, Lizzy. *August Strindberg: the spirit of revolt; studies and impressions,* pp. 311-314.

Matthews, Honor. *The primal curse,* pp. 124, 128-133, 135, 144.

Milton, John R. "The Esthetic Fault of Strindberg's *Dream Plays.*" *Drama Rev.,* vol. 4, no. 3 (Mar., 1960.), pp. 108-116.

Scanlon, David. "*The Road to Damascus,* Part One: A Skeptic's Everyman." *Modern Drama,* vol. 5, no. 3 (Dec., 1962), pp. 344-351.

Sokel, Walter. *The writer in extremis, pp. 34-36,* 155.

Sprinchorn, Evert, ed. *The genius of the Scandinavian theater,* pp. 271-274, 583-598.

Styan, J.L. *The dark comedy,* 2nd ed., pp. 69, 119-122.

Vincentia, Sister M.O.P. "Wagnerism in Strindberg's *The Road to Damascus.*" *Modern Drama,* vol. 5, no. 3 (Dec., 1962), pp. 335-343.

Williams, Raymond. *Drama from Ibsen to Eliot,* pp. 110-118.

The Saga of the Folkungs (Folkungasagan)

Johnson, Walter. *Strindberg and the historical drama,* pp. 75-93.

Lind af Hageby, Lizzy. *August Strindberg: the spirit of revolt; studies and impressions,* pp. 297-298.

Steene, Birgitta. "Shakespearean Elements in Historical Plays of Strindberg." *Comparative Literature,* vol. 11, no. 3 (Summer, 1959), pp. 209-220.

Strindberg, August. *Open letters to the intimate theater,* pp. 136-137, 249-253, 303.

Samum

Lind af Hageby, Lizzy. *August Strindberg: the spirit of revolt; studies and impressions,* pp. 219-220.

The Secret of the Guild

Johnson Walter. *Strindberg and the historical drama,* pp. 58-68.

Lind af Hageby, Lizzy. *August Strindberg: the spirit of revolt; studies and impressions,* p. 142.

The Spook Sonata

Downer, Alan S. *The art of the play,* pp. 321-326.

The Stronger

Lind af Hageby, Lizzy. *August Strindberg: the spirit of revolt; studies and impressions,* pp. 222-223.

Swanwhite (Svanevit)

Strindberg, August. *Open letters to the intimate theater,* pp. 13, 143, 299, 305.

There Are Crimes and Crimes (Brott och Brott)

Allen, James L., Jr. "Symbol and Meaning in Strindberg's *Crime and Crime.*" *Modern Drama,* vol. 9, no. 1 (May, 1966), pp. 62-73.

Benston, Alice N. "From Naturalism to the *Dream Play:* A Study of the Evolution of Strindberg's Unique Theatrical Form." *Modern Drama,* vol. 7, no. 4 (Feb., 1965), pp. 382-398.

Bentley, Eric. "The Ironic Strindberg." *In:* Sprinchorn, Evert, ed. *The genius of the Scandinavian theater,* pp. 599-603.

Bentley, Eric. *The playwright as thinker,* pp. 174-178.

Ellehauge, Martin. *The position of Bernard Shaw in European drama and philosophy,* p. 144.

Lind af Hageby, Lizzy. *August Strindberg: the spirit of revolt; studies and impressions,* pp. 309.

Sprinchorn, Evert, ed. *The genius of the Scandinavian theater,* pp. 271-274, 599-603.

Styan, J.L. *The dark comedy,* 2nd ed., pp. 72-73, 118.

MORNA STUART

Traitor's Gate

Dent, Alan. *Preludes and studies,* pp. 174-175.

ARIANO SUASSUNA

Auto da Compadecida

Ratcliff, Dillwyn F. "Folklore and Satire in a Brazillian Comedy." *Hispania,* vol. 44, no. 2 (May, 1961), pp. 282-284.

HERMANN SUDERMANN 1857-1928

General

Bockstahler, O.L. "Sudermann and Ibsen." *German Q.,* vol. 5, no. 2 (Mar., 1932), pp. 54-57.

Dukes, Ashley. *German dramatists* pp. 68-78.

Garten, H.F. *Modern German drama,* pp. 30-34.

Heller, Otto. *Studies in modern German literature,* pp. 107-115.

Mainland, William F. "Hermann Sudermann." *In:* Natan. A., ed. *German men of letters,* vol. 2 (1963), pp. 33-53.

The Battle of the Butterflies (Die Schmetterlingsschlacht)

Heller, Otto. *Studies in modern German literature,* pp. 56-59.

Witkowski, Georg. *German drama of the nineteenth century,* pp. 157-158.

The Destruction of Sodom (Sodoms Ende)

Ellehauge, Martin. *The position of Bernard Shaw in European drama and philosophy,* pp. 22-23, 267-269.

Heller, Otto. *Studies in modern German literature,* pp. 37-45.

Witkowski, Georg. *German drama of the nineteenth century,* pp. 155-156.

Fritzchen

Heller, Otto. *Studies in modern German literature,* pp. 63-65.

Happiness in a Nook (The Vale of Content) (Das Gluck im Winkel)

Heller, Otto. *Studies in modern German literature,* pp. 53-56.

Miller, Nellie Burget. *The living drama,* pp. 267-269.

Home (Heimat) (Magda)

Bauland, Peter. *The hooded eagle,* pp. 9-10, 14, 54.

Ellehauge, Martin. *The position of Bernard Shaw in European drama and philosophy,* pp. 10, 70-71.

Heller, Otto. *Studies in modern German literature,* pp. 45-53.

MacCarthy, Desmond. *Drama,* pp. 79-83.

Miller, Nellie Burget. *The living drama,* pp. 265-266.

Shaw, George Bernard. *Shaw's dramatic criticism (1895-98),* pp. 169-173.

Witkowski, Georg. *German drama of the nineteenth century,* pp. 156-157.

Honor (Die Ehre)

Ellehauge, Martin. *The position of Bernard Shaw in European drama and philosophy,* pp. 141-142.

Heller, Otto. *Studies in modern German literature,* pp. 30-37.

Witkowski, Georg. *German drama of the nineteenth century,* pp. 152-155.

It's a Man's World (Das Ewig-Mannliche)

Heller, Otto. *Studies in modern German literature,* pp. 65-67.

Johannes

Heller, Otto. *Studies in modern German literature,* pp. 67-77.

Witkowski, George. *German drama of the nineteenth century,* pp. 158-159.

The Joy of Living (Es Lebe das Leben)

Bauland, Peter. *The hooded eagle,* pp. 11-12, 24.

Heller, Otto. *Studies in modern German literature,* pp. 92-102.

St. John's Fire (Johannisfeuer)

Heller, Otto. *Studies in modern German literature,* pp. 83-92.

Der Sturmgeselle Sokrates

Heller, Otto. *Studies in modern German literature,* pp. 103-107.

Witkowski, Georg. *German drama of the nineteenth century,* p. 160.

Teja

Heller, Otto. *Studies in modern German literature,* pp. 59-62.

The Three Heron Plumes (Die Drei Reiherfedern)

Heller, Otto. *Studies in modern German literature,* pp. 77-83.

Witkowski, George. *German drama of the nineteenth century*, p. 159.

The Witches Ride

Hobson, Harold. *Theatre*, pp. 125-127.

JULES SUPERVIELLE 1884-1960

La Belle au Bois Dormant

Knowles, Dorothy. *French drama of the inter-war years, 1918-39*, pp. 191-192.

Bolivar

Knowles, Dorothy. *French drama of the inter-war years, 1918-39*, p. 193.

Robinson

Knowles, Dorothy. *French drama of the inter-war years, 1918-39*, p. 192.

Shéhérazade

Knowles, Dorothy. *French drama of the inter-war years, 1918-39*, p. 192.

Le Voleur d'Enfants

Knowles, Dorothy. *French drama of the inter-war years, 1918-39*, p. 192-193.

ERWIN SYLVANUS 1921-

Dr. Korczak and the Children (Korczak und Seine Kinder)

Coenen, F.E. "The "Modern German Drama." *In:* Hammer, Carl, Jr., ed. *Studies in German literature*, pp. 112-113.

Wellwarth, G.E. "Introduction." *In:* Benedikt, M., and G.E. Wellwarth, eds. *Postwar German theatre*, pp. xvi-xvii.

JOHN MILLINGTON SYNGE 1871-1909

General

Barnett, Pat. "The Nature of Synge's Dialogue." *English Literature in Transition (1880-1920)*, vol. 10 (1967), pp. 119-129.

Bickley, Francis. *J.M. Synge and the Irish dramatic movement*, pp. 9-31, 47.

Boyd, Ernest. *Ireland's literary renaissance,* pp. 316-321, 332-335.

Casey, Helen. "Synge's Use of the Anglo-Irish Idiom." *English J.,* vol. 27, no. 9 (Nov., 1938), pp. 773-776.

Clement, K.E. "John Millington Synge." M.A., University of Colorado, 1927.

Corkery, Daniel. *Synge and Anglo-Irish literature,* pp. 65-122.

Coxhead, Elizabeth. *J.M. Synge and Lady Gregory,* pp. 7-24.

Ellis-Fermor, Una. *The Irish dramatic movement,* pp. 163-186.

Estill, Adelaide D. "The sources of Synge." Ph.D., University of Pennsylvania, 1937.

Fraser, G.S. *The modern writer and his world,* pp. 204-206.

Gassner, John. *The theatre in our times,* pp. 217-224.

Greene, David Herbert. "The drama of J.M. Synge; a critical study." Ph.D., Harvard University, 1943.

Gregory, Isabella Augusta (Lady). *Our Irish theatre,* pp. 119-139.

Hoare, Dorothy M. *The works of Morris and of Yeats in relation to early saga literature,* pp. 105-110.

Howe, P.P. *J.M. Synge, a critical study,* pp. 100-125, 178-213.

Howland, Kathleen. "Synge: a tragic life imposes a tragic drama." M.A., University of Kansas, 1950.

Knight, G. Wilson. *The golden labyrinth,* pp. 322-325.

Krause, David. "The Rageous Ossean." *Modern Drama,* vol. 4 no. 3 (Dec., 1961), pp. 268-291.

Krutch, Joseph Wood. *"Modernism" in modern drama,* pp. 93-98.

Lamm, Martin. *Modern drama,* pp. 302-306, 312-314.

Lucas, F.L. *The drama of Chekhov, Synge, Yeats and Pirandello,* pp. 149-166.

McKinley, C.F. "John Millington Synge." Ph.D., Trinity College, Dublin. 1950-51.

Malone, Andrew E. *The Irish drama,* pp. 147-148, 155-156.

Miller, Nellie Burget. *The living drama,* pp. 337-339.

Montague, Charles E. *Dramatic values,* pp. 1-15.

Newlin, Nicholas. "The language of Synge's plays: the Irish element." Ph.D., University of Pennsylvania, 1950.

O'Donovan, Michael. *A short history of Irish literature,* pp. 146, 167, 168, 170, 171-172, 175-176, 177, 183-189, 191, 194.

Peacock, Ronald. *The poet in the theatre,* pp. 105-116.

Price, A.F. "The art of John Synge." M.A., University of London, 1951-52.

Price, Alan. "Synge's Prose Writings: A First View of the Whole." *Modern Drama,* vol. 11, no. 3 (Dec., 1968), pp. 221-226.

Saddlemyer, Ann. "A Share in the Dignity of the World: J.M. Synge's Aesthetic Theory," *In:* Skelton, Robin, ed. *The world of W.B. Yeats,* pp. 241-253.

Saddlemyer, Ann. "Rabelais versus A Kempis: The Art of J.M. Synge." *Komos: A Quarterly of Drama and Arts of the Theatre,* vol. 1 (1967), pp. 85-96.

Salerno, Henry F. *English drama in transition, 1880-1920,* pp. 415-416.

Setterquist, Jan. *Ibsen and the beginnings of Anglo-Irish drama. I. John Millington Synge,* pp. 9-15, 76-91.

Strong, L.A.G. "John Millington Synge." *Bookman* (U.S.A.), vol. 73 (Apr., 1931), pp. 125-136.

Williams, Harold. *Modern English writers,* pp. 206-217.

Williams, Raymond. *Drama from Ibsen to Eliot,* pp. 154-174.

Woods, Anthony S. "Synge Stayed At Home By the Fireside." *Catholic World,* vol. 141 (Apr., 1935), pp. 46-52.

Deirdre of the Sorrows

Barnet, Sylvan, ed. *The genius of the Irish theater,* pp. 151-154.

Bickley, Francis. *"Deirdre." Irish Rev.* (July, 1912).

Bickley, Francis. *J.M. Synge and the Irish dramatic movement,* pp. 40-47.

Boyd, Ernest. *Ireland's literary renaissance,* pp. 330-332.

Casey, Helen. "Synge's Use of the Anglo-Irish Idiom." *English J.,* vol. 27, no. 9 (Nov., 1938), pp. 773-776.

Corkery, Daniel. *Synge and Anglo-Irish literature,* pp. 205-228.

Coxhead, Elizabeth. *J.M. Synge and Lady Gregory,* pp. 21-22.

Fackler, Herbert V. "J.M. Synge's *Deirdre of the Sorrows:* Beauty Only." *Modern Drama,* vol. 11, no. 4 (Feb., 1969), pp. 404-409.

Ganz, Arthur. "J.M. Synge and the Drama of Art." *Modern Drama,* vol. 10, no. 1 (May, 1967), pp. 57-68.

Gassner, John. *The theatre in our times,* pp. 221-223.

Green, David H. "Synge's Unfinished *Deirdre."* *PMLA,* vol. 63, no. 4 (Dec., 1948), pp. 1314-1321.

Heilman, Robert B. *Tragedy and melodrama,* pp. 39-40.

Howe, P.P. *J.M. Synge, a critical study,* pp. 84-99.

Lucas, F.L. *The drama of Chekhov, Synge, Yeats and Pirandello,* pp. 225-237.

Malone, Andrew E. *The Irish drama,* pp. 154-155.

Orel, Harold. "Synge's Last Play: 'And A Story Will Be Told Forever.'" *Modern Drama,* vol. 4, no. 3 (Dec., 1961), pp. 306-313.

Price, Alan. *Synge and Anglo-Irish drama,* pp. 191-215.

Setterquist, Jan. *Ibsen and the beginnings of Anglo-Irish drama. I. John Millington Sunge,* pp. 71-75, 78, 82-84.

Styan, J.L. *The elements of drama* pp. 126-129, 257-260.

Williams, Raymond. *Drama from Ibsen to Eliot,* pp. 164-168.

In the Shadow of the Glen

Beerbohm, Max. *Around theatres,* pp. 314-319.

Boyd, Ernest. *Ireland's literary renaissance,* p. 321.

Dorcey, Donal. "The Big Occasions." *In:* McCann, Sean, ed. *The story of the Abbey Theatre,* pp. 130-133.

Howe, P.P. *J.M. Synge, a critical study,* pp. 43-51.

Lucas, F.L. *The drama of Chekhov, Synge, Yeats and Pirandello,* pp. 167-180.

Malone, Andrew E. *The Irish drama,* pp. 148-150.

Setterquist, Jan. *Ibsen and the beginnings of Anglo-Irish drama. I. John Millington Synge,* pp. 16-26, 38, 79, 85, 88. *II. Edward Martyn,* pp. 94-95.

The Playboy of the Western World

Bickley, Francis. *J.M. Synge and the Irish dramatic movement,* pp. 38-40.

Boyd, Ernest. *Ireland's literary renaissance,* pp. 326-329.

Cohn, Ruby, ed. *Twentieth-century drama,* pp. 93-94.

Corkery, Daniel. *Synge and Anglo-Irish literature,* pp. 179-204.

Cowell, Raymond. *Twelve modern dramatists,* pp. 57-59.

Coxhead, Elizabeth. *J.M. Synge and Lady Gregory,* pp. 18-21.

Cusack, Cyril. "A Player's Reflections on *Playboy." Modern Drama,* vol. 4, no. 3 (Dec., 1961), pp. 300-305.

Dorcey, Donal. "The Big Occassions." *In:* McCann, Sean, ed. *The story of the Abbey Theatre,* pp. 133-140.

Gallaway, Marian. *The director in the theatre,* pp. 90-132, 217-220.

Gassner, John. *The theatre in our times,* pp. 537-543.

Greene, David H. *"The Playboy* and Irish Nationalism." *J. of English and Germanic Philology, vol. 46 (1947)* pp. 199-204.

Greenwood, Ormerod. *The playwright,* pp. 192-197.

Gregory, Isabella Augusta (Lady). *Our Irish theatre,* pp. 109-118, 169-252, 280-305.

Hawkes, Terence. "Playboys of the Western World." *Listener,* vol. 74, no. 1916 (Dec., 16, 1965), pp. 991-993.

Henn, T.R. *The harvest of tragedy,* pp. 204-205.

Henry, P.L. *"The Playboy of the Western World." Philogica Pragensia,* vol. 8, nos. 2-3 (1965), pp. 189-204.

Howe, P.P. *J.M. Synge, a critical study,* pp. 61-76, 168-177.

Johnson, Wallace H. "The Pagan Setting of Synge's *Playboy." Renascence,* vol. 19 (1967), pp. 119-121, 150.

Kavanagh, Peter. *The story of the Abbey Theatre from its origins to the present,* pp. 57-60, 70-71, 93-96.

Kronenberger, Louis. *The thread of laughter,* pp. 284-288.

Lamm, Martin. *Modern drama,* pp. 310-312.

Lucas, F.L. *The drama of Chekhov, Synge, Yeats and Pirandello,* pp. 201-224.

McLean, Hugh H. "The Hero as Playboy." *Univ. of Kansas City Rev.,* vol. 21, no. 1 (Autumn, 1954), pp. 9-19.

Malone, Andrew E. *The Irish drama,* pp. 100-104, 109, 111-112, 151-153.

O'Casey, Sean. "John Millington Synge." *In:* O'Casey, Sean. *Blasts and benedictions,* pp. 39-40.

Pearce, Howard D. "Synge's *Playboy* as Mock-Christ." *Modern Drama,* vol. 8, no. 3 (Dec., 1965), pp. 303-310.

Podhoretz, Norman. "Synge's *Playboy:* Morality and the Hero." *Essays in Criticism,* vol. 3, no. 3 (July, 1953), pp. 337-344.

Price, Alan. *Synge and Anglo-Irish drama,* pp. 161-180.

Reinert, Otto, ed. *Drama; an introductory anthology* (alternate ed), pp. 696-701.

Salerno, Henry F., ed. *English drama in transition, 1880-1920,* pp. 416-419.

Setterquist, Jan. *Ibsen and the beginnings of Anglo-Irish drama. I. John Millington Synge,* pp. 52-70, 78, 79, 81-82, 91.

Sidnell, M.J. "Synge's *Playboy* and the Champion of Ulster." *Dalhousie Rev.,* vol. 45, no. 1 (Spring, 1965), pp. 51-59.

Spacks, Patricia Meyer. "The Making of the *Playboy." Modern Drama,* vol. 4, no. 3 (Dec., 1961), pp. 314-323.

Styan, J.L. *The dark comedy,* 2nd ed., pp. 131-132, 261, 271.

Styan, J.L. *The elements of the drama,* pp. 57-63.

Synge, J.M. *In:* Cole, Toby, ed. *Playwrights on playwriting,* pp. 201-203. (Reprinted from *The complete works of John M. Synge* (New York: Random House, 1935), pp. 3, 177-78.)

Tynan, Kenneth. *Tynan right and left,* p. 41.

Williams, Raymond. *Drama from Ibsen to Eliot,* pp. 162-164.

Riders to the Sea

Allison, Alexander W., ed. *Masterpieces of the drama,* 2nd ed., pp. 505-506.

690

Beerbohm, Max. *Around theatres,* pp. 314-319.

Bickley, Francis. *J.M. Synge and the Irish dramatic movement,* pp. 34-37.

Boyd, Ernest. *Ireland's literary renaissance,* pp. 321-323.

Combs, William W. "J.M. Synge's *Riders to the Sea:* A Reading and Some Generalizations." Michigan Academy of Science, Arts, and Letters, *Papers,* vol. 50 (1965), pp. 599-607.

Corkery, Daniel. *Synge and Anglo-Irish Literature,* pp. 135-146.

Coxhead, Elizabeth. *J.M. Synge and Lady Gregory,* pp. 14-16.

Heilman, Robert B. *Tragedy and melodrama,* pp. 38-39, 40, 72, 80, 82.

Henn, T.R. *The harvest of tragedy,* pp. 202-203.

Howe, P.P. *J.M. Synge, a critical study,* pp. 51-60.

Lamm, Martin. *Modern drama,* pp. 306-309.

Lucas, F.L. *The drama of Chekhov, Synge, Yeats and Pirandello,* pp. 181-188.

Malone, Andrew E. *The Irish drama,* p. 150.

Miller, Nellie Burget. *The living drama,* pp. 339-340.

Nicoll, Allardyce. *British drama,* pp. 271-274.

O'Casey, Sean. "John Millington Synge." *In:* O'Casey, Sean. *Blasts and benedictions,* pp. 37-39.

Price, Alan. *Synge and Anglo-Irish drama,* pp. 181-191.

Setterquist, Jan. *Ibsen and the beginnings of Anglo-Irish drama. I. John Millington Synge,* pp. 27-39, 78, 79-80, 88.

The Shadow of the Glen

Bickley, Francis, *J.M. Synge and the Irish dramatic movement,* pp. 32-34.

Corkery, Daniel. *Synge and Anglo-Irish literature,* pp. 123-134.

Coxhead, Elizabeth. *J.M. Synge and Lady Gregory,* p. 14.

Ganz, Arthur. "J.M. Synge and the Drama of Art." *Modern Drama,* vol. 10, no. 1 (May, 1967), pp. 57-68.

Greene, David H. *"The Shadow of the Glen* and the Window of Ephesus." *PMLA,* vol. 62, no. 1, part 1 (Mar., 1947), pp. 233-238.

Kronenberger, Louis. *The thread of laughter,* pp. 282-283.

O'Casey, Sean. "John Millington Synge." *In:* O'Casey, Sean. *Blasts and benedictions,* pp. 36-37, 39, 40.

Price, Alan. *Synge and Anglo-Irish drama,* pp. 118-126.

Styan, J.L. *The dark comedy,* 2nd ed., pp. 130-131.

Williams, Raymond. *Drama from Ibsen to Eliot,* pp. 156-159.

The Tinker's Wedding

Boyd, Ernest. *Ireland's literary renaissance,* pp. 323-324.

Corkery, Daniel. *Synge and Anglo-Irish literature,* pp. 147-152.

Coxhead, Elizabeth. *J.M. Synge and Lady Gregory,* p. 16.

Ganz, Arthur. "J.M. Synge and the Drama of Art." *Modern Drama,* vol. 10, no. 1 (May, 1967), pp. 57-68.

Greene, David H. *"The Tinker's Wedding,* a Revaluation." *PMLA,* vol. 62, no. 3 (Sept., 1947), pp. 824-827.

Howe, P.P. *J.M. Synge, a critical study,* pp. 76-84.

Kronenberger, Louis. *The thread of laughter,* 283-284.

Lucas, F.L. *The drama of Chekhov, Synge, Yeats and Pirandello,* pp. 189-191.

Malone, Andrew E. *The Irish drama,* pp. 153-154.

Price, Alan. *Synge and Anglo-Irish Drama,* pp. 127-137.

Setterquist, Jan. *Ibsen and the beginnings of Anglo-Irish drama. I. John Millington Synge,* pp. 40-42, 80-81, 88.

The Well of the Saints

Bickley, Francis. *J.M. Synge and the Irish dramatic movement,* pp. 37-38.

Boyd, Ernest. *Ireland's literary renaissance,* pp. 324-325.

Corkery, Daniel. *Synge and Anglo-Irish literature,* pp. 153-178.

Coxhead, Elizabeth. *J.M. Synge and Lady Gregory,* pp. 17-18.

Ganz, Arthur. "J.M. Synge and the Drama of Art." *Modern Drama,* vol. 10, no. 1 (May, 1967), pp. 57-68.

Howe, P.P. *J.M. Synge, a critical study,* pp. 33-43.

Lucas, F.L. *The drama of Chekhov, Synge, Yeats and Pirandello,* pp. 192-200.

Malone, Andrew E. *The Irish drama,* pp. 150-151.

Price, Alan. *Synge and Anglo-Irish drama,* pp. 138-161.

Setterquist, Jan. *Ibsen and the beginnings of Anglo-Irish drama. I. John Millington Synge,* pp. 43-51, 81, 88.

Styan, J.L. *The dark comedy,* 2nd ed., p. 111.

Williams, Raymond. *Drama from Ibsen to Eliot,* pp. 160-162.

RABINDRANATH TAGORE 1861-1941

King of the Dark Chamber

Brustein, Robert. *Seasons of discontent,* pp. 44-45.

ROBERTO A. TALICE

General

Jones, W.K. *Behind Spanish American footlights,* pp. 174-175.

JEAN TARDIEU 1903-

General

Esslin, Martin. *The theatre of the absurd,* pp. 168-176.

Hatzfeld, Helmut. *Trends and styles in twentieth-century French literature,* p. 277.

Kuhn, Reinhard. "The Debasement of the Intellectual in Contemporary Continental Drama." *Modern Drama,* vol. 7, no. 4 (Feb., 1965), pp. 454-462.

Pronko, Leonard C. *Avant-garde: the experimental theater in France,* pp. 155-158.

The A. B. C. of Our Life (L'A. B. C. de Notre Vie)

Wellwarth, George. *The theatre of protest and paradox,* pp. 88-89.

The Apollo Society (Le Société Apollon)

Wellwarth, George, *The theatre of protest and paradox,* pp. 92-93.

693

Conversation-Sinfonietta

Wellwarth, George. *The theatre of protest and Paradox,* pp. 93-94.

The Information Bureau (Le Guichet)

Wellwarth, George. *The theatre of protest and paradox,* pp. 89-92.

The Keyhole (La Serrure)

Wellwarth, George. *The theatre of protest and paradox,* pp. 94-95.

The Lovers in the Metro (Les Amants du Metro)

Wellwarth, George. *The theatre of protest and paradox,* pp. 95-97.

One Way for Another (Un Geste pour un Autre)

Wellwarth, George. *The theatre of protest and paradox,* p. 94.

The Rite of Night (Le Sacre de la Nuit)

Wellwarth, George. *The theatre of protest and paradox,* p. 86.

Useless Courtesy (La Politesse Inutile)

Wellwarth, George. *The theatre of protest and paradox,* pp. 87-88.

Who Is There? (Qui Est La?)

Wellwarth, George. *The theatre of protest and paradox,* pp. 86-87.

SAMUEL ALBERT TAYLOR 1912-

The Happy Time

Sievers, W. David. *Freud on Broadway,* pp. 433-434.

AHMET KUTSI TECER 1901-

The Neighborhood (Kösebasi)

Halman, Talat S. "A Turkish Play in English." *Books Abroad,* vol. 40 (1966), pp. 160-161.

HERMAN TEIRLINCK 1879-

General

Mallinson, Vernon. *Modern Belgian literature, 1830-1960,* pp. 165-167.

ANDRES TERBAY *See* Sarah, Roberto

CARLOS TERRON 1913-

General

Pandolfi, Vito. "Italian Theatre Since the War." *Tulane Drama Rev.,* vol. 8, no. 3 (Spring, 1964), p. 99.

DYLAN THOMAS 1914-1953

Under Milkwood

Ackerman, John. *Dylan Thomas, his life and work,* pp. 67, 99, 170-183.

Daiches, David. "The Poetry of Dylan Thomas." *In:* Cox, C.B., ed. *Dylan Thomas: a collection of critical essays,* pp. 23-24. (Reprinted from Daiches, David. *Literary essays* (Oliver and Boyd, Ltd., 1956).)

Dupee, F.W. *"The King of the Cats."* and other remarks on writers and writing, pp. 196-198.

Hawkes, Terence. "Playboys of the Western World." *Listener,* vol. 74, no. 1916 (Dec., 16, 1965), pp. 991-993.

Holbrook, David. "A Place of Love: *Under Milk Wood."* *In:* Cox, C.B., ed. *Dylan Thomas: a collection of critical essays,* pp. 99-116. (Reprinted from Holbrook, David. *Dylan Thomas and poetic dissociation* (Southern Illinois University Press, 1964). *Also in:* Holbrook, David. *Llareggub revisited.*

Korg, Jacob. *Dylan Thomas,* pp. 176-178.

Manly, Frank. "The Text of Dylan Thomas' *Under Milk Wood."* *Emory University Q.,* vol. 20, no. 2 (Summer, 1964), pp. 131-144.

Rea, J. "A Topographical Guide to *Under Milk Wood." College English,* vol. 25 (1964), pp. 535-542.

Styan, J.L. *The dark comedy,* 2nd ed., pp. 114-115, 235, 289, 294.

Wells, Henry W. "Voice and Verse in Dylan Thomas' Play." *College English,* vol. 15, no. 8 (May, 1954), pp. 438-444.

Williams, Raymond. "Dylan Thomas's Play for Voices." *In:* Cox, C.B., ed. *Dylan Thomas: a collection of critical essays,* pp. 89-98. (Reprinted from *Critical Q.,* vol. 1 (Spring, 1959), pp. 18-26.)

SAM THOMPSON 1916-1965

General

Hogan, Robert. *After the Irish renaissance,* pp. 100-102.

695

JAMES THURBER 1894-1961

General

Gould, Jean. *Modern American playwrights,* pp. 151-154.

Morsberger, Robert E. *James Thurber,* pp. 154-159.

The Male Animal

Gilder, Rosamond. "Brain and Brawn, Broadway in Review." *Theatre Arts,* vol. 24 (Mar., 1940), pp. 158-162.

Krutch, Joseph Wood. "Review of *The Male Animal.*" *Nation,* vol. 150 (Jan. 20, 1940), pp. 81-82.

Morsberger, Robert E. *James Thurber,* pp. 54, 87, 102, 105, 126-135, 137-141, 147-151, 153, 155, 157, 179, 197.

Stroud, Beverley Jean. *An analysis and production book of The Male Animal,* Unpublished M.A. Thesis, Ohio State Univ., 1950.

WALLACE THURMAN 1902- (William Jourdan Rapp, co-author)

Harlem

Abramson, Doris E. *Negro playwrights in the American theatre, 1925-1959,* pp. 32-38, 41-43.

CESAR TIEMPO

See Zeitlin, Israel

FRANCISCO TOBAR GARCIA 1928-

General

Jones, W.K. *Behind Spanish American footlights,* pp. 318-319.

ERNST TOLLER 1893-1939

General

Bauland, Peter. *The hooded eagle,* pp. 78-82, 93, 111-115, 126, 142, 160.

Beckley, Richard. "Ernst Toller." *In:* Natan, A., ed. *German men of letters,* vol. 3 (1964), pp. 85-104.

Garten, H.F. *Modern German drama,* pp. 107, 134, 138-147.

Hatfield, Henry. *Modern German literature,* pp. 76-78.

Sokel, Walter. *The writer in extremis,* pp. 180, 190, 196-197, 200-201, 230-231.

Willibrand, W.A. "Ernst Toller's Ideological Skepticism." *German Q.,* vol. 19, no. 3 (May, 1946), pp. 181-186.

Willibrand, W.A. "The Timely Dramas of Ernst Toller." *Monatshefte,* vol. 39, no. 3 (Mar., 1947), pp. 157-169.

Bibliography

Spalek, John M. *Ernst Toller and his critics; a bibliography.*

The Blind Goddess (Adapted by Denis Johnson with title Blind Man's Buff)

Williamson, Audrey. *Contemporary theatre, 1953-1956,* pp. 94-96.

Bloody Laughter (Hinkemann) (Also known as The Red Laugh and Brokenbrow)

Bauland, Peter. *The hooded eagle,* pp. 79, 111-112, 231n.

Beckley, Richard. "Ernst Toller." *In:* Natan, A., ed. *German men of letters,* vol. 3 (1964), pp. 97-98.

Block, Anita. *The changing world in plays and theatre,* pp. 207-209.

Garten, H.F. *Modern German drama,* pp. 143-144.

Draw the Fires (Feuer aus den Kesseln)

Beckley, Richard. "Ernst Toller." *In:* Natan, A., ed. *German men of letters,* vol. 3 (1964), p. 97.

The Machine Wreckers (Die Maschinenstürmer)

Bauland, Peter. *The hooded eagle,* pp. 97, 113-114.

Beckley, Richard. "Ernst Toller." *In:* Natan, A., ed. *German men of letters,* vol. 3 (1964), pp. 95-96.

Block, Anita. *The changing world in plays and theatre,* pp. 204-207.

Garten, H.F. *Modern German drama,* pp. 142-143.

Toller, Ernst. In: Cole, Toby, ed. *Playwrights on playwriting,* pp. 222-223. (Reprinted from "My Works." translated by Marketa Goetz in *The Tulane Drama Rev.* (Mar., 1959), pp. 99-106 passim.)

Man and the Masses (Masse-Mensch)

Bauland, Peter. *The hooded eagle,* pp. 78, 79, 80-82, 93.

Beckley, Richard. "Ernst Toller." *In:* Natan, A., ed. *German men of letters,* vol. 3 (1964), pp. 93-94.

Block, Anita. *The changing world in plays and theatre,* pp. 18-19, 196-204.

Garten, H.F. *Modern German drama,* pp. 141-142.

Greenwood, Ormerod. *The playwright,* pp. 129, 131-135.

Sokel, Walter. *The writer in extremis,* pp. 195-196, 197-200, 203-204.

Toller, Ernst. In: Cole, Toby, ed. *Playwrights on playwriting,* pp. 220-222. (Reprinted from "My Works." translated by Marketa Goetz in *The Tulane Drama Rev.* (Mar., 1959), pp. 99-106 *passim.*)

No More Peace (Nie Wieder Friede!)

Bauland, Peter. *The hooded eagle,* p. 114.

Die Schwalbenbuch

Beckley, Richard. "Ernst Toller." *In:* Natan, A., ed. *German men of letters,* vol. 3 (1964), pp. 98-99.

Such is Life! (Hoppla, Wir Leben!)

Garten H.F. *Modern German drama,* pp. 144-145.

Loving, Pierre. "A Note on Ernst Toller." *Dial,* vol. 86 (Mar., 1929), pp. 205-210.

Toller Ernst. *In:* Cole, Toby, ed. *Playwrights on playwriting,* pp. 223-227. (Reprinted from "My Works." translated by Marketa Goetz in *The Tulane Drama Rev.* (Mar., 1959), pp. 99-106 *passim.*

Williams, Raymond. *Drama from Ibsen to Eliot.* pp. 179-184.

Transfiguration (Die Wandlung)

Beckley, Richard. "Ernst Toller." *In:* Natan, A., ed. *German men of letters,* vol. 3 (1964), pp. 85-93.

Garten, H.F. *Modern German drama,* pp. 139-140.

Sokel, Walter. *The writer in extremis,* pp. 180-183, 187, 188-189, 198.

Toller, Ernst. *In:* Cole, Toby, ed. *Playwrights on playwriting.* pp. 218-220. (Reprinted from "My Works," translated by Marketa Goetz in *The Tulane Drama Rev.* (Mar., 1959), pp. 99-106 *passim.*)

ALEKSEI NIKOLAEVICH TOLSTOI 1882-1945

General

Macleod, Joseph. *Actors cross the Volga,* pp. 130, 133, 247, 287.

LEO NIKOLAYEVITCH TOLSTOI 1828-1910

General

Lavrin, Janko. "Tolstoy and Nietzsche." *In:* Lavrin, J. *Studies in European literature,* pp. 131-155.

The Fruits of Enlightenment

Ellehauge, Martin. *The position of Bernard Shaw in European drama and philosophy,* pp. 61-62.

Perry, Henry Ten Eyck. *Masters of dramatic comedy and their social themes,* pp. 336-338.

Light Shines in Darkness

Balmforth, Ramsden. *The problem-play and its influence on modern thought and life,* pp. 28-33.

Ellehauge, Martin. *The position of Bernard Shaw in European drama and philosophy,* pp. 309-310.

Lamm, Martin. *Modern drama,* pp. 190-193.

The Living Corpse

Baring, Maurice. *Punch and Judy and other essays,* pp. 327-332.

Hamilton, Clayton. *Seen on the stage.* pp. 145-150.

Lamm, Martin. *Modern drama,* pp. 188-190.

The Powers of Darkness

Ellehauge, Martin. *The position of Bernard Shaw in European drama and philosophy,* pp. 125-126.

Hamilton, Clayton. *Seen on the stage.* pp. 150-153.

Lamm, Martin. *Modern drama,* pp. 182-185.

Redemption

Bertensson, Sergei. "The History of Tolstoy's Posthumous Play." *American Slavic and East European Rev.,* vol. 14, no. 2 (1955), pp. 265-268.

The Root of All Evil

Lamm, Martin. *Modern drama,* pp. 185-188.

JOSEPH TOMELTY 1911-

General

Hogan, Robert. *After the Irish renaissance,* pp. 99-100, 102, 105-108.

Is the Priest at Home?

Hogan, Robert. *After the Irish renaissance,* pp. 107-108.

JEAN TOOMER 1894-

General

Fullinwider, S.P. "Jean Toomer: Lost Generation or Negro Renaissance." *Phylon,* vol. 27 (1966), pp. 396-403.

Turner, Darwin T. "The Failure of a Playwright." *College Language Association J.* (Morgan State Coll., Baltimore), vol. 10 (1967) pp. 308-318.

JOSEF TOPOL

The Carnival

Tigrid, Pavel. "Frost and Thaw: Literature in Czechoslovakia." *East Europe,* vol. 15, no. 9 (Sept., 1966), p. 10.

The Cat on the Rails

Tigrid, Pavel. "Frost and Thaw: Literature in Czechoslovakia." *East Europe,* vol. 15, no. 9 (Sept., 1966), p. 10.

DAN TOTHEROH

Moor Born

Sievers, W. David. *Freud on Broadway,* pp. 306-307.

SOPHIE TREADWELL

Hope for a Harvest

Himelstein, Morgan Y. *Drama was a weapon, the left-wing theatre in New York 1929-1941,* pp. 151-152.

Machinal

Brustein, Robert. *Seasons of discontent,* pp. 36-39.

Sievers, W. David. *Freud on Broadway,* pp. 90-91.

SERGEI MIKHAILOVICH TRETIAKOV 1892-

Roar China

Block, Anita. *The changing world in plays and theatre,* pp. 367-374.

Himelstein, Morgan Y. *Drama was a weapon, the left-wing theatre in New York 1929-1941,* pp. 127-128.

IVAN SERGEEVICH TURGENEV 1818-1883

General

Keefer, Lubov. "The Operetta Librettos of Ivan Turgenev." *Slavic and East European J.,* vol. 10 (1966), pp. 134-154.

The Bachelor

Valency, Maurice. *The breaking string,* pp. 41-42.

A Month in the Country

Dent, Alan. *Preludes and studies,* pp. 148-149.

Perry, Henry Ten Eyck. *Masters of dramatic comedy and their social themes,* pp. 328-331.

Valency, Maurice. *The breaking string,* pp. 42-45.

ROBERT TURNEY

Daughters of Atreus

O'Hara, Frank H. *Today in American drama,* pp. 38-52.

MILAN UHDE

King Vavra (Král Vávra)

Den, Petr. "Notes on Czechoslovakia's Young Theater of the Absurd." *Books Abroad,* vol. 41, no. 2 (Spring, 1967), pp. 159-160.

MIGUEL DE UNAMUNO Y JUGO 1864-1936

General

Ayllón, Cándido. "Experiments in the Theatre of Unamuno, Valle-Inclán, and Azorin." *Hispania,* vol. 46 (1963), pp. 49-56.

Ungerer, Gustav. "Unamuno and Shakespeare." *In:* Bleiberg, German and E. Inman Fox, eds. *Spanish thought and letters in the twentieth century,* pp. 513-532.

FRITZ VON UNRUH 1885-

General

Garten, H.F. *Modern German drama,* pp. 123, 134-138, 139, 188 note.

A Race (Ein Geschlecht)

Garten, H.F. *Modern German drama,* pp. 135-137.

Square (Platz)

Garten, H.F. *Modern German drama,* pp. 137-138.

RODOLFO USIGLI 1905-

General

Anderson Imbert, Enrique. *Spanish-American literature: a history,* pp. 511-512.

Franco, Jean. *The modern culture of Latin America,* pp. 208-209, 233-234.

Jones, W.K. *Behind Spanish American footlights,* pp. 497, 501, 502-504, 506, 510, 511.

Ragle, Gordon. "Rodolfo Usigli and His Mexican Scene." *Hispania,* vol. 46 (1963), pp. 307-311.

The Impersonator (El Gesticulador)

Anderson Imbert, Enrique. *Spanish-American literature: a history,* pp. 511-512.

Franco, Jean. *The modern culture of Latin America,* pp. 209, 234, 274.

PETER USTINOV 1921-

General

Lumley, Frederick. *New trends in 20th-century drama,* pp. 304-306.

Lumley, Frederick. *Trends in 20th-century drama,* pp. 213-214.

Ustinov, Peter. "Talking to F. Galle." *In:* Richards, Dick. *The curtain rises,* pp. 13-16.

The Love of Four Colonels

Bentley, Eric. *The dramatic event,* pp. 86-89.

Sievers, W. David. *Freud on Broadway,* pp. 445-446.

The Moment of Truth

Hobson, Harold. *The theatre,* pp. 93-98.

Photo Finish

Lumley, Frederick. *New trends in 20th-century drama,* pp. 305-306.

Sainer, Arthur. *The sleepwalker and the assassin, a view of the contemporary theatre,* pp. 34-36.

ALBERTO VACAREZZA 1888-1959

General

Jones, W.K. *Behind Spanish American footlights,* pp. 138-140.

San Antonio de los Cobres

Jones, W.K. *Behind Spanish American footlights,* p. 138.

RAMON MARIA DEL VALLE-INCLAN 1866-1936

General

Marquerie, Alfredo. "A Centenary of Spanish Theatre." *Topic: A Journal of the Liberal Arts* (Wash. and Jeff. College, Wash., Penn.), no. 15 (Spring, 1968), pp. 35-37.

Ayllón, Cándido. "Experiments in the Theatre of Unamuno, Valle-Inclán, and Azorin." *Hispania,* vol. 46 (1963), pp. 49-56.

Ely, Barbara Fay. "The problem of Spain, as interpreted in the works of Don Ramon del Valle-Inclán." *Dissertation Abstracts,* vol. 23 (1963), 4355-4356 (Tulane).

Hardison, Felicia. "Valle-Inclán and Artaud: Brothers Under the Skin." *Educational Theatre J.,* vol. 19, no. 4 (Dec., 1967) pp. 455-466.

Lima, Robert. "Valle-Inclán: The Man and His Early Plays." *Drama Critique,* vol. 9, no. 2 (1966), pp. 69-78.

Zahareas, Anthony al (1967), pp. 3-23.d Gerald Gillespie. "Ramon Maria del Valle-Inclán: The Theatre of Esperpentos." *Drama Survey,* vol. 6 (1967), pp. 3-23.

Divine Words

Benedikt, M., and G.E. Wellwarth. *Modern Spanish theatre, an anthology of plays,* pp. 2-3.

La Reina Castiza

Greenfield, Summer M. "Stylization and Deformation in Valle-Inclán's *La reina castiza." Bulletin of Hispanic Studies,* vol. 39 (1962), pp. 78-89.

ANTON VAN DE VELDE 1895-

General

Mallinson, Vernon. *Modern Belgian literature, 1830-1960,* pp. 167-168.

JOHN VAN DRUTEN 1901-1957

The Voice of the Turtle

Hobson, Harold. *Theatre,* pp. 105-107.

Young Woodley

Sievers, W. David. *Freud on Broadway,* p. 410.

SUTTON VANE 1888-1963

Outward Bound

Balmforth, Ramsden. *The problem-play and its influence on modern thought and life,* pp. 121-140.

JEAN-CLAUDE VAN ITALLIE 1935-

America Hurrah (Three one-act plays)

Gassner, John. "Broadway in Review," *Educational Theatre J.,* vol. 19, no. 1 (Mar., 1967), pp. 81-82.

Gottfried, Martin. *A theater divided; the postwar American stage,* pp. 301-302.

Lester, Elenore. "...Or the Wave of the Future?" *The New York Times* (June 30, 1968), Sec. 2, p. 3.

JEAN VAUTHIER

General

Beaujour, Michel. "An Introduction to the Theatre of Jean Vauthier." *Yale French Studies,* vol. 28 (Spring-Summer, 1962), pp. 125-131.

Guicharnaud, Jacques. *Modern French theatre from Giraudoux to Genet* (rev. ed.), pp. 169-172, 177, 286, 321, 341-342, 361-362.

Hatzfeld, Helmut. *Trends and styles in twentieth-century French literature,* pp. 277-278.

Captain Bada (Le Capitaine Bada)

Knapp, Bettina L. "Torn Dialogues...Torn and Lacerated Dialogues...Jean Vauthier." *Modern Drama,* vol. 9, no. 1 (May, 1966), pp. 40-53.

Pronko, Leonard C. *Avant-garde: the experimental theater in France,* pp. 159-160.

The Character Against Himself (Le Personnage Combattant) (Fortissima)

Bishop, Thomas. *Pirandello and the French theater,* pp. 139-140.

Flanner, Janet. *Paris journal, 1944-1965,* pp. 310-311.

Knapp, Bettina L. "Torn Dialogues...Torn and Lacerated Dialogues...Jean Vauthier." *Modern Drama,* vol. 9, no. 1 (May, 1966), pp. 40-53.

Pronko, Leonard C. *Avant-garde: the experimental theater in France,* pp. 160-163.

The Dreamer (Le Reveur)

Knapp, Bettina L. "Torn Dialogues...Torn and Lacerated Dialogues...Jean Vauthier." *Modern Drama,* vol. 9, no. 1 (May, 1966), pp. 40-53.

A. VELODIN

General

Revutsky, Valerian. "Velodin's Two Plays." *Canadian Slavonic Papers,* vol. 7 (1965), pp. 223-234.

The Appointment (Naznacenie)

Ferrer, Olga P. "Theater in the U.S.S.R.: Summer of 1964." *Books Abroad,* vol. 39, no. 3, p. 301.

PEDRO JORGE VERA 1912-

General

Jones, W.K. *Behind Spanish American footlights,* pp. 314-315.

GIOVANNI VERGA 1840-1922

General

Goldberg, Isaac. *The drama of transition,* pp. 141-145.

LOUIS VERNEUIL 1893-

General

Knowles, Dorothy. *French drama of the inter-war years, 1918-39,* pp. 279-280.

PAUL VIALAR 1898-

Les Hommes

Knowles, Dorothy. *French drama of the inter-war years, 1918-39,* pp. 158-159.

BORIS VIAN 1920-1959

General

Guicharnaud, Jacques. *Modern French theatre from Giraudoux to Genet* (rev. ed.), pp. 160, 180-184, 194, 344, 362.

The Empire Builders (Les Batisseurs d'Empire)

Esslin, Martin. *The theatre of the absurd,* pp. 177-179.

The Generals' Tea Party

Hope-Wallace, Philip. *"The Generals' Tea-Party." Guardian,* no. 37,432 (Nov. 12, 1966), p. 6.

Lambert, J.W. "Vian not Viable." *Times,* no. 7486 (Nov. 13, 1966) p. 25. "M. Vian's Generals Fail to Survive Carnage." *Times,* no. 56,787. (Nov., 12, 1966), p. 13.

"Paris Enjoys Fun at Generals' Expense." *Times,* no. 56,557 (Feb. 16, 1966), p. 17.

GORE VIDAL 1925-

General

White, Ray Lewis. *Gore Vidal.*

The Best Man

Brustein, Robert. *Seasons of discontent,* pp. 108-110.

White, Ray Lewis. *Gore Vidal,* pp. 100-104.

On the March to the Sea

White, Ray Lewis. *Gore Vidal,* pp. 105-108.

Romulus

Brustein, Robert. *Seasons of Discontent,* pp. 132-133.

White, Ray Lewis. *Gore Vidal,* pp. 108-110.

Visit to a Small Planet

White, Ray Lewis. *Gore Vidal,* pp. 96-100.

ALFRED DE VIGNY 1797-1863

Chatterton

Friedman, Martin B. "Vigny's use of Chatterton in *Stello.*" *Revue de Littérature Comparée,* vol. 38, no. 2 (Apr.-June, 1964), pp. 262-263.

JEAN VILAR

General

Lenoir-Kingham. "Jean Vilar Interviewed: Documents, plays and play-documents?" *World Theatre,* vol. 14, no. 3 (May-June, 1965), pp. 280-289.

Oppenheimer Case

Michalski, John. "German Drama and Theater in 1965." *Books Abroad,* vol. 40 (1966), pp. 137-138.

CHARLES VILDRAC 1882
(real name Charles Messager)

General

Bissel, C.H. "The Dramatic Art of Charles Vildrac." *French Rev.,* vol. 10 (1937), pp. 480-490.

Daniels, May. *French drama of the unspoken,* pp. 126-129, 140-143.

Knowles, Dorothy. *French drama of the inter-war years, 1918-39,* pp. 124-125.

Moore, Harry T. *Twentieth-century French literature to World War II,* pp. 129-130.

L'Air du Temps

Daniels, May. *The French drama of the unspoken,* pp. 139-140.

La Brouille

Knowles, Dorothy. *French drama of the inter-war years, 1918-39*, pp. 123-124.

Madame Beliard

Daniels, May. *The French drama of the unspoken*, pp. 136-138.

Knowles, Dorothy. *French drama of the inter-war years, 1918-39*, pp. 123.

Michel Auclair

Krutch, Joseph Wood. "Tenderness and Truth." *Nation*, vol. 120 (Mar. 25, 1925), pp. 344-355.

Theatre Arts, vol. 8 (Jan., 1924), pp. 13-18.

Le Pelerin

Daniels, May. *The French drama of the unspoken*, pp. 134-136.

The Steamer Tenacity (Le Paquebot Tenacity)

Daniels, May. *The French drama of the unspoken*, pp. 129-134.

Knowles, Dorothy. *French drama of the inter-war years, 1918-39*, pp. 122-123.

Young, Stark. *S.S. Tenacity.*" *New Republic*, vol. 29 (Jan. 25, 1922), p. 251.

DINKA VILLARROEL 1909-

General

Jones, W.K. *Behind Spanish American footlights*, p. 238.

Jones, W.K. "New Life in Chile's Theatre." *Modern Drama*, vol. 1, no. 1 (May, 1959), pp. 61-62.

XAVIER VILLAURRUTIA 1903-1950

General

Jones, W.K. *Behind Spanish American footlights*, pp. 501-502, 504.

Moreno, Antonio. "Xavier Villaurrutia: The Development of His Theatre." *Hispania*, vol. 43 (Dec., 1950), pp. 508-514.

ROGER VITRAC

Le Camelot

Knowles, Dorothy. *French drama of the inter-war years, 1918-39,* p. 86.

Le Coup de Trafalgar

Knowles, Dorothy. *French drama of the inter-war years, 1918-39,* pp. 85-86.

Les Demoiselles du Large

Knowles, Dorothy. *French drama of the inter-war years, 1918-39,* p. 86.

Victor, or All Power to the Children

Clurman, Harold. *The naked image,* pp. 211-213.

Gascoigne, Bamber. "A Time When Anything Goes." *Observer,* no. 9032 (Aug. 9, 1964), p. 20.

Gross, John. "Darkness Risible." *Encounter,* vol. 23, no. 4 (Oct., 1964), pp. 41-43.

Hobson, Harold. "Laughter and Subversion." *Times,* no. 7369 (Aug. 9, 1964), p. 23.

Hobson, Harold. "Waiting for *Victor.*" *Times,* no. 7367 (July 26, 1964), p. 29.

Hope-Wallace, Philip. *"Victor* at the Aldych." *Guardian,* no. 36,729 (Aug. 7, 1964), p. 7.

Knowles, Dorothy. *French drama of the inter-war years, 1918-39,* pp. 83-85.

MARTIN WALSER 1927-

General

Lumley, Frederick. *New trends in 20th-century drama,* pp. 357-359.

The Black Swan (Der Schwarze Schwan)

Lumley, Frederick. *New trends in 20th-century drama.* p. 358.

The Detour

Lumley, Frederick. *New trends in 20th-century drama,* p. 358.

Oaktree and Angora (Also called The Rabbit Race) (Eiche und Angora)

Garten, H.F. *Modern German drama,* pp. 266-267.

Lumley, Frederick. *New trends in 20th-century drama,* pp. 357-358.

ROBERT WALSER 1878-1956

General

Wilbert-Collins, Elly. *A bibliography of four contemporary German-Swiss authors: Friedrich Durrenmatt, Max Frisch, Robert Walser, Albin Zollinger.*

EUGENE WALTER 1874-1941

The Easiest Way

Gassner, John. "Introduction." *Best plays of the early American theatre from the beginning to 1916,* pp. xliii-xlv.

Phillips, Elizabeth C. *Modern American drama,* pp. 49-53, 54-55.

DOUGLAS TURNER WARD

General

Mitchell, Loften. *Black drama,* pp. 209-211, 215-216.

Day of Absence

Downer, Alan S. "Total Theatre and Partial Drama: Notes on the New York Theatre, 1965-1966." *Q. J. of Speech,* vol. 52, no. 3 (Oct., 1966), pp. 234-235.

Happy Ending

Downer, Alan S. "Total Theatre and Partial Drama: Notes on the New York Theatre, 1965-1966." *Q. J. of Speech,* vol. 52, no. 3 (Oct., 1966), p. 234.

THEODORE WARD

Big White Fog

Abramson, Doris E. *Negro playwrights in the American theatre, 1925-1959,* pp. 92-93, 109-117, 157-159.

Our Lan'

Abramson, Doris E. *Negro playwrights in the American theatre, 1925-1959,* pp. 117-135, 163-164.

Mitchell, Loften. *Black drama,* pp. 133-134.

ROBERT PENN WARREN 1905-

All the King's Men: A Play

Bohner, Charles H. *Robert Penn Warren,* pp. 99-100.

DAVID WASHBURN

The Love Nest

Sainer, Arthur. *The sleepwalker and the assassin, a view of the contemporary theatre,* pp. 60-64.

KEITH WATERHOUSE 1929-

General

Gillett, Eric. "Regional Realism: Shelagh Delaney, Alun Owen, Keith Waterhouse and Willis Hall." *In:* Armstrong, William A., ed. *Experimental drama,* pp. 197-203.

PETER WATLING

Indian Summer

Hobson, Harold. *The theatre now,* pp. 112-117.

FRANK WEDEKIND 1864-1918

General

Corrigan, Robert W., ed. *Masterpieces of the modern German theatre,* p. 222.

Dukes, Ashley. *Modern dramatists,* pp. 95-113.

Ellehauge, Martin. *The position of Bernard Shaw in European drama and philosophy,* pp. 157-163, 179-180.

Garten, H.F. *Modern German drama,* pp. 87-96.

Gittleman, Sol. "Frank Wedekind and Bertolt Brecht: Notes on a Relationship." *Modern Drama,* vol. 10, no. 4 (Feb., 1968), pp. 401-409.

Hatfield, Henry. *Modern German literature,* pp. 61-64.

Heuser, Frederick W.J. "Gerhart Hauptmann and Frank Wedekind." *Germanic Rev.,* vol. 20 no. 1 (Feb., 1945), pp. 54-68.

Hill, Claude. "Wedekind in Retrospect." *Modern Drama,* vol. 3, no. 1 (May, 1960), pp. 82-92.

Natan, Alex. "Frank Wedekind." *In:* Natan, A., ed. *German men of letters*, vol. 2, pp. 103-129.

Sokel, Walter. *The writer in extremis,* pp. 57-63.

Spalter, Max. Brec*ht's tradition,* pp. 113-135.

Wedekind, Frank. "The Art of Acting: A Glossary." *In:* Corrigan, Robert W., ed. *Masterpieces of the modern German theatre,* pp. 223-233. (Reprinted from Corrigan, Robert W., ed. *The modern theatre,* N.Y., Macmillan, 1964.)

Westervelt, William O. "Frank Wedekind and the search for morality." *Dissertation Abstracts,* vol. 27 (1967), 3886A (So. Calif.).

The Awakening of Spring (Frühlings Erwachen)

Bauland, Peter. *The hooded eagle,* pp. 43-45, 47, 175.

Block, Anita. *The changing world in plays and theatre,* pp. 39-44.

Dukes, Ashley. *Modern dramatists,* pp. 101-106.

Hill, Claude. "Wedekind in Retrospect." *Modern Drama,* vol. 3, no. 1 (May, 1960), pp. 82-92.

Kayser, Wolfgang. *The grotesque in art and literature* pp. 131-132.

Natan, Alex. "Frank Wedekind." *In:* Natan, A., ed. *German men of letters,* vol. 2, pp. 104-110.

Sokel, Walter. *The writer in extremis,* p. 97.

Spalter, Max. *Brecht's tradition,* pp. 116-123.

Bismarck

Ellehauge, Martin. *The position of Bernard Shaw in European drama and philosophy,* pp. 317-319.

Censorship (Die Zensur)

Ellehauge, Martin. *The position of Bernard Shaw in European drama and philosophy,* pp. 157-163.

Spalter, Max. *Brecht's tradition,* p. 130.

Death and the Devil

Mueller, Carl Richard. "Introduction." *In:* Mueller, C.R., *Frank Wedekind: the Lulu plays.*

Spalter, Max. *Brecht's tradition,* p. 181.

Earth Spirit (Erdgeist - Part I of Lulu)

Bauland, Peter. *The hooded eagle,* pp. 33, 47-48, 169.

Ellehauge, Martin. *The position of Bernard Shaw in European drama and philosophy,* pp. 146-148.

Hill, Claude. "Wedekind in Retrospect." *Modern Drama,* vol. 3, no. 1 (May, 1960), pp. 82-92.

Kayser, Wolfgang. *The grotesque in art and literature,* pp. 132-133.

Mitchell, D. "The Character of Lulu: Wedekind's and Berg's Conceptions Compared." *Music Rev.,* vol. 15 (1954), pp. 268-274.

Mueller, Carl Richard. "Introduction." *In:* Mueller, C.R., tr. *Frank Wedekind: the Lulu plays.*

Natan, Alex. "Frank Wedekind." *In:* Natan, A., ed. *German men of letters,* vol. 2, pp. 110-115.

Sokel, Walter. *The writer in extremis,* pp. 61-62, 152.

Spalter, Max. *Brecht's tradition,* pp. 123-128, 129-130.

Franziska

Ellehauge, Martin. *The position of Bernard Shaw in European drama and philosophy,* pp. 180-183.

Natan, Alex. "Frank Wedekind." *In:* Natan, A., ed. *German men of letters,* vol. 2, pp. 118-120.

Die Gutgeschnittene Ecke

Ellehauge, Martin. *The position of Bernard Shaw in European drama and philosophy,* pp. 122-123.

Hidalla, or Karl Hetmann, the Dwarf-Giant (Karl Hetmann, der Zwergriese)

Dukes, Ashley. *Modern dramatists,* pp. 106-112.

Ellehauge, Martin. *The position of Bernard Shaw in European drama and philosophy,* pp. 179, 265-266.

Sokel, Walter. *The writer in extremis,* p. 59.

Spalter, Max. *Brecht's tradition,* pp. 134-135.

Das Höhere Leben

Ellehauge, Martin. *The position of Bernard Shaw in European drama and philosophy,* pp. 121-122.

Die Junge Welt

Ellehauge, Martin. *The position of Bernard Shaw in European drama and philosophy,* p. 66.

King Nicolo, or Such Is Life (König Nicolo, oder So Ist Leben)

Sokel, Walter. *The writer in extremis,* pp. 58-59.

Spalter, Max. *Brecht's tradition,* pp. 132-133.

Marquis von Keith

Natan, Alex. "Frank Wedekind." *In:* Natan, A., ed. *German men of letters,* vol. 2, pp. 115-118.

Spalter, Max. *Brecht's tradition,* pp. 133-134.

Music

Spalter, Max. *Brecht's tradition,* pp. 131, 133.

Oaha

Ellehauge, Martin. *The position of Bernard Shaw in European drama and philosophy,* pp. 150-151.

Pandora's Box (Die Büchse der Pandora - Part II of Lulu)

Hill, Claude. "Wedekind in Retrospect." *Modern Drama,* vol. 3, no. 1 (May, 1960), pp. 82-92.

Mitchell, D. "The Character of Lulu: Wedekind's and Berg's Conceptions Compared." *Music Rev.,* vol. 15 (1954), pp. 268-274.

Mueller, Carl Richard. "Introduction." *In:* Mueller, C.R., *Frank Wedekind: the Lulu plays.*

Natan, Alex. "Frank Wedekind." *In:* Natan, A., ed. *German men of letters,* vol. 2, pp. 110-115.

Sokel, Walter. *The writer in extremis,* p. 96.

Spalter, Max. *Brecht's tradition,* pp. 128-130.

The Quick Painter

Spalter, Max. *Brecht's tradition,* pp. 115-116.

Simpson

Ellehauge, Martin. *The position of Bernard Shaw in European drama and philosophy,* pp. 173-176.

The Tenor (Die Kammersänger)

Ellehauge, Martin. *The position of Bernard Shaw in European drama and philosophy,* p. 161.

Sokel, Walter. *The writer in extremis,* p. 57.

Spalter, Max. *Brecht's tradition,* p. 133n.

Wetterstein Castle

Spalter, Max. *Brecht's tradition,* pp. 133-134n.

The Young World

Spalter, Max. *Brecht's tradition,* p. 114.

GUNTHER WEISENBORN 1902-

General

Coenen, F.E. "The Modern German Drama." *In:* Hammer, Carl, Jr., ed. *Studies in German literature,* p. 115.

PETER WEISS 1916-

General

Cohn, Ruby. *"Theatrum Mundi* and Contemporary Theater." *Comparative Drama,* vol. 1 (1967), pp. 28-35.

Lumley, Frederick. *New trends in 20th-century drama,* pp. 247-253.

Milfull, John. "From Kafka to Brecht: Peter Weiss's Development Towards Marxism." *German Life and Letters,* vol. 20 (1966), pp. 61-71.

Wager, Walter. "Peter Weiss." *In:* Wager, Walter, ed. *The playwrights speak,* pp. 189-196.

Weiss, Peter. (Interview with Walter Wager.) *In:* Wager, Waltcr, ed. *The playwrights speak,* pp. 196-197, 207-211.

The Investigation (Die Ermittlung)

Anonymous. *Times Literary Supplement* (London) (Feb. 10, 1966), p. 103.

Carmichael, Joel. "German Reactions to a New Play About Auschwitz." *American-German Rev.,* vol. 32, no. 3 (Feb., Mar., 1966), pp. 30-31.

Cohn, Ruby. "Theatre Abroad." *Drama Survey,* vol. 5, no. 3 (Winter, 1966-67), p. 290.

Lumley, Frederick. *New trends in 20th-century drama,* pp. 252-253.

Michalski, John. "German Drama and Theater in 1965." *Books Abroad,* vol. 40 (1966), p. 138.

Weiss, Peter. (Interview with Walter Wager.) *In:* Wager, Walter, ed. *The playwrights speak,* pp. 199-207, 211-212.

Weigenstein, Roland H. "Theatre." *American-German Rev.,* vol. 32, no. 2 (Dec., 1965), pp. 33-35.

Zipes, Jack D. "Documentary Drama in Germany: Mending the Circuit." *Germanic Rev.,* vol. 42, no. 1 (Jan., 1967), pp. 49-62.

The Persecution and Assassination of Marat as Performed by the Inmates of the Asylum of Charenton Under the Direction of the Marquis de Sade (Marat/Sade)(Die Verfolgung und Ermordung Jean Paul Marats Dargestellt Durch die Schauspielgruppe des Hospizes zu Charenton Unter Anleitung des Herrn de Sade)

Bauland, Peter. *The hooded eagle,* pp. 220-224.

Beaujour, Michel. "Peter Weiss and the Futility of Sadism." Yale French Studies, vol. 35 (1965), pp. 114-119.

Brook, Peter. "An Introduction to Weiss's *The Persecution and Assassination of Jean Paul Marat...*" *In:* Seltzer, Daniel, ed. *The modern theatre, readings and documents,* pp. 285-287. (From Weiss, Peter, *The persecution and assassination...* London, Atheneum, 1965.)

Clurman, Harold. *The naked image,* pp. 117-122.

Cohn, Ruby. *"Marat/Sade:* An Education in Theatre." *Educational Theatre J.* vol. 19, no. 4 (Dec., 1967), pp. 478-485.

Downer, Alan S. "Total Theatre and Partial Drama: Notes on the New York Theatre, 1965-1966." *Q. J. of Speech,* vol. 52, no. 3 (Oct., 1966), pp. 227-229.

Gassner, John. "Broadway in Review." *Educational Theatre J.,* vol. 18, no. 1 (Mar., 1966), pp. 60-62.

Gottfried, Martin. *A theater divided; the postwar American stage,* pp. 11, 120, 152, 203-204.

Lumley, Frederick. *New trends in 20th-century drama,* pp. 249-252.

Marowitz, Charles, ed. *Theatre at work,* pp. 183-184.

Moeller, Hans-Bernhard. "German Theater 1964: Weiss' Reasoning in the Madhouse." *Symposium,* vol. 20 (1966), pp. 163-173.

Oliver, William I. *"Marat/Sade* in Santiago." *Educational Theatre J.,* vol. 19, no. 4 (Dec., 1967), pp. 486-501.

Pronko, Leonard C. *Theater East and West,* pp. 175-177.

Schechner, Richard, ed. *"Marat/Sade* Forum." *Tulane Drama Rev.,* vol. 10, no. 4 (Summer, 1966), pp. 214-237.

Sontag, Susan. Agains*t interpretation and other essays,* pp. 163-174.

Sontag, Susan. *"Marat/Sade/*Artaud." *In:* Seltzer, Daniel, ed. *The modern theatre, readings and documents,* pp. 400-409. (From Sontag, Susan. *Against interpretation,* N.Y., Farrar, 1965.)

Triesch, Manfred. "Peter Weiss, Marat and De Sade." *American-German Rev.,* vol. 30, no. 6 (Aug.-Sept., 1964), pp. 9-11.

Triesch, Manfred. "Peter Weiss: The Murder of Marat." *Books Abroad,* vol. 39, no. 1 (Winter, 1965), pp. 27-29.

Weiss, Peter. (Interview with Walter Wager.) *In:* Wager, Walter, ed. *The playwrights speak,* pp. 197-199, 200-201, 211.

Weiss, Samuel A. "Peter Weiss's *Marat/Sade." Drama Survey,* vol. 5, no. 2 (Summer, 1966), pp. 123-130.

The Tower

Wellwarth, G.E. "Introduction." *In:* Benedikt, M., and G.E. Wellwarth, eds. *Postwar German theatre,* pp. xxv-xxvi.

FRANZ WERFEL 1890-1945

General

Bauland, Peter. *The hooded eagle,* pp. 68, 74, 83-91, 92, 138-140, 150-153, 155, 160, 161, 173.

Fox, W.H. "Franz Werfel." *In:* Natan, A., ed. *German men of letters,* vol. 3 (1964), pp. 107-125.

Garten, H.F. *Modern German drama,* pp. 111-115.

Krugel, Fred. "Franz Werfel and Romanticism." *Seminar: A Journal of Germanic Studies* (Victoria Coll., Toronto; and Newcastle U., New South Wales), vol 3 (1967), pp. 82-102.

Politzer, Heinz. "Franz Werfel: Reporter of the Sublime." *Commentary,* vol. 9 (Jan.-June, 1950), pp. 272-274.

Puckett, Hugh W. "Franz Werfel's Mission." *Germanic Rev.,* vol. 22, no. 2 (Apr., 1947), pp. 117-125.

Slochower, Harry. "Franz Werfel and Sholom Asch: The Yearning for Status." *Accent,* vol. 5, no. 2 (Winter, 1945), pp. 73-82.

Werner, Alfred. "The Strange Life and Creed of Franz Werfel." *Judaism,* vol. 4, no. 2 (spring, 1955), pp. 142-148.

The Eternal Road (Der Weg der Verheissung)

Bauland, Peter. *The hooded eagle,* pp. 138-140.

Young, Stark. *Immortal shadows,* pp. 189-192.

Goat Song (Bocksgesang)

Bauland, Peter. *The hooded eagle,* pp. 85-88.

Garten, H.F. *Modern German drama,* pp. 113-114.

Scharbach, Alexander. "Irony in Franz Werfel's Expressionistic Drama *Bocksgesang.*" *Modern Drama,* vol. 2, no. 4 (Feb., 1960), pp. 410-416.

Smith, Winifred. "The Dying God in the Modern Theatre." *Rev. of Religion,* vol. 5 (March, 1941), pp. 265-269.

Jacobowsky and the Colonel (Jacobowsky und der Oberst)

Bauland, Peter. *The hooded eagle,* pp. 150-153.

Fox, W.H. "Franz Werfel." *In:* Natan, A., ed. *German men of letters,* vol. 3 (1964), pp. 113-115.

Klarmann, Adolf D. "Allegory in Werfel's *Das Opfer* and *Jacobowsky and the Colonel.*" *Germanic Rev.,* vol. 20, no. 3 (Oct., 1945), pp. 195-217.

Juarez and Maximilian

Bauland, Peter. *The hooded eagle,* pp. 89-91.

Mirror Man (Spiegelmensch)

Block, Anita. *The changing world in plays and theatre,* pp. 134-137.

Garten, H.F. *Modern German drama,* pp. 112-113.

Das Opfer

Klarmann, Adolf D. "Allegory in Werfel's *Das Opfer* and *Jacobowsky and the Colonel." Germanic Rev.,* vol. 20, no. 3 (Oct., 1945), pp. 195-217.

Schweiger

Bauland, Peter. *The hooded eagle,* pp. 88-89.

Ling, Harold. "Franz Werfel's *Schweiger." Monatshefte für Deutschen Unterricht,* vol. 28, no. 4 (Apr., 1936), pp. 168-172.

Temptation (Versuchung)

Sokel, Walter. *The writer in extremis,* p. 124.

Die Troerinnen (Based on Euripides' The Trojan Woman)

Garten, H.F. *Modern German drama,* pp. 111-112.

ARNOLD WESKER 1932-

General

Amis, Kingsley. "Not Talking About Jerusalem." *Spectator* (Aug. 10, 1962), p. 190.

Brown, John Russell. "Introduction." *In:* Brown, John Russell, ed. *Modern British dramatists, a collection of critical essays,* pp. 12-14.

Chiari, J. *Landmarks of contemporary drama,* pp. 115-118.

Cohen, Mark. "The World of Wesker." *Jewish Q.* (London: Winter, 1960-61), p. 45.

Findlater, Richard. "Plays and Politics." *Twentieth century* (London: Sept., 1960), pp. 235-241.

Fletcher, John. "Confrontations: II. Arnold Wesker, John Arden, and Arthur Adamov." *Caliban,* vol. 4 (1967), pp. 149-159.

Garforth, John. "Arnold Wesker's Mission." *In:* Marowitz, Charles, ed. *Encore reader,* pp. 223-230. (Reprinted from *Encore* (May, 1963).)

Gascoigne, Bamber. *Twentieth-century drama,* pp. 198-200.

Goodman, Henry. "The New Dramatists, 2: Arnold Wesker." *Drama Survey,* vol. 1, no. 2 (Oct., 1961), pp. 215-222.

Gordon, Giles. "Arnold Wesker." *Transatlantic Rev.,* vol. 21 (1966), pp. 15-25. (Interview.)

Hall, Stuart. "The First Five Years." *In:* Marowitz, Charles, ed. *Encore reader,* pp. 214-217. (Reprinted from *Encore* (Nov. 1961).)

Kitchin, Laurence. "Drama with a Message: Arnold Wesker." *In:* Armstrong, William A., ed. *Experimental drama,* pp. 169-185. *Also in:* Brown John Russell, ed. *Modern British dramatists, a collection of critical essays,* pp. 71-73; 80-82. (From Armstrong, W.A. *Experimental drama,* London, Bell, 1963.)

Leech, Clifford. "Two Romantics: Arnold Wesker and Harold Pinter." *In:* Brown, John Russell, and Bernard Harris, eds. *Contemporary theatre,* pp. 11-31.

Jones, A.R. "The Theatre of Arnold Wesker." *Critical Q,* vol. 2, no. 4 (Winter, 1960), pp. 366-370.

Lumley, Frederick. *New trends in 20th-century drama,* pp. 273-279.

Page, Malcolm. "Whatever Happened to Arnold Wesker?: His Recent Plays." *Modern Drama,* vol. 11, no. 3 (Dec., 1968), pp. 317-325.

Ribalow, Harold U. "The Plays of Arnold Wesker." *Chicago Jewish Forum* (Winter, 1962-63), pp. 127-131.

Rothberg, Abraham. "East End, West End: Arnold Wesker." *Southwest Rev.,* vol. 52 (1967), pp. 368-378.

Wager, Walter. "Arnold Wesker." *In:* Wager, Walter, ed. *The playwrights speak,* pp. 269-276.

Wellwarth, George. *The theatre of protest and paradox,* pp. 52, 197, 221, 234-243, 244, 255, 274.

Wesker, Arnold. (Interview given to Simon Trussler in 1966.) *In:* Marowitz, Charles, ed. *Theatre at work,* pp. 78-95.

Wesker, Arnold. (Interview with Walter Wager.) *In:* Wager, Walter, ed. *The playwrights speak,* pp. 279-290.

Wesker, Arnold. "Let Battle Commence." *In:* Marowitz, Charles, ed. *Encore reader,* pp. 96-103. (Reprinted from *Encore* (Nov., 1958).)

Winegarten, Renee. "Arnold Wesker: Is Sincerity Enough?" *Jewish Observer and Middle East Rev.* (London: Apr., 19, 1963), pp. 18-19.

Billy Liar (Adapted by Keith Waterhouse and Willis Hall)

Tynan, Kenneth. *Tynan right and left,* pp. 19-20.

Chicken Soup and Barley

Fraser, G.S. *The modern writer and his world,* pp. 235-236.

Kitchin, Laurence. "Drama with a Message: Arnold Wesker." *In:* Brown, John Russell, ed. *Modern British dramatists, a collection of critical essays,* pp. 79-80. (From Armstrong, W.A. *Experimental drama.)*

Kitchin, Laurence. *Mid-century drama,* pp. 216-218.

Lumley, Frederick. *New trends in 20th-century drama,* pp. 274, 275-276.

Ribalow, Harold U. *Arnold Wesker,* pp. 34-41.

Spencer, Charles. "Arnold Wesker as a Playwright." *Jewish Q.* (London: Winter, 1959-60), pp. 40-41.

Tynan, Kenneth. *Tynan right and left,* pp. 32-33.

Wellwarth, George. *The theatre of protest and paradox,* pp. 235-236, 238, 255.

Wesker, Arnold. (Interview given to Simon Trussler in 1966.) *In:* Marowitz, Charles, ed. *Theatre at work,* pp. 79-83, 89, 92-93.

Chips with Everything

Brustein, Robert. "The Backwards Birds." *New Republic* (Oct. 19, 1963), pp. 28, 30-31.

Brustein, Robert. *Seasons of discontent,* pp. 198-200.

Chapman, John. *"Chips With Everything* Strong, Penetrating, Crisp, Well Staged." *New York Daily News* (Oct. 2, 1963), p. 64.

Chapman, John. "Two Strong New Dramas: *Luther* and *Chips With."* *Sunday News* (Oct. 20, 1963), Sec. Two, p. 1.

Clurman, Harold. "Theatre." *Nation* (Oct. 26, 1963), pp. 267-268.

Cohen, Mark. "Impersonal Hero." *Jewish Q.* (London: Autumn, 1962), pp. 48-49.

Coleman, Robert. *"Chips* Is Amusing, Moving." *New York Mirror* (Oct. 2, 1963), p. 31.

Dennis, Nigel. "What Though the Field Be Lost?" *Encounter* (Aug. 1962), pp. 43-45.

Gascoigne, Bamber. "Goodbye, Mr. Chips." *Spectator* (May 11, 1962), p. 621.

Gellert, Roger. "Chips and After." *New Statesman* (May 11, 1962). p. 685.

Hewes, Henry. "Keep the Home Fires Frying." *Saturday Rev.* Oct. 19, 1963), p. 30.

Kerr, Walter. *"Chips With Everything."* *New York Herald Tribune* (Oct. 2, 1963), p. 18.

Kerr, Walter. "Magic Over Matter." New York, *The Sunday Herald Tribune Magazine* (Oct. 27, 1963), p. 25.

Lewis, Emory. *"Chips with Everything."* *Cue* (Oct. 12, 1963), p. 15.

Lumley, Frederick. *New trends in 20th-century drama,* pp. 276-277.

McClain, John. "Lively Play About RAF." *New York Journal-American* (Oct. 2, 1963), p. 27.

McGuiness, Frank. "Culture With Chips." *London Mag.* (London: July, 1962), pp. 48-50.

Marriott, R.B. *"Chips With Everything* Is Wesker's Best." *Stage and Television Today* (London: May 3, 1962), p. 13.

Matthews, Honor. *The primal curse,* pp. 193-194.

Nadel, Norman. *"Chips* Has Everything." *New York World-Telegram and Sun* (Oct. 2, 1963), p. 43.

Newsweek (Oct. 14, 1963), p. 72.

Plays and Players (London, July, 1962), pp. 20-23, 50. (Reviews of London Production).

Popkin, Henry. "Class War With Everything." *New Leader* (Oct. 28, 1963), pp. 31, 32.

Ribalow, Harold U. *Arnold Wesker,* pp. 58-75.

Rosselli, John. "The Wesker Twist." *Reporter* (Sept. 3, 1962), pp. 48-51.

"Sheep That Don't Say Baa." *Time* (Oct. 11, 1963), pp. 72-73.

Sigal, Clancy. *"Chips with Everything."* *Queen* (london: May 15, 1962), p. 10.

Smith, Michael. "Wesker's *Chips."* *The Village Voice* (Oct. 10, 1963), pp. 15, 18-19.

Taubman, Howard. "Life with R.A.F. Trainees." *The New York Times* (Oct. 2, 1963), p. 49.

Tynan, Kenneth. *Tynan right and left,* pp. 119-121.

Watts, Richard, Jr. "Another Striking British Drama." *New York Post* (Oct. 2, 1963), p. 68.

Watts, Richard, Jr. "Paradox in *Chips with Everything.*" *New York Post* (Oct. 20, 1963), p. 15.

Wellwarth, George. *The theatre of protest and paradox,* pp. 241-243.

Wesker, Arnold. (Interview given to Simon Trussler in 1966.) *In:* Marowitz, Charles, ed. *Theatre at work,* pp. 89-92.

Wesker, Arnold. (Interview with Walter Wager.) *In:* Wager, Walter, ed. *The playwrights speak,* pp. 276-278.

The Four Seasons

Lumley, Frederick. *New trends in 20th-century drama,* pp. 277-278.

Page, Malcolm. "Whatever Happened to Arnold Wesker?: His Recent Plays." *Modern Drama,* vol. 11, no. 3 (Dec., 1968), pp. 321-322, 325.

Ribalow, Harold U. *Arnold Wesker,* pp. 85-90.

Wesker, Arnold. (Interview given to Simon Trussler in 1966.) *In:* Marowitz, Charles, ed. *Theatre at work,* 87-88, 94-95.

I'm Talking About Jerusalem

Fraser, G.S. *The modern writer and his world,* pp. 233-235.

Ribalow, Harold U. *Arnold Wesker,* pp. 52-57.

Tynan, Kenneth. *Tynan right and left,* pp. 37-39.

Wellwarth, George. *The theatre of protest and paradox,* pp. 235, 238-239.

The Kitchen

Kitchin, Laurence. "Drama with a Message: Arnold Wesker." *In:* Brown, John Russell, ed. *Modern British dramatists, a collection of critical essays,* pp. 74-79. (From Armstrong, W.A. *Experimental drama,* pp. 174-182.)

Lumley, Frederick. *New trends in 20th-century drama,* p. 174.

Ribalow, Harold U. *Arnold Wesker,* pp. 28-33.

Tynan, Kenneth. *Tynan right and left,* pp. 81-82.

Wellwarth, George. *The theatre of protest and paradox,* pp. 239-241.

Wesker. Arnold, (Interview given to Simon Trussler in 1966.) *In:* Marowitz, Charles, ed. *Theatre at work,* pp. 81, 89-91.

Woodroofe, K.S. "Mr. Wesker's *Kitchen." Hibbert J.,* vol. 62, no. 246 (Apr., 1964), pp. 148-151.

Menace (Television play)

Ribalow, Harold U. *Arnold Wesker,* pp. 94-96.

Taylor, John Russell. "Mr. Wesker's *Menace." Listener* (London: Dec. 12, 1963), p. 1001.

Roots

Balliett, Whitney. "Maybe." *The New Yorker,* (Mar. 18, 1961); pp. 126-127.

Brien, Alan. "Theatre, London." *Theatre Arts* (Dec., 1959), pp. 20, 22.

Brustein, Robert. "Fragments from a Cultural Explosion." *New Republic,* vol. 144 (Mar. 27, 1961), pp. 30-31.

Brustein, Robert, *Seasons of discontent, pp. 48-49.*

Cowell, Raymond. *Twelve modern dramatists,* pp. 103-105.

Fraser, G.S. *The modern writer and his world,* pp. 236-238.

Hatch, Robert. "Arise, Ye Playgoers of the World." *Horizon* (July, 1961), pp. 116-118.

Hatch, Robert. "Theatre." *Nation* (Mar. 25, 1961), p. 272.

Kitchin, Laurence. "Drama with a Message: Arnold Wesker." *In:* Brown, John Russell, ed. *Modern British dramatists, a collection of critical essays,* pp. 73-74. (From Armstrong, W.A. *Experimental drama.*)

Kitchin, Laurence. *Mid-century drama,* pp. 112-114.

Latham, Jacqueline. *"Roots:* A Reassessment." *Modern Drama,* vol. 8, no. 2 (Sept., 1965), pp. 192-197.

Mander, John. *The writer and commitment,* pp. 194-211.

Ribalow, Harold U. *Arnold Wesker,* pp. 42-51.

Spencer, Charles. "Arnold Wesker as a Playwright." *Jewish Q.* (London: Winter, 1959-60), pp. 40-41.

Styan, J.L. *The dark comedy,* 2nd ed., pp. 166-167.

Time (Mar. 17, 1961), p. 42.

Tynan, Kenneth. *Tynan right and left,* p. 35.

Wellwarth, George. *The theatre of protest and paradox,* pp. 234-238.

Wesker, Arnold. (Interview given to Simon Trussler in 1966.) *In:* Marowitz, Charles, ed. *Theatre at work,* pp. 79-82, 88.

Their Very Own and Golden City

Page, Malcolm. "Whatever Happened to Arnold Wesker?: His Recent Plays." *Modern Drama,* vol. 11, no. 3 (Dec., 1968), pp. 322-325.

Ribalow, Harold U. *Arnold Wesker,* pp. 76-84.

Wesker, Arnold. (Interview given to Simon Trussler in 1966.) *In:* Marowitz, Charles, ed. *Theatre at work,* pp. 80, 82, 85, 87-88, 92-94.

JOHN WEXLEY

They Shall Not Die

Block, Anita. *The changing world in plays and theatre,* pp. 251-263.

Brown, John Mason. *Two on the aisle,* pp. 211-212.

Himelstein, Morgan Y. *Drama was a weapon, the left-wing theatre in New York 1929-1941,* pp. 130-133.

EDITH WHARTON 1862-1937

Ethan Frome (Adapted by Owen and Donald Davis)

O'Hara, Frank H. *Today in American drama,* pp. 34-39.

PATRICK WHITE 1912-

A Cheery Soul

Brissenden, R.F. "The Plays of Patrick White." *In:* Christesen, Clement Byrne. *On native grounds; Australian writing from the Meanjin Q.,* pp. 182-183. (From *Meanjin Q.,* vol. 23, no. 3 (1964).)

The Ham Funeral

Brissenden, R.F. "The Plays of Patrick White." *In:* Christesen, Clement Byrne. *On native grounds; Australian writing from the Meanjin Q.,* pp. 175-180. (From *Meanjin Q.,* vol. 23, no. 3 (1964).)

Loder, Elizabeth. *"The Ham Funeral:* Its Place in the Development of Patrick White." *Southerly,* vol. 23, no. 2 (1963), pp. 78-91.

Night on Bald Mountain

Brissenden, R.F. "The Plays of Patrick White." *In:* Christesen, Clement Byrne. *On native grounds; Australian writing from the Meanjin Q.,* pp. 183-186. (From *Meanjin Q.,* vol. 23, no. 3 (1964).)

The Season at Sarsaparilla

Brissenden, R.F. "The Plays of Patrick White." *In:* Christesen, Clement Byrne. *On native grounds; Australian writing from the Meanjin Q.,* pp. 181-182. (From *Meanjin Q.,* vol. 23, no. 3 (1964).)

JOHN WHITING 1917-

General

Chiari, J. *Landmarks of contemporary drama,* pp. 126-127.

Fry, Christopher. "The Plays of John Whiting." *Essays by divers hands,* vol. 34 (1966), pp. 36-54.

Gascoigne, Bamber. *Twentieth-century drama,* pp. 202-203.

Lumley, Frederick. *New trends in 20th-century drama,* pp. 257-260.

Lumley, Frederick. *Trends in 20th-century drama,* pp. 214-216.

Lyons, Charles R. "The Futile Encounter in the Plays of John Whiting." *Modern Drama,* vol. 11, no. 3 (Dec., 1968), pp. 283-298.

O'Connor, Garry. "The Obsessions of John Whiting." *Encore,* vol. 11, no. 4 (July-Aug., 1964), pp. 26-36.

Trewin, J.C. "Two Morality Playwrights: Robert Bolt and John Whiting." *In:* Armstrong, William A., ed. *Experimental drama,* pp. 107-119.

Whiting, John. (Interview with Tom Milne and Clive Goodwin, first published in *Encore* in 1961.) *In:* Marowitz, Charles, ed. *Theatre at work,* pp. 10-11, 21-35.

The Devils

Gassner, John. "Broadway in Review." *Educational Theatre J.,* vol. 18, no. 1 (Mar., 1966), pp. 62-63.

Hurrell, John Dennis. "John Whiting and the Theme of Self-Destruction." *Modern Drama,* vol. 8, no. 2 (Sept., 1965), pp. 134-141.

Lumley, Frederick. *New trends in 20th-century drama,* pp. 259-260.

Lyons, Charles R. "The Futile Encounter in the Plays of John Whiting." *Modern Drama,* vol. 11, no. 3 (Dec., 1968), pp. 285, 290-297.

Taylor, John Russell. "The Early Fifties." *In:* Taylor, John Russell, ed. *Modern British dramatists, a collection of critical essays,* p. 23. (From Taylor, J.R. *Anger and after,* London, Methuen, published as *The angry theater,* N.Y. Hill and Wang, 1962.)

Tynan, Kenneth. *Tynan right and left,* pp. 71, 73.

Whiting, John. (Interview with Tom Milne and Clive Goodwin, first published in *Encore* in 1961.) *In:* Marowitz, Charles, ed. *Theatre at work,* pp. 28, 46.

Gates of Summer

Whiting, John. (Interview with Tom Milne and Clive Goodwin, first published in *Encore* in 1961.) *In:* Marowitz, Charles, ed. *Theatre at work,* pp. 24-26, 29.

Marching Song

Baxter, Kay M. *Contemporary theatre and the Christian faith,* pp. 56-64.

Hurrell, John Dennis. "John Whiting and the Theme of Self-Destruction." *Modern Drama,* vol. 8, no. 2 (Sept., 1965), pp. 134-141.

Taylor, John Russell. "The Early Fifties." *In:* Taylor, John Russell, ed. *Modern British dramatists, a collection of critical essays,* pp. 22-23. (From Taylor, J.R. *Anger and after,* London, Methuen, published in *The angry theater,* N.Y., Hill and Wang, 1962.)

Whiting, John. (Interview with Tom Milne and Clive Goodwin, first published in *Encore* in 1961.) *In:* Marowitz, Charles, ed. *Theatre at work,* pp. 24-25, 26, 29, 32, 34.

Williamson, Audrey. *Contemporary theatre, 1953-1956,* pp. 26-29.

Saint's Day

Hoefer, Jacqueline. "Pinter and Whiting: Two Attitudes Towards the Alienated Artist." *Modern Drama,* vol. 4, no. 4 (Feb., 1962), pp. 402-408.

Hurrell, John Dennis. "John Whiting and the Theme of Self-Destruction." *Modern Drama,* vol. 8, no. 2 (Sept., 1965), pp. 134-141.

Milne, Tom. "The Hidden Face of Violence." *In:* Taylor, John Russell, ed. *Modern British dramatists, a collection of critical essays,* pp. 38-46. (From *Encore,* vol. 7, no. 1 (1960), pp. 14-20.) *Also in:* Marowitz, Charles, ed. *Encore reader,* pp. 118-120, 123.

Taylor, John Russell. "The Early Fifties." *In:* Taylor, John Russell, ed. *Modern British dramatist, a collection of critical essays,* pp. 21-22. (From Taylor, J.R. *Anger and after,* London, Methuen, published as *The angry theater,* N.Y., Hill and Wang, 1962.)

Trewin, J.C. "Two Morality Playwrights: Robert Bolt and John Whiting." *In:* Armstrong William A., ed. Exp*erimental drama,* pp. 107-114.

Whiting, John. (Interview with Tom Milne and Clive Goodwin, first published in *Encore* in 1961.) *In:* Marowitz, Charles, ed. *Theatre at work,* pp. 22-24, 26-28, 30, 32, 47.

OSCAR WILDE 1854-1900

General

Archer, William. "Pinero, Jones, and Wilde." *In:* Freedman, Morris, ed. *Essays in the modern drama,* pp. 107-121. (Reprinted from *The old drama and the new* by William Archer, c. 1923 by Dodd, Mead; renewal copyright 1950 by Frank Archer.)

Bentley, Eric. *The playwright as thinker,* pp. 154-157.

Brockett, O.G. "J.T. Grein and the Ghost of Oscar Wilde." *Q. J. of Speech,* vol. 52, no. 2 (Apr., 1966), pp. 131-138.

Ellmann, Richard. "Oscar and Oisin." *In:* Ellmann, R. *Eminent domain,* pp. 9-27.

Freedman, Morris. "The Modern Tragicomedy of Wilde and O'Casey." *College English,* vol. 25, no. 7 (Apr., 1964), pp. 518-522, 527.

Gregor, Ian. "Comedy and Oscar Wilde." *Sewanee Rev.,* vol. 74, no. 2 (Apr.-June, 1966), pp. 501-521.

Henderson, Archibald. *European dramatists,* pp. 253-320.

Knight, G. Wilson. *The golden labyrinth,* pp. 305-307.

Krutch, Joseph Wood. *"Modernism" in modern drama,* pp. 43-48.

Miller, Nellie Burget. *The living drama,* pp. 292-295.

Montague, Charles E. *Dramatic values,* pp. 172-186.

Norwood, Gilbert. *Euripides and Shaw with other essays,* pp. 60-62.

Salerno, Henry F. *English drama in transition, 1880-1920,* pp. 141-144.

San Juan, Epifanio. *The art of Oscar Wilde,* pp. 131-140, 196-204.

Shanks, Edward. *Second essays on literature,* pp. 206-212.

Wadleigh, Paul Custer. "Form in Oscar Wilde's comedies: a structural analysis." *Dissertation Abstracts,* vol. 23 (1962), 2257 (Indiana).

Williams, Harold. *Modern English writers,* pp. 227-229.

Bibliography

Mason, Stuart. (Christopher Millard) *Bibliography of Oscar Wilde.* London, B. Rota (new ed.)

The Duchess of Padua

San Juan, Epifanio. *The art of Oscar Wilde,* pp. 105-110, 129, 133.

The Florentine Tragedy

San Juan, Epifanio. *The art of Oscar Wilde,* pp. 108-110, 129, 133.

An Ideal Husband

Ganz, Arthur. "The Divided Self in the Society Comedies of Oscar Wilde." *Modern Drama,* vol. 3, no. 1 (May, 1960), pp. 16-23.

Gregor, Ian. "Comedy and Oscar Wilde." *Sewanee Rev.,* vol. 74, no. 2 (Apr.-June, 1966), pp. 509-512.

Kronenberger, Louis. *The thread of laughter,* pp. 216-220.

San Juan, Epifanio. *The art of Oscar Wilde,* pp. 165-179, 199, 201, 203.

Shaw, George Bernard. *Shaw's dramatic criticism (1895-98),* pp. 4-6.

The Importance of Being Earnest

Barnet, Sylvan, ed. *The genius of the later English theater,* pp. 247-248.

Bentley, Eric. *The playwright as thinker,* pp. 140-145.

Brown, John Mason. *Seeing more things,* pp. 206, 209-210, 215-220, 225.

Foster, Richard. "Wilde as Parodist: A Second Look at *The Importance of Being Earnest.*" *College English,* Vol. 18, No. 1 (Oct., 1956), pp. 18-23.

Freedman, Morris. "The Modern Tragicomedy of Wilde and O'Casey," *College English,* vol. 25, no. 7 (Apr., 1964), pp. 518-527.

Freedman, Morris. *The moral impulse,* pp. 63-65, 69.

Ganz, Arthur. "The Meaning of *The Importance of Being Earnest.*" *Modern Drama,* vol. 6, no. 1 (May, 1963), pp. 42-52.

Gielgud, Sir John. "Introduction to *The Importance of Being Earnest.*" *In:* Barnet, Sylvan, ed. *The genius of the later English theater,* pp. 518-523.

Gregor, Ian. "Comedy and Oscar Wilde." Sewanee *Rev.,* vol. 74, no. 2 (Apr.-June, 1966) pp. 501, 513-521.

Kronenberger, Louis. *The thread of laughter,* pp. 222-225.

McCarthy, Mary. *Sights and spectacles 1937-1956,* pp. 106-110.

McCarthy, Mary. "The Unimportance of Being Oscar." *In:* Corrigan, Robert, ed. *Laurel British drama: the nineteenth century,* pp. 399-402. (Reprinted from McCarthy, Mary. *Sights and spectacles: theatre chronicles.*)

Mikhail, W.H. "The Four-Act Version of *The Importance of Being Earnest."Modern Drama,* vol. 11, no. 3 (Dec., 1968), pp. 263-266.

Salerno, Henry F. *English drama in transition, 1880-1920,* pp. 144-145.

San Juan, Epifanio. *The art of Oscar Wilde,* pp. 133, 138, 180-196, 203.

Shaw, George Bernard. *Shaw's dramatic criticism (1895-98),* pp. 18-20.

Styan, J.L. *The elements of drama,* pp. 20-25, 142-146.

Toliver, Harold E. "Wilde and the Importance of 'Sincere and Studied Triviality.'" *Modern Drama,* vol. 5, no. 4 (Feb., 1963), pp. 389-399.

Wadleigh, Paul C. *"Earnest* at St. James' Theatre." *Q. J. of Speech,* vol. 52, no. 1 (Feb., 1966), pp. 58-62.

Lady Windermere's Fan

Brooks, Cleanth. *Understanding drama,* pp. 43-45, 54-56, 63-66, 73-82.

Brown, John Mason. *Seeing more things,* pp. 209-214, 217.

Freedman, Morris. "The Modern Tragicomedy of Wilde and O'Casey." *College English,* vol. 25, no. 7 (Apr., 1964), pp. 518-527.

Freedman, Morris. *The moral impulse,* pp. 65-67, 71.

Ganz, Arthur. "The Divided Self in the Society Comedies of Oscar Wilde." *Modern Drama,* vol. 3, no. 1 (May, 1960), pp. 16-23.

Gregor, Ian. "Comedy and Oscar Wilde." *Sewanee Rev.,* vol. 74, no. 3 (Apr.-June, 1966), pp. 502-507, 509.

Kronenberger, Louis. *The thread of laughter,* pp. 213-216.

Mikhail, W.H. "Oscar Wilde and His First Comedy." *Modern Drama,* vol. 10, no. 4 (Feb., 1968), pp. 394-396.

Miller, Nellie Burget. *The living drama,* pp. 295-296.

San Juan, Epifanio. *The art of Oscar Wilde,* pp. 140-154.

La Sainte Courtisane

San Juan, Epifanio. *The art of Oscar Wilde,* pp. 110-113, 126, 129.

Salome

Brockett, O.G. "J.T. Grein and the Ghost of Oscar Wilde." *Q. J. of Speech,* vol. 52, no. 2 (Apr., 1966), pp. 131-138.

Ellmann, Richard. "Oscar and Oisin." *In:* Ellmann, R. *Eminent domain,* pp. 23-24.

Hamilton, Clayton. *Seen on the stage,* pp. 122-124.

San Juan, Epifanio. *The art of Oscar Wilde,* pp. 8-9, 113-130.

A Woman of No Importance

Ganz, Arthur. "The Divided Self in the Society Comedies of Oscar Wilde." *Modern Drama,* vol. 3, no. 1 (May, 1960), pp. 16-23.

Gregor, Ian. "Comedy and Oscar Wilde." *Sewanee Rev.,* vol. 74, no. 2 (Apr.-June, 1966), pp. 507-509.

Jameson, Storm. *Modern drama in Europe,* pp. 131-135.

Kronenberger, Louis. *The thread of laughter,* pp. 220-222.

San Juan, Epifanio. *The art of Oscar Wilde,* pp. 154-165, 202-203.

THORNTON WILDER 1897-

General

Alder, Henry. "Thornton Wilder's Theatre." *Horizon,* vol. 12, no. 68 (Aug., 1945), pp. 89-98.

Bogard, Travis. "The Comedy of Thornton Wilder." *In:* Bogard, Travis, and Oliver, William I., eds. *Modern drama; essays in criticism,* pp. 355-363, 370-373. (Reprinted from Wilder, Thornton. *Three plays,* N.Y., Harper and Row, 1962.) Also in: Kernan, Alvin B., ed. *The modern American theater,* pp. 52-69. (Reprinted from *Three plays by Thornton Wilder* (Introduction); (N.Y., Harper and Row, 1962). *Also in:* Meserve, Walter J., ed. *Discussions of American drama,* pp. 51-66.

Broussard, Louis. *American drama...,* pp. 92-103.

Corrigan, Robert W. "Thornton Wilder and the Tragic Sense of Life." *Ed. Theatre J.,* vol. 13, no. 3 (Oct., 1961), pp. 167-173 Also in: Freedman, Morris, ed. *Essays in the modern drama,* pp. 311-319. (Reprinted from *Educational Theatre J.,* vol. 13.)

Cowley, Malcolm. "The Man Who Abolished Time." *Saturday Rev.,* vol. 36, no. 40 (Oct. 6, 1956), pp. 13-14, 50-52.

Fergusson, Francis. *The human image in dramatic literature,* pp. 41-43, 50-60.

Fergusson, Francis. "Search for New Standards in the Theatre." *Kenyon Rev.,* vol. 17, no. 4 (Autumn, 1955), pp. 593-596.

Fergusson, Francis. "Three Allegorists: Brecht, Wilder, and Eliot." *Sewanee Rev.,* vol. 64 (Fall, 1956), pp. 553-573.

Firegaugh, Joseph J. "The Humanism of Thornton Wilder." *Pacific Spectator,* vol. 4, no. 4 (Autumn, 1950), pp. 426-438.

Four Quarters, vol. 16, no. 4 (May, 1967), Thornton Wilder Number.

Frenz, Horst. "American Playwrights and the German Psyche." Bd. 10, (Apr. 1961), pp. 170-178.

Frenz, Horst. "The Reception of Thornton Wilder's Plays in Germany." *Modern Drama,* vol. 3, no. 2 (Sept., 1960), pp. 123-137.

Fuller, Edmund. "Reappraisals, Thornton Wilder: The Notation of the Heart." *American Scholar,* vol. 28, no. 2 (Spring, 1959), pp. 210-217.

Fulton, A.R. "Expressionism—Twenty Years After." *Sewanee Rev.,* vol. 52, no. 3 (Summer, 1944), pp. 398, 411-413.

Fussell, Paul Jr. "Thornton Wilder and the German Psyche." *Nation,* vol. 186, no. 18 (May 3, 1958), pp. 394-395.

Goldstein, Malcolm. "Thornton Wilder." *In: Dow*ner, Alan S., ed. *The American theater today,* pp. 60-63, 70-72.

Gould, Jean. *Modern American playwrights,* pp. 204-224.

Guthrie, Tyrone. "The World of Thornton Wilder." *In:* Kernan, Alvin B., ed. *The modern American theater,* pp. 45-51. (Reprinted from *The New York Times Magazine* (Nov., 27, 1955), pp. 26-27, 64-68.) *Also in:* Guthrie, T. *In various directions,* pp. 110-118.

Haberman, Donald. *The plays of Thornton Wilder, a critical study,* pp. 11-14, 74-92, 93-114, 115-125.

Isaacs, Edith J.R. "Thornton Wilder in Person." *Theatre Arts,* vol. 27, no. 1 (Jan., 1943), pp. 21-30.

Lewis, Flora. "Thornton Wilder at 65 Looks Ahead—and Back." *N. Y. Times Mag.* (Apr. 15, 1962), pp. 28-29, 54, 56, 58.

Lumley, Frederick. *New trends in 20th-century drama,* pp. 324-327.

Parmenter, Ross. "Novelist into Playwright." *Saturday Rev., vol.* 18, no. 7 (June 11, 1938), pp. 10-11.

Popper, Hermine I. "The Universe of Thornton Wilder." *Harpers Mag.,* vol. 230 (June, 1965), pp. 72-78, 81.

Twitchett, E.G. "Mr. Thornton Wilder." *London Mercury,* vol. 22, no. 127 (May, 1930), pp. 32-39.

Vos, Nelvin. *The drama of comedy: victim and victor,* pp. 32-38, 47-52.

Weales, Gerald. "Unfashionable Optimist." *Commonweal,* vol. 67, no. 19 (Feb. 7, 1958), pp. 486-488.

Wilder, Thornton. "A Passion and a Platform for Two." *In:* Oppenheimer, George, ed. *The passionate playgoer,* pp. 231-238 (Reprinted from Wilder's preface to *Three plays,* N.Y., Harper, 1957.) *Also in: Harpers Mag.,* vol. 215 (Oct., 1957), pp. 48-51, *and* Frenz, Horst, ed. *American playwrights on drama,* pp. 120-126.

Wilder, Thornton. "Some Thoughts on Playwriting." *In:* Cassell, Richard A. *What is the play?* pp. 644-651. (From *The intent of the artist,* ed. by Augusto Centeno, Princeton Univ. Pres, 1941.)

Bibliography

Kosok, Heinz. "Thornton Wilder: A Bibliography of Criticism." *Twentieth Century Literature,* vol. 9 (1963), pp. 93-100.

The Alcestiad

Haberman, Donald. *The plays of Thornton Wilder, a critical study,* pp. 39-53, 82-84, 91, 99, 111.

The Angel That Troubled the Waters

Haberman, Donald. *The plays of Thornton Wilder, a critical study,* pp. 29, 93-94.

A Happy Journey to Trenton and Camden

Haberman, Donald. *The plays of Thornton Wilder, a critical study,* pp. 103-104.

Life in the Sun

Hartley, Anthony. "Festival Blues." *Spectator,* vol. 195 (Sept. 2, 1955), p. 305.

The Long Christmas Dinner

Littell, Robert. "Plays by Thornton Wilder, *The Long Christmas Dinner* and Other Plays." *Saturday Rev.,* vol. 8, no. 21 (Dec. 12, 1931), p. 366.

Vos, Nelvin. *The drama of comedy: victim and victor,* pp. 36-37.

The Matchmaker

Bogard, Travis. "The Comedy of Thornton Wilder." *In:* Bogard, Travis, and Oliver, William I., eds. *Modern drama; essays in criticism,* pp. 368-370. (Reprinted from Wilder, Thornton. *Three plays,* N.Y., Harper, 1962.)

Cassell, Richard A. *What is the play?* pp. 247, 306-307.

Goldstein, Malcolm. "Thornton Wilder." *In:* Downer, Alan S., ed. *The American theater today,* pp. 66-68.

Hewitt, Barnard, "Thornton Wilder Says 'Yes.'" *In:* Cassell, Richard A. *What is the play?* pp. 701-705. (From *Tulane Drama Rev.,* vol. 4, no. 2 (Winter, 1959), pp. 110-114.)

Voaden, Herman, ed. *Human values in the drama,* pp. x, xiv-xv, 96-100, 189-195.

Vos, Nelvin. *The drama of comedy: victim and victor,* pp. 42-43.

The Merchant of Yonkers (Later revised as The Matchmaker, and still later as the musical Hello, Dolly!)

Bauland, Peter. *The hooded eagle,* p. 136.

Haberman, Donald. *The plays of Thornton Wilder, a critical study,* pp. 18, 19-24, 68-69, 70, 79-81, 99, 117, 127-136.

Our Town

Ballet, Arthur H. "In Our Living and in Our Dying." *English J.,* vol. 15, no. 5 (May, 1956), pp. 243-249.

Bogard, Travis. "The Comedy of Thornton Wilder." *In:* Bogard, Travis, and Oliver, William I., eds. *Modern drama; essays in criticism,* pp. 363-365. (Reprinted from Wilder, Thornton. *Three plays,* N.Y., Harper and Row, 1962.)

Broussard, Louis. *American drama...,* pp. 95-99.

Brown, John Mason. *Two on the aisle,* pp. 187-193.

Brown, John Mason. "Wilder: *Our Town." Saturday Rev.,* vol. 32, no. 32 (Aug. 6, 1949), pp. 33-34.

Brown, John Mason. "Wilder's *Our Town." In:* Brown, John Mason. *Dramatis personae,* pp. 79-84.

Cohn, Ruby, ed. *Twentieth-century drama,* pp. 277-278.

Eastman, Fred. *Christ in the drama,* pp. 113-119.

Fergusson, Francis. *The human image in dramatic literature,* pp. 52-56, 59.

Goldstein, Malcolm. "Thornton Wilder." *In:* Downer, Alan S., ed. *The American theater today,* pp. 64-66.

Groff, Edward. "Point of View in Modern Drama." *Mod. Drama,* vol. 2, no. 3 (Dec. 1959), pp. 280-281.

Haberman, Donald. *The plays of Thornton Wilder, a critical study,* pp. 14-17, 20, 24, 35, 36-37, 38, 56-59, 62-64, 66-67, 69, 71, 75-79, 82, 84-85, 87, 91-92, 99, 107-108.

Hagopian, John V., and Martin Dolch. *Insight I: analysis of American literature,* pp. 264-270.

Hewitt, Barnard. "Thornton Wilder Says 'Yes.'" *In:* Cassell, Richard A. *What is the play?* pp. 705-708. (From *Tulane Drama Rev.,* vol. 4, no. 2 (Winter, 1959), pp. 114-117.)

Hidden, Norman. "A School Play." *English,* vol. 14, no. 84 (Autumn, 1963), pp. 231-233.

Kohler, Dayton. "Thornton Wilder." *English J.,* vol. 28, no. 1 (Jan., 1939), pp. 1-11.

Lewis, Allan. *American plays and playwrights of the contemporary theatre,* pp. 68-71.

McCarthy, Mary. *Sights and spectacles 1937-1956,* pp. 26-29.

Nathan, George Jean. *Theatre book of the year, 1943-44,* pp. 205-206.

Sawyer, Julian. "Wilder and Stein." *Saturday Rev.,* vol. 26 (Apr. 17, 1943), p. 27.

Scott, Winfield Townley. "*Our Town* and the Golden Veil." *Virginia Q. Rev.,* vol. 29, no. 1 (Winter, 1953), pp. 103-117.

Sievers, W. David. *Freud on Broadway,* pp. 255-258.

735

Stephens, George D. *"Our Town* - Great American Tragedy?" *Modern Drama,* vol. 1, no. 4 (Feb., 1959), pp. 258-264.

Vos, Nelvin. *The drama of comedy: victim and victor,* pp. 38-42.

Plays for Bleecker Street

Simon, John. *Hudson Rev.,* vol. 15 (Summer, 1962), pp. 268-270.

Pullman Car Hiawatha

Haberman, Donald *The plays of Thorton Wilder, a critical study* pp. 35-36, 62.

Queens of France

Haberman, Donald. *The plays of Thornton Wilder, a critical study,* pp. 104-105.

The Skin of Our Teeth

Balliett, Carl Jr. "The Skin of Whose Teeth, Part III." *Saturday Rev.,* vol. 26, no. 1 (Jan. 2, 1943), p. 11.

Bates, Esther Willard. "In Defense of Thornton Wilder." *Saturday Rev.,* vol. 26, no. 1 (Jan. 2, 1943), p. 11.

Bauland, Peter. *The hooded eagle,* pp. 157-158.

Bogard, Travis. "The Comedy of Thornton Wilder." *In:* Bogard, Travis, and Oliver, William I., eds. *Modern drama; essays in criticism,* pp. 366-368. (Reprinted from Wilder, Thornton. *Three plays,* N.Y., Harper and Row, 1962.)

Broussard, Louis. *American drama...,* pp. 99-103

Campbell, Joseph, and Henry M. Robinson. "The Skin of Whose Teeth? The Strange Case of Mr. Wilder's New Play and *Finnegan's Wake." Saturday Rev.,* vol. 25, no. 51 (Dec. 19, 1942), pp. 3-4. (Same title, Part 2) "The Intention Behind the Deed." *Saturday Rev.,* vol. 26, no. 7 (Feb. 13, 1943), pp. 16, 18-19.

Clurman, Harold. *Lies like truth,* pp. 38-40.

Cubeta, Paul M. *Modern drama for analysis,* pp. 577-586.

Fergusson, Francis. *The human image in dramatic literature,* pp. 56-59, 68, 69.

Fleming, Peter. *Spectator,* vol. 177 (Sept. 20, 1946), p. 287.

Goldstein, Malcolm. "Thornton Wilder." *In:* Downer, Alan S., ed. *The American theater today,* pp. 68-70.

Haberman, Donald. *The plays of Thornton Wilder, a critical study,* pp. 24-27, 35-36, 38, 41, 56-57, 59-61, 65, 69-73, 82, 91, 99, 108-111, 117-122.

Heilman, Robert B. *Tragedy and melodrama,* pp. 82, 107-108.

Hewitt, Barnard. "Thornton Wilder Says 'Yes.'" *In:* Cassell, Richard A. *What is the play?* pp. 708-711. (From *Tulane Drama Rev.,* vol. 4, no. 2 (Winter, 1959), pp. 117-120.)

Hodge, Francis. "German Drama and the American Stage." *In:* Shaw, LeRoy R., ed. *The German theatre today, pp. 83-*88.

Lewis, Allan. *American plays and playwrights of the contemporary theatre,* pp. 71-72.

McCarthy, Mary. *Sights and spectacles 1937-1956,* pp. 53-56.

Nathan, George Jean. *Theatre book of the year, 1942-43,* pp. 132-136.

Redfern, James. *Spectator,* vol. 174 (May 25, 1945), p. 474.

Sievers, W. David. *Freud on Broadway,* pp. 258-261.

Smith, Harrison. "The Skin of Whose Teeth: Part 2." *Saturday Rev.,* vol. 25, no. 52 (Dec. 26, 1942), p. 12.

Thompson, Alan Reynolds. *The dry mock,* pp. 68-69.

Vos, Nelvin. *The drama of comedy: victim and victor,* pp. 43-47.

Wilson, E. "The Antrobuses and the Earwickers." *Nation,* vol. 156, no. 5 (Jan. 30, 1943), pp. 167-168.

Sloth

Haberman, Donald. *The plays of Thornton Wilder, a critical study,* pp. 17-18.

Such Things Only Happen in Books

Haberman, Donald. *The plays of Thornton Wilder, a critical study,* pp. 18-19.

The Trumpet Shall Sound

Fergusson, Francis. *The human image in dramatic literature,* p. 51.

Haberman, Donald. *The plays of Thornton Wilder, a critical study,* pp. 29-31, 34, 64, 87, 90.

CHARLES WILLIAMS 1886-1945

General

Roston, Murray. *Biblical drama in England from the Middle Ages to the present day,* pp. 291-293.

The Death of Good Fortune

Spanos, William V. *The Christian tradition in modern British verse drama,* pp. 166-171.

Grab and Grace

Spanos, William V. *The Christian tradition in modern British verse drama,* pp. 170-171, 177-179.

The House by the Stable

Spanos, William V. *The Christian tradition in modern British verse drama,* pp. 170-176, 178-179.

The House of the Octopus

Spanos, William V. *The Christian tradition in modern British verse drama,* pp. 295-304

Judgment at Chelmsford

Spanos, William V. *The Christian tradition in modern British verse drama,* pp. 68-80.

Seed of Adam

Spanos, William V. *The Christian tradition in modern British verse drama,* pp. 155-166.

Thomas Cranmer of Canterbury

Spanos, William V. *The Christian tradition in modern British verse drama,* pp. 104-124.

EMLYN WILLIAMS 1905-

General

Taylor, John Russell. *The rise and fall of the well-made play,* pp. 147-148.

The Corn Is Green

Eastman Fred. *Christ in the drama,* pp. 78-86.

738

Himelstein, Morgan Y. *Drama was a weapon, the left-wing theatre in New York 1929-1941,* pp. 212-213.

He Was Born King

Dent, Alan. *Preludes and studies,* pp. 84-88.

The Late Christopher Bean

MacCarthy, Desmond. *Drama,* pp. 255-260.

The Light of Heart

Dent, Alan. *Preludes and studies,* pp. 177-179.

Night Must Fall

O'Casey, Sean. *The green crow,* pp. 48-56.

Trespass

Hobson, Harold. *Theatre,* pp. 109-111.

TENNESSEE WILLIAMS 1914-

General

Adler, J.H. "The Rose and the Fox: Notes on the Southern Drama." *In:* Rubin, L.D., and R.D. Jacobs, eds. *South: modern Southern literature in its cultural setting,* pp. 349-375.

Allsop, Kenneth. "Tennessee Williams and the Albatross." *In:* Richards, Dick. *The curtain rises,* pp. 88-92.

Atkinson, Brooks. "His Bizarre Images Can't Be Denied." *New York Times Book Rev.* (Nov. 26, 1961), pp. 1, 36.

Barksdale, Richard K. "Social Background in the Plays of Miller and Williams." *College Language Assn. J.,* vol. 6 (Mar., 1963), pp. 161-169.

Birney, Earle. "North American Drama Today: A Popular Art?" *Transactions of the Royal Society of Canada,* vol. 51, Series iii, Sec. 2 (June, 1957), pp. 31-42.

Brandt, George. "Cinematic Structure in the Work of Tennessee Williams." *In:* Brown, J.R., and Bernard Harris, *American theatre,* pp. 162-187.

Brooks, Charles. "The Comic Tennessee Williams." *Q. J. of Speech,* vol. 44, no. 3 (Oct., 1958), pp. 275-281.

Brooks, Charles. "William's Nebulous Nightmare." *Hudson Rev.,* vol. 12 (Summer, 1959), pp. 255-260.

Buell, John. "The Evil Imagery of Tennessee Wllliams." *Thought,* vol. 38 (1963), pp. 167-189.

Callaghan, Barry. "Tennessee Williams and the Cocaloony Birds." *Tamarack Review,* no. 39 (1966), pp. 52-58.

Callahan, Edward F. "Tennessee Williams' Two Worlds." *North Dakota Q.,* vol. 25 (1957), pp. 61-67.

, Carroll, Sidney. "A Streetcar Named Tennessee." *Esquire,* vol. 29 (1948), p. 46.

Casty, Alan. "Tennessee Williams and the Small Hands of the Rain." *Mad River Rev.* (Dayton, Ohio), vol. 1, no. 3 (1965), pp. 27-43.

, Chiari, J. *Landmarks of contemporary drama,* pp. 142-146.

Clurman, H. *Lies like truth,* pp. 72-86.

Coffey, Warren. "Tennessee Williams: The Playwright as Analysand." *Ramparts,* vol. 1, no. 3 (1962), pp. 51-58.

DaPonte, Durant. "Tennessee Williams' Gallery of Feminine Character." *Times Literary Supplement* (London), vol. 10 (1965), pp. 7-26.

DaPonte, Durant. "Tennessee's Tennessee Williams." *Univ. of Tennessee Studies in Humanities,* no. 1 (1956), pp. 11-17.

Dobson, Eugene Jr. "The reception of the plays of Tennessee Williams in Germany." *Dissertation Abstracts,* vol. 28 (1967), 226A-27A (Ark.).

Donahue, Francis. *The dramatic world of Tennessee Williams.*

Downer, Alan S. "Mr. Williams and Mr. Miller." *Furioso,* vol. 4 (Summer, 1949), pp. 66-70.

Downer, Alan S. *Recent American drama,* pp. 28-34.

Downer, Alan S. "The Two Worlds of Arthur Miller and Tennessee Williams." *In:* Seltzer, Daniel, ed. *The modern theatre, readings and documents,* pp. 410-422. (Reprinted from *Princeton Alumni Weekly,* vol. 52, no. 5 (Oct. 20, 1961).)

Duprey, Richard A. "Tennessee Williams' Search for Innocence." *Catholic World,* vol. 189, no. 1, 131 (June, 1959), pp. 191-194.

Dusenbury, Winifred L. *The theme of loneliness in modern American drama,* pp. 134-154.

Falk, Signi. "The Profitable World of Tennessee Williams." *Modern Drama,* vol. 1, no. 3 (Dec., 1958), pp. 172-180.

Falk, Signi. *Tennessee Williams.*

Fedder, Norman J. "The influence of D.H. Lawrence on Tennessee Williams." *Dissertation Abstracts,* vol. 14 (1963), 742-743. *New York University.*

Fedder, Norman J. *The influence of D.H. Lawrence on Tennessee Williams,* pp. 9-15, 54-62, 120-126.

Flaxman, Seymour L. "The Debt of Williams and Miller to Ibsen and Strindberg." *Comparative Literature Studies* (Special Issue, 1963), pp. 51-60.

Frenz,. Horst, and Ulrich Weisstein. "Tennessee Williams and His German Critics." *Symposium,* vol. 14, no. 4 (Winter, 1960), pp. 258-275.

Funke, Lewis, and John E. Booth. "Williams on Williams." *Theatre Arts,* vol. 46 (Jan., 1962), pp. 17-19.

Ganz, Arthur. "The Desperate Morality of the Plays of T. Williams." *American Scholar,* vol. 31 (1962), pp. 278-294.

Gascoigne, Bamber. *Twentieth-century drama,* pp. 166-173.

Gassner, John. *Theatre at the crossroads,* pp. 77-91.

Gassner, John. *The theatre in our times,* pp. 348-352.

Gassner, Jonn. "Tennessee Williams: Dramatist of Frustration." *College English,* vol. 10, no. 1 (Oct., 1948), pp. 1-7.

Glicksberg, Charles I. "Depersonalization in the Modern Drama." *Personalist,* vol. 39 (Spring, 1958), pp. 158-169.

Goldstein, Malcolm. "Body and Soul on Broadway." *Modern Drama,* vol. 7, no. 4 (Feb., 1965), pp. 411-421.

Goodman, Randolph. *Drama on stage,* pp. 274-278.

Gould, Jean. *Modern American playwrights,* pp. 225-246.

Green, William. "Significant Trends in the Modern American Theatre." *Manchester Rev.,* vol. 8 (1957), pp. 65-78.

Hall, Peter. "Tennessee Williams: Notes on the Moralist." *Encore,* vol. 4 (Sept.-Oct. 1957), pp. 16-19.

Heilman, Robert B. "Tennessee Williams: Approaches to Tragedy." *Southern Rev.,* vol. 1, n.s., no. 4 (Oct., 1965), pp. 770-790.

Highet, Gilbert. "A Memorandum: From: Lucius Annaeus Seneca; To: Tennessee Williams; Subject: Horror." *Horizon,* vol. 1 (May, 1959), pp. 54-55.

Isaac, Dan. "Big Daddy's Dramatic Word Strings." *American Speech,* vol. 40 (1965), pp. 272-278.

Isaac, D.B. "In Defence of Tennessee Williams." *Religious Education,* vol. 53 (Sept., 1958), pp. 452-453.

Jackson, E.M. *The broken world of Tennessee Williams.*

Jackson, E.M. "Music and Dance as Elements of Form in the Drama of Tennessee Williams." *Revue d'Histoire du Theatre,* vol. 15 (July, 1963) pp. 294-302.

Jackson, Esther M. "The Problem of Form in the Drama of Tennessee Williams." *College Language Assn. J.,* vol. 4 (1960) pp. 8-21.

Jackson, Esther M. "Tennessee Williams." *In:* Downer, Alan S., ed. *The American theater today,* pp. 73-84.

Jones, Robert Emmet. "Tennessee Williams' Early Heroines." *Modern Drama,* vol. 2, no. 3 (Dec., 1959), pp. 211-219.

Keating, Edward M. "Mildew on the Old Magnolia." *Ramparts,* vol. 1, no. 3 (1962), pp. 69-74.

Kernan, Alvin. "Truth and Dramatic Mode in the Modern Theatre: Chekhov, Pirandello, and Williams." *Modern Drama,* vol. 1, no. 2 (Sept., 1958), pp. 101-114.

Kerr, W. *Pieces at eight,* pp. 125-134.

Kitchin, Laurence. *Mid-century drama,* pp. 63-69.

Krutch, Joseph W. *The American drama since 1918,* pp. 325-327, 329-330.

Krutch, Joseph Wood. *"Modernism" in modern drama,* pp. 123-130.

Lewis, Allan. *American plays and playwrights of the contemporary theatre,* pp. 53-65.

Lewis, R.C. "A Playwright Named Tennessee." *New York Times Mag.* (Dec. 7, 1947), pp. 19, 67, 69-70.

Lewis, Theophilus. "Freud and the Split-Level Drama." *Catholic World,* vol. 187 (May, 1958), pp. 98-103.

Lumley, Frederick. *New trends in 20th-century drama,* 183-194, 317, 319.

Lumley, Frederick. *Trends in 20th-century drama,* pp. 187-191.

Magid, Marion. "The Innocence of Tennessee Williams." *Commentary,* vol. 35 (Jan., 1963), pp. 34-43. (Reprinted in Freedman, Morris, ed. *Essays in the modern drama,* pp. 280-293.)

Mannes, Marya. "The Morbid Magic of Tennessee Williams." *Reporter,* vol. 12, no. 10 (May 19, 1955), pp. 41-43.

Oppenheimer, George, ed. *Passionate playgoer,* pp. 246-254, 342-356, 588-591.

Peterson, William. "Williams, Kazan, and the Two Cats." *New Theater Magazine* (Bristol) vol. 7, no. 3 (1967), pp. 14-20.

Phillips, Elizabeth C. *Modern American drama,* pp. 118-120, 121-122.

Popkin, Henry. "The Plays of Tennessee Williams." *Tulane Drama Rev.,* vol. 14, no. 3 (Mar., 1960), pp. 45-64.

Popkin, Henry. "Williams, Osborne, or Beckett?" *New York Times Book Rev.* (Nov. 13, 1960), pp. 32-33.

Powers, Harvey M., Jr. "Theatrical Convention: The Conditions of Acceptability." *Bucknell Rev.,* vol. 7, no. 1 (1957), pp. 20-26.

Rogoff, Gordon. "The Restless Intelligence of Tennessee Williams." *Tulane Drama Rev.,* vol. 10, no. 4 (1966), pp. 78-92.

Roth, Robert. "Tennessee Williams in Search of a Form." *Chicago Rev.,* vol. 9 (Summer, 1959), pp. 86-94.

Sagar, K.M. "What Mr. Williams Has Made of D.H. Lawrence." *Twentieth-Century* vol. 168, no. 1002 (Aug., 1960), pp. 143-153.

Sharp, William. "An Unfashionable View of Tennessee Williams." *Tulane Drama Rev.,* vol. 6, no. 3 (Mar., 1962), pp. 160-171.

Sharpe, Robert Boies. *Irony in the drama,* pp. 191-194.

Sievers, W.D. *Freud on Broadway,* pp. 370-388.

Spevac, Marvin. "Tennessee Williams: The Idea of the Theatre." *Jahrbuch fur Amerikastudien,* no. 10 (1965), pp. 221-231.

Styan, J.L. *The dark comedy,* pp. 217-226.

Styan, J.L. *The dark comedy,* 2nd ed., pp. 76, 106, 118, 215-217, 292, 208-214.

"Talk With a Playwright." *Newsweek,* vol. 53 (Mar. 23, 1959), pp. 75-76.

Taylor, Harry. "The Dilemma of Tennessee Williams." *Masses and Mainstream,* vol. 1 (Apr., 1948), pp. 51-56.

Taylor, William E. "Tennessee Williams: Academia on Broadway." *In:* Langford, R.E., ed. *Essays in modern American literature,* pp. 90-96.

Tischler, Nancy M. *Tennessee Williams.*

Tynan, K. "American Blues: The Plays of Arthur Miller and Tennessee Williams." *Encounter,* vol. 2, no. 5 (May, 1954), pp. 13-19. *Also in:* Kernan, Alvin B., ed. *The modern American theater,* pp. 34-44. (Reprinted from Tynan, K. *Curtains* (Atheneum, 1961).)

Tynan, K. *Curtains,* pp. 257-266.

Vowles, Richard B. "Tennessee Williams and Strindberg." *Modern Drama,* vol. 1 no. 3 (Dec., 1958), pp. 166-171.

Vowles, Richard B. "Tennessee Williams: The World of His Imagery." *Tulane Drama Rev.,* vol. 3, no. 2 (Dec., 1958), pp. 51-56.

Wager, Walter. "Tennessee Williams." *In:* Wager Walter, ed. *The playwrights speak,* pp. 213-224.

Waters, Arthur B. "Tennessee Williams: Ten Years Later." *Theatre Arts,* vol. 39 (1957), pp. 72-73.

Weales, Gerald. *American drama since World War II,* pp. 18-39.

Weales, Gerald. *Tennessee Williams,* pp. 5-42.

Weissman, Philip. "Psychopathological Characters in Current Drama: A Study of a Trio of Heroines." *American Imago,* vol. 17 (1961), pp. 271-288.

Weissman, Philip. "Tennessee Williams Presents His POV (point of view)." *New York Times Magazine* (June 12, 1960), p. 12.

Whiting, John. "A Glare of Intimacy." *Spectator,* vol. 208 (Mar. 30, 1962), p. 418.

Williams, Raymond. *Modern tragedy,* pp. 115, 119-120.

Williams, Tennessee. (Interview with Walter Wager.) *In:* Wager, Walter, ed. *The playwrights speak,* pp. 224-237.

Williams, Tennessee. "The World I Live In." (Tennessee Williams Interviews Himself.) *In:* Goodman, Randolph. *Drama on stage,* pp. 293-295. (Reprinted from *The Observer* (Apr., 7, 1957).)

Bibliography

Carpenter, Charles A., Jr., and E. Cook. "Addenda to Tennessee Williams: A Selected Bibliography." *Modern Drama,* vol. 2 (Dec., 1959), pp. 220-223.

Dony, Nadine. "Tennessee Williams: A Selected Bibliography." *Modern Drama,* vol. 1 (Dec., 1958), pp. 181-191.

At Liberty

Weales, Gerald. "Tennessee William's 'Lost Play.'" *American Literature,* vol. 37 (1965-66), pp. 321-323.

Baby Doll (Film)

Brandt, George. "Cinematic Structure in the Work of Tennessee Williams." *In: American theatre,* pp. 167-168.

Dusenbury, Winifred. *"Baby Doll* and the Ponder Heart." *Modern Drama,* vol. 3 (1961), pp. 393-395.

Fedder, Norman J. *The influence of D.H. Lawrence on Tennessee Williams,* p. 100.

Hewes, Henry. "The Boundaries of Tennessee." *Saturday Rev.,* vol. 39 (Dec. 29, 1956), pp. 23-24.

Knight, A. *"SR* Goes to the Movies." *Saturday Rev.,* vol. 39 (Dec. 29, 1956), pp. 22-23.

Scott, N.A., Jr. "Reviews. Movies: The *Baby Doll* Furor." *Christian Century,* vol. 74 (Jan. 23, 1957), pp. 110-112.

Battle of the Angels

Falk, S.L. *Tennessee Williams,* pp. 59-65.

Lewis, Allan. *American plays and playwrights of the contemporary theatre,* pp. 61-62.

Nelson, B. *Tennessee Williams,* pp. 55-63.

Quirino, Leonard. "Tennessee Williams' Persistent *Battle of Angels."* *Modern Drama,* vol. 11, no. 1 (May, 1968), pp. 27-39.

Sievers, W. David. *Freud on Broadway,* p. 371.

Tischler, N.M. *Tennessee Williams,* pp. 73-89, 234-240.

Camino Real

Bentley, Eric. *The dramatic event,* pp. 107-110.

Bentley, Eric. "Essays of Elia." *New Republic,* vol. 128 (Mar. 30, 1953), pp. 30-31.

Brandt, George. "Cinematic Structure in the Work of Tennessee Williams." *In: American theatre,* pp. 179-181.

Broussard, Louis. *American drama...,* pp. 111-116.

Clurman, Harold. *Lies like truth,* pp. 83-86.

Clurman, Harold. *Nation,* vol. 176 (Apr. 4, 1953), pp. 293-294.

Falk, S.L. *Tennessee Williams,* pp. 120-130.

Fedder, Norman J. *The influence of D.H. Lawrence on Tennessee Williams,* pp. 95-97.

Glicksberg, Charles I. "The Modern Playwrights and the Absolute." *Queen's Q.,* vol. 65 (Autumn, 1958), pp. 459-471.

Hewes, Henry. "Tennessee Williams - Last of Our Solid Gold Bohemians." *Saturday Rev.,* vol. 36 (Mar. 28, 1953), pp. 25-27.

Jackson, E.M. *The broken world of Tennessee Williams,* pp. 110-128.

Kazin, Alfred. "Psychoanalysis and Contemporary Literary Culture." *Psychoanalysis and the Psychoanalytic Rev.,* vol. 45, no. 4 (1958), pp. 41-51.

Miller, Jordan Y. *American dramatic literature,* pp. 139-141.

Nathan, George Jean. *Theatre in the fifties,* pp. 109-112.

Nelson, B. *Tennessee Williams,* pp. 172-184.

Sievers, W. David. *Freud on Broadway,* pp. 385-388.

Tischler, N.M. *Tennessee Williams,* pp. 179-196.

Tynan, K. *Curtains,* pp. 173-176.

Watt, David. *Spectator,* vol. 198 (Apr. 12, (1957), p. 488.

Williams, Tennessee. "Foreword to *Camino Real." In:* Meserve, Walter J., ed. *Discussions of American drama,* pp. 138-140. Cole, Toby, ed. *Playwrights on playwriting,* pp. 277-281. Reprinted from Tennessee Williams, Foreword and Afterword, *Camino Real* (New York: New Directions, 1953, pp. viii-xiii. Published in the *New York Times* on Sunday, March 15, 1953.)

Williams, Tennessee. "Foreword. . .And Afterword." *Theatre Arts,* vol. 38 (Aug. 1954) pp. 34-35.

746

Wolf, Morris Philip. "Casanova's portmanteau: a study of *Camino Real* in relation to the other plays and stories of Tennessee Williams, 1945-1955." *Dissertation Abstracts,* vol. 20, 2817 (Georgia), 1960.

Cat on a Hot Tin Roof

Bentley, Eric. *New Republic,* vol. 132 (Apr. 11, 1955), p. 28.

Brandt, George. "Cinematic Structure in the Work of Tennessee Williams." *In: American theatre,* pp. 171-173.

Downing, Robert. "From the *Cat*-Bird Seat: The Production Manager's Notes on *Cat on a Hot Tin Roof." Theatre Arts,* vol. 14 (1956), pp. 46-50.

Dukore, Bernard F. "The Cat Has Nine Lives." *Tulane Drama Rev.,* vol. 8, no. 1 (Fall, 1963), pp. 95-100.

Falk, S.L. *Tennessee Williams,* pp. 102-113.

Fedder, Norman J. *The influence of D.H. Lawrence on Tennessee Williams,* pp. 98-100.

Finkelstein, Sidney. *Existentialism and alienation in American literature,* pp. 214-215.

Funatsu, Tatsumi. "A Study of *Cat on a Hot Tin Roof." Kyusha American Literature* (Fukuo-ka, Japan), no. 2 (May, 1959), pp. 33-39.

Gardner, R.H. *The splintered stage; the decline of the American theater, pp. 89-93.*

Hethmon, Robert. "The Foul Rag-and-Bone Shop of the Heart." *Drama Critique,* vol. 8, no. 3 (Fall, 1965), pp. 94-102.

Hurley, Paul J. "Tennessee Williams: The Playwright as Social Critic." *Theatre annual, 1964,* vol. 21, pp. 40-56.

Lolli, Giorgio. "Alcoholism and Homosexuality in Tennessee Williams' *Cat on a Hot Tin Roof." Q. J. of Studies on Alcohol,* vol. 17 (1956), pp. 543-553.

Magid, Marion. "The Innocence of Tennessee Williams." *In:* Freedman, Morris, ed. *Essays in the modern drama,* pp. 281-293. (Reprinted from *Commentary,* (Jan., 1963).)

Miller, Arthur. "The Shadows of the Gods: A Critical View of the American Theater." *Harper's Mag.,* vol. 217 (Aug., 1958), pp. 41-43.

Nelson, B. *Tennessee Williams,* pp. 200-222.

Rosselli, John. "A Moral Play." *Spectator,* vol. 196 (Mar. 2, 1956), p. 284.

Sacksteder, William. "The Three Cats: A Study in Dramatic Structure." *Drama Survey,* vol. 5, no. 3 (Winter, 1966-67), pp. 252-266.

Styan, J.L. *The dark comedy, 2nd ed.,* pp. 76-77, 108, 211-214, 296.

Tischler, N.M. *Tennessee Williams,* pp. 197-218.

Tynan, K. *Curtains,* pp. 202-204.

Young, Vernon. "Social Drama and Big Daddy." *Southwest Rev.,* vol. 41, no. 2 (Spring, 1956), pp. 194-197.

The Garden District

Tischler, N.M. *Tennessee Williams,* pp. 245-262.

Tynan, K. *Curtains,* pp. 278-280.

The Glass Menagerie

Beaurline, Lester A. *"The Glass Menagerie:* From Story to Play." *Modern Drama,* vol. 8, no. 2 (Sept., 1965), pp. 142-149.

Bluefarb, Sam. *"The Glass Menagerie:* Three Visions of Time." *College English,* vol. 24 no. 7 (Apr., 1963), pp. 513-518.

Brandt, George. "Cinematic Structure in the Work of Tennessee Williams." *In: American theatre,* pp. 181-187.

Brown, John Mason. *Saturday Rev.,* vol. 28 (Apr. 14, 1945), pp. 34-36.

Brown, John Mason. *Seeing things,* pp. 224-230.

Cohn, Ruby, ed. *Twentieth-century drama,* pp. 333-334.

Cubeta, Paul M. *Modern drama for analysis,* pp. 270-275.

Dusenbury, Winifred L. *The theme of loneliness in modern American drama,* pp. 136-140.

Falk, S.L. *Tennessee Williams,* pp. 72-80.

Fedder, Norman J. *The influence of D.H. Lawrence on Tennessee Williams,* pp. 73-79.

Gottfried, Martin. A theater *divided; the postwar American stage,* pp. 248-250.

Hagopian, John V., and Martin Dolch. *Insight I; analysis of American literature,* pp. 272-280.

Heilman, Robert B. *Tragedy and melodrama,* pp. 120-120.

Krutch, Joseph Wood. *Nation,* vol. 160, no. 15 (Apr. 14, 1945), pp. 424-425.

Lid, R.W., ed. *Plays, classic and contemporary,* pp. 441-442.

Nelson, B. *Tennessee Williams,* pp. 97-112.

Nolan, Paul T. "Two Memory Plays: *The Glass Menagerie* and *After the Fall." McNeese Rev.,* (McNeese State Coll., La.), vol. 17 (1966), pp. 27-38.

Reinert, Otto, ed. *Modern drama; nine plays,* pp. 444-449.

Sievers, W. David. *Freud on Broadway,* pp. 372-374.

Stein, Roger B. *"The Glass Menagerie* Revisited: Catastrophe Without Violence." *Western Humanities Rev.,* vol. 18, no. 2 (Spring, 1964), pp. 141-153.

Tischler, N.M. *Tennessee Williams, pp. 91-116.*

Young, Stark. *Immortal shadows,* pp. 249-253.

Young, Stark. *"The Glass Menagerie." In:* Oppenheimer, George, ed. *The passionate playgoer,* pp. 588-591.

I Rise in Flame Cried the Phoenix

Fedder, Norman J. *The influence of D.H. Lawrence on Tennessee Williams,* pp. 47-54.

The Milk Train Doesn't Stop Here Anymore

Brustein, Robert. *Seasons of discontent,* p. 129.

Fedder, Norman J. *The influence of D.H. Lawrence on Tennessee Williams,* pp. 117-119.

Gottfried, Martin. *A theater divided; the postwar American stage,* pp. 255-256.

Grande, Brother Luke M. "Tennessee Williams' New Poet-Prophet." *Drama Critique,* vol. 6, no. 2 (Spring, 1963), pp. 60-64.

Lewis, Allan. *American plays and playwrights of the contemporary theatre,* pp. 60-61.

Simon, John. "Theatre Chronicle." *Hudson Rev.,* vol. 16, no. 1 (Spring, 1963), pp. 87-89.

The Night of the Iguana

Adler, Jacob H. *"Night of the Iguana:* A New Tennessee Williams?" *Ramparts,* vol. 1, no. 3 (1962), pp. 59-68.

Brandt, George. "Cinematic Structure in the Work of Tennessee Williams." *In: American theatre,* pp. 169-170, 171-173.

Brustein, Robert. *New Republic,* vol. 146 (Jan. 22, 1962), pp. 21-23.

Brustein, Robert. *Seasons of discontent,* pp. 126-129.

Clurman, Harold. *The naked image,* pp. 126-128.

Fedder, Norman J. *The influence of D.H. Lawrence on Tennessee Williams,* pp. 109-117.

Forrey, Robert. "Tennessee Williams." *Mainstream,* vol. 15, no. 8 (Aug., 1962), pp. 62-64.

Gilman, Richard. "Williams as Phoenix." *Commonweal,* vol. 75, no. 18 (Jan. 26, 1962), pp. 460-461.

Kerr, Walter. *The theater in spite of itself,* pp. 252-255.

Leon, Ferdinand. "Time, Fantasy, and Reality in *Night of the Iguana."* *Modern Drama,* vol. 11, no. 1 (May, 1968), pp. 87-96.

Lewis, Allan. *American plays and playwrights of the contemporary theatre,* pp. 58-60.

Simon, John. "Theatre Chronicle." *Hudson Rev.,* vol. 15, no. 1 (Spring, 1962), pp. 120-121.

Orpheus Descending (Revision of Battle of Angels)

Alvarez, A. "Hurry On Down." *New Statesman,* vol. 57 (May 23, 1959), pp. 721-722.

Brien, Alan. *Spectator,* vol. 202 (May 22, 1959), pp. 725-726.

Falk, S.L. *Tennessee Williams,* pp. 130-136.

Fedder, Norman J. *The influence of D.H. Lawrence on Tennessee Williams,* pp. 63-73.

Gardner, R.H. *The splintered stage; the decline of the American theater,* pp. 119-120.

Gassner, John. *Theatre at the crossroads,* pp. 223-226.

Hatch, Robert. *Nation,* vol. 184 (Apr. 10, 1957), pp. 301-302.

Justice, Donald. "The Unhappy Fate of the 'Poetic.'" *Poetry,* vol. 93 no. 6 (Mar., 1959), pp. 402-403.

Lewis, Allan. *The contemporary theatre,* pp. 288-289.

Nelson, B. *Tennessee Williams,* pp. 224-239.

Tischler, N.M. *Tennessee Williams,* pp. 232-243.

Watts, Richard, Jr. "Orpheus Ascending." Theatre Arts, vol. 42, no. 9 (Sept., 1958) pp. 25-26.

Period of Adjustment

Brustein, Robert. *Seasons of discontent,* pp. 117-119.

Clurman, Harold. *Nation,* vol. 191 (Dec. 3, 1960), pp. 443-444.

Falk, S.L. *Tennessee Williams,* pp. 136-142.

Fedder, Norman J. *The influence of D.H. Lawrence on Tennessee Williams,* pp. 106-109.

Gascoigne, Bamber. *Spectator,* vol. 208 (June 22, 1962), pp. 823, 826.

Gassner, John. *Educational Theatre J.,* vol. 13 (Mar., 1961), pp. 51-53.

Hatch, Robert. "Human Beings and Substitutes." *Horizon,* vol. 3 (Mar., 1961), pp. 102-103.

Nelson, B. *Tennessee Williams,* pp. 136-142.

Simon, John. "Theatre Chronicle." *Hudson Rev.,* vol. 14, no. 1 (Spring, 1961), pp. 83-84.

Tischler, N.M. *Tennessee Williams,* pp. 280-290.

The Rose Tattoo

Beyer, William H. "The State of the Theatre: Hits and Misses." *School and Society,* vol. 73 (Mar., 10, 1951), pp. 181-183.

Brien, Alan. *Spectator,* vol. 202 (Jan. 23, 1959), pp. 103, 105.

Brown, John Mason. "Seeing Things: Saying it with Flowers." *Saturday Rev., of Lit.,* vol. 34 (Mar., 10, 1951), pp. 22-24. (Reprinted in *As they appear,* pp. 161-166.)

Downer, Alan S. *Fifty years of American drama, 1900-1950,* pp. 145-147.

Dupee, F.W. "Literature on Broadway." *Partisan Rev.,* vol. 18 (May, 1951), pp. 333-334.

Falk, S.L. *Tennessee Williams,* pp. 96-102.

Fedder, Norman J. *The influence of D.H. Lawrence on Tennessee Williams,* pp. 92-95.

Gottfried, Martin. *A theater divided; the postwar American stage,* pp. 252-254.

Ken, Walter. *Commonweal,* vol. 53 (Feb. 23, 1951), pp. 492-494.

Nelson, B. *Tennessee Williams,* pp. 158-165.

Sievers, W. David. *Freud on Broadway,* pp. 383-385.

Simpson, Alan. *Beckett and Behan and a theatre in Dublin,* pp. 138-167.

Tischler, N.M. *Tennessee Williams,* pp. 167-177.

Something Unspoken

Brien, Alan. *Spectator,* vol. 201 (Sept. 26, 1958), pp. 401-402.

Clurman, Harold. *Nation,* vol. 186 (Jan. 25, 1958), pp. 86-87.

Gassner, J. *Theatre at the crossroads,* pp. 226-228.

Stairs to the Roof

Nelson, B. *Tennessee Williams,* pp. 67-74.

A Streetcar Named Desire

"Backstage at *Streetcar* Provides Own Drama, Too." *In:* Goodman, Randolph. *Drama on stage,* pp. 315-316. (From *Chicago Sun-Times* (Jan. 16, 1949).)

Bentley, Eric. "Back to Broadway." *Theatre Arts,* vol. 33 (Nov., 1947), p. 14.

Berkman, Leonard. "The Tragic Downfall of Blanche Du Bois." *Modern Drama,* vol. 10, no. 3 (Dec., 1967), pp. 249-257.

Brandt, George. "Cinematic Structure in the Work of Tennessee Williams." *In: American theatre,* pp. 173-179.

Brown, John Mason. *Saturday Rev.,* vol. 30 (Dec. 27, 1947), pp. 22-24.

Brown, John Mason. *Seeing more things,* pp. 266-272.

Brown, John Mason. "Southern Discomfort: Tennessee Williams' *Streetcar.*" *In:* Brown, John Mason. *Dramatis personae,* pp. 89-94.

Brustein, Robert. "America's New Culture Hero: Feelings Without Words." *Commentary, vol. 25, no.* 2 (Feb., 1958), pp. 123-129.

Clurman, Harold. *Lies like truth,* pp. 72-80.

Downer, Alan S. *Fifty years of American drama, 1900-1950,* pp. 102-104.

Downer, Alan S. "Mr. Williams and Mr. Miller." *Furioso,* vol. 4, no. 3 (Summer 1949), pp. 66-68.

Dusenbury, Winifred L. *The theme of loneliness in modern American drama,* pp. 140-143.

Falk, S.L. *Tennessee Williams,* pp. 80-90.

Fedder, Norman J. *The influence of D.H. Lawrence on Tennessee Williams,* pp. 85-88.

Gardner, R.H. *The splintered stage; the decline of the American theater,* pp. 111-115, 117-118.

Gassner, John. *The theatre in our times,* pp. 355-363. *Also in:* Bogard, Travis, and Oliver William I., eds. *Modern drama; essays in criticism,* pp. 374-384.

Goodman, Randolph. "Blanche Du Bois; an Interview With Jessica Tandy." *In:* Goodman, Randolph. *Drama on stage,* pp. 304-307.

Goodman, Randolph. "Blanche Du Bois on Stage and Screen; An Interview with Vivien Leigh." *In:* Goodman, Randolph. *Drama on stage,* pp. 307-311.

Goodman, Randolph. "Designing and Lighting *Streetcar;* An Interview with Jo Mielziner." *In:* Goodman, Randolph. *Drama on stage,* pp. 312-314.

Goodman, Randolph. *Drama on stage,* pp. 278-289, 291-293.

Gottfried, Martin. *A theater divided; the postwar American stage,* pp. 250-254.

Heilman, Robert B. *Tragedy and melodrama,* pp. 113, 121-122, 148, 159, 160.

"Here's News! *Streetcar* Has a Ballet." *In:* Goodman, Randolph. *Drama on stage,* pp. 314-315. (From *New York Herald Tribune* (Nov. 7, 1948).)

Hurrell, John D., ed. *Two modern American tragedies: reviews and criticism of "Death of a Salesman" and "A Streetcar Named Desire."*

Kazan, Elia. "Notebook for *A Streetcar Named Desire.*" In: Oppenheimer, George, ed. *The passionate playgoer,* pp. 342-356. (Reprinted from Cole, Toby. *Directing the play,* pp. 296-310.) *Also in:* Cole, T., and H.K. Chinoy, eds. *Directors on directing,* pp. 364-379 and Goodman, Randolph. *Drama on Stage,* pp. 295-304.

Kernan, Alvin. "Truth and Dramatic Mode in the Modern Theater: Chekhov, Pirandello and Williams." *Modern Drama,* vol. 1 (Sept. 1958), pp. 111-114.

Krutch, Joseph W. *The American drama since 1918,* pp. 330-331.

Krutch, Joseph Wood. *"Modernism"* in modern drama, pp. 126-130.

Krutch, Joseph Wood. *Nation,* vol. 165, no. 25 (Dec. 20, 1947), pp. 686-687.

Law, Richard A. *"A Streetcar Named Desire* as Melodrama." *Criticism* vol. 14 (1964) pp. 2-8 Also in: *English Record,* vol. 14, (Feb., 1964), pp. 2-8.

Leaska, Mitchell A. *The voice of tragedy,* pp. 279-285.

Lewis, Allan. *The contemporary theatre,* pp. 290-291.

McCarthy, Mary. *Sights and spectacles 1937-1956,* pp. 131-135.

Nelson, B. *Tennessee Williams,* pp. 130-154.

Phillips, Elizabeth C. *Modern American drama,* pp. 120-121.

Ridell, Joseph N. *"A Streetcar Named Desire*—Nietzsche Descending." *Modern Drama,* vol. 5, no. 4 (Feb., 1963), pp: 421-430.

Sievers, W. David. *Freud on Broadway,* pp. 376-380.

Smith, R.D. *New Statesman,* vol. 38 (Oct. 22, 1949), p. 451.

Styan, J.L. *The dark comedy,* 2nd ed., pp. 77, 107, 112, 210, 211, 214-216, 264, 273.

Thomas, Eugene A. "A Streetcar to Where." *Wingover,* vol. 1, (Fall-Winter, 1958/59), pp. 30-31.

Tischler, N.M. *Tennessee Williams,* pp. 134-149.

Weissman, Philip. *Creativity in the theater,* pp. 176-189.

Weissman, Philip. "Psychopathological Characters in Current Drama: A Study of a Trio of Heroines." *Amer. Imago,* vol. 17, no. 3 (Fall, 1960), pp. 271-288.

Wilmer, Harry A. "Psychiatrist on Broadway." *American Imago,* vol. 12 (1955), pp. 157-178.

Suddenly Last Summer

Brien, Alan. *Spectator,* vol. 201 (Sept. 26, 1958), pp. 401-402.

Clurman, Harold. *Nation,* vol. 186 (Jan. 25, 1958), pp. 86-87.

Driver, Tom F. "Accelerando." *Christian Century,* vol. 75, no. 5 (Jan. 29, 1958), pp. 136-137.

Falk, S.L. *Tennessee Williams,* pp. 96-102.

Fedder, Norman J. *The influence of D.H. Lawrence on Tennessee Williams,* pp. 100-102.

Funatsu, Tatsumi. "A Study of *Suddenly Last Summer." Fukuoka Univ. Rev. of Literature and Science,* vol. 7, (Mar. 1963), pp. 341-362.

Gardner, R.H. *The splintered stage; the decline of the American theater,* pp. 115-117, 121.

Gassner, John. *Theatre at the crossroads,* pp. 226-228.

Hayes, Richard. "An Infernal Harmony." *Commonweal,* vol. 68, no. 9 (May 30, 1958), pp. 232-233.

Hewes, Henry. "The Boundaries of Tennessee." *In:* Oppenheimer, George, ed. *The passionate playgoer, pp. 250-254.*

Hurley, Paul J. *"Suddenly Last Summer* as Morality Play." *Modern Drama,* vol. 8, no. 4 (Feb., 1966), pp. 392-402.

Hurt, James R. *"Suddenly Last Summer:* Williams and Melville." *Modern Drama,* vol. 3, no. 4 (Feb., 1961), pp. 396-400.

Johnson, Mary L. "Williams' *Suddenly Last Summer,* Scene One." *Explicator,* vol. 21 (1963), Item 66.

Justice, Donald. "The Unhappy Fate of the 'Poetic.'" *Poetry,* vol. 93, no. 6 (Mar., 1959), pp. 402-403.

Nelson, B. *Tennessee Williams,* pp. 244-259.

Tischler, N.M. *Tennessee Williams,* pp. 249-262.

Summer and Smoke (Film)

Brandt, George. "Cinematic Structure in the Work of Tennessee Williams." *In: American theatre,* pp. 170-171.

Brooking, Jack. "Directing *Summer and Smoke:* An Existential Approach." *Modern Drama,* vol. 2, no. 4 (Feb., 1960), pp. 377-385.

Brown, John Mason. "People Versus Characters." *Saturday Rev.,* vol. 31, (Oct. 30, 1948), pp. 31-33.

Clurman, Harold. *Lies like truth,* pp. 80-83.

Falk, S.L. *Tennessee Williams,* pp. 90-94.

Fedder, Norman J. *The influence of D.H. Lawrence on Tennessee Williams,* pp. 88-92.

Gassner, John. *Theatre at the crossroads,* pp. 218-223.

Jackson, E.M. *The broken world of Tennessee Williams,* pp. 137-140.

Krutch, Joseph Wood. *Nation,* vol. 167, no. 17 (Oct. 23, 1948), pp. 473-474.

Nelson, B. *Tennessee Williams,* pp. 120-129.

Sievers, W. David. *Freud on Broadway,* pp. 380-382.

Stavrou, Constantine N. "The Neurotic Heroine in Tennessee Williams." *Literature and Psychology,* vol. 5, no. 2 (1955), pp. 26-34.

Tischler, N.M. *Tennessee Williams,* pp. 151-163.

Tynan, Kenneth. *Spectator,* vol. 187 (Dec. 7, 1951), p. 772.

Sweet Bird of Youth

Brandt, George. "Cinematic Structure in the Work of Tennessee Williams." *In: American theatre,* pp. 168-169.

Brustein, Robert. "Sweet Bird of Success." *Encounter,* vol. 12, no. 6 (June, 1959), pp. 59-60.

Brustein, Robert. "Williams' Nebulous Nightmare." *Hudson Rev.,* vol. 12, no. 2 (Summer, 1959), pp. 255-260.

Clurman, Harold. *The naked image,* pp. 123-126.

Clurman, Harold. *Nation,* vol. 188, no. 3 (Mar. 28, 1959), pp. 281-283.

Driver, Tom F. *New Republic,* vol. 140 (Apr. 20- 1959), pp. 21-22.

Dukore, Bernard F. "American Abelard: A Footnote to *Sweet Bird of Youth.*" *College English,* vol. 26, no. 8 (May, 1965), pp. 630-634.

Falk, S.L. *Tennessee Williams,* pp. 155-162.

Fedder, Norman J. *The influence of D.H. Lawrence on Tennessee Williams,* pp. 102-105.

Gassner, John. *Educational Theatre J., vol.* 11 (May, 1959), pp. 122-124.

Gassner, John. *Theatre at the crossroads,* pp. 228-231.

Hays, Peter L. "Tennessee William's Use of Myth in *Sweet Bird of Youth:" Educational Theatre J.,* vol 18, no. 3 (Oct., 1966), pp. 255-258.

Jackson, E.M. *The broken world of Tennessee Williams,* pp. 148-150.

Kerr, Walter. *The theatre in spite of itself,* pp. 247-252.

Lewis, Allan. *American plays and playwrights of the contemporary theatre,* pp. 54-57.

Nelson, B. *Tennessee Williams,* pp. 260-274.

Roulet, William M. *"Sweet Bird of Youth:* Williams' Redemptive Ethic." *Cithera,* vol. 3, no. 2 (1964), pp. 31-36.

Tischler, N.M. *Tennessee Williams,* pp. 263-274.

Tynan, K. *Curtains,* pp. 306-309.

27 Wagons Full of Cotton (Adapted for film as Baby Doll)

Falk, S.L. *Tennessee Williams,* pp. 49-59

This Property Is Condemned

Weissman, Philip. "Psychopathological Characters in Current Drama: A Study of a Trio of Heroines." *American Imago,* vol. 17, no. 3 (Fall, 1960), pp. 271-288.

You Touched Me (Adapted from a story by D.H. Lawrence)

Falk, S.L. *Tennessee Williams,* pp. 66-69.

Fedder, Norman J. *The influence of D.H. Lawrence on Tennessee Williams,* pp. 79-85.

Gilder, Rosamond. "Poetry, Passion and Politics." *Theatre Arts,* vol. 29 (Nov., 1945), pp. 618-621.

Nelson, B. *Tennessee Williams,* pp. 92-96.

Sievers, W. David. *Freud on Broadway,* pp. 375-376.

Tischler, N.M. *Tennessee Williams,* pp. 120-130.

Weales, Gerald. "Tennessee Williams Borrows A Little Shaw." *Shaw Rev.,* vol. 8, no. 2 (May, 1965), pp. 63-64.

Young, Stark. "At the Booth." *New Republic,* vol. 113 (Oct. 8, 1945), p. 469.

WILLIAM CARLOS WILLIAMS 1883-1963

A Dream of Love

Worth, Katharine J. "The Poets in the American Theatre." *In: American theatre,* pp. 101-102.

Many Lovers

Weales, Gerald. *American drama since World War II,* pp. 195-197.

Worth, Katharine J. "The Poets in the American Theatre." *In: American theatre,* pp. 99-101.

Tituba's Children

Worth, Katharine J. "The Poets in the American theatre." *In: American theatre,* pp. 97-99.

EDMUND WILSON 1895-

Beppo and Beth

Paul, Sherman. *Edmund Wilson,* pp. 101-105, 150, 158, 171.

The Crime in the Whistler Room

Paul, Sherman. *Edmund Wilson,* pp. 31, 40-46, 50, 101, 103.

Cyprian's Prayer

Paul, Sherman *Edmund Wilson,* pp. 8, 81, 181, 192, 199-200.

The Little Blue Light

Paul, Sherman. *Edmund Wilson,* pp. 5-6, 8, 153, 164, 181, 188-189, 192-199, 214, 220.

This Room and This Gin and These Sandwiches

Paul, Sherman. *Edmund Wilson,* pp. 31, 47-50, 56, 101.

FRANK WILSON

Brother Mose

Abramson, Doris E. *Negro playwrights in the American theatre, 1925-1959,* pp. 54-59, 86.

LANFORD WILSON

This Is the Rill Speaking

Gottfried, Martin. *A theater divided; the postwar American stage,* pp. 300-301.

MORTON WISHENGRAD

The Rope Dancers

Gassner, John. *Theatre at the crossroads,* pp. 161-164.

STANISLAW IGNACY WITKIEWICZ 1885-1939

General

Gerould, Daniel C. "Introduction." *In:* Witkiewicz, Stanislaw I. *The Madman and the Nun and other plays,* pp. xxiii-liii.

Grabowski, Zbigniew A. "S.I. Witkiewicz: A Polish Prophet of Doom." *The Polish Rev.,* vol. 12, no. 1 (Winter, 1967), pp. 39-49.

Kott, Jan. "Foreword." *In:* Gerould, Daniel C., and C.S. Durer, eds. *The Madman and the Nun and other plays by Stanislaw Ignacy Witkiewicz,* pp. v-xv.

Milosz, Czeslaw. "S.I. Witkiewicz, A Polish Writer for Today." *Tri-Quarterly,* no. 9 (Spring, 1967), pp. 143-154.

Puzyna, Konstanty. "The Prism of the Absurd." *Polish Perspectives,* vol. 6, no. 6 (June, 1963), pp. 36-44.

Tarn, Adam. "Plays." *Polish Perspectives,* vol. 8, no. 10 (Oct., 1965), p. 8.

Toeplitz, Krzysztof T. "Avant-Garde with Tradition." *Poland,* American ed., no. 4 (Apr., 1965), pp. 28-31.

KARL WITTLINGER

Do You Know the Milky Way? (Kennen Sie die Milchstrasse?)

Bauland, Peter. *The hooded eagle,* pp. 213-214.

FRIEDRICH WOLF

General

Garten, H.F. *Modern German drama,* pp. 189-191.

Professor Mamlock

Bauland, Peter. *The hooded eagle,* pp. 120-122.

Himelstein, Morgan Y. *Drama was a weapon, the left-wing theatre in New York 1929-1941,* pp. 101-102.

Sailors of Cattaro (Die Matrosen von Cattaro)

Bauland, Peter. *The hooded eagle,* p. 120.

Block, Anita. The changing world in plays and theatre, pp. 210-212.

Himelstein, Morgan Y. *Drama was a weapon, the left-wing theatre in New York 1929-1941,* pp. 61-63.

THOMAS WOLFE 1900-1938

Concerning Honest Bob

McElderry, B.R. "Thomas Wolfe: Dramatist." *Modern Drama,* vol. 6 (1963-64), pp. 1-11.

Deferred Payment

McElderry, B.R. "Thomas Wolfe: Dramatist." *Modern Drama,* vol. 6 (1963-64), pp. 1-11.

Mannerhouse

McElderry, B.R. "Thomas Wolfe: Dramatist." *Modern Drama,* vol. 6 (1963-64), pp. 1-11.

The Return of Buck Gavin

McElderry, B.R. "Thomas Wolfe: Dramatist." *Modern Drama,* vol. 6 (1963-64), pp. 1-11.

The Third Night

McElderry B.R. "Thomas Wolfe: Dramatist." *Modern Drama,* vol. 6 (1963-64), pp. 1-11.

Welcome to Our City

McElderry, B.R. "Thomas Wolfe: Dramatist." *Modern Drama,* vol. 6 (1963-64), pp. 1-11.

EGON RAUL WOLFF 1926-

General

Jones, W.K. *Behind Spanish American footlights,* p. 239.

A Touch of Blue (La Niña Madre) (La Polla)

Jones, W.K. *Behind Spanish American footlights,* p. 239.

MAXINE WOOD

On Whitman Avenue

Mitchell, Loften. *Black drama,* pp. 126-127.

HERMAN WOUK 1915-

The Caine Mutiny Court Martial

Bentley, Eric. *The dramatic event,* pp. 191-194.

Sievers, W. David. *Freud on Broadway,* pp. 440-441.

RICHARD WRIGHT 1908-1960

General

Brignano, Russell C. "Richard Wright: the major themes, ideas, and attitudes in his works." *Dissertation Abstracts,* vol. 28 (1967), 666A-67A (Wis.).

Margolies, Edward L. "A critical analysis of the works of Richard Wright." *Dissertation Abstracts,* vol. 27 (1966), 1829A-30A (N.Y.U.).

Zietlow, Edward R. "Wright to Hansberry: the evolution of outlook in four Negro writers." *Dissertation Abstracts,* vol. 28 (1967), 701A (U. of Wash.).

Daddy Goodness

Kloman, William. "Moses Gunn: A Brilliant Black Star." *The New York Times* (June 16, 1968) Sec. 2, pp. 1, 3.

The Long Dream (Adapted by Ketti Frings)

Mitchell, Loften. *Black drama,* pp. 184-185.

Native Son (Adapted by Richard Wright and Paul Green)

Abramson, Doris E. *Negro playwrights in the American theatre, 1925-1959,* pp. 136-155, 160-163.

Himelstein, Morgan Y. *Drama was a weapon, the left-wing theatre in New York 1929-1941,* pp. 120-122.

Mitchell, Loften. *Black drama,* pp. 109, 114-115, 116.

Sievers, W. David. *Freud on Broadway,* pp. 319-321.

Young, Stark. *Immortal shadows,* pp. 223-226.

JACK B. YEATS 1871-1957

In Sand

Hogan, Robert. *After the Irish renaissance,* p. 44.

Skelton, Robin. "Unarrangeable Reality: The Paintings and Writings of Jack B. Yeats." *In:* Skelton, Robin, ed. *The world of W.B. Yeats,* pp. 264.

La La Noo

Barnet, Sylvan, ed. *The genius of the Irish theatre,* pp. 212-214.

Hogan, Robert. *After the Irish renaissance,* pp. 43-44.

Skelton, Robin. "Unarrangeable Reality: The Paintings and Writings of Jack B. Yeats." *In:* Skelton, Robin, ed. *The world of W.B. Yeats,* pp. 262-263.

The Scourge of the Gulph

Skelton, Robin. "Unarrangeable Reality: The Paintings and Writings of Jack B. Yeats." *In:* Skelton, Robin, ed. *The world of W.B. Yeats,* pp. 256-257.

WILLIAM BUTLER YEATS 1865-1939

General

Ayling, Ronald W. "W.B. Yeats on Plays and Players." *Modern Drama,* vol. 9, no. 1 (May, 1966), pp. 1-10.

Baksi, Pronoti. "The Noh and the Yeatsian Synthesis." *Rev., of English Literature* (Leeds), vol. 6, no. 3 (1964), pp. 34-43.

Bentley, Eric. *The playwright as thinker,* pp. 187-189.

Bradbrook, M.C. *English dramatic form,* pp. 123-142.

Bradford, Curtis B. *Yeats at work,* pp. 169-173.

Brogunier, Joseph. "Expiation in Yeats' Late plays." *Drama Survey,* vol. 5, no. 1 (Spring, 1966), pp. 24-36.

Bushrui, S.B. *Yeats' verse plays: the revisions 1900-1910,* pp. 209-226.

Byars, John A. "Yeats' Introduction of the Heroic Type." *Modern Drama,* vol. 8, no. 4 (Feb., 1966), pp. 409-418.

Chiari, J. *Landmarks of contemporary drama,* pp. 83-85.

Chislett, William. "On the Influence of Lady Gregory on William Butler Yeats." *In:* Chislett, William. Moderns *and near-moderns,* pp. 165-167.

Clark, David R. *W.B. Yeats and the theatre of the desolate reality,* pp. 13-25, 104-108.

Clark, David R. "W.B. Yeats and the Drama of Vision." *Arizona Q.* vol. 20, no. 2 (Summer, 1964), pp. 127-141.

Clarke, David R. "Yeats and the Modern Theatre." *Threshold,* vol. 4, no. 2 (1960), pp. 36-56.

Dasgupta, Pranabendu. "The 'Subjective Tradition': A Comparative Analysis of the Dramatic Motives in the Plays of W.B. Yeats and Rabindranath Tagore." *Dissertation Abstracts,* vol. 27 (1967), 4245A (Minn.)

Davis, Dorothy R. "Parallelism between classical tragedy and the tragedy of William Butler Yeats." Ph.D., Boston University, 1937.

Desai, Rupin W. "A Note on 'Yeats on the Possibility of an English Poetic Drama.'" *Modern Drama,* vol. 11, no. 4 (Feb., 1969), pp. 396-399.

Dupee, F.W. *"The King of the Cats" and other remarks on writers and writing,* pp. 42-48.

Ellis-Fermor, Una. *The Irish dramatic movement,* pp. 91-116.

Ellmann, Richard. *Eminent domain.*

Ellmann, Richard. *Yeats: the man and the masks.*

Gaddis, Marilyn. "The Purgatory Metaphor of Yeats and Beckett." *London Magazine,* vol. 7, no. 5, pp. 33-46.

Gassner, John. *The theatre in our times,* pp. 226-233.

Henn, T.R. "The Poetry of the Plays." *In:* Henn, T.R. *The lonely tower,* pp. 272-296.

Hethmon, Robert H. "Total Theatre and Yeats." *Colorado Q.,* vol. 15, no. 4 (Spring, 1967), pp. 361-377.

Hoare, Dorothy M. *The works of Morris and of Yeats in relation to early saga literature,* pp. 76-100, 111-133.

Hogan, Robert. *After the Irish renaissance,* pp. 147-151.

Hubbell, Lindley Williams. "Yeats, Pound and No Drama." *East-West Rev.,* vol. 1, no. 1 (Spring, 1964), pp. 70-78.

Ishibashi, Hiro. *Yeats and the Noh: types of Japanese beauty and their reflection in Yeats' plays.* Ed. by Anthony Kerrigan. (Yeats Centenary Papers, 1965).

Kennelly, Brendan. "The Heroic Ideal in Yeats' Cuchulain Plays." *Hermathena,* (101 (1965), pp. 13-21.

Kersnowski, Frank L. "Portrayal of the Hero in Yeats' Poetic Drama." *Renascence,* vol. 18, no. 1 (Fall, 1965), pp. 9-15.

Knight, G. Wilson. *The golden labyrinth,* pp. 325-329.

Krause, David. "O'Casey and Yeats and the Druid." *Modern Drama,* vol. 11, no. 3 (Dec., 1968), pp. 252-262.

Lamm, Martin. *Modern drama,* pp. 293-302.

Lucas, F.L. *The drama of Chekhov, Synge, Yeats and Pirandello,* pp. 241-280, 344-355.

Malone, Andrew E. *The Irish drama,* pp. 42-52.

Mercier, Vivian. "In Defense of Yeats as a Dramatist." *Modern Drama,* vol. 8, no. 2 (Sept., 1965), pp. 161-166.

Miller, Nellie Burget. *The living drama,* pp. 331-333.

Moore, John R. "Cuchulain, Christ, and the Queen of Love: Aspects of Yeatsian Drama." *Tulane Drama Rev.,* vol. 6, no. 3 (Mar., 1962), pp. 150-159.

Murphy, Daniel J. "Yeats and Lady Gregory: A Unique Dramatic Collaboration." *Modern Drama,* vol. 7, no. 3 (Dec., 1964), pp. 322-328.

Nicoll, Allardyce. *British drama,* pp. 313-315.

O'Casey, Sean. "Ireland's Silvery Shadow." *In:* O'Casey, Sean. *Blasts and benedictions,* pp. 182-187.

O'Connor, Frank. "A Lyric Voice in the Irish Theatre." *In:* Barnet, Sylvan, ed. *The genius of the Irish theatre,* pp. 354-358.

O'Connor, Frank. *A short history of Irish literature,* pp. 163-182.

Parkinson, Thomas. "The Later Plays of W.B. Yeats." *In:* Bogard, Travis, and Oliver, William I., eds. *Modern drama; essays in criticism,* pp. 385-393.

Peacock, Ronald. *The poet in the theatre,* pp. 117-128.

Popkin, Henry. "Yeats as a Dramatist." *Tulane Drama Rev.,* vol. 3, no. 3 (Mar., 1959), pp. 73-82.

Prior, Moody E. *The language of tragedy,* pp. 326-340.

Pronko, Leonard C. *Theatre East and West,* pp. 71-73.

Reid, Benjamin L. "William Butler Yeats and generic tragedy." Ph.D., University of Virginia, 1957.

Saddlemyer, Ann. "The Heroic Discipline of the Looking-Glass: W.B. Yeats' Search for Dramatic Design." *In:* Skelton, Robin, ed. *The world of W.B. Yeats,* pp. 87-103.

Saddlemyer, Ann. "Worn Out with Dreams: Dublin's Abbey Theatre." *In:* Skelton, Robin, ed. *The world of W.B. Yeats,* pp. 104-132.

Salerno, Henry F. *English drama in transition, 1880-1920,* pp. 387-389.

Saul, George Brandon. *Prolegomena to the study of Yeats' plays.*

Schrickx, W. "On Giordano Bruno, Wilde and Yeats." *English Studies,* vol. 45: Supplement, 1964. (Presented to R.W. Zandvoort on the occasion of his 70th birthday.), pp. 257-264.

Sena, Vinod. "Yeats on the Possibility of an English Poetic Drama." *Modern Drama,* vol. 9, no. 2 (Sept., 1966), pp. 195-205.

Sidnell, M.J. "John Bull's Other Island—Yeats and Shaw." *Modern Drama,* vol. 11, no. 3 (Dec., 1968), pp. 245-251.

Starkie, Walter. "Yeats and the Abbey Theatre." *In:* Starkie, W., and A. Norman Jeffares. *Homage to Yeats 1865-1965,* pp. 3-39.

Steiner, George. *The death of tragedy,* pp. 316-319.

Stewart, J.I.M. *Eight modern writers,* pp. 338, 391-393, 394-395, 398.

Stucki, Yasuko. "Yeats' Drama and the No: A Comparative Study in Dramatic Theories." *Modern Drama,* vol. 9, no. 1 (May, 1966), pp. 101-122.

Torchiana, Donald T. *W.B. Yeats and Georgian Ireland.*

Ure, Peter. "Yeats Hero on the World Tree: Yeats' Plays." *English* (London), vol. 15, no. 89 (Summer, 1965), pp. 169-172.

Ure, Peter. "The Plays." *In:* Donoghue, Denis. *An honoured guest,* pp. 143-164.

Vendler, Helen Hennessy. "Yeats, Changing Metaphors for the Other World." *Modern Drama,* vol. 7, no. 3 (Dec., 1964), pp. 308-321.

White, H. "A study of W.B. Yeats as a dramatist, with special reference to his treatment of the ideas formulated in *A Vision.*" M.A., University of Leeds, 1956-57.

Williams, Harold. *Modern English writers,* pp. 197-198.

Williams, Raymond. *Drama from Ibsen to Eliot,* pp. 205-222.

Worth, Katharine J. "Yeats and the French Drama." *Modern Drama,* vol. 8, no. 4 (Feb., 1966), pp. 382-391.

Zwerdling, Alex. *Yeats and the heroic ideal.*

At the Hawk's Well

Bradford, Curtis B. *Yeats at work,* pp. 174-216.

Donoghue, Denis. *The third voice: modern British and American verse drama,* pp. 50-54, 61.

Ellmann, Richard. "Ez and Old Billyum." *In:* Ellmann, R. *Eminent domain,* p. 72.

Lucas, F.L. *The drama of Chekhov, Synge, Yeats and Pirandello,* p. 326.

Mills, John G. "W.B. Yeats and Noh." *Japan Q.,* vol. 2 (1955), pp. 496-500.

Rajan, Balachandra. *W.B. Yeats, a critical introduction,* pp. 23, 95, 96-98, 135.

Sandberg, Anna. "The Anti-theatre of W.B. Yeats." *Modern Drama,* vol. 4, no. 2 (Sept., 1961), pp. 131-137.

Stewart, J.I.M. *Eight modern writers,* pp. 350, 391, 393-394, 408.

Stucki, Yasuko. "Yeats' Drama and the No: A Comparative Study in Dramatic Theories." *Modern Drama,* vol. 9, no. 1 (May, 1966), pp. 116-118.

Calvary

Ellmann, Richard. "Oscar and Oisin." *In:* Ellmann, R. *Eminent domain,* pp. 22-23.

Flannery, James W. "Action and Reaction and the Dublin Theatre Festival." *Educational Theatre J.,* vol. 19, no. 1 (Mar., 1967), pp. 72-80.

Gose, Elliott B., Jr. "The Lyric and the Philosophic in Yeats' *Calvary." Modern Drama,* vol. 2, no. 4 (Feb., 1960), pp. 370-376.

Jeffares, A. Norman, ed. *In excited reverie, a centenary tribute to William Butler Yeats, 1865-1939,* pp. 311-312.

Lucas, F.L. *The drama of Chekhov, Synge, Yeats and Pirandello,* pp. 331-332.

Prior, Moody E. *The language of tragedy,* pp. 335-38.

Rajan, Balachandra. *W.B. Yeats, a critical introduction,* pp. 103-105.

Roston, Murray. *Biblical drama in England from the Middle ages to the present day,* pp. 266-269.

Stewart J.I.M. *Eight modern writers,* pp. 391-395.

The Cat and the Moon

Jeffares, A. Norman, ed. *In excited reverie, a centenary tribute to William Butler Yeats, 1865-1939,* pp. 311-312.

Lucas, F.L. *The drama of Chekhov, Synge, Yeats and Pirandello,* pp. 333.

Stewart, J.I.M. *Eight modern writers,* p. 398.

Cathleen ni Houlihan

Boyd, Ernest. *Ireland's literary renaissance,* pp. 150-151.

Jeffares, A. Norman, ed. *In excited reverie, a centenary tribute to William Butler Yeats, 1865-1939,* pp. 168, 195-196, 204, 221, 226-228.

Lucas, F.L. *The drama of Chekhov, Synge, Yeats and Pirandello,* pp. 294-298.

Rajan, Balachandra. *W.B. Yeats, a critical introduction,* pp. 52.

Stewart, J.I.M. *Eight modern writers,* pp. 325-326, 394.

Suss, Irving D. "Yeatsian Drama and the Dying Hero." *South Atlantic. Q.,* vol. 54 (1955), pp. 369-380.

Countess Cathleen

Beerbohm, Max. "In Dublin." *In:* Barnet, Sylvan, ed. *The genius of the Irish theatre,* pp. 344-347.

Boyd, Ernest. *Ireland's literary renaissance,* pp. 146-147, 150.

Clark, David R. "Vision and Revision: Yeats' *The Countess Cathleen." In:* Skelton, Robin, ed. *The world of W.B. Yeats,* pp. 158-176.

Dorcey, Donal. "The Big Occasions." *In:* McCann, Sean, ed. *The story of the Abbey Theatre,* pp. 126-129.

Ellmann, Richard. "The Hawklike Man." *In:* Ellmann, R., *Eminent domain,* pp. 31-32.

Gregory, Isabella Augusta (Lady). *Our Irish theatre,* pp. 20-25.

Henn, T.R. *The harvest of tragedy,* 205-206.

Jeffares, A. Norman, ed. *In excited reverie, a centenary tribute to William Butler Yeats, 1865-1939,* pp. 57, 196-202.

Lucas, F.L. *The drama of Chekhov, Synge, Yeats and Pirandello,* pp. 281-289.

Orel, Harold. "Dramatic Values, Yeats and *The Countess Cathleen.*" *Modern Drama,* vol. 2, no. 1 (May, 1959), pp. 8-16.

Rajan, Balachandra. *W.B. Yeats, a critical introduction,* pp. 24-27, 50.

Stewart, J.I.M. *Eight modern writers,* pp. 301, 302, 303, 330.

The Death of Cuchulain

Henn, T.R. *The harvest of tragedy,* pp. 211-212.

Lucas, F.L. *The drama of Chekhov, Synge, Yeats and Pirandello,* pp. 339-343.

Pearce, Donald. "Yeats' Last Plays: An Interpretation." *J. of English Literary History* (ELH), vol. 18, no. 1 (Mar., 1951), pp. 67-76.

Rajan, Balachandra. *W.B. Yeats, a critical introduction,* pp. 158, 166-169.

Stewart, J.I.M. *Eight modern writers,* pp. 408-409.

Suss, Irving D. "Yeatsian Drama and the Dying Hero." *South Atlantic.* vol. 54 (1955), pp. 369-380.

Deirdre

Boyd, Ernest. *Ireland's literary renaissance,* pp. 160-162.

Bushrui, S.B. *Yeats' verse plays: the revisions 1900-1910,* pp. 120-167.

Clark, David R. *W.B. Yeats and the theatre of desolate reality,* pp. 26-42.

Jeffares, A. Norman, ed. *In excited reverie, a centenary tribute to William Butler Yeats, 1865-1939,* pp. 204-205.

Lucas, F.L. *The drama of Chekhov, Synge, Yeats and Pirandello,* pp. 313-321.

Rajan, Balachandra. *W.B. Yeats, a critical introduction,* pp. 47, 60-64, 95, 167.

Salerno, Henry F. *English drama in transition, 1880-1920,* pp. 389-390.

Slattery, Sister Margaret Patrice. *"Deirdre,* The 'Mingling of Contraries' in Plot and Symbolism." *Modern Drama,* vol. 11, no. 4 (Feb., 1969), pp. 400-403.

Stewart, J.I.M. *Eight modern writers,* pp. 335-337.

Ure, Peter. "Yeats' *Deirdre."* *English Studies,* vol. 42 (1961), pp. 218-230.

Diarmuid and Grania

Saddlemyer, Ann. "All Art Is a Collaboration? George Moore and W.B. Yeats." *In:* Skelton, Robin, ed. *The world of W.B. Yeats,* pp. 220-222.

The Dreaming of the Bones

Boyd, Ernest. *Ireland's literary renaissance,* p. 165.

Brogunier, Joseph. "Expiation in Yeats' Late Plays." *Drama Survey,* vol. 5, no. 1 (Spring, 1966), pp. 24-26, 27, 34, 36.

Clark, David R. *W.B. Yeats and the theatre of desolate reality,* pp. 43-59.

Clark, David R. "Nishikigi and Yeats' *The Dreaming of the Bones."* *Modern Drama,* vol. 7, no. 2 (Sept., 1964), pp. 111-125.

Lucas, F.L. *The drama of Chekhov, Synge, Yeats and Pirandello,* pp. 328-331.

Rajan, Balachandra. *W.B. Yeats, a critical introduction,* pp. 101-103.

Salvadori, Corinna. *Yeats and Castiglione, poet and courtier,* pp. 48-49.

Stewart, J.I.M. *Eight modern writers,* pp. 391-395.

Suss, Irving D. "Yeatsian Drama and the Dying Hero." *South Atlantic Q.,* vol. 54 (1955), pp. 369-380.

Fighting the Waves

Stewart, J.I.M. *Eight modern writers,* pp. 385, 394.

Four Plays for Dancers

Stewart, J.I.M. *Eight modern writers,* pp. 338, 391, 393, 395.

A Full Moon in March

Bentley, Eric. "Yeats as a Playwright." *Kenyon Rev.,* vol. 10, no. 2 (Spring, 1948), pp. 196-208.

Bradford, Curtis B. *Yeats at work,* pp. 268-293.

Donoghue, Denis. *The third voice: modern British and American verse drama,* pp. 55-61.

Rajan, Balachandra. *W.B. Yeats, a critical introduction,* pp. 115, 160-162.

Stewart, J.I.M. *Eight modern writers,* pp. 402-404.

The Green Helmet

Boyd, Ernest. *Ireland's literary renaissance,* pp. 162-163.

Bushrui, S.B. *Yeats's verse plays: the revisions 1900-1910,* pp. 168-208.

Jeffares, A. Norman, ed. *In excited reverie, a centenary tribute to William Butler Yeats, 1865-1939,* pp. 202-204.

Lucas, F.L. *The drama of Chekhov, Synge, Yeats and Pirandello,* p. 324.

The Herne's Egg

Lucas, F.L. *The drama of Chekhov, Synge, Yeats and Pirandello,* p. 337.

Moore, John R. "Cold Passion: A Study of *The Herne's Egg." Modern Drama,* vol. 7, no. 3 (Dec., 1964), pp. 287-298.

Pearce, Donald. "Yeats' Last Plays: An Interpretation." *J. of English Literary History (ELH),* vol. 18, no. 1 (Mar., 1951), pp. 67-76.

Rajan, Balachandra. *W.B. Yeats, a critical introduction,* pp. 162-164, 169.

Stewart, J.I.M. *Eight modern writers,* pp. 404-405, 408.

Ure, Peter. "Yeats' Hero-Fool in *The Herne's Egg." Huntington Library Q.,* vol. 24, no. 2 (Feb., 1961), pp. 125-136.

The Hour Glass

Boyd, Ernest. *Ireland's literary renaissance,* pp. 152-153.

Donoghue, Denis. *The third voice: modern British and American verse drama,* pp. 46-50.

Lucas, F.L. *The drama of Chekhov, Synge, Yeats and Pirandello,* pp. 307-308.

Parker, J. Stewart. "Yeats' *The Hour Glass.*" *Modern Drama,* vol. 10, no. 4 (Feb., 1968), pp. 356-363.

Stewart, J.I.M. *Eight modern writers,* pp. 329.

Ure, Peter, Yeats and the Two Harmonies." *Modern Drama,* vol. 7, no. 3 (Dec., 1964), pp. 237-255.

The Island of Statues

Berryman, Charles. *W.B. Yeats, design of opposites,* pp. 81-86.

Jeffares, A. Norman, ed. *In excited reverie, a centenary tribute to William Butler Yeats, 1865-1939,* pp. 70-71, 74-75, 79-85, 88-89, 94-95, 97.

The King of the Great Clock Tower

Lucas, F.L. *The drama of Chekhov, Synge, Yeats and Pirandello,* pp. 333-336.

Rajan, Balachandra. *W.B. Yeats, a critical introduction,* pp. 152, 158-160, 169.

Stewart, J.I.M. *Eight modern writers,* pp. 402-404, 407, 409.

The King's Threshold

Beerbohm, Max. *Around theatres,* pp. 314-319.

Black, Haskell M. "Yeats' *The King's Threshold;* The Poet and Society." *Philological Q.,* vol. 34 (1955), pp. 206-218.

Boyd, Ernest. *Ireland's literary renaissance,* pp. 156-158.

Bushrui, S.B. *Yeats' verse plays: the revisions 1900-1910,* pp. 73-119.

Lucas, F.L. *The drama of Chekhov, Synge, Yeats and Pirandello,* pp. 298-301.

Rajan, Balachandra. *W.B. Yeats, a critical introduction,* pp. 47, 52-54.

Salvadori, Corinna. *Yeats and Castiglione, poet and courtier,* pp. 20, 68-70, 83, 85.

Stewart, J.I.M. *Eight modern writers,* pp. 293, 330-332.

Ure, Peter. "Yeats and the Two Harmonies." *Modern Drama,* vol. 7, no. 3 (Dec., 1964),pp. 237-255.

The Land of Heart's Desire

Boyd, Ernest. *Ireland's literary renaissance,* pp. 148-150.

Lucas, F.L. *The drama of Chekhov, Synge, Yeats and Pirandello,* pp. 290-294.

Miller, Nellie Burget. *The living drama,* pp. 333-335.

Stewart, J.I.M. *Eight modern writers,* pp. 304-307.

On Baile's Strand

Barnet, Sylvan, ed. *Eight great tragedies,* pp. 324-327.

Boyd, Ernest. *Ireland's literary renaissance,* pp. 158-160.

Bushrui, S.B. *Yeats' verse plays: the revisions 1900-1910,* pp. 39-72.

Henn, T.R. *The harvest of tragedy,* pp. 136-137, 206-208.

Lucas, F.L. *The drama of Chekhov, Synge, Yeats and Pirandello,* pp. 308-312.

Rajan, Balachandra. *W.B. Yeats, a critical introduction,* pp. 12, 45, 50, 54-58, 60, 106.

Stewart, J.I.M. *Eight modern writers,* pp. 332-335.

Suss, Irving D. "Yeatsian Drama and the Dying Hero." *South Atlantic Q.,* vol. 54 (1955), pp. 369-380.

Ure, Peter. "Yeats and the Two Harmonies." *Modern Drama,* vol. 7, no. 3 (Dec., 1964), pp. 237-255.

The Only Jealousy of Elmer

Boyd, Ernest. *Ireland's literary renaissance,* pp. 164-165.

Cohn, Ruby, ed. *Twentieth-century drama,* pp. 148-150.

Lucas, F.L. *The drama of Chekhov, Synge, Yeats and Pirandello,* pp. 326-328.

Rajan, Balachandra. *W.B. Yeats, a critical introduction,* pp. 98-101.

Salvadori, Corinna. *Yeats and Castiglione, poet and courtier,* pp. 37-38, 42, 78-79.

Scanlon, Sister Aloyse. "The Sustained Metaphor in *The Only Jealousy of Elmer.*" *Modern Drama,* vol. 7, no. 3 (Dec., 1964), pp. 273-277.

Stewart, J.I.M. *Eight modern writers,* pp. 391, 394.

Stucki, Yasuko. "Yeats' Drama and the No: A Comparative Study in Dramatic Theories." *Modern Drama,* vol. 9, no. 1 (May, 1966), pp. 111-120.

Suss, Irving D. "Yeatsian Drama and the Dying Hero." *South Atlantic Q.,* vol. 54 (1955), pp. 369-380.

The Player Queen

Berryman, Charles. *W.B. Yeats, design of opposites,* pp. 37-38, 86-94.

Mercier, Vivian. "In Defense of Yeats as a Dramatist." *Modern Drama,* vol. 8, no. 2 (Sept., 1965), pp. 161-166.

Stewart, J.I.M. *Eight modern writers,* pp. 337, 396-398, 404.

The Pot of Broth

Boyd, Ernest. *Ireland's literary renaissance,* pp. 151-152.

Stewart, J.I.M. *Eight modern writers,* p. 325.

Purgatory

Bradbrook, M.C. *English dramatic form,* pp. 123-142.

Bradford, Curtis B. *Yeats at work,* pp. 294-304.

Brogunier, Joseph. "Expiation in Yeats' Late Plays." *Drama Survey,* vol. 5, no. 1 (Spring, 1966), pp. 29-36.

Clark, David R. *W.B. Yeats and the theatre of desolate reality,* pp. 85-103.

Dorcey, Donal. "The Big Occasions." *In:* McCann, Sean, ed. *The story of the Abbey Theatre,* pp. 154-155.

Gaskell, Ronald. *"Purgatory." Modern Drama,* vol. 4, no. 4 (Feb., 1962), pp. 397-401.

Henn, T.R. *The harvest of tragedy,* pp. 209-211.

Jeffares, A. Norman, ed. *In excited reverie, a centenary tribute to William Butler Yeats, 1865-1939,* pp. 121-122.

Lightfoot, Marjorie J. *"Purgatory* and *The Family Reunion:* In Pursuit of Prosodic Description." *Modern Drama,* vol. 7, no. 3 (Dec., 1964), pp. 256-266.

Lucas, F.L. *The drama of Chekhov, Synge, Yeats and Pirandello,* pp. 337-339.

Mercier, Vivian. "In Defense of Yeats as a Dramatist." *Modern Drama,* vol. 8, no. 2 (Sept., 1965), pp. 161-166.

Moore, John Rees. "An Old Man's Tragedy—Yeats' *Purgatory" Modern Drama,* vol. 5, no. 4 (Feb., 1963), pp. 440-450.

Pearce, Donald. "Yeats' Last Plays: An Interpretation." *J. of English Literary History (ELH),* vol. 18, no. 1 (Mar., 1951), pp. 67-76.

Prior, Moody E. *The language of tragedy,* pp. 339-340.

Rajan, Balachandra. *W.B. Yeats, a critical introduction,* pp. 164-166, 169.

Reinert, Otto. *Drama: an introductory anthology,* pp. 473-475.

Reinert, Otto, ed. *Modern drama; nine plays,* pp. 311-313.

Stewart, J.I.M. *Eight modern writers,* pp. 405-408.

Unterecker, John. "The Shaping Force in Yeats' Plays." *Modern Drama,* vol. 7, no. 3 (Dec., 1964), pp. 345-356.

Warschausky, Sidney. "Yeats' Purgatorial Plays." *Modern Drama,* vol. 7, no. 3 (Dec., 1964), pp. 278-286.

The Resurrection

Baird, Sister Mary Julian, RSM. "A Play on the Death of God: The Irony of Yeats' *The Resurrection." Modern Drama,* vol. 10, no. 1 (May. 1967), pp. 79-86.

Berryman, Charles. *W.B. Yeats, design of opposites,* pp. 94-99.

Bradford, Curtis B. *Yeats at work,* pp. 237-267.

Flannery, James W. "Action and Reaction at the Dublin Theatre Festival." *Educational Theatre J.,* vol. 19, no. 1 (Mar., 1967), pp. 72-80.

Mercier, Vivian. "In Defense of Yeats as a Dramatist." *Modern Drama,* vol. 8, no. 2 (Sept., 1965), pp. 161-166.

Rajan, Balachandra. *W.B. Yeats, a critical introduction,* pp. 90, 156-157.

Roston, Murray. *Biblical drama in England from the Middle Ages to the present day,* pp. 269-274.

Stewart, J.I.M. *Eight modern writers,* pp. 368-369, 399-401, 403.

The Shadowy Waters

Boyd, Ernest. *Ireland's literary renaissance,* pp. 155-156.

Bushrui, S.B. *Yeats' verse plays: the revisions 1900-1910,* pp. 1-38.

Clark, David R. "Aubrey Beardsley's Drawing of the 'Shadows' in W.B. Yeats' *The Shadowy Waters." Modern Drama,* vol. 7, no. 3 (Dec., 1964), pp. 267-272.

Clark, David R. "W.B. Yeats: *The Shadowy Waters* (Ms. Version). Half the Characters Had Eagles' Faces." *In:* Skelton, Robin, and David R. Clark, eds. *Irish renaissance,* pp. 26-55.

Donoghue, Denis. *The third voice: modern British and American verse drama,* pp. 32-46, 54-55.

Lucas, F.L. *The drama of Chekhov, Synge, Yeats and Pirandello,* pp. 302-306.

Rajan, Balachandra. *W.B. Yeats, a critical introduction,* pp. 40-44.

Stewart, J.I.M. *Eight modern writers,* pp. 322-324, 330, 332, 389.

Ure, Peter. "Yeats and the Two Harmonies." *Modern Drama, vol. 7,* no. 3 (Dec., 1964), pp. 237-255.

Sophocles' King Oedipus

Stewart, J.I.M. *Eight modern writers,* pp. 398-399.

The Unicorn from the Stars

Boyd, Ernest. *Ireland's literary renaissance,* pp. 153-155.

Harper, George M. "The Reconciliation of Paganism and Christianity in Yeats' *Unicorn from the Stars." In:* Bryan, Robert A. *et al. All these to teach: essays in honor of C.A. Robertson,* pp. 224-236.

Lucas, F.L. *The drama of Chekhov, Synge, Yeats and Pirandello,* pp. 321-323.

Mercier, Vivian. "Douglas Hyde's 'Share' in *The Unicorn from the Stars." Modern Drama,* vol. 7, no. 4 (Feb., 1965), pp. 463-465.

Stewart, J.I.M. *Eight modern writers,* pp. 327-329, 367.

Suss, Irving D. "Yeatsian Drama and the Dying Hero." *South Atlantic Q.,* vol. 54 (1955), pp. 369-380.

Where There Is Nothing

Boyd, Ernest. *Ireland's literary renaissance,* pp. 153-155.

Stewart, J.I.M. *Eight modern writers,* p. 327.

The Words upon the Window Pane

Barnet, Sylvan, ed. *The genius of the Irish theater,* pp. 194-197.

Bradford, Curtis B. *Yeats at work,* pp. 217-236.

Brogunier, Joseph. "Expiation in Yeats' Late Plays." *Drama Survey,* vol. 5, no. 1 (Spring, 1966), pp. 26-29, 30, 35.

Clark, David R. *W.B. Yeats and the theatre of desolate reality,* pp. 60-84.

Stewart, J.I.M. *Eight modern writers,* pp. 401-402.

Warschausky, Sidney. "Yeats' Purgatorial Plays." *Modern Drama,* vol. 7, no. 3 (Dec., 1964), pp. 278-286.

LEONIDAS YEROVI 1881-1917

General

Jones, W. K. *Behind Spanish American footlights,* p. 268.

PHILIP YORDAN 1914-

Anna Lucasta

Mitchell, Loften. *Black drama,* pp. 113, 122-123, 135, 147.

Hobson, Harold. *Theatre,* pp. 155-157, 161-164.

STARK YOUNG 1881-1963

The Saint

Sommers, John J. "The Critic as Playwright: A Study of Stark Young's *The Saint.*" *Modern Drama,* vol. 7, no. 4 (Feb., 1965), pp. 446-453.

ISRAEL ZANGWILL 1864-1926

General

Knight, G. Wilson. *The golden labyrinth,* pp. 318-321.

FEDERICO ZARDI 1912-

General

Pandolfi, Vito. "Italian Theatre Since the War." *Tulane Drama Rev.,* vol. 8, no. 3 (Spring, 1964), pp. 99-101.

ISRAEL ZEITLIN 1906-
(pseud. Cesar Tiempo)

General

Jones, W.K. *Behind Spanish American footlights,* pp. 176-177.

Pan Criollo

Jones, W. K. *Behind Spanish American footlights,* p. 176.

BERNARD ZIMMER

General

Knowles, Dorothy. *French drama of the inter-war years, 1918-39,* pp. 132-133.

Bava l'Africain

Knowles, Dorothy. *French drama of the inter-war years, 1918-39.* pp. 131-132.

Pauvre Napoleon

Knowles, Dorothy. *French drama of the inter-war years, 1918-39,* pp. 132.

Le Veau Gras

Knowles, Dorothy. *French drama of the inter-war years, 1918-39,* pp. 129-130.

Les Zouaves

Knowles, Dorothy. *French drama of the inter-war years, 1918-39,* pp. 130-131.

ALBIN ZOLLINGER 1895-1941

Bibliography:

Wilbert-Collins, Elly. *A bibliography of four contemporary German-Swiss authors: Friedrich Dürrenmatt, Max Frisch, Robert Walser, Albin Zollinger.*

LEONID ZORIN

The Deck (Paluba)

Ferrer, Olga P. "Theater in the U.S.S.R.: Summer of 1964." *Books Abroad,* vol. 39, no. 3, (Summer, 1965), p. 300.

CARL ZUCKMAYER 1896-

General

Bauland, Peter. *The hooded eagle,* pp. 109, 122-124, 156, 160.

Boeninger, Helmut. "A Play and Two Authors: Zuckmayer's Version of Hauptmann's *Herbert Engelmann." Monatshefte für Deutschen Unterricht,* vol. 46, no. 6 (Nov., 1954), pp. 339-345.

Coenen, F.E. "The Modern German Drama." *In:* Hammer, Carl, Jr., ed. *Studies in German literature,* pp. 109-110.

Glade, Henry. "The Motif of Encounter in Zuckmeyer's Dramas." *Kentucky Foreign Lang. Q.,* vol. 10 (1963), pp. 183-190.

Hatfield, Henry. *Modern German literature,* pp. 115-116.

Loram, I.C. "Carl Zuckmayer: An Introduction." *German Q.,* vol. 27 (1954), pp. 137-149.

Loram, Ian C. "Carl Zuckmayer—German Playwright in America." *Educational Theatre J.,* vol. 9 (1957), pp. 177-183.

Moore, Harry T. *Twentieth-century German literature,* pp. 45-46, 138-139, 153.

Peppard, Murray B. "Moment of Moral Decision: Carl Zuckmayer's Latest Plays." *Monatshefte für Deutschen Unterricht,* vol. 44, no. 1 (Nov., 1952), pp. 349-356.

Rook, Sheila. "Carl Zuckmayer." *In:* Natan, ed., German men of Letters, vol. 3, pp. 209-233.

The Captain from Kopenick (Der Hauptmann von Köpenick)

Bauland, Peter. *The hooded eagle,* pp. 109, 123.

The Cold Light (Das Kalte Licht)

Peppard, Murray B. "Carl Zuckmayer: Cold Light in a Divided World." *Monatshefte,* vol. 49, no. 3 (March, 1957), pp. 121-129.

The Devil's General (Das Teufels General)

Bauland, Peter. *The hooded eagle,* pp. 123-125.

Glade, Henry. "Carl Zuckmayer's *The Devil's General* as Autobiography." *Modern Drama,* vol. 9, no. 1 (May, 1966), pp. 54-61.

Peppard, Murray B. "Moment of Moral Decision: Carl Zuckmayer's Latest Plays." *Monatshefte,* vol. 44, no. 7 (Nov., 1952), pp. 349-356.

Weltmann, Lutz. "Two Recent German Plays." *German Life and Letters,* vol. 2 (1949), pp. 158-163.

Williamson, Audrey. *Contemporary theatre, 1953-1956,* pp. 87-88.

Der Gesang im Feuerofen

Peppard, Murray B. "Moment of Moral Decision: Carl Zuckmayer's Latest Plays." *Monatshefte,* vol. 44, no. 7 (Nov., 1952), pp. 349-356.

Herbert Engelmann

Boeninger, Helmut. "A Play and Two Authors, Zuckmayer's Version of Hauptmann's *Herbert Engelmann." Monatshefte,* vol. 44, no. 7 (Nov., 1952), pp. 341-348.

Spahr, Blake L. "A Note on *Herbert Engelmann." Monatshefte,* vol. 46, no. 6 (Nov., 1954), pp. 339-345.

STEFAN ZWEIG 1881-1942

Jeremiah (Adaptation of Zweig's Jeremias)

Bauland, Peter. *The hooded eagle,* pp. 115-116.

Garten, H.F. *Modern German drama,* pp. 125-126.

Himelstein, Morgan Y. *Drama was a weapon, the left-wing theatre in New York 1929-1941,* pp. 142-143.

INDEX
—
Play Titles

800

INDEX
—
Critics

819

The Machine Wreckers (Die Maschinensturmer) Ernst Toller, 697

Man and the Masses (Masse-Mensch) Ernst Toller, 698

Man with the Portfolio Alexis Faiko, 216

The Mask and the Face (Mask and Face (La Maschera e il Volto) Luigi Chiarelli, 158

Miracle at Verdun (Wunder um Verdun) Hans von Chlumberg, 159

Mirror Man (Spiegelmensch) Franz Werfel, 718

The Mob William Somerset Maugham, 416

Mourning Becomes Electra Eugene O'Neill, 516

Mr. & Mrs. So-and-So (Monsieur et Madame Un Tel) Denys Amiel, 19

Mrs. Warren's Profession George Bernard Shaw, 645

On the Rocks George Bernard Shaw, 646

Paradise Lost Clifford Odets, 474

Peace on Earth George Sklar and Albert Maltz, 664

The Processional John Howard Lawson, 382

Red Rust Vladimir Kirchon and Andre Uspenski, 374

Roar China Sergei Mikhailovich Tretiakov, 701

Sailors of Cattaro (Die Matrosen von Cattaro) Friedrich Wolf, 760

Sickness of Youth (Krankheit der Jugend) Ferdinand Bruckner, 134

Squaring the Circle Valentin Katayev, 365

Stevedore Paul Peters and George Sklar, 531

Strange Interlude Eugene O'Neill, 520

They Shall Not Die John Wexley, 725

Waiting for Lefty Clifford Odets, 475

The Weavers (Die Weber) Gerhart Hauptmann, 293

What Price Glory? Maxwell Anderson, 29

Wings over Europe Robert Nichols and Maurice Brown, 456

Yegor Bulychov Maxim Gorki, 276

Yes, My Darling Daughter Mark Reed, 557

Young Love Samson Raphaelson, 554

Block, Toni
On: George Bernard Shaw, 606

Bloomfield, B.C.
Bibliography Wystan Hugh Auden, 59

Bluefarb, Sam
The Glass Menagerie Tennessee Williams, 748
The House of Bernarda Alba (La Casa de Bernarda Alba) Federico Garcia Lorca, 238

Boas, F.S.
Saint Joan George Bernard Shaw, 649

Boas, Guy
On: Sean O'Casey, 459

Bockstahler, O.L.
On: Henrik Ibsen, 315
On: Hermann Sudermann, 683

Bode, Carl
On: John Osborne, 523

Boeninger, Helmut
On: Carl Zuckmayer, 778
Herbert Engelmann Carl Zuckmayer, 779

Bogard, Travis
On: Thornton Wilder, 731
Anna Christie Eugene O'Neill, 494
The Matchmaker Thornton Wilder, 734
Our Town Thornton Wilder, 734
The Skin of Our Teeth Thornton Wilder, 736

Boggs, W. Arthur
All My Sons Arthur Miller, 426

Bohner, Charles H.
All the King's Men Robert Penn Warren, 711

Bolt, Robert
On: Robert Bolt, 113
Flowering Cherry Robert Bolt, 113
Gentle Jack Robert Bolt, 113
A Man for All Seasons Robert Bolt, 114
The Thwarting of Baron Bolligrew Robert Bolt, 114
The Tiger and the Horse Robert Bolt, 115

Bondy, L.S.
On: Paul Claudel, 160

Bonosky, Phillip
The Blacks (Les Negres) Jean Genet, 247

Boorsch, Jean
On: Jean Cocteau, 168

Booth, John E.
On: Edward Albee, 6

Booth, John E., and Lewis Funke
On: Tennessee Williams, 741

Bordinat, Philip
Uncle Vanya (The Wood Demon) (Dyadya Vanya) Anton Pavlovich Chekhov, 157

Duerksen, Roland A.
On: George Bernard Shaw, 609
Duffin, H.C.
On: George Bernard Shaw, 609
Dukes, Ashley
On: Bjornsterne Bjornson, 111
On: Eugene Brieux, 132
On: Anton Pavlovich Chekhov, 150
On: John Galsworthy, 232
On: Maxim Gorki, 275
On: Gerhart Hauptmann, 287
On: Hermann Heijermans, 295
On: Henrik Ibsen, 315
On: Maurice Maeterlinck, 398
On: George Bernard Shaw, 609
On: August Strindberg, 670
On: Hermann Sudermann, 683
On: Frank Wedekind, 711
The Awakening of Spring (Fruhlings Erwachen)
Frank Wedekind, 712
Blanchette Eugene Brieux, 132
Ghetto Hermann Heijermans, 295
The Good Hope (Op Hoop van Zegen)
Hermann Heijermans, 295
Hidalla, or Karl Hetmann, the Dwarf-Giant (Karl Hetmann, der Zwerg-griese) Frank Wedekind, 713
Justice John Galsworthy, 233
The Lower Depths Maxim Gorki, 275
Maternite Eugene Brieux, 132
Monna Vanna
Maurice Maeterlinck, 402
Mourning Becomes Electra
Eugene O'Neill, 516
Ora et Labora
Hermann Heijermans, 295
The Philanthropists (Les Bienfaiteurs)
Eugene Brieux, 132
The Seagull (Chayka)
Anton Pavlovich Chekhov, 155
The Three Daughters of Monsieur Dupont (Les Trois Filles de M. Dupont) Eugene Brieux, 132
The Three Sisters (Tri Sestry)
Anton Pavlovich Chekhov, 156
Dukore, Bernard F.
On: Bertolt Brecht, 119
On: Harold Pinter, 534
On: George Bernard Shaw, 610
The Apple Jack Gelber, 242
The Bald Soprano (La Cantatrice Chauve) Eugene Ionesco, 343
The Brig Kenneth H. Brown, 133
Cat on a Hot Tin Roof
Tennessee Williams, 747
The Connection Jack Gelber, 243
The Creditors
August Strindberg, 673

The Dance of Death
August Strindberg, 673
The Dutchman Le Roi Jones, 359
The Homecoming Harold Pinter, 538
How He Lied to Her Husband
George Bernard Shaw, 638
The Lesson (La Lecon)
Eugene Ionesco, 348
Major Barbara
George Bernard Shaw, 640
Play Samuel Beckett, 87
The Simpleton of the Unexpected Isles
George Bernard Shaw, 653
Sweet Bird of Youth
Tennessee Williams, 756
The Threepenny Opera (Die Dreigroschenoper)
Bertolt Brecht, 129
Tiny Alice Edward Albee, 12
Waiting for Godot (En Attendant Godot) Samuel Beckett, 90
Who's Afraid of Virginia Woolf?
Edward Albee, 13
Dunkel, Wilbur D.
On: George Bernard Shaw, 610
Dupee, F.W.
On: William Butler Yeats, 763
Look Back in Anger
John Osborne, 526
The Rose Tattoo
Tennessee Williams, 751
The Three Sisters (Tri Sestry)
Anton Pavlovich Chekhov, 156
Under Milkwood
Dylan Thomas, 695
Dupler, Dorothy
On: George Bernard Shaw, 610
Duprey, Richard A.
On: Edward Albee, 7
On: Paddy Chayefsky, 149
On: Murray Schisgal, 599
On: Tennessee Williams, 740
Mrs. Dally William Hanley, 285
Slow Dance on the Killing Ground
William Hanley, 285
The Subject Was Roses
Frank D. Gilroy, 261
Who's Afraid of Virginia Woolf?
Edward Albee, 13
Duran, Manuel
On: Federico Garcia Lorca, 236
Duran, Manuel, and Michael Nimetz
On: Jacinto Benavente, 102
On: Jose Echegaray, 201
Durrenmatt, Friedrich
On: Friedrich Durrenmatt, 195
Frank V—Opera of a Private Bank (Frank V—Oper Einer Privatbank) Friedrich Durrenmatt, 197
The Visit (Der Besuch der Alten Dame)
Friedrich Durrenmatt, 199

874

On: Albert Camus, 138
On: Paul Claudel, 161
On: Jean Cocteau, 168
On: Roland Dubillard, 192
On: Marguerite Duras, 193
On: Armand Gatti, 241
On: Jean Genet, 244
On: Michel de Ghelderode, 253
On: Jean Giraudoux, 262
On: Eugene Ionesco, 339
On: Henry De Montherlant, 442
On: Armand Salacrou, 572
On: Jean-Paul Sartre, 582
On: Georges Schehade, 597
On: Jean Vauthier, 704
On: Boris Vian, 706
The Blacks (Les Negres)
 Jean Genet, 248
La Maison d'Os
 Roland Dubillard, 192
Naives Hirondelles
 Roland Dubillard, 192
The Screens (Les Paravents)
 Jean Genet, 251
The Unknown Women of Arras (L'Inconnue d'Arras)
 Armand Salacrou, 574
Waiting for Godot (En Attendant Godot) Samuel Beckett, 92
Gump, Margaret
On: Eugene O'Neill, 482
The Hairy Ape Eugene O'Neill, 506
Gunvaldsen, K.M.
The Master Builder (Bygmester Solness) Henrik Ibsen, 328
The Sunken Bell (Die Versunkene Glocke) Gerhart Hauptmann, 292
Gustafson, Alrik
Rosmersholm Henrik Ibsen, 330
Guth, Hans P.
The Visit (Der Besuch der Alten Dame) Friedrich Durrenmatt, 200
Guthrie, Tyrone
On: Thornton Wilder, 732
Gutkke, Karl S.
The Wild Duck (Vildanden) Henrik Ibsen, 333
Haakonsen, Daniel
On: Henrik Ibsen, 316
Haberman, Donald
On: Thornton Wilder, 732
The Alcestiad Thornton Wilder, 733
The Angel That Troubled the Waters Thornton Wilder, 733
A Happy Journey to Trenton and Camden Thornton Wilder, 733
The Merchant of Yonkers Thornton Wilder, 734
Our Town Thornton Wilder, 735

Pullman Car Hiawatha Thornton Wilder, 736
Queens of France Thornton Wilder, 736
The Skin of Our Teeth Thornton Wilder, 737
Sloth Thornton Wilder, 737
Such Things Only Happen in Books Thornton Wilder, 737
The Trumpet Shall Sound Thornton Wilder, 737
Hackett, Francis
On: George Bernard Shaw, 612
Anna Christie Eugene O'Neill, 494
Hagopian, John V.
Death of a Salesman Arthur Miller, 432
Hagopian, John V. and Martin Dolch
All My Sons Arthur Miller, 427
Beyond the Horizon Eugene O'Neill, 495
Death of a Salesman Arthur Miller, 432
The Glass Menagerie Tennessee Williams, 748
Our Town Thornton Wilder, 735
Hahn, Paul
On: Armand Salacrou, 572
Hahn, Vera T.
On: Eugene O'Neill, 482
Hainsworth, J.D.
On: John Arden, 50
Happy Haven John Arden, 51
Serjeant Musgrave's Dance John Arden, 53
The Workhouse Donkey John Arden, 54
Hale, Edward E., Jr.
Monna Vanna Maurice Maeterlinck, 402
Hales, John
On: George Bernard Shaw, 612
Hall, Peter
On: Tennessee Williams, 741
Hall, Philip G.
Mourning Becomes Electra Eugene O'Neill, 517
Hall, Stuart
On: Arnold Wesker, 720
Halline, Allan G.
On: Maxwell Anderson, 21
Halman, Doris F.
On: Eugene O'Neill, 482
Halman, Talat S.
The Neighborhood (Kosebasi) Ahmet Kutsi Tecer, 694
Halpern, Martin
On: William Vaughn Moody, 447
The Death of Eve William Vaughn Moody, 447

Mother (Matka) Karel Capek, 145
The Outlaw (Loupeznik)
   Karel Capek, 146
R.U.R. Karel Capek, 146
*The White Plague (The Power and
   Glory) (Bila Nemoc)*
   Karel Capek, 146
Harper, George M.
   The Unicorn from the Stars
   William Butler Yeats, 775
Harris, Ainslie
   On: Maxwell Anderson, 21
Harris, Frank
   On: George Bernard Shaw, 612
   The Apple Cart
   George Bernard Shaw, 624
   Mrs. Warren's Profession
   George Bernard Shaw, 645
   The Philanderer
   George Bernard Shaw, 648
   Saint Joan
   George Bernard Shaw, 650
   Widowers' Houses
   George Bernard Shaw, 655
Harris, Harold J.
   On: George Bernard Shaw, 612
Harris, Kenneth E.
   On: Maxwell Anderson, 22
Harris, Leonard
   On: Michel de Ghelderode, 253
   Hop, Signor!
   Michel de Ghelderode, 256
Harris, Wendell V.
   On: Edward Albee, 7
Harrison, George B.
   On: George Bernard Shaw, 612
Hart-Davis, Rupert
   Awake and Sing Clifford Odets, 472
Hartley, A.A.
   On: Henry De Montherlant, 442
Hartley, Anthony
   The Big Knife
   Clifford Odets, 473
   The Crucible
   Arthur Miller, 429
   King Ubu (Ubu Roi)
   Alfred Jarry, 354
   Life in the Sun
   Thornton Wilder, 734
Hartley, Lodwick, and Arthur Ladu
   On: George Kelly, 367
Hartley, Lois
   On: Edgar Lee Masters, 412
   Althea Edgar Lee Masters, 412
   The Bread of Idleness
   Edgar Lee Masters, 413
   Eileen Edgar Lee Masters, 413
   The Leaves of the Tree
   Edgar Lee Masters, 413
   The Locket
   Edgar Lee Masters, 413

Maximilian
   Edgar Lee Masters, 413
Trifler
   Edgar Lee Masters, 413
Hartman, Murray
   On: Eugene O'Neill, 482
   On: August Strindberg, 671
   Desire Under the Elms
   Eugene O'Neill, 498
   More Stately Mansions
   Eugene O'Neill, 515
   On: Jean Anouilh, 34
Harvey, J.
   Antigone Jean Anouilh, 37
   *Ardele, or The Daisy (Ardele, ou La
   Marguerite)* Jean Anouilh, 38
   *Becket, or The Honor of God (Becket,
   ou L'Honneur de Dieu)*
   Jean Anouilh, 39
   Colombe (Mademoiselle Colombe)
   Jean Anouilh, 40
   *Dinner with the Family (La Rendez-
   vous de Senlis)*
   Jean Anouilh, 40
   The Ermine (L'Hermine)
   Jean Anouilh, 41
   *Eurydice (Point of Departure) (Legend
   of Lovers)* Jean Anouilh, 41
   Fading Mansions (Romeo et Jeannette)
   Jean Anouilh, 42
   *The Fighting Cock (L'Hurluberlu, ou
   Le Reactionnaire Amoureux)*
   Jean Anouilh, 42
   The Lark (L'Alouette)
   Jean Anouilh, 43
   Medea (Medee)
   Jean Anouilh, 43
   Ornifle, ou Le Courant d'Air
   Jean Anouilh, 44
   Poor Bitos (Pauvre Bitos)
   Jean Anouilh, 44
   *The Rehearsal (La Repetition, ou L'A-
   mour Puni)*
   Jean Anouilh, 45
   *Traveller Without Luggage (Le Voy-
   ageur sans Bagage)*
   Jean Anouilh, 46
   *The Waltz of the Toreadors (La Valse
   des Toreadors)* Jean Anouilh,
   47
Harvey, Lawrence E.
   *Waiting for Godot (En Attendant
   Godot)* Samuel Beckett, 92
Harvitt, Helene
   *Becket, or The Honor of God (Becket,
   ou L'Honneur de Dieu)*
   Jean Anouilh, 39
Haslam, Gerald W.
   Awake and Sing
   Clifford Odets, 472

935

Edward Estlin Cummings, 182
Norrish, P.J.
On: Henry De Montherlant, 443
Norton, Roger C.
The Difficult Man (Der Schwierige)
Hugo Von Hofmannsthal, 305
Waste Harley Granville-Barker, 277
Norwood, Gilbert
On: St. John Emile Clavering Hankin,
284
On Henrik Ibsen, 317
On: Eugene O'Neill, 486
On: George Bernard Shaw, 617
On: Oscar Wilde, 728
Ann Leete
Harley Granville-Barker, 277
Caesar and Cleopatra
George Bernard Shaw, 629
The Devil's Disciple
George Bernard Shaw, 632
The Eldest Son John Galsworthy,
232
Fountain George Calderon, 137
Justice John Galsworthy, 233
The Madras House
Harley Granville-Barker, 277
The Silver Box John Galsworthy,
233
The Voysey Inheritance
Harley Granville-Barker, 277
Waste Harley Granville-Barker, 277
Norwood, W.D., Jr.
On: Luigi Pirandello, 542
Novick, Julius
Bless the Child
Bernice Blohm and Adelaide Bean,
112
Fire John Roc, 567
Poor Bitos (Pauvre Bitos)
Jean Anouilh, 44
Nugent, Robert
Break of Noon (Partage de Midi)
Paul Claudel, 163
Nydahl, Bertil
The Highway August Strindberg, 678
Oberg, Arthur K.
On: Edward Albee, 8
Death of a Salesman Arthur Miller,
434
Krapp's Last Tape Samuel Beckett,
87
A Taste of Honey Shelagh Delaney,
187
OBrien, Charles H.
Luther John Osborne, 527
O'Brien, Justin
On: Samuel Beckett, 77
Queen After Death (La Reine Morte)
Henry De Montherlant, 446

O'Callaghan, John
Endgame (Fin de Partie)
Samuel Beckett, 84
O'Casey, Sean
On: Anton Pavlovich Chekhov, 151
On: Noel Coward, 178
On: Maxim Gorki, 275
On: Lady Isabella Augusta Gregory,
282
On: Henrik Ibsen, 317
On: Sean O'Casey, 461
On: George Bernard Shaw, 617
On: William Butler Yeats, 764
Afore Night Come David Rudkin,
571
*The Bald Soprano (La Cantatrice
Chauve)* Eugene Ionesco, 344
Bedtime Story Sean O'Casey, 462
The Birthday Party Harold Pinter,
536
The Bishop's Bonfire
Sean O'Casey, 462
Cavalcade Noel Coward, 178
Cock-A-Doodle Dandy
Sean O'Casey, 463
Design for Living Noel Coward, 179
Entertaining Mrs. Sloane
Joe Ordway, 523
Juno and the Paycock
Sean O'Casey, 464
Night Must Fall Emlyn Williams,
739
On the Rocks
George Bernard Shaw, 647
Ours Thomas William Robertson,
565
The Playboy of the Western World
John Millington Synge, 690
The Plough and the Stars
Sean O'Casey, 466
A Resounding Tinkle
Norman Frederick Simpson, 663
Riders to the Sea
John Millington Synge, 691
The Shadow of the Glen
John Millington Synge, 692
The Silver Tassie Sean O'Casey, 468
Too True To Be Good
George Bernard Shaw, 654
*Waiting for Godot (En Attendant
Godot)* Samuel Beckett, 94
Within the Gates Sean O'Casey, 470
O'Connor, Frank
On: William Butler Yeats, 764
Exiles James Joyce, 361
O'Connor, Garry
On: John Whiting, 726
O'Connor, Patricia
On: Gregorio Martinez Sierra, 409
The Double Story of Doctor Valmy

Spalter, Max
  On: Bertolt Brecht, 121
  On: Karl Kraus, 377
  On: Frank Wedekind, 712
  *The Awakening of Spring (Fruhlings
    Erwachen)* Frank Wedekind,
    712
  Baal Bertolt Brecht, 122
  *The Caucasian Chalk Circle (Der
    Kaukasische Kreidekreis)*
    Bertolt Brecht, 123
  Censorship (Die Zensur)
    Frank Wedekind, 712
  Death and the Devil
    Frank Wedekind, 712
  *Drums in the Night (Trommeln in der
    Nacht)* Bertolt Brecht, 124
  Earth Spirit (Erdgeist-Part I of Lulu)
    Frank Wedekind, 713
  *The Exception and the Rule (Die
    Ausnahme und die Regel)*
    Bertolt Brecht, 124
  Die Fackel Karl Kraus, 378
  Galileo (Das Leben des Galilei)
    Bertolt Brecht, 124
  *The Good Woman of Setzuan (Der
    Gute Mensch von Sezuan)*
    Bertolt Brecht, 125
  *Hidalla, or Karl Hetmann, the Dwarf-
    Giant (Karl Hetmann, der Zwer-
    griese)* Frank Wedekind, 713
  *In the Jungle of Cities (In the Swamp
    of the Cities) (Im Dickicht der
    Stadte)* Bertolt Brecht, 125
  *King Nicolo, or Such Is Life (Konig
    Nicolo, oder So Ist Leben)*
    Frank Wedekind, 714
  *The Last Days of Mankind (Die
    Letzten Tage der Menschheit)*
    Karl Kraus, 378
  *The Life of Edward the Second of
    England (Leben Eduards des
    Zweiten)* Bertolt Brecht, 126
  A Man's a Man (Mann Ist Mann)
    Bertolt Brecht, 126
  Marquis von Keith
    Frank Wedekind, 714
  The Measures Taken (Die Massnahme)
    Bertolt Brecht, 126
  *Mother Courage and Her Children
    (Mutter Courage und Ihre Kinder)*
    Bertolt Brecht, 128
  *Mr. Puntila and His Hired Man, Matti
    (Herr Puntila und Sein Knecht Matti)*
    Bertolt Brecht, 126
  Music Frank Wedekind, 714
  *Pandora's Box (Die Buchse der Pan-
    dora-Part II of Lulu)*
    Frank Wedekind, 714
  The Private Life of the Master Race

  *(Fear and Misery of the Third
    Reich) (Furcht und Elend des
    Dritten Reich)*
    Bertolt Brecht, 128
  The Quick Painter
    Frank Wedekind, 714
  *The Resistable Rise of Arturo Ui (Der
    Aufhaltsame Aufsteig des Arturo Ui)*
    Bertolt Brecht, 128
  *The Rise and Fall of the City of
    Mahagonny (Aufsteig und Fall
    der Stadt Mahagonny)* Bertolt
    Brecht, 128
  *The Roundheads and the Peakheads
    (Die Roundkopfe und die Spitzkopfe)*
    Bertolt Brecht, 129
  *Saint Joan of the Stockyards (Die
    Heilige Johanna der Schlachthof)*
    Bertolt Brecht, 129
  The Tenor (Die Kammersanger)
    Frank Wedekind, 715
  *The Threepenny Opera (Die Dreigro-
    schenoper)* Bertolt Brecht, 129
  Wetterstein Castle
    Frank Wedekind, 715
  The Young World
    Frank Wedekind, 715
Spanos, William V.
  The Acts of Saint Peter
    Gordon Bottomley, 115
  Christ's Comet
    Christopher Hassall, 287
  The Cocktail Party
    Thomas Stearns Eliot, 207
  The Coming of Christ
    John Masefield, 412
  The Death of Good Fortune
    Charles Williams, 738
  The Elder Statesman
    Thomas Stearns Eliot, 209
  The Family Reunion
    Thomas Stearns Eliot, 211
  Grab and Grace
    Charles Williams, 738
  The House by the Stable
    Charles Williams, 738
  The House of the Octopus
    Charles Williams, 738
  Judgment at Chelmsford
    Charles Williams, 738
  Murder in the Cathedral
    Thomas Stearns Eliot, 214
  The Old Man of the Mountains
    Norman Nicholson, 456
  The Rock Thomas Stearns Eliot, 214
  Seed of Adam Charles Williams, 738
  The Shadow Factory
    Anne Ridler, 565
  A Sleep of Prisoners
    Christopher Fry, 230

BOOKS INDEXED

√ABEL, LIONEL. *Metatheatre, a new view of dramatic form.* New York, Hill & Wang, 1963. *809.2 A*

√ABRAMSON, DORIS E. *Negro playwrights in the American theatre, 1925–1959.* New York, Columbia University Press, 1969. *812.09 A*

√ACKERMAN, JOHN. *Dylan Thomas, his life and work.* London, Oxford University Press, 1964. *921 T*

op ADAMCZEWSKI, ZYGMUNT. *The tragic protest.* The Hague Nijhoff, 1963.

ADAMS, ROBERT M. *Strains of discord: studies in literary openness.* Ithaca, Cornell University Press, 1958.

√ADEMA, MARCEL. *Apollinaire.* London, William Heinemann, 1954.

√ADERETH, MAXWELL. *Commitment in modern French literature, a brief study of "Littérature Engagée" in the works of Péguy, Aragon, and Sartre.* London, Gollancz, 1967.

√AGATE, JAMES. *The English dramatic critics.* New York, Hill & Wang, 1958.

op ALEXANDER, DORIS. *The tempering of Eugene O'Neill.* New York, Harcourt, Brace & World, 1962.

ALLISON, ALEXANDER W., ed. *Masterpieces of the drama.* 2nd ed. New York, Macmillan, 1966.

√ALLSOP, KENNETH. *The angry decade.* London, Peter Owen, 1964.

American Contributions to the Fifth International Congress of Slavists. Sofia, September 1963. 2 vols. (SPR 50) The Hague, Mouton, 1963.

AMERICAN-SCANDINAVIAN FOUNDATION, New York. *Scandinavian studies, essays presented to Dr. Henry Goddard Leach on the occasion of his eighty-fifth birthday.* Edited by Carl F. Bayerschmidt and Erik J. Friis. Published for the American-Scandinavian Foundation by the University of Washington Press, Seattle, 1965.

√ANDERSON, MAXWELL. *The essence of tragedy, and other footnotes and papers.* Washington, D. C., Anderson House, 1939.

op ———. *Off Broadway: essays about the theatre.* New York, William Sloan Associates, 1947.

ARMATO, ROSARIO P., and JOHN M. SPALEK, eds. *Medieval epic to the "Epic Theater" of Brecht, essays in comparative literature.* Los Angeles, University of Southern California Press, 1968. *(University of Southern California Studies in Comparative Literature, I)*

op ARMSTRONG, WILLIAM A. *Experimental drama.* London, G. Bell, 1963.

———. *Sean O'Casey.* London, Longmans, Green, 1967. *(British Council. Writers and their work, no. 198)*

Aspects of Drama and the theatre; five Kathleen Robinson lectures delivered in the University of Sydney 1961–63. Sydney, Sydney University Press; London, Methuen, 1965.

ATKINS, JOHN. *Graham Greene.* New York, Roy Publishers, 1958.

AUDEN, WYSTAN HUGH. *The Dyer's hand, and other essays.* New York, Random House, 1962.

AYLEN, LEO. *Greek tragedy and the modern world.* London, Methuen, 1964.

BAILEY, MABEL D. *Maxwell Anderson: the playwright as prophet.* New York, Abelard-Schumann, 1957.

BAKER, JAMES R. *William Golding; a critical study.* New York, St. Martin's Press, 1965.

BALDNER, R. E., ed. *Proceedings, Pacific Northwest conference on foreign languages. Eighteenth annual meeting, March 17–18, 1967. Volume 18.* Victoria, B. C., University of Victoria Press.

BALMFORTH, RAMSDEN. *The problem-play and its influence on modern thought and life.* London, Allen & Unwin, 1928.

BANNISTER, WINIFRED. *James Bridie and his theatre.* London, Rockliff, 1955.

BAREA, ARTURO. *Lorca: the poet and his people.* Translated by Isla Barea. New York, Harcourt-Brace, 1958.

BARING, MAURICE. *Punch and Judy and other essays.* New York, Doubleday, 1924.

BARNES, HAZEL E. *The literature of possibility.* Lincoln, University of Nebraska Press, 1959.

BARNES, RONALD E. *The dramatic comedy of William Somerset Maugham.* The Hague, Mouton, 1968. *(Studies in English Literature, vol. 32)*

BARNET, SYLVAN, ed. *Eight great tragedies.* New York, New American Library, 1957.

———, ed. *The genius of the Irish Theater.* New York, New American Library, 1960.

———, ed. *The genius of the later English theater.* New York, New American Library, 1962.

BARZUN, JACQUES. *The energies of art: studies of authors classic and modern.* New York, Harper, 1956.

BATES, SCOTT. *Guillaume Apollinaire.* New York, Twayne Publishers, 1967. *(World Authors Series, 14)*

BAULAND, PETER. *The hooded eagle: modern German drama on the New York stage.* Syracuse, N. Y., Syracuse University Press, 1968.

BAXTER, KAY M. *Contemporary theatre and the Christian faith.* Nashville, Abington Press, 1965.

BEACH, JOSEPH. *The making of the Auden canon.* Minneapolis, University of Minnesota Press, 1957.

Beckett at 60, a festschrift. London, Calder and Boyars, 1967.

BEERBOHM, MAX. *Around theatres.* London, Rupert Hart-Davis, 1953.

BEHRMAN, S. N. *The suspended drawing room.* New York, Stein & Day, 1965.

BENEDIKT, MICHAEL, and GEORGE E. WELLWARTH. *Modern Spanish theatre, an anthology of plays.* New York, Dutton, 1968.

———. *Postwar German theatre, an anthology of plays.* New York, Dutton, 1967.

BENTLEY, ERIC. *Bernard Shaw*. 2nd British ed. London, Methuen, 1967.

————. *The dramatic event, an American chronicle*. New York, Horizon Press, 1954.

————. *Father's day*. New York, Istituto Italiano di Cultura, 1968.

————. *The playwright as thinker*. Cleveland and New York, World Publishing Company, 1964.

————. *The theatre of commitment and other essays on drama in our society*. New York, Atheneum, 1967.

————, ed. *The genius of the Italian theatre*. New York, New American Library (a Mentor Book), 1964.

————, ed. *The storm over The Deputy*. New York, Grove Press, 1964.

BERCHAN, RICHARD. *The inner stage; an essay on the conflict of vocations in the early works of Paul Claudel*. East Lansing, Michigan State University Press, 1966.

BERMEL, ALBERT, ed. *The genius of the French theatre*. New York, New American Library, 1961.

BERRYMAN, CHARLES. *W. B. Yeats, design of opposites*. New York, Exposition Press, 1967.

BICKLEY, FRANCIS. *J. M. Synge and the Irish dramatic movement*. London, Constable; Boston and New York, Houghton Mifflin, 1912.

BIERMAN, JUDAH. *The dramatic experience*. Englewood Cliffs, N. J., Prentice-Hall, 1958.

BIGSBY, C. W. E. *Confrontation and commitment, a study of contemporary American drama, 1959–1966*. Columbia, Mo., University of Missouri Press, 1968.

BISHOP, THOMAS. *Pirandello and the French theatre*. New York, New York University Press, 1960.

BLAU, HERBERT. *The impossible theatre*. New York, Macmillan, 1964.

BLOCK, ANITA. *The changing world in plays and theatre*. Boston, Little, Brown, 1939.

BLOCK, HASKELL M., and HERMAN SALINGER, eds. *Creative vision; modern European writers on their art*. New York, Grove Press, 1960.

BOGARD, TRAVIS, and WILLIAM I. OLIVER, eds. *Modern drama; essays in criticism*. New York, Oxford University Press, 1965.

BOHNER, CHARLES H. *Robert Penn Warren*. New York, Twayne Publishers, 1964.

BORRAS, F. M. *Maxim Gorky and writer; an interpretation*. Oxford, Clarendon Press, 1967.

BOYD, ERNEST. *Ireland's literary renaissance*. Reprint of 1922 ed. New York, Barnes & Noble, 1968.

BRADBROOK, MURIEL CLARA. *English dramatic form*. New York, Barnes & Noble, 1965.

————. *Ibsen, the Norwegian, a revaluation*. New edition. Hamden, Conn., Archon Books, 1966.

BRADFORD, CURTIS B. *Yeats at work*. Carbondale, Southern Illinois University Press, 1965.

BRECHT, BERTOLT. *Brecht on theatre: the development of an aesthetic*. New York, Hill & Wang, 1964.

✓BRERETON, GEOFFREY. *Principles of tragedy, a rational examination of the tragic concept in life and literature.* Coral Gables, University of Miami Press, 1968.

BRINSER, AYERS. *The Respectability of Mr. Bernard Shaw.* Cambridge, Harvard University Press, 1931.

✓BRITTEN, NORMA A. *Edna St. Vincent Millay.* New York, Twayne Publishers, 1967.

✓BROOKS, CLEANTH, ed. *Tragic themes in Western literature.* New Haven, Yale University Press, 1955.

✓BROOKS, CLEANTH, and ROBERT B. HEILMAN. *Understanding drama.* New York, Holt, 1948.

ℛ BROUSSARD, LOUIS. *American drama, contemporary allegory from Eugene O'Neill to Tennessee Williams.* Norman, University of Oklahoma Press, 1962.

ℛ BROWN, JOHN MASON. *Broadway in review.* New York, W. W. Norton, 1940.

✓———. *Dramatis personae; a retrospective show.* New York, Viking, 1963.

⅋ℛ ———. *Seeing more things.* New York, McGraw-Hill, 1948.

———. *Still seeing things.* New York, McGraw-Hill, 1950.

✓ ———. *Two on the aisle.* New York, W. W. Norton, 1938.

ℛ ———. *Upstage: the American theatre in performance.* New York, W. W. Norton, 1930.

✓ ———. *The worlds of Robert E. Sherwood, mirror to his times 1896–1939.* New York, Harper & Row, 1965.

✓ BROWN, JOHN RUSSELL, ed. *Modern British dramatists, a collection of critical essays.* Englewood Cliffs, Prentice-Hall, 1968.

⅋ BROWN, JOHN RUSSELL, and BERNARD HARRIS, eds. *American theatre.* London, Edward Arnold, 1967. (Stratford-Upon-Avon Studies, 10)

———, eds. *Contemporary theatre.* New York, St. Martin's Press, 1962.

⅋ BROWNE, ELLIOTT MARTIN. *The making of a play; T. S. Eliot's 'The Cocktail Party'.* Cambridge, Cambridge University Press, 1966.

✓BRUSTEIN, ROBERT. *Seasons of discontent.* New York, Simon & Schuster, 1965.

✓ ———. *The theatre of revolt; an approach to the modern drama.* Boston, Little, Brown, 1962.

✓ BÜCHNER, GEORG. *Complete plays and prose.* New York, Hill & Wang, 1963.

———. *Danton's death.* San Francisco, Chandler, 1961.

✓ ———. *Woyzeck and Leonce and Lena.* San Francisco, Chandler, 1962.

BÜDEL, OSCAR. *Pirandello.* New York, Hillary House, 1969. (Studies in Modern European Literature and Thought)

✓BURNSHAW, STANLEY, ed. *Varieties of literary experience,* New York, New York University Press, 1962.

ℛBURTON, RICHARD. *Bernard Shaw, the man and the mask.* New York, Henry Holt & Co., 1916.

⅋ ℛBUSHRUI, S. B. *Yeats's verse plays: the revisions 1900–1910.* Oxford, Clarendon Press, 1965.

✓CAMBON, GLAUCO, ed. *Pirandello: a collection of critical essays.* Englewood Cliffs, Prentice-Hall, 1967.

CAPUTI, ANTHONY, ed. *Modern drama; authoritative texts of The Wild Duck, Three Sisters, The Devil's Disciple, A Dream Play, Desire Under the Elms, Henry IV, [with] backgrounds and criticism.* New York, W. W. Norton & Co., 1966.

✓CARPENTER, FREDERIC I. *Robinson Jeffers.* New York, Twayne Publishers, 1962.

CASSELL, RICHARD A., and HENRY KNEPLER. *What is the play?* Glenview, Ill., Scott, Foresman, 1967.

CATTAUI, GEORGES. *T. S. Eliot.* Tr. by Claire Pace and Jean Stewart. London, The Merlin Press, 1966.

₂ₚ CAUDWELL, CHRISTOPHER. *Studies in a dying culture.* London, Lane, 1947.

✕ CHANDLER, FRANK WADLEIGH. *The contemporary drama of France.* Boston, Little, Brown, 1921.

✓CHAPPELOW, ALLAN, ed. *Shaw the villager and human being: a biographical symposium.* New York, Macmillan, 1962.

ₒₚCHESTERTON, G. K. *Bernard Shaw.* 7th ed. New York, Devin-Adair, 1950.
✓————. *George Bernard Shaw.* London, John Lane, 1910.

ℛ CHIARI, JOSEPH. *The contemporary French theatre; the flight from naturalism.* New York, Macmillan, 1959.

ℛ ————. *Landmarks of contemporary drama.* London, Herbert Jenkins, 1965.

ᵐCHICK, EDSON M. *Ernst Barlach.* New York, Twayne Publishers, 1967. *(World Authors Series, 26)*

CHISLETT, WILLIAM, JR. *Moderns and near-moderns; essays on Henry James, Stockton, Shaw, and others.* Freeport, N. Y., Books for Libraries, 1967. *(Essay Index Reprint Series)*

ₒₚ CHRISTESEN, CLEMENT BYRNE. *On native grounds; Australian writing from the Meanjin Quarterly.* Selected with a preface by C. B. Christesen. Sydney, Angus & Robertson, 1968.

ℛ CHURCH, RICHARD. *British authors.* London, Longmans, Green, 1948.

ₒₚ CLARK, BARRETT H. *Continental drama of today.* New York, Holt, 1914.
✓————. *Eugene O'Neill.* New York, Dover, 1947.
ₒₚ ————. *An hour of American drama.* Philadelphia, Lippincott, 1930.
————. *Maxwell Anderson, the man and his plays.* New York, Samuel French, 1933.
✓————. *A study of the modern drama; a handbook for the study and appreciation of the best plays, European, English, and American, of the last half century.* New York, London, Appleton, 1925.

ₒₚ CLARK, DAVID R. *W. B. Yeats and the theatre of desolate reality.* Chester Springs, Pa., Dufour Editions, 1965.

ₒₚCLARKE, DAVID WALDO. *Modern English writers.* London, Longmans, Green, 1948.

✓CLARKE, WINIFRED. *George Bernard Shaw; an appreciation and interpretation.* Altrincham, England, J. Sherratt, 1948.

✓CLURMAN, HAROLD. *Lies like truth; theatre reviews and essays.* New York, Macmillan, 1958.
✓————. *The naked image; observations on the modern theatre.* New York, Macmillan, 1966.

ₒₚ COATES, J. B. *Leaders of modern thought.* London, Longmans, Green, 1947.

COATS, R. H. *John Galsworthy as a dramatic artist.* New York, Scribner's, 1926.

✓COBB, CARL W. *Federico Garcia Lorca.* New York, Twayne Publishers, 1967.

COCTEAU, JEAN. *The difficulty of being.* New York, Coward-McCann, 1967.

COE, RICHARD N. *Ionesco.* New York, Barnes & Noble, 1961.

————. *Samuel Beckett.* New York, Grove Press, 1964.

————. *The vision of Jean Genet.* London, Peter Owen, 1968.

✓COHEN, ROBERT. *Giraudoux; three faces of destiny.* Chicago, University of Chicago Press, 1968.

COHN, RUBY, ed. *Casebook on Waiting for Godot.* New York, Grove Press, 1967.

COHN, RUBY, and BERNARD F. DUKORE, eds. *Twentieth century drama: England, Ireland, the United States.* New York, Random House, 1966.

✓COLBOURNE, MAURICE. *The real Bernard Shaw.* New York, Philosophical Library, 1949.

COLE, TOBY, ed. *Playwrights on playwriting: the meaning and making of modern drama from Ibsen to Ionesco.* New York, Hill & Wang, 1960.

✓COLE, TOBY, and H. K. CHINOY, eds. *Actors on acting.* New York, Crown, 1949.

COLEMAN, ARTHUR P. *Humor in the Russian comedy from Catherine to Gogol.* New York, AMS Press, 1966.

COLLINS, ARTHUR SIMONS. *English literature of the twentieth century.* London, University Tutorial Press, 1951.

COOK, ALBERT. *Prisms, studies in modern literature.* Bloomington, Indiana University Press, 1967.

CORKERY, DANIEL. *Synge and Anglo-Irish literature.* Cork University Press, 1955.

✓CORRIGAN, ROBERT W., ed. *Comedy: meaning and form.* San Francisco, Chandler, 1965.

————, ed. *Laurel British drama; the nineteenth century.* New York, Dell Publishing Company, 1967.

————, ed. *Masterpieces of the modern French theatre.* New York, Collier Books, 1967.

————, ed. *Masterpieces of the modern German theatre.* New York, Collier Books, 1967.

————, ed. *Masterpieces of the modern Italian theatre.* New York, Collier Books, 1967.

————, ed. *Masterpieces of the modern Spanish theatre.* New York, Collier Books, 1967.

————, ed. *The new theatre of Europe.* New York, Dell Publishing Co., 1962.

————. *Theatre in the twentieth century.* New York, Grove Press, 1963.

CORRIGAN, ROBERT W., and JAMES L. ROSENBERG, eds. *The context and craft of drama.* San Francisco, Chandler, 1964.

COURTNEY, WILLIAM LEONARD. *The idea of tragedy in ancient and modern drama.* New York, Russell & Russell, 1967.

COWASJEE, SAROS. *O'Casey.* New York, Barnes & Noble, 1966.

COWELL, RAYMOND. *Twelve modern dramatists.* Oxford, Pergamon Press, 1967.

✓COWLEY, MALCOLM, ed. *After the genteel tradition: American writers since 1910.* New York, Norton, 1937.

✓Cox, C. B., ed. *Dylan Thomas: a collection of critical essays.* Englewood Cliffs, N. J., Prentice-Hall, 1966.

✓COXHEAD, ELIZABETH. *J. M. Synge and Lady Gregory.* London, Longmans, Green, 1962.

⟩ℓ CRUICKSHANK, JOHN. *Montherlant.* Edinburgh and London, Oliver & Boyd, 1964.

✓CUBETA, PAUL M. *Modern drama for analysis.* 3rd ed. New York, Holt, Rinehart & Winston, 1962.

ℴℓ CURTIS, ANTHONY. *New developments in the French theatre. (The Masque, no. 8)* London, The Curtain Press, 1948.

D'AMATO, GUY ALBERT. *Portraits of ideas.* Boston, Christopher, 1947.

ℴℛ DANIELS, MAY. *The French drama of the unspoken.* Edinburgh, at the University Press, 1953.

DARLINGTON, WILLIAM AUBREY. *J. M. Barrie.* London, Blackie, 1938.

————. *Literature in the theatre, and other essays.* New York, Holt, 1933.

————. *Through the fourth wall.* New York, Brentano's, 1922.

✓DAVIES, MARGARET. *Apollinaire.* Edinburgh and London, Oliver & Boyd, 1964.

ℴℓ DEBUSSCHER, GILBERT. *Edward Albee, tradition and renewal.* Brussels, American Studies Center, Royal Library of Belgium, 1967.

ℴᵐ DEMBO, L. S. *Nabokov, the man and his work.* Madison, University of Wisconsin Press, 1967.

✓DEMETZ, PETER, ed. *Brecht.* Englewood Cliffs, N.J., Prentice-Hall, 1962.

DENT, ALAN. *Preludes and studies.* London, Macmillan, 1942.

DESELINCOURT, AUBREY. *Six great playwrights: Sophocles, Shakespeare, Moliére, Sheridan, Ibsen, Shaw.* London, Hamilton House, 1960.

ℛᵐDICK, BERNARD F. *William Golding.* New York, Twayne Publishers, 1967.
635 ℨⁱᵇ *(English Author Series, no. 51)*

✓DOBRÉE, BONAMY. *The lamp and the lute, studies in seven authors.* 2nd ed. London, Frank Cass, 1964.

DONOGHUE, DENIS. *The third voice; modern British and American verse drama.* Princeton, Princeton University Press, 1959.

✓DONOGHUE, DENIS, and J. R. MULRYNE, eds. *An honoured guest; new essays on W. B. Yeats.* London, Edward Arnold, 1965.

✓DOWNER, ALAN S. *American drama and its critics.* Chicago, The University of Chicago Press, 1965.

57 ℛ✓————. *The art of the play.* New York, Holt, 1955.

✓————. *Fifty years of American drama 1900–1950.* Chicago, Henry Regnery Co., 1951.

✓————. *Recent American drama.* Minneapolis, University of Minnesota Press, 1961. *(University of Minnesota Pamphlets on American Writers, Number 7)*

✓DOWNER, ALAN S., ed. *The American theater today,* New York, Basic Books, 1967.

√DUCLAUX, MARY. *Twentieth century French writers.* Freeport, N. Y., Books for Libraries, Inc., 1966.

√DUKES, ASHLEY. *Modern dramatists.* London, F. Palmer, 1911.

ᴄᴿDUPEE, FREDERICK WILCOX. *"The King of the Cats", and other remarks on writers and writing.* New York, Farrar, Straus & Giroux, 1965.

√DURAN, MANUEL, ed. *Lorca: a collection of critical essays.* Englewood Cliffs, N. J., Prentice-Hall, 1962.

DUSENBURY, WINIFRED L. *The theme of loneliness in the modern American drama.* Gainesville, University of Florida Press, 1960.

EASTMAN, FRED. *Christ in the drama.* New York, Macmillan, 1947.

ᴏᴾEATON, WALTER P. *The drama in English.* New York, Scribner's, 1930.

√EHRENBURG, ILYA. *Chekhov, Stendhal, and other essays.* New York, Knopf, 1963.

ᵇ⁷⁰ₑ₄ ᵐELIOT, THOMAS STEARNS. *Poetry and drama.* Cambridge, Harvard University Press, 1951.

ELLEHAUGE, MARTIN. *The position of Bernard Shaw in European drama and philosophy.* New York, Haskell House, 1966.

√ELLIS-FERMOR, UNA. *The Irish dramatic movement.* London, Methuen, 1954.

√ELLMANN, RICHARD. *Eminent domain: Yeats among Wilde, Joyce, Pound, Eliot, and Auden.* New York, Oxford University Press, 1967.

√————. *Yeats: the man and the masks.* New York, Macmillan, 1948.

ELTON, OLIVER. *Essays and Addresses.* London, Longmans, 1939.

√EMANUEL, JAMES A. *Langston Hughes.* New York, Twayne Publishers, 1967. *(United States Authors Series, no. 123)*

√ENGEL, EDWIN A. *The haunted heroes of Eugene O'Neill.* Cambridge, Harvard University Press, 1953.

ᴏᴾ ENGLISH INSTITUTE. *Ideas in the drama; selected papers from the English Institute.* Edited with a foreword by John Gassner. New York, Columbia University Press, 1964.

ᴿERLICH, VICTOR. *The double image: concepts of the poets in Slavic literatures.* Baltimore, Johns Hopkins Press, 1964.

√ERVINE, ST. JOHN. *Bernard Shaw, his life, work, and friends.* New York, Morrow, 1956.

Essay annual, 1933–40, a yearly collection of significant essays, personal, critical, controversial, and humorous; ed. by E. A. Walter. 8 vols. Chicago, Scott Foresman, 1933–40.

¹⁸⁶¹/ᴇ⁸ᴿESSLIN, MARTIN. *The theatre of the absurd.* Garden City, Doubleday, 1961.

√————, ed. *Samuel Beckett; a collection of critical essays.* Englewood Cliffs, N. J., Prentice-Hall, 1965.

ᴏᴾ EVANS, GARETH LLOYD. *J. B. Priestley—the dramatist.* London, Heinemann, 1964.

ᴿEVERETT, BARBARA. *Auden.* Edinburgh and London, Oliver & Boyd, 1964. *(Writers and Critics, ed. by A. Norman Jeffares.)*

√EWEN, FREDERIC. *Bertolt Brecht, his life, his art and his times.* New York, Citadel, 1967.

ᴏᴾ FABRICIUS, JOHANNES. *The unconscious and Mr. Eliot: a study in expressionism.* Copenhagen, Nyt Nordisk, 1967.

FALCONIERI, JOHN V. *Spanish American literature.* Detroit, Wayne State University Press, 1963.

FALK, DORIS V. *Eugene O'Neill and the tragic tension.* New Brunswick, Rutgers University Press, 1958.

FALK, EUGENE H. *Renunciation as a tragic focus: a study of five plays.* Minneapolis, University of Minnesota Press, 1954.

FALK, SIGNI L. *Tennessee Williams.* New York, Twayne Publishers, 1961.

FEDDER, NORMAN J. *The influence of D. H. Lawrence on Tennessee Williams.* The Hague, Mouton, 1966.

FERGUSSON, FRANCIS. *The human image in dramatic literature.* Garden City, Doubleday, 1957. (Anchor Books)

————. *The idea of a theater.* Garden City, New York, Doubleday, 1953.

FIELD, ANDREW. *Nabokov, his life in art.* Boston, Little, Brown & Co., 1967.

FINKELSTEIN, SIDNEY. *Existentialism and alienation in American literature.* New York, International Publishers, 1965.

FISKIN, A. M. I., ed. *Writers of our years.* Denver, Denver University Press, 1950. (Denver University Studies in Humanities, no. 1)

FLANNER, JANET (GENET). *Paris journal, 1944–1965.* New York, Atheneum, 1965.

FLETCHER, JOHN. *Samuel Beckett's art.* London, Chatto & Windus, 1967.

FLEXNER, ELEANOR. *American playwrights: 1918–1938.* New York, Simon and Schuster, 1938.

FLOAN, HOWARD R. *William Saroyan.* New York, Twayne Publishers, 1966. *(United States Authors Series, 100)*

FORCE, WILLIAM M., ed. *Orestes and Electra, myth and dramatic form.* Boston, Houghton Mifflin, 1968.

FORSTER, EDWARD M. *Two cheers for Democracy.* New York, Harcourt, 1951.

FOWLIE, WALLACE. *Age of surrealism.* New York, Swallow Press, 1950.

————. *André Gide: his life and art.* New York, Macmillan, 1965.

————. *Dionysus in Paris; a guide to contemporary French theater.* New York, Meridian Books, 1960.

————. *A guide to contemporary French literature from Valèry to Sartre.* New York, Meridian Books, 1957.

————. *Jean Cocteau; the history of a poet's age.* Bloomington, Indiana University Press, 1966.

FRANCO, JEAN. *The modern culture of Latin America: society and the artist.* New York, Praeger, 1967.

FRASER, GEORGE SUTHERLAND. *The modern writer and his world.* New York, Praeger, 1965.

FRAZER, WINIFRED DUSENBURG. *Love as death in The Iceman Cometh.* Gainsville, University of Florida Press, 1967.

FREEDMAN, MORRIS. *The moral impulse; modern drama from Ibsen to the present.* Carbondale, Southern Illinois University Press, 1967.

————, ed. *Essays in the modern drama.* Boston, Heath, 1964.

FREEMAN, JOHN. *The moderns; essays in literary criticism.* London, Robert Scott, 1916.

√FRENCH, WARREN, ed. *The thirties: fiction, poetry, drama.* Deland, Fla., Everett Edwards, 1967.

√FRENZ, HORST, ed. *American playwrights on drama.* New York, Hill & Wang, 1965.

FRIEDMAN, MAURICE. *To deny our nothingness.* New York, Delacorte Press, 1967.

√FRIEDMAN, NORMAN. *E. E. Cummings, the growth of a writer.* Carbondale, Southern Illinois University Press, 1964.

√FULLER, EDMUND. *George Bernard Shaw: critic of western morale.* New York, Scribner, 1950.

GAGEY, EDMOND M. *Revolution in American drama.* New York, Columbia University Press, 1947.

ℓℓ GARDNER, RUFUS HALLETTE. *The splintered stage; the decline of the American theater.* New York, Macmillan, 1965.

√GARTEN, HUGH F. *Modern German drama.* 2nd ed. London, Methuen, 1964.

1861 63 √GASCOIGNE, BAMBER. *Twentieth century drama.* London, Hutchinson & Co., 1962.

√GASSNER, JOHN. *Directions in modern theatre and drama.* New York, Holt, Rinehart and Winston, 1965.

√ ———. *Theatre at the crossroads; plays and playwrights of the mid-century American stage.* New York, Holt, Rinehart & Winston, 1960.

√ ———. *The theatre in our times.* New York, Crown, 1954.

√ ———, ed. *O'Neill: a collection of critical essays.* Englewood Cliffs, Prentice-Hall, 1964.

625 G3 √GASSNER, JOHN, ed., and MOLLIE GASSNER. *Best plays of the early American theatre from the beginning to 1916.* New York, Crown, 1967.

ℓℓ GERGELY, EMRO JOSEPH. *Hungarian drama in New York.* Philadelphia, University of Pennsylvania Press, 1947.

ℓℓ ℳℓ GHEON, HENRI. *The art of theatre.* New York, Hill & Wang, 1961.

2020 τ55 √GILDER, ROSAMOND, ed. *Theatre Arts anthology.* New York, Theatre Arts Books, 1950.

ℓℓ ℓ GILROY, FRANK D. *About those roses, or how not to do a play and succeed and the text of The Subject Was Roses.* New York, Random House, 1965.

√GLICKSBERG, CHARLES I. *The self in modern literature.* University Park, Pennsylvania State University Press, 1963.

√ ———. *The tragic vision in twentieth-century literature.* Carbondale, Southern Illinois University Press, 1963.

ℓℓ GOLDBERG, ISAAC. *The drama of transition, native and exotic playcraft.* Cincinnati, Stewart Kidd Company, 1922.

√GOLDEN, JOSEPH. *The death of Tinker Bell: the American theatre in the 20th century.* New York, Syracuse University Press, 1967.

ℓℳ GONZÁLEZ PEÑA, CARLOS. *History of Mexican literature.* University Press in Dallas, Southern Methodist University, 1943.

√ GOODMAN, RANDOLPH. *Drama on stage.* New York, Holt, Rinehart and Winston, 1961.

√ GOTTFRIED, MARTIN. *A theater divided; the postwar American stage.* Boston, Little, Brown, 1967.

√ GOULD, JEAN. *Modern American playwrights.* New York, Dodd, Mead, 1966.

GRANT, VERNON W. *Great abnormals; the pathological genius of Kafka, van Gogh, Strindberg and Poe*. New York, Hawthorne Books, 1968.

GRAY, JAMES. *Edna St. Vincent Millay*. Minneapolis, University of Minnesota Press, 1967. (*Univ. of Minnesota Pamphlets on American Writers, no. 64*)

GRAY, RONALD. *The German tradition in literature*. London, Cambridge University Press, 1965.

GREEN, PAUL. *Dramatic heritage*. New York, French, 1953.

GREENWOOD, ORMEROD. *The playwright; a study of form, method, and tradition in the theatre*. London, Sir Isaac Pitman & Sons, 1950.

GREGORY, ISABELLA AUGUSTA. *Lady Gregory's Journals, 1916–1930*. (Ed., L. Robinson). London, Putnam, 1946; New York, Macmillan, 1947.

——. *Our Irish theatre, a chapter of autobiography*. New York, G. P. Putnam's Sons, 1913.

GRENE, DAVID. *Reality and the heroic pattern, last plays of Ibsen, Shakespeare, and Sophocles*. Chicago, University of Chicago Press, 1967.

GROSSVOGEL, DAVID I. *Four playwrights and a postscript: Brecht, Ionesco, Beckett, Genet*. Ithaca, Cornell University Press, 1962.

——. *The self-conscious stage in modern French drama*. New York, Columbia University Press, 1958.

GUICHARNAUD, JACQUES. *Modern French theatre from Giraudoux to Beckett*. New Haven, Yale University Press, 1961.

——. *Modern French theatre from Giraudoux to Genet*. Rev. ed. New Haven, Yale University Press, 1967. (*Yale Romantic studies, second series, 7*)

GURKO, MIRIAM. *Restless spirit; the life of Edna St. Vincent Millay*. New York, Crowell, 1962.

GUTHKE, KARL S. *Modern tragicomedy*. New York, Random House, 1966.

GUTHRIE, TYRONE. *In various directions; a view of theatre*. New York, Macmillan, 1965.

HACKETT, FRANCIS. *On judging books*. New York, John Day Company, 1947.

HAGOPIAN, JOHN V., and MARTIN DOLCH. *Insight I; analysis of American literature*. Frankfurt-am-Main, Hirschgraben-Verlag, 1962.

HALPERN, MARTIN. *William Vaughn Moody*. New York, Twayne Publishers, 1964. (*United States Authors Series, 64*)

HAMBURGER, MICHAEL. *Reason and energy: studies in German literature*. New York, Grove Press, 1957.

HAMILTON, CLAYTON. *Conversations on contemporary drama*. New York, Macmillan, 1924.

——. *Seen on the stage*. New York, Henry Holt, 1920.

HAMM, GERALD. *The dramas of Philip Barry*. Philadelphia, University of Pennsylvania Press, 1948.

HAMMER, CARL, ed. *Studies in German literature*. Baton Rouge, Louisiana State University Press, 1963. (*Louisiana State University studies. Humanities series, no. 13*)

HARDING, DENYS CLEMENT WYATT. *Experience into words; essays on poetry*. London, Chatto & Windus, 1963.

✓HARRIS, FRANK. *Bernard Shaw.* New York, Simon and Schuster, 1931.

✓HARRISON, GEORGE BAGSHAWE. *Major British writers.* 2 vols. New York, Harcourt, 1954.

ᵒᵖHARTLEY, LODWICK and ARTHUR LADU, eds. *Patterns in modern drama.* New York, Prentice-Hall, 1948.

ₒₚ ℛ,ᵐHARVEY, JOHN. *Anouilh; a study in theatrics.* New Haven, Yale University Press, 1964.

ℛHASSAN, IHAB. *The literature of silence; Henry Miller and Samuel Beckett.* New York, Alfred A. Knopf, 1967.

✓HATFIELD, HENRY. *Modern German literature: the major figures in context.* London, New York, St. Martin's Press, 1966.

✓HATHORN, RICHMOND YANCEY. *Tragedy, myth, and mystery.* Bloomington, Indiana University Press, 1962.

✓HATZFELD, HELMUT. *Trends and styles in twentieth century French literature.* Revised and enlarged edition. Washington, D. C., The Catholic University of America Press, 1966.

ℛHEBBLETHWAITE, PETER. *Bernanos; an introduction.* New York, Hillary House, 1965.

ℛHEILMAN, ROBERT BECHTOLD. *Tragedy and melodrama, versions of experience.* Seattle, University of Washington Press, 1968.

HELLER, OTTO. *Prophets of dissent: essays on Maeterlinck, Strindberg, Nietzsche and Tolstoy.* New York, Knopf, 1918.

————. *Studies in modern German literature; Sudermann, Hauptmann, women writers of the nineteenth century.* Boston, Ginn and Company, 1905.

HENDERSON, ARCHIBALD. *European dramatists.* New York, Appleton, 1926.

ℛ ————. *George Bernard Shaw: man of the century.* New York, Appleton, 1956.

✓————. *Table-talk of G. B. S.; conversations on things in general between George Bernard Shaw and his biographer.* New York, Harper & Bros., 1925.

1892 H4 ✓HENN, THOMAS RICE *The harvest of tragedy.* London, Methuen, 1956.

✓————. *The lonely tower: studies in the poetry of W. B. Yeats.* 2nd ed. London, Methuen, 1965.

HENRY, DAVID D. *William Vaughn Moody, a study.* Boston, Bruce Humphries, Inc., 1934.

HEPPENSTALL, RAYNER. *The double image, mutations of Christian mythology in the work of four French Catholic writers of to-day and yesterday.* London, Secker & Warburg, 1947.

✓HILL, HERBERT, ed. *Anger, and beyond; the Negro writer in the United States.* New York, Harper & Row, 1966.

✓HIMELSTEIN, MORGAN Y. *Drama was a weapon, the left-wing theatre in New York 1929–1941.* New Brunswick, N. J., Rutgers University Press, 1963.

ᵐHINCHLIFFE, ARNOLD P. *Harold Pinter.* New York, Twayne Publishers, 1967. *(English Author Series, no. 51)*

✓HINGLEY, RONALD. *Chekhov, a biographical and critical study.* London, George Allen & Unwin, 1966.

ₒₚHIRAI, MASAO, and E. W. F. TOMLIN, eds. *T. S. Eliot, a tribute from Japan.* Tokyo, Kenkyusha, 1966.

HOARE, DOROTHY M. *The works of Morris and Yeats in relation to early saga literature.* London, Cambridge University Press, 1937.

HOBSON, HAROLD. *The French theatre of today.* London, Harrap, 1953.

————. *Theatre.* London, Longmans, Green, 1948.

————. *The theatre now.* London, Longmans, Green, 1953.

HOFFMAN, FREDERICK J. *Samuel Beckett: the language of self.* Carbondale, Southern Illinois University Press, 1962.

HOGAN, ROBERT. *After the Irish Renaissance: a critical history of the Irish drama since The Plough and the Stars.* Minneapolis, University of Minnesota Press, 1967.

————. *The independence of Elmer Rice.* Carbondale, Southern Illinois University Press, 1965.

————. *Seven Irish plays, 1946–1964.* Minneapolis, University of Minnesota Press, 1967.

HONIG, EDWIN. *García Lorca.* Norfolk, New Directions, 1944.

HOWE, PERCIVAL PRESLAND. *J. M. Synge, a critical study.* London, Martin Secker, 1912.

HUDSON, DEREK, ed. *English critical essays, twentieth century; second series.* London, Oxford University Press, 1958.

HUDSON, LYNTON. *The twentieth-century drama.* London, Harrap, 1953.

HUGHES, LANGSTON. *Five plays by Langston Hughes.* Edited with an introduction by Webster Smalley. Bloomington, Indiana University Press, 1968.

HURRELL, JOHN D. *Two modern American tragedies, reviews and criticism of "Death of a Salesman" and "A Streetcar Named Desire."* New York, Scribner's, 1961.

ILLINOIS UNIVERSITY, DEPARTMENT OF ENGLISH. *Studies by members of the English Department, University of Illinois, in memory of John Jay Parry.* Urbana, University of Illinois, 1955.

IMBERT, ENRIQUE ANDERSON. *Spanish-American literature: a history.* Translated by John V. Falconieri. Detroit, Wayne State University Press, 1963.

INTERNATIONAL COMPARATIVE LITERATURE ASSOCIATION. *Actes du congrès. Proceedings of the 4th congress.* Ed. by Francois Jost. 2 vols. Fribourg, 1964. The Hague, Mouton, 1966.

IRVINE, WILLIAM. *The universe of G. B. S.* New York, McGraw-Hill, 1949.

ISHIBASHI, HIRO. *Yeats and the Noh: types of Japanese beauty and their reflection in Yeats' plays.* Cleveland, World Publishing Company, 1968.

JACKSON, ESTHER M. *The broken world of Tennessee Williams.* Madison and Milwaukee, The University of Wisconsin Press, 1965.

JACKSON, ROBERT LOUIS, ed. *Chekhov, a collection of critical essays.* Englewood Cliffs, N. J., Prentice-Hall, 1967.

JACOBSEN, JOSEPHINE, and WILLIAM R. MUELLER. *Ionesco and Genet, playwrights of silence.* New York, Hill & Wang, 1968.

————. *The testament of Samuel Beckett.* London, Faber & Faber, 1966.

JAMES, HENRY. *The scenic art.* New York, Hill & Wang, 1957.

JAMESON, STORM. *Modern drama in Europe.* London, W. Collins Sons, 1920.

JARRY, ALFRED. *Selected works of Alfred Jarry.* Edited by Roger Shattuck and Simon Watson Taylor. New York, Grove Press, 1965.

KOSLOW, JULES. *Sean O'Casey, the man and his plays.* New York, The Citadel Press, 1966.

KOSTELANETZ, RICHARD, ed. *The new American arts.* New York, Horizon Press, 1965.

KRONENBERGER, LOUIS. *The thread of laughter; chapters on English stage comedy from Jonson to Maugham.* New York, Alfred A. Knopf, 1952.

———, ed. *George Bernard Shaw: a critical survey.* Cleveland, World Publishing Company, 1953.

KROPOTKIN, P. *Russian literature.* New York, Benjamin Blom, 1967. (Reprint. First published 1905 by McClure, Phillips & Co.)

KRUTCH, JOSEPH WOOD. *The American drama since 1918.* New York, George Braziller, 1957.

———. *"Modernism" in modern drama.* Ithaca, Cornell University Press, 1953.

LAGERKVIST, PÄR. *Modern theatre; seven plays and an essay.* Lincoln, University of Nebraska Press, 1966.

LAING, ALLAN M., ed. *In praise of Bernard Shaw.* London, Müller, 1949.

LAMM, MARTIN. *Modern drama.* Translated by Karin Elliott. Oxford, Basil Blackwell, 1952.

LANGFORD, RICHARD E., GUY OWEN, and WILLIAM E. TAYLOR, eds. *Essays in modern American literature.* Deland, Fla., Stetson University Press, 1963.

LANGNER, LAWRENCE. *G. B. S. and the lunatic: reminiscences of the long, lively and affectionate friendship between George Bernard Shaw and the author.* New York, Atheneum, 1963.

LA NOUVELLE REVUE FRANÇAISE. *From the N. R. F.* Edited by Justin O'Brien. New York, Farrar, Straus & Cudahy, 1958.

LAVRIN, JANKO. *Nikolai Gogol (1809–1852), a centenary survey.* London, Sylvan Press, 1951.

———. *Studies in European literature.* London, Constable, 1929.

LAWSON, JOHN HOWARD. *The theory and technique of playwriting.* New York, Putnam, 1936.

LEASKA, MITCHELL A. *The voice of tragedy.* New York, Robert Speller & Sons, 1963.

LEVIN, RICHARD. *Tragedy: plays, theory, and criticism.* New York, Harcourt, Brace and World, 1960.

LEWIS, ALLAN. *American plays and playwrights of the contemporary theatre.* New York, Crown, 1965.

———. *The contemporary theatre.* New York, Crown, 1962.

LEWISOHN, LUDWIG. *Drama and the stage.* New York, Harcourt, 1922.

———. *Expressionism in America.* New York, Harper, 1932; rev. ed., *The story of American literature.* New York, Modern Library, 1939.

LID, RICHARD WALD, comp. *Plays, classic and contemporary.* Philadelphia, Lippincott, 1967.

LIFSON, DAVID S. *The Yiddish theatre in America.* New York, Thomas Yoseloff, 1965.

LIMA, ROBERT. *The theatre of García Lorca.* New York, Las Américas, 1963.

LIND AF HAGEBY, LIZZY. *August Strindberg: the spirit of revolt; studies and impressions.* New York, Appleton, 1913.

✓LINDENBERGER, HERBERT. *Georg Büchner.* Carbondale, Southern Illinois University Press, 1964.

LINKLATER, ERIC. *The art of adventure.* London, Macmillan, 1948.

LOGGINS, VERNON. *I hear America . . . Literature in the United States since 1900.* New York, Crowell, 1937.

LONG, CHESTER CLAYTON. *The role of nemesis in the structure of selected plays by Eugene O'Neill.* The Hague, Mouton, 1968. *(Studies in American Literature, vol. VIII)*

LUCAS, FRANK LAURENCE. *The drama of Chekhov, Synge, Yeats, and Pirandello.* London, Cassell, 1963.

✓LUMLEY, FREDERICK. *New trends in twentieth century drama.* London, Barrie and Rockliff, 1967.

✓————. *Trends in 20th century drama.* 2nd revised edition. London, Barrie & Rockliff, 1960.

LUPPÉ, ROBERT DE. *Albert Camus.* Translated from the French by John Cumming and J. Hargreaves. London, Merlin Press, 1966.

LUYBEN, HELEN L. *James Bridie: clown and philosopher.* Phildelphia, University of Pennsylvania Press, 1965.

LYONS, CHARLES R. *Bertolt Brecht, the despair and the polemic.* Carbondale, Southern Illinois University Press, 1968.

McCANN, SEAN, ed. *The story of the Abbey Theatre.* London, New English Library, 1967.

————, ed. *The world of Sean O'Casey.* London, New English Library, 1966.

MacCARTHY, DESMOND. *Drama.* London, Putnam, 1940.

————. *Theatre.* New York, Oxford University Press, 1955.

✓McCARTHY, MARY. *Sights and spectacles, 1937–1956.* New York, Farrar, Straus & Cudahy, 1956.

McCOLLOM, WILLIAM G. *Tragedy.* New York, Macmillan, 1957.

McELROY, DAVIS DUNBAR. *The study of literature; an existential appraisal.* New York, Philosophical Library, 1965.

✓McFARLANE, JAMES WALTER, ed. *Discussions of Henrik Ibsen.* Boston, Heath, 1962.

MacIVER, ROBERT MORRISON. *Great moral dilemmas: in literature, past and present.* New York, Institute for Religious and Social Studies (dist. by Harper), 1956.

MACKWORTH, CECILY. *Guillaume Apollinaire and the cubist life.* New York, Horizon, 1963.

MACLEOD, JOSEPH. *Actors cross the Volga: a study of the 19th century Russian theatre and of Soviet theatres in war.* London, Allen & Unwin, 1946.

✓McNEIR, WALDO F., ed. *Studies in comparative literature.* Baton Rouge, Louisiana State University Press, 1962. *(Louisiana State University Studies, Humanities Series, no. 11).*

✓MALLINSON, VERNON. *Modern Belgian literature, 1830–1960.* London, Heinemann, 1966.

✓MALONE, ANDREW E. *The Irish drama.* New York, Scribner's, 1929.

MANDER, JOHN. *The writer and commitment*. Philadelphia, Dufour Editions, 1962.

MANDER, RAYMOND, and JOE MICHENSON, compilers. *Theatrical companion to Shaw*. London, Rockliff, 1954; New York, Pitman, 1955.

MANHEIM, LEONARD and ELEANOR MANHEIM, eds. *American playwrights of today*. New York, Dodd, Mead, 1929.

MANTLE, BURNS. *Contemporary American playwrights*. New York, Dodd, Mead, 1938.

MARBLE, ANNIE RUSSELL. *The Nobel Prize winners in literature*. New York, Appleton, 1925.

MARCEL, GABRIEL. *The existential background of human dignity*. Cambridge, Harvard University Press, 1963.

MAROWITZ, CHARLES, ed. *The Encore reader*. London, Methuen, 1965.

MAROWITZ, CHARLES and SIMON TRUSSLER, eds. *Theatre at work; playwrights and productions in the modern British theatre*. London, Methuen, 1967.

MARSH, EDWARD O. *Jean Anouilh. Poet of Pierrot and Pantaloon*. London, Allen, 1953.

MARSH, RICHARD M. *T. S. Eliot, a symposium*. London, Editions Poetry, 1948.

MATTHEWS, HONOR. *The primal curse, the myth of Cain and Abel in the theatre*. New York, Schocken Books, 1967.

MATUSKA, ALEXANDER. *Karel Capek: an essay*. London, Allen & Unwin; Prague, Artia, 1964.

MAUROIS, ANDRÉ. *From Proust to Camus; profiles of modern French writers*. Garden City, N. Y., Doubleday, 1966.

MAYNE, FRED. *The wit and satire of Bernard Shaw*. London, Edward Arnold, 1967.

MEISEL, MARTIN. *Shaw and the nineteenth century theater*. Princeton, N. J., Princeton University Press, 1963.

MERCHANT, W. MOELWYN. *Creed and drama*. Philadelphia, Fortress Press, 1966.

MERSAND, JOSEPH E. *The American drama since 1930; essays on playwrights and plays*. New York, Modern Chapbooks, 1949.

———. *Plays the thing; enjoying the plays of today*. New York, Modern Chapbooks, 1941.

MESERVE, WALTER J., ed. *Discussions of American drama*. Boston, D. C. Heath, 1965.

MEYER, MICHAEL. *Henrik Ibsen; the making of a dramatist, 1828–1864*. London, Rupert Hart-Davis, 1967.

MICKLE, ALAN D. *Studies on six plays of Eugene O'Neill*. New York, Liveright, 1929.

MILLER, ARTHUR. *Death of a salesman*. Text and criticism, edited by Gerald Weales. New York, The Viking Press, 1967.

MILLER, JORDAN Y. *American dramatic literature: ten modern plays in historical perspective*. New York, McGraw-Hill, 1961.

———. *Playwright's progress: O'Neill and the critics*. Chicago, Scott, Foresman, 1965.

MILLER, NELLIE BURGET. *The living drama, historical development and modern movement visualized; a drama of the drama.* New York, The Century Co., 1924.

✓MITCHELL, LOFTEN. *Black drama; the story of the American Negro in the theatre.* New York, Hawthorne Books, 1967.

✓MONTAGUE, CHARLES EDWARDS. *Dramatic values.* Garden City, N. Y., Doubleday, Page & Co., 1925.

✓MOORE, HARRY T. *Twentieth-century French literature since World War II.* Carbondale, Southern Illinois University Press, 1966.

————. *Twentieth-century French literature to World War II.* Carbondale, Southern Illinois University Press, 1966.

————. *Twentieth-century German literature.* New York, Basic Books, 1967.

MORRIS, LLOYD R. *Postscript to yesterday; America: the last fifty years.* New York, Random House, 1947.

✓MORSBERGER, ROBERT E. *James Thurber.* New York, Twayne Publishers, 1964. *(United States Author Series, No. 62)*

✓MOSES, MONTROSE J., and JOHN MASON BROWN, eds. *The American theatre as seen by its critics, 1752–1934.* New York, Norton, 1934.

℞ MOSKOWITZ, SAMUEL. *Explorers of the infinite; shapers of science fiction.* Cleveland, World Publishing Company, 1963.

✓ MOSS, LEONARD. *Arthur Miller.* New York, Twayne Publishers, 1967. *(United States Authors Series, No. 115)*

MUELLER, CARL RICHARD, translator. *Frank Wedekind: The Lulu plays.* New York, Fawcett World Library, 1967.

1892 H7 ✓MULLER, HERBERT J. *The spirit of tragedy.* New York, Knopf, 1956.

MUNK, ERIKA, ed. *Stanislavski and America.* New York, Hill & Wang, 1966.

3525
I 5156 28 ✓MURRAY, EDWARD. *Arthur Miller, dramatist.* New York, Frederick Ungar, 1967.

3529 046 ————. *Clifford Odets: the thirties and after.* New York, Frederick Ungar,
277 1968.

MYERS, HENRY ALONZO. *Tragedy: a view of life.* Ithaca, N. Y., Cornell University Press, 1956.

✓NABOKOV, VLADIMIR. *Nikolai Gogol.* New York, New Directions, 1961.

✓NAIK, M. K. *W. Somerset Maugham.* Norman, University of Oklahoma Press, 1966.

343 N32 ✓NATAN, ALEX, ed. *German men of letters. Vols. 1–3.* London, Oswald Wolff, 1961–1964.

2266
N 3732 ✓NATHAN, GEORGE JEAN. *Theatre book of the year, 1948–1949.* Toronto, McClelland, 1949.

℞ ————. *Theatre in the fifties.* New York, Knopf, 1953.

✓NATHAN, LEONARD E. *The tragic drama of William Butler Yeats. Figures in a dance.* New York, Columbia University Press, 1965.

3545 ✓NELSON, BENJAMIN. *Tennessee Williams: the man and his work.* New York,
5365 279 Obolensky, 1961.

✓NELSON, ROBERT JAMES. *Play within a play; the dramatist's conception of his art: Shakespeare to Anouilh.* New Haven, Yale University Press, 1958. *(Yale Romantic Studies, 2nd ser., 5)*

NETHERCOT, ARTHUR HOBART. *Men and supermen: the Shavian portrait gallery.* Cambridge, Harvard University Press, 1954.

NICOLL, ALLARDYCE. *British drama.* 5th ed. rev. New York, Barnes and Noble, 1962.

NORMAN, CHARLES. *E. E. Cummings, a biography.* New York, E. P. Dutton & Co., 1967.

NORWOOD, GILBERT. *Euripides and Shaw with other essays.* London, Methuen, 1921.

O'CASEY, SEAN. *Selected plays of Sean O'Casey.* New York, Braziller, 1954.

———. *Blasts and benedictions, articles and stories by Sean O'Casey.* Selected and introduced by Ronald Ayling. London, Macmillan, 1967.

———. *The green crow.* New York, George Braziller, 1956.

O'CONNOR, FRANK. *A short history of Irish literature: a backward look.* New York, Putnam's, 1967.

O'CONNOR, PATRICIA WALKER. *Women in the theater of Gregorio Martinez Sierra.* New York, The American Press, 1966.

O'HARA, FRANK H. *Today in American drama.* Chicago, University of Chicago Press, 1939.

OHMANN, RICHARD. *Shaw, the style and the man.* Middletown, Conn., Wesleyan University Press, 1962.

OLDSEY, BERNARD S. and STANLEY WEINTRAUB. *The art of William Golding.* Bloomington, Indiana University Press, 1968.

OLSON, ELDER. *Tragedy and the theory of drama.* Detroit, Wayne State University Press, 1961.

OPPENHEIMER, GEORGE, ed. *The passionate playgoer; a personal scrapbook.* New York, Viking Press, 1958.

OXENHANDLER, NEAL. *Scandal and parade: the theater of Jean Cocteau.* New Brunswick, Rutgers University Press, 1957.

PALMER, JOHN. *Studies in the contemporary theatre.* Boston, Little, Brown, 1927.

PARIS REVIEW. *Writers at work; The Paris Review interviews. Third series.* Introduced by Alfred Kazin. New York, Viking Press, 1967.

PAUL, SHERMAN. *Edmund Wilson; a study of literary vocation in our time.* Urbana, University of Illinois Press, 1965.

PEACOCK, RONALD. *The poet in the theatre.* New York, Harcourt, Brace, 1946.

PERRY, HENRY TEN EYCK. *Masters of dramatic comedy and their social themes.* Cambridge, Harvard University Press, 1939.

PHELPS, WILLIAM LYON. *Essays on modern dramatists.* New York, Macmillan, 1926.

PHILLIPS, ELIZABETH C., and DAVID ROGERS. *Modern American drama.* New York, Monarch Press, 1966. *(Monarch Notes and Study Guides)*

PRICE, ALAN. *Synge and Anglo-Irish drama.* London, Methuen, 1961.

PRIOR, MOODY E. *The language of tragedy.* New York, Columbia University Press, 1947.

PRONKO, LEONARD CABELL. *Avant-garde: the experimental theater in France.* Berkeley, University of California Press, 1962.

————. *Eugene Ionesco.* New York, Columbia University Press, 1965. *(Columbia Essays on Modern Writers, Number 7)*

————. *Theater East and West, perspectives toward a total theater.* Berkeley, University of California Press, 1967.

————. *The world of Jean Anouilh.* Berkeley, University of California Press, 1961.

PURDOM, CHARLES BENJAMIN. *A guide to the plays of Bernard Shaw.* London, Methuen, 1963.

QUINN, ARTHUR HOBSON. *Literature of the American people; an historical and critical survey.* New York, Appleton, 1951.

RABKIN, GERALD. *Drama and commitment.* Bloomington, Indiana University Press, 1964.

RAGHAVACHARYULU, DHUPATY V. K. *Eugene O'Neill, a study.* Bombay, Popular Prakashan, 1965. (Distributed in the U.S. by Humanities Press)

RAHV, PHILIP. *Image and idea.* New York, New Directions, 1959. (New Directions Paperback, no. 67)

————. *The myth and the powerhouse.* New York, Farrar, Straus & Giroux, 1965.

————, ed. *Modern occasions.* New York, Farrar, Straus & Giroux, 1966.

RAJAN, BALACHANDRA. *W. B. Yeats, a critical introduction.* London, Hutchinson University Library, 1965.

RALEIGH, JOHN H. *The plays of Eugene O'Neill.* Carbondale, Southern Illinois University Press, 1965.

RECHCIGL, MILOSLAV, JR., ed. *The Czechoslovak contribution to world culture.* The Hague, Mouton, 1964.

REINERT, OTTO, ed. *Drama, an introductory anthology.* Boston, Little, Brown, 1961.

————, ed. *Drama; an introductory anthology.* Alternate edition. Boston, Little, Brown, 1964.

————, ed. *Modern drama; nine plays.* Boston, Little, Brown, 1966.

RIBALOW, HAROLD U. *Arnold Wesker.* New York, Twayne Publishers, 1965.

RICE, ELMER. *Minority report; an autobiography.* New York, Simon and Schuster, 1963.

RICHARDS, DICK. *The curtain rises; an anthology of the international theatre.* London, Leslie Frewin, 1966.

RICHARDSON, RUTH. *Florencio Sanchez and the Argentine theatre.* New York, Instituto de las Espanas, 1933.

ROPPEN, GEORG. *Evolution and poetic belief, a study in some Victorian and modern writers.* Oslo, Oslo University Press, 1956. *(Oslo Studies in English, no. 5)*

ROSSET, B. C. *Shaw of Dublin: the formative years.* University Park, Pennsylvania State University Press, 1964.

ROSTON, MURRAY. *Biblical drama in England from the Middle Ages to the present day.* Evanston, Northwestern University Press, 1968.

ROWE, KENNETH THORPE. *A theatre in your head.* New York, Funk & Wagnalls, 1960.

ROY, EMIL. *Christopher Fry.* Carbondale and Edwardsville, Southern Illinois University Press, 1968. *(Crosscurrents/Modern Critiques)*

RUBIN, LOUIS D. and ROBERT D. JACOBS, eds. *South: modern Southern literature in its cultural setting.* New York, Doubleday, 1961.

RUSSELL, LEONARD, ed. *English wits.* London, Hutchinson, 1953. (Reissue of 1940 publication)

RUTENBERG, MICHAEL E. *Edward Albee: playwright in protest.* New York, DBS Publications, 1969.

SADDLEMYER, ANN. *In defence of Lady Gregory, playwright.* Dublin, The Dolmen Press, 1966.

SAINER, ARTHUR. *The sleepwalker and the assassin, a view of the contemporary theatre.* New York, Bridgehead Books, 1964.

SALACROU, ARMAND. *Three plays by Armand Salacrou: The World is Round, When the Music Stops, Marguerite.* Minneapolis, University of Minnesota Press, 1967. *(Minnesota Drama Editions, no. 4)*

SALAVERRI, VICENTE A. *Florencio Sanchez, the man and the dramatist.* New York, Inter-America, 1921.

SALERNO, HENRY F., ed. *English drama in transition, 1880–1920.* New York, Pegasus, 1968.

SALVADORI, CORINNA. *Yeats and Castiglione, poet and courtier; a study of some fundamental concepts of the philosophy and poetic creed of W. B. Yeats in the light of Castiglione's Il Libro Cortegiano.* Dublin, Allen Figgis, 1965.

SAMELSON, WILLIAM. *Gerhart Herrmann Mostar: a critical profile.* The Hague, Mouton, 1966. *(Studies in German Literature, vol. 6)*

SANDERSON, JAMES L., ed. *Media, myth and dramatic form.* Boston, Houghton Mifflin, 1967.

——, ed. *Oedipus, myth and dramatic form.* Boston, Houghton Mifflin, 1968.

——, ed. *Phaedra and Hippolytus, myth and dramatic form.* Boston, Houghton Mifflin, 1966.

SAN JUAN, EPIFANIO, JR. *The art of Oscar Wilde.* Princeton, Princeton University Press, 1967.

SARTRE, JEAN-PAUL. *Saint Genet, actor and martyr.* New York, Braziller, 1963.

SAUL, GEORGE BRANDON. *Prolegomena to the study of Yeats' plays.* Philadelphia, University of Pennsylvania Press, 1958.

SAYLER, OLIVER M. *Our American theatre.* New York, Brentano's, 1923.

SCHWARTZ, ALFRED, JR. *Hugo von Hofmannsthal: three plays.* Detroit, Wayne State University Press, 1966.

SCHWARZ, EGON, HUNTER G. HANNUM, and EDGAR LOHNER, eds. *Festschrift fur Berhard Blume: Aufsätze zur deutschen und europaischen Literatur.* Gottingen: Vandenhoeck & Ruprecht, 1967.

SCOTT, NATHAN A. *Samuel Beckett.* New York, Hillary House, 1965.

——, ed. *Man in the modern theatre.* Richmond, John Knox Press, 1965.

SELTZER, DANIEL, ed. *The modern theatre, readings and documents.* Boston, Little, Brown, 1967.

SETCHKAREV, VSEVOLOD. *Gogol: his life and works.* New York, New York University Press, 1965.

SETTERQUIST, JAN. *Ibsen and the beginnings of Anglo-Irish drama. I. John Millington Synge; II. Edward Martyn.* 2 vols. Upsala, Lundequistska Bokhandeln, 1951–1960. *(Upsala Irish Studies, II & V.)*

SHANKS, EDWARD. *Second essays on literature.* London, W. Collins Sons & Co., 1927.

℟ SHARP, WILLIAM. *Studies and appreciations.* Freeport, N.Y., Books for Libraries, 1967. (Reprint of 1912 ed.) *(Essay Index Reprint Series)*

✓SHARPE, ROBERT BOIES. *Irony in the drama; an essay on impersonation, shock and catharsis.* Chapel Hill, University of North Carolina Press, 1959.

✓ SHATTUCK, ROGER. *The banquet years.* New York, Harcourt, Brace, 1958.

✓SHAW, GEORGE BERNARD. *The quintessence of Ibsenism.* 3rd edition. London, Constable, 1926.

℟ ———. *The rationalization of Russia.* Edited by Harry M. Geduld. Bloomington, Indiana University Press, 1964.

℟ ———. *Shaw's dramatic criticism (1895–98).* A selection by John F. Matthews. New York, Hill & Wang, 1959.

2654 S56 ✓SHAW, LEROY R. *The German theatre today: a symposium. Austin,* University of Texas Press, 1963.

℟ SHIPLEY, JOSEPH T. *The art of Eugene O'Neill.* Seattle, University of Washington Bookstore, 1928.

✓SHUMAN, ROBERT BAIRD. *Robert E. Sherwood.* New York, Twayne Publishers, 1964. *(United States Author Series, no. 58)*

✓ ———. *William Inge.* New York, Twayne Publishers, 1965.

351 S5 SIEVERS, WIEDER DAVID. *Freud on Broadway.* New York, Hermitage House, 1955.

✓SIMMONS, ERNEST J. *Introduction to Russian realism; Pushkin, Gogol, Dostoevsky, Tolstoy, Chekhov, Sholokhov.* Bloomington, Indiana University Press, 1965.

✓ SIMON, MYRON, and THORNTON H. PARSON, eds. *Transcendentalism and its legacy.* Ann Arbor, University of Michigan Press, 1966.

✓SIMONSON, HAROLD P. *Zona Gale.* New York, Twayne Publishers, 1962. *(United States Authors Series, no. 18).*

SIMPSON, ALAN. *Beckett and Behan and a theatre in Dublin.* London, Routledge & Kegan Paul, 1962.

℟ 5907 S4 SKELTON, ROBIN, ed. *The world of W.B. Yeats; essays in perspective.* Published for the University of Victoria, British Columbia, by the Adelphi Bookshop, Victoria, Canada, 1965.

SKELTON, ROBIN, and DAVID R. CLARK, eds. *Irish Renaissance: a gathering of essays, memoirs, and letters from The Massachusetts Review.* Dublin, The Dolmen Press, 1965.

✓SKINNER, RICHARD DANA. *Eugene O'Neill; a poet's quest.* New York, Longmans, 1935; Russell & Russell, 1964.

———. *Our changing theatre.* New York, Dial, 1931.

Skrifttradisjon og litteraturmal: Artikler og avhandlinger i utvalg. Festskrift i anledning av professor dr. Trygve Knudsens 70 ars dag 23 juni 1967. Oslo: Universitetsforlaget.

✓SLONIM, MARK L'VOVICH. *Soviet Russian literature; writers and problems, 1917–1967.* New York, Oxford University Press, 1967.

SLOTE, BERNICE, ed. *Literature and society: nineteen essays by Germaine Brée and others.* Lincoln, University of Nebraska Press, 1964.

——, ed. *Myth and symbol; critical approaches and applications.* Lincoln, University of Nebraska Press, 1963.

SMITH, HUGH A. *Main currents of modern French drama.* New York, Henry Holt, 1925.

SMITH, JOSEPH PERCY. *The unrepentant pilgrim; a study of the development of Bernard Shaw.* Boston, Houghton Mifflin, 1965.

SMITH, MAXWELL A. *Jean Giono.* New York, Twayne Publishers, 1966. *(World Authors Series, No. 7)*

SOKEL, WALTER H. *The writer in extremis: expressionism in twentieth-century German literature.* Stanford, Stanford University Press, 1959.

SONTAG, SUSAN. *Against interpretation and other essays.* New York, Farrar, Straus & Giroux, 1966.

SPALTER, MAX. *Brecht's tradition.* Baltimore, The Johns Hopkins Press, 1967.

SPANOS, WILLIAM V. *The Christian tradition in modern British verse drama: the poetics of sacramental time.* New Brunswick, N.J., Rutgers University Press, 1967.

SPRINCHORN, EVERT, ed. *The genius of the Scandinavian theater.* New York, New American Library, 1964.

SQUIRES, RADCLIFFE. *The loyalties of Robinson Jeffers.* Ann Arbor, University of Michigan Press, 1956.

STANFORD, WILLIAM BEDELL. *The Ulysses theme; a study of the adaptability of a traditional hero.* 2nd ed. Oxford, Basil Blackwell, 1963.

STARKIE, WALTER. *Jacinto Benavente.* New York, Oxford University Press, 1924.

——. *Luigi Pirandello, 1867–1936.* Berkeley, University of California Press, 1965.

STARKIE, WALTER, and A. NORMAN JEFFARES. *Homage to Yeats 1865–1965, papers read at a Clark Library Seminar, October 16, 1965.* Los Angeles, Clark Memorial Library, University of California, 1966.

STEDMAN, JANE W. *Gilbert before Sullivan: six comic plays by W. S. Gilbert.* Chicago, University of Chicago Press, 1967.

STEINER, GEORGE. *The death of tragedy.* New York, Knopf, 1961.

STEWART, JOHN INNES MACINTOSH. *Eight modern writers.* Oxford, Clarendon Press, 1964.

STRINDBERG, AUGUST. *Open letters to the intimate theater.* Translations and introductions by Walter Johnson. Seattle, University of Washington Press, 1966.

STYAN, J. L. *The dark comedy.* London, Cambridge University Press, 1962.

——. *The dark comedy; the development of modern comic tragedy.* 2nd edition. London, Cambridge University Press, 1968.

——. *The elements of drama.* London, Cambridge University Press, 1960.

SUTTON, GRAHAM. *Some contemporary dramatists.* New York, Doran, 1925.

TATE, ALLEN, ed. *T. S. Eliot; the man and his work.* New York, Delacorte Press, 1966.

TAYLOR, JOHN RUSSELL. *Anger and after; a new guide to the new British drama.* London, Methuen, 1963.

⸺. *The rise and fall of the well-made play.* London, Methuen, 1967.

The Theatre Annual. Cleveland, Western Reserve University Press, 1953–1961.

Theatre; the annual of the Repertory Theatre of Lincoln Center. Edited by Barry Hyams. Volume 1. New York, The Center, 1964.

Theatre; the annual of the Repertory Theatre of Lincoln Center. Edited by Barry Hyams. Volume 2. New York, Hill & Wang, 1965.

THODY, PHILIP. *Jean Genet, a study of his novels and plays.* New York, Stein & Day, 1969.

THOMPSON, ALAN REYNOLDS. *The anatomy of drama.* Berkeley, University of California Press, 1946.

⸺. *The dry mock, a study of irony in drama.* Berkeley, University of California Press, 1948.

THORPE, WILLARD. *American writing in the twentieth century.* Cambridge, Harvard University Press, 1960.

TIUSANEN, TIMO. *O'Neill's scenic images.* Princeton, Princeton University Press, 1968.

TORCHIANA, DONALD T. *W.B. Yeats and Georgian Ireland.* Evanston, Northwestern University Press, 1966.

TRILLING, DIANA. *Claremont essays.* New York, Harcourt, 1964.

TULANE DRAMA REVIEW. *Theatre in the twentieth century.* New York, Grove Press, 1963.

TURNELL, MARTIN. *Graham Greene: a critical essay. (Contemporary Writers in Christian Perspective)* Grand Rapids, Mich., William B. Eerdmans, 1967.

TURQUET-MILNES, GLADYS ROSALEEN. *Some modern Belgian writers; a critical study.* New York, Robert M. McBride, 1917.

TYNAN, KENNETH. *Tynan right and left, plays, films, people, places and events.* New York, Atheneum, 1967.

UNGER, LEONARD. *T. S. Eliot, moments and patterns.* Minneapolis, University of Minnesota Press, 1966.

VALENCY, MAURICE. *The breaking string, the plays of Anton Chekhov.* New York, Oxford University Press, 1966.

VIDAL, GORE. *Rocking the boat.* New York, Dell, 1951.

VOADEN, HERMAN, ed. *Human values in the drama.* Toronto, The Macmillan Co. of Canada, 1966.

VOLPE, EDMOND L. and MARVIN MAGALANER, eds. *An introduction to literature: drama.* New York, Random House, 1967.

VOS, NELVIN. *The drama of comedy: victim and victor.* Richmond, John Knox Press, 1966.

WAGER, WALTER, ed. *The playwrights speak.* New York, Delacorte Press, 1967.

WALCUTT, CHARLES C. *American literary naturalism, a divided stream.* Minneapolis, University of Minnesota Press, 1956.

WALKLEY, ARTHUR BINGHAM. *Drama and life.* New York, Brentano's, 1908.

WARD, ALFRED CHARLES. *Bernard Shaw.* 4th ed. London and New York. Published for the British Council and the National Book League by Longmans, Green, 1960. *(Bibliographical series of supplements to British Book News on Writers and their Work, no. 1)*

WARREN, LESLIE ALEC. *Modern Spanish literature, a comprehensive survey of the novelists, poets, dramatists, and essayists from the eighteenth century to the present day.* London and New York, Brentano's, 1929.

WATERMAN, ARTHUR E. *Susan Glaspell.* New York, Twayne Publishers, 1966.

WATON, HARRY. *The historic significance of Eugene O'Neill's Strange Interlude.* New York, Worker's Educational Institute, 1928.

WATSON-WILLIAMS, HELEN. *André Gide and the Greek myth, a critical study.* Oxford, Clarendon Press, 1967.

WEALES, GERALD. *American drama since World War II.* New York, Harcourt, Brace & World, 1962.

———. *Religion in modern English drama.* Philadelphia, University of Pennsylvania Press, 1961.

———. *Tennessee Williams.* Minneapolis, University of Minnesota Press, 1965. *(Pamphlets on American Writers, Number 53)*

WEGNER, ROBERT E. *The poetry and prose of E. E. Cummings.* New York, Harcourt, Brace & World, 1965.

WEIGAND, HERMANN J. *Surveys and soundings in European literature.* Princeton, Princeton University Press, 1966.

WEISSMAN, PHILIP. *Creativity in the theater; a psychoanalytic study.* New York, Basic Books, 1965.

WEISSTEIN, ULRICH. *Max Frisch.* New York, Twayne Publishers, 1968.

WELLEK, RENÉ. *Essays on Czech literature.* The Hague, Mouton, 1963.

WELLWARTH, GEORGE. *The theatre of protest and paradox.* New York, New York University Press, 1964.

WEST, ALICK. *George Bernard Shaw, "A Good Man Fallen Among Fabians."* New York, International Publishers, 1950.

WHIPPLE, THOMAS K. *Spokesmen, modern writers, and American life.* New York, Appleton, 1928.

WHITBREAD, THOMAS B., ed. *Seven contemporary authors; essays on Cozzens, Miller, West, Golding, Heller, Albee, and Powers.* Austin, University of Texas Press, 1966.

WHITE, RAY LEWIS. *Gore Vidal.* New York, Twayne Publishers, 1968.

WIENER, LEO. *The contemporary drama of Russia.* Boston, Little, Brown, 1924.

WILLIAMS, HAROLD. *Modern English writers: being a study of imaginative literature, 1890–1914.* London, Sidgwick & Jackson, 1919.

WILLIAMS, RAYMOND. *Drama from Ibsen to Eliot.* London. Oxford University Press, 1952.

———. *Drama in performance.* London, Frederick Muller, 1954.

———. *Drama in performance.* New ed. New York, Basic Books, 1968.

———. *Modern tragedy.* Stanford, Stanford University Press, 1966.

WILLIAMSON, AUDREY. *Bernard Shaw: man and writer.* New York, Crowell-Collier, 1963.

———. *Contemporary theatre, 1953–1956.* London, Rockliff, 1956.

WILSON, COLIN. *Religion and the rebel.* Boston, Houghton Mifflin, 1957.

WITKIEWICZ, STANISLAW IGNACY. *The madman and the Nun and other plays.* Ed. and translated by Daniel C. Gerould and C.S. Durer. Seattle, University of Washington Press, 1968.

WITKOWSKI, GEORG. *The German drama of the nineteenth century.* New York, Holt, 1909.

WOODBRIDGE, HOMER. *G. B. Shaw, creative artist.* Carbondale, Southern Illinois University Press, 1963.

WOOLLCOTT, ALEXANDER. *Enchanted aisles.* New York, Putnam, 1924.

World literatures. Pittsburgh, University of Pittsburgh Press, 1956.

YOUNG, STARK. *Immortal shadows.* New York, Scribner's, 1948.

ZABEL, MORTON DAUWEN. *Literary opinion in America.* New York, Harper, 1951.

ZWERDLING, ALEX. *Yeats and the heroic ideal.* New York, New York University Press, 1965.